MW01132046

Case Studies in Public Budgeting and Financial Management

PUBLIC ADMINISTRATION AND PUBLIC POLICY

A Comprehensive Publication Program

Executive Editor

JACK RABIN
Professor of Public Administration and Public Policy
School of Public Affairs
The Capital College
The Pennsylvania State University—Harrisburg
Middletown, Pennsylvania

ANNALS OF PUBLIC ADMINISTRATION

Case Studies in Public Budgeting and Financial Management

Second Edition, Revised and Expanded

edited by

Aman Khan
Texas Tech University
Lubbock, Texas, U.S.A.

W. Bartley Hildreth
Wichita State University
Wichita, Kansas, U.S.A.

CRC Press
Taylor & Francis Group
Boca Raton   London   New York

CRC Press is an imprint of the
Taylor & Francis Group, an **informa** business

The first edition was published by Kendall/Hunt Publishing Company (Dubuque, Iowa), 1997.

Library of Congress Cataloging-in-Publication Data
A catalog record for this book is available from the Library of Congress.

ISBN: 0–8247–0888–1

This book is printed on acid-free paper.

Headquarters
Marcel Dekker
270 Madison Avenue, New York, NY 10016
tel: 212–696–9000

The publisher offers discounts on this book when ordered in bulk quantities. For more information, write to Special Sales/Professional Marketing at the headquarters address above.

To
Terri Khan
and
Rhonda Hildreth

Foreword

Working with friends is always a pleasure, but commenting on an outstanding product of friends is a greater pleasure. I have known Professors Aman Khan and W. Bartley Hildreth for many years. I now even occupy the same position at LSU that Professor Hildreth previously occupied. Over those years, I worked with them on several projects and found a great deal of joy in contributing with them to an improving literature of public budgeting and financial management. In the case of Professor Khan, I also was his colleague for several years and enjoyed his always positive approach to life's challenges. For both Professors Khan and Hildreth, we have shared experiences with the American Society for Public Administration. We contributed to that organization in various ways including organizing panels and doing the many tasks necessary in making a living organization significant to our profession.

I was pleased to see this book in print. For over a decade, I have had a textbook on public budgeting and financial management in print. My book is in its fourth edition. A textbook must provide an overview of its subject and thus it must omit much of the richness of the subject to achieve clarity. In contrast, a book of case studies provides a very good sample of the richness of detail associated with this complex and exciting subject. For example, this book covers case studies on a county using target-based budgeting, cash management practices of a local government, the local politics of pension investment, and financing a recycling facility through a public–private enterprise. Budgeting is the nexus of politics and public management. These case studies illustrate that important and often under-appreciated fact with a richness of information.

For the inquiry of public budgeting and financial management to continue to advance and be useful to the professional community of which it is a part, empirical studies are essential. We are awash in prescriptive theories on how to do better budgeting and financial management. To build more useful theories we must have a keen appreciation of the practice of budgeting and financial management. Case studies and comparative empirical research are the means to enhance our empirical understanding of practice. This work by Professors Khan and Hildreth is a major step forward in improving both our teaching materials and our empirical information on this subject. We owe these editors and all the contributors a very large thank you.

Thomas D. Lynch
Baton Rouge, Louisiana, U.S.A.

About the New Edition

With its modest success since it was first published in 1994, we felt that it was time to make some additional changes in the book—add a few new chapters to reflect some of the recent developments in the field and revise some that we felt could provide new insights to old problems. The new edition includes twenty-four new chapters, including some that were published elsewhere before, and six revisions or updates. We also decided to keep many of the chapters from the first edition because we thought they were interesting, covered areas that are still current, and can serve a useful learning purpose for our students.

We are certain that we could have added many more chapters and introduced many more topics, but it would still not have covered everything there is to be included. No amount of space can cover every single topic that one needs to learn. It is simply not feasible, but recognizing this need is critical to the learning process, and, in the end, makes any discipline worth pursuing. We hope the new edition will receive the same amount of interest as did its predecessor.

No book can claim to have addressed or fulfilled every single need of its readers, but all try to capture, to the extent possible, the essence of the discipline without losing sight of the objectives set out in the first place. The primary objective of this book is to help the students of public budgeting and financial management have a better grasp of the discipline through an understanding of real-world problems and how they are addressed. It is not quite as simple to comprehend the range or the breadth of problems one will encounter in the real world by studying a handful, but this book should give our readers a glimpse of what they are likely to experience. To the extent that it helps even a single student understand that, we should consider our effort worthwhile.

Aman Khan and W. Bartley Hildreth

Acknowledgments

This book is the product of collaborative efforts of many individuals, without whose support and active participation this book would have never seen the light of day. We owe it to the contributors more than anybody else. Thanks are also due to several colleagues at Texas Tech, in particular Clarke Cochran, Charles Fox, and Murray Havens for their generous support and encouragement for the project. A study of this nature would have never been completed without the support of numerous individuals from various public organizations, who contributed immensely by giving their time to furnish data and other information used in these cases. In many instances, they went beyond their professional courtesy to extend a helping hand by going over the findings and helping many of us in the process not get carried away in our analysis or recommendations. They deserve our heartfelt appreciation. We would also like to take this opportunity to thank Russell Dekker, Paige Force, and Jennifer Paizzi of Marcel Dekker, Inc. for their wonderful support and cooperation throughout the production process and beyond. It was a pleasure working with them.

Finally, and in spite of our best effort and of those mentioned above, it is quite possible that errors will have found their way into the book. The responsibility, in this case, will be ours—the editors.

Contents

Contents

PART II FINANCIAL MANAGEMENT

A. Accounting, Auditing, and Financial Reporting

B. Financial Management Practices

Contributors

Laurie W. Adams Louisiana State University, Baton Rouge, Louisiana, U.S.A.

Troy Albee Office of Budget and Evaluation, City of Myrtle Beach, South Carolina, U.S.A.

Alan Blankley Western Michigan University, Kalamazoo, Michigan, U.S.A.

Robert Boydston Tennessee State University, Nashville, Tennessee, U.S.A.

Richard C. Brooks Department of Accounting, College of Business and Economics, West Virginia University, Morgantown, West Virginia, U.S.A.

Richard W. Campbell University of Georgia, Athens, Georgia, U.S.A.

Michael Campenni Public Administration Program, Department of Political Science, Texas Tech University, Lubbock, Texas, U.S.A.

K. Lee Carter University of North Carolina, Chapel Hill, North Carolina, U.S.A.

Edward J. Clynch Department of Public Administration, Mississippi State University, Mississippi State, Mississippi, U.S.A.

Charles Coe MPA program, Department of Political Science and Public Administration, North Carolina State University, Raleigh, North Carolina, U.S.A.

Dan Durning University of Georgia, Athens, Georgia, U.S.A.

C. Nelson Easterling Governmental Consultant, Florida, U.S.A.

Sandra M. Emerson California State University, Pomona, California, U.S.A.

William A. Firestone Rutgers University, New Brunswick, New Jersey, U.S.A.

Howard Fleeter School of Public Administration, Ohio State University, Columbus, Ohio, U.S.A.

Dana Forgione University of Baltimore, Baltimore, Maryland, U.S.A.

John P. Forrester U. S. General Accounting Office, Washington, D. C., U.S.A.

Robert J. Freeman Department of Accounting, College of Business Administration, Texas Tech University, Lubbock, Texas, U.S.A.

Margaret E. Goertz University of Pennsylvania, Philadelphia, Pennsylvania, U.S.A.

Merl Hackbart Martin School of Public Administration, University of Kentucky, Lexington, Kentucky, U.S.A.

Arie Halachmi Tennessee State University, Nashville, Tennessee, U.S.A.

Rebecca Hendrick Department of Public Administration, University of Illinois, Chicago, Illinois, U.S.A.

W. Bartley Hildreth Hugo Wall School of Urban and Public Affairs, Wichita State University Wichita, Kansas, U.S.A.

Natalee Hillman University of Pittsburgh, Pittsburgh, Pennsylvania, U.S.A.

Kay Hofer MPA Program, Department of Political Science, Southwest Texas State University, San Marcos, Texas, U.S.A.

Jesse W. Hughes Department of Accounting, College of Business Administration, Old Dominion University, Norfolk, Virginia, U.S.A.

Craig L. Johnson School of Public and Environmental Affairs, Indiana University, Bloomington, Indiana, U.S.A.

Aman Khan Department of Political Science, Public Administration Program, Texas Tech University, Lubbock, Texas, U.S.A.

Frank U. Koehler College of Public Affairs & Community Services, University of Nebraska, Omaha, Nebraska, U.S.A.

Thomas P. Lauth School of Public and International Affairs, The University of Georgia, Athens, Georgia, U.S.A.

Suzanne Leland Department of Political Science, University of North Carolina, Charlotte, North Carolina, U.S.A.

Thomas D. Lynch Public Administration Institute, Louisiana State University, Baton Rouge, Louisiana, U.S.A.

Susan A. MacManus University of South Florida, Tampa, Florida, U.S.A.

Patrick W. Manion† Deputy City Manager, City of Phoenix, Arizona, U.S.A.

Herbert A. Marlowe, Jr. University of Florida, Gainesville, Florida, U.S.A.

Thomas W. Matteo New York University, New York, New York, U.S.A.

Jerry McCaffery School of Business and Public Policy, Naval Postgraduate School, Monterey, California, U.S.A.

Jerome B. McKinney Graduate School of Public and International Affairs, University of Pittsburgh, Pittsburgh, Pennsylvania, U.S.A.

---

† Deceased.

John L. Mikesell School of Public and Environmental Affairs, Indiana University, Bloomington, Indiana, U.S.A.

Gerald J. Miller Graduate program in Public Administration, Rutgers University, Newark, New Jersey, U.S.A.

Patti A. Mills College of Business Administration, Department of Accounting, Indiana State University, Terre Haute, Indiana, U.S.A.

Rowan Miranda* Office of Management and Budget, City of Pittsburgh, Pennslyvania, U.S.A.

Jennie L. Mitchell Department of Accounting, Saint Mary-of-the-Woods College, Saint Mary-of-the-Woods, Indiana, U.S.A.

John E. Mutty School of Business and Public Policy, Naval Postgraduate School, Monterey, California, U.S.A.

Ronald C. Nyhan Florida Atlantic University, Boca Raton, Florida, U.S.A.

David B. Pariser Department of Accounting, College of Business and Economics, West Virginia University, Morgantown, West Virginia, U.S.A.

Terry K. Patton University of Wisconsin, Oshkosh, Wisconsin, U.S.A.

James R. Ramsey† Department of Economics, Western Kentucky University, Bowling Green, Kentucky, U.S.A.

B.J. Reed College of Public Affairs & Community Services, University of Nebraska, Omaha, Nebraska, U.S.A.

William C. Rivenbark University of North Carolina, Chapel Hill, North Carolina, U.S.A.

Ellen Rosell‡ University of Central Florida, Orlando, Florida, U.S.A.

David H. Rosenbloom Department of Public Administration, American University, Washington, D.C., U.S.A.

Bernard H. Ross Department of Public Administration, American University, Washington, D.C., U.S.A.

Michael W. Shelton Office of Budget and Evaluation, City of Myrtle Beach, South Carolina, U.S.A.

Robert W. Smith Department of Political Science, Clemson University, Clemson, South Carolina, U.S.A.

Alan Walter Steiss Department of Urban & Regional Planning, Virginia Polytechnic Institute and State University, Blacksburg, Virginia, U.S.A.

Current Affiliations
* Government Finance Officers Association, Chicago, Illinois, U.S.A.
† University of Louisville, Louisville, Kentucky, U.S.A.
‡ MPA Program, Department of Government, New Mexico State University, Las Cruse, New Mexico, U.S.A.

Jeffrey M. Stonecash   Department of Political Science, Syracuse University, Syracuse, New York, U.S.A.

Theodore J. Stumm   Texas Tech University, Lubbock, Texas, U.S.A.

Kurt Thurmaier   Department of Political Science, Public Policy and Administration Program, Iowa State University, Ames, Iowa, U.S.A.

Joseph P. Viteritti   New York University, New York, New York, U.S.A.

L. Lee Walker   School of Public Administration, Ohio State University, Columbus, Ohio, U.S.A.

Charles W. Washington   School of Urban and Public Administration, Florida Atlantic University, Boca Raton, Florida, U.S.A.

Patricia Wigfall   Department of Public Administration, North Carolina Central University, Durham, North Carolina, U.S.A.

Katherine G. Willoughby   Andrew Young School of Policy Studies, Georgia State University, Atlanta, Georgia, U.S.A.

C. Kurt Zorn   School of Public and Environmental Affairs, Indiana University, Bloomington, Indiana, U.S.A.

Introduction

Organizing a case book on public budgeting and financial management presents a number of interesting challenges. There are several reasons for this. First, the literature on public budgeting and financial management is vast and constantly growing, a fact that is clearly evidenced in the number of books and periodicals that are now devoted to the discipline. Second, interest in the discipline is wide and diverse. One could easily find topics that range from simple analytics of budget behavior, to pure calculus of investments of public funds, to decisions involving capital facilities location. Yet there is an underlying thread that ties them all together into a coherent body of knowledge that is dynamic and, at the same time, has direct practical significance. Third, but not least, is the fact that, despite the remarkable growth the discipline has experienced in recent years, public budgeting and financial management still remain an eclectic discipline, relying heavily on politics, economics, finance, and management for substantive growth. This should be regarded as a welcome challenge for any discipline that has the potential to grow from the richness of other fields with long history and tradition.

The book is divided into two parts, each part further divided into sections. Part I, devoted to public budgeting, addresses several key topics that have become an integral part of contemporary public budgeting: political economy of public budgeting, budget management practices, and budgeting under financial stress. Part II focuses on financial management with an emphasis on accounting, auditing, and financial reporting; financial management practices; and financial management under budgetary stress. Virtually all of the cases are based on real life and every effort has been made by the contributors to present them in a simple, easy-to-understand manner without sacrificing substance or factual rigor. Most of the cases have been drawn from recent experiences to ensure that the readers are able to relate to them easily.

REVIEW OF CONTENTS

The cases accompanying each part of the book are organized in an orderly fashion and associated with the chapter most characteristic of the problem the book would require the readers to address. This structure should also help assigning the cases for use with any other text, if so desired. A unique feature of the book is that each case begins with a brief background discussion of the problem, followed by a description of the concept or concepts that underlie the problem, the case analysis, and, in some cases, recommendations, thus providing an interesting learning framework that combines principles with practice.

The first five cases contained in Part I, Chapters 1 through 5, lay out the foundation of the book. The primary focus of these chapters is on the interaction of politics and economics, and how that interaction affects public budgeting and the challenges it poses for budget decision makers. The first of these cases, "The Political Economy of City Life Cycles: A Comparative Analysis of Services, Expenditures, and Revenues," analyzes the life cycles of a cross section of cities, thirty-five altogether, including some new and some old. Based on the original work of R.D. Norton and his life cycle theory of urban political economy, where the author tried to explain differentiations in the functional responsibilities of local jurisdictions through a historical analysis of their developmental patterns, the study observed significant difference in the service mix, spending patterns, and revenue sources of older and younger cities. Older cities, according to the study, offer a broad mix of services, with the most dramatic differences among redistributive and safety functions, and notable differences in public works and administrative services.

The second case, "Equity and Budgetary Analysis: Determining Fair Shares of Local-Option Sales Tax Revenue," discusses the perennial dispute between different levels of government over the distribution of revenue, in particular of a shared local-option sales tax. This case demonstrates how apparently simple disputes, especially those involving the distribution of resources where there are clear winners and losers, are not easily resolved. It also shows that no one definition of fairness could be universally accepted as the one that should guide the distribution of these revenues and suggests that one needs to examine the issue carefully, determine the purpose of the tax, and then adopt a definition of fairness that seems most reasonable. The third case, "Waste Not, Want Not: School Finance Reform and Educational Equity in New Jersey," provides another example of controversy over equity issue in school finance reform. The case challenges, with good empirical support, the conventional wisdom that state funds provided to poor districts are wasted on salary increases, administrative featherbedding, and reduction in local property taxes. On the contrary, the findings of the study show that funds spent on poor districts are not wasted and that, on average, rich school districts still spend more and have more administrative personnel than poor districts.

In "Confidence, Competence, and Clientele: Norm Maintenance in Budget Preparation," the chapter focuses on budget development in the typical Wildavsky tradition as a dialogue between claimants and reviewers as they try to articulate demands and justify needs. The process illustrates how difficult it is to develop and maintain the norm of competence in budgeting. The last case in this series, "The Political Economy of Outsourcing," explores the decision to outsource government services, whether by privatization or by contracting out with other governments, and the resulting consequences that go beyond the traditions of measuring efficiency and effectiveness, and the simple mathematics of "make or buy" analysis. The consequences, as the case shows, are manifestly political, strategic, operational, and financial.

The next set of cases presented in Part I can be divided into four distinct categories: *budget execution, budget management systems, budget analysis,* and *capital budgeting.* Together, these cases constitute the core of what can be loosely defined as "budget management practices." The next case, "Issues in Budget Execution," discusses the principles and procedures of budget execution along with some emergent issues affecting the execution process at the federal level. Although the issues are discussed in the context of federal budget execution, one could easily extrapolate them to state and local budgeting.

Chapters 7 through 12 present some of the more commonly used budget management systems, from program budgeting ("Do Program Budgets and Performance Indicators Influence Budget Allocations? An Assessment of Mississippi Budgeting"), to performance budgeting ("Performance Budgeting in Florida: To Muddle or Not to Muddle, That is the Question"), to zero-base budgeting ("Implementing and Managing Zero-Base Budgeting"), to target-based budgeting ("Target-Based Budgeting in Lincoln County"), to strategic budgeting ("Strategic Planning and Budgeting in the "New Texas:" Putting Service Efforts and Accomplishments to Work"), to outcome-based budgeting ("Transition to Outcome-Based Budgeting: The Case of Missouri's Department of Revenue and Milwaukee, Wisconsin"). Budget management systems have a long history that goes back at least to the Progressive Reform Movement of the late nineteenth century, which culminated in the development, among other things, of the well-known line-item budgeting system. As the budgetary problems facing governments became complex over the years, the need for better and more efficient management systems also became acute. The number of systems developed since then has increased significantly. Today, there is hardly a government that does not use a budget management system of one form or another. The six cases included here provide a good account of how governments and agencies play a balancing act in trying to cope with their budgetary needs through careful use of these systems.

The next two chapters, Chapters 13 and 14, discuss the role analytical tools play in public budgeting, especially those related to budget forecasting, forecasting process, and budget analysis. The chapter "Forecasting the General Fund Budget of a Local Government" shows how simple forecasting tools such as regression analysis could be used to forecast long-term revenues and expenditures. Perhaps more important than that is the scenario these forecasts produce for a local government in terms of budget deficit and surplus, and an exploration of the options that are available to government to deal with a problem. In the next case, "Revenue Forecasting," the chapter examines the legal, economic, political, and technical elements of the budget process to predict the general fund revenue of a state government. The highlight of the model is how the authors use a systems approach to explain the forecasting process and how it affects the final outcome (i.e., the forecasts). The lessons learned from both of these cases should be useful in establishing, fine tuning, and evaluating budget forecasts. The next case, "Parties, Professionalism and Changing Budget Battles in New York: 1950–1997," analyzes how budget battles are fought along party lines. Citing the experience of New York, the study reestablishes the age-old argument that parties, as broad aggregations of differing sets of interests, serve as the primary vehicle for representing differing views of taxation and spending issues. All budgets belong to one of two categories: operating or capital. In the last few years, there has been a resurgence of interest in capital budgeting. Capital budgeting for roads, bridges, buildings, vehicles, and equipment is crucial to the economic growth and development of a community. Without this basic infrastructure, most governments will find it difficult to sustain the revenue base they need to provide the necessary services. Yet investments in this vital area of government have been declining in recent years.

The three cases specifically devoted to capital budgeting, Chapters 16 through 18, deal with three topics that frequently appear together: capital budgeting practices, capital programming, and capital financing. In the first of these cases, "Capital Budgeting Practices in Local Governments: A Comparative Study of Two States," the chapter explores the capital budgeting practices among local governments in the states of Louisiana and North Carolina. By isolating the key features of similarity and dissimilarity between capital budgeting practices in the two states, the study discerns the common influences on the use of capital budgeting and examines any differences that may exist, and speaks to the significance of those differences. The unending questions of how best to finance capital improvements in the face of declining revenues are discussed in the next two chapters. In "Procedures for Programming and Financing Capital Improvements," for instance, the chapter illustrates a set of procedures and guidelines appropriate to the formulation of a capital improvements program in terms of various financing options, ranging from pay-as-you-go to borrowing to the use of capital reserve funds. In "Can the Riverside Community Afford a Massive Debt-Financed Capital Improvements Program?" on the other hand, the chapter addresses the question of debt affordability. It highlights the typical debt burden borne by a government and calculates its debt service requirements for capital improvement plans, followed by estimates of results from alternative revenue policies and their implications for government.

The chapter, "Budget Analysis: A Study in the Budgetary Practices of a Small Community," provides an interesting assessment of budgetary practices of a local government, from its budget management system to an analysis of its revenues and expenditures. The chapter also provides a critique of the government's overall budgetary practice in view of the criteria used by Government Finance Officers Association (GFOA) when rating a government budget. In a different vein, Chapter 20 discusses the "Budgeting for Unincorporated Area Services." This is an area of budgeting that has been seriously overlooked in the literature. The case studied in this chapter highlights the peculiar problems faced by a government in deciding the appropriate sources to be used to provide the needed infrastructure and programs to residents in its unincorporated area. In doing so, it affords the reader an opportunity to understand the legal and fiscal decisions made by a government in selecting from a set of policy alternatives the most appropriate policy to budget for the provision of services in the unincorporated area for its citizens.

The remaining cases within Part I focus on budgeting under financial stress. The last two decades have been saturated with all kinds of with budgetary problems, which often forced governments to devise difficult alternatives, sometimes with unanticipated consequences. The five cases presented in this section, Chapters 21 through 25, discuss the most frequently suggested means used by governments to deal with some of these budgetary problems. In the first of these cases, "The Collapse of Fiscal Home Rule in the District of Columbia," the chapter provides a critical analysis of the causes and consequences of fiscal problems of a city that changed within a span of twenty-two years from a state of home rule independence to almost fiscal bankruptcy. The perilous financial condition presented in the study provides a vivid picture of financial mismanagement, political brinkmanship, and poor administrative control, and how all this contributed to the financial predicament that left the city without much hope. The next chapter, "City—County Consolidation: The Case of the Illusive Cost Savings," raises serious questions about the real benefit of consolidation. The end result of any consolidation is cost savings, but there is a trade-off between savings resulting from efficiency in consolidation and equity. There are also questions of effectiveness and accountability. When budgets are consolidated across jurisdictions, these questions can produce conflicting results, as the chapter amply demonstrates, invalidating any efforts that prompt consolidation.

The discussion on the means to deal with declining budgets is continued into the next case, "Innovations in Public Budgeting: Applying Organizational Development Processes to Downsizing," which examines how to successfully apply a simple theoretical model of organizational development (OD) and culture to deal with the problem of cutbacks, or downsizing, as some would like to call it. The case reports the processes and interventions in some detail and provides a summary of what can be gained from such an approach. In "Cutback Management in Georgia: State Agency Responses to Fiscal Year 1992 Budget Reductions," the chapter examines the responses of state agencies to a sudden and severe revenue shortfall which necessitated cutbacks in agency operating budgets. Based primarily on interviews with principal budget officers of Georgia executive branch agencies and selected officials in the state's Office of Planning and Budget, the study provides a clear understanding of state budgeting and cutback management in government. The final chapter in this group, "The Struggle for Better Budgets: The Curious Case of the Legislative Conference System in New York State," evaluates the state's experience with a revamped budget process, in particular its conference committee system, that many believed to be initially ineffective. Using anecdotal information, news accounts, interviews, public documents, and relevant budget literature, the chapter concludes that the use of the conference committee system, a common practice in many states, is a "failure" and that the "fix" is not addressing the principal reason behind late state budgets—politics.

Part II of the text concentrates on financial management. Financial management has become increasingly important in government. Its activities transcend all departments and agencies, while providing the mechanisms for managerial planning, control, and evalua-tion. The recent changes in government finance, especially those related to shrinking revenue, have brought management of a government's financial affairs to primary impor-tance. Not only have resources shrunk, but, more important, taxpayers are demanding greater efficiency and accountability from their government for every tax dollar they spend. Consequently, financial management has become the principal means for effectively handling tax dollars and their corresponding usage. What is becoming more evident in today's government is that financial management is as much a *management* as it is a finance function. Every program a government undertakes requires commitments of finan-cial resources, making the finance manager's role a crucial one. How finances are managed, controlled, and planned may eventually determine how policy makers make other deci-sions.

Another important role financial management plays in government is accountability. The information produced and dispersed by finance managers is vital to both internal and external operations of a government. Internally, financial management produces informa-tion that is critical to the decisions legislators and administrators make on policy formula-tion. Externally, it produces information that is as important to governmental oversight agencies, citizens, creditors, and insurers as it is to the financial stability of the governmen-tal entity. This is clearly evident in the first five chapters of Part II, Chapters 26 through 30, which present cases involving accounting, auditing, and financial reporting.

With the introduction of the double-entry accounting system and formal reporting procedures some years ago, government accounting and financial reporting practices have reached a new level of sophistication. Governments today are expected to use accounting and reporting procedures that are uniform across the board to ensure effective evaluation of their financial performance. In spite of this, evidence exists of widespread noncompli-ance with these standards. The most common form of noncompliance is the use of cash basis reporting, as opposed to accrual or modified accrual basis of reporting prescribed by Generally Accepted Accounting Principles (GAAP).

The first case, "Cash Basis Financial Reporting for Local Government: A Compari-son with GAAP," takes up the issue by introducing cash basis financial reporting as practiced by a small government, then addressing the relationship of cash basis reporting to an operating budget, and finally explaining how it differs from GAAP. Since there is no GAAP for cash basis reporting, the study suggests that the accounting principles used and the format of financial statements often vary across governments even within the same state. The second case, "Changes for Governmental Financial Reporting," examines the changes all reporting procedures will have to go through in the coming years under the new statement 34 issued by the Governmental Accounting Standards Board (GASB). The need for the new system grew out of the belief that the current state of governmental financial reporting is antiquated because it does not provide information to assist users in the assessment of long-term financial health. The new system is expected to fill this gap. Not only that, it is also expected to provide readers with information to assess operational accountability that is lacking under the current reporting structure. The third case, "Financial Analysis of the City of Mesquite, Texas, Using Comprehensive Annual Financial Reports," provides a thorough analysis of financial performance based on the current system of reporting. Although the new system will produce additional information that the current reporting system does not contain, the methods suggested in the study, nevertheless, will be useful for similar analysis elsewhere.

The fourth case in this series, "Governmental Audit Recommendation Follow-up Systems: Implementing Recommendations Effectively," presents a framework for a audit recommendation follow-up system. While auditing has become a common vocabulary in financial management practices of government, very little attention has been given to audit recommendation follow-up. The *Government Auditing Standards* (GAS) requires that all auditing reports contain recommendations that governments can use to improve their management operations. An audit follow-up system essentially monitors the progress the audited government makes in implementing these recommendations. This case examines the need for such a system by systematically analyzing the recommendations a government has received, and then explaining what these recommendations mean in the context of financial management and accountability. In the next case, "Benchmarking and Cost Accounting: The North Carolina Approach," the chapter illustrates the importance of benchmarking as a management tool to promote process improvement. One of the weaknesses of benchmarking is that it lacks a set of generally accepted criteria by which service costs can be compared. The chapter shows how the accuracy and comparability of performance and cost data can serve as ingredients of benchmarking and financial measurement.

Chapters 31 through 45 of the book deal with a set of topics that form the nuts and bolts of financial management in government. They also include some recent developments in financial management tools and practices. The case "Comparative Analysis of Key Governmental Financial Indicators" evaluates the financial performance of two compatible governments in terms of their spending and taxing policies as well as the degree of comparability in their resource, cash, and debt management policies. The study uses these comparisons to isolate areas where significant difference exists and to measure the extent of this difference.

The series of chapters continues with a discussion of financial accountability in "Financial Performance Monitoring and Customer-Oriented Government." While accountability can be measured in many different ways, the chapter provides a customer-oriented approach in which a government actively solicits community (customer) involvement in financial decision making. By involving the public in the policy process, the government elevates the importance of the customers (i.e., the public's understanding of financial problems, the alternatives to deal with those problems, and their boundaries).

In "Determining the Full Cost of Residential Solid Waste Services," the chapter shows how the concepts of full and differential costing can be applied in government.

Although these concepts are nothing new, their application to government has been limited. Using the experience of residential solid waste services, the chapter demonstrates how these concepts, when applied properly, could improve both service provisions and accountability in government. In "Reengineering Financial Management: Pittsburgh's Unisource 2000 Project," the chapter demonstrates the importance of reengineering as a tool that can be used to deal with persistent financial problems. The case, in particular, shows how the city of Pittsburgh has pursued process engineering, using information technology to radically redesign its budgeting and accounting systems.

The next four cases focus on two of the most important financial management functions in government, namely cash and debt management. Both of these functions are the essence of what a government primarily does to manage its financial resources. In "Learning from Experience: Cash Management Practices of a Local Government," the chapter presents a simple example of cash management practices of a local government and the problems it encounters in the process. The primary objective of cash management is to have enough cash available to a government to meet its payment obligations that arise from normal operations during a fiscal year, and to ensure that any idle balance that remains is kept to a minimum. The chapter discusses the extent to which the government has been successful in achieving these objectives through a variety of efforts that range from cash budgeting, to management of cash flows, to investment of idle balances. It also offers a number of recommendations that could be realistically implemented by the government without making any changes in the existing management structure. The next chapter, "The Evolution of Debt Management Policy and Program: A Case Study of Kentucky," traces the development of a centralized debt management policy of a government in response to the need to enhance efficiency and management process. Reduced federal financial support, as the case argues, created the need for the government to issue more debt to finance infrastructure and other public investments which led to greater legislative scrutiny and more public pressure to intelligently respond to debt management. The net result is the evolution of a professional staff and the establishment of a centralized, innovative office that permits the government to manage this important public policy issue.

In the last few years governments have been actively seeking out financial tools, instruments, and measures that traditional practices would not have permitted. There are two apparent reasons for this emerging trend: the proliferation of new and sophisticated financial instruments, especially those related to investment of funds, and relative prosperity of many of these governments that allow them the flexibility to venture into a world of enormous financial promise, but also of disaster. In "The Orange County Debacle: Where Irresponsible Cash and Debt Management Practices Collide," the chapter presents a classic example of such a disaster. It provides a succinct analysis of the financial bankruptcy that became the hallmark of Orange County, California, resulting primarily from irresponsible financial decision making that ultimately cost the government $1.5 billion in losses. In "The Gordian Knot of a Project Revenue Bond Default," the chapter presents an opposite situation, where prudent judgment and effort helped a government reorganize its bond default. The study examines how successful use of a workout (where the bondholders and the issuer attempt to resolve their differences) can help resolve a bond default. The differences, in this instance, arose because of the complexity surrounding the arrangements under which the bonds were issued. The bond default discussed in the study is different from the traditional defaults in which a government fails to meet its obligations. This one is labeled as "technical" since all principal and interest payments were made on time, although from sources not anticipated in the original financing.

Government bonds, like those issued by the private sector, are rated. A higher rating reflects a government's ability to meet its financial obligations on time and also its ability to attract investors who are willing to pay a higher premium for its bonds. Since the rating agencies do not disclose the factors they take into consideration in the rating process, governments can only hope to do their utmost to improve the likelihood of getting a better rating. In "Obtaining a Better Bond Rating: A Case Study," the chapter advocates a proactive approach that would, according to the study, entail establishing a "back and forth" relationship with a rating agency, whereby a government would take the initiative to keep the agency abreast of its financial policy as well as of any new developments that highlight changes and improvements.

The next six cases in this section deal with procurement policies, contracting out for services, management of risks, pension funds, and enterprise fund operations, as well as ethical concerns in financial management, an emerging issue that has not received much attention in the financial management literature. In "Procurement Dilemmas: Social Policies Versus Pure Competition—The Case of Vendor Preferences," the study presents the dilemmas confronting public finance specialists charged with setting, implementing, evaluating, and defending government procurement policies. The focus here is on vendor preference policies, especially those promoting the purchase of in-state or locally-produced goods and services and those encouraging purchases from small businesses and firms owned by women, racial and ethnic minorities, and the handicapped. The next chapter, "Risk Management," provides a bread-and-butter approach to risk management. It also shows how a fairly common set of events can lead to a new catastrophe. The chapter, in particular, looks at the Supreme Court's role in assessing liability in a risk management case, while tracing the evolution of shifting legal responsibilities of local governments to effectively deliver services to citizens. The chapter "The Politics of Pension Investment Returns" analyzes the implications for a public pension system that produces financial loss resulting from poor investment returns. Looking into the nature of the loss, the case first identifies the types of investment portfolios the pension system maintained, then addresses the pension system's delegation of investment decisions to an internal money manager, and finally highlights the political implications of pension investment decisions.

In "Promises and Pitfalls of Contracting for Public Services: The LAWA Case," the chapter focuses on emerging trends in procurement policies by tracing the historical promises and pitfalls that have come to define public service contracting in the twenty-first century. It describes the experiences of the Los Angeles World Airport (LAWA) with purchase of service contracts. The exploration of LAWA's approach provides insight on how managers meet the community's needs for efficiency and equity by capitalizing on contracting for public services.

In "Enterprise Fund Operation in a West Texas City," the chapter examines the enterprise operations of a government that uses a variety of enterprise funds to provide a wide range of services. The study reviews the enterprise fund structure and operations, examines these operations to determine whether problem areas exist, and then provides a set of options for solving these problems along with some considerations which may affect the choice of solutions. The final case in this section, "Ethical Issues Facing Private, Not-for-Profit Hospitals in the United States: The Case of the Methodist Hospital System," looks at how financial pressures often lead to resistance to charity care services, shifting the ultimate burden to government. Drawing on a legal case, the study shows how, when under pressure, the charitable institution and the government resort to accounting gimmicks to defend their positions.

Managing financial activities under budgetary stress is just as difficult as managing budgets under poor financial management conditions. In "Financial Management Under Budgetary Stress," the chapter discusses the general fiscal problems faced by a government and how its financial management initiative assisted in controlling the government expenditures. It also suggests a number of expenditure reduction initiatives adopted by the government and the budget agency, emphasizing the financial management plan initiative. Perhaps the biggest financial management problem under budgetary stress is the one faced by poor school districts. Public schools, especially those located in poor and disadvantaged areas, are hard-pressed to provide quality education for lack of adequate resources. In "The Richmond Unified School District Default: COPs, Bankruptcy, Default, State Intervention, and Epilogue," the chapter looks at an extreme example of fiscal stress where a school district literally defaults. By examining the events leading up to the default, the default, and the aftermath of the default, the case provides insights into the workings of the municipal bond market, the use of exotic financial techniques, the fragile relationship between a state and its local governments, the problems of a continuing operating deficit, and the need for clear fiscal control.

Another recent measure to deal with the problem of public finance resulting from declining revenues is to use tax abatement, especially property tax abatement, as an incentive to attract and retain business and related activities in a political jurisdiction. Tax abatements, if properly applied, have the potential to generate substantial revenues for a government through rapid economic growth. In "Property Tax Abatement: A Case Study of San Marcos, Texas," the chapter identifies a number of factors that are both essential and realistic that can be used to evaluate the tax abatement policy of a government. The chapter examines the interrelationship of property tax abatement and assessment, and measures the impact of this relationship using the criteria developed earlier.

The last two chapters in the book, Chapters 49 and 50, are devoted to an area of budgeting and financial management that has been receiving wide attention in the literature in recent years. Privatization of public services, public–private partnership, and, of late, "reverse privatization" have become the *sine qua non* of public management studies as governments continue to grapple with the problems of efficiency, productivity, and declining revenues. In "Financing a Recycling Facility Through a Public–Private Partnership," the chapter looks anew at public–private partnership as a means of providing public services in the face of declining government revenue. It analyzes this partnership through a competitive request for proposals (RFP) process leading to the selection of a firm to build and operate a cost-effective materials recycling facility. The case meticulously details the negotiation process and final contract with the firm to determine the net financial impact to the government. It also examines the operational stipulations that help ensure that the facility can be profitable, while safeguarding the government revenue stream from extreme fluctuations in the market. In the final case, "The Chickens Come Home to Roost: The Publicization of Private Infrastructure," the chapter looks at a thirty-year public–private partnership in infrastructure that failed a community when the private partner declared bankruptcy and abandoned its infrastructure commitments, forcing the public partner to inherit the problem. This is a new development in the public–private partnership; no proper term is available to describe a failed relationship, or no adequate strategies available that a partner could use to assume the responsibility without facing the challenges from a tax-resistant but service-demanding citizenry. The study carefully traces the development of the partnership and the causes for its collapse, and evaluates the challenges to the government in undertaking its former partner's delivery system.

Case Studies in Public Budgeting and Financial Management

1

The Political Economy of City Life Cycles

A Comparative Analysis of Services, Expenditures, and Revenues

Joseph P. Viteritti and Thomas W. Matteo
New York University, New York, New York, U.S.A.

More than a decade has passed since R. D. Norton proposed his life cycle theory of urban political economy. Based on an empirical analysis of thirty American cities, Norton explained differentiations in the functional responsibilities of local jurisdictions through a historical analysis of their developmental patterns.[1] Using the 1860–1920 period as a point of demarcation, Norton found that the older industrial cities of the Northeast and North Central states tend to have a more extensive range of service responsibilities and a stronger commitment to social welfare functions than the younger cities of the South and Southwest. He traced the variations to the policy outputs of governing regimes that prevailed during the formative period of the respective cities' public agenda.

According to Norton, older industrial cities that were controlled by political machines responded to the social needs and demands of immigrant populations with a generous assortment of services, a large portion of which were redistributive in nature. Cities of the South and Southwest developed their policy agendas in the context of political regimes that were middle class-based. Their constituents were less dependent on public resources and preferred a mix of local services that was not so burdensome to the taxpayer. Norton also identified a pattern of territorial annexation that influenced the demography and political economy of cities. He found state annexation laws to be more restrictive in northern states where legislatures sought to protect the boundaries of middle class suburbs. The result was to leave behind an urban population with limited residential mobility that was more dependent on public goods and services.

Because of their history of generosity with regard to service provision, the older cities remained attractive destinations for successive generations of immigrant and migrant groups who arrived with acute social needs. Thus local politics kept these cities locked into a redistributive service and fiscal agenda. These older northern cities became less attractive to middle class residents and corporations seeking to avoid higher taxes. Thus

Reprinted from: *Public Budgeting and Financial Management*, 1994, 6(4), 518–541. Copyright 1994 by Pr Academics Press.

many sought alternatives.[2] And beyond the more proximate suburbs, additional choices became available with the birth of newer more cost-conscious cities.[3] The continuing demand to administer redistributive programs in the face of declining revenues became a serious source of fiscal stress among the older industrial cities.[4]

Norton's data covered the 1970 and 1976 fiscal years.[5] This chapter updates and expands Norton's analysis by studying the fiscal policies of thirty-five cities for the 1991 fiscal year. Given the serious fiscal crises that afflicted many of the older industrial cities during the mid-1970s, is there any evidence of a change in course among them? Is there still a major difference between the fiscal policies of older and newer cities?

OBJECTIVES

Specifically, this chapter addresses the following research questions:

1. Do older industrial cities that are concentrated primarily in the North and North Central regions offer a wider assortment of local services than those younger cities found in the South, West, and Southwest?
2. Do the older cities spend more per capita on services than the younger ones?
3. Do older cities spend proportionately more of their operating budgets on "redistributive services?"[6]
4. Do older cities spend proportionately more on debt service? Debt service can be viewed here as either a symptom or a cause of stress.[7]
5. Do the older (and bigger) cities spend proportionately more on administrative overhead? Here we are particularly interested in determining whether the larger older cities suffer from "diseconomies of scale."[8]
6. Do older cities impose higher per capita taxes on their constituents? Stein found that older cities do tax more and relates it to spending for certain redistributive services.[9]
7. Do the older cities exhibit different revenue sources than the younger counterparts? Here we are especially concerned with determining whether younger cities derive a larger proportion of their revenues from user fees, as is often suggested.[10] For example, California was among those states that led the way in imposing user fees for services in an attempt to keep property taxes down.

A three-step approach was adopted in order to address these issues concerning the services, expenditures, and revenues of the thirty-five cities being studied. First, in order to define service patterns, an instrument utilized in a 1988 national survey by the International City Management Association (ICMA) was adapted and sent to each city.[11] Second, both the expenditure and revenue budgets for the 1991 fiscal year in each city were obtained and analyzed. Finally, telephone interviews were conducted with senior officials in each city. These extensive conversations served two purposes: they assured cooperation in completing the modified ICMA instrument, and they helped us to better understand and compare various budgeting categories and formats.

FINDINGS

Among the thirty-five cities studied, sixteen were grouped in the category of older industrial cities. (See Tables 1 through 4.) All but two of these (Oakland and San Francisco)

Table 1 Profile

	Population	Square miles	Density	Budget
Old cities				
Average	1,131,061	96	9,477	3,251,182,590
Baltimore	736,014	79	9,317	1,755,309,723
Boston	574,282	47	12,167	1,363,040,000
Buffalo	357,870	50	7,157	517,148,969
Chicago	2,783,726	228	12,204	5,445,587,506
Cincinnati	364,040	78	4,667	768,297,570
Cleveland	505,616	79	6,400	788,215,000
Detroit	1,027,974	136	7,581	2,329,314,000
Minneapolis	368,383	55	6,686	888,701,661
Newark	275,221	24	11,468	853,675,176
New York	7,322,564	322	22,755	28,224,624,729
Oakland	372,242	53	6,971	682,990,000
Philadelphia	1,585,577	136	11,659	3,627,789,500
Pittsburgh	369,879	55	6,677	777,193,440
St. Louis	396,685	61	6,461	825,269,930
San Francisco	723,959	47	15,502	2,681,830,986
Toledo	332,943	84	3,954	489,933,250
Young cities				
Average	569,302	287	3,034	1,092,849,714
Albuqerque	384,736	95	4,037	791,173,049
Atlanta	394,017	132	2,996	1,827,476,207
Austin	465,622	106	4,393	1,329,065,469
Charlotte	395,934	157	2,523	728,764,778
Denver	467,610	111	4,228	1,471,778,299
Ft. Worth	447,619	277	1,616	675,324,645
Honolulu	871,100	621	1,404	1,037,571,848
Houston	1,630,553	573	2,846	2,325,346,799
Indianapolis	741,952	352	2,108	1,123,647,683
Jacksonville	672,971	760	886	2,372,906,299
Miami	358,548	34	10,546	727,817,730
Nashville	510,784	533	958	949,825,453
Oklahoma City	444,719	621	716	430,120,763
Omaha	335,795	99	3,382	432,091,298
Portland	418,470	103	4,051	1,102,482,183
San Diego	1,110,549	329	3,376	1,463,973,816
Tucson	405,390	99	4,103	807,564,633
Tulsa	367,302	187	1,964	510,800,707
Virginia Beach	393,069	259	1,519	656,412,902

are from the Northeast and North Central states. The remaining nineteen are counted among the younger cities. All but two of the latter group (Honolulu and Indianapolis) are located in the South, the West, or the Southwest. With some modifications, the data generally support the findings that are generated by Norton and other contributors to the research literature mentioned above. It shows that there are real differences in the service mix, spending patterns, and revenue sources of older and younger cities. These findings

Table 2 Services

City services	Old (%)	Young (%)
Public works	87	82
Residential solid waste collection	100	95
Comm. solid waste collection	47	58
Solid-waste disposal	93	84
Street repair	100	100
Arterial repair	80	84
Snow plowing/sanding	93	63
Traffic engineering	93	89
Bridge repair	87	89
Recycling	100	79
Permits	100	95
Wastewater treatment	67	89
Water supply	87	89
Air resources	73	63
Environmental management	87	74
Trade licenses	87	58
Inspection/code enforcement	100	95
Public safety	87	67
Crime prevention	100	100
Highway patrol	47	42
Fire prevention/supp.	93	100
Emergency medical services	100	89
Traffic control/park. enforcement	80	100
Vehicle towing/storage	93	95
Emergency 911 system	93	95
Jails	87	53
Probation	100	37
Board of corrections	100	0
Juvenile justice	67	21
Health and human services	66	47
Sanitary inspection	87	53
Animal control	67	58
Child welfare	47	42
Aging	73	42
Family services	60	47
Youth services	47	58
Hospitals	40	32
Public health programs	87	53
Drug/alcohol treatment	67	42
Mental health/retard.	47	21
Homeless services	80	68
Potters field	87	26
Public housing	73	68
Parks and recreation	55	57
Parks	100	95
Museums	53	63
Botanical gardens	67	63
Zoos	40	58

(continued)

Table 2 Continued

City services	Old (%)	Young (%)
Art centers	33	53
Historical society	40	21
Libraries	73	74
Sports commission	33	26
Support functions	87	80
Building maintenance	100	100
Fleet management	100	100
Payroll	100	100
Personnel	100	100
Labor relations	100	79
Municipal supplies	93	89
TV/radio stations	53	47
Reproduction center	93	84
Public relations/information	80	79
Tax collections	87	63
Tax appeals	80	63
Audits	93	95
Actuary	87	53
Computer services	100	100
Legal services	100	100
Consumer affairs	33	37
Retirement system	73	74
Economic development	62	63
Ports and trade	47	42
Business development	87	84
International trade	53	63
Education	47	34
Elementary/secondary	73	63
University	20	5
Total	77	67

underscore the redistributive fiscal policies that distinguish older cities from younger jurisdictions.

Profile

In addition to their geographical locations, older and younger cities are distinguished from each other by population density. (See Table 1.) The older cities have an average population of 1,131,061 (718,294 without New York). For younger cities the average population is 569,302. The average size of the older cities is 96 square miles: the average size of the newer cities is 287 square miles. Older cities therefore have an average population density of 9,477 people per square mile (8,591 without New York), while in younger cities the population density is only 3,034 people per square mile. These differences in density are consistent with Norton's thesis on territorial annexation, which portrayed older northern cities as less capable of expanding their boundaries. Because their state legislators were

Table 3 Expenditures

	Budget (per capita)	Police		Fire		Education		Parks		Debt service		Administrative overhead		Redistributive services	
		(%)	per capita	(%)	per capita	(%)	per capita	(%)	per capita	(%)	per capita	(%)	per capita	(%)	per capita
Old															
Average	2,309	9.20	203	5.06	112	40.47	873	2.11	47	6.07	144	18.25	266	12.79	254
Baltimore	2,385	10.37	247	5.14	123	39.97	953	1.88	45	6.61	158	13.08	187	15.04	215
Boston	2,373	9.35	222	6.35	151	28.25	670	0.86	20	6.55	156	15.76	268	20.39	347
Buffalo	1,445	8.88	128	6.89	100	58.42	844	1.01	15	5.66	82	na	na	3.27	20
Chicago	1,956	11.79	231	4.64	91	41.00	802	2.94	57	11.69	229	18.01	208	11.65	134
Cincinnati	2,110	3.72	79	4.44	94	36.47	770	2.89	61	10.41	220	14.71	197	8.31	111
Cleveland	1,559	14.31	223	7.09	111	58.91	918	3.26	51	1.65	26	13.17	84	6.79	44
Detroit	2,266	12.32	279	3.34	76	39.67	899	5.28	120	1.54	35	24.86	340	15.46	211
Minneapolis	2,412	6.11	147	3.17	76	32.33	780	4.62	112	10.59	255	13.68	223	8.01	131
Newark	3,102	7.60	236	5.15	160	49.32	1,530	0.53	16	2.91	90	13.00	204	6.77	106
New York	3,854	5.75	222	2.32	89	22.91	883	0.44	17	9.82	378	12.86	382	42.19	1,254
Oakland	1,835	13.94	256	7.77	143	40.26	739	2.91	53	3.22	59	26.72	293	7.05	77
Philadelphia	2,288	8.94	204	3.20	73	37.41	856	0.79	18	7.54	173	27.01	387	23.66	339
Pittsburgh	2,101	7.20	151	5.31	112	55.36	1,163	1.96	41	4.91	103	22.87	215	0.00	0
St. Louis	2,080	10.18	212	3.01	63	43.08	896	1.28	27	3.84	80	na	na	1.97	23
San Francisco	3,704	7.17	266	5.89	218	14.10	522	2.21	82	4.94	183	17.87	569	32.64	1,039
Toledo	1,472	9.63	142	7.23	106	50.01	736	0.96	14	5.31	78	21.86	161	1.37	10

Young

Average	2,045	7.67	142	4.75	86	35.87	705	2.37	45	5.75	106	14.37	181	4.99	72
Albuqerque	2,056	6.76	139	3.29	68	43.18	888	2.37	49	6.38	131	14.66	171	9.26	108
Atlanta	4,638	5.20	241	3.08	143	21.72	1,008	2.03	94	3.79	176	11.92	433	0.20	7
Austin	2,854	4.07	116	3.42	98	24.65	704	1.42	40	4.29	122	14.29	307	14.39	310
Charlotte	1,841	4.96	91	3.81	70	51.33	945	1.62	30	12.42	229	na	na	1.95	17
Denver	3,147	5.35	168	3.07	97	36.71	1,156	2.38	75	3.26	103	11.17	223	16.49	329
Ft. Worth	1,509	8.08	122	5.11	77	40.15	606	1.92	29	7.67	116	10.39	94	1.82	16
Honolulu	1,191	10.82	129	4.29	51	24.26	289	5.36	64	8.99	107	15.48	140	5.26	47
Houston	1,426	10.74	153	6.54	93	36.08	515	1.13	16	6.40	91	11.50	105	5.98	55
Indianapolis	1,514	5.61	85	3.36	51	29.67	449	1.99	30	3.07	46	na	na	5.38	57
Jacksonville	3,526	5.48	193	2.71	95	32.51	1,146	0.72	25	2.62	92	na	na	1.83	43
Miami	2,030	11.27	229	6.01	122	45.84	930	1.48	30	3.34	68	15.66	172	2.62	29
Nashville	1,860	6.99	130	4.14	77	26.14	486	1.67	31	6.64	123	na	na	11.88	163
Oklahoma City	967	14.64	142	14.11	136	31.66	306	2.16	21	7.03	68	26.59	176	0.24	2
Omaha	1,287	7.37	95	5.64	73	46.39	597	4.60	59	6.12	79	10.54	73	0.22	1
Portland	2,635	6.62	174	4.84	127	31.58	832	2.63	69	3.01	79	9.92	179	0.33	6
San Diego	1,318	10.46	138	4.48	59	43.76	577	3.04	40	2.54	33	19.33	143	0.33	2
Tucson	1,992	6.69	133	3.10	62	36.41	725	3.31	66	4.07	81	na	na	5.54	70
Tulsa	1,391	8.38	116	6.52	91	35.62	495	2.79	39	6.53	91	na	na	2.11	19
Virginia Beach	1,670	6.16	103	2.74	46	43.95	734	2.35	39	11.11	186	15.31	143	8.91	83

Table 4　Revenues

	Residential tax		Commercial tax		Income tax		Sales tax		Other taxes		Miscellaneous revenue		State/federal aid		Total revenue	
	(%)	per capita	(%)	per capita	(%)	per capita	(%)	per capita	(%)	per capita	(%)	per capita	(%)	per capita	(%)	per capita
Old																
Average	6.99	131	11.21	233	15.13	195	2.38	51	8.37	161	31.29	524	24.60	480	99.98	1,776
Baltimore	13.99	334	11.91	284	6.81	162	0.00	0	4.51	107	23.05	550	39.74	948	100	2,385
Boston	11.42	271	26.65	633	0.00	0	0.00	0	3.52	84	29.97	711	28.43	675	100	2,373
Buffalo	6.58	110	9.59	160	0.00	0	7.48	125	3.46	58	11.25	188	61.63	1,027	100	1,667
Chicago	9.45	109	14.17	164	0.00	0	4.31	50	22.99	265	37.97	438	11.10	128	100	1,154
Cincinnati	2.31	31	2.09	28	33.38	448	0.00	0	0.00	0	52.43	703	9.79	131	100	1,341
Cleveland	3.78	24	7.75	50	58.50	375	0.00	0	1.92	12	15.45	99	12.48	80	100	641
Detroit	4.02	76	3.73	71	14.46	274	0.00	0	6.03	114	40.69	771	31.09	589	100	1,894
Minneapolis	6.37	104	20.33	332	0.00	0	3.00	49	3.42	56	45.87	749	21.01	343	100	1,633
Newark	7.36	116	15.63	246	0.00	0	0.00	0	7.58	119	34.61	544	34.52	543	100	1,572
New York	2.82	109	22.85	881	11.01	424	8.92	344	12.88	496	9.45	364	32.07	1,236	100	3,854
Oakland	9.92	113	6.62	76	0.00	0	0.00	0	15.14	173	41.52	474	26.81	306	100	1,143
Philadelphia	7.44	104	7.80	109	43.95	612	3.13	44	14.16	197	5.55	77	17.96	250	100	1,392
Pittsburgh	10.78	227	16.17	340	13.15	276	0.00	0	15.14	318	14.11	296	30.65	644	100	2,101
St. Louis	2.88	34	2.88	34	20.27	240	7.43	88	7.55	89	58.20	689	0.80	9	100	1,184
San Francisco	9.35	309	9.35	309	0.00	0	3.78	125	14.26	472	43.65	1,445	19.61	649	100	3,310
Toledo	3.33	26	1.86	15	40.54	316	0.00	0	1.34	10	36.95	288	15.98	125	100	780

Young

Average	10.84	137	12.29	159	1.28	28	11.27	11	5.68	72	45.17	678	13.48	203	100	1,396
Albuqerque	5.90	69	3.78	44	0.00	0	10.60	124	3.36	39	46.09	539	30.27	354	100	1,169
Atlanta	3.10	113	4.65	169	0.00	0	0.00	0	8.88	322	75.55	2,743	7.82	284	100	3,631
Austin	2.95	64	6.89	148	0.00	0	5.48	118	0.16	3	81.52	1,753	3.00	64	100	2,151
Charlotte	24.93	149	22.55	135	0.00	0	0.00	0	16.50	98	18.60	111	17.43	104	100	597
Denver	3.54	70	6.37	127	0.00	0	21.33	425	7.89	157	41.84	833	19.03	379	100	1,992
Ft. Worth	14.19	133	18.81	176	0.00	0	9.50	89	1.13	11	48.85	456	7.52	70	100	934
Honolulu	18.98	173	23.20	211	0.00	0	0.00	0	13.96	127	39.95	364	4.01	37	100	911
Houston	10.53	96	15.79	144	0.00	0	13.51	123	5.89	54	53.41	487	0.87	8	100	912
Indianapolis	15.69	275	25.60	448	6.31	111	0.00	0	11.55	202	27.33	478	13.51	237	100	1,750
Jacksonville	12.00	286	15.00	357	18.00	428	0.00	0	0.00	0	30.00	714	25.00	595	100	2,380
Miami	6.78	75	18.30	203	0.00	0	0.00	0	0.07	1	67.83	754	7.03	78	100	1,112
Nashville	16.45	226	22.72	312	0.00	0	20.45	281	0.00	0	14.38	198	25.99	357	100	1,374
Oklahoma City	8.98	48	3.85	20	0.00	0	36.08	191	9.72	51	35.91	190	5.46	29	100	530
Omaha	10.81	76	16.22	114	0.00	0	25.56	179	10.33	72	32.57	229	4.51	32	100	702
Portland	10.76	194	9.93	179	0.00	0	0.00	0	0.00	0	69.25	1,248	10.06	181	100	1,802
San Diego	7.26	54	8.53	63	0.00	0	11.78	87	3.02	22	63.31	469	6.10	45	100	741
Tucson	1.33	17	1.84	23	0.00	0	17.58	223	2.78	35	44.40	562	32.07	406	100	1,267
Tulsa	5.19	47	2.23	20	0.00	0	38.15	342	4.37	39	47.70	428	2.36	21	100	896
Virginia Beach	26.66	445	7.16	120	0.00	0	4.09	68	8.25	13	19.65	328	34.18	571	100	1,670

more determined to preserve demographic patterns in adjacent suburbs, older cities were not permitted to expand in response to population growth. As poorer racial minorities migrated to these urban centers from the South and abroad and the white middle class began to flee to the suburbs, substantial demographic changes occurred in the northern cities.

As might be expected from their bigger size, older cities, on average, have larger operating budgets. Given the fact that the older cities became somewhat restrictive environments for the urban poor, it is also reasonable to expect that these jurisdictions would have more extensive service demands placed upon them, which in turn would generate higher per capita costs for conducting business. In fact our data show population density to be strongly correlated with per capita spending for redistributive services, police, and administrative overhead.[12]

Services

Using the ICMA instrument as a basis, our survey covers seventy public services that are divided into seven categories. The categories include public works, public safety, health and human services, parks and recreation, administrative support services, economic development, and education. The results of the survey indicate that as a group, the older cities provide a larger percentage of the services listed. (See Table 2.) Specifically, older cities provide 77% of the total services listed, while younger cities provide 67%. Most of the difference is accounted for in four particular categories: public works, public safety, health and human services, and administrative support functions.[13] Differences in parks and economic development are minimal.

As a group, the older cities provided 87% of the services listed in the public works category, whereas the younger cities delivered 82% of these services. The older cities provided 87% of the services listed in the public safety category; in the younger cities the figure was 67%. In the area of health and human services the older cities made 66% of the services available, while the younger cities made only 47% of these services available. And finally, older cities performed 87% of the support services, while younger cities performed 80% of these services.

On the whole these results are consistent with the expectations set in the work of Norton and others. A rich assortment of public works programs is part of a long-standing service tradition in older industrial cities. It is representative of the kind of public commitment that allowed these urban centers to employ immigrant populations and develop into centers of manufacturing and commerce.[14] And now as these cities age, their crumbling infrastructures necessitate further investment and higher infrastructure costs.

The priority given to administrative support services may have a more complex explanation. Once again we might point to the more generous service tradition in older cities. However, as we later examine actual expenditures, it is suggested that, as a function of size (measured in terms of population and budget), older cities may require a more complex support structure for their service delivery systems than younger cities do.

Of all seven service categories observed, the most dramatic differences between the older and younger cities are in two areas: public safety and health and human services. The commitment to public safety, particularly policing, has well planted historical roots in local government. However, it is the growing need for expanded crime-related programs that most likely explains the dramatic differences in this service area between older and younger jurisdictions. Crime is a function of socioeconomic determinants, and as older cities evolved as the depository of poorer, more restricted populations the demand for safety-related services increased.[15]

Closely related to the crime issue is a host of social problems that drive the need for programs in the health and human services category. Commonly defined as redistributive in nature by Norton and others (e.g., Peterson and Shefter) these are the areas of government involvement that are among the most costly to provide. As the literature suggests, they are a continuing source of fiscal stress for cities with an eroding revenue base. They point to the most dramatic difference in the service menus of older and younger cities.

Expenditures

Older cities spend somewhat more per capita than younger cities (See Table 3). The average per capita spending for older cities, including expenditures for education, is $2309. That for younger cities is $2045.[16] As might have been predicted from the mix of services, there are greater differences in how cities spend their money than in what they spend. While our comparison of expenditures by category was not so extensive as our survey of services, the results are still revealing. Our expenditure analysis focused on four basic municipal services (police, fire, education and parks) and three categories of other outlays (redistributive services, debt service, and administrative overhead). The two groups of cities were compared in terms of both per capita spending by category and the proportion of their respective budgets dedicated to each category. These factors measure different phenomena. Per capita spending for an item is an indicator of cost; its proportion of the budget measures its place among spending priorities.

The one service area in which there are no clear distinctions in either the share of spending or the amount of spending is parks. This confirms the findings in the service survey. Although there are not notable differences between older and younger cities in the proportion of their budgets dedicated to police and fire services, older cities spend considerably more for both police ($203 vs. $142 per capita) and fire ($112 vs. $86). For reasons noted above, this is consistent with the larger mix of protective services offered by older cities.

There are notable differences in both the share and the amount of their budgets that older and younger cities spend on elementary and secondary education. Older cities devote a larger percentage (40.47% vs. 35.87%) of their expenditures and more per capita ($873 vs. $705) on education. Since a portion of educational services (compensatory programs) is allocated on the basis of social indicators of need, this pattern of spending tends to reinforce the redistributive policy agenda of older cities.

Older cities spend considerably more per capita on both debt service and administrative overhead, although the proportion of expenditures allocated to these categories is more similar. Older cities spend $144 per capita on debt service, as compared to $106 within younger municipalities. Again, such spending might be characterized as both a source and a symptom of fiscal stress. It is consistent with the stronger focus on public works in the older cities. Per capita spending for administrative overhead in older cities is $266, whereas in newer cities it is $181.[17] This speaks again to the more complex service delivery systems of older industrial cities and to the diseconomies of scale associated with their size.

As may have been predicted from the existing research literature and the data summarized above on service mixes, the most dramatic difference between the spending policies of older and younger cities is found in the area of redistributive services. Older cities spend 12.79% of their operating budgets on redistributive services, while younger cities spend only 4.99% of their operating budgets on redistributive services. The average per capita expenditure for redistributive services in older cities is $254, in younger cities it is $72. As stated above, given the relatively large financial burden associated with these services, they go a long way toward explaining the fiscal stress experienced by our older industrial cities. Further analysis indicates that among older cities there is a significant correlation between total spending and the percentage of dollars dedicated to redistributive services.[18] While much of the difference in redistributive services is driven by demographics (older cities have more dependent populations), it may also, to some extent, be a function of state policy. Cities in the Northeast, for example, are more likely to be required to pay a share of the services that involve federal matching grants (e.g., Aid to Families with Dependent Children and Medicaid). In other regions, where younger cities are, the states pay a full share of the matching grants, absolving localities of responsibility for costs.

Revenues

Older cities do impose higher taxes on their constituents than younger cities. (See Table 4.) Counting residential property taxes, commercial property taxes, sales taxes, and other taxes, the average per capita tax charge for older cities is $771. The per capita tax figure for the younger cities is $514. These higher taxes are consistent with the higher spending.

An examination of the tax structure also reveals some notable differences. Older cities derive a smaller portion of their revenues from residential property taxes (6.99% vs. 10.84%), but per capita charges in this category are nearly the same ($131 vs. $137). While the two groups derive a similar portion of their revenues from commercial property taxes, the older cities raise more per capita from this source ($233 vs. $159). In a sense these patterns are understandable since older cities have had more time to develop a commercial tax base. They also point to a certain irony, however, since younger cities are often perceived as havens from high personal taxes. But these facts only tell part of the story.

Nine of the sixteen older cities and two of the nineteen newer cities have an income tax. On the whole, therefore, older cities derive 15.13% ($195 per capita) of their revenues from income taxes as opposed to 1.28% ($28 per capita) in the younger cities. Seven of sixteen older cities have a sales tax, as opposed to twelve of the nineteen younger cities. On the whole, older cities derive 2.38% ($51 per capita) of their revenues from sales taxes; for younger cities the figure is 11.27% ($118 per capita).

Older cities rely more heavily on a variety of taxes beyond the usual property, sales, and income taxes, whereas younger cities are more inclined to generate revenue from nontax sources. Older cities receive 8.37% of their revenue from "other taxes" at a rate of $161 per capita, while younger cities get 5.68% of their receipts from this source at a rate of $72 per capita. This contributes greatly to the higher tax burden in older cities.

As much as 45.17% of the revenues in younger cities comes from nontax sources, compared to 31.29% in older cities. This amounts to on average $678 per capita in younger cities and $524 per capita in older cities. A large part of the revenues in this category come in the form of user fees. Further analysis indicates that there is an inverse relationship between miscellaneous revenue sources and residential property taxes in younger cities.[19] Nevertheless, when the per capita revenues from nontax sources are added to the per capita costs for all taxes, then the per capita burden to support local services among older and newer cities is substantially narrowed ($1295 for old, $1192 for new).

The final and crucial difference between the revenue sources of older and newer cities is found in the category of intergovernmental aid. Older cities, on average, receive $480 per capita in state and federal aid. It accounts for 24.60% of their revenues. Newer cities get $203 per capita in state and local aid, which amounts to 13.48% of their revenues. It is this intergovernmental aid, much of which is need-driven, that has historically supported the redistributive fiscal agenda of older cities. Likewise, the loss of federal aid since the appearance of the "new federalism" has contributed to the fiscal stress of both city and state governments over the last decade.[20]

SUMMARY AND CONCLUSION

On the whole, the data from this thirty-five-city study supports Norton's findings that distinguish the political economies of the older industrial cities of the North from the younger cities of the South, West, and Southwest, with some modification. There is a measurable difference in the amount of services made available in these two groupings, but there are even larger differences in the mix of services. Older cities offer a broader menu of activities in the areas of public works, public safety, and administrative support services. As predicted by Norton and others, however, the most dramatic difference is found in those redistributive services that are included in the health and human services category.

Older cities spend more per capita on local services than their younger counterparts, and they also seem to expend their resources quite differently. Newer cities tend to direct their spending priorities toward basic municipal services (e.g., police, fire, education, and parks). As anticipated by the service patterns, older cities spend proportionately more on redistributive services (e.g., health, hospitals, welfare, and housing). As Peterson and Shefter have explained, this is a major source of fiscal stress for older cities with a limited and shrinking revenue base. Among basic services analyzed, older cities also spend more per capita on police, fire, and education, all of which can be tied to the same socioeconomic variables that influence redistributive costs.

Older cities spend more on debt service and administrative overhead. The former may be both a function and an outcome of fiscal stress. The latter is to some extent a function of size and complexity of the respective service delivery systems. It may also be explained in terms of the way administrative organizations are historically established by accretion rather than design, making it difficult if not impossible to eliminate bureaucratic units that no longer have utility or purpose.

Older cities do impose larger tax burdens than newer ones. These differences are somewhat modified, however, when various forms of other local revenues are added to the equation that impose a financial burden on constituents. The structure of taxes between the two groups of cities also differs considerably. Older cities are much more dependent on commercial property taxes than residential property taxes, perhaps making them a less desirable place to do business. While newer cities do get a larger portion of their revenues from residential property taxes, the per capita charges imposed on homeowners are similar. Nevertheless, one could certainly make a case that the latter factor has not been sufficiently highlighted in the calculations of public choice theorists.

We should finally note with regard to taxes that at least on the basis of our sample, older cities are more likely to levy an income tax, while the younger group is somewhat more inclined toward a sales tax.

One of the greatest sources of revenue for the older cities remains intergovernmental aid. This emphasizes how the older industrial cities of America remain dependent upon the federal and state governments to pursue their long-standing redistributive agenda. Given the precarious vulnerability of local and regional economies in the northeastern and central states, it points to the growing need for the federal government to assume a greater share of responsibility if redistributive politics and economics are to remain part of the urban agenda.

REVIEW QUESTIONS

1. What is Norton's original life cycle theory of urban political economy? What did he find in his empirical analysis?
2. What are the sources of the data used by the present authors in the study? Are the data the same as those used by Norton? Does that influence their findings?
3. Do the findings of the current study conform to Norton's original theory? If so, discuss how? If no, explain what contributed to the differences.
4. Based on Norton's original theory and the current findings, how would you explain the differences between old cities and young cities regarding the expenditure and revenue patterns?
5. Using the life cycle theory of urban political economy, explain the different activities between old cities and young cities.

NOTES

1. Norton, R. D. (1979). City Life Cycles and American Urban Policy. New York: Academic. Norton divides his study cities into three categories: older industrial include New York, Chicago, Philadelphia, Boston, Pittsburgh, St. Louis, San Francisco, Baltimore, Cleveland, Buffalo, Detroit, and Cincinnati; younger cities include Atlanta, Denver, Columbus, Dallas, Houston, Indianapolis, Jacksonville, Memphis, Nashville, Phoenix, San Antonio, and San Diego; anomalous cities include Kansas City, Los Angeles, Milwaukee, New Orleans, Seattle, and Washington.
2. See Tiebout, C. M. (1956). A pure theory of local expenditures. Journal of Political Economy, 65, 416–424; Buchanan, J. (1971). Principles of fiscal strategy. Public Choice, 4, 1–16. For a critical assessment of public choice theory, see Cebula, R. J. (1980). Voting with one's feet: A critique of the evidence. Regional Science and Urban Economics, 10, 91–107.
3. Miller, G. (1981). Cities by Contract. Cambridge: Harvard University Press.
4. See Peterson, P. E. (1989). City Limits. Chicago: University of Chicago, Press; Shefter, M. (1985). Fiscal Crisis, Political Crisis. New York: Basic Books; Nathan and Adams also found a disproportionate incidence of fiscal hardship among Northeast and North Central cities. See Nathan, R. P. and Adams, C. F. (1976). Understanding central city hardship. Political Science Quarterly, 91,

47–62; and (1989). Four perspectives on urban hardship. Political Science Quarterly, *104*, 483–508.

5.   Norton's findings on city service and spending patterns, and their contributions to fiscal stress have been replicated by other economists. See, for example, Bahl, R. W. (1984). Financing State and Local Government in the 1980's. New York: Oxford University Press; Bradbury, K. L., Downs, A. and Small, K. A. (1982). Urban Decline and the Future of American Cities. Washington, DC: Brookings Institution; Ladd, H. F. and Yinger, J. (1989). America's Ailing Cities: Fiscal Health and the Design of Urban Policy. Baltimore: Johns Hopkins University Press; Bahl's 1969 comparative study of city expenditures actually predated Norton's. See Bahl, R. W. (1969). Metropolitan City Expenditures: A Comparative Analysis. Lexington, KY: University of Kentucky Press. For a comparative analysis of city revenues that appeared at approximately the same time as the Norton book, see MacManus, S. A. (1978). Revenue Patterns in U.S. Cities and Suburbs: A Comparative Analysis. New York: Praeger.

6.   Redistributive services here refer to health, hospitals, welfare, and housing.

7.   See Fuchs, E. R. (1992). Mayors and Money: Fiscal Policy in New York and Chicago. Chicago: University of Chicago Press; Pammer, W. J. (1990). Managing Fiscal Stress in Major American Cities. New York: Greenwood.

8.   Empirical support for the concept of "diseconomies of scale" is long-standing, and can be found in two bodies of literature. Organizational research in both the public and private sectors indicates that as organizations grow a larger proportion of their resources is devoted to coordinative and administrative functions. See Melman, S. (1951). The rise of administrative overhead in the manufacturing industries of the United States 1899–1947. Oxford Economic Papers, *3*, 62–112; Hendershot, G. E. and James, T. F. (1972). Size and growth as determinants of administrative-production ratios in organizations. American Sociological Review, *37*, 140–153; Kasarda, J. (1974). The structural implications of social system size. American Sociological Review, *39*, 19–28. The economics literature is a bit more tenuous. It suggests that economies or diseconomies in size are a function of specific types of service. See Hirsch, W. (1959). Expenditure implications of metropolitan growth and consolidation. Review of Economics and Statistics, *41*, 232–242; Ostrom, V., Tiebout, C. M., and Warren, C. (1961). The organization of government in metropolitan areas: A theoretical inquiry. American Political Science Review, *55*, 831–842; Bish, R. (1971). The Political Economy of Metropolitan Areas, Chicago: Markham; Pack, H. and Pack, R. (1978). Metropolitan fragmentation and local public expenditures. National Tax Journal, *31*, 349–361; Ladd and Yinger, op. cit. See also Bunch, B. S. and Strauss, R. P. (1992). Municipal consolidation: An analysis of the financial benefits for fiscally distressed small municipalities. Urban Affairs Quarterly, *27*, 615–629.

9.   Stein, R. M. (1985). Market maximization of individual preferences and metropolitan service responsibility. Urban Affairs Quarterly, *25*, 86–116. Stein confirmed Norton's use of the age variable as a predictor of city services and spending. Using the SMSA as a unit of analysis, however, he found that age is a predictor of spending for only three of five redistributive services: health, hospitals, and federal welfare. He found spending for housing and municipal welfare to be correlated with city tax burdens.

10. See, for example, Netzer, D. (1992). Differences in reliance on user charges in American state and local government. Public Finance Quarterly, *20*, 499–511; Forrester, J. P. and Spindler, C. J. (1990). Assessing the impact on municipal resources of the elimination of general revenue sharing. State and Local Government Review, *22*, 73–93; Plant, J. F. and White, L. G. (1982). The politics of cutback budgeting: An alliance building perspective. Public Budgeting & Finance, *2*, 65–71.

11. ICMA. (1988). Special Report: Service Delivery in the 90's, Alternative Approaches for Local Governments, Washington, DC: International City Management Association. The ICMA survey had been mailed to 4,870 local governments. Its major categories of service included public works, public safety, health and human services, parks and recreation, and support functions. We added to our survey instrument economic development, education, and debt service.

12. Using a Pearson test we found density to correlate with per capita spending in the following services: for redistributive services r = .77, P = .000, for police r = .64, P = .000; for administrative overhead r = .58, P = .001.

13. There are also differences between older and younger cities in the provision of educational services (old, 47%; young, 34%). This is largely a function of governance, that is, whether the city has a fiscally independent or dependent school system. See also Ref. 16.

14. See Teaford, J. (1984). The Unheralded Triumph. Baltimore: Johns Hopkins University Press.

15. See Ladd and Yinger, op. cit. See also Ref. 12.

16. Cities differ as to whether they have dependent school systems supported through the municipal budget or independent school systems supported through self-generated funds. Our expenditure analysis does not distinguish between cities on this basis. Instead it measures total spending to include public education. If one excludes public education from the total, older cities show a $1436 per capita spending rate, while for newer cities it is $1340.

17. The following cities do not have data available on administrative overhead: Buffalo and St. Louis (old) and Charlotte, Indianapolis, Jacksonville, Nashville, Tucson, and Tulsa (new).

18. Total spending for all cities correlates with the percentage of dollars dedicated to redistributive services, where r = .69, P = .000. Among older cities total per capita spending correlates with per capita spending for redistributive service, where r = .93, P = .000.

19. The Pearson correlation between miscellaneous revenue and residential property taxes indicates r = .70, P = .000.

20. See Carnevale, J. T. (1988). Recent trends in the financing of the state and local sector. Public Budgeting & Finance, *8*, 33–48.

2

Equity and Budgetary Analysis
Determining Fair Shares of Local-Option Sales Tax Revenue

Dan Durning and Richard W. Campbell
University of Georgia, Athens, Georgia, U.S.A.

Analysis is an increasingly important part of the budgetary process, providing information that contributes to informed decisions. A government's budget is the product of numerous policy decisions, made over many years, about what services it will provide and who will pay for them. Such budgetary policy decisions distribute both the benefits and financial burdens of government, and they usually involve difficult choices among competing claims on government resources. When allocating benefits and burdens, elected policy makers consider the political implications of their decisions, but beyond that they also are expected to be concerned about the economic efficiency and the equity effects of their decisions.

The efficiency of alternative policies that provide benefits and impose costs can usually be analyzed well by budget analysts and others trained in public finance and economics. Using formal benefit-cost analysis, the analysts can even suggest which programs should be included in the budget to maximize net social benefits. However, both analysts and decision makers have more difficulty using analytic methods to determine which expenditures and taxes are fairer than their alternatives. When they try to compare the equity of alternative expenditures and taxes, they face many competing measures of equity but no method to determine definitively which is the "right" or best measure.

In the case study described in this chapter, fairness is the key issue in a dispute between city government officials and county government officials over the distribution of a revenue source important to both: a shared local-option sales tax. Claiming the present distribution of the sales tax revenue is unfair, county government leaders are demanding that the county government get a larger share. City government officials reject that demand, arguing that the present tax split is as fair as possible.

In the role of a consulting budget analyst from outside the area, you have been requested to provide advice to both county and city officials on what you think would be an equitable distribution of local-option sales tax (LOST) revenue. As you analyze this issue, you will have to come to grips with competing definitions of equity, the practical impacts of using one definition of equity rather than alternative definitions, and the distributional impacts of differing choices of equity measures. Also, you have to think about the political context of your analysis and the details of implementing any recommendations you make.

THE CASE: THE SALES TAX DISPUTE BETWEEN THE CITY OF GREENLIGHT AND ORANGE COUNTY, GEORGIA

The leaders of the Orange County government are fussing with leaders of the city of Greenlight over the distribution of the one-cent LOST revenues collected in Orange County. Greenlight is the county seat of and only city in Orange County.

The LOST was approved by voters in 1983 and went into effect on January 1, 1984. As provided by state law in Georgia (where the local governments are located), after the referendum, the legislative bodies of Greenlight and Orange County negotiated an agreement on the division of LOST revenue between the two governments. The terms of this agreement were spelled out in a "distribution certificate" signed by the chief executives of both governments. Like many other Georgia local governments, Greenlight and Orange County agreed to split the revenue, based roughly on population. Each would get half of the LOST revenues, reflecting the fact that at the time about half of the county residents lived in Greenlight and the remainder elsewhere. (See Table 1.)

County officials were concerned with the distribution of LOST revenues right from the start, and part of their concern involved the population-based formula. Over time they became increasingly frustrated with the distribution of LOST revenues, which they believed were based on a population formula that did not reflect reality. During the debate in the mid-1980s city officials repeatedly cited 1986 estimates that the city's population was increasing while the population in the unincorporated area of the county was holding steady. Since then, however, the 1990 census shows that the population mix has changed, but not as the 1986 estimates had suggested; much of the county's population growth has occurred in the unincorporated area of the county while the city's population actually declined. (See Table 1.)

Rather than their relative populations, they could have based the distribution of LOST revenues on any other principle they chose. For example, in some counties, local governments split the revenue based on the shares of total property taxes paid by the residents of each city, with the county share based on the property taxes paid by residents

Table 1 Information About Greenlight and Orange County

	1980 population	1986 population	1990 population	Percentage nonwhite	Per capita income	Percentage rent	Average value of house
Greenlight	4,833	6,640	4,737	55.8	$4,662	34.2	$28,900
Unincorporated county	5,462	5,460	9,400	—	—	—	—
Entire county	10,295	12,100	14,137	41.7	$5,421	25.2	$31,200

Note: Orange County figures include Greenlight residents. All numbers except the estimated 1986 population and actual 1990 population are from the 1980 census. The average value of houses is in 1980 dollars. The 1986 population figures are state government estimates. Figures on the percentage nonwhite, per capita income, percentage renting, and the average value of a house were not available for the unincorporated area of the county.

of unincorporated parts of the county. Others factored into the distribution agreement such things as the shares of total tax digest or shares of total expenditures. Still others used population, but weighted the population shares so that city residents were also treated as county residents (which, of course, they are). In some counties, the distribution of the LOST revenue was negotiated with side deals in which one or another local government agreed to take on additional functions in return for a larger share of the revenue. These different distribution agreements could be made because the state legislation authorizing the LOST left it up to the local governments in each county adopting the tax to agree to a mutually acceptable distribution agreement or lose the tax.

The LOST yields Orange County's local governments an extraordinarily large amount of LOST revenue because the county is the site of a large Georgia Power Company electricity plant, which pays a use tax (like a sales tax) on the coal it burns. In 1989, LOST revenues in Orange County were about $2 million. Of that, Georgia Power paid about $1.6 million. As agreed, half of the revenue was distributed to Greenlight and half to the Orange County government.

State Legislation Concerning the Use of LOST Revenues

The state legislation creating the LOST required that it be imposed only in counties in which voters approved it. It also mandated that in the second year the tax was collected all of the revenue was to be used to roll back city and county property taxes. At least in that year, the LOST revenue was to provide tax relief, not to give the local governments additional revenue. The legislation was less explicit about whether LOST revenues had to be distributed as property tax rollbacks after the second year, but did require local governments to show on their property tax bills the amount of the tax rollback resulting, at least theoretically, from the LOST revenue.

The state association representing county governments maintained that legislation authorizing the LOST required that the revenues be used *only* to roll back property taxes. The city association disagreed, and the dispute had not been clarified by state courts. In any case, it would be difficult to determine for sure if the sum of a government's LOST and property tax revenues was greater than the property tax revenues would have been if no LOST were imposed. No one can know the amount of property tax revenues that would have been collected in the absence of a LOST.

The Debate about the Distribution Agreement

Within eighteen months after the Orange County LOST went into effect, the leaders of the county government asked that the agreement be renegotiated. They asserted that the sales tax distribution was unfair because it was counter to both the intention of state law concerning the use of LOST revenues and to promises made to Orange County voters during the campaign for approval of the sales tax. They argued that state law requires LOST revenues be used only to roll back property taxes, not for financing new or expanded services, such as those being provided with LOST revenue by Greenlight. Also, they pointed out the promises made in a newspaper advertisement signed by both county commissioners and city council members in November 1983.

> Why should we levy a 1% tax? Georgia Law requires that property taxes be reduced by the amount collected except for the first year. *This is the only reason—property*

tax reduction. . . . Who benefits? *All Taxpayers*, the City and County will not receive
one additional penny from this tax! [emphasis in the original].

On September 3, 1985, the attorney for the Orange County commissioners wrote a
letter to the mayor and city council of Greenlight in which he asked them to consider
changing the division of the LOST revenue from 50/50 to 60/40. He stated, "This would
help all the citizens of Orange County, both incorporated and unincorporated areas."

Over two years later, in November 1987, the Orange County manager wrote the
mayor and council on the same topic: "It is the intention of the Orange County Board of
Commissioners to come to an equitable distribution of the one percent optional sales tax.
. . . [T]he [County] Commissioners feel an 80% County and 20% City split would be
equitable."

In February 1989, the chairman of the Orange County Board of Commissioners
asked the mayor to join the county in appointing "a Citizens Committee comprised of three
members representing the County and three members representing the City to recommend a
fair split based on a mathematical approach considering overall ad valorem taxes paid,
costs and benefits along with the current population estimates." After little progress was
made on this proposal, the chairman argued the county's position in a letter to the editor
of the local newspaper.

> A distribution formula which could have been and perhaps should have been applied
> considering the factors of budget size and [tax] digest distribution would be a compari-
> son of the property values within and without the city limits. Currently, this would
> equate to about 84% county and 15% city. Adjustments could be made after a considera-
> tion of the value of benefits and services obtained from each government and for state
> and federal mandated activities. . . . I believe in doing what is just and right. I believe
> also the vast majority of our citizens respect the rights of others and are fair-minded,
> God fearing people. I ask that people of Greenlight recognize that they will receive a
> further reduction in their county ad valorem taxes if a fairer distribution is agreed upon.

In August 1989, the chairman wrote a long letter to the mayor of Greenlight, again
outlining the county's position.

> The purpose and goal of the sales tax legislation was to provide equally to each citizen
> some relief from ad valorem taxes through a dollar for dollar rollback. The sales tax
> agreement between the City and County when it was written and as it exists today,
> does not reflect the intentions of the legislation, nor is it equally fair to all taxpayers.
> . . . The situation that exists today allows that portion of the population that lives in
> the incorporated area to pay 16% of the ad valorem taxes and to receive benefit of
> 58.8% of the rollback. . . . A sizeable portion of the sales tax revenue is being used
> to supplement [city services]. The end result is that the taxpayers in the unincorporated
> areas are subsidizing the services of the incorporated areas.

At various times, the county officials pointed out that the county government has
to provide services to the huge Georgia Power electricity plant, located several miles from
Greenlight. In addition, they noted that a boom in the construction of vacation homes
around a lake in the unincorporated part of the county was adding to the county's service
burden. They pointed out that none of the service costs of the power plant or of the part-
time residents in vacation homes were reflected in the distribution of the LOST revenues.

City officials fended off the demands to change the sales-tax distribution. In October
1985, the mayor responded to the letter from the county by asking, "[W]hat fairer way
could one imagine than a distribution based on population?" In addition, he wrote

> There seems to be some misconception among some of the members of your board
> that the City of Greenlight is going to get rich on the 1% Sales tax money. Nothing
> could be further from the truth. We will simply be able to do some things we could
> not afford to do before.

Again in 1987, the mayor responded to letters from the county by writing, "We
conclude that the present split is just and adequate for all concerned, as closely divided
as is reasonably possible." In 1989, under increasing pressure from the county government
to change the distribution formula, the mayor and the entire city commission wrote the
Orange County Board of Commissioners a long letter rejecting any change. Key parts of
that letter include the following:

> There has always been some ridiculous notion by some of the former commissioners
> and some of you that the City has more money than it knows what to do with. This
> is not the case now nor has it ever been. Since 1983–84 the City has been able to make
> major changes upgrading our waste water systems and our water systems including the
> building of two new water tanks. Without these improvements, none of the new indus-
> tries that have located recently in our county would or could have come. . . .
>   None of the [alternative] proposed sales tax percentage splits . . . are fair. To
> think the City could simply adjust its budget by any of these [lower] percentages is
> totally ridiculous. It is obvious you have no thought or consideration as to the financial
> difficulties that would be imposed upon the City should your proposal be agreed to.
> You are interested in only one thing: take as much from the city as you can. They will
> manage.

City officials maintained that the distribution is fair because it is based on population,
like the LOST distribution formulas in most other counties. They said that because half
of the people in Orange County live in Greenlight, the city should get half of the LOST
revenue. They noted that the county's share is distributed mostly as tax rollbacks to the
richest taxpayers in the county—those with the land and property of the greatest value.
Thus, if the county were to get more of the LOST revenues, most of it would go to Georgia
Power and other wealthy landowners, not to middle-income homeowners. In effect, LOST
revenues would be shifted largely from poor- and middle-income households living in the
city (a majority of whom are racial minorities) to Georgia Power and other affluent landowners in the county.
    Also, city leaders argued that it would be unfair to take away the city's LOST
revenue because the city depends on it to pay off the capital debt it incurred for its water
system. The city entered into this debt based on the expectation that it would have LOST
revenues to pay it off. If it lost the sales tax revenues, it would have to raise taxes, probably
dramatically. About 4 mills of property tax would be needed to make up for each $100,000
of LOST revenues shifted from the city to the county.

Local Government Finances in Greenlight and Orange County

The 1989 Greenlight budget totaled about $1.5 million, which excluded enterprise funds
for water, sewer, and garbage pickup services. City residents paid no city property tax
because its share of the LOST revenue "rolled it back" to zero. Also, city residents enjoyed
water and garbage pickup services at low rates because LOST revenues were used to
subsidize the enterprise fund services.

The city government would have needed a property tax of 41.21 mills to raise as much money as the LOST revenue. Before the sales tax was enacted, city residents paid 12 mills of city property tax and 7 mills of county property tax.

The 1989 county budget was near $5.5 million. All county residents (including those living in the city) paid 11.5 mills of county property tax. They got a 4.31 mill rollback in taxes. Thus, at least theoretically, the county property tax would have been 15.81 mills if the LOST had not been adopted.

Table 2 shows the assessed taxable value (the tax digest) for the city of Greenlight and the unincorporated parts of Orange County. From this tax digest, it is easy to see the importance of the Georgia Power's electricity generating plant for the county government. The assessed value of the plant is nearly half of the total assessed value of property in unincorporated areas.

It should be kept in mind that the county government collects property taxes on property in both unincorporated Orange County and in Greenlight. Thus, the 1989 county tax digest totalled $232,946,453.

Unhappy County Campers

Despite efforts by the county government to convince the city to renegotiate the agreement, the 50–50 split remains in effect. Although the county leaders abhor the distribution agreement, state law did not permit them to force the city to negotiate a change. In fact, state law had no provisions for changing the distribution; once the formula was adopted, it apparently was set forever.

In the late 1980s, some unhappy county residents threatened to file a suit to challenge the LOST revenue distribution. Also, during that time, the County Board of Commissioners tried to call a referendum on the question of whether or not the sales tax should be revoked. They hoped that voters would approve an end to the LOST (and the distribution agreement), then later they (the voters) would approve reinstating the LOST and a new distribution agreement would be negotiated.

Table 2   Assessed Taxable Value in Greenlight and Orange County

	City of Greenlight	Unincorporated Orange County
Locally assessed real property	$16,463,548	$97,893,090
Total personal property	6,284,393	5,312,718
Total motor vehicle	4,827,719	13,076,177
Total mobile home	134,672	1,633,452
Total public utility assessment	1,573,231	96,581,386[a]
Total gross digest	29,283,563	214,496,823
Exempt property	5,118,897	5,715,036
Total taxable property value	$24,164,666[b]	$208,781,787

[a] Most of this property is owned by the Georgia Power Company.

[b] The taxable value is 40% of the assessed value of property. To calculate how much revenue a mill of property tax would raise for the city of Greenlight, multiply $24,164,666 times .001. To calculate how much a mill of property tax would raise for Orange County, add the total taxable property value for both Greenlight ($24,164,666) and Orange County ($208,781,787) and multiply that amount times .001.

CASE ANALYSIS: BUDGET ANALYSIS WITH EQUITY AS A CRITERION

This case asks a budget or policy analyst to suggest either a fair distribution of the LOST revenues or an approach to finding a distribution that is acceptably fair to both governments. As with any analysis in which equity is a major criterion, this task is difficult for one main reason: no one measure of fairness can be proven to be superior to all alternative measures. Because of that, the analyst lacks a definitive "yardstick" to use in comparing alternative distributions to identify the "best" one. Thus, when evaluating the equity of alternatives, analysts can argue that one is more or less fair than others, but cannot prove that it is.

In addition, the case is complicated by other factors, including the following:

Because this is a zero-sum issue, every dollar gained by one government is lost by the other. As a result, equity considerations are complicated by political considerations. A redistribution of funds would mean fewer services or higher taxes for one government and more services or lower taxes for the other. The elected officials who can deliver the latter are more likely to be re-elected than those associated with the former.

Details complicate the larger equity question. For example, the city government based some of its capital expenditures on the expectation that it would receive the same sales tax revenues in the future that it had received in the past. If those revenues are taken away, it will have to impose substantial additional property taxes on residents who, on average, are poorer than noncity residents.

The city can refuse to renegotiate the agreement. To overcome that refusal, the county has threatened to force a referendum to get rid of the sales tax. It is not clear if that threat is enough to induce the city to act, or whether the county should try to make deals with the city to lessen the impact of changing the distribution—deals that would avoid the loss of the sales tax or the cost of a lawsuit.

The complexity of the analytic task leads to an important question: What can a budget or policy analyst do to help policy makers confront such a complex issue? Our answer is that analysts could provide great assistance through one or both of two services: (1) structuring the issue so that the competing choices and their consequences are clear to decision makers and the public, and (2) organizing and participating in a process designed to help the parties to the dispute work out an agreement that both will view as fair. In the sections that follow, we discuss how these types of assistance could be provided.

Structuring the Issue and Informing the Policy Makers

Typically, budget/policy analysts are taught to analyze policy issues using a series of steps adopted from systems analysis. For example, Weimer and Vining (1992) suggest a series of tasks for analyzing a problem to be solved and then another series for comparing alternatives to find the best solution. They urge analysts to work nonlinearly, performing tasks as information becomes available or as epiphanies strike. Thus, their model envisions these tasks as a structure for the work to be done, but the work can be performed iteratively or in any sequence the analyst chooses.

Such a modified systems analysis approach would likely be a good guide for the analyst assisting Greenlight-Orange County. Using such a guide, the analytic tasks would include

Understanding the context of the issue. An analyst can be effective only if he or she understands the history of the issues, the contentions of the competing sides, the structure of power in the local government, and the personal dimensions of the dispute.

Identifying and defining the problem. It is important to address these questions: Is the status quo unacceptable? If so, why? What is the nature of the problem that makes a change in policy desirable?

Determining the goals of the policy. If some problem exists, then a policy change will be designed to achieve—or come closer to achieving—public policy goals. So to determine which action, if any, is needed, it is necessary to determine the purpose of the action.

Selecting specific measures to be used to compare alternatives to determine how well they achieve the policy goals. Such measures often include the efficiency, effectiveness, equity, and political feasibility of policies. These concepts must be operationalized so that explicit comparisons can be made. When multiple criteria are used, it may be necessary to establish priorities among them, perhaps by assigning them different weights.

Identifying a set of reasonable alternative ways of reaching the goals.

Gathering the information needed to compare the alternatives based on the chosen criteria.

Providing analysis to decision makers on how the different alternatives compare based on the criteria, and if appropriate, recommend a preferred alternative based on the analysis.

In this case, it is clear that equity is a key criterion to be used to compare alternatives. In the discussion that follows we provide some information related to equity and to several of the analytic steps noted above. First, we examine whether or not there is a problem with the existing distribution. Then we suggest different measures of equity that could reasonably be used to compare alternatives and identify the distribution method that likely would be preferred if a given measure of equity were selected as the one that should guide the distribution decision. Finally, we determine the consequences associated with one alternative method of distributing the LOST.

Is There a Problem with the Present Distribution Method?

To begin the analysis, a budget analyst would explore the nature of the problem. To do so, he or she would talk to city and county officials to get their perspectives, but also would employ one of the most powerful tools available to analysts, long division. Both methods would provide insights into the issue of whether or not the existing LOST distribution is fair.

The arguments of city and county officials have been summarized in the case, and they should be carefully considered by the analyst. In addition, the case provides data that permit the analyst to examine more closely who is getting how much from the present LOST distribution. According to these data, in 1989 both local governments received half of the $2 million in LOST collected in Orange County. As shown in Table 3, that distribution resulted in a $166 per capita share for city residents and $165 per capita share for residents in unincorporated areas. Although on the surface that distribution of shares seems fair, a deeper examination of it might yield a different conclusion.

To probe the distribution more deeply, it might be helpful to answer the following question: Does a per capita distribution of LOST revenues result in city and noncity

Table 3 Estimated Per Capita Shares of 1989 LOST Revenues

Benefit recipients	City share	County share	1986 population (est.)	Per capita share
City residents	$1,000,000	$100,000[a]	6,640	$166
Noncity residents	0	$900,000	5,460	$165

[a] We assume that city residents get a share of the county LOST benefits approximately in proportion to their share of the total tax digest. About 10.4% of the county tax digest consists of property in Greenlight.

residents getting (1) equal shares of property tax rollbacks or (2) an equal amount of services financed by LOST revenues? The information discussed below provides persuasive evidence that the answer to both questions is no.

If LOST revenue is used mainly for property tax rollbacks, the owners of property in the city received a much greater benefit in 1989 than owners of property outside the city. As shown in Table 4, the owners of city property received a 45.52 mill rollback of their combined city and county property taxes compared to a 4.31 mill rollback for owners of noncity property. The reason for this differential is clear; over half of the county's residents live in Greenlight (according to the 1986 estimates), but only about 10% of the assessed value of property in the county is located in the city. As a result, over half of the LOST revenues in 1989 were distributed to the owners of property, making up only 10% of the tax digest.

Assuming LOST revenues are used for rollbacks, of the $900,000 rollback in 1989 noncity property taxes, $416,266 was provided to utilities, mainly the Georgia Power Company, which pay 46.3% of the property taxes collected from owners of noncity property in Orange County. The remainder of the rollback went to other property owners.

If LOST revenues are used primarily to pay for services, fairness might be achieved if each government received LOST revenue shares that represented equal dollars per unit of service demand. Using that definition of fairness, a per capita distribution of LOST revenues would be fair if residential population is a good measure of the demand or need for services. In that case, service need is a direct function of residential population, so adding 100 residents to an area would add 100 units of service need or demand. In that situation, a government with half of the residential population could argue that it should receive half of the LOST revenues to pay for half of the service need per unit of demand to be satisfied with the revenues. In many counties, including Orange, focusing only on residential population as the basis of service need ignores other factors that create the need for public services. For example, in Greenlight-Orange County, local governments

Table 4 Property Tax Rollback with Present LOST Revenue Distribution

	Rollback amount	Tax digest	Mills reduction
City residents	$1,100,000	$24,164,666	45.52
Noncity residents	900,000	208,781,787	4.31

Note: Mills reduction is calculated as [(rollback amount/tax digest)(.001)].

provide services not only to residents (those who live there), but also to the Georgia Power Company plant that pays much of the sales tax collected in the county; daytime visitors and workers, including commuters who have homes in one location and work in others; part-time residents with vacation homes in the county; and businesses and industries that require more services than residents. Thus, local governments with identical residential populations may have very different service needs, and a per capita distribution may not reflect those needs.

This brief analysis indicates that the distribution of LOST revenues between Greenlight and Orange County may not be fair to some taxpayers living outside Greenlight. At a minimum, it provides a reason for examining more closely whether changes in the distribution method are needed, and if so, what method would be better.

Different Measures of Equity

When considering whether or not the existing LOST distribution is fairer than alternative distributions, it is essential to determine how equity in this case might be measured, or in other words, how the equity criterion could be operationalized to be used to compare different distribution methods. Various definitions of equity have been suggested by different authors, including Savas (1978) and Stone (1988), who were writing for policy analysts and researchers. Savas, for example, differentiates between several types of equity, including equal outputs, equal inputs (per district, per unit area, or per capita), equal satisfaction of demand (equal inputs per unit of demand, equal inputs per complaint, and equal inputs per politically weighted complaints), and equal payments (for equal amounts of service or for equal ability to pay). Stone offers a similar topology of equity definitions, differentiating between three main types of equity:

> Horizontal equity, meaning equal treatment (e.g., inputs, outputs, satisfaction of demand) for people of the same rank.
> Vertical equity, meaning unequal treatment of people of different ranks; that is, some groups of people deserve larger shares because of their circumstances.
> Process equity, concerned with how decisions to distribute benefits and burdens are made. Stone quotes Robert Nozick (1974), who argues that "a distribution is just if it came about by a voluntary and fair process."

Stone (1988: 41) writes that "one major divide in the great debate about equity" is whether distributions should be judged by criteria of process or by criteria concerned about who gets what.

Although Savas and Stone provide different ways of viewing equity, neither can tell analysts what measure of fairness they should use to determine if some expenditure or tax—or, in this case, the distribution of tax revenue—is equitable. Ultimately, the selection of an equity measure must be based on value judgements, which usually should be made by the people with the legitimacy to make them: elected officials. However, budget analysts can present arguments that some approaches are fairer than others and can provide evidence about who will be helped and harmed by the adoption of alternative measures of equity.

Goals of the LOST and Measures of Fairness

To compare alternative distribution methods, it seems important first to address a core issue: What is the main purpose of this policy instrument? How did the state legislature intend for local governments to use LOST revenues: to reduce property taxes, to help

Table 5 Distribution Methods Associated with LOST Purposes and Measures of Fairness

Purpose of the LOST	Measures of fairness	Appropriate distribution method
Property tax relief	Amount of property tax relief received by each property taxpayer	All revenue to county government; county mills reduced the same number for each property taxpayer
	Amount of property tax relief as a percentage of property tax burden	Government shares based on percentage of property tax revenues paid by residents of each local government in county
	Proportion of sales tax paid	Government shares based on income, wealth, or other indicators of sales taxes paid
Finance services	Governmental shares of services financed by LOST revenues	Each local government gets share based on its share of county population (county government gets share based on percentage of population outside cities)
	Percentage of services provided by local governments	Government shares based on each local government's percentage of total tax digest or total expenditures or on point of sale
	Percentage of services provided by local governments (weighted)	Government shares based on each weighted population or tax digest, or on point of sale
Redistribute revenues	Horizontal equity in distribution of rollbacks or services	Property tax credits for lower-income households

local governments pay for additional services, or to help poorer residents? In Table 5 we suggest related measures of fairness for each of the three competing LOST goals. Then we propose the distribution method that likely would be most appropriate for each measure of fairness.

For example, if the purpose of the LOST is to provide property tax relief, horizontal equity may be achieved if each property taxpayer receives the same reduction in property tax mills. Alternatively, equity may be achieved if each property taxpayer receives the same *percentage* reduction in property taxes. This second alternative recognizes the fact that city dwellers pay property taxes to both the city and county governments, and they will pay proportionally higher property taxes than comparable property owners living in unincorporated areas even if they get the same millage reduction.*

If the purpose of the LOST revenue is to pay for additional services, horizontal equity may be achieved by allotting each local government shares based on shares of services financed by LOST revenues (Savas's equal inputs per capita or per government; we discussed above why equal inputs per capita may not be fair). Alternatively, the LOST revenue could be divided based on the percentage of service need or demand met by the local governments (equal inputs per service need). Using this second definition of equity, the distribution of service need would have to be measured and the distribution of LOST revenues would be based on that. Possible measures of service need include shares of total tax digest, total governmental expenditures, and the point of sales tax collections. For example, it could be argued that the best unit of measure for service need is the tax digest; that is, the need for services increases directly as the dollar value of property increases. If true, shares of LOST revenues should be distributed between the governments according to their share of the total tax digest.†

A third LOST policy goal could be to redistribute revenues. That purpose could be achieved by giving property tax credits only to lower-income households. Such a distribution would have horizontal equity if households with the same income or wealth received the same tax credits regardless of whether they live in or outside the city.

Identifying the Consequences of Different Methods of Distributing LOST Revenues

Once alternative measures of fairness and related distribution methods have been identified, it is possible to carry out the next phase of the work—to examine the consequences of each alternative being considered. Several consequences could be identified. We suggest that the first cut of the analysis focus on the financial consequences and address the issue of how different distributions of LOST revenues would affect relevant interest groups. Specifically, it seems important to determine how the LOST revenues would be distributed (1) among county taxpayers living inside and outside Greenlight, and (2) between the city and county governments.

We will leave it to the student-analyst to select the most promising methods and determine their consequences. We will illustrate with one example how this work might be done, however, and what information could be provided to policy makers.

While Greenlight officials might balk at such an assumption, let us assume that we decided that the state legislature intended for LOST revenues to be used to provide property tax rollbacks. If so, the distribution of revenues between the city and county governments should make little difference to leaders of either government because the LOST revenues

---

* For example, assume the owner of city property pays a property tax rate of 5 mills to the city government and 15 mills to the county government. The owner of property outside the city pays only the 15 mills to the county government. If LOST revenues provided each property with a 5-mill rollback, the owner of city property would get a 25% reduction while the owner of noncity property would get a 33.3% reduction. An alternative rollback method would be to reduce the millage rates of each by the same percentage. For example, a fixed 20% rollback would mean a 4-mill rollback for the owner of city property and a 3-mill rollback for the owner of county property.

† This distribution method, however, would ignore the fact that city property is also located in the county. If that fact were taken into account, the LOST revenue distribution would be based on the following formulas:

City government share = city tax digest/adjusted county tax digest

County government share = city + noncity tax digest/adjusted county tax digest

Adjusted county tax digest = 2(city tax digest) + noncity tax digest

will simply be passed on to taxpayers. To make sure the rollbacks are distributed fairly, all of the LOST revenues could be provided to the county government, which would administer the rollbacks. The rollbacks could be either the same amount per dollar of assessed value or the same percentage per dollar of assessed value.

If the rollbacks were to be the same amount per dollar of assessed value, each Orange County property taxpayer in 1989 could have received a rollback of 8.596 mills. That rollback can be calculated as follows. First determine how much a one-mill rollback would reduce property tax collections. Given the total county tax digest of $232,946,453, a one-mill reduction in the tax rate would mean that tax collections would fall by $232,946. (Multiply the tax digest by .001.) Then, by dividing the property tax reduction resulting from a one-mill rollback into the LOST revenues ($2,002,408/232,946), it can be determined that an 8.596 millage reduction could be financed by the $2,002,408 in LOST revenues.

In Table 6, we show how the LOST revenues would have been distributed in 1989 among city and noncity residents if based on shares of tax digest. This method of distribution would have directed most of the LOST revenues to owners of property outside the city. Also, it would have increased the benefits of the LOST revenues for utilities from an estimated $481,099 with the present distribution to $843,737. The owners of city property would have received less than 20% of the LOST revenues that they actually received in 1989.

After calculating the financial consequences of this and other alternative methods of distributing LOST revenues, it is essential to consider some of the advantages and disadvantages associated with each. For example, the use of equal millage rollbacks appears to treat property owners equally, but also raises some difficult questions. Does it make sense to take money (as allocated by the existing LOST revenue distribution) from city residents, many of whom are poor, to give to the Georgia Power Company, a giant public utility? Aside from giving more LOST revenues to Georgia Power, this method of distribution would shift money from city residents and property taxpayers to county property taxpayers, who on average are more affluent than city residents. Is that fair or wise? On the other hand, is it fair to give low-income residents of the city more benefits from the LOST than are given to low-income noncity residents, as happens with the existing per capita distribution method?

Table 6 Distribution of LOST Revenues as Property Tax Rollback Assuming Equal Rollback Per Dollar of Assessed Value of Property

Benefits to	Tax digest	Mills	Total rollback	Percent	1986 population	Per capita shares
City property owners	$24,164,666	8.596	$207,720	10.4	6,640	$31.3
Noncity property owners	$208,781,787	8.596	$1,794,688	89.6	5,460	$328.7
Total	$232,946,453		$2,002,408	100.0		
City property owners (without utilities)	$22,591,435	8.596	$194,196	9.7	6,640	$29.2
Noncity property owners (without utilities)	$112,200,401	8.596	$964,475	48.2	5,460	$176.6
Utilities	$98,154,617	8.596	$843,737	42.1	—	—
Total	$232,946,453		$2,002,408	100.0		

We leave it to the student-analyst to wrestle with these and other complicated questions associated with the different distribution methods. It should be quickly clear that there are no right answers to most of the questions we have raised. The analyst's work must thus be judged by how well the alternatives are analyzed so that decision makers are provided with complete information about the implications of either continuing with the present distribution method or switching to an alternative method.

Suggesting a Process for Solving the Sales Tax Dispute

Instead of or in addition to the analysis of alternative methods of distributing LOST revenues, an analyst may assist his or her client by helping set in motion a process that would enable the city and county leaders to negotiate a mutually satisfactory agreement, one that meets a definition of "process equity" as mentioned earlier. Such an agreement would require creative thought, side deals, compromise, and open minds, and it seems unlikely that such an agreement could be made without the involvement of facilitators or analysts from outside the county or perhaps a mediator to finally resolve the dispute.

For example, the analyst might suggest that the city and county immediately set up a negotiating committee, and outline who would be on the committee and how they would be chosen. If such a committee were appointed, the analyst might suggest some ideas to serve as starting points for finding an acceptable compromise. Some possible suggestions might include the following:

> Because residents of unincorporated Orange County pay higher property taxes than they did in 1983 (before the sales tax was adopted), the city would agree that city residents would have no net reduction in (city and county) millage from the 1983 levels. It would levy enough city mills to make the total property millage equal to 19 mills, the city's millage prior to passage of the sales tax. The tax revenue raised from the city millage would be transferred to the county for its use.
>
> The city would agree to freeze its sales tax revenue. It would agree that it would not receive, for a specified number of years, an amount in excess of its sales tax revenue in 1989 (or 1988, or whatever year seems best). It would distribute to the county any dollar amount of sales tax above the base-year revenues.
>
> The city and county government would propose adjustments to the per capita distribution of property tax revenue based on expenses that are not reflected well by the population proportion. For example, the city might show how much it spends, in excess of the amount it is reimbursed, on water services that directly benefit county residents and request an adjustment for those expenditures. The county could request an adjustment for its expenditures on the services it provides to households who have dwellings in Orange County, but because they are not full-time residents, do not show up in the official population figures. Also, it could request an adjustment based on its expenditures for the services it provides to Georgia Power. The mediation committee would examine these claims and make adjustments to the distribution agreement to reflect these extraordinary expenditures that are not fully represented in the population figures.
>
> Perhaps the city and county could find some way that any payments from the city to the county (as described above) would be used by the county to replace some existing user charges or be provided in the form of a per-household tax rebate so that the benefits would be distributed primarily to households. If the tax relief

were in the form of property tax rollback, most households in unincorporated Orange County would receive only a minor property tax reduction—no matter how large the county's share of the sales tax. Only a reduction in fees or a direct per-household tax rebate would provide households in unincorporated areas with significant tax reductions and help equalize the tax benefits going to comparable households inside and outside Greenlight.

By working as a staff person in this type of process, the analyst would help facilitate the search for a mutually acceptable agreement. This type of participatory policy analysis would require different approaches and skills than the traditional analytic approach. (See Durning, 1992.)

SUMMARY AND CONCLUSION

In this case study, we described an apparently simple dispute between a city and county government over the distribution of tax resources. When the dispute is examined closely, however, it is shown to be one that cannot easily be solved. Like most fights for resources, any change in the distribution of LOST revenues will give additional funds to the winners and take funds from the losers.

When confronting this issue, analysts and decision makers quickly realize that the basic issue is fairness, and they find no one definition of fairness that will be universally accepted as the one that should guide the distribution of these revenues. Their challenge is thus to examine the issue carefully, determining the purpose of the LOST revenues and adopting a definition of fairness that seems the most reasonable to them and the contending parties. Alternatively, they may help resolve the dispute by serving as a mediator or by assisting in a process designed to help the city and county leaders find a compromise that is mutually acceptable.

The issues raised in this case have broad applicability. The distributional and political considerations alluded to above would be relevant to analysis associated with taxation decisions generally and are not limited to the local-option sales tax. Moreover, while this case involves one community in one state, local governments across the country are experiencing fiscal pressure from decreases in federal aid and citizen resistance to increases in property tax levies. As local governments continue to strive for diversification of their revenue bases, options on state sales and income taxes are likely to become more common, and how the revenue from these sources is distributed is likely to receive more attention from policy makers.

REVIEW QUESTIONS

1. Assume that the time is early 1991, after the 1990 census results have been released, instead of 1990. How would the 1990 census information likely be used in the debate about the distribution of LOST revenue and how should it be used in the analysis?
2. How should the following issues affect the analysis of the LOST revenue distribution? What is the relation between who pays the LOST and who gets the benefits of the LOST? What redistribution of government benefits or burdens

results from raising taxes through LOST instead of through property taxes? Who wins and who loses?

3. How likely is the city to agree to renegotiate the LOST distribution agreement? Suggest how the county might be able to force the city to renegotiate. Consider both internal (government to government) and external (bringing outside pressure to bear) approaches. What role, if any, should an analyst play in helping to persuade the city to renegotiate the agreement?

4. The state legislation authorizing the LOST does not indicate that the LOST revenue should be used to aid lower-income households by reducing their tax burdens or providing them with additional services. Despite that, do you think that the distribution method should reflect a goal of helping lower-income households more than higher-income households and businesses? If so, why and how would it affect your analysis? Should it affect your analysis?

5. What do you think is the main justification that the present distribution method did not count the residents of Greenlight as also being the residents of Orange County? What are the arguments for and against changing the distribution so that the county share reflects the entire population of the county?

6. Given the difficulty in achieving a consensus locally to change the distribution formula, what should the state role be? Should it require that local governments negotiate a formula every five (or ten) years? Should it impose a formula? Should it impose a negotiation process that would require a mediator?

7. Assume the year is 1990 (before the 1990 census results are available) and you are an experienced budget and policy analyst from outside Orange County who has been asked as a consultant to conduct an unbiased, objective analysis of this problem and to suggest a method or framework for solving it. What advice would you give to the city and county governments on how this dispute should be solved? Be sure to support that advice with appropriate analysis.

REFERENCES

Durning, D. W. (1992). *Distributing Georgia's General-Purpose Local-Option Sales Tax Revenues. An Examination of the Present Policy and Some Options*. Athens: Carl Vinson Institute of Government.

Durning, D. W. (spring 1993). Participatory policy analysis in a social service agency: A case study. *Journal of Policy Analysis and Management*, 21(2), 297–322.

Nozick, R. (1974). *Anarchy, State, and Utopia*. New York: Basic Books.

Savas, E. S. (April 1978). On equity in providing public services. *Management Science*, 24(8), 800–808.

Stone, D. (1988). *Policy Paradox and Political Reason*. Glenview, IL: Scott, Foresman/Little, Brown College Division.

Weimer, D. and Vining A. (1992). *Policy Analysis: Concepts and Practice*. Englewood Cliffs, NJ: Prentice Hall.

3

Waste Not, Want Not
School Finance Reform and Educational Equity in New Jersey

William A. Firestone
Rutgers University, New Brunswick, New Jersey, U.S.A.

Margaret E. Goertz
University of Pennsylvania, Philadelphia, Pennsylvania, U.S.A.

School finance equity suits have become a fact of life in many states. Recently equal numbers of suits have been resolved by state supreme courts in favor of plaintiffs suing to increase funding to poor districts and the state defending the status quo. Cases are still pending or have been acted on by lower courts in another 19 states (Harp, 1995). The acrimony resulting when legislatures must respond to court mandates is often extreme. In 1990, when New Jersey's Supreme Court declared the state's school funding system unconstitutional for the second time in twenty years, then-governor Florio and the Democratic legislature moved quickly to respond to the challenge by passing the Quality Education Act (QEA). That law increased state aid by almost 25%, established a moderate foundation for each student in the state, and phased out general aid to wealthy school districts. It also changed the way the state compensated districts for the higher costs of educating disadvantaged students, applied more stringent caps to school budgets, and limited overall growth in state aid by linking it to changes in per capita income. Within two years, the Republicans won control of both houses of the legislature by substantial margins as well as control of the executive branch.

The debate over the QEA led to charges that the state funds directed to poor school districts would be wasted in increased teacher salaries, administrative featherbedding, and taxpayer relief. At the same time, loss of state funds to wealthy districts would undermine the quality of the state's "lighthouse" programs. To explore these concerns, we conducted a three-year study of the state's richest and poorest districts. We asked how the QEA affected school district resource allocation. How much money was directed to taxpayer relief? How much went to educational expenditures? We also examined how school finance

Reprinted from: *Public Budgeting and Financial Management*, Summer 1996, 8(2), 224–246. Copyright 1996 by PrAcademics Press.

reform affected the size, composition, and salaries of districts' professional staffs. Finally we examined whether QEA narrowed disparities in spending and staff between rich and poor districts.

DATA SOURCES (Methodology)

Data come from two sources. The first comprises quantitative and qualitative data collected on a sample of twelve school districts between 1990–1991 and 1993–1994 (Firestone et al., 1994a; 1994b). The sample included six "special needs" districts—the poor urban school districts targeted by the New Jersey Supreme Court's mandate for expenditure equalization. Four "transition aid" districts—the state's wealthiest school districts that were to lose their minimum aid over a four-year period; and two "foundation aid" districts—non-special-needs districts that qualify for equalization aid and generally fall between the special needs and transition aid districts in per-pupil wealth. The sample was selected to provide variation in district size and geographic location, as well as relative property wealth. In 1990–91, the special needs districts in this sample had a student population that was 71–98% minority and property wealth that ranged from 10–65% of the state average. They spent between $5,000 and $6,700 per pupil. In contrast, the transition aid districts were 13–20% minority, had property valuations that ranged from 140–250% of the state average, and spent between $7,500 and $9,300 per pupil.

The second data source is the New Jersey State Department of Education's consolidated staff report, which contains the salary, educational attainment, and teaching experience of all certificated staff in the state (teachers, administrators, and educational services personnel).

USE OF NEW STATE FUNDING

Bush Jr.
Clinton

Between 1990–1991 and 1993–1994, state aid increased by $885 million to $4.4 billion, a 25% increase. Aid for the "regular education" program—foundation aid—increased by $814.4 million, and aid for categorical programs—special education, bilingual education, at-risk aid, and transportation aid—grew another $457.1 million. These increases were offset by a *reduction* in teacher retirement costs of $415 million due to the refinancing of teacher pensions.

About half (51.3%) of these new aid dollars were allocated to the 30 special needs districts in the state. This level of allocation is not surprising, as the special needs districts received 42% of state aid for current and capital expenditures the year prior to the QEA. In dollar terms, these poor districts received an additional $652.7 million in aid in the three-year period (1990–1991 to 1993–1994) a 61.3% increase over 1990–1991.

Past research on intergovernmental grants for education showed that increases in general aid are used in part for property tax relief. Odden and Picus (1992) reviewed studies showing that school districts increased educational expenditures between 50 and 85 cents for every additional dollar of general state aid. These studies did not look at the impact of the large increases in state aid that resulted from new school funding formulas. When Goertz (1979) examined district response to New Jersey's first major school finance reform, the Public School Act of 1975, she found that districts that received substantial increases in state aid (exceeding 25% of their budgets) spent on average 84% of their new

Table 1 Changes in Education Revenues Per Pupil, by Category (Fiscal Year 1990–1991 to 1993–1994)

District	Change in state aid		Change in local revenues[a]		Change in total revenues	
	Amount	Percent	Amount	Percent	Amount	Percent
Special needs districts (N = 6)	$2,770	68	−$206	−7	$2,564	40
Transition aid districts (N = 3)	0	0	$1,005	13	$1,005	11

[a] Total general fund revenues.
Source: *School District Advertised Budgets* (spring 1992, spring 1994). Figures for 1990–1991 based on actual expenditures; for 1993–1994 based on revised appropriations.

funds on education. The remaining dollars were used to reduce property tax rates by an average of 20%. Low-spending and low-wealth districts directed relatively more of their new funds to education than did those that were more affluent and higher spending.

Table 1 shows changes in education revenues in our sample districts from 1990–1991 to 1993–1994. State aid increased 68% in the six special needs districts, with a range of increases running from 42–116%. Five of the six (all but SN5)[1] allocated nearly all of their new aid to education expenditures, increasing that category between 29–63% in three years (an annual growth rate of 9–18%). Four of these five used the remaining dollars to reduce their property taxes by a small amount. The fifth district (SN6) raised its property taxes substantially. SN5 allocated more aid to property tax relief. A provision of the QEA requiring districts to contribute a "fair share" to support local schools placed a floor on how much tax relief special needs districts could take under QEA.

The four transition aid districts had small changes in state aid, ranging from a loss of 6% aid to an increase of 4%. Since state aid represents less than 10% of these districts' budgets, the dollar changes were also small, ranging from an increase of $43 per pupil to a loss of $55 per pupil. Not surprisingly, these districts raised their local taxes so they could maintain growth in their school budgets of between 2% and 6% a year. When the QEA was enacted, suburban districts feared that the legislation's more restrictive budget caps would force them to "level down" the quality of their educational programs. We found, however, that only one of the four transition aid districts in our sample spent the amount allowed in their caps. Tight economic times, coupled with taxpayer discontent and budget defeats at the polls, led the other districts to develop much more austere budgets than in the past.

Table 2 shows the percentage of increased expenditures allocated to each of six major spending categories: (1) *direct educational expense*—the sum of instruction, attendance and health services, student body activities, and special education and other special needs programs; (2) *plant operation and maintenance*; (3) *transportation*; (4) *fixed charges and other expenses*—the sum of administration, community services, sundry accounts, and insurance costs; (5) *tuition* paid for out-of-district placements; and (6) *capital outlay*.[2] We exclude TR4 from this analysis because it had a program budget, and figures comparable to the line item budgets in the other districts were not available for both years. We also exclude SN6 because we had incomplete data for 1990–1991.

Table 2   Changes in Education Expenditures Per Student, by Category (Fiscal Year 1990–1991 to 1993–1994)

	Special needs districts (N = 5)		Transition aid districts (N = 3)	
	Amount	Percent	Amount	Percent
Current and capital expenditures	$2,632	–	$1,203	–
Direct educational expenditures[a]	1,350	51	743	62
Operations/maintenance	244	9	214	18
Transportation	61	2	13	−1
Fixed charges and other[b]	437	17	420	35
Tuition	197	7	108	9
Capital outlay	278	11	153	13

[a] Direct education expenses are defined as the sum of the following budget items: instruction, attendance and health services, student activities, and special education, and other special needs programs.
[b] Fixed charges and other are the sum of budget lines for administration, community services, sundry accounts, and insurance costs. It excludes teacher retirement and social security costs.
Source: *School District Advertised Budgets* (spring 1992; spring 1994). 1990–1991 figures based on actual expenditures; 1993–1994 based on revised appropriations.

Regardless of district type, about half the increased funds were used for *direct educational expenditures*. Among the special needs districts, two targeted 44–46% of their new dollars to this category, and two targeted 53–57%. Two of the three transition aid districts allocated a similar share of its increased funds to this category—54–56%. One transition aid district spent 83% of its new dollars this way. Both types of districts also had to use substantial portions of their new dollars for *fixed costs*. The percentages ranged from 14–31% among the special needs districts, and 18–44% among the transition aid districts.

The special needs districts spent an average of 8% of their new dollars on *operation and maintenance*, and another 11% on *capital outlay*. In contrast, two of the transition aid districts reduced their spending in this area to direct more dollars into direct education expenses (TR2) or fixed costs (TR1). All three of the transition aid districts increased their spending on capital outlay, but only TR1 devoted a substantial portion of its increased funds to this category of expenditure.

In dollar terms, spending on the direct education expense category increased between $1018 and $2104 per pupil in the special needs districts, about twice as much as that in the transition aid districts (with the exception of TR2). The special needs districts spent relatively more on capital outlay and on operation and maintenance than did the transition aid districts. Spending in the latter category remained stagnant or decreased in the transition aid districts.

It is not surprising to find the special needs districts increasing their investment in facilities and equipment in the early years of the QEA. Years of tight budgets had resulted in extensive deferred maintenance (and hard use) of school buildings and pent-up demands for instructional equipment. For example, SN2 had already developed a wide variety of education and social support programs in the years preceding the QEA. Although it had a very large percentage of students from families in which English was not the native language, it met state standards for the percentage of ninth graders passing the state's high school graduation test on the first try. On the other hand, partly in response to community opposition to extensive investment in education, buildings were in sorry shape, and the district had no room to house growing enrollments and expanded programs, such as pre-school programs. While this district used much of its increase from the QEA for instructional purposes, it made a major investment in improving its facilities. In addition, SN4 had also had a difficult time convincing its overburdened and increasingly elderly taxpayers to fund improvements to its schools. Along with other state funds, QEA dollars were used to bring schools up to building code, modernize science laboratories, and build libraries for its elementary schools.

IMPACT OF FUNDING CHANGES ON EDUCATIONAL STAFF

This section examines how funding changes in the first three years of the QEA affected staffing levels and distribution in the special needs and transition aid districts in New Jersey. We focus on personnel for two reasons. First, the largest portion of school district budgets goes to salaries (Raimondo, 1994); therefore much of how resource allocation decisions affect instruction is through the purchase of personnel. Second, there was considerable suspicion that new funds to urban districts would be misspent. Some feared that new money would be directed to raising already high teacher salaries. In fact, negotiated salary settlements were in the 8% range in the years before the passage of QEA, and teacher salaries were well above the national average. In 1990–1991, the average teacher salary in New Jersey was $38,411, 116% of the national average (NCES, 1994). The other concern was that urban districts would waste funds by hiring administrators who would not directly help students.

Studies of earlier school finance reforms in California (SB 90) and New Jersey (Chapter 212) found that districts that received large increases in state aid under these reforms did not spend a disproportionate amount of these funds on salaries for existing teachers. In California, districts that received at least a 15% increase in revenues spent 85% of these new dollars on additional instructional personnel and instructional materials (Kirst, 1977). New Jersey school districts that received large increases in aid (at least 25% of their budgets) also increased the number of classroom teachers and nonteaching instructional personnel (Goertz, 1979). At the same time, salary increases in these districts stayed below the state average in the first two years of the reform.

Using data from the state-certificated staff files (teachers, administrators, and educational services personnel), we ask how districts allocated funds between salary increases for existing staff and the hiring of new staff, whether special needs districts raised their salaries more than did their more affluent neighbors, whether or not higher salaries helped purchase stronger staff in terms of experience and formal education, and how fiscal changes affected the mix of staff that districts employ.

Salary Increases vs. New Staff

To determine how much money was spent on raises and new staff, we first computed the total increase in salaries from 1990 to 1993. Next, we computed the average salary increase and multiplied that by the number of people on staff in 1990 to get the total salary increase.

The amount spent on new personnel was the difference between the total salary increase and the amount spent on raises.

Statewide, transition aid and special needs districts increased their spending on salaries for certified staff about the same amount per pupil, $775 in the former and $756 in the latter. The special needs districts put somewhat less money into salary increases, however ($637 per pupil vs. $697 in the transition aid districts) and more into new hires ($119 in special needs districts vs. $78 in wealthy districts). The special needs districts put 16% of new salary dollars into new staff while the wealthy districts spent 10% in the same way.

Our sample districts (which were somewhat poorer and lower spending than the total group of special needs districts, and which were somewhat wealthier and higher spending than the average transition aid district) show a more extreme response. The sample special needs districts increased per-student spending on all salaries by $835 per pupil or about 10% more than the full thirty special needs districts, while our wealthy districts increased salary spending by $580 per pupil, or about 25% less. Still, the sample special needs districts put even less into salary increases ($570) and more into hiring new staff ($268, almost a third of the new money) than the thirty special needs districts. The sample transition aid districts put essentially the same amount into salary increases ($634) as the thirty special needs districts. In fact they put so much into raises that they had to reduce staff to make up the difference; funding for staff actually declined $90 per pupil.

While raising salaries so much that staff had to be let go seems irrational, wealthy districts had relatively little short-run discretion. All professional salaries in these districts were geared to teacher contracts that were agreed to for three-year periods. As a result, patterns of raises followed decisions made before the QEA went into effect. District TR3, for instance, reached a settlement with its teachers in 1990–1991, the year before the QEA, that gave teachers annual salary increases of 8.2%. When QEA was passed the next year, the state capped increases on its budget to 6% per year, thus for two years the district would have had to get special voter approval to raise its budget enough to cover its contract. When a new agreement was reached beginning in the 1993–1994 school year, increases were set in the 4.2–4.8% range. Generally, as settlements were reached during this later period, the rate of salary increases went down in both transiton aid and special needs districts, but there were often discontinuities for a few years that forced districts—especially the wealthier ones that had lower budget caps and little support to override those caps—to reduce staff to balance the budget.

Salary Changes

Table 3 shows salary increases for teachers and administrators during the study period. Throughout the state, there was a remarkable consistency in raises during this period. The annualized salary increase was around 5.5% for both personnel categories in both transition aid and special needs districts. Figures are about comparable for the sample districts. What also remained consistent was the salary gap between transition aid and special needs districts. In 1990, teachers in transition aid districts made about 13% more than did those in special needs districts, and the difference was just about the same in 1993. The gap for administrators, while somewhat larger (almost 16%), remained just as stable during this time period. Salary differences were larger in the sample (a 24% difference in salaries between teachers in transition aid and special needs districts and a 27% difference for administrators), however, than in comparable districts statewide.

Table 3 Change in Salaries (1990–1993)

	1990	1993	Annual increase (%)
Panel A: teachers			
State			
Special needs	$37,606	$44,370	5.67
Transition aid	42,614	50,296	5.68
Sample			
Special needs	35,643	41,971	5.60
Transition aid	44,533	51,889	5.23
Panel B: administrators			
State			
Special needs	57,925	68,033	5.51
Transition aid	67,104	78,626	5.42
Sample			
Special needs	53,968	63,755	5.71
Transition aid	69,142	80,791	5.33

While these salary differentials between poor and wealthy districts may be attributable in part to differences in experience and education, personal background factors do not fully explain the variation. Using regression analysis, we determined that throughout the state the average salary difference between teachers in transition aid and special needs districts was $3,271, after controlling for differences in experience and education. The difference for administrators is even higher, $9249, and relatively more of the difference in salaries is explained by district wealth and less by personal characteristics than is true for teachers.

Differences in salaries across districts seemed to affect the quality of the teaching force. The superintendent of the smallest poor district in our sample, a district with one of the lowest average teaching salaries in the state, complained that his district had been the training ground for the surrounding districts for years. Teachers would begin in his district and after two or three years move to a neighboring district that offered higher salaries. This anecdotal evidence is borne out by an examination of staff backgrounds. Statewide, teachers had an average of fifteen years of experience in the poor special needs districts as opposed to seventeen years in the wealthy transition aid districts. More transition aid district teachers had masters' degrees (52%, as opposed to 31% in the special needs districts). The difference in experience between administrators in transition aid and special needs districts is essentially negligible, but that in the highest level of education is noticeable; more than twice as many administrators in wealthy districts (20%) hold doctorates than in special needs districts (9%). The patterns in our sample districts are quite similar.

Personnel Changes

While the districts allocated similar levels of new funds to personnel, the special needs districts invested more heavily than transition aid districts in new staff. In what categories of staff did the districts invest their new funds? This section provides a broad overview of changes in personnel from 1990 to 1993, and then presents more specific analyses for teachers and administrators.

Overview

The special needs districts in our sample increased staff across the board, with the greatest expansion in educational services personnel (14%); the number of teachers and administrators increased by 7% and 8%, respectively. The transition aid districts in the sample increased salaries during this time more than they increased funding on staff overall, so they had to reduce staff. Generally, they held the line on teachers (1% increase) while reducing educational services staff somewhat (5%) and substantially shrinking the number of administrators (25%).

Once again, the degree of change in our sample is somewhat more extreme than in the state as a whole, but we find the same patterns when examining all of the special needs and transition aid districts. Statewide, special needs districts increased their educational services personnel by 11% and teachers by 5% while actually reducing the number of administrators by 2%. Meanwhile, the transition aid districts statewide had a slightly larger increase of teachers (3%) and smaller reduction of administrators (a still noticeable 10%), while actually increasing educational services staff by 3%.

The picture suggested by these percentage changes is overly positive for both transition aid and special needs districts, however, because it does not take enrollment growth into account. During the three years of the study, student enrollment increased 6% in the sample of special needs districts. As a result, the apparently large growth in educational support staff (almost 100 persons across the six districts) was essentially eaten up by population growth, leading to an increase of only 0.65 staff per 1,000 students. Similarly, an increase of 374 teachers only enhanced the number of teachers per 1,000 students by 0.39, and the ratio of administrators per 1,000 students only went up 0.12. The sample special needs districts thus essentially held the line in staffing.

Meanwhile the student population increased 9% in our sample transition aid districts. Although the change in number of teachers was minuscule, the number per 1,000 students actually declined by 5.35. Meanwhile the decreases in administrators and educational services personnel were 2.94 and 1.08 per 1,000 students, respectively.

Statewide, growth was not as pronounced as in the study districts, but it was still a noticeable 3% in the thirty special needs districts and 7% in the 108 transition aid districts. Because of the lower average growth rate, the full set of special needs districts was somewhat more successful in increasing the ratio of teachers to students (increase of 0.84 per 1,000 students), actually cut administrators (reduction of 0.35 per 1,000 students), and increased educational services staff (0.65 per 1,000 students). In the transition aid districts, the ratios of staff to students fell, but at smaller rates than in sample ones (i.e., 2.69 teachers per 1,000 students, 1.33 administrators, and 0.27 support staff).

These averages hide important variation among districts within each category, however. In fact, only three special needs districts in the sample (SN3, SN4, SN6) showed a net increase in staff when enrollment is taken into account (Table 4). Two (SN1, SN5) had a net loss of staff when small staff increases were overwhelmed by large enrollment growth. Their stories are similar to one wealthy district (TR2). In one special needs district (SN2) and one transition aid one (TR4), enrollment growth and staff increases essentially cancelled out. Finally, two transition aid districts (TR1, TR3) were hit by a combination of staff reductions and enrollment growth. Thus, even some special needs districts experi-

Table 4 Comparison of Changes in Teachers per 1,000 Students with Changes in Teachers and Enrollment Growth (1990–1993)

	Change per 1,000 students	Staff growth (%)	Enrollment growth (%)
SN 1	−4.91[a]	3.72[a]	12.13[a]
SN 2	1.21	8.47	6.61
SN 3[b]	5.81[b]	10.58[b]	1.69[b]
SN 4[b]	9.71[b]	13.41[b]	−0.68[b]
SN 5	−4.66[a]	2.92[a]	10.01
SN 6	4.73[b]	9.07[b]	2.45[b]
TR 1	−8.60[c]	−2.24[c]	9.96[c]
TR 2	−3.91[a]	7.65[a]	13.20[a]
TR 3	−11.19[c]	−0.60[c]	17.31[c]
TR 4	0.08	1.31	1.18

[a] District in which staff additions were overwhelmed by enrollment growth.
[b] District in which staff growth and enrollment stability allowed real staff growth.
[c] District in which absolute staff shrinkage and enrollment growth substantially shrank staff.

enced a net reduction in staff, and transition aid and special needs districts alike that increased staff were not able to do so at a rate that kept pace with student growth.

The districts that increased staff responded to a variety of local priorities. For instance, SN3 added 137 teachers (11% increase), seventeen administrators (10%), and fifty educational services staff for a whopping 32% increase. One of the poorest districts in the country, its administration had a vision of making its schools into integrated social services centers to help overcome the economic depression and family dislocation so prevalent in surrounding neighborhoods. To that end, it initiated two elementary programs that called for the expansion of social services staff (social workers, psychologists, etc.) in schools. At the same time, SN3 initiated an integrated social services center in high schools with district funds. The district also started an alternative school for especially difficult middle school-aged children.

SN3 increased services at the elementary level beyond the introduction of social services-oriented programs. Most new staff were placed at that level. Some were hired to expand the number of full-day kindergartens; others were new librarians placed in schools that were getting libraries for the first time. The district also placed at least one mentor teacher in each school to help beginning teachers and others who needed to improve their instruction and added assistant principals at the secondary level.

Some special needs districts initiated new programs even when staff increases did not keep up with enrollment growth. In SN5, preschool enrollment almost doubled from 219 to 412 students between 1990 and 1993; and the district, lacking space in its own schools, placed classrooms in available space in low-income housing projects. In the process, it added about thirty early childhood education teachers.

The transition aid districts that lost staff in relation to the number of students reallocated personnel. For instance, TR3, which seemed to have the largest loss, was actually overwhelmed by massive growth, a three-year 17% expansion in the number of students with a 21% increase in grades K–3. Essentially the number of staff stayed the same, but people were released to help hire more regular classroom teachers. Some of these changes might be seen as a reduction of waste. For instance, eight permanent substitutes were let go. These people had been hired primarily to coach sports teams and were not given regular teaching assignments. Other staff members were supports to the regular program. In 1992–1993, the district laid off three half-time teachers in the school for grades 4 and 5 as well as teachers of physical education, creative arts, and the academic enrichment program in the middle school. The district also sent a teacher who had been assigned as the audiovisual coordinator back to the classroom. These changes did impact on services somewhat. For instance, there was an initial dislocation in the use of audiovisual materials in the high school until a technician was hired.

In TR1, the changes in staff–student ratios were not as large as in TR3, but this district actually lost staff—including nine teachers, a 2% reduction. It also reduced the number of administrators by seven (18%), and educational services staff by six (8%). These figures actually obscure a redirection of staff. In 1991–1992, the district reduced its high school staff by twenty after consolidating two separate schools in one new building. It was able to do so in part because high school enrollments were essentially stagnant. During the three years of the study, however, K–3 enrollments increased 16%, and the district was able to hire some new teachers to address this growth.

Teachers

A central question for any effort that wants to use state funding to improve instruction is how districts allocate teachers. Table 5 provides information on how districts changed their teaching force during the three years after passage of QEA and what teachers' assignments were in 1993 at the end of the three-year period. In our sample special needs districts, the numbers of teachers increased in almost every category identified, especially in the art, music, and foreign languages areas. The major exception is in business and home economics, in which a statewide reduction appears underway. Here SN4 broke with the statewide pattern, adding two business education teachers as part of its effort to increase the availability of electives in the high school. In addition, there was no change in staffing of non-special education categorical and vocational programs. These overall changes in the six districts are similar to, but more extreme than, patterns of change found in the thirty special needs districts statewide.

The transition aid districts held the line in most areas. In the one area, in which they cut back—business and home economics—the reductions were substantially larger than in the special needs districts. What appears to be a large increase in the "other"—non-special education categorical and vocational—classification in fact represents an increase of six teachers in addition to the forty-two already working in these areas. This growth was primarily in TR2 and TR3, districts with large enrollment increases.

Administrators

In the last decade, there has been concern that school districts in general, and urban districts in particular, have an excessive number of administrators. New Jersey citizens feared that QEA funds would be used to bloat what they believed were already excessive administrative staffs. Overall, these fears seemed misplaced in both the rich and poor districts of New Jersey. Statewide, the proportion of certified staff that were administrators in 1990–1991 was quite small and essentially identical in both transition aid and special needs districts (8% in each). Among our sample districts, the proportion of administrators was slightly higher in the special needs districts—ranging from a low of 8% to a high of 10%—and slightly lower in the transition aid ones—ranging from 6–9%. It is thus hard

Table 5   Status and Change in Selected Categories of Teachers

| | Special needs | | Transition aid | |
	Change (%)	Teachers per 1,000 students	Change (%)	Teachers per 1,000 students
Type of teacher				
	Sample			
All	07	70.65	01	67.97
Classroom[a]	07	45.69	01	48.97
Art, music, foreign language	18	4.67	−03	8.10
Business, home economics	−08	2.40	−25	1.53
Special education[b]	11	9.43	11	6.31
Other[c]	−01	8.46	14	3.06
Librarians	04	1.22	08	1.79
	State			
All	05	70.21	03	72.34
Classroom[a]	05	45.46	03	51.15
Art, music, foreign language	09	4.66	01	8.23
Business, home economics	−05	2.33	−25	1.53
Special education[b]	09	8.90	11	7.60
Other[c]	00	8.86	−06	3.83
Librarians	05	1.22	01	1.96

[a] Self-contained regular education and bilingual education classroom teachers.
[b] Teachers in self-contained special education classrooms.
[c] These are largely teachers in special education and ESI resource rooms, compensatory education programs, and vocational programs.

to argue that New Jersey's schools are overstaffed with administrators or that the problem is particularly pervasive in urban districts.

Among the sample special needs districts, there was a slight growth in the number of administrators, primarily at the building level (10% increase in the number of principals and 28% increase in the number of assistant principals). These districts differed from the statewide pattern, in which there was a very slight reduction in the number of administrators. This reduction was led by a shrinking of central offices and somewhat offset by growth at the building level.

The wealthy districts experienced a substantial reduction in administrators, and here our sample districts show a statewide phenomenon in accentuated form. Generally, wealthy districts reduced the number of administrators, especially in the lower-level, central office area. Our sample districts followed this pattern, but with somewhat deeper cuts, especially at the central office level.

There are important differences in how transition aid and special needs districts use administrators. Statewide the poorer districts assign relatively more administrators to the building level than the central office; 44% of the special needs districts' administrators are in buildings in special needs districts as opposed to 40% in wealthy ones. These differences probably reflect the larger size of urban schools in general, and particularly the high schools. The poor, urban schools may also hire more assistant principals to help maintain order. Finally, the central office staffs of the transition aid districts are relatively larger overall than are those of the poorer districts. This difference may be due to differences in average district size: 9,200 students in special needs districts and only 1,800 in transition aid districts; thus the smaller transition aid districts would be expected to have proportionately more central office staff.

CONTINUING DISPARITIES

After three years, disparities in spending, while shrinking, still remained. Table 6 shows spending by major categories in our sample districts in 1993–1994. The gap in total current and capital outlay expenditures per pupil has closed from more than $4000 in 1990–1991 to $1323 in 1993–1994. Differences in per-pupil spending for direct education expenses also narrowed; in 1993–1994, the four transition aid districts spent, on average, $925 per pupil more than the average of the six special needs districts. A combination of dollar growth in the special needs districts and shifts in how districts allocated their funds resulted in more even spending in the categories of operation and maintenance and capital outlay. In fact, the special needs districts in the sample were, on average outspending the transition aid districts by $193 per pupil in this area. The special needs districts remained more heavily burdened by tuition to support students in out-of-district special education placements, however.

These figures do not take into account differences in student need across the two types of districts. In spite of greater student need, the special needs districts still had fewer

Table 6   Changes in Education Expenditures per Student by Category (Fiscal Year 1990–1991 to 1993–1994)

District	Current and capital expenditures	Direct educational expenditures[a]	Operations and maintenance	Transportation and other	Fixed charges and other[b]	Tuition	Capital outlay
SN 1	$8,036	$4,260	$745	$234	$1,270	$1,208	$271
SN 2	8,787	4,847	630	234	2,045	551	365
SN 3	9,003	5,245	1,098	335	1,414	432	414
SN 4	8,123	4,741	727	215	1,592	936	489
SN 5	7,729	4,630	986	241	1,238	349	252
SN 6	10,066	5,326	881	360	2,243	675	521
TR 1	9,446	5,765	988	533	1,533	350	277
TR 2	9,525	6,394	1,048	98	1,618	319	48
TR 3	8,151	4,799	967	459	1,647	207	72
TR 4	9,347	6,113	917	171	1,410	159	370

[a] Direct education expenses are defined as the sum of the following budget line items: instruction, attendance and health services, student body activities and special education and other special needs programs.
[b] Fixed charges and other are the sum of budget lines for administration, community services, sundry accounts, and insurance costs. It excludes teacher retirement and social security costs.
Source: School District Advertised Budgets (spring 1992, spring 1994). Figures for 1990–1991 based on actual expenditures; that for 1993–1994 based on revised appropriations.

resources overall and for their direct education programs. One way to adjust for differences in student need is to examine differences in the districts' "local levy budget"—a budget that excludes spending on all categorical programs. The average local levy budget for the special needs districts in our sample was $6458, compared to $8050 for the transition aid districts. Statewide, on average $1445 per pupil separated the thirty special needs districts from the 108 transition aid districts ($6816 vs. $8261).

Changed disparities in staffing after three years of QEA were influenced by a complex interaction of financial inputs, salary agreements, and demographic changes. At the end of three years, the staffing pattern in these districts reflected their different clienteles. Both sets of districts had about the same number of teachers overall (Table 5). The mix of teachers differed considerably, however. Transition aid districts committed more teachers to the regular classroom and nearly twice as many teachers to academic and cultural enrichment programs, such as art, music, and foreign languages. The transition aid districts also had 60% more librarians per 1,000 students than did the special needs districts. The special needs districts had more staff in programs for low-achieving and non-college-bound students, most notably non-special-education categorical programs (e.g., compensatory education), and vocational programs, including business and home economics. Indeed, without the staffing made available by special programs (and through federal and state categorical aid), students in poor districts would have access to substantially fewer teachers than would students in wealthier ones.

In addition, teachers in special needs districts continued to have less experience, less formal education, and lower pay on average than their peers in transition aid districts. While salary differentials are explained in part by differences in experience and education, a significant part of the difference is driven by variations in district wealth.

Contrary to popular belief, special needs districts were not top-heavy with administrators. In 1993–1994, the thirty special needs districts employed slightly fewer administrators per 1,000 students than did the transition aid districts (7.02 vs. 7.39), and in spite of their greater education needs, the special needs districts had the same number of educational services personnel per 1,000 students than the wealthier communities (8.84 vs. 8.70).

SUMMARY AND CONCLUSION

In this chapter we have examined the response of special needs and high-wealth districts to a major funding change in New Jersey. Contrary to popular belief (but not to earlier research), the special needs districts did not "waste" their new state aid dollars on property tax relief, excessive salary increases, or padded administrative roles. Instead, they used their dollars in ways that met the needs of their students and districts. This meant increased spending on facilities and capital equipment, educational support service personnel, and teachers in expanded academic areas, such as art, music, and foreign language. The new funds they received were not sufficient to erase years of dollar and programmatic inequities, however. In spite of increased investment in staff, students in special needs districts still have fewer classroom teachers and considerably less access to teachers of art, music, and foreign language, as well as to librarians, than those in wealthy districts.

Meanwhile, the state's wealthy communities are facing pressures from enrollment increases, stagnant state aid, and weary taxpayers. While the high-wealth communities continue to provide an educational program that is the model for the state (and the state supreme court), the trends reported here raise a warning flag; continued enrollment growth without expanded fiscal support from the state or local taxpayers may begin to limit the broad range of education offerings that have been taken for granted in these school districts.

Finally, our findings are consistent with, and add to, a small but growing body of research on local district response to state school finance reform. Adams (1994) and Picus (1994), for example, also found that low-wealth districts that benefited from recent school finance reforms in Kentucky and Texas, respectively, used these funds for educational purposes.

REVIEW QUESTIONS

1. Define equity. What does equity mean in the context of school finance and educational reform? What is the net benefit of equity measures on education in general?
2. What kinds of data do the authors use to measure reform and equity? Are the data sufficiently representative of the population? Why?
3. What are the major differences between poor and rich districts? What are the effects of these differences on education?
4. Besides salary increases, where else do the districts spend their money? Why?
5. How does school finance reform affect the size, composition, and salaries of districts' professional staffs?

NOTES

1. Individual districts are referred to by SN for special needs (or poor, urban) and TR for transition aid (or wealthy) and a number referring to the specific district.
2. We have included capital outlay in these analyses for two reasons. One is technical. When the state changed its accounting system in 1993–1994 to conform to generally accepted accounting principles (GAAP), it moved certain categories of capital outlay expenditures from the instructional to the capital outlay category. We thus need to look at both categories to measure real change between 1990–1991 and 1993–1994. Second and more important, we found that several of our special needs districts used new aid dollars to address years of neglect in their facilities and to purchase much needed technology. These expenditures will show up in the capital outlay accounts.

REFERENCES

Adams, J. E. Jr. (1994). Spending school reform dollars in Kentucky: Familiar patterns and new programs, but is this reform? *Educational Evaluation and Policy Analysis, 16*, 375–390.

Firestone, W. A., Goertz, M. E., Nagle, B., and Smelkinson, M. F. (1994a). Where did the $800 million go? The first year of New Jersey's Quality Education Act. *Educational Evaluation and Policy Analysis, 16*, 359–373.

Firestone, W. A., Natriello, G. J., and Goertz, M. E. (1994b). The QEA: Myth & reality *New Jersey Reporter, 24*, 16–25.

Goertz, M. E. (1979). *Money and Education: How Far Have We Come? Financing New Jersey Education in 1979*. Princeton, NJ: Educational Testing Service, Education Policy Research Institute.

Harp, L. (1995). Recent finance activity follows disparate patterns. *Education Week, 14*, 11–15.

Kirst, M. W. (1977). What happens at the local level after school finance reform? *Policy Analysis, 3*, 301–324.

National Center for Education Statistics (NCES). (1994). *Digest of Education Statistics, 1994*, (NCES 94–115). Washington, DC: U.S. Government Printing Office.

Odden, A. O. and Picus, L. O. (1992). *School Finance: A Policy Perspective*, New York: McGraw-Hill.

Picus, L. O. (1994). The local impact of school finance reform in four Texas school districts, *Educational Evaluation and Policy Analysis, 16*, 391–404.

Raimondo, H. J. (1994). *How Much for Administration? Expenditure Priorities Across New Jersey School Districts, FY90–91*, New Brunswick, NJ: Rutgers University, Eagleton Institute of Politics.

4

Confidence, Competence, and Clientele
Norm Maintenance in Budget Preparation

Jerry McCaffery
Naval Postgraduate School, Monterey, California, U.S.A.

Aaron Wildavsky's *Politics of the Budgetary Process* has brilliantly captured the essence of the dialogue that takes place between those who budget and those who review budgets. His observation that it takes more than numbers to be successful in budgeting is still true three decades later; his identification of confidence, competence, and clientele as pervasive themes in the budget process is still persuasive, and his identification of contingent strategies (e.g., making a profit or workload as a means of articulating need in the budget dialogue), is still eminently useful. Wildavsky noted "several informants put it in almost identical words, 'It's not what's in your estimates, but how good a politician you are that matters.' Being a good politician, these officials say, requires essentially three things: cultivation of an active clientele, the development of confidence among other governmental officials and skill in following strategies that exploit one's opportunities to the maximum. Doing good work is viewed as part of being a good politician."[1] This chapter applies Wildavsky's analysis to a midlevel bureaucratic setting at the fleet level in the Department of Navy. These budgets have been built and reviewed at lower levels and will be reviewed and consolidated again at the Department of Navy, Department of Defense, and Office of Management and Budget levels.

Wildavsky's original discussion of budgeting described the federal government when most of its spending was still discretionary, before it became a checkwriter for entitlements and other mandatory payments. In the 1990s budgeting in the Department of Defense may be compared to Wildavsky's description of federal domestic spending in the late 1950s, with its struggles over agency-centered routines as opposed to current federal budgets, which focus on multiple baseline forecasts and the sticky expenditures[2] involved in paying out what is required by changing demographic patterns and various economic factors—factors outside the scope of agency control. Consequently, although this discussion takes place deep within the Department of Navy organization, no matter how unfamiliar the

---

This chapter is dedicated to the memory of Aaron Wildavsky (1930–1993) whose work has had such a great influence on so many who have studied budgeting.

reader is with defense budgeting, those who have a responsibility for agency budgeting will immediately recognize the outlines of this budget discussion.

BACKGROUND

This is a study of a budget review hearing that occurred at the comptroller's level in the U.S. Pacific Fleet (CINCPACFLT) in May 1990.[3] The purpose of this hearing was to begin the FY 92 budget review process by discussing execution of the 1990 budget, reviewing the FY 91 budget base currently under discussion in Congress, and giving guidance on subordinant unit budgets to be submitted to CINCPACFLT in June for FY 92. The hearing made these units consider elements of both budget preparation and budget execution.

The process was dominated by expectations of increasingly scarce resources. In May 1990, Congress was debating additional defense budget reductions beyond what the president had suggested. As a result of discussion over how big these cuts should be, expectations at CINCPACFLT were that future years would see substantial across-the-board reductions as well as some vertical cuts in specific programs. CINCPACFLT intended to pass that message down to its subordinant units, hence the intent of the review was to make sure the fat was out of the unit budgets and that the units were prepared to present tight and accurate budgets for the lean years to come.

A secondary goal for the budget analysis of CINCPACFLT in these hearings was to encourage units to build an executable budget. This was somewhat of a deliberate departure from tradition, since control numbers[4] were usually handed down from the CINCPACFLT budget office to the subordinant units at the start of the fiscal year and the subordinant commands then executed their budgets in accordance with those numbers. Generally, they were not permitted to transfer money between control number accounts (e.g., travel to maintenance), when one account had a surplus and another a shortage. In this year of fast and downward change, another purpose of the hearings was to introduce to the subordinant commands the idea that in this year they could transfer money between accounts, especially if it established a budget structure that would enable them to execute their programs in the coming years when they might not be given transfer authority or have the dollars to transfer. This was to be seen as a one-time opportunity to "fix" unit budget structures so they were synchronized with their operational needs—what the budget analysts referred to as developing an executable fiscal plan.

The hearings were meant to enhance the budget preparation process by ensuring that units

1. Prepared a budget that would be an executable fiscal plan. Thus the question was often asked "will you be able to execute this budget, or are you just giving us back our control numbers."
2. Justified all budget changes, all increases or decreases, and that the justifications were adequate. One question that appeared again and again concerned the length of a budget justification. The answer was that two words was too short, but that more than a paragraph (about 50 words) was too long since the Department of Navy budget office (NAVCOMPT) would never read it, and that "you have to get their attention in the first couple of lines."
3. Understood that the program (work plan) drove the numbers and that the budget process was not just an exercise in manipulating lots of little numbers.

4. Understood that resources were scarce and that they were expected to find and solve their own budget problems and that the budget cost framework they created in this budget process would set the framework for the budget process the following year. They were told that if the budget were just a piece of paper that they had done for the CINCPACFLT budget office, then they had wasted a lot of time.

The hearings lasted four days. Each unit was scheduled separately, with some hearings taking all day and others only half a day. Each hearing opened with a statement about the importance of using the budget as a management tool—an executable business plan—and then proceeded to a warning about how "tight" money would be this year and in the foreseeable future. A representative of each unit made an opening statement and then the analysts for CINCPACFLT addressed questions to the unit representative about his or her own area in each budget. The unit was usually represented by the assistant comptroller for that unit and one or two budget analysts.

Just as in Miles law, which stipulates that where you stand depends on where you sit, budget claimants are expected to take certain positions and budget analysts others. They also have expectations about how the other should behave. In these hearings, the claimant units showed great surprise that the comptrollers expected them to turn in a budget that was a plan that differed from the control numbers. After all, CINCPACFLT had given them the control numbers as part of the budget development process at the start of the year and the budget claimants thought that they would be pleased to get them back in the final product. Telling the claimants to change the control numbers to make the budget executable was not a position the claimants had anticipated the budget office would take.

In addition to these new dimensions, other problems of a more traditional nature kept recurring during the review. A checklist of these would include:

1. The usual technical considerations—for example, average salary fluctuations; inconsistent entries on different forms, one form identifying a reduction of 18 people, another specifying 11; and incorrect entries, e.g., civilian positions entered on the wrong line.

2. The usual analytical thrusts—is this a one-time or continuing expense; how can support costs increase when the number of ships is decreasing; if you can live with a low number in 1991 and 1993, why should there be a high number in 1992.[5]

3. A series of policy guidances that developed out of the give and take of the budget hearing—make this a real work plan; justify changes, because NAVCOMPT[6] will look; say the right thing . . . not defer spare parts, but transfer to the Naval Reserve budget; show your budget decreases; remember that numbers tell two stories: ask yourself what someone could make of these numbers: if FY 92 is up, then you have to justify why you got by in FY 91 and can not get by in FY 92. Without adequate justification, the increase in FY 92 "is just fat." Look for linked categories; consumables is directly proportional to parts. The two should be linked together (move up or down together). Avoid bad words; for example, travel is a bad word: "NAVCOMPT does not like to see an increase in travel, so we need to see justification. An increase in travel really runs up a red flag."

The rest of this chapter will be concerned with the roles, decision rules, and strategies for budget presentation and review that occurred in this budget review process.

SUBMARINES (SUBPAC)

SUBPAC's theme was articulated early in the hearing with its opening statement: "We are different," they said. This was a suggestion that the whole budget system ought to treat them differently, or perhaps that the budget system was inappropriate to their concerns. "Operating tempo has no meaning for us, because when we tie up submarines we have to pay utility bills which we do not pay when we are under way . . . (since electricity is generated by the nuclear reactor)." A budget strategy to reduce the operating costs of the fleet is to decrease operating tempo by tieing up ships, which decreases steaming time, which decreases the amount of fuel used and hence fuel costs as well as other associated costs. SUBPAC was different in that it was funded out of the budget activity for strategic forces and many in the Navy believed that it was the ballistic missile submarines that persuaded the Russians to keep the peace during the years of the Cold War.

The CINCPACFLT analysts did not challenge this opening statement since there are many in the Navy who agree with it. What CINCPACFLT did do was reinforce the legitimacy of doing a budget review on SUBPAC by opening a discussion of a typical budget issue where SUBPAC was at fault; SUBPAC was underexecuting its budget in spare parts so CINCPACFLT warned that "It is hard to go in and ask for $10 million when you are executing at $4 million." The message here was twofold: first, you are just like anyone else when it comes to the potential for typical budget errors and thus our role in review is legitimate and second, there is no additional money for underexecutors.

SUBPAC argued that it was underexecuting only because of the lag in credits from the accounting system when parts were turned in. This turned into a complex argument, but the budget role had been sent; in the context of being told that there was no additional money for people who underexecute budgets, SUBPAC had been told it was not unique.

A series of technical criticisms re-enforced this message.

Firefighting/personal safety: "You can't cut these, you know these are two of your highest priorities . . . so make sure you do not submit high priorities as cuts."

Be alert to one-time costs in a specific year: "make sure you take it (one-time costs) out the next year."

Be realistic: "no 'nice to do's,' only 'must do's' (projects)."

Watch for blips and explain them (e.g., a trend line that runs FY 88 $400, FY 89 $400, FY 90 $400, FY 91 $800, FY 92 $400). (In this example, FY 91 is a blip.) "You have to give us a reason for that blip." SUBPAC argued the blip was a control number that had been passed through to it traceable up the chain of command to NAVCOMPT: "You gave us that control number." CINCPACFLT responded by saying "Well, then you have to tell us what you are not going to do the next year, or what you did in 91 that you didn't do in 90. You have to explain that blip. Besides, a control is a starting point, not an ending point."

When price adjustments are made, make sure they get put in the right line: "We lose money that way."

Make sure your changes show up in narrative justification. All changes have to be justified.

"You show funding going down, but you show you are going to be under way more days. You'll have to explain that." The response was that "we had our operators (submarine captains) actually count days under way," so this was a better indicator. CINCPACFLT responded that SUBPAC ought not to change performance criteria unless it had a good reason, but if it changed them, then they "have to put it in the budget narrative, so that people do not jump on us." This was a warning that CINCPACFLT's work was reviewed by others, and hence helped legitimize its role as well as justify any "hard line" it might seem to be taking.

The numbers for the same item on two different schedules do not agree: "This is maybe a typo or a rounding error, but the numbers for program and pricing growth on these two forms do not agree, and they should. It is not a lot, but it does get into important areas of the budget, like utilities. Since you are the only unit in this budget account, this will stick out like a sore thumb." The problem here is that one number was right and one wrong, and they should have been the same. If the discrepancy were to go to the budget review stage, a budget analyst will automatically pick the lower number and cut the higher to make it conform to the lower. The analyst may even cut below the lower since this kind of error seems to indicate either the budgeting unit does not know what it is doing or is treating the budget system with disrespect.

"Per diem average costs jump by $10, but there is no justification for it. First chop (review), you lose the $10. So if it is in there, you must justify it."

One program had a profile where FY 89 was $800, FY 90 was $600, and FY 91 was $140. The FY 91 seemed inadequate: "This is a bad profile. Can you *execute* at this level . . . What is the absolute minimum you have to have to execute (this program)?" The response was that this was a staff category, and while it was not very popular, the money was for communications for orders involving launching nuclear missiles in the event of war; "these are the guys who communicate with the guys who shoot the missiles. The Joint Chiefs of Staff still have to talk to these guys." This identified the item as supercritical, perhaps what Wildavsky would have called a crisis item. It is also interesting to note that the budget office analysts acted as guardians here in attempting to ensure that the unit had enough money to execute the function. Although the inclination to cut was always present, the budget office felt a greater responsibility to make sure the unit could execute its most important programs when it was truly important to do so. The decision on when to do what was often based on information that emerged from the dialogue between the unit budgeteers and the analysts.

As this hearing proceeded, the SUBPAC budgeteers became irritated by the level of detail of review and at one point one said: "I want to come back when AIRPAC comes to see if they have to justify $5,000 to $10,000 items. Why do we have to justify (something that is) .5% of our budget?"

One CINCPACFLT analyst responded: "We often get questions about $2,000 items from NAVCOMPT." Another said: "we may get questions on it from NAVCOMPT, but if we are pre-armed, we won't have to pass the questions on to you." A third analyst added: "This budget line is by itself; things stick out." The "it's so small" argument was thus detoured. Wildavsky has identified well the it's so small and absorb it as contingent strategies. Here the CINCPACFLT analysts were quick to defend attacking small items because it is often from the small inconsistencies that budget analysts find large differences in program directions or intentions, or a "camel's nose," a program that starts small and has huge consequences in future years when political support might make it unstoppable.

After several more technical errors were discussed, in which associated budget categories moved in different directions or in which numbers that should have been the same from different schedules were not the same, the comptroller said:

"The day is over when you have a budget which is just a piece of paper. You have to stand behind it and execute it. You have to look at it to see that it is properly balanced (e.g. steaming hours go up, fuel should go up) and justifiable the way it is shown."

SUBPAC was thus urged to treat its budget as a live document—a business plan—that it was really going to execute.

In various parts of the hearing, the budget analysts followed through on this philosophy. One cautioned *against* a large cut in travel: "Is that a realistic reduction in travel? Maybe you ought to take a look at this, because we will cut it if we have to cut travel."

The probing to see what was behind a change was unrelenting and usually ended with a warning to justify changes; budget claimants also learned that decreases had to be justified, and justified with more than just a few words. How much justification was required was more problematical: "for a decrease of $200,000, four words is not enough." But then, where there was no justification at all was even worse: "What program are you going to decrease (next year) that you had (this year). You did not justify the decrease from one year to the next, so I will go back to the current year and take the money away, too." This is a way of working from the future into the present as well as penalizing the claimant in the current year for not writing justification in his budget for the future year.

Review went from the very detailed to the more general. At the detail end, the typical errors appeared—forms that did not "crossfoot,"[7] numbers that should have been the same, annualization incorrectly done, one-time programs continued. These were sometimes introduced apologetically: "This looks nit-picky, but it is really not . . . it gets me into other issues. Your spreadsheet shows decreases in all other items, but fuel goes up . . . Why is that?"

Another issue had to do with the cost of contractor support of computer wargames. The program and budget exhibits reported different numbers. The CINCPACFLT analyst suggested that just saying the number of war games would be reduced was not good enough: "need to say what percentage of the contract we would be supporting if $\times$ dollars were taken away . . . to try to stop questions from NAVCOMPT."

The claimant responded: "Wargames do not track to dollars . . . it is man hours provided that make costs fluctuate . . . I have to be careful about providing that kind of data in budgets because it is 'business sensitive' information." Here the claimant alerts CINCPACFLT to the possibility that full provision of information in budget documents might be illegal, because it would allow another contractor to gain inside information; if the contractor knew what the full cost of this budget item was going to be, he could fix his bid to be just under the budget cost and get the contract.

The budget analyst replied: "We cannot have the number of wargames provided go up and down and funds not fluctuate. NAVCOMPT will ask." Notice the emphasis on trend analysis—looking at a line over time—and the expectation that program variations ought to lead to funding variations. These were two fundamental concepts that the budget analysts always used, looked for, and asked questions about. The statement that NAVCOMPT would ask was both a legitimization of the question asked by the CINCPACFLT budget analysts, and their role. It was also the truth; NAVCOMPT would ask.

AIRPLANES (AIRPAC)

The introduction to the AIRPAC hearing was much the same as SUBPAC; it emphasized that there was no midyear money so it would be AIRPAC's responsibility to take care of its hard core unfunded requirements and that the problem was going to get worse. Thus was the stage set.

AIRPAC basically operates the aircraft carriers, air wings, and air stations of the Navy in the Pacific and in the western United States. Its mission is to see that its pilots and planes are ready, so it has extensive training tasks. It also must provide for equipping planes. In the Navy, the configuration of a weapons system—an airplane—is defined through the programming and budgeting process. The budget process tends to answer pricing, timing, and execution questions with precise dollar figures for a specific year in budget execution and the following year in the budget under development. The budget process is guided by the comptroller of the Navy and his staff, abbreviated almost every-where to NAVCOMPT.

The programming process is dominated by a set of offices called resource sponsors. These resource sponsors have lifetime responsibility for the various parts of the Navy (assets), from training to personnel to submarines, no matter where the assets are used and no matter what stage of development those assets are in. Traditionally, the three most important resource sponsors have been those for surface ships, airplanes, and submarines.[8] The resource sponsor is a key decision maker in the programming process and is responsi-ble for the shape of the resource. If it is an airplane, the resource sponsor determines the kind, what it should do, and how it should be configured and deployed. The resource sponsor is rather like a rental car company; it buys a mix of cars, configures them to the idea of what is necessary for the market and updates the car fleet with the passage of time. The resource sponsor is the lifetime owner of that asset. The Pacific Fleet is like the car renter who possesses and uses the car but is not responsible for long-term strategic management of the group of assets[9]. It is necessary to understand a little about this process for this hearing, because there are sometimes disagreements between the resource sponsor and the budget office chain of command over how the assets (aircraft) should be used and how much will be required in the budget to fly and maintain those assets in any particular budget year. The resource sponsor and the budget office often disagree over timing, if nothing else, since the budgeteers have to react to the immediate pressures of cost and timing of aircraft purchases and modifications for each budget year while the resource sponsor is concerned with the total inventory of aircraft and all it takes to fly and maintain them over time. This is partially a tension between single-year budgeting and multiyear planning and between operating budgets and capital budgeting processes.

The resource sponsor's input occurs in the annual programming process, called the POM[10], which creates and updates a series of planning documents that describe the requirements of the Navy over a six-year horizon, but without the pricing precision or annual timing of the budget process. The resource sponsor for airplanes plans for all air assets and operations, including the flying hour program which dictates how many hours will be spent flying each year. The budget then costs this out in precise detail. AIRPAC is responsible to two masters here, one for executing its flying hour program[11] and one for executing the budget.

In this instance, AIRPAC had discussed the flying hour program with its sponsor and had received certain guarantees from it about what would be in the POM for flying hours and hence what it could ask for in the budget for flying hours. Some of this detail was not in agreement with what CINCPACFLT saw as the resource constraint it had to operate under, however, the resource sponsor had been more generous with the flying hour program than the CINCPACFLT budget analysts believed was realistic.

The AIRPAC budget presenter chose to make a very brief opening statement, stating only that he would prefer to get to the details of his budget. As the hearing developed, a better strategy might have been to admit that he had reviewed his numbers and realized that it would be a bad year for AIRPAC because workload demands appeared to outrun resources but that AIRPAC's resource sponsors stood firm on several key points, including executing the flying hour program. AIRPAC could thus have pleaded that it was between a rock and a hard place and would appreciate all the help it could get from the analysts at CINCPACFLT. AIRPAC did not make that argument.

The hearing opened with a program that was growing and would be fully operational in the following year. The CINCPACFLT analyst asked: "Has anything been done to eliminate unnecessary expenses in this program?" He wanted an example to show that the program manager had "really looked at this to see what we can do without if we get cut. The justification has to speak to cost efficiencies made to keep costs in line." AIRPAC's response was that a multimillion dollar building had already been built and that the program was growing. CINCPACFLT responded: "We need to highlight this to Washington so we can say 'hey we do not have money to fund this program when it comes on line in 1992.' "

AIRPAC argued that they had just received word from its program sponsor that resources were included in the POM, which was due to be released the following week. The budget analysts were skeptical, noting that this sponsor did not have a lot of money and may not have had the resources to fix the program. AIRPAC argued it had been fixed. Since the POM was not out yet, nobody knew the truth and AIRPAC had to argue what it had been told in good faith. Reluctantly, CINCPACFLT gave in: "Well, if your sponsor has fixed the POM, we may be all right."

AIRPAC's response was brief: "I guarantee he has." The budget analysts remained skeptical, however, saying. "We'll see." What the budget analysts feared was that the final decisions in the programming process might have removed the funding from the POM or planning document final draft where funding had been promised to AIRPAC. The AIRPAC request could have been sacrificed to a higher, and later developing priority, hence the "we'll see" response. For example, under the stress of a declining defense budget, the resource sponsor for airplanes could decide at the last moment and despite previous promises to buy more spare parts and fewer flying hours. This discussion marked the first time in the hearings in which the resource sponsor was introduced in direct opposition to the budget office and its perceived mission. AIRPAC did not give any ground in this issue because it thought it was right, and it would be proved right by subsequent events. Moreover, although the resource sponsor was in a different chain of command, he was senior in rank to the admiral who directed the budget office (NAVCOMPT), thus if the issue were given high enough visibility, AIRPAC might well get a favorable outcome, unless the issue went to the secretary of navy and he backed the budget admiral. In the present moment, AIRPAC had the blessing of a senior admiral to do what it was doing, even if the budgeteers at CINCPACFLT argued to the contrary.

The next phase of the hearing concerned some of the usual budget trivia: a 38% pay raise, which could only have been a typo, missing justification when a transfer was made from one program to another (AIRPAC: "We do show it on the reprogramming exhibit"; analyst: "Every exhibit should stand by itself"), and the usual search for "fat": "You took money out of this account; why did you have a surplus there."

AIRPAC was admonished that even when CINCPACFLT itself changed the control numbers it was up to AIRPAC to "come back and tell us what you are going to do" (how it would accommodate the cuts or changes or protest if it could not.) This brought the argument back to the opening dialogue.

AIRPAC(AP) "It's hard for us bean counters to do that" (forecast operational decisions that will be made in response to comptroller dollar cuts).

CINCPACFLT(CP): "I assume you talked with your admiral about this budget."

AP: "They reject the cut."

CP: "Well, find something else to cut. What you suggested [in the budget] is unacceptable up the line . . . so find something else. Not everything is a gold watch[12] . . . be brave."

AP: "The admiral does not want to cut something [a program or vertical cut] and see that others haven't made the same cut [suffered equally]."

CP: "Well, if he feels he is being treated inequitably, he can appeal. The flying hour program [the meat of this budget] has got to come down."

The flying hour program would not be discussed until later, however, and not in depth at that. The next series of activities illustrated the usual budget concerns, pay raise numbers that did not agree, pricing incorrectly transferred, inadequate justification. Once again a philosophical difference surfaced in this account, rising out of a detail on one form.

AP: "Well, we have to get back to the control number, don't we?"

CP: "We want you to rebalance this between accounts so that you have an executable document . . . because we are going to hold you to it."

AP: "We thought we had to come to the controls."

CP: "Bottom line, you did . . . but we all work hard on this and we want to know it stands for something . . . What did you do in the past when you just budgeted back to control numbers? Did you make up your own business plan [internal plan]?"

AP: "Yes . . . for example I make up my own station plans. Then we would come to you where we had to do reprogramming." This was an admission that the AIRPAC staff routinely developed operating plans for its air stations and then translated them into budget documents at the appropriate time. This meant running one information system for work planning and another for budget planning. CINCPACFLT was trying to sell the budget as a business or management plan that could be used for both budgeting and work planning. With a small operation, operating two sets of plans is acceptable; with a larger operation, the fear is that one plan or the other will suffer in quality. CINCPACFLT's budget office feared it was the budget planning that was suffering and did not see why AIRPAC could not create one process that would drive both work planning and budgeting. It was clear, at least to AIRPAC, that its number one priority was executing the flying hour program, not doing the budget.

This was followed by a discussion of the methodology for making air station plans and led into review of another account, in which control numbers seemed to cause some problems.

CP: "Looks like you are overexecuting travel."

AP: "It is a control number problem."

CP: "What is your real number . . . what is your real execution document plan number . . . How do you know you are doing good or bad against what you know you are going to do? . . . You do it backwards . . . You should make a plan that will allow you to execute what you need to do and then make a budget . . . If you had sat down at the beginning of the year and made a real financial plan, you would not be in the position of saying you are going to overexecute your travel by 50%."

AIRPAC was silent. The budget analyst added: "I want you to put together the budget you think you can execute at the beginning of the year."

AP: "We have to come to our sponsor's flying hour schedule. Your control numbers are not our only guidance." (Guidance does not mean advice in this context; it means targets.)

CP: "Well, fight the flying hour battle right up front."

AP: "You cannot make a flying hour program for FY 93 in FY 90."

CP: "Yes, you can . . . that does not mean it will not change twelve times."

AIRPAC did not respond to this.

CP: "What would you do if you lost an additional $50 million?"

AP: "Cut squadrons . . . part of this is due to the fact that operators [line administrators] still believe they will get midyear relief."

The hearing concluded with another discussion of the flying hour program; after all, this was the central issue in this budget. Finally, one CINCPACFLT budget analyst noted in a conciliatory manner: "What we are trying to do is to make sure that anything that goes to NAVCOMPT does not come back with a mark [cut] because we missed something . . . we are trying to get a budget here that we can stand behind and support." Explaining the level of detailed scrutiny, another of the analysts said "NAVCOMPT told us it was extremely important that our op-32's [a key budget form] be perfect."

There was a clear mismatch in this hearing. AIRPAC admitted in essence to running two sets of books, one with the CINCPACFLT numbers in it and one with their real plans in it. That could be rectified. On a deeper philosophical level, AIRPAC challenged the budget process when it claimed to be unable to project a flying hour program three years in the future. Probably what it meant to say was that it did not want to make such projections in an era in which steep funding declines were obviously going to happen until it saw others bite the bullet too. There was a high level of conflict in this hearing, different from the usual budget admonitions, which usually relate to wrong numbers and inadequate justifications. This was primarily caused by the fact that both sides argued about the flying hour program, but both realized that the real decision on this issue would have to be made later in Washington by higher-ranking officers representing the budgeting and Navy air communities.

CINCPACFLT

The supporting units in the administrative division of CINCPACFLT also were reviewed. Since the budget office was part of this unit there was an extra imperative for the budgeting unit's home to be tested at least as severely as the other units.[13] The opening statement stressed the harsh fiscal climate and then emphasized that what the budget office wanted was a budget as balanced as it could be between resources and program needs and that there would be no money for unfunded requirements, so "reprogram if you have left a high priority unfunded out of the budget." In addition to the now familiar decision rules, some new rules were identified.

Find the actor who benefits; if it is not CINCPACFLT exclude it from the budget or charge them back in some way, but get it off your budget.

Drop a program that has a history of being unfunded by higher levels: "Are we putting the money in and losing it every year? If it is not supported in the next budget, then we should take it out."

Make sure promises are kept and that budget claimants realize they made a promise: "When they pound on my door on 1 October (at the start of the fiscal year) saying 'you didn't recognize my deficiency (budget needs),' I want to be able to say 'we saw you; you had some good consolidations[14]; they made sense; now go do them.' "

Beware crossing trend lines: "how can you increase by three people each year, but have a decrease of $80,000? In a few more years they will be free."

Check average salary for the unit: "there is $300,000 that sticks out like a sore thumb . . . that is $64,000 apiece; that is too high an average salary for this unit."

Make sure your starting number is correct: "I checked this year's number for this year against last year's number for this year. What you show as last year's number is incorrect. If you start right, then the changes will be right."

Do what you say: "you told me [in the narrative] the change was in vehicle rental support, so I checked it and did not find it . . . that will make analysts ask questions about the program."

Use the right numbers: "your program forms and your budget forms have different numbers for the pay raise. Which is right?"

In this case, the analyst continued by suggesting how the right number could be found.

Challenge the unusual number: "FY 90 and FY 92 look comparable; FY 91 looks out of place; it is $50,000 more than FY 89 and FY 90. Which is the real base? You have to convince me that FY 91 is the real number."

Claimant: "We are in deep trouble [in this account]."

BA: "Looking at the numbers, I cannot tell whether you are in deep trouble in FY 90 or just fat in FY 91."

Weed out the unfunded requirements that won't sell: "CINCPACFLT is decreasing ships, but you are not decreasing funding and your unfunded requirements are not decreasing."

Let the operators—those captains and admirals who command the line operations of the Navy—make the decisions, but make them stick with them: "operators have to decide how much training time is enough; financial guys cannot make this decision."

A good scrub (tight budget) prevents end runs: If we can say this is a hard core program (no 'nice to do's,' just 'must do's'), then we can turn back the $1 call[15] by the operators (line administrators) to their admiral that gets a good budget decision reversed.

Link changes to PBDs (program budget decisions made at the secretary of defense level) but explain the PBD: "When a program budget decision is made that changes one of your accounts, tell us the logic of the PBD, don't just tell us the PBD Number . . . unless it is a crosscutting PBD that is obviously understandable [e.g., 4% inflation adjustment for fuel]."

This was basically a budget technician's hearing, in which most of the questions involved perfecting the technical aspects of the budget, and was very different from the AIRPAC budget. The general discussion at the conclusion of this hearing focused on the claimant's difficulty in finding historical records to explain changes in budget items and about how much justification was enough. The claimant asked how much narrative should be provided since one claimant had "pages and pages." The CINCPACFLT budget analyst replied:

"Well, pages won't get it. What you need is the meat . . . just one paragraph [holding thumb and forefinger apart] . . . we don't have time to read pages and pages. If you don't get us [our attention] in the first two lines, it is gone [the money is cut]."

As CINCPACFLT's own claimancy, part of the thoroughness of this review was driven by the perceived need to be "above suspicion" so no accusations could be made that the budget office had "gone easy" on its own claimancy. The other driver was the recognition that everyone should suffer in a cutback environment.

SUMMARY AND CONCLUSION

At the conclusion of the hearing the analysts told one claimant it had done a good job on its basic budget document. The claimant responded by saying it had created a budget team that actually moved into a separate room away from the phones in the afternoons and did nothing but the budget—that it "worked hard on it," but there were difficult questions to answer, basic questions that even senior people could not answer. Thus, even specialists in budgeting sometimes found it necessary to set themselves apart from their normal budget work to gear up for the annual budget review.

The hearings were intensive training sessions in getting budget claimants to say what they needed and to say what they meant. Time and again budget claimants used contingent strategies (e.g., fire safety training). Time and again reviewer and claimant became involved in sorting out the right numbers and the right forms from the multiplicity of numbers and forms required by the process. All of this was reminiscent of Wildavsky's *Politics*. Time and again budget claimants referred to their clienteles within the Navy, but so did the budget reviewers; their clientele was the Navy budget office. In the discussion of the AIRPAC budget, AIRPAC brought in the demands of its resource sponsor as a clientele strategy and CINCPACFLT invoked NAVCOMPT as its clientele. SUBPAC referred to the Joint Chiefs of Staff as a clientele strategy when pressed on a communications account. While Wildavsky's original concept of clientele as a ubiquitous strategy leaned in the direction of clienteles external to the bureaucracy and evoked images of interest groups and lobbies, in this instance the clienteles invoked were internal to the bureaucracy.

Wildavsky also discussed competence and the confidence in others of one's ability as a budget person. What was interesting from this example is how difficult upholding this norm is. People may be born with an aptitude for numbers, but budgeting requires more than that. Budgeting is difficult to do. It takes great analytic ability and an ability to think how others will respond to your numbers and proposals. Just ensuring that the numbers are displayed correctly and on different forms is difficult. In fact some forms are designed to expose players who are not careful with their numbers or not painstaking in handling data. Being competent is difficult; being seen as competent given the multiplicity of forms and schedules is even more difficult. Budget forms require closure, but they also invite error. A surprising amount of effort is required to maintain the ethic of competence. It was not surprising, then, to see how much time was spent in coaching and teaching during the budget process. There is little that is inherently knowable in the budget process, and even experienced professionals can be taught to do better.

Insofar as contingent strategies are concerned, it was somewhat surprising to see how seldom "crisis" strategies were invoked. The casual observer might think this would be a natural strategy for defense budgeteers, but just as in other professional budget arenas, emotional appeals to a defense crisis do not hold much leverage within the professional community. Everyone seemed to know when a suggested program cut would really harm a vital program, and no extra emotion was needed in those instances. Moreover, when a cut threatened damage to a key element of a program, both claimant and analyst explored the ramifications with great care. The burden of clearly articulating the need rested with the claimant, as it always does in budgeting.

It was also surprising to see how much of budget analysis involved trend line analysis. Analysts assumed that if they could graph a five-year pattern of budget numbers and knew just a little bit about the program, the trend line would tell them something. Often the lowest number in the trend line became the analyst's starting point; the claimant was obliged to defend numbers higher than that number.

Budgetary technology has changed since the original *Politics*. Much of the work for these hearings was based on computer printouts and spreadsheets, sometimes piled half a foot high on the table. However, computers did not solve any problems other than basic manipulation of data, valuable enough in itself, but all of the decision making surrounding the schedules and the review of those decisions was a human process done by experts in their areas, some to propose a budget, others to review those proposals. What was also illustrated time and again was that even experts do not know everything, because expertise is compartmentalized and because issues grow and change over time and present themselves in different ways in different years, and some issues change even within the year during the course of the budget process. Moreover, even subject matter experts have to be coached to make the best case for themselves and their programs. That, in essence, was the purpose of these budget hearings.

REVIEW QUESTIONS

1. How can the same numbers tell two different stories?
2. What is the difference in having confidence and others having confidence in you in budgeting? How does one purchase confidence?
3. How have computers changed the budget process?
4. Do budget reviewers have too much power?
5. What contingent strategies did you see in this case study?
6. Which is better: telling people the right number or teaching them how to find the right number; telling them what to say or teaching them to think about how others will review their proposals?
7. What is an executable fiscal plan? What are some things that prevent a budget from being an executable fiscal plan?
8. How long should a justification be? Why?

NOTES

1. See Wildavsky A. *The Politics of the Budgetary Process*. Boston: Little, Brown (1964) (4th ed, 1984, pp. 64–65). For more on strategies see McCaffery J. Strategies for achieving budgetary goals in J. Perry (ed.) (1989). *Handbook of Public Administration*, San Francisco: Jossey-Bass. pp. 290–301.

2. See Schick, A. *Constraints on the Capacity to Budget*. Washington, DC; Urban Institute Press, (1990) Chap. 4 and 6.

3. These hearings were between budget claimants and budget analysts representing the line operators of the Pacific Fleet and the commander in chief of the Pacific Fleet, abbreviated as CINCPACFLT. The three units herein described are the budget offices for airplanes, submarines, and the administrative unit for CINCPACFLT. Space precludes the examination of other units. The budget chain of command runs from the Navy budget office (NAVCOMPT) to the budget office at CINCPACFLT to the type commands (e.g., AIRPAC representing airplanes) to local bases. All do budgets representing the needs of their line operators, those uniformed personnel and civilians who operate the navy. At the fleet level, people will tell you that the Atlantic Fleet and the Pacific Fleet are the Navy. The budgets under discussion are mainly operations and maintenance accounts, since the Navy does not budget at this level for military personnel or major weapons systems or research and development expenses. None of the numbers in this manuscript are real numbers, but the profiles are accurate. The quoted dialogue was intended to provide a sense of the budgeting arena and was constructed from notes taken at the hearings. In this chapter CINCPACFLT is used to identify the fleet budget office and the analysts who work in it; the budget analysts of the units under review are identified as they appear: for example, AIRPAC stands for the budget analysts who represent the airplane budget claimant.

4. Control numbers relate to the legally authorized budget number as passed by Congress for various items, programs, and accounts.

5. With the prior year actuals (FY 89), this year's budget (FY 90), the budget that was in Congress (FY 91), and preparations for a budget for the next two years (FY 92, FY 93), it was not unusual to see analysts examining five-year budget profiles. Only the FY 92 budget would go to the appropriation committees, but the authorizing committees asked for a two-year budget, hence the consideration of FY 92 and FY 93.

6. In the course of the hearings, notice how often NAVCOMPT, the Department of Navy budget office, is introduced into the discussion as a way of legitimizing the action the CINCPACFLT budget office is recommending.

7. Crossfoot is an antique budget expression dating at least to the 1960s. The totals of a schedule when added down and added across should add to the same number in the lower right-hand corner. It is an arithmetic check that became particularly important with program budgets, which showed programs across the page (in columns) and objects of expenditures going down the page (in rows).

8. Although all naval functions have a resource sponsor, the sponsors for aircraft, submarines, and ships have most of the money and are seen as the most important. Sometimes they are referred to as the "barons." In 1993, a reorganization

was undertaken to improve co-ordination and co-operation of these offices and to emphasize joint military missions, but they still remain more important than other resource sponsors.

9. Picture the submarine resource sponsor saying to the Pacific and Atlantic fleets: "Here are your submarines. Use them well, but do not break them. They will have to last us awhile."

10. The acronym comes from the first letter of the documents produced in the programming process (i.e., program objective memoranda).

11. This includes training and operational flying. AIRPAC calculates pilot hours and aircraft flight costs. There is a direct relationship in combat aircraft between the number of hours flown by pilots and accident rates, which vary somewhat by type of aircraft. Pilots who fly too few hours due to fiscal constraints get rusty and have accidents, just as those who fly too much under combat conditions.

12. A gold watch is slang for offering up the most popular program to be cut, like turning off the lights on the Washington Monument, another contingent strategy Wildavsky identified.

13. Generally budget and comptroller units in the Navy take extra pains to be both frugal and efficient; if they are going to severely test other budgets, they must also prove that their budgets are above reproach. In this way they increase others' confidence in them as competent, as Wildavsky suggests.

14. In this case, consolidations refers to ideas discussed by a claimant during the budget process to meet budget needs (deficiencies) by combining services or functions rather than asking for more budget money.

15. This is a reference to a cheap telephone call that may cause a complicated and large budget decision to be reversed.

5

The Political Economy of Outsourcing

Arie Halachmi and Robert Boydston
Tennessee State University, Nashville, Tennessee, U.S.A.

Outsourcing—contracting out and privatization of public services*—has been advocated as an alternative means of providing necessary services while reducing the size and the cost of government operations. As pointed out by Halachmi and Holzer (1993), some writers suggest that the use of alternative providers is a promising way to improve productivity, while others view outsourcing as an irresponsible abdication of important government roles. While the debate about the advantages and disadvantages of contracting out goes on, the threat of contracting out is emerging as another tool in the arsenal of budget negotiators. The option of contracting out thus introduces a new twist to the political economy of the budgetary process. It adds to this process the pressures from and the involvement of new interested parties that argue not only about the desired levels of services (like the traditional participants in the process), but also about the mechanics of delivering the service. Thus, for example, budget analysts and legislators must now hear not only the arguments of administrators, civil servants, and service recipients, but also those of current and potential alternative service providers. Such would-be contractors use sharp marketing skills to influence public opinion in favor of outsourcing plans with promises of greater economy, better service, and cost containments that prevent the need for future tax increases.

This chapter revolves around a true case study. The case study brings to light financial, power, and political issues that influence the outsourcing decision. A review of these issues is important in analyzing the case.

ISSUES IN OUTSOURCING

The most visible outsourcing issues are normally financial. Proponents contend that outsourcing is one means to providing more efficient, reliable, and quality government ser-

---

This case was prepared for class discussion rather than to illustrate proper or improper management of public policy, and may not represent the views of the authors' organizational affiliations.

* While privatization involves contracting with the private sector to provide public services, contracting out can involve agreements with either private or public sector organizations (such as other governmental units) to provide these services.

65

vices (outputs) at the lowest total cost (inputs). In this government version of the corporate "make or buy" decision, the issue of a cost analysis usually becomes that of avoiding costs by having the private sector provide the service (Kelley, 1984). This depends upon accurately identifying total and unit costs, a purpose often not facilitated by government budgeting and accounting systems. It also depends upon equating public and private outputs for a given service serving a similar set of customers; in other words, "comparing apples to apples" when looking at proposed services. The evidence indicates that outsourcing economy depends upon a competitive environment, maintained accountability, emphasis on ends rather than means, and clear specification of the performance the government expects from the supplier (Donahue, 1989).

A second issue in outsourcing is the difference in the roles played in the budgetary process by individuals wielding political power (i.e., those with the ability to influence decisions) and those with electoral mandate (i.e., individuals who were able to win an election). As revealed by our case, having either one of these powers is not enough for assuming the other. Public agencies do not function in a political vacuum. The political context (i.e., the political environment) can determine which decision options are viable and which are not. The carving of the budgetary pie reflects the roles that are played by both types of participants. The number of slices approximates the number of mandates given out by the polity. The size of each slice, relative to the total size of the whole pie, approximates the distribution of political power. Other variables, such as political history, organizational culture, and the ability to foster or join winning coalitions, determine the final distribution of resources. Thus, whether or not an elected official can influence important budgetary decisions is a function of many factors. The ability to influence the allocation of resources in turn influences the official's ability to be re-elected or successful in carrying out subsequent projects. By the same token, brokers who yield political influence may be able to manipulate administrative processes and affect individual decisions, but may not be able to secure election results. The implications of this fact—that having either political power or an electoral mandate is not a sufficient condition for exercising the other—are important for preserving a democratic system of government. However, is this fact conducive to rational allocation of scarce resources, to ranking priorities, or for solving potential conflict between the general will (i.e., what most people want in the short run) and the general welfare (what is in the best interest of a polity in the long run)?

A third issue in outsourcing is an important but sometimes overlooked aspect of contracting out: the possibility that when a single element of an administrative unit is contracted out the economic and political viability of that unit or some of its other functions may become questionable. The resulting change in the nature and distribution (or allocation) of the overhead for carrying it out is not without consequences. These include

Financial consequences. Outsourcing by its very nature, changes the amount and distribution of revenues, direct costs, and indirect costs. When a service is being outsourced some of the "old" overhead is gone and is considered as "savings," while other elements of the old overhead must be redistributed among the remaining functions. Furthermore, some of the old overhead is replaced with "new" overhead related to negotiating, implementing, managing, and overseeing the outsourcing contract. This new overhead may appear in other parts of the organization. Without very good accounting and cost measurement procedures, however, the expenditures related to the new overhead may not be weighed against the alleged outsourcing savings in order to reveal the true merit of the decision to contract out.

Operational consequences. Contracting out may affect the performance of other administrative units and how they carry out their own mission. In other words, a decision to contract out may affect organizational capacity in ways that are different from the impact of the decision not to contract out.

Strategic political power consequences. Since what government does and how it does it has political implications, a decision to contract out may change the relevant power matrix. Therefore outsourcing changes the context of subsequent decisions about contracting and allocation of resources. The loss of the responsibility for any government service diminishes the power and autonomy of the official who used to oversee it. It may trigger (or at least facilitate) suggestions of outsourcing even more activities, thus changing the posture of the involved official. From being on the offense (i.e., making legitimate claims for additional resources) such an official may find himself or herself on the defense (i.e., attempting to shield previous allocation levels from further cuts).

Outsourcing can have an adverse influence on the political clout of elected officials who remain accountable for a contracted service without the dividends that result from being able to control it. However, it can boost the political fortunes of others who are in a position to influence the development, award, or oversight of the outsourcing contract. Such an influence may determine the actual administrative capacity of a government entity. To use an analogy from the world of personal computers, the order in which programs are loaded in the computer's memory determines which applications will have priority in using system resources, including the overhead needed to load and run the application. Changing the list of programs loaded or the order in which they load can change each program's ability to access needed resources (especially memory), thus determining which programs are loaded and how they behave when running. Failing to load a program can thus free up resources, but may also cause other programs to run erratically or not at all. Thus, even if the arithmetic sum of the memory required by a given group of applications is less than the memory that is installed on the computer, some may not be able to load. In other words, the program that determines what other programs are to be loaded, in what order, and what their characteristics should be when they load is the program that determines the capacity of that computer. In a similar fashion organizational capacity can be determined by those individuals who can influence what functions stay in-house as the responsibility of which administrative unit, which activities can be outsourced, and the terms for the contract.

In the case under consideration, organizational capacity is influenced not only by changes in the stream of expenditures but also by changes in the stream of revenues that correspond to the terms of the contract. These changes in turn leverage the ability of the organization (a local authority in our case) to sustain a given level of service or mix of services. Revenues lost when a service is outsourced may have contributed to the underwriting of direct or indirect costs of other services. Thus, outsourcing may generate financial pressures on those other services. This is often the case when revenues are based on full cost, average cost, or cost plus (not merely marginal direct cost) and are not legally earmarked. For instance, if such program revenues are deposited into a government's general fund where they (with revenues from many other sources) are pooled to fund a wide variety of governmental functions, programs, and services, their loss subsequent to outsourcing effectively reduces the revenues to support administrative and operational overhead or shifts that overhead burden onto other revenue sources.

In addition to the above, for the student of public productivity outsourcing brings many of the traditional questions about politics and administration and how being responsive to pressures from within and from the outside may influence performance. In addition, contracting out revives the old dilemma of optimizing the delivery of one function (i.e., spatial optimization or suboptimization) without reducing overall performance at the system level and how to optimize at the system level without compromising performance of any one of its subsystems.

OUTSOURCING IN COUNTY GOVERNMENT: A CASE STUDY

Background

The sheriff's office is one of the many departments of the moderately large urban county government. The office, established by state law, is headed by the sheriff, popularly elected in a countywide partisan election. The duties of the office, as defined in the county charter, are to house pre- and posttrial inmates, provide security for the courts, and serve civil and criminal process (legal papers such as warrants, subpoenas, and levies) in the county. Notably absent from these duties are any involving law enforcement: such duties are performed by a separate police department under the county executive.

The county executive is the most visible of the other political actors in the county. He or she is popularly elected in a nonpartisan election that is held about a year after the sheriff's election. In addition, a large part-time county council is elected in nonpartisan district elections at the same time as the county executive. Other local political actors include the judges of the state criminal courts for the county, the judges of the state civil courts for the county, the county courts, and the court clerks of the two state court systems. All of the judges and court clerks are elected by the public in partisan elections. Those partisan elections follow primaries in which voters can vote in either party's primary without declaring party affiliation. In fact, Democrats have held most of these offices as long as anyone can remember, and partisan politics is not a big factor in the county's governance.

The fiscal year (FY) begins on July 1 and ends the following June 30, with the FY identified by the calendar year in which it ends (e.g., FY 1993 began on July 1, 1992 and ended on June 30, 1993). The county executive is charged by the county charter with the responsibility of preparing and submitting the annual operating budget to the council in May. The council must then pass a balanced budget before the fiscal year begins on July 1. It is the responsibility of the county executive, through his finance department, to monitor and control expenditures to assure compliance with the budget. Departments and elected offices are bound by charter to operate within that budget. Formal budgetary authority thus remains with the county executive.

Elected officials, however, are elected by the same public in at-large elections as the county executive, so they tend to view themselves as under less executive control than most county departments. The historical attitude of various county executives has been nonconfrontational; traditionally they have rarely tried to dictate policies to other elected officials.

At the time of this case, the most stable and powerful political institutions in the county were the county executive and the sheriff's office. For eighteen years the sheriff and his office provided the county with a variety of services. As previously noted, he ran the jail, provided court officers and juries with meals, and delivered warrants for the courts. These core functions led to other somewhat unique indirect services, however such as picking up litter around streets and churchgrounds at the request of council members and citizens (an outgrowth of a community services program that put inmates to work for the county), using inmate work crews to help other departments in special projects (cleanups, moves, etc.), using inmate-staffed jury kitchens to serve meals to members of the council before their meetings (although paying for the food itself with contributions from those fed and with political funds), and operating a roadside brush removal program similar to one operated by the county roads department. Extraofficial activities included helping churches charities, not-for-profit organizations, and candidates for other political offices raise funds by sponsoring and catering barbecues on their behalf; creating and putting up political signs; giving rides to the polls; having other politicians' and officials' cars washed; and helping out other officials with various services. The county's premier political event of the year was a sheriff-hosted informal dinner that was virtually required attendance for anybody who held or aspired to county office. In short, the old sheriff was much more than the county's jailer.

That political power of the sheriff was reflected in his budget. Table 1 shows the sheriff's budget as a percentage of the total budget and in comparison to various grouping of other annual allocations.

During his tenure from FY 1972 to FY 1990, Sheriff Ossman's budget grew faster than the budget of any of the other reference groups (i.e., the police department, all other elected officials, all other justice administration departments, the general fund, or the total budget for all governmental funds).

For eighteen years, Sheriff Ossman was arguably the pre-eminent politician in the county (with his only close competition being the county executive). His victories in the quadrennial elections became almost routine, winning with 55% of the vote in 1986 elections. Throughout 1986 and 1987, the primary issue in county corrections was the overcrowding of the county jail that resulted from the state's refusal to accept convicted felons (which itself was the result of a lawsuit over the constitutionality of the state prison system). Then, in 1988, as the sheriff was publicizing the strain that the state inmate population was putting on county jail facilities, allegations began to surface about the propriety of repair contracts.

Table 1 Sheriff's Operating Budget as a Percentage of Various Budget Groupings

Fiscal year	1972	1989	1990	1991	1992	1993	1994
All elected officials	26.4	42.1	42.9	39.7	40.4	44.5	43.6
Police department	18.2	29.2	30.8	28.0	30.2	37.7	36.9
All justice-related departments	12.1	18.7	19.4	17.8	18.7	21.9	21.5
All general fund departments	1.9	3.9	4.1	3.7	3.9	4.7	4.6
All governmental type funds	0.9	2.1	2.2	2.0	2.2	2.6	2.6

Source: County financial records (1972–1994).

The initial allegations soon broadened into a general investigation of the sheriff's procurement habits, his relationships with vendors, and his alleged use of employees for personal and political activities on county time. The investigations by the county grand jury, county auditors, state auditors, the IRS, and the FBI made almost daily news throughout 1989, and sheriff's office employees began to be indicted.

Also in 1989, an unrelated countywide efficiency study recommended eliminating the sheriff's office (among others) and consolidating its duties into the police department. Although this was unconstitutional, it added pressure on the office.

With the 1990 elections approaching, the allegations of corruption in the sheriff's office became the central campaign issue. In September 1989, Joe Nesbitt, a former federal law enforcement agent, announced his candidacy. Nesbitt organized his campaign around some very powerful slogans: depolitization of the sheriff's office, cutting the size of the county's contribution to its budget by $1 million, and ending alleged corruption and nepotism.

As the sheriff lost staff (through normal attrition, indictment, and resignation), he rehired Chuck Denney as his chief deputy. Denney had worked for Ossman in the 1970s, but had been employed elsewhere since 1979. Denney opposed the efficiency study's proposals to terminate the office and privatize certain functions, including its warrant division.

In early 1990, the sheriff was indicted on several counts by a federal grand jury. In May 1990, Nesbitt defeated Ossman in the Democratic primary. Since the county government always had been a sound Democratic institution, the primary virtually assured Nesbitt's election in August. At the end of May, Ossman retired and applied for his pension, leaving Denney in charge. Nesbitt suggested that the council appoint him acting sheriff immediately, but the state attorney general confirmed that the chief deputy became acting sheriff pending the results of the August general election.

At about the same time, the county submitted its annual operating budget. Although Nesbitt offered to discuss the budget with the council, the formal hearing was conducted by interim sheriff Denney, who was by this time a lame duck. The proposal for the sheriff's office was a status quo (or continuation) budget of $16.2 million. During council deliberations, Denney advised the council that the office could operate with a budget of $15.3 million. The council made a further cut of $1.1 million (made, according to one council member, to reflect the newly elected sheriff's vow to save $1 million). The result was a final budget of $14 million, or a 13.4% cut from the status quo budget.

In July, Ossman vacated his offices and accepted a plea bargain that included a five-year prison term and a fine. The August general election saw Nesbitt win with 70% of the vote.

Nine hours after taking office, Nesbitt fired seventy of the office's 440 employees, eliminated twenty-five positions, hired his son, along with some former employees who had resigned late in the Ossman administration as upper-level managers, and before long promoted his son to chief deputy. He also ended the long-standing practice of serving dinner to the council before its weekly meetings as well as some of the other perks provided by the former sheriff. Much effort was spent sorting out records (with only mixed success) and bringing order and reforms to what years of controversy had made a troubled office.

Despite cutting $700,000 in food costs, partially because of apparently unrestrained spending by the recently departed administration, the spring of 1991 found Nesbitt facing the possibility that his budget would be overspent by $700,000 to $980,000. Rather than ask the council to appropriate additional funds, Nesbitt initiated cost-saving measures, including pay cuts for many employees and mandatory leave without pay for all. This upset the judges of the criminal court, whose court officers were paid by Nesbitt and subject to the proposed cuts. The judges protested, asking the county executive to transfer the court officers from Nesbitt's budget to theirs. Under such pressure, Nesbitt had no choice but to rescind the proposed cuts in court officers' salaries.

As this occurred, the county was preparing its budget for FY 1992. The budget raised the allocation to the sheriff's office by $950,000 for inflation and increased salary costs (budget additions received by all departments). It also added $1.2 million to fund compliance with an agreement to end a federal lawsuit dealing with jail overcrowding, and deducted $800,000 to transfer court officers from the sheriff's budget to the criminal court. The sheriff was allocated a total of $15.4 million, and authorized staffing went to 471 positions, reflecting the addition of the court-ordered guards but removal of the court officers.

The Warrant Division

In addition to incarceration, a primary sheriff's office activity is the service of process—legal papers such as civil warrants, eviction notices, property levies, protection orders, and repossessions. These services are provided for courts and litigants in return for a fee set by state statute. In 1992 the sheriff's office served 175,000 such papers. According to the sheriff's office, this cost about $2 million; the county's financial records reflect a cost of about $1.3 million (not including fringe benefits). The division deposited $1.3 million in corresponding process service fees as revenues to the general fund, from which the division (and the entire sheriff's office) was funded. Fees were received only upon successful service of the process. Although it was generally considered that the warrants division was a money-making operation, revenues actually covered only the costs of salaries and operating expenses, and not the fringe benefits of employees (see Table 2).

Table 2 Warrant Division Budget Summary (in Thousands of Dollars)

Fiscal year	1989	1990	1991	1992	1993	1994
Gross salaries	$1,012	$1,192	$1,010	$1,114	$1,157	$1,212
Operating expenses (excluding capital)	286	238	172	177	181	208
Subtotal	1,298	1,430	1,181	1,291	1,337	1,420
Estimated fringes (at 35% of salaries)	354	417	353	390	405	424
Total (excluding capital)	1,652	1,847	1,534	1,681	1,742	1,844
Revenues	1,288	1,230	1,228	1,196	1,037	1,211
Profit or loss (excluding fringes)	(9)	(200)	46	(94)	(300)	(209)
Profit or loss (including fringes)	(363)	(617)	(307)	(484)	(704)	(633)

Totals may not add due to rounding. Source: County financial records.

The Outsourcing Decision: Warrantco, Inc.

In February of 1991, Denney, who had been dismissed with other Ossman's deputies when Nesbitt took office, joined other former deputies and other persons in forming Warrantco, Inc., a private business whose product would be the service of process for lawyers and the courts. On February 6, Denney proposed to contract with the county for the purpose of serving civil warrants. Unbeknown to the sheriff the proposal circulated among members of the county council, the state courts, and the county court judges for about two weeks. Denney was going to use former employees of the warrants division under Ossman to do what they did before but this time not as public employees. Denney used Nesbitt's campaign rhetoric about privatization and contracting out for greater efficiency in support of his proposal. Specifically, Denney suggested that Warrantco would actually serve a greater percentage of process given to them and would serve it faster than the warrant division—two primary areas of complaint about the warrant division that practicing attorneys had brought to the attention of local judges. Since process service fees were set by state law, Warrantco claimed it would make money through greater efficiency without actually raising costs to litigants.

Upon learning about the Denney proposal, Sheriff Nesbitt fired back with some revelations of his own. First he informed the judges, attorneys, and public that some employees of Warrantco had criminal records and that sheriff's deputies would not be available to enforce warrants that could (or would) not be served by Warrantco. Second, he pointed out that he had to fire one of his employees who was caught doing work for Warrantco on county time using a county computer. Third, he alleged that under Ossman the sheriff's office maintained two lists for the warrant service. A "red" list included attorneys and collection agencies that contributed to Ossman's fund-raising activities. Warrants that were initiated by those who made the red list were served promptly. Lesser contributors were blacklisted and got poor service from the warrant division. Nesbitt went on to secure the support of the state sheriff association against the move to outsource the service or any legislative effort to facilitate it.

The support of the state sheriff association was important since the county court judges were not sure that privatization of the service was permissible under the current law. They directed a question to the state's attorney general and were assured that there was nothing in the law to prevent them from using a private contractor. However, there was nothing to assure them that the law would not be changed in the future under pressure from other counties' sheriffs who would be threatened by this precedent.

On March 6, 1991, a local newspaper signaled the end of this outsourcing initiative when it suggested that while it was not clear if the privatization of the warrant services would improve their efficiency it would definitely result in a loss of revenues for the county. There was additional concern that a private process service company would get the easy higher-fee assignments, leaving more difficult or lower-fee service to whatever remained at the sheriff's warrant division. This concern reflected that of county financial analysts, who were afraid that the warrant division's operating loss would only become larger if Warrantco siphoned off more revenues than expenses from the county budget. Furthermore, since judges could by law compel the sheriff to serve process, the warrant division would have to remain in some form and (contrary to the sheriff's statement) the division would have to serve warrants that could (or would) not be served by Warrantco.

Although the state courts had amended their rules of court to permit the use of private process servers, one of the county court judges found an obscure section of the

> **County Courts—Process Service**: The sheriff, his duly appointed deputy, or any person appointed by a judge of the court for such purpose, shall be empowered to serve regular process, writs, and papers issued by said court with the same authority and power provided for such service in the state civil and criminal courts. Any person specifically appointed for such purpose under this section shall serve without compensation.

charter that appeared to prohibit private process servers in county court cases from being paid for such services. This seemed to end the issue in the county courthouse.

As the issue of the privatization of the warrant services was fading away the county contracted with the American Brig Company (ABC) to run a new detention center. This actually had been planned during Ossman's administration and confirmed by the council (over Nesbitt's objections) immediately after the 1990 election. The facility opened in the spring of 1992, when state felons were transferred out of county jails and into the new ABC facility. This caused closure of a county jail facility at the beginning of FY 1993. At the same time the sheriff's accounts ballooned due to reimbursement payments for housing state inmates that flowed from the state through the sheriff's office to ABC.

In March 1992 the idea of eliminating the sheriff's office surfaced again. A member of the county council asked the county department of law to research the possibility of transferring various functions from the sheriff's office to the police department or other county agencies. Redistribution of the sheriff's office functions among other units was expected to facilitate greater efficiency and generate additional savings by payroll reductions.

Trouble for the sheriff's office continued into the following year. The county executive, not satisfied with the quality of information he had concerning the sheriff's office operations, recommended a FY 1994 sheriff's office budget equal in dollars to that of FY 1993, with two exceptions. First, funds were added to cover cost increases due to increased inmate populations and increased per diem payments scheduled in the original contract between ABC and the county. The increased costs were offset by increased reimbursements from the state. Second, the budget for the pretrial probation program was transferred to the courts' budget. This transfer was in response to complaints from the judges that the sheriff was inadequately and improperly operating the program. The council approved the county executive's recommendations.

In June 1993, a month before the beginning of the new fiscal year and while the county was holding its last-minute negotiations of the budget for FY 1994, the county department of law asked the sheriff to give back $8,400 worth of blue emergency lights he had just purchased for ten of his cars. Blue lights, the department said, were restricted by a 21-year-old court ruling to law enforcement agencies—a function exercised in the county by the police department, not the sheriff's office. The sheriff complied.

Epilogue

Three years after the changing of the guard at the sheriff's office, the following appeared in a local newspaper:

> Once upon a time, a High Sheriff named Ossman built a powerful and rich kingdom on a foundation of barbecue and services to the Council of Dukes. In those days, any

Duke of the County Council whose vassals needed services did not need to request them from the Executive Emperor, but could petition the High Sheriff. The Sheriff would have his indentured servants provide the services free to those Dukes who supported and defended his kingdom, thus earning the vassals' favor for both the Sheriff and the Duke. Alas and alack, the Sheriff's hand was caught in the vassal-financed barbecue sauce, and he was sent to the dungeon. But woe to the Dukes, who must again depend on the Emperor for their vassals' services. Then cometh the new High Sheriff who, although his kingdom is the subject of rebellions and incursions, also sends indentured servants to service the Dukedoms. And so again some of the Dukes are beginning to join in the support and defense of the new High Sheriff's kingdom.

DISCUSSION

What happens when a local authority is presented with the option of contracting out a service that used to be a key element of its sheriff's office? The "do-it-yourself or buy" dilemma is not a new one to budget analysts in the public sector, yet dealing with it is still very difficult. What at first glance appears to be a financial decision in fact involves more than rational economic analysis as the sole consideration for rank ordering the different options. Financial managers and budget analysts cannot ignore the political context in which the choice is made, nor can they afford to overlook the broad policy and organizational implications of choosing one option over the other.

This chapter describes the circumstances leading a group of former sheriff's employees to form a company for providing the local court system with services that were customarily provided by the sheriff's office. The case provides the basic data for calculating the monetary (but not the policy or political) implications of allowing the sheriff to continue the provision of the said services and of outsourcing. Such analysis is a first step toward assessment of the economic rationale for a change or for keeping the status quo. However, this rationale can support—but not substitute for—the political rationale for deciding in favor of one or the other. The reason is that in the public sector political efficiency is more potent than economic efficiency (Halachmi, 1977; 1979).

This case suggests that considerations of economy are not enough for making the case for or against contracting out a specific service. Legal constraints or political opposition (e.g., from those that stand to lose political clout as they lose control over the operation, the personnel that are involved in carrying it out, and stakeholders with other monetary or tangible interests) can derail a proposed contract. The case points out that in addition to the discreet analysis of the specific issue the analyst must also examine whether outsourcing is consistent with other policies of the local authority for determining whether or not the saving in one place (e.g., the sheriff's office) may not be offset by new overhead costs for administration of the contract elsewhere. In addition, the case illustrates how the proposal of outsourcing one service may open the door to the possibility of outsourcing others or create the perception that the proposed move is only the first step of a calculated political maneuver that may lack economic justification. Convincing public opinion that political rather than economic considerations are behind the move to abolish a whole administrative unit through outsourcing and/or consolidation with other functions can doom such an idea. The case thus demonstrates that economic efficiency is meaningful only when it is politically feasible; the political context is as important as the consideration of efficiency, and the successful public financial manager must be aware of both issues.

SUMMARY AND CONCLUSION

You have reviewed the circumstances leading a group of former employees to form a company that would provide, on a privatized basis, the same services they had formerly provided internally as government employees. This case has shown that the economics of the move toward privatization are no more important than the political considerations of government officials, that analysis must also examine whether or not outsourcing is consistent with other governmental policies, and that an analysis must be aware not only of the savings in one place (i.e., the sheriff's office), but also of the possibility of new or shifted revenue and cost patterns (e.g., for administration of the contract). The case further illustrates how with the consideration of each additional function for outsourcing there is an increased momentum to consider the outsourcing of the remaining ones. This in turn may explain why department heads are motivated to resist the outsourcing of any function, including those they consider as burdens.

REVIEW QUESTIONS

1. What are the immediate and what are the long-term benefits and costs of outsourcing an existing service according to this case? Are they consistent with the writing of other proponents and opponents of privatization and contracting out?
2. Can the outsourcing of one service reduce the ability of the sheriff's office to carry out any one of its other duties in an effective and efficient manner? Is the sheriff's office providing nonmandatory services that interfere with the delivery of the mandatory ones? If the answer to the second question is yes, explain why the sheriff wants to continue this service when he was willing to do away with others. If the answer to the first question is yes, should the local authority consider the outsourcing of the other service(s) as well or should it drop the whole issue?
3. Given the nature of its mission should the sheriff's office be involved or encouraged to (1) generate revenues for the county or (2) underwrite its own operations? Should the sheriff have any control over how revenues his office generates are being collected (e.g., set rates for different recipients) or how they are used? If the answer to 1 or 2 is no, outline the reason for your answer and explain why you think the department could survive in the long run as a cost center.
4. The sheriff is an elected official but the local authority is underwriting the cost of most of his or her activities as a regular item in the local budget. Under these circumstances what are the implications of a discrepancy between fiscal responsibility and political accountability?
5. Is contracting out with other government agencies (either within the same government or in another government) a promising solution when outsourcing a public service to private providers is deemed questionable, inappropriate, or in poor taste? Assuming that there are no legal constraints that bar such agencies from providing the service in question, what are the considerations for selecting one agency over the other?

6. Was the data presented sufficient to support an outsourcing decision? If not, what was missing? What should some of the performance measures/indicators be if the decision is to try a contracted service for a limited period before making the final decision whether to outsource or not? Can such an experiment provide sufficient data for making the choice?

7. The county was in the hands of Democrats for many years. Given this background, how would the attractiveness of a contracting-out proposal be influenced by the presence of a strong union, partisan politics, a civil service, or other non-employment-at-will systems in the sheriff's office? Of an appointed sheriff?

8. In such a diversified and decentralized environment, how does a government perform strategic planning? How does it manage the transfunctional "suprasystems" (Stahl and Bounds, 1991) that by nature involve and affect a number of departments without being under the control of any one (such as justice administration processes that involve police, prosecutors, public defenders, the courts, court clerks, incarceration, parole, and other organizationally independent departments and units)? Who are the stake holders in such suprasystems, and what are their interests? How (and to what extent) does the budget analyst consider these interests and incorporate them into a budget recommendation?

9. Since 1992, process service costs have risen and fees have fallen. How might such growing losses affect the political calculus? What actions might concerned stakeholders take?

10. How is this case consistent or inconsistent with various theories of (1) the "budget maximizing bureaucrat" as presented by Niskanen (1971; 1975; 1991) or any other economic models of bureaucracy, and (2) principal–agent models as presented by Stein (1990) or Miranda (1992; 1994).

REFERENCES

Donahue, J. D. (1989). *The Privatization Decision: Public Ends, Private Means*. New York: Basic Books.

Halachmi, A. (April 1979). Introducing the concept of feasibility in class. *Teaching Political Science*, 6(3), 291–310.

Halachmi, A. (1977). Feasibility analysis and custom made planning. *Indian Journal of Public Administration*, 30(1), 139–148.

Halachmi, A. and Holzer, M. (1993). Towards a competitive public administration. *International Review of Administrative Sciences*, 59, 29–45.

Kelley, J. T. (1984). *Costing Government Services: A Guide for Decision Making*. Washington, DC: Government Finance Research Center of the Government Finance Officers Association.

Miranda, R. A. (1992). *Privatizing City Government: Explaining the Adoption and Budgetary Consequences of Alternative Service Delivery Arrangements*, unpublished doctoral dissertation. Chicago: Harris Graduate School of Public Policy Studies, University of Illinois at Chicago.

Miranda, R. (1994). Privatization and the budget-maximizing bureaucrat, *Public Productivity and Management Review*.

Niskanen, W. A. (1971). *Bureaucracy and Representative Government*. Chicago: Alladin Atherton.

Niskanen, W. A. (1975). Bureaucracies and politicians, *Journal of Law and Economics*, 18, 617–644.

Niskanen, W. A. (1991). A reflection on bureaucracy and representative government. In A. Blais and S. Dion (eds). *The Budget Maximizing Bureaucrat: Appraisals and Evidence*. Pittsburgh: Pittsburgh University Press. pp. 13–31.

Stahl, M. J. and Bounds, G. M. (1991). *Competing Globally Through Customer Value: The Management of Strategic Suprasystems*. Westport, CT: Quorum.

6

Issues in Budget Execution

Jerry McCaffery and John E. Mutty
Naval Postgraduate School, Monterey, California, U.S.A.

Budgeting is Planning, Implementing is management

While the act of budgeting is a planning process, budget execution is a management process. Budget preparation is planning for policy accomplishment, and budget execution is managing the budget plan for policy implementation. Bernard Pitsvada suggests budget execution is "that phase of the budget cycle in which agencies actually obligate or commit funds in pursuit of accomplishing programmatic goals."[1] Following plans made in the budget preparation cycle, employees or contractors are engaged, materials and supplies are purchased, contracts are let, and capital equipment is purchased. All the minutiae of administration necessary to realize those programs, plans, and activities are presented in the budget process. While much can be observed in budget making as a result of the openness of the legislative budget process with its hearings, debates, and votes based on executive budget documents and various legislative analyses, only parts of the budget execution process are observable to outsiders. Actions that require legislative approval or notification are observable: thus impoundments, rescissions and deferrals, reprogrammings, and certain transfers may be studied at the federal level. Gross breaches in propriety, program inefficiency, and even fraud, waste, and misuse of funds may be seen in audits, General Accounting Office studies, and inspector general reports, reported in congressional hearings, or unearthed as items of interest by the news media. The ordinary routines of budget execution, however, are usually carried out far from the spotlight of public attention, and the crises that make up much of the day-to-day lives of account administrators and program managers are slowly buried under an accumulating mass of detail as the fiscal year rolls on. Even players within an agency see little of this budget execution process as it unfolds, unless it affects their own program. While there is an assumption that the budget will be executed as planned once it is approved and that this is a relatively simple task compared to preparing and passing the budget, the reality of administrative life is quite different. A substantial portion of budget execution is driven by the necessity of rescuing careful plans from unforeseen events and emergencies and unknowable contingencies. At the end of the year, in the aggregate and on average, budget execution may appear to have been a matter of uninteresting routine constrained by obscure and arcane rules and procedures and dominated by financial control procedures, but it is unlikely to have appeared so uneventful to the department budget officer and his staff or the manager charged with carrying out the program.

Despite great attention paid to budget execution in the last decades by practitioners, the academic literature is still largely focused on budget preparation. There is a substantial body of literature developing on budget execution under other titles,[2] however, and leading texts now discuss cash management and investment, debt administration, and tax administration, pension funds, risk management, capital budgeting and bonds, and property management as well as budget preparation.[3] In this chapter we extend the study of budget execution to reflections on how the Department of Defense (DOD) administers its main supporting expense account, operations and maintenance (O&M). We examine resource commitment patterns and then we reflect on some of the issues managers confront in solving the tension between control and flexibility. Our intent is to show the turbulence that exists in budget execution, while illustrating some of the rules and constraints DOD managers must cope with in this turbulent environment.

BACKGROUND

All systems have set rules and procedures to help guide the jurisdiction through budget execution. In the federal government, once an appropriation is passed, the Treasury issues a warrant for the amount of money to be spent during the year. The Office of Management and Budget (OMB) apportions this amount to each agency. Each agency head then uses allotments to delegate to subordinates the authority to incur a specific amount of obligations. These allotments may be further subdivided into allocations by lower administrative levels. Following these allotments and allocations, obligations can be incurred (e.g., a contract let) and outlays can be paid when the work or service is completed or the equipment is delivered. The apportionment, allotment, and allocation processes are the actual planning for when funds will be spent, by quarter or month and by administrative level.[4] Taken from the Department of Energy budget execution manual, Exhibit I describes many of the federal mechanisms that control budget execution. Some of these are department-specific; some apply to all federal agencies. Their scope also indicates the complexity of budget execution.

Exhibit 1   Legal Bases for Budget Execution

1. Article 1, Section 9, of the Constitution of the United States, which states that, "No money shall be drawn from the Treasury, but in Consequence of Appropriations made by Law" and upon which the apportionment and Treasury warrant process is based.
2. Title 31, United States Code (U.S.C.), Section 1301, "Application of Appropriations," which restricts the expenditure of funds to the purposes for which they are appropriated.
3. Title 31, U.S.C. Sections 1341, 1342, the "Anti-Deficiency Act," which states that no federal officer or employee may authorize government obligations or expenditures in advance of or in excess of an appropriation, unless otherwise authorized by law, and that no federal officer or employee may accept voluntary services except as authorized by law.
4. Title 31, U.S.C., Section 1512, "Apportionment and Reserves," which provides the legislative basis for the apportionment process by requiring, except as otherwise provided, that all appropriations and funds available for obligation be apportioned.

5. Title 31, U.S.C., Section 1514, "Administrative Division of Apportionments," which requires establishment of administrative control of funds designed to restrict obligations against an appropriation or fund to the amount of the apportionment or reapportionment, and that the agency head be able to fix responsibility for the creation of any obligation in excess of an apportionment or reapportionment.

6. Title 31, U.S.C., Section 1517, "Prohibited Obligations and Expenditures," which prohibits making or authorizing expenditures or obligations in excess of available apportioned funds, or amount permitted by regulations under Section 1514, and requires the reporting of violations of this section to the president and the Congress.

7. The "Budget and Accounting Procedures Act of 1950," which defines the legal basis for the issuance of appropriation warrants by the secretary of the treasury, who is responsible for the system of central accounting and financial reporting for the government as a whole.

8. "Congressional Budget and Impoundment Control Act of 1974," which establishes the fiscal year to commence on 10–1 (Title 31, U.S.C., Section 1102), and prescribes the rescission and deferral process (Title 2, U.S.C., Sections 681–688).

9. Title 31, U.S.C. Section 1535, "Agency Agreements" (commonly referred to as the "Economy Act"), which authorizes a federal agency to place reimbursable agreements for work or services with other federal agencies.

10. Section 111 of the Energy Reorganization Act of 1974, as amended, Public Law 93–438, which cites provisions and limitations applicable to the use of operating expenses, expenditures for facilities and capital equipment, new project starts, and the merger of funds.

11. Section 659 of the Department of Energy Organization Act of 1977, Public Law 95–91, which allows the secretary, when authorized in an appropriation act for any fiscal year, to transfer funds from one appropriation to another, providing that no appropriation is either increased or decreased by more than 5% for that fiscal year.

12. Annual authorization and appropriation acts, which may contain specific guidance on department funding as well as limitations on reprogramming, restructuring, and appropriation transfer actions.

13. OMB Circular No. A-34, "Instructions on Budget Execution," of 10–18–94, which provides instructions on budget execution, including apportionments, reapportionments, deferrals, proposed and enacted rescissions, systems for administrative control of funds, allotments,

14. Treasury Fiscal Requirements Manual, volume I, Section 2040, which prescribes the procedures to be followed in the issuance of treasury appropriation warrants.

15. DOE 4300.2C, Non-Department of Energy Funded Work (Work for Others), of 12-28-94, which establishes policies, procedures, and responsibilities for authorizing non-DOE funded work.

16. "Government Accounting Office Policy and Procedures Manual for Guidance of Federal Agencies," Title 7, Fiscal Procedures, of 5-18-93, which provides guidance related to agency fiscal processes and financial systems.

Source: Ref. 5.

In his classic text on budgeting, Jesse Burkhead states that budget execution is an executive responsibility;[6] however, he observes, in the United States history is replete with instances in which the legislative body has intervened in execution to modify decisions it has previously made to influence administrative actions and to interpose independent checks on specific transactions.[7] Burkhead divides techniques for budget execution into two groups, financial and administrative. Financial controls are directed at the various accounts used to record government transactions for both receipts and expenditures. Administrative controls refer to the normal events of budget execution as they are experienced in the daily lives of most administrators and have to do with executing and adjusting the budget plan that was developed and refined in the executive branch and reviewed and approved in the legislative branch. Burkhead observes that the goals of budget execution involve preserving legislative intent, observing financial limitations, and maintaining flexibility at all levels of administration.[8]

These themes were reflected in research reported in 1983 by Bernard Pitsvada, who examined the flexibility federal agencies have in budget execution in terms of object classification, appropriation structure, contingency appropriations, emergency provisions, and reprogramming authority.[9] Pitsvada suggested that object classification serves accounting and control purposes, but that planning and management purposes are not well served by object classification. He observed that no agency in the federal government prepared a budget solely in object format, but that object data were provided to Congress with programmatic budget data in order to support agency requests because Congress found it easier to understand. Pitsvada further suggests that in budget execution, object classification generally leaves agencies with great flexibility to shift funds around to meet needs within or between categories. Pitsvada states that funds can be shifted from personnel salaries to purchase supplies and equipment if there is a surplus in the personnel account, and funds can be shifted from the utility account to communications, if for example "a successful energy conservation campaign reduces the original requirement for utilities."[10] Pitsvada states that these transfers among various objects of expenditure occur at thresholds below those at which Congress would have to be notified. Pitsvada adds that, in general, Congress intercedes with specific constraints only if an agency has "performed in a manner that displeases Congress."[11] Pitsvada concludes that the paradox of budget execution involves agencies, which feel they must have more flexibility to meet changing needs, and Congress, which feels that unless it exercises meaningful control over execution it is not performing its most vital constitutional power, the power or the purse. Pitsvada calls for more study of budget execution because it is of fundamental importance: "It is, after all, the entire reason that agencies prepare and justify budgets and Congress enacts them."[12] He laments that budget execution remains the most neglected area of budget research and that this paucity of research has existed for many decades,[13] probably because budget execution is such a "diverse complicated field that is filled with complex details."[14]

The tension over the correct amount of control and flexibility in budget execution remains. Recently observers have suggested that too much control, and controls of the wrong kind, impair program efficiency,[15] but with the growth in size of the federal budget making any small percentage errors into large dollar errors, the necessity for controls that ensure fiscal propriety contains powerful practical and symbolic value. Where managers might prefer more flexibility, the public insists that public monies be safeguarded, even if this results in more control than might be strictly necessary. In this chapter we do not examine the interface between Congress and DOD, but rather the routine administration of the O&M account in DOD and the turbulence that DOD managers face as they administer accounts and implement programs. As Pitsvada suggests, certain transfers can be and are made, but there is also a multitude of constraints with which managers must cope in this turbulent environment.

DON/DOD BUDGET EXECUTION PATTERNS

Table 1 describes the obligation rate of the DOD O&M account. This account is analogous to the supporting expense category in most other budgets; it funds everything from bombs to bullets, steaming hours to flying hours, yellow tablets to yellow paint. It does not fund military personnel, weapon systems procurement, or research and development. This account is closely watched, for it is a major contributor to training and readiness and to the ability of DOD to go places and do things. It is also closely watched when new missions emerge or budget reductions are necessary. To assume a new unbudgeted mission in the national interest within a fiscal year often means finding money in the O&M accounts and spending it, with the reimbursement coming later. When quick budget reductions are needed, the O&M account is often the first target, because it is usually spent in one year and a dollar reduction means a dollar of saving in the particular year, whereas the ship procurement account may require $20 of reductions to get $1 of reduction in the current year because ship construction is a multiple year account. In sum, the O&M account, which averages over 35% of the DOD appropriation,[16] is a sensitive and important account that funds much of the daily business of DOD. By the same token, it requires close and skillful management.

Mark Kozar studied the DOD O&M account over fourteen fiscal years (FY 1977 through FY 1990) and found O&M account managers obligating over 99% of their funds before the appropriation expired at the end of the year.[17] This is a remarkable performance

Table 1 Percentage of O&M Monthly Obligation (1977–1990)

Month	DOD	Air Force	Army	Navy
October[a]	11.235	14.192	9.188	11.69
November	8.018	8.52	8.059	7.736
December	7.346	6.815	7.968	7.212
January[b]	10.048	10.526	9.117	10.814
February	7.165	6.224	7.851	7.429
March	7.223	6.251	7.979	7.166
April[b]	9.083	9.399	8.209	9.69
May	6.708	6.159	7.046	6.445
June	6.726	5.881	7.141	6.49
July[b]	8.778	9.324	8.113	8.525
August	6.887	6.173	7.276	6.67
September	10.616	10.662	12.473	9.319
Total	99.833	100.13	100.42	99.186

Note: Percentages exceed 100 due to rounding; [a]start of fiscal year; [b]first month of quarter.

by these fund managers, given legal constraints and penalties against overspending.[18] Within this orderly pattern of commitment of resources, however, there were quarterly and monthly variations, and variations among the military departments. In general, the first and last months of the FY are the highest months. October generally surges as a result of new contracts being let. The summer is low as year-end positioning takes place and then September is high as managers rush to spend their funds on what had been planned for and those new needs that have arisen.

In the introduction to *Reinventing Government*, Osborne and Gaebler state that the federal budget system encourages managers to waste money:

> "If they don't spend their entire budget by the end of the fiscal year, three things happen: they lose the money they have saved; they get less next year; and the budget director scolds them for requesting too much last year. Hence the time honored rush to spend all funds by the end of the fiscal year."[19]

Data from Kozar's study seem to support the rush to spend funds at the end of the fiscal year. The data in Table 1 are presented in a monthly format for DOD and the military departments.[20] Not only are there quarterly and monthly variations, but obligation rates also vary by military department, particularly in the first month of the fiscal year.

Figure 1 clearly demonstrates the cyclical nature of those obligations. October, the first month of the fiscal year, is the highest. Then the first month of the next three quarters is high, but lower than October, with average obligation rates decreasing during the fiscal year. September, the last month of the fiscal year, represents a significant surge, exhibiting an obligation rate only slightly lower than October.

There are two legal bases for these patterns. The first may be found in the U.S. Code, Title 31, Section 1512, Apportionment and Reserves, which states that an appropriation available for obligation for a definite period should be apportioned to prevent obligation or expenditure at a rate that would indicate a necessity for a supplemental or deficiency appropriation for the period. An appropriation subject to apportionment may be apportioned by months, calendar quarters, operating seasons, or other time periods.

Operations and Maintenance appropriations are apportioned by calendar quarters by the OMB under the authority of Title 31, Section 1513. The apportionments, available on a cumulative basis unless reapportioned by OMB, are based on input from the military departments through the secretary of defense. According to Title 31, Section 1514, the secretary of defense is then responsible for enacting regulations to administratively control and divide the apportionment. The system is designed to limit obligations to the amount

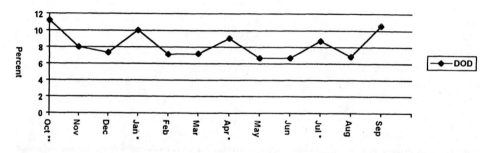

Figure 1 O&M monthly obligations (1977–1990)

apportioned, to fix responsibility for violations of the apportionments, and to provide a simple way to administratively divide the appropriation between commands. Apportionments are an effective tool for preventing too rapid an obligation of total funds at any point in the fiscal year. Because funds are available on a cumulative basis, however, apportionments are better able to prevent obligation surges at the beginning of the fiscal year than at the end of the fiscal year.[21] The data in Figure 1 clearly show an end-of-year spending surge. When compared to the actual average obligation rate of the last month of each of the first three quarters (7.098%), September's rate of 10.616% is 49.6% higher.

The second legal basis for these patterns may be found in Title 31, Section 1502 of the U.S. Code, which states that the balance of an appropriation or fund limited for obligation to a definite period is available only for payment of expenses properly incurred during the period of availability or to complete contracts properly made within that period of availability and obligated consistent with Section 1501. A balance remaining in an appropriation account at the end of the period of availability must be returned to the general fund of the Treasury, according to this section. This is reiterated annually in the general provisions of the DOD Appropriations Act, which typically states that "no part of any appropriation contained in this Act shall remain available for obligation beyond the current fiscal year, unless expressly so provided herein."

As a matter of practice, the budget execution box in which the funds administrator is forced to work is bounded by appropriation life, appropriation size, and the penalties associated with either over- or underspending. The first quarter surge reflects the award of annual service contracts, which must be in place for the entire fiscal year but cannot be awarded until money is appropriated and allocated for a new fiscal year. The second and third quarters each starts with a surge as quarterly allocations are received in the first month. Overall spending, however, is tempered by the realization that funds must last for the entire fiscal year. Some funding is held in reserve for unknown contingencies. That funding is held until the end of the fourth quarter, when it is spent on those contingencies, or more likely, to cover requirements deferred from earlier in the year. In either case, the money *is* spent.

With few exceptions, any unobligated funds are lost when the O&M appropriation expires at the end of the fiscal year. This gives managers a very strong incentive to spend all available funds and explains the 99% obligation rate and the September surge. The obligation rate data indicate that DOD managers are highly skilled at obligating funds before the end of the fiscal year and commit a lot of funds quickly in September despite numerous rules and provisions designed to forestall this process and prevent abuses in commitments of funds. After all, DOD managers must find valid current fiscal year needs to legally justify obligating the funds before the remaining obligational authority expires.

Undoubtedly some of these September purchases help meet needs in the next fiscal year and thus by supporting purchases other than current fiscal year needs, funds can be freed up in the next fiscal year which is, in September, less than 30 days away.[22] Managers in the O&M accounts know they are managing a multiple-year stream of resources. Replacing inventory or beginning a ship or aircraft overhaul are examples of obligations the manager may take at the end of the current fiscal year to meet fiscal burdens that he certainly would have had to meet in the next fiscal year. The O&M account is not a neat and orderly world; prices and inflation rates change, commodity prices fluctuate, and operating tempos change from what was anticipated. Fund managers must adjust to these changes. This means that they pay the bills they must when they must, such as service contracts that come due at the first of the year and in the first month of each quarter, and then hold back a little on other items that can be postponed until later in the year.

For example, although it is a small percentage of the total funds, the item for "equipment" in the Department of Navy O&M appropriation shows a large peak in obligations near the end of the fiscal year.[23] This category includes items such as motor vehicles, furniture, machinery, data-processing equipment, armaments, instruments, and appliances. Overall, an average of 41% of O&M Navy equipment obligations occurred during August and September.[24]

This pattern is understandable from the point of view of budget managers. The equipment purchase category constitutes a source of flexibility. If a piece of equipment scheduled for replacement is still operational, the unit may be willing to delay replacing it until closer to the end of the fiscal year. Then if no higher priority need appears, the unit may purchase the item or items previously budgeted. By accepting uncertainty and delaying certain purchases, the financial manager provides some slack, which may help reduce the impact of unpredictable events upon him.

Toward the end of one fiscal year, O&M managers are also positioning themselves for the next fiscal year by examining actions they can take in this year that will help them meet the burdens of the following year. During the 1980s, the time period covered in Table 1, both the Army and the Marine Corps consistently held large training exercises in the fall. Fund managers may have prepared for these exercises by starting their maintenance ramp-up in September for the operations, which typically lasted from mid-September to mid-November in the United States and in Europe. This buildup then appears as a surge in September obligations for operations for when the main burden falls in the next fiscal year. If this phenomenon happened between May and June, it would be unremarkable; since it happens at the end of the fiscal year, it is noticed.

Execution Processes and Problems

The problems associated with budget execution highlight the old saw, "where you stand on an issue depends on where you sit at the time."[25] The layers of management faced by a comptroller in the federal government can severely limit the options available to make the adjustments needed to correct an emergent problem. Typically, the higher the level, the more control an organization has over its own resources, yet the nature and size of the problems also change with the various levels. For example, when the DOD receives the funds apportioned by OMB, it in turn allocates those funds to the various military departments and defense agencies within its jurisdiction. Typically a portion of those funds are withheld to accommodate either known or potential problems. If funding for programs has been appropriated but not authorized, that money may be withheld pending negotiations with the authorizing committees. Similarly, those programs that received funding in excess of the president's budget request may have the additional funds withheld as a source of funding for contingencies. When operations in Bosnia became more expensive than anticipated and additional moneys were not appropriated by Congress, DOD developed a rescission list that in large part consisted of those programs added by Congress that were either not in the president's budget request or were increased over the amount requested. While these actions provided some flexibility at the department level, they had the opposite effect at lower levels. Those programs that had anticipated the additional funding now had to proceed with the uncertainty associated with any rescission list; that is, when will the list be submitted and if submitted, will it be approved? At the very least,

Table 2   Manageability of Budget Execution Issues

	Level		
Issue (problem)	Local	Headquarters	Agency
Taxes (administrative)	1	2	3
Timeliness	1	2	2
Discretionary dollars	1	2	2–3
Color of money	1	1	1–2
Politics	1	1	2
Flexibility	1	2	2
Management information systems	2	2	2

any actions must be delayed until the end of the process. If Congress does not approve the rescission, an already late allocation will be even later. If the rescission is approved, there will be no funding at all. Given that the Congress has 45 days to approve a rescission after the president proposes it, the funds will not be available for obligation, at the earliest, until one to two quarters into the fiscal year.

The following sections discuss some of the issues that are common to all levels of budget execution. While they are common, however, they affect each of the levels to a differing degree. Table 2 provides an indication of who is affected by what and how much flexibility they have to respond to the problem at their level. Each of the issues will be discussed later.

Table 2 assigns a number to each of the above issues (problems), to its manageability. Such manageability typically varies with the level at which the problem is experienced: 1 = little ability to control at this level; 2 = some ability to control at this level; and 3 = a great deal of ability to control at this level.

Taxes (Administrative)

With the exception of the lowest level, at nearly every level of control funds administrators have the tendency to shave a "little off the top" to accommodate either known or anticipated contingencies.[26] These taxes can range from those imposed by Congress, such as the 2% reduction applied to all Department of the Navy procurement and research and development programs in FY 1997 to pay for a shortfall in the defense business operations fund, to a 1–2% withhold by the Department of the Navy to all O&M accounts, to a base commanding officer keeping a small percentage of his operating funds in reserve until the end of the fiscal year.[27] While each of these taxes may be known early in the year, each requires an adjustment to the level of spending that had been justified in the budget planning phase. Because budgeting for contingencies is not allowed and budget submissions are scrubbed to eliminate excess funding, a tax by definition means that the money received at the lower levels is less than that required. Additionally, if the "contingency" does not materialize, the money that had been set aside will likely be released late in the fiscal year, requiring additional perturbations to the revised plan that is now being executed.

Timeliness

All budgets are premised on a spending plan that assumes receipt of funds at a certain time. In a perfect world, Congress would finish deliberations in time to pass authorization and appropriations bills by the first of October. Treasury would be ready to issue its warrants, and OMB would be ready to apportion the money on the first day of the fiscal year, with the receiving agencies following closely behind. In that the first step rarely occurs on time, none of the follow-on steps can be timely either.[28] This entails adjustments to the plans upon which the budgets were approved. In the case of a continuing resolution authority (CRA), Congress typically specifies not only the level of spending but also imposes other restrictions (e.g., no spending on new program starts). Spending levels are normally limited to prior year rates or the lower of the House or Senate versions of the appropriations bill (assuming that a conference between the House and Senate has not yet taken place.) For a program that is fairly new, reverting to a spending profile that matches that of the previous year may require laying off employees, postponing tests, and delaying contract awards. Over the course of the previous fiscal year, a new program typically will have hired additional people, started testing, and increased the rate of spending in other areas. If the program must revert to a pre-expansion level of spending because of a CRA, inefficiencies, additional start-up costs, and other money "sumps" will be the inevitable result, requiring program restructures and perhaps additional funding. Whenever funding is not received when it is anticipated, budget execution is affected.[29]

Discretionary Dollars

The more control one has over the dollars allocated to his programs, the easier it is to execute a budget. The control over the dollars depends on the amount and the level of specificity tied to each dollar. If X employees must be paid Y dollars and Y dollars are all that are available, there are no discretionary dollars. Unless someone leaves, there is no flexibility to accommodate changes in work requirements or pay for promotions, give bonuses, or take other appropriate actions. If a comptroller has access to Y + Z dollars, however he has the ability to pay overtime, hire temps, or hire additional workers should the workload dictate. The availability of discretionary dollars typically is directly proportional to the level of management. This is not surprising, given the increase in the level of aggregation at the higher levels. If there are 1000 employees in a major organization, accommodating the departure and replacement of twenty-five employees across the organization is relatively simple. At a lower level, however, the replacement of two employees out of a twenty person workforce could cause major problems. Moreover, with no turnover this unit manager accrues no slack in his personnel account to use to meet unforeseen needs.

Color of Money

Money is appropriated for the DOD in specific categories, each having specific rules and limitations. The categories or appropriations restrict the manner in which a budget can executed. While all dollars are green, these restrictions make the use of these dollars so different they might as well be different colors. For example, the O&M appropriation has a one-year life and finances the cost of ongoing operations (e.g., base operations, civilian personnel salaries, maintenance of property, and training). Aircraft procurement has a three-year life and finances the procurement of aircraft and related supporting programs. Military construction has a five-year life and finances the purchase of land and construction of facilities. The restrictions on each of these appropriations effectively create legal boundaries that put the budget manager in a budgetary box with walls that are difficult to breach.

The ability to move money from one box to another is normally beyond the control of the funds administrator. Should one box have too little money and another too much, it is not a simple matter of shifting money from one to the other; that can only be accomplished within the restrictions imposed by such mechanisms as reprogrammings, transfers, supplemental appropriations, and concomitant glacial approval processes, first within the executive branch and then within Congress. This would be equivalent to receiving your paycheck divided into categories such as food, clothing, housing, and transportation. Suppose you were invited out to dinner and therefore had that meal's allocation available for something else. Maybe you would like to take advantage of a sale on tires for the car. If you were working under rules similar to those imposed by the federal government, spending that food money on tires (which might save you three times as much in the long run) would require you to get approval from your banker and employer—in writing. Similarly, if you just wanted to save that money for a nice meal in a restaurant next month—sorry; that food money was only good for this month.

Political

While there is no question that the budget formulation and approval process has political dimensions, it might be surprising to find that the budget execution process is also affected, albeit from a distance. In gross terms, any congressional pork item has the potential to change a budget plan. Assuming a zero sum game, if Congress adds three C-130 aircraft to the president's budget request, the C-130 program manager has to make changes to adjust for the additional aircraft in everything from the quantity of training materials to the amount of support equipment. Additionally, some other portion of the budget must be decremented to pay for the additional aircraft, causing perturbations to programs unrelated to the C-130 program.

Oftentimes decisions are made with respect to suppliers, both foreign and domestic, that have less to do with military requirements than with political considerations. Nuclear submarines are constructed in two domestic shipyards, ostensibly to maintain an "industrial base", even though a single shipyard has the capacity to build all the required submarines. Using two shipyards may increase costs and delay contract awards, but it also ensures that workers from two states and many more congressional districts are employed. Buying products overseas to satisfy commitments to foreign governments certainly affects the execution process when language concerns, exchange rates, and security issues are factored in. Requirements to hire minority firms, buy American, ensure that fighter aircraft fit both men and women, all have political origins, and all affect budget execution. Additionally, program managers may adopt political strategies to enhance the life of their programs. For example, ensuring that contracts are let in as many congressional districts as possible may enhance the attractiveness of the program in Congress, but it also will complicate the execution of the program by increasing the number of contracts and contractors.

Flexibility

Flexibility in the budget execution process means the ability to make adjustments within the resources that have been allocated. As with discretionary dollars, the higher the level of management, the greater the degree of flexibility. At the local level, dollars for maintenance and repair are typically not tied to specific buildings or projects. The local manager can decide to use dollars to fix a leaking roof or paint a building; he may not have the flexibility to do both. If money is appropriated to construct a new building, there is essentially no option other than to build that building, even if repairing another building would be more useful. The flexibility thus depends on the amount of money available as well as the specificity with which it is authorized and appropriated. Even "commonsense" decisions are sometimes restricted. For example, in 1988, a program manager for a missile program negotiated a contract that would have allowed him to procure eight more missile for the same amount of money. He could not sign that contract without prior congressional approval, however, because the missiles were line-item appropriated with a specific quantity specified. While it seems to make sense to buy the additional missiles, some Congressmen may argue against it on the grounds that only the original number of missiles was necessary and any money saved should be put elsewhere. In sum, congressional approval of such changes is neither quick nor certain.

Management Information Systems

Finally, the comptroller is somewhat at the mercy of his management information system to provide specifics on funds available, funds obligated, and funds expended. The days of manual ledger sheets are long gone. As with any system, the quality of the inputs directly affects the quality of the outputs. Frequently the comptroller has little or no control over the inputs. Those inputs may be made in distant field activities, in a contractor's facility, or not at all. His system may not be compatible with the systems of other activities that he deals with, which in turn means manual intervention with all of its attendant errors. In 1993, the DOD had 270 financial management information systems. It also had $24 billion of unmatched disbursements,[30] that is, bills had been paid but who had been paid and out of what account they had been paid could not be determined. Contractors were not demanding payments, so it was logical to assume that they had been paid, yet how they had been paid and how much they had been paid was a mystery. Errors ranged from simple numerical transpositions (not surprising when strings of manually entered numbers and letters were as long as sixteen characters); to funds being paid out of the wrong appropriation or the wrong year. Records at the local (execution) level seldom matched those at the headquarters level. Executing a budget without precisely knowing the status of one's funds would give even the most cavalier comptroller nightmares.

SUMMARY AND CONCLUSION

Financial managers must meet the challenges of a turbulent environment, but their discretion is circumscribed by custom, rules, congressional intercessions, and fundamentally, law. The Anti-Deficiency Act, the common name for Title 31, Sections 1341, 1349, 1350, 1512–14, and 1517–19, prevents managers from obligating more funds than are available and from obligating funds before an appropriation is enacted unless provided for by a continuing resolution. Title 31, Section 1341 includes limits on the expenditure and obligation of funds and states that an officer or employee of the U.S. government may not make or authorize an expenditure or obligation exceeding the amount available in an appropriation for the expenditure or obligation, or involve the government in a contract or obligation for the payment of money before an appropriation is made unless authorized by law.

Penalties for those who break this law are substantial; administrative discipline and criminal penalties can include suspension without pay, removal from office, fines up to

$5,000, and imprisonment for two years.[31] The same penalties apply to officials who authorize exceeding apportionments, allotments, or operating budgets. Some scholars have argued that the laws and rules that surround financial management substantially decrease mission performance, efficiency, and effectiveness. Jones and Thompson argue that controls on budget execution ought to be tailored to the type of good produced, with simple and homogeneous goods relying on after-the-fact controls (ex post) and complex and new goods relying on before-the-fact controls (ex ante). Differentiation would also occur by type of organization and degree of probable competition to produce the good. Ultimately a more appropriate and effective, and less costly set of controls would be developed.[32] Until this happens federal financial managers will have to cope with a turbulent environment and compendious constraints that inhibit entrepreneurial behavior while punishing illegal actions.

REVIEW QUESTIONS

1. What are the most significant differences between budget preparation and budget execution? In the same vein, what do you think are the most important parts of the legal framework surrounding budget execution?

2. What is the paradox in budget execution? How much say should the legislature have in budget execution?

3. For what are apportionments and allotments used?

4. What options does a manager have to find money for emergencies within the fiscal year?

5. How does a continuing resolution appropriation work? What are its benefits and costs?

6. How does the federal budget system encourage managers to waste money? Is there a year-end spending rush in the DOD? If so, is this good or bad?

7. Do all the military departments show the same obligation rate? What are the differences and what causes them?

8. How does the ability to manage funds change with the administrator's level in the organization? Which is better to be—higher up or lower down? Of the management issues, which do you think are the most difficult for the manager to handle?

9. To what extent do you think the laws and rules surrounding budget execution impair mission performance and lead to inefficiency? What solution do you see in this problem?

NOTES

1. See Pitsvada, B. (summer 1983). Federal budget execution. *Public Budgeting and Finance*, 3(2), 83–101; see p. 87.

2. For example, recently *Public Budgeting and Finance* has carried such articles as "Local Government Reserve Funds" (C. Tyer, summer 1993); "State and Corporate Cash Management" (K. Mattson, M. Hackbart and J. Ramsey, winter 1990); "Surviving a Revenue Collapse" (R. Gould, winter 1990); "Federal Financial Management Control Systems" (W. B. Hildreth, spring 1993); and

"The Impact of State Rainy Day Funds in Easing State Fiscal Crises During the 1990–1991 Recession" (R. Sobel and R. Holcombe, fall 1996).

3. See Mikesell J. *Fiscal Administration*. Chicago: Dorsey; (1986). Lynch, T. (1995). *Public Budgeting in America*. Englewood Cliffs, NJ: Prentice Hall.

4. For more detail on the federal budget execution process, see OMB circular A-34.

5. The source for this exhibit is the Department of Energy. (1996). *Budget Execution Manual*, DOE M 135.1–1. Office of the Chief Financial Officer, Budget Execution Branch, CR-131.

6. See Burkhead, J. (1959). Budget execution. In *Government Budgeting*. New York: Wiley. pp. 340–356.

7. See Note 6, p. 341. Historically, Burkhead noted, there has been a strong decentralized component in the United States, particularly at state and local levels. Burkhead quotes A. E. Buck on the reason for this "agencies were often arranged in a haphazard and disjointed fashion, their administrative officers, in many instances not being even remotely under executive control or supervision . . . Although the executive might prepare a satisfactory financial plan for the legislative body under these circumstances, he could not hope to be able to enforce the plan once it had been adopted" (Ref. 6, p. 342).

8. See Note 6, p. 342.

9. See Note 1.

10. Note 1; see the discussion on p. 85.

11. Note 1, p. 86.

12. Note 1, p. 100.

13. Note 1, p. 84.

14. Note 1, p. 100.

15. See Jones, L. R. and Thompson, F. (1994). *Reinventing the Pentagon*. San Francisco: Jossey-Bass; especially Chapt. 6, Redesigning control systems, pp. 155–193.

16. See Perry, W. J. (March 1996). *Annual Reprot to the President and Congress*. Washington, DC: USGPO, p. B-1.

17. See Kozar, M. J. (Dec. 1993). *An Analysis of Obligation Patterns for the Department of Defense Operations and Maintenance Appropriations*. master's thesis, Naval Postgraduate School, Monterey, CA, p. 73.

18. For further discussion of these end-of-year patterns, see Kozar M. and McCaffery, J. (Oct. 1994). DOD O&M obligation patterns: Some reflections and issues. *Navy Comptroller*, 5(1), 2–13.

19. Gaebler, T. and Osborne, D. (1993). *Reinventing Government*. New York: Penguin, p. 3.

20. The data in Table I are derived from Note 17, Appendix A, from the following tables: "O&M Total Obligations," pp. 132–133, "O&M Air Force," pp. 126–127, "O&M Army," pp. 120–121 and "O&M Navy," pp. 116–117. Fourteen years of monthly obligation data provided by the Defense Finance and Accounting Service for 11 Department of Defense O&M accounts were studied for the fiscal years 1977 through 1990.

21. See Note 18, p. 3.

22. By law, it is illegal to use current-year money to meet next year's needs, the money must be obligated to meet needs that arise in the current year. The

actual outlay of funds may happen in the following year. For example, in 1984 GAO found that DOD industrial funds illegally carried O&M funds over to the next fiscal year. Reporting to the chairman of the House Appropriations Committee, GAO reported that the six DOD industrial fund activities carried over about $35.7 million from FY 1982 to 1983 through the improper use of industrial funds, extending the life of one-year appropriations that would have otherwise expired. The primary causes for the improper carryover of funds were the lack of a legitimate current need for the good or service and the failure of the industrial activity to start the work before the end of the fiscal year. These actions violate Title 31, Section 1502 and the general provisions of the DOD Appropriation Acts. See Improper Use of Industrial Funds by Defense Extended the Life of Appropriations Which Otherwise Would Have Expired (June 1984) GAO Report AFMD-84–34. Washington, DC: USGPO.

23. Note 18, p. 10. Although this is a small account, the profile is striking. In FY 89 50.8% of this account was spent in the last quarter and 41.3 in the last two months, FY 90 saw 49.1 and 41.8, FY 91 saw 66.7 and 57.4, and FY 92 saw 57.0 and 46.5, respectively. It seems clearly to have been used as an emergency bank.

24. Note 18, p. 19.

25. This is often called Miles law, attributed to a famous Department of Agriculture budget officer, Jerry Miles, who supposedly defended conflicting statements by indicating that he had now assumed a different role.

26. Legal authority to establish reserves rests in Title 31, Section 1512, Apportionments and Reserves. Section 1512 states that in apportioning of reapportioning an appropriation, a reserve may be established only (1) to provide for contingencies; (2) to achieve savings made possible through or by changes in requirements or greater efficiency of operation, or (3) as specifically provided by law. A reserve established under this subsection may be changed as necessary to carry out the scope and objectives of the appropriation concerned.

27. Kozar and McCaffery found varying practices in the three military departments. In the early 1990s it was customary for the chief of naval operations to hold back a 2% reserve at the beginning of the year; the army chief of staff had a similar contingency policy, holding back about 5% of his O&M funds, or $100 million. Differing from Army and Navy practices, the Air Force chief of staff held back no reserve funds in this account. Normally these reserve funds would be given back to subordinate commands based on new needs during the middle-of-the-year budget review. At the same time, commands that were underexecuting their budget might well have money taken from them to be given to others that were perceived as more needy, or they might be told to pick up the pace of execution. See Note 18, p. 10.

28. All appropriation bills were passed on time in 1948, 1976, 1988, 1994, and 1996. During the period studied in Table I, DOD appropriations were passed on time in 1976, 1977, and 1988.

29. Even a slightly delayed appropriation may have large consequences for a project: "If the weather during the winter and spring precludes work on an outside project, funding and subsequent contract delay in the first quarter of the fiscal year may force some projects to be delayed for considerably longer periods of time than one might have predicted, given the length of time covered

by short term funding legislation." The same administrator commented that late appropriations were not a problem for other accounts and programs he had to administer, unless an increase in program scope was planned—thus does he reflect the essence of the budget execution dilemma: some things roll on as planned, others do not. See Note 18, p. 12.

30. Note 16, p. 107.
31. The penalties are described in Sections 1349 and 1350 of the Anti-Deficiency Act, Title 31.
32. To pursue this argument see Jones, L. R. and Thompson, F. (spring 1986) reform of budget execution control. *Public Budgeting and Finance*, 6(1), 33–49; Jones, L. R. and Bixler, G. (1992). *Mission Financing to Realign National Defense*. Greenwich, CT: JAI; Note 15, especially Chap. 6.

7

Do Program Budgets and Performance Indicators Influence Budget Allocations?

An Assessment of Mississippi Budgeting

Edward J. Clynch
Mississippi State University, Mississippi State, Mississippi, U.S.A.

At the beginning of the twentieth century, operating agencies submitted spending requests directly to the legislature without formal executive approval. Budget formats often differed, which made agency comparison impossible. For example, one agency might use five object classifications and another agency seven. With the governor out of the loop, legislators were forced to estimate revenues produced by taxes and fees, a step necessary to set the ceiling for aggregate spending. Once the legislature passed appropriations bills, agencies spent money with little if any executive oversight. As America moved through the twentieth century, freewheeling legislative-centered budgeting ceased to serve as the operating norm. Budget reform at all levels of government has centralized budgetary and financial management functions under the executive branch.

Early reformers advocated an executive budget process in which agencies submit requests to the executive, the executive analyzes and reviews the requests, the executive prepares a unified budget for submission to the legislature, and this budget operates as the basis of legislative consideration. Reformers envisioned strong executive budget powers as a gubernatorial tool to overcome the diffusion of executive authority between elected officials and independent boards and commissions. Change advocates also expected the executive document to give administrators the upper hand in budget struggles with the legislature (Cleveland, 1915; Willoughby, 1918). Beginning in the 1920s and 1930s many states gave governors strong budget powers, and reformer aspirations came to fruition. A strong executive budget provides governors with leverage over other statewide elected officials and independent boards and commissions. Since all budget requests flow through the governor's office, the executive budget sets the agenda for legislative consideration and significantly influences the content of appropriation bills (Abney and Lauth, 1989).

Generally, both conservative and liberal reformers endorsed executive budgeting. Both groups believed governors, elected by all the people, would use budget proposals to advocate spending priorities that reflected citizen wishes. Both groups expected a fiscal dividend, since executives would hold the costs of government services in check. Conservatives envisioned using this money for lower taxes while liberals anticipated employing these resources for additional worthy public sector endeavors. According to both camps, strong governors would consider the extent to which programs had achieved their stated goals when making funding decisions. Reformers pushed program budgeting, since it is difficult to determine program efficiency or program effectiveness with data displayed in an object classification format (Rubin, 1994).

Currently, forty-seven governors assume sole responsibility for preparing a budget document for legislative consideration*. Mississippi's governors were marginal budget players until the 1983 Mississippi State Supreme Court "separation of powers" decision (*Allain et al.* v. *State of Mississippi*, 1983). Today the state's top elected official prepares a budget proposal to submit to the legislature and holds exclusive responsibility for budget execution. At the same time, the legislative leadership in the form of the Joint Legislative Budget Committee (JLBC) also prepares and submits a budget proposal. Not surprisingly, the legislature tends to disregard the governor's budget and uses the JLBC budget as its working document during the session. To avoid confusion and duplication, Mississippi operates with budget guidelines developed jointly by the governor and the JLBC (Clynch, 1986).

In Mississippi, the limited gubernatorial control over budget decisions also results from the percentage of the general funds consumed by agencies that report to the governor (gubernatorial agencies). Until a 1988 executive reorganization, gubernatorial agencies accounted for only 3% of the general fund budget. After 1988, this figure increased to 21%. As Abney and Lauth (1989) note, governors use their formal powers to influence budget allocations. In Mississippi, governors could impact gubernatorial agency budget requests by reviewing and approving their budget proposals before submission to the JLBC.

Hypothesis 1: Governors preapprove the budgets of gubernatorial agencies before these documents are submitted to the JLBC.

Traditionally, most states budgeted by major object classifications, such as personnel and equipment, or by detailed line items, such as the salary for each authorized position and the amount recommended for each approved device. During the last twenty-five years many governors attempted to increase their leverage over budget decisions by adding program formats and analytic mechanisms to their state's budgeting process (Botner, 1985; Lee, 1997; Lauth, 1987). Budgeting by program involves identifying the cost of similar activities carried out for a defined purpose, such as administration or children's nutrition. Program budgets greatly enhance policy making, particularly when coupled with output data showing "efficiencies or productivity," meaning the average cost of each unit of service performed (e.g., clients served, tests conducted, number of persons trained), and outcome data indicating the average cost of each unit of a result achieved (e.g., number of persons graduated, percentage increase in test scores). A program budget with cost and impact indicators increases the likelihood of budget decisions based on efficiency and effectiveness criteria and reduces the probability of decisions simply reflecting bargained agreements (Gosling, 1992, Lee and Johnson, 1998; Lynch, 1995). Evidence exists that

---

* Both the governor and legislative leadership submit a budget proposal in Mississippi and Texas. In South Carolina a budget control board composed of the governor, other elected executive officials, and legislative leaders submits a budget.

adopting a programmatic budget format changes the focus of budget consideration from object classification items to more programmatic topics (Pettijohn and Grizzzle, 1997).

Recently the performance budget movement spread to many states that added efficiency and effectiveness measures (Broom, 1995; Posner, 1993; Sheffield, 1996). Mississippi's governors thus may use their power to develop budget guidelines to require program and analytic information in agency budget requests.

Hypothesis 2: Mississippi governors added program components and analytic mechanisms to budget guidelines in order to focus the budget debate and allocation decisions on program priorities and program performance.

Previous studies clearly demonstrate that legislators want details to maintain control (Schick, 1971). Lawmakers often resist efforts to eliminate line items and object classifications. These detailed formats focus the budget debate and allocation decisions on financial accountability and control of agency actions. (Lee, 1997; Schick, 1971). Nevertheless, Congress and many state and local legislative bodies accepted the executive budget as a way to improve legislative oversight of agency spending. Given the complexity of revenue estimation, many legislators willingly gave this task to governors. Lawmakers also recognized their inability to exercise oversight to make sure that agency spending conformed with legislative intent. Governors were granted the authority to monitor spending for compliance (Schick, 1971). In Mississippi, the 1983 separation of powers decision gave governors oversight over agency spending. In addition, legislation mandates that the governor and the JLBC share revenue-estimating responsibilities. Clearly, the existence of a separate legislative budget-writing committee creates the opportunity for legislators to add financial accountability and control items.

Hypothesis 3: The JLBC added object classification control mechanisms to focus the budget debate and allocation decisions on issues of financial accountability and control of agency actions.

Changes in state budgeting over the last quarter century suggest that governors expect to increase leverage over budget outcomes through the use of performance measures. Many scholars caution that efforts to integrate performance indicators into budget decision making have found very limited success, however (Joyce, 1993; Lauth, 1987; Posner, 1993; Lu, 1998). Agency budget requests include performance measures for programs, but budget allocators ignore them and use other factors to make decisions, such as incremental increases. Lack of success in other states suggests that Mississippi budgeters are not likely to use analytic information to shape budget allocations.

Hypothesis 4: Program and analytic information incorporated into the budget has limited impact on budget allocations.

This chapter attempts to accomplish four goals: (1) to determine the extent to which governors make an effort to shape budgets of gubernatorial agencies and to assess gubernatorial success in this endeavor; (2) to outline and assess the informational changes in Mississippi's budget guidelines initiated by governors; (3) to outline and assess the informational changes in Mississippi's budget guidelines initiated by the JLBC, and (4) to assess the impact of performance indicators on budget allocation decisions.

THE EVOLVING MISSISSIPPI BUDGET PROCESS

Mississippi's budget format retains a line-item, object classification quality, but the last fifteen years have seen the addition of several program elements, including performance indicators. Agencies receive budget guidelines in June and must submit their budget request no later than September 1. Figure 1 displays the form presented by agencies for their total budget request, a document that remains essentially unchanged since 1983 (Mississippi Legislative Budget Office and Governor's Budget Office, 1998). Agencies submit actual expenditures for the last completed fiscal year, the estimated expenses for the current spending year, money requested for the following fiscal year, and the amounts by which individual requests differ from the current year's estimated spending. Agencies must segment their budgets into major object classification categories, such as personnel services, contractual services and subdivide each object classification into line items. Section II of Figure 1 lists funding sources that support the agency's budget, including money from the general fund, federal dollars, and resources from other funds, most of which are self-generated through user fees. Section III records personnel information consisting of the number of authorized positions, the daily average number of employees, and the daily average number of vacant positions.

Table 1 lists all the information items in the 1983 agency budget requests (Mississippi Commission on Budget and Accounting, 1983). The detailed requests reflected a desire to keep agencies financially accountable and under legislative control. Budget requests contain large amounts of detailed information focusing on resource inputs. At the same time budget analysts did not receive costs broken down by program. No data delineated either the cost of a unit of service provided or the results achieved by the agency. Budget summary information included the total agency requests (Figure 1) and separate forms that display desired increases for new money needed to continue existing services because of such things as inflation, money to expand the scope of ongoing services, and money to add new services. In 1983 agencies also submitted forms containing detailed information about each object classification. Much of this information enhanced control of agency activities. For instance, the travel form catalogues each trip taken, including the name of the employee and the cost. Another item under contractual services lists professional fees and individuals hired through personal service contracts. Agencies also detailed the sources of money for each object classification category and listed each source and amount of non-general-fund money.

Table 2 arrays the information added to budget requests since the Allain decision (Mississippi Legislative Budget Office and Governor's Budget Office, 1984–1993).* *All* information requests required in 1983 remain in place today. In fact, during the last decade most years brought requirements for new information. Expanded budget requests created new demands for agencies and budget reviewers alike. As the decade progressed, budget analysts found themselves facing a wider and wider collection of information. Meaningful review was made more difficult by the small number of analysts assigned to each budget office. The twelve budget analysts who worked together as one unit in 1983 were divided

---

* The information included in this section was gleaned from several anonymous interviews conducted during the summer of 1993 and 1998. The author thanks all of these persons for their help with this project.

3 The information for Table 2 was gleaned from an analysis of the separate budget instructions issued by the JLBC's LBO and the governor's budget office for 1984, and from the joint and supplemental instructions issued by these offices for 1985–1998.

State of Mississippi
Form MBR-1 (1998)

ORIGINAL _____
REVISED _____
DATE FILED _____

AGENCY	ADDRESS		CHIEF EXECUTIVE OFFICER		
	(1) Actual Expenses FY Ending June 30, 1998	(2) Estimated Expenses FY Ending June 30, 1999	(3) Requested For FY Ending June 30, 2000	(4) Requested Increase (+) or Decrease (-) FY 2000 vs. FY 1999 (COL. 3 vs. COL. 2)	
				AMOUNT	PERCENT
I. A. PERSONAL SERVICES:					
1. Salaries, Wages & Fringe Benefits (Base)					
a. Additional Compensation					
b. Proposed Vacancy Rate (Dollar Amount)			( )		
c. Per Diem					
Total Salaries, Wages & Fringe Benefits					
2. Travel					
a. Travel & Subsistence (In State)					
b. Travel & Subsistence (Out-of-State)					
c. Travel & Subsistence (Out-of-Country)					
Total Travel					
B. CONTRACTUAL SERVICES (Schedule B):					
a. Tuition, Rewards & Awards					
b. Communications, Transportation & Utilities					
c. Public Information					
d. Rents					
e. Repairs & Service					
f. Fees, Professional & Other Services					
g. Other Contractual Services					
h. Data Processing					
i. Other					
Total Contractual Services					
C. COMMODITIES (Schedule C):					
a. Maintenance & Const. Materials & Supplies					
b. Printing & Office Supplies & Materials					
c. Equipment Repair Parts, Supplies & Accessories					
d. Professional & Scientific Supplies & Materials					
e. Other Supplies & Materials					
Total Commodities					
D. CAPITAL OUTLAY:					
1. Total Other Than Equipment (Schedule D-1)					
2. Equipment (Schedule D-2)					
a. Automobiles, Station Wagons, Trucks & Other Vehicles					
b. Road Machinery, Farm & Other Working Equipment					
c. Off. Machines, Furniture, Fixtures & Equipment					
d. IS Equipment (Data Processing & Telecommunications)					
e. Equipment - Lease Purchase					
f. Other Equipment					
Total Equipment					
E. SUBSIDIES, LOANS & GRANTS: (Schedule E)					
1. Total Subsidies, Loans & Grants					
TOTAL EXPENDITURES					
II. BUDGET TO BE FUNDED AS FOLLOWS:					
Cash Balance-Unencumbered					
General Fund Appropriation (Enter General Fund Lapse Below)					
Federal Funds					
Other Funds (Specify):					
Less: Estimated Cash Available Next Fiscal Period					
TOTAL. (same as total of A through E above)					
GENERAL FUND LAPSE					
III. PERSONNEL DATA					
Number Positions Authorized in Appropriation Bill — a.) Full Perm.					
b.) Full T-L					
c.) Part Perm.					
d.) Part T-L					
Average Annual Vacancy Rate (Percentage) — a.) Full Perm.					
b.) Full T-L					
c.) Part Perm.					
d.) Part T-L					

Approved by _____
    Official of Board or Commission

Budget Officer _____

Phone Number _____

Submitted by _____
                Name

Title _____

Date _____

Figure 1 Mississippi budget request form.

Table 1   Information Included in 1983 Agency Budget Requests

Budget summary information
    Total agency request—Uses object classification breakdowns (see Figure II)
    Continuation request—New money requested for each object classification to continue existing
       services
    Expansion request—New money requested for each object classification to expand existing
       services
    New activities request—New money requested for each object classification to carry out new
       services
Detailed information about object classifications
    Personnel services
       List of salaries for authorized positions
       Cost of overtime money requested and use of overtime
       Cost of implementing position reclassifications approved by the state personnel board
       Cost of new positions being requested
    Travel
       List of trips in state and out of trips made with name of person traveling and the cost of the trip
    Contractual services
       List of space rented, including cost
       List of professional fees paid
       List of personal service contracts paid
    Commodities
       Details of commodity purchases in addition to the information provided on the form showing
         the total budget request
    Capital outlay
       List with cost of requested land purchases
       List with cost of building construction and building remodeling projects
    Subsidies/loans/grants
       List of payments to individuals
       List of payments to private organizations who have contracts to provide services
       List of payments to other governmental units (mostly local governments)
Sources of money to fund agency requests
    Amount and percentage of each object classification funded by
       The general fund
       Special funds (listed separately)
       Listing of each source and amount of federal money expected to come to the agency
       Listing of each source and amount of self-generated money (i.e., user fees) expected to come to
         the agency
Other information
    List of board or commission members, including appointment date, appointing person, and term of
       office

between the legislative budget office (LBO) the governor's office of budget and fund management (BFM). Seven stayed in the legislature, and five transferred to the governor's staff.

    Beginning in 1985 the two budget offices issued joint instructions, with each office having the option of asking for supplemental information. During the last thirteen years, the joint guidelines incorporated many information requests that first appeared in supplemental

Table 2 Additions in Budget Information Required in Mississippi Agency Budget Requests (1984–1998)

Joint Legislative Budget Committee	Joint forms	Governor
		Allain
	1984	
List object classification increases by program in priority order	No joint form	List funding increases by program
	1985	
Provide list of professional service contracts	List object classification increases by program in priority order	Agencies define programs and provide program breakdowns
Provide a vehicle inventory list		Narrative required for each program
	1986	
	Agencies given program designations and asked to budget by programs designated with object classification breakdowns in each program budget	
	Narrative required for each program	
	Provide list of professional fees	
	Provide a vehicle inventory list	
	1987	
	No changes	
		Mabus
	1988	
		Pilot program
		Output indicators consisting of number of service units
		Completed and program efficiencies showing average cost per service unit
		Program outcome indicators that indicate the extent the program achieved its objectives
	1989	
	Agencies provide summary of program measures, including at least one performance	List nonrecurring costs each program; list increases by inflation separately; show administrative costs allocated to each program
	Output measure and one outcome measure per designated program; provide more indicators if possible	Agencies reporting to the governor ordered to request standstill budget requests
	Provide a list of leases and lease purchases	

Table 2 Continued

Joint Legislative Budget Committee	Joint forms	Governor
	1990 Separate listing for special fund and federal money by major object classifications	
	List out-of-country travel separately	
	1991 No changes	
		Fordice
	1992 Specify general and special fund reductions made in current year budget recission	Agencies reporting to the governor presubmit their budgets in advance with explanations of program costs and benefits and justifications for changes in spending; also asked to suggest funding alternatives
	1993	
Pilot program for five agencies	Prioritize increases in designated programs by showing program objective classification increases	Presubmission by gubernatorial continues
Modify program designations if necessary		
Replaces request for "summary of key performance indicators and measures" with	Indicate impact of 3% general fund reduction on object classifications and on designated programs	
1. Program output measures (e.g., volume service units produced, people served)		
2. Program outcome measures of program effectiveness (e.g., increase in customer satisfaction)		
3. Where possible, data on subprogram spending for each object classification and subprogram output and outcome measures		
	1994 Legislatively mandated	Presubmission for gubernatorial agencies continues
	1. Performance indicators for each designated program	
	2. Performance targets in appropriation bills	
	3. Strategic plan to accompany budget proposal	
	4. Agencies may include performance indicators subprograms	

Table 2   Continued

Joint Legislative Budget Committee	Joint forms	Governor
	Budget office changes	
	1. Provide information on spending changes by object classification for each designated program	
	a. Identify nonrecurring items dropped from request	
	b. Identify midyear funding increases	
	c. Identify new money requests	
	d. Include narrative justifying changes	
	2. Detailed commodity request	
	1995	
	No changes	Presubmission for gubernatorial agencies continues
	1996	
	No changes	Presubmission for gubernatorial agencies continues governor:mandated agency spending caps to free money for cut in the "marriage penalty"
	1997	
	No changes	Presubmission for gubernatorial agencies continues agencies limited to 4% growth
	1998	
	No changes	Governor does not issue presubmission instructions to gubernatorial agencies

instructions. Conservative Bill Allain (1983–1987), liberal Ray Mabus (FYs 1988–1991), and extreme conservative Kirk Fordice (1992 to present) all left their mark on budget requests.

The Allain Era

Governor Allain showed more interest in holding the line on taxes than budget reform, but he supported the efforts of his budget staff to carry the program ball in order to hold spending in check. Throughout his term, the JLBC only initiated a few changes, all of which added budget details to enhance legislative control. During 1984, the only year in which agencies received two sets of request guidelines, both the governor and the JLBC mandated that agency requests link funding increases to programs. The governor asked for a listing of funding increases by program, and JLBC called on agencies to catalog each program's object classification increases in priority order. For instance, the health department itemized the preventive health services program and asked for an increase in commodities to cover vaccine costs (Mississippi Department of Health, 1984).

The 1985 joint forms incorporated the JLBC's program increase system. During this year, the gubernatorial supplemental instructions directed agencies to define programs and to divide their requests for new money along programmatic lines. Additionally, the gubernatorial guidelines required agencies to discuss funding needs for individual programs in the budget narrative. Conversely, 1985 supplemental legislative guidelines added two control items, a list of professional contractors, and a vehicle inventory. In 1986, the joint budget instructions incorporated all 1985 gubernatorial and JLBC supplemental items. During the 1985 budget cycle, many agencies included a large number of programs in their budgets, which made analysis difficult. As a result, in 1986 the two budget offices and each agency agreed on three to five designated programs. Most of these designations remain in use today. In 1987 the election year put change on hold. In fact, outgoing governor Allain did not submit a budget proposal, a task which by state law fell to new governor Ray Mabus.

The Mabus Era

Governor Mabus and his top lieutenants were more interested in educational reform than budget reform. Moving as much money as possible into elementary and secondary education without a tax increase served as his top budget priority. Nevertheless, the Mabus years produced more programmatic budget mechanisms, and these were viewed as possible tools for freeing up money for education. One person who worked as an analyst in the Mabus budget office noted that "there were a lot of fire drills, a lot of efforts to try new things." Like liberal reformers at the turn of the century, the governor hoped to use the budget process as a device to shift resources to priority programs.

Since he took office in early January and the law required submission of his proposal by January 31, the first Mabus budget simply reflected minor modification to the already released JLBC document. During 1988, his second year, Governor Mabus created a fifteen-agency pilot program. Pilot agencies were expected to develop performance indicators that reported outputs such as the number of service units completed or number of clients served, efficiencies such as the average cost per unit of services delivered, and outcome indicators that showed the degree to which the program achieved its objective. For example, performance output data for a master of a public administration (MPA) program could include such measures as the number of students enrolled and/or the number of classes taught. Budgeters could measure an MPA program's efficiency by totaling faculty salaries and other operating costs and dividing this amount by the number of students enrolled and/or the number of classes taught. For example, a program spending $200,000 with fifty students costs $4000 per student. Outcome indicators could display the percentage of MPA graduates employed in public and nonprofit professional positions. In Mississippi, many pilot agencies lacked the data or expertise to develop output, efficiency, and outcome measures. In many cases, information did not exist that reflected the number of clients served analogous to the number of students taught or showed the impact of an agency's activities similar to the percentage of graduates placed in appropriate professional positions. Even if this kind of information existed, agencies usually lacked the information needed to compute such efficiencies as the cost per client served.

In 1989 the joint budget forms incorporated a scaled-back version of the pilot program requirements. Agencies were expected to add output indicators, but they possessed some leeway since only output was required for each designated program. As carried out, spending units did not provide efficiencies. Budget guidelines also did not require data on the percentage of targeted results or outcomes actually achieved. At the request of the JLBC, the joint forms also incorporated the financial accountability requirement to list leases and lease purchases.

In 1989 the BFM also issued supplemental instructions that requested additional object classification details. Agencies were asked to identify nonrecurring costs, to determine increases due to inflation, and to allocate central administrative expenditures among designated programs.

The Mabus administration also issued separate instructions to agencies reporting to the governor, which consumed 21% of the general fund budget. The governor ordered these departments to rework their budget requests and to limit their submission to the same dollars as last year. This process created resentment among the JLBC, especially since these agencies recalled their original requests from the LBO. The revised asking budgets placed all new money in a separate document entitled "wish list." During the JLBC budget hearings these agencies were chastised by the lieutenant governor for not following the format of the joint request form (Elliott, 1989).

The 1990 budget season saw no additional requests from the governor or the legislative leadership. None of the 1989 gubernatorial supplemental items were added to the joint forms, perhaps reflecting the animosity between Governor Mabus and the JLBC. Furthermore, Mabus did not place dollar ceilings on the budget requests of agencies reporting to the governor. The joint forms did grow, however, with the addition of two pieces of financial accountability information added by the JLBC. The legislative side required agencies to show how they divided federal and special fund money among object classifications (personnel, equipment, etc.) and to list out-of-country travel undertaken by employees. (See Figure 1).

In 1991, an election year, no changes occurred in the information requested. As occurred during the Allain years, the professional budget staff demonstrated more interest in changing budget practices than Governor Mabus and his top political appointees. When reforms failed to produce noticeable additional resources for education, the governor placed less emphasis on program budgeting. The budget office staff was reduced to only five people, who lacked the person power to conduct a comprehensive review of all budgets. Mississippi's legislative-dominated process limited Mabus' ability to use budgeting as a tool to change spending patterns. During the Mabus years, the JLBC continued its concern with legislative oversight and control and added only accountability items.

The Fordice Era

Governor Kirk Fordice brought his conservative low-tax, low-spend agenda to office. During his two terms as governor, Fordice has pushed for spending cuts to generate money for tax reductions. Unlike many conservative reformers, however, he has not advocated programmatic and analytic mechanisms as tools to identify slack resources. Nonetheless, he cooperated with the JLBC in developing some alternations in the budget process, a dramatic change from the confrontations of the later Mabus years. For the most part,

Fordice focused his energies on limiting gubernatorial agency spending through a preapproval process, and he let the JLBC place additional items into the joint forms at will.

Like Mabus in early 1988, Fordice did not have time to refine the budget process during his initial two months in office. He followed his predecessor's lead and compiled minor revisions to the already released legislative leadership budget proposal. In mid-1992, however, Fordice took a leaf from the Mabus playbook and instituted a preapproval process for agencies reporting to the governor. He asked gubernatorial agencies to delineate the costs and benefits of each program, to justify changes in spending, and to suggest alternative funding sources such as user fees or privatizing services. Unlike Mabus, Fordice's budget staff explained to the LBO and the JLBC any gubernatorial changes made in agency requests during the preapproval process. In 1992 the joint gubernatorial—JLBC forms included one additional information request. Agencies were asked to identify cuts in object classification items that occurred during the 1991 midyear budget reduction, a step not taken in the past when midyear decreases took place.

In 1993, the JLBC and its staff took the lead in requiring additional programmatic information in agency budget proposals. At the request of Lieutenant Governor Eddie Briggs, several JLBC members and the LBO staff visited budget officials in Texas to learn about the Lone Star State's performance budget. Like Fordice, Briggs was elected as a Republican, but was not a close ally of Fordice.* As lieutenant governor, he assigned state senators to committees and appointed committee chairs. In addition he cochaired the JLBC with the speaker of the House. Briggs, a former state senator, believed that performance indicators could identify low-performing programs. Unlike Fordice, he believed that analytical budget mechanisms could identify slack resources for tax reductions, a view similar to early conservative reformers.

In 1993, the LBO added additional information requirements to the joint forms with the concurrence of the governor's budget office. Agencies prioritized their increases in their designated programs, including increases for object classifications consumed by these programs. The joint instructions also asked departments to show how they would distribute a 3% cut among designated programs and among object classifications at the agencywide level. Cuts could be uneven among programs. For example, program A could be cut by 1% and program B by 6%. This information provided a map if cuts proved necessary during the session because of a reduced revenue estimate or if cuts in approved budgets needed to take place during the spending year due to revenue shortfalls.

The JLBC took the lead in 1993 and established a pilot program covering five agencies. These agencies were asked to modify program designations if necessary to impart a more precise blueprint of functional costs and to include output and outcome indicators for each program, such as the number of persons served (output) and the percentage of satisfied clients (outcome). Where possible, pilot agencies were asked to identify subprograms and to provide subprogram object classification breakdowns, output indicators, and outcome data.

Performance budget measures were incorporated into the budget request process in 1994 by legislative mandate. The Mississippi Budget and Performance Strategic Planning

---

* Governor Fordice and Lieutenant Governor Briggs did not get along during the four years that they served together. The lieutenant governor functions as the acting governor when the governor is out of state. During one year Fordice was away on a trip and Briggs added items to the "call" for a legislative special session. Fordice removed the items upon his return. When both men were running for re-election in 1995, the lack of support from Fordice contributed to Briggs's defeat.

Act codified the use of performance indicators (State of Mississippi, 1994). Budget requests must include for each program performance measures that have been developed jointly by the agency, the BFM and the JLBC's LBO. In addition to performance items included in the pilot program, the 1994 law added efficiencies, the cost per unit of output as a performance indicator. For example, the department of transportation needs to show the cost per mile of highway maintenance. For the twenty-one largest state agencies, which consume 77% of the general fund budget, the statue requires the placement of performance indicators in agency appropriation bills. By 1998 appropriation bills displayed data from three time points: the last completed fiscal year, the current fiscal year, and targets for the upcoming fiscal year. In addition, a strategic plan that includes performance targets for five years and an agency evaluation of success in meeting performance goals for the last two years must accompany the budget proposal. Agencies are allowed to submit as many performance indicators as possible, but for the twenty-one units with legislative benchmarks or targets, the list must include these indicators.

The legislature receives the JLBC budget proposal, which includes performance indicators for programs operated by the twenty-one agencies with legislative benchmarks. Appropriation subcommittee chairs set targets for the upcoming year, often in consultation with other committee members. The agency budget proposal for the next year will include data that compare the target and actual performance. Every six months budget analysts also receive reports on agency progress that compare actual performance to targeted performance. Budget reviewers and legislators thus could determine whether or not agencies were reaching their performance targets.

The addition of performance measures did not signal a complete shift to programmatic concerns. The JLBC also added financial accountability requirements to the joint forms in 1994 Agencies now complete a form for each designated program that summarizes one-time expenses in the current appropriation bill, changes in authorized spending during the current fiscal year, and requests for new money in the upcoming fiscal year. An example is found in Figure 2 which shows that agencies divide their program allocations by object classifications and show the funding sources supporting each object classification category. The beginning balance is adjusted upward for any new money acquired and downward for any nonrecurring expenditures. Once agencies make these changes, any new money requested is added to this adjusted total. Almost all escalations during the spending year steam from additional federal funds. The general fund does not change during the fiscal year without action by the legislature. This form serves several functions. First, budget reviewers are informed about any new federal money coming into the agency that may free up general fund money for other purposes. Second, budget reviewers are informed about nonrecurring expenses. This information provides the budget reviewer with information about money that may be used for other expenses without increasing the agency appropriation.

In 1994 through 1997, the governor's budget office continued to receive and review presubmissions from the agencies reporting to the governor. In 1996 Governor Fordice used the preapproval process to cap spending increases of gubernatorial agencies in order to free up money for a tax cut that reduced the "marriage penalty." Similar to the federal level, Mississippi's income tax forced married couples to pay more in taxes than two single persons with the same combined income. For gubernatorial agencies, the JLBC only recommended the amount requested. The legislature changed the state income tax deductions to reduce the marriage penalty. In 1998 Governor Fordice did not issue any presubmission instructions to gubernatorial agencies. With the exception of the 1996 cap

State of Mississippi
Form MBR-1 (1998)

ORIGINAL _____
REVISED _____
DATE FILED _____

AGENCY	ADDRESS		CHIEF EXECUTIVE OFFICER	
	(1)	(2)	(3)	(4)
	Actual Expenses FY Ending June 30, 1998	Estimated Expenses FY Ending June 30, 1999	Requested For FY Ending June 30, 2000	Requested Increase (+) or Decrease (-) FY 2000 vs. FY 1999 (COL. 3 vs. COL. 2)
				AMOUNT / PERCENT
I. A. PERSONAL SERVICES:				
1. Salaries, Wages & Fringe Benefits (Base)				
a. Additional Compensation				
b. Proposed Vacancy Rate (Dollar Amount)			( )	
c. Per Diem				
Total Salaries, Wages & Fringe Benefits				
2. Travel				
a. Travel & Subsistence (In State)				
b. Travel & Subsistence (Out-of-State)				
c. Travel & Subsistence (Out-of-Country)				
Total Travel				
B. CONTRACTUAL SERVICES (Schedule B):				
a. Tuition, Rewards & Awards				
b. Communications, Transportation & Utilities				
c. Public Information				
d. Rents				
e. Repairs & Service				
f. Fees, Professional & Other Services				
g. Other Contractual Services				
h. Data Processing				
i. Other				
Total Contractual Services				
C. COMMODITIES (Schedule C):				
a. Maintenance & Const. Materials & Supplies				
b. Printing & Office Supplies & Materials				
c. Equipment Repair Parts, Supplies & Accessories				
d. Professional & Scientific Supplies & Materials				
e. Other Supplies & Materials				
Total Commodities				
D. CAPITAL OUTLAY:				
1. Total Other Than Equipment (Schedule D-1)				
2. Equipment (Schedule D-2)				
a. Automobiles, Station Wagons, Trucks & Other Vehicles				
b. Road Machinery, Farm & Other Working Equipment				
c. Off. Machines, Furniture, Fixtures & Equipment				
d. IS Equipment (Data Processing & Telecommunications)				
e. Equipment - Lease Purchase				
f. Other Equipment				
Total Equipment				
E. SUBSIDIES, LOANS & GRANTS: (Schedule E)				
1. Total Subsidies, Loans & Grants				
TOTAL EXPENDITURES				
II. BUDGET TO BE FUNDED AS FOLLOWS:				
Cash Balance-Unencumbered				
General Fund Appropriation (Enter General Fund Lapse Below)				
Federal Funds				
Other Funds (Specify):				
Less: Estimated Cash Available Next Fiscal Period				
TOTAL (same as total of A through E above)				
GENERAL FUND LAPSE				
III. PERSONNEL DATA				
Number Positions Authorized in Appropriation Bill a.) Full Perm				
b.) Full T-L				
c.) Part Perm				
d.) Part T-L				
Average Annual Vacancy Rate (Percentage) a.) Full Perm				
b.) Full T-L				
c.) Part Perm				
d.) Part T-L				

Approved by _____
        Official of Board or Commission

Budget Officer _____

Phone Number _____

Submitted by _____
                        Name

Title _____

Date _____

Figure 2   Detailed funding changes during the current fiscal year.

for the marriage penalty tax cut, the JLBC generally ignored caps on gubernatorial agency requests. These agencies were asked to provide information about additional needs during budget hearings. As his second term winds to a close, Governor Fordice, like Governor Mabus, seems to recognize the marginal roles that governors play in Mississippi budgeting.

Since 1994 the JLBC has not added any budget information requirements. Several factors contributed to this lack of activity. First, the LBO needed to work with agencies to refine performance indicators. Second, significant year-to-year revenue growth reduced pressure to ask for additional information that might identify areas to reduce spending.

CHANGES IN MISSISSIPPI'S BUDGET FORMAT: AN ASSESSMENT

Do Governors Shape Spending by Gubernatorial Agencies Through the Preapproval Process?

Evidence does not support hypothesis 1; governors experienced only limited success in shaping spending of gubernatorial agencies through the preapproval process. Governor Allain made no attempt to control gubernatorial agency submissions to the JLBC. His lack of effort stemmed from the fact that gubernatorial agencies only consumed 6% of the general fund budget during his term. Governor Mabus used the preapproval process in an effort to shift money to public education, but the JLBC rebuffed his efforts to limit gubernatorial agency requests. Governor Fordice concentrated his budget-shaping efforts on gubernatorial agencies. He attempted to gain JLBC acceptance of his preapproval changes by telling the committee about his alterations to initial gubernatorial agency proposals. Fordice's intervention proved successful during one budget year when the preapproval process limited these agency requests and freed up money for a small tax cut, but this mechanism showed limited success during Fordice's years in office. The JLBC sometimes asks gubernatorial agencies for supplemental requests when their budget requests do not cover obvious needs. In 1998 the governor did not even issue preapproval budget instructions to gubernatorial agencies.

Do Mississippi Governors Add Program Components and Analytic Mechanisms to Budget Guidelines in Order to Focus the Budget Debate and Allocation Decisions on Program Priorities and Program Performance?

Evidence supports hypothesis 2; of the three governors two added program components and analytic information to agency budget requests. Unlike its 1983 counterpart, the 1998 budget request form asks for program and analytic information. As Table 2 makes clear, Governors Allain and Mabus emerged as the major program initiators. These two governors and their budget staffs developed program components that were introduced through supplemental instructions in 1985 and 1988 and were added to the joint guidelines in subsequent years. Allain initiated the first program components incorporated into the Mississippi budget agency request guidelines. Mabus undertook efforts to enhance program budgeting. He started a pilot program that required a few agencies to submit performance data. The requirement that each agency program include one output and outcome measure represents the only enduring direct program legacy from the Mabus years. Indirectly, Mabus', efforts in regard to performance indicators helped pave the way for the performance process started by the JLBC in 1993. With Fordice, the expectation that he would advocate more programmatic and analytic mechanisms proved untrue. Fordice let the JLBC alter the budget format while he concentrated on limiting gubernatorial agency spending.

Does the Legislative Joint Budget Committee Add Object Classification Control Mechanisms to Focus the Budget Debate and Allocation Decisions on Issues of Financial Accountability and Control of Agency Actions?

Evidence also partially supports hypothesis 3; the JLBC added an array of object classification control mechanisms during the last fifteen years to focus the budget debate and allocation decisions on issues of financial accountability and control of agency actions, but the JLBC also incorporated performance indicators into the budget process. In part, increased computerized management information capabilities made it possible for agencies to generate details such as professional fees paid, out-of-country employee trips, lease agreements, and vehicle inventories. The major indicator of JLBC concern with accountability and control derives from legislative insistence that agencies include object classification breakdowns in their program requests. During the last fifteen years Mississippi budget guidelines added budgets for designated agency programs, a list of prioritized program increases, a prioritized enumeration of potential 3% program reductions, and detailed dollar change information for each program. In each of these instances agencies must provide object classification details. For instance, if the College of Veterinary Medicine request budget lists an increase in swine research as a program priority, this document must also indicate the object classifications items (personnel, equipment, etc.) that make up this program enhancement. Clearly, Mississippi fits the pattern found in other states in which legislators try to maintain control through detailed budgets.

The JLBC demonstrated its accountability and control orientation over the past fifteen years, but this legislative committee also brought performance budgeting to Mississippi. The JLBC's 1993 pilot program and the 1994 legislatively initiated Mississippi Performance Budgeting and Strategic Planning Act represent deviations from the control orientation. Under the leadership of the lieutenant governor, the JLBC assumed the lead in bringing performance indicators to Mississippi. Contrary to the pattern found in most jurisdictions, the legislative leadership instituted output, efficiency, and outcome measures to increase the potential for budget decisions based on program efficiency and effectiveness.

Do Program and Analytic Information Incorporated into the Budget Impact Budget Allocations?

The addition of program information brings us to hypothesis 4, which assumes that Mississippi will not differ from other jurisdictions. In essence, this hypothesis states that program and analytic information incorporated into the budget will have a limited impact on budget allocations. Evidence seems to confirm this initial expectation. One person knowledgeable about Mississippi budgeting indicated that he knows of no examples in which changes in the JLBC recommendation or appropriation subcommittee action resulted in agency budget increases or decreases because of performance indicators. As one budgeter put it, "money is the focus of budget reviews. Using a book as an analogy, money is the book and performance measures are the footnotes." Mississippi program and performance information engender limited impact over budget allocation decisions for several reasons.

First, the LBO reports that 142 program designations are spread across Mississippi government (Mississippi Joint legislative Budget Committee, 1992). When these designations represent fairly distinctive undertakings, knowledgeable budget reviewers can probably make judgments about program efficiency and effectiveness even without precise output and outcome measures. A few program designations meet this criterion. For instance, the Department of Archives and History uses such program designations as historic properties, historic preservation efforts, and the state historical museum (Mississippi Department of Archives and History, 1998). Unfortunately, many of Mississippi's program designations function as holding companies for several operating programs. As a result, actual programs are not reviewed. For example, the Medicaid agency uses two programs that receive general fund money, medical services for the needy and administrative services. Each "program" represents several wide-ranging activities (Mississippi Division of Medicaid, 1998). The health department designates six programs, which the agency divides into thirty-one subprograms. While health includes subprogram narratives and performance indicators such as listing the number of service units performed, the dollars spent on subprograms are not reported. For instance, the health department budget uses persons screened and treated for sexually transmitted diseases as a performance indicator for its "sexually transmitted disease program." The health department reported that 36,608 persons received diagnostic treatment services in 1996, but there is no way from the budget data to determine the average cost of a test. The lack of measured results prevents ascertaining the impact on public health in a measurable way. Given federal reporting requirements, the health department could provide this information if requested, but the budget offices limit the number of designations to control the amount of information required to review (Health Budget Request, 1998).

The overall composition of Mississippi's budget format represents a second reason why performance indicators generate limited influence over allocation decisions. Current program budgets also include nonprogram details that enhance accountability and control. Program requests are broken down into such object classifications as personnel and equipment. This information permits reviewers to shift their focus from total program costs and questions about program efficiency and effectiveness to operating details for financial accountability purposes. This detail gives budget reviewers greater potential control over lower-level agency activities.

Mississippi grafts performance indicators onto this control-oriented format. Rather than eliminate object classification and line-item details and create a format that displays lump sum program totals accompanied by performance data, Mississippi adds performance measures as supplements to existing budget information. Small budget review staffs found it impossible to assume the added burden of comparing performance indicators across departments. Comfortable with such things as object classification data, busy budgeters ignored the new information and based decisions on object classification data.

A third reason why performance indicators fail to influence spending decisions concerns the completeness and accuracy of agency indicators. Table 3 displays an example of agency benchmarks for the College of Veterinary Medicine from this unit's 1999 budget request, submitted in the summer of 1998. The indicators are drawn from the designated program budget for the animal health center, the hospital section of the school. The actual figures (1997) come from the last completed fiscal year, the estimated number (1998) from the current fiscal year, and the targets represent changes expected in the next fiscal

Table 3 Program Measures for the College of Veterinary Medicine's Animal Health Center

	1997 actual	1998 estimated	1999 projected
Program outputs			
Cases managed	7654	7500	7600
Number of hours of student clinical training	182,208	175,000	175,000
Clinical research funds	105,218	110,000	120,000
Program efficiencies			
Average revenue per clinical case	150	150	150
Consultation hours per clinical case	350	365	365
Program outcomes			
Percentage increase/decrease in community wellness program	30%	No change	No change
Percentage increase/decrease in consultation hours	5%	No change	No change

year (1999). The vet school's appropriation bill contains the targets for 1999 from the budget request. The reader may observe several characteristics from Table 3. The animal health center developed several program outputs or units of service delivered. The efficiencies or cost per unit of service do not match the outputs. Revenue per clinical case represents the only efficiency tied to a listed output. Efficiencies include the cost of a consultation hour per clinical case, but no analogous output appears. At the same time efficiencies are not included for clinical research funds and the number of hours of student clinical training. The program outcomes displayed do not deal with results, but instead show changes in outputs. Changes in the community wellness program and consultation hours represent changes in the amount of services provided and not the results of services.

A relevant question concerns whether or not the animal health center indicators are typical of programs in other agencies. Table 4 suggests the answer is yes. Table 4 displays the results of an analysis of performance measures prepared by the twenty-one largest agencies in 1998. As can be seen, almost all agencies included output indicators. Only 6% of the agencies included efficiencies for all programs, while 78% included these data for some programs but not for all programs. Only 3% included outcomes for all programs, while 38% included this indicator for some but not all programs. In many instances budget requests included outputs labeled as outcomes. In essence, some performance indicators reflect outputs, some reflect efficiencies, and very few represent program outcomes.

Table 4 Mississippi Performance Indicators (Percentage)

Program outputs			Program efficiencies			Program outcomes		
All	Some	None	All	Some	None	All	Some	None
94	6	0	6	78	16	6	38	55

Note: Number of cases 21.

The lack of complete information inhibits the use of performance indicators as decision-making tools.

The absence of a validation process illustrates a fourth limitation to the use of performance indicators in spending allocation decisions. Agencies are not asked to verify the accuracy of their data, and thus questions of correctness exist. Budgeters are not likely to use indicators to compare agency performance and allocate resources if questions exist about the validity of the information. As one budgeter put it, "Performance indicators will not provide reliable information until the numbers are audited for accuracy."

Political reality also limits the utility of performance measures. Performance measures that include unit costs of clients served and/or unit costs of results achieved highlight trade-offs between programs when one is funded and one is not. In effect, measures point out that more of they means less of the z. Object classifications for the whole agency do not show explicit trade-offs between programs.

MISSISSIPPI'S PROSPECTS FOR FULL-BLOWN PROGRAM BUDGETING

Mississippi moved in the direction of program budgeting with performance measures, but the current system limits these tools in budget decision making. A review of the information provided by agencies raises serious doubts about the ability of budgeters to make choices based on the analysis of programs. In many cases program designations serve as holding companies for several subprograms. Most agency budget requests contain dollar breakdowns only for designated holding company programs and not subprograms. Conversely, performance indicators are tied to subprograms. Holding company program designations, such as the health department's chronic illness and disease prevention, may be useful for making macro decisions that allocate resources among major functional areas, but budget analysts cannot assess subprograms to determine efficiency and effectiveness, even informally. Experienced analysts exercising seasoned judgment still require budget data for subprograms to make reasoned choices.

The lack of verifiable performance measures creates another obstacle to tying budget decisions to efficiency and effectiveness indicators. Many writers stress the difficulty in developing outcome measures for public sector programs, given the wide range of factors impacting program results. For instance, does an increase in sexually transmitted diseases suggest a failed program? The answer may be no if factors beyond the control of the health department lead to more intercourse among teenagers.

The lack of gubernatorial commitment to program budgeting with performance measures and the control orientation of the JLBC also limited the development of meaningful program budgeting. Mississippi government generated a number of program innovations, but neither governors nor legislative leaders viewed developing program budgets or verifiable performance measures as a priority. Wildavsky questions the feasibility and desirability of making budget decisions based on analytical information instead of bargained agreements (Wildavsky, 1984). Clearly, Mississippi's governors and legislative leaders seem to agree. Despite budget innovations, both conservative and liberal governors pursued policy agendas that gave only limited attention to creating a program format with meaningful efficiency and effectiveness indicators.

Mississippi's chief executives tend to give low priority to developing a full-blown program budgeting system. Governor Allain's major interest in budgeting concerned keeping spending in line with existing taxes. Governor Mabus made education spending a priority. While his administration tried ambitious pilot programs, he emphasized education reform and not budget reform. Budget directors came and went, creating a lack of continuity. At the end of the Mabus term only five persons remained on the budget staff, including the director. During the budget review process just prior to the 1991 election, a nonprogram concern dominated deliberations. Governor Mabus wanted to set up a statewide leasing system to cut costs and to use the fiscal dividend for education. When Mabus lost the election, the statewide lease plan faded away.

Governor Fordice's budget concerns consisted of cutting spending, privatizing as many programs as possible, and cutting taxes. For gubernatorial agencies, Fordice tried to use the preapproval process as a cost control mechanism. At the same time, he accepted any changes to budget guidelines developed by the JLBC and its LBO. Unlike many conservatives, he did not view the budget format content as relevant to his government reduction goals.

By the same token, the JLBC and its legislative colleagues do not envision in-depth program evaluation as part of the budget process. Despite the recent performance measurement effort, it appears that the well-documented desire of legislators to control agencies through detailed input information clearly exists in Mississippi. Numerous detailed information requirements provide opportunities to exercise oversight. Object classification breakdowns within program budgets extended legislative control to lower levels of agencies. If Mississippi's agency budget requests only consisted of lump sum program budgets, then budget reviews would by necessity focus on programs instead of resources inputs, but legislators would not be able to micromanage agency spending.

Given the mechanical obstacles and attitudes of elected officials, why the continuing push to refine performance and result indicators? Simply put, Mississippi is following the strategy noted by Lauth of making the budget format compatible with program evaluation (Lauth, 1987). If agency budget requests include programs with performance indicators that are linked dollars, the state auditor and the professional and well-respected staff of the program audit unit of the legislature—the Performance, Evaluation and Expenditure Review Committee—will be in a position to evaluate programs. Politics drives budget decisions that are reached through bargained agreements. At the same time, Mississippi strives to make its budget format compatible with program evaluation, which will be done outside the budget process. The next decade will see Mississippi agency budgets with more useful analytical information, but it is doubtful that the state will implement full-blown program budgeting.

REVIEW QUESTIONS

1. Governors seem more interested in program budgeting and performance indicators than legislators. Why is this usually the case? Does Mississippi's dual budget proposal system limit the state's ability to adopt program budgeting with performance indicators?
2. Meaningful program designations are critical to program budgeting. What impediments exist to the development of meaningful program designations?
3. Why do agencies find it difficult to develop output, efficiency, and outcome indicators?

4. Mississippi legislative leaders seem more interested in data displaying resources spent on object classification categories than program data. Why do legislators often feel this way?

5. What do elected officials gain if agency budget requests only show program breakdowns instead of object classifications? What do officials lose by substituting program information for object classification details?

REFERENCES

Allain et al v. State of Mississippi By and Through Allain. 441 So. 2D 1339 (Nov. 23, 1983).

Broom, C. A. (winter 1995). Performance-based government models: Building a track record. *Public Budgeting and Finance*, 3–17.

Cleveland, F. A. (Nov. 1915). Evolution of the budget idea in the United States. *Annals of Political and Social Science, 62*, 15–35.

Clynch, E. J. (spring 1986). Budgeting in Mississippi: Are two budgets better than one? *State and Local Government Review*, 49–55.

Clynch E. J. (1991). Mississippi: Does the governor really count? In E. J. Clynch and T. P. Lauth (eds.), *Governor, Legislators and Budgets: Diversity Across the American States*, New York: Greenwood. pp. 125–136.

Elliott J. (1989). Fiscal officer told to revise estimates. *Starkville, MS Daily News*, Sept. 15.

Gosling, J. J. (1997). *Budgetary Politics in American Governments*. New York: Garland.

Joyce, P. G. (winter 1993). Using performance measures for federal budgeting: Proposals and prospects. *Public Budgeting and Finance*, 4–17.

Lauth, T. P. (spring 1987). Budgeting and productivity in state government: Not integrated but friendly. *Public Productivity Review, 4*, 21–32.

Lee, R. D. Jr. (March/April 1997). Developments in state budgeting: Trends of two decades. *Public Administration Review, 57*, 133–140.

Lee, R. D. Jr. and Johnson, R. W. (1998). *Public Budgeting Systems*. Rockville, MD: Aspen.

Lu, H. (summer 1998). Performance budgeting: Why is it still inviable? *Journal of Public Budgeting, Accounting, and Financial Management, 10*, 151–172.

Lynch, T. D. (1995). *Public Budgeting in America*, 4th ed. Englewood Cliffs, NJ: Prentice-Hall.

Mississippi Department of Archives and History. (1998). *Budget Request for Fiscal Year 2000*. Jackson, MS.

Mississippi Commission on Budget and Accounting. (1983). *Budget Request Forms for Fiscal 1985*. Jackson, MS.

Mississippi Department of Health. (1984). *Budget Request for Fiscal 1986*. Jackson, MS.

Mississippi Department of Health. (1998). *Budget Request for Fiscal 2000*. Jackson, MS.

Mississippi Division of Medicaid. (1998). *Budget Request for Fiscal 2000*. Jackson, MS.

Mississippi Governor's Office. (1984). *Budget Instructions/Forms for Fiscal Year 1986*. Jackson, MS.

Mississippi Joint Legislative Budget Committee. (1992). *The Mississippi Budgeting Process*. Jackson, MS.

Mississippi Legislative Budget Office. (1984). *Budget Instructions/Forms for Fiscal Year 1986*. Jackson, MS.

Mississippi Legislative Budget Office and Governor's Budget Office. (1985–1993). *Budget Instructions/Forms for Fiscal Years 1987–1995*. Jackson, MS.

Mississippi State University College of Veterinary Medicine. (1998). *Budget Request Fiscal 2000*. Mississippi, State MS.

Pettijohn, C. D. and Grizzle, G. A. (1997). Structural budget reform: Does it affect budget deliberations? *Journal of Public Budgeting, Accounting and Financial Management, 9*, 26–45.

Posner, P. L. (1993). *Performance Budgeting: State Experiences and Implications for the Federal Government.* General Accounting Office Report (GAO/AFMD-93–41).

Rubin, I. S. (Sept. 1994). Early budget reformers: Democracy, efficiency, and budget reforms, *American Review of Public Administration, 24,* 229–252.

Schick, A. (1971). *Budget Innovation in the States.* Washington, DC.: Brookings Institution.

Sheffield, S. R. (Oct. 1996). Performance indicators in state government: Florida's performance-based program budgeting. Paper delivered at the Southeastern Conference of Public Administration, Miami.

State of Mississippi. Mississippi Performance Budget and Strategic Planning Act of 1994. *Mississippi Code.* Section 27–103–139.

Wildavsky, A. (1984). *Politics of the Budgetary Process,* 4th ed. Boston: Little, Brown.

Willoughby, W. F. (1918). *The Movement for Budgetary Reform in the States.* New York: Appleton.

8

Performance Budgeting in Florida
To Muddle or Not to Muddle, That is the Question

C. Nelson Easterling
Governmental Consultant, Florida, U.S.A.

In its September 26, 1995, edition, *Financial World* (FW) proclaimed: "Florida gets FW's vote for the most promising performance measurement system—though it still has a long way to go" (Barrett and Greene, 1995: 43).

Financial World's comment is accurate in both regards. First, Florida's law is a comprehensive effort to overcome the weaknesses of earlier reform efforts and finally implement a dramatic change by moving to results-oriented budgeting. This law may determine whether rational-comprehensive budgeting can overcome the "art of muddling through" of incremental budgeting that Lindblom (1959) described and lauded. It certainly can provide the basis for making muddling through more comprehensive, more rational, and more informative, despite the continued support and approbation incremental budgeting receives as the best that can be expected from governmental leaders (White, 1994).

Second, FW is correct in its assessment of the potential for failure. Several major obstacles are yet to be overcome, including the weaknesses that caused Florida's history of failed reform attempts and Florida's traditional biennial turnover of legislative leadership.

The first part of this chapter will describe Florida's history of reform failure and discuss the causes of these failures. The second part will describe the legislation and its process of debate and eventual passage. The third part will analyze the current efforts at implementation and the obstacles being faced. Finally, the likelihood of success will be discussed and the potential causes of yet another failure will be detailed.

BUDGET REFORM IN FLORIDA

Budget reform began in the United States in the early days of this century with the adoption of the executive budget system and has grown to a frenetic pace in the last decade before

Reprinted from: *Journal of Public Budgeting, Accounting, and Financial Management*, Winter 1999, 11(4), 559–577. Copyright 1999 by PrAcademics Press.

the end of this millennium. Although the executive budget had been in use in many European countries for several decades, it was first adopted in a few American cities at the end of the nineteenth century. It gained popularity in the early part of this century and was adopted at the federal level in 1921 (Axelrod, 1995). The executive budget was seen as a major reform at the national level because it took what had been a desultory and fractured process of budget formulation and created a unified system that placed the responsibility for creating budget requests and implementing legislative appropriations in a single pair of hands.

Florida also adopted this reform effort in 1921, although the responsibility for submitting budget requests was placed in a collegial body called the Budget Commission made up of the governor, the treasurer, and the comptroller (Klay, 1994). All of these officials were independently elected and shared responsibility with other elected cabinet officials in many areas of executive government. It was not until 1969 that the governor was given singular responsibility for overseeing the preparation of budget requests (Chapter 69–106, Laws of Florida). This was done by establishing the governor as the chief budget officer and placing the responsibility for overseeing budget preparation and implementation in the division of budget that was housed in the Department of Administration, the secretary of which was appointed by the governor.

It was also this 1969 reform legislation that saw Florida embark on its second phase of budget reform when it established an effort to implement the Programming, Planning, and Budgeting System (PPBS). Although the 1969 reform in Florida did not abolish the use of the standard line-item approach to the appropriations bill, the statute provided that the Department of Administration was given the authority to develop instructions for agencies to follow in preparing their legislative budget requests.

The intent of the legislation was clear, and the department followed up on this intent by issuing new instructions that established new formats and required additional information to be reported. Program components were established as the building blocks of agency requests, and the new information that was to be developed would report on "workload analysis and performance standards" (governor's recommended budget for the biennium 1969–71, p. 990). Prior to this time, the only performance information had been presented in the text of narrative justifications for requested increases in appropriations. By fiscal year (FY) 1973, specific program measures, including workload and efficiency measures, were required on standardized forms. Beginning in FY 1974–1975, the basic form and measures to be reported for the legislative budget requests had been settled. Further, the form developed for that year has been used in its basic form from that year until the present with only minor and occasional variations.

At the beginning of the 1973 reform effort a staff was assembled to develop the program components and assist agencies with the development of program measures. The original staff office was housed in the division of planning, a sister organization to the division of budget in the Department of Administration. In 1974, this group was transferred to the division of budget to better integrate the reforms into the standard budget request. Despite the efforts of this section, the quality of program measures was uneven in the early days. Although there were agencies that were developing meaningful and useful measures, not all agencies were as successful in developing measures of such quality that could be used in a rational-comprehensive budget system.

During the early 1970s, however, neither the governor nor the legislature reinforced the efforts of the more aggressive agencies by using the measures that were adequate for budget decisions. Discussions with staff of all three entities involved (the agencies, the division of budget, and the legislative appropriations staff) demonstrated a classic chicken-and-egg debate. Budget analysts in the appropriations committees said they did not use the measures because too many of them were inadequate. Agency staff claimed they had developed many good measures but had ceased to expend much effort on them because no one used them; if they had no value to the decision makers, they had no value to the agency. Analysts in the division of budget shrugged and said there was a little truth on both sides, and they hoped to overcome all objections.

In 1977, the legislature placed into statute the requirement that "workload and other performance indicators required by the department" be included in every budget request (Section 4, Chapter 77–352, Laws of Florida), and the governor's recommended budget for FY 1977–1978 and 1978–1979 did include some performance measures for some budget entities. These measures were presented under the title "Summary of Workload" and included not only the level of workload the agency said would be accomplished with the level of funding they requested, but also included the governor's assessment of the level of workload his recommendations would support.

At the end of the appropriations process in 1977, however, the legislature did not report on the level of workload or any other measure that was contained in the actual appropriations. The measures included in the FY 1978–1979 governor's recommendations were also apparently ignored by the legislature. This led Turnbull (1979) to report that the appropriations bills were being developed around line-item decisions just as they had been before the reform effort had begun ten years earlier.

The election of Bob Graham as governor in 1978 reinvigorated the reform effort. In the 1979 session of the legislature, he pushed through a reorganization bill that placed the budget function within the executive office of the governor and merged many of the planning functions that had been in the division of budget into a new office of planning and budget. The purpose of this reorganization was to rekindle the reform efforts of PPBS and to integrate planning and budgeting with the intent of creating a budget system that would end with performance-based budgets.

Performance measures were a large part of Graham's efforts. In his first budget recommendations (for the biennium 1979–1981) not only did he increase the number of program measures contained in his recommendations, he broke them down into program components. In those cases in which the governor recommended less funding than an agency had requested, he reported both the measures the agencies proposed and the level that could be accomplished with his recommended level of funding. He continued to include these program measures in his recommendations for the second biennium of his administration (1981–1983). As a matter of fact, his second biennium recommendations contained measures that were the results of a major effort to develop and use relevant, quantitative measures in the budget process.

The legislature passed a biennium appropriations act in the 1979 session. It did not include any program measures, nor did any of the work papers that were transmitted to the executive branch include any program measures. When the legislature passed a massive amendment to the second year of appropriations in the 1980 session, it again failed to respond to the proposed workload and outcome measures the governor had proposed. The legislature did not pass a biennial budget for the next biennium; instead it returned to the practice of passing single-year appropriations acts, while continuing to require the agencies to submit biennium requests and the governor to submit biennium recommendations. [It was not until 1991 that the legislature amended the budget statute to put everyone on an annual budget process (Chapter 91–109, Laws of Florida).] During that time, the legislature never reported on the level of program activity or accomplishment that was intended to be funded by the appropriations act.

Discussions with legislative appropriations staff indicated the legislative committees simply did not use any of the proposed measures in their deliberations. Staff members said they did not have time to contemplate changes in the level of performance that would follow from last-minute adjustments in appropriation line items that were being made in the last, frantic hours of conference on the budget.

After the second biennium, Governor Graham stopped proposing programmatic levels and performance in his recommendations. He and his staff were not pleased with the measures that had been developed and decided an interim phase was needed in their efforts at budget reform (Polivka and Osterholt, 1985). The decision was made to develop performance agreements between the governor and his agency heads. This was intended to bridge the gap between the integration of planning and budgeting and the eventual use of program-performance measures in a rational-comprehensive budget system.

Although the budget law of Florida continues to require programmatic budgeting and performance measures, essential elements of PPBS reform, the efforts to implement that reform expired in the mid-1980s. Governor Graham's performance contracts continued to be developed and signed during his administration, but his effort to restore performance accountability to the budget process lapsed and was not reinstituted.

During the time of the earlier reform efforts, the legislature took very little interest in overseeing the actual implementation of the appropriations acts. No active steps were taken to ensure the success of the budget laws they were writing. When PPBS was originally endorsed, the size of the legislative staff was small and inadequate for such an oversight role. By the time the reform ended, however, there were several hundred substantive and appropriations staff members available for this function. There is no indication, however, of any enthusiasm for reform among that group.

In 1989, the legislative leadership again invoked a desire to make government more responsive and accountable to elected officials and the citizens when the newly elected speaker of the House of Representatives, Tom Gustafson, proposed a modified version of the zero-based budget reform. Mr. Gustafson proposed a periodic evaluation of every program in state government be conducted by outside evaluators. The original proposal would have evaluators from the big eight certified public accounting firms perform major reviews of each state agency and its programs on a rotating basis. The evaluators would be under contract to the legislature and would recommend reduction, elimination, or continuation of each program reviewed. The proposed reduction or recommendation would be the new base appropriation for that program. It would take an affirmative action on the part of the legislature to restore the program to the pre-existing level of funding.

Speaker Gustafson asked the Senate majority leader and former appropriations chairman, Jack Gordon, to assist him in developing the concept and sponsoring implementing legislation in the Senate. Senator Gordon rejected the idea that private citizens and out-of-state evaluators could, in essence, set the base budget for programs in Florida. He also was skeptical about the exclusive use of contract evaluators for this effort. He proposed a modified General Accounting Office concept in which the legislature would set up an office within its branch of government that would hire a core staff of professional evaluators. This small staff, designated the Office of Policy Analysis and Agency Review (PAAR), would then have a duty to conduct the periodic reviews with assistance from outside experts and evaluators. There would be a fixed timetable that would ensure a review of every program every seven years. An additional duty of this office would be to analyze and comment on the reliability and validity of program measures agencies were required to use in their legislative budget requests.

Throughout the 1989 legislative session this concept was debated in each chamber and passed the House only to die in the Senate. In 1990, the measure was again debated in both chambers. Minor adjustments were made, and a funding source was created to guarantee the fiscal resources needed to carry out the mandate of the legislation. The funding source was a small assessment against the various trust funds that exist in Florida state government. The final bill passed both chambers and was signed into law by the governor. It never went into effect.

Legislative staff, especially in the Senate, was strongly opposed to the law. This group argued that the provisions requiring the joint legislative auditing committee to hire an interim director be held in abeyance because of pending elections in the fall. The chair of the Senate Appropriations Committee was the Democratic president-designee, and the Republican Senate president-designee was the immediate past chair of the committee. They were convinced and asked the auditing committee to wait.

By the time the Democratic designee was formally elected president in November, there was a substantial revenue problem in the state. During the 1991 legislative session, a major revenue package was passed, and a Senate amendment to that bill repealed the funding source for the PAAR office. The reform therefore was never implemented.

Although the 1991 legislative session saw the demise of one budget reform effort, it also saw the beginning of three others. One initiative was again sponsored by Senator Jack Gordon, chair of the Committee on Health and Rehabilitative Services (HRS) Reorganization, which had been established to oversee the separation of the elderly affairs programs from the Department of HRS. This committee proposed legislation that would require the HRS to develop and implement unit cost budgeting over a term of five years (Chapter 91–158, Laws of Florida). The legislation was designed to "Ensure that information be provided to decision makers so that resources are allocated to programs . . . that achieve desired performance levels" (Chapter 91–158, Laws of Florida, p. 1465). This effort continued for three years as an independent project in the department and was then transferred to the agency budget office. Although some who worked on the original project report that it became bogged down in minutia, it is still the foundation for the performance budgeting efforts of the department.

The second reform initiative was brought forth by the committees on education in the legislature. This provided a new level of budget and administrative flexibility in the university system and required the board of regents to establish processes for systematic and ongoing evaluations of the quality and effectiveness of the universities (Chapter 91–55, Laws of Florida).

The third reform initiative was championed by Governor Chiles and provided budget flexibility. In his first state of the state address on March 5, 1991, the governor laid out his plan for a budget process that would end micromanagement by the legislature and the governor. In response to his proposal, the legislature provided for a one-year pilot project in the Department of Revenue (DOR) and the Division of Workers Compensation in the Department of Labor and Employment Security (DLES). This pilot project provided for relaxation of bureaucratic rules on personnel management and budget implementation. In lieu of these controls, an oversight board was created to monitor the efforts and accomplishments of the experiment. The project was extended by the 1992 and 1993 legislatures for both entities. The DOR however, was more active in developing performance reviews and analyses of processes than was DLES.

During the summer following the end of the 1993 legislative session, the governor's budget office asked the DOR to redirect efforts to performance measurement as a means of developing a basis for performance budgeting. Staff from the DOR, the governor's office of planning and budget (OPB), and the House Committee on Governmental Operations worked together for several months developing a program structure and performance measures to be used in a proposed performance budgeting bill. At the same time, the president pro tempore of the Senate, Pat Thomas, was preparing to assume the presidency of the Senate and was developing his agenda for the 1994 session. At the top of this agenda was a commitment to prepare legislation for budget reform.

THE GOVERNMENT ACCOUNTABILITY AND PERFORMANCE ACT OF 1994

With little knowledge of what the other chamber was doing, the Senate and the House of Representatives began the process of developing a performance budgeting system in the fall of 1993. The House was working with the governor's office to draft legislation that would implement a performance-based budgeting system based on the activities being conducted with the DOR. The Senate had appointed a select committee on governmental reform, with one of its missions being a review of the legislation that created the PAAR office and the role that office should play in any reforms to be proposed. In addition, the senate president had given the chairman of the appropriations committee the charge to work with the select committee on governmental reform to develop a budget reform package that would change the process from one concerned primarily with inputs to one that was based on the results that accrue from the expenditure of inputs and that would allow the allocation of scarce funds to achieve maximum results.

Early in the 1994 session, both chambers had drafted legislation to implement a performance budgeting system in Florida. While the House bill was more comprehensive and complete than the original Senate bill, it was clear that both chambers were prepared to debate and pass major budget reform legislation.

At this point, there was substantial agreement on what was needed to achieve success with the reform effort. Both chambers agreed that everyone involved in the planning, budgeting, and evaluation process had to be involved in all aspects of the proposed system. It was also clear to everyone that the magnitude of the change being proposed would require a multiyear process that would bring a few agencies into the system each year. The essential elements of the changes were the designation of programs that had a unified purpose and the development of measures to accurately reflect the activities and results of each program. There was agreement that a legislative organization outside the actual legislative and appropriations process would need to be established to provide a central clearing house and repository or "institutional memory" that could learn from early mistakes and provide guidance throughout the process. Although there was general agreement on these important issues, however, the process of preparing legislation that contained the details of these agreements proved more difficult than most had anticipated.

Although both chambers talked of the need to provide administrative flexibility in exchange for the creation and use of performance measures that provided more information on the activities and results of the programs, two major conflicts arose. The first concerned the Senate bill and the perception in the House that it did not provide enough flexibility to the agencies to achieve the eventual goals. The second was the concern by the House that the Senate bill was too rigid in its requirement that the programs and measures be constructed in such a way that they could be used in the process of allocating scarce funds between competing programs. It was not until the lieutenant governor, the president of the senate, and the speaker of the House re-established their personal involvement in the legislation that movement was restored. The leaders instructed their respective staffs to get together and draft compromise language that all could agree would meet the mutual objectives of the leadership. The final days of the session saw many drafts of different sections of the bill before a final document was put together and passed by unanimous vote in the House and with only one dissenting vote in the Senate.

The final bill provided for the conversion from incremental, line-item budgeting to performance budgeting over a seven-year period, beginning in FY 1994–1995 and ending in FY 2001–2002. As each agency was scheduled to convert, it would be required to propose a set of programs that would be implemented within that agency. Such a proposal was to be made after consultation with the legislative appropriations and appropriate substantive committees as well as the executive office of the governor (EOG). The EOG was given thirty days to confer with the respective legislative committees and then approve, disapprove, or modify the list of programs.

Subsequent to approval of the program structure, each agency would be required to submit a list of performance measures, including outputs, outcomes, and baseline data for review by EOG. The EOG then had thirty days to confer with the respective legislative committees and the Office of Program Policy Analysis and Government Accountability (OPPAGA) before approving or disapproving the measures. The bill also clearly stated that the final approval of all programs, performance measures, and standards would be made by the legislature through the appropriations process.

The OPPAGA had been created by transferring the performance auditing function from the office of auditor general to create a new entity reporting directly to the joint legislative auditing committee. The OPPAGA assumed most of the duties previously established for PAAR, and it was given the additional responsibility of being the repository of technical expertise and institutional memory for performance budgeting.

For those programs that had measures approved by the legislature, funds would be appropriated under the bill in a lump sum for operations instead of in the many line-item categories that had been used in the past. The program administrator would then be required to allocate these funds to existing appropriation categories for the purposes of expending the funds. The administrator could move the funds within categories at his or her own discretion, however, without approval of the EOG or legislative committees. The funds could not, however, be moved between programs without going through traditional budget amendment procedures.

The performance measures adopted by the legislature and the quantification of the expected level of achievement would be placed in the appropriations bill for each program. Programs could request amendment to the levels of expectation by providing EOG with justification for the adjustment. In such cases, EOG would review the request and provide copies of the proposed changes to the legislative committees for review and possible objection. If there were no objections, EOG could approve the requested change. Similarly, the agencies could request adjustments to the program structures and the performance measures. These requests also had a formal method of review and approval that required all the participants to reach a consensus.

THE IMPLEMENTATION PROCESS

Performance budgeting was going to be difficult to implement. Many entities—legislative committee staff, the governor's budget office, agency leaders and budgeters, and legislators themselves—had to be willing to be full participants. Establishing a meaningful program structure was the first step, and it had to be done with care and caution. Developing performance measures that clearly communicated the purpose, effectiveness, and efficiency of the program was a most arduous enterprise and would require enormous dedication and effort by all the participants. Finally, all had to be kept focused on the purpose of the reform—to better communicate with citizens as well as governmental decision makers what government was accomplishing with scarce resources.

In the best of times, with the easiest of reforms, implementation is the key to eventual success. No matter how well designed the legislation is, if there are failures or unresolved difficulties in the implementation strategy, there is the likelihood of failure.

When developing an implementation strategy for a complex and radical reform issue such as performance budgeting, in which the legislation contains compromises that some elements of each chamber resent, the possibility for success is substantially diminished. The deliberative body that passed the legislation recessed and left the implementation to others. In this case, it left the most difficult part of the reform process to a set of players that were not in complete accord on the specifics of implementation. The staff of the governor's office and House of Representatives had worked closely to develop one concept. The staff of the Senate, at best a reluctant participant in the reform movement, served a leadership that had a distinctly different concept than that of the governor and House. Agency professionals and OPPAGA staff did not understand precisely what the legislature wanted. Each group had preconceived ideas that were different not only from each other, but differed from those of the political leadership as well.

As with any piece of legislation, this bill is subject to interpretation. Some of the ambiguity was deliberate. It is not easy, and frequently not wise, to try to write specific implementation strategies into legislation. The statutory authority must be vague in some sense. Statutes are relatively permanent and must have some flexibility in their wording for future adjustments to changing exogenous conditions. Unfortunately, this ambiguity provides cover for those who wish to revisit decisions and compromises that went against their predilections. That is one of the problems being faced in the current implementation phase of this legislation. The people who wanted a system that would be more of a performance audit system are not supporting those people who insisted that the new system have utility annually in the appropriations process.

The second major implementation problem has been studied by Kravchuk and Schack (1996). They tell us no measurement system can be meaningful unless the program structure is rational. Programs must not be aggregations of unrelated activities and interrelationships. Specifically, their comments on this point are well stated:

> Where subsystems are sufficiently diverse as to embrace fundamentally different activities, their interlinkages will be minimal (or nonexistent). Consequently, their aggregation for purposes of management, measurement, and control probably is ill-advised (Kravchuk and Schack, 1996: 353).

Agencies perceive the new system as a method of shedding layers of outside control. They have seized upon the promise of flexibility as if it were the purpose of the reform instead of a tool to gain reform, and they have embarked upon a path that may well doom the effort to the same fate as all those that preceded it. Many of the agencies have taken the position that the programs they wish to have approved for lump-sum budgeting are at a very high level. For example, the Department of Transportation (DOT) has requested only three programs for a department with 10,550 employees and a budget of $3.1 billion. One program was entitled "transportation systems development." This proposed program is made up of such diverse activities as public transportation, planning, traffic operations, and right-of-way acquisition. Currently, this proposed program comprises four budget entities and is in excess of seventy line-item appropriations. The department wants to trade that level of fiscal control for one lump sum for operations and several specific product categories. The department has proposed eight output measurement indicators to explain this one program's deliverables.

At the time the legislation was passed, the professional staff of the appropriations committees knew that DOT had an existing structure for budgeting purposes of four budget entities and twenty-three program components with 112 specific line-item appropriations. Each program component had been established after much review and consideration of the activities of the department, and each had a defined objective. These components met the definition of a program under the new legislation. The existing program components could have been a good place to start with the development of new programs, but the department insisted on more "flexibility." The department has also recommended fourteen output measures for its three proposed programs. These measures are quite similar to the objectives that accompanied the program component structure within the current budget format and system. If each of these fourteen outputs represented a different program for budgeting purposes, achievement of the intent of the legislation would be much nearer.

The third implementation problem is related to the types and uses of measures. During the debate on the legislation it was generally agreed that any measure adopted for use in performance budgeting must also have utility for the agency managers in overseeing the internal activities of the programs. It was important to avoid the creation of one set of performance or activity measures that would be reported in the budget process and another set of measures that the agency would use internally.

Related to this problem is the proper use of output and outcome measures. Both are needed for high-level executive decisions on programmatic issues and for allocation decisions in the legislative budget system. Outputs must be the measures used for direct evaluation of program activity and will drive allocation decisions. Since all public programs are driven by the need to accomplish some external social goal, however, outcomes must be developed that relate to the outputs. These must be monitored to ensure that programs are achieving the societal effects intended. Outcomes should not, however, be used to evaluate programs or for allocation decisions. Doing so has been found to be destructive of the process. Outcomes are generally beyond the direct control of the program. The program cannot, therefore, be held accountable for failing to achieve them.

The fourth implementation problem comes from nonspecificity in the use of budgeting terminology. "Performance budgeting" and "performance measurement" have been used to describe many different systems. These range from the establishment of benchmarks and use of performance measures to monitor results in Oregon and Minnesota (Broom and McGuire, 1995) to the use of performance measures to set budgets and manage programs in Sunnyvale, California (Osborne and Gaebler, 1992), and in Indianapolis, Indiana (Anderson, 1993). In Florida, the intent was to follow the lead of Sunnyvale and Indianapolis. There was a clear understanding that Florida would move toward the contract budgeting model of these two cities. Unfortunately, many people involved in the implementation phase have read of earlier and less dramatic uses of these budgeting concepts and assume Florida can only move as far as Oregon or Minnesota.

The final implementation problem is that of continuity. The actors who approved this legislation are no longer active in its development. Legislatures, especially part-time, citizen legislatures, are known for weak oversight of executive functions. This weakness is even more noticeable in the oversight of new, innovative, and difficult programs. Legislators are willing to pass that problem off to others. Their job is to pass laws, not to execute them. Even when implementation of such a central reform as performance budgeting is at risk, it is difficult to keep the legislature focused. Before new laws become effective, these actors are being bombarded by new problems their constituents bring to them for resolution. In addition, Florida rotates its legislative leadership every two years. The specific persons who fought for this reform are no longer in a position to urge others to expend the energy and political capital necessary to accomplish its goals.

The problem of continuity will be exacerbated when limits on legislators begin in the year 2000. After that time no legislator may serve for more than eight consecutive years. All legislative continuity will then reside almost exclusively with committee staff. Whether or not they will become supporters of this reform is in doubt. The OPPAGA staff will have a vested interest in making the reform work. Other staff may not. Staff of the substantive committees may see this effort as just another reform that adds to their workload and is doomed to failure. Senior appropriations staff may resist the reform because it is foreign to their training and experience.

The university system is probably the best hope for overcoming the potential lack of support from staff. As new MPA graduates enter the workforce of the legislature, OPB, and the agencies, they should bring with them a new appreciation for the strengths and promises of performance budgeting.

THE PROBABILITY OF SUCCESS

Individually, each of these problems bodes ill for the success of this budget reform effort. Together, they present a challenge that will require substantial effort and perservance by the political leaders of the state. All were foreseen, however, and most of them were addressed in the legislation itself. The first three problems are impacted positively by the requirement that numerous participants be involved in the development of program structures and performance measures. It was the intent to have substantive committee staff be the repository of expertise in program structure since they know the authorizing legislation for the programs best. Measures and programs would have to be approved by the appropriations committees on the basis of utility for decision making. The OPPAGA was to create basic performance budgeting expertise and advise the less knowledgeable legislative and executive staff on the nature of the system and the experiences of others, both in Florida and in other states. The number and diversity of experts involved in implementation, coupled with the detailed process required for implementation, was thought to be the best guarantee that the requisite ambiguity in the law could be overcome and that the clear intent could be achieved.

The fourth problem was addressed by defining terms in the law and specifying the purpose of the reform in such a manner that it would be clear that the Florida law exceeds the budget reform purposes of most other state laws. Florida law is clear. The intention is to adopt the model of Sunnyvale, California, not the Oregon model. Further, internal communications clearly indicate the intent of this reform is to allow Florida to move to a budget system in which the legislature "contracts" with agencies for provision of a certain level of services to the citizens of the state (Easterling, 1993; Boyd, 1994).

The final problem was addressed by the Senate president after the legislation became law. He appointed three members of the Senate appropriations committee to oversee the implementation of the reforms. Unfortunately, his term in office was not extended as expected, and the informal oversight committee dissolved. In addition, the primary forces in the House either left the House immediately after the session in which the law was passed or have left in the ensuing years. The success of the reform is thus in doubt.

The ability to implement such a dramatic reform in a democracy has been reviewed and found to be quite difficult (Schedler, 1994). Florida may be in the process of demonstrating that it is equally improbable in a state with a part-time legislature, especially one with a tradition of rotating its leadership. Nevertheless, the safeguards written into the law have at least provided a greater opportunity for reform than ever before in Florida. The process is proceeding. It has made progress. The mistakes and weaknesses are reparable. All that is needed is a renewed involvement by the people who are the eventual users, the legislators and the citizens.

The ultimate fate, however, rests in the hands of the legislature. Rosenthal (1986) has documented two eras of strong legislative leadership in Florida that he called "golden eras." This reform could be the hallmark of the third. If Florida's current legislative leadership is equal to that in the earlier golden eras. Florida will enter the twenty-first century with a new tool to serve the political officials of the state in their efforts to lead and inform the citizens. If they are not, Florida will likely enter the next century on the heels of yet another failure and will continue to "muddle through" with incremental and misleading budgets.

REVIEW QUESTIONS

1. Define performance budgeting. How does it differ from other more commonly used budgeting systems? What are its advantages and disadvantages?
2. Florida has a long history of failed budgetary reforms. What are the causes of these reform failures? What can the government do to correct the problem?
3. Performance budgeting is often difficult to implement. Why? What can a government do to successfully implement performance budgeting? Which institution is the key to successful implementation? How?
4. How common are the obstacles faced by the state of Florida in implementing performance budgeting? Why?

REFERENCES

Axelrod, D. (1995). *Budgeting for Modern Government*, 2nd ed. New York: St. Martins.
Anderson, B. (1993). Using activity-based costing for efficiency and quality. *Government Finance Review, 8(3)*, 7–9.
Barrett, K. and Greene, R. (Sept. 26 1995). State of the states—Tick, tick, tick. *Financial World, 64(20)*, 36–60.

Boyd, F. A. (1994). Government Performance and Accountability Act of 1994: The Unrealized Potential. unpublished manuscript used as basis for speeches and oped articles.

Broom, C. A. and McGuire, L. B. (1995). Performance-based government models: Building a track record. *Public Budgeting and Finance, 15(4)*, 3–17.

Easterling, C. N. (1993). Budget Reform, unpublished memorandum to Florida Senate appropriations committee chair, Senator Ken Jenne.

Klay, W. E. (1994). Planning and budgeting. In R. Chackerian (ed.), *The Florida Public Policy and Management System: Growth and Reform.* pp. 189–210. Tallahassee, FL: Florida Center for Public Management.

Kravchuk, R. S. and Schack, R. W. (1996). Designing effective performance-based management systems under the Government Performance and Results Act of 1993. *Public Administration Review, 56(4)*, 348–358.

Lindblom, C. A. (1959). The science of muddling through. *Public Administration Review, 19(2)*, 79–88.

Osborne, D. and Gaebler, T. (1992). *Reinventing Government.* New York: Penguin.

Polivka, L. and Osterholt, B. J. (1985). The governor as manager: Agency autonomy and accountability. *Public Budgeting and Finance, 5(4)*, 91–104.

Rosenthal, A. B. (1986). The state of the Florida legislature. *Florida State University Law Review, 14(2)*, 399–431.

Schedler, K. (1994). Performance measurement in a direct democratic environment: Local performance in Switzerland. *Public Budgeting and Finance, 14(4)*, 36–53.

Turnbull, A. B. (1979). The Florida appropriations process. In H. P. Tuckman (ed.), *Financing Florida State Government*, pp. 359–381. Tallahassee, FL: Policy Sciences Program.

White, J. (1994). (Almost) nothing new under the sun: Why the work of budgeting remains incremental. *Public Budgeting and Finance, 14(1)*, 113–134.

9

Implementing and Managing Zero-Base Budgeting

Jerome B. McKinney
University of Pittsburgh, Pittsburgh, Pennsylvania, U.S.A.

The first record of zero-base budgeting (ZBB) application in the public sector occurred in the Department of Agriculture in 1964, mainly because of Secretary Orville Freeman's interest in budgeting (Schick, 1977:12–3). This attempt was short-lived in spite of top-level support. Each responsibility center charged with budgeting functions fought to further its priorities while ignoring the goals, objectives, priorities, and instructions of the department. Among the problems contributing to ZBB's failure to take hold in the Department of Agriculture included short lead time for budget preparation and massive paperwork. Despite the failed implementation of ZBB, it motivated the department's top management to initiate more comprehensive examination of budgeting decisions and encouraged the involvement of all levels of operating managers' in the budgetary process.

Momentum for ZBB in the public sector began when the state of Georgia (under then-governor Carter), the city of Garland, Texas, and a few other entities implemented it during the early 1970s. When Jimmy Carter was elected president in 1976, his support for ZBB in the federal government infused new enthusiasm about ZBB in government. A number of especially attractive features were then being emphasized, such as effective planning and control and efficient allocation of scarce budgetary resources, clearly setting forth the benefits to be gained versus the costs to be incurred for each program or activity undertaken. In ZBB every dollar allocation is required to stand or fall on its merit. Each increment or unit of cost for an activity or program requested must generate an equal or greater increment of benefit. Zero-base-budgetary requires constant matching of costs versus benefits; no program or activity can be continued simply because a budget request is made.

Excitement about ZBB was heightened because it promised superior resource allocation, allowing trade-offs among competing budget demands. The rational and systematic process of ZBB permits the different levels of management to fund prioritized undertakings. Both the qualitative and quantitative information generated allows managers to evaluate programs from a holistic perspective, indicating how each contributes to the goal or purpose of the organization. Moreover, ZBB encourages planning before the budgeting phases begin, enabling clear guidelines to be decided upon prior to budget preparation.

This chapter explores the rationale that gives rise to ZBB, including sunset legislation, downsizing, and the reinvention movement in government. There are five sections to this chapter. The first contains an overview and context of ZBB. In the next, the process and mechanics of ZBB are examined, exploring helpful ways to minimize implementation problems. The subsequent section reviews the promises and reality of ZBB. In the section offer that the differences between old and new ZBB are examined. The final section contains the summary and concluding observations.

ZBB: PROCESS AND MECHANICS

Before implementing the ZBB process, an organization is required to clearly identify its goals, objectives, and structure. At the initiating stage, an organization cannot apply ZBB without a clear understanding of its structure and adaptability. For this reason it is essential to know at the outset if an existing organization is amenable for the installation of ZBB. If not, what organizational, programmatic, and present changes can be effectively instituted and what planned changes are needed for the future? The organization should have in place a framework that links operations planning (short-range objectives) and long-range planning (or what is typically called strategic planning). Answers to the following questions must be sought: What are the outcomes that are being sought? What technology will be used? Who are the users for whom the information system is being designed? What are the types of linkages between the existing management system and the ZBB process? What are the specific implementation strategies that would be followed? Additional long-range questions to which consideration should be given are: "Where is the organization presently headed? Where should it be headed? Is it moving in the right direction?" (Mckinney, 1979:67).

The ZBB Process

Figure 1 presents a synopsis of the basic steps involved in the ZBB process. *Step 1* requires a clear articulation of *goals and objectives*. While this step has often been neglected in traditional ZBB, it is critical if the organization is to become more focused in linking and fully utilizing ZBB. Goal articulation gives top management an instrument that can be used to state relative priorities and provide general guidelines for all participants. In the typical governmental entity, broad policy or mission is set by the legislature, although the determination and implementation of short-range and long-range plans are developed and carried out by elected and appointed executives (e.g., president, mayor, county commissioner, and city manager). Ideally, preliminary goals and objectives are articulated by top management and passed on to middle- and lower-level managers for their review and potential modification, allowing the bottom-up management system to operate. Once a meeting of the minds has been achieved, the next step can begin.

To help us understand how goals and objectives may be linked to the ZBB budget, a review of the linkage of the goals and objectives in a city department of housing is presented in Table 1. As Table 1 shows, the objectives are articulated with specificity to facilitate identification of results that can be measured quantitatively and qualitatively. Management at all levels must engage in this function so that (1) performance can be measured, (2) program and activities can be continuously monitored, and (3) postevaluation and feedback can occur. Table 1 links five performance indicators: (1) need/demand indicates the quantity of unsafe housing to which attention must be given; (2) workload shows the amount of unsafe housing that needs to be demolished; (3) efficiency/productivity

Levels of
Management   Top   Middle   Lower

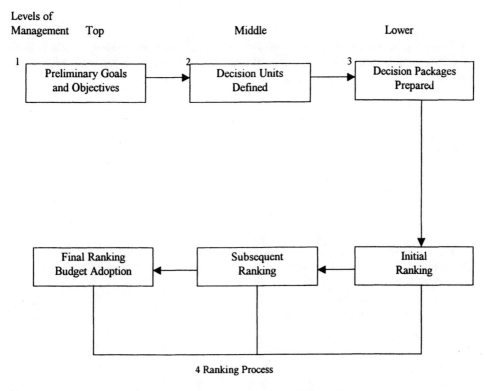

Figure 1   Overview of ZBB process:*Source*: McKinney J 1995, p 5.

indicates per-unit demolition completed for each unit of resource used or consumed; (4) effectiveness indicates the number and percentage of safe housing; and (5) sustainability indicator is the extended time horizon over which the percentage of unsafe housing units continues to decline.

Examination of the objectives of the housing demolition program in Table 1 shows that: (1) each objective is achievable within the budget year, (2) quantitative workload measures are provided, allowing the assessment of the operation's efficiency, (3) impact measures (measures of effectiveness) are obtainable, and (4) measures of sustainability can be established.

Step 2 involves the selection of *decision units*. With preliminary goals and objectives defined, top management can now identify the organization's activities or responsibility areas and the persons charged with carrying each activity. Top management can sit down with program managers and define *decision units*, a responsibility area in which budget requests are prepared.

Decision units are typically budget units located at the point of which costs are accumulated and budgetary decisions are made. The decision unit may be a specific activity such as street cleaning, or a grouping of existing and proposed related activities called programs (e.g. street maintenance) that management views or identifies as meaningful for planning and budget purposes. In summary, a decision unit may be a program or an

Table 1   City Department of Housing: Demolition of Unsafe Housing

Objectives
   1.   To clean 10% of structures that are vacant and deteriorated beyond repair by fiscal year end.
   2.   To level 15% of buildings that pose a potential health or safety hazard by fiscal year end.
Activities
   1.   Determining the conditions of the homes
   2.   Demolishing unsafe housing
Evaluation measurements
   Need/demand
      Number of homes considered vacant and deteriorating
      Number of homes declared unsafe
      Number of inspections requested
      Number of homes requiring public aid to repair
      Number of homes requiring demolition
   Workload measurement
      Number of houses to be demolished
      Number of acres to be cleared of demolished buildings
      Number of inspections to be made
      Number of man-hours to be expended in demolishing and inspecting
   Efficiency/productivity
      Number of homes inspected per inspector
      Cost per home inspected
      Number of homes demolished
      Cost per home demolished
   Effectiveness
      Percentage increase or decrease of substandard housing units in city
      Percentage reduction in accidents related to unsafe buildings
      Percentage of abandoned buildings actually demolished
   Sustainability
      Extent to which vacant structures deterioration have been stabilizing or
      declining over a specified time
      Duration of time over which unsafe homes have been declining

organizational entity with common and measurable objectives for which budget requests are prepared and individual accountability can be assigned (Mckinney, 1979:75).

Since each decision unit is viewed as a responsibility center, there must be a manager who can make decisions about spending and the quality of work. A decision unit may be a line item, a project, an activity, a program, or an entire organization, depending on the level of management responsible for the preparation of the decision packages.

In most cases, decision units are formed in existing organizational structures. This is especially true in those cases in which planning, programming, and budget systems (PPBS) have been operating. It provides a logical structure that can easily accommodate ZBB. The fit or correspondence with the existing structure has the advantage of making the linkage with the accounting system. Where new decision units must be designed, the accounting linkage must be effectively incorporated.

Locating decision units tends to be more troublesome initially in those agencies that have not experimented with program budget or PPBS. It is important to keep in mind that decision units are organized by top management to achieve control over scarce budgeting resources. The design of the information-gathering system and the location of decision units thus should always be geared toward higher-level management. Ideally, decision units should be at the level in the organizational structure that minimizes paperwork and provides optimum opportunity for review. An example from Mt. Lebanon, Pennsylvania, would help us to clarify the ZBB process.

Step 3 is the level at which *decision packages* are prepared. It is here that the preliminary goals and objectives are developed into concrete budget requests. To effectively prepare decision packages, lower-level managers must clearly understand articulated goals and objectives when they design decision packages to deliver the appropriate or intended outputs and results. Because the decision package preparation takes place at the point of which initial options for budget allocations and ranking occur, it (decision package) becomes the building block for ZBB. In other words, this is the point at which agreed-upon goals, objectives, output units, quality, guidelines, and funding levels of agencies' activities are operationalized into concrete decision packages or increments of service, as shown in Tables 2 and 3. Among the information that the decision manager needs is projected inflation rate, top management priorities, personnel ceilings, impacting laws, and desired quality levels. This knowledge facilitates communication and helps to bring about budget projection consistency.

Decision package is a request document indicating in monetary terms the amount of resources a manager would like to have. It provides sufficient information about an activity, function, or operation, permitting managers to obtain informed judgment about the allocation of resources. Importantly, the information must be organized to allow management to rank each decision package with competing activities.

Because of its pervasive role in influencing resource allocation and priority of budget decision, as previously noted decision package is the basic building block in the ZBB process. Each decision is ideally required to have at least three decision packages, except in those cases in which a program or activity level is mandated. In such cases only one decision package is produced. Typically at least three decision packages are prepared. They are the minimum-level increment; the base or current level, and the advanced or enhanced level. Decision packages are prepared at the lowest operational level possible where the best cost-benefit information is available.

There are five basic steps that are involved in the formulation and preparation of a decision package: (1) a description of existing operations and available resources, (2) a clear definition of the purpose or goal of each function or activity to aid in measuring outputs and results, (3) evaluation of alternate ways or means of achieving objectives, (4) specification of the benefits to be achieved at each funding increment (also known as level

Table 2   Decision Unit–Increment Matrix

Increments/ decision unit	1	2	3	4	5	Totals
Golf course	$201,460	$138,120	$14,000	$6,880	$5,000	$365,460
Sanitary sewers	43,500	13,000	54,200	84,600	16,000	211,300
Civic activities	4,820	7,140	28,230	19,600	12,000	71,790

Source: Adapted from Mt. Lebanon, Pennsylvania, 1998a.

Table 3 Civic Activities

The civic activities function provides physical services for various community activities and celebrations that are supported but not directly sponsored by Mt. Lebanon. Services are offered for various holiday celebrations and to community organizations and groups for special events.

1996 actual: $61,358
1997 budget: $57,500

1998 service level options

S/L rank	S/L cost	Cum. cost
1	$4,820	$4,820
2	7,140	11,960
3	28,230	40,190
4[a]	19,600	59,790
5	12,000	71,790
6	5,100	76,890
7	13,000	89,890

Service level narrative
1. *Basic activities.* Provides preparation and cleanup for the West Penn Tennis Tournament and
   preparation and setup of voting equipment and polling places.
2. *Holiday celebration.* Civic activity support to include Washington Road Christmas decorations
   and Christmas tree preparation at Cyclops Building and Beverly Road business district. Includes
   funds for decorative lighting repair and replacement.
3. *Fourth of July.* Complete arrangements for the July 4 celebration, including, part-time help, en-
   tertainment, and fireworks. Provides $10,000 in revenue.
4. *Community activities (current level).* Includes summer concert series, barricades for block parties and parades, farmer's market, and preparation and cleanup for special events.
5. *Security cameras.* Installation of security cameras and equipment in the access area between
   Washington Road and the Port Authority Transit (PAT) station.
6. *Mt. Lebanon Day of Caring.* A one-day event matching community volunteers with fixed-income elderly and disabled residents who need help maintaining and improving their properties.
7. *First Night celebration.* Provides support to the First Night Mt. Lebanon Organization; nonal-
   coholic New Year's Eve party for the entire family, food booths, children's activities, parade, and
   fireworks.

[a] Indicates current service level.
Source: Mt. Lebanon, Pennsylvania, 1998b.

of effort or service) and the consequence that will result from nonfunding, and (5) definition
of performance measures.

While it may not be readily obvious, evaluation of alternative ways or methods have
important implications for ZBB. It is this activity that aids significantly in initiating and
accessing productivity. By questioning existing ways of doing things, it provides the
incentive and potential for innovation. The alternative approach requires that managers
(1) review operations and explore different ways of achieving selected decision packages,

and (2) consider the level of effort (see Table 3; service or increment level 5 costs $12,000 and the cumulative cost $71,300) at which the activity can be performed—"In theory, selecting the alternative method for performing an activity is more important than the identification of level of efforts, because selection of the wrong alternative will make it difficult if not impossible to achieve the most productive outcome" (McKinney, 1979: 78). for the resources expended. A number of alternatives may be employed, including contracting out as opposed to performing the task in-house. If the total commitment for achieving the best cost-benefit outcome is followed, the alternative selected might require that the manager's job be eliminated. Ranking is another critical activity in ZBB.

Step 4, the final action in the ZBB process, begins with ranking the decision packages. To avoid aimless discussion and minimize conflict in the ZBB selection process, advance agreement on a ranking methodology is imperative. A ranking standard improves discipline and the opportunity for reaching quick and rational decisions. Three of the ranking methods that have been widely used are as follows (Austin and Cheek, 1979:74). (1) the single criterion approach, which ranks packages on one indicator, such as return on investment (ROI) in a profit-oriented organization or surplus creation in a public organization, (2) the consensus approach, which allows key managers to discuss and vote on each package in a ranking committee, and (3) a major category approach that groups budgeting packages with defined grouping, such as core management, legal mandates, support systems, and strategic programs. Most governmental units follow the consensus approach. Step 4 follows the ranking process activity, as shown in Figure 1. This is a very important step, as it begins the ranking or the formal prioritizing process at the lower management level. As decision packages are developed, they are ranked and sent upward to the next management levels for ranking until top management makes the final selection, as shown in Figure 1.

Generally speaking, priority ranking begins as soon as the decision packages have been completed. When this step is done effectively, it can produce the most productive outcome consistent with prioritized needs. This step requires multiple participants at all levels of the hierarchy to participate in the ranking process in determining budget priorities for the agency, as shown in Figures 1 and 2. The lower-level managers are the most knowledgeable individuals in the ZBB process, as they are charged with providing and initially ranking all decision packages. (When all these packages or increments are added together they equal the total budget.) At successive levels in the ranking process, managers must be motivated to pass on the best decision packages with their attendant performance indicators. Properly done, the ranking process determines which proposed activities will be funded. Ranking allows resource allocations to be effectively made. This approach requires deranking of program, function, or activity in descending order of priority based on benefits to be gained for each spending level. As shown in Tables 2 and 3, the decision packages are priority ranked in descending order of importance. Decision package 1 thus has a higher priority than decision package 2.

After decision unit managers rank their packages within their division or between divisions or departments of the organization, as suggested in Figure 2, the consolidated decision packages are reviewed until a final ranking is made. At some point in the process, top management will know generally the budget "cutoff point"; that is, the total budget fund that will be available for allocation. It is only then that the final decision makers are in a position to determine which packages will be funded and which will not. All decision packages above the cutoff point are funded and those below are not.

| Division | Decision Units | Initial Rankings | Consolidated Rankings | Final Ranking |

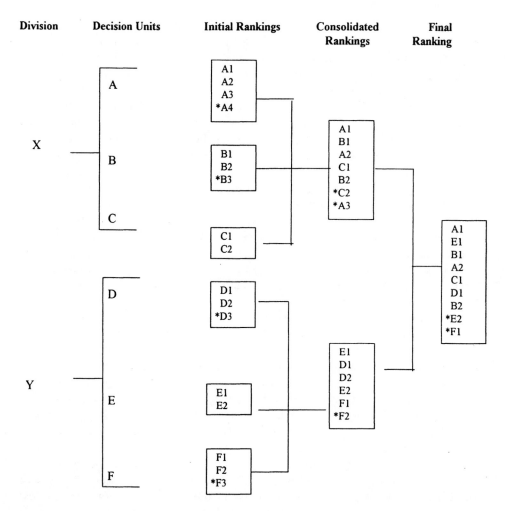

Figure 2   The ranking process: a consolidation of decision packages (with budget cutoffs).

Mt. Lebanon and the ZBB Process

The Borough of Mt. Lebanon is a progressive upper-middle-class suburban community with a population of just over 33,000 people, outside the city of Pittsburgh. When Mt. Lebanon implemented ZBB in 1979, it developed a transitional- or hybrid-type budget. The Mt. Lebanon model parallels the traditional four-step ZBB process (see Figure 1) that was adopted in most jurisdictions.

Selection of Goals and Objectives

Unlike the traditional ZBB model, in which goals and objectives are articulated on a yearly basis, Mt. Lebanon assumes the goals and objectives of the prior year are the operating guides. Top management thus does not articulate yearly initial goals. Instead, lower-level managers developing decision packages are permitted to modify prior year goals and objectives to fit their (lower-level managers) perceived need for change. Lower-level managers make incremental changes to reflect new realities.

Because goals and objectives are not explicitly articulated yearly, it tends to make linkage with results slightly more difficult. This is especially so in Mt. Lebanon as it typically focuses on such outputs, such as miles of street to be paved, and not on the quality or impact of work completed. In terms of the five performance indicators shown in Table 1, Mt. Lebanon's ZBB system does not parallel the five indicators. While need and demand indicators for specific activities are informally assessed by lower-level managers, they are not explicitly identified in their ZBB budget. Both workload and efficiency/productivity measures are often identified. Quality, impact, and sustainability measures are not included, however.

Selection of Decision Units

Decision unit selection in Mt. Lebanon normally follows the traditional departmental organizational lines. For instance, a large department, such as the police department, performs a number of activities in which budget decisions are made in such areas as administration, support services, and field services. Each of these major activities becomes a decision unit or responsibility center, requiring the manager to account to the police chief for spending and work output. This allows the decision units in the police department to effectively link budgeting and accounting in the ZBB system.

Decision units typically comprise a number of decision packages or projected increments of expenditures, as shown in Table 2. Table 2 identifies three decision units (golf course, sanitary sewers, and civic activities) from the Mt. Lebanon ZBB budget. It further shows that as an increment is reviewed and funded, the next sequential increment is placed in competition with the preceding ones. According to Table 2, increment 1 is the minimum level. (It is the least acceptable amount of resources necessary to maintain the service integrity.) The dark partitioning lines in the table identify the increment level or decision package selected in this decision unit. For example, in the golf course decision unit, decision package or increment level 2, costing $138,120, is selected. The total cost for the decision package at increment level 2 is $339,580 (includes increment 1, with a cost of $201,460, plus increment 2, with a cost of $138,120). When a decision package is selected, the total cost of the package always includes all prior increments costs, including the one selected. In the golf course decision unit, for example, if increment 5 were selected, the total cost would be $365,460. This includes increments 1 to 5. All increments beyond level 3 are considered advanced or an enhanced level.

A budget is prepared once the decision units (in Table 2, the golf course, sanitary sewers, and civic activities) have been identified and synchronized with the accounting and other data collection, providing specific instructions regarding the budget preparation.

Selection of Decision Packages

This step of the process in Mt. Lebanon closely follows the model shown in Figure 1. Lower-level managers prepare all initial decision packages. Since managers are at liberty to modify the prior year goals and objectives to fit existing or changed conditions, they are in an ideal position to influence what happens to decision packages that will be passed up to the next level for review.

Once decision units have been selected, determination of the decision package is thus the next step. Decision packages are then developed, typically having at least three service levels or increments—minimum or basic, current, and advanced levels. In Table 3, civic activities (decision unit) provide seven service levels of increments or decision

Table 4 Mt. Lebanon Budget: Calendar of Events (1998)

Date	Event
June 13	Managers decision units due
July 21	Salary figures to departments
August 20	Cost figures to finance
August 25–September 4	Departmental reviews
September 8–10	Ranking
October 13	To printer
November 1	Release

packages. The asterisked increment is the current or existing decision package, costing $59,790 or the cumulative amount for this level was accepted and funded in 1997. In 1998 the fifth service level or increment (costing $71,790, or the cumulative amount for this level) was the amount accepted and funded.

A review of Mt. Lebanon ZBB budget format (see Table 3) shows that each service level (S/L), the associated incremental level of cost for each S/L, and the cumulative level (cum.) are identified. Next, the service-level narrative is provided for each increment level, explaining actions and activities that will take place. The reader thus knows what to expect from each level of service, including the dollar amounts and general guidelines to permit monitoring of service-level accomplishments. (See Table 3.)

Each incremental service level or decision package contains sufficient cost information and description of the projected inputs and general outputs that allow managers to rank them based on the ranking criteria articulated yearly. The calendar of budget events for Mt. Lebanon is shown in Table 4. It provides an easy-to-follow timetable for ZBB preparation.

The fact that lower-level managers can incrementally change prior years' goals and objectives to fit new and changing priorities has the potential positive impact to: (1) minimize the time devoted to goal setting, (2) minimize miscommunication, (3) foster effective bottom-up management decision making, and (4) empower lower-level managers in the ZBB decision-making process to effectively participate in budget resource allocation.

Unlike the traditional ZBB system that articulates goals and objectives, Mt. Lebanon provides a description of existing operations and available resources. As noted earlier, the lack of goals and objectives articulation makes it somewhat difficult to make direct measurement linkages. Additionally, no evaluation of alternative ways of achieving goals and objectives is presented. Because alternative approaches for implementing decision packages are not employed, Mt. Lebanon may not always realize the most productive use of resources. Finally, a review of Table 3 shows that benefits to be delivered for each level of service are not presented.

Ranking Decision Packages

Table 3 also shows the ranking process for Mt. Lebanon, which generally follows the traditional ZBB model. Unlike traditional ZBB, however, in which clearly articulated goals and objectives are effectively accommodated and blended with the ranking criteria, Mt. Lebanon allows lower-level managers to informally modify goals and objectives and blend them with deranking criteria that have been initially stated by the borough commis-

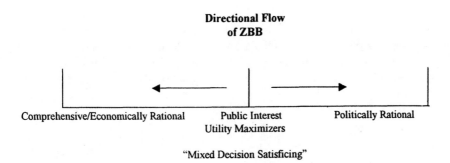

Figure 3   ZBB and decision making. *Source*: Adjusted from McKinney, (1995): 122.

sioners and agreed upon by all participants. Managers must keep the following criteria in mind when ranking decision packages: (1) perceived health, welfare, and safety satisfaction of the citizens; (2) statutory, charter, and contractual commitments required to be met, (3) informal desired quality level, and (4) desired cost-effectiveness (not normally made explicit). In terms of the ranking approaches discussed earlier, Mt. Lebanon employs a hybrid approach, including the consensus and aspects of the major category grouping aspects (Figure 2).

As shown in Figure 2, Mt. Lebanon's three ranking levels are typical of the ZBB process. The manager at each decision level, such as civic activities in Figure 3, initiates the ranking process. At the second level, the city manager acts as the committee of one that does the ranking. The final ranking is done by the borough commissioners, including the city manager and an outside observer, typically a student intern. The participation of the student intern is perhaps unique to Mt. Lebanon.

The Traditional Implementation Model and Mt. Lebanon

When Mt. Lebanon implemented ZBB in 1979, it developed a transitional- or hybrid-type budget. It was a mixture of ZBB and traditional line-item budget. The hybrid approach facilitates a smooth transition to the adapted ZBB model. The major restraining factor, particularly in Mt. Lebanon, was the skill of the staff who had to be trained before ZBB could be effectively implemented. Tables 2 and 3 show that Mt. Lebanon follows the traditional ZBB approach that requires three service levels—minimum or basic, current, and advanced levels. Goal articulation, which is the first step in the ZBB implementation process, is not emphasized. As shown in Table 3, Mt. Lebanon's decision package provides only a general description. The next step requires the identification of decision units.

Of particular note is that Mt. Lebanon has maintained its detailed line-item budget structure as a subcomponent of the ZBB budget. In each decision unit, the decision package such as the golf course, Table 3 service level 2, the $138,000 cost is broken down into line items in a budget appendix identifying such input items as supplies, labor, travel, and utilities. Maintaining this crosswalk (conversion of line item into ZBB activities or program) is useful when queries are made at public budget hearings. Additionally, the public can easily relate to and understand a budget that facilitates better communication, allowing the public to follow the exchanges on budget matters.

The ZBB is successful in Mt. Lebanon because it has kept the process simple, maintaining effective communication, cooperation, and team spirit among all those involved in preparing and managing the budget. The budget is constructed on the basis of prioritized community needs and not simply on revenue expectation. The budget is thus priority-driven. After Mt. Lebanon's needs have been prioritized, the budget is pared down to meet revenue expectations. This strategy aids policy makers in focusing attention on priority policy issues. Budget prepares in Mt. Lebanon ask that ZBB implementers keep a few simple points in mind if success is to achieved.

1. Implementers need to carefully identify what, who, and how services are to be provided in the most cost-effective manner possible. To achieve this objective one should examine alternative ways (a weak link in the Mt. Lebanon ZBB, as noted) for the service to be undertaken prior to preparing the proposed budget.
2. An effective monitoring system is maintained to assess expenditure and the progress of service delivery on a continuous basis.
3. It views training as an imperative for implementation and preparation.
4. Participants are always ready to modify the ZBB process whenever the situation dictates.

Like the Rex Hospital ZBB approach, the Mt. Lebanon ZBB system shows how each entity implemented ZBB to fit its organizational needs. Mt. Lebanon's hybrid system (a combination of ZBB and the line-item budget) stresses dollar accountability and control of functions and activities. Only minimum stress is put on outputs and impacts. Mt. Lebanon does not emphasize goal linkage to such performance indicators as need, workload, productivity, and effectiveness measures, as shown in Table 1. Additionally, Mt. Lebanon does not feel the need to explain the consequences of not funding a decision package; to analyze the alternative ways for implementing a decision package; and to explain the justification for selecting the decision package to be implemented.

NEW PROMISES AND REALITY

This section focuses attention on the contrast between ZBB theory and practice. Despite the new enhanced methodology that ZBB provides, implementers tend to be content with marginal or incremental changes that adopt the ZBB format but continue the traditional decision-making budget allocation approach. It minimizes the ZBB impact while reinforcing the status quo.

Traditional budgeting emphasizes such inputs as yearly increasing cost increments, accounting categories, namely personnel, materials, and equipment. Programmatic priorities, end results, or outcomes are not emphasized. Little effort is made to relate inputs and outputs. By contrast, ZBB clearly articulates the basic operating assumptions on which the budget is based. The ZBB relates inputs, outputs, and results in terms of the cost required to achieve activities or programmatic objectives.

The ZBB assumes every activity begins at zero: "Every function of every department is questioned. Existing programs are scrutinized as much as expanded or new programs. The entire budget is viewed as a series of supplemental requests with a theoretical base of zero. And each supplement must be analyzed" (Mt. Lebanon, Pennsylvania, 1997: A-1). Each responsibility manager is required to defend all existing budgetary allocations before the new period funds are allocated. Allocation of funds for the new period occurs only after each activity or function is evaluated and ranked on the basis of costs and benefits.

The ZBB focuses mainly on short-range goals. It is a bottom-up approach involving all management levels. Unlike traditional budgeting, managers are given a "range of choices to facilitate priority setting in the establishment of funding levels" (McKinney, 1979:61). This system does not allow subordinates to send up budgetary requests on a take-it-or-leave-it basis; ZBB requires that at least three options be proposed for every budgetary request made.

As a rational approach to budget resource allocation, ZBB systematically links planning and budgeting and encourages review processes sufficient to evaluate each organization's programmatic activities, both new and proposed. Because of the flexibility and clear articulation of costs and benefits, ZBB facilitates effective resource allocation.

Zero-base-budgeting proponents view the process as a hard-nosed set of management techniques that are aimed at transforming budget making, creating an instrument that maximizes productivity while it minimizes expenditure. Because all undertakings are evaluated prior to budgetary allocation, it is an efficient means for preventing and checking the growth and size of bureaucracy while increasing responsiveness and accountability. The promises made by ZBB are many; they have been organized in a number of categories. The most prominent are reviewed.

Decision Making

Zero-base-budgeting facilitates top-level managers to allocate resources more efficiently. It promotes development of management skills in decision making while fostering effective superior subordinate communication and interaction. Zero-base-budgeting forces participants to focus on the necessity of choice as a key element in budgeting. Importantly, it forces decisions to be made at that point in the organization where the quality of information is greatest. Additionally, it provides a rational means for settling resource allocation conflicts.

Planning

Zero-base-budgeting has the potential for facilitating and integrating goal setting, incremental analysis, alternative analysis, cost-benefit analysis, and performance measurement. Zero-base-budgeting has the potential for fostering better linkage between its short-range and long-range goals. Alternative evaluation emphasis fosters a creative mode of thinking. Zero-base-budgeting flexible orientation fosters the opportunity for contingency planning.

Productivity Monitoring and Evaluation

Zero-base-budgeting's emphasis on detailed program analysis strongly encourages efficiency and productivity, especially at the decision-making level. The prioritized focus of the system promotes efficient resource allocation. Zero-base-budgeting facilitates reduction in spending levels without reducing the quantity and quality of service. Because of the linkage among inputs, outputs, results, and the required monitoring system, ZBB provides the opportunity to take timely corrective action.

Information, Communication, and Participation

Zero-base-budgeting provides all levels of management with better information to appraise capabilities of subordinates. Because of the quality of information exchanged through the channels, it gives each level of management, especially top management, greater insight into the details of subordinates. This provides practical aid for promoting greater line management commitment to budget decision making.

Operating Premises

The assumptions, though unexamined, are that everyone fully understands the premises on which ZBB is based. In reality many of the assumptions underlying ZBB's validity have not been proved. The view is that all decisions are measurable in qualitative and quantitative terms for which alternatives can be identified with complete calculation of cost-benefit relationships. It is thus both practical and desirable to allocate resources, starting from zero. The assumption is made that ZBB's decentralized management system promotes responsible management commitment by permitting lower-level management to make critical significant budgetary allocation (the bottom-up approach). Finally, the view is accepted that the decentralized system has built-in incentive to induce participants to exchange the best available information up the hierarchy, facilitating effective budget allocation. Rex Hospital is one of the recent adopters of ZBB, providing its experience, promises, and premises of ZBB.

The New Implementation Emphasis: The Rex Hospital Model

The Rex Hospital in Raleigh, North Carolina, applies the ZBB model to reduce rising costs and increase opportunity to generate a surplus. To smooth the transition and aid continuity in moving to the ZBB model, Rex involved line managers at the ZBB initiating stage. The ZBB application at the Rex Hospital shows that it can be highly flexible and adaptable.

Line managers are motivated to prepare justification packages for traditional budgetary units and budget types, such as expense, capital, and revenue budgets. Ranking is not done in the traditional ZBB style, however Instead, it is done by a committee that evaluates the justification of packages in accordance with established planning assumptions and budgetary targets. Based on the committee's assessment, recommendations are made to top management, which makes final allocation decisions.

The justification for eliminating traditional ranking in the Rex Hospital case is to maintain the familiar line-item framework. Because line-item budgets stress inputs such as supplies, personnel, and travel costs, the (line-item budgets) cannot easily be linked with outputs and results, which ZBB emphasizes. Rex Hospital did not have to change format as it made sure that participants in the ZBB process understood how the existing line-item budget system could be used to move from where they were to achieve the desired cost savings goal in the ZBB model. The point is made that the budget committee's ability to interact with all participants allows it to make its decision with a holistic perspective. Because of its simplicity, the line-item budget facilitates the participation of all managers making budgetary decisions. If ZBB is to be most useful, Rex Hospital strongly suggests that an *organizational assessment* be systematically undertaken as a first step. This means giving attention to such aspects as leadership, organizational culture, support structures, and timing.

Rex Hospital is a not-for-profit 394-bed hospital. A few years prior to Rex Hospital's adoption of the ZBB innovation, Rex was forced to implement a 15% rate increase compared to the consumer price Index (CPI), which was 4.0% and the medical consumer price index (MCPI), which was 7.7% (Person, 1998:3–4). The 100-year-old institution had long prided itself as a high-quality, low-cost health provider; thus the steep increase in hospital costs was philosophically unacceptable. This was happening at a time in which Medicare was instituting cost constraints for its prospective payment system. This was particularly critical to Rex, since Medicare patients constituted 40% of the hospital workload. Although Rex was still the preferred provider for a number of major medical plans in its serving area, the hospital officials felt that it could not continue to negotiate favorable future contracts if it could not find an effective means to control rate and cost increases (Person, 1998:4).

Demographic factors were dictating demand, bringing increasing numbers of sicker and older patients to Rex. Additionally, there was partial shortage of skilled people. Capital expenditures were being driven by "technological imperative" (Person, 1998:4). To maintain physicians' and patients' confidence, Rex had to meet the competitive pressure. Rex's search to find the instrument or technique to "analyze and address the cost situation hospital-wide" led to the implementation of ZBB.

During the year following the implementation of ZBB, Rex was able to achieve opportunities for cost reduction in the areas of service consolidations, recoganizations, hiring, purchase deferrals, automation, and subcontracting. The rate of increase was held to 7.0%, representing reduction of more than 50%. Its cost rise was below the MCPI by 85%. By 1994 Rex's rate of increase had fallen to 4.0%. Rex's drive for rate reduction is expected to continue until the rate increases at least equal the inflation rate.

Rex's experience demonstrates that ZBB is an important means for permitting health care industries to understand and control costs. Zero-base budgeting forced Rex to analyze and justify every proposed expenditure increase: (1) it dictated the change and adaptation to the new austerity environment: (2) resource allocations were made on a prioritized basis to meet the fiscal constraints and limitations, and (3) Rex was able to hold down costs while improving service quality to the community. Once the ZBB system had been established, it proved to be a flexible and an analytical means to aid vitally in forcing changes, facilitating informed matching between ends and means, enhancing the opportunity to move away from "non-value added activities to higher priorities; permitting managers to meet and deal with uncertain and unpredictable environment" (Person, 1998).

SUMMARY AND CONCLUSION

The new emphasis is put on linkage of inputs to outputs and results (see Table 1) instead of having a particular ZBB format. Stress is put on maximally achieving articulated priorities. As evidenced from the Rex Hospital, planning, budgeting, and decision making are integrated, allowing a timely and effective flow of information, communication, participation, monitoring, and evaluations. The new emphasis mobilizes and directs all efforts toward the productive achievement of stated goals and objectives. The new approach deemphasizes format and seeks to maximally realize articulated priorities.

There is no one single model of ZBB that is followed; each organization adapts ZBB to fit its specific situation. The reasons for using ZBB vary widely, minimizing the uniformity in the application of ZBB.

The implementation of ZBB has been prominent for its divergence between theory and practice. Although ZBB was praised for its innovative and rational emphasis, in practice it has been highly conservative, status quo-oriented, and highly political. The use of cost-benefit analysis was seldom operationalized as a norm. Zero-base-budgeting promised an integrative system, as practiced by Rex Hospital planning was seldom realized. Top-level management's goal setting as ZBB's indispensable first step most often was not followed, as Mt. Lebanon clearly demonstrates. The role of ranking that is so critical to ZBB for "rooting out inefficiencies and eliminating duplications" (Lerson, 1998:104) was seldom applied consistently to achieve the results anticipated. Among the factors helping to impede ZBB's success included the following:

1. Unmanageability of the large volume of information that the system generates. Because the ZBB system is bottom up, the mass amount of information has to be processed by the lower-level manager, who may not have the appropriate incentive to send the highest quality of information up the hierarchy.
2. Haphazard definition of decision units has made comparability difficult.
3. There is a inexplicable criterion to systematically apply the ranking criteria.
4. There is a lack of feedback between levels of management.
5. There is a lack of incentives to encourage lower-level managers to complete priorities.
6. There is confusion about measurement indicators workload because outputs and impacts were not used consistently.

Like most innovation ZBB must compete with and successfully penetrate the existing budgetary routines. Zero base budgeting has not succeeded in achieving this objective. The rationality emphasis of ZBB fails to give institutional politics a significant role in the allocation of scarce resources. Zero base budgeting failed to achieve a balance between *political rationality* and economic rationality, as shown in Figure 3. The short-term tactical orientation of ZBB does not effectively accommodate broader long-range objectives. Where ZBB has survived, it has been due to attention that has been given to training of participants, establishing a simplified and unified philosophy, accepting a long-term horizon before expecting success, and accommodating environmental and political influences in resource allocation.

Typically ZBB's failure has been associated with a lack of discipline and commitment. Zero base budgeting has been seen as a quick-fix budget reduction panacea. Most often little care has been given to the implementation of the system. Zero base budgeting was oversold and viewed as a means of supplanting traditional budgeting. The specific accountability being sought was never clearly articulated (McKinney, 1996:176): "ZBB came at a time when pressures were great to reduce government spending. It forced public sector budget makers to face a problem that had become a continuing concern. Regularized budget reduction was a major departure from traditional practices which expect budgets to be an upward and incremental spiral" (McKinney, 1996: 177).

REVIEW QUESTIONS

1. It is often said that ZBB is concerned more with short-term outlook and cost-effectiveness. Explain why this is so.

2. Because ZBB requires that a number of options be given to higher-level managers, it creates greater opportunities to effectively downsize an agency. Explain.
3. ZBB is often described as a bottom-up approach to budgeting. What does this mean and how does it apply to the concept of ZBB?
4. It is said that ZBB employs the national mode in decision making. What advantages and disadvantages are there to this approach?
5. It is said that ZBB is an ideal mode for achieving effective resource allocation and promoting maximum productivity. Explain.
6. What are some of the practical problems ZBB has experienced in the process of implementation? Discuss and be specific.

REFERENCES

Austin, L. A. and Cheek, L. M. (1979). *Zero-Base Budgeting*. New York: AMACOM.
McKinney, J. B. (1979). *Understanding ZBB: Promise and Reality*. Chicago: Public Policy Press.
McKinney, J. B. (1995). *Understanding ZBB & TQM: Promise and Reality*. Clinton, MD: Public Policy Press.
Mckinney, J. B. (1996). The status and evaluation of ZBB: The American experience. In K. S. Moon (ed), *Public Policy-Making and Budgeting Issues*, Taegu, Korea: Kyung Look National University Press.
Mt. Lebanon, Pennsylvania. (1997). *1988 Budgeting Manual*. Finance Office.
Mt. Lebanon, Pennsylvania. (1998). *Manager's Proposed Budget*. pp. 25, 29, 40–41.
Mt. Lebanon, Pennsylvania. (1998). *Manager's Recommended Budget*. p. 30.
Person, M. M. III. (1998). *The Zero-base Hospital*. Chicago: Health Administration Press.
Schick, A. (Spring 1977). Zero-based budgeting and sunset: Redundancy or symbiosis? *Bureaucrat*, *6*.

BiBLIOGRAPHY

Charlebois, R. (1993). Downsizing in the public sector—One approach. *CMA Mag. 67 (6)*, 29.
Cutt, J. (1994). Public Non-Profit Budgeting. The Evolution and Application of Zero-Base Budgeting. Toronto: Institute of Public Administration of Canada.
Doost, R. (1992). Zero-based control system: It can work in good times and in bad. *CPA Journal*, *62 (6)*, 72–73.
Duffy, M. F. (1989). ZBB, MBO, PPB, and their effectiveness within the planning marketing process *Strategic Management Journal*, *10 (2)*, 163–173.
Goertz, R. K. (1993). Target-based budgeting and adaptations to fiscal uncertainty, *Public Productivity and Management Review*, *16 (4)*, 425–429.
Hill, W. D. (1977). Implementing Zero-Base Budgeting: The Real World, A Case Study. Oxford, OH: Planning Executive Institute.
McKinney, J. B. (1979). Understanding ZBB: Promise and reality, charless, IL.: Public Policy Press pp. 1–3.
Schick, A. (1977). Zero base budgeting and sunset: Redundancy or symbiosis, *Bureaucrat, 6* (spring) 12–13.
Schick, A. (1973) *Zero-Base Budgeting: A Practical Management Tool for Evaluating Expenses*, New York: J Wiley.
Williams, J. J. and Hinings, C. R. (1988) A note on matching control system implications with organizational characteristics: ZBB and MBO revisited, *Accounting Organizations and Society*, *13 (3)*, 191–198.

10

Target-Based Budgeting in Lincoln County

Frank U. Koehler and B.J. Reed
University of Nebraska, Omaha, Nebraska, U.S.A.

Much has been written about how city governments go about the process of budgeting resources and expenditures. Surprisingly little, however, has been written about the budgeting process in counties. This is true despite the fact that over 3,000 counties operate in forty-eight states (Salant, 1991). While a number of new initiatives to study county government have occurred in recent years (Menzel, 1992), information about county processes and operations remains limited.

Similarly, our knowledge and understanding of the use of target-based budgeting (TBB) at the local level is also quite limited. Research has been done on the application of this budgeting approach in a few cities, but we know little about its broader application in counties (Rubin, 1991).

The objective of this case study is to explore the application of TBB in a midwestern metropolitan county. Of particular interest is how a county's legal and political environment affects the budgeting process and the advantages and disadvantages of target budgeting in such an environment. While the event discussed really took place, all names and locations are fictitious.

PROBLEM BACKGROUND AND DISCUSSION

The Case of Lincoln County: Target Budgeting in County Government

County governments have been a part of the American tradition since the earliest colonial settlements (Salant, 1991). Recently, states have increasingly looked to counties to provide additional services, resulting in changes to their structure of operation and in their roles and responsibilities (Gurwitt, 1989). County governments in most cases serve as agents of state government and historically have provided a wide range of services primarily focused on public safety, social services, and public works. Metropolitan counties are finding these traditional functions expanding rapidly. Responsibilities ranging from affordable housing, AIDS, solid waste management, cable TV, and refugee resettlement now

145

threaten to overwhelm county officials. Many of these duties have been mandated by federal and state governments and cannot be shifted to other jurisdictions.

In this period of increased demands for services, most county governments remain heavily dependent on property taxes and direct state support (Ebel, 1991). While cities have increasingly diversified their revenue base, most counties have remained tied to inelastic taxes and relatively flat levels of state support. One major change in resources over the past twenty years has been a substantial increase in support from user charges and miscellaneous general revenue (Ebel, 1991).

These dual trends of increasing demands for assistance and restricted revenue sources have forced counties to face increasingly difficult policy decisions about what services to provide and how to pay for them. Budgeting practices play an important role in how county officials manage the financial stress these dual trends create. A survey of budgeting practices in the mid-1980s indicated that almost 60% of local governments continue to use the traditional line-item budgeting format (O'Toole and Marshall, 1987). This survey pointed to an increased likelihood that counties will move away from the line-item approach in the future and toward such alternatives as performance, program, zero-based, and target-based approaches.

Target-based budgeting is a variation of zero-based budgeting and is used to place overall limits on spending requests of departments and agencies (Rubin, 1991). Irene Rubin has identified larger cities, such as Cincinnati, Tampa, Rochester and Phoenix, that have incorporated TBB into their process. Target-based budgeting expenditure levels are determined by forecasts of revenue levels that will exist during the fiscal year. Based upon these revenue projections departments are given a "target" expenditure level from which to work. This level is usually a percentage of the previous year's expenditure amount. The percentage may be allocated across the board or vary from department to department. Departments provide goods and services at or below that ceiling limit. Certain costs that are mandated are automatically included and certain minimum levels of service activity are assumed to meet the mandate requirements. Beyond these costs, managers have discretion to shift funding between and among various activities under their control. They may also have discretion in how they meet those service levels. Capital and operating items may be given separate target levels or they may be included in the overall target level.

The success of TBB is linked to a number of factors, such as the following:

Accurate revenue projections and capable oversight to eliminate budget "games" that attempt to sacrifice popular items to increase the target base amount
Accurate assessments of service-level responsibilities of individual departments
An honest accounting of mandated costs into the target levels that are set

Rubin notes potential problems with TBB, including the "tendency to obscure service level reductions that have to be made in other areas in order to fund new . . . initiatives" and the potential to limit reallocations among departments (Rubin, 1991, p. 12).

The Case of Lincoln County: History and Background

Demographics

Lincoln County consists of a mix of the state's largest urban area and prime rural and agricultural lands. With a current population of 415,000, it represents one-fourth of the state's population. Eleven percent of the population is African American, 3% is Hispanic, and 3% consists of other minorities.

Employment opportunities exist in a variety of fields, including food processing, health, education, manufacturing, and other service industries. Unemployment tends to be below the national average and is currently 4%. Median family income is $37,000 and per capita income is approximately $14,700. Less than 11% of the population has income below the poverty rate.

Political Background

The county is supervised by and operated under the general direction of a board of commissioners consisting of five members (frequently referred to as the commission). As in most states, several of the county departments are under the complete and independent direction of elected officials. The commissioners have also established departments with appointed directors (e.g. Department of Corrections, Department of Roads). They have also appointed a county administrator who has management responsibility for the departments with appointed directors. These are generally referred to as the "departments" and "department heads," as contrasted to the elected agency heads, who are referred to as the "elected officials." The commissioners have also created a position of budget officer. That appointed officer and the administrator supervise the budget process and provide needed coordination with elected officials on an as-needed basis.

Lincoln County politics have seen little conflict, especially for a county with a growing urban core. Elections are partisan, but offices are retained by individuals for extended periods of time. Incumbents generally work well together regardless of party affiliation. This continuity has encouraged informal communication and procedures and a sense of everyone understanding the needs of everyone else. In addition, policy issues have been relatively routine. Revenue sources have been growing with the growth of the community, and therefore budgets have grown with minimal constraints.

The Changing Political and Economic Environment

Several major events during the late 1980s helped shape the county's finances and budget procedures. These included

> The county and its region experienced the recession affecting other parts of the United States. The county responded by becoming actively involved in development finance and making major commitments in infrastructure projects designed to enhance the community's economic viability.
>
> County commissioner decisions were now recognized as having greater significance for the entire community. The print and electronic media significantly increased their coverage, and thereby increased citizen awareness.
>
> Political "reformers" successfully promoted changing the structure of the county commission from an at-large to a ward system with seven commissioners effective in the next fiscal year. The goal was to achieve "better representation," and in particular, to enhance the possibility of electing a minority commission member.
>
> Court decisions on challenges to the property tax system required the county to make significant refunds of property taxes during the previous two budget years.
>
> The state legislature adopted a number of budgetary constraints, including a requirement for a 0% lid on property tax increases. The lid could only be exceeded by a supermajority vote of the commission.
>
> Anticipating the need to make reductions, the county in the previous year adopted an early retirement program to be accepted by employees before the end of the calendar year.

The Case of Lincoln County: Budgeting Practices

Historic Budgeting Practices in Lincoln County

The Lincoln County government budget process reflected the high degree of comfort among the several actors while also incorporating legal requirements of the state and initiatives unique to Lincoln County.

State law provided the board of county commissioners with two levels of authority to control agency budgets and expenditures. They could control in detail the operations of the departments they reported to the commissioners (e.g., Department of Roads, Department of Social Services); however, they could only control budget totals for the elected officials (e.g., county sheriff, county attorney). Over a period of years, the county accommodated itself in a unique manner. First, it adopted a line-item budget procedure to develop, review, and approve all budget requests. Appropriations were made, as allowed by state law, on a lump-sum basis for each department. Department heads reporting to the county administrator and the county commissioners were required to comply with line-item budgets or obtain approval for changes. Elected officials, however, had total flexibility and could expend their funds based on their own best judgment and without regard to the line-item requests originally submitted. Second, by the mid-1970s, the county developed techniques to limit the flexibility of elected officials. Gradually, a number of budgetary line items were removed from departmental control and transferred to separate budget functions under the administrator's control. These included such items as purchase of vehicles, fringe benefits, insurance, communication costs, and computer and software systems. Purchases in these joint areas were controlled by the administrator with the advice of a committee representing the affected departments. Departments therefore, could not forego capital or operating expenses in order to employ additional personnel or provide salary increases. Expenditures under the direct control of department heads and elected officials are now primarily limited to personnel and day-to-day operating supplies and services.

Prior to the mid-1970s, the state required that the county appropriate or authorize expenditures by resolution and levy taxes to support those expenditures. At that time, the state adopted a local government budget act that required

That the county adopt a budget by a specific date
That specific historical and projected information be included in the budget
That budget hearings be held prior to the adoption of the budget and dictated the
   type of information to be required in the notice of the hearing

The "old boys" network functioned fairly well during the years of gradually increasing revenues and operating expenses, with all the players maintaining their base and receiving a fair share of the growth.

The Case of Lincoln County: Applying Target Budgeting

To the Sheriff's Budget

In the spring it became clear that "business as usual" would not take place. Mandated costs for social service programs and union-negotiated salary and benefit increases were rapidly increasing. At the same time, state-mandated caps on property tax increases and a political climate strongly opposed to tax increases were placing considerable pressure on the budget process for the coming year.

The traditional budget calendar for the fiscal year beginning July 1 operated in the following manner:

April 1—The budget administrator issued a call letter on behalf of the county finance committee providing guidelines and historical information.

May 30—Agencies submitted their estimate of own-source revenues and their expenditure budget request. Budget requests for hundreds of thousands of dollars or even millions of dollars were submitted with a brief one-page letter of transmittal stating in essence that "There has been inflation, our employees need a pay increase of x%, and we need a budget in the amount requested."

May/June—Budget officer assembled information, made own revenue estimates, adjusted "departments" as appropriate, identified changes, submitted information, and estimated the surplus or deficit to the finance committee.

July—Finance committee reviewed budget material, possibly adjusted after informal contacts with elected officials, and submitted to county commission.

August—county commission reviewed, set and conducted public hearing, adopted budget, appropriated funds, set property values, and set tax rate.

It is in this budgetary and political environment that the sheriff developed and submitted his budget request to the county administrator. Several key players were involved in the actions and decisions in this case. They are

Marge Anderson—long-time member of the board of commissioners, chair of the board, and member and chair of the finance committee. Ms. Anderson had been active in county political circles for several years and worked well with all involved in county politics, regardless of party affiliation. Ms. Anderson is chief executive officer of a small privately owned company. Ms. Anderson and the other commissioners faced an election in the fall of the year.

Sam Marsden—Member of the board of commissioners and the finance committee, but with shorter tenure than Ms. Anderson. Mr. Marsden is an attorney-at-law.

David Strong—County administrator, former county budget officer, member of the finance committee, and an accountant in background. County departments report to and are responsible to Mr. Strong. Elected officials are independent of the county administrator. They do participate in the budget process, accounting procedures, and similar processes controlled or supervised by Mr. Strong, however, Mr. Strong acts as primary staff for the county commissioners and the finance committee.

Sheri Wilson—County budget officer, member of the finance committee, and former accountant with one of the county departments.

Ray Ramsey—Sheriff, long-term law enforcement officer, very aware politically, forceful personality, but generally a low-key team player in county politics.

Tami Daniels—Chief deputy sheriff, long-term deputy sheriff, holder of a masters' degree in public administration, training advocate, and actively trying to apply public administration principles.

The Media—The *Regional Star* and several television and radio stations had provided limited coverage on county issues prior to the late 1980s. County issues had been perceived as rather mundane until the county became involved in such exciting issues as economic development, considered eliminating some health services, and faced the tensions of budget reductions.

Table 1 Lincoln County Sheriff's Budgets

Prior year 5	$4,035,000	
Prior year 4	$4,472,000	10.83%
Prior year 3	$4,742,000	6.04%
Prior year 2	$5,053,000	6.56%
Prior year 1	$5,465,000	8.15%

Source: Deputy sheriff, Lincoln County.

The Shaping of the County Sheriff's Budget

During the five-year period ending with the previous year's budget, the sheriff's budget increased an average of 7.9% annually, as shown in Table 1.

Prior to the beginning of the current budget calendar, the county, through its labor negotiating team, agreed with the deputy sheriff's union to provide 4% wage pay rate increases, a night shift differential, and increased uniform allowances.

Also prior to the budget call, the county administrator and the equipment and computer committees allocated $110,000 to replace vehicles and $50,000 for new computer software for the sheriff's office.

On April 5, the county administrator issued the budget call directing that budget submissions provide for no increase over the previous year's budget *and* that the budget request include a narrative identifying reductions of either 5% or 10% from the previous year's budget in case they were needed. In essence, this represented the county's first effort at TBB.

Tami Wilson and Sheriff Ramsey developed a budget request that provided for no reduction in staff, incorporated the increases required by the new union contract, and requested comparable increases for management and supervisory personnel. The brief letter of justification addressed the fact that their request was almost entirely for personnel, that any reductions in personnel would represent a reduction in services, and that management and supervisory personnel were entitled to raises at least comparable to those provided the union. No reference was made to possible reductions of 5% or 10%. The budget requested an increase of over $430,000.

The budget officer and the county administrator proceeded with review and evaluation of all budget requests and advised the finance committee that marginal budget cuts or revenue adjustments would not be a viable option. Drastic cuts or revenue increases would be necessary. Initial reactions were to consider a property tax increase to reduce the amount of the cuts. While discussing preliminary budget approval with the other commissioners, however, Marge Anderson announced that she would not vote for any property tax increase. The other commissioners, who also were running for re-election in November, declined to vote for a property tax increase unless the vote was unanimous. The preliminary budget was approved and set for hearing the budget required that "law enforcement" agencies stay within the previous year's budget (i.e., a "target" budget amount equal to the previous year) and that other agencies be funded at 97% of the previous year's budget. The finance committee was charged with communicating this information to the agencies. The county commissioners on the finance committee were assigned to contact individual elected officers while staff would contact the "departments." The finance committee members were under the impression that Commissioner Anderson had contacted the sheriff and his response was "Do what you have to do." Sheriff Ramsey later stated that he had not discussed the budget decision with Commissioner Anderson and did not receive any information about the potential impact of the target budget for his department. The budget hearing was held as scheduled and the revised budget adopted.

Sheriff's Ramsey's routine activities were shattered by a call from budget officer Wilson requesting information on how to allocate $431,000 in reductions. Ramsey and Deputy Chief Daniels proceeded to evaluate the impact of the cut and develop a strategy to recoup as much of the reduction as possible. Only $31,000 in reductions that would have limited impact were identified, leaving $400,000 of major cuts to address. They concluded that they would have to lay off one civilian and sixteen deputy sheriffs. Services identified by the sheriff and deputy chief that would be reduced or eliminated were (1) drug abuse resistance education (D.A.R.E.) program, (2) the training sergeant, (3) the investigative units, (4) participation in a federally funded cooperative program with other metropolitan law enforcement, (5) the vehicle origination identification program, and (6) a 20% reduction in patrol programs.

Sheriff Ramsey decided that his only recourse was to build support for restoring the cuts and increasing funding above the target amount by going around the formal process and seeking as much public support as possible. He conducted a news conference and expressed concern about the impact on the school system due to loss of the D.A.R.E. program. He also discussed potential reductions in safety and security that would result from reduced staff. Press coverage was extensive, with many school officials expressing concern over the loss of programs aimed at reducing drug use among children. Sheriff Ramsey avoided direct public criticism of the commissioners, but made it clear that the final decision to restore these programs rested with the county board.

After several days of front page newspaper stories highlighting the negative impacts caused by the loss of services in the sheriff's office, Ramsey and Daniels met with Anderson, Marsden, Strong, and Wilson to develop a compromise limiting the impact on law enforcement services. Among the agreed-upon changes were the following:

> The sheriff would not purchase any vehicles and the county would use $110,000 of vehicle money for sheriff's office salaries.
> The sheriff would postpone $50,000 in data processing investments and that amount would be allocated to sheriff's office salaries.
> Savings from the county reduction in force (RIF) policy would be used to hire replacement personnel.
> The sheriff would institute additional fees and the revenues therefrom could also be used for additional personnel.

The Case of Lincoln County: The Aftermath

The current year process led to a county budget that basically held the line. Significant distortions occurred in resource allocation, however, having major implications for future budgets. They are as follows:

1. At the sheriff's direction Tami Daniels instituted an internal zero-based budget approach to reallocate resources between cost centers and maximize productivity. The sheriff plans to submit extensive and substantive justification for his current request.

2. The compromises increased the sheriff's "base" for current budget year personnel decisions by at least $100,000, an increase of approximately 1.8%, while other units were granted no increase or received reductions.
3. The sheriff's vehicle requirement for the current year's budget will be at least 50% greater than normal, requiring an additional $60,000 compared to other years.
4. Data processing requirements in the amount of $50,000 will need to be included in the current year's budget.
5. The sheriff replaced some RIF uniformed personnel with civilian personnel, thereby achieving some short-term and long-term savings.
6. The sheriff reduced the availability of prisoner transport for prisoner convenience activities. This resulted in some efficiencies by combining trips, some reduced services to prisoners, and some transfer of transportation cost to the corrections department.

Budgeting in Lincoln County: The Lessons Learned

This case points to a number of unique aspects of budgeting for county governments. First, counties act as agents of the state and therefore encounter a number of mandated costs and service requirements that other units of local government do not face. Second, elected county boards have limited control over the budgetary expenditures of other elected officials within county government. Elected sheriffs, assessors, treasurers and so forth have an atypical position vis-à-vis the county board. They have direct responsibility to the voters that appointed departments do not have. This makes it both legally and politically difficult to "control" the budget of these officials' departments even though overall revenue and expenditure decisions may be set by the board.

These unique features of county government also affect the application of TBB. Elected policy boards and mayors in cities are able to enforce discipline on individual departments to ensure budget "games" are not played in an attempt to get around targets that are set. The same cannot be said of county boards and elected executives. County boards lack control over what actual services departments with elected heads provide.

Rather than applying TBB as a "top-down" approach, county boards and elected officials have to develop collaborative approaches that lead to a shared set of target levels. On the other hand, TBB is particularly suited to county government because it recognizes the decentralized nature of decision making among departments with elected heads. By acknowledging that the authority for service delivery resides at the departmental level, TBB provides a budgetary framework that is responsive to the legal and political environment of county government.

Lincoln County made several errors in its application of TBB. Target-based budgeting requires a precise definition of a base which must include a recognition of increases to that base that are outside the control of the department. There was little systematic review of factors that might impact the target level other than the previous year's expenditure levels. Elements such as new mandates from state and federal government or other externally created costs were not included. In the case of the county sheriff's budget, the target level failed to include negotiated salary increases for the sheriff's deputies. By moving capital expenditure items such as vehicles and computer equipment out of the department's budgetary control, the county commissioners reduced the discretion of the departments to shift between capital and operating expenditures. As a result the sheriff's budget consisted almost totally of personnel costs, making the omission of mandated salary increases a major factor limiting the options available.

Also, a last-minute decision on the part of county commissioners to oppose additional revenue in the form of a property tax increase led directly to the predicament faced by the county. This decision came as a surprise to the county administrator and to the other elected officials. Earlier identification of the board's intentions concerning tax increases would have given more lead time to adjust for the impact on expenditures.

Poor communication between the county commissioners and the sheriff caused many of the problems in applying TBB. Little explanation was provided to the sheriff's office about how TBB worked and how it would impact its budget preparation. Using a top-down approach, the commissioners and staff gave the target figure to the sheriff without discussing the effect such a decision would have on staffing and service levels. By the time the sheriff was informed of the decision, the legal process had been completed and little could be done to alter the overall county budget expenditure level. This left little maneuvering room other than to enlist external pressure on the county commissioners to reallocate from the existing budget to make up for the shortfall.

Finally, neither the Lincoln County board nor the sheriff's department had developed a formal analysis of service levels or outcome measurement system to link the target budget amount to a particular level of service delivery or performance. Rubin argues that TBB works best with such a component (Rubin, 1991, p. 13).

SUMMARY AND CONCLUSION

This case provides the reader with a glimpse of how county governments carry out the budget process and the potential use of TBB at this level of local government. Counties play an important role in the delivery of services at the local level. This role is changing dramatically, and with this change come increasing pressures to provide more services with fewer resources.

The case reveals that TBB may be an effective approach to budgeting at the county level, but only if it is adapted to the unique characteristics of county government. Particularly important is understanding the significant role that elected officials play at the departmental level. Also, those implementing TBB need to recognize the constraints placed on these departments through state and federal requirements that mandate certain programs and services.

REVIEW QUESTIONS

1. Although Lincoln County's decision to try target-based budgeting was not based on an evaluation of different theoretical approaches to budgeting, to what extent does the county's effort conform to TBB budget theory?
2. Was Lincoln County's approach to budgeting shaped by management, control, or planning expectations? Explain.
3. Was Lincoln County's use of TBB successful or unsuccessful? What factors contributed to that success or failure?
4. What steps, if any, should have been taken by the key actors in the case to make the budget process more effective?

5. How did the legal relationship between the county board and the sheriff's department affect the implementation of target budgeting?
6. What strategies did the sheriff's office employ to improve its budgetary position? Were they successful? Why or why not?

REFERENCES

Ebel, R. D. (1991). A profile of county finances. *Intergovernmental Perspectives*, 17(1), 16.

Gurwit, R. (April 1989) Cultures clash as old-time politics confronts button-down management. *Governing*, 42–48.

Menzel, D. C. et al. (March/April, 1992). Setting a research agenda for the study of the American county. *Public Administration Review*, *52*(2).

O'Toole, D. E. and Marshall, J. (Oct 1987). Budgeting practices in local government: The state of the Art. *Government Finance Review, 3*(5), 11–16.

Rubin, I. (Fall, 1991). Budgeting for our times: Target base budgeting. *Public Budgeting & Finance, 11* (3).

Salant, T. J. (Winter 1991). County governments: An overview. *Intergovernmental Perspectives 17*(1), 6.

11

Strategic Planning and Budgeting in the "New Texas"

Putting Service Efforts and Accomplishments to Work

Texas Governor's Office of Budget and Planning
Austin, Texas, U.S.A.

TEXAS GOVERNMENT AND PERFORMANCE MEASURES

Overview of Texas State Government

Texas state government is unusual in its substantially decentralized executive functions. Texas is one of twelve states that do not have a cabinet structure.[1] The executive branch consists of over 200 state agencies and institutions of higher education (collectively referred to as "agencies" hereafter). While eight executive agencies are run by statewide elected officials, most are governed by boards or commissions appointed by the governor. Since members are appointed to staggered terms that may cross over gubernatorial terms, a new governor does not usually appoint the majority of a board for several years. Under this system of a "plural executive" and staggered appointments, agencies have significant autonomy from executive oversight, making it difficult for a governor to implement changes in policy upon taking office.

The Texas Constitution also limits legislative oversight of agencies. The Texas legislature is part-time, meeting in regular session for 140 days every two years. Legislative budget policy is initiated by the Legislative Budget Board (LBB). The ten-member LBB consists of the lieutenant governor and the speaker of the house, who each appoint four members from their house. The lieutenant governor, as the chair and the only statewide elected official on the LBB, exercises considerable influence over budgetary issues.

The Legislative Budget Office (LBO) provides staff support to the LBB. It prepares and presents budget recommendations to the LBB and the legislature. The budget chairs in the house and senate typically introduce the LLB-drafted budget as the starting point for the appropriations bill.

Traditionally, the governor presents a budget to the legislature, but it is frequently a policy budget, stating spending and policy priorities. It does not contain specific line items of appropriation and does not serve as an appropriations bill.

Reprinted from: *International Journal of Public Administration,* 1995, 18(2&3), 409–441. Copyright 1995 by Marcel Dekker, Inc.

The governor and the LBB share budget execution authority, which allows changes to agency appropriations during the interim. The governor does have authority to veto line items in the budget bill passed by the legislature. The governor is also constitutionally designated as the state's chief planning officer.

(SEA)

The relatively autonomous nature of Texas state agencies acts as a barrier to accountability. Service efforts and accomplishments (SEA) reporting is an important tool to provide the accountability needed for good government.

The Texas Experience with Performance Measures

The use of SEA indicators in Texas, where they have historically been referred to as performance measures, predates the GASB report.[2] Beginning in the mid-1970s, Texas replaced its object of expense budget with a program-based format. The object of expense budget made appropriations for specific expenditure items such as capital, travel, and personnel, regardless of the programs for which the funding was used. The new format used programs, rather than objects of expense, as the line items of appropriation.

To support the new format, a program evaluation function was created within the LBO. The program evaluation unit worked with agencies to develop performance measures. As early efforts in this area, most measures focused on workload or inputs (e.g., number of license applications). Performance measures were monitored through detailed reporting by the agency to the legislature and governor.

This system of budgeting and measurement provided better insight into agency programs, organization, and operations. While lawmakers made some use of this information in the legislative decision-making process, it was used primarily by budget staff. Measures were not classified and there was no formal structure or system for linking performance measurement and budgeting. The measures were weighted toward those useful to staff and agencies in highlighting their workloads and outputs.

The decline of the state's fiscal health in the early 1980s provided impetus for improving the performance measurement system. The LBO developed standard measures of administrative and operational efficiency, using them for all agencies which they were applicable (e.g., administration as a percentage of budget, administrative cost per employee, average cost per licensee). While the measures allowed tracking of an agency's performance over time, lack of consistency in defining and calculating these measures limited their usefulness for comparison across agencies. In the late 1980s, the LBO initiated the Measures Improvement Project to develop measures of service outcomes and unit costs that moved Texas toward a system based on outcome measures.

DEVELOPMENT OF THE STRATEGIC BUDGETING SYSTEM

Initial Steps by the House Appropriations Committee

In writing the 1992–1993 biennial budget, two efforts championed by reform-minded members of the house appropriations committee were precursors of change in the budget process. The first effort focused on planning for outcomes of government initiatives. The committee directed the state's fourteen health and human service agencies to prepare a single strategic plan and budget that coordinated initiatives across agencies and reflected the relationship among common planning data, appropriate resources, and desired outcomes. The result was the first explicit attempt to influence the budget by focusing on outcomes of programs and the effect of budgetary decisions on those outcomes.[3]

The second effort linked performance with budget flexibility. At the initiative of house appropriations committee members the final 1992–1993 appropriations bill included key performance targets for each agency. These were included in the agency's bill pattern in an informational rider.[4] Performance measures, classified as either "outcomes" or "outputs," were developed for every agency program, including administration. To allow agencies to meet the targets with diminishing resources, more budgetary flexibility was provided. Transferability among line items increased from 10–35% for most agencies. Institutions of higher education and elected officials received their appropriations in a single line item, allowing complete flexibility.

A Budget Reform Plan from the Lieutenant Governor

With the ink hardly dry on the 1992–1993 state budget, Lieutenant Governor Bob Bullock submitted a proposal to the LBB and the governor to entirely revamp the budget process. He proposed scrapping the program-based budgeting system in favor of a simplified "performance-based budgeting system."[5] Emphasis and practice would move from "slicing the revenue pie and delivering the money" to using performance targets incorporated in the recently passed appropriations bill to monitor state agency performance.[6] Periodic reviews and an automated monitoring system would compare agency results with performance targets. The 1994–1995 budget would incorporate performance elements, and funding decisions would be made based on achievement of performance goals. Outcomes were to drive appropriations and funding levels, with rewards for achievement and penalties for failure.

Leadership staff and agency directors were assigned to two task forces to help implement the budget overhaul. One was assigned to design the automated budget monitoring system. The second, the interagency performance budgeting panel, was to develop a new budget system, designing the format, levels of detail, and mechanisms to assure that all funding sources were tied to desired results and outcomes.

Performance budgeting had a clear endorsement from the leadership but there were no existing blueprints for building a system from which decisions could be made. The key was found in a separate initiative advanced by Governor Ann W. Richards, establishing a statewide strategic planning effort.

A Strategic Planning Initiative from the Governor

Upon taking office in 1991, Governor Richards pledged to make state government more accountable and customer-focused. In *Blueprint for the "New Texas"*, a broad outline of her policy goals, she noted that state government had become reactive; it was responding to court orders or federal mandates and not planning to meet long-term needs. To "build . . . a 21st Century Texas," state government had to plan today for the needs of the future. She called for a statewide initiative in which all state agencies would develop strategic plans and "establish goal and performance criteria so we can evaluate their effectiveness."[7]

Governor Richards's strategic planning initiative became law with the passage of house bill (HB) 2009.[8] The legislation was designed to stimulate state government to move beyond incremental thinking to a more holistic perspective; to rise above the organi-

zational view to a global, public vision; and to transcend traditional functional and programmatic considerations to reach a more integrated system of governance and service
delivery.

The bill required the governor, in cooperation with the LBB, to set goals for each
functional area of state government. Drawing from those goals, each of the state's 200-
plus state agencies was required to submit a six-year strategic plan to the governor's office
and LBB. After receiving the agency plans, the governor and the LBB were to prepare a
statewide strategic plan.

Implementing HB 2009

To implement HB 2009, the state leaders and their staffs needed a fundamental understanding of strategic planning. In the fall of 1991, leadership staff researched existing Texas
state agency strategic planning efforts and those of other states. A small steering committee
was formed, composed of staff from the two state budget offices and the offices of the
lieutenant, governor, speaker, and comptroller. The Council of Governor's Policy Advisors
provided training for the steering committee and the budget offices, covering strategic
planning principles and the experiences in other key states.

While the statute only required setting statewide goals, leadership staff decided
that establishing simple statements of the vision, mission, and philosophy of Texas state
government were an important starting point for the process. Drafting these statements
was one of the more time-consuming and thoughtful parts of the process. These elements
were published as *Texas Tomorrow*[9] in January 1992 as the first step in a strategic planning
process that involved every state agency.

The vision statement served as a guiding light, establishing a common purpose. The
statement of philosophy expressed the values underlying state government service. Key
principles were for the first time succinctly and forcefully enumerated. The mission statement classified the basic functions of state government into five broad areas, allowing
each state agency to identify a place for their services within the basic functions. Each of
the five broad areas was further defined by a series of goal statements. These elements
are shown in Appendix A.

Definition of Strategic Planning Elements: The Texas Template

Many state agencies in Texas had experience in strategic planning. The Department of
Transportation used its ten-year strategic plan to identify future traffic patterns and propose
new highway projects. Other agencies used the planning process to foster communication
between divisions, to link management with employees, and to conduct need assessments
of client groups. In order that budget staff and others could evaluate and compare plans
across agencies, it was necessary to establish a template that did not unduly disrupt existing
agency planning processes while still providing the proper guidance for less experienced
agencies.

Using the guidelines in HB 2009 and the results of research into other state and
agency plans, the steering committee designed a Texas strategic planning template (Figure

Figure 1   Key elements of the Texas strategic planning template. *Statewide elements; **agency, specific element.

1). The elements at the top are broad and poetic, flowing down to the specific and quantifiable.

The purpose of each of the agency strategic planning elements is described below.

Mission statement.   The first step in an agency's planning process, after reviewing the statewide elements in *Texas Tomorrow*, was to arrive at a concise statement of purpose. The mission statement was to answer the following questions:

Who are we and whom do we serve?

What are the basic purposes for our existence as an agency and what basic problems are we established to address?

What makes us and our purpose unique?

Is the mission in harmony with the agency's basic enabling statute?

The statement should be short enough to remember, yet broad enough to convey information.

Philosophy.   As part of the governor's focus on customer service, agencies were asked to draft a philosophy statement. The philosophy statement expresses the core values and operating principles of an agency and its employees and defines the relationship between the agency and its stakeholders—its consumers or clients, the community it regulates, and for some, the general public. The philosophy defines basic approaches to management, organizational values, and rules of behavior.

External-internal assessment.   An agency turns from the lofty to the concrete in conducting its external-internal assessment. The assessment is designed to identify both opportunities for and obstacles to achieving the agency mission. Relevant factors are identified both within and from outside the agency. The assessment serves as a reality check for the agency and aids in sorting out factors affecting performance.

Goals.   Goals represent the ends toward which an agency directs its efforts. Goals are still broad but are more specific than the agency mission and philosophy. The goals may seem disparate, reflecting the different responsibilities of an agency. An agency's goals are few in number, even for a large agency, because of their nonspecific nature.

Objectives.   Objectives are subsets of goals and represent quantified statements of all or part of a goal. Objectives require specific actions within a specific time frame. The aim may be to accomplish an objective within the biennium or even beyond the six-year planning horizon. Objectives are tracked using outcome measures.

Strategies.   Strategies are operational statements that specifically define a way to accomplish an objective. There can be many strategies supporting an objective. Strategies are tracked using output measures.

The broad elements—mission, philosophy, and goals—are critical steps in each agency's plan. Developing these elements forces the agency to take a detached, global view of its operations and the public benefit those operations provide and to state those operations and benefits concisely. These elements also demonstrate that the diverse functions an agency performs fit within a bigger picture. The state's general services agency has taken such pride in its mission statement that it is posted in all state buildings to emphasize customer service to its employees and the public.

Through the mission, philosophy, and goals, an agency can present all the expected results of its efforts, even those results that are not easily quantified or cost-effectively measured. These broad elements also lay the foundation for developing the specific and measurable objectives and strategies that reflect an agency's efforts.

Role of Performance Measures in Strategic Planning

In the Texas strategic planning process, two service accomplishment indicators, outcomes and outputs, quantify agency progress toward their goals. Goals are quantified by objectives and measured by outcomes. Outcome measures state the public benefits associated with each objective, allow for evaluation of an agency's progress in achieving them, and provide the basis to assess whether or not an agency is functioning effectively. Strategies are measured by outputs. Output measures track an agency's workload. Combined with data on expenditures, output measures help assess an agency's efficiency.

Outputs and outcomes are linked. A certain level of output has a corresponding impact on outcomes. Determining the relationship between agency outputs and outcomes is difficult. While Texas has considerable experience with performance measures, it may take several years to satisfactorily define these linkages.

Including some SEA indicators as an explicit part of strategic planning brought new importance to the use of performance measures in Texas. The strategic planning initiative provided the impetus for re-evaluating existing agency measures. The initiative offered an opportunity to correct classifications and to develop more meaningful measures.[10] Board members and constituent groups gained more familiarity with performance measures and used them more.

IMPLEMENTATION OF "STRATEGIC BUDGETING"

Linking Budget Reform and Strategic Planning

As the strategic planning template was being finalized, it became obvious that the ends for the strategic planning initiative and the budget reform proposal held much in common:

Table 1 Linking Strategic Planning and Performance Budgeting

Strategic planning		Performance measures		Budget
Mission philosophy				
Internal–external assessment				
Agency goals			⇒	Bill pattern element
Objectives	⇒	Outcome measures: Quantifiable results measuring how the public is benefitted by the agency meeting the objective	⇒	Bill pattern element
			⇒	Performance targets
Strategies	⇒	Output measures: Quantity of agency workload and work product as it pursues its strategies	⇒	Line items of appropriation
			⇒	Performance targets
		Efficiency measures: Agency workload unit costs or time for completion		
		Explanatory or input measures: External factors relating to agency operations		

improved accountability, improved resource allocation, and greater focus on public benefits. The interagency budget reform panel proposed, and leadership agreed, that strategic planning elements should also serve as key elements in budget reform.

Since measures were integrated into agency strategic plans, they were the obvious link between the strategic plans and a performance-based budget system. Agency planning structures took on new implications for agencies and budget offices.

Table 1 illustrates the linkages between strategic planning and budgeting. Agency strategic plans are the basis for their appropriations requests. Ideally, an agency's budget request is the amount it needs to meet the performance targets for the first two years of its strategic plan.

Strategies serve as the line items in the appropriations bill. Output measures identify the workload associated with a particular strategy and the line item is the estimated cost of meeting this workload target.

Since measures were to be used in evaluating performance and determining appropriations, much hinged on arriving at workable agency planning and budget structures and valid measures. Combining planning and budgeting was a difficult exercise because most of the elements of a well-crafted strategic plan are not stated in technical or operational terms, while writing a budget is a technical, operations-oriented enterprise.

In reviewing the initial agency strategic plan submissions, the budget offices negotiated or mandated changes to many agencies' strategic planning structures so they would also work as budget structures. One of the more common changes was to reduce the number of strategies by condensing planning structures, (i.e., stating general strategy directions). Since strategies were to be the line items of appropriation, these reductions were necessary so that an agency would not have hundreds of line items. Objective statements were also frequently changed. Many were too broad and could not be quantified. The budget offices required that they be rewritten so specific targets could be drawn from them.

While necessary for linking the planning and budgeting systems, these revisions often caused considerable tension. Merging strategic planning and budget reform cost some of the poetry and flexibility of the planning initiative. Agencies, particularly those with experience in strategic planning, had invested a great deal of human capital in their plans, making them resistant to changes imposed by the budget offices. For many agencies, publicizing their strategic plans exposed them to pressure and criticism from constituency groups and state policy makers. Agencies resented the budget office requirements to restructure their plans to blend with the budget format.

Once negotiations over planning and budget structures and measures were completed, agencies received formal approval of the budget and planning structure from the LBO and the governor's budget office. Strategies and measures in these structures were used by the agencies in their budget requests.

In keeping with the emphasis on performance and outcomes, one significant change in the budget structure was to drop agency administration as a separate item of appropriation. There were no specific administrative strategies since administration is not an outcome-oriented effort of an agency. Agencies were to allocate administrative costs across their strategies.

Using the Strategic Budgeting System to Write a State Budget

To encourage legislators to focus on the performance and results of agency programs, the LBO and the governor reduced the number of forms required for the budget request process (Table 2). Rather than devote their time to filling out forms, state leadership wanted agencies to focus on how the public's dollars translated into public benefits.

In their appropriations request, agencies were asked to cost-out each strategy with estimates of corresponding output and outcome targets. The format was designed to provide state budget writers with information to determine the impact of different levels of funding on services. Appendix B is a condensed sample of the *strategy request form*. It shows the detail required by the budget offices for each strategy.

Agencies were required to indicate the priority order for their strategies on the *priority allocation table*. Perhaps the single most controversial aspect of the strategic budgeting system, this table ranked agency strategies and showed the impact on performance measures at different increments of funding.[11] From an agency's perspective, communicating priorities in a public document was uncomfortable. Agencies resisted choosing among client groups, yet for state policy makers and their staffs, the priority tables offered the greatest insight into individual agency priorities, showing how each agency would exercise discretion at different funding levels and how the public would be affected.

The strategic planning template includes only GASB service accomplishment indicators. The budget request instructions added the service effort indicator and inputs, as well as efficiency and explanatory measures. Explanatory indicators display other factors that affect agency performance. Efficiency indicators relate the proportion of inputs to an outcome or output.

Table 2 Strategic Budgeting Compared to Program Budgeting

	Old program budget system	New strategic budget system
Number of budget request submissions	Agencies filed two budget requests: one in June and a revised one in October.	Agencies file one budget request in the early fall.
Range of funding options	Agencies prepared four levels of funding, ranging from famine to feast.	Agencies submit request based on funding necessary to meet its strategic plan, but must rank each strategy in priority order.
Number of forms required	Budget instructions totaled 125 *legal-sized* pages and required completion of 23 separate forms.	Budget instructions total 35 *letter-size* pages (plus a 28-page appendix) and require only five forms; capital budget requires 20 pages and two forms.
Agency training	Agencies were given little formal training in completing their budget forms in this mature budget system.	Governor's Budget Office and the LBB staff held several workshops for agencies to walk through the forms.

In writing the 1994–1995 appropriations bill, the legislature used the performance measures to make some budget decisions. One of the governor's key initiatives, immunizations for all Texas children, benefitted from the use of efficiency and outcome measures. The Department of Health demonstrated the long-term cost-effectiveness of immunizing children. This new initiative was fully funded while other higher unit cost programs were scaled back. Similarly, the house appropriations committee relied heavily on the priority allocation table developed by the health and human services commissioner to add $800 million to the highest-priority health and human services strategies. The Department of Insurance successfully used its priority allocation table to direct legislatively mandated reductions to lower-priority strategies.

In other instances, performance information was not a factor in the final decision-making process. Legislators often did not explicitly discuss performance measures when making budgetary decisions. For most agencies, changes in the levels of funding did not cause changes in the performance measures. The appropriations bill delegates authority to the LBO to make revisions in the interim.

In the 1994–1995 appropriations bill, an agency's bill pattern consists of the strategic planning structure for that agency: its goal statements, objectives, outcome measures, strategies, and output measures, as well as efficiency measures and, in some cases, explanatory measures. Performance targets are listed with the dollar appropriations.

Agencies are expected to meet these performance targets with the funding provided. Recognizing that conditions can change during the biennial fiscal period, there is flexibility in the relationship between targets and appropriations. Agencies have authority to transfer up to 35% from one line item of appropriation to another, enabling them to adjust their budget to best achieve their performance targets. Additionally, the appropriations bill rider that authorizes the LBO to adjust performance targets for the changes in funding levels will also allow adjustments for changes in conditions.

Agencies are required to file quarterly reports with the leadership and budget offices "analyzing the performance and operational efficiency of each funded objective and strategy as indicated by the agency's efforts in attaining stated outcome, output and efficiency targets." The reports compare actual with projected performance.[12]

A new rider in the appropriations act authorizes the LBB or the governor to penalize or reward an agency for its performance. The rider states that agencies "shall make every effort to attain the designated key performance target levels associated with each item of appropriation." The rider adds that if agencies do not meet established performance targets, a budget execution order may be proposed to provide "positive incentives/reward" or "negative incentives/redirection" (i.e., penalties).[13]

EVALUATION OF THE STRATEGIC BUDGETING SYSTEM

Texas has designed and implemented a comprehensive budget and planning system that incorporates SEA indicators and reporting. As a result, there have been numerous requests for information or presentations on the Texas system. The following evaluation of the system and conclusions drawn from that analysis are intended to help others incorporating SEA reporting into planning and budgeting processes.

As agencies discovered in the strategic planning process, it is logical to measure success as steps toward expected outcomes. The governor's office of budget and planning adopted a similar approach to measure the success of the strategic budgeting system. While many conclusions are tentative at this time, a number of observations can be made.

Evaluation Criteria and Methodology

Five criteria were selected to evaluate the strategic budgeting system: quality of process, degree of integration, improved resource allocation, increased accountability, and improved public trust.

The methodology for evaluating the new system included: small evaluation groups, consisting of staff from a diverse set of state agencies; interviews with legislators involved in the budget process; and comparison of measures and line items in the appropriations acts written under the old and new systems.

The following evaluation looks at the effect of the strategic budgeting system on agencies and on executive-level and legislative-level decision making. In examining the effect of the new system on agencies, key questions included the following. Has the new system improved agency planning? To what extent was it used? Has it improved agency accountability? Has it improved allocation of resources within the agency? Has it improved public trust in how the agency uses resources? In examining the statewide effect, key questions included the following. Has the new system improved the governor's and legislature's ability to plan and thereby avoid crises? Has it improved resource allocation decisions? Has it improved state leadership's accountability for use of tax dollars? Has public trust in state government improved?

Evaluation Results

Quality of Process: How Effectively Was the Strategic Budgeting Process Implemented?

The evaluation group participants generally agreed that the strategic planning process was valuable. The process increased intraorganizational communication and improved understanding of role and mission. Many agencies included board members, all levels of agency employees, and constituent groups in a process that examined agency mission, objectives, and results. Including SEA indicators in the planning structure caused agencies to evaluate their effectiveness, in some cases for the first time. Agency staff members commented that the process of determining outcomes was useful. Examination of outputs and strategies focused attention on whether or not the most efficient means were being employed to achieve agency objectives. The benefits of the strategic planning process were strongest in relatively new agencies or agencies that had experienced a recent change in leadership.

Agencies with a less enthusiastic view of the strategic planning process were those with existing strategic planning systems, those that felt that there were already enough administrative demands on them, or those that viewed this process as another budget drill. Agencies with existing strategic plans were concerned about the effect a centrally imposed process would have on the value of their existing systems.

Many agencies were disappointed that the leadership offices did not put more effort into developing and distributing the statewide plan. This was perceived as an indication of a lack of statewide acceptance of the process. Plans are being made to establish a better process to develop the next statewide strategic plan. This plan is likely to contain SEA indicators for tracking the state's progress in meeting its goals.

During the development stages of strategic planning, experienced planners warned against linking strategic planning and budgeting, at least in the first planning cycle. They argued that the strategic value of the plan would be undermined by the inclusion of operational elements. Even before negotiating budget structures with the budget offices, some planning ideas were compromised in order to be compatible with budget requests.

Despite these problems, the linkage worked for most state agencies. The link gave urgency to the process and forced planners and budgeters to work together, which was not standard practice in many agencies. By providing the means to quantify planning elements in a budgeting system focused on performance, SEA indicators provided the crucial mechanism to link plans and budgets.

While the strategic planning process was invaluable in focusing agencies on outcomes and results, developing meaningful and cost-effective indicators proved to be the most difficult aspect of the strategic budgeting system. Some agency representatives commented that the indicators included in the current appropriations act are only marginally better than those in the previous appropriations act. Legislative intent had been to reduce the number of measures for each agency and collect data more reflective of the agency's mission and goals. The actual result was even a few more measures, some requiring long-term and expensive data collection and some not particularly relevant to the individual agencies. There is strong consensus that SEA indicators can be improved.

Degree of Integration: To What Extent Has the Strategic Budgeting Process Been Integrated into Agency Management and Decision Making and Legislative Decision Making?

The strategic budgeting system was used by many agencies to improve programs, operations, and management. The legislature used the system to write an appropriations act. Anecdotal evidence from agency discussions indicates the system is a useful management tool for many agencies. Some agencies reorganized around their strategic plans. Other agencies integrated measures into their employee and management evaluation and reward systems. Agencies that viewed the strategic budgeting process as another budget drill, however, saw less value in integrating the system into their operations.

Legislative budget staff used the tools of the new system in writing the original budget submitted to the legislature. The legislature continued to focus less on inputs and more on the results of agency programs. There seemed to be less discussion of "how many clerks were necessary to a particular function." The performance budgeting tools provided by the SEA indicators (e.g., efficiency measures and performance levels associated with funding levels shown in agency priority allocation tables) were explicitly used to make some budgetary decisions. While the use of these tools was less than might have been anticipated, increased familiarity with the tools should further their future use.

Agency staff expressed deep concern over how SEA indicators will be integrated in a reward and penalty system. Still unclear is how such a system will be implemented. Adequacy, reliability, and cost-effectiveness were among the budget office criteria for good SEA indicators. These criteria are not met for some of the current performance measures. Agencies are concerned that their projections, as well as the measures themselves, are not reliable enough to determine rewards and punishments. Agencies are also concerned about the balance between accountability and cost. In the small group discussions, one agency representative noted, "We're spending less and less time on our mission and more and more on data collection."

Better Resource Allocation: To What Extent Did the Strategic Budgeting System Improve Resource Allocation at Both the Statewide and Agency Level?

On the whole, the new system proved useful as a resource allocation tool for both the agencies and the legislature. The system seemed to have more utility for agencies and for legislative and governor's budget staff than for legislators, however, and it seemed to be more useful in some instances than in others. Agencies indicated that the planning process and priority allocation table were effective tools to establish and communicate their resource allocation priorities. Many agencies produced detailed, well-thought-out priorities as a result of analyzing agency mission and objectives. Other agencies were hesitant to produce detailed priorities for fear they would be used to make budget cuts or would alienate constituency groups.

The governor and legislators often had their own priorities in making budget decisions, and some agencies felt that the priority allocation tables were largely ignored by these decision makers. One large agency, when requested to identify areas for budget cuts, responded that the priority allocation table was the appropriate source for that information. Many agencies indicated that lower priorities, and even new programs, were funded while higher priorities went begging.

As a measure of changes produced by the process, the governor's office of budget and planning staff compared budget structures under the old budgeting system and the new strategic budgeting system to determine the number of line items that were different. In the over 100 agencies analyzed, 56% of the line items were new. Almost one-third of the agencies had a completely new set of line items. Another third saw at least a 50% change in line items. These changes indicate that, despite the stress to the planning process, linking the budget and planning initiatives did allow agency initiatives to be implemented. The state's largest agencies, some of which viewed strategic planning as simply another budget drill, did not see significant change in their line-item structure. The state's transportation, criminal justice, education, and mental health and mental retardation agencies all had a change, of less than 20%.

Increased Accountability: Are State Agency Personnel More Accountable to Their Governing Boards, Agencies More Accountable to the Legislature and Governor, and the Legislature and Governor More Accountable to the Public?

Performance measurement has been used for many years as an accountability tool in Texas. Refining performance measurement by including the GASB SEA indicators improved the oversight tools available to the legislature, governor, and governing boards.

Agencies are more accountable to all stakeholders because the quality of the performance measures improved. Agencies hailed as a positive development the exclusion of a set of administrative cost efficiency indicators that had been applied to each agency in the previous appropriations act. Despite the improvements, there is consensus that there is room for further improvement of indicators.

Not all government services lend themselves easily to measurement, particularly outcome measurement. The outcomes of some services, such as education, are difficult to measure in the short term. Other services, such as research, are difficult or too expensive to quantify and measure. The goal-setting part of the strategic planning process provides an opportunity for an agency and its employees to define a particular effort as being worthy of recognition, regardless of whether or not it can be measured.

The governor's office of budget and planning staff reviewed the changes in most of the SEA indicators in the appropriations acts. While there was little net change in the total number of indicators, nearly 77% of the indicators were new. There was some reclassification of indicators (e.g., outcome to efficiency). The number of outcome measures decreased by nearly 45% because administrative efficiency measures, inappropriately classified as outcomes in the previous appropriations act, were eliminated and because nonadministrative efficiency measures were reclassified. Over 76% of the remaining outcome measures are new, reflecting substantial discussion of appropriate outcomes.

There was a 19% increase in the number of output measures. While 71% of all output measures are new, again reflecting improved focus on agency efforts, the increase is largely attributable to the development of output measures for programs that had none in the previous appropriations act.

For the first time, correctly defined efficiency measures are included. Reclassification accounts for 13% of these measures.

Improved Public Trust: To What Extent Has Implementation of the Strategic Budgeting System Improved Public Trust in the Business of State Government?

Eventually, improvements in the above criteria should contribute to an increase in public trust in the effectiveness and efficiency of the operations of state government. Since the process improved agency interaction with constituency groups and the quality of indicators, it is expected to improve public trust. There is no existing mechanism to gauge public trust in Texas government. It is too soon to know the impact strategic budgeting will have in this area.

Conclusions

The experience of Texas provides several conclusions about the effective use of SEA indicators and reporting.

SEA indicators are most effective when combined with a broader planning initiative. SEA indicators and strategic planning are necessary complements. Despite experience using performance measures, it was not until the state embarked on a broad-scale strategic planning effort that performance measurement was brought to the forefront. The strategic planning initiative provided impetus to review and correct the classification of measures and to discuss their validity and reliability. While SEA indicators are critical to quantify movement toward achieving strategic goals, the strategic planning structure filled gaps where quantification is not possible or practical.

The planning process is as important as the plan itself. Good strategic planning provides many benefits. One benefit is a document that clearly communicates the goals and expectations of the organization and delineates how to achieve them. Another no less important benefit is the process of creating the plan. Done correctly, strategic planning involves all of the individuals in an organization, from front-line workers and clerical staff to senior management and governing boards. Effective strategic planning brings together all the experiences and energies of an organization and channels them toward a positive end.

The process of thinking about outcomes and outputs was one of the most important benefits of the planning process. The SEA indicators required quantification of ideas. Using SEA indicators forced agencies to think in concrete as well as abstract terms.

Effective planning requires that priorities be established. Government is in a period of diminishing resources. Priorities for spending are needed. The SEA indicators, particularly outcome indicators, are an effective tool for making tough resource allocation decisions.

Merging planning and budgeting has costs as well as benefits. The SEA indicators provided the key link between the planning and budget systems in Texas. Agencies were forced—at least superficially, and substantively in most cases—to coordinate their planning and budgeting efforts. Imposing budget requirements on strategic planning resulted in loss of some agency initiatives and some of the poetry of the planning process.

SEA indicators provide a tool for performance-based budgeting. Texas linked SEA indicators and reporting to budget line items in an effort to appropriate funds based on performance. An agency is expected to meet a specific performance target with the funding provided. To allow agencies to meet performance targets, they are provided budgetary flexibility. This freedom creates the need for good accountability tools. SEA reporting is the tool Texas has chosen.

Outcomes are more important to the public than outputs. One finding of GASB's initial report on SEA indicators was that emphasis should be placed on outcome measurement as opposed to outputs.[13] Some of the motivation behind Texas' strategic planning initiative was to demystify government and to better educate the public about what state government does. Outcome measures are more important in this effort because they define how the public benefits from government initiatives.

Outcome measures are difficult to tie to the budget. There is great pressure to set lofty targets, but if SEA outcome indicators are to be used for budgeting decisions, they must be realistic. If measures are to be used to formulate decisions concerning resource allocation, targets must reflect the real effects of government initiative. While Texas has moved in that direction, measures must be refined and data validated to improve confidence in linking budget to outcomes.

The job is never done. Performance measurement in Texas made a giant leap forward with use of the GASB SEA classification system. All parties agree that indicators can still be improved. It will take time to establish baselines and trends from which to draw meaningful information for making hard decisions about agency programs and operations.

ACKNOWLEDGMENTS

This chapter represents a group effort by staff of the governor's office of budget and planning. Principal authors were Dale Craymer, Patricia Hall, Karen Sayles, and Karl Urban. Significant contributions were made by other staff, including Edward Baldwin, Rebecca Martin, Ara Merjanian, Tina Mills, and Mani Rao. We wish to acknowledge and thank John Blanton and Chad McManus of the governor's office and Mary Gerdes of the LBO for the technical assistance without which the chapter would not have been possible.

APPENDIX A: THE VISION, PHILOSOPHY, AND MISSION OF TEXAS

Our vision: We envision a Texas where all people have the skills and opportunities they need to achieve their individual dreams; a Texas where people enjoy good health, are safe and secure from harm, and share a quality standard of living; a Texas where we and future generations can enjoy our bountiful natural beauty and resources.

Our philosophy: Public service is a public trust. As public servants we take pride in the service we provide for our fellow citizens. We will be open, ethical, responsive, accountable and dedicated to the public we serve—providing legendary customer service. We will foster a working environment free of bias and respectful of the individual. We will operate efficiently and spend the public's money wisely.

Our mission: The mission of Texas state government is: . . . to provide educational opportunities for all its people; . . . to protect and enhance the health, well-being and productivity of all Texas; . . . to preserve the state's environment, and ensure wise, productive use of the state's natural resources; . . . to build a solid foundation for social and economic prosperity; and . . . to ensure the safety of our communities.

---

* Each of these mission statements contained several goal statements, such as: "Every child will start school ready to learn."

APPENDIX B: STRATEGY REQUEST FORM (CONDENSED FROM ORIGINAL)

Appendix B   Strategy Request Form (condensed from original)

Agency Code	Agency Name	Prepared By	Date	Statewide Goal Code
Code:	STRATEGY:			
Code:	AGENCY GOAL:			
Code:	OBJECTIVE:			

Code		Budgeted 1993	Requested 1994	Requested 1995
	Outcome Measures:			
	Output Measures:			
	Objects of Expense: Total, Objects of Expense			
	Method of Financing:			
	Total, Method of Financing			
Number of Positions (FTE):				

Strategy Description and Justification:

External/Internal Factors Impacting Strategy:

Codes		Budgeted 1993	Requested 1994	Requested 1995
	Efficiency Measures:			
	Explanatory Measures:			

REVIEW QUESTIONS

1. What is unique about Texas government? Why did the state need to implement the new "strategic budgeting" system? How does the new system differ from the old one?

2. Describe the development of the new strategic budgeting system in Texas and discuss the roles of various government institutions in this process. Which institution played the major role?

3. What are the key elements of the Texas strategic budgeting system? What role does performance measurement play in this?

4. How did the state implement the new system? What were the results of implementation? Looking at the evaluation results, would you say that the system was successfully implemented? Why or why not?

NOTES

1. Council of State Government, *The Book of the States*, 1992–1993 ed., p. 53. Lexington, KY: Council of State Governments.
2. Hatry, H. P., Fountain, J. R. Jr., Sullivan, J. M., and Kremer, L., eds. (1990). *Service Efforts and Accomplishments: Its Time Has Come*. Norwalk, CN: Governmental Accounting Standards Board.
3. During the period the house appropriations committee was working with the health and human service agencies, the Council of Governors' Policy Advisors published *Getting Results: A Guide for Government Accountability*. The book's publication was timely. Legislative, agency, and executive budget and policy analysts were all working on the very issues addressed by the book; Brizzuis, J. A. and Campbell, M. D. (1991). *Getting Results: A Guide for Governmental Accountability*, Washington, DC: Council of Governors' Policy Advisors.
4. HB 1, (1991). *General Appropriations Act.*, Acts of the Seventy-second Texas Legislature, Austin.
5. Bullock, B. (1991). *Draft Proposal: Performance and Achievement Based Budgeting*. Austin, TX: Texas Lieutenant Governor's Office.
6. Bullock, B. (1991). Press release. Austin, TX: Lieutenant Governor's Office.
7. Richards, A. W. (1991). *Blueprint for a "New Texas"* pp. 31–2. Austin, TX: Texas Governor's Office.
8. HB 2009, (1991). Acts of the 72nd Texas Legislature, regular session, Austin.
9. Texas Governor's Office. (Jan. 1992). *Texas Tomorrow*, Austin.
10. During the seventy-second legislature, the Texas state auditor's office audited performance measure reporting by selected agencies. This audit revealed that measures in the 1992–1993 appropriations act were not properly classified by GASB definitions. The legislature had created the measures before publication of the GASB report. See Texas State Auditor. (Feb. 1992). *Accurate and Appropriate Performance Measures are the Foundation of Tomorrow's Texas*. SAO Report Number 2-044. Austin.
11. Agencies are encouraged to divide each strategy into discrete funding increments called strategy options to indicate priorities in amounts of funding less than those necessary to completely meet a performance target in its strategic plan. This is because it may be more important to an agency to partially fund many strategies instead of fully funding only a few.
12. SB 5, *General Appropriations Act.* Acts of the Seventy-Third Legislature, Regular Session, Austin, TX, p. V 66.
13. SB 5, *General Appropriations Act.* Acts of the Seventy-Third Legislature, Regular Session, Austin, TX, p. V 95–6.

12

Transition to Outcome-Based Budgeting
The Case of Missouri's Department of Revenue and Milwaukee, Wisconsin

John P. Forrester
U.S. General Accounting Office, Washington, D.C., U.S.A.

Rebecca Hendrick
University of Illinois, Chicago, Illinois, U.S.A.

Governments are always searching for ways to budget more effectively, and because of the political and fiscal pressures, the principals responsible for implementing the changes usually phase them in slowly and incrementally. At least this is what conventional budgetary wisdom might suggest. In this chapter, one state and one local governmental setting will be examined to show what some governments go through in searching for a new budget process and how such a change can be implemented effectively. The new budgeting process for both governments is fundamentally outcome-based budgeting in which both governments are striving to dramatically alter their budgeting process, either in specific areas or governmentwide, in a relatively short period of time.

First present background on outcome-based budgeting (OBB) as part of a comprehensive system of managerial reforms being implemented at the federal government and many state and local governments. The actual cases, including one local government (Milwaukee, Wisconsin) and one state government (Missouri Department of Revenue), are contrasted and compared. Finally, lessons are offered to help guide future reforms.

OUTCOME-BASED BUDGETING: WHAT IS IT?

What is OBB? This relatively new approach to governmental budgeting does not have one unique format but is a collection of principles and practices that are part of a larger set of managerial reforms that have been taking place in this country at all levels of government since the early 1990s. These budgeting and management reforms are rooted

---

* Evidence of these trends at the national level include the Governmental Performance and Results Act of 1993, the National Performance Review (1993a; 1993b), and the Chief Financial Officer's Act of 1990 (Jones and McCaffery, 1992; 1993). Such trends at the local level were fueled to a great degree by the concept of "reinventing government" (Osborne and Gaebler, 1992).

Note: The views presented here are those of the authors and do not necessarily represent the views of the author's institutions.

in practices that began in the private sector and later were adopted by the public sector, such as total quality management, re-engineering, and strategic planning. These reforms also have much in common with the "new public management" (NPM) reforms that began in 1980s in the United Kingdom, Australia, and New Zealand. Over time, the reforms have evolved into a comprehensive system of public sector administration that includes changes in budgeting, management, and organizational structure as well as new definitions of accountability (Kettl, 1997; Thompson, 1993).

Similar to past budgeting and management reforms in the United States, such as PPBS, ZBB, and management by objectives, OBB tends to focus budgetary decisions at the programmatic level, incorporate measures of performance (especially outcomes), and be guided by objectives. Unlike these historic reforms, however, which did not live up to the original promises of linking performance and budgeting, the popular sentiments among academics and practitioners alike is that OBB in conjunction with the system of reforms holds more promise for making government more effective, responsive, and accountable. Although descriptions of OBB may vary slightly, its key features usually include the following (Lynch and Lynch, 1996; Cothran, 1993):

Programmatic budget format
Stated programmatic goals and objectives (usually determined through a strategic planning process)
Regular and systematic measurement of programmatic outcomes and performance (effectiveness and efficiency in meeting goals and objectives), which includes measures of citizen satisfaction
Lump sum or block grant budget authority, which is granted based on evidence of achievement of goals and objectives
Greater managerial flexibility in determining how to allocate budget to achieve goals and objectives

The primary objective of OBB is to infuse agency personnel with the incentives, discretion, information, tools, training, and opportunity to be productive, to achieve results, and to respond effectively to organizational uncertainties. The budget basically is seen as a contract with managers to meet specific goals and objectives, giving them the flexibility and options to achieve outcomes in the manner they believe is best. As a result, government agencies focus their efforts on program effectiveness and efficiency, and they reduce their preoccupation with inputs, structure, rules, and procedures. On another level, as Ingraham and Kettl (1992) indicate, this budgeting approach is expected to promote macro-level control and long-term perspectives among upper-level administrators and policy makers and to reduce their inclination to micromanage.

If implemented in full, OBB budget authority is lump-sum and represents an upper limit on spending. Within this limit, administrators are expected to achieve specified objectives as measured by outcome or performance indicators. This process can be facilitated through strategic planning, which encourages agencies to establish broad-based missions and goals and to identify internal and environmental conditions that can affect their operations and ability to be successful.

---

* Lump-sum budgetary authority should not be confused with "target-based budgeting," in which an agency's base budget is assigned according to what it received in the previous year or what is necessary to provide the current level of services. Additional amounts are allocated based on specific proposals the agency makes for enhancement, growth, and improvements to efficiency and effectiveness (Cope, 1995).

To make planning easier and the OBB process work as intended, managers and controllers will need information on performance, efficiency, and service coverage, while policy makers and administrators will need information on program quality and effectiveness. The success of OBB also depends upon balancing management flexibility with fiscal control, by which traditional procedural constraints and rules (e.g., allotments, vouchers, preauditing procedures) are to some extent replaced with mechanisms for monitoring and assessing programs' effectiveness. Such evaluations serve as key sources of information to hold the agencies accountable to the public for results and outcomes rather than inputs and efforts.

Just how successful OBB and related reforms might be in the long run is not clear. It is somewhat premature to expect concrete results from reforms in the United States with respect to improved governmental performance, efficiency, and accountability. In the next section, two case studies of OBB are presented—for the city of Milwaukee, Wisconsin, and for the Missouri Department of Revenue. Both organizations have recently undertaken and are still in the process of OBB budgetary reform. Together they illustrate the variety of political, financial, and organizational factors that may lead to reform and how successful reforms are implemented.

CASE STUDIES

Milwaukee, Wiscosin

When Milwaukee's Mayor Norquist assumed his position in 1988, he was the city's first new mayor since the early 1960s. With this change came a new centralization of authority and power, a sense of urgency to address external threats and alter a likely future chain of events, the appointment of key reform-minded personnel, and generally, opportunities for significant reform. Norquist and his new administration seized the opportunity and indeed undertook sweeping budgetary, organizational, and managerial reforms.

Prior to 1988, power in Milwaukee was very fragmented. The mayor had minimal authority over departmental heads, who reported to either the city's common council (CC) or semi-independent commissions. On the day Norquist was sworn in changes in state statute bestowed upon the office many of the privileges of a strong mayor that were not available to prior officeholders, including the ability to appoint all nonelected departmental heads. Four elected departmental heads (of noncabinet departments) were to remain outside the mayor's appointing authority, including the comptroller, city attorney, treasurer, and the chief municipal judge. Although the mayor controls the budget of noncabinet departments, the full-time comptroller has authority over and responsibility for the revenue side of the budget.

Prior to becoming mayor, Norquist was a state senator and chair of the state assembly finance committee, which familiarized him with many budgeting and related managerial issues. It also gave him contact with experts in these fields and people skilled in these areas in both branches of state government. As mayor, Norquist drew many of his appointees from this population. He and his appointees recognized that the first year and budget of an administration often provides the best opportunity to institute major reforms, and they took advantage of this. The mayor left many of the administrative details of reform to his key appointees, choosing instead to focus on the macro issues and building political support for his objectives (Reimer, 1997).

Initial Phase: The Reform Begins

The first leg of the reform that emerged from the honeymoon arose because the administration took advantage of the community's belief in a pending crisis and drew on the ideas of community leaders. Until the early 1980s, Milwaukee had not experienced the level of crime, unemployment, and overall urban decay seen in other "rust belt" cities. The government was fiscally healthy, having sound fiscal policies, low debt, and low per capita service costs relative to other large cities (but high relative to the suburbs). Significant problems were looming on the horizon, however: per capita income was declining, crime was rising, increasing numbers of residents and employers were fleeing to the suburbs, and relative property values were declining throughout the city. If they continued and if actions were not taken, these trends would eventually devalue Milwaukee's existing assets and weaken its remaining strengths.

To build support for his reforms and to generate ideas and identify key items for change, Norquist drew on the Committee on the Future of Milwaukee. The committee was assembled in May of 1988, just over a month after he took office, and consisted of fifty-one community leaders. It was directed to set timetables for the next two years, establish priorities for policy initiatives, determine policy goals, and identify challenges and opportunities facing Milwaukee in four issue areas—spending and taxes, economic development, neighborhood preservation and safety, and education (Committee for the Future of Milwaukee, 1988). Given the current fiscal environment, Norquist and his staff determined that the issues raised by this committee could be addressed by focusing city government administration and service delivery on achieving results and reducing costs. The budget seemed to be an effective instrument for initiating these changes. Through Norquist's first two budgets, the administration was able to reorganize and downsize the bureaucracy, reduce costs, and increase productivity. These changes were facilitated by a combination of factors, including the chief executive's newfound authority over cabinet-level departments, the instability that usually accompanies fundamental changes in the rules that govern political and the roles played by participants, the feelings of good will, accommodation, and expectation that exist after an election of a new chief executive (especially after, twenty-six years), and the administration's quick actions to take advantage of these conditions (Benson et al., 1995).

The new administration's honeymoon ended in 1989, and officials realized that the changes produced in the first two budgets could not be pursued indefinitely. The administration wanted to continue with budget and management reform, also recognizing that future reforms would require more fundamental changes in governmental operations, but they were somewhat uncertain about how to proceed. Based on the advice and guidance of a strategic planning consultant from the private sector and drawing heavily from the experience and knowledge of other key officials, the administration began to articulate a plan for a system of future reforms in the city. The first step was to examine the city's overall objectives, identify appropriate strategies for achieving the objectives, and more fully examine services from both management and budgeting perspectives (Reimer, 1997; Kinney, 1995a).

Second Phase: Citywide Planning and Fiscal Reform

The second leg of the reform, which began late in 1990, was to develop a broadly scoped strategic plan. The administration began by trying to iron out a strategic fiscal plan, and in time produced a citywide strategic plan. As envisioned, the strategic fiscal plan was to serve as the basis for the fiscal component of the overall strategic plan, and was to be used in identifying crucial internal strengths and weaknesses and external threats and opportunities (SWOTS), and strategic issues related to the city's fiscal health. Based on this analysis, the city defines (1) its fiscal goal, to ensure the long-term fiscal stability and integrity while serving the needs of its residents and promoting an equitable distribution of costs, and (2) its objectives, to include pursuing policies of sound fiscal management, obtaining appropriate financing for services, and providing appropriate services in a cost-effective manner (*Milwaukee's Fiscal Outlook and Strategies for the Future*, 1991).

The next step was to construct a citywide strategic plan that expands the discussion of the city's SWOTS, goals, and strategies beyond fiscal concerns to cover the range of issues and factors that affect the city and that are of concern to its stakeholders. The city's budgeting office conducted an extensive analysis of the external and internal environment, and based both on that analysis and discussions between the mayor and his cabinet, seven strategic issues were identified: public health and safety; stakeholder assurance (jobs, housing, and neighborhoods); education and literacy; the environment, transportation, and infrastructure; internal management; public finance and taxation; and economic development. Similar to the strategic fiscal plan, the citywide strategic plan outlined strategic objectives across the seven strategic issues, as well as major strategies, timetables, and agency responsibilities for achieving the objectives (*Strategic Plan: Issues and Actions*, 1992).

Examining the initial reforms and planning initiatives politically and their intended impact on city government, the changes brought about by the first two budgets seemed to shake the bureaucracy, or at least to continue destabilizing the rules and roles of the bureaucracy that began with the transformation to a strong mayoral system. The new dynamics helped to infuse the bureaucracy with a greater willingness to accept change and an increased ability to accommodate change, both of which were preconditions for the citywide strategic plan. The plan laid the groundwork for more comprehensive procedural reforms, helped place the reforms in a larger context, and helped minimize the tendency to see change as a "hostile takeover" or an end in itself (Daun, 1997; Kinney, 1995a).

System 94 and Departmental Strategic Planning

With the citywide strategic plan in place, the next hurdle was to develop a strategy for getting the departments to buy into the plan, operationally and managerially. The solution of top administrators was to bring strategic planning down to the departmental level, possibly lower, and to link budgeting and management decisions. They did this through a reform strategy referred to as *System 94*. Specifically, *System 94* called for (1) developing a citywide strategic plan (already in place); (2) developing departmental strategic plans; (3) specifying their programmatic objectives and creation of outcome indicators; (4) incorporating internal management indicators; and (5) replacing departmental budget requests with administratively determined allocations (Benson et al., 1995; Kinney, 1995b).

The development of strategic plans at the department level has occurred with some variance, largely because departments differed in both their planning proficiencies and their perceived needs for planning. Some departments began strategic planning, or at least training for strategic planning, as early as 1991. This was true for departments that expected they would be required to submit a strategic plan as part of their 1994 budget, had prior exposure to or knowledge of strategic planning, or had administrators with close ties to the private sector. Not surprisingly, noncabinet departments lagged in their strategic planning efforts (Reimer, 1997).

To guide the departments in the new procedures and educate them about the overall reform effort, the Budget and Management Division (BMD) provides instructions, work-

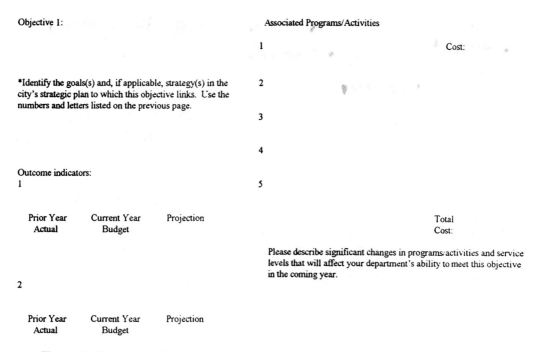

Objective 1:   Associated Programs/Activities

                                                         1   Cost:

*Identify the goals(s) and, if applicable, strategy(s) in the   2
city's strategic plan to which this objective links. Use the
numbers and letters listed on the previous page.
                                                         3

                                                         4

Outcome indicators:
1   5

Prior Year   Current Year   Projection   Total
Actual   Budget   Cost:

                                    Please describe significant changes in programs/activities and service
                                    levels that will affect your department's ability to meet this objective
                                    in the coming year.
2

Prior Year   Current Year   Projection
Actual   Budget

Figure 1 Programs and activities worksheet. *Note*: Departments are expected to fill out this worksheet for every objective.

sheets, and diagrams. Figures 1–3 present the basic contents of three budgetary and planning worksheets that require departments to identify strategic objectives, outcome indicators, associated program activities, program goals and measures, and activity or program costs broken down by object of expenditure (*From BMD-10*, 1996). Figures 4 and 5 present diagrams that the department uses to relate the different reform components, concepts, and budgeting and management tools up and down the organization (Langhoff and Pingle, 1997; Benson et al., 1995).

Another important component of System 94 was the use of preliminary budget allocations at the beginning of the budget process rather than relying on departments to develop their budget requests independently. Each department's aggregate allocation is based on inflation and other priorities, and then departments submit their budget worksheets (see Figures 1–3), which arrange their allocations according to objectives. To help departments reduce their resource demands, the BMD also outlines procedures for both prioritizing services according to strategic plans and grouping services based on whether they might be eliminated or consolidated (Benson et al., 1995; Kinney, 1995b; Langhoff and Pingle, 1996).

For several reasons, the administration decided to implement System 94 as quickly as possible. First, much of the reform work had already been completed—the city had in place a viable citywide strategic plan. Second, the city could readily draw on existing research on and other governments' experiences with performance measures and expenditure-control budgeting. Equally as important, running two budgeting systems at once would be difficult at best, and on the political side was the press, who paid little attention to the

Program/activity and objective totals should match totals stated on the BMD-10. While a breakdown of non-O&M costs is not required at this time, departments should be prepared to provide a breakdown upon request by BMD.

Objective 1:

Program/Activity: 1:   2:   3:   4:   5:

O&M
Salaries
Fringe Benefits
Supplies and Materials
Equipment & Facility Rent
Services
Equipment
Other

O&M TOTAL

Non-O&M
Capital Projects
Grant Funded
Reimbursables

NON-O&M TOTAL

Program/Activity Total

OBJECTIVE TOTAL

Figure 2 Departmental funding by objective and program activity worksheet. *Note*: Departments are expected to fill out this worksheet for every objective.

changes. By not having to address concerns of the press, the administration had time to fully implement System 94, weather any mistakes and negative feedback, and produce some concrete, positive results.*

Early Impacts and Results
Most departments have worked to comply with the reforms. Some noncabinet departments, however (and even some cabinet departments), continue to function under the old budgeting system, as demonstrated by their habit of submitting requests that exceed their budget allocations and by their poorly developed strategic plans and outcome indicators (Kinney, 1995a). Departments that demonstrate they can use the new system effectively are given increased flexibility over how funds are used, and some have had this authority and freedom

---

* Although it is too early to determine the outcome, current events within the CC suggest that the administration's honeymoon with the CC regarding the reforms may be over. Some members of the CC have taken issue with imposing these budget procedures on community-based organizations which receive, in total, approximately 28 million (about 40% of total grants funds received by the city). These members, who are primarily from the inner city, feel that the reforms will hurt their constituents disproportionately.

OBJECTIVE 1:

Program/Activity: 1:
  Goal:
  Program Measures:

Program/Activity: 2:
  Goal:
  Program Measures:

Program/Activity: 3:
  Goal:
  Program Measures:

Program/Activity: 4:
  Goal:
  Program Measures:

Program/Activity: 5:
  Goal:
  Program Measures:

Figure 3 Departmental program evaluation summary by objective. *Note*: Departments are expected to fill out this worksheet for every objective.

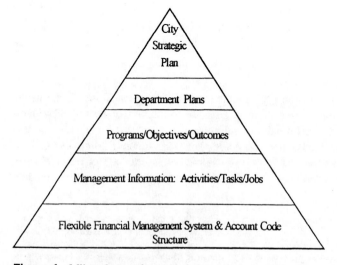

Figure 4 Milwaukee performance information pyramid.

Figure 5 Management and budgeting model.

extended to personnel and procurement practices. The administration expects the decentralized planning and budgeting process to change the regulatory relationship it has with departments to one that is steering-or guidance-oriented. The change is also expected to reduce tendencies to micro-manage (Reimer, 1997; Lawrence, 1997).

At least two successes, one financial and one organizational, appear to be associated with the reforms. Although the city has increased charges significantly, its tax rate relative to the nineteen other communities in Milwaukee County has decreased from 133% of the metropolitan average in 1988, the second highest rate in the county, to 123% of the average, the ninth highest in the county. Also, many departments have seen their service delivery and performance improve and their demand for inputs decline. For example, the percentage of responses to fires in under five minutes has increased from the 80s to the low 90s, property assessment appeals have declined by 70%, and the operating budgeting for the Department of Public Works has decreased by 17% (*Proposed Plan and Executive Budget Summary*, 1997; Public Policy Forum, 1989; 1997).

Not all has been glorious, however. There have been problems with implementing the reforms. For instance, budgets have not always been tightly linked to departmental plans, and departmental plans have not necessarily been fitted to the citywide strategic plan. The quality of objectives and outcome indicators developed by units differs greatly, reflecting the need for a standardized language to discuss programmatic performance and impacts and the need to improve staff training and knowledge in OBB. Moreover, much of the data needed to estimate the impacts of agency programs are not available. The first set of problems has been attributed to the predominately top-down approach to citywide planning, an approach that excluded several departmental managers from the reform process. The latter problems are associated primarily with implementing performance monitoring and impact assessment, and to some extent are technical problems that can be resolved with time, attention, and resources. Both sets of problems currently are being addressed.

Performance measurement and impact assessment are crucial to implementing the final and possibly the most fundamental of the features of OBB in Milwaukee—that of appropriating dollars based on achieving objectives and measurable targets. These efforts represent the next stage of budgeting and management reform for the city, which tentatively has been christened "Monitoring Milwaukee" (Benson et al., 1995). The next few years should prove interesting as Milwaukee begins to tackle this phase of outcome budgeting.

Missouri Department of Revenue

Reform in the Missouri Department of Revenue (DOR) began in 1993. The department had a deplorable track record with the legislature, the press, and the public, and in 1993 the decision was made to make improvements, beginning with the budgeting process. The reform effort was guided by a departmentwide strategic planning process that was supported at the top and included employees at all levels. The result was a proposed detail-based budget reform that depended upon reorganization, new appropriation language, and a level of trust between the legislature and the department that was, well, unheard of. Not only did the department get the budgetary flexibility it desired to improve the administration, management, and implementation of the department mission, but the legislature got what it wanted—increased programmatic and fiscal accountability and a more economically run department.

Currently, DOR is divided into four commissions—highway reciprocity, tax, state lottery, and the motor vehicle commissions—and five divisions—the director and deputy director offices and four support offices. The significant budget reforms affected the commissions and the divisions (in addition to the director) and thus the remaining discussion addresses only these units. The director has the responsibility for appointing the directors of DOR's divisions and chairs the reciprocity commission, but the governor appoints separately the commissioners for the tax, state lottery, and motor vehicle commissions, none of whom report to the director of DOR. The organizational structure of the divisions and commissions within DOR directly affect the way resources are budgeted; all resources appropriated for DOR are DOR monies, but the director has direct control over budgets only for divisions, not for commissions.

DOR's Need for Change: Accountability and Flexibility

The current director of DOR was appointed in April of 1993, about six months before the budget was due to the governor's office of administration (OA). Having been educated as an accountant/auditor and employed as a private sector auditor, she had the knowledge and experience necessary to take on the budgetary responsibilities of DOR. Within the first few months of her tenure, a few telltale signs signaling the "need" for both budgetary and organizational reform within DOR became very clear. First, budget request numbers given to her did not "add up." Salary figures, for instance, were not the real salaries paid out but instead were averages. If you earned $45,000 but the salary range for your position was between $45,000 and $55,000, then the budgeted figure was $50,000, since it was the average. Second, members of the legislature expressed to her their historical distrust of DOR budgetary figures. In part this was because DOR's budget numbers historically did not add up and partly because the legislature did not believe DOR representatives played it straight in budget hearings. Third, appropriations were very detailed, so much so that they cost the state a lot of money. In her desire to use state resources wisely, one of her objectives, then, was to get the legislature to change the appropriation language to grant DOR more flexibility.

The budget process in DOR had run amuck and the question was how to fix it. The fix, to increase administrative flexibility over the administration of resources, would not likely be easy because DOR had already shown by its actions that it was not very accountable. The solution, then, had to address *both* flexibility and accountability. The solution was in part a statewide budgetary reform effort (macro in scope) and was in part specific to DOR (micro in scope). The discussion that follows shows how flexibility and accountability were addressed both at the state level and at the departmental level.

COMAP: The Fix Becomes Part of a Larger Statewide Strategy

The biggest push for statewide agency budgetary reform may have come from the Governor's Commission on Management and Productivity, commonly referred to as COMAP. COMAP included members of the public and private sectors working together to make the state more productive and more effectively managed. Two of COMAPs working units, the organizational planning task force (OPTF) and the organizational planning committee (OPC), were primarily responsible for identifying a need for statewide reform and structuring a policy to address the budgetary problem. A third group, the Missouri Interagency Planning Council (IPC), created by the governor, was charged with leading the strategic planning implementation process, "the basis for program implementation and the allocation of state resources" (*Missouri Integrated Strategic Planning Model and Guidelines*, 1995: 1). The action plan developed by the OPC tied the strategic planning and performance (outcome-based) budgeting process, especially through its advocacy of performance standards and measures. The OPC produced the following:

1. A draft executive order that established the IPC, issued by the governor on April 26, 1995. Beginning with the 1996–1997 budget year, the planning and budgeting processes are to be linked, thereby increasing accountability by placing greater emphasis on benefits and results rather than activities and workloads.
2. Refinements to the planning principles, the integrated process, and the strategic planning model, emphasizing a customer focus, an integrated planning and budgeting process statewide, and an appropriations process to be based on outcome measures (*Missouri Integrated Strategic Planning Model and Guidelines*, 1995: 5).
3. A framework (see Figure 6) that would help the integrated strategic planning process clarify the direction, structure, and measurement of the reform effort. This would include a new budget request form (program decision item analysis form 5) and a set of planning guidelines that link the planning and budgeting processes (*Missouri Integrated Strategic Planning Model and Guidelines*, 1995: 4). From the committee's perspective, a successful strategic planning process within and across agencies must be structured so that staff members at all levels "have input into the strategic planning process and determination of outcomes and objectives" (*Missouri Integrated Strategic Planning Model and Guidelines*, 1995: 11).

Each product has come to be key to budgetary reform both for the DOR and for the state generally.

DOR's Self-Analysis: A Bottom-Up Approach

As a complement to the macro reforms proposed by COMAP for a statewide-oriented fix, DOR undertook efforts of its own that tailor the statewide fix to its needs. During the seven months following her appointment, the director of DOR, with cooperation from the governor's OA, house appropriations, and senate appropriations, met to propose a detailed study of the operations of each division and find projects that could be streamlined or

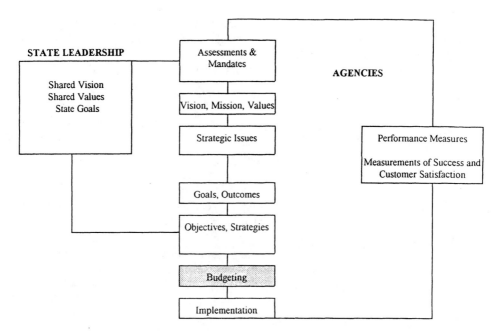

Figure 6   Conceptual framework for integrated strategic planning in Missouri, *Source: Missouri Integrated Strategic Planning Model and Guidelines*, 1995.

greatly changed to generate cost savings or more effectively managed operations. (See Backer, 1994: 1, 2). On November 9, 1993, the group completed a final draft proposal for the study, which they called a "detailed base budget review" (DBBR).

The proposed review indicated that whatever reforms would be forthcoming should be fairly broad in scope and possibly very comprehensive. According to the proposal, the resulting budget should clearly reflect an organizational structure, allow analysis of the impact of changes in budgeting resources, and focus only on the five operating divisions of DOR. The team members to conduct the analyses, provide information, and assist the general assembly in the detailed base review included one person from each of the OA, the house appropriations and senate appropriations committees, and various divisions within DOR.

Structure of the DBBR Reform

Through the DBBR process, DOR proposed projects that were expected to be (and that have become) fiscally beneficial to the state and managerially beneficial to the department. In the first DBBR, for instance, the department identified fourteen projects that were anticipated to save the state $740,000 per year, generate for the state up to $3,000,000 per year, free up as many as twenty-eight full-time positions, and reduce costs by $354,000. More important for the department, through the process, management gained the flexibility that it wanted to cut positions, shift personnel, streamline management, and improve services. For example, in the division of taxation and collection the proposed projects (e.g., a general reorganization and consolidation of the taxpayer services bureau into the collections bureau) were expected to result in the elimination of management and management support positions and decrease overtime costs, saving the department over $200,000 per year.

One of the more unconventional reforms occurred in the Division of Information Systems (DIS). The seemingly innocuous proposal was to increase the number of temporary employees during the busy tax season, thereby permitting the department to eliminate its need to contract out "overloads." The problem, however, was that DIS's 1994 appropriations bill was too strictly worded to permit DIS to transfer the related costs from E&E (expense and equipment account) to PS (personal services account) for this purpose (Backer, 1994: 12). Moreover, the state does not allow monies appropriated for one division or program to be transferred to another division or program. What DOR was requesting, in effect, was permission to receive a lump-sum appropriation that it could use however and wherever it felt the money was needed most, rather than the very detailed line-item appropriation that it had received for years. Wow! The DOR was given this authority, despite the dismal reputation that the department earned over several years; it seems to be a direct result of the department officials' conviction in reform and their ability to convince others of the need for it. This flexibility, however, was not to be unchecked.

By way of the agreement, the DOR's director, as a "direct price" for its leeway, offered to provide on a monthly basis the legislative oversight committees' assurances of accountability to the DBBR. A DBBR monthly report is given in Figure 7. The monthly reports provide the legislature the detailed information it needs about the project initially and upon its completion to assess accountability.

To complement the DBBR reform and based on the recommendations of COMAP and on feedback from executive agencies, the OA has implemented a new budget request form (Form 5), a core personal service reallocation review, and a budget responsiveness proposal to hold all state agencies, including DOR, accountable for the resources they use and the objectives they are to accomplish. Form 5 was developed "to assist in integrating the strategic plan with the budget allocation of resources . . . for both core and new decision items." (See Figure 8.) The performance (outcome) measures included in the document are to play an important role in providing departmental accountability to citizens and to the legislature. Departments, including DOR, also are to conduct a core personnel review, in where agencies are encouraged to identify ways to reduce the state's workforce while maintaining a high level of service. (See Figure 9.) In addition, they are encouraged to identify ways to make the budget more responsive to managers in a dynamic environment. All three forms are sent as attachments to the governor's budget instructions to the agencies.

SUMMARY AND CONCLUSION

What can we learn from DOR's and Milwaukee's OBB reforms? While the results are by no means conclusive, there is reason to believe that seemingly rational types of reforms are very possible. The key seems to be whether or not the agency is ready for the reform. In both cases, reforms were approached in the context of the government's management and political culture. Simply put, a reform will not succeed if it does not fit with the organization and its routines; it has a chance to succeed if it does. The success of both reforms depended upon a critical self-assessment and a strategic planning effort that seems to be missing in most reported reform efforts. The governments also were equipped and willing to use the available technology for budgetary and performance purposes.

Division/Director: Taxation and Collection
Project Number: A4
Project Name: Correspondence Tracking and Generation System (CTG)
Bureau/Responsible Administrator: End Users Computing Services
Date Submitted: June 1, 1994

1. **Problem Statement:** The Division of Taxation and Collection generates approximately 17,000 pieces of correspondence per month. The turnaround time offered to users of the various typing/word processing pools within the Division has increased to an unacceptable level. The maintenance and retrieval of files necessary to correspond with taxpayers has become unmanageable. A system is needed that would allow users to produce their own correspondence when needed and to maintain that correspondence in an easily accessible form without consuming the limited storage space within their working areas.

2. **Proposed Resolution:**

   a. Description: A mainframe based system that uses shell documents completed by tax analysts has been developed by the Department's Information Systems Division. This system is being designed, customized and implemented by Division of Taxation and Collection personnel. This system will decrease response time for the generation of correspondence and provide an electronic filing and retrieval system for all correspondence generated by the various bureaus.

   b. Cost/Source of Funding: No additional appropriation is required.

   c. Estimated Time for Implementation: December 1994 for the Division of Taxation and Collection.

3. **Anticipated Results:**

   a. The requirement for word processing staff should be reduced. Two to three employees are expected to be available for reassignment to be available for reassignment to more productive projects within the Department during fiscal year 1995.

   b. Implementation of this system should reduce turnaround time on taxpayer inquiries and billings. The Division currently plans to reassign available employees to collections activities to increase productivity and collections.

4. **How Measured:**

   a. Budgeted positions will be identified and adjusted in accordance with relevant detailed base procedures.

   b. Backlog and production reports will measure the improvements in turnaround times. The Division also plans to track the productivity of employees who are freed up and transferred to perform other collections activities.

5. **Detailed Implementation Plan:**

Action Item	Estimated Start Date	Estimated Completion Date
a. Implement CTG within the Tax Administration Bureau.	03/01/94	09/30/94
b. Implement CTG in Taxpayer Services Field Offices within the Collections Bureau.	04/01/94	09/30/94
c. Implement CTG within the Central Processing Bureau.	09/01/94	12/31/94

Figure 7 DOR detailed base budget review monthly report.

Division/Director: Taxation and Collection
Project Number: A4
Project Name: Correspondence Tracking and Generation System (CTG)
Bureau/Responsible Administrator: End Users Computing Services
Month/Year Reviewed: December 1994
Date Submitted: February 1, 1995

1. **Implementation Status:** The Correspondence Tracking and Generation (CTG) project is complete for the Division and Taxation and Collection. Division personnel continue to maintain the system.

2. **Measurement of Results and Benefits:**

Month	Number of Users	Letters Generated
December 1994	201	13,005
November 1994	197	12,172
:		
May 1994	156	13,184

The implementation of CTG has helped the Division dramatically improve its response time to taxpayer correspondence. The following chart compares the Collections Bureau's response time for December 1991 to December 1994.

Tax Type	December 1991	December 1994	Percent of Total
Individual Income	83 days	16 days	63%
Withholding	60 days	38 days	20%
Sales/Use	27 days	32 days	16%
Corporate	27 days	17 days	1%

Figure 7 *Continued.*

Both reforms occurred in phases, organizationwide and departmental, and in each case administrative support and lower-level bureaucratic participation were used to facilitate personal ownership of the reforms. With the ownership and a buy-in to the change, officials in both settings were more willing to ask tough questions and make equally tough organizational changes.

Politics too is important, but it seems to be more of a regulating factor than the key determinant. In Milwaukee the council role was much less direct and intense than that played by the appropriations and budgeting committees in Missouri. This seemed to be due largely to the different reputations of the governmental units affected by the change. The other difference was the role of the press. In Milwaukee the press was silent, while in Missouri, again largely due to the past performance of the department, the press reported (quite favorably) on the budgetary changes underway. Also, perhaps because of the press, governments seem to pay more attention to the outcomes of their service delivery.

The cases suggest that at least some governments see value in being effective at what they do and see the budgetary process as a means for helping them do that. These governments are willing to ask tough questions, including the following:

1. What is the relationship between the organization's budget and its culture?
2. How can the budget reform be implemented to ensure its success? Also, what is success?
3. Should the reform be comprehensive in scope or should it be piecemeal?
4. Why undertake the reform?
5. Is the organization ready to fundamentally and openly question its goals and objectives?
6. Does the government have the capacity to implement these reforms?

1. **STRATEGIC ISSUE AND REFERENCE, AND GOALS**
    Strategic issues are those internal or external challenges to the agency's mission, direction, policies, way of doing business, or culture. Strategic planning focuses on achievement of the best "fit" between the agency and its environment. Agencies should have developed a set of strategic issues as they prepared their plan. This box should simply be a statement of the strategic issue. Where necessary, agencies may instead use the form to describe the operational issue that is being addressed. If the issues can be summarized in key word phrases the box can be filled out in that manner. The box should also contain a reference to the strategic plan so that the reader has a place to go to obtain more detailed information.

    Goals chart the future direction of an agency. The goal development process begins to focus the agency's actions toward clearly defined purposes. Goals specify where the agency wants to be in the future. Goals are broad, issue-oriented statements that reflect the realistic priorities of the agency. For the budget process, goals are generalized, directional statements of an intended purpose (i.e., to improve, increase, maintain, decrease, provide) and are qualitative and not usually quantified.

2. **EXPLANATION, RATIONALE, AND OUTCOMES**
    Agencies should use this box to explain, define, and describe the problem in specific terms. It is important to explain how the decision item is related to the strategic issue. Outcomes are statements of exactly what result is being pursued by the agency. They are the desired results, future conditions, or impacts of agency action or policy. Outcomes are the resulting effect of the use or application of an output from which a desired level of quality/effectiveness can be determined. Agencies should describe the positive impact that will result from funding the decision item or the negative impact if the item is unfunded.

3. **OBJECTIVES AND STRATEGIES**
    Agencies should state their objectives and the strategies that will be used to attain them. Agencies should identify all of the objectives related to new decision item requests. For core decisions [sic] items agencies can identify selected high priority objectives and strategies if appropriate.

    Objectives are statements of specific initiatives to be accomplished. An agency's objectives are derived from its goals and are the basis for allocation of resources. The objective should provide:
    •a concise statement of what should be accomplished (specifically),
    •how much will be accomplished (quantity),
    •when it will be completed (deadline), and
    •by whom will it be completed (responsibility).

    Strategies are specific courses of action that will be undertaken by the agency to accomplish its goals and objectives. While an objective indicates what the agency must do, a strategy indicates how the particular objective or set of objectives will be achieved. To develop strategies, the agency determines how best to achieve the results intended by the objectives. The budget request should provide a narrative statement of an approach to achieve each objective.

4. **OUTCOME MEASURES**
    Outcome measures are expressed in quantifiable form and indicate the degree to which an agency is achieving its outcome and goals. An outcome measure is based on existing or collectable data which will be used for measuring outcome success or achievement, including customer satisfaction. The Division of Budget and Planning is interested in working with agencies in selection of these measures. Examples of outcome measures include:
    •Rate of infant mortality per 1,000 live births

Figure 8   Form 5: Program decision item analysis.

•Number of acres of private land protected through development and delivery of private land management plans
•Landowner satisfaction with private land management plans
•Cases of vaccine-preventable diseases
•Employer satisfaction with recently hired college graduates ...

5. **OUTPUT MEASURES**
    Output measures are numerical data showing the quantity of services provided or goods produced by the program. Examples of output measures include:
    •Collections generated by a program
    •Number of pre-sentence investigations completed
    •Number of program participants
    •Number of applications processed each month...

6. **COST EXPLANATION**
    Budget analysts and members of the General Assembly that review agency budgets need to understand how the request has been put together. Agencies need to describe the detailed calculations and assumptions that have been used to derive the request. Data sources should be cited to allow budget analysts to review the methodology used by the agency. Where necessary, agencies should explain the rationale for fund splits. In addition, agencies should identify one-time costs in detail.

Figure 8 *Continued.*

LEVEL 1	NAME OF DECISION ITEM:			PAGE
LEVEL 2				
LEVEL 3	DECISION ITEM RANK		OF	
LEVEL 4				
LEVEL 5	DECISION ITEM NO.			

		Fiscal Year 1996	Fiscal Year 1997	Fiscal Year 1998	Fiscal Year 1999
1.	**STRATEGIC ISSUE AND REFERENCE** - Summarize the strategic issue. Reference to strategic plan (page number). **GOALS** - In what direction does the agency want to be headed?				
2.	**EXPLANATION, RATIONALE, AND OUTCOMES** - Define and describe the problem in specific terms. How is the decision item related to the strategic issue? What outcomes are being pursued? Describe the positive impact funding this decision item will have on the problem. Describe the negative impact not funding this item will have on the problem.				
3.	**OBJECTIVES** - Describe what will be done, how much will be accomplished, and the timetable for measurement. **STRATEGIES** - How will the objective be accomplished?				
4.	**OUTCOME MEASURES** - Identify and quantify proposed outcome measures that will measure success. Note other budget items or assumptions affecting these outcomes.	Fiscal Year 1996	Fiscal Year 1997	Fiscal Year 1998	Fiscal Year 1999
5.	**OUTPUT MEASURES** - Identify and quantify the services to be provided.	Fiscal Year 1996	Fiscal Year 1997	Fiscal Year 1998	Fiscal Year 1999
6.	**COST EXPLANATION** - Describe the detailed calculations and assumptions used to derive this request, including breakdown and justification for any splits between funds. Identify data sources. Identify one-time costs in detail.				

Figure 8 *Continued.*

GR Core Personal Service Reallocation Target

3% = _____   Dept _____

FY 1997 HB Section	Appropriation Description	FY 1997 Approp.-Dept. Core Reductions or Transfers	FTE	FY 1997 Planned Spending	FTE	Potential FY 1998 Core Reallocation for pay plan	FTE	Impact

TOTALS

Figure 9 FY 1998 general revenue core personal service reallocation review.

Answers to these questions may lead to a change in policy and program focus and to adoption of new ways of thinking. These changes, though difficult in the short run, are likely to lead to new possibilities for the organization.

REVIEW QUESTIONS

1. What is outcome-based budgeting (OBB)?
2. What makes OBB different from other budget reforms?
3. Based on the experiences of the Missouri Department of Revenue (DOR) and the city of Milwaukee, what political, financial, and organization factors may precipitate OBB reform?
4. What obstacles did Milwaukee and the DOR face as they undertook OBB reform? Could these obstacles have been avoided?
5. What is a successful budget reform? How are successful reforms implemented? How do we know if OBB succeeds or fails?
6. Extrapolating from your knowledge of federal budgeting, what are the prospects of successfully implementing OBB at the federal level?

REFERENCES

Benson, D., Gultry, J., Kreklow, S., Metz, D., and Agostini, S. J. (1995). Performance budgeting: The milwaukee experience. paper presented at the 17th Annual Conference of the Association of Policy Analysis and Management, Washington, DC.

Memorandum from M. E. Ward to department directors. Fiscal Year 1998 Budget Instructions. (July 3, 1996).

Committee for the Future of Milwaukee. (1988). *Final Report.*

Cope, G. Hahn. (1997). Budgeting for performance in local government. *Municipal Yearbook, 1995.* Washington, DC: ICMA.

Cothran, D. A. (1993). Entrepreneurial budgeting: An emerging reform? *Public Administration Review, 53 (5)*, 445–454.

Daun, M. (1997). Interviewed on Jan. 29.

Form BMD-10. (1996). Milwaukee: Department of Administration, Division of Budget and Management.

(1992) *Strategic Plan: Issues and Actions.* Department of Administration, Office of Strategic Planning.

Ingraham, P. and Kettl, D. F. (1992). *Agenda For Excellence: Public Services in America.* Chatham, NJ: Chatham House.

Jones, L. R. and McCaffery, J. eds. (1992). Symposium: Federal financial management reform, part I. *Public Budgeting and Finance, 12 (4)*, 70–106.

Jones, L. R. and McCaffery, J. eds. (1993). Symposium: Federal financial management reform, part I. *Public Budgeting and Finance, 13 (1).*

Kettl, D. F. (1997). The global revolution in public management: Driving themes, missing links, *Journal of Public Policy Analysis and Management, 16 (3)*, 446–462.

Kinney, A. S. (1995a). Interviewed on Jan. 24.

Kinney, A. S. (1995b). Oct: Mission, management, and service delivery: Integrating strategic planning and budgeting in Milwaukee. *Government Finance Review*, 7–11.

Langhoff, G. and Pingle, J. (1997). *Putting the Plans Together: Integrating the City's Strategic Plan with Departmental Plans and Budgets.* Department of Administration, Division of Budget and Management.

Lawrence, J. (1997). Interviewed on Feb. 19.

Lohman, J. (1997). Interviewed on Jan. 6.

Lynch, T. D. and Lynch, C. (1996). Twenty-first century budget reform: Performance, entrepreneurial, and competitive budgeting. *Public Administration Quarterly, 20 (3)*, 254–284.

Milwaukee's Fiscal Outlook and Strategies for the Future. (1995). Department of Administration, Budget and Management Division.

July 1995. *Missouri Integrated Strategic Planning Model and Guidelines.*

National Performance Review. (Sept. 1993a). *From Red Tape to Results: Creating a Government That Works Better and Costs Less.* Office of the Vice President; Washington, DC: http://www.npr.gov/library/nprrpt/annrpt/sysrpt93/mission.htm.

National Performance Review. (Sept. 1993b). *Mission Driven, Results-Oriented Budgeting.* Washington, DC: Office of the Vice President; http://www.npr.gov/library/nprrpt/annrpt/sysrpt93/mission.htm.

Osborne, D. and Gaebler, T. (1992). *Reinventing Government.* Reading, MA: Addison-Wesley.

Proposed Plan and Executive Budget Summary. (1997). Department of Administration, Budget and Management Division.

Public Policy Forum. (1989). Milwaukee: *Spending and Taxing in the Milwaukee Metropolitan Area.*

Public Policy Forum. (1997). Milwaukee: *Spending and Taxing in the Milwaukee Metropolitan Area.*

Reimer, D. (1997). Interviewed on July 9.

State of Missouri, Office of Administration, Division of Budget & Planning. *FY 1997 Executive Budget: Budget Summary*; http://www.state.mo.us/oa/bp/exesum97/a01.htm.

State of Missouri, Office of Administration, Division of Budget & Planning. *FY 1998 Budget Summary Governor's Letter of Introduction*; http://www.state.mo.us/oa/bp/budget98/govlet.htm.

State of Missouri, Office of Administration, Division of Budget & Planning. *FY 1998 Budget Summary: Review of the Fiscal Year 1997 Budget & the Economic Outlook*; http://www.state.mo.us/oa/bp/budget98/review.htm.

State of Missouri, Office of Administration, Division of Budget & Planning. *FY 1998 Budget Summary: Review of the Fiscal Year 1997 Budget & the Economic Outlook*; http://www.state.mo.us/oa/bp/budget98/review.htm.

State of Missouri, Office of the Lieutenant Governor, Council on Efficient Operations. (Sept. 1996) *1996 Annual Report.*

Thompson, F. (1993). 'Matching responsibilities with tactics: Administrative controls and modern government. *Public Administration Review, 53(4)*, 303–314.

Ward, M. (March 5, 1997). presentation to one author's public budgeting and taxation class.

13

Forecasting the General Fund Budget of a Local Government

The City of Pleasantville

Aman Khan
Texas Tech University, Lubbock, Texas, U.S.A.

Forecasting has become an integral part of public budgeting in recent years. Long-range forecasts in particular are now required by many local and state governments to be included as part of their normal budget process. This is due in part to the fact that government revenues in most instances have not been able to keep pace with the demand for services. This battle between rising demand for services on the one hand and a frequent shortage of funds to provide support for such services on the other has often forced governments into increasingly narrow operating budgets. Having a long-range forecast of revenues and expenditures can avert the problem by identifying the levels of services at which the expenditures of a government will not exceed its revenues (Forrester, 1991).

Long-range forecasts are also important in aiding decisions regarding the funding of long-term debt. Many of a government's cherished capital improvement, redevelopment, and public welfare projects and programs require financing over a very long period of time. Long-range forecasts of revenues and expenditures can reduce the risk of funding long-term debt. Perhaps the most important benefit of long-range forecasts is that it allows a government to test the implications of alternative policies before placing them into effect. Successful policy makers must have an interest in going beyond the present and seriously looking into options that may be necessary to deal with problems in the future. Without long-range forecasts of revenues and expenditures, most decision makers will find it difficult to grasp those options.

This chapter discusses the budget forecasting practices of a local government which, to maintain its anonymity, we will call Pleasantville. In particular, the objective here is to present a six-year revenue and expenditure forecast for the general fund (GF) of the government. The chapter is divided into five sections. The first section presents some background information about the community. The next section II discusses the current forecasting practices of the government, while the one after that, the heart of the chapter, presents the models used and the rationale for using them. The subsequent section discusses the forecast results, while the final section concludes the chapter with some general observations on the future budgetary situation of the government.

BACKGROUND INFORMATION

The city of Pleasantville has a very special need for long-range revenue and expenditure forecasts. The city is in a situation where it is becoming more and more important to find ways to provide services while staying within the revenue limits of the government. It has major investments in the infrastructure system and has increased its share of services in recent years. The city is also a frequent recipient of transplanted residents who require services above and beyond what is required of most governments. This places additional responsibility on the government to find ways to provide services to meet the needs of its citizens. The following provides some background information about the city—its demographic, economic, and financial conditions.

Pleasantville is a midsize southeastern city with a population of approximately 368,000 people. After some initial increases in the early 1990s, the population has been declining in recent years, but at a decreasing rate, meaning that the growth rate will eventually stabilize. The city enjoys a diverse ethnic and racial mix. It also has a large population of prime working age individuals. The largest segment of the population, 38.97%, is the 30–50 age cohort, which is consistent with the overall growth pattern of the surrounding communities. In addition to its size and growth, there are indications that the quality of the labor force in the city and the surrounding communities has been rising recently. Employment in the city represents roughly about 20% of the total employment. Service, commerce, finance, and government account for the majority of jobs in the city. Other sectors with significant employment include transportation, construction, and real estate.

Personal income for the city has grown at about the same rate as the nation over the last several years, although its per capita income has run at about 3% higher than the national average. Mean household income for the city has also been at par with the national average in recent years. As with all statistics, however, income statistics must be viewed in light of the general economic and demographic composition. Since a higher proportion of the city's population has relatively stable and high-income potentials, it is expected that the income data will reflect this effect in the future.

As for city finance, property taxes represent the single most important source of revenue. Over the years both gross and net assessed value of real and personal property have been increasing at a reasonably consistent rate.* For instance, between 1990 and 1997 total gross assessed value increased by more than 228.24%, from $4.566 billion to $10.421 billion (Table 1). The corresponding increase for net assessed value for the same years was 238.18%, up from $3.984 billion in 1990 to $9.489 billion in 1997 (not shown in Table 1). It is the real property, however, that represents the largest proportion of the city's taxable base (nearly 88.84% in 1995). Personal property values, on the other hand, have declined somewhat in the last eight years, from 18.02% of the total assessed value in 1990 to 11.06% in 1997.

Although it has slowed down somewhat in recent years, overall property tax still remains the dominant source of income for the government, accounting for 47.06% of total receipts in 1997. Business and excise tax is the second most important source of

---

* Net assessed values are calculated by subtracting homestead and other exemptions from the gross assessed values for a given year.

Table 1 Distribution of Gross Assessed Values: Real and Personal Properties (in Thousands of Dollars)

	1980	1985	1990	1995	1997
Personal	380,278	672,697	822,729	1,158,212	1,210,435
Percent	18.63	19.09	18.02	11.95	11.06
Real	1,727,513	2,851,310	3,743,051	8,538,398	9,210,476
Percent	81.37	80.91	81.98	88.05	88.84

Source: Comprehensive annual financial reports of the city.

revenue, accounting for 21.20% in 1997. It has been one of the most consistent sources of city revenue over the years. This is followed by intergovernmental revenue, accounting for 14.43% in 1997. Intergovernmental revenue has experienced considerable decline in recent years due to reduction in federal grants and assistance (Table 2). Although state support has been forthcoming, it has not been able to fully replenish the lag created by the decline in federal revenue. Other important sources of revenue are miscellaneous charges and business licences and permits.

The demographic trend discussed earlier indicates that the city has been losing its population for the past several years, although gradually, along with some reductions in taxable income. This presents two challenging situations for the government: (1) the general operating costs continue to increase in spite of the decreasing trend in population growth and (2) a reduced revenue base may force the government to raise the property tax even higher, which is fast nearing its cap. Table 3 shows the per capita expenditure growth for the city by major categories between 1985 and 1997. According to Table 3, the population has declined by 3.16% since 1995, while per capita expenditure rose by 30.49%. When per capita expenditures are adjusted for the percentage decline in population, the figure translates to a 56% increase, or 18.67% per year over the three-year period (from 1995 to 1997). This is a much higher rate of increase than what one would consider to be the norm for an average city (Moody's, 1997).

One of the more effective ways to evaluate the general financial condition of a government is to look at its annual balance sheet. Balance sheets list a government's assets, liabilities, and fund balances by individual funds or fund groups. Table 4 presents the city GF balances for 1987, 1992, and 1997, including its assets and liabilities. As

Table 2 Percentage distribution of revenues (by Major Sources)

	1985	1990	1995	1997
Property tax	39.323	42.672	47.238	47.058
Business and excise tax	21.837	23.700	22.362	21.198
Intergovernmental revenues	19.528	12.476	13.926	14.429
Business licenses and permits	5.503	5.635	3.389	3.429
Miscellaneous	13.809	15.099	13.085	13.388
Total	100.00	100.00	100.00	100.00

Source: Comprehensive annual financial reports of the city.

Table 3 Per Capita Expenditure: Selected Services [PCCE] Selected Services [$]

	1985	1990	1995	1997
Public safety	89.958	152.980	262.318	304.033
Solid waste	28.661	41.732	60.005	126.986
Public improvements	20.795	32.991	39.403	52.111
General government	18.684	29.706	46.576	52.549
Culture and recreation	11.404	21.262	22.766	26.812
Total PCCE	$169.502	$278.671	$431.068	$562.490
Population	336,000	347,000	380,000	368,000

Source: Comprehensive annual financial reports of the city.

Table 4 shows, the city's total assets increased from $4.944 million in 1987 to $17.863 million in 1992. From 1992 to 1997, however, it increased by a meager $255,000. The asset increase for the first five years seems to have come principally from an increase in pooled cash and investment, from $4.087 million to $14.294 million. Interestingly enough, for the years between 1992 and 1997, it decreased by about $3 million, which raises some concern about a possible cash flow problem. Another concern for liquidity comes from the fact that the city's receivables are almost negligible compared to its cash position, meaning that any decline in cash position is bound to have some speculations about its future financial condition.

Table 4 Assets, Liabilities, and Fund Balance, Year Ended, December 31 (in Millions of Dollars)

	1987	Percentage change	1992	Percentage change	1997
Assets					
Pooled cash and investment	4.087	249.743	14.294	−18.812	11.605
Receivables					
Taxes	0.483	316.977	2.014	−43.595	1.136
Accounts	0.374	269.519	1.382	−66.787	0.459
Other funds	—	—	—	9,431.428	3.336
Other governments	—	—	—	1,060.156	1.485
Deposits and other expenses	—	—	—	—	0.097
Total assets	4.944	261.307	17.873	1.427	18.118
Liabilities					
Vouchers and accounts payable	1.247	140.337	2.997	−53.420	1.396
Accrued expenses	0.974	262.012	3.526	−9.841	3.179
Deferred revenue	1.745	16.332	2.030	−7.044	1.887
Refundable deposits	—	—	1.196	−69.300	0.503
Total liabilities	3.968	146.067	9.759	−28.630	6.965
Fund balance	0.978	728.630	8.104	37.623	11.153

Source: Comprehensive annual financial reports of the city.

Table 5 Short-Run Liquidity Measures (Year Ended, December 31, 1997)

	1990	1995	1997
Current ratio	1.246	2.204	1.491
Net working capital	$0.978M	$8.104M	$12.153M

Source: Comprehensive annual financial reports of the city.

The short-term liquidity ratios also present a mixed signal (Table 5). The current ratios show a decrease in the city's liquidity, suggesting the likelihood of its inability to meet short-term obligations. On the other hand, an analysis of net working capital indicates reasonable operating liquidity, judging by the positive increases.

The importance of maintaining sufficient liquidity is to protect the creditors and other lending institutions. Ideally, there should be a "reference value" against which the existing level could be compared. Since no such measure was used here as to the minimum requirement for the city, it was not possible to determine the exact nature of its operating liquidity.

CURRENT FORECASTING PRACTICES

For the budget in general, the city uses a very basic approach to estimate its revenues and expenditures. For instance, the largest single source of revenue, ad valorem property tax, is estimated for the budget by applying a millage rate to a certification of property value for the city. The county appraiser notifies the city of the real value of personal property in the city sometime during the early phases of budget planning (usually before June). Using this appraised value as well as the budget policy of the city administration and the budget requests of the various departments, a millage rate is then proposed.

Revenue collected from the franchise fees is determined by means of the numbers and types of electrical and telephone hookups in the city, both presently and for the upcoming year. The utilities provide for the city the current hookup numbers and types. Both time series trend analysis and quantitative methods are used to estimate future hookups and usage of utilities. Building permits are an important variable in these estimates.

Intergovernmental transfers, which constitute a significant source of city revenue, are determined based on past experience and individual judgements. For instance, the budget department relies on notification from the contributing government about the amount it will receive in the coming year. Since the notifications can vary from year to year, it increases the uncertainty in predicting the revenue the city is going to receive. Another important source of revenue for the GF is transfer from other funds, generally known as "nonrevenues" or "interfund transfers." Information on these amounts is determined through negotiations among the departments and the administration.

In fact, city revenues and expenditures, in particular the former, are not estimated consistently using any formal methodological approach. Revenues are expected to follow the general trend experienced in the recent past, and both millage rates and expenditures

---

* See the chapter by Khan and Stumm in this book.

are adjusted during the budget proposal process. The consequence of this is that it forces the government to be more short-term-oriented in planning its service operations.

This study provides a modest alternative to the current practices of the city by offering a simple regression (causal modeling) approach to forecasting its revenues and expenditures. The advantage of using regression analysis is its ability to discover the effect the various economic and noneconomic factors will have on the forecast. To the extent that these models are successful in explaining that effect, they can be used to predict the future revenues and expenditures of a government with a certain degree of reliability (Bretschneider and Gorr, 1987; Pindyck and Rubinfeld, 1991). As noted earlier, the forecasting is restricted to the GF budget of the city.

FORECASTING GENERAL FUND REVENUES AND EXPENDITURES

This section discusses the models used in the study to forecast the GF revenues and expenditures of the city along with a set of statistics that are typical of the method used. Data for the study came from several sources, including (1) the budgets of the city, (2) comprehensive annual financial reports, (3) city business reports, (4) the county profile of economic growth, (5) state statistical abstracts, and (6) the U.S. Bureau of Labor statistics reports. In keeping with the standard practice for statistical analysis, data were cleaned for inconsistencies before running the regression equations (Zorn, 1982). Each equation was individually tested for statistical reliability, given by minimum standard errors of estimate, high t values, high coefficient of determination, and other factors, such as low multicollinearity and serial correlation.

Revenue Forecasts

Revenue forecasts for the study are based on an analysis of eighteen years of budget history. Several individual projections are made and aggregated into five broad categories consistent with the principal sources of revenue for the government: (1) property tax revenue, (2) business and excise taxes, (3) intergovernmental revenue, (4) business licenses and permits, and (5) miscellaneous charges and other sources of revenue. Of these, property taxes alone make up for more than 47% of the total GF revenue. Also, as noted before, business and excise taxes (which mostly include franchise fees, local option gasoline taxes, and fines and forfeitures) account for nearly 21% of the revenue. Intergovernmental revenues account for 14%, business licenses and permits for another 4%, while the miscellaneous other charges and revenue sources make up for the remaining 14%.

The revenue projections are based on several assumptions: (1) the tax rate will not change (i.e., it will remain constant for the forecast period), (2) the historical trends and relationships will continue unchanged, at least for the forecast period, and (3) the general projections made here are correct within the conditions underlying the model and the equations used. In other words, if the model conditions or the conditions of the real world change, the future values of these forecasts will also change.

Property Tax Revenue (PTR)

Property tax revenue is projected by a simple formula that takes into consideration the net value of taxable property and the current millage rate. The net value of taxable property is computed by adjusting for the homestead exemption from the gross value. The model first forecasts the net values of taxable property, which are then plugged into the equation to forecast the PTR.

$$PTR = \left(\{[(NVTP)(0.95)]/1000\} \times MR\right)$$
$$NVTP = 1223.3660 + 481.7977 \ TIME$$
$$\qquad\quad (209.5845) \quad (19.3623)$$
$$R^2 = 0.9748; \ F = 619.1785; \ D-W = 0.4793; \ MAD = 7.05$$

where PTR is the property tax revenue, NVTP is the net value of taxable property, MR is the millage rate, R^2 is the coefficient of determination, SEE is the standard error of estimate, F is the F ratio, D-W is the Durbin–Watson statistic, MAD is the mean absolute deviation, and the numbers within the signs of aggregation represent the standard errors of the regression coefficients. (Note that we could have used MAPE, but MAD turned out to be a better measure for backcasting in this case.)

Discussion. As noted earlier, the city receives the lion share of its revenue from property taxes. Property tax revenue for 1997 was $88.138 million. The projected figure for 1998 is $91.676 million, which represents a 4.01% increase over a twelve-month period. It is expected to increase to $103.425 million in 2003. Since the tax rate is assumed to remain constant for the forecast period, the growth in property tax revenue is largely due to the growth in net assessed value of property.

Business and Excise Tax (BEXT)
The equation for BEXT is self-explanatory; it is defined as a function of the city population and the real county personal income. The county personal income data were used because they produced a much better fit than either the state or the national personal income data, which makes sense because of proximity.

$$BEXT = -106.8300 + 147.3780 \ CPOP + 12.0638 \ RCPI$$
$$\qquad\qquad (16.0992) \quad (65.0353) \qquad\qquad (1.8505)$$
$$R^2 = 0.9181; \ F = 84.0797; \ D-W = 0.7754; \ MAD = 2.28$$

where BEXT is the business and excise tax, CPOP is the city population, RCPI is the real county personal income, and the rest of the terms are the same as before.

Discussion. Business and excise tax, which is the second largest source of GF revenue, consists of franchise fees, utility fees, and local option gasoline tax (LOGT). These fees are levied on a corporation or individual by the city in return for granting a privilege, sanctioning a monopoly, or permitting the use of public property. Revenue collected from business and excise tax in 1997 was $42.445 million and is expected to remain around that figure through 2000. The projected growth for 2003 is about $47.148 million.

Intergovernmental Revenue (IGR)
Intergovernmental revenue primarily consists of state grants and subsidies. This also in-cludes the city's share of sales tax collection and support from the county government. The LOGT, which appears as part of IGR in city annual budgets, is incidentally reported as part of the BEXT in the annual financial report. To avoid this confusion, they are

excluded from the computation of this revenue here, as can be seen from the following expressions:

$$IGR = [(FAST + CSSTC) - LOGT] \tag{1}$$

$$FAST = 4.3955 + 1.2705 \text{ TIME} \tag{2}$$
$$\quad (1.3440) \quad (0.1242)$$
$$R^2 = 0.8674; F = 104.6949; D-W = 1.1061; MAD = 1.89$$

$$CSSTC = [(GSSTC)(0.100)](0.15759172) \tag{3}$$

$$GSSTC = 169.5396 + 0.1173 \text{ SSTR} \tag{4}$$
$$\quad (24.8662) \quad (0.0085)$$
$$R^2 = 0.9267; F = 189.6872; D-W = 0.3401; MAD = 1.54$$

$$LOGT = 53.8629 - 133.9527 \text{ CPOP} \tag{5}$$
$$\quad (7.5991) \quad (20.5358)$$
$$R^2 = 0.9341; F = 42.5481; D-W = 1.9353; MAD = 0.4987$$

where IGR is the intergovernmental revenue, FAST is the federal and state transfer, CSSTC is the city share of sales tax collections, GSSTC is the county sales tax collections, LOGT is the local option gasoline sales tax, SSTR is the state sales tax revenue, and the rest of the terms are the same as before.

Discussion. Forecasts for IGR are obtained in two stages. First, individual equations for FAST, GSSTC, and LOGT were estimated. The results of these equations are then plugged back into the expression for IGR to forecast the future revenue. Note that revenue from CSSTC comprises about one-eighth of the total GF revenue. The computation of CSSTC is based on a formula that allocates to the city a portion of the GSSTC. On the other hand, the GSSTC was obtained by fitting an equation that uses SSTR as the explanatory variable. The estimated values are then multiplied by a fixed percentage to obtain the city share of sales tax revenue. Finally, the equation for LOGT was estimated using city population as the explanatory variable. It should be pointed out that LOGT was created only recently; as such, data were not available for all eighteen years. In spite of this limitation, however, the equation seems to have produced good results, as evidenced by the various regression statistics. Revenues from intergovernmental sources in 1997 were $27.320 million, which are expected to increase to $31.790 million in fiscal year 2001 and to approximately $37.133 million in 2003.

Business Licenses and Permits (BLPs)

The idea behind the BLP forecasting equation is straightforward. In this equation, BLPs are determined as a function of real county personal income and the consumer price index (CPI). Earnings from this source are expected to remain constant around the 1997 figure for at least a couple of years, by all the indications given by the economy of the city.

$$BLP = -1.0562 + 0.6868 \text{ RCPI} + 0.0064 \text{ CPI}$$
$$\quad (1.4470) \quad (0.3155) \quad (0.0028)$$
$$R^2 = 0.9136; F = 79.2892; D-W = 0.9798; MAD = 0.2344$$

where BPL stands for business licenses and permits, RCPI is the real county personal income, and CPI is the consumer price index, and the rest of the terms are the same as before.

Discussion. Revenue from business licenses and permits, which covers a very small percentage of the total GF revenue, is of two basic types. Professional and occupational licenses are required for the privilege of engaging in certain trades, occupations, and other activities. These fees are used to cover the cost of administration, inspection, and enforcement of health, security, and safety standards established by the city. Permits, such as building permits, provide revenue that is used to cover the inspection of construction within the city to ensure compliance with safe building codes. In 1997, contribution from BLPs was $6.082 million, which is expected to grow to $6.917 million in 2000 and to about $7.429 in 2003.

Fines and Forfeitures (FAF)

The FAF forecasting equation is expressed as a simple linear time trend with a lag of one. It is the best possible equation that could be fitted with the available data. Several alternative models were tried, but the lag of time seems to explain the relationship better (although not by an overwhelming amount). This may be due to the fact that although it is recognized as a distinct source of revenue, it constitutes a very a small percentage of the total revenue of the city. It is therefore unlikely that changes in the behavior of any of the explanatory variables used here will have any serious effect on it.

$$FAF = 0.8401 + 0.0657 \text{ TIME } (-1)$$
$$(0.1536) \quad (0.0150)$$
$$R^2 = 0.5612; F = 19.1838; D-W = 2.1674; MAD = 1.32$$

where FAF stands for fines and forfeitures and the rest of the terms are the same as before.

Discussion. Fines are generally imposed on statutory offenses and collected in the form of confiscated property, pollution control fines, and court fees, among other things. Forfeits, on the other hand, are revenue produced from confiscation of deposits or bonds that are held as performance guarantees. Together these revenues add up to about 1% of all GF revenues. In 1997, the city collected about $2.439 million, which is expected to increase to $2.351 million by 2003.

Miscellaneous Charges and Revenue Sources (MCRS)

Like the BLP model, the MCRS equation is a simple linear time trend, but without a lag. As before, the advantage of using time as an explanatory variable is that it minimizes the forecast error variance because the values of the forecast period of the explanatory variable are known with certainty. Looking at the results, it appears to have produced a good fit.

$$MCRS = -7.0621 + 1.8012 \text{ TIME}$$
$$(3.7212) \quad (0.2459)$$
$$R^2 \; 0.9148; F = 53.6531 ; D-W = 2.1788; MAD = 0.27$$

where MCRS stands for miscellaneous charges and revenue sources, and the rest of the terms are the same as before.

Discussion. Revenue in this category includes contributions from all those sources that are not listed in the above categories. Examples of charges include photos, reports, zoning map sales, ordinances, and microfilming, as well as charges for computer printouts, engineering services, and public hearing fees. Miscellaneous charges and revenue sources also include interest earned on investments, contracts, and notes, plus revenue from the sale of fixed assets or from compensation for losses of fixed assets, such as insurance proceeds. The MCRS contribution to GF revenue in 1998 was $25.857 million, which is expected to increase to $30.763 million in 2000 and to about $36.167 million in 2003.

Expenditure Forecasts

Expenditure forecasts are based on an eleven-year analysis of expenditures by major expense categories and accounts. These accounts are: (1) personnel services, (2) operating expenses, (3) capital outlays, and (4) special programs and accounts. As before, simple regression models are used to determine the future values of these variables. Unlike the revenue forecasts, however, expenditure forecasts are built on an additional assumption that the future values of these variables depend on their lagged value(s). In other words, past expenditure patterns would provide good information about the future. This procedure, which has been applied to two of the four expenditure forecasts, is known as the "first differencing autoregressive" technique.

City Personnel Services (CPS)

As indicated, the CPS forecasting equation is a function of its lagged values. In other words, lagged values are used to forecast the future values of the variable. The observed statistics for the estimated model seem to indicate a good fit of the data.

$$CPS = 15.0404 + 0.9448 \ CPS \ (-1)$$
$$(7.6867 \quad (0.0633)$$
$$R^2 = 0.9654; \ F = 222.9980; \ D-W = 1.6734; \ MAD = 4.05$$

where CPS stands for city personnel services and the rest of the terms are the same as before.

Discussion. Personnel services constitute the largest segment of the city expenditure categories, accounting for almost 75% of the total budget. In 1997, the total amount expended on personnel services was $158.440 million, which is expected to grow to about $172.934 million in 2001 and to $183.623 million in 2003.

City Operating Expenses (COE)

The equation for COE is simple. In addition to the lagged operating expenses, this equation also uses the city population as an explanatory variable. The equation as a whole appears to be a good fit, reflecting a growth pattern that is commensurate with its recent growth trend.

$$COE = -31.7238 + 0.5344 \ COE \ (-1) + 126.8361 \ CPOP$$
$$(3.5678) \quad (0.1159) \quad (51.8370)$$
$$R^2 = 0.9039; \ F = 32.9089; \ D-W = 2.7667; \ MAD = 2.24$$

where COE stands for city operating expenses, CPOP is the city population, and the rest of the terms are the same as before.

Discussion. Operating expenses are the second most important category on the expenditure side of the budget, accounting for almost 15% of all expenses. Operating expenses in 1997 were $34.235 million, which would decline to $31.894 million in 1999, partly due to city efforts to control its (expenditure) growth. Future projection of operating expenses further indicates a continuation of this trend, at least for the forecasting period.

City Capital Expenses (CCE)

The CCE equation is defined in terms of inflation rate and its lagged values. The justification for including inflation as an explanatory variable is that capital expenditures include a long-term commitment of resources. Resources committed for this purpose must therefore be discounted by an appropriate rate to find out what they are worth in today's terms (to justify the expenditure). Inflation, although not a good measure, is frequently used for this purpose. Looking at the observed results, the equation seems to be a good fit.

$$CCE = -0.0577 + 0.1343 \text{ INFR } (-1)$$
$$(0.1945) \quad (0.0290)$$
$$R^2 = 0.7542; F = 21.4750; D-W = 2.6143; MAD = 0.98$$

where CCE stands for city capital expenses, INFR is the inflation rate, and the rest of the terms are the same as before.

Discussion. Capital improvement costs constitute a very small fraction of total GF expenditure. With the exception of the years 1990–1991 and 1991–1992, capital expenses have never been more than $1 million (not a very desirable choice) a year, reaching as low as $285,000 in 1995. The projection for 2003 shows only a marginal growth of about $50,000. Although there is a need for major capital improvements, the city does not have enough surpluses in the general fund to accommodate this need. Using debt finance for capital improvements is a common practice, but because of the millage rate being so close to the cap, it prohibits the city from getting into this situation.

Special Programs and Accounts (SPAC)

The SPAC is a simple equation of linear time trend, where lagged values have been used instead of simple time for a better fit. The results from the fitted equation show an upward trend in the expenses of this account. The high R^2 and low standard errors reflect the stability of the method.

$$SPAC = 4.8780 + 1.4216 \text{ TIME } (-1)$$
$$(0.8939) \quad (0.1440)$$
$$R^2 = 0.9241; F = 97.3645; D-W = 2.9601; MAD = 1.21$$

where SPAC stands for special programs and accounts and the rest of the terms are the same as before.

Discussion. This is a catchall category that uses approximately 10% of the GF expenditure. The largest single account in this category was solid waste, which after experiencing some operating losses, was moved from the GF to the enterprise fund during the 1996–1997 fiscal year. Important among the activities in this category are expenses for the contingent fund, communications services, reserve pension plan, and reserve self-insurance fund. Total SPAC expenses for 1997 were $17.518 million, which is expected to increase to $21.937 million in 2001 and to $24.780 million in 2003.

GENERAL FUND SURPLUS AND DEFICIT

As a general rule, city governments are not allowed to have budget deficits. This is particularly true for the GF. Most governments at the state and local level are restricted by law

Table 6 GF Budget Forecast (in Millions of Dollars)

	1998	1999	2000	2001	2002	2003
Revenues						
PTR	91.6758	94.6333	99.0289	103.4245	107.7563	112.1519
BEXT	39.3505	40.6399	41.9293	43.5884	45.3812	47.1481
IGR	29.9658	30.6794	31.7899	33.5295	35.4268	37.1332
BLP	6.5395	6.7264	6.9166	7.1003	7.2872	7.4291
FAF	2.0222	2.0879	2.1536	2.2192	2.2849	2.3506
MCRS	27.1610	28.9622	30.7634	32.5646	34.3659	36.1671
Total	196.7148	203.7291	212.5817	222.4265	232.4893	242.3800
Expenditures						
CPS	154.4425	160.9593	167.1165	172.9338	172.4301	183.6230
COE	33.3362	32.5133	31.8198	31.1955	30.9265	30.9510
CCE	0.5547	0.6381	0.6751	0.6581	0.6085	0.6913
SP&A	17.6722	19.0938	20.5154	21.9370	23.3586	24.7802
Total:	206.0056	213.2045	220.1268	226.7244	233.3237	240.0455
Surplus/(deficit)	(9.2908)	(9.4754)	(7.5451)	(4.2979)	(0.8344)	(2.3345)

not to have any deficit in their GFs. A budget deficit is the difference between revenues and expenditures. Table 6 presents a brief summary of the estimated revenues and expenditures for the GF of the city through 2003. According to Table 6, GF expenditures are projected to exceed revenues in each of the forecast years, with the exception of 2003.

The deficits are expected to be much higher for 1998 and 1999, and are expected to decline gradually. By the end of 2002, the GF is expected to have a deficit that is substantially lower than any of the previous years. By the end of 2003, the deficit is expected to disappear, producing a negligible surplus. For instance, the deficit for 1998 is estimated to be $9.29 million, followed by $9.47 in 1999, $7.55 in 2000, and so on. What these deficit figures essentially mean is that the projected revenues for the city would not be sufficient to sustain the projected growth in the costs of city services, especially during the early years of the forecast period.

Although they are not permitted, GF deficits are nothing new to the city. There were instances of occasional deficits in the past, but the current trend indicates a lingering pattern that raises some serious concern about the city's overall fiscal soundness. If the revenue projections remain reliable and the city fails to control its expenditure growth, then it is more than likely that this deficit will not disappear by 2003. There are a number of things the city can do to correct the problem, however, in particular taking a more proactive approach. The following provides two sets of strategies the city might find useful to deal with the current problem.

Short-Term Strategies

The forecasts for 1998 and 1999 have clearly identified a potential problem for the city's GF. It is not, however, a major crisis given by the size of the deficit, but nevertheless, a trend is emerging that is not healthy by any definition of fiscal soundness. A simple and commonsense approach would be to carefully monitor the revenue and expenditure growth for the next several years. There are several ways in which this can be accomplished: (1)

do not undertake any new projects unless they are mandated or absolutely necessary, (2) limit inventory purchases to the level required to maintain existing levels of services (this will free up some money), (3) pursue an aggressive policy to increase interest income from prudent and timely investments of available funds, (4) minimize overtime whenever possible, both for essential and nonessential services, (5) make a conscious effort to hold the expenditures to about 98% of the current budget (this would release about $5 million, which could be made available to help reduce the projected deficit for 1999), and (6) as a last resort, raise the property tax, which will be difficult because the millage rate is already close to the cap. To do so, the city will probably have to have state approval.

It is not possible to suggest a service reduction plan in the study since this would require a more thorough and exhaustive analysis of the all the expenditure programs. At the same time, it may be worthwhile to develop a plan that would look into the possibility of per capita reduction in a step-by-step fashion.

Long-Term Strategies

In the long term, the city can pursue a set of policies that are broader in scope but would put it into a more balanced path toward fiscal solvency. For instance, it can develop a productivity improvement program through evaluation of alternative methods of service provision. It can also strive to recover increased service delivery costs through new user fees where appropriate or by revising the existing charges to reflect the full cost of recovery. Although it may require some serious commitment on the part of the administration, it can try to make an effort to increase the fund balance to about 10% of the budget to offset the rising expenditure growth. It can also try to reduce the increased demand for services through expanded cooperation with neighborhood groups, business establishments, outside agencies, and volunteer organizations, especially in the areas of recreation, crime, and fire protection. Finally, it can try to provide the services in a more cost-effective manner by undertaking innovative measures and technological improvements. This may require investments in new equipment, employee incentives, and training.

If properly pursued the strategies suggested above should have the effect of maintaining the existing levels of services currently provided by the city. The measures are not difficult, but they rely on efforts that will reduce costs and improve productivity, gradually shifting toward more stable and recurring revenue sources.

SUMMARY AND CONCLUSION

This study is the first of its kind that the city of Pleasantville has developed to forecast its GF revenues and expenditures. It is hoped that the city would continue to update and expand this study in the future. There are many different courses of action that the city can pursue to develop a capability similar to the one used here. The ideal approach would be to develop a 'permanent forecasting team' with individuals who have been instrumental in developing this study and who have a sound understanding of the problem and techniques. Another alternative would be to engage 'consulting firms' familiar with forecasting models for local government studies. The cost of such studies could be enormous, however, especially for small governments.

Regardless of who is responsible for doing a budget forecast, the general approach to forecasting remains essentially the same: (1) the choice of major revenue and expenditure items to be projected, (2) creation of a new time series representing those major revenue and expenditure items and an explicit statement of the sources or base of those items as well as their collection procedures, (3) timing and explanation of all discontinuities or exceptions contained within the data, and (4) acquisition of socioeconomic and demographic data from appropriate sources. Perhaps more important than the results a forecasting study produces is the judgment the decision makers must use regarding how to use the forecasts. To conclude, it must be emphasized that forecasting models are nothing but tools used to produce results that are valid only within the limits of the models used. Decision makers must be aware of this and must use proper judgments in making the best use of the forecasting results. Failure to do so may not only affect the future revenues and expenditures of a government but also the quality of life that follows from those decisions.

REVIEW QUESTIONS

1. Why is forecasting important in budget decision making in government? What can a government do to improve its forecasting practices? Why is it necessary to use forecasts with caution?
2. Looking at the general background of Pleasantville, what can you say about its overall financial situation? Does it give the impression that the community is heading toward any financial problem? Why? Why not? Did the forecasting help the community to realize the potential problem?
3. What is the difference between a time series and an econometric forecast? Under what circumstances should a government use one as opposed to the other (or both) in a single study?
4. What are the advantages and disadvantages of using a single equation as opposed to a multiequation model in budget forecasting? Was the author justified in using single equation models? Why? Why not?
5. A quick review of GF forecasts for Pleasantville indicates that the city is going to encounter some financial problems in the near future. Do you agree with the strategies suggested in the case study? What other strategies would you recommend? Why?

REFERENCES

Bretschneider, S. and Gorr, W. (1987). "State and local government revenue forecasting". In S. Makridakis and W. Wheeright (eds.), *The Handbook of Forecasting: A Manager's Guide*, New York. pp. 118–134.
Forrester, J. (1991). "Multi-year forecasting and municipal budgeting." *Public Budgeting & Finance, 11 (2)*, 47–61.
Moody's Investors Service. (1997). *Selected Indicators of Municipal Performance*. New York.
Pindyck, R. S. and Rubinfeld, D. L. (1991). *Econometric Models and Economic Forecasts*. New York: McGraw-Hill.

14

Revenue Forecasting

Howard Fleeter and L. Lee Walker
Ohio State University, Columbus, Ohio, U.S.A.

The foundation of any budget process, public or private, is the forecasting of the revenue available to support the activities of the government or business for the budget period. For state governments, the task of forecasting revenues is particularly difficult because of the many independent and largely uncontrollable variables that influence the revenues realized from a particular source. Complicate the difficulty of accurate forecasting of revenues with the requirement that the budget must be balanced at the conclusion of the fiscal year[1] and you begin to realize why it is so important to understand and pay attention to both the process and outcomes of revenue forecasting.

While each of the fifty states has unique revenue forecasting processes, we will, for the purposes of this case study, focus on Ohio's process. The discussion of Ohio's revenue forecasting process and the outcomes of that process will be useful in your understanding the general nature of revenue forecasting. It will provide you with some insight into the strengths and weaknesses of the various methods used in Ohio which may be used independently or in combination to enhance any revenue forecasting effort. Ohio is typical of many states. For instance

It relies on a wide variety of revenue sources.
Its primary sources of revenue are tax collections and federal funds.
Its process includes input from private sector economists and national econometric forecasting services.
It uses estimation tools such as simulation, regression, and trend analysis models.
It uses two independent forecasts, one produced by the administration and one by the nonpartisan and independent Legislative Budget Office (LBO).
It has a monitoring and revision process that provides the governor and legislative leadership with the most accurate and reliable information available to make informed decisions regarding compliance with Ohio's balanced budget requirement.

In this chapter we describe and discuss Ohio's budget forecasting process and comment on the strengths and limitations of such a process and its outcomes. The first part of this chapter will describe the legal, economic, and political factors that define and influence Ohio's revenue forecasting process. The second part will examine the outcomes of Ohio's revenue forecasting process for the period from FY (fiscal year) 1987 through

209

FY 1993. The third section will look at the political and practical limits of revenue forecasting. The conclusion will provide a summary of good revenue forecasting practices.

OHIO'S REVENUE FORECASTING PROCESS

Legal Factors

Ohio's constitution provides that no appropriation may be made for a period longer than two years. Current law provides that the state operate in a fiscal biennium which includes two fiscal years each of which commences on July 1 and ends on June 30. The governor of Ohio is required by law to submit to the legislature a balanced budget proposal in late January of odd numbered years (except when a newly elected governor is, by law, given an extension). The constitution requires the General Assembly to "provide for raising revenue, sufficient to defray the expenses of the state, for each year, and also a sufficient sum to pay the principal and interest as they become due on the state debt."[2] This provision precludes the state from ending a fiscal year or a biennium in a deficit. The state may not borrow money except where specifically authorized by the constitution.

The law provides that if the governor determines that actual revenues and fund balances will not be sufficient to cover the anticipated fiscal year expenditures, he or she shall by executive order reduce spending in order to avoid ending the fiscal year with a deficit.

The General Assembly, consisting of a 99-member house of representatives and a 33-member senate, has the sole responsibility for authorizing state expenditure limits or appropriations. The governor, however, may eliminate a legislatively enacted spending appropriation through a line-item veto. The veto may be overridden by a three-fourths vote of both houses of the General Assembly.

Ohio's general revenue fund budget represents approximately 50% of the total (all funds) state budget. The general revenue fund portion of the budget is made up of those taxes and other revenue sources that are not designated by statute or the constitution to a specific purpose or program. For example, the general revenue fund budget does not include the revenues of the gasoline tax, which are constitutionally earmarked for highway purposes only.

The general revenue fund is supported primarily by five tax sources: (1) the personal income tax, (2) the auto sales tax, (3) the general or nonauto sales tax, (4) the corporate franchise tax, and (5) the public utility tax. These five tax sources represent about 66% of the general revenue fund, or roughly 33% of the total budget. Federal matching funds earned as a result of state spending on the medicaid and AFDC (Aid for Dependent Children) programs represent 23% of the general revenue fund and are forecast on the basis of caseload and cost of services projections, as well as the anticipated state and federal share of the projected costs of the programs. The medicaid and AFDC forecasts are jointly developed by the Department of Human Services and the Office of Budget and Management in a coordinated but separate forecasting effort that is then incorporated into both the revenue and spending aspects of the state budget. An error in these forecasts has a double effect on the budget since these forecasts play a role in the projections of both the revenue and the spending component of the budget. (Although interesting, complex, and important, the process of the medicaid and AFDC forecasts is beyond the scope of this discussion.) The remaining 11% of the general revenue fund is made up of various smaller tax sources, earnings on investments, and license and fee income.

While the state has to forecast revenues from all sources, to simplify our review of this process we will focus on the projection of revenues from the five major tax sources. Indeed, these sources are also where the state focuses most of its efforts.

Economic Factors

Ohio is the seventh largest state in terms of population.[3] Manufacturing remains the core of Ohio's economy; however, the greatest growth in employment in recent years, consistent with national trends, has been in the nonmanufacturing sector. In addition, agriculture and related businesses continue to be an important element of the Ohio economy. Ohio ranks eleventh among the states in farm crops marketed and nineteenth in livestock sales.[4]

Ohio ranks eighth among the states in the size of its general revenue fund receipts and thirty-sixth on a per capita basis. In terms of state taxes collected, Ohio again ranks eighth and is thirty-fourth on a per capita basis.[5]

Typical of the industrial midwest, economic activity in Ohio is cyclical, tracking in many instances the national economy.

Political Factors

The governor of Ohio has traditionally relied on two cabinet agencies, the Office of Budget and Management (OBM) and the Department of Taxation, to prepare the revenue estimates. Each agency has a director appointed by the governor and confirmed by the senate. The staffs of the agencies, however, are primarily civil service, professional staff who tend to have careers spanning transitions between governors and changes in politics.

Revenue forecasting is a year-round and continuous activity of these agencies. The cycle begins with a revenue forecast in the fall of even-numbered years, prior to the presentation of the governor's two-year budget proposal to the legislature enacted in January of odd-numbered years. As the new budget planning cycle begins the state is continuously monitoring the current forecast and comparing the forecast to actual revenues in the current biennium to ensure that the budget will end the fiscal year in the black, as required by the constitution.

The revenue forecast prepared in the fall of even-numbered years for the governor's budget proposal projects revenues through the remaining six months of the current biennium and for the following twenty-four-month budget period. These forecasts project revenues from six to thirty months into the future.

In addition to the executive branch forecasting activities, Ohio has an independent and nonpartisan legislative budget office (LBO), which produces a revenue forecast for the same time frame. The state legislature also has a partisan staff that works directly for the elected representatives and senators. This staff reviews the revenue forecasts and advises their employers as to the strengths and weaknesses of the forecasts.

Recent History of Legal, Economic, and Political Factors Impact

In 1981, the state created the budget stabilization fund (BSF) for the purposes of cash and budgetary management. One of the stated benefits of creating the BSF was to provide a cushion to protect state programs from drastic reductions as a result of overly optimistic revenue projections or unanticipated costs that must be absorbed by the general revenue fund. The BSF cannot be used for new programs or as an enhancement to current antici-pated revenues.

After the national recession of the early 1980s, Ohio, following the national trend, experienced a period of economic growth stretching from about 1984 through 1989. This relatively healthy economic period coupled with careful planning and good management decisions, allowed actual revenue collections above estimates to be deposited into the BSF beginning in FY 1985. Additional deposits were made in FYs 1986 through 1989.

The national economic slowdown contributed to Ohio's general revenue fund collec-tions falling below the forecasted levels commencing in FY 1990. The lower than expected revenues combined with the higher than expected spending in the human service and health care entitlement programs triggered two executive orders to reduce spending and a transfer of money from the BSF into the general revenue fund in order to avoid a FY 1991 deficit.

The July 1991–June 1993 biennium revenue forecast anticipated a no- or slow-growth economy and therefore projected low growth in the major revenue sources and increased spending in the entitlement programs. In anticipation of these double trouble factors, the FY 1992 and 1993 budgets funded most programs at a no-growth level and still planned an additional transfer from the BSF to the general revenue fund in order to balance the budget at the end of the year. This transfer would, if needed at the anticipated level, exhaust the BSF.

Even this conservative forecast proved too optimistic, however, and in December of 1991 and again in July of 1992, in the face of revenue collections continuing to fall below estimates, the exhaustion of the BSF and entitlement spending continuing to grow above projected level, the governor ordered additional spending reductions. The total 1991–1992 executive-ordered reductions below planned spending levels now totaled over $600 million. Rather than face even deeper reductions in planned spending levels, the legislature in December of 1992 enacted almost $200 million in annual revenue enhance-ments, including broadening the base of the sales tax to previously untaxed services and increased tax rates on alcohol, soft drinks, and cigarettes.[6]

Politically, the legislature and the governor promised, when the FY 1993 budget balancing bill was passed, that no additional taxes would be required to support the July 1993–June 1995 biennium budget. That promise, preceded by four years of overly optimis-tic revenue estimates, placed the executive and legislative revenue estimators in a highly sensitive position as they began the FY 1994–1995 revenue estimating process.

Ohio's Forecasting Process

Ohio's forecasting process starts with the convening of a council of economic advisors. These advisors are volunteer private sector economists who are asked by the budget director to share with the state their unique insights into the economic future of Ohio. First convened in 1983, the group represents a cross section of Ohio's manufacturing sector, utilities, insurance and financial institutions, and agricultural industry. Ranging from ten to twelve participants, the council membership has remained fairly stable over the past ten years and two governors.

The members are provided with economic forecasts from three national forecasting services (DRI, WEFA, and Blue Chip) prior to the meeting and are asked to provide to OBM, prior to the meeting, their own quarterly forecasts of eleven key economic indica-tors[7] for the next thirty-month period. The advisors share their individual forecasts based

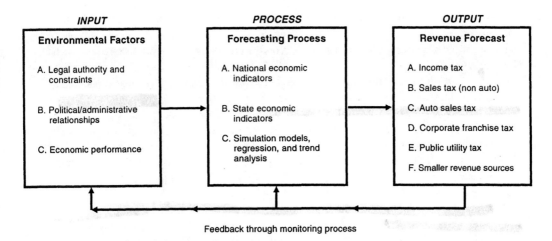

Figure 1 Revenue forecasting relationships.

on the understanding that the state will not release the individual forecasts and will publicly release only the consensus forecast developed at the council meeting. The individual forecasts, however, provide the state and the advisors with important information as to the viability of the consensus forecast. For example, if the individual forecasts are so similar that the consensus forecast is also similar to them it is considered much more likely to be accurate than a consensus forecast obtained from individual forecasts with great variation among them. The advisors' mix of optimistic and pessimistic forecasts are helpful bounds of the likely future state of the economy, hence the smaller the range among the individual forecasts the greater the confidence in the consensus forecast.

The consensus forecast has traditionally been developed in a one-day session with the economic advisors, OBM, the tax department, LBO, and key legislative leadership and governor's office staff. Governor Voinivich, Ohio's current governor, has raised the visibility of the process considerably by attending the advisor's meetings himself rather than sending key staff.

Each advisor is provided a summary sheet with all the individual advisors' forecasts and the national forecasts. This information is provided by quarter for the thirty-month period under consideration. The morning is devoted to each member explaining his or her forecast, the underlying assumptions, and the level of confidence in the forecast. In the afternoon, a consensus forecast is developed through an informal discussion among the advisors. The consensus forecast projects eleven economic indicators for the remaining six months of the current fiscal year and the upcoming twenty-four months of the new biennium, or in other words, for thirty months into the future. This two-part process allows the advisors and the state to benefit from the individual advisor's expertise in the morning discussion. The development of the consensus forecast tempers any individual advisor's bias with the input of the other advisors. The process thus provides the participants with both the individual insight of the advisors and a buffering of individual bias in the group formulation of the consensus forecast.

While the consensus forecast process focuses on annual trends, the forecast must also pinpoint turning points in economic activity. The projection of the timing of a recovery or downturn will not only affect the accuracy of the forecast but will also determine in which fiscal year or biennium the predicted change will impact the budget. It is these judgments as to exactly when a period of economic growth will turn into an economic downturn (or a downturn into a period of growth) that cause the revenue forecasts to be so volatile.[8]

The OBM and the tax department staff use the consensus forecast indicators as the starting point to forecast the revenues for the major tax sources. The personal income tax revenues are forecast using a simulation model. The simulation model is based on a sample of Ohio tax returns. The model sample is updated periodically to reflect changes in the tax laws. Based on the consensus forecast of the gross change in Ohio personal income and adjusting for deductions, credits, exemptions, and other filing changes, the tax liability is projected for each return in the sample. The sample is then extrapolated to simulate the entire population and generate an estimate.

The sales tax, both auto and nonauto, and the corporate franchise tax are projected using regression analysis. The public utilities tax and most smaller tax sources are projected using a trend analysis assuming in each case that historical growth rates and patterns will continue.

These forecasts produce baseline estimates. The baseline estimates project revenues based on current law and tax rates. Proposed changes in the tax laws are shown as adjustments (plus or minus) to the baseline estimates.

The staff's estimates typically project a range of high, medium, and low anticipated revenues by source. These estimates are reviewed by the budget director and the tax commissioner prior to being shared with the governor. The final estimates, which include the governor's input and a judgment as to where in the forecasted range to peg the anticipated revenues by source, are shared with the legislature and the general public in January concurrently with the release of the governor's biennial budget proposal.

Meanwhile, LBO has been simultaneously developing an independent revenue estimate based on the same consensus forecast. The LBO estimates are released shortly after the governor's budget. The LBO estimates and the executive estimates are presented in similar formats to allow easy identification of similarities and differences. The house, at its discretion, may use as a basis for its budget decisions the executive revenue estimate or the LBO revenue estimate, or pick and choose elements of both of the estimates. The senate has the same option during its budget deliberations.

By tradition, the executive and LBO revenue estimates are not revised during the house and senate budget deliberations. The economic advisors are reconvened in the spring for a final revision of the economic forecast. This forecast and the revised executive and LBO revenue estimates are shared with the joint house–senate conference committee in June. This revision allows the governor and legislative leadership the benefit of the most up-to-date estimates of future revenues. The conference committee may use as a basis for its budget decisions either the revised executive or the revised LBO, or pick and choose elements of both revised revenue estimates. The June revision process provides the conference committee with an opportunity to make any necessary spending and/or revenue adjustments prior to recommending a final budget bill to the two houses of the General Assembly and the governor for approval.

Both OBM and LBO continually monitor the performance of actual revenue sources and compare the actual performance to the estimates on a monthly basis (see Figure 2). The monthly monitoring process is useful over time to understand the validity of the estimates and most important, to provide the governor and the legislative leadership with early warning indicators of any significant variations between actual and estimated reve-

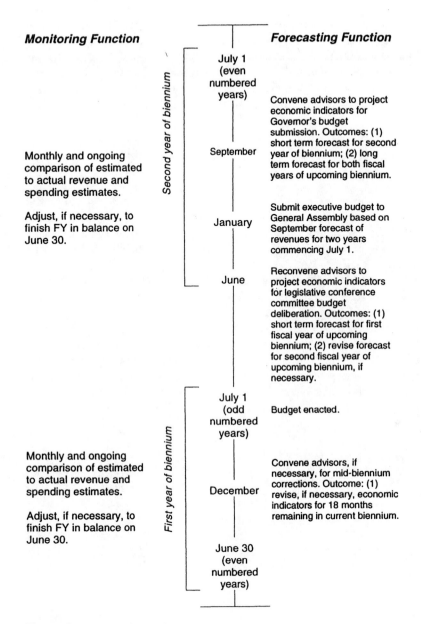

Figure 2 Revenue forecasting process.

nues so that adjustments can be formulated, and if necessary, implemented to ensure compliance with the no-deficit-spending provisions of the constitution. Each monthly estimate, however, needs to be taken into consideration with the prior and the next month's estimates to account for minor timing variations (e.g., a deposit on the first of the month rather than the last day of the prior month).

Traditionally, the economic advisors are brought back together in a midbiennium review of the estimates in the winter of the first year of the biennium. At that time, a new forecast and subsequently new estimates are developed, if necessary. The governor and legislative leadership confer as to the need for adjustments to bring the budget into conformance with the new estimates. The ultimate responsibility to ensure that the budget is in balance at the close of the fiscal year, however, is the governor's. If spending is outpacing actual revenues and fund balances and the legislature is not inclined to raise additional revenues the governor must order and implement spending reductions.

OHIO'S FORECAST OUTCOMES (1987–1993)

A good forecast should be accurate and unbiased. While the vagaries of the economy and individual behavior preclude 100% accuracy, a useful, unbiased forecast should have equal likelihood of erring by overestimation as by underestimation. Table 1 summarizes the accuracy of forecasting general revenue fund tax revenues in the state of Ohio over the period encompassing FYs 1987–1993.[9]

While in dollar terms the errors are as high as $303 million for the short forecast and $483 million for the long forecast (both shortfalls), in percentage terms the forecasting process has been rather accurate in Ohio over this time frame. Comparison of the accuracy of the long and short forecasts reveals that the short forecast is more accurate in four of the six cases. This is consistent with conventional wisdom, which suggests that longer-range forecasts will be less accurate because of greater uncertainty in economic conditions. It is also apparent that revenues were underestimated in the first three years of the period and overestimated in the last three years. Overall, the mean percentage error over the time frame is near zero for both the long and short forecasts. The actual and forecast revenues

Table 1   Accuracy of Ohio General Revenue Fund Tax Revenues

Fiscal year	Actual revenues (millions)	Short forecast (millions)	Error (%)	Long forecast (millions)	Error (%)
1987	$7549	$7256	3.9	$7636	−1.2
1988	$8024	$7835	2.4	$7758	3.3
1989	$8697	$8432	3.1	$8214	5.6
1990	$9048	$9146	−1.1	$9031	0.2
1991	$9053	$9116	−0.7	$9548	−5.5
1992	$9422	$9622	−2.1	$9673	−2.7
Mean percentage error (1987–1992)			0.9		−0.1
Absolute value mean percentage error			2.2		3.1

Note: Percentage error is computed $\dfrac{\text{actual} - \text{forecast}}{\text{actual}} \times 100$

Mean percentage error averages the positive and negative errors of the six years. This averaging provides some insight as to whether or not the forecasts have tended to err in one direction or the other over time. Mean absolute value percentage error averages the absolute value of the errors, regardless of the direction of the error. This approach provides a measure of the average magnitude of the errors. Because the mean percentage error procedure offsets negative and positive errors, these values will always be equal or less than the mean absolute percent errors.

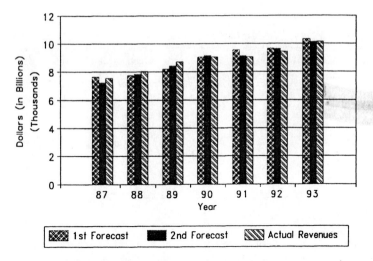

Figure 3 Total tax revenues (1987–1993).

are depicted in Figure 3. (In Figure 3 forecast 1 refers to the long forecast and forecast 2 refers to the short forecast).

Examination of the five major tax sources provides further insight regarding the accuracy of revenue forecasting in Ohio. Figure 4 depicts the distribution of tax revenues by source over the period 1987–1993. The general (nonauto) sales tax and the personal income tax are shown to be the largest sources of revenue as well as the most rapidly increasing sources. The corporate franchise tax exhibits a slight increase in the middle of the period, while taken as a group the public utility, the auto sales, and all other taxes are relatively flat over the time frame.

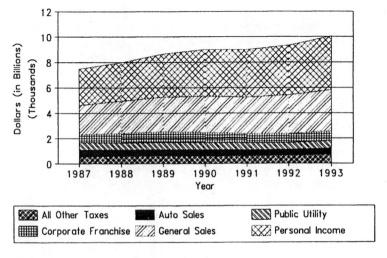

Figure 4 Actual tax revenues by source.

Table 2 Accuracy of Tax Revenues by Source (1987–1992)

Revenue source	Percentage of tax revenues	Short forecast		Long forecast	
		Mean absolute error (%)	Mean error (%)	Mean absolute error (%)	Mean error (%)
Personal income	39.8%	3.8%	2.2%	5.2%	2.4%
Nonauto sales	31.7%	2.0%	1.5%	4.5%	3.5%
Corporate franchise	9.1%	5.7%	−3.9%	8.6%	−6.4%
Public utility	6.6%	2.6%	−1.0%	14.8%	−12.3%
Auto sales	6.1%	3.2%	−2.0%	10.5%	−5.9%
All other taxes	6.8%	2.5%	2.2%	11.8%	−2.0%
Total taxes	100%				

Table 2 examines the accuracy of forecasts of each of the five major tax revenue sources in Ohio. A number of key findings are evident when the tax sources are disaggregated. First, short-term forecasts are clearly more accurate than long-term forecasts for each of the revenue sources examined. Second accuracy of long-term forecasts for the two largest revenue sources, personal income taxes and nonauto sales taxes, are more accurate in percentage terms than are the forecasts for the other revenue sources. This is because these taxes are broad-based, providing the forecasting advantage of sheer size with the smoothing of behavior over a large number of taxpayers. These tax sources are thus less susceptible to distortions caused by the behavior of a small number of taxpayers. Third the corporate franchise tax is shown to be the most difficult tax to predict in the short term. This is most likely attributable to the manipulation of corporate profits through discretionary spending and accounting techniques. Finally, forecast errors in individual revenue sources tend to offset one another. Over the time period examined here income and nonauto sales taxes were underestimated while the other smaller revenue sources were overestimated.

Complete annual data on revenues and estimates for each tax source are provided in Table 3, where forecast 1 refers to the long forecast and forecast 2 refers to the short forecast. The data clearly reveal steady increases in personal income tax revenues and in general (nonauto) sales tax revenues, both of which tracked well with the forecast revenues. The auto sales tax exhibits declining revenues, which were not predicted by the long forecast, while the corporate franchise tax is noticeably volatile in both actual and projected revenue. Utility taxes were subject to a three-year period of substantial overestimation in the long-term forecast. As utility revenues are forecast using trend analysis, these errors are most likely attributable to extrapolations deriving from particularly extreme weather in 1985. The errors were corrected in the short forecast. Finally, the category of all other taxes was subject to long-term forecast overestimates in excess of $100 million dollars in both 1990 and 1991. These errors are derived almost entirely from excessive estimates of cigarette tax revenues based on the expectation of a cigarette tax increase that never took place. Again, the short forecasts account for this circumstance.

THE POLITICAL AND PRACTICAL LIMITS OF REVENUE FORECASTING

Having analyzed the degree of precision with which Ohio has forecast general revenue fund tax payments it is fruitful to explore the sources of errors and limits on forecasting

Table 3 Predicted and Actual GRF Tax Revenues by Category (Fiscal Years 1986–1995)

	Year	GSALES	ASALES	PINCOME	CORPFRN	Utility	ALLOTHR	TOTLREVS
Forecast 1	1986	2127.8	481.1	2765.5	664.1	730.0	450.8	7219.3
Forecast 2	1986	NA						
Actual	1986	2136.2	555.8	2587.1	669.3	634.3	483.4	7066.1
Forecast 1	1987	2277.4	501.8	2994.6	627.7	785.0	449.5	7636.0
Forecast 2	1987	2224.3	579.0	2683.5	676.8	604.3	488.2	7256.1
Actual	1987	2286.8	582.1	2900.8	664.8	605.9	508.1	7548.5
Forecast 1	1988	2303.6	587.3	2783.5	868.3	673.3	541.5	7757.5
Forecast 2	1988	2406.7	596.9	2858.9	845.9	574.1	552.5	7835.0
Actual	1988	2553.3	531.8	3015.0	797.7	552.2	573.8	8023.8
Forecast 1	1989	2434.8	616.0	2995.8	921.7	692.4	553.0	8213.7
Forecast 2	1989	2683.6	530.0	3220.1	850.0	561.3	587.0	8432.0
Actual	1989	2735.8	524.6	3394.4	892.0	561.9	589.9	8698.6
Forecast 1	1990	2798.5	537.3	3527.1	890.4	560.0	717.5	9030.8
Forecast 2	1990	2872.5	521.0	3669.6	929.9	560.5	592.5	9146.0
Actual	1990	2875.6	527.6	3660.2	812.5	585.1	587.2	9048.2
Forecast 1	1991	2950.4	545.1	3742.2	946.8	559.5	713.9	9547.9
Forecast 2	1991	2905.0	475.0	3805.0	765.0	576.8	589.1	9115.9
Actual	1991	2895.7	483.3	3728.3	769.0	578.2	598.4	9052.9
Forecast 1	1992	3098.1	526.7	4100.2	753.7	587.5	606.4	9672.6
Forecast 2	1992	3092.5	505.8	4006.6	811.1	588.1	617.7	9621.8
Actual	1992	3060.8	493.9	3911.2	761.6	550.2	644.1	9421.8
Forecast 1	1993	3271.0	563.7	4433.9	830.2	595.1	623.9	10317.8
Forecast 2	1993	3305.6	513.6	4176.5	825.9	613.1	682.3	10135.6
Actual	1993	3258.1	515.6	4226.6	801.4	615.3	707.3	10124.3
Forecast 1	1994	3591.3	557.7	4518.1	928.7	627.3	728.8	11018.9
Forecast 2	1994	NA						
Actual	1994	NA						
Forecast 1	1995	3818.3	585.1	4839.4	983.9	638.4	726.6	11659.8
Forecast 2	1995	NA						
Actual	1995	NA						

accuracy with which any forecaster must grapple. Vasche and Williams identify five principle sources of error in state revenue forecasts.[10] Errors in national and state forecasts of economic conditions, in model specification of revenue sources, revisions in data, statistical error margins, and errors in estimated timing of payments will all result in errors in forecast revenues.

Link Between Economic Indicators and Forecasting Outcomes

Much attention has been given to the development of a consensus forecast of economic indicators and to the overall accuracy of the resulting revenue forecasts, but little has been done to analyze the relation between indicator forecast accuracy and revenue forecast

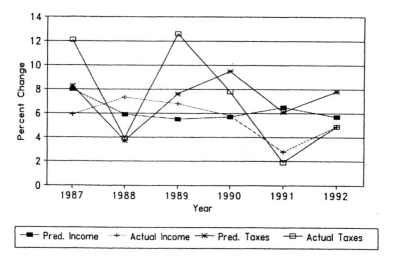

Figure 5 Percentage growth personal income and tax revenues (1987–1992).

accuracy. Figures 5–7 depict forecasts and outcomes of the three largest revenue sources along with predictions and outcomes of key economic indicators pertinent to each revenue source. Tax revenue predictions and outcomes have been converted to percentage growth terms to provide comparability with the economic indicators.[11] It is important to note that the economic indicators are tabulated on a calendar year basis while the revenue forecasts occur over a fiscal year time frame. A complete listing of predicted and actual economic indicator values is provided in Table 4.

Figure 5, which compares personal income tax revenues with growth in Ohio personal income reveals that variation in both forecasts and outcomes of personal income

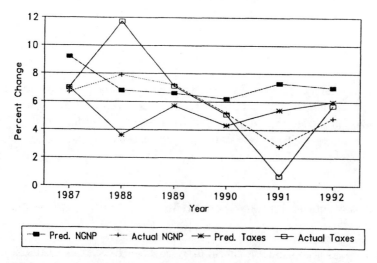

Figure 6 Percentage growth sales tax revenue vs. nominal GNP (1987–1992).

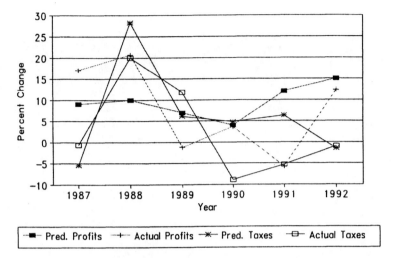

Figure 7 Percentage growth in corporate franchise taxes and profits (1987–1992).

growth is much less than the variability in income tax revenues. Tax revenue growth fluctuates from 2–12%, while actual income growth is in the range of 4.5–7% in all but one year. This is an example of how changes in the tax code (seven in the last seven years) can weaken the relationship between economic indicators and tax revenues. This also underscores the importance of adjusting the simulation model used to predict income tax revenues to reflect changes in both the state and federal tax codes.[12]

Figure 6, which compares nonauto sales tax revenues with growth in nominal GDP (national), reveals quite a different pattern, which predictions and outcomes of the indicator and the revenue source track one another rather closely.[13] Predictions of nominal GDP and sales tax revenues are more closely aligned with each other than with the actual outcomes of GDP and tax revenue growth. The same is true of the actual outcomes. The regression-based model of forecasting appears to work rather well in this case.

Figure 7, comparing corporate franchise tax revenues and corporate profits, reveals yet a third pattern. In this case, forecasts of each variable show less fluctuation than do the actual outcomes. Actual corporate profits vary much more widely than do the forecasts, as do actual corporate franchise taxes in relation to estimates. This pattern is likely due to the inherent difficulties in forecasting profits (and hence tax revenues), which are highly dependent on discretionary decisions by corporations over yearly profit levels.

As the simulation and regression models directly use particular economic indicators in their forecasting process, distinguishing the extent to which errors in indicators as opposed to errors in forecasting models contribute to errors in revenues forecast would be an interesting enterprise. One possibility would be to plug actual values of economic indicators into the forecasting models and see how accurate the resultant revenue forecasts are. By controlling for one source of error, this would allow assessment regarding how much statistical and modeling error remains after the model inputs have been determined. This process, which requires access to OBM and LBO personnel and computer accounts, was beyond the scope of this study.

Table 4 Predicted and Actual Economic Indicators (Calendar Years 1986–1995)

	Year	RGDP	NGDP	USPINC	OHPINC	CPI	GNPDL	CPROFIT	USCARS	Housing	USUNEMPL	OHUNEMPL
Forecast 1	1986	2.2	7.3	7.4	6.7	5.0	5.0	−5.0	10.2	1.50	7.6	9.6
Forecast 2	1986	2.6	5.4	5.4	4.5	2.0	2.1	8.5	11.1	1.88	7.0	8.3
Actual	1986	2.7	5.4	6.0	4.8	1.9	2.7	5.3	11.4	1.81	7.0	8.1
Forecast 1	1987	4.0	9.2	8.5	8.0	5.0	5.0	9.0	10.5	1.70	7.3	9.4
Forecast 2	1987	2.1	5.9	5.8	4.9	3.3	3.1	19.7	10.7	1.75	6.9	8.1
Actual	1987	3.4	6.7	6.8	5.9	3.6	3.3	17.1	10.3	1.63	6.2	7.0
Forecast 1	1988	3.2	6.8	6.8	5.9	3.5	3.5	10.0	11.1	1.78	6.7	7.8
Forecast 2	1988	3.8	7.2	7.2	6.5	4.1	3.3	8.5	10.5	1.47	5.5	6.2
Actual	1988	3.9	7.9	7.2	7.3	3.9	4.1	20.7	10.6	1.49	5.5	6.0
Forecast 1	1989	2.7	6.6	6.6	5.5	3.8	3.8	7.0	10.7	1.70	6.7	7.7
Forecast 2	1989	2.5	6.7	7.0	6.4	4.6	4.1	5.0	10.0	1.40	5.7	6.5
Actual	1989	2.5	7.2	7.5	6.8	4.8	4.6	−1.3	9.9	1.38	5.3	5.6
Forecast 1	1990	1.8	6.2	6.5	5.7	4.9	4.3	4.0	9.8	1.35	6.0	6.9
Forecast 2	1990	0.9	5.1	5.9	5.0	5.4	4.2	−2.5	9.3	1.20	5.5	5.7
Actual	1990	0.8	5.2	6.5	5.8	5.4	4.3	3.6	9.5	1.21	5.5	5.7
Forecast 1	1991	3.0	7.3	7.3	6.5	4.5	4.2	12.0	10.5	1.50	5.6	6.3
Forecast 2	1991	−0.5	3.2	4.0	3.2	4.0	3.7	6.0	8.7	1.10	6.7	6.8
Actual	1991	−1.2	2.8	3.5	2.8	4.2	4.0	−5.8	8.4	1.02	6.8	6.5
Forecast 1	1992	3.5	7.0	6.5	5.7	3.6	3.5	15.0	9.5	1.30	6.4	6.4
Forecast 2	1992	1.8	4.4	4.5	4.0	3.0	2.6	15.0	8.4	1.20	7.5	7.2
Actual	1992	2.1	4.8	4.8	4.9	3.0	2.6	12.3	8.4	1.21	7.4	7.2
Forecast 1	1993	2.7	6.5	6.0	5.5	4.0	3.8	5.0	9.3	1.40	5.9	5.9
Forecast 2	1993	2.5	5.2	4.9	4.5	2.8	2.6	16.0	9.0	1.30	7.2	7.0
Actual	1993	2.9	5.5	4.7	4.1	12.0	2.6	2.9	8.7	1.30	6.8	6.5
Forecast 1	1994	2.9	5.9	5.5	5.0	3.5	2.9	9.0	9.5	1.35	6.8	6.4
Forecast 2	1994	NA										
Actual	1994	NA										
Forecast 1	1995	2.8	6.0	6.0	5.5	3.5	3.1	5.0	9.7	1.35	6.5	6.2
Forecast 2	1995	NA										
Actual	1995	NA										

SUMMARY AND CONCLUSION

A forecast cannot be 100% precise. Ohio's process, however, suggests that there are a number of practices that can acknowledge the political environment in which the process exists and enhance the credibility and usefulness of the revenue forecasting outcomes. A good forecast is one upon which decision makers are comfortable relying to make political and policy judgments involving resource allocation decisions for the budget period.

In his 1990 article, Shkurti[14] provides a list of criteria that he concludes should be incorporated in a revenue forecasting process to enhance the credibility of the process and guard against the common pitfalls of political and/or personal bias creeping into the forecast. Ohio has incorporated many of these criteria into its revenue forecasting process. They include the following.

Economic Assumptions

Ohio's considers the economic council's assumptions regarding Ohio's economy in light of national forecasts. If the Ohio forecast is not consistent with the national forecasts a plausible state or regional explanation is sought. Careful attention is paid to the forecasting of turning points in the business cycle.

The council members' expertise is used in areas in which their expertise is appropriate. Their personal biases are minimized through the development of a consensus forecast.

Estimating Techniques

Ohio's forecasting models are appropriate and objective without being unnecessarily complicated.

The variables used in the models are consistent with the assumptions about the state and national economies.

The historical data are reviewed and adjusted by the state's professional staff to remove one-time variations.

Independent alternative forecasts are provided by LBO in a form that facilitates comparison.

Monitoring, Evaluation, and Revision

Ohio has a mechanism established to report actual versus forecast revenues on a monthly basis and an established revision procedure.

Presentation

In Ohio, the presentation of the executive and LBO revenue estimates to the legislature explains the advisory council's economic assumptions and the staff-generated individual revenue source estimates; describes the probable range of error for each estimate; and highlights the differences and relative risks of both the executive and LBO forecast.

Other

The use of the economic council to generate economic indicators and the reliance on professional state staff and statistical models to generate the revenue estimates helps to keep the forecast process and outcomes free of inappropriate political influence and manipulation by top management and public officials.

When staff, management, or public officials make judgment calls they are clearly identified and described.

Assumptions about ending balances are explicit, including both the general revenue fund balance and the balance, if any, in the BSF.

The one element identified in the Shkurti article that Ohio has not yet developed is a process to evaluate past forecasts to determine why errors, if any, occurred and identify possible mechanisms for fine tuning the process based on these understandings.

Every revenue forecasting process has to be designed to meet the individual needs and work within the resources available for the entity using the process. In this chapter, we have looked at a variety of elements of the process used in Ohio and evaluated the outcomes of that process. The lessons learned from the review of Ohio's process will be useful in establishing, fine tuning, or evaluating any public revenue forecasting process with an eye toward producing acceptable outcomes.

REVIEW QUESTIONS

1. Using the information in Table 3, analyze, by graphing, the historical data for actual auto sales tax revenues. Is this source of revenue a good candidate for trend analysis? Why or why not? What economic indicators would be useful in predicting the auto sales tax revenues?
2. What methods would you suggest Ohio implement to evaluate ex post the accuracy of its revenue estimating process? Discuss the strengths and weaknesses of the methods you have suggested.
3. Beginning in FY 1985, the state deposited revenues above estimates into the BSF. By FY 1987, the BSF had a positive balance of $262.4 million or 2.7% of the GRF. Additional deposits were made in FY 1988 and FY 1990, bringing the BSF balance to $364.4 million or 3.15% of the GRF. Withdrawals from the fund in FYs 1991 and 1992 reduced the BSF balance to 0. What impact, if any, would the data suggest the BSF had on the state's revenue forecasts?
4. Figure 6 depicts the relationship between prediction and outcomes of nominal GNP growth and growth in the nonauto sales tax. Many economists posit a constant "marginal propensity to consume" a fraction of personal income. How do the prediction and outcome of personal income growth over the period 1987–1992 act in relationship to the nonauto sales tax revenue pattern?

NOTES

1. Vermont is the only state without a balanced budget requirement. National Conference of State Legislatures (1988). *Legislative Budget Procedures in the 50 States.* (Denver: NCSI, pp. 19–20.

2. Ohio Constitution. Article XII, Section 4.

3. *Statistical Abstracts of the United States.* U.S. Bureau of the Census (1990).

4. *Statistical Abstracts of the United States.* U.S. Bureau of the Census. (1990).

5. *Governmental Finances in 1988–1989.* (U.S. Bureau of the Census.)

6. The sales tax on soft drinks is being tested through a court challenge on the premise that the Ohio sales tax exempts taxation of retail sales of food and that soft drinks are a food.

7. The eleven indicators forecast are real GDP, nominal GDP, U.S. personal income growth, Ohio personal income growth, CPI, GDP price deflator (1982 = 100). U.S. corporate profits before taxes, total U.S. car sales U.S. housing starts. U.S. unemployment, and Ohio unemployment. Prior to 1992, GNP was used rather than GDP. Forecasts and actual outcomes of these variables for calendar year 1987–1995 are provided in Table 4.

8. Shkurti, W.A. "User's guide to state revenue forecasting." *Public Budgeting and Finance*, Spring 1990, 89.

9. For an earlier look at Ohio's forecasting-process see: Shkurti, W. 1989. The politics of state revenue forecasting in Ohio, 1984–1987: A case study and research implications. *International Journal of Forecasting*, 5, 361–371.

10. Vascha J. D. and Williams B. Spring 1987 Optional government budgeting contingency reserve funds. *Public Budgeting and Finance*: 66–82.

11. The long forecast was used because these predictions are made at the same time for each year of a biennium. Percentage growth calculations used the short forecast of the preceding year as the basis for the percentage change forecast in the first year of a biennium, and computed the percentage change between the first and second year for the second year of a biennium.

12. Changes in the federal tax code impact Ohio income tax revenues because federaly adjusted gross income is the basis of the Ohio income tax.

13. Nominal rather than real GDP was selected here because general sales tax revenues are dependent on the gross value of goods purchased rather than on the inflation-adjusted value.

14. Shkurti, W. (spring 1990). A user's guide to state revenue forcasting. *Public Budgeting and finance: 92–93.*

15

Parties, Professionalism, and Changing Budget Battles in New York (1950–1997)

Jeffrey M. Stonecash
Syracuse University, Syracuse, New York, U.S.A.

"The enduring issues of politics revolve around taxes and spending" (Key, 1949: 309). Lower-income and liberal groups want more programs and need more tax revenue to pay for the programs. Conservatives want fewer programs and lower taxes. There are also significant differences of opinion about who should pay taxes. Liberals tend to favor progressive tax systems, while conservatives are far more willing to tolerate regressive ones.

Political parties are often seen as central to debates over the role state governments should play. As broad aggregations of differing sets of interests parties have the potential to serve as the primary vehicles for representing differing views on taxation and spending issues. Democrats may serve as advocates for lower-income interests—more programs and taxes to pay for them—and Republicans as advocates of the more affluent—less government and lower taxes. This chapter studies and analyzes how budget battles are fought along these lines of arguments, especially as they relate to the budget of the state of New York.

PARTIES AND BUDGET DEBATES

Contrary to what may seem natural, the actual record of party behavior is often mixed with regard to the expectations mentioned above. Sometimes parties do present party platforms that differ in ways we might expect—Democrats supporting more liberal positions and Republicans supporting more conservative positions (Paddock, 1992)—but other times parties control institutions and do not advocate the goals we might expect. Democrats often control a legislative house and are not advocates of more social programs or tax increases. Republican control of a legislative house often is not associated with proposals for program cuts and tax decreases.* There are even times when parties directly contradict

---

* In New York during the 1980s Republicans controlled the senate and regularly supported the status quo on taxes.

our expectations. During the early 1960s Republicans in New York and other states enacted tax increases. During the mid-1980s and the 1990s Democrats advocated tax cuts. When parties are in the minority there is often equally puzzling behavior. We sometimes witness parties in the minority opposing majority party positions, such as tax increases supported by Republicans, even though it would seem the majority position would help the constituents of the minority party. In these cases it appears the minority party is seeking just to find a way to criticize the majority party.*

The studies of actual policy enactments by parties are also mixed. Some studies indicate that Democrats do enact increases in taxes and do support more funding for welfare and education (Jennings, 1979; Brown, 1995). In many states, however, Democratic or Republican control has had no systematic impact on tax or welfare expenditure levels (Dye, 1984). Hansen's findings about state tax increases during the Great Depression illustrate the puzzle that emerges from much of this research (1983). Most (70%) tax increases took place when Democrats held power, but 30% took place when Republicans held power, and many instances of Democratic control did not result in changes in taxes.

These examples suggest that Democrats and Republicans cannot be presumed to consistently adopt the policy positions we might expect. Parties often seem to be just trying to win elections (without any connection to substance), and not winning elections to do anything substantive (Schlesinger, 1985). While we might expect Democrats and Republicans to help create a continuing dialogue about how much government should do and who should bear the burden, their role in creating this debate seems erratic at best.

While there are reasons to be puzzled by the role of parties, much of our puzzlement may be a product of our expectations. Our expectations about parties regularly ignore context. Most of our state-level studies presume that parties are ideological and mechanical pursuers of unvarying policy goals. Democrats are expected to raise taxes and spending, regardless of context, and Republicans are expected to lower spending and taxes, regardless of context. These presumptions about parties and the role of context are questionable (Sundquist, 1983: 327). If we are to understand party behavior we must begin with the party situation and the context. These matters must be examined and not assumed.

This study examines the role parties play in state budget debates about spending and taxes from 1950–1997 in New York. The concern is with the positions taken by gubernatorial and legislative "parties" on issues of spending and taxes. The context of parties has changed considerably over that time. The concerns here are to identify those contextual conditions that affect party behavior, consider how they might have affected party behavior in New York, and assess how parties have responded.

PARTIES AND POLITICAL CONTEXT

Parties cannot just be presumed to be collections of mechanical ideologues who announce policies different from the opposing party. We often presume that the collection of elected

---

* New York legislative parties, which are the primary concern of this analysis, illustrate this. We generally presume that Democrats will be advocates for lower-income interests and want more tax revenue for programs, yet during the 1950s. The Democrats, the minority party in each house of the legislature, often criticized the slightest suggestion of a tax increase by Republicans, who bore the responsibility to pass a budget. Such behavior suggests that parties, particularly when they are in the minority, react to majority party positions in terms of the political advantage that may result from opposition (the possibility of looking good by opposing taxes) rather than emphasize only the needs of their constituents.

politicians who constitute the "Democratic party" represent very different constituencies from those elected officials who constitute the "Republican party," but it is often the case that the general electoral bases of the parties do not differ significantly (Erikson, et al., 1993: 40; Gimpel, 1996), and class and race, for example, may not have much effect on which party wins seats (Stonecash, 1987–1988; Stonecash, 1997c). Even within a party the gubernatorial and legislative wings of the party may have very different electoral bases (Stonecash, 1992). If parties are to adopt differing positions, an essential condition is that they represent different constituencies. If politicians represent differing constituents and desire to be re-elected [which has increasingly become the case (Ray, 1976; Jewell, 1988; Stonecash, 1993)], then differing policy concerns are likely to be expressed.

Politicians also interact with their context. They may represent different constituencies and have differing convictions, but their desire to be re-elected leads them to pay attention to the political climate.* Politicians monitor and react to political context and adjust their positions as the climate changes. The interest here is in the long-term changes in context that can affect the goals politicians pursue. Changes may occur in the general mood of the electorate and in the resources politicians have to assist them in formulating their goals.

Changes in "political climates" are continual in American politics. It is widely argued that the 1950s were a time in which government was not expected to widely intervene in society. In contrast, the 1960s, were a time in which expectations about the possible benefits of government action increased. Sometime during the 1970s this optimism and support eroded. Since then decline for government activism has declined (Edsall and Edsall, 1991). Another crucial contextual condition involves the economy. If the state economy ceases to grow, then state revenue continues to diminish. If state taxes and spending are seen as a hindrance to growth, then politicians may be less inclined to advocate high levels of government taxing and spending.

If there are shifts in political moods and in the condition of the state economy, these shifts should affect the positions parties adopt. When public support for government is increasing, Democrats can be expected to be advocates for spending and tax increases. When that support declines, however, and Democrats sense there is less support for these positions, Democrats may well shift to trying to restrain cuts. Likewise, when public support for government is increasing, Republicans may feel comfortable with modest increases in spending and taxes, but when that support declines they can be expected to be much stronger advocates of cuts.

Finally, the ability of a party to formulate and argue for policy positions is affected by the staff available to legislators. The greater staff levels are, the greater the capability of legislators to translate their general concerns into specific positions. Staff resources do not create goals, but they do facilitate the pursuit of the partisan goals (Thompson, 1986–1987). A legislative party with staff can create its own revenue and spending estimates. It can formulate its own tax proposals for changes in tax laws.

The New York Situation

All these factors are relevant for New York. Party bases differ in the state, but there have been significant shifts in the electoral bases of the gubernatorial and legislative wings of

---

* This is not to argue that politicians are without principle and simply change their positions as the political winds shift, as Mayhew suggests (1974); rather, the argument is that liberals shade to the middle when the political mood drifts conservative and conservatives shade to the middle when the political mood drifts liberal.

the parties. The national changes in political climate have also affected New York, and perhaps have been accentuated by the long-term economic decline in the state. The ability of the parties to formulate specific spending and tax proposals has also been significantly affected by the emergence of a large legislative staff that can thoroughly review gubernatorial budgets, formulate economic forecasts, and prepare specific tax and spending proposals.

Parties

In many ways the electoral bases of the parties have been stable and different. There is no poll data over time to indicate party bases, but it is possible to define the party bases using geographical groupings, which coincide with demographic differences. Using that approach, there are some consistent differences between the parties. The legislative parties indicate some of the continuities. The senate has been held for every year except 1966–1967 by the Republican party. The party wins the bulk of its seats in suburban and rural/small town areas outside New York City. There is concern for New York City, however, because the party has generally had five to six of its members from New York City (Stonecash, 1994a) and these seats provide the party with a majority. The party is conservative, but with some moderate leanings because of the New York City seats and because some suburban Republicans are not strong conservatives.

The assembly Democrats, on the other hand, have experienced two significantly different eras. Their situation was relatively stable within each era. Prior to 1974 the party was generally in the minority (except 1966–1969). The party was composed largely of New York City Democrats, most of whom were liberal. The 1974 election gave Democrats the majority, which they have held since then. The most important change has been the expansion of the party's base since 1975. There has been a significant increase in the proportion of seats within the party from outside New York City. The crucial matter is that the party became the majority party only because of its seats outside New York City. The party had to respect the views of its new, less liberal members, if it was to remain in the majority. The party base shifted from being primarily New York City-based to a statewide urban party with several suburban legislators. That broader composition changed the party from primarily a liberal, urban, New York City party to a more moderate party. The party is more liberal than senate Republicans, but comprises liberals, moderates, and even a few conservatives.

The gubernatorial wings of the parties have also experienced change. Until 1994, Republican governors were able to win elections only by doing well in New York City (Stonecash, 1989). This led Republican candidates to be largely moderate. Nelson Rockefeller, a Republican governor who generally had a Republican legislature, was often an advocate of social programs, and depended on New York City for votes more than his legislative party. The situation of Republican governors changed with the 1994 election, when Republican George Pataki was able to win with less than 30% of the vote in New York City. His electoral base was primarily in upstate and suburban areas around New York City. He no longer had a heavy dependence on New York City, and had less need to focus on improving his voting percentage in New York City (Stonecash, 1997b).

Democrats faced a different but more stable situation. New York City is heavily Democratic, but even with 40% of the state's population, it does not provide enough votes to elect a Democrat. Democrats have always had to win upstate urban areas and do reasonably well in the suburbs around New York City to win. That political situation has been stable over time. This dependence on areas outside New York City has moderated the stances taken by Democratic governors.

Expectations

These party bases and the changes in them should produce some very specific differences in behavior. Republicans in the legislature should be more conservative than Democrats. Republicans are likely to be more interested in restraining taxes, and in school aid, given their suburban base, and less interested in social programs. Democrats, while more likely to be supportive of social programs and taxes, are likely to be more moderate after the 1970s because of their reliance on legislators outside New York City. Republican and Democratic governors should also be expected to differ, but with limited differences because each party has had to do well in areas outside their primary base to win. The exception is the Republican governor George Pataki, who won with very little support in New York City.

Political Climate and Economic Change

New York experienced essentially the same shifts in political climate that the rest of the country experienced, except that economic decline may have accelerated the shift. As with the rest of the country, there were increased expectations that government should be more active during the 1960s (Connery and Benjamin, 1979). The decline in support for government, spending, and taxes was accentuated in New York by the fiscal crisis in the mid-1970s of the state and New York City. Both levels had expenditure levels above revenues for several years, and were finally unable to finance the continuation of these practices (McClelland and Magdovitz, 1981: 61–129). The state was also losing jobs (Alba and Trent, 1986), and state taxes were well above the national average (Stonecash, 1994c). Along with the long-term decline of economic growth in the state, there were also several recessions, which prompted questions of whether or not the state should cut spending and growth to cope with the situation (Stonecash, 1994d). This combination of conditions resulted in a shift from government doing more to trying to find a way to lower expenditures and taxes (Dwyre, et al., 1994).

PARTY AND SPENDING PROPOSALS

Each budget cycle requires spending and tax decisions. The governor is constitutionally obligated to make a budget proposal in late January, and the legislative parties react to that proposal. The concern here is with the initial and public positions taken by governors. The initial position of governors may be intended only as an initial bargaining position, and may not reflect what is really desired. The real goal of the parties may be revealed in the intense negotiations that take place when the budget is finally passed. The concern here, however, is with the public positions that governors present to the public prior to the final bargaining. The initial public positions taken by party leaders receive extensive media coverage and broadly define party images. Even if the final bargaining positions were of interest, they are traditionally not publicly revealed in New York during the last stages of the relatively private negotiations. It is also not possible to discern "real" positions from outcomes, because it is difficult to know what specific concessions were made by the governor and the legislative leaders during the final stages of negotiations.

Table 1 presents an overview of budget proposals by governors since 1950. The results are presented by party and then by era. For each year the budget proposed during that year (for the upcoming fiscal year) is compared to the budget for the prior year. For example, in January and February of 1965 the governor proposed a budget for the

Table 1 Governor's Budget Proposals, by Party (1950–1997) and by Era

Governor's proposal	Republicans	Democrats
Number of proposals	24	23
Average percentage increase (all years)	8.4	7.3
1950–1974 (10.3 avg.)	9.5	11.7
1975–1995 (5.6 avg.)	.9	6.3
Proposals	N = 24	n = 23
1950–1974 (n = 25)	n = 21	n = 4
Reductions (4%)	4.8	0
0–5% increase (20%)	23.8	0
5.1% plus increase (76%)	71.4	100.0
1975–1997 (n = 22)	n = 3	n = 19
Reductions (25%)	33.3	5.3
0–5% increase (35%)	66.7	36.8
5.1% plus increase (40%)	0	57.9

1965–1966 fiscal year. That proposed budget (not the final enacted budget) is compared to the enacted budget for the prior year to determine the extent and nature of the change proposed by the governor. To eliminate the effects of inflation, all budgets (both enacted and proposed) are expressed in real dollars, and then the prior budget is subtracted from the proposed budget. The difference is then divided by the prior to express the proposed change as a percentage of the prior in real dollars. Table 1 first presents average changes, and then groups the proposed changes into reductions, 0–5% increases, and increases of 5.1% or more.

If all years are considered together, Republicans (8.4%) average larger budget increases than Democrats (7.3%). Eras are very important, however. The average increase before 1975 is 9.9, while after that the average is 5.6. The political climate changed and it became less acceptable to propose large increases. To assess the role of party, then, we need to compare Republicans and Democrats within eras. Increases were greater prior to 1975, but did Democrats propose larger increases? Increases were less after 1975, but did Democrats still propose relatively larger increases? As Table indicates, within each era Democrats did propose larger increases than Republicans. For the initial era, Republicans proposed increases averaging 9.7% while Democrats proposed increases averaging 11.7%. After 1974 Republican increases averaged .9% while Democratic increases averaged 6.3%.

LEGISLATIVE PARTIES AND REACTIONS

Once executive budgets are submitted, the legislative parties have the option to react. The reactions of the legislative parties were taken from *New York Times* stories.* Responses

---

* This source, of course, may not accurately reflect party positions. Journalists may not regard party reactions as sincere, and may not report them. A party may be in the minority and the reactions may not be seen as having any consequence, so they may not be reported. To try to minimize these possibilities, an additional check was conducted by using the archives of the Albany *Times Union*. After each year was checked in the *New York Times*, the recorded party positions were checked against *Times Union* stories to see if the same positions were reported. While the two newspapers did not report events in the same way there was considerable overlap of information, suggesting that the *Times* could be relied upon for information about party positions.

Table 2 Legislative Party Responses to Budgets by Party Proposing Budget and by Era

	Cut spending	No change	Increase spending and/or cut tax
All years			
Republicans	41.3	32.6	26.1
Democrats	8.7	41.3	50.0
By era			
1950–1974			
Republicans	54.2	41.7	4.1
Democrats	16.0	48.0	36.0
1975–1997			
Republicans	27.3	22.7	50.0
Democrats	0	33.3	66.7
By party of governor and era			
Democratic response			
Republicans (50–74)	19.1	38.1	42.9
Republicans (95–97)	0	0	100.0
Republican response			
Democrats (55–58)	100.0	0	0
Democrats (75–94)	32.6	26.3	42.1

were coded as to whether the legislative party sought a cut in spending, no change in the proposed budget, increased spending with tax cuts, increased spending, or a tax increase. For the period of 1950–1965 the Democrats were the minority party in both houses, so their party position could have emerged from the house or the assembly. Some years the primary position taken came from one house and other years from the other house. There were no cases in which there was a significant discrepancy between the positions emerging from the two houses.

The responses of the legislative parties are shown in Table 2. Since 1950 Republicans have been more likely to advocate cuts in spending (41.3% of the years), while Democrats have been much more likely to advocate spending increases and tax increases (50% of the years, with most of their responses focusing on the need for more spending). The pattern holds within different eras. During the 1950–1974 era, Republicans advocated cuts in spending in over half of their responses (54%), while Democrats did so in only 16% of their responses. In the 1975–1997 era, Republicans advocated cuts in 27.3% of their responses, while Democrats never did. In general, the legislative parties behave as we often presume; Republicans are more likely to propose spending cuts, while Democrats are both less likely to propose spending cuts and more likely to propose increasing spending and raising taxes. The shift from the political climate of expansive government (pre-1974) to that of less support (post-1974) appears to have to have affected the proposals governors make. The legislative Democrats, however, have continued to serve as advocates of increased spending. It is important, of course, to note that after 1974 Democrats were facing budget proposals that increased spending less, and therefore they may have felt more of an obligation to increase spending in response to these smaller increments. Indeed, the statements from Democratic legislative leaders after 1975 indicate that they recognized that there was less support for government and that they had to adjust to that reduced support in formulating responses to gubernatorial budget proposals. Despite that, Democrats still were much more likely than Republicans to advocate spending increases before and after 1975.

The significant matter is how the opposing party in the legislature responds to gubernatorial proposals. The last part of Table 2 indicates responses as reactions of Democrats to Republican governors and those of Republicans to Democratic governors. When Republican governors proposed budgets (almost all during the 1950s–1960s and involving increases in spending), Democrats made suggestions for reductions in only 25% of the cases. When Democrats proposed budgets (almost all involving increases in spending), Republicans always responded with responses of cuts from 1955–1958, and in a third of the cases from 1975–1994.

The differences between the parties endure, with Republicans more likely to support cuts in spending and Democrats more likely to support increases in spending. Political eras also matter. Since 1975 all governors have proposed smaller budget increases. Despite that change, the relative differences between the legislative parties in the positions they have taken on the budget have persisted. Parties continue to take differing positions on aggregate budget issues.

ENDURING DIFFERENCES AND INCREASING CONFLICT IN THE BUDGET PROCESS

While there is continuity in party positions across time, there is not continuity over time in the budget process in New York. The budget process has become more conflictual and protracted. Since the 1950s the budget has taken longer and longer to enact. The state has a constitutional deadline to pass a budget by April 1 of each year. If it is late, state aid to localities cannot be distributed and money cannot be borrowed. Figure 1 indicates the number of days the budget has been passed before or after that deadline since 1950. It is has been passed later and later since 1950.

Why, if stability of party positions has occurred, has negotiating a budget become more difficult? The answer appears to lie in the argument of Thompson about the role of professionalism and its interaction with partisanship. He argues that legislative staff do not create goals, but facilitate the pursuance of partisan goals (Thompson, 1986–1987). To the extent that staff and legislative resources increase, the ability of parties to formulate and pursue policy goals also increases.

The New York legislature has changed greatly since 1950. Beginning in the 1960s the legislature began a steady increase in staff levels and in the general level of the budget (Stonecash, 1993 and 1994b). Staff office space and computer capacities were increased (Benjamin and Nakamura, 1991: xiv–xxvi). The staff of the fiscal committees increased a great deal, economists were hired, and computer capabilities were developed (Dawson, 1990). This gave the legislature the ability to challenge gubernatorial revenue estimates. As has occurred with legislatures across the country since the 1950s, the New York legislature has a greater capacity to conduct its own analyses and generate its own policy proposals. It is now much more capable of playing a significant role in budget decisions.

These changes accelerated by 1970 in New York. The legislature was very frustrated with the extent to which the Republican governor Nelson Rockefeller dominated them. Rockefeller continually proposed a series of tax increases during the late 1960s with the legislature felt it had little ability to critique. In response the legislative leaders supported

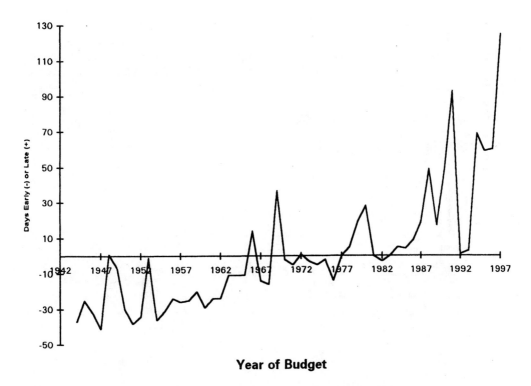

Year of Budget

Figure 1   New York budget passage: days budget early or late (1944–1996).

increases in the legislative budget to hire more staff. This support for increased staff has persisted across time. (See interviews in Benjamin and Nakamura, 1991.) A particular concern was to increase the staffs of the fiscal committees so legislative leaders would have the ability to counter gubernatorial proposals (Dawson, 1990). Figure 2 indicates how much the legislative budget has increased over time and how much of that increase was due to things other than legislative salaries. As Figure 2 indicates, the 1970s and 1980s resulted in an enormous increase in the resources devoted to legislative staff.

The availability of staff has had a significant influence on budget and tax debates. With increased resources, the legislative staff began in the 1980s (Balutis, 1975) to generate studies on the state economy ("Plain Talk About Improving the Economy of New York," Senate, 1980; "Toward a Blueprint for Economic Survival," Assembly, 1981) and on the impact and burden of taxes ("The Effects of the Corporate, Sales, and Property Taxes on Business Locational Decisions," 1984; "The State Personal Income Tax: Taxation of the Family and Low Income Relief," 1984; "Who Pays New York Taxes," 1985). There were proposals about how to respond to the declining fiscal situation of the state and the reform of the budget process ("Tax Programs and Fiscal Policy Priorities," Assembly, 1986; "Fiscal Change Financial Sense," Assembly, 1989). Each house now generates its own revenue estimates so the legislature can compete in the game of projecting revenue. The assembly, for example, regularly publishes documents such as "New York State Economic and Revenue Forecasts 1990–91 and 1991–92." The senate contracts with the Wharton School for revenue estimates. This additional staff has allowed the legislature, and particu-

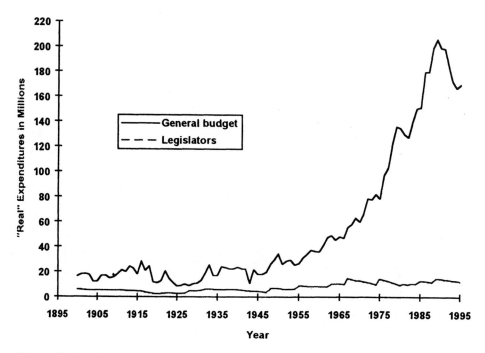

Figure 2   The New York legislative budget, in real dollars, (1900–1996; spending on legislators and general budget).

larly the Democrats, to challenge revenue estimates of the governor and to generate specific information about the impact of taxes.

The availability of staff has also allowed the legislature to propose much more specific tax proposals than in prior eras.* The legislative parties argued about the fairness of taxes during the 1950s–1970s, but they did not generate specific alternatives to the existing system or to gubernatorial proposals. That changed in the mid-1980s. The revision of the federal tax code prompted states to decide whether or not to revise their own tax codes (Dwyre et al., 1994). The responses of the assembly and senate were to propose very specific proposals to counter a gubernatorial proposal. Legislative Democrats differed from legislative Republicans in two ways. Democrats wanted to cut taxes less than Republicans, and they wanted the personal income tax system to end up being more progressive than Republicans. The assembly leadership took another significant step forward in making the legislature a significant actor during this session. For the first time the assembly created a brochure about the tax proposal and mailed it statewide in an attempt to present its position and make it prominent.

Events in the next decade created more situations in which the legislative parties had to make choices about spending and taxes. The state had continual deficits, and Republicans and the business community argued that taxes were too high and should be

---

* There are no stories from *The New York Times* for the 1950s–1970s that report detailed tax proposals from the legislature. Legislators complained about the level of proposed increases, but there are no stories of detailed counterproposals.

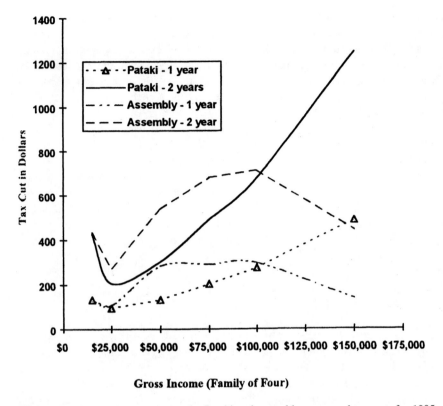

Figure 3 Contrasting tax proposals: Pataki and assembly–proposed tax cuts for 1995 and 1996.

cut. Faced with this situation, Democrats, across three different speakers, continued to argue that if tax levels were to be cut, there should increases in the income taxes on the most affluent. Finally, faced with a conservative Republican governor in 1995 who proposed a tax cut, the Democrats responded to his tax cut proposal with an alternative tax cut, which would have been much more progressive in its impact. The assembly Democrats were able to use econometric models to project the specific tax savings by income level from the alternative proposals for several years in the future, allowing them to match the governor in reporting on the likely impacts of change. Figure 3 presents the expected reductions in tax obligations under the alternative proposals and indicates how specific the legislative parties were able to be in their response. The important change of the last decade is that the legislative parties have now developed the ability to formulate very specific proposals to be considered during the budget process.

These legislative resources mean the legislative parties are able to project the consequences of change and stake out very specific positions that represent their party interests. This is a very significant change from the 1950s. Interviews with legislators and staff from that era indicate that governors presented budgets, and the legislature, with little ability to analyze and dissent, passed budgets relatively quickly and without extensive change. Now the legislature is able to present counterproposals in many areas and to even develop initiatives before the budget process begins. The development of the capability to present alternatives creates the possibility of a more contentious process.

This potential has been realized because of professional and partisan conditions within the legislature. Professionally, more and more legislators are making this their sole job and are staying longer in the legislature (Stonecash, 1997a). The decisions they make are probably more serious to them than they were in the 1950s, and they are less likely to comply with leadership directives than they were in the 1950s. This makes legislators more likely to hold out for what they want or can get than in the past. The existence of a staff with the capability to research gubernatorial proposals and to do studies for legislators—surely propelled by the emergence of career legislators—has given them a greater ability to express their own interests.

At the same time that this greater capability developed, divided partisan control emerged as an enduring institutional condition. Democrats took control of the assembly in 1974 following Watergate and have held control since then. Republicans have held the senate continuously, except for two years following the 1964 Republican disaster of Barry Goldwater. This divided control has meant the institutionalization of the development of alternative proposals. It has also meant that regardless of what party holds the governorship, the opposing party has the power within the legislature to obstruct the governor.

SUMMARY AND CONCLUSION

In conclusion, the combination of legislators more concerned about staying in the legislature, shaping legislative outcomes, and achieving greater legislative capability, and of persisting divided control has reshaped the budget process. It is now a process dominated by disputes about revenue projections and by detailed policy proposals and arguments about the consequences of specific changes. It now takes much longer to reach agreements about budgets. These changes have produced a process widely disparaged in the press for the delays in enacting a budget, but it is a process that involves more serious discussions of policy alternatives than occurred in the 1950s.

Political parties and career legislators have driven these changes. The Democrats and Republicans differ on spending in ways we might expect over the years. What has changed has been the ability of legislators to pursue these differing interests. Governors now find themselves facing legislative parties ready to criticize budget proposals in great detail, to present alternatives, and to hold out for changes that serve their goals. The budget process is a richer and more thorough one. It is also one that takes longer, and it is unlikely that will change.

REVIEW QUESTIONS

1. Most of our attempts to understand the role of parties on budgets presume that their role is invariant—Democrats always do one thing and Republican do another. How does this analysis suggest that the policy goals of parties can vary by era, and why would these policy goals vary?

2. The role of increased staff also affects parties in that it can affect their ability to pursue their goals. What do the changes in New York tell us about how staff have affected the ability of legislative parties to pursue goals over time?

3. What do increased staff levels do to the extent of partisan conflict and the ability to reach agreement on budgets, and why does that effect occur?

4. Greater legislative staff increases can change the balance of power between the legislature and the governor. How did increased staff in New York change that balance and what did it do to the speed with which budget agreements have been reached?

5. Would you conclude that the quality of policy debate between the executive and legislative branches has improved or diminished over time in New York, and why would you offer that judgment?

REFERENCES

Alba, R. and Trent K. (1986). Population loss and change in the north: An examination of New York's migration to the sunbelt. *Social Science Quarterly*, *67*, 690–706.

Balutis, A. P. (1975). The budgetary process in New York: The role of the legislative staff. In A. P. Balutis (ed.), *The Political Pursestrings*. Beverly Hills: Sage Publications.

Benjamin, G. and Nakamura, R. T. (1991). *The Modern New York Legislature: Redressing the Balance*. Albany, Nelson, A. Rockefeller Institute.

Brown, R. D. and Wright, G. C. (1992). Electoral polarization in the American states. *American Politics Quarterly*, *20(4)*, 411–426.

Connery, R. H. and Benjamin, G. (1979). *Rockefeller of New York*. Ithaca, NY: Cornell University Press.

Dawson, C. S. Jr. (1990). The power of the purse in transition: An investigation of the New York state legislature's increasing budgetary power from a developmental perspective. unpublished dissertation, Albany, NY: Department of Public Administration.

Dye, T. R. (1984). Party and policy in the states. *Journal of Politics*, *46*, 1097–1116.

Dwyre, D., O'Gorman, M., Stonecash, J. M. and Young, R. (1994). Disorganized politics and the have-nots: Politics and taxes in New York and California. *Polity*, *27(1)*, 25–47.

Edsall, T. B. and Edsalll M. D. (1991). *Chain Reaction: The Impact of Race, Rights, and Taxes on American Politics*. New York: Norton.

Erikson, R. S., Wright, G. C. and McIver, J. P. (1993). *Statehouse Democracy*. New York: Cambridge University Press.

Gimpel, J. L. (1996). *National Elections and the Autonomy of American State Party Systems*. Pittsburgh: University of Pittsburgh Press.

Hansen, S. (1983). *Taxation Without Representation*. New York: Praeger.

Jennings, E. T. (1979). Competition, constituencies, and welfare policies in American states. *American Political Science Review*, *73*, 414–429.

Jewell, M. (1988). The effect of incumbency on state legislatures. *Legislative Studies Quarterly*, *13*, 495–514.

Key, V. O. Jr. (1949). *Southern Politics*. New York: Knopf.

Mayhew, D. R. (1974). *The Electoral Connection*. New Haven: Yale University Press.

McClelland, P. D. and Magdovitz, A. L. (1981). *Crisis in the Making: The Political Economy of New York State Since 1945*. Cambridge: Cambridge University Press.

Paddock, J. (1992). Inter-party ideological differences in eleven state democratic parties, 1956–1980. *Western Political Quarterly*, *45(3)*, 751–160.

Ray, D. (1976). Voluntary retirement and electoral defeat in eight state legislatures. *Journal of Politics*, *38*, 426–433.

Schlesinger, J. A. (1985). The new American political party. *American Political Science Review*, *79*, 1152–1169.

Stonecash, J. M. (1987–1988). Inter-party competition, political dialogue, and public policy: A critical review. *Policy Studies Journal*, *16(2)*, 243–262.

Stonecash, J. M. (1989). Political cleavage in gubernatorial and legislative elections: The nature of inter-party competition in New York elections, 1970–1982. *Western Political Quarterly, 42(1)*, 69–81.

Stonecash, J. M. (1991). Observations from New York: The limits of 50-state studies and the case for case studies. *Comparative State Politics, 12(4)*, 1–9.

Stonecash, J. M. (1992). Split constituencies and the impact of party control. *Social Science History, 16(3)*, 455–477.

Stonecash, J. M. (1993). The pursuit and retention of legislative office in New York, 1870–1990: Reconsidering sources of change. *Polity, XXVI(2)*, 301–315.

Stonecash, J. M. (1994a). Political parties and partisan conflict. In J. M. Stonecash, J. K. White, and P. Colby (eds), *Governing New York State*, pp. 83–101 Albany: SUNY Press.

Stonecash, J. M. (1994b). The legislature: The emergence of an equal branch. In J. M. Stonecash, J. K. White, and P. Colby (eds), *Governing New York State*, pp. 149–193 Albany: SUNY Press.

Stonecash, J. M. (1994c). Taxes and policy debates in New York State. In J. M. Stonecash, J. K. White, and P. Colby (eds), *Governing New York State*, pp. 235–241. Albany: SUNY Press.

Stonecash, J. M. (1994d). The revenue problem: Revenue fluctuations and forecasting, New York State, 1950–1990, A. Khan and W. B. Hildreth (eds), *Case Studies in Public Budgeting and Financial Management*, pp. 153–163. Dubuque, IA: Kendall/Hunt.

Stonecash, J. M. (1997a). The rise of the legislature, In S. F. Liebschutz (ed.), *New York Politics and Government*. Lincoln, NE: University of Nebraska Press.

Stonecash, J. M. (1997b). Parties, elections, and political debate in New York. In S. F. Liebschutz (ed.), *New York Politics and Government*. Loncoln, NE: University of Nebraska Press.

Stonecash, J. M. (1997c). Political cleavage in state legislative parties. presented at the 1997 New York State Political Science Association Meetings, New York City, April.

Sundquist, J. L. (1983). *Dynamics of the Party System*. rev. ed. Washington, DC: Brookings Institution.

Thompson, J. (1986–1987). State legislative reform: Another look, one more time, again. *Polity, 19(1)*, 27–41.

16

Capital Budgeting Practices in Local Governments

A Comparative Study of Two States

Patricia Wigfall
North Carolina Central University, Durham, North Carolina, U.S.A.

Thomas D. Lynch
Louisiana State University, Baton Rouge, Louisiana, U.S.A.

where in constitution does it say this?

One function of government is to provide, on a collective basis, that which cannot be achieved by individual action. According to Alan Steiss, this statement reflects two basic government activities: first, safeguarding the public through the regulation of individual actions; and second, providing all citizens public facilities and services (Steiss, 1978). The second activity underscores one of the principal functions of government, which is to procure and maintain public facilities and services for the public good. Local governments account for the largest proportion of public capital expenditures with significant investments in transportation, water supply storage and distribution, wastewater collection and treatment, and other facilities (Millar, 1998). In 1993 direct capital outlays in local governments in the United States totaled $86 billion, of which $22 billion was for school construction and $14 billion for utility capital outlays. Roads, sewage, water, and housing construction made up the remainder (Lee and Johnson, 1998).

Ironically, public demand for government services continues to increase as the public seeks to limit government spending by capping and even rolling back taxes. According to the Government Finance Officer's Association (GFOA), the magnitude and severity of the fiscal crisis of the major American cities have "eclipsed the problems of the smaller government units. Although their problems are perhaps not so dramatic, they too encounter increased pressure on available resources" (GFOA, 1984). Capital budgeting therefore is an important tool not only for critical public policy decision making, but also for the management of limited resources.

This study explores the capital budgeting process among local governments in the states of Louisiana and North Carolina. By isolating key features of similarity and difference between capital budgeting methods in selected cities in the two states, the study's objectives are to (1) discern the common influences on the use of capital budgeting in city and county governments in Louisiana and North Carolina, and (2) examine any differences that may exist and speak to the significance of those differences. This empirical study is suggestive of capital budgeting as it exists at the local level in the United States.

STUDY BACKGROUND

The literature on capital budgeting practices in local governments is scanty, especially in terms of definition, models, and political import. Several classifications of the literature on capital budgeting are identified, however: (1) "how to" manuals, (2) behavioral studies of capital budgeting, and (3) case studies of government programs, capital budgeting and planning, financial analysis, and determinants of capital budgeting (White, 1978). While the largest portion of the literature falls under the heading of manuals, another rapidly growing segment of the literature is in the area of case studies. Although case studies are useful, their exclusive focus on a single entity or agency renders them inadequate for testing budgeting theories or drawing general conclusions about capital budgeting (Rubin and Babbie, 1995).

The American Society of Planning Officials (ASPO), in cooperation with other organizations, is largely responsible for a new and growing segment of the literature in capital budgeting and planning (American Society of Planning Officials, 1977). According to Michael White, the society's empirical approach in studying capital programming and growth management crystallizes capital budgeting conceptually (White, 1978).

While a significant number of public and not-for-profit organizations are using capital budgeting strategies in making decisions relating to capital projects, public sector capital budgeting practices are influenced by concerns that are unique to the public sector (Sekwat, 1994). Analytical work in costing items accurately is critical in the current climate of taxpayer revolts because inadequate analytical tools handicap government's ability to make sound investment decisions and to market its debt effectively. In addition, concern for equity and efficiency make quantifying benefits difficult. Economic considerations and other external intervening variables, such as political influence and societal demands, must exceed the costs for a project to be acceptable using rational analysis. Unlike the private sector, which simply uses profit as the yardstick to measure a project's worthiness, the public sector must consider collective worth beyond dollars.

Decisions concerning public investments are difficult to make because the projects are usually intangible and hard to quantify. Accounting systems in public organizations often lack systematic provisions for the depreciation of assets. In addition, planning is often inadequate to integrate the capital items with the structural needs of a community. Careful and deliberate capital improvement plans (CIPs) covering a fiscal year period are essential to coordinate the work and finances over time (Lynch, 1995). The investigation of capital budgeting practices that are reported in this study addresses some of these problems.

White enumerates a litany of areas that need more research in capital budgeting (White, 1978). Unfortunately, even though a little more than two decades have passed since his critique of the literature, his research agenda still needs to be done. This study is one step toward meeting his research agenda. Based on a survey of 153 local governments in North Carolina and Louisiana in which capital budgeting practices are compared, this analysis builds on the recent work of Alex Sekwat and develops a reliable and extensive knowledge base on local government budgeting practices. In addition, it standardizes the definition of terms to achieve a meaningful comparative analysis across the states, regions, and country. To our knowledge, the Sekwat study and this analysis are unique because there is so little empirical information that exists on comparative capital budgeting procedures, especially on the local governments researched. Hopefully, this study will encourage others to investigate other local governments, and in so doing, create a better basis of comparative analysis.

The objective of this examination is to determine if similarities in capital budgeting practices exist and to reveal differences, if any, between Louisiana and North Carolina. Fiscal crises and crumbling infrastructures are still major problems facing local governments today. This comparative analysis examines how Louisiana and North Carolina rated the condition of their basic infrastructure facilities in order to explore possible impacts of their existence on governmental procedures and policies in the two states. Are there commonalties in how local governments in Louisiana and North Carolina cope with these challenges and pressures? If differences exist in how they address problems of infrastructure, what are the key dissimilarities?

The study focuses on two key questions that explore determinants of capital budgeting. The first question is what the nature of capital budget preparation is in the two states. Specifically, how many localities in Louisiana and North Carolina prepare these budgets annually? The second question is how similar the states are in deciding how often to prepare capital budgets in considering such factors as risk and uncertainty, receipt and size of intergovernmental grants, and evaluation and selection techniques of capital projects.

PROFILE OF LOCAL GOVERNMENTS

The study looks at sixty-four parish governments in Louisiana and eighty-nine cities in North Carolina (populations equaling or exceeding 5,000). To illustrate the comparability of the cities, this analysis looks at several general characteristics: (1) population, (2) income, (3) education, and (4) items that reflect the nature of capital budgeting. Tables 1 through 3 show how the two states compare in terms of demographic attributes.

As Table 1 shows, Louisiana's mean population is clearly larger than North Carolina's. This finding was not unexpected, as parishes tend to be larger than cities. The comparison of levels of income and education, shown in Tables 2 and 3, reveal that the two states are very much alike in these characteristics. North Carolina's mean income is less than $2,000 higher than that for Louisiana. Similarly, the level of college graduates for North Carolina is only 7% higher than in Louisiana.

Table 1 Population (Household) of Local Governments

State	Mean population
Louisiana	286,047
North Carolina	22,168

Source: Census of Population and Housing (1990).

Table 2 Income (Household) of Local
Governments

State	Mean income
Louisiana	25,969
North Carolina	27,168

Source: Census of Population and Housing (1990).

This study also examines several dimensions of comparability of the two states in terms of attributes that reflect the nature of capital budgeting for Louisiana and North Carolina. Tables 4 through 8 indicate levels of similarity for budget preparation, size of capital budgets, how capital expenditures are handled, and intergovernmental funding. Of primary interest in this study is the annual preparation of a separate capital budget.* Not all governments in the study prepare a capital budget each year, but there is not a significant difference in the frequency in developing capital budgets in Louisiana and North Carolina. As Table 4 indicates, while approximately a third of local governments in both states prepare separate capital budgets each year, a significant proportion—56% in Louisiana and 39% in North Carolina—never develop a separate capital budget.

The size of capital expenditures helps to differentiate capital expenditures from current ones. Despite some differences between Louisiana and North Carolina, the distribution of the size of capital budgets or expenditures in Louisiana and North Carolina is very similar. Table 5 shows that the greatest similarities in capital budget size exist for two budget categories—those with annual budgets of less than $1 million and budgets of $10 million to $49 million. This dimension's similarity is encouraging because it suggests that capital budgeting practices in the two states are parallel.

How local governments handle capital expenditures gives us useful information about their capital budgeting practices. While a higher proportion of governments in North Carolina than in Louisiana handle capital expenditures by merging into an annual operating budget (distributed throughout) than by other practices, those in Louisiana make use of several approaches in reporting capital expenses, two of which reflect high degrees of similarity between the two states. Table 6 indicates that almost one-third of local governments in both states prepare separate capital budgets each year and about a fourth in both states merge capital expenditures into one part of the operating budget.

Table 3 Education (25 Years and Older)

State	Bachelor degree or higher (%)
Louisiana	12
North Carolina	19

Source: Census of Population and Housing (1990).

* A capital budget is a document prepared separately from an annual budget to take account of long-term expenditures of government.

Table 4 Preparation of a Separate Capital Budget

State	Annually	Often	Sometimes	Rarely	Never
Louisiana	28	3	6	6	56
North Carolina	29	5	5	11	39

Table 5 Size of Capital Budgets

State	$0–$999,999	$1,000,000–$9,999,999	$10,000,000–$49,000,000	$50,000,000–$99,999,999	$100,000,000 or greater
Louisiana	41	28	13	6	13
North Carolina	33	47	15	3	3

Table 6 How Capital Expenditures Are Handled

State	Prepare separate capital budget annually	Merge into entire annual operating budget	Merge into one section of the operating budget	Include in CIP
Louisiana	28	31	28	13
North Carolina	39	53	25	3

Table 7 Receipt of Intergovernmental Grants

State	Federal Yes	Federal No	State Yes	State No
Louisiana	50	50	81	19
North Carolina	47	53	48	52

Table 8 Size of IGR Grants

State	$0–$999,999	$1,000,000–$9,999,999	$10,000,000–$49,999,999	$50,000,000–$99,999,999	$1000,000,000 or greater
A. Federal grants					
Louisiana	28	16	1	0	0
North Carolina	28	18	0	3	3
B. State grants					
Louisiana	41	3	6	3	0
North Carolina	38	10	1	0	0

Comparison of the two states in terms of intergovernmental funding indicates almost equal levels of federal grant allocations, but as Table 7 shows, rather strong differences are revealed for state funding. Eighty percent of Louisiana's local governments receive state grants, while just under 50% of those in North Carolina do.

The size of intergovernmental grants for Louisiana and North Carolina are markedly similar. Table 8 shows that most local governments in both states are in the lowest range of intergovernmental grant size, with state grants being used more than federal grants. Twenty-eight percent of local governments in Louisiana and North Carolina receive federal grants specifically earmarked for capital expenditures amounting to less than $1 million. Approximately 40% in both states receive state grants in the same category of grant size.

ANALYSIS OF SPECIFIC CAPITAL BUDGETING PRACTICES

This section looks at factors critical to capital budgeting practices and how these factors influence the preparation of capital budgets. Comparisons reveal strong similarities. Both states considered stimulating economic development, identifying essential capital projects, and guiding the development of new capital projects, as always being influential in capital budgeting preparation. The two states are almost identical in how other factors affected the capital budgeting process. Balancing the budget, observing state statutes, and achieving equity in debt financing have some degree of impact on the capital budgeting process. Clear disparities, however, are shown for how intergovernmental funding "always" influenced capital budgeting preparation in the two states. As Table 9 shows, a fourth of Louisiana's local governments consider receiving federal and state grants to be influential in the capital budgeting process. In contrast, the effect of IGR funding for North Carolina is almost negligible; however, the two states are closer in similarity in how IGR funding "sometimes" influenced capital budgeting decisions. Table 9 also indicates that over a third of local governments in both states look at federal and state grants as sometimes influencing capital budgeting decisions. Factors such as following state statutes, balancing the budget, and guiding new projects, similarly always impact capital budget preparation.

In addition to the above, the study also looks at such issues as linkages between infrastructure and capital budgeting practices; the condition of such capital projects as

Table 9 Influences on the Preparation of Capital Budgets

State	State statute	Achieve equity in debt financing	Balance the budget	Identify essential capital projects	Guide new projects	Stimulate economic development	Obtain federal grants	Obtain state grants
Always								
Louisiana	22	13	28	41	34	44	25	25
North Carolina	23	14	29	50	39	35	1	1
Sometimes								
Louisiana							31	31
North Carolina							43	41

library and solid waste facilities, professional training and the experience of individuals participating in the capital budgeting process, risk and uncertainty in capital budgeting decisions; use of capital improvement programs; and instruments used in financing and evaluating capital projects. For instance, while a significant proportion of local governments in both states indicates the good condition of some facilities, differences exist in how local governments in the two states rate the condition of specific capital facilities.

As Table 10 indicates, Louisiana and North Carolina are most similar in their ratings of public libraries and solid waste disposals. A little less than half of the governments in both states considers these facilities to be in good condition. Twice the proportion of local governments in Louisiana rate hospitals, jails, police and fire facilities, and public parks as being in good condition as in North Carolina cities.

The formal professional training and experience that individuals bring to capital budgeting decision making bears heavily on the outcome of this process. Table 11 shows comparisons of the official position of the individuals in Louisiana and North Carolina upon whose data we relied for this study. A high degree of similarity exists between the two states in who responded to the questions in the study. For Louisiana and North Carolina, most respondents report official titles of budget director, finance officer, auditor, or treasurer.

The attention to risk management at the time of capital investment is also considered in this case study. Table 12 shows that for local governments that consider risk and uncertainty in making capital budgeting decisions, North Carolina does so more often than Louisiana. Conversely, Louisiana has a higher proportion of local governments that do not use risk and uncertainty in capital decision making.

Comparisons of official involvement shed light on the job categories of individuals who are assigned capital budgeting responsibilities. Table 13 indicates that at least one-fourth to a third of local governments in Louisiana and North Carolina always include several officials—the city/county commissioner, budget officer, treasure, sheriff, city/county clerk, public works director, and mayor. Disparities between Louisiana and North Carolina are shown for the involvement of city and county commissioners and budget finance officers. North Carolina is twice as likely to involve those particular officials than Louisiana.

Table 14 shows that North Carolina uses CIP in greater percentages than Louisiana. As indicated in Table 14 almost half of Louisiana parishes are without a CIP.

The type of methodology used in financing capital projects becomes important in this analysis because of its linkage to how the projects are prioritized. Comparisons of the types of methods used to finance capital projects or facilities offer additional information on the general budgeting practices of the two states. Table 15 shows that by far the most frequently used methodology to finance capital projects or facilities in both Louisiana and North Carolina were put-option bonds and zero-coupon bonds.* The two states are also similar in their utilization of tax increment financing.

Table 16 shows that both Louisiana and North Carolina use payback period and benefit-cost ratio as the primary tools by which they evaluate and/or select capital budget-

---

* The put-option method presents the buyer with the option of requiring the bond to be paid off at specified intervals. Under the zero-coupon plan, maturity must be reached and both principal and interest are paid at once before interest is paid out (Lee and Johnson, 1998).

Table 10 "Good" Condition Rating of Infrastructure Facilities

State	Hospitals	Jails	Public libraries	Police/fire facilities	Public parks	Solid waste disposals
Louisiana	50	51	41	40	36	41
North Carolina	25	24	47	22	16	33

Table 11 Official Position of Study's Respondent

State	Budget director or finance officer	Administrator or manager	Auditor or treasurer	Other position
Louisiana	41	6	31	22
North Carolina	36	1	45	17

Table 12 Consideration of Risk and Uncertainty

State	Yes	No
Louisiana	44	56
North Carolina	67	33

Table 13 Official Involvement (Always)

State	City/county commissioner	Budget officer	Treasurer	Sheriff	City/county clerk	Public director works	Mayor
Louisiana	28	25	25	31	27	22	25
North Carolina	54	51	24	30	24	27	34

Table 14 Capital Improvement Plan

State	Yes	No
Louisiana	56	44
North Carolina	76	24

Table 15 Methodology of Financing Capital Projects and Facilities

State	General obligation bonds[a]	Reserve bonds	Revenue bonds	Tax increment financing	Zero coupon bonds	Put option bonds
Louisiana	16	9	34	81	78	81
North Carolina	95	48	18	75	82	81

[a] Includes backing by property tax, sales tax, and other revenue sources.

Table 16 Evaluation/Selection Techniques for Capital Projects

State	Payback period	Benefit-cost ratio	Net present value	Interval rate of return	Accounting rate of return
Primary techniques					
Louisiana	16	41	3	3	3
North Carolina	42	54	14	4	3
Secondary techniques					
Louisiana	28	25	22	9	9
North Carolina	25	26	33	19	18

ing projects in greater proportion than for other primary evaluation techniques. Table 16 indicates slight differences between the two states in the degree to which payback periods are used, but they are more similar in utilizing benefit-cost analysis. Greater similarity exists between the two states for secondary methods of evaluation and selection. Again, payback period, benefit-cost ratio, and net present value are similar for both states. About a fourth of local governments in both states use payback period and benefit-cost ratio as secondary methods of evaluation and selection. One-third of local jurisdictions in North Carolina use net present value as a secondary technique. A very small percentage of local governments in both states either "never used" the techniques or did not note which tools they use. These are not shown in Table 16.

EVALUATION OF THE STUDY

The central question in the present study is whether or not local governments in these states share common practices of capital budgeting, and if differences are revealed, in what part of the capital decision-making process they appear. Sound capital budgeting practices can be seen as increasing the abilities of administrative officials and administrators to be both more efficient and accountable (Lynch and Lynch, 1995). The discussion of the study's background emphasizes the critical nature of capital investment decisions at the local level, particularly those relating to the frequency of capital budget preparation, quality of infrastructure facilities, role of official involvement, influence of risk and uncertainty, and CIP. The results of this study suggest that only about a third of Louisiana and North Carolina local governments annually prepare a capital budget and over one-half in each state has a capital improvement plan in place. This indicates that many and not enough local administrators have some knowledge of those techniques.

Although Louisiana and North Carolina are alike in their assessments of public libraries and solid waste disposals, the types of facilities that show the greatest divergence perhaps provide the most useful information about the differences in their priorities. For example, the fact that half of Louisiana's local governments indicate hospitals and jails to be in good condition compared to only a fourth of those in North Carolina with similar ratings, reflects Louisiana's emphasis on health and crime capital investments. At the same time, this finding points to North Carolina's possible inattention to these types of capital priorities. Similarly, North Carolina rates police and fire facilities as being in good shape in half the proportion of Louisiana. Interestingly, North Carolina's assessments are somewhat inconsistent with the study's findings regarding official involvement, which we discuss in more detail below. While North Carolina and Louisiana involve their sheriffs in capital budgeting decisions in equal proportion, the former gives good ratings to police and fire facilities and jails in half the proportion of Louisiana. An assumption is that the disparities in these ratings indicate different perspectives on how public safety and citizen protection should be enhanced through capital investment. Clearly, differences in the perspectives of actors in the capital budgeting process guide the kinds of values that go into the decisions regarding the capital projects selected for funding.

The differences may be due to the differences in the perspectives of officials rather than differences in governance. When the two states are compared along the dimension of official involvement, both Louisiana and North Carolina include several officials, such as treasurer, sheriff, city or county clerk, and public works director. All are involved in the capital budgeting process in very similar proportions.

A somewhat different indicator of individual influence is the study's examination of the role of official position in the capital budgeting process. The typical job classification in Louisiana is finance officer, treasurer, or auditor, but almost all of the local governments in Louisiana use the perspectives of financial specialists of some sort. The North Carolina respondent is much more likely to be an administrator or manager. (Some of the job titles listed under "other" included assistant city manager and administrative manager). Finance specialists with possibly more narrow views may bring different perspectives to the process than generalists, such as managers and administrators, with broader views and possibly less certainty of some accounting details. The differences in capital budgeting practices may be attributable to differences in the perspectives of officials rather than to differences in governance.

Consideration of risk and uncertainty are important in budget decision making. The conscious awareness of risk management at the time of capital investment is examined in this study, and there is some dissimilarity between the two states. North Carolina governments considered risk and uncertainty in making decisions about individual capital projects in greater proportion than Louisiana. Conversely, more governments in Louisiana than in North Carolina do not include risk and uncertainty in capital budgeting decision making.

The presence of a CIP suggests that a local government has both the commitment and knowledge to develop long-range capital investment strategies. Eighty percent of states in the United States and more than 60% of city and county governments have CIPs or budgets (Lee and Johnson, 1998). The study's results show that a majority of both states had a CIP during the year of the study. A more substantial majority of local governments in North Carolina had a CIP in place.

Funding for capital expenditures from intergovernmental sources is important to local governments, as they may be unwilling to commit to major capital projects if state or federal funding is uncertain. Although local governments may only be required to raise a small portion of the total cost of a capital project, that commitment may become overwhelming for them. The comparison indicates that just about half of local governments in both states receive federal funding that was allocated specifically for capital expenditures during the fiscal year of this study. Differences, however, do exist for state funding. In North Carolina federal and state grants are received in equal proportions, while a much higher proportion of Louisiana governments receive state grants that are earmarked for capital projects during the same fiscal year.

For both Louisiana and North Carolina, state statutes are less influential on capital budgets than some other factors. This suggests that state political directives may be perceived as being less significant than assumed. The perspectives of the individual preparing the budget indicate that state law is not highly influential on their local government behavior.

SUMMARY AND CONCLUSION

This study examines the capital budgeting process among local governments in Louisiana and North Carolina.* The comparative analysis reveals interesting similarities in capital budgeting practices between the two states. This study's findings reveal that Louisiana and North Carolina are very much alike in how annual capital budgets are prepared at the local level. Similarities are also indicated for how the two states use CIPs in the selection of methods to finance capital projects and in the receipt of federal funding. Commonalities in capital budgeting decision making are also exemplified by the relatively strong role that sheriffs play in the capital budgeting process in both states. Differences are also revealed in our comparative analysis. While the receipt of federal funding is proportionately similar in the two states, state funding is received in higher proportions at the local level in Louisiana. This research also found differences in the type of official involvement in capital budgeting practices. Louisiana uses finance specialists more than North Carolina in local-level capital budgeting decision making. On the other hand, North Carolina's local governments consider risk and uncertainty more in making capital budgeting decisions than Louisiana. How the two states prioritize capital projects is indicative of another key disparity; Louisiana's emphasis on capital investments in health and crime contrasts with both North Carolina's inattention to these local government policy areas and its priority on public library investments. Several suggestions are offered to address the shortcomings this research reveals.

Local governments in Louisiana and North Carolina need to make three primary changes in terms of their capital budgeting practices. First, they need to learn and apply more sophisticated budgeting techniques. The reliance of both states on sheriffs to an important degree to make capital budgeting decisions suggests that local political factors influence decision making more than technical budgeting expertise. Second, more governments at the local level should use CIPs. This study reveals that local governments in Louisiana use CIPs far less frequently than those in North Carolina, which suggests the possibility of inefficient local-level planning, especially in Louisiana. Third, individuals who are officially involved in making local government budgeting decisions need professional training. The fact that North Carolina and Louisiana use the auditor or treasurer more in budget decision making indicates that professional training needs to be expanded to other local government administrators. Although professionally trained auditors and treasurers are important, other local officials are involved in budget decision making and they also need the advantages of a professional education.

---

* The authors would like to thank Professor Aman Khan for his comments on the initial drafts of the chapter.

REVIEW QUESTIONS

1. Why is capital budgeting important at all levels? What were the important differences in the study between Louisiana parishes and North Carolina cities? Do you think the fact that the comparison is between parishes (counties) and cities might make a difference? Explain your answer.

2. In looking at the tables, do you think that the level of professionalism in the two states might explain some of the differences?

3. Does the fact that federal and state grants are available to local governments seem to influence the capital budgeting process? If yes, in what ways? What may explain the differences between the two states?

4. Notice the importance of the sheriff in local politics. Why do you think this is true? What might account for the differences between the two states?

5. What is the importance of sophistication in capital budgeting based on what you can determine from the case study's findings? What did you use to define sophistication in capital budgeting? Justify your answer.

6. What are the differences between governments that prepare capital budgets annually and those that do not?

7. What is the significance of prescriptive theory on the development of capital budgets? What may account for the difference between the two states?

8. Develop a possible descriptive theory of the development of capital budgets. Why did you select the key independent variables in our theory?

REFERENCES

American Society of Planning Officials (ASPO). (1977). *Local Capital Improvements and Development Management: Literature Synthesis.* (Washington, DC: U.S. Department of Housing and Urban Development.

Census of Population and Housing. (1990). *Summary: Social, Economic and Housing Characteristics for the U.S.* Washington, D.C.: Bureau of the Census.

Doss, C. B., Jr. (1987). The use of capital budgeting procedures in U.S. cities. *Public Budgeting and Finance.* 7(3).

Government Finance Officer's Association. (1984). *Blueprints for Change.* Chicago: GFA.

Lee, R. D. and Johnson, R. (1989; 1998). *Public Budgeting Systems.* Rockville, MD: Aspen.

Lynch, T. D. (1995). *Public Budgeting in America.* 4th ed. Englewood Cliffs, NJ: Prentice Hall.

Lynch, T. D. and Lynch, C. F. (1995). The state of capital budgeting in Louisiana's cities. Paper presented at the International Conference of the Academy of Business Administration, Wimbly, England, June 20–24.

Millar, A. (1988). Selecting capital investment projects for local governments. *Public Budgeting and Finance,* 8(3).

Rubin, A. and Babbie, E. (1995). *Research Methods for Social Work.* Pacific Grove, CA: Brooks/Cole.

Sekwat, A. (1995). *Capital Budgeting in American County Government: Analysis of Current Practices.* Ann Arbor, MI. UMI Dissertation Services.

Steiss, A. W. (1978). *Local Government Finance: Capital Facilities Planning and Debt Administration.* MA: Lexington.

Stone, J. B. (1993). Public entrepreneurship. a paper presented at the Southeastern Conference on Public Administration, Cocoa Beach, FL, Oct. 7.

U.S. Conference of Mayors and U.S. Department of Housing and Urban Development. (1980). *A Mayor's Financial Management Handbook.*

White, M. J. (1978). Capital budgeting. In *State and Local Government Finance Management: A Compendium of Current Research.* J. E. Peterson and M. F. Laffey (eds.), Washington, D.C. Municipal Finance Officer's Association.

17

Procedures for Programming and Financing Capital Improvements

Alan Walter Steiss
Virginia Polytechnic Institute and State University, Blacksburg, Virginia, U.S.A.

Two fundamental responsibilities of government stem from the broad objective to "promote the general health, safety, morals, and public welfare": (1) regulations to ensure that the action of individuals will not be detrimental to the general public, and (2) provision of public services and facilities for the mutual benefit of all or a majority of citizens. The imposition of regulations and controls in the public interest is as old as history itself. Of more recent origins, the provision of public facilities and services has become widely accepted as a basic responsibility of government in contemporary society. Segments of the public may complain when taxes are increased to provide new schools or to expand public welfare programs. It is generally acknowledged, however, that significant economies can be achieved by such government activities—economies that could not be derived if each citizen had to provide for these facilities and services on an individual basis. The availability of public facilities can have a profound effect on the form and functioning of a community. Capital facilities represent very large investments of public resources, usually exert their effects over a period of many decades, and are not easy to modify once built. A systematic planning effort is therefore vital in making decisions about the programming and financing of such facilities.

PAY-AS-YOU-GO FINANCING

For many years, public officials held that the only appropriate financing method was to pay for capital facilities improvements out of current revenues—to "pay as you go." This approach is more economical in the long run since the cost of borrowed money can be eliminated. It is often suggested that when taxpayers feel the costs more immediately, the programming of capital improvements and the commitment of public revenues for these improvements will be handled more efficiently. In the pursuit of "efficiency," however, many public officials have foregone the basic objective of effectiveness, that is, of providing critically needed public improvements in a timely manner.

   The feasibility of a pay-as-you-go approach largely depends upon two factors: the nature of the community and the character of the anticipated expenditures. Once the infrastructure of a community has been established, it may be easier to finance required improvements out of increased tax revenues than is the case in communities experiencing rapid growth. A pay-as-you-go approach is also more feasible when capital expenditures are recurrent, either as to purpose or amount (e.g., the paving of streets, or the acquisition of neighborhood parks to serve new residential areas).

On the other hand, the pay-as-you-go approach may place an undue burden on present taxpayers to finance future improvements from which they may not fully benefit in the present. Excessive commitment to pay-as-you-go financing may prevent a jurisdiction from doing those things that really need to be done. Projects may be too costly to be carried out if financed only by annual tax revenues. In point of fact, few governments have the capability to finance vital public facilities strictly on a pay-as-you-go basis.

It may thus be argued that public projects providing services over many years should be paid for by people according to their use or benefit—that is, should be financed on a "pay-as-you-use" basis. Achieving user-benefit equity may require that the financing burden be spread over the life of the improvement with the borrowed funds repaid over a period of many years.

BORROWING

The power to borrow is one of the most important assets of state and local government. By borrowing, taxpayers are relieved of part of their immediate tax burden, which is shifted to future taxpayers. In so doing, however, tax liabilities are increased because of the interest charged on the borrowed funds. The general assumption is that future economic and population growth will offset the increased liability, making the payment of debt service (principal and interest) more feasible.

Borrowing may also be based on the assumption that inflation will make repayment easier. As inflation erodes the real value of the dollar, the actual burden of a given debt declines. A locality that issued thirty-year bonds in 1970 was paying debt service in 1999 with dollars worth perhaps one-third their initial value. Unless one's crystal ball is unfailing accurate, however, relying on inflation to lift the burden of debt can sometimes be a risky strategy.

In general, long-term borrowing is appropriate under the following conditions: (1) where the project will not require replacement for many years, such as a city hall, public health facility, or sewage disposal plant; (2) where the project can be financed by service charges to pay off debt service commitments; (3) where needs are urgent for public health and safety purposes or other emergency reasons; (4) where special assessment bonds are the most feasible means of financing improvements; (5) where intergovernmental revenues may be available on a continuous basis to guarantee the security of the bonds; and (6) for financing projects in newly annexed areas or areas of rapid expansion in which the demands on local tax resources are comparatively large and unforeseen.

Like all governmental powers, the capacity to borrow must be used with critical regard for its justifiable purposes and with a clear understanding of its safe and reasonable limits. A sound borrowing policy is one that seeks to conserve rather than exhaust credit. The ability to borrow when necessary on the most favorable market terms is an objective that applies to governments just as it does to business and industry.

CAPITAL RESERVE FUNDS

Financing capital facilities through a reserve fund (sometimes called a capital reserve) can be thought of as the opposite of borrowing in that the timetable is reversed. A portion of current revenue is invested each year in order to accumulate sufficient funds to initiate some particular project in the future. The amount S of a reserve fund created by a fixed investment N placed annually at compound interest r for a term of n years can be expressed by the following formula:

$$S = \frac{N\,[(1 + r)^n - 1]}{r}$$

An investment of $10,000 each year for ten years at 6% interest will thus yield a reserve fund of $131,800. Conversely, the amount N that must be placed annually at compound interest r for a term of n years to create a reserve fund S may be calculated by the following formula:

$$N = \frac{(S) \times r}{[(1 + r)^n - 1]}$$

Should the objective be to develop a reserve fund of $2 million at the end of ten years, an investment of $151,736 per year at 6% would be required.

Debt Financing and Administration

A bond is a promissory note ensuring that the lender will receive periodic payments of interest (at some predetermined rate), and at maturity (the due date), repayment of the original sum (principal) invested. A ten-year bond for $2 million with a 7% interest rate will thus pay the bondholders $140,000 in interest each year (usually in semiannual installments), and at the end of ten years, the $2 million will be repaid. Although referred to as "municipal" bonds, this broad investment category includes bonds issued by any political subdivision—cities, counties, school districts, or special purpose districts—public agency, authority, commission, state, territory, or possession of the United States.

Interest earned on municipal bonds is exempt from federal taxation, and usually from state taxes in the state in which the bond is issued. As a consequence, municipal bonds carry lower interest rates than taxable corporate bonds. This tax exemption, in effect, is a federal subsidy that reduces borrowing costs for local governments. In April 1988, the Supreme Court overruled a 1895 precedent by holding that the Constitution does not protect state and local governments against federal taxation of the interest received by holders of their bonds. The chairmen of the Senate and House tax-writing committees, however, immediately went on record that the Court's decision was not expected to prompt Congress to impose any new taxes on municipal bonds.

Municipal bonds possess three significant features in addition to their tax-exempt status:

1. The *security* of municipal bonds is generally considered second only to that of federal government bonds.
2. Municipal bonds have high *marketability*, assuring that investors can always sell them if they wish to do so.

3. The *diversity* of municipal bonds enables investors to obtain bonds in geographic areas and at maturities of their preference.

TYPES OF BONDS

General obligation bonds are backed by the "full faith, credit, and taxing power" of the issuing government. For many investors, general obligation bonds are seen as the most secure of the municipal issues, since the issuing authority has the power to levy taxes to meet debt service requirements. There are practical limits in the levying of taxes, however. In effect, the security of general obligation bonds is based upon the economic resources of taxpayers in the issuing jurisdiction.

Special tax or *special assessment bonds* are payable only from the proceeds derived from a special tax (e.g., highway bonds payable from a gasoline tax) or from a special assessment levied against those properties that benefit from the facilities constructed (e.g., for curbs and gutters in certain residential areas). The rising cost of special assessment bonds in recent years, however, has resulted in the majority of such bonds additionally being secured by a pledge of full faith and credit, making them general obligation bonds.

Revenue bonds are backed by a pledge of revenues to be generated by the facility being financed. These bonds do not carry the full faith and credit pledge. Revenue bonds are often used to construct toll roads and bridges, parking structures, sewage treatment plants, and other facilities that have fairly predictable revenue-generating capacities.

Municipal bonds can also be classified into two general types according to the method of redemption: term bonds and serial bonds. *Term bonds* become due in a lump sum at the end of the term of the loan. All bonds in the issue reach maturity and must be paid off at the same time. The lump-sum principal payment is met by making annual payments to a *sinking fund*. (See Table 1.) When invested at compound interest, these annual payments should produce the amount of principal required at maturity. Frequent actuarial computations are required to determine the adequacy of sinking funds to meet

Table 1 Debt Service Charges on $1 Million for Ten-Year Term Bonds (Sinking Fund Earning at 4.5%)

Year	Outstanding principal	Interest rate (%)	Interest payment	Sinking fund payment	Annual payments	Sinking fund accumulation
1	1,000,000	5.00	50,000	81,379	131,379	81,379
2	1,000,000	5.00	50,000	81,379	131,379	166,420
3	1,000,000	5.00	50,000	81,379	131,379	255,287
4	1,000,000	5.00	50,000	81,379	131,379	348,154
5	1,000,000	5.00	50,000	81,379	131,379	445,200
6	1,000,000	5.00	50,000	81,379	131,379	546,613
7	1,000,000	5.00	50,000	81,379	131,379	652,589
8	1,000,000	5.00	50,000	81,379	131,379	763,335
9	1,000,000	5.00	50,000	81,379	131,379	879,064
10	1,000,000	5.00	50,000	81,379	131,379	1,000,000
Totals			$500,000	$813,788	$1,313,788	

principal payments at maturity. Some states do not permit the issuance of bonds for which the principal is funded solely through a sinking fund. With proper investment safeguards, however, term bonds do offer some advantages. Term bonds may serve to finance public utilities and other enterprises that do not have established earning records.

Serial bonds are retired by annual installments directly from tax revenues, or in the case of revenue bonds, from income earned by the facility. Serial bonds have simpler retirement requirements and offer greater flexibility in marketing and in arranging the debt structure of the jurisdiction. There are two types of serial bonds: annuity serials and straight serials.

With *annuity serials*, the debt service payment is approximately the same each year (as with a home mortgage). The portion of the annual payment devoted to interest is higher in the early years of the issue but declines as payments toward principal are made (as the outstanding principal is retired). *Straight serial bonds* require annual payments of principal of approximately equal amounts. Interest payments are large in the early years and decline gradually as the bonds approach maturity. A payment schedule for straight serial bonds, with interest calculated at 6% over ten years on a declining principal, is shown in Table 2. Also shown in Table 2 is the payment schedule for an annuity serial bond, with interest calculated at 6% on the outstanding principal for the life of the loan. Note that the total

Table 2 Debt Service Charges on $1 Million for Ten Years

Year	Outstanding principal	Principal payment	Interest payment	Total debt service
Straight serial bonds (6% on declining principal)				
1	1,000,000	100,000	60,000	160,000
2	900,000	100,000	54,000	154,000
3	800,000	100,000	48,000	148,000
4	700,000	100,000	42,000	142,000
5	600,000	100,000	36,000	136,000
6	500,000	100,000	30,000	130,000
7	400,000	100,000	24,000	124,000
8	300,000	100,000	18,000	118,000
9	200,000	100,000	12,000	112,000
10	100,000	100,000	6,000	106,000
Total		$1,000,000	$330,000	$1,330,000
Annuity serial bonds (6% on outstanding principal)				
1	1,000,000	75,868	60,000	135,868
2	924,132	80,420	55,448	135,868
3	843,712	85,425	50,623	135,868
4	758,467	90,360	45,508	135,868
5	668,107	95,782	40,086	135,868
6	572,325	101,528	34,340	135,868
7	470,797	107,620	28,248	135,868
8	363,177	114,077	21,791	135,868
9	249,100	120,922	14,946	135,868
10	128,178	128,177	7,691	135,868
Total		$1,000,000	$358,680	$1,358,680

debt service cost of a straight serial is less than that of an annuity serial issued at the same rate of interest.

NEW FIDUCIARY AND FISCAL INSTRUMENTS

The municipal bond market traditionally has been supported by large institutional investors, such as fire and casualty insurance companies. More recently, however, many of these institutions have curtailed their municipal bond buying, resulting in significant increases in interest costs as bond issuers have been forced to make yields more attractive to investors who may be unwilling to lock into fixed returns, feeling uncertain about inflation, tax liabilities, and yield curves. As a consequence, a number of new fiduciary and fiscal instruments have been devised.

In traditional serial bonds, each maturity has the same interest (coupon) rate payable over the life of the bond. *Stepped coupon bonds*, on the other hand, use a maturity schedule in which interest rates start at lower levels and progressively increase to higher levels. The increase in interest payments each year is intended to provide a hedge against inflation and thus make the bonds more marketable. The issuing government may schedule more bonds to mature in early years because of the lower interest rates, thereby lowering the average life of the issue. The ten-year stepped coupon bond shown in Table 3, for example, retires 61% of the bonds issued in the first four years, distributing the remaining 39% over the next six years in decreasing increments. The $15,000 in bonds issued with a ten-year maturity earn 10.45% in interest each year for ten years, the $50,000 in bonds with nine-year maturity earn 9.55% in interest for nine years, and so forth.

Zero-coupon bonds take advantage of federal tax laws that entitle bondholders who forego tax-free income over the life of their investment to receive tax-exempt capital gains upon maturity. Zero-coupon bonds sell at substantial discounts from the face value (or par) because they pay no interest. By paying the face value upon maturity, however, they offer significant capital gains. For example, a seventeen-year zero-coupon bond with a face value of $1000 might be purchased at a significant discount of $150. If held to

Table 3 Ten-Year Stepped Coupon Bond Issue

Year	Outstanding principal	Principal payment	Interest rate (%)	Interest payment	Annual debt service
1	1,000,000	175,000	3.50	57,660	232,660
2	825,000	160,000	4.25	51,535	211,535
3	665,000	145,000	5.00	44,735	189,735
4	520,000	130,000	5.75	37,485	167,485
5	390,000	115,000	6.50	30,010	145,010
6	275,000	100,000	7.25	22,535	122,535
7	175,000	75,000	8.00	15,285	90,285
8	100,000	50,000	8.75	9,285	59,285
9	50,000	35,000	9.55	4,910	39,910
10	15,000	15,000	10.45	1,560	16,560
Totals		$1,100,000		$275,000	$1,275,000

maturity (e.g., seventeenth years), this investment would provide a tax-free capital gain of $850. According to the IRS, this return on investment represents $50 in tax-exempt income each year ($850 divided by seventeen-years). When the economy loses momentum and interest rates decline, zero-coupon bonds tend to outperform other fixed-income issues.

Compound interest bonds (also called accumulators, municipal multipliers, or capital appreciation bonds) return to the investor at maturity the principal plus interest compounded at a rate specified at the time the bond is issued. For example, a fifteen-year compound interest bond, issued for $1000 with a 5% interest rate, would yield $2078.93 at maturity. Unlike zero-coupon bonds, which sell at a discount, these bonds sell at face value. An investor in compound interest bonds, however still pays much less for the bond than it would be worth at maturity. This type of bond combines the investment-multiplying power of compound interest with the income-sheltering feature of traditional tax-exempt bonds.

The issuing jurisdiction must make payments to a sinking fund that are structured to earn a sufficient sum to cover the accumulated interest and principal costs. At some point during the term of a compound interest bond, the issuing jurisdiction may begin to make interest payments. The total annual payments are much higher, however, because interest must now be paid on the interest that has accumulated as additional capital (principal).

The yield (interest paid by the issuer) on *flexible interest* or *variable rate bonds* changes over the life of the bond, based on some interest index printed on the bond itself. This feature stands in contrast to the traditional fixed-rate bond for which the interest rate remains constant, while the market value of the bond changes when interest rates rise or fall. The interest index most often used is the average weekly rate of U.S. Treasury bills or bonds issued during the preceding interest period. The floating rate for a short-term flexible interest bond, for example, might be pegged at 67% of the average weekly rate for a Treasury bill, while the rate for a longer-term issue might be set at 75% of the average weekly rate on thirty-year Treasury bonds. This approach provides stability for both the issuer and the bondholder throughout the life of the bonds, particularly during times of interest rate volatility.

A *tender option bond* offers the investor the option of submitting the bond for redemption before maturity, usually five years after the date of issue or on any anniversary date thereafter. In return for this option, the issuer pays a lower rate of interest (usually about 1% less than for conventional bonds of the same maturity), and consequently, the jurisdiction's cost is lower. Tender option bonds may also be issued with a simultaneous "call" date, on which the issuer can call in and pay off the bonds. The issuer and the bondholder thus have equal rights to cash in the bonds when market conditions and interest rates are favorable. If interest rates go down, such bonds will likely be called in by the issuing government. Conversely, if interest rates go up, the bondholders can "tender their option" to be paid at face value by the issuer.

Detachable warrant bonds give the holder the right at some future date to purchase more of the same securities to which the warrant is attached at the same price and rate of return as the original bond. In exchange for that right, the issuer pays a lower rate of interest (about 0.5% less) than that offered on otherwise comparable securities. The marketability of such bonds depends on the opinion of prospective buyers as to anticipated fluctuations in interest rates. If interest rates rise, the savings to the issuer become real because of the initial lower interest cost. If the rates fall, the opposite is true.

In recent years, state and local governments have had to develop capital financing programs that are more responsive to their overall financial conditions and fiscal policies than traditional general obligation and revenue bonds. The emergence of more innovative approaches stems from the willingness of state and local governments to accept and deal with the uncertainty of future markets for financing capital facilities. More conventional approaches should not be abandoned, however, unless officials are satisfied that sufficient benefits will accrue when compared to the risks. Practical concerns are also part of the equation, including the political acceptability of such approaches, the ability of government to structure and manage these more creative financing mechanisms, and the laws that govern capital financing. Interest payments are still the cost that governments must pay for using the money of others. Careful application of new financing techniques, however, may uncover some real opportunities or provide capital resources than otherwise would be unavailable.

CASE STUDY FOR THE CITY OF RURBANA

The growth in population over the past fifteen years has placed considerable demands on the educational facilities of the city of Rurbana. In response to these pressures, the board of education replaced the traditional primary–secondary school system (i.e., K through 8 and 9 through 12) with a three-tiered approach: (1) kindergarten through sixth grade, (2) middle schools (grades 7, 8, and 9), and (3) senior high schools (grades 10, 11, and 12). This shift permitted the space needs for grades K through 6 to be accommodated within the former primary schools. It necessitated the construction of two new middle schools, however: George Washington Middle School and Thomas Jefferson Middle School, both opened in 1995. John F. Kennedy High School was opened in the past year, and the former Rurbana Memorial High School was converted into a middle school. Two new elementary schools have also been opened in the past seven years, bringing to fifteen the number of K through 6 schools in the city.

As shown in Table 4, the physical plant of Rurbana's public school system currently includes 570 classrooms. Applying a standard of thirty students per classroom, these facilities have the capacity to house 17,100 students. Current school enrollments record 17,426 students, distributed as follows:

K through 6:	9110
7, 8, and 9:	4232
10, 11, and 12:	4084

Table 4   Current School Facilities

Grade level	Schools	Classrooms	Capacity
K through 6 (elementary school)	15	300	9,000
7, 8, and 9 (middle school)	3	140	4,200
10, 11, and 12 (high school)	2	130	3,900
Totals	20	570	17,100

The current facilities are eleven classrooms short of meeting the thirty student per class-room standard. The major deficit (six classrooms) is at the high school level.

A recent directive from the state board of education mandates that in order to continue to receive maximum state support, all public school systems must maintain a standard of not more than twenty-five students per classroom. In other words, a maximum of 14,250 students can be accommodated in the current classroom inventory of Rurbana if this state standard is to be met. School districts have been given six years to meet the standard.

Stanley Farkel, a senior planner in the department of planning and budget, was given the responsibility for working with the board of education in the coordination of the educational facilities component of the city's six-year capital improvements program (CIP). Although the board of education established operating policies and procedures for the city's school system, the operating and capital budgets for education must be approved by the city council.

Building on previous population estimates, Farkel prepared the following six-year enrollment projections:

K through 6:   9350
7, 8, and 9:   3950
10, 11, and 12:   5300

To meet the state board of education standards, 374 classrooms (or an additional seventy-four classrooms) would be required at the K through 6 level. Farkel concluded that this need could be best met by building three new elementary schools. Two of these schools are already on the drawing board, each with twenty-classroom capacities; a third new school would be designed with a twenty-five-room capacity. Farkel proposed that the remaining nine-classroom deficit be accommodated through the use of temporary classrooms. This "interim plan" will permit these temporary facilities to be provided where the needs are most evident while retaining the flexibility for possible future expansion when funds are available.

The projected enrollment levels of 3945 students at the middle school level would dictate the construction of eighteen additional classrooms (to be added to existing schools). The projection of high school enrollment (5300) would require the addition of eighty-two classrooms over the current inventory. The school board had earlier proposed the construction of a new sixty-five-classroom high school to be available for use by the end of the six-year programming period. The school board argued that this size facility would be required to maintain a balance in the high school system of Rurbana.

Current costs for various classroom types are shown in Table 5. It is estimated that construction costs will increase at a rate of 6% per year over the next ten years. In other

Table 5   Cost Estimates for Classroom Facilities

Type	Capacity	First-year cost	Second-year cost	Third-year cost
Elementary (new school)	25	$129,965	$137,763	$146,030
Elementary (addition)	25	$93,700	$99,322	$105,281
Middle school (new school)	25	$148,700	$157,622	$167,079
Middle school (addition)	25	$104,745	$111,030	$117,692
High school (new school)	25	$149,450	$158,417	$167,922
High school (addition)	25	$111,650	$118,349	$125,450

words, as a consequence of inflation, it is anticipated that a classroom costing $129,965 today to construct as part of a new elementary school will cost approximately $146,030 two years from now (i.e., $129,965(1.06)(1.06) = $146,030). These cost calculations include all supporting facilities appropriate to a given type of classroom (additional versus new facility), such as halls, offices, lavatories, and so on, Figures for new schools also include estimates of basic site development costs. Land acquisition costs, however, must be funded separately.

Before decisions could be made regarding the timing and method of financing these new facilities, it was necessary for Farkel to determine the debt margin and the debt service limits that might prevail during the programming period. Under recently mandated practices of full value assessment, the debt limit for the city of Rurbana has been established at 2% of the assessed value of all real property within Rurbana. The debt limit for the current fiscal year is approximately $64 million. The city of Rurbana cannot have more than $64 million in debt (principal) outstanding in any given fiscal year. Educational facilities accounted for approximately 53% of the total debt limit during the last fiscal year. The city council has adopted an objective to maintain the long-term debt commitments for schools at no more than 50% of the total debt limit for the municipality.

Rurbana has a fairly substantial debt margin for educational facilities, as may be seen from Table 6. In the current capital budget, the principal outstanding for educational facilities totals $26,078,650. The educational debt limit of $32,000,000 is projected to increase by approximately 6% per year during the programming period as a consequence of increases in the assessed value of real property.

The second constraint on debt service is based on the notion that a jurisdiction should be able to retire its indebtedness within twenty years (or at a rate of 5% per year). Therefore this rule of thumb holds that the amount of funds required to retire 5% of the outstanding principal plus cover the total annual interest requirements should not exceed 25% of a normal annual budget. Since Rurbana has elected to issue bonds for shorter time periods, the rule of thumb has been appropriately modified to reflect the need to liquidate the city's indebtedness within fifteen years. As shown in Table 6, this heuristic translates into an annual debt service limit of $4,000,000, or 12.5% of the current total debt limit.

Table 6   Summary of Outstanding Debt Obligations for Educational Facilities

Category	Capital Budget	Capital Improvements Programming Period				
		Year 1	Year 2	Year 3	Year 4	Year 5
Total Principal Outstanding	$26,078,650	$23, 405,314	$20,652,028	$17,814,699	$14,889,023	$12,510,475
Principal Payments	$ 2,773,218	$ 2,853,168	$ 2,937,211	$ 3,025,558	$ 2,478,429	$ 2,576,057
Interest Payments	$ 1,322,516	$ 1,190,766	$ 1,054,922	$ 914,775	$ 770,104	$ 649,477
Total Debt Service	$ 4,095,734	$ 4,043,934	$ 3,992,134	$ 3,940,334	$ 3,248,534	$ 3,225,534
Sinking Fund	$ 1,061,026	$ 1,207,344	$ 1,359,516	$ 1,517,774	$ 1,682,362	$ 1,857,532
Educational Debt Limit	$32,000,000	$33,920,000	$35,955,200	$38,112,512	$40,399,263	$42,823,218
Debt Margin*	$ 6,982,376	$ 11,722,030	$16,662,688	$21,815,587	$27,192,602	$32,170,275
Debt Service Limit**	$ 4,000,000	$ 4,240,000	$ 4,494,400	$ 4,764,064	$ 5,049,908	$ 5,352,902

* Equals Debt Limit plus Sinking Fund minus Total Principal Outstanding
** Equals 12.5% of Debt Limit

Table 7   Interest Rates on Various Types of
School Bond Issues

Type	Maturity	Interest rate (%)
Straight serial	10	6.00
Straight serial	15	5.75
Straight serial	20	5.50
Term bond	10	5.50
Term bond	15	5.25
Term bond	20	5.00
Annuity serial	10	5.85
Annuity serial	15	5.60
Annuity serial	20	5.35
Deferred principal	15	5.50
Deferred principal	20	5.00
Stepped coupon	10	5.50
Stepped coupon	15	5.30

While these constraints are not legally binding in terms of state enabling legislation, they do reflect sound principles of public finance. Accordingly, the Rurbana city council has adopted these guidelines in connection with decisions regarding capital commitments for education.

Examining the data in Table 6, Farkel determined that the overall debt limit on educational facilities would not constitute a binding constraint on further borrowing. The limit on annual debt service was not being met in the current capital budget, however. The debt service payments of $4,095,734 required to support the commitments in the current capital budget is in excess of the annual debt service limit by nearly 2.4%.

As a general rule, bonds with different durations (or maturity dates) carry different interest rates, as shown in Table 7. Bonds with longer maturities often carry lower interest rates because the total interest accruing to these bonds is greater over the period for which principal is outstanding, thereby making them attractive to certain investors. The total debt service costs of bonds with longer maturities, however, are higher for the issuing jurisdiction. The objective is therefore to determine the bond issue with the shortest duration that meets other debt parameters.

In view of this situation and mindful of the city council's strong desire to adhere to these guidelines, Farkel recommended that additional borrowing be deferred until year 2 of the CIP. Using the interest rates on various types of school bond issues, as shown in Table 8, he further proposed that a fifteen-year stepped coupon bond for $2,920,600 be issued to finance the construction of Woodrow Wilson Elementary School as a twenty-classroom facility.

Farkel calculated that a fifteen-year stepped coupon bond, carrying an average interest rate of 5.3%, would add $351,110 to the debt service charges for year 2 of the CIP. (See Table 9.) When added to the continuing commitment of $3,992,134, shown in Table

Table 8   Debt Service Costs for Various Bond Issues to Finance the Construction of Woodrow Wilson Elementary School ($2,920,600)

Type	Total debt service	First-year debt service
Stepped coupon bond with 10-year maturity @ 5.50% average interest rate	$3,803,773	$518,202
Stepped coupon bond with 15-year maturity @ 5.30% average interest rate	$4,158,973	$351,110
Straight serial with 15-year maturity @ 5.75% interest	$4,264,075	$362,641
Annuity serial with 15-year maturity @ 5.60% interest	$4,393,550	$292,903
Term bond with 15-year maturity @ 5.25% interest (4% sinking fund)	$4,487,842	$299,189
Straight serial with 20-year maturity @ 5.50% interest	$4,607,247	$306,663
Annuity serial with 20-year maturity @ 5.35% interest	$4,818,990	$146,030
Term bond with 20-year maturity @ 5.00% interest (4% sinking fund)	$4,827,228	$241,361

Table 9   15-year stepped coupon bond issue (Woodrow Wilson Elementary School)

Year	Outstanding principal	Principal payment	Interest rate (%)	Interest payment	Annual debt service
1	2,929,600	208,000	3.40	143,110	351,110
2	2,712,600	206,000	3.62	136,037	342,037
3	2,506,600	204,000	3.84	128,580	332,580
4	2,302,600	202,000	4.06	120,746	322,746
5	2,100,600	200,000	4.28	112,545	312,545
6	1,900,600	198,000	4.50	103,985	301,985
7	1,702,600	196,000	4.72	95,075	291,075
8	1,506,600	195,000	4.94	85,824	280,824
9	1,311,600	194,000	5.16	76,191	270,191
10	1,117,600	192,000	5.38	66,180	258,180
11	925,600	190,000	5.60	55,851	245,851
12	735,600	187,800	5.82	45,211	233,011
13	547,800	185,200	6.04	34,281	219,481
14	362,600	182,600	6.26	23,095	205,695
15	180,000	180,000	6.48	11,664	191,664
Totals		$2,920,600		$1,238,374	$4,158,974

Table 10 Fifteen-Year Annuity Serial Bond Issue (Harry S. Truman Elementary School)

Year	Outstanding principal	Principal payment	Interest rate (%)	Interest payment	Annual debt service
1	3,095,800	137,109	5.60	173,365	310,474
2	2,958,691	144,787	5.60	165,687	310,474
3	2,813,903	152,895	5.60	157,579	310,474
4	2,661,008	161,458	5.60	149,016	310,474
5	2,499,551	170,499	5.60	139,975	310,474
6	2,329,051	180,047	5.60	130,427	310,474
7	2,149,004	190,130	5.60	120,344	310,474
8	1,958,874	200,777	5.60	109,697	310,474
9	1,758,097	212,021	5.60	98,453	310,474
10	1,546,077	223,893	5.60	86,581	310,474
11	1,322,184	236,432	5.60	74,042	310,474
12	1,085,753	249,672	5.60	60,802	310,474
13	836,081	263,653	5.60	46,821	310,474
14	572,427	278,418	5.60	32,056	310,474
15	294,009	294,009	5.60	16,465	310,474
Totals		$3,095,800		$1,561,310	$4,657,110

6, the total debt service would be $4,333,244, within the projected annual debt service limit, leaving a margin of $151,156. The total debt service cost of this new bond issue would be $4,158,974. A stepped coupon bond with a ten-year maturity and an average interest rate of 5.5% would carry a total debt service of $3,803,773, or $355,201 less than the recommended bond. (See Table 8.) The first-year debt service of $518,202 for this stepped coupon bond cannot be accommodated within the annual debt service limit established by the city council, however.

A fifteen-year annuity serial bond (5.6% interest rate) for $3,095,800 is proposed for year 3 of the CIP to finance the construction of Harry S. Truman Elementary School. The total debt service cost of this issue would be $4,657,110. (See Table 10.) A fifteen-year straight serial bond with a 5.75% interest rate would cost $139,834 less in total debt service than the proposed annuity bond. The annual debt service limit will not permit the substantially higher first-year debt service required by a straight serial bond, however.

Gerald R. Ford Elementary School is proposed to be built in year 4 of the CIP, financed by a fifteen-year straight serial bond for $4,101,945. The total debt service on this bond over the fifteen years would be $5,988,840. (See Table 11.)

The eighteen rooms to be added to existing middle schools are scheduled for construction in year 4 at a cost of $2,380,300. Farkel proposed that these additional classrooms be financed by a ten-year annuity serial bond, with a 5.85% interest rate and total debt service of $3,211,121.

The seventeen rooms beyond the proposed sixty-five high school classrooms required to accommodate the projected high school enrollment can be provided through additions to the existing high schools. The room additions would be financed through a twenty-year annuity serial bond for $2,396,250, to be issued in year 4.

The construction of a new sixty-classroom high school—the final recommended addition to the current educational facility inventory—presented a greater problem. Defer-

Table 11   Fifteen-Year Straight Serial Bond Issue (Gerald Ford Elementary School)

Year	Outstanding principal	Principal payment	Interest rate (%)	Interest payment	Annual debt service
1	4,101,945	273,463	5.75	235,862	509,325
2	3,828,482	273,463	5.75	220,138	493,601
3	3,555,019	273,463	5.75	204,414	477,877
4	3,281,556	273,463	5.75	188,689	462,152
5	3,008,093	273,463	5.75	172,965	446,428
6	2,734,630	273,463	5.75	157,241	430,704
7	2,461,167	273,463	5.75	141,517	414,980
8	2,187,704	273,463	5.75	125,793	399,256
9	1,914,241	273,463	5.75	110,069	383,532
10	1,640,778	273,463	5.75	94,345	367,808
11	1,367,315	273,463	5.75	78,621	352,084
12	1,093,852	273,463	5.75	62,896	336,359
13	820,389	273,463	5.75	47,172	320,635
14	546,926	273,463	5.75	31,448	304,911
15	273,463	273,463	5.75	15,724	289,187
Totals		$4,101,945		$1,886,895	$5,988,840

ring this project to year 5 of the CIP would result in an estimated construction cost of $13,000,000. The debt service heuristic will not permit any earlier financing through borrowing, however, Farkel therefore recommended that a capital reserve fund be established to accumulate $7 million over the next five years (beginning with the current capital budget). This fund would require annual payments of $1,215,433 at the beginning of the fiscal year, earning interest compounded at 4.75%. (See the capital reserve accummulation in Table 13.)

A bond issue for $6 million to build Rurbana Memorial High School can be placed as a twenty-year annuity serial at 5.35%. A twenty-five-year straight serial bond at a interest rate of 4.5% would actually cost $474,745 less in total debt service than the proposed twenty-year annuity serial. Here again, the substantially higher debt service required in the initial years of a straight serial bond cannot be accommodated within the annual debt service limit established by the city council.

All of the existing and proposed capital commitments for the next six years are summarized in Table 12. The new commitments, including the funding from general revenues for the land acquisition program for the proposed new construction, are shown in Table 12. The additional items to be financed from general revenues (pay-as-you-go financing), including temporary classroom facilities, are also shown. It should be noted that a decision was made to acquire twenty temporary classrooms (at $60,000 each) to provide more immediate relief to the current overcrowded conditions in the elementary and high schools. Ten of these units will be financed out of the current capital budget, with five more being acquired in each of the next two years. Table 13 provides an overall summary of obligations for educational facilities and represents an updated version of Table 6.

Table 12 Current and Projected Obligations for Educational Facilities: City of Rurbania

Facility	Capital Budget	Capital Improvements Programming Period				
		Year 1	Year 2	Year 3	Year 4	Year 5
George Washington Middle School	$2,560,000	$1,920,000	$1,280,000	$640,000	Retired	Retired
$6,400,000 straight	$640,000	$640,000	$640,000	$640,000		
serial/10-yrs. @ 4.5%	$115,200	$86,400	$57,600	$28,800		
Expansion of Administration Building	$896,592	$764,777	$626,372	$481,046	$328,454	$168,233
$1,364,000 annuity serial	$131,815	$138,405	$145,326	$152,592	$160,222	$168,233
10-years @ 5.00%	$44,830	$38,239	$31,319	$24,052	$16,423	$8,412
John F. Kennedy High School	$7,493,618	$6,573,253	$5,606,870	$4,592,168	$3,526,730	$2,408,021
$10,000,000 annuity	$920,365	$966,383	$1,014,702	$1,065,437	$1,118,709	$1,174,645
serial/ 10-yrs. @ 5.00%	$374,681	$328,663	$280,344	$229,608	$176,337	$120,401
Theodore Roosevelt High School–Addition	$2,430,000	$2,160,000	$1,890,000	$1,620,000	$1,350,000	$1,080,000
$4,050,000 straight serial	$270,000	$270,000	$270,000	$270,000	$270,000	$270,000
15-yrs. @ 5.00%	$121,500	$108,000	$94,500	$81,000	$67,500	$54,000
Thomas Jefferson Middle School	$3,443,580	$3,134,482	$2,809,157	$2,466,752	$2,106,370	$1,727,069
$5,000,000 annuity serial	$309,098	$325,325	$342,405	$360,381	$379,301	$399,215
15-yrs. @ 5.25%	$180,788	$164,560	$147,481	$129,504	$110,584	$90,671
Patrick Henry Elementary School	$1,800,000	$1,600,000	$1,400,000	$1,200,000	$1,000,000	$200,000
$4,000,000 straight serial	$200,000	$200,000	$200,000	$200,000	$200,000	$200,000
20-yrs. @ 4.75%	$85,500	$76,000	$66,500	$57,000	$47,500	$9,500
Abraham Lincoln Elementary School	$5,454,860	$5,252,801	$5,039,629	$4,814,733	$4,577,467	$4,327,152
$6,000,000 annuity serial	$202,059	$213,172	$224,896	$237,266	$250,315	$264,083
20-yrs. @ 5.50%	$300,017	$288,904	$277,180	$264,810	$251,761	$237,993
Athletic Fields $2,000,000 term bonds	$2,000,000	$2,000,000	$2,000,000	$2,000,000	$2,000,000	$2,000,000
15-yrs. @ 5.00% with	$99,882	$99,882	$99,882	$99,882	$99,882	$99,882
4.00% sinking fund	$100,000	$100,000	$100,000	$100,000	$100,000	$100,000
Woodrow Wilson Elementary School (20 rooms)			$2,920,600	$2,777,490	$2,641,452	$2,512,872
$2,920,600 stepped coupon			$143,110	$136,038	$128,580	$120,746
15-yrs. @ 5.30%			$208,000	$206,000	$204,000	$202,000
Harry S. Truman Elementary School (20 rooms)				$3,095,800	$2,958,691	$2,813,904
$3,095,800 annuity serial				$137,109	$144,787	$152,895
15-yrs. @ 5.60%				$173,365	$165,687	$157,579

(continued)

Table 12 Continued

Facility	Capital Budget	Capital Improvements Programming Period				
		Year 1	Year 2	Year 3	Year 4	Year 5
Gerald Ford Elementary School (25 rooms)					$4,101,945	$3,828,482
$4,101,945 straight serial 15-yrs. @ 5.75%					$273,463 $235,862	$273,463 $220,138
Middle School Addition (18 rooms)					$2,380,300	$2,198,435
$2,380,300 annuity serial 10-yrs. @ 5.85%					$181,865 $139,248	$192,504 $128,608
High School Addition (17 rooms)					$2,396,250	$2,290,123
$2,396,250 annuity serial 15-yrs. @ 5.60%					$106,127 $134,190	$112,070 $128,247
Rurbania Memorial High School						$6,000,000
$7,000,000 annuity serial 20-yrs. @ 5.35%						$174,846 $321,000
Capital Reserve for New High School $1,215,433@ 4.75% over 5 years	$1,215,433	$1,215,433	$1,215,433	$1,215,433	$1,215,433	
Land Acquisition General Revenues	$600,000	$1,100,000	$1,300,000	$600,000	$600,000	
Capital Equipment Replace. General Revenues	$1,400,000	$1,512,000	$1,632,960	$1,763,597	$1,904,685	$2,057,059
New Capital Equipment General Revenues	$1,200,000	$1,512,000	$1,849,000	$2,212,800	$2,606,000	$3,030,400
Temporary Classrooms General Revenues	$600,000	$324,000	$349,920			

SUMMARY AND CONCLUSION

The approach that Stan Farkel adopted illustrates a set of procedures appropriate to the formulation of a capital improvements program. Initial needs were identified by the board of education. Based on both established standards and projections of the target population, these needs were then translated into facility costs for various time periods.

The city council adopted CIP guidelines to establish the operational parameters within which various alternative solutions could be explored. The choice among the available options reflect both the established limits as to total commitments and the need to maintain flexibility for assuming additional commitments in the future.

Although the recommendations proposed by Stan Farkel may not necessarily represent the optimal strategy for financing these projects, they afford the flexibility required

Table 13 Summary of Obligations for Educational Facilities

Category	Capital Budget	Capital Improvements Programming Period				
		Year 1	Year 2	Year 3	Year 4	Year 5
Total Principal Outstanding	$26,078,650	$23,405,314	$23,572,628	$23,687,989	$29,367,661	$31,354,292
Principal Payments	$2,773,218	$2,853,168	$3,080,321	$3,298,705	$3,313,251	$3,602,581
Interest Payments	$1,322,516	$1,190,766	$1,262,922	$1,294,140	$1,649,091	$1,778,549
Total Debt Service	$4,095,734	$4,043,934	$4,343,244	$4,592,846	$4,962,342	$5,381,130
Pay-As-You-Go Financing	$5,015,433	$5,663,433	$6,347,313	$5,791,830	$6,326,118	$5,087,459
Total Capital Outlay	$9,111,167	$9,707,367	$10,690,557	$10,384,675	$11,288,459	$10,468,589
Sinking Fund	$1,061,026	$1,207,344	$1,359,516	$1,517,774	$1,682,362	$1,857,532
Capital Reserve	$1,273,166	$2,606,808	$4,003,797	$5,467,143	$7,000,000	
Educational Debt Limit	$32,000,000	$33,920,000	$35,955,200	$38,112,512	$40,399,263	$42,823,218
Debt Margin	$6,982,376	$11,722,030	$13,742,088	$15,942,297	$12,713,964	$13,326,458
Debt Service Limit	$4,000,000	$4,240,000	$4,494,400	$4,764,064	$5,049,293	$5,352,902
Debt Service Margin	($95,734)	$196,066	$151,156	$171,218	$87,566	($28,227)

to incorporate all of the identified needs on a priority basis with the minimum violation of the basic CIP guidelines. It should be noted from Table 13 that the total debt service in the final year of the CIP is slightly in excess of the projected debt service limit. This amount ($28,227), however, is not particularly critical, given the assumptions underlying the projected debt service limit and the time frame of these commitments.

This case study illustrates some problems that may be encountered in dealing with a self-imposed annual debt limit. In the long run, the city council could save public funds in terms of interest charges by affording some latitude as to the debt service that can be assumed in a given fiscal year (e.g., by permitting the $6 million required to build Rurbana Memorial High School to be financed through a straight serial bond issue).

Some greater flexibility might also be attained by refunding some of the outstanding bonds to free up an additional annual debt margin. The $1,350,000 in straight serial bonds outstanding in year 4 of the CIP, for example, issued to finance the additions to Theodore Roosevelt High School, might be refunded in combination with the proposed bonds to construct an additional seventeen rooms as part of the further high school expansion. A fifteen-year annuity serial bond issue for $3,750,000 (at 5.6%) would cost $5,641,200 in total debt service. While this refunded issue would cost Rurbana approximately $128,500 more than the two issues taken separately, the refunding would provide a sufficient annual debt margin in year 5 of the CIP to finance the proposed $6 million bond issue for the new high school through a twenty-year straight serial bond, thereby creating a substantial savings in total debt service.

REVIEW QUESTIONS

1. What are some of the advantages of financing capital improvements on a "pay-as-you-go" basis? What are some of the drawbacks?
2. Under what conditions is long-term borrowing by local governments most appropriate? What is the primary rule of a sound borrowing policy?

3. What are the four most significant features that municipal bonds possess?
4. What is the basic difference between a general obligation bond and other types of bonds that a municipality might issue?
5. What are the distinguishing characteristics of an annuity serial bond, a straight serial bond, and a term bond?
6. What are some of the advantages to issuing jurisdictions of stepped coupon and zero-coupon bonds?
7. What is the primary purpose of such CIP guidelines as the debt margin and the annual debt service limit?
8. How might the refunding of outstanding bonds be used to provide greater flexibility in the bond strategy adopted by a local government?

18

Can the Riverside Community Afford a Massive Debt-Financed Capital Improvements Program?

W. Bartley Hildreth
Wichita State University, Wichita, Kansas, U.S.A.

Gerald J. Miller
Rutgers University, Newark, New Jersey, U.S.A.

A community is limited in what it can afford to pay for public purposes. It is unclear where the breaking point is between affordability and the lack thereof. Public officials as well as taxpayers, however, confront this issue time and time again. Recently, two Riverside County taxing jurisdictions sharing the entire county as the tax base—the combined city–county government and the county school board—separately announced capital improvement plans that together required over $802 million in *local* tax-supported bonds. While there are other countywide taxing and borrowing jurisdictions (e.g., a recreation and parks district), these were the only two that publicly presented plans for tax-supported bonds to finance capital improvements. On the basis of typical debt capacity ratios the community appeared able to support the bonds, but on further inquiry the plans imposed enormous burdens on the taxpaying community, perhaps more than the community could afford.

This case addresses the nature of debt affordability. Typical debt burden indicators are given. The case then calculates debt service requirements for the respective governments' capital improvement plans, estimates the results from alternative revenue policies, and draws the implications for the community to afford the combined debt levels.

TYPICAL DEBT BURDEN INDICATORS

Local governments can identify a long list of capital improvement needs, most with a great deal of justification and political support. In many governments, the legal capacity to borrow accommodates more debt. A set of measures, termed debt capacity ratios, are often proffered as an alternative to legal capacity in gauging the limits of borrowing. Since repaying debt places a burden on taxpayers, capacity is best determined by comparing economic and demographic data with the amount of outstanding debt. Common measures for evaluating relative debt burdens are debt per capita and debt to full valuation of taxable property.

Key to calculating debt burdens is the definition of debt. *Direct net debt* represents gross debt less all revenue bonds, other self-supporting debt, and cash flow notes. *Overall net debt* is the sum of direct net debt and the proportionate share of the debt of other local governmental units that overlap the debt-issuing one. So, if a city is a part of a county, the overall net debt for the city is its own amount, plus a share of the county's outstanding debt (defined as the percentage of the property base that the city comprises of the county). An overall debt figure gives the total burden imposed by all local debt-creating jurisdictions on a given property base.

A measure of the proportionate amount of debt borne by each resident is *per capita debt*, determined by dividing the amount of outstanding debt (defined as either direct net debt or overall net debt) by population. A rationale for this measure is that capital improvement needs often increase as the population grows. In such situations, if the growth of long-term debt is proportionate to the increased demands of a rising resident population, then debt ratios will not change significantly. When long-term debt increases faster than the rate of population growth, however, debt levels may reach or exceed the residents' ability to pay. An underlying assumption is that residents perceive that their individual tax burden is distributed fairly.

As of the end of the last year, the Riverside city–county government had $61 of per capita net direct debt and $90 of per capita net overall debt (again defined as the combined debt of all the other political jurisdictions that constitute a burden on the same geographic area, such as the school system). The direct debt figures were well below the national median of $207 for counties approximately the same size of Riverside. Based on its population, Riverside could add $64 million in debt before it reached this national median per capita figure. Riverside maintained an overall debt per capita level well below the national median of $816, thus giving an indication that significant levels of new local debt could be accommodated if the ratio were the only limit.

A second debt ratio, alternatively termed debt burden or *debt to property value*, measures the burden of debt on a government's ad valorem (property) tax base. The amount of outstanding debt is divided by the aggregate full value of property. This provides an indication of the burden that debt places upon all property owners within a particular jurisdiction. The property tax base serves as a proxy for local wealth, and therefore reflects to some degree the capacity to provide public services.

A comparison of Riverside debt to full property valuation yielded similar results as the per capita debt analysis. The ratio of Riverside direct debt to the tax base was 0.2% in 1988, or 0.3 percentage points below the national median of 0.5%. Using overall debt as a guide, Riverside recorded a figure of 0.3%, a ratio significantly below the national median of 2.4% for similar-sized counties.

Each of these ratios—debt per capita and debt to property value—presume that the debt burden is distributed somewhat equitably among the population and across the total real property wealth of the community. When measured by both of the typical measures of debt capacity, Riverside showed the ability to handle a higher debt burden. In Riverside, however, over 90% of the taxable base for property taxes falls on nonresidential taxpayers, namely rental property and business and industry. What happens to the affordability equation when the tax burden is not borne equally by all the major taxpaying segments of the community? Riverside is a community faced with this type of problem.

This case presents an analysis of the community's debt affordability. Both the school board staff and the city–county government's fiscal experts supported their respective spending plans. Since they represent separate political jurisdictions, neither group sought to total the combined price of these spending plans. This analysis seeks to rectify that oversight. Fundamentally, this case study calculates the tax implications of local borrowing plans, therefore aiding a determination of debt affordability.

LOCAL FISCAL CONDITIONS AND KEY ASSUMPTIONS

In calculating the impact of financing plans, several assumptions regarding taxing and borrowing in Riverside had to be made. Some of the key assumptions used in the study were

> 1 mill ad valorem tax levied countywide yields about $1.08 million that is available to the taxing jurisdiction.
>
> 1/2 cent sales (and use) tax imposed countywide produces $20 million in collections.
>
> $1 million par value of serial bonds for twenty years at an 8% coupon rate, structured to achieve level debt service, equals $104,000 in debt service requirements per year.

The property tax base in Riverside County was approximately $14 billion of estimated actual value (excluding $2.1 billion of industrial exemptions and $175 million other exempt properties). In terms of assessed value—assessed value is approximately 11% of the total estimated actual value—the tax base was $1.53 billion. This 11% figure is a blend of a residential property assessment ratio of 10% of market value and all other properties at 15% of market value. The state constitution provides for a homestead exemption granted to all homeowners of $7,500 of assessed value (effectively shielding the first $75,000 of property value from tax). As a result, the total taxable value was only $1.08 billion (meaning that approximately 70% of total assessed value was taxable).

To modify the homestead exemption would have the following results:

> A reduction to $5,000 of assessed value would gain $95.2 million in taxable value, so 1 mill would yield $95,000 in taxes, assuming a 100% collection rate.
>
> A reduction to $2,500 of assessed value would gain $246.7 million in taxable value (or $246,700 per 1 mill).

As a result of the generous homestead exemption, approximately 90% of the property tax bill was borne by nonresidential taxpayers. In fact, the top ten taxpayers held 19.3% of the taxable value in the county. The top taxpayer alone accounted for almost 7.5% of the total tax base. For homeowners, only about 22,000 of the 82,403 homesteads were exposed to countywide property taxes as a result of the homestead exemption.

A change in revenue policy requires more than a decision by the local governing body. Changing the homestead exemption requires approval by the state legislature and the voting public, something that politicians have been loath to advocate for years. A property tax levy (such as a dedicated levy to pay off bonds) requires a vote of the electorate in the jurisdiction. To restore a one-half-cent sales tax rate after its expiration date requires a vote of the electorate. To increase the existing sales tax rate requires legislative approval and then voter approval.

The calculations in this study do not address operating millages or the cost of operating all the proposed new public facilities and improvements, nor does this study cover the relative costs-to-benefits of the capital projects; the capital plans are accepted as authoritative lists of needs structured by whatever evaluation principles guide such decisions.

The report strictly focuses on the revenue policy impact of two governments' announced capital acquisition plans.

HORIZON PLAN

To identify capital improvement needs in some systematic manner is the purpose of long-range comprehensive planning tied to scenarios regarding a community's future development. The Riverside city–county government developed a comprehensive land use and development plan following a voter-approved change in the local government charter that was heavily supported by civic and business interests. The name given this project was the Horizon Plan. A consulting team of planners, engineers, architects, and investment bankers worked on the plan for about two years at a cost of $1 million. In a move designed to narrow the scope of work (thereby saving contract fees), school facilities were not analyzed, thus excluding them from the schedule of needs. Also excluded were capital projects that were in the traditional scope of responsibilities of two small incorporated towns located within the outlying corners of the county.

As presented in 1991, the Horizon Plan included a schedule of needs from 1992–2010, totaling $1.133 billion. The plan relied on generous assumptions regarding federal and state funding, resulting in a need for $516 million in local funding. After excluding the listed wastewater capital improvements of $176 million for the entire planning period since those projects were presumed to be financed through rate increases and an existing dedicated sales (and use) tax for sewer improvements, the plan left approximately $340 million of needs for local tax-based funding.

The Horizon Plan's strategy for financing the first five years of the capital program was to seek voter approval to continue existing, but expiring, taxes [i.e., property taxes supporting one of the last voter-approved capital improvement bonds (the "1965 bonds") and the three-year pay-as-you-go street improvement sales (and use) tax set to expire in mid-1993]. The Horizon Plan did not present a financing plan for the rest of the planning period to 2010, due to the highly variable nature of those plans.

The yearly requirements to finance the Horizon Plan debt service schedule are displayed in Table 1. To arrive at this table the tax yield was calculated from the existing, but expiring, revenue sources (i.e., the existing property tax levies for the 1965 bonds and the street improvement sales tax), which could provide funds for new debt service. This flow of funds was used to fund, under a level debt service rule, debt service for a set of twenty-year serial bonds. These bonds were calculated using an estimated annual coupon interest rate of 8%, the same assumptions used by the Horizon Plan's financial advisor. All wastewater projects were excluded from the entire program for the reasons stated earlier.

The matching of available revenue to the Horizon Plan schedule of needs would fund $215 million of identified local (non-wastewater) capital projects covering the years 1992–1998. This consisted of four series of general obligation bonds totaling $18.648 million. The issuance of sales tax-backed revenue bonds totaling $196,368,000 was to take place as soon as the proposed sales tax election was official. Financing Horizon Plan needs for the 1999–2010 period required the projection of debt service for twelve consecutive debt issues matched to yearly needs specified in the Horizon Plan. This cumulative bond sizing exercise resulted in an estimated $127 million of bonds. In summary, financing the entire schedule of Horizon Plan locally funded projects required an estimated

Table 1 Horizon Plan Debt Service (Par = $342,013,000)

	Property tax General obligation Bonds					Sales tax Revenue bonds	
Year	Series 1 $3,703,000 total	Series 2 $3,860,000 total	Series 3 $6,085,000 total	Series 4 $5,000,000 total	Series 5–17[a] $127,000,000 total	Series 1 $196,365,000 total	Series grand total
1992	382,653						382,653
1993	380,653	393,169				20,000,000	20,773,822
1994	380,653	393,169				20,000,000	20,773,822
1995	380,653	393,169				20,000,000	20,773,822
1996	380,653	393,169				20,000,000	20,773,822
1997	380,653	393,169	620,595			20,000,000	21,394,417
1998	380,653	393,169	620,595	520,000		20,000,000	21,914,417
1999	380,653	393,169	620,595	520,000	1,856,100	20,000,000	23,770,517
2000	380,653	393,169	620,595	520,000	3,548,767	20,000,000	25,463,184
2001	380,653	393,169	620,595	520,000	5,103,900	20,000,000	27,018,317
2002	380,653	393,169	620,595	520,000	6,738,133	20,000,000	28,652,550
2003	380,653	393,169	620,595	520,000	7,721,500	20,000,000	29,635,917
2004	380,653	393,169	620,595	520,000	8,545,700	20,000,000	30,460,117
2005	380,653	393,169	620,595	520,000	9,315,633	20,000,000	31,230,050
2006	380,653	393,169	620,595	520,000	10,022,200	20,000,000	31,936,617
2007	380,653	393,169	620,595	520,000	10,874,167	20,000,000	32,788,584
2008	380,653	393,169	620,595	520,000	11,627,867	20,000,000	33,542,284
2009	380,653	393,169	620,595	520,000	12,293,667	20,000,000	34,208,084
2010	380,653	393,169	620,595	520,000	12,994,000	20,000,000	34,908,417
2011	380,653	393,169	620,595	520,000	13,034,200	20,000,000	34,948,617
2012		393,169	620,595	520,000	13,023,000	20,000,000	34,556,764
2013			620,595	520,000	13,039,000		14,179,595
2014			620,595	520,000	13,032,400		14,172,995
2015			620,595	520,000	13,027,000		14,167,595
2016			620,595	520,000	13,034,600		14,175,195
2017				520,000	13,035,800		13,555,800
2018					13,027,400		13,027,400
2019					11,051,200		11,051,200
2020					9,385,400		9,385,400
2021					7,833,200		7,833,200
2022					6,182,200		6,182,200
2023					5,251,800		5,251,800
2024					4,427,000		4,427,000
2025					3,668,000		3,668,000
2026					2,972,800		2,972,800
2027					2,114,400		2,114,400
2028					1,363,800		1,363,800
2029					696,600		696,600
Total DS	$7,615,060	$7,863,380	$12,411,900	$10,400,000	$259,841,434	$400,000,000	$698,131,774

Note:

* Excludes wastewater capital program, which is presumed to be financed through existing sales taxes and rate increases.

** Projected debt service for twelve consecutive debt issues (1999 to 2010) matched to Plan needs.

Par values are, in order, in millions of 1990 dollars, $19.5, $16.385, $15.2, $15, $9.2, $8.1, $7.5, $6.8, $8.5, $7.3, $6.6, and $6.9.

$342 million of par value bonds. The grand total debt service on these bonds amounted to $698 million for the entire planning period.

SCHOOL BOARD PLANS

The Riverside County School Board, a separate political jurisdiction, had before it the superintendent's proposal for $460 million in capital spending. The proposal would have built three new schools, rehabilitated or replaced the existing 101 schools, added new classrooms to eliminate the use of temporary buildings and emergency classrooms—such as closets and stages—provided additional room for the next ten years of growth, and housed a prekindergarten program (that had not yet gained board approval). The capital proposal neither addressed the extensive busing program nor the prospect for approval by the federal district court, as required under a long-running court order.

In a debt strategy driven by cash needs, the school staff prepared and presented the yearly debt service schedules for $460 million of bonds (shown in Table 2). Unlike the city–county's plan, the school plan was not based on the use of existing tax policy since

Table 2 School District Capital Improvements Plan Debt Service (Par = $460,415,000)

	1991 issue	1992 issue	1993 issue	1994 issue	1995 issue	1996 issue	1997 issue	Total debt service
1992	3,831,406							3,831,406
1993	4,950,925	6,440,925						11,391,850
1994	4,948,468	6,438,318	6,440,925					17,827,711
1995	4,943,456	6,431,606	6,438,318	6,938,968				24,752,348
1996	4,940,306	6,425,206	6,431,606	6,932,256	6,938,968			31,668,342
1997	4,933,437	6,423,150	6,425,206	6,925,856	6,932,256	6,938,968		38,578,873
1998	4,927,268	6,414,662	6,423,150	6,923,800	6,925,856	6,932,256	6,938,968	45,485,960
1999	4,925,831	6,408,968	6,414,662	6,915,312	6,923,800	6,925,856	6,932,256	45,446,685
2000	4,918,350	6,400,100	6,408,968	6,909,618	6,915,312	6,923,800	6,925,856	45,402,004
2001	4,914,050	6,396,893	6,400,100	6,900,750	6,909,618	6,915,312	6,923,800	45,360,523
2002	4,906,962	6,388,187	6,396,893	6,892,737	6,900,750	6,909,618	6,915,312	45,310,459
2003	4,896,312	6,378,012	6,388,187	6,884,418	6,892,737	6,900,750	6,909,618	45,250,034
2004	4,890,937	6,370,012	6,378,012	6,879,437	6,884,418	6,892,737	6,900,750	45,196,303
2005	4,884,481	6,357,831	6,370,012	6,866,631	6,879,437	6,884,418	6,892,737	45,135,547
2006	4,875,781	6,349,918	6,357,831	6,859,643	6,866,631	6,879,437	6,884,418	45,073,659
2007	4,863,675	6,334,725	6,349,918	6,846,925	6,859,643	6,866,631	6,879,437	45,000,954
2008	4,856,612	6,325,506	6,334,725	6,836,925	6,846,925	6,859,643	6,866,631	44,926,967
2009	4,843,043	6,310,325	6,325,506	6,822,900	6,836,925	6,846,925	6,859,643	44,845,267
2010	4,831,418	6,297,243	6,310,325	6,812,912	6,822,900	6,836,925	6,846,925	44,758,648
2011	4,819,800	6,279,131	6,297,243	6,795,025	6,812,912	6,822,900	6,836,925	44,663,936
2012		6,263,662	6,279,131	6,782,106	6,795,025	6,812,912	6,822,900	39,755,736
2013			6,263,662	6,761,831	6,782,106	6,795,025	6,812,912	33,415,536
2014				6,746,681	6,761,831	6,782,106	6,795,025	27,085,643
2015					6,746,681	6,761,831	6,782,106	20,290,618
2016						6,746,681	6,761,831	13,508,512
2017							6,746,681	6,746,681
Total DS	96,902,518	127,434,380	127,434,380	137,234,731	137,234,731	137,234,731	137,234,731	900,710,202

Note: Debt service is stated in current dollars.

the school board had no outstanding bonded debt, having just retired its last general obligation bonds out of accumulated debt service reserve funds.

In its plan, the school board anticipated issuing $50 million to $70 million in bonds in seven yearly increments. This total of $460 million in desired capital improvements can be compared to an existing, balance sheet value of $172 million for all general fixed assets in land, buildings and improvements, as well as furniture and equipment! In short, the school board planned to expand greatly the physical asset base of the school system and raise taxes to the level necessary to generate the funds. This was at a time when the school staff had not presented to, or gained, school board approval for the new schools or decided which existing facilities would be replaced or improved.

THE COMBINED SPENDING PLANS AND REVENUE POLICIES

The combination of the proposed city–county Horizon Plan and the school's capital plan, plus the existing city–county bond levy, is shown in Table 3, along with the revenues generated under existing revenue policies. Table 3 incorporates a property tax rate set at 1988 levels of 5.51 mills for bond repayment, comprising 3.42 mills for existing city–county bonds and 2.09 for the school board. An alternative scenario would have been to use the 1990 tax levy of 2.70 mills for the city and zero for the school board. To do so, however, would have penalized the school board for retiring its last bonds out of debt service funds and avoiding the imposition of the last year of the voted tax levy. This decision by the school board saved taxpayers money. For the purpose of this analysis, therefore, the subjective decision to fix current tax policy at 1988 levels for both taxing jurisdictions resulted in a tax bill higher than at the time of the analysis (thereby making the "current" tax policy really a rollback to a higher tax period, but at least it did not penalize the school system for its fiscal acumen).

There were other key assumptions in the existing revenue policy scenario. The homestead exemption was assumed to continue at the existing level ($7,500 of assessed value). The sales tax was assumed to stay at the one-half-cent tax level, which was to become available for voter renewal in mid-1993 (upon expiration of the existing three-year pay-as-you-go street improvement program). According to city–county records, sales tax collections grew an average of about 1% over the five preceding years. In following the lead of the Horizon Plan's financial advisor, however, this project assumed only $20 million in sales tax proceeds in each of the future years.

Comparing total revenues from existing tax policies to total debt service needs revealed significant deficits—shown in the next to last column. Avoiding such deficits required new revenue sources, assuming the debt issuance plans were not changed.

To cover the yearly deficits brought on by debt service, new property tax millages were required. Given the assumption that 1 mill would generate about $1.1 million in tax receipts, the millage rate in the last column floats to cover each year's shortfall—when debt service needs exceed revenues. As demonstrated, millage levels would have to increase substantially, and quickly, to service all the bonds envisioned under the two governments' plans. The rate increases would hover from 40 to 49 mills into the second decade of the twenty-first century.

Table 3   Combined Capital Plans Under Property Tax-Dependent Revenue Policies

Year	County GO debt	Horizon Plan DS	School plans DS	Levy set @ 5.51 HE = $7500	1/2 cent sales tax	Total revenues	Total DS needs	Revenues minus needs	Additional millage required for debt service
1992	3,457,761	382,653	3,831,406	5,800,000		5,800,000	7,671,820	(1,871,820)	1.7
1993	3,064,593	20,773,822	11,391,850	5,800,000	10,000,000	15,800,000	35,230,265	(19,430,265)	17.9
1994	3,062,705	20,773,822	17,827,711	5,800,000	20,000,000	25,800,000	41,664,238	(15,864,238)	14.6
1995	3,065,038	20,773,822	24,752,348	5,800,000	20,000,000	25,800,000	48,591,208	(22,791,208)	20.9
1996	3,069,954	20,773,822	31,668,342	5,800,000	20,000,000	25,800,000	55,512,118	(29,712,118)	27.2
1997	2,449,359	21,394,417	38,578,875	5,800,000	20,000,000	25,800,000	62,422,651	(36,622,651)	33.5
1998	1,331,850	21,914,417	45,485,962	5,800,000	20,000,000	25,800,000	68,732,229	(42,932,229)	39.2
1999		23,770,517	45,485,962	5,800,000	20,000,000	25,800,000	69,256,479	(43,456,479)	39.7
2000		25,463,184	45,485,962	5,800,000	20,000,000	25,800,000	70,949,146	(45,149,146)	41.2
2001		27,018,317	45,485,962	5,800,000	20,000,000	25,800,000	72,504,279	(46,704,279)	42.6
2002		28,652,550	45,485,962	5,800,000	20,000,000	25,800,000	74,138,512	(48,338,512)	44.1
2003		29,635,917	45,485,962	5,800,000	20,000,000	25,800,000	75,121,879	(49,321,879)	44.9
2004		30,460,117	45,485,962	5,800,000	20,000,000	25,800,000	75,946,079	(50,146,079)	45.7
2005		31,230,050	45,485,962	5,800,000	20,000,000	25,800,000	76,716,012	(50,916,012)	46.4
2006		31,936,617	45,485,962	5,800,000	20,000,000	25,800,000	77,422,579	(51,622,579)	47.0
2007		32,788,584	45,485,962	5,800,000	20,000,000	25,800,000	78,274,546	(52,474,546)	47.8
2008		33,542,284	44,926,968	5,800,000	20,000,000	25,800,000	78,469,252	(52,669,252)	48.0
2009		34,208,084	44,845,268	5,800,000	20,000,000	25,800,000	79,053,352	(53,253,352)	48.5
2010		34,908,417	44,845,268	5,800,000	20,000,000	25,800,000	79,753,685	(53,953,685)	49.1
2011		34,948,617	44,845,268	5,800,000	20,000,000	25,800,000	79,793,885	(53,993,885)	49.2
2012		34,556,764	39,755,737	5,800,000	20,000,000	25,800,000	74,312,501	(48,512,501)	44.2
2013		14,179,595	33,415,537	5,800,000	20,000,000	25,800,000	47,595,132	(21,795,132)	19.8
2014		14,172,995	27,085,643	5,800,000	20,000,000	25,800,000	41,258,638	(15,458,638)	14.1
2015		14,167,595	20,290,618	5,800,000	20,000,000	25,800,000	34,458,213	(8,658,213)	7.9
2016		14,175,195	13,508,512	5,800,000	20,000,000	25,800,000	27,683,707	(1,883,707)	1.7
2017		13,555,800	6,746,681	5,800,000	20,000,000	25,800,000	20,302,481	5,497,519	0.0
2018		13,027,400		5,800,000	20,000,000	25,800,000	13,027,400	12,772,600	0.0
2019		11,051,200		5,800,000	20,000,000	25,800,000	11,051,200	14,748,800	0.0
2020		9,385,400		5,800,000	20,000,000	25,800,000	9,385,400	16,414,600	0.0
2021		7,833,200		5,800,000	20,000,000	25,800,000	7,833,200	17,966,800	0.0
2022		6,182,200		5,800,000	20,000,000	25,800,000	6,182,200	19,617,800	0.0
2023		5,251,800		5,800,000	20,000,000	25,800,000	5,251,800	20,548,200	0.0
2024		4,427,000		5,800,000	20,000,000	25,800,000	4,427,000	21,373,000	0.0
2025		3,668,000		5,800,000	20,000,000	25,800,000	3,668,000	22,132,000	0.0
2026		2,972,800		5,800,000	20,000,000	25,800,000	2,972,800	22,827,200	0.0
2027		2,114,400		5,800,000	20,000,000	25,800,000	2,114,400	23,685,600	0.0
2028		1,363,800		5,800,000	20,000,000	25,800,000	1,363,800	24,436,200	0.0
2029		696,600		5,800,000	20,000,000	25,800,000	696,600	25,103,400	0.0
								(670,408,686)	

Note: The levy is set at 1988 levels or 3.42 mills (for county) and 2.09 mills (for schools). The homestead exemption is assumed to remain at its present level.

BROADLY BASED REVENUE POLICIES

Actions to broaden the revenue base were examined. Table 4 shows the combined capital plans under more broadly based revenue policies. Table 4 assumed a property tax levy set at 1988 levels (as in the early tables), removal of the homestead exemption (thereby taxing the first dollar of every homestead, not just the market value over $75,000), and an increase in the sales tax rate to a full 1% (requiring voter renewal as well as a change in purpose for the soon-to-expire one-half-cent tax, plus state approval for another one-half-cent tax). Debt service needs were left unchanged from the earlier tables. Despite a

Table 4 Combined Capital Plans Under More Broadly Based Revenue Policies

Year	County GO debt	Horizon Plan DS	School plans DS	Levy set @ 5.51 HE = 0%	1 cent sales tax	Total revenues	Total DS needs	Revenues minus needs	Additional millage required for debt service
1992	3,457,761	382,653	3,831,406	8,400,000		8,400,000	7,671,820	728,180	0.0
1993	3,064,593	20,773,822	11,391,850	8,400,000	40,000,000	48,400,000	35,230,265	13,169,735	0.0
1994	3,062,704	20,773,822	17,827,711	8,400,000	40,000,000	48,400,000	41,664,237	6,735,763	0.0
1995	3,065,038	20,773,822	24,752,348	8,400,000	40,000,000	48,400,000	48,591,208	(191,208)	5.6
1996	3,069,954	20,773,822	31,668,342	8,400,000	40,000,000	48,400,000	55,512,118	(7,112,118)	10.1
1997	2,449,359	21,394,417	38,578,875	8,400,000	40,000,000	48,400,000	62,422,651	(14,022,651)	14.5
1998	1,331,850	21,914,417	45,485,962	8,400,000	40,000,000	48,400,000	68,732,229	(20,332,229)	18.5
1999	0	23,770,517	45,485,962	8,400,000	40,000,000	48,400,000	69,256,479	(20,856,479)	18.8
2000		25,463,184	45,485,962	8,400,000	40,000,000	48,400,000	70,949,146	(22,549,146)	19.9
2001		27,018,317	45,485,962	8,400,000	40,000,000	48,400,000	72,504,279	(24,104,279)	20.9
2002		28,652,550	45,485,962	8,400,000	40,000,000	48,400,000	74,138,512	(25,738,512)	21.9
2003		29,635,917	45,485,962	8,400,000	40,000,000	48,400,000	75,121,879	(26,721,879)	22.6
2004		30,460,117	45,485,962	8,400,000	40,000,000	48,400,000	75,946,079	(27,546,079)	23.1
2005		31,230,050	45,485,962	8,400,000	40,000,000	48,400,000	76,716,012	(28,316,012)	23.6
2006		31,936,617	45,485,962	8,400,000	40,000,000	48,400,000	77,422,579	(29,022,579)	24.0
2007		32,788,584	45,485,962	8,400,000	40,000,000	48,400,000	78,274,546	(29,874,546)	24.6
2008		33,542,284	44,926,968	8,400,000	40,000,000	48,400,000	78,469,252	(30,069,252)	24.7
2009		34,208,084	44,845,268	8,400,000	40,000,000	48,400,000	79,053,352	(30,653,352)	25.1
2010		34,908,417	44,845,268	8,400,000	40,000,000	48,400,000	79,753,685	(31,353,685)	25.5
2011		34,948,617	44,845,268	8,400,000	40,000,000	48,400,000	79,793,885	(31,393,885)	25.5
2012		34,556,764	39,755,737	8,400,000	40,000,000	48,400,000	74,312,501	(25,912,501)	22.0
2013		14,179,595	33,415,537	8,400,000	40,000,000	48,400,000	47,595,132	804,868	0.0
2014		14,172,995	27,085,643	8,400,000	40,000,000	48,400,000	41,258,638	7,141,362	0.0
2015		14,167,595	20,290,618	8,400,000	40,000,000	48,400,000	34,458,213	13,941,787	0.0
2016		14,175,195	13,508,512	8,400,000	40,000,000	48,400,000	27,683,707	20,716,293	0.0
2017		13,555,800	6,746,681	8,400,000	0	8,400,000	20,302,481	(11,902,481)	13.1
2018		13,027,400		8,400,000	0	8,400,000	13,027,400	(4,627,400)	8.5
2019		11,051,200		8,400,000	0	8,400,000	11,051,200	(2,651,200)	7.2
2020		9,385,400		8,400,000	0	8,400,000	9,385,400	(985,400)	6.1
2021		7,833,200		8,400,000	0	8,400,000	7,833,200	566,800	0.0
2022		6,182,200		8,400,000	0	8,400,000	6,182,200	2,217,800	0.0
2023		5,251,800		8,400,000	0	8,400,000	5,251,800	3,148,200	0.0
2024		4,427,000		8,400,000	0	8,400,000	4,427,000	3,973,000	0.0
2025		3,668,000		8,400,000	0	8,400,000	3,668,000	4,732,000	0.0
2026		2,972,800		8,400,000	0	8,400,000	2,972,800	5,427,200	0.0
2027		2,114,400		8,400,000	0	8,400,000	2,114,400	6,285,600	0.0
2028		1,363,800		8,400,000	0	8,400,000	1,363,800	7,036,200	0.0
2029		696,600		8,400,000	0	8,400,000	696,600	7,703,400	0.0
								(341,608,685)	

Note: The levy is set at 1988 levels or 3.42 mills (for county) and 2.09 mills (for schools). The homestead exemption is assumed to be zero.

broader-based revenue scenario, the prospect for higher property taxes remained. The top tax rates stayed in the range of 20–25 mills, however, instead of the 39–49 mills under the earlier existing revenue scenario.

SUMMARY AND CONCLUSION

In conclusion, existing revenue levels of property and sales taxes do not support the two organizations' capital plans in the period originally planned. Even upon assuming that the property tax homestead exemption was eliminated and the voters agreed to dedicate a full

1% sales tax (both highly unlikely in the current political environment), significant millage increases would still be needed to finance the two plans within the original period.

Affordability could be achieved by a slower schedule of bond sales and greater coordination among debt issuers. To do so would require a re-examination of projects and the establishment of new priorities, not just within the school board's plans, but between public schools and all the other public improvements contained in the Horizon Plan. A new operating premise of competition for scarce tax dollars would replace the intended strategy of expanding the tax levels to accommodate the full capital appetite.

Uncontrolled and uncoordinated debt from the various jurisdictions within the county's boundaries can result in rapid increases in the area's overall debt, therefore overburdening taxpayers and affecting credit quality. Bond rating agencies view coordinated debt management favorably and recognize the credit quality enhancement flowing from intergovernmental cooperation.

Efforts to broaden the tax base would help all parts of the community bear the costs of needed capital improvements. A heavier tax burden often results in a heightened sense of accountability over public taxing and spending decisions.

Higher debt levels can affect the local bond rating. Riverside has a low level of outstanding debt, but a concentrated economy. How these contradictory factors influence local bond ratings is subject to debate. Officials have to exercise caution, however, because a higher cost of borrowing (brought on by a lower bond rating) means less money placed into local capital improvements and more money sent out of the community in interest payments to bondholders.

REVIEW QUESTIONS

1. What would be the impact of growth in the taxable property tax base and in the sales tax base? What if the assumption of 8% coupon interest rates on bonds turned out wrong? To what degree do these assumptions offset each other? How does an analyst handle alternative scenarios?
2. On a practical level, how realistic were the combined plans given the changes in tax policy required to support those plans?
3. If you were a taxpayer in Riverside, how would you vote on the tax levies required to fully implement these plans? Explain your position. Would it change your vote if you were a senior executive of the top taxpaying firm in Riverside? A renter of housing? An owner of a home valued at less than $75,000? A parent with a public school student?
4. While the largest taxpayer accounted for almost 7.5% (or $118 million) of the total taxable value in the county, it owned other industrial property (at $129 million in taxable value) exempt under a state-controlled ten-year industrial tax exemption. Other large industrial companies in the county enjoyed similar tax advantages. A coalition of citizens and unions organized to improve "tax justice" noted that such corporations "have the best deal in town when it comes to property taxes. A corporation that is lucky enough to pay tax on one-half, one-third, or one-fifty of its property value ought to be leading the charge to raise the millage a bit to improve school conditions in its own back yard." Instead, the top taxpayers supported efforts to test the affordability of the school's capital plan. What do you think about the tax justice of this situation?
5. What could the school board and the mayor-council do to improve the coordination of their respective government's capital plans?

6. Given the plans to issue large amounts of debt and the inability of existing tax policy to support the debt, requiring a substantial increase in property taxes, a question arises as to how this might influence the bond rating. A bond rating is an independent credit quality assessment intending to measure the probability of the timely repayment of principal of and interest on municipal securities. In the market, the higher the credit quality, the lower the cost of borrowing. The two most prominent bond rating services, Moody's Investors Service and Standard & Poor's Corporation, say they look at many factors before deciding on a rating. Standard & Poor's *Ratings Guide* (1979), however, states: "We consider an issuer's economic base the most critical element in the determination of a municipal bond rating."

   In the article "Credit Ratings and General Obligation Bonds: A Statistical Alternative" by S. R. Wilson, vice president of public finance for an investment banking firm, and published in *Government Finance Review* (June 1986), the author used a random sample of municipalities to study factors affecting a bond rating. Of four sets of variables—debt, financial condition, management, and economy—he found

   > Only economic variables show any real discriminating ability. The largest taxpayer and 10 largest taxpayers variables, which are intended to measure the concentration and dependence of the local economy, are significant. . . . The results . . . indicate that Moody's considers the strength of the local economy to be the single most important factor in assigning a GO (general obligation) bond rating.

   As to the often cited debt capacity ratios of debt per capita and debt to local property value, Wilson observed they showed "no logical pattern."
   One way to apply Wilson's findings is to see how bond ratings decline with increases in the concentration of the property tax base. He reported mean values for the ten largest taxpayers by rating category.

Rating	Mean value of the top 10 taxpayers as percentage of tax base
Aaa	10.6%
Aa1-Aa	11.4%
A1	13.9%
A	19.7%
Lower	20.4%

   In comparison, 19.3% of the taxable assessed value in Riverside County was held by the top ten taxpayers. The city–county government's bond rating is consistent with this discriminating variable. Wilson's research suggests that higher property tax rates on a concentrated tax base threaten the general obligation bond rating.
   Compare the implications of this research finding with the results from applying typical debt capacity indicators. What does all of this mean for the Riverside community?

7. Can the Riverside community afford a massive debt-financed capital improvements program?

19

Budget Analysis

A Study in the Budgetary Practices of a Small Community

Michael Campenni and Aman Khan
Texas Tech University, Lubbock, Texas, U.S.A.

The re-emphasis upon local government as the primary provider of public goods and services has served to focus attention upon the lower levels of government finance and budgeting as never before. Over the last quarter century, local government expenditures have increased at a higher average annual rate than the GNP or the federal government's spending (Aronson and Hilley, 1986: ix). This shift in emphasis has been accompanied by an explosive growth in local governmental responsibilities as the federal and state governments continue to decentralize and divest responsibility under the new federalism. In essence, the role of local government has exploded as it attempts to fill the vacuum created by the continued retrenchment of the national and state governments. This new reality has crippled some local governments while others have adapted remarkably well. The key to successfully meeting these new financial challenges lies in the budgetary process.

A budget has multiple purposes. For most of this century and to a large extent still, control was the primary use of a budget. The use of a budget as a control mechanism ensures that revenues are expended according to an established set of priorities or policies. Accountability becomes the primary goal of the budgetary process. A second objective of budgeting has been management. The use of a budget for management purposes manifests itself in an emphasis upon the attainment of efficiency and economy in reaching goals and objectives. The third purpose behind budgeting concerns planning. When planning is of major importance the emphasis centers upon rationality in the decision-making process. Every budget contains all three of these elements to some degree. The key to understanding any budget analysis is in recognizing how these considerations are prioritized. The goal of this chapter is to illustrate these relationships by analyzing the budget of a small southwestern city.

SAMPLEVILLE: CITY AND BUDGET BACKGROUND

Sampleville is the largest municipal entity in Smith County* and is the county seat. It is located in the northeastern quadrant of the state near the border. It is the largest municipal

---

* The city and county names have been changed but represent an actual locale.

entity in the middle of an area encompassing 20,000 square miles and serving the needs
of over 200,000 people. Sampleville has a population of 43,000 people, approximately
80% of the Smith County population. The population of Sampleville has grown by about
16% in this decade and by approximately 60% in the last quarter century. The population
of Sampleville is 72.8% white (including Hispanics), 7% black, and 19% Asian and other,
with the overall ethnic diversity remaining stable. The percentage of Hispanics is 26.8%.
In terms of age, 29.7% of the population is under 18, 58% is 18 to 64 years old, and just
over 12% is 65 years or older. The adult population is heavily skewed toward the ages
of 18 to 34. This is the result of the presence of a large U.S. Air Force base and two
local colleges. The current employable civilian workforce in Sampleville is approximately
22,000. The current unemployment rate is approximately 1000 workers, or 4.5% of the
workforce. This low unemployment rate has resulted in 8% increases in wages in recent
years (U.S. Bureau of the Census, 1996).

Smith County leads the state in agricultural production, raises more beef than any
other region of the state, and is the second largest dairy producer. Feed mills, grain storage,
commodity brokerages, and implement dealers are also major economic players in the
area. The rail line running through Sampleville is the busiest east–west rail bed in the
nation, and Sampleville is the home of a major railroad facility. Sampleville is home to
major manufacturing, distribution, and transportation entities as well as some oil and gas
production (Sampleville Chamber of Commerce).

Sample Air Force Base, however, remains the cornerstone of Sampleville's economy.
Established in 1942, the base has continually been the site of a large military establishment.
It is presently home to over 12,000-military personnel, dependents, and civilian employees.
The base brings to the area a large economic stimulus, as well as providing a pool of
skilled labor. A side benefit of the base is the large community of retired servicemen and
women it brings to the area. The retired military community brings a significant degree
of economic affluence and stability to the city. In addition, military retirees bring a diverse
set of skills and trades that are often in short supply in smaller towns.

Sampleville has a poorly diversified economy. It consists of the following sectors.
The largest sector, by far, is government, at 42%. The second largest sector is retail, at
18%. This is closely followed by services, at 25%, and agriculture, at 10%. Manufacturing,
financial services, and construction, the smallest sectors, each constitutes about 5%. There
have been some notable changes in these sectors, with Sampleville successfully "growing"
the manufacturing, services, and retail sectors in recent years. Sampleville anticipates a
future in which the base may be downsized or closed. It is with this thought that the city
has pursued a policy of aggressive economic growth and diversification (U.S. Bureau of
the Census, 1996).

Sampleville and Smith County were the first—and one of only two locales statewide—to implement the Local Economic Development Act. This program allows for
special incentive packages to be developed to encourage specific types of businesses to
relocate or start up in the area. Essentially, this program allows for the issuance of industrial
revenue bonds (IRBs) to offer carefully controlled land, buildings, and infrastructure incentive packages to companies involved in manufacturing, distribution, or value-added processing. The IRB financing mechanism is used to acquire land, buildings, and equipment
that is then sold by installment, or leased, to the business. Sampleville also courts economic
development through the aggressive use of several other mechanisms, which include the
state's Development Incentive Act and the Sampleville Industrial Development Corporation (Sampleville Chamber of Commerce).

In summary, the city of Sampleville has a poorly diversified economic base. The city remains dependent upon the government services sector to a large extent. In order to minimize the impact of possible base downsizing, the city has embarked upon a mission of economic development and diversification. The political considerations behind Sampleville's economic diversification programs have had a major impact upon the Sampleville budget.

Administrative and Service Structure

The city of Sampleville was incorporated in 1909 in anticipation of the state's being granted statehood in 1912. For the first sixty or so years after incorporation, Sampleville experimented with various forms of the mayoral–alderman form of government. On November 2, 1971, Sampleville adopted the council/manager form of government. This system continues in place to this day. The Sampleville city council consists of eight members elected by district for two-year periods and a mayor elected at large. The city council appoints the city manager and hires various administrators and department heads. Ultimately, the city manager is the chief administrative officer of the government and is responsible for day-to-day operations. Other important administrative officers involved in the budget process include the city attorney, the city secretary, the city budget director, the municipal judge, and the heads of the operating departments.

Sampleville provides a full range of governmental and community services. These include public safety, street construction and repair, parks and recreation, planning, zoning, building and codes enforcement, sanitation and sewage, and a municipal court system. In line with its growth agenda, the city of Sampleville has aggressively pursued a policy of enhanced capacities for city services, overbuilding its police, fire, water, wastewater, and solid waste facilities. This allows for controlled growth while collecting revenues from the state and outlying rural areas through the sale of surplus capacities. More recently added responsibilities include a housing agency, public health, welfare, and economic development. The city also operates an airport, a golf course, a cemetery, and a conventions bureau.

The elected leaders of the city of Sampleville and their appointed directors and officers work all year on the budget—forecasting, lobbying for funds from federal, state, and interagency sources, planning capital projects, and working on myriad other details. Revenue sources—taxes, fees, intergovernmental transfers, user charges and borrowings—must be identified and matched to expenditures. In turn, these expenditures both discretionary and required, must be carefully scrutinized. The budget process is overshadowed by a series of political, legal, and economic constraints.

The mayor with his or her citywide constituency and the council members with their district constituencies must develop a budget that meets the needs of the entire city. Professional administrators and city department operating heads also have diverse constituencies. They represent, in turn, their agencies and departments, programs required by federal and state law, and their citizen and client groups.

The functions of local government involve the production and distribution of public goods and services and the regulation of citizen activities. The financial systems utilized by government are designed to promote accountability, responsibility, control, efficiency, and in a democracy, equity. Accountability, responsibility, and control refer to the systems and constraints placed upon public managers to ensure that resources are used only in an authorized manner. Efficiency refers to how well the local government provides cost-effective public goods and services. Equity refers to the elimination of disparities between taxpayers in terms of services provided and revenues collected. For the most part, the city of Sampleville's first priority is fiscal conservatism and accountability (Petersen and Strachota, 1991: 437).

The Sampleville Budget

Budgeting is perhaps the single most important function of local government. This fact notwithstanding, however, no two entities approach budgeting in exactly the same manner; there are always variations in timing and process. Despite these variations, all budgets do possess some common elements. Among these elements are the establishment of a budget cycle and calendar. The budget cycle and the budget calendar refer to two separate but interconnected phenomena. The budget cycle refers to a four-phase process of preparation, appropriation, implementation, and evaluation. The preparation phase of the cycle includes an almost constant process of planning, often overlapping a number of budget years. Subsequently, budget cycles are often stagger-stepped with budget years. Budget calendars, on the other hand, represent the budget-building phases within one year's budget. The Sampleville budget is essentially developed over a number of phases and steps, both formal and informal. The Sampleville city budget runs from July 1 through June 30.

Almost as soon as a current year's budget is implemented, preparatory work begins on the next year's budget. Forecasting and setting priorities represent the first step in creating a budget. Sampleville's city administrators present preliminary estimates of revenues and necessary or basic expenditures to the city council in the early part of the year. Sampleville uses a simplified form of forecasting revenues and expenditures known as trending. Trending involves various averaging methods and some informed judgments as its basis (Lynch, 1995: 142). Generally, projections of three to five years are made at this time. Included in these projections are forecasts of general fund revenues, basic necessary minimum expenditures, and potential financial issues, such as the issuance or retirement of bonds or other obligations. Administrators also present some preliminary plans and recommendations at this time.

This first phase of forecasting is crucial because all other decisions pertaining to the budget are based upon the forecast of anticipated revenues and necessary expenditures. The second stage in the planning cycle revolves around the city council. After the preliminary forecast is presented to the council, members, on an individual and ad hoc basis, develop a policy agenda. The agenda includes priorities, issues, and expenditure goals. This agenda is transmitted via the city manager and city budget director to the operating departments in February. It is at this time that a budget calendar is established.

During March the departments prepare a series of necessary and discretionary budget requests that are based upon the policy guidelines of the council and their own recommendations. These requests are prioritized and are then coordinated by the city budget director and city manager into a preliminary budget proposal that includes a refined but not final revenue forecast. This revenue forecast includes estimates of potential state and federal funding as well as funding from semipublic agency sources. This budget proposal is presented to the council in early April.

Throughout the month of April, the council debates the budget in closed session and often requests alternatives and additional information from the budget director and/ or department heads. Preliminary public hearings are held in early May to secure citizen input. Final deliberations and adjustments are then made to the budget. A finalized budget

Table 1 Budget Process—City of Sampleville

Planning
  Preliminary forecasts and data presented to initial council
  Guidelines presented to city manager
  Budget calendar established
  Budget proposal formulated
Appropriations
  Preliminary council hearings
  Legal notices posted
  Open budget sessions held
  Council approval
Implementation
  Start of fiscal year
Evaluation
  Monthly reports
  Council meetings

is presented in open session during the first week of June and forwarded to the state for approval by the Department of Finance and Administration. The open sessions occur after legal notices are published concerning the proposed budget and tax rates. The budget is formally adopted by the city council through the passage of an appropriations bill. Included in this bill are the tax levy rates. The approved budget with legally set revenues and authorized appropriations goes into effect on July 1. (This process is outlined in Table 1.)

From this implementation point, the city manager and/or budget director present periodic reports to the council, state, and various governmental and nongovernmental agencies on expenditures and revenues. These reports in turn provide the continuing basis for the next year's budget. The final phase of the budget cycle revolves around the careful monthly monitoring of revenues and expenditures. During this process, budget expenditures are closely compared to actual expenditures. Variations between the two must be carefully examined in order to adjust appropriations, if necessary. The city council may transfer funds within departments within any fund; however, the state department of finance and administration must clear any revisions that alter fund aggregates. Revenue shortfalls thus must be quickly discovered and expenditures adjusted.

Budget Management Systems

It is only since the advent of modern public administration after World War II that budget management has become a science in itself. Prior to the modern era, budgeting most often was characterized as a "shopping list" approach to governance. It wasn't until the latter part of the twentieth century that reasoning and efficiency entered budgeting considerations with the development of budget management systems. There are several different budgeting systems available to a governmental entity. Each has significant strengths and weaknesses. Line-item budgets, for instance, emphasize fiscal accountability. In this type of budgeting system literally every dollar is accounted for. The disadvantage to this type of budgeting lies in its "failure to see the forest for the trees." Despite this, however, line-item budgeting remains part of most systems. Program budgeting approaches the issue by defined areas of control or responsibility. The resulting emphasis is upon the ends rather than the means. Unfortunately program budgeting has serious weaknesses in terms of accountability. A refinement to program budgeting is performance budgeting. Performance budgeting stresses results against some predetermined benchmark. Various other budgeting systems combine two or more approaches. Examples of these include planning, programming budgeting (PPB), zero-based budgeting (ZBB), target budgeting (TB), strategic budgeting (SB), and management by objective (MBO).

Sampleville has begun to utilize a form of zero-based budgeting (ZBB). Zero-based budgeting essentially starts with the premise that each year's budget should be a wholly self-contained package with little or no reference to earlier budgets. The primary advantage to ZBB is that all expenditures have to be justified anew each year. The primary disadvantage to ZBB is that it creates tremendous workloads, as previous policies and programs have to be continually reviewed and justified. The city of Sampleville, with a relatively small budget and a commitment to fiscal conservatism, finds ZBB a useful technique, especially with the changing financial conditions associated with the air base.

At the heart of ZBB is the preparation of decision packages. These packages represent some minimum necessary spending coupled with a series of alternatives or supplemental requests. These various packages are then prioritized into budget requests, first by departments and then by the city manager. Ultimately, the proposed budget is reprioritized at the council level for the final time. In essence, therefore, ZBB starts at the lower levels of administration and works upward. As such, it is a "bottom-up" approach. This is in contrast to the more prevalent top-down systems (Aronson and Hilley, 1986: 187).

Four major problems are associated with the use of ZBB. First, the more complex the governance unit, the greater the number of potential decision packages to consider. In essence, this allows for a considerable degree of discretion by managers and loss of control by the legislative authorities. Second, an increasing amount of expenditures at all levels is uncontrollable. Third, priorities are essentially political decisions and are oftentimes difficult to discern. Finally, ZBB is a difficult system in which to incorporate various grant packages.

The ZBB system used by Sampleville begins with a review of the previous year's budget expenditures and a projection of the next year's revenues by the city manager, the city's budget director, and the finance staff. This material forms the basis of early spending guidelines for the department heads' requests and supplemental requests. All budget requests, including current personnel and basic operating expenses, are reviewed yearly. Although ZBB stresses a "new" budget every year, certain realities constrain the use of ZBB. While revenue projections and prior budget expenditures do not form the basis of the new budget, Sampleville's administrators do use them to help establish starting points. The city uses ZBB to effectively control expenditure growth. The primary objective of ZBB is to scrutinize and justify each departmental expenditure. Sampleville's council members originally instituted ZBB to control hidden revenues and expenditures and eliminate carryovers.

In discussions with Sampleville's administrators, the following factors were emphasized as forming the basis of budget guidelines each year. First and most important, a determination is made concerning the level of necessary services, such as fire, police protection, street repair, and sanitation. Second, a determination is made concerning the city's capital needs. Third, a review of projected revenues is made. Fourth, a mix of likely revenues is agreed upon. Fifth, a review of the impact of various expenditures and revenues is made. Finally, some preliminary decisions are made concerning a broad budget outline.

ANALYSIS OF REVENUE AND EXPENDITURE

At the heart of the budgeting process lies the need for an understanding of what financial resources are available and how these same resources will be allocated. Governmental income is known as revenue; as it is spent it becomes expenditures. Any budget's construction must start with a detailed look at what monies are available to finance the activities of government. Revenues are based upon the legal capacity of an entity to levy taxes and collect fees and by the entity's economic condition.

Revenues

For the most part, Sampleville generates revenues from six major sources. These are taxation, the sale of public services, the sale of property, intergovernmental transfers, borrowing, and increasingly the application for and utilization of funds from semipublic and private sources. Sampleville's main sources of revenue are taxation, the sale of public services, and intergovernmental transfers. Unlike most other cities, Sampleville's revenues are subject to major fluctuations because of the impact of the air base's operations. Over the last several years, deployments and base mission modifications have impacted Sampleville's revenues several times. This has necessitated major changes, such as fund transfers and borrowings on several occasions.

Like much of the nation, Sampleville has been fortunate in the last several years in terms of its economy. This in turn has produced an increasing stream of revenues without increasing tax rates. Table 2 shows the aggregate revenues for the current budget year and the five previous years. Time series averaging generates the projected revenues for the budget year ending June 30, 2001.

As Table 2 shows, taxes as a source of revenue have been remarkably consistent at 62–64%. Service fees and charges have also been remarkably consistent at 21–24% of the total. There have been, however, some fluctuations between the other revenue sources. These fluctuations mostly revolve around changes in state and federal funding transfers as programs expand or end. A good example of this are the state funds made available for road maintenance.

Table 2   Aggregate Revenues—City of Sampleville

Budget year ending	Aggregate revenues	Percentage change from previous year
06/30/95	18,398,376	—
06/30/96	19,186,803	4.2
06/30/97	18,889,651	−1.55[a]
06/30/98	20,211,654	6.9
06/30/99	1,219,874	9.9
06/30/00 (projected)	22,922,235	3.6
06/30/01 (projected)	23,978,950	4.6

[a] Administrators credit the deployment of the local air base wing to Bosnia for the drop-in revenues.

Table 3 Aggregate Expenditures—City of Sampleville

Budget year ending	Aggregate expenditures	Percentage change from previous year
06/30/96	$27,297,476	—
06/30/97	25,552,372	−6.8%
06/30/98	25,285,921	−1.1%
06/30/99	26,670,986	5.5%
06/30/00 (estimated)	31,160,313	16.8%
06/30/901 (projected forecast)	32,282,084	3.6%

Note: Forecasted by method of averages.
Source: City of Sampleville.

Expenditures

Expenditures consist of expenses, including personnel and operating costs, a percentage of capital outlays, and bond payments. In the most current budget year, the year ending June 30, 2000, the single greatest expenditure is for personal services, at 39.4%. The second largest expenditure is operating expenses, at 20.9%. These are followed by contracted expenses, at 15.5%, commodity costs, at 5.5%, and debt service, at 5.3%. The balance of expenditures goes for capital equipment. This is shown in Table 3.

As Table 3 shows, at the aggregate level there has been a 14.2% growth in expenditures from the budget year ending June 30, 1996, through the current budget year. Much of the growth in expenditures can be attributed to the surge in personnel costs (18.7%) and operating expenses (18.4%). At least part of this can be attributed to the remarkably high wage increases in the Sampleville area (8% per annum).

Analysis by Funds

Sampleville has organized its accounts on the basis of funds and account groups, each of which is considered a separate accounting entity. Sampleville has several types of funds within each fund type. Subsequently, the activities of each fund are accounted for with its own set of self-balancing accounts that include its assets, liabilities, equity, revenues, and expenditures. Sampleville operates three fund types and two account groups, which contain seven separate funds. These include: the general fund, the special revenue funds, the trust funds, the capital projects funds, the enterprise funds, the internal service funds, and the debt services fund. The general fund, the special revenue funds, the capital projects funds, and the debt services funds are governmental fund types. These are the funds through which most governmental type functions are usually financed.

The General Fund

The general fund is by far the largest single fund. It comprises the city's general operating expenses and is financed by tax revenues, fees and charges, and certain lesser miscellaneous sources of income. It accounts for all the city's finances except for those required to be accounted for in another fund. For the fiscal year ending June 30, 2000, the general fund had projected revenues of $9,661,407 and projected expenditures of $11,433,262 (see

Table 4 General Fund Revenues—City of
Sampleville

Year	Amount	Percentage change
1995	8,152,276	—
1996	8,443,476	3.57
1997	8,744,428	3.56
1998	8,970,946	2.59
1999	9,913,025	10.50
2000	9,661,407	−2.54
2001	10,014,048	3.65

Note: General revenues are down in 1999 as a result of lost
interest and cash reserves on deposit at the La Caixa
Bank in Barcelona, Spain 2001 estimated using
method of averages.

Table 4). The general fund has grown from revenues of $8,152,276 in the 1995 budget
year, a growth of 18.5%.

The general fund receives its revenue from a variety of sources, including property
tax, sales and use taxes, intergovernmental transfers, service charges, minor taxes, and fund
transfers. By far the greatest proportion of this year's general fund revenues is provided by
taxes. In the budget ending June 30, 2000, 84% of the general fund came from taxes, 10%
came from service charges and fees, and 6% came from grants and other sources.

The revenue sources for the general fund have remained remarkably constant since
1995. The major tax component of the general fund revenues is the gross receipt from
sales tax. This has grown from $5,600,000 in 1995 to $6,761,250 projected in the current
budget year. Despite this 21% increase over the last five years, however, the gross receipts
tax has remained constant at the 68–69% level of general fund revenues. The sales tax
rate for the city is 6.1875%. Of this, the city retains 2.6625%. The city has another .25%
of legislated authorization in reserve. Due to Sampleville's expanding economy, the gross
sales tax receipts are projected to increase by 5% per annum for the foreseeable future.

The property tax revenues have grown from $494,994 in 1995 to $566,685 in the
current year, an increase of 14%. Property taxes have declined slightly in total importance
over this period, however. The city of Sampleville has a remaining 3.55 mill of legislated
authorization on its property tax rate. With a total property valuation of $254,000,000,
this could generate another $900,000 in revenues per year. The Sampleville property tax
rate has remained constant at .003725 since at least 1996. Total property tax revenues are
expected to increase each year by about 5%. Per capita property tax revenues, however,
are expected to remain at the $23–$25 range. This remains well below the state average
and helps to keep home ownership affordable.

Two other factors have had a major impact upon general fund revenues in the time
period 1995–2000. First, the city's share of gasoline taxes has been absorbed by the state.
This represents a loss of $300,000 per year from the general fund revenues. This money
has been replaced by state paving district funds and other direct state grants. Second,
ambulance service fees have grown from $185,000 in 1995 to $569,000 in 2000. This
300% increase is the result of dramatically higher fees and not demographics.

The ZBB system utilized by Sampleville results in the distribution of specially designated revenues into the general fund in an inconsistent manner. Revenue sources are often not assigned to the same funds consistently over time. These revenues include: occupational licenses, business licenses and permits, franchise fees, hotel and accommodation taxes, and various types of permits. Other sources include golf green fees, golf cart rentals, swimming pool revenues, beverage permits, and alcohol consumption taxes. These sundry taxes make up about 10% of the city's internally generated revenues. In the 2000 budget year they amounted to about $2 million, a figure that has remained fairly constant since 1995. The general fund, however, did show a great deal of consistency in revenue growth throughout the period of analysis. Sampleville city administrators do a poor job of revenue forecasting. The differences between actual and forecasted revenues were significant, ranging up to about 10%. Specific revenue forecasts of individual taxes also fluctuated by significant levels. This caused an overuse of fund transfers, which fluctuated quite widely by year. This is primarily a function of the nature of ZBB systems.

In the budget year ending June 30, 2000, approximately 10% of all revenues come from direct intergovernmental transfers, as the federal and state governments transferred greater responsibilities to local governments. In the budget year ending June 30, 1996, less than 4% came from direct transfers. This represents a 250% increase over the last five years. Additionally, the state and federal governments provide direct funding for various cooperative endeavors, such as airport funding, which appear as notes to the budget but are not directly included.

By far the largest department included under the general fund is the police department, at 40% of general fund expenditures. In the budget year ending June 30, 2000, police department expenditures are scheduled to be $4,468,616. This represents an increase of 16% over the 1996 police budget. The single largest percentage of these expenditures is the personnel costs associated with its eighty-one employees. In the current year these are projected to be $3,373,648, or 75% of the total departmental expenses. This in turn represents an increase of 18% in associated personnel costs since 1996. The other major expenditures in the police budget are contractual services at $721,318 and commodities at $195,400. Contractual services include education and training costs, maintenance items, and various forms of liability insurance, which cost $315,120 per year.

The second largest set of expenditures in the general fund are those of the fire department, scheduled in the June 30, 2000, budget at $3,387,899 or 30% of the general fund. This represents an increase of about 16% over the expenditures in the June 30, 1996, budget. In much the same manner as the police department, personnel expenses of $2,911,662, covering sixty-five employees, are the largest single departmental expense at 86%. Ironically, in the fire department personnel expenses are only up about 2% over the past five years as compared to the 18% increase in the police department.

As one can see from the above police and fire department discussions, a large part of the budget expenditures in the general fund are relatively fixed as necessary. Regardless of the use of ZBB, a significant part of any municipal budget is not easily subject to much change.

The other governmental type funds are significantly smaller than the general fund. They include special revenue funds, capital project funds, and debt service funds. Special revenue funds are used to account for the proceeds of specific revenue sources, which by law are restricted to specific expenditures. Capital projects funds are used to account for revenues and expenditures tied to the acquisition, construction, or renovation of major capital facilities. Debt service funds are used to account for revenues and expenditures tied to the payment of general long-term debt and interest.

Proprietary Funds

Proprietary funds are used to account for operations that are organized as self-supporting activities. As a small city, Sampleville has less capacity for providing public services, such as electricity. Subsequently, Sampleville's proprietary funds are smaller and less significant sources of income for the city than elsewhere. Sampleville maintains two proprietary type funds: an internal service fund and an enterprise fund. Internal service funds are established to account for the financing of goods and services exchanged between city departments on a cost-reimbursement basis. Enterprise funds are used to account for operations that are similar to private business services. These operations involve providing goods and services to the public in exchange for user fees.

Enterprise Funds. Enterprise funds are used to provide citizens with a variety of services in a businesslike manner. This allows for the provision of services to citizens without higher taxes. Some examples of services provided by Sampleville through enterprise type activities are transit services, recreational activities, airport services, cemetery, water, sewer, and solid waste. Furthermore, the user fees collected often help finance other activities of local governments.

The largest source of enterprise funds for Sampleville comes from sanitation services. Sanitation services have revenues of $2,437,850 for the budget year ending June 30, 2000. This represents a 55% growth in sanitation services since the budget ending June 30, 1996. Table 5 shows how sanitation revenues have grown since the mid-1990s. Sampleville's sanitation services have been significantly overbuilt. This allows the city to serve as a contractor for county and air base solid waste services. This has generated some unexpected income for the city. Of the total revenues included in the department of sanitation budget, 86% is generated by user fees, 11% from a special gross sales tax levy, and 13% from grants. This has remained fairly consistent over the last five budget years.

The second largest source of user fees comes from the wastewater department. Wastewater has total revenues of $1,426,911 in the budget year ending June 30, 2000. This represents a 10.9% increase over the $1,285,900 in revenues generated by that department in the budget year ending June 30, 1996. Unlike solid waste, the outlying areas do not contract with Sampleville for wastewater treatment.

Table 5 Sanitation Revenue—City of Sampleville

Budget year ending	Revenues	Percentage change
6/30/95	1,562,500	—
6/30/96	1,572,500	0.60%
6/30/97	1,572,500	0.00%
6/30/98	1,892,946	20.40%
6/30/99	1,990,238	5.14%
6/30/00	2,437,850	22.49%
6/30/01 (projected)	2,674,321	1.09%

Note: Forecast by method of averages.
Source: City of Sampleville.

Budget Variance

The Sampleville budget has a great deal of variance between projected revenues and expenditures and the actual budget numbers. This represents lost opportunities for both the city and its citizens. For example, poor revenue forecasting impacts the city's tax rates, necessitating undue burdens upon citizens and businesses. These same monies, needlessly collected as taxes, could be used to expand capital investment or be spent on consumer goods. This in turn would eventually add to the city's coffers as increased sales tax and property tax monies. Furthermore, tax rates can impact business development and property improvements. Similarly, overestimating expenditures can lead to poor cash management as funds are needlessly left idle rather than being used to generate investment returns or pay down debt. Table 6 illustrates the variance between projected revenues and expenditures and the actual budget numbers.

The general fund for the year ending June 30, 1999, had budgeted revenues of $10,332,874.00 and actual revenues of $ 11,520.718.00. This represents a variance of $1,187,844.00, or an underestimation of revenues of 11.5%. In this same year, general fund expenditures were budgeted at $11,649,887.00, with actual expenditures coming in at $10,534,040.00. This represents an overestimation of expenditures by $1,115,847.00, or a variance of 9.5%. The total variance in the general fund between actual revenues and expenditures thus was $2,303,691.00, or about 22%. This same pattern of gross underestimation of revenue and overestimation of expenditures repeated itself in the special revenue

Table 6 Budget Variances for Major Fund Types (Budget Ending June 30, 1999)

Excess or deficiency	Revenues	Expenditures
General fund		
Budget	$10,332,874	$11,649,887
($1,317,013)		
Actual	11,520,718	10,534,040
9 86,678		
Variance	1,187,844	1,115,847
2,303,691		
Special revenue funds		
Budget	7,053,957	6,656,369
397,588		
Actual	7,712,318	5,143,240
2,569,078		
Variance	658,361	1,513,129
2,171,490		
Capital projects funds		
Budget	1,845,404	7,477,905
(5,632,501)		
Actual	1,143,344	6,354,395
(5,211,451)		
Variance	(702,060)	(5,211,451)
(421,056)		

Source: Sampleville annual final report.

funds as well. There the estimated revenues of $7,053,957 were dwarfed by actual revenues of $7,712,318; a difference of $658,361, or about 9.5%. The budgeted expenditures of $6,656,369 were $1,513,129 more than the actual expenditures of $5,143,240, representing a difference of almost 30%. The total difference between actual revenues and actual expenditures in the special revenue funds amounted to $2,569,078. The capital projects fund also showed serious differences between the budgeted and actual numbers. These large variances between budgeted and actual revenues and expenditures are a cause for major concern.

BUDGET DOCUMENT AND EVALUATION

As we mentioned earlier, budgeting represents the single most important function of local government. Included in the budget process are instruments of control and accountability, but most important, budgeting represents a communications device among citizens, policy makers, and administrators. A budget should include financial information, policy information, and the structures of government so that citizens can understand what services are being provided for them and at what cost. A good budget should follow certain criteria in its presentation.

Government Finance Officers Association Criteria

The Government Finance Officers Association (GFOA) provides a set of criteria* for the presentation of a budget. The GFOA essentially views budgets as policy briefs, operations outlines, and communications devices as well as financial documents. For a GFOA award, budgets must meet a number of criteria. In the area of policy, budgets should include a statement that provides a comprehensive overview of goals, objectives, and strategies. A good budget document should explain the processes used in its creation. Furthermore, the budget should discuss changes in policies from preceding years, explain the how and why behind those changes, and discuss how the changes are to be implemented and monitored.

The budget document should also explain the type of accounting system it uses, whether GAAP, modified accrual, or cash. It should explain the fund types and funds, revenues and sources, financial structures, and operating procedures. It should include information concerning the past and projections about the future. It should discuss capital improvements and debt. In essence, the budget should be a comprehensive statement concerning the financial operation of the city. As such, it should explain the relationships among departments, organizational units, managers, and programs. It should specify the degree of discretion allowed to the various managers. It should outline performance objectives for the various subunits of government and the timetables for accomplishing them.

According to the GFOA, the most important function of a budget is that of communication. The document should be readily available to the public and in a manner, that is easily understood by people with limited expertise with public finance. Subsequently, it should avoid overly technical language. It should include a table of contents, a glossary of key terms, and definitions and explanations, which would allow a reasonably informed reader to understand it. It should include graphs and charts to illustrate and explain key

---

* The information contained in this section is drawn from the GFOA (2000).

trends and relationships. In summary, the budget should provide a blueprint of the city's operations and finances.

The GFOA budget awards guidelines are divided into four broad areas and twenty-six individual criteria. Of these twenty-six criteria, the GFOA considers thirteen to be mandatory for an award-caliber budget presentation. These criteria essentially provide an outline for conscientious budget administrators to follow.

The Budget as a Policy Document

At its most basic level, a budget essentially represents a set of goals and priorities—policies, if you will—attached to a spending plan. Unlike the U.S. Congress or the various state legislatures, which utilize a constant stream of bills and proposals with their attendant publicized committee hearings and votes to implement and direct policy, city councils operate mostly outside the view of the public. The only concise statement of any city council's policies is its budget document. Subsequently, if local government is to be truly democratic, it must deliver a budget document that clearly articulates its policies and priorities to its citizenry. To this end, the GFOA requires that the budget document include a budget message that specifies and prioritizes policy issues and goals. This message should include any changes of issues and goals from preceding years.

To augment this mandatory requirement, the GFOA recommends that:

1. The budget document should include a coherent statement of long-term budgetary policies and goals. This statement should explain long-term budget practices and how these practices should help the budgeting entity meet its goals.
2. The budget document should explain the budgetary process itself. This explanation should include the important steps, phases, and dates in the budget-making process.
3. The budget document should outline the basic policies, objectives, and goals of government. This outline should include linkages between short-term objectives and longer-term goals.
4. The budget document should explain how policies will be implemented and how their effects will be measured.

The Sampleville budget documents do not contain any information as to the city's priorities or goals. In fact, it doesn't contain any type of budget message whatsoever. The document does not contain any information concerning the budget process, important dates in the budget-making calendar, or how the budget figures were arrived at. The Sampleville budget fails to conform to any of the GFOA criteria concerning the budget as a policy document. Sampleville administrators generate a basic document that barely conforms to the statutory requirements of the state.

The Budget as a Financial Plan

As a rule, the citizenry holds the city council accountable through the electoral process. the council in turn holds the city's administration accountable for its actions through its adherence to the policies and guidelines set in the budget. Subsequently, the budget serves as a measurement of the effectiveness of the city government's financial planning. For the citizenry to evaluate the council's performance and the council to measure the administration's effectiveness, sufficient data must be supplied in the budget document to form the basis of an informed judgment. The GFOA considers the following financial criteria as mandatory for an award. First, the budget document should present a summary of all the major revenues and expenditure areas. This should include all major sources of financing. In other words, the document should provide an overview of the total financial resources relied upon by the city.

Second, the budget document should provide summaries of revenues and expenditures for prior year actual, current year budget (current year actual if available), and the proposed year. In other words, the budget document should provide a basis of historical comparison for financial trends. Third, the budget document should discuss major revenue sources and the assumptions underlying the projections of estimated revenues and any discernible revenue trends. Fourth, the budget document should include any change or projected change in fund balances. This discussion should also address how surpluses and deficits are to be handled. Fifth, the budget document should discuss debt issues. This discussion should cover the relationship between outstanding debt and current financial operations, as well as the degree of outstanding debt versus the legal debt ceiling. Finally, the budget document should explain the basis of fund budgeting used; whether GAAP, cash, modified accrual, or some other method. The document should explain how this relates to the accounting method used in the *Certified Annual Financial Report*.

The GFOA recommends that the following information also be included to facilitate an understanding of the budget document as a financial plan. First, the budget document should explain the financial structures and organization of the city government. This explanation should include an outline of the major fund types, their purposes, and the resources allocated to them. Second, the budget document should include a discussion of capital expenditures and projects. This discussion should include a listing of appropriations for capital acquisition purposes and information concerning how capital spending might (or will) impact the current operating budget.

The Sampleville budget includes information concerning the previous year, the current year, and the proposed year. The information comes in the form of tabular accounting columns, however, which are hard for laypersons to comprehend. The Sampleville budget document does not provide any information as to the underlying assumptions for revenue projections or any historical trends or data. The budget document does not discuss any contingency planning or debt issues. The budget document fails to provide sufficient information from which the average citizen can measure the city administration's effectiveness or the city's financial condition. The Sampleville budget fails to conform to the GFOA criteria for the document to serve as a financial plan.

The Budget as an Operations Guide

Most people are unaware of the structure of their city's government. Unlike the national government, which is a topic of instruction throughout the formal education process, city government is rarely studied or discussed. Subsequently, the citizenry has little knowledge of how to judge the effectiveness of city government or to even access its appropriate agents. To this end, the GFOA requires that budget documents should first provide an organizational chart for the entire governmental entity. This chart should highlight the structural and functional organization of the city's administration. Second, the budget document should have a discussion of personnel and staffing. This should include a schedule or summary of personnel and/or staffing positions, as well as a discussion of any reorganization or changes from prior to current and planned budget years.

The GFOA also recommends that the budget document should describe the major organizational units, their activities, their functions, and the services they provide. The document should also specify the discretionary authority assigned to each major unit manager. Finally, the budget document should include objective performance measures and/or targets and timetables wherever appropriate. This will allow for a comparison of results versus expenditures and some objective criteria to measure governmental performance.

The Sampleville budget document lists the city's authorized personnel positions and the people in the key manager in positions and their salaries. It does not however, provide an organizational chart for the city or a description of the responsibilities assigned to any position. The document does not include any discussion of actual or proposed personnel and staffing changes, nor does it provide any objective criteria to measure the various missions and responsibilities assigned to the city's organizational units.

The Budget as a Communications Device

At the base of the GFOA criteria lies the premise that the citizens have a right to know about their city government, its policies, and its effectiveness. The budget document represents the single best opportunity to communicate this crucial information. Subsequently, the GFOA requires first that the budget document should include a cover or transmittal letter and either a table of contents or an index. This allows the uninformed citizen to quickly locate the desired information. Second, the budget document should include simple, easy to comprehend graphs and charts that serve to communicate key information quickly to the untrained viewer. Finally, the budget document should describe the process for preparing, reviewing, and adopting the budget. It should also include a discussion of the procedures available for amending the document. In essence, this gives the citizen some potential access to the process.

To help facilitate the use of these criteria the GFOA recommends first that the budget document provide summary information, including an overview of major budgeting issues and trends. This allows the citizen reader to grasp the important facts presented in the budget. Second, the budget document should include a glossary of key terms to facilitate its understanding, even by a layman. Third, the budget document should include cross-references, tables, schedules, and narratives to aid readers in understanding its content. Fourth, the document should be presented in such a manner that a layman could easily comprehend its content. It should be reader-friendly and written in a nontechnical manner. The budget document should also include supplemental data that describe the budgeting entity, the community, and the population it serves. Finally, the budget document should include in its discussion any other financial material, plans, and processes that may impact the city's current financial operations.

Most cities do not submit their budget documents to the GFOA for review. This is especially true of smaller cities, such as Sampleville. The GFOA criteria represent a dedicated effort to move budgeting into a modern civic-minded era, however. Any city, regardless of size, can aspire to present its budget in the most professional manner. Adhering to the GFOA criteria represents a step in this direction.

The Sampleville budget document is not written in an easy to comprehend manner. It does not provide any narrative, charts, graphs, or summaries. The document does not have an index, a glossary of key terms, or a table of contents. The Sampleville budget document is designed to conform to the state-required minimums and nothing more. The budget document is almost intentionally obtuse. The citizens of Sampleville would not have any idea of the city's organization, policies, or financial condition based upon their budget document.

RECOMMENDATIONS

The city of Sampleville has a poor budget by GFOA standards. The documents are poorly prepared and difficult for a layman to understand. While the city uses ZBB as an accounting system, this would not be apparent from the budget document itself. City policies, goals, and objectives are not readily apparent. The following recommendations should serve to improve the Sampleville budget presentation and structure:

Recommendation 1. The city's budget documents should conform to the GFOA criteria. The budget documents should include an overview of the budgetary process, information concerning the budget system being used, and the budget calendar. Citizens should know how the budget is created. They should know what particular budgeting system is being followed and why. They should have an idea of the timetable being followed so that they can make timely contributions and comments.

Recommendation 2. The city should include a statement of its policy objectives and prioritize them. Citizens delegate responsibility to their elected leaders for making decisions on their behalf. There needs to be a comprehensive statement of what actions and decisions are being made for them by their elected representatives, however.

Recommendation 3. The city should present information that illustrates the present state of the city's finances, an estimate of the city's midterm finances, and some long-term projections. In essence, the citizens should have ready access to the same type of information that the state department of finance and administration has and its own council members possess. That way, the citizens can make informed judgments of how good a job the city is doing.

Recommendation 4. The city should provide information on revenues and tax rates, expenditures, and reserves. Furthermore, this information should be presented in the manner of trends starting from the immediate past and projecting into the future. Some basis of comparison should be provided for citizens to see how well their city measures up to other similar municipalities.

Recommendation 5. The city should provide a set of objectives and goals and some criteria to measure their attainment. Citizens should be provided with enough information to judge the level of effectiveness of the city's administration.

Recommendation 6. The city should conform to the GFOA criteria even if it does not wish to submit the budget for GFOA award consideration. The city's budget is virtually impossible for a layman to understand. The budget comes across as intentionally obtuse and misleading. The budget document should be written in an easy to comprehend format utilizing simple graphs, charts, and narratives. The document should include a glossary, a table of contents, and cross-referencing.

Recommendation 7. The city should adjust its budget management system to include elements of programming and performance. The use of ZBB as a standalone management system is impractical and misleading. Sampleville should use

ZBB as a management philosophy, but since 70–75% of the budget is fixed, the city should use a PPB management system. It should also incorporate performance measures.

Recommendation 8. The variance between actual and budgeted revenues and expenditures is excessive. It shows a poor grasp of underlying assumptions, planning, and or projections. The variance is undoubtedly having major impacts upon planning and budgeting. The city should seek competent outside help to create better budgeting processes.

SUMMARY AND CONCLUSION

The city of Sampleville adopted a zero-based budgeting system to implement fiscal conservatism in its operations. The use of ZBB has allowed Sampleville to tightly curtail its expenditures and debt. The city is highly concerned with these factors due to the uncertainties associated with its air base operations. It is because of its fear of base downsizing that Sampleville has embarked upon a program of diversification and economic development.

The city of Sampleville may well have increased its control over fiscal affairs through the use of ZBB. Much of its budget is essentially fixed, however. Subsequently, ZBB generates considerably more effort on the part of city employees than the resulting control may be worth. The use of ZBB also may have political ramifications. The areas in which ZBB has been used creates civic conflicts. For example, inconsistent funding to the library results in poor collections and frustrated patrons. Inconsistent funding for street maintenance gives the impression of a city divided into have and have-nots. Finally, budgets should truly represent long-term planning; ZBB by definition is a short-term instrument. It would be worthwhile for Sampleville to use a mixed system, perhaps incorporating elements of ZBB into a PPPB system. This would have the advantage of introducing consistency, accountability, and performance measures into a system sorely in need of this.

Sampleville city budgets are not generally in accordance with generally accepted accounting principals (GAAP). Few municipalities are. This failure to conform to GAAP results in conflicting interpretations of the current financial condition of the city. By simple budgetary analysis, Sampleville shows remarkable fiscal strength. By converting the Sampleville budget to GAAP standards, however, several glaring problems arise. First, the city seriously misestimates revenues through all its fund types. For example, the general fund underestimated revenues by approximately 10% in the most recently audited year. Second, the city relies upon excessive use of transfers to compensate for its poor forecasting. Third, the city maintains excessive funds on deposit and much of the funds are held in category 3 accounts. The city holds cash and cash equivalents of close to $21 million (the equivalent of one year's expenditures). While the airbase necessitates the maintenance of larger cash reserves than normal, this may be excessive. It would behoove the city to use some of this money for paying down its long-term debt.

The city of Sampleville does not utilize GFOA criteria in its budget process. The budget barely meets the standards of the state's department of finance and administration for its content. The budget does not lend itself to easy interpretation or analysis. The budget of the city of Sampleville seems to be designed to discourage civic participation in the budgetary process.

REVIEW QUESTIONS

1. Discuss the importance of the budgetary process. What are the different uses of a budget?
2. Discuss the various types of budget systems. What is zero-based budgeting? Why is it used?
3. What is a budget calendar? What is a budget cycle? How do they interrelate?
4. How do the various economic background factors impact a city's budget process?
5. What are revenues? What are the major revenue sources for city government? How does the local economy interact with revenues?
6. Discuss the impact of fixed expenses upon a city's budget. How does this affect the use of ZBB?
7. What is budget variance? Why is excessive budget variance to be avoided? How can budget variance impact a city's budget?
8. What are the major criteria of the GFOA for a budget-award presentation? Why does the GFOA advocate the use of these criteria?

REFERENCES

Aronson, J. R. and Hilley, J. C. (1986). *Financing State and Local Governments.* Washington, DC: Brookings.

Aronson, J. R. and Schwartz, E. eds. (1975). *Management Policies in Local Government Finance.* Washington, DC: ICMA.

Banks, P. (1999). Sampleville, city of the plains. *Southern New Mexico Online Magazine.*

City of Sampleville. *Annual Budgets 1995–2000.*

Finley, L. K. (1989). *Public Sector Privatization.* Westport, CT: Greenwood.

Government Finance Officers Association (GFOA). (2000). *Distinguished Budget Presentation Awards Program.* Chicago: GFOA.

Haveman, R. H. and Margolis, J. (1977). *Public Expenditure and Policy Analysis.* New York: Rand McNally.

Ingram, R. et al. (1991). *Accounting and Financial Reporting for Governmental and Non-Profit Organizations.* New York: McGraw Hill.

Lynch, T. D. (1995). *Public Budgeting in America.* Englewood Cliffs, NJ: Prentice-Hall.

Moak, L. L. and Millhouse, A. M. (1975). *Local Government Finance.* Chicago: MFOA.

Petersen, J. E. and Strachota, D. R. (1991). *Local Government Finance.* Chicago: GFOA.

Winfrey, J. C. (1973). *Public Finance.* New York: Harper & Row.

20

Budgeting for Unincorporated Area Services

Charles W. Washington
Florida Atlantic University, Boca Raton, Florida, U.S.A.

County governments across the United States are administrative units of state governments. These 3,043 governments vary in size, structure, and powers granted to them by their respective state government (U.S. Department of Commerce, 1992: 1). Some counties are governed under home-rule charters designed by citizen charter commissions and approved by referendum of the local population. Others simply operate as administrative arms of the state government governed by general and special legislation passed by their state legislature.

Urban county governments of 50,000 population or more, especially in the South, typically comprise several incorporated municipalities with an unincorporated area outside the incorporated municipalities. These counties are faced with the challenge of budgeting to provide both countywide services that benefit all citizens and specific services to meet the needs of those who live in the unincorporated area. Unincorporated area residents are governed by an elected board of county commissioners, county legislative council, county board of supervisors, or similar body identified differently by state. The revenue options available to counties are typically less than those available to incorporated municipalities unless the state constitution, specific state statute, statewide referendum, judicial decision, or charter home-rule permits otherwise (Gold and Richie, 1993: 12–13). The options for providing government services to unincorporated area citizens include incorporation of the area, annexation by an existing incorporated government, interlocal agreement, city–county separation, as in the state of Virginia, city–county consolidation, urban or municipal service districts, special taxing districts, or the use of revenue-raising instruments targeted only at the unincorporated area residents to pay for the services they receive (Bowman and Kearney, 1990: 315–339).

In Broward County, Florida, the unincorporated area comprises a municipal service district. This means residents of the unincorporated area are considered by the county to live in a service district that is provided services that would otherwise be provided by a municipality if the area were incorporated or annexed by an existing municipality. The primary budgetary problem for the county is that of selecting the appropriate revenue measures that are equitable to those citizens living in the unincorporated area while taking into consideration their economic well-being, service needs, and service costs.

This chapter has two objectives: (1) to highlight the peculiar problems faced by an urban county government in deciding the appropriate revenue sources to be used to provide needed infrastructure and program services to residents in its unincorporated area; and (2) to afford the reader an opportunity to understand, review, and critique the legal and fiscal decisions made by Broward County in selecting from a set of policy alternatives the most appropriate policy to properly budget for the provision of services to unincorporated area citizens.*

PROBLEM BACKGROUND AND DISCUSSION

Broward County, Florida was established in 1915 as an administrative subdivision of the state operating under the general laws of the state of Florida. In 1974 the residents of the county approved the Broward County charter, to become effective January 1, 1975. This brought home rule to the county and established an elective county commission/administrator form of government. This form of government consists of a seven-person county commission elected by district and an appointed county administrator (Charter of Broward County, 1974: 4–7). The 1,196 square mile county encompasses twenty-eight incorporated municipalities within its borders. The 1990 population of the county was 1,278,384, with 1,125,659 citizens living in the incorporated municipalities within the county. Seven cities comprise 44% of the total county population. Twenty-one percent of the population is age 65 or older.

Approximately 12% (or 152,725) of the county's population lives in the unincorporated area. These citizens receive their municipal-type services from the county government. This raises the following budgetary questions for the county administrator and the board of county commissioners. How shall these services be financed? To what extent should the ad valorem property tax is used to finance the cost of such services? If the ad valorem property tax is used, what millage rate should apply? Should services be paid for by fees, charges, or special assessments? (Adrian and Press, 1972: 389–392). If fees are used, what constitutes an equitable fee compared to fees charged by incorporated municipalities? How much bonded indebtedness should be incurred by the county in order to provide services to the unincorporated areas? (Lamb and Rappaport, 1980: 94–100).

In preparing the 1991–1992 fiscal year budget, Broward County was faced with the challenge of providing services to several "pockets" of the unincorporated area throughout the county. Because the unincorporated area is not located within any incorporated municipality, the county is the responsible government to provide these services. The ability to pay for the services demanded differs by pockets, or areas within the unincorporated area. It is therefore useful to refer on occasions to the unincorporated pockets of the county as unincorporated areas, although in the aggregate, these different areas or pockets comprise the unincorporated area of the county. The demand for and cost of services tend to vary according to the location of the pockets of the unincorporated area. To adequately provide resources in the county budget to pay for unincorporated area services requires knowledge of the magnitude of the needs.

---

* These objectives could not have been achieved without the cooperation and information provided by John Canada and Marci Gelman, director and senior analyst, respectively, of the Broward County Office of Budget and Management Policy.

UNINCORPORATED AREA NEEDS

The unmet needs of the unincorporated area in Broward County for fiscal year 1991–1992 were primarily municipal-type services provided via the municipal service district, infrastructure or capital needs, and the need to pay certain mandatory program cost increases due to inflation. The municipal service district programs included police and fire protection and prevention, parks and recreation, building permitting and code enforcement, subdivision inspection, canal maintenance that is not provided by another district, garbage collection, and some street lighting. The infrastructure needs included stormwater management projects, fire protection equipment, and a communications system. The major needs are briefly described below.

Police and Fire Protection

Broward County provides police protection to its unincorporated area via the Broward County Sheriff's Department. In 1979 the District Court of Appeals of Florida, Fourth District, affirmed that road patrol and related services can be funded by countywide revenues such as the ad valorem property tax (*Alsdorf* v. *Broward County*, 1979). This permitted the county to use a broad-based tax to provide services to residents of the unincorporated area.

The fire protection needs of the unincorporated area include maintaining a replacement schedule for aging fire trucks and equipment and relocating certain fire stations from deteriorating trailers intended for temporary use to more permanent locations. This requires building new fire stations to keep up with the current demand for fire protection services.

Broward County operates fifteen fire stations in the unincorporated area staffed by paid and volunteer firefighters. Fire protection services are funded by a special assessment that is assessed owners of particular properties who benefit from specific services, improvements, or projects (Reed and Swain, 1990: 33). In 1987, the county issued bonds to replace aging fire trucks and equipment. No additional funds have been allocated for fire equipment replacement. An annual allocation of $600,000 is necessary to maintain a replacement schedule of two or three trucks annually, depending on the type of equipment, to lower maintenance costs and to ensure an effective fleet.

Parks and Recreation

Providing and maintaining neighborhood parks comprise one of the most expensive services in the unincorporated area. The county's comprehensive plan calls for three acres of neighborhood parkland per thousand population. Currently there is a need to develop a community park in one of the county's westmost unincorporated areas—Weston, a developer community. The construction and maintenance of the park would require a sizeable commitment on the part of the developer and a county contribution of approximately $1.6 million. The resource yield from impact fees applying to developers will not be sufficient to purchase and develop the required land. In addition, the county has placed several park rehabilitation projects on hold because of insufficient resources to complete them.

Building and Permitting

Broward County assures the enforcement of the South Florida building code requirements for new construction in the unincorporated area and issues building permits. The expenses for these and other municipal-type services, including school crossing guards, are incorporated in the municipal service district fund, a special purpose fund supported by either a special assessment or specifically levied fees.

Garbage Collection

Under contract with the county, private garbage collection services are provided to residents of the unincorporated area. Garbage is picked up twice per week, and trash is picked up six times per year. Residents are charged a garbage assessment fee for this service. Providing and maintaining a countywide recycling program, charging tipping fees to fund the household hazardous waste program, and operating a materials recovery facility and trash transfer stations (all countywide programs) have an impact on the fees charged for garbage collection.

Stormwater Management Projects

The stormwater management projects include stormwater or drainage projects that control the quantity and quality of stormwater drainage. Planned stormwater management projects consisted of $60 million worth of drainage needs not supplied by special districts within the county. These needs existed in built-out communities that could not support the level of special assessments or stormwater utility fees that would be necessary to recover the full cost of the drainage projects. The county's comprehensive plan called for spending $10 to $11 million on the construction of these stormwater management projects by 1994 in order to be in compliance with the minimum requirements of the plan. To meet this target at least $2.5 to $2.8 million would have to be allocated annually to fund the comprehensive plan projects over the next four years.

The budget office estimated that the cost for assessing the current condition of the stormwater drainage system to assure that existing and planned projects meet U.S. Environmental Protection Administration standards for quality of stormwater runoff would be over $1 million, and if retrofitting the system is required to meet EPA standards, additional millions may be required.

Mandatory Requirements

Mandatory requirements that needed to be met in the unincorporated area consisted of keeping pace with inflationary impacts on retirement expenses and rising per unit cost of services caused by increased annexation activities of surrounding municipalities. As annexation occurs fewer unincorporated area residents remain. This reduces the size and economic capacity of the remaining residents to pay the increasing cost of municipal-type services within the remaining unincorporated area.

Table 1 Unincorporated Area Dollar Value of Annual Unmet
Capital Needs (in Millions of Dollars), Fiscal Years 1991–1992

	Amount
Drainage/stormwater management	$ 2.8
Fire equipment replacement	.6
Communications for unincorporated area agencies	.4
Total[a]	$ 3.8

[a] Total unmet needs were actually higher; they include municipal
service district services, mandatory expenses, and the above unmet
capital needs.
Source: Office of Budget and Management, Internal Analysis, Broward
County, Florida.

Capital Needs

The estimated annual unmet capital or infrastructure needs of the unincorporated area are
listed in Table 1.

REVENUE SOURCES AND EXISTING TAX STRUCTURE

The capacity to generate revenues from the unincorporated area depends primarily on the
municipal service district (MSD) ad valorem property tax, which is a tax on the assessed
value of property in the area. The revenue from the ad valorem property tax results from
the taxable assessed value of property (assessed value minus $25,000 homestead exemp-
tion) times a millage rated* (Mikesell, 1991: 292–294). Other revenues come from fees,
charges, and special assessments. These include utility taxes, cable TV franchise fees, and
MSD assessments. The county seeks to use fees and charges in an equitable fashion.

The county levied a 1.3 Msd millage rate in fiscal year 1991 against the taxable
assessed value of property within the unincorporated area to provide municipal services
such as neighborhood parks, building permitting and zoning enforcement, development
review, waterway management, school crossing guards, and lighting of major roadways.
This millage rate raised approximately $5,500,000, which is approximately 22% of the
resources required to provide ongoing MSD operations.

The cable TV franchise fees are derived from 3% of the basic installation cost and
any basic and optional services. The electric franchise fees are generated from a 6% fee
charged to the electric company per contract, from which the electric company subtracts
its tax obligation. If the property tax obligation is less than the yield from the franchise
fee, the company will have to pay some of the obligation and has the right to pass on the
difference in the form of a special charge to customers in order to generate funds to pay
the remaining portion of the assessed franchise fee.

---

* A millage rate is a rate of taxation based on the payment of $1 of taxes per $1,000 of taxable assessed valuation
of real property. For example, five mills is equivalent to $5 per $,1000 dollars of taxable assessed valuation
of property.

Fees and MSD assessments are paid by only the users of a specific service and not by all residential and business property owners. These fees and assessments are expected to generate certain amounts of revenue and consist of several measures. Building and zoning fees (which are affected by building and zoning permits, actions of the board of adjustments and appeals, code enforcement fees, and municipal inspection fees) are expected to generate $3 million. Water resources contract fees, principally aquatic spray fees, are expected to generate $55,000. Parks and recreation fees are expected to generate $15,000 in building rentals.

Fire protection service assessments, which are based on the type of building, are expected to generate approximately $10.4 million, plus an additional estimated $200,000 for providing emergency fire protection services to the Seminole Indians located in Broward County. The nonad valorem special assessment is included on the tax bill of unincorporated area residents. The fire protection assessment for fiscal year 1991 was $110 annually per residential unit. Commercial properties were charged in proportion to the size of the facility. The per resident charge for fire protection, translated into a millage rate, equals roughly 2.4 mills.

Garbage collection revenues are raised from a mandatory assessment on each homeowner at the rate of $190.53 and represents a 2.53 millage rate on a property with a taxable assessed value of $75,000. This assessment generates approximately $7,550,690.

Impact fees, which are charges levied on land developers typically in growing areas in the unincorporated area, are another source of revenues. These fees yield only limited revenues, however, and cannot be used for renovation or rehabilitation purposes. The revenue produced can only be used for new capital expenditures. Furthermore, the economic well-being of residents of the unincorporated area is typically such that these residents are unable to support special assessments sufficient to provide both MSD services or operations and infrastructure or capital needs. If a utility tax were levied, the revenues from the tax would have the potential for providing additional revenues for infrastructure (capital) improvements necessary to meet certain comprehensive plan requirements and certain federal mandates. At the start of the budget preparation year, utility taxes did not appear to be a viable alternative for raising the necessary revenues to provide unincorporated area services.

CURRENT ISSUES AND POLICY OPTIONS

The problem faced by Broward County was how to finance within legal constraints the needed services in the unincorporated area as equitably as possible compared to the tax burden found in municipal governments within the county. Keeping in mind the vertical and horizontal equity principles related to taxes and fees, the county's task was to decide whether the costs of services in the unincorporated area should be distributed according to the benefits received by individuals or based on their ability to pay. Both approaches focus on the individual, who must ultimately bear the cost of the services received.

"The benefits-received approach is a quasi-market approach," which requires only those who receive the benefits from the service to pay for them (Mikesell, 1991: 220–221). It also prevents some individuals from benefitting from the service at the expense of others as in a "pure" public or social good, because the only beneficiaries are those who pay. (Musgrave and Musgrave, 1973: 52–60; Herber, 1975: 22–43; Rosen, 1988: 81–82). The benefits-received approach has its difficulties, however. The first is knowing what share of total benefits from a service an individual receives so that costs can be properly allocated. To the extent that fees and charges can be attached to specific services this difficulty can be overcome. The second difficulty is less easy to overcome. It is the difficulty of achieving a redistribution of affluence or wealth through a tax system to help low-income individuals. The benefits-received approach, utilizing fees and charges, does not accomplish this. Setting the appropriate price to charge in a fee structure in county government is not influenced the same way market forces influence pricing in the private sector, in which competitors can take advantage of changing market pricing systems (Swiss, 1991: 179–180).

The ability-to-pay approach seeks to assign the burden of the cost of government services to individuals based on the costbearing or taxbearing capacity as measured by income or affluence under particular circumstances (Musgrave and Musgrave, 1973: 204–206; Mikesell, 1991: 221). Implementing an ability-to-pay approach requires careful consideration of both horizontal and vertical equity. Horizontal equity seeks to assign to individuals in equal economic circumstances an equal tax or cost burden for the receipt of services (Rosen, 1988: 331–334). Alternatively stated, individuals with equal affluence will pay equal taxes for the consumption of public services. When the services are packageable and measurable, however, this principal applies more to the rate of tax burden or to the payment of costs based on amount of consumption of the particular service (Mikesell, 1991: 222). Vertical equity seeks to place different tax or cost burdens on individuals in different economic circumstances. Increasing the amount of taxes paid or the cost paid for a service based on increased income or higher levels of affluence is only part of the equation. To be equitable, such fee or tax must take into consideration the proportion of affluence or income consumed by the tax or cost burden placed upon the individual. Such burden may be classified as progressive if the rate or proportion of income or affluence consumed in taxes or costs rises as income or affluence rises. It is regressive if the proportion or rate of taxes or cost of services falls as affluence or income rises, and is proportional if the taxes paid or cost of services is constant whether affluence or income remains the same, rises or falls (Reed and Swain 1990: 86–87). Deciding whether and how much to rely on fees, charges, ad valorem taxes, or bonded indebted would therefore take place in the context of equity considerations.

LEGAL ISSUES CLARIFICATION

Based on past practices, Broward County's policy options for providing unincorporated area services included raising the MSD ad valorem property tax rate; increasing fees and charges for garbage collection, fire protection, building and zoning permits, water resources, and parks and recreation services; and increasing franchise fees. The county could also look for some other revenue source, such as bonded indebtedness for capital projects and a utility tax on electric, telephone, or other utility services.

The two new policy options were issuing general obligation bonds and levying a utility tax. The issuance of general obligation bonds, approved by referendum solely within the unincorporated area of the county, raised certain legal and other questions. Could the county legally issue general obligation bonds to fund infrastructure needs only in the unincorporated area? How general would the general obligation bonds have to be? Could the burden for repayment be limited only to the ad valorem property taxes paid by unincorporated area residents? The utility tax raised similar questions. First, did the county have the legal authority to levy such a tax in the incorporated area? Could the tax apply only to utility consumption by residents in the unincorporated area? Finally, could the funds be used for municipal-type purposes only within the unincorporated area?

General Obligation Bonds

Before moving forward with a fully developed proposal to the board of county commissioners through the county manager, the office of budget and management policy (OBMP) secured from the county attorney an interpretation of the legality of proposing either the bonded indebtedness approach or a tax on utilities.

The county attorney's opinion was that under authority of Section 125.01, Florida Statutes, and Article VII, Section 9(b) of the Florida Constitution, it was legally permissible for the county to hold a general obligation bond referendum solely within the unincorporated area and to issue such bonds for the purposes the county intended.

Section 125.01(I) (q) 1, Florida Statutes, authorized a county to establish municipal service taxing units for any part or all of the unincorporated area of the county, within which may be provided recreation services and facilities, drainage, and other essential facilities and municipal services from funds derived from the charge of a fee or special assessment for such services within the unincorporated area only. The statute also provided the authorization for all counties to levy additional taxes, within the limits fixed for municipal purposes, within the municipal service taxing unit or district. This latter flexibility is also affirmed by Article II, subsection 9(b) of the Florida Constitution. Legal authority was also found in the charter of Broward County, which authorized Broward County to accomplish municipal purposes within its unincorporated area through the creation of special municipal taxing units (Charter of Broward County, 1974).

In 1978 the Florida Supreme Court validated bonds issued by the Pasco County municipal service taxing unit (MSTU) (*Speer* v. *Olson*, 1978), since the bonds were issued to finance a water and sewer system for the benefit of the residents of the unincorporated area of the county. The bonds issued pledged for repayment both net revenues of the water and sewer system and ad valorem taxes to be levied and collected in the MSTU. (i.e., the unincorporated area affected) The supreme court of Florida also held that since Chapter 125, Florida Statutes, authorized the issuance of general obligation bonds and since the bonds in the case of Pasco County pledged both net revenues and ad valorem taxes, it was necessary to hold a bond election as part of the local authorization process. This meant calling a special election by the residents of the MTSU for the purpose of securing approval of the bond issue.

Utility Tax

With respect to the legality of the county imposing a utility tax on residents in the unincorporated area, the county attorney reported that, pursuant to Section 166.231, Florida Statutes, it was legal for the county to impose such a utility tax within the unincorporated area of the county. Section 166.231 provides generally that a municipality may levy a tax on the purchase of electricity, metered or bottled gas (natural liquefied petroleum gas or manufactured gas), fuel oil, water service, and telecommunication. This provision of the Florida Statutes did not conflict with Article VII, subsection 9(a) of the Florida Constitution (*Constitution of the State of Florida*, 1968), entitled "Local taxes." This section of the constitution authorizes counties, school districts, municipalities, and special districts to levy ad valorem taxes and permits them, as may be authorized by general law, to levy other taxes, for their respective purposes, except ad valorem taxes on tangible personal property and any taxes prohibited by the Florida Constitution.

The Florida Constitution (1968), Article VIII, subsection 1(g), entitled "Charter Government," grants counties operating under charters to have all powers of local self-government not inconsistent with general law, or with special law approved by vote of the electors. This confirming authority is consistent with Section 1.03 of the charter of Broward County, which states that, "Unless provided to the contrary in this Charter, Broward County shall have all powers of local self-government not inconsistent with general law, or with special law approved by vote of the electors" (Charter of Broward County, 1974: 4).

In 1972, in the case of *State ex rel. Volusia County* v. *Dickinson*, the Florida Supreme Court upheld the ability of a charter county to levy any tax not inconsistent with general or special law, as is permitted municipalities. In its ruling the court stated: "When Section 1(g), Article VIII and Section 9(a), Article VII are read together, it will be noted that charter counties and municipalities are placed in the same category for all practical purposes," and that "unless precluded by general or special law, a charter county may without more authority of existing general law impose by ordinance any tax in the area of its tax jurisdiction a municipality may impose" (*State ex cel. Volusia County* v. *Dickinson*, 1972).

POLICY OPTIONS

Once the legal opinions were provided to the OBMP by the county attorney, the OBMP conducted its analysis in preparation for its selection of a policy proposal to submit to the board of county commissions in the form of a proposed ordinance.

Option 1: The Bond Referendum

Having analyzed and separated the MSD's operations from the capital improvement needs, the OBMP produced an estimated total revenue of approximately $29.3 million (approximately $25.5 million for MSD services and $3.8 million for unmet capital needs). The bond referendum option could be used to fund MSD or capital needs or both. This option would be accepted or rejected on the basis of its potential revenue yield, political feasibility, and relative fairness in fiscal burden compared to other municipalities within the county. Use of the bond referendum approach to fund infrastructure needs would require public referendum approval of specific capital projects listed on the ballot.

The critical data in considering this option included comparing the existing ad valorem property tax millage rate paid by citizens in the unincorporated area to the rate paid by residents in incorporated municipalities within the county. The data in Table 2 show these differences.

The millage rate for the unincorporated area in 1991 was 1.3081, 3.07 mills below the average rate levied in surrounding municipalities and 4.7 mills below the highest millage rate levied by a municipality within the county. Most municipalities levied a tax on utilities ranging from 5–10%. Only seven did not levy a some form of utility tax.

Option 2: Increase the Property Tax and Levy Utility Tax

The second policy option was to propose a substantial increase in the property tax rate *and* implement a utility tax in the unincorporated area. The property tax rate would increase

Table 2 Comparative Millage Rates and Fees Charged Unincorporated Area and Municipalities as of January 1991

Jurisdiction	Millage rate	Percentage utility tax[a]		
		Electric	Phone	Other
County				
Unincorporated area	1.3081	—	—	—
Fire assessment	2.3590	—	—	—
Total	3.6671	—	—	—
Municipalities				
Coconut Creek	3.3566	8%	8%	8%
Cooper City	4.2700	10%	10%	—
Coral Springs	4.3485	10%	10%	10%
Dania	5.7800	10%	10%	10%
Davie	5.0500	9%	7%	9%
Deerfield Beach	5.0000	—	—	—
Lauderdale	5.1055	10%	7%	10%
Hallandale	5.7956	10%	10%	10%
Hillsboro Beach	4.0620	—	—	—
Hollywood	5.8542	10%	7%	10%
Lauderdale by the Sea	4.1182	—	—	—
Lauderdale Lakes	1.7500	—	—	—
Lauderhill	3.2500	5%	10%	—
Lazy Lakes	2.2625	—	—	—
Lighthouse Point	3.5134	10%	10%	10%
Margate	4.6963	8%	8%	8%
Miramar	4.6140	10%	10%	10%
North Lauderdale	4.3414	10%	10%	10%
Oakland Park	4.9512	10%	10%	10%
Parkland	4.6000	7%	10%	7%
Pembroke Park	1.7521	—	—	—
Pembroke Pines	3.7968	10%	10%	10%
Plantation	2.4900	10%	10%	10%
Pompano Beach	6.0405	10%	10%	10%
Sea Ranch Lakes	5.8500	10%	10%	10%
Sunrise	5.0900	10%	10%	10%
Tamarac	5.2033	—	—	—
Wilton Manors	5.6902	10%	7%	10%
Average	4.3797	9%	8.7%	9.6%

[a] Some cities charge up to 10% in franchise fees on monthly utility bills.
Source: Office of Budget and Management, Internal Analysis, Broward County, Florida.

from 1.3 mills to 2.51 mills (93.0% increase) by adding .94 mills for capital needs and .27 mills for the projected increased cost of the MSD operations. In addition, a utility tax of approximately 4% would be imposed on residents in the unincorporated area, with an estimated revenue yield of $4 million per year.

The rationale for proposing a utility tax is that it would make the unincorporated area tax structure more comparable to the tax structure of surrounding municipalities. The

Table 3 Projected Combined Effects of Utility and Property Tax

	Annual utility tax	Additional annual property tax
Taxpayer 1		
$75 average monthly utility bill	$36	—
$50,000 taxable property value	—	$47
Taxpayer 2		
$100 average monthly utility bill	$48	—
$75,000 taxable property value	—	$70
Taxpayer 3		
$150 average monthly utility bill	$72	—
$100,000 taxable property value	—	$94

Source: Office of Budget and Management, Internal Analysis, Broward County, Florida.

impact of the utility tax would still be less expensive to unincorporated area residents than to municipal residents, however. The tax could also offer flexibility to the county if it wished to stabilize fire assessments and millage rates in future years. The specific anticipated impact of the 4% utility tax and an increase in property taxes on typical taxpayers in the MSD is illustrated in Table 3.

Option 3: Impose a Utility Tax Only

The third policy option was to choose a particular utility to tax and apply the appropriate rate. The utilities seriously considered by the county were electric and telecommunications. The data used to arrive at a recommendation are summarized below.

State law permits the county to levy a tax at any rate up to and including 10% on local (intrastate) telecommunications and up to and including 7% on long-distance (interstate) telecommunications services. The tax can apply to the purchase of telecommunication services defined as the monthly recurring customer service charges (Florida Statutes, Section 166.231 and Section 203.012). The county is also permitted to allow 1% of the amount of the taxes collected to be taken by the collecting agent in the form of a deduction for remittance. The telecommunications tax would be paid every month on a recurring basis and not in a lump sum. The tax also allows the county to expand its tax base if it were to include beepers and cellular telephones, thus allowing it to raise more revenues with a lower rate.

The potential yield from a telecommunications tax is indicated by the figures in Tables 4 and 5. Considering first a 10% tax on local telecommunication services, the monthly net tax revenue would approach $90,000. This estimate is based on a first-quarter month's revenue, selected at random from the files of Southern Bell, the state's telephone carrier. Applying a 10% tax to the estimated monthly revenue of $899,224 and accounting for 1% of the revenues retained by Southern Bell for collecting the tax, the county would realize a monthly revenue of $89,023. Annualized, this amount comes to $1,068, 276. (See Table 4.) Applying the 7% maximum tax to both long-distance and local telecommunications services yields a projected monthly revenue of $112,508, using March 1990

Table 4 Projected Revenue from
Telecommunications Tax Based on Single Month
(March 1990) Revenue Annualized

Total taxable revenue	$ 899,224
10% tax	89,922
1% retained by Southern Bell	899
Net tax	$ 89,023
Annualized	12
	$1,068,276

Source: Office of Budget and Management, Internal
Analysis, Broward County, Florida.

Table 5 Projected Revenue from Telecommunications
Tax, Local and Long-Distance Service Based on Single
Month (March 1990) Revenue Annualized

Local taxable revenue	$ 899,224
South Florida long-distance revenue	724,273
Total revenue	1,623,497
7% tax	113,644
1% retained by Southern Bell	1,136
Net tax revenue	112,508
Annualized revenue	12
Total tax revenue	$1,350,096

Source: Office of Budget and Management, Internal Analysis,
Broward County, Florida.

Table 6 Projected Revenue from Electric Utility Tax—Annual
Revenue Data (1989)

Type of usage	Revenue
Residential	$62,332,902
Commercial	28,578,542
Industrial	3,411,112
Street/highways and public authorities	1,143,734
Miscellaneous service	505,698
Total taxable revenue	$95,971,988
10% tax	$ 9,597,198

Source: Office of Budget and Management, Internal Analysis, Broward
County, Florida.

Table 7 Estimated Utility Tax Receipts (in Thousands) per Tax Rate

	Estimated annual revenue	Tax rate and estimated utility tax receipts				
		1%	3%	5%	7%	10%
Electric	$100,000	$1,000	$3,000	$5,000	$7,000	$10,000
Local phone service	10,800	108	324	540	756	1,000
Local and interstate phone service	39,500	395	1,185	1,975	2,765	—
Water	10,000	100	300	500	700	1,000
Natural gas	1,100	11	33	55	77	110

Source: Office of Budget and Management, Internal Analysis, Broward County, Florida.

monthly revenues as the reference point. Potential annual revenue is an estimated $1,350,096. (See Table 5.)

The county's electricity tax option permits a tax levy on the purchase of electricity at a rate of up to 10% of payments received by the seller of the taxable service. The electric tax is more progressive compared to the telecommunications tax because larger homes, reflecting greater affluence, tend to consume greater amounts of electricity. The consumption of electricity also seems more stable in periods of economic changes, except that there will be variations in peak usage during summer months in Florida. Using data from Florida Power and Light Company, the state's major provider of electricity, the county projected annual revenues from an electric utility tax at 10% per annum. Based on twelvemonth data ending December 28, 1989 (end of billing period), projected revenue from the electric utility tax is shown in Table 6.

In deciding which option to propose, the OBMP did a projection of utility revenues from unincorporated area residents based on different utility tax rates. Table 7 shows the results of this analysis.

The maximum tax rate allowed by law to be levied on electric, local telephone, water, and natural gas services is 10%. A maximum of 7% is permitted to be levied on long-distance telephone service. The maximum amount of annual tax revenue to be potentially realized from each tax source, given various rates, is shown in Table 7.

RESULTS

The OBMP considered the various options available to the county and the accompanying issues of equity and fairness in the imposition of fees, charges, or a utility tax on phone services, gas, water, or electricity. It weighed these choices against the advantages and disadvantages of increasing the MSD ad valorem property tax rate to fund ongoing MSD operations and $3.8 million in unmet capital needs. After considering the potential revenue yield and political advantage of exercising the various options, the director of the OBMP, through the county manager, recommended that the board of county commissioners approved a 4% tax only on electricity and increase the MSD millage rate from 1.3 mills to 1.6 mills. The manager emphasized that the fiscal year 1992 budget for the unincorporated area would focus primarily on unmet capital needs such as fire equipment replacement

($.6 million), public safety communications system ($.4 million), and maintenance of ongoing MSD operations, including mandated inflationary increases.

Several elements contributed to the manager's rationale for the proposal. First, it was necessary to state the priorities the county would address given the limited resources and taxpayers' resistance to tax increases in general and strong resistance to property tax increases in particular. Second, a 1% tax on electricity would be more productive than the same rate levied on any other utility. A 1% tax on electricity would raise approximately $1 million annually, compared to $.5 million annually from a 1% tax on water, phone services and natural gas combined. It would take a 3% tax on all allowable utilities—water, telecommunication, gas and fuel oil—to raise the same resources as a 4% tax on electricity only. Third, a tax on electricity was considered to be more progressive and less regressive than each of the other utility taxes on taxpayers. This position is supported by the fact that the amount of electricity consumed by a residential unit is directly related to the size or square footage of the residential unit and the number of electrical amenities the residents use, such as air conditioning, pool pumps, and other luxuries. Fourth, a tax on electricity was considered the easiest to administer. Administrative costs would be low because electricity is sold to consumers by a single provider, as contrasted with water services that are sold to unincorporated area residents by many different municipalities and private utilities.

The county rejected the bonded indebtedness approach because proposing a bond issue would entail a public referendum and a considerable amount of work to educate the public about the need to approve the bond issue. This would isolate the issue of raising money, interpreted to mean tax increases, and allows for greater opposition more generally than attaching the provision of a service for a specific fee to those who use the service.

Following budget hearings in August and early September, the board of county commissioners approved a millage rate increase of .27 mill and adopted the Broward County Public Service Tax Ordinance.' This ordinance was adopted on September 26, 1991. Its provisions would apply to all purchases of electricity occurring on or after November 1, 1991. It would levy and impose a public service tax at a rate of 4% on the payments received by the seller on each and every purchase of electricity within the unincorporated area of Broward County. The tax is to be charged and collected at the time of sale by the seller of electricity within the unincorporated area of the county. The seller of electricity is required to report and pay over to the revenue collection division of the county, on or before the second Monday of each calendar month, all public of service taxes levied and collected during the preceding calendar month. Any purchaser willfully failing or refusing to pay the tax, any seller who has not elected to pay the tax for the purchaser, or any seller who violates the ordinance may be punished by a maximum fine of $500 or by imprisonment for a period not to exceed sixty days or both. Recognized churches in the state of Florida that purchase electricity exclusively for church purposes are exempt from the public service tax levied by the ordinance (Broward County, 1991).

The success of the initial tax and the magnitude of unmet infrastructure and operational needs influenced the county to later increase the utility tax. In September 1993 the board of county commissioners approved an increase in the electric utility tax from 4–10%, effective October 1, 1993 (Broward County, 1993).

SUMMARY AND CONCLUSION

This case study demonstrates how a range of local government concerns converge when addressing the budgetary issue of how to provide services to unincorporated area residents.

These issues include such matters as needs definition, legal and jurisdictional authority, equity, and appropriate and most productive revenue sources. Providing adequate unincorporated area services requires first that the county possess appropriate home-rule, statutory, or constitutional authority to act as a municipality with respect to its local fiscal affairs. This means it must possess a range of authorized revenue options. This was made possible by a provision in Florida's Constitution that counties operating under home-rule charters have all the powers of local self-government not inconsistent with general state law. The state supreme court made this provision clear when it ruled that "the charter county could impose those taxes which a municipality could levy under general law" (*State ex rel. Volusia County* v. *Dickinson*, 1972). This meant that Broward County could exercise an option to levy a tax typically used by municipalities to provide services to its unincorporated area.

In addition to appropriate constitutional-legal authority and a range of revenue options, decisions about which revenue option to choose must be based on comparative analysis of revenue yields and tax burden effects. This requires the administrator to take into consideration equity effects, tax incidence, and the relevance of public budgeting and public finance concepts such as horizontal and vertical equity, progressivity, regressivity, benefits received, and ability to pay.

REVIEW QUESTIONS

1. How equitable was the decision made by the county manager to propose a 4% electric utility tax on residents of the unincorporated area?
2. Discuss the significance of constitutional and legal authorization for county governments faced with the need to provide services to unincorporated area residents.
3. Given the new 4% utility tax, how much better or worse off are unincorporated area residents compared to residents living within the surrounding municipalities with respect to tax burden?
4. If you were the county manager, would you have made a different policy recommendation for financing the needs of the unincorporated area? If yes, what recommendations would you have made and why?
5. What arguments would you use to support the use of general obligation bonds to obtain funds to provide infrastructure needs in the unincorporated area?
6. Assume you are the public relations officer for the county and draft a press release describing the rationale for the budgetary policy changes necessary to provide adequate services to the unincorporated area for fiscal year 1991–92.
7. Based on the information provided in this case, construct a table of projected costs by program area and projected revenues by revenue source.

REFERENCES

Adrian, C. R. and Press, C. (1972). *Governing Urban America*. New York: McGraw-Hill.
Aisdorf, et al. v. *Broward County*. App., 372 So. 2d 695 (Fla. 4th DCA 1979).
Bowen, A. O. and Kearney, R. C. (1990). *State & Local Government*. Boston: Houghton Mifflin.
Broward County. (1993). Ord. no. 91–31. 1991 and ord. no. 93–31.

Charter of Broward County Florida. (1974) as amended.

Constitution of the State of Florida. (1968) as amended.

Florida Statutes. Sections 125.01, 166.231, and 203.012.

Gold, S. D. and Richie, S. (1992). State policies affecting cities and countries in 1992. *Public Budgeting & Finance*, 13, 12–14.

Herber, B. P. (1975). *Modern Public Finance: The Study of Public Sector Economics.* Homewood, IL: Irwin.

Lamb, R. and Rapport, S. P. (1980). *Municipal Bonds: The Comprehensive Review of Tax Exempt Securities and Public's Finance.* New York: McGraw-Hill.

Mikesell, J. L. (1991). *Fiscal Administration: Analysis and Applications for the Public Sector.* Pacific Grove, CA: Brooks/Cole.

Musgrave, R. A. and Musgrave, P. B. (1973). *Public Finance in Theory and Practice.* New York: McGraw-Hill.

Reed, B. J. and Swain, J. W. (1990). *Public Finance Administration.* Englewood Cliffs, NJ: Prentice Hall.

Rosen, H. S. (1988). *Public Finance.* 2nd ed. Homewood, IL: Irwin.

Speer v. *Olson.* 367 So. 2nd 207 (Fla. 1978).

State ex rel. Volusia County v. *Dickinson.* 269 So. 2d 9 (Fla. 1972).

Swiss, J. E. (1991). *Public Management Systems: Monitoring and Managing Government Performance.* Englewood Cliffs, NJ: Prentice Hall.

U.S. Department of Commerce. Bureau of the Census. Government units in 1992. *Census of Governments.* Washington, DC: U.S. GPO. preliminary report, GC92–1(P).

21

The Collapse of Federal Fiscal Home Rule in the District of Columbia

An Analysis of Municipal Financial Conditions

Craig L. Johnson and John L. Mikesell
Indiana University, Bloomington, Indiana, U.S.A.

How did the government of the District of Columbia, the capitol city of the strongest economy in the world, manage in twenty-two years to go from home rule independence to pending fiscal bankruptcy under congressional receivership? The causes are several, including the constraints under which the D.C. government operated, the peculiar nature of the D.C. economy, and the fiscal mismanagement reflected in an unwillingness to make politically difficult but fiscally necessary choices. Its financial condition—its ability to pay its bills in full and on time while maintaining the levels of service demanded by it citizens—was so imperiled that congressional action was imperative. It lacked short-run liquidity, the ability to raise cash to meet immediate needs, long-run fiscal balance, and the ability to raise revenue sufficient to cover the expenditure plans appropriate to the service needs of its citizenry. By exploring the perilous financial condition of the district-and how it got there, students of public finance, citizens of the district, and the American public may enter the twenty-first century with a better understanding of this national embarrassment.

THE ESSENTIAL FACTS: DISTRICT OF COLUMBIA GOVERNMENT

The U.S. Constitution establishes the fundamental dependence of the District of Columbia. Congress, by Article 1, Section 8, clause 17, "shall have the power . . . to exercise exclusive legislation in all cases whatsoever, over such district (not exceeding ten miles square) as may, by cession of particular States, and the acceptance of Congress, become the seat of Government of the United States." The district is therefore different from any state—it has no reserved powers and was not part of those United States that conceived the federal government. Furthermore, it differs from other cities because it has no overlapping state government with some degree of ultimate responsibility for its operations. The district is governmentally beholden to the Congress alone. Indeed, it is so beholden that one of the thirteen annual appropriation bills passed by Congress and signed into law by the president is the budget of the district; therefore above all other governmental actions by the people of the district and their elected officials there lies a supercity council—the Congress of the United States.

The district has had some degree of self-government and some capacity to deal with its own finances, however, the district was created in 1791 and has served as the capital of the United States since 1800. Four different structures of government have been in place since then.

1. Commissioners: From its inception until November 3, 1967, three commissioners appointed by the president administered the district.
2. Mayor–council: From 1967 to 1973, a mayor–commissioner and a nine-member council governed the district. All were appointed by the president with the approval of the Senate, however.
3. Home rule: Following the passage of the Home Rule Act of 1973 by Congress on December 23, 1973, the citizens of the district approved a home rule charter,[1] giving them an elected mayor and thirteen-member council. Congress retained final control over budgetary and legislative matters.
4. Congressional receivership: On April 17, 1995, the District of Columbia Financial Responsibility and Management Assistance Authority (hereinafter the "authority") was established by Congress, effectively stripping the mayor and council of all power over the district's financial affairs for an indeterminate period of time.

CONTRIBUTORS TO THE COLLAPSE: THE ECONOMY OF THE DISTRICT OF COLUMBIA

Financial condition is a general concept that is operationalized by specifying a series of latent constructs and their indicator variables.[2] For example, one the most important aspects of a government's financial condition is its *economic base*. Economic base is a latent construct; it has no real substantive meaning in and of itself, and it gets its meaning from concrete variables associated with the economy. Such economic indicator variables as *unemployment rate* and *personal income* provide an indication of the strength of the economic base. In this case study we use indicator variables to inform our understanding of the critical latent constructs associated with financial condition. The indicator variables are commonly ratios, such as per capita income (personal income divided by population), that are analyzed over time to help determine if particular trends exist (e.g., a growing or declining economy). This type of analysis uses financial condition in dictators to uncover specific areas of fiscal, economic, and demographic stress that may be structural in nature and that require immediate and effective administrative attention.

The economic base is one of the most critical elements in determining the financial condition of a government. The evaluation of the economic base is complex and takes into account many factors, including trends in *population, employment, earnings, industry diversity* and *economic growth*, and community *property-based wealth*.

From 1986 to 1995 the district suffered a substantial loss in *population*.[3] The outmigration is primarily middle-income, professional households headed for the nearby suburbs of Maryland and Virginia, leaving behind a bifurcated city consisting conspicuously of a disproportionate number of wealthy and poor people. Inevitably, this has negatively impacted government resources.

The poor have placed greater and greater demands on expenditures for social services, while the heart of the revenue base—middle-income taxpayers has shrunk. This fiscal imbalance places a great strain on existing resources and requires frugal and prudent management. It is clear that actions must be taken to slow down and eventually reverse the outmigration trend. If not, it will inevitably have long-term disastrous consequences. Overall, the district is not a poor community. Figure 1 compares *per capita income* for the district and the United States from 1986–1995. The district has a higher per capita income than the United States, and the gap has grown since 1986. Indeed, per capita income grew in the district every year except from 1990–1991. Based on this indicator of economic strength, it appears that the community has substantial revenue-raising ability.

Another measure of the economic base is *employment*, both the *unemployment rate* and *number of people employed* (Table 1). The district's unemployment rate declined from 11.7% in 1983 to 5.1% in 1987, but was up to 8.9% in 1995. Although still suffering from a much higher unemployment rate than the Washington SMSA or the United States, the district has a better employment picture in 1995 than in 1983. The number employed, however, tell a different story and must be analyzed to gain a more complete picture of the unemployment figures.

The number employed in the civilian labor force in the district in 1995 (258,000) is fewer than that in 1983 (287,000), indicating that the labor force base contracted over the twelve years, while job growth increased significantly in the Washington SMSA and the United States. Indeed, the reduction in the district's unemployment rate stems largely from the decrease in its labor force, not from an increase in job creation. This indicates

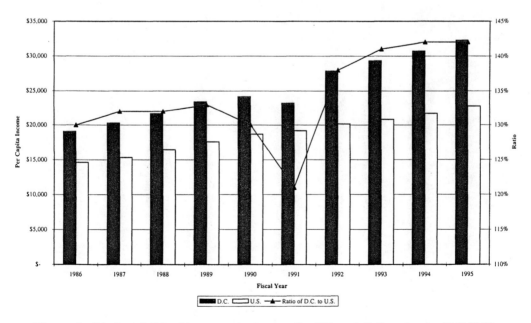

Figure 1 District of Columbia per capita income for U.S. and D.C. and ratio (D.C./U.S.); 1986–1995) *Source*: Bureau of Economic Analysis, U.S. Department of Commerce.

Table 1 Employment and Unemployment in the Civilian Labor Force, Washington, D.C., Washington SMSA, and the Nation (1983–1995)

	1983	1984	1985	1986	1987	1988	1989	1990	1991	1992	1993	1994	1995
Washington, D.C.													
Labor force	325,000	320,000	324,000	323,000	332,000	332,000	315,000	298,000	282,000	308,000	319,000	314,000	283,400
Number employed	287,000	291,000	296,000	298,000	315,000	315,000	299,000	278,000	260,000	282,000	292,000	289,000	258,000
Number unemployed	38,000	29,000	28,000	25,000	17,000	17,000	16,000	20,000	22,000	26,000	27,000	26,000	25,000
Unemployment rate	11.7%	9.1%	8.6%	7.7%	5.1%	5.1%	5.1%	6.7%	7.7%	8.4%	8.5%	8.2%	8.9%
Washington SMSA[a]													
Labor force	1,783,000	1,915,400	1,851,000	2,041,000	2,073,000	2,139,000	2,216,100	2,209,787	2,228,960	2,262,700	2,549,384	2,585,308	2,564,741
Number employed	1,690,000	1,840,400	1,782,000	1,970,000	2,003,000	2,076,000	2,156,600	2,134,412	2,128,660	2,150,600	2,432,718	2,479,036	2,458,199
Number unemployed	93,000	75,000	69,000	71,000	70,000	63,000	59,500	75,375	100,000	112,200	116,666	106,272	106,542
Unemployment rate (S.A.)	5.2%	3.9%	3.7%	3.5%	3.4%	2.9%	2.7%	3.4%	4.5%	5.0%	4.6%	4.1%	4.2%
United States													
Labor force[b]	111,500	116,162	115,461	117,834	119,865	121,669	123,869	124,784	125,303	126,982	128,040	131,056	132,304
Number employed (nonag.)[b]	100,834	102,888	107,150	109,597	112,440	114,996	117,342	117,914	116,877	117,598	119,306	123,060	124,908
Number unemployed[b]	10,717	8,191	8,312	8,237	7,425	6,701	6,528	6,874	8,426	9,384	8,374	7,996	7,494
Unemployment rate (S.A.)[b]	9.6%	7.1%	7.2%	7.0%	6.2%	5.5%	5.3%	5.5%	6.7%	7.4%	6.8%	6.1%	5.6%

[a] Washington SMSA data from the Bureau of Labor Statistics on subnational data.
[b] In thousands. S.A. = Seasonally adjusted
Source: District of Columbia, Department of Employment Services, Area Labor Summary Metropolitan Washington, D.C., and U.S. Department of Labor Statistics, Employment and Earnings.

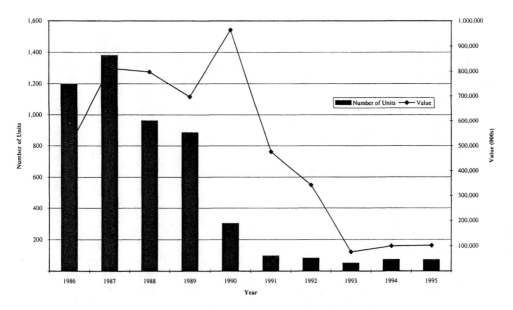

Figure 2 District of Columbia total construction (units and value); 1986–1995). *Source*: Department of Finance and Revenue, Federal Deposit insurance Corporation Data Book. Washington, D.C.

that economic activities that lead to sustained job creation were all but absent from the district from 1983–1995.

Figure 2 illustrates that the construction industry has been in a precipitous free fall since 1987, and that remarkably, construction activity virtually stopped from 1991–1995. The lack of any meaningful construction activity since 1990 clearly has deepened the district's fiscal problems. Moreover, the district government's failure to sustain a capital projects construction program has attenuated the problem. The district authorized $1.5 billion in 1986 and $8.5 billion in 1987 for new capital projects, but nothing for 1998–2002.

Table 2 shows a breakdown of *employment by industry* for the district from 1983–1994. Unfortunately, over 40% of district employment is concentrated in government jobs, federal predominately, but local government accounted for 48,700 jobs in 1994. While this overreliance on government employment may seem odd for a major city, it should be kept in mind that the district is a political construct, set up for political purposes with no consideration for economic concerns. Government *is* the district's home industry and carrying out the nation's political business *is* its reason for being. In contrast, most big cities are economic constructs; they exist and grow because of their strategic economic importance or decline because of the loss thereof.

The estimated *full market value of property* in a community is a measure of the community's wealth, is a signal of the health of the local economy, and can be an important part of local government fiscal capacity. Figure 3 provides a graph of the *total assessed valuation of real property*, adjusted for inflation, in the district from 1984–1995.[4] The assessed value of real property in the district increased in real terms from 1984–1992,[5] and then dropped each year thereafter. This implies that property wealth in the district actually increased from 1984–1992, but has since decreased.[6] The major hit to the district's

Table 2 District of Columbia, Employment by Industry, Annual Average Data

Calendar year	1983	1984	1985	1986	1987	1988	1989	1990	1991	1992	1993[c]	1994[c]
Federal government	208.3	210.3	215.5	213.2	214.5	214.5	217.7	220.4	223.5	230.8	230.0	217.4
District government[a]	45.4	45.3	46.7	48.8	51.4	53.2	52.1	52.6	51.7	51.2	50.9	48.7
Other government	5.2	5.0	4.9	4.9	4.8	4.8	4.8	4.8	4.6	4.5	4.4	4.7
Services	194.2	203.7	212.7	219.2	230.8	242.7	253.4	260.3	255.5	255.6	256.4	261.4
Wholesale/retail	58.8	62.5	62.7	62.7	62.9	64.9	63.5	61.8	57.6	54.7	53.2	52.8
Finance, real estate, insurance	34.5	34.8	34.8	36.6	35.9	34.8	33.5	33.7	34.5	33.7	31.6	31.1
Transportation and communication	25.8	26.1	25.4	24.9	24.5	25.2	24.5	24.0	23.4	23.2	21.4	20.7
Construction and manufacturing	24.3	26.0	28.4	29.7	30.7	29.7	30.2	30.2	26.0	23.0	22.5	22.0
Mining[b]	0.1	0.1	0.1	0.1	0.1	0.1	0.1	0.1	0.1	0.1	—	—
Total[b]	596.6	613.8	631.2	640.1	655.6	669.9	679.8	687.9	676.9	676.8	670.4	658.8

Note: Estimates (in thousand) are benchmarked to ES-202 data for the first quarter of the most current year; thus they are subject to revisions during subsequent benchmarkings.

[a] Annual average of all district employment, including summer and seasonal workers.

[b] Excludes self-employed, unpaid family members, domestic workers, and foreign government personnel.

[c] Revised from previously published data.

Source: D.C. Department of Employment Services, Area Labor Summary, Metropolitan Washington, D.C.

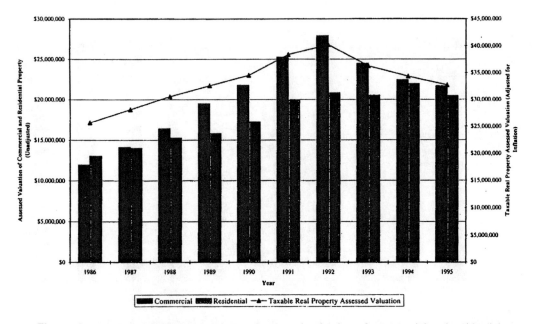

Figure 3   District of Columbia, total annual assessed valuation of commercial and residential property (unadjusted) and taxable real property assessed valuation (adjusted for inflation) 1986–1995) *Source*: Department of Finance and Revenue, Federal Deposit Insurance Corporation Data Book. Washington, D.C.

property tax base, its basic source of fiscal wealth, was in commercial real estate, which declined 20% in just three years, as shown in Figure 3. Residential real estate assessed valuation was basically stagnant from 1992–1995, but suffered a loss in value when adjusted for inflation.

If the government is overreliant on property taxes to fund its expenditures, the gutting of its commercial real estate base will prove deleterious to revenue stability. A decline in overall property values is likely a symptom of underlying problems that may be systemic and long-term in nature, such as the decline or relocation of a major industry or large employer, or an epidemic drug and safety problem.

CONTRIBUTORS TO THE COLLAPSE: THE PUBLIC FINANCES OF THE DISTRICT

The revenue structure and the economic base determine the government's capacity to provide services and pay its bills. The revenue structure can be evaluated in terms of *revenue base stability*, *growth*, *diversity*, and *elasticity*. Our analysis must also include *tax administration* concerns as well.

Figure 4 shows district *revenue* in constant dollars from 1986–1995. Total revenues in 1995 are running around 1988 levels.[7] While there has been some real revenue growth over this time period, despite, or perhaps because of tax rate increases, the revenue base does not produce a stable amount of revenue. Given the substantial exogenous demands

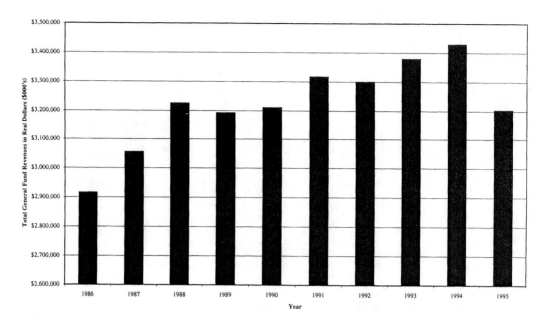

Figure 4   District of Columbia, total general fund revenues in real dollars (1986–1995) *Source*: Office of the Budget, Office of the Controller, Washington, D.C.

on the expenditure side of the budget, its precarious revenue situation places great fiscal stress on the district. Figure 5 illustrates *revenues per capita*, changes in revenue relative to population size. A look at this ratio over time captures the changing burden of raising revenue placed on each citizen. Revenues per capita grew substantially from $4500 in 1986 to $7600 in 1995, indicating that the revenue burden on district residents has become more onerous.

The *diversity of revenue sources*, as shown for 1995 in Figure 6, is critically important for the district because it has such a limited economic base and has always been reliant on the Congress for a significant portion of its revenue. The share of taxes to total revenue has increased in absolute terms since 1986, but has declined from a high of 63% in 1989 to 56% in 1995. The district raises most of its revenue from a diversified tax base that includes property, general sales and excise, income and franchise, and other taxes.

The district's tax potential is constrained, however, because of its large number of tax-exempt entities. This prohibits the district from fully tapping its potential reservoir of tax revenue sources. The property tax base is constrained because 55% of real property in the district is exempt from taxation because it belongs to the federal government or other tax-exempt organizations.[8] The sales tax base is restricted because half of all sales in the district are to tax-exempt organizations, and the income tax base has substantial untapped potential because the district is specifically prohibited by Congress from taxing nonresident income earned in the district. This prohibition results in 60% of the income earned in the district being exempt from district income taxation. All states and many cities have the right to tax income earned in their jurisdiction by both residents and nonresidents.

The *percentage of federal revenues to total revenues* declined from 1986 to 1989, but has picked up and is 35%, or $1.6 billion, in 1995. (See Figure 7.) Federal revenues

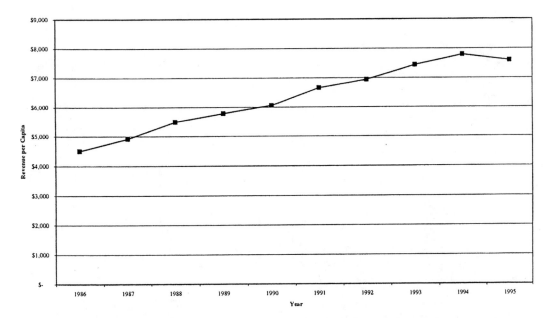

Figure 5 District of Columbia, total revenue (GAAP basis) per capita (1986–1995) *Source*: Office of the Budget. Office of the Controlle, Washington, DC and Federal Bureau of the Census, Current Population Series P-24–1024.

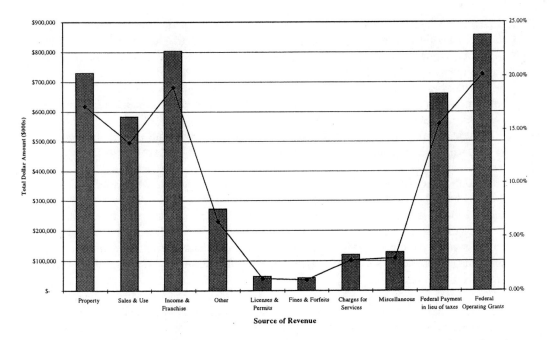

Figure 6 District of Columbia, cross Section of all revenue sources and as percentage of total revenues for 1995 *Source*: Office of the Budget, Office of the Controller. Washington, DC.

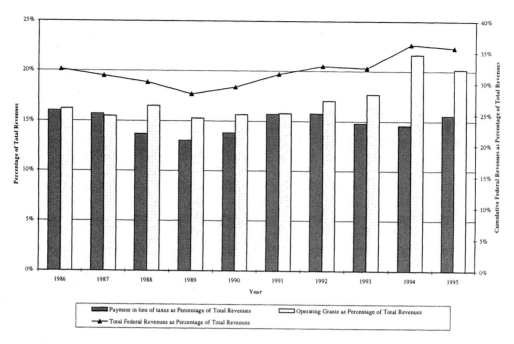

Figure 7 District of Columbia, federal revenues as percentage of total revenues (1986–1995) *Source*: Office of the Budget, Office of the Controller, Washington, DC.

come in two forms; federal operating grants and a federal payment in lieu of taxes, as shown in Figure 8. Federal operating grants have grown markedly since 1986, but the federal payment in lieu of taxes has remained stagnant since 1991.[9] The lack of any real growth in the federal payment in lieu of taxes places an undue strain on an extraordinarily limited tax base. The district has responded by levying high rates on all its tax bases, which has contributed to its outmigration and makes it unable to retain and attract private businesses (Table 3).

Table 4 is a snapshot of the *distribution of individual income taxpayers* in 1991 and 1994 that provides a glimpse into why the district's fiscal problems are somewhat intractable. The number of taxpayers declined by 41,875 over this brief period of time, from 283,549 to 241,674. The number of taxpayers with incomes under $50,000 declined, while those with incomes $50,000 and above increased. Moreover, those taxpayers with incomes above $50,000 are shouldering a greater percentage of the tax burden. This appears to bear out the district's contention that its tax base is more progressive than in past, but progressivity, an equity measure, should not be misunderstood to represent tax base strength. The district's individual income tax base may be more progressive, but it is not any stronger.

Expenditures are a rough measure of the cost of providing services demanded by the electorate. The pattern of expenditures should be consistent with the ability and willingness of the electorate to pay for services. Expenditure patterns should be stable and substantially under the discretion of the government to ensure flexibility in the face of changing demands.

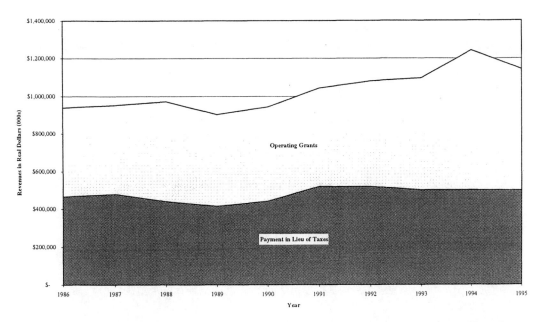

Figure 8 District of Columbia, federal revenues in real dollars (1986–1995) *Source*: Office of the Budget, Office of the Controller, Washington, DC.

Figure 9 indicates that from 1986–1995 total expenditures grew in nominal terms, but are basically flat when adjusted for inflation, indicating that expenditure growth is under control. Nevertheless, *expenditures per capita* increased from $4330 to $7583 over the same time frame, providing evidence that the expenditure burden has increased.

The district spends almost 60% of its budget on public safety, criminal justice, and so-called human support services, a total of over $2.3 billion in 1995. Human support services have experienced the most rapid growth. The district is responsible for many services traditionally provided at the state or county levels of government [higher education, Medicaid, Aid to Families with Dependent Children (AFDC), hospitals]. For example, the district is responsible for 100% of nonfederal Medicaid expenditures, unlike other municipalities, which usually pick up a minor share of the liability with the state government picking up the lion's share. In FY 1994, Medicaid expenditures in the district increased by almost $300 million, crippling the district's budgetary plans.

While district government is overstaffed, as pointed out by "The Report of the Commission on Budget and Financial Priorities" (1990), headed by Alice Rivlin,[10] the citizens of the district are dependent on government employment because private sector employment is limited and insufficient. Its service sector has grown modestly since 1983, but every other sector has declined. The district's employment base must be strengthened and diversified. Strong, long-term financial performance cannot be built upon a weak and deteriorating economic base. The elimination of unnecessary public sector jobs is required to improve administrative efficiency and to reduce the tax burden, but any sincere, substantive attempt to improve the long-term financial condition of the district must include private sector job creation as a primary component. Having the district government as employer of last resort, however, spells fiscal disaster.

Table 3 District of Columbia, Changes to Major Tax Rates (1986–1995)

| Fiscal year | Property[a] | | | | | | Sales and use | | Income and receipts[e] | | Gross receipts |
| | Real | | | | | Personal | General[b] | Selective Cigarettes[c] motor fuel[d] | Individual | Business | Public utility[f] |
	Owner occupied	Tenant occupied	Hotels	Improved	Unimproved						
1986	1.22	1.54	1.82	2.03	2.03	3.10	0.0600	0.33	.02–.11	0.1050	0.067
1987									.06–.1		
1988									.06–.095	0.1025	
1989	1.06										
1990	0.96		1.85	2.15	3.29			0.18			
1991								0.30		0.1050	0.097
1992						3.40		0.70			
1993					5.00			0.65		0.1025	
1994											0.100
1995							0.0575			0.0998	

[a] Per $100 of assessed value.
[b] Per $1 of sales.
[c] Per pack.
[d] Per gallon.
[e] Per $1 of taxable income.
[f] Per $1 of gross receipts.
Source: Department of Finance and Revenue, Washington, D.C.

Table 4 District of Columbia, Distribution of Individual Income Taxes (Years Ended December 31, 1991 and 1994)

| | 1991 | | | 1994 | | |
Income levels	Percentage of total taxes collected	Number of taxpayers	Percentage of taxpayers	Percentage of total taxes collected	Number of taxpayers	Percentage of taxpayers
Under $5,000	0.3%	13,899	4.9%	0.2%	9,142	3.8%
$5,000 to $9,999	1.6%	33,814	11.9%	1.1%	24,566	10.2%
$10,000 to $14,999	3.7%	40,350	14.2%	2.7%	30,668	12.7%
$15,000 to $24,999	14.5%	79,935	28.2%	10.5%	60,674	25.1%
$25,000 to $49,999	32.7%	81,137	28.6%	30.0%	75,653	31.3%
$50,000 to $99,999	23.2%	26,261	9.3%	27.7%	30,717	12.7%
Over $100,000	24.0%	8,153	2.9%	27.8%	10,264	4.2%
Total	100.0%	283,549	100.0%	100.0%	241,684	100.0%

Source: Department of Finance and Revenue. 1991 and 1994 Returns with Taxable Income.

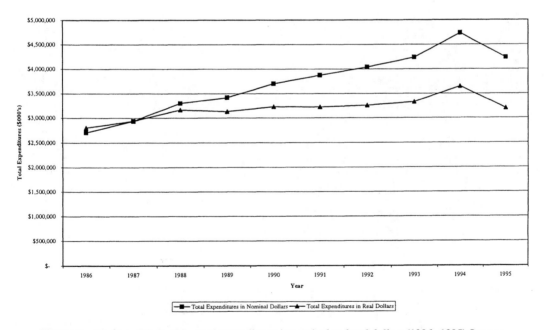

Figure 9 District of Columbia, total expenditures in nominal and real dollars (1986–1995) *Source*: Office of the Budget, Office of the Controller, Washington, DC.

Table 5 District of Columbia General Fund, Actual Revenues and Expenditures (Fiscal Years 1986–1995; GAAP Basis)

	1986	1987	1988	1989	1990	1991	1992	1993	1994	1995
Revenues										
Taxes										
Property	$488,849	$541,211	$609,425	$710,766	$737,138	$881,878	$903,319	$1,011,663	$811,009	$730,343
Sales and use	432,969	459,418	468,942	507,169	546,823	531,004	524,750	504,735	557,474	584,107
Income and franchise	689,763	782,574	847,611	896,563	905,224	891,587	708,085	730,519	800,868	804,355
Other	72,954	90,464	95,934	90,100	89,942	67,263	248,146	310,935	300,702	272,236
Total taxes	1,684,535	1,873,667	2,021,912	2,204,598	2,279,127	2,371,732	2,384,300	2,557,852	2,470,053	2,391,041
Licenses and permits	31,850	31,907	31,601	33,069	32,285	32,997	41,856	44,564	49,098	47,583
Fines and forfeits	39,528	38,569	41,594	45,511	48,542	53,026	51,860	51,845	48,107	42,447
Charges for services	117,585	134,531	124,943	125,756	139,554	148,810	148,723	138,156	137,361	120,033
Miscellaneous	34,897	24,076	129,664	93,490	98,431	125,323	122,952	112,012	127,628	128,008
Intergovernmental										
Payment in lieu of taxes	450,265	479,500	459,500	453,800	506,966	625,231	643,772	635,930	647,930	660,000
Operating grants	456,421	473,157	555,197	532,967	575,357	628,370	695,616	759,845	960,708	855,308
Total revenues	$2,815,081	$3,055,407	$3,364,411	$3,489,191	$3,680,262	$3,985,489	$4,089,079	$4,300,204	$4,440,885	$4,244,420
Expenditures										
Current										
Government direction and support	123,759	136,320	148,194	147,014	153,766	155,541	142,265	136,630	129,601	131,001
Economic development and regulation	211,038	239,248	251,594	258,969	275,225	289,644	263,003	285,249	286,722	258,514
Public safety and justice	743,224	813,947	886,537	928,983	1,040,924	1,043,279	1,057,508	1,067,374	1,106,555	1,069,910
Public education system	507,003	554,411	627,393	658,857	713,372	736,652	754,009	754,104	796,138	759,973
Human support services	875,757	954,434	1,258,995	1,097,031	1,212,370	1,342,828	1,411,451	1,636,871	1,874,348	1,349,991
Public works	238,624	250,667	265,980	270,089	287,094	294,484	289,587	303,366	276,964	249,202
Employment benefits (deduction)	(181,402)	(210,156)	(353,854)	(169,653)	(234,595)	(273,006)	(219,517)	(295,232)	(73,542)	75,688
Debt service										
Principal	39,505	53,416	66,630	71,743	84,922	97,792	128,917	151,675	139,515	157,308
Interest	145,104	145,495	148,783	153,555	162,050	177,452	204,181	193,641	186,878	184,510
Fiscal charges	3,440	2,913	1,916	3,550	7,878	9,677	7,260	5,755	7,020	3,077
Total expenditures	2,706,052	2,940,695	3,302,168	3,420,138	3,703,006	3,874,343	4,038,664	4,239,433	4,730,199	4,239,174

Excess of revenues over expenditures	109,029	114,712	62,243	69,053	(22,744)	111,146	50,415	60,771	(289,314)	5,246
Other financing sources (uses)										
Proceeds (payment) of General fund recovery bonds	—	—	—	—	—	336,605	—	—	—	—
Refunding bonds	442,810	248,297	100,159	194,903	—	—	272,244	1,063,322	407,410	—
Refunded debt	(424,756)	(239,398)	(83,703)	(166,524)	—	—	(261,077)	(929,738)	(369,080)	—
Refunding charges	(14,826)	(8,840)	(16,456)	(29,312)	—	—	(2,238)	(127,769)	(38,330)	—
Loases	—	—	—	—	—	—	—	10,920	—	—
Operating Transfers in (Out)										
Capital projects fund	(9,136)	(17,897)	(481)	5,813	(13,146)	(23,119)	12,323	1,352	7,356	—
General hospital fund	(48,350)	(42,423)	(41,930)	(44,430)	(49,993)	(59,510)	(69,010)	(58,768)	(46,735)	(56,735)
Convention center fund	(8,521)	(6,261)	(6,758)	(8,597)	(10,603)	(11,139)	(12,550)	(13,250)	(12,512)	(38,078)
Lottery and games fund	40,000	40,100	42,500	53,000	48,875	45,700	48,500	66,875	69,050	85,100
University fund	(67,715)	(70,215)	(71,667)	(74,310)	(74,958)	(73,495)	(73,495)	(67,796)	(66,449)	(49,961)
Housing finance fund	(1,234)	(1,350)	(1,825)	(29)	(778)	(547)	(355)	—	—	—
Pension fund	2,752	3,563	3,639	4,902	5,161	7,518	8,358	—	—	—
Straplax	—	—	—	1,000	—	—	584	1,847	—	—
Water and sewer	—	—	—	—	—	—	28,287	—	3,177	—
Total other financing sources (uses)	(88,976)	(94,424)	(76,522)	(63,584)	(95,442)	222,013	(48,429)	(53,005)	(46,113)	(59,674)
Excess (deficiency) of revenues over (under) expenditures and other uses	20,053	20,288	(14,279)	5,469	(118,186)	333,159	1,986	7,766	(335,427)	(54,428)
Fund balance (deficit), at Oct. 1	(244,934)	(224,881)	(204,593)	(218,872)	(213,403)	(331,589)	1,570	3,556	11,322	(324,106)
Fund balance (deficit), at Sept. 30	$(224,881)	$(204,593)	$(218,872)	$(213,403)	$(331,589)	$1,570	$3,556	$11,322	$(324,105)	$(378,534)

Note: In thousands of dollars.
Source: Office of the Budget, Office of the Controller, Washington, D.C.

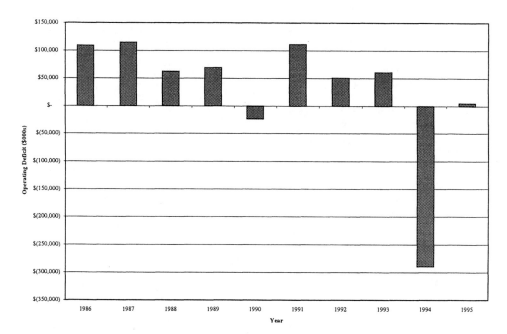

Figure 10 District of Columbia, operating deficit (1986–1995) *Source*: Office of the Budget, Office of the Controller, Washington, DC.

The general fund operating surplus or deficit, shown in accounting records as the *excess of revenues over (under) expenditures*, is a measure of financial performance from operations during the fiscal year. The district ran operating surpluses in every fiscal year since 1986 except 1990 and 1994 (Figure 10, Table 5). The *operating deficit* was $22.744 million in 1990 and jumped to $289.315 million in 1994. The 1994 operating deficit was primarily the result of the $200.654 million decrease in property tax revenue and the $237.477 million increase in human support services.[11]

The 1994 operating deficit resulted in a negative fund balance of −$324,105. This wiped out the benefits derived from bonding out the FY 1990 $331.589 million negative fund balance with the 1991 $336.605 million recovery bonds Issuance of the 1991 general fund recovery bonds gave the district some breathing room to fundamentally restructure its operations and bring the district into fiscal balance by eliminating the persistently large *fund balance* deficits.[12]

The fund balance deficit is much larger than the operating deficit because the district is responsible for many enterprises outside the general fund. As shown in Figure 11, these enterprises—the general hospital fund, the convention center fund, the university fund—regularly operate in the red and require large infusions of cash from the general fund in order to survive. They have drained the district for a cumulative total loss of over $1.3 trillion between 1986–1995.

CONTRIBUTORS TO THE COLLAPSE: DEBT MANAGEMENT AND PENSIONS

Debt securities are financial instruments that represent a pledge to fulfill a contractual obligation; the borrower promises to repay the lender the amount borrowed plus interest

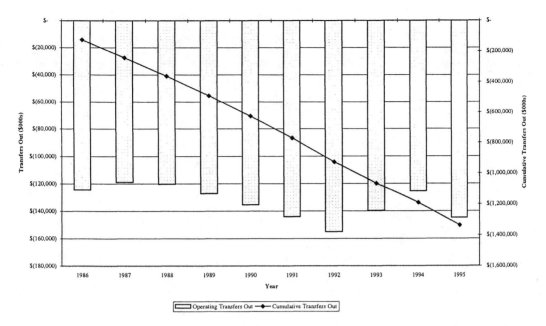

Figure 11 District of Columbia, operating transfers out (1986–1995) *Note*: Transfers out include transfers to the general hospital fund, the convention center fund, and the university fund. *Source*: Office of the Budget, Office of the Controller. Washington, DC.

over some specified period of time. The amount of money necessary to pay principal and interest is termed debt service. Governments issue debt to finance long-term capital investment projects and short-term cash flow needs. The district's debt portfolio is unique since it consists of U.S. Treasury loans in addition to standard municipal general obligation and revenue bonds.

Short-term debt instruments, usually notes or commercial paper, have a stated maturity of thirteen months or less and are usually issued to meet cash flow needs. Borrowing money to finance an operating deficit should be kept to an absolute minimum. It is not uncommon for governments to borrow to meet unexpected cash shortfalls resulting from differences in the timing in the receipt of revenues and the payment of expenditures, but such borrowing should be a rare event, not a recurring one. In addition, the amount of short-term borrowing, which by definition is debt that is to be paid with current year revenues, should be only a small percentage of total revenues.

The district traditionally issues tax revenue anticipation notes (TRANs) to pay general expenses during the fiscal year in anticipation of the receipt of certain revenues by the end of the fiscal year. The TRANS must be repaid no later than the last day of the fiscal year in which they are issued, but they may be renewed or rolled over into the following fiscal year. Table 6 shows district short-term borrowing from 1987–1996.[13] The data show a pattern of short-term borrowing as a matter of strategic financial management.[14] In most years, the amount of borrowing takes up a large portion of general fund revenues, indicating that the district is financing its operating budget with debt proceeds. Moreover, the two years that show zero TRANS outstanding result from the district bonding out its recurring deficit, issuing long-term debt to repay short-term debt by issuing

Table 6   District of Columbia, Short-Term Borrowings (Fiscal Years 1987–1996; in thousands of dollars)

	1987	1988	1989	1990	1991	1992	1993	1994	1995	1996[a]
Maximum proceeds of tax revenue anticipation notes (TRANS)	$150	$150	$250	$250	$300	—	—	$200	$250	$220[b]
Maximum amount of tax revenue anticipation notes outstanding as a percentage of general fund revenues[a] (TRANS)	4.9%	4.5%	7.2%	6.8%	7.5%	0.0%	0.0%	7.3%	7.3%	4.9%[c]

Note: Does not include short-term borrowings from the U.S. Treasury in fiscal years 1995 and 1996, which totaled $146.7 million and $379 million, respectively.

[a] Based on general fund revenues calculated in accordance with generally accepted accounting principles; numbers for fiscal year 1996 are projected, based on budgeted revenue figures.

[b] Figures for fiscal year 1996 are projections and assume no additional notes will be issued.

[c] In fiscal year 1996, the calculation is based on a gross budget amount.

the 1991 $336 million TRANS.[15] Rather than alleviating the district's structural imbalance, this action turned a bad short-term situation into a worse longer-term situation.

Long-term debt instruments, or bonds, have maturities greater than thirteen months and are generally sold to finance capital improvements, although they may also be sold to augment the cash positions of state and local governments. The district's total long-term debt to be repaid from the general fund, general obligation, and U.S. Treasury debt, peaked at $3.65 billion in 1994. The U.S. Treasury funds the construction of capital projects with long-term loans that are unsecured general obligations of the district. In addition, under D.C. Code Section 47–3401 the district has the legal authority to borrow funds from the U.S. Treasury to finance general expenses. This provision has not been utilized since 1983 (U.S. General Accounting Office, 1994), however. The Home Rule Act prohibits the district from issuing long-term general obligation bonds if the amount of debt service (principal and interest) in any fiscal year on all outstanding long-term general obligation and treasury loans exceeds 14% of estimated revenues of the fiscal year in which the debt is issued (D.C. Code Section 47–313).

Debt burden is commonly analyzed by calculating and interpreting the meaning of certain *debt ratios*. Debt ratios are comparative statistics that show the relationship between outstanding debt and such important measures as tax base, income, and population. The relative size of the debt burden is measured by the *debt per capita* ratio. The burden of debt on a government's tax base is measured by the *debt-to-property-value* ratio. The value of a jurisdiction's property is an implicit measure of the stock of government wealth and reflects its ultimate capacity to service debt.[16] The *debt-to-personal-income* measure is a commonly used measure that also reflects the government's ability to service its debt by comparing personal income in a jurisdiction to its outstanding debt. We also use *debt service as a percentage of total expenditures* to measure the debt service burden on the government's operating statement. This represents the amount of money the government has implicitly chosen not to spend on other expenditures, such as human support services.

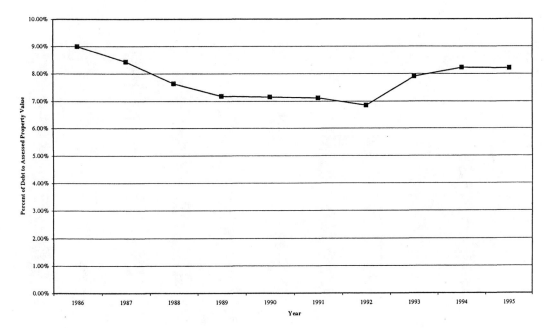

Figure 12 District of Columbia, debt to assessed property value (1986–1995) *Source*: Office of the Budget, Office of the Controller. Washington, DC.

Figure 12 shows that the general obligation *debt-to-property-value* ratio has remained between 7–9% from 1986–1995. It has not increased significantly over the years, despite the district's fiscal problems, but it is still very high relative to other cities. The Moody's median for similarly sized cities is 3.8% (Moody's Investors Service, 1995). In contrast, *debt per capita* (Figure 13) has almost doubled since 1986, from $3,700 to slightly over $6,000. The Moody's median for this ratio is $1,476, which implies that district residents are under the yoke of an oppressive debt burden. Moreover, outstanding *debt to personal income* has hovered around the 20% mark since 1986, which is well above industry benchmarks.

Debt service as a percentage of total expenditures is around 8% in 1995, as shown in Figure 14. This indicates that 8% of the district's budget, a figure moderately above what is considered prudent, cannot be spent on providing services and must be used to pay interest and retire principal when due. Moreover, it indicates that district management does not have sufficient flexibility over the expenditure side of its operating statement.

Part of the cause of this financial management inflexibility is due to the district's *debt repayment schedule*. Figure 15 shows that the district's long-term debt repayment schedule is very front-loaded—more debt service is payable sooner rather than later, including $75.3 million of U.S. Treasury debt. Clearly, the repayment schedule should be stretched out to provide the district with some current budgetary relief.

Employee pension plans place a significant long-term liability on governments. Ideally, a government's pension plan should be fully funded, meaning that there are sufficient funds for paying future retirement benefits, calculated on an *actuarial basis*. If the pension plans are not at least approximately fully funded, it places a significant burden on the

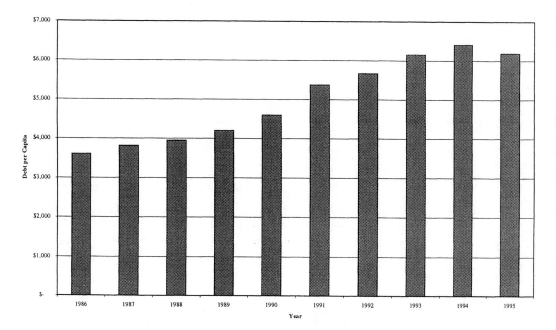

Figure 13 District of Columbia, debt per capita, (1986–1995) *Source*: Office of the Budget, Office of the Controller. Washington, DC.

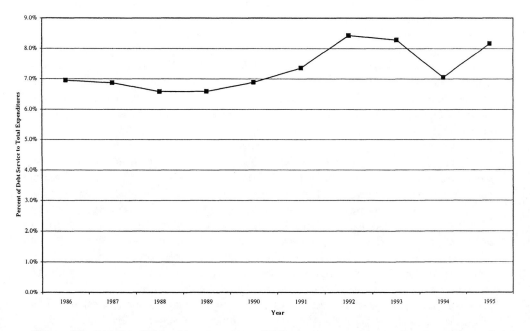

Figure 14 District of Columbia, percentage of debt service to total expenditures (1986–1995) *Source*: Office of the Budget. Office of the Controller. Washington, DC.

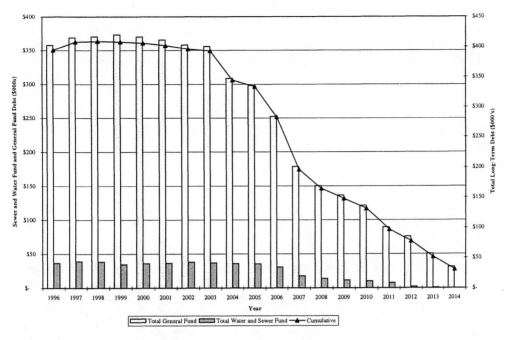

Figure 15 District of Columbia, repayment schedule for long-term debt (1996–2014) *Source*: Office of the Controller. Washington, DC.

government's finances in the future and raises concerns of intergenerational inequities by which current and future beneficiaries may place an undue burden on current and future taxpayers.

When the district was given home rule, the federal government passed the unfunded pension benefit actuarial liability of $1.9 billion and future funding responsibility to the district. As of September 30, 1995, the district had an unfunded pension benefit obligation of $4.6 billion, or 56% of its total pension benefit obligation. The district's pensions were never funded according to actuarial principles, by which sufficient moneys are set aside each year to ensure that adequate funds are available to meet pension obligations in the future, rather, the federal government set up the district's pension system on a pay-as-you-go basis. Since the pension system has always been a defined benefit plan (as opposed to a defined contribution plan), the federal government made annual payments to cover the annual benefit payments. After home rule, federal contributions to the pension fund were never intended to reduce underfunding; rather, they were intended to partially fund the continuation of the pay-as-you-go approach. The policy of underfunding pension obligations has resulted in a ballooning unfunded liability and cash flow problems that have forced the district to defer its pension fund contributions on numerous occasions.

REFORM INITIATIVES

Thus far we have presented an analysis of the district's financial condition through most of 1995. Since then two major federal reform initiatives have been developed, passed by

Congress and deployed in the district. The remaining sections of the chapter outline these initiatives, focusing on the components of the reforms that are designed to fundamentally change the organizational and leadership structure of the district. Such reforms are intended, among other things, to turn around the district's financial condition and restore its ability to deliver services to its residents. The question of whether these efforts will be successful or not remains unanswered.

The reforms are presented with minimal accompanying discussion. The reader should use the financial condition analysis presented earlier and other information at her disposal to analyze and evaluate the reform initiatives. The reader should evaluate the probability that the full implementation of the reforms will be effective at improving the district's structural financial condition.

THE CONGRESSIONAL RECEIVERSHIP: WHO DOES WHAT TO WHOM?

In the face of the fiscal, economic, demographic, and political problems facing the district, in April 1995 Congress established the District of Columbia Financial Responsibility and Management Assistance Authority (the authority) with the enactment of the District of Columbia Financial Responsibility and Management Assistance Act of 1995 (the authority act). The authority was established to improve the management of the district's resources by, among other things:

> Eliminating budget deficits and cash shortfalls
> Ensuring efficient and effective service delivery
> Enhancing access to public capital markets
> Ensuring long-term financial, fiscal, and economic viability
> Examining the structural relationship between the district government and the federal government
> Reviewing the financial impact of activities of the district before the activities are implemented or submitted for congressional review

The authority act establishes a control period beginning in FY 1996 and running for an unlimited duration, but for a minimum of four years, during which the district is effectively placed in receivership under authority control. During the control period, the authority is required to

> Approve the district's annual financial plans and budgets for the applicable fiscal year and the next three consecutive years or submit to Congress a recommended alternative financial plan and budget
> Review acts of the council to ensure their consistency with the approved financial plan and budget
> Review certain contracts and leases proposed to be entered into by the District
> Approve all short-term and long-term borrowing of the district

If the mayor or council rejects any recommendation of the authority, then the mayor or council must state in writing the reasons for the rejection. Despite any such objection, the authority may take such action as it deems appropriate to adopt and implement its recommendations after consulting with Congress. Moreover, the authority has been given certain powers to recommend to Congress disapproval of legislation adopted by the council. If the mayor and the council do not submit budgets that do not have operating deficits that make substantial progress in reducing the district's accumulated fund balance deficit, the authority must develop its own budget that does so and the mayor is required by law to implement it. The district is also required to substantially revise the presentation of its enterprise funds in its budget document.

Since the Home Rule Act of 1973, the mayor was in charge of the administration of the financial operations of the district. The authority act of 1995 and the district's 1996 appropriation act establish the office of the chief financial officer and remove day-to-day control over the district's financial operations from the mayor and transfer financial control to the chief financial officer (CFO). The CFO is appointed by the mayor with the concurrence of the council and the authority and cannot be removed by the mayor during a control year. During a control year, the district's CFO is responsible for

> Preparing the financial plan and budget of the district for use by the mayor
> Assuring that all financial information presented by the mayor is consistent with the requirements of the authority;
> Submitting to the council a financial statement of the district government
> Supervising and assuming responsibility of the assessment of all property subject to assessment and special assessment
> Supervising and assuming responsibility for levying and collecting all taxes, fees, and other revenues
> Preparing with the approval of the authority annual estimates of all revenues of the district and quarterly re-estimates
> Supervising and assuming responsibility for financial transactions to ensure adequate control of revenues and resources and to ensure that appropriations are not exceeded
> Certifying all contracts prior to execution as to the availability of funds
> Implementing appropriate procedures and instituting programs to improve budget, accounting, and personnel control systems
> Maintaining systems of accounting and internal control and the custody of all public funds

In addition, Congress cemented CFO control over district financial operations by providing the CFO with widespread authority over key administrative appointments. The administrative heads and personnel of the office of the treasury, the office of the controller, the office of the budget, the office of financial information services, and the department of finance and revenue are appointed by, serve at the pleasure of, and are under the direct control and supervision of the CFO.

THE FEDERAL REFORM PLAN: TOO MUCH OR NOT ENOUGH?

Apparently, the federal government viewed the authority act as only a precursor of things to come. On January 14, 1997, the Clinton administration unveiled a comprehensive reform plan for the district entitled the National Capital Revitalization and Self-Government Improvement Plan, which was enacted by Congress in August 1997 with only slight modifications. The federal revitalization plan for the district is sweeping and fundamentally changes the nature of district governance and redefines its relationship with the federal government.

In terms of annual budgetary fiscal matters, the changes required by the revitalization plan include

Requiring a balanced budget in FY 1998

Requiring federal government financing of $400 to $500 million of the district's accumulated deficit

Immediately reducing the annual federal payment to $140 million from $660 million and eliminating the federal payment completely in the future

Authorizing the district to borrow up to $300 million over ten years from either the U.S. Treasury or the municipal market to finance its deficit

Requiring any federal contribution to be used to repay any money owed to the U.S. Treasury

The major change made by the federal revitalization plan to the general administration of the district government involves

Stripping the mayor of control over the nine largest city agencies and shifting control to the authority

It also requires the authority to hire consultants to develop plans for reforming the nine major agencies[17] and gives the authority both the right to confirm directors of the nine agencies and the sole power to fire directors. The major changes made by the federal revitalization plan to financial administration involve the federal government assuming responsibility for an array of district functions, including

Taking over $1.4 billion in spending to operate prisons and courts and $885 million for prison renovation

Assuming responsibility for the district's approximately $5 billion unfunded pension liability (district is responsible for setting up a new pension plan for current employees

Reducing the district's Medicaid contribution to 30% from 50%

Authorizing the district CFO to contract with private firms for tax administration and collection services

The major changes made by the federal revitalization plan to debt management include[18]

Providing authority to do negotiated sales on general obligation bonds

Expanding revenue bond provisions to include several additional classes of authorized debt

Creating the ability to sell bond anticipation notes (BANs) with maturities up to three years

Increasing the borrowing limit to 17% of revenues from 14%

CONCLUSION

The District of Columbia has never been a truly free and independent fiscal entity. It has always been—and perhaps always will and should be—dependent on the Congress for its revenue lifeline. The Congress has always reserved ultimate control over the district's budgetary and legislative affairs. Control and responsibility go hand in hand, therefore the Congress is at least equally responsible for the failure of the district's brief flirtation with limited home rule.

Notwithstanding this, fiscal mismanagement under limited autonomy is as much a disservice to district residents and the nation as fiscal mismanagement under full autonomy. There also can be no doubt that district government officials have poorly managed the district and underserved district residents for an extended period of time.

REVIEW QUESTIONS

1. Evaluate the pros and cons of the Home Rule Act of 1973 in terms of giving the district the ability to govern its own fiscal affairs.
2. What actions should the district government have taken to pre-empt a complete federal takeover of its financial and administrative affairs?
3. Identify the strengths and weaknesses of the district's economic base and fiscal structure.
4. Suggest some reforms to the district's handling of its enterprise funds.
5. Critically evaluate the federal government revitalization plans for the district. Address the following major questions:
   a. Will it be effective in the short-run? In the long-run?
   b. Does it adequately remedy the district's major structural problems?
   c. Is it fair to all stakeholders?
   d. Is it likely to improve the relationship between the federal government and the district government?
6. What is the purpose behind creating a separate authority and CFO structure? Why have they been given their specific powers?
7. Should the district have the same access to the federal Treasury as an official federal government department or agency?
8. U.S. congressional committees have always been responsible fore overseeing the district and legally authorizing and appropriating the district's budget, even under home rule. If this is the case, then how did the district get into such dire fiscal straits in the first place?
9. Should the district have been allowed to issue the 1991 general fund recovery bonds? Evaluate the district's debt issuance and debt management practices according to the principles of efficiency, effectiveness, accountability, and equity.

NOTES

1. Formally, the District of Columbia Self-Government and Governmental Reorganization Act, Public Law (PL) 93–198.
2. For comprehensive discussions of the variables involved in financial condition analysis see Berne and Schramm, 1986; Groves and Valente, 1994.
3. District population peaked at 802, 178 in 1950. The 1970s saw the most rapid losses, during which the district's population declined from 757,000 to 638,000.
4. According to the district, it assesses property at 100% of market value.

5. Some of the property value growth in the late 1980s and early 1990s may be due more to inflated assessments, designed to keep tax revenues up, than to any real increase in local real estate prices.

6. While the 17.5% drop in property value from 1992–1995 has had an adverse impact on district resources, it is consistent with the negative trend in taxable property value for most large cities, which was 9%.

7. A one-time accounting change in 1993 shifted the real property tax year from June 30 to September 30. That inflated fiscal year 1993 property tax revenue (three more months) and reduced FY 1994 revenue (three fewer months).

8. The Report of the Commission on Budget and Financial Priorities of the District of Columbia (1990).

9. The annual federal payment, $660 million for FY 1996, now goes directly to the authority "on behalf" of the district.

10. The report states that the "District has approximately 40 percent more staff per 10,000 population than the average of 12 (similar) cities" and that, "the Commission believes total staff should be reduced by approximately 6,000 positions."

11. The FY 1993 reported surplus includes the aforementioned inflated property tax revenues due to the change in the tax year. Without the additional three months of revenue from the accounting change, the district would have reported a $165 million operating deficit in FY 1993.

12. This problem did not begin in 1991. Upon granting the district limited autonomy in 1973, the Congress left the district with a $284 million accumulated deficit (U.S. General Accounting Office, 1996).

13. Please note that the 1995 and 1996 figures do not include $146.7 million and $379 million, respectively, in short-term borrowing (advances) from the U.S. Treasury. From 1939–1983 the district regularly received Treasury advances to meet short-term cash requirements for general expenses. The district is currently able to requisition an advance of funds up to the amount of the advanced federal payment to the district. Among the numerous conditions the district must meet to receive the advance is that it is unable to access the public credit markets. Such a requirements is expensive. While the fiscal discipline imposed by public credit markets can only help improve the financial condition of the district, the substantial costs of issuing public debt places an avoidable strain on already strapped district government coffers.

14. To meet cash flow needs, the district also regularly borrows internally from its capital projects fund, and has deferred payments to vendors.

15. The total amount of outstanding TRANS at any time is limited to 20% of the district's total expected revenue for the fiscal year. This limit is too permissive.

16. A similar measure that compares flows is the *debt-service-to-personal income* ratio. This ratio measures expenditure outflows for debt service to money inflows in the jurisdiction.

17. These agencies include administrative services, employment services, public works, human services, health, consumer and regulatory affairs, fire and emergency medical services, corrections, and housing and community development.

18. The revitalization plan also eliminates capital taxes on investments in impoverished areas and provides middle-income first-time home buyers with a $5000 tax credit.

REFERENCES

Berne, R. and Schramm R. (1986). *The Financial Analysis of Governments*. Englewood Cliffs, NJ: Prentice-Hall.

Bond Buyer. (1997). District of Columbia revitalization plan (HR 1963). *Bond Buyer*, July 7.

Groves, S. M. and Valente, M. G. (1994). *Evaluating Financial Condition*. Washington, DC: International City/County Management Association.

Moody's Investors Service. (1995). *1995 Medians: Selected Indicators of Municipal Performance*. New York: Public Finance Department.

Morris, V (1997). Control board has the power; now it has to exercise it; Congress passes plan to revitalize city. *Washington Times*, Aug. 1.

Morris, V. (1997). Control board starts cabinet shuffle; three fired; nine named 30-day chiefs. *Washington Times*, Aug. 6.

Resnick, A. B. (1997). Federal reform plan's contribution helps give D.C. a "fighting chance." *Bond Buyer*, Aug. 29.

Resnick, A. B. (1997). District of Columbia would be given more fiscal help under budget pact. *Bond Buyer*, July 31.

Resnick, A. B. (1997) Raters like Clinton's D.C. proposal but await details. *Bond Buyer*, Jan. 21.

The Report of the Commission on Budget and Financial Priorities of the District of Columbia. (1990). *Financing the Nation's Capital*. November.

U.S. Code Service. (1995). *Public Law 104–8*. 104th Congress, 1st Session. Lawyers Cooperative Publishing. April 17.

U.S. General Accounting Office (1994). *District of Columbia: Information on the District's Debt*. (GAO/AIMD-95-19). November.

U.S. General Accounting Office (1996). *District Government: Information on Its Fiscal Condition and the Authority's First Year of Operations*. (GAO/T-AIMD-96–126) July 9.

U.S. House of Representatives. (1997). HR 1963. *National Capital Revitalization and Self-Government Improvement Act of 1997*. Lexis-Nexus. 1997 Bill Tracking. July 31.

Vise, D. and Chandler, C. (1997) Clinton proposes U.S. run many D. C. services. *Washington Post*, Jan. 14.

22

City–County Consolidation
The Case of the Illusive Cost Savings

Suzanne Leland
University of North Carolina, Charlotte, North Carolina, U.S.A.

Kurt Thurmaier
Iowa State University, Ames, Iowa, U.S.A.

When over 60% of the voters of Wyandotte County and Kansas City, Kansas (WyCo/ KCK), voted in 1997 to consolidate the city and county governments into a unified city/ county structure, they also swept the entire slate of reform candidates into the positions of mayor/county administrator and councilors on the unified government board (UGB). The decision to consolidate was remarkable considering that it passed on the first-ever vote on the issue and that it passed by a wide margin. Although the first city–county consolidation occurred in New Orleans in 1805, there have been hundreds of subsequent consolidation attempts in the United States, but only about thirty that have been successful.

There are several reasons why a grassroots effort was formed to consolidate the governments of WyCo/KCK, including high tax rates, population loss, declining incomes, and a need for improved service provision (Consolidation Study Commission, 1997). The reform coalition effectively persuaded voters that the long-term fiscal stress experienced by the city could be more effectively addressed in a consolidated government structure. Inherent in the argument was the notion that improving the fiscal health of the county government would require a major reform of the county's budget. Reformers presented the arguments in terms of efficiency, effectiveness, equity, and accountability.

CASE BACKGROUND

Wyandotte County had the highest property tax rate in the state of Kansas. Moreover, KCK had the highest property taxes in the Kansas City metropolitan region. Consequently, KCK citizens and businesses pay 32% more than the average of other Kansas cities in the region. The KCK chamber of commerce cited this as one of the key factors deterring people from choosing KCK as a place to buy a home or operate a business: "This community is facing an economic crisis and has lost its competitive edge to the point that families and businesses choose not to locate here and leave in alarming numbers" (Chamber of Commerce, 1996). This problem was exacerbated by steadily declining federal aid to cities and counties. This meant that not only were property taxes the highest in the region, but hope for future relief was bleak.

According to the U.S. Census Bureau, the KCK population declined by an estimated 7225 people between 1990 and 1996, an average loss of over 2000 residents per year. This decline was more serious considering that KCK had annexed 5000 additional residents in Piper Township. When such population losses occur, sales tax and property tax revenues are directly affected, and the tax burden was borne by a smaller population base. Population loss and the decline of the real estate market go hand in hand. In the area of residential development over the past five years, a total of 718 new homes have been built in KCK. During this same period, however, 1538 units have been demolished. This means that KCK actually destroyed 865 more homes than it built (Bruns, 1996).

According to the 1990 U.S. census data, per capita income was $10,478 in KCK and $15,465 in Wyandotte County. These are among the lowest in the state. The 1990 census data indicate that more than 23,000 of the 150,000 Wyandotte County residents are receiving food stamps, representing a 45% increase since 1990. In addition, the unemployment rate for KCK (6.4% in 1996) was the highest in the state (Chamber of Commerce, 1996).

The following case illustrates how budget reform was an integral part of the effort to consolidate WyCo/KCK. Facing severe and continued fiscal stress, WyCo/KCK citizens demanded a fundamental restructuring of their local governments. One of the primary outcomes was a complete reform of the county budget and its consolidation into the city's budget, yielding increased accountability for how county taxes were spent and by whom.

THE CENTRAL ISSUES: EFFICIENCY, EFFECTIVENESS, EQUITY, AND ACCOUNTABILITY

Historically, until the 1960s academics typically agreed that metropolitan reform such as city–county consolidation was desirable. These arguments were based on the theory that the central city should constitute the sole governing unit and be the central service provider for a total metropolitan area. Proponents argued that increasing the size of urban governmental units via consolidation would be associated with improved output of public services, increased technical efficiency, increased responsibility of local officials, and increased confidence among citizens about their ability to influence public policy (Parker, 1992). Scholars in the following three decades (1960–1990), however, cast doubt on the theory of consolidation and concluded that these benefits never materialized (Tiebout, 1956; Ostrom et al., 1961). This not only diminished the attention of scholars in the area of city–county consolidation, it also slowed the number of city–county consolidation attempts in the United States.

The Renewed Promise of Consolidation

Proponents of a new metropolitan movement emerged in the 1990s arguing that a consolidated local government would increase efficiency via economies of scale that reduce the cost of government. They argue that the urban problem is the existence of a large number of independent jurisdictions within a single metropolitan area (Dolan, 1990; Rusk, 1993). In addition to these traditional arguments they add something new; metropolitan consolidation can help fiscally strapped central cities at a time when federal aid to cities had all but disappeared.

Effectiveness

Metropolitan reformers argue that consolidation is more effective for local government. First, in almost all cases fragmented governments are overlapping governments. Where there are overlapping jurisdictions and functions it is difficult for citizens to sort out which services come from which entity and what the price is that they pay for them. In many cases such confusion means that citizens may not be able to discern whether or not they are indeed getting the services they desire.

The state of Kansas has more than 3892 governmental entities. Only four other states have more—California, Illinois, Pennsylvania, and Texas (Dewitt, 1995). This is an incredible number of governments per citizen if you take into account that Kansas has a much smaller population than any of the other four states. Before consolidation, there were eighteen governmental entities within Wyandotte Country alone, and it is geographically the smallest county in the state.

The Wyandotte County reformers argued that consolidation would avoid duplication of services and reallocate resources so that the most desirable programs could be delivered as efficiently and effectively as possible. Consolidating duplicative services such as planning, zoning, and building inspections would also provide for more effective service delivery, eliminating citizen confusions over jurisdictions and variable processes. A reformed budget and management process would also install performance measurements and other professional administrative techniques to boost program effectiveness.

Efficiency

Metropolitan reformers are interested in finding a more technically efficient solution than government fragmentation because of two national trends: the devolution of responsibilities to states and localities and the overall decline of central cities. In the 1980s national policy called for New Federalism, a legacy left from the Nixon era and resurrected by President Reagan. New Federalism fundamentally changed the role of local governments in the policy-making arena (Wright, 1988). As Reagan addressed the 1980 Republican National Convention he defined his view of New Federalism: "Everything that can be run more effectively by state and local government we shall turn over to state and local governments, along with funding sources to pay for it." This philosophy was based on the belief that state and local governments should control domestic spending and such programs as economic development. This was a sharp contrast to the way things had been done in the past, where typically the federal government was responsible for carrying out administration and funding (Elazar, 1984). While responsibilities were shifted, funding support for local governments declined.

With more responsibilities and less federal aid, and a constituency depending upon the maintenance of existing services, local governments are faced with the option of increasing revenues, cutting services, becoming more efficient, or using some combination of the three. Since raising taxes is politically unpopular and citizens are generally unwilling to tolerate a cut in the services they receive, increasing technical efficiency seems to be the most popular path for approaching this dilemma (DeWitt, 1995). Reformists such as Town and Lambert (1987) argue that technological efficiency can be achieved by reducing governmental fragmentation through consolidating city and county functions.

The fragmented governmental structure in Wyandotte County allowed for duplication and few economies of scale. Consolidation advocates argued that duplicative services, such as street, road, and bridge maintenance; park maintenance; economic development; recreation opportunities; and such administrative services as purchasing, were raising the cost of government in WyCo/KCK. A new unified city and county government would have the opportunity to become more technically efficient by ridding itself of duplicative services and achieving economies of scale by centralizing several administrative and support functions, such as payroll, word processing, budgeting, and personnel.

Equity

In addition to efficiency arguments, the reformists advocate consolidation for equity reasons. The equity argument hinges on two interrelated demographic phenomena, racial segregation and income inequalities. Both problems were accentuated with the changes that occurred in America at midcentury. Since the 1950s, the idealized style of living has been suburban, not urban. The flight of the population to the suburbs from urban areas is the key contributor to the decline of central cities (Rusk, 1994; 1995). African Americans and other minority groups were excluded from the suburban lifestyle in two ways. The majority could not afford to move to the suburbs, and those that could faced discrimination when trying to purchase a home in largely white neighborhoods. Because of urban sprawl, the nation's metropolitan communities are now largely segregated. Upper and middle-income whites live in the suburbs and lower-income whites and African Americans live in the central cities (Rusk, 1994; 1995).

Rusk (1994; 1995) makes the case that metropolitan consolidation and annexation forces suburbanites to help pay for the central cities they have abandoned. This is fair, he argues, because those who live in the suburbs still enjoy the benefits of the central city. Those cities that include their own suburbs are able to grow and to maintain a wealthier tax base. Those cities that cannot grow because of restrictive state laws or an unwillingness of the suburban population to merge with the central city are "inelastic cities." These cities have reached what Rusk calls "the point of no return." Such a city typically has lost more than 20% of its population since the 1950s (some as high as 40%); minority populations typically have exceeded more than 30% of the city's population makeup; and the income of city residents has fallen to 70% or less of suburban incomes (Rusk, 1994). Fiscal considerations include heavy reliance on short-term debt, high taxes, and decline of services. Kansas City, Kansas, is on Rusk's list of such cities.

Wyandotte County, Kansas, is rather small and compact, with only three municipalities: Kansas City, Bonner Springs, and Edwardsville. For mainly political reasons, the latter two municipalities were excluded from the potential consolidation, and the only new territory to be added via consolidation was the 2.7-square-mile Loring area (DeWitt, 1995). This case thus represents something of an outlyer to Rusk's idea that racial and income equality could be achieved by combining the inner city and suburbs. The WyCo/KCK situation is not a case of bridging segregated municipal boundaries.

On the other hand, racial politics was an important factor in the consolidation debate. In part, there was a widespread sense that the county's machine politics ensured minority representation on the county commission, proportional to its population (about 30%), but the reform coalition studied the politics of past consolidations and learned their lessons (Marinovich, 1997). In particular, successful consolidations had involved minority interests in the consolidation process and guaranteed them voices in the new government. In that regard, the district boundaries for the proposed unified board of commissioners were drawn in such a way that minority representation was highly probable for 20% of the council seats and would likely increase to 30% or more in the near future, given the changing racial demographics of other districts within the county. In essence, this maintained the proportional representation minorities had in the old city government, and reduced it slightly from the 30% enjoyed on the old county commission. The WyCo/KCK case thus is not about bridging segregated municipal boundaries, as discussed by Rusk, but about preserving racial representation within the reformed government structure.

Accountability

Reformers have also used citizen accountability as the driving force in the move to consolidate a city and county. Fragmented governments involve duplication and confusion. Citizens are unsure of which entity is responsible for their problems. Entities can blame each other when things go wrong to avoid accountability altogether. In addition, consolidation reformers often tackle unreformed government, in which political patronage dispenses public employment and services and the budget is difficult to read and understand. Such practices artificially raise the costs of government by providing superfluous or undesirable services. The process of consolidation involves drawing up a new structure to eliminate duplication and confusion and a budget process that permits citizens to hold their elective officials accountable for tax and expenditure decisions.

For example, city–county consolidation in Jacksonville/Duvall County, Florida, was a case of both an unreformed city and an unreformed county whose unresponsiveness to citizen demands led to a total breakdown in local government. Problems associated with both governments included the inability to secure adequate funds, an increasing crime rate, blight and traffic congestion in the central city, and ballooning suburban areas without adequate planning (Urban Action Clearing House, 1968). In 1959, school accreditation was threatened, the city fire marshal threatened to close some old buildings as hazards, and the county commissioners remained unresponsive. In 1964, the Southern Association of Colleges and Schools struck Jacksonville from its approved list, which sent the town into an uproar. In addition to an unresponsive county government, the cost of government in the city was rapidly rising: "In 1950, Jacksonville's 204,000 citizens had $116 per person spent for government. In 1965, there were only 198,000 Jacksonville citizens, and government was costing them $479 a piece, an increase of 300 percent" (Martin, 1968:8). On August 8, 1967, voters approved consolidating the city and county into a newly reformed entity that included term limits, a professional administrator, and the conversion of several previously elected positions to merit-based appointments. The Jacksonville case had several similarities with the WyCo/KCK consolidation effort.

Following legislative authorization, Kansas governor Bill Graves appointed a consolidation study commission (CSC) composed of five members balanced for partisanship (three Democrats, two Republicans), race (one black, one Hispanic, three whites), and personal backgrounds (from a pastor to a banker). The commission was staffed by an executive director appointed by the governor and academics from the University of Kansas. The staff members[1] work was thus to be highly professional and nonpartisan, and their information and recommendations were to be considered by a commission representative of the principal interests in the county, racially, economically, and politically.

Over the course of several months, the CSC heard presentations from various country and city officials, citizens, and expert consultants and reached a similar conclusion: that the answer to the financial and other woes of WyCo/KCK lay in a renewed structure of government that would provide greater accountability for budget and personnel systems.

As one citizen advised the commission (Vrabac, 1997), it is one thing to look for duplication between city and county departments to find the "most obvious means of reducing costs." The real work of finding efficiencies requires a consideration of the "interactions between departments . . . understanding the flow of work . . . [and] reducing labor costs." Mr. Vrabac noted that the stakes were high: "We are counting on you to set in motion a revival, whereby our city and county can more ably compete with our neighbors in the metropolitan area—compete for better jobs and better and safer residential areas and schools. We need to change the image that our city had been saddled with: an image of machine politics, favoritism, and urban decay."

These candid remarks from a citizen spoke directly to an issue that the study commission members were loath to mention publicly but that underlay much of their work. The issue of machine politics and the associated problem of favoritism was the real theme of the consolidation study. While the residents of Wyandotte Country, including Kansas City, had a common understanding that machine politics rules the county government, it was difficult to directly identify it. There were two principal sources of obscurity: the county budget and the county personnel system. The two were understandably connected. The word on the street was that you could get hired for a county job if you were connected, and salaries and funding sources were not a problem (Alm, 1996). How does a government reformer bring this kind of practice into the open light of public scrutiny?

The CSC's assignment of analyzing the benefits and costs of consolidation increasingly focused on the problems of integrating the unreformed county government with the reformed city government to increase accountability. The commission approached the problem in two tracks. First, it commissioned a classification study of the county personnel, including a comparison with the city's classification system. The goal was a portrait of the personnel structure of the potential consolidated government. This was accomplished to some degree and is available from the study commission files, although it is beyond the scope of this chapter (Lewinsohn, 1996). The focus of this case is on the second track, a study of the city and country budgets, with the goal of creating a portrait of the consolidated budgets. The budget study also had the important objective of identifying areas of overlap and redundancy.

BUDGET CONSOLIDATION FOR WYANDOTTE COUNTY–KANSAS CITY KANSAS

Budget reform has been an important element of government reform since the beginning of this century. The creation of the executive budget process in cities, states, and then the U.S. government shifted power to chief executives from legislative bodies. The previous practice of individual departments pleading their separate budgets with individual legislative committees was replaced with a unified, comprehensive executive-branch budget presented to the legislature by the chief executive. In cities, the executive budget reform complemented the introduction of city manager forms of government. Willoughby (1927) and other reformers of the time argued that budget reform was essential to public administration reform. In particular, Willoughby argued, the budget format "determines in no small degree the whole character of the appropriation and accounting system of government" (p. 455). These reformers were keen on introducing "efficiency" measures into government administration, and they argued that an executive budget promoted clear executive priorities, efficient administration, and accountability to the public for how and why taxes were spent (Rubin, 1998).

Although some of the early reformers urged a program or performance budget format, the line-item budget format became popular because it emphasized controlling expenditures. Subsequent periods of budget reform have used performance budget formats to emphasize management concerns and program budget formats to emphasize planning and policy concerns (Schick, 1966; Grizzle, 1986). Despite the continued repetition of the argument that budget format influences the kinds of budget deliberations taken and subsequently budgetary outcomes, very little empirical research has tested the argument. Grizzle reviewed extant literature and found "conflicting results about the effect of format upon legislative deliberations" (Grizzle, 1986: 63). Grizzle then tested the argument with deliberations from state legislative committees in Florida and North Carolina, finding that budget "format is, as budget reform proponents have assumed, an important factor influencing the nature of budget deliberations. . . . [although] format is not the only factor and, at least in this study, does not explain a majority of the variation in orientation among legislative appropriations committee meetings" (p. 67). The budget analysis conducted for the Wy Co/KCK consolidation study commission represents a good illustration of the argument that different budget formats shape the kinds of budgetary discussions held by elected officials.

Searching for Cost Savings

The Wyandotte County budget was a traditional line-item budget, with minimal programmatic formatting. The 1996 budget document identified basic budgets for most departments and listed budgets for most funds. Capital outlay (equipment and improvements) expenses were included for each program area. The "program" structure was confusing, however, and important information was either lacking or buried within other budget lines. Consequently, the county budget failed miserably as a device to communicate the costs of providing various county services; there were no overall summaries of revenue and expenditure information, no narrative explanations of recent trends, and no explanations of changes in department budgets. More important, many general fund departments were grouped into one budget table (WyCo, 1996: 52–53), including the finance department, law librarian, medical contracts, and surveying. In addition, "other funds" within the general fund lumped together risk management, county fair premiums, county equipment, and employee benefits, among other budget lines.

The inclusion in this lump sum appropriation of various employee benefits proved to be the most difficult problem for consolidating the county and city budgets. For example, while the county budget pages ostensibly presented the costs of the county sheriff, this excluded many of the employee benefit costs that would accrue to the sheriff's operations in a program format. Allocating "overhead" line items to the appropriate county program was not entirely possible without a conversion on a position-by-position basis. Such a task was beyond the time and personnel limits authorized for the budget study. Instead, the goal was modified to allocate these overhead costs to a budget function area (e.g., public works). This was acceptable in part because the functional level was best for comparing county and city activities. The basic formula was to divide the total amount in these overhead lines by the number of county Full-Time Equivalent positions (FTE), and then allocate the costs to functional budget areas based on the FTE count in each functional area. It was imprecise, but acceptable for the purposes of the study.

The KCK, budget, on the other hand, was formatted as a program budget, and also retained a degree of line-item detail and personnel positions for each program. It had repeatedly received the *Distinguished Budget Award* from the Government Finance Officers Association (GFOA). This meant that it met a rigorous set of criteria in four areas: financial accountability, policy content, operations measurement, and communications. The 1996 KCK budget was thus used as the template for the consolidated budget analysis because it permitted a consolidation of county and city expenditures by program area. The consolidated budget model was created to provide study commissioners with a view of what a consolidated city–county budget would look like by functional area. In the process, the study was expected to identify overlapping programs that could be targeted for cost-cutting measures in a consolidated government.

The reorganization of the county budget proceeded with two efforts. As son be seen in Table 1, the first task was organizing the appropriate line items into a program line, such as the public safety program. One component of this was building maintenance ($1,693,014 in Table 1). The county budget actually combined maintenance costs for

Table 1 Example from County Budget Reorganization Worksheet

Category		1996 Budget	Funding	Amount	Explanation
Wyandotte County, All Funds Budget Composition, 1996 (Reallocated accounts version).					
Category		*1996 Budget*	Funding	Amount	Explanation
Public Safety		$ 18,920,539		$34,390	juvenile center maintenance
Sheriff/Jail		7,009,822		871,451	courthouse maintenance
Sheriff		1,055,201	General	787,173	county justice center maintenance
Jail		3,843,263	General	$1,693,014	Total
Medical Contract Dept.		750,000	Other	173,160	
Emergency Medical (Jail)		50,000	General	7,000	
Juvenile Detention		965,686	Segregated/ Grants	236,802	
Jail Commissary		172,000	Enterprise	6,400	
Detention Business Office		173,672	General	7,500	
Building Maintenance		$ 1,693,014	Miscellaneous	16,600	
District Attorney		1,565,209	General	4,230	
District Coroner		101,953	General	54,500	probation
House Arrest		312,453	Enterprise	23,000	
Community Corrections		1,561,866	Grants	31,000	
County Grants		1,146,636	Grants	533,500	juvenile
County Civil Process Servers		404,420	General	7,920	
Internal Security		140,000	General	13,050	
Police Services		42,000	General	670,000	
District Court Conveying		14,300	General	100,000	state cases
Pretrial Investigators		6,408	Other	1,884,662	Total
Unified Court System		$ 1,884,662	General	75,000	sex offenses
Sex Offenses		75,500	Miscellaneous	500	sex predator
Employee Benefits/Hospitalization		$ 2,962,296	General	$ 75,500	Total

seven different facilities in the county budget into a programmatic line called facilities management (WyCo, 1996: 27). The revised county budget (reallocated on functional criteria) disaggregated this budget line across the public safety, facilities maintenance/ garage, and social services budget areas.

Some of the components of other programmatic areas were also line items in other county "departments" and had to be disaggregated and reallocated. Other programmatic lines were complied from several different funds, such as the $75,500 for the sex offenses subprogram in public safety. (See Table 1.) The employee benefits/hospitalization line item ($2,962,296) is an aggregation of seven different numbers, including workers' compensation costs, based on the different departments included under the public safety functional area.

The reallocation tasks of the county budget were mostly unnecessary for the city budget. The city budget was already formatted as a program budget. Employee benefit costs and other overhead items were already allocated to the appropriate budget program area. The one exception was workers' compensation costs. Following the logic used in the county budget, these costs were divided by the total number of positions and then allocated to program costs accordingly. As was the case with the county, this was somewhat imprecise, since one might expect higher costs for the police positions than the city clerk's positions. Overall, however, it provided an acceptable level of approximation for purposes of the consolidation study. As seen in Table 2, the city budget format also encouraged a comparison of operating funds, other (nongeneral) funds, and capital budget costs for each program area.

As expected, there were some county functional areas that were not present in the city budget, especially regarding social services. Likewise, some city functions were not present in the county budget. New functional areas, such as social services, were created in the county budget to encompass unique programs.

Table 2 Example from City Budget Reorganization Worksheet

Operating Budget Composition: Kansas City, Kansas All funds: 1996			1996 Budget	of which: Operating (Gen Fund)	Other Funds	Capital Budget
Category						
Public Safety			$ 53,039,134	$ 52,217,233	$ 821,901	$ 1,951,855
	Police		28,552,550	28,286,550	266,000	1,070,155
	Fire		22,254,300	22,254,300		807,200
	Civil Service		20,000	20,000		
	Municipal Court		569,000	569,000		
	Emergency Management		926,901	371,000	555,901	74,500
	Workers Compensation (Public Safety group)		716,383	716,383		
of which:	Operating Budgets (Gen Fund)		$ 52,217,233			
of which:	Other Funds		821,901			
of which:	Capital Budget		1,951,855			

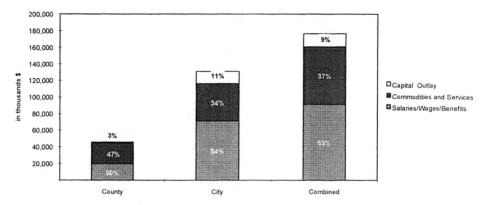

Figure 1   City, county, and combined budgets (1996).

Comparative and Consolidated Views

The reorganized county budget was then fitted to the framework of the city budget structure by functional area. This step permitted an analysis that compared and contrasted the various functions of the city and county and the potential range—and costs—of functions of a consolidated government.

Three features stood out from the budget analysis. First, as seen in Figure 1, the county budget was relatively small compared to the city. The $52 million county budget was only a third of the $131 million city budget. In addition, the county's capital outlay budget was a mere 3% of its expenditures, compared to 11% of the city's budget. The shape of the consolidated budget was consequently dominated by the city's budget.

The second comparative feature was that public safety was a major share of both the city and county budgets. As seen in Figure 2, public safety accounted for 42% of city and 36% of county expenditures. In the combined budget, it accounted for 39% of the budget. This was a particularly important issue for the business community, whose 1996 chamber of commerce study used comparative cost evidence to argue that the KCK expenditures were substantially higher than for neighboring communities and required significant reductions. (Chamber of Commerce, 1996: 5–7).

This was not a likely area for fruitful inefficiency searches due to consolidation, however The sheriff and police departments' functions had essentially been consolidated previously in response to a court order that closed the KCK jail. The major portion of the county's public safety activity was related to the sheriff's role running the county jail, which already kept municipal prisoners. It also included the county court system. The principal duty of traffic enforcement and other nonjail law enforcement activities was mainly a city police department responsibility, accounting for over half of the city's public safety budget. The city's fire department services accounted for most of the other half of that portion of the budget.*

The third comparative feature of the combined budget analysis was that administrative costs were higher in the county than in the city as a proportion of the respective

---

* Fire department costs were the principal target of the chamber of commerce study (1996, 7).

Kansas City, Kansas

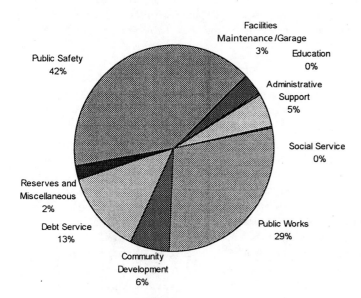

Wyandotte County

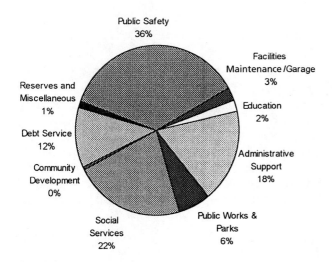

Figure 2   1996 expenditures.

budgets. Administrative support accounted for only 5% of the city budget, but 18% of the county budget. Lest one jump to the "AHA!" as some observers were wont to do, it was important that the 18% administration in the county budget be examined carefully. First, it included the county's unique tax collection and administration function, a full 35% of the administrative support budget. This compared to finance and budget accounting for only 22% of the city's administrative support budget. The county's unique election function (including county clerk) accounted for another 12% of the administrative support budget. Each of these functions was unique to the county; deducting them from the administrative support budget reduced that functional area to only 9% of the total county budget. Significantly, however, that was *still* nearly *twice* the size of the city's budget.

What Does It Mean?

The traditional line-item budget used in Wyandotte County may have lived up to its reputation for limiting budgetary conflict, but ultimately it failed the long-term interests of county residents. To the extent that it reduced conflict by limiting public scrutiny of spending allocations across programs, it also postponed the day in which the county would face difficult choices about spending priorities. To the extent that it reduced conflict by allowing department heads to add personnel at will with great flexibility in salary levels, it also hastened the day in which the county could no long sustain the weight of its bureaucracy in the face of more economical administrations in neighboring communities.

The steps to financial health and economical administration were not immediately laid bare by the consolidated budget analysis presented to the commission; rather, the picture had a more impressionist quality to it. The functions of each government were outlined and the range of functions of the consolidated government were arrayed in the landscape, but the areas for trimming the fat in the county and city governments were hidden in the shadows, awaiting a detailed analysis that comes from a budget process that emphasizes transparency and comprehensive evaluations of departmental budget requests.

DISCUSSION: SUMMARY AND CONCLUSSION

In July 1998, the unified government (UG) of WyCo/KCK approved the first (fiscal year 1999) combined city and county budget of $198.4 million. The amount was about $3 million less than the previous budget estimate for 1998. It also represented a 3% reduction in expenditures in the combined budgets of the city and county. The budget cut sixty vacant jobs and reduced property tax rates 3%. The UG budget director told the unified board of commissioners, "We're holding the line ... It's a bare bones budget with no decreases in services and few increases in services" (Nicely, 1997). Only a few persons spoke at the brief public hearing before the budget was adopted. The commission approved it with little comment except to commend the budget director and his staff for their work. The total cost of the UG per citizen was set at $989, with $426 per person for public safety (43% of the budget), $314 for community services (32% of the budget), and $171 for policy and administration (17% of the budget).

Speaking to a Kansas legislative review committee in September 1998, the new county administrator, Dennis Hays, reported that the transition to a consolidated government would be complete by June 1999. The process of merging city and county staffs continued. A new management structure was put in place on July 2, 1998, and a staff reorganization plan was due back to the UG commission in October 1998. Over 100 FTE positions had been left open in the transitional county and city organizations, mainly to cut costs. Efficiency gains included county park rangers working with police in patrolling camps and park maintenance personnel sharing equipment and supplies with maintenance crews for the city golf course. Organizational restructuring had reduced the number of units reporting to the county administrator from thirty to seven, and performance budgeting goals had been set for all departments. The major changes he reported, however, concerned the unified policy-making focus of the UG and the ability to link the budget with a strategic plan of who in the UG would be doing what, and how.

The Role of Budget Reform in Increasing Accountability

Rubin and Stein (1990) note that cities with deteriorating economies are likely to want a more activist government, putting pressure on the budget process to create flexibility and policy responsiveness within severe revenue constraints: "If the existing budget process is not up to the task, and if the technical capacity is already in place, there may be a determined push to modernize the budget process" (p. 420). This would seem to be a factor present in the KCK case.

The UG is reforming the budget process so that the entire consolidated budget is subjected to the scrutiny of a central budget staff that reports to a chief executive. The county's financial accounting staff has been integrated into the city's budget and finance staff. The county's departmental budget requests are being subjected to rigorous scrutiny and review by the city's professional budget staff in the same way that city departmental requests have been examined. The executive budget process is forcing activities of the former county units to compete for limited resources in a transparent budget process. Perhaps most important, the new process is guided by a fairly powerful chief executive who was given a substantial leadership role in the new UG.

This was particularly important since the charter of the new UG requires the unified board of commissioners to

> target a minimum of 8% reduction in per capita costs of daily operations over a five year period based on 1997 budget figures (an estimated $8.7 million savings). These savings will be targeted at 2% per year after the first year of transition (Consolidation Study Commission, 1997: 8).

Success will require a careful and systematic review of all programs, a process that will be facilitated by the reformed budget and budget process the city had already been using. Broadening the scope of the reformed budget process to encompass the county's programs was seen as the best hope for bringing full accountability to the citizens.*

Metropolitan Consolidation Success = E³ + A

In the end, Wyandotte County was successfully consolidated with KCK because the county government was eventually characterized as looking more like a rogue city department that was essentially beyond the control of the reformed city government structure and particularly the chief executive. In essence, the budget for 28% of the combined city and county governments was "uncontrollable" with respect to strategic planning and priorities, as well as personnel and budget practices.

The successful consolidation of WyCo/KCK harkens back to the earliest days of budget reform. The Progressives and then the Taft Conservatives both sought budget

---

* There are important differences between the two cases that should be noted, however. First, St. Louis was already a unified city/county government, but one that remained essentially "unreformed," particularly with respect to the municipal budget process. On the other hand, KCK was a reformed city with a chief executive that was combining with an unreformed county.

reform to increase government efficiency, mainly through decreasing costs for current programs (Rubin, 1992). In language echoed ninety years later in Kansas, the early budget reformers argued that efficiency was impossible when the budget process was opaque, protecting program funding from scrutiny and preventing the chief executive from establishing priorities and allocating resources accordingly (Rubin, 1992: 20).*

Ultimately, the issues of efficiency, effectiveness, and equity were insufficient factors for the successful consolidation. Accountability became the central issue in the KCK/WyCo debate, much as it did in the early years of budget reform. It was upon the issue of government accountability that a broad coalition was formed, internally and externally, to reform the city/county government structure.

The hoped-for gains in efficiency and effectiveness depend upon the UG board being able to establish a strategic vision that incorporates all of the city/county government activities and the political fortitude to allocate budget resources to them according to their priorities. The new UG structure is designed to protect equity and promote accountability. Such goals are the hallmark of the historical movement for budget and government reform.

REVIEW QUESTIONS

1. What were some of the symptoms of fiscal distress in WyCo/KCK? Why did the image problems exacerbate these?
2. What arguments did the consolidation reform commission use to persuade voters that consolidation would improve the fiscal health of the economy?
3. In your opinion, which core value of public administration (efficiency, effectiveness, accountability, or equity) was most influential in persuading voters to approve consolidation?
4. In what ways do budget formats promote or diminish accountability in this case? Are there alternatives to budget reform that would also bring greater accountability to the county government?
5. The authors argue that *Metropolitan consolidation success* $= E^3 + A$ To what extent is the A in the formula dependent upon the relationship between budget reform and personnel reform in this case?

REFERENCES

Alm, R. (1996). Hiring? I guess it's all relative. *Kansas City Star*, Jan. 11: 8.
Banfield, E. C. (1974). *The Unheavenly City Revisited*. Boston: Little, Brown.

---

* In another important parallel between this case and the historic roots of budget reform, academics and pracademics were more instrumental in the methods of early budget reform than the business community (Rubin, 1992). Much of the work on consolidation reform was performed by academics and pracademics, largely from the Edwin O. Stene public administration program at the University of Kansas (KU), wellknown for its emphasis on local government scholarship, and particularly for its emphasis on the reformed council–manager form of government. It is not an accident that the KU public administration program supplied three faculty members, two graduate students, and one highly respected alumnus to the reform effort. The credentials of the research team were respected in the region and within the political arena. The KU faculty had already been instrumental in helping KCK craft a code of ethics as part of its internal reform effort.

Bish, R. and Ostrom V. (1973). *Understanding Urban Government: Metropolitan Reform Reconsidered.* Washington, DC: American Enterprise Institute.

Boyne, G. (1992). Is there a relationship between fragmentation and local government costs? A
comment on Drew Dolan. *Urban Affairs Quarterly, 26,* 28–45.

Bruns, T. (1996). *Consolidation of Governments in KCK and Wyandotte County: A Vision for
Growth of our Future.* report presented by the KCK councilman to the consolidation study
commission, Sept. 25, 1996.

Chamber of Commerce. (1996). Revenue study Report. Kansas City, KS: Chamber of Commerce.

Consolidation Study Commission (1997). Final recommendations for the consolidation of the governments of Wyandotte County and Kansas City, Kansas. submitted to the state legislature and
the governor, Jan. 13.

DeWitt, J. (1995). *Metropolitan Government Reform: A Case Study of Potential Governmental
Consolidation Within Wyandotte County, Kansas.* master's thesis. Lawrence, KS: University
of Kansas.

Dodge, W. R. (1996). *Regional Excellence: Governing Together to Compete Globally and Flourish
Locally.* Washington, DC: National League of Cities.

Dolan, D. A. (1990). Local government fragmentation: Does it drive up the cost of government?
Urban Affairs Quarterly, 26 (1), 28–45.

Dowding, K., John, P. and Biggs, S. (1994). Tiebout: A survey of empirical literature. *Urban Studies,
31 (4/5),* 767–797.

During, D. (1995). The effects of city–county consolidation: The perspectives of United Government
Employees in Athens–Clarke County, Georgia. *Public Administration Quarterly, fall,*
272–297.

Elazar, D. J. (1984). *American Federalism: A View from the States* 3rd ed. New York: Harper and
Row.

Fisher, R. C. (1996) *State and Local Public Finance.* 2nd ed. Chicago: Irwin.

Grizzle, G. A. (1986). Does budget format really govern the action of budget markers? *Public
Budgeting and Finance, 6(spring),* 60–70.

Hawkins, B. and Hendrick, R. M. (1994). Do county governments reinforce city–suburban inequities? A study of city and suburban service allocations. *Social Science Quarterly, 75 (4),*
755–769.

Krumholz, N. (1997). Regionalism redeux. *Public Administration Review, 57 (1).*

Lewinsohn, T. (1996). Salary survey: Wyandotte County, Kansas City, and Board of Public Utilities.
Wyandotte–Kansas City, KS: Consolidation Study Commission.

Lowery, D. (1997). Public choice, consumer sovereignty, and quasimarket failure: Toward a neopro-
gressive theory of urban institutions. Paper presented at the Midwest Political Science Association, Chicago, Illinois.

Lowery, D. and Lyons, W. (1989). The impact of jurisdictional boundaries: An individual-level test
of the Tiebout model. *Journal of Politics, 51 (1),* 73–97.

Marinovich, C. S. (1997). Anatomy of a merger: Kansas City, Kansas–Wyandotte County, talk to
Kansas City chapter of the American Society for Public Administration, Oct. 22.

Martin, R. (1968). *Consolidation: Jacksonville–Duval County: The Dynamics of Urban Political
Reform.* Jacksonville, FL: Convention Press.

Nicely, S. (1997). Column. Kansas City Star. May 2: p. 1. Local section.

Oates, W. E. (1972). *Fiscal Federalism.* New York: Harcourt Brace Jovanovich.

Ostrom, E. (1972). Metropolitan reform propositions derived from two traditions. *Social Science
Quarterly, 53,* 474–493.

Ostrom, V., Tiebout, C. and Warren, R. (1961). The organization of government in metropolitan
areas—A theoretical inquiry. *American Political Science Review, 55,* 831–842.

Ostrom, V. Bish R. and Ostrom, E. (1988). *Local Government in the United States.* San Francisco:
Institute for Contemporary Studies.

Pack, H. and Pack, J. R. (1977). Metropolitan fragmentation and suburban homogeneity. *Urban Studies*, *14*, 191–201.

Parker, L. (1992). Rethinking consolidation: A note on decentralization. *Partnerships for Governing in the Twentieth Century: The Proceedings of the Wichita Assembly*. Wichita, KS: Wichita Assembly Series, Wichita State University.

Peterson, P. (1993). The changing urban scene: 1960–1990 and beyond. In Ed. H. Cisneros, *Interwoven Destinies: Cities and the Nation*, New York: Norton.

Percy, S. L., Hawkins, B. and Maier, P. (1995). Revisiting Tiebout: Moving rationales and Interjurisdictional relocation. *Urban Affairs Quarterly*, *19*, 431–446.

Pierce, N. R. (1993). *City-States: How Urban America Can Prosper in a Competitive World*. Washington DC: Seven Lock Press.

Rafuse, R. Jr. (1991). *Financing local government*. In (eds.) *J. E. Petersen and D. Strachota Local Government Finance Concepts and Practices*, Chicago: Government Finance Officers Association of the United States and Canada.

Reining, H. Jr (1970). Symposium on Governing Megacentropolis. *Public Administration Review*, *30 (Sept./Oct.*, 473–520.

Reschovsky, A. (1979). Residential choice and the local public sector: An alternative test of the "Tiebout hypothesis." *Journal of Urban Economic*, *6*, 501–520.

Rubin, I. (1992). Early budget reformers: Democracy, efficiency and budget reforms, paper presented at meeting of the American Political Science Association, Chicago, Illinois.

Rubin, I. S. and Stein, L. (1990). Budget reform in St. Louis: Why does budgeting change? *Public Administration Review, 50 (July/Aug.)*, 420–427.

Rusk, D. (1994). Bend or dies: Inflexible state laws and policies are dooming some of the country's central cities. *State Government News* (Feb.), 6–10.

Rusk, D. (1995). *Cities Without Suburbs*. 2nd ed. Washington, DC: Woodrow Wilson Center Press.

Rusk, D. (1997). Opening address for the Mid-America Regional Conference. Jack Reardon Civic Center, Kansas City, Kansas, April 30.

Schick, A. 1966. The Road to PPB: The Stages of Budget Reform. *Public Administration Review* 26 (December): 243–58.

Tiebout, C. (1956). A Pure theory of Local Government Expenditures. *Journal of Political Economy,* 44 (October): 416–424.

Town, K. and Lambert, C. (1987). *The Urban Consolidation Experience in the United States*. Atlanta: Research Atlanta.

Urban Action Clearing House. (1968). Jacksonville, Florida, merges city and county governments. Washington, DC: Chamber of Commerce of the United States.

Vrabac, D. (1997). Remarks from a Citizen's Testimony. Wyandotte County/Kansas City, Kansas Consolidation Commission Public Hearings.

Wright, D. (1988). *Understanding Intergovernmental Relations* 3rd ed. Pacific Grove, CA: Brooks/Cole.

Zimmermann, J. F. (1970). Metropolitan reform in the U.S.: An overview. *Public Administration Review (Sept./Oct.)*, 531–543.

23

Innovations in Public Budgeting
Applying Organizational Development Processes to Downsizing

Herbert A. Marlowe, Jr.
University of Florida, Gainesville, Florida, U.S.A.

Ronald C. Nyhan
Florida Atlantic University, Boca Raton, Florida, U.S.A.

This chapter examines how to successfully apply one theoretical model of organizational development (OD) and organizational culture, the cognitive model, through theoretically consistent (i.e. cognitive), interventions to solve the organizational problem of downsizing in a public agency. Downsizing is occurring ring in a variety of organizational settings. Handled improperly, there can be enormous organizational and human costs. This study conceptualizes downsizing as essentially a cognitive problem in organizational strategy. In this study OD is defined as processes that facilitate an organization developing a more adaptive schemata. The key characteristic of these processes is that they are inclusionary, designed to strengthen the capability of the organization itself to use these processes, and assume the organization possesses the requisite knowledge and skill to solve the problem. The interventions used to facilitate this change are primarily cognitive in nature; survey feedback, attribute weightings, group problem solving (problem definition/alternatives generation/weightings), small group discussions, and extended conversations. The organizational problem to which the OD process was applied was also primarily a cognitive one—how to substantially downsize a government entity in the face of an approximate 13% budget shortfall.

The study reports the processes and interventions in detail and provides a summary of what can be gained from such an approach. The cognitive model of OD as schemata change was found to be a viable and useful approach to organizational downsizing in the public sector.

ORGANIZATIONAL DEVELOPMENT AS A BASIS FOR BUDGETING INTERVENTIONS

The field of OD has expanded dramatically since its origins in the 1940s and 1950s (Hammons, 1982; Weisbord, 1987). It is international in scope (Adler, 1983; Bate, 1990), is applied to a wide variety of organizational problems, (Pati and Salitore, 1989; McDaniel et al., 1987; Maurice et al., 1980), and is considered technologically and professionally significant for solving practical management problems (Fitzgerald, 1987; Buller, 1988; Walter, 1984).

If is to continue to make creative advances, one required step is the development of theoretically based interventions that address critical organization problems. Only when OD interventions are seen as contributing to the solution of core problems will they be valued by senior executives and policy makers. In presenting a cognitive approach to OD, Bartunek and Moch (1987) argue that OD has focused on behavioral changes "without specifically addressing how organizational members understand themselves and their organization" (p. 484). They present the concept of schemata as a way to rectify this omission. Schemata are cognitions, interpretations or ways of understanding events. Schemata serve a data reduction function by enabling individuals to identify entities and specify relationships among these entities. Schemata guide and give meaning to behavior by suggesting implications of certain actions and making certain events meaningful. The role of the OD practitioner is to help an organization recognize its schemata and evaluate the viability of that schemata.

In this study OD is defined as processes that facilitate an organization developing a more adaptive schemata. The key characteristic of these processes is that they are inclusionary, are designed to strengthen the capability of the organization itself to use these processes, and assume the organization possesses the requisite knowledge and skill to solve the problem. The interventions used to facilitate this change are primarily cognitive in nature: survey feedback, attribute weightings, group problem solving (problem definition/ alternatives generation/weightings), small group discussions and extended conversations. The organizational problem to which the OD process was applied in this study was also primarily a cognitive one—how to substantially downsize a government entity in the face of an approximate 13% budget shortfall.

PROBLEM BACKGROUND AND DISCUSSION

Palm Beach County Government (PBCG) provides regional governance to one of the nation's fastest growing counties. The county's population has increased 150% since 1970. During the past five years the county grew at the rate of 101.7 persons per day, or 26%. The current population is approximately 900,000, with projections of 1.4 million by the year 2020. The current operating budget is $1.39 billion, of which $600 million are general operating funds. Over the last five years the operating budget has increased by $215 million, or 68%. The PBCG provides a wide variety of services, including law enforcement, fire protection, conservation and resource management, public improvements, libraries, health and welfare, parks and recreational facilities, transportation, planning and zoning, water utilities, and general administrative services. Four thousand seven hundred employees work for the Board of County Commissioners (BCC) and an additional 2300 for the sheriff and the other constitutional officers. County constitutional offices, also called "row officers," are those elected county officials, exclusive of county governing board members, whose duties and responsibilities are constitutionally or statutorily based. The BCC approves the budgets for the constitutional officers but does not participate in their development. For the past fifteen years, each fiscal year has brought for the most part larger budgets and increased staffing to the operational and support departments. Any budget difficulties, primarily related to national economic recessions, had been handled through postponement of capital projects, short-term hiring freezes, or elimination of a few positions.

The 1991–1992 fiscal year (FY) budget was projected to be dramatically different, however. The FY 1992 forecast indicated that $70 million in additional taxes would be necessary to maintain existing service levels. Since the BCC did not support any increase in taxes, staff had to devise a strategy to downsize government to meet a shortfall of this dimension. A $50 million cost reduction goal was set for those functions reporting directly to the BCC, and a $20 million goal was established for the constitutional officers.

For the first time, PBCG was faced with a serious examination of what functions it should continue to perform. The high growth rates of the county and the expansion of governmental services to meet the needs of a growing and increasingly diverse citizenry had created a serious set of tensions within PBCG. The organization had changed from a rather small, informal, rural government to a large urban bureaucracy. Control processes were now more sophisticated and operations were more impersonal. The organization's own internal attempts to transform itself, coupled with numerous changing demands from an external environment, had created a high level of frustration among the management staff (senior executives and department heads).

From the perspective of OD theory, the problem to be solved was a cognitive one—how to rethink PBCG to a smaller entity. The methods to arrive at a solution to this problem had to meet several requirements: (1), in order for the rethinking of PBCG to occur, the existing organizational schemata had to be replaced—downsizing rather than growth was the new organizing framework. The OD interventions had to allow for the development of this new downsizing schemata. (2), The methods had to encourage development of, and be consistent with, new schemata about participation and empowerment. (3), The problem had a real-time deadline. (4) The methods had to be carried out in full public view. (5) The methods had to surface any other assumptions or schema that would stand in the way of solving the problem.

Step One: Redefining the Budget Process

The first step in the redefined budget process was to conduct a retreat for the management staff. During the retreat a number of hypotheses regarding organizational functioning were presented to the management staff. The management staff discussed the hypotheses and the underlying data and based on their experience and knowledge of PBCG accepted or rejected the hypotheses. The empirical findings and the management staff's comments during the retreat convinced the county administrator to adopt management practices that would be more inclusionary and open. Through such practices it was hoped that the management staff would develop a more coherent and unified vision (i.e., schemata) of the organization's needs and future direction. As a result, a number of task teams were formed to further address the needs and issues identified in the retreat. The task teams met and developed a series of recommendations to improve management practices. The vast majority of these were accepted by the county administrator. The work of these task teams culminated during a time frame in which PBCG's budget office was finalizing projections of the major budget shortfall. At this point there were two new languages being spoken in the organization: increased inclusionary management practices and fiscal and program cutback.

The major challenge the county administrator faced at this point was how to engage in the very difficult task of program reductions in a manner this was consistent with the culture of inclusion and participation he wanted to foster in the organization. To meet this challenge he formed a design and process management team. This team designed and facilitated a process to meet the twin goals of budget balancing and fostering a participative culture (Appelbaum et al., 1989; Greenhalgh, 1982; Kilman, 1989; Schein, 1990). This process is described in the following section.

Step Two: The Budgeting Downsizing Decision Process

The design of the budgeting downsizing decision process began with a meeting between the design team, the administrator, and the director of the Office of Finance, Management and Budget (OFMB). In this meeting a key decision was made—program reductions would be made differentially rather than across the board. While the implications of this decision were not fully understood by any of the parties to it at this time, it was clear that the number of decisions had geometrically increased. Now, instead of budget balancing being a technical accounting task to find the required across-the-board percentage reduction, each program area would have to be evaluated. Discussion and development of the criteria and processes to do this would comprise much of the next two months.

Once the decision to use differential reductions was made, the design team began its work. Its tasks were threefold.

1. Design and manage a process that would allow the policy group (BCC) to take a strategic view of the downsizing and budget reduction process. All parties involved did not want the BCC to have to make piecemeal decisions but to be able to view each decision within a holistic context.
2. Design and manage a process that would allow the BCC to differentiate the value (according to criteria to be developed) of each of the PBCG's 180 major programs.
3. Design and manage a process that would elicit ideas and suggestions throughout the organization and in which the decision process would be explicit, open to review and comment, and appropriately inclusionary

the Administrator believed firmly that the actions of the management staff during the budget process would send a clear message to the rest of the organization about how serious he and his fellow executives were about such concepts as participation, empowerment, creativity, and initiative.

Given these tasks, the design team developed the process outlined in Table 1 and illustrated in Figure 1. The process was highly fluid, being continually modified to meet changing requirements. As both Table 1 and Figure 1 show, the process was highly interactive and participatory. Prior budget processes (shown on the left side of Figure 1) had occurred as discrete events that involved minimal interaction among three of the four key actors in the process. Department heads (operational managers) prepared their budgets, had them reviewed by the senior executive in charge of their department, and then submitted them to OFMB. The OFMB would resolve any problems it had with the departments directly and involve the senior executives only if there was an unresolvable conflict. These resolved budgets (for twenty-eight departments) would then go to the BCC en masse. The BCC would then have a series of meetings within a three-week span to review and approve the budget. Through this process only the most controversial items came to the BCCs'

Table 1 Overview of Budget Downsizing Process

Date	Event/intervention	Operational objective	Culture/schemata goal	OD process goal	OD technology	Key actors
November 1990	$70 million deficit projection	Balance budget	—	—	—	Management team (MT), Office of Finance, Mgmt and Budget (OFMB)
November	Design team formed	Design process to balance budget	Develop new schema	Model participation, build trust	—	Design team (DT)
November	Process design	Process design and review, scheduling	Develop "core mission" schema	Develop action research model	Group problem solving (GPS)	DT
November–December 10	Development of major budget strategies	Model 1 of strategy matrix	Develop "systems as whole" schema	Practice participation, teamwork	GPS	OFMB, MT, DT
December 15	Retreat with department heads	Begin budget work	Challenge continued growth schema	Model participation, empowerment	Survey feedback, structured interaction	Department heads (DH), DT
January 5, 1991	Preparation for first budget retreat	Develop date and agenda for retreat	Challenge growth schema, develop "core mission" schema	Design structure to allow interaction and schema examination	GPS	DT, OFMB, MT, county administrator (CA)
January 30, 31	First budget retreat	Develop model 2 of strategy matrix	Same as above plus downsizing schema	Build trust, BCC group cohesiveness	Survey feedback utility, focused interaction	Board of County Commissioners (BCC), MT, DH, OFMB, DT, CA
February–April	Subsequent budget retreats	Develop final model	Clarify "core mission" and downsizing schemas	Same as above plus strengthen group decision making	Survey feedback utility, focused interaction	BCC, DH, OFMB, CA

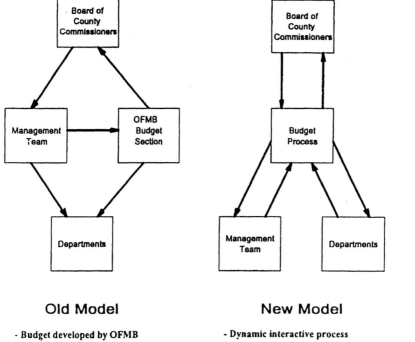

Old Model

- Budget developed by OFMB
- BCC does not see budget until final hearing
- Limited feedback and interaction

New Model

- Dynamic interactive process
- On-going feedback and communication
- Budget catalyst for synergistic interaction
- OFMB serves as a staff resource only

Figure 1   Information flow patterns of the old and new budget process.

attention. The new process (shown on the right side of Figure 1) made the budget processes the center point of a prolonged interaction among the BCC, senior executives, and department heads. The OFMB staff became technical resources to all three groups. This higher level of interaction, comprising a five-month period, provided a much greater opportunity for the development of shared organizational schemata. It should be noted that the entire process was covered by the press, was the subject of editorial comment in the local papers, and elicited public reaction by constituents of programs whose budgets were substantially reduced. The process was conducted in a highly political and public context. The capability for continuous change therefore was a requirement.

The overall methodology of the budget downsizing strategy was to facilitate an extended conversation among the management staff and the policy makers about PBCG. This extended conversation took the form of an action research model: initial questions or hypotheses, data collection and analysis, results feedback, decision/action/further questions. The major stages of this conversation were

1.   *Initial development of overall strategies.*   The design team developed a list of overall strategies for budget balancing. In order to meet the task requirement that the rethinking process be holistic, these strategies were arrayed in a strategy matrix, which is shown in Table 2. These strategies were discussed in a series of meetings with the senior executives and the department heads. They served

Table 2 Budget Strategy Matrix Summary

Budget strategies		Model 1 dollars (in thousands)	Model 9 dollars (in thousands)
County staff goal—$50,000,000			
B-1	Hiring freeze	3,000	3,000
B-2	Reduction travel and office exp.	200	200
C-1	Salary freeze	1,300	3,900
D-1	Reorganization	1,100	1,100
D-2	Level of service	10,000	9,325
D-3	Efficiency measures	3,000	3,600
E-1	Privatization—oustodial	0	670
E-2	Privatization—motor pool towing	181	62
E-3	Privatization—body shop	77	77
E-5	Reassign costs—HCD/county home	0	130
E-6	Reassign costs—medicaid/HCD	0	120
E-7	Reassign costs—ERM	—	222
E-8	Overmatch of grant programs	0	250
G-1	Road program	0	3,000
G-2a	Fire—rescue staffing. Sta. 34	420	420
G-2b	Fire—rescue, South County Rescue	(75)	(210)
G-2c	Defer capital proj. (fire/rescue)	—	9,500
G-2d	Fire rescue staffing	—	(530)
G-3	Timing of library projects	0	317
G-4	Combine biminate library projects	0	0
G-5	Parks	500	500
G-6	General capital	6,000	5,300
G-7	Juvenile detention facility	0	0
G-8	Defer purch. replace EQ. (pub. saf.)	—	170
G-9	Eliminate funding—automation enhance	—	700
H-1	Revenue enhancements	4,000	3,831
I-1	Affordable housing	—	1,000
I-2	Median beautification	—	0
I-3	Franchise fee	—	200
I-4	Revised supplemental	—	1,592
I-5	Reassigned costs—Agriculture	—	35
I-6	Reassigned costs—engineering	—	470
I-7	Reassigned costs—parks and recreation	—	50
I-8	Reassigned costs—public safety	—	239
Total reduction, county staff		29,703	49,240
Shortfall from goal		20,297	760
Constitutional officers goal—$20,000,000			
All constitutional officers		12,000	—
A1	Sheriff	—	12,600
A2	Property appralser	—	538
A3	Supervisor of elections	—	150
A4	Tax collector	—	—
A5	Clerk of court			
Total reduction, constitutional officers		12,000	13,288
Shortfall from goal		8,000	6,712
Residual property tax increase		$28,297	$7,472

as a mechanism to present staff's hypotheses about downsizing and budget reductions to the BCC. The BCC then accepted, rejected, or requested modification of the hypothesis. As the BCC decided on each hypothesis, this in turn generated other strategies or hypotheses by the management staff. The matrix became the heuristic device to test which downsizing model the BCC could accept on policy and political grounds.

2. *Development of a schema for differential program reductions.* One of the most difficult problems to solve was how to develop a method to differentially target programs for reduction. All parties involved recognized the truth of the adage "one person's fat is another's bone," and that there were constituent groups for these services. To make this process as rational and reasonable as possible while avoiding the vagaries of political influence, the management staff and the design team developed a new schema, "core mission." The core mission was defined as a basic and fundamental service critical to the organization. It was assumed that services could then be ranked on a unidimensional scale from core (10) to peripheral (1) and that a reasonable degree of consensus could be built on the ranking of those services.

3. *Challenging the schemata of continued growth.* The critical thinking about downsizing PBCG had to be done by the department managers. If they simply applied an across-the-board strategy to their departments, a true rethinking of PBCG would not have occurred. As long as they assumed a model of continued growth, an across-the-board strategy would be preferable. This strategy would allow them to simply cut back this year and then restore in future years. To challenge the schemata of continued growth two actions were taken. First, in a meeting with the department heads the director of OFMB explained the components of the project budget shortfall and its implications for budget out-years, which were even worse. Second, in this same meeting, the administrator introduced the schema of core mission as the guideline for the department heads to use in preparing their budget reduction plans. Across-the-board strategies were explicitly rejected by the administrator. Third, department heads were instructed to prepare three levels of budget reduction scenarios (5%, 10% and 15%) as well as reorganization plans to reduce staffing by 10%. Since these were reduction levels far exceeding anything in the experience of the department heads, it was hoped this action, coupled with the OFMB director's comments, would challenge their continued growth assumptions.

To foster a holistic view of the process, management staff members were asked in a premeeting survey to look beyond their own areas of responsibility and identify any service or function within PBCG that could be merged, downsized, or eliminated. As a second part of this meeting, these survey results were presented. These results were discussed by the group as a whole. Significant information in and of itself, it was also hoped this discussion would stimulate development of the downsizing schemata.

The goal of this meeting was to communicate the seriousness of the budget problem and the commitment of the administrator to a participatory problem-solving process. The administrator encouraged department heads to involve as many of their staff members as possible in developing budget plans and to think creatively in the process. Both the survey feedback technique and the group discussion techniques were designed to facilitate a reassessment of the continued growth schema as well as demonstrate the administrator's commitment to a participative model.

4. *Program prioritization activity* While department heads were developing budget reduction scenarios, the design team was preparing a weighting process through which the senior executives and the BCC could indicate their program priorities. Based on these results, differential reduction targets would be set. The process used to arrive at the final results was a modified delphi using the schema of core mission. Each program (the 300 separate county programs were aggregated into 180 major programs for this activity) was rated on its centrality to the core mission using a five-point scale that ranged from clearly core mission to "nice, but optional." Senior executives and the BCC rated programs individually and anonymously. Those programs in which there was a significant rating difference (perceptually, not statistically) between the BCC and the senior executives were isolated for further discussion during the BCC's first budget retreat.

5. *Management staff review of department budgets.* Without reference to the program rating results the senior executives reviewed the proposed reductions of each department. Two questions were asked: "Are we comfortable with these cuts or has the department gone too far?" and If we are comfortable, "could further cuts be made?" These results were used to generate an initial budget cut number that could be placed in the strategy matrix.

6. *BCC budget retreat.* The results of the preceding stages 4 and 5 were presented to the BCC in a two-day retreat. Those programs in which there were significant differences between BCC and staff ratings were explained. After the presentation and discussion of the key differences, BCC members and the management staff rerated those programs. Beginning on the second day the BCC was presented with a strategy book outlining the various strategies (and options within those strategies). These were summarized in the matrix of Table 2, which was projected onto an overhead screen using Lotus 1-2-3. Beginning with a shortfall of $70 million, each strategy was presented. When the BCC made its decision an appropriate amount was subtracted from the $70 million figure. By the end of the second day (model 9) the BCC had agreed upon approximately $63 million in cuts. All functions directly under the control of the county staff had met 98.48% of their cost-cutting goal. The constitutional officers, who were not active participants in the process, met 66.44% of their goal. The total impact on the county was a $7,472,000 property tax increase.

7. *Analysis of downsizing strategy.* With the BCC's reratings of programs, ratings were translated into approximate budget cuts required of each department to meet the overall dollar target. These results were provided to the department heads. Those departments that had not met the percentage reduction targeted by the BCC were required to make additional reductions, while those whose reductions exceeded the BCC targets were allowed to reinstate items. Once this was complete the targeted budget reductions closely paralleled the BCC priority ratings.

8. *Management staff downsizing revisions.* At this point the schemata of continued growth was no longer experienced as a viable way to interpret reality. Downsizing was now the operative schema. Department heads were allowed to revisit their proposed budgets based on a more precise targeted level. The management staff reviewed and approved or disapproved these revised downsiz-

ing plans. The new downsizing projections were then placed in the strategy matrix.

9. *Final review and approval.* By this point, (five months after the first two-day budget retreat) the interaction between the BCC and the management staff had clearly changed the guiding schemata from growth to downsizing. The BCC requested a final retreat to look at the "whole picture" once more before finalizing its decisions. During this retreat additional strategies were presented that not only allowed the BCC to make the final reductions but to also develop a reserve for unanticipated expenses. The process had succeeded in rethinking PBCG to a smaller organization that could operate within the budgetary restrictions.

SUMMARY AND CONCLUSION

The purpose of this study was to examine how to successfully apply one theoretical model of OD, the cognitive model, through theoretically consistent (i.e., cognitive) interventions to solve a significant organizational problem. The process generated a number of questions and insights. Some were philosophical questions about the role of government while others were at the more technical level of how the process could be improved. There were two key schemata that the process had to address. The first was the assumption of continued growth. The second was that key budget decisions would be made without the input of affected parties. Whether or not these schemata changed can be best judged by the behaviors of the parties involved.

With respect to the assumption of continued growth the first budget retreat appeared to be the key breakpoint. Up to that point the assumption was that the BCC would increase taxes. By the end of the first retreat it was clear this was not an option the BCC was going to readily take. Anecdotal evidence that the continued growth schemata had changed was a sensitivity to budget concerns that surfaced almost immediately after the first retreat. Furthermore, the BCC's rating of programs challenged the values placed on many of those programs by staff. Discussion of agenda items in official board meetings was frequently predicated by statements such as "in light of budget pressures" or "because of budget pressures." This was not language that was in use prior to the first budget retreat.

Whether the schema of inclusion was firmly established is more difficult to determine. At a behavioral level, decisions were made in the open with full opportunity for input. All meetings were public. When the senior executives convened to review the work of department heads it was done with the foreknowledge of the department heads. During the budget retreat the department heads made presentations to the BCC if their strategies were questioned. If behind-the-scenes decision making and closed door meetings occurred, the design team was not made aware of them. While staff reactions to such drastic reductions have been negative, there is a general consensus among staff that they were included in the process.

Finally, the interventions can be judged successful from the perspective that the budget was balanced without tax increases in a manner that was acceptable to the policy makers.

The process also led to two important lessons about the application of OD interventions. One is that there is a delay between the rejection of an existing organizational schemata, the acceptance of a new one, and behavioral action. Even after the cognitive acceptance of downsizing, there was not an immediate attempt to identify and address the actions required by this new schema. A second lesson learned is that a shift in organizational schemata is an oscillating process, requiring a prolonged period of time. The design team had initially planned for a two-month period of budget retreats. In the end five months were required. During that time period issues were revisited several times. Decisions were changed. It appears this rethinking process is necessary for a group to develop a shared schemata.

Based on the study findings, the model of OD as schemata change is a viable and useful approach to guide interventions and budgeting strategies. This study, however, raises issues of the timing and process of schemata change that should be addressed in further research.

REVIEW QUESTIONS

1. What are the pitfalls of engaging in an iterative dialogue with elected officials and special interest groups in the budget development process? How should you "control" the agenda?
2. Drawing on your own experiences, delineate the advantages and disadvantages of inclusive, participatory decision making in the budget process.
3. What additional OD interventions should be considered after the approval of a budget requiring downsizing?
4. What are the advantages and disadvantages of alternative budgeting strategies, such as "across-the-board" reductions and zero-based budgeting?
5. Describe the competing strategies of the different schemata in this case study.
6. Based on this information in this case study, discuss the circumstances under which OD interventions should be used in subsequent budgeting years.
7. What alternative strategies could have been used to better involve constitutional officers in the budget process?

REFERENCES

Adler, N. J. (1983). Organization development in a multicultural environment. *Journal of Applied Behavioral Science, 19*, 349–365.

Appelbaum, S. H., Simpson, R. and Shapiro, B. T. (1987). The tough test of downsizing. *Organizational Dynamics, 16*, 68–79.

Bartunek, J. M. and Moch, M. K. (1987). First-order, second-order, and third-order change and organization development interventions: A cognitive approach. *Journal of Applied Behavioral Science, 23*, 483–500.

Buller, P. F. (1988). For successful strategic change: Blend OD practices with strategic management. *Organizational Dynamics, winter*, 42–54.

Fitzgerald, T. H. (1987) The OD practitioner in the business world: Theory versus reality. *Organizational Dynamics, 15*, 21–33.

Greenhalgh, L. (1982). Maintaining organizational effectiveness during organizational retrenchment *Journal of Applied Behavioral Science, 18*, 155–170.

Hammons, J. O. (1982). Organization development: An overview. In J. O. Hammons, (ed.), *Organization Development: Change Strategies*, San Francisco: Jossey-Bass.

Kilmann, R. H. (1989). A completely integrated program for creating and maintaining organizational success. *Organizational Dynamics, 18,* 4–19.

Maurice, M., Sorge, A., and Warner, M. (1980). Societal differences in organizing manufacturing units. *Organization Studies, 1,* 59–86.

McDaniel, R. R., Thomas, J. B., Ashmos, D. P., and Smith, J. P. (1987). The use of decision analysis for organizational design: Reorganizing a community hospital. *Journal of Applied Behavioral Science, 23,* 337–350.

Pati, G. C. and Salitore, R. A. (1989). The resurrection of a rust-belt service organization. *Organizational Dynamics, 18,* 33–51.

Porras, J. I. and Hoffer, S. J. (1986). Common behavior changes in successful organization development efforts. *Journal of Applied Behavioral Science, 22,* 477–494.

Schein, E. H. (1990). A general philosophy of helping: Process consultation. *Sloan Management Review, spring* 57–62.

Walter, G. A. (1984). Organizational development and individual rights. *Journal of Applied Behavioral Science, 20,* 423–439.

Weisbord, M. R. (1987). *Productive Workplaces.* San Francisco: Jossey-Bass.

24

Cutback Management in Georgia

State Agency Responses to Fiscal Year 1992 Budget Reductions

Katherine G. Willoughby
Georgia State University, Atlanta, Georgia, U.S.A.

Thomas P. Lauth
The University of Georgia, Athens, Georgia, U.S.A.

This case study examines the responses of Georgia state agencies to a sudden and severe revenue shortfall that necessitated cutbacks in agency operating budgets. Based primarily on interviews conducted in the fall of 1991 with the principal budget officers of Georgia executive branch agencies and selected officials in the state's Office of Planning and Budget (OPB), the study seeks to enhance our understanding of state budgeting and cutback management in government.[1]

FOCUS OF INQUIRY

What is at stake in cutback management? Under the most ideal circumstances, government agencies have sufficient resources to continue existing programs, including cost increases normally associated with program continuation, and to initiate selected new programs. The primary focus of the budget process is on program development, or increments beyond the base. In normal times, government agencies are typically able to continue what is already being done and engage in a limited amount of program growth. Resources are expanding fast enough to accommodate increased costs associated with program continuation, and some—but not all—of the demands for program and service expansion (Schick, 1980: 120). When available resources are insufficient to cover the costs associated with program continuation, however, and it is nearly impossible to fund new programs, agencies are forced to engage in cutback management. Under these circumstances a few highly favored new initiatives may be funded, but the main task of budgeters is to find an acceptable balance between the demand for funds and available resources (Schick, 1980: 123). The primary focus of the budget process is the base, or the reduced base, rather than increments. On the resources side, balance may be achieved by identifying new revenue sources or increasing the yields of existing sources. On the program and services side, it may be achieved by a variety of techniques falling under the general heading of cutback management.

There is an extensive literature on cutback management (Hovey, 1981; Levine, 1978; 1979; Levine, et al., 1981a; 1981b), but empirical studies have focused on either the federal government (Rubin, 1985) or local governments (Levine, et al., 1981a; Rubin, 1982). Such research specific to cutback management in the states is fairly limited. Druker and Robinson (1993) surveyed human resource and budget officers from the fifty states regarding financial conditions and personnel management strategies in periods of shortfall. Their research considered cutback strategies related to state personnel and employment only, however, Grizzle and Trogen (1994) examine fiscal stress in the state of Florida during the 1989 recession and describe the cutback budgeting strategies of the executive and legislative branches to accommodate such stress. Their research considers both personnel and programmatic changes to the state budget. Grizzle and Trogen (1994: 520) conclude that the short-term fixes to the budget that dealt with revenue decline from 1989 to 1991 do not bode well for future budget balancing in their state. While this research outlines some cutback budgeting outcomes within a few specified agencies, it does not provide an overall assessment of how agencies attempted to cope with revenue decline. The present case provides an empirical examination of state-level agency responses to cutback directives on the part of the chief executive. Levine (1979: 182–183) points out the need for research on the management of fiscally stressed public organizations, starting with an inventory of techniques and case studies of their application. This case adds to that inventory.

FISCAL STRESS IN GEORGIA

From 1975 to 1990, Georgia experienced real growth in revenue collections, which enabled the state to fund not only a continuation of current services, but also program and activity expansion, without having to raise state taxes (Lauth, 1991: 56–57). A national recession contributed to severe shortfalls in 1991 that forced Georgia, like many states, to cut the budget. The general assembly was called into a special session in the summer of 1991 to reduce the state's $7.9 billion fiscal year (FY) 1992 budget by $415 million ($-$5.3%). Table 1 shows the size of each state agency's budget reduction. In order to achieve budget reduction objectives, several governmentwide spending restrictions were imposed, and state agencies were required to initiate additional cost-cutting measures. In contrast to the decisions made in other states, tax increases were rejected as a deficit reduction alternative in Georgia.[2]

The budget situation in Georgia at the beginning of FY 1992 required state agencies to engage in cutback management. What did they do? First, some steps were mandated by OPB as part of a governmentwide effort to bring demands into alignment with available resources. Second, state agencies engaged in a variety of techniques dictated by their individual circumstances. The purpose of this case is to identify the budget reduction techniques used by state agencies and to assess the overall agency approaches for coping with fiscal stress.

LITERATURE REVIEW

The literature on cutback management is largely descriptive of causes (Hovey, 1981) and speculative about potential effects (Levine, 1978; 1979), and as noted earlier, there have

Table 1 Agency Budget Reductions, Fiscal Year 1992 Special Session

Agency	Amended appropriation (August 1991)	Change from original appropriation (%)
Legislature	21,686,449	−7.8
Audits	15,180,703	−5.8
Judicial	56,773,178	−1.3
Administrative Services	31,717,982	−9.5
Agriculture	34,796,808	−8.8
Banking and Finance	6,918,628	−0.7
Community Affairs	13,357,577	−4.8
Corrections	480,012,708	−9.9
Defense	4,821,635	−6.8
Education	2,797,511,028	−2.9
Forestry Commission	32,678,095	−7.5
Georgia Bureau of Investigation	35,506,683	−4.6
Governor	19,876,458	−4.0
Human Resources	1,026,923,450	−4.8
Industry and Trade	15,495,602	−6.9
Insurance	12,150,922	−9.2
Labor	16,173,541	−2.5
Law	8,475,028	−6.0
Medical Assistance	828,029,708	−1.5
Natural Resources	62,820,656	−12.1
Public Safety	92,161,956	−5.1
Public School Employee Retirement	9,851,433	−9.7
Public Service Commission	6,789,997	−9.1
Board of Regents	870,736,522	−8.2
Revenue	67,242,842	−11.2
Secretary of State	22,998,550	−6.1
Soil and Water Conservation	1,709,299	−4.6
Student Finance Commission	21,882,053	−7.4
Teachers' Retirement System	3,950,000	0.0
Technical and Adult Education	118,631,375	−7.6
Transportation	426,020,626	−15.1
Veterans' Services	20,972,949	−3.8
Workers' Compensation Board	8,554,436	−2.6
GO Debt Sinking Fund	342,591,218	−2.7
Guaranteed Revenue Debt Fund	5,000,000	NA
Total	$7,540,000,095	−5.2

Source: Committee on Conference Report on HB I-EX, Aug. 1991.

been very few empirical studies that consider the strategies for dealing with revenue shortfalls in public organizations. Levine (1978; 1979) describes the major decisions faced by managers of an organization in decline as (1) deciding whether to resist or smooth change, (2) selecting tactics for resisting or smoothing the change, and (3) deciding how and where to make resource cuts within the organization. A dominant theme in the cutback management literature is the equity versus efficiency trade-off inherent in implementing budget cuts, with across-the-board cuts representing the former and targeted cuts representing the latter (Levine, 1978; 1979). A second important theme is the impact of cutbacks on personnel, including morale problems, diminished creativity, and the effects of layoff policies based on seniority (Levine, 1978; 1979).

In an analysis of four cities, Levine et al. (1981a) demonstrated the importance of politics as an intervening factor between reduced budgets and cutback responses. In testing the retrenchment management decisions postulated by Levine, the authors describe an "orderly retrenchment" as one in which management (1) attempted to smooth rather than resist the cutback, (2) developed a multiyear plan for dealing with the effects of the cutback rather than acknowledging only short-term effects, and (3) imposed targeted rather than across-the-board cuts. In a study of selected New York City agencies, Glassberg (1978) identifies the important role of leadership when organizations face decline. Levine et al. (1981b) conclude from their study of Cincinnati and Oakland that political centralization helps in the management of retrenchment.

In an analysis of five federal government agencies, Rubin (1985) suggests that federal agencies can be cut back, but management improvement cannot simultaneously occur. Rubin reports that cutbacks resulted in uncertainty, disruption, low morale, reduced quality of work life, and reduced productivity. Similarly, Grizzle and Trogen's (1994) assessment of cutback budgeting in Florida emphasizes that often short-term fixes to the budget win out over more politically sensitive, long-term solutions to support fiscal health in government. Their research highlights the battle between the executive and legislative branches regarding how best to accommodate cuts in periods of decline.

RESEARCH QUESTIONS AND METHOD

According to Levine (1979: 182), fiscally stressed organizations must make decisions about confronting, planning, targeting, and distributing cuts. In the present case, did Georgia managers resist impending budget reductions or seek to smooth the impact on agency personnel and programs? Did they implement across-the-board cuts, distributing the pain evenly among all agency units, or was the budget crisis used to justify targeted reductions in poorly performing programs, programs of marginal value, or programs serving politically weak constituencies? In other words, did they utilize what is commonly known as rational decison making (Lauth, 1987b; Lindblom, 1959; 1979; Schick, 1971)? Did they acquiesce in deep cuts initially with the expectation of building back organizational capacity at a later date or did they seek to take small cuts so as to minimize the short-term impact of the budget reductions? What was the mix of program versus personnel reductions? Specifically, what activities were terminated (Brewer, 1978)? What projects were deferred? Were any operations privatized (Hovey, 1981; Lewis and Logalbo, 1980)? What low-cost or no-cost labor was used? What labor-saving techniques were introduced (Hovey, 1981: 85)? What gains were made in efficiency? What was done to reduce or ration demand for services?

Information about the management of fiscally stressed state agencies was obtained through elite interviews (Dexter, 1970). Interviews were conducted in the fall of 1991 with the principal budget officer of Georgia executive branch agencies (n = 29).[3] The interview protocol consisted of questions about the agency and the professional background of the agency budget officer, and then progressed through a series of questions related

Table 2 Cutback Strategies: Georgia State Agencies (Fall 1991)

Cutback strategy	Agencies implementing strategy (%) (N = 29)
Institute hiring freeze	96
Initiate layoffs	86
Request purchase freeze and/or cuts	86
Request travel freeze and/or cuts	75
Give up vacant positions	71
Reduce activities, services, programs	71
Initiate efficiency measures	57
Eliminate activities, services, programs	50
Consolidate activities, services, programs	32

specifically to their interpretation of gubernatorial directives concerning revenue shortfall and to their strategies for accommodating the request for budget cuts. Interviews were conducted by both researchers, with one questioning the agency budget officer and the second taking notes. Interviews ranged in length from forty-five minutes to two hours, but on average lasted approximately one hour. Interview notes were transcribed as soon after agency visits as possible. Researchers then cross-checked for accuracy of understanding and consistency of interpretation. All quotes from budget officers are from the interview notes. Content analysis of interview notes provides the data for Table 2.

Georgia is a useful case because the fiscal stress experienced in FY 1992 was an aberrant event that can be isolated for investigation and because until now empirical studies of cutback management have focused predominantly on the national government and local governments. In addition, we are able to build upon the previous research that has been done on the Georgia budget process (Lauth, 1978; 1979; 1984; 1985; 1986; 1987a; 1987b; 1988; 1990), and while in-depth individual state studies are not substitutes for multistate studies (Jewell, 1982), such research can serve as reality checks on the speculative literature on cutback management. This case study contributes to an understanding of how cutback management actually worked in Georgia in FY 1992, provides a basis for future comparative studies of cutback management in the states, and serves as a check on the nonempirical cutback management literature.

FINDINGS

In a memorandum dated July 12, 1991, Governor Zell Miller stipulated to state agency heads

> I want you to assume a 10% reduction in the state fund appropriation to your department. The purpose of this action is to provide me the largest array of budget reduction options possible throughout all of State Government. I am not planning to recommend a 10% State budget reduction. To reach this objective you should prepare a list of the programs and service delivery activities that you would either eliminate or significantly scale back if this appropriation level were approved by the General Assembly. . . . This list should include a definition of the program or service delivery and the dollar savings

and position count that would be effected with your action. A logical assumption is that these identified programs will represent the lowest priorities of your department and its governmental mission.

Along with this memorandum, budget officers received suggested expenditure reduction initiatives from the director of the OPB. This memorandum served as "more detailed guidance and instruction" concerning gubernatorial directives regarding cuts. The director specifically discussed furloughs (later ruled unconstitutional),[4] hiring and purchase freezes, and travel curtailment.

Defensiveness and Protectiveness

Given this mission, how did Georgia's budget officers react? The initial responses by state agencies to these directives from the governor and OPB suggest some defensiveness or protectiveness on their part, especially when comparing their agency to others in state government. Most sought to explain the unique aspect(s) of their agency that influenced their use of particular cutback strategies. For example, two officers noted that

> We have undergone budget reductions the last couple of years. There is less fat in this agency compared to others.

> We don't have programs we can eliminate as all we do is mandated.

Many budget officers suggested that their agency's unusual funding mechanism either protected them from suggested cuts or at least provided justification for slight or marked departure from gubernatorial direction.

> We are self-sufficient and self-supporting. Our operations are funded out of investment income.

> We provide investment services . . . In our case, a personnel cut could [result in] a loss of $100 million a day.

> Our operating budget is entirely self-supporting. We pay for our operating budget through user fees and contracts with the federal government.

> Really, 85% of our revenues are generated through user fees . . . so we are a bit different from other state agencies that are funded out of general revenues.

> In our case, we have a special funding situation where we assess fees and collect money, deposit it in the General Treasury, and draw down on the balance.

> Dedicated revenues offer some protection for our agency. Really, we are comparatively efficient for the money, considering the machinery and outputs of this organization.

The protection from cuts afforded by federal funding was also mentioned.

> Comparatively speaking, we are pretty nonpolitical . . . our predominant provider of funds is the federal government.

> We are a stand alone agency with predominant fiscal support from the federal government.

> Eighty-two to 86% of our budget is federal dollars while the remaining comes from the state plus fees and assessments. Also, the types of funds received by the federal

government are different from other agencies in that they are collected directly by us, yet go to the Treasury.

Finally, some officers alluded to both the nature of their agency's programs and activities and the public's understanding of such activities as contributing to the cut strategies that were implemented.

> We are the marketing department for the state. We generate revenue for Georgia. So, if you cut this budget, there are fewer resources for us to bring in revenue, and revenue inflow [to the state] declines.

> [Compared to other agencies] we are at a disadvantage because we just take money from people. We do not have what people want, what legislators want, no programs, per se. When legislators have money for facilities and programs, they do not think of us.

> During the last few years [our agency] has really downsized, even though the perception persists that we have grown by leaps and bounds.

> There is a perception in general that we are high paid folks over here. It is really difficult to articulate what we are about [to those unfamiliar with our agency].

To Smooth or Resist

While many of the budget officers interviewed sought to frame their agency as special or unique when compared to others in state government, most expressed a desire to smooth rather than resist the cuts requested.

> Last December, our Director, in anticipation of reductions, froze within-grade increases. He tried to anticipate reductions and act before the last minute. He prohibited out-of-state travel and limited in-state travel. He has been trying to stay one step ahead of cuts, so we can handle them.

> We knew that financial problems were coming. Our Director froze all hiring immediately and we didn't fill vacant positions.

> We have good communication with OPB and our analyst. We submitted [cut] packages and reviewed them with the governor. We also submitted an amendment to the August report which offered a bit more flexibility with the RIF process.

> Our public school activity is in good financial shape and we told the state. "You need the money now, and we are in good shape, [so] you take it."

Cutback Strategies

Georgia agencies considered a variety of cutback strategies. A content analysis of interview transcripts yields information in Table 2 that identifies the percentage of all state agencies in which agency budget officers noted implementing various cutback strategies. Not surprisingly, given the directives from OPB, all agencies save one (96%) instituted an immediate hiring freeze. That agency (teacher's retirement system) reported that as a "stand-alone" corporation, it did not formally freeze hiring. Other self-sustaining agencies (e.g., Georgia Student Finance Commission and employees retirement), however, adhered to the hiring freeze policy as a symbolic gesture to the governor of being team players.

Layoffs (used by 86% of agencies) and reductions in purchasing (used by 86% of agencies) are the second most popular strategies for realizing the 10% reduction request. Budget officers said that when possible layoff of temporary help, political appointees, and voluntary separations and retirements were sought before instituting involuntary separations. Generally, agencies responded to what one budget officer referred to as the governor's call to "slash state bureaucracy" in the form of personnel cuts, particularly midlevel management. Their adherence to the hiring freeze and use of layoffs attests to recognition of this gubernatorial preference.

> With a large portion of our budget in personal services, and the governor's agenda to downsize government, I guess this is what you expect.

> The focus of the governor's cuts was initially mid-level management. It was our understanding that his agenda was to reduce filled positions. We have 41 positions in this office alone and we sent three people out the door.

> We felt that Governor Miller wanted "to see bodies in the water." OPB had political reasons for cutting—an agenda from Miller to cut positions.

> We lost 12 positions in 1991 and expect to lose eight positions in 1992–1993. While six of these will slide into other activities, two on the management/consultant level will be eliminated.

Several officers indicated that the layoffs actually provided the opportunity to prune the organization, a difficult challenge in fiscally plentiful times.

> While layoffs did not hurt our agency that much, they certainly hurt those people we let go. But it did speed up the process of getting rid of people we would have anyway.

> From an organizational standpoint, the initial cuts and layoffs did improve productivity a bit. In fact, this round of cuts took care of some "cleaning house" from the growth experienced in the 1980s.

One officer believed that the recession in fact worked to the advantage of the governor, stating "the economic impact of the recession fell into [the governor's] plan concerning downsizing. State government had expanded far beyond logic."

The elimination, reduction, or deferral of purchases included office supplies as well as equipment, maintenance, telecommunications, motor vehicles, computer hardware and software, per diem fees on contracts, and real estate rentals and purchases. The nature of the agency's functions dictated purchasing freezes and cuts. For instance, in this area the department of corrections reduced supplies to inmates (shirt allotments were reduced from four to three per inmate); the department of industry, trade, and tourism cut purchases for advertising; and veterans' services put off the replacement of a nurse call system in one of its hospitals.

Travel freezes were utilized by 75% of the agencies. The most common consideration of this cutback strategy was to keep travel to what is mandated, such as attendance at conferences for certification purposes. Along with the reduction in the number of conferences attended, much out-of-state and in-state travel for regulatory, training, or field service purposes was reduced or discontinued.

Giving up vacant positions and reducing programs and services closely follows travel cuts as a means to whittle budgets. Almost three-quarters (71%) of the agencies took advantage of one or both of these cutback strategies. A few managers who anticipated future budget cuts and "shored up" vacancies to provide a safety net nevertheless felt cheated when these positions and the money to fund them were taken.

> It seems that economizers were shafted as vacancies were eventually taken away. We were penalized for freezing hiring because we lost the vacancies [in the end].

One officer, however, noted that "on our own initiative, we stopped filling vacancies and spaces of those who left. Shoring up our resources in this way paid off for us when the cuts came down. In total, we [only] realized a three percent cut from the special session."

Reductions in programs and/or services were fairly common among the agencies and were related to agency functions, like cuts associated with purchasing. The Department of Agriculture reduced the hours of operation of the state's, farmers' markets. The secretary of state's office closed the archives one day a week. Medical assistance changed reimbursement rates, resulting in a reduction in benefits. As in the case of layoffs, some reductions were welcomed by agencies; that is, the governor's directives only speeded up the process.

Efficiency measures were implemented by a little over one-half (57%) of the agencies. The most prominent means of increasing efficiency and thereby reducing costs was running equipment and vehicles longer. Providing service and maintenance of equipment and vehicles internally was also a means to save money. Other efforts included reducing patrol mileage (public safety and public service commission), increasing class size and greater use of part-time instructors (board of regents), and reducing the use of fax machines (revenue). While small efficiencies, such as letting supplies run down, or allowing "permissive activities to fall by the wayside," were mentioned by most fiscal officers, few felt that any real savings could be gained by such measures. According to one officer, "efficiency measures are really 'chump change' and have a morale cost to them." Additionally, most of those running equipment and vehicles longer cited the associated risk to the employees who use the older cars and to those to which equipment/vehicles are then surplused (such as to local governments that acquire state patrol vehicles).[5]

When discussing efficiency measures, the issue of user fees was addressed by many of the budget officers. Aside from those agencies predominantly funded by user fees or otherwise self-supporting (e.g., administrative services, student finance commission, and workers' compensation), nine agencies had budget officers who discussed the potential of user fees in alleviating future fiscal ills, at least concerning the functioning of their department. For example, the department of agriculture has the ability to institute fees and/ or licenses for many types of manufacturers and dealers, consumer protection inspections, bottlers, produce weightings, and seed, grain, and feed. Specially, this budget officer noted a motor fuel inspection fee to generate more revenue: "There is talk of assessing it per gallon rather than per pump." Other agencies considering reassessing presently mandated fees or instituting new ones included the forestry commission, Georgia Bureau of Investigation, department of natural resources, public service commission, department of revenue, office of the secretary of state, soil and water conservation commission, and department of transportation.

Exactly one-half (50%) of Georgia agencies eliminated services and/or programs, while about one-third (32%) provided for consolidation of services, programs, or activities. There is a consistent rationale among the budget officers concerning elimination of services and/or programs. Those most likely to be abolished include programs providing oversight, accreditation, or public relations functions, services not mandated (e.g., the publication and distribution of informational brochures), those that do not bring in revenue, and those that can be provided by another level of government (even if of lesser quantity and/or quality). Not surprisingly, those last added to the agency's responsibilities. For instance, the department of agriculture eliminated its animal protection program, which licenses pet dealers and inspects premises. According to the budget officer of this department, "this was the last thing to be added on in terms of services provided by Agriculture and therefore the first to go. Also, this program generated no revenue in terms of no incoming fees for inspections and licensing."

Consolidation often occurred where duplication of activity existed. For example, the department of administrative services closed seven vehicle rental locations without cutting the service entirely. Likewise, the forestry commission closed two of three reforestation nurseries. The department of human resources did a great deal of downsizing, such as reducing county administrative staff and collapsing county administrative functions into multicounty operations. Other avenues for consolidating activities and functions included the development of clerical pools (agriculture) and cutting the number of patrolling shifts (public safety). Finally, the merit system of personnel administration provided the sole instance of dramatic function change due to the fiscally stressed environment. Their applicant services division became outplacement.

Agency Characteristics and Use of Strategies

Having investigated the cutback strategies implemented by state agencies, it is instructive to consider the nature of each organization and determine if agency characteristics influenced guidance received from OPB or the cutback strategies eventually employed. Georgia's agencies can be divided into two budget share categories, large and small. Six agencies comprise approximately 85% of the total state budget for FY 1992 and are thus termed "large." These include: corrections (6.8%), education (36.5%), human resources (13.7%), medical assistance (9.9%), regents (12.0%), and transportation (6.4%). The rest of the agencies are lumped into the "small" category, with budget shares ranging from less than 0.01% to almost 2% of the total budget.

Of the large agencies, 100% received only general guidance from OPB about making cuts.[6] Of the small agencies, most (82%) received similar guidance, yet four agencies (18%) did receive detailed guidance about cuts. The secretary of state's office, the soil and water conservation commission, technical and adult education, and veterans' services were the only agencies reporting that they received specific directives from OPB regarding where to make spending cuts. Comments by these budget officers indicate different reasons for such directed attention on the part of OPB. One noted that they were working with "new people" in OPB who may not have had a full understanding about their department's activities and functions. Likewise, another indicated a perception on the part of OPB that its agency was administratively top-heavy and duplicative, thereby the governor requested positions over programs. Another indicated a concerted effort on the part of OPB to downsize the organization to facilitate the possibility of folding the agency into a larger one in the future. Nevertheless, regarding OPB direction on cuts in general, most officers seem to agree with one who suggested that, "I think they [OPB] wanted to get ideas [about cuts] from us. I think they asked for ten percent so that they could pick and choose five percent in cuts."

While directives about cuts to agencies by OPB were predominantly across the board, internal decisions about cuts were more likely to be guided by agency perceptions of what was available—agencies cut where they could; that is, if their activities and functions were personnel-intensive, positions were cut (as in administrative services and forestry). Where equipment and maintenance were a major part of the budget, such as in defense, those suffered most. Program-intensive agencies, such as corrections, community affairs, education, and human resources, often were reduced to mandated activities only. At industry, trade, and tourism, advertising was cut even though it is a potential revenue-generating devise. Most budget officers indicated that the cuts made for the governor at this time sliced any and all fat from their agency. According to one officer, "if we had to come up with [any more cuts], we would be getting into the bone." Another summed up the sentiment of the majority of officers, "I say, if you want more cut, you'll have to be the bad guy and come and get it yourself."

SUMMARY AND CONCLUSION

Our investigation of responses by Georgia agencies to FY 1992 budget reductions provides support for Levine's postulates of cutback management strategies and behaviors. Interview data identify a predominantly cooperative spirit among the Georgia budget officers. When faced with the need to make reductions, most sought to smooth rather than resist. Nearly all budget officers exhibited some degree of protectiveness when discussing the activities, programs, and services of their agencies, but none remained obstinate when faced with the governor's request for reductions. Much of the defensiveness of Georgia budget officers seems to reflect traditional behavior as described by Wildavsky (1984); that is, these budget officers are willing to support the chief executive up to a point while defending the unique qualities of their agency and its contributions made to the public at large. For the most part, the budget officers provided an array of choices to the governor and OPB that could be included as part of total cuts. These budget officers followed OPB directives regarding the hiring freeze as well as travel and purchase cuts, and acknowledged the governor's preference for pruning personnel first where possible.[7]

During the period under study, most Georgia budget officers sought to address cuts by focusing on the resource intensive areas within their particular agency or department (personnel, equipment and maintenance, programmatic, etc.). As interview data demonstrate, most budget officers cut where they could in areas that would realize the greatest dollar savings. Nevertheless, as Table 2 illustrates, the relatively small number of agencies that consolidated or eliminated activities, programs, or services attests to the lack of any immediate fundamental change in the traditional activities of state government in Georgia as a results of these cuts. Considering Levine's postulate of an equity and efficiency trade-off, equity may have been an issue the governor sought to address by initially targeting personnel, specifically midlevel management, for reduction throughout state government. Neither equity nor efficiency seemed to be of great interest to budget officers when determining where to cut, however. One budget officer did suggest that certain employees may be more protected in a cutback atmosphere, stating

> The RIF [reduction in force] process compounds the problem of status related to job retention. For instance, military service is a consideration for some and can help in maintaining employment when cuts begin to be made.

The majority of budget officers, however, were more likely to consider the cutback atmosphere as an opportunity to weed out inefficient personnel. Also, there were several instances in which technological advancement was coupled with personnel layoffs to meet the governor's request. In effect, many spending reductions merely sped up previously considered management strategies to cut costs and increase efficiency. Such behavior coincides a bit with findings from Lewis and Logalbo (1980) that indicate that fiscally stressed environments can foster innovation. In fact, in our case most budget offices did not consider that their agencies could expect to lose "the best and the brightest" with the reductions, although many questioned future recruitment capacity should Georgia state government remain in a fiscally stressed environment.

In summary, Georgia agencies did not deny the reality of a fiscal problem and resist budget reductions. They recognized fiscal exigencies and sought to minimize adverse impacts on their organizations. Governor Miller was successful during this cutback period because of the overwhelming—although not enthusiastic—participation of the budget officers. No one wanted to give up resources, yet most wanted to be included as a team players in achieving a balanced budget.[8] Some budget reductions actually fostered techno-logical advancement, thereby increasing agency capabilities, while reducing personnel. Ironically, the few agencies with organizational slack seemed to be able to weather the cuts with less adverse impact than those already operating more efficiently.

Budget reformers may be disheartened by the lack of rational analysis evident in most cutback strategies in this case. The rational budgeting model posits that systematic analysis of productivity and performance can and should be used to allocate resources during periods in which new resources are available and to target budget reductions during periods of fiscal stress when proposed spending exceeds available resources. In Georgia, budget officers understood the vulnerable spots in their budgets. When asked for money and positions, they came up with requested amounts from the least disruptive places. Generally, these officers used short-term, satisficing strategies rather than long-term, op-timizing strategies.

This does not mean that rational analysis cannot work. In fact, some Georgia budget officers illustrate that past application of rational analysis can influence cutback strategy in times of fiscal stress. On the other hand, for many of the budget officers, rational analysis did not come into play when determining cuts. Essentially, it is not expected that rational analysis is conducted during periods of fiscal stress, although the fruits of such analysis are most helpful then. Ultimately, in the absence of rational analysis, agencies muddle through (Lindblom, 1959), making cuts where they can and doing what is good enough to weather the fiscal storm. The fiscal crisis that necessitated the FY 1992 budget cuts in Georgia did not last very long, and the strategy of muddling through worked reasonably well for agencies. If the short-term fiscal crisis had turned into a chronically depressed fiscal condition, however, muddling through would not work and more rational budget cutting strategies would be required.

Postscript: A Return to Relative Normalcy

The FY 1993 General Appropriations Act of $8.5 billion represented an increase of 7% over the FY 1992 reduced appropriations and an increase of 2.8% over the initial FY 1992 appropriation. Revenue collections in the years since FY 1992 have grown by an average of more than 8% and have been sufficient to sustain annual appropriations. This suggests that Georgia quickly entered a period of sustained financial recovery and that the FY 1992 budget reductions were an isolated event. Because the FY 1992 revenue shortfall had a reasonably clear beginning and end, however, we have been afforded a rare opportunity to learn about cutback management strategies in state government.

REVIEW QUESTIONS

1. What fiscal conditions produce the need for cutback management? What is at stake in cutback management?
2. What governmentwide steps were taken in Georgia to bring projected spending into alignment with available resources?
3. Did Georgia agency managers resist or seek to accommodate impending budget reductions? Did they employ across-the-board or targeted budget cuts? What was the mix of personnel versus program reductions?
4. Can cutback management be used to achieve management improvement objectives?
5. To what extent was there evidence that agency budget officials used rational analysis in making cutback decisions?
6. What can you learn from this case about the relationship between fiscal management and organization behavior?

NOTES

1. The authors thank the budget officials of the state of Georgia who so generously gave their time and information to this study. The information reported here would not have been possible without their cooperation.
2. In the 1992 session, the Georgia General Assembly enacted new fees and fee increases related to driving in the state. Fees for drivers' licenses, annual tag fees, and motor vehicle title fees were increased. A new impact fee, based on a vehicle's value, was passed charging owners of cars brought into the state.
3. The term agency is used here in the generic sense to include all those executive branch entities that for budgetary purposes are accorded separate consideration. Budget officers from those listed below were interviewed for this study. Sixteen are designated as departments, and the remainder are designated as boards, commissions, offices, or systems. Two agencies that receive no direct state appropriations, the Georgia Finance and Investment Commission and the Public Employees Retirement System, were excluded from consideration. Only the department of law declined to participate in the study.

Administrative	Employee	Merit	Teacher retirement
services	retirement	Natural resources	Technical and adult
Agriculture	Forestry	Public safety	ed.
Banking and	GBI	Public service	Transportation
finance	Human resources	Regents	Veterans' services
Community	Industry and trade	Revenue	Workers'
affairs	Insurance	Secretary of state	compensation
Corrections	Labor	Soil and water	
Defense	Medical	Student finance	
Education	assistance		

4. A state superior court ruling of July 26, 1991, held that if the governor had based the furlough plan on a stated desire to produce efficiency in state government, the action probably would have been legal because the 1962 budget act allows the

governor to supervise and manage the OPB. Because the governor presented the plan as an effort to bring about a temporary budget cut before the special session of the general assembly, however, the action amounted to an infringement on the general assembly's authority to amend the appropriations act.

5. A handful of budget officers mentioned technological advancement resulting from the cutbacks experienced. Comments included

> Because of cuts, we have been pressed to advance our technological abilities.

> The cuts have required that we make some technological advances sooner than planned.

> Our staff reduction has been facilitated with an upgrade in technology. Major conversions for computers have been made.

Examples of agencies experiencing such advancement include corrections, which implemented perimeter electronic detection systems (PEDS) in a majority of facilities in an effort to do away with manned tower watches. Likewise, the forestry commission intensified the phasing out of fire tower personnel by shifting to airplane monitoring of forests. Both revenue and the secretary of state's office considered updating computers. Each budget officer noted that the use of technology over personnel would lead to greater efficiency of operations as well as dollar savings.

6. In the FY 1992 amended budget report presented to the Georgia General Assembly in August 1991, for reductions to budget unit B of the board of regents, the governor recommended reductions in force for the marine extension service of nine unclassified positions and for the cooperative extension service of 390 unclassified positions, for a total estimated full-year savings of approximately $14.3 million. While such a recommendation is indeed specific, the budget officer of the board of regents made no direct mention of it. He did note that regents makes up 12% of the total state budget yet served as 19% of the "solution" as a result of the August session. He added that "the institutions took a great hit because you can't cut K through 12 and you can't cut debt service. And, the Regents is not locked in by federal mandates and/or matching funds."

7. While the budget officers complied with the governor's initial call for 10% reductions, few generated the 5% contingency plan also requested. Most seemed to agree with one budget officer who stated, "concerning the five percent contingency plan, I thought it wouldn't go, so I didn't plan for it." Given the fiscal environment at the time, budget officers responded realistically to the governor's call for spending cuts. They exhibited the disbelief or denial that Levine calls the Tooth Fairy syndrome, however, when confronted with a request for additional cuts in the future.

8. Few budget officers conceived of taking advantage of the midyear adjustment or supplemental budget available in Georgia. In fact, some felt to do so would only result in a greater loss of resources due to the attendant scrutiny of their budget required of such a request.

REFERENCES

Brewer, G. D. (1978). Termination Hard choices—harder questions. *Public Administration Review*, *38*, 338–344.

Dexter, L. A. (1970). *Elite and Specialized Interviewing*. Evanston, IL: Northwestern University Press.

Druker, M. J. and Robinson, B. D. (1993). States' responses to budget shortfalls: Cutback management techniques. In *Handbook of Comparative Public Budgeting and Financial Management*, T. D. Lynch and L. L. Martin Ed. New York: Marcel Dekker. pp. 189–206

Glassberg, A. (1978). Organizational responses to municipal budget decreases. *Public Administration Review*, *38*, 325–332.

Grizzle, G. A. and Trogen, P. C. (1994). Cutback budgeting in Florida: Causes, approaches, and consequences. *Southeastern Political Review*, *22*, 503–523.

Hovey, H. A. (1981). Cutback management in state government. *State Government*, *54*, 82–86.

Jewell, M. E. (1982). The neglected world of state politics. *Journal of Politics*, *44*, 638–657.

Lauth, T. P. (1978). Zero-based budgeting in Georgia state government: Myth and reality. *Public Administration Review*, *38*, 420–430.

Lauth, T. P. with Rieck, S. C. (1979). Modifications in Georgia zero-base budgeting procedures: 1973–80. *Midwest Review of Public Administration*, *13*, 225–238.

Lauth, T. P. (1984). Methods of agency head selection and gubernatorial influence over agency appropriations. *Public Administration Quarterly*, *7*, 396–409.

Lauth, T. P. (1985). Performance evaluation in the Georgia budgetary process. *Public Budgeting and Finance*, *5*, 67–82.

Lauth, T. P. (1986). The executive budget in Georgia. *State and Local Government Review*, *17*, 56–64.

Lauth, T. P. (1987a). Exploring the budgetary base in Georgia. *Public Budgeting and Finance*, *7*, 72–87.

Lauth, T. P. (1987b). Budgeting and productivity in state government. *Public Productivity Review*, *41*, 21–32.

Lauth, T. P. (1988). Mid-year appropriations in Georgia: Allocating the surplus. *International Journal of Public Administration*, *11*, 531–550.

Lauth, T. P. (1990). The governor and the conference committee in Georgia. *Legislative Studies Quarterly*, *15*, 441–453.

Lauth, T. P. (1991). Georgia: Shared power and fiscal conservatives. In E. J. Clynch and T. P. Lauth (eds.), *Governors, Legislatures, and Budgets: Diversity Across the American States*, pp. 53–62. Westport, CT: Greenwood.

Levine, C. H. (1978). Organizational decline and cutback management. *Public Administration Review*, *38*, 316–325.

Levine, C. H. (1979). More on cutback management: Hard questions for hard times. *Public Administration Review*, *39*, 179–183.

Levine, C. H., Rubin, I. S., and Wolohojian, G. G. (1981a). *The Politics of Retrenchment: How Local Government Manage Fiscal Stress*. Beverly Hills, CA: Sage.

Levine, C. H., Rubin, I. S., and Wolohojian, G. G. (1981b). Resource scarcity and the reform model: The management of retrenchment in Cincinnati and Oakland. *Public Administration Review*, *41*, 619–628.

Lewis, C. W. and Logalbo, A. T. (1980). Cutback principles and practices: A checklist for managers. *Public Administration Review*, *40*, 184–188.

Lindblom, C. E. (1959). The science of muddling through. *Public Administration Review*, *19*, 79–88.

Lindblom, C. E. (1979). Still muddling, not yet through. *Public Administration Review*, *39*, 517–526.

Schick, A. (1971). *Budget Innovations in the States*. Washington, DC: Brookings Institution.

Schick, A. (1980). Budgetary adaptations to resource scarcity. In *Fiscal Stress and Public Policy*. C. H. Levine and I. Rubin ed. pp. 113–134. Beverly Hills, CA: Sage.

Rubin, I. S. (1982). *Running in the Red*. Albany, NY: State University of New York Press.

Rubin, I. S. (1985). *Shrinking the Federal Government*. New York: Longman.

Wildavsky, A. (1984). *The Politics of the Budgetary Process*. 4th ed. Boston: Little, Brown.

25

The Struggle for Better Budgets
The Curious Case of the Legislative Conference System in New York State

Robert W. Smith
Clemson University, Clemson, South Carolina, U.S.A.

The 2000–2001 fiscal year was the sixteenth consecutive year that New York State experienced a late state budget. What was even more disheartening than sixteen straight years of budgets approved after the official April 1 start date of the fiscal year was the expectation that the fourteenth year was to be the last year of tardy budgets. A new budget process was put in place during the 1998–1999 fiscal year and was adopted to put an end to chronically late budgets in New York.

This chapter examines New York's experience with a revamped budget process that many observers conclude is already a short-lived experiment. Early in 1997 both houses of the state legislature agreed to adopt a new approach to improve a tardy and cantankerous budget process. By concurrent resolution, the assembly and senate created a general conference committee and a subcommittee structure to reconcile differences between the houses to present a consensus budget back to the governor for final approval.

The use of conference committees in the budget process is not new and is utilized by the federal government and most state governments. The use of such a process in New York State, however, represented a major shift in the historical budget process, which involved closed door meetings between the three major political leaders of the state: the governor and the majority leaders of the senate (upper house) and the assembly (lower house). The move to a more open and participative budget process was intended to forge a consensus that would result in swifter passage of the state budget and mollify growing citizen discontent about budgeting in New York State.

This chapter relies on anecdotal information, news accounts, interviews, public documents, and relevant budget literature to examine the phenomenon of the conference committee in New York more as a lesson in politics than an exercise in budget reform. In particular, it summarizes the historical budget process in New York State, describes the financial and political problems with business as usual, explains the use of conference committees in government, describes the state's implementation of the conference system, and closes with some observations about the future of budgets in New York State. This chapter concludes that the use of the committee system in New York is a failure and that the "fix" is not addressing the major reason behind late state budgets—politics. The chapter also suggests an alternative approach to achieve a more timely, accountable, and democratic budget process for the citizens of New York in the twenty-first century.

LEGISLATIVE CONFERENCE SYSTEMS IN CONTEXT

The use of a conference committee process is not new to state legislatures or to Congress. The system for resolving difficult political issues in legislatures has been a consensus-building process in use for over 200 years. In fact, conference committees date back to 1789 and were used to resolve differences between bicameral state legislatures (Oleszek, 1978: 181). Conference committees are used not only for resolving differences on major substantive legislative issues, but also for reconciling appropriations or setting budgetary or fiscal parameters at both the state and federal levels.

Early congressional conference committees were clouded in obscurity because most of their meetings were held in secret. In the 1970s, congressional procedures were drastically reformed and the committee process was opened and records were made public (Lowi and Ginsberg, 1998: 186). If there is a hallmark of the conference committee it can be identified as the ability of a small number of conferees to resolve difficult political issues in the relative calm and orderly forum offered by the conference committee. Reaching consensus among nine to thirteen legislators is much less problematic than agreement between 535 often boisterous members of Congress.

A more implicit role for conference committees is their symbolic use as vehicles for broad-based participation. Being named as a conferee on an important piece of legislation is a coveted role in both Congress and state legislatures. An individual legislator "in" on the final negotiations presumably has a great deal of influence on what is included and not included in the legislation, hence the individual legislator is perceived to be an influential player in the public policy process. The inclusion of a variety of legislators in the conference committee also carries important symbolism, however. By presenting a broad-based conference committee, the legislative body itself is perceived to be inclusive and participatory in the consensus-building process. It is these two roles that legitimize the conference committee system as both practical and politically expedient.

What is not evidenced by the public at large is the power wielded by conference committees, the exclusivity of the process, and the oftentimes rigid process that guides the work of these committees. Selection of who participates in conference committees is largely a measure for the leadership of the majority party in each house in the legislature. Seniority in Congress and the statehouses has been, and continues to be, a criterion for selection; however, expertise in particular subject/policy areas is also important for selection as a conferee.

Bargaining, however, is the stuff of conference committees. Majority party leadership clearly determines the direction and work of the conference committee. Adherence to respective house positions is a very important factor in determining what agreements or amendments are acceptable or not. Moreover, conference committees are typically established under a set of procedural rules that determine the type and substance of amendments and even the approval process of the conference report, which provides the details of the final agreement.

Curiously, in New York State the conference committee system as a vehicle for compromise between both houses of the legislature did not exist prior to 1995. After passage of a permanent joint rule a conference committee was created to extend the speed limit on the New York State Thruway (New York State Assembly, 1997: 2). Differences over legislation are hammered out in New York the way they have been handled for centuries, the good old-fashioned way—three men in a room.

Typically, major legislation and budgets were agreed to as part of a three-way negotiation featuring the governor, the speaker of the assembly, and the senate majority leader; there was no need for conference committees. Party conferences took their place, and were the means for resolving differences. Deals were hammered out in this majority party forum, which had the votes to pass the bills in its own house of the legislature. Next, legislative leaders sat down with the governor to work out legislation or a budget acceptable to all parties. The agreement was then ratified in a party-line vote in both houses: "Both houses have committees, but they hardly serve as points of entry for the public or even rank and file members" (Gurwitt, 2000: 25). The New York experiment with conference budget committees therefore is truly historic, albeit wrought with problems.

THE NEW YORK BUDGET PROCESS IN BRIEF

New York State has a well-established executive budget process that features the chief executive of the state, the governor, presenting executive budget recommendations to the state legislature for approval. The governor is required by the constitution to seek and coordinate requests from agencies of the state government, develop a complete plan of proposed expenditures and revenues available to support them (balanced budget), and submit a budget to the legislature along with the appropriation bills and other legislation to carry out budgetary actions. Under state finance law, the governor is changed with managing the budget throughout the fiscal year (New York State, 1999: 548). The Division of the Budget (DOB) is the agency charged with developing the executive budget and implementing the budget for the balance of the fiscal year.

The state's fiscal year begins on April 1 and ends on March 31. While fiscal years vary from state to state, New York is only one of five states that have a fiscal year start other than July 1 (Axelrod, 1995: 24). The actual budget process is structured in stages and begins nine months earlier with agency budget preparation, formal requests, and DOB review. The next distinct stage in the process includes the period for gubernatorial review and executive budget decision making. The next stage involves the submission of the budget to the legislature for review and adoption. The final stage, budget implementation, occurs over the course of the fiscal year. The entire budget process takes approximately twenty-seven months, until the expiration of the state comptroller's (state's chief finance officer) authority to honor vouchers against the previous year's appropriations.

In order to understand the nature of budget reforms in New York, it is necessary to focus on the legislative review/adoption stage that involves extensive negotiation between both houses of the legislature and the governor. The legislative adoption stage is where problems and politics have arisen and delays occur. The executive submits the appropriation bills to the legislature's two main fiscal committees, the senate finance committee and the assembly ways and means committee, which analyze the executive proposals, hold hearings, and eventually enact the bills.

In a state well versed in partisan politics, however, the three main players in a budgetary context have been divided along partisan political lines, by upstate versus downstate dynamics, by urban versus rural differences, and by a host of other issues that have divided the political structure of the state over the years. For the past several years both the governor and the senate majority leader or the governor and assembly speaker have been from the same political party. The other party has controlled the other house of the legislature. Historically cantankerous three-way budget negotiations take place between these three leaders and their representatives. Ever since the adoption of the executive budget system in the state in the 1920s these three leadership positions have negotiated the state's budget (Kerker, 1984: 36). Each of the majority parties in the legislature strives to maximize funding for their programs and perks for their respective members. Often substantial gulfs exist between the parties, making budget agreements almost impossible. This legacy continues to the present day; Republican governor George Pataki, Republican senate majority leader Joe Bruno, and Democratic assembly speaker Sheldon Silver are the main players negotiating the current state budget.

PROBLEMS, PITFALLS, AND POLITICS

This exclusive and hierarchical budget system has been characterized as a process of three men in a room and is reminiscent of the backroom politics of Tammny Hall for which New York is so infamous (Ginsberg et al., 1999: 38). Indeed, backroom politics appears to be alive and well in the New York State budget process. Partisan-based budget negotiations have been the primary reason New York has run late state budgets in the past sixteen consecutive years and overall, the twenty-third out the past twenty-five years (Dao, 1997: C6). Many budget observers cite the size and complexity of the state budget as the reason for difficult negotiations. (The 2000–2001 state budget totaled some $77 billion.) Any cursory review of news accounts over the last two decades, however, reveals the real reason state budgets are chronically late. Partisan politics, petty bickering, and wrangling over funding levels that occur between legislative leaders and the governor are synonymous with late state budgets.

An obvious question to ask, however, is So what? If New York State experienced late state budgets for the last quarter century, what impact if any has this had on the state functioning as one of the world's largest economies? The answer on the surface is that the state continues to operate, bills are paid, services are provided, taxes are collected, and government seems to function. Below the surface, however, the real answer is that late state budgets cost the state and its citizens millions of dollars. New York State adds more than $60 million annually in interest costs attributable to the delay, adding to its significant debt load (Breslin, 1997: B4). The implications for public finance are clear, but so are the ramifications for accountability of the budget process to citizens in a democracy. The end product of any public budget in a constitutional democracy is a budget responsible to the people.

With estimated annual costs in the millions, late state budgets have financial impacts resulting from borrowing to fund transfer payments, local grants-in-aid, revenue sharing, and a variety of local government and service providers. If the budget process is delayed, aid payments must still be provided to these entities. Moreover, local governments must borrow to cover operating expenses until state aid is approved.

Over the years New York State has gotten very good at dealing with late state budgets by a variety of fiscal maneuvering and budgetary procedures. The most notable is the passage of emergency appropriations covering state operations and local aid portions of the budget for a specified period of time. The latest twist has been the use of so-called two-week extenders during the 1999–2000 budget negotiations (Precious, June 21, 1999: A6). It was thought that a two-week time frame during which legislators would have to return to the state capitol of Albany for a vote would prompt lawmakers to a hastier resolution. This allows for government to function even though a budget is still not in place.

Even with these accommodations, however, the state's fiscal watchdog, comptroller Carl McCall (a Democrat), predicted that during the 1999–2000 fiscal year, school districts would face an "unprecedented problem" because school districts are heavily dependent upon state aid. They would have to purposely underestimate how much state aid they will be receiving (Precious, July 13, 1999: B1). Moreover, the state's inability to deal with the budget problems has resulted in the state receiving one of the lowest credit ratings over the years from the major municipal ratings services, such as Standard and Poor's and Moody's (Axelrod, 1995: 124).

Late budgets are having an impact on taxpayers in the form of increased costs and uncertainty of funding streams, but has this outcry led to widespread citizen protests? Surprisingly, the perennially late state budget has never manifested itself into widespread opposition in terms of political fallout. A recent poll commissioned to look at a number of statewide issues, however, revealed that New Yorkers might have finally had enough of the late state budgets. In a 1999 Siena College poll, 68% of the respondents believed that passage of a timely state budget was very important, while another 26% felt it was somewhat important (Odato, August 13, 1999: B2). Overall, approval ratings for the governor and legislators fell to 50 and 49%, respectively. This displeasure with the process is not confined to New York. In California, the approval of budgets has gone well beyond the constitutionally provided deadline date of June 30. A poll conducted in 1997 revealed that 83% of those surveyed believed the budget delay caused serious problems for the state (Marelius, 1997: A6).

Politically speaking, voters rarely hold legislators or governors responsible for late state budgets. In 1996, when the budget was enacted 104 days late, all but three of the more than 145 incumbents who sought re-election won their races; "the average voter doesn't make the late State budget an issue," said state comptroller Carl McCall, and "The public has simply come to accept this" (Hammond, 1999: A1).

As a response to the growing public discontent over state budget delays, the legislature was prompted to action in 1997. Threatened by a legacy of budget impasses that might take its toll in upcoming elections and widespread discontent of rank and file members of the legislature (upset because they were relegated as bystanders to three-men-in-a-room negotiations), a new budget process was adopted. The new process was similar to the conference committee concept used by the federal government and state governments. It was thought this process would open participation and result in more timely budgets for New York State.

ADOPTING THE CONFERENCE COMMITTEE CONCEPT

With the 1996 and 1997 state budgets more than 100 days late, eyes turned toward a process in use by the federal government. It was costing New York State millions of dollars annually in interest costs, all attributable to the budget delays (Breslin, 1997: B4). The senate majority leadership turned to a conference committee process as a possible solution to the protracted stalemate and delay.

The assembly majority leadership also called for a joint assembly/senate conference committee to spur stalled budget negotiations. They noted that over the previous two years conference committees had proven to be valuable tools for the senate and assembly to resolve a handful of issues. In 1995, a conference committee was utilized to extend the 65 mph speed limit on the state's thruway. Another conference committee was used in the 1996 session to compromise on a series of issues: providing minimum maternity care and coverage, giving small city school districts the power to vote on school budgets, and creating a pesticides registry. Again in 1997, a conference committee featured representatives of the senate and the assembly negotiating low-cost power alternatives for business development in New York (New York State Assembly, 1997: 2). An attractive feature of the conference committee process was the provision for public input. This public input and scrutiny would finally be included in what historically were closed-door state budget negotiations.

The conference committee approach was endorsed by Democratic state comptroller Carl McCall, who urged lawmakers "to begin an open dialogue on policy issues that are preventing budget enactment" (Silver, 1999: 1). Newspapers and interest groups from across the state applauded the maneuver. Those officially supporting the effort were the League of Women Voters, the *Albany Times Union*, the *Daily Gazette*, the *Syracuse Herald Journal*, *Newsday*, and the Business Council of New York (Hammond, 1999: A1).

What was the conference committee structure to look like? Conference committees were envisioned as a framework for reconciling differences between two very different spending bills in the assembly and the senate. In many respects, New York was finally catching up with the rest of the country. In fact, the only states not to use conference committees for budget negotiations are Delaware, Nebraska, and Oregon (New York State Assembly, 1997: 2).

Indeed, it was the federal conference committee model that served as the basis for New York's foray into conference committees for budget resolution. In February of each year the president submits to Congress a budget for the fiscal year beginning on October 1. Congressional action on the president's budget can be thought of as a series of distinct actions. Among these actions are the passage of budget resolutions, annual appropriations, authorizing legislation, and reconciliation bills. These actions are linked together through the conference committee process, which resolves differences between the House of Representatives and the U.S. Senate, yet the concept of a conference committee has a much broader application as a congressional mechanism to resolve differences between the House and Senate on a variety of bills. The leadership of both houses determines the composition of the conference committees, and the size of the committee may vary. Typically conference committees include the relevant standing committee chair and ranking minority member (Longley and Oleszek, 1989).

From an operational perspective, language agreed to in both bills presented for conference negotiation cannot be deleted or changed. Although attention is meant to be focused on major spending differences in bills, negotiations can involve all aspects of the legislation. Committee proceedings are open to the public unless closed by a vote of the entire House. At the conclusion of the process, two reports are issued. One is a conference report containing actual bill language and the other report is a statement explaining the changes. The House and the Senate then vote on conference reports.

This framework is mirrored in the states that have adopted the process. Conference committees are established for resolution of budget differences, and typically have members appointed from the fiscal committees of each house. In many states membership is restricted to a defined number of conferees. Most states use a small number of committee members, however (e.g., California has anywhere from three to six members from each house). The numbers of conference committees are often established based on the number of appropriations bills. In states such as Michigan there are a number of appropriation bills, so each bill must have a conference to reconcile differences. In states such as Wisconsin or South Carolina there is one appropriation bill, which requires only one conference committee. In most instances, majority approval of the conference committee report is usually required before the report can be acted upon by the full legislature. The conference report can take the form of a formal report similar to the federal model or merely reflect amendments to the original appropriations bills. The use of conference committees is both consistent and widespread across state government (Straayer, 1996: 4–22).

In their definitive study of conference committees in Congress, Longley and Oleszek (1989) thoroughly examined the political, organizational, and procedural changes that have occurred over the years and highlight the motivations and incentives that drive conferees in what they describe as "bicameral politics." In addition, it has been noted that the conference committee that wrote the final language of the historic 1986 tax overhaul, the so-called conference committee of two (Senate finance chairman Bob Packwood and House ways and means chair Dan Rostenkowski), was "among the most inaccessible, exclusive parts of the legislative process" (Hook, 1991: 210), hence while the conference committee process holds hope for forging consensus and facilitating openness of the budgetary process, for New York with its tradition of closed and exclusive budget negotiations, the fit was problematic from the start with no guarantees for openness or accountability. The New York State legislature nonetheless moved aggressively to embrace the new mechanism.

THE NEW YORK STATE BUDGET CONFERENCE COMMITTEE

During 1998 the New York State legislature created a joint conference committee to resolve differences between appropriations bills passed by each house of the legislature. That resolution helped pave the way for the legislature to negotiate and pass the 1998–1999 budget. The conference committee consisted of five members from each house. Meetings were open to the public. The final product of committee deliberations was in the form of a written report setting forth the recommendations of the committee and included specific bill language that would implement the recommendations. The report had to be approved by a majority vote of each house's delegation on the committee (New York State Legislature, 1997).

Governor Pataki released his proposed budget for the 1998–1999 fiscal year on January 20, 1998. The assembly started the process of passing appropriations bills on March 16. The senate completed the passage of its budget bills on March 24, 1998. To resolve differences between both sets of budget bills, a general budget conference committee was created. The conference committee in turn established nine budget subcommittees. These subcommittees began deliberating on March 31 (one day before the end of the fiscal year) and concluded their work on April 9. The subcommittees were created to focus on budget provisions in such substantive functional areas as education and economic development. On April 8, both houses of the legislature began passing conference-produced budget bills, and on April 14 the budget was enacted (Precious, June 21, 1999: A6).

The general conference committee established spending targets for each of the sub-committees and was responsible for the final reconciliation with the financial plan. The general committee consisted of ten members (five from the senate and five from the assembly). Subcommittees were created in the areas of higher education, taxes and economic development, health, mental health, transportation, environment and housing, public protection, human services, education, and general government and local assistance (Kolbert, 1998: B1). Appointments to the subcommittees were based on a seniority system. For the 1998–1999 fiscal year the revised legislative budget process tackled an executive budget proposal of more than $71 billion. The general conference committee and its nine subcommittees involved some ninety legislators who were previously cut out of the negotiating process. An agreement was reached on April 14, just fourteen days beyond the budget deadline. The process seemed to have achieved more broad-based participation and produced a timelier budget.

THE CONFERENCE COMMITTEE THAT WASN'T?

Despite a process that was more inclusive and more timely, the state budget for 1998–1999 was far from concluded. The legislative stage of the budget concluded, but the budget still had to go back to the governor for final approval. Governor Pataki vetoed in excess of $1.6 billion in certain line-item appropriations from the legislature's approved budget (Hammond, 1999: A1). With a backdrop of political charges, the governor maintained that the budget agreed to by the legislature was dangerously out of balance and would threaten the progress made in the early years of his administration. It had been reported that many of the cuts occurred in programs supported primarily by assembly Democrats. His veto angered members of both the senate and the assembly and cast a shadow over the historic agreement and process.

With the introduction of the executive budget in January of 1999, an environment of frustration and negativity enveloped the budget process for the 1999–2000 fiscal year. Because of the threat of yet another gubernatorial veto, the assembly Democrats postponed participating in the conference process until the governor promised not to veto the agreed-to legislative budget. Moreover, the process was stalled as early as March 1999 because the governor and legislative leaders could not agree on the amount of revenue that would be available to the state going into the budget year. The governor balked in July of 1999, agreeing to resubmit the approved legislative budget under his sponsorship—which would prevent his veto of the proposal. Under this makeshift arrangement, hastily-called-for and disorganized conferences were convened to consider the proposals. The budget was finally adopted on August 7, leading to the fifteenth consecutive year of late state budgets. Indeed, the term the conference committee that wasn't is a more accurate descriptor for the 1999–2000 budget, since the bulk of the details had already been worked out in traditional fashion between the governor and two legislative leaders well in advance (Precious, June 21, 1999: A6). Business as usual prevailed despite the existence of a conference committee process.

Even with the improved conference committee process in predictable fashion the 2000–2001 budget was late again (Odato, May 3, 2000: A1). Prospects for timely passage of the 2001–2002 budget are just as dismal. Sources in the DOB report that the conference system will likely be used again in a similar fashion for the upcoming fiscal year (Anonymous Interview, 2000), yet in November 1999, senate majority leader Joe Bruno and assembly speaker Sheldon Silver announced plans for budget reforms that would extend beyond the dysfunctional conference committee concept.

NEXT STEPS FOR THE BUDGET?

The failure of the conference committee process in New York State was echoed in sentiments expressed at the close of the 1999–2000 budget battle. The majority leader described the budget process as "exasperating. It is frustrating. It is unconscionable that we can't fix it" (Hammond, 1999: A1).

The prospects for on-time passage of the 2001–2002 state budget are gloomy. Over the years, the state has considered a number of proposals to encourage the passage of timely state budgets. One of the latest gimmicks was tied to a legislative pay increase for state legislators agreed to in December of 1998. In exchange for the pay increase, legislators agreed that their salaries would be withheld and placed in a non-interest-bearing escrow account until a state budget was approved (Hernandez, 1999: B5). This plan was in effect for the 1999–2000 fiscal year. That budget year witnessed state lawmakers go unpaid until August when an agreement was finally reached. This was the first provision of its kind in the nation. A number of Democratic legislators sued on the grounds the governor could not coerce legislators into agreeing to a state budget. In a six-to-one ruling the state court of appeals (the state's highest court) ruled that the agreement was neither coercive nor unconstitutional. Nonetheless, the legislative pay penalty did nothing to improve the timeliness of a budget (Hernandez, 1999: B5).

Other legislative proposals have emerged over the years, including proposals for an alternative budget to be enacted if agreement is not reached, automatic resignations of legislative leaders if the budget is not passed on time, and a referendum on a state budget that is automatically placed on the ballot if the budget is not enacted on time (Hammond, 1999: 1). Although these proposals were greeted with skepticism and never reached the legislature's floor for a vote, the proposals reflect the frustration of many lawmakers with the process.

Because late state budgets continue even after the conference committee reforms, legislative leaders felt compelled to offer another series of proposals to address the problem. The senate majority led the charge by proposing comprehensive reform legislation aimed at addressing fiscal stability and accountability. The plan calls for

1. A November 15 start to negotiations between the legislature and the governor on revenue and expenditure limits
2. Early budget submission date for the governor's executive budget of January 15
3. Consensus revenue forecasting between the legislature and the governor by March 1 of each year
4. A general conference committee process that would commence on March 16
5. A change in date of the fiscal year from April 1 to May 1 to accommodate the negotiating phase
6. Provision of a default budget so if the budget were not in place by May 1 the budget in place for the current fiscal year would be automatically adopted
7. Other structural reforms (e.g., a reserve fund, multiyear fiscal impact statements) (Bruno, 1999)

402   Smith

The assembly advanced a plan of its own:

1. Opening state agency budget requests to the public.
2. Beginning the negotiations and revenue estimation process on November 15.
3. Providing a multiyear financial plan over four years.
4. Beginning the legislative hearing process by February 15 (at least one to two months early).
5. Having consensus process decide receipts disbursements and reserves. (The state comptroller would intercede if no agreement were reached.)
6. Adopting a congressional model calling for legislative resolutions and a formal conference committee process.
7. Changing the start of the fiscal year to June 1.
8. Providing for a contingency budget to be put into effect by May 15 if agreement on a budget is not reached. (The current budget would be adopted.)
9. Providing for multiple appropriation bills after the current-year budget is enacted.
10. Providing for public disclosure, plain language provisions, onl2ine access to budget documents, and inclusion of performance measures.
11. Establishing a budget reform task force to look at constitutional or statutory changes to improve the budget process (Silver, 1999).

Not to be outdone, Governor Pataki introduced a program bill in 2000 in relation to legislative action on the budget (Governor's Program Bill, S. 12215-02-0). The bill requires.

1. A Consensus revenue forecasting conference and issuance of a joint report on March 10 of each year
2. The legislature place the financial plan impact report on members' desks prior to voting on budget bills
3. Changes in the use of cash surplus, guidance on enactment of revenue bills, and stipulations on dates for the above-proposed changes (Governors' Program Bill, 2000 memorandum)

The prospects for passage of these or elements of the proposals by both houses of the legislature are unlikely. It is clear that the reality of an institutional budget problem has led to some of the most dramatic actions and proposals for reform in recent history, and notwithstanding the 2000–2001 budget, the prospects for meaningful reform may have been heightened by the realization that for the last six years New York State lawmakers have produced the five latest state budgets in the state's history—the last two the latest by any state since the Great Depression (Perez-Pena, 2000: B6).

There is little reason to expect that the state legislature or governor will make any dramatic changes to the process, however, particularly in view of the continuing partisan legal battle between the Republican governor and the Democratic assembly speaker. The governor and speaker are still fighting over the $1.6 million in gubernatorial vetoes from 1998–1999. The appellate division of the New York court system dismissed the speaker's lawsuit in June of 2000. In a three-to-two vote the court stated it did not want to get into the middle of a political fight (Odato, July 25, 2000: A1). The speaker plans to appeal, hence the conference committee process will likely continue as a paper mechanism that has resulted in very little change to the historically late and costly state budget process in New York.

SUMMARY AND CONCLUSION

The purpose of this chapter was not to compare the conference committee concept between New York and other states or the federal government. This chapter did not offer an empirical treatment of the utility of conference committees for public budgeting; neither did it present a treatise on the budget process in New York. (Each of these dimensions would be fruitful areas for future research, however.) Instead, this case study attempted to focus on the politics of budgeting as the perennial enemy of on-time budgets and fiscal responsibility in New York State. Anecdotal evidence assembled in this chapter confirms that the budgetary process is indeed part and parcel of the political process. The focus of budget reforms in New York State was more on the mechanics of the budget approval process than on the political motivations behind budget agreements. The conference committee process attempted to bring openness and accountability to the process while ignoring the political basis behind the allocation decisions of public resources. The expectations were that this conference process would lead to timely state budgets. It is clear that openness and inclusiveness do not lead to better, timely, or accountable budgets, however.

The significant reforms in the budget process did not lead to any meaningful changes precisely because they ignored the fundamental role of politics in budgeting. This occurred despite the substantial research that exists in the area of political influences on the budgetary process [e.g., by Wildavsky (1988) and Fenno (1966) at the federal level and Gosling (1992) at the state and local levels]. Any meaningful reforms must therefore examine, accommodate, or change the wrangling and gamesmanship that occurs in budgetary politics.

The only way to produce better budgets is to produce better politics and better politicians. Thought of in this light, the struggle to produce better budgets can be thought of as another form of the struggle to help preserve democracy. Both struggles will be successful only when politicians are held responsible for policies and accountable to citizens. This lack of accountability in the 2000–2001 budget is best expressed in a *New York Times* editorial that stated "This entire budget package suffers from the secret way it was developed" (Editorial, 2000). There are no straightforward solutions, but by ignoring the reality that budgeting is a political process the struggle for better budgets will be akin to the search for the Holy Grail in the Empire State. The fix for budgetary responsibility, openness, timeliness, and accountability in New York lies in the recognition that in its purest form budgeting involves the allocation of public resources as articulated by the citizens of the government. Budgets are the stuff that constitutes the very essence of democracy. Indeed, for budget reform to succeed in New York State it must embrace and accommodate this political dimension. The budget battle then becomes how to reform the political decision-making process, not the mechanics and trappings of a contrived budgetary process. For democracy in the twenty-first century it is the politics of budgeting that must be reformed, not the budgeting subject to politics.

REVIEW QUESTIONS

1. Discuss the obstacles presented by a legislative budget conference committee system from the viewpoint of the governor, assembly majority leader, and senate majority leader. How might you overcome those obstacles?

2. If you were governor, what role, if any, should you play on budget conference committees?
3. Provide a critique of the legislative budget conference system as an individual state legislator.
4. Will rationality ever replace politics in budgetary decisions? How can rationality be introduced into the budgetary decision process?
5. Is democracy best served by an inclusive decision-making system, such as the mechanism offered by the legislative budget conference committees?
6. Whose decision is "final" in the budget conference system?
7. Compare New York's experience with similar mechanisms or processes in your home state.
8. Should legislators be penalized for their inability to pass on-time budgets? For other budgetary failures?
9. Why should the governor, the courts, or other interest groups have *any* say in the legislature's control of the public purse?
10. Design a legislative budget conference system using elements of the reform proposals presented in the chapter and adopting other reforms you think make sense.

REFERENCES

Anonymous interview. (Jan. 10, 2000). New York State Division of the Budget.

Axelrod, D. (1995). *Budgeting for Modern Government*. New York: St. Martin's.

Breslin, N. (Aug. 3, 1997). Blame the process for late state budget, editorial. *Albany Times Union*, p. B4.

Bruno, J. (Dec. 20, 1999). Senator Bruno announces budget reform plan. press release. Albany, NY.

Dao, J. (March 31, 1997). Budget lateness is a form of realism. *New York Times*, p. C6.

Editorial. (April 20, 2000). *New York Times*.

Fenno, R. F. (1966). *The Power of the Purse*. Boston: Little, Brown.

Ginsberg, B., Lowi, T., and Weir, M. (1999). *We the People*. New York: Norton.

Gosling, J. L. (1992). *Budgetary Politics in American Governments*. New York: Longman.

Gurwitt, R. (2000). Yesterday's legislature. *Governing*, *14*, 26–29.

Hammond, W. F. (Aug. 8, 1999). Little hope of change. *Sunday Gazette*, p. A1.

Hernandez, R. (Oct. 15, 1999). Court backs law docking legislators. *New York Times*, p. B5.

Hook, J. (1991). CQ roundtable: The modern Congress' smoke-filled room. *Congressional Quarterly Weekly Report*, *49*(3), 210.

Kerker, R. (1984). *The History of the Executive Budget in New York State*. Albany, NY: New York State Division of the Budget.

Kolbert, E. (March 26, 1998). Budget panel offers touch of the comical. *New York Times*, p. B1.

Longley, L. D. and Oleszek, W. J. (1989). *Bicameral Politics: Conference Committees in Congress*. New Haven, CT: Yale University Press.

Lowi, T. J. and Ginsberg, B. (1998). *American Government: Freedom and Power*. New York: Norton.

Marelius, J. (Aug. 26, 1997). Californians are fed up with late state budget, poll shows. *San Diego Union-Tribune*, p. A6.

New York State Assembly. (1997). *Conference Committees on the Budget*. Albany, NY, pp. 2–5.

New York State. (1999). *Executive Budget 1999–2000*. Albany, NY, p. 543–577.

New York State. (2000). *Governor's Program Bill S. 12215-02-0*. Albany, NY.

New York State. (2000b). *Governor's Program Bill 2000 Memorandum*. Albany, NY.

New York State Legislature. (1997). Joint rule II. *Permanent Joint Rules of the Senate and the Assembly*. Albany, NY.

Odato, J. M. (Aug. 13, 1999). Late state budget shakes up job ratings. *Albany Times Union*, p. B2.

Odato, J. M. (May 3, 2000). Spending plan on the way. *Albany Times Union*, p. A1.

Odato, J. M. (July 25, 2000). Silver likely to appeal dismissal of lawsuit. *Albany Times Union*, p. A1.

Oleszek, W. J. (1978). *Congressional Procedures and the Public Policy Process*. Washington, DC: Congressional Quarterly Press.

Perez-Pena, R. (Jan. 12, 2000). Their best behavior. *New York Times*, p. B6.

Precious, T. (June 21, 1999). Critics call Pataki's and Silver's political jaunts inappropriate amid late state budget. *Buffalo News*, p. A6.

Precious, T. (July 13, 1999). Late state budget posing risk of hikes in school taxes. *The Buffalo News*, July 13 p. B1.

Silver, S. (Nov. 3, 1999). *Assembly leadership advances 11-point budget reform proposal*. (press release). Albany, NY.

Straayer, J. A. (1996). How prevalent are state legislative conference committees? *Comparative State Politics*, *17* (April), 4–17.

Wildavsky, A. (1988). *The New Politics of the Budgetary Process*. Glenview, IL: Scott, Foresman.

26

Cash Basis Financial Reporting for Local Government
A Comparison with GAAP

Patti A. Mills
Indiana State University, Terre Haute, Indiana, U.S.A.

Jennie L. Mitchell
*Saint Mary-of-the-Woods College, Saint Mary-of-the-Woods, Indiana,
U.S.A.*

Accounting and financial reporting have become an integral part of local governmen[t]
make this reporting more relevant and reliable, an increasing number of states are requ[ir]
that local units follow the reporting standards established by the Governmental Accoun[ting]
Standards Board (GASB) in preparing financial statements (Ingram and Robbins, 198[7]
Notwithstanding these efforts, there are still wide variations in the accounting princip[les]
or standards used for financial reporting at the local government level. Studies indic[ate]
that the rate of noncompliance with accounting principles generally accepted as appropri[ate]
by the accounting profession is higher in the public sector than in the private sector (Bailey,
1993).

This lack of compliance with generally accepted accounting principles (GAAP) is
likely to continue. Unlike in the private sector, the Securities and Exchange Commission
has no authority to mandate standards for local government reporting, nor can it sanction
public accounting firms associated with non-GAAP financial statements of a government
entity. Moreover, the courts have yet to resolve whether a third party has the right to sue
a state or local government based on errors or omissions in financial statements (Bailey,

---

* The GASB is a private sector organization responsible for developing governmental accounting concepts and
standards. It is funded by the Financial Accounting Foundation, which also supports the Financial Accounting
Standards Board (FASB). Since its founding in 1984, the GASB has been the chief source of generally accepted
accounting principles (GAAP) for state and local government units. GASB statement no. 1, "Authoritative
Status of NCGA Pronouncements and AICPA Industry Audit Guides," issued in July 1984, established certain
previously published pronouncements as the basis for GAAP. These included "Pronouncements and Interpretations of the National Council on Governmental Accounting," the industry audit guide *Audits of State and Local
Government Units*; published by the American Institute of Certified Public Accountants (AICPA), and AICPA
statements of position on governmental accounting. Thus far, the GASB has issued twenty-three statements
of governmental accounting standards.

1993). In light of these factors, many states and localities have been unwilling to devote the resources necessary to produce GAAP basis financial information, or to follow GAAP in all aspects of its financial reporting.*

The most common exception to GAAP basis financial statements is cash basis reporting. When strictly applied as a comprehensive basis of accounting, cash basis reporting accounts only for cash receipts and disbursements (i.e., revenues are recognized or recorded as cash is received and expenditures are recognized as cash is disbursed) Accordingly, the activity statement summarizes receipts and disbursements for the period. In contrast, GAAP prescribes the modified accrual basis for recording governmental revenues and expenditures. Under modified accrual, which is a combination of both cash and accrual basis concepts, revenues are recognized when they are susceptible to accrual (i.e., when they are both measurable and available to finance current expenditures). Expenditures are recognized when they are incurred, since they are usually measurable when the liability arises.

Although the GASB and other authoritative bodies do not consider the cash basis, or any non-GAAP basis, appropriate for reporting by state and local governments, the conceptual simplicity of the cash basis has made it a popular choice for many local units, especially in states that have not mandated GAAP basis reporting. Another major factor promoting cash basis reporting are local government accounting systems. During the fiscal year, most local units account for revenues and expenditures—and may also prepare their budgets—on a cash basis. They may also be required by law to prepare special purpose non-GAAP financial statements, schedules, and reports during the year or at year end. Under these circumstances, it is simply easier and less costly to prepare cash basis statements rather than convert to GAAP for financial reporting purposes.

The purpose of this chapter is twofold: to serve as a general introduction to cash basis financial reporting, which has hitherto received little attention in the literature; and to compare this method with GAAP basis financial reporting. To this end, we describe cash basis financial reporting as it is practiced in a small city in Indiana, the city of Harriss;[†] address the relation of cash basis financial statements to an operating budget; and explain differences from GAAP. A small municipality in Indiana was chosen because the state is one of several in the United States in which cash basis financial reporting is widely used at the local government level.

Please note that there are no generally accepted standards established for cash basis financial reporting. Consequently, the accounting principles used and the format of financial statements will vary across local governments. The city of Harris illustrates one approach. Another point to remember is that even though a unit departs from the modified accrual basis of accounting, it may still adhere to other aspects of GAAP for financial reporting purposes. The city of Harris is an example of this practice.

THE REPORTING ENTITY

Regardless of the comprehensive basis of accounting, the scope or extent of the entity to be reported on must be defined. In practice, this can be a daunting task, because of the

---

* In 1987, there were at least thirteen states that did not require GAAP basis financial reporting for one or more types of local government. For a listing, see Ingram and Robbins (1987); 14

[†] The name of the municipality used in this case is fictional. The cash basis financial statements are taken from the annual report of an actual city in Indiana.

many activities, joint ventures, board, and other bodies often associated with government operations. Fortunately, GAAP (Governmental Accounting Standards Board, 1991 GASB 14) provides criteria for determining which organizations and component units make up the reporting entity. According to GASB-14, the financial reporting entity consists of "(a) the primary government, (b) organizations for which the primary government is financially accountable, and (c) other organizations for which the nature and significance of their relationship are such that exclusion would cause the reporting entity's financial statements to be misleading or incomplete." The "nucleus" of the financial reporting entity is the primary government. States, general purpose local governments, and certain special-purpose governments, such as school or park districts, are primary governments.

Although component units are considered part of the reporting entity, GASB-14 requires that financial information for such units be presented in a separate column on the combined financial statements of the reporting entity. Financial information of a component unit can be "blended" with that of the primary government if the unit is in substance part of the primary government. The purpose of this "discrete presentation" is to enable financial statement users to distinguish information concerning the primary government from that of the component units.

In the present case, the city's financial statements include all municipal operations, but exclude the Harris Housing Authority and the Harris Public Library. These organizations were excluded from the reporting entity because they are funded independently from the city, are separate legal entities, and are governed by their own boards. In addition, the city has no influence over their daily operations or budgets. In this example, the reporting entity consists only of the primary government, therefore there is no discrete presentation of component units in the financial statements.

FUND STRUCTURE

Where cash basis accounting is employed, it is still possible, and in many jurisdictions required, to use funds to report on the entity's financial position, in this case regarding cash and investments and results of operations. According to GAAP (National Council on Governmental Accounting Statement 1 [NCGA-1], "Governmental Accounting and Financial Reporting Principles"), a fund is a separate accounting entity with its own set of accounts, which is segregated in order to ensure that certain government functions and activities are performed and accounted for. Indeed, financial statements may be prepared for each fund as well as for the government unit as a whole. There are three categories of funds—governmental, proprietary, and fiduciary—each of which is divided into fund types. The categories and types of funds are explained below.

> *Governmental funds.* Governmental funds are used to account for the collection and disbursement of resources that support a unit's general activities. These include general government operations (general fund); specific mandated activities (special revenue funds); acquisition or construction of major capital facilities (capital projects funds); and servicing of general long-term debt principal and interest (debt service funds).
> *Proprietary funds.* There are two types of proprietary funds, enterprise funds and internal service funds. Enterprise funds are used to account for activities operated and financed as private sector enterprises, where the goods or services are provided

to the general public on a user charge basis. Internal service funds account for goods and services provided by one department or agency to other departments or agencies within the governmental unit.

Fiduciary funds. Fiduciary funds are used to account for resources held on behalf of outside parties, other governmental units, or other funds within the same unit. Expendable trust funds, nonexpendable trust funds, pension trust funds, and agency funds are types of fiduciary funds.

GAAP basis fund accounting systems also include two other accounting entities, the general fixed assets account group and the general long-term debt account group. These entities are not funds but accounts, and are used to record long-lived fixed assets and long-term debt, respectively. In a cash basis fund accounting system, the two account groups may be omitted and information concerning long-lived fixed assets and long-term debt is not reflected on the financial statements. In the annual report of the city of Harris, this information is included in the notes to the financial statements rather than incorporated in the statements.

The kind of structure described above is reflected in the city's fund accounting system, which has the following fund categories, fund types, and funds:

Governmental funds
   General fund
   Special revenue funds
      Highway
      Local road and street
      Cemetery
      Accident reports training
      Police firearms training
      Department of redevelopment
      Economic development commission
      Park and recreation
      Community development
      Swimming pool
      George Craig Park
      Park and recreation nonreverting
   Debt service funds
      Redevelopment bonds
      Judgment loan I
      Judgment loan II
      Obligation loan—municipal garage construction
   Capital project fund
Proprietary funds
   Enterprise funds
      Water utility
      Sewage utility
      Golf course
      Sanitation
Fiduciary funds
   Trust funds
      Pension trust funds

Police pension
Firefighters pension
Nonexpendable trust fund
Cemetery
Agency fund

FINANCIAL STATEMENTS

GAAP Basis Reporting

GAAP (National Council on Governmental Accounting Statement 1, "Governmental Accounting and Financial Reporting Principles)* prescribes the content of the comprehensive annual financial report (CAFR) required of each governmental reporting entity. At the minimum, the CAFR should contain an introductory section, consisting of title page, table of contents, letter of transmittal, and any other introductory materials; a financial section, made up of the auditor's report; general purpose financial statements for the government unit as a whole (combined statements); combining statements, or financial statements for each fund type, and any individual fund and account group statements; and a statistical tables section. For the most part, the CAFR of the city of Harris conforms to these requirements. It differs markedly from GAAP, however, in the form and content of the financial statements.

The basic statements for GAAP basis financial reporting, called the general purpose financial statements (GPFS), include the following:

Combined balance sheet—All fund types and account groups
Combined statement of revenues, expenditures, and changes in fund balances—All governmental fund types
Combined statement of revenues, expenditures, changes in fund balances—budget and actual—general and special revenue funds
Combined statement of revenues, expenses, and changes in retained earnings (or equity)—All proprietary fund types
Combined statement of cash flows—All proprietary fund types

The combined statements serve as an overview and show cumulative information for each fund type. The combined statements are supported by combining statements, which are prepared for each fund type and provide information for the component funds within each class.

The city of Harris reports on a non-GAAP basis and accordingly has not compiled the above statements. For comparative purposes, we have created the principal GAAP basis statement, a "combined balance sheet—all fund types and account groups" for the city of Harris. (See Table 1.) Note that this statement incorporates general fixed assets and general long-term debt, information that is confined to the notes in the city's cash basis reports.

---

* The National Council on Governmental Accounting (NCGA) was established in 1974 by the Municipal Finance Officers Association to develop accounting standards for state and local governments. The NCGA was succeeded in 1984 by the GASB, which adopted NCGA statements as continuing in force until superseded.

Table 1 City of Harris Combined Balance Sheet All Fund Types and Account Groups (December 31, 1993)

	Government fund types				Proprietary fund types	Fiduciary fund types		Account groups		Totals (memorandum only)
	General	Special revenue	Debt service	Capital projects	Enterprise	Trust funds	Agency funds	General fixed assets	General long-term debt	December 31,1993
Assets										
Cash and investments	(161,921)	34,222	104,150	54,219	214,152	134,810	20,936			400,568
Accounts receivable					178,982					178,982
Interest receivable			638		852					1,490
Taxes receivable	7,212	3,331	2,566			2,223				15,332
Due from federal government	3,250	1,184								4,434
Due from other funds	16,315									16,315
Inventories					12,680					12,680
Prepaid expenses and deposits					23,445					23,445
Property, plant and equipment										0
utility property, at cost less accumulated depreciation					583,500					583,500
General fixed assets										0
Land								110,195		110,195
Building								316,134		316,134
Improvements other than buildings										0
Machinery and equipment								389,991		389,991
Assets under capital lease								437,120		437,120
Amount available in debt service funds									104,150	104,150
Amount to be provided for general long-term debt									6,303,351	6,303,351
Total Assets	(135,144)	38,737	107,354	54,219	1,013,611	137,033	20,936	1,253,440	6,407,501	8,897,687

Liabilities										
Accounts payable	96,671	23,711	7,891		24,768					153,041
Accrued wages payable	8,505	4,958			4,320					17,783
Contracts payable			125,678							125,678
Due to state							2,314			2,314
Payroll withholdings payable							18,622			18,622
Other liabilities						68,315				68,315
Due to other funds						16,315				16,315
Interest payable				27,893						27,893
General obligation bonds payable								5,000		5,000
Revenue bonds payable								5,975,000		5,975,000
Notes payable								153,189		153,189
Capital leases								274,312		274,312
Total liabilities	105,176	28,669	133,569	27,893	29,088	84,630	20,936	6,407,501	0	6,837,462
Fund equity										
Investment in general fixed assets									1,253,440	1,253,440
Retained earnings					984,523					984,523
Fund balances										
Reserved for encumbrance	9,850	7,600								17,450
Reserved for debt service				79,461						79,461
Unreserved (deficit)	(250,170)	2,468	(79,350)			52,403				(274,649)
Total Fund Equity	(240,320)	10,068	(79,350)	79,461	984,523	52,403	0	0	1,253,440	2,060,225
Total liabilities and fund equity	(135,144)	38,737	54,219	107,354	1,013,611	137,033	20,936	6,407,501	1,253,440	8,897,687

Table 2 City of Harris, Combined Statement of Receipts, Disbursements, Cash, and investments, All Governmental, Proprietary, and Fiduciary Fund Types as of and for the Year Ended December 31, 1993

	Governmental fund types				Proprietary fund type	Fiduciary fund types		Totals (memorandum only)
	General	Special revenue	Debt service	Capital projects	Enterprise	Trust funds	Agency funds	
Cash and investments	(152,168)	28,754	78,373	38,384	186,939	58,873	34,685	273,840
Operating receipts								
Taxes	769,369	178,226	44,784			156,700		1,149,079
Licenses and permits	6,703							6,703
Intergovernmental	66,921	199,350		60,558		117,432		444,261
Charges for services	101,478	45,133						146,611
Fines and forfeits	10							10
Enterprise—operating					2,469,171			2,469,171
Miscellaneous	38,588	3,174				153		41,915
Total operating receipts	983,069	425,883	44,784	60,558	2,469,171	274,285		4,257,750
Enterprise—nonoperating					1,569,132			1,569,132
Transfers in	297,724				0	3,528		301,252
Agency fund additions							1,372,587	1,372,587
Total receipts	1,280,793	425,883	44,784	60,558	4,038,303	277,813	1,372,587	7,500,721
Operating disbursements								
General government	474,761	68,080						542,841

							Total
Public safety	592,816	525					593,341
Highways, streets, and roadways		188,262					188,262
Culture and recreation	34,050	151,233					185,283
Capital outlay				44,723			44,723
Retirement and pensions					201,876		201,876
Debt service							
Principal		9,000	13,331				22,331
Interest, agent fees		3,315	5,676				8,991
Enterprise							
Operating					1,727,073		1,727,073
Equipment and Improvements					142,135		142,135
Total operating disbursements	1,101,627	420,415	19,007	44,723	1,869,208	201,876	0	3,656,856
Enterprise							
Nonoperating					1,188,286		1,188,286
Debt service principal					184,000		184,000
Debt service—interest					471,872		471,872
Other disbursements	185,391						185,391
Transfers out	3,528				297,724		301,252
Agency fund deductions						1,386,336	1,386,336
Total disbursements	1,290,546	420,415	19,007	44,723	4,011,090	201,876	1,386,336	7,373,993
Excess (deficiency) of total receipts over (under) total disbursements	(9,753)	5,468	25,777	15,835	27,213	75,937	(13,749)	126,728
Cash and investments, 12/31/93	(161,921)	34,222	104,150	54,219	214,152	134,810	20,936	400,568

Cash Basis Financial Statements

In lieu of the combined balance sheet, the combined activity statements, and the combined statement of cash flows, the city of Harris has provided a single overview activity statement—'combined statement of receipts, disbursements, cash, and investment balances—all governmental, proprietary, and fiduciary fund types'—that summarizes cash transactions for the period. The statement appears as Table 2. The combined statement is supported by combining statements for the special revenue funds (Table 3), debt service funds, enterprise funds, and trust funds.

Unlike GAAP basis statements, there is no separate balance sheet. Under strict cash basis accounting, any such statement would be relatively brief. There is no accounting recognition of accruals (i.e., amounts to be paid or received) such as the wages payable and taxes receivable appearing on the GAAP basis balance sheet. Similarly, there is no recognition of the two types of deferrals: assets resulting from prepayment of expenses, and liabilities resulting from revenues received in advance of services. Amounts due to or from other funds or other units of government, which appear as "due from other funds," "due to other funds," "due from federal government," and "due to state" on the GAAP basis statement, are also omitted. Other GAAP basis elements that disappear under strict cash basis accounting are fund equity, defined as the excess of assets over liabilities (or of liabilities over assets if a fund deficit exists), and reservations of fund equity, which represent restrictions on excess assets. In the present case, the beginning and ending balances of cash and investments, the only balance sheet items shown, are simply incorporated in the summary of cash transactions.

For the most part, the combined statement of the city of Harris is formatted like a GAAP basis statement. Note that in both the GAAP basis and cash basis statements the information is presented in columns, with a separate column for each fund type. The different fund categories and fund types are shown across the top of the statement. There is also an optional totals column. The body of the cash basis statement is configured in the following manner, which is similar to a GAAP basis operating statement:

> Cash and investment balances—beginning of the period
> Operating receipts
> Nonoperating receipts, other receipts, and transfers in
> Total receipts
> Operating disbursements
> Nonoperating disbursements, other disbursements, and transfers out
> Total disbursements
> Excess of total receipts over (under) total disbursements
> Cash and investment balances—end of period

Rather than receipts and disbursements, the GAAP basis operating statement would report revenues and expenditures, recognized on the modified accrual basis. It would also show beginning and ending fund balances in place of cash and investment balances.

Within the cash basis statement, receipts are classified by fund and source (taxes, licenses and permits, fines, etc.), and disbursements by fund and function (general governmental services, public safety, highway and streets, etc.). These classifications are also used in a GAAP basis operating statement for revenues and expenditures. Please note that in many jurisdictions, budgets are prepared using object class classifications (personal services, supplies, capital outlay, etc.). Where this is the case, budgeted disbursements will need to be reclassified according to function in order to compare actual to budgeted

Table 3 City of Harris, Combining Statement of Receipts, Disbursements, Cash, and Investment Balances, Special Revenue Funds as of and for the Year Ended December 31, 1993

	Motor vehicle highway	Local road and street	Cemetery	Accident report	Police firearms training	Department of re development	Economic development commission	Parks and recreation	Swimming pool	Parks and recreation nonreverting	Community development	G. Craig Park	Totals
Cash and investments, 1/1/93	(1,561)	23,868	(13,923)	8,025	202	14,681	29,362	(18,356)	(15,587)	271	1,241	531	28,754
Operating receipts													
Taxes			79,009					90,513					178,226
Licenses and permits													
Intergovernmental	171,406	27,944				8,704							199,350
Charges for services			5,489	649				5,236	32,980	369			45,133
Fines and forfeits					410								
Miscellaneous	397		242				1,058	565	10	226	626	50	3,174
Total operating receipts	171,803	27,944	84,740	649	410	8,704	1,058	96,314	32,990	595	626	50	425,883
Operating disbursements													
General government			68,080										68,080
Public safety					525								525
Highways, streets, and roadways	168,678	19,584											188,262
Culture and recreation								104,969	46,238	26			151,233
Debt service													
Principal						9,000							9,000
Interest, agent fees						3,315							3,315
Total operating disbursements	168,678	19,584	68,080	0	525	12,315	0	104,969	46,238	26	0	0	420,415
Excess (deficiency) of total receipts over (under) total disbursements	3,125	8,360	16,660	649	(115)	(3,611)	1,058	(8,655)	(13,248)	569	626	50	5,468
Cash and investments, 12/31/93	1,564	32,228	2,737	8,674	87	11,070	30,420	(27,011)	(28,835)	840	1,867	581	34,222

amounts. The GAAP basis statement "combined statement of revenues, expenditures, changes in fund balances—budget and actual" incorporates such a comparison for both the general and special revenue funds.

An important feature of the cash basis statement is the presence of parentheses around cash and investment balances, which indicates a negative amount. In particular, negative amounts appear as the beginning and ending balances of cash and investments in the general fund. In the general fund, the negative beginning balance for cash and investments indicates that in past years disbursements for general fund activities exceeded receipts earmarked for the general fund. Such deficiencies accumulate and are carried over to subsequent reporting periods unless offset by an excess of receipts. The combination of the negative beginning balance and the excess of disbursements for the current period has produced a negative ending balance for cash and investments in the general fund for 1993, which will appear as the beginning balance for 1994. In sum, the general fund is overdrawn. The combining statement in Table 3 shows that the swimming pool fund and the park and recreation fund among the special revenue funds are also overdrawn.

It is important to note that negative amounts in one fund may not represent an actual bank overdraft. In the present case, the totals column reveals that at the end of 1993 the reporting entity as a whole had $400,568 in cash and investments. The overdrafts are still cause for concern, however, because they indicate that the funds have been or are "over budget" (See below.) Typically, local governments have no statutory authority to overdraw funds.

The GAAP basis balance sheet tells a fuller and more distressing story concerning the financial position of the city. The parentheses surrounding the amount for total fund equity indicate that the general fund is in deficit (i.e., that the total of all fund liabilities exceeds fund assets). The fund equity has two components: a portion representing encumbrances or outstanding purchase commitments and the unreserved portion, which is in deficit. Normally any unreserved fund balance represents a margin of safety for the unit, enabling it to meet unexpected expenditures or to reduce future budget requests. The city of Harris no longer has such a cushion for general government operations. Moreover, the GAAP basis balance sheet shows that the capital projects fund is also in deficit, primarily because of a heavy burden of debt. The cash basis statement itself gives little clue as to the precarious position of this fund.

NOTES TO THE FINANCIAL STATEMENTS

Notes are an integral and important part of all financial statements, providing informative disclosure beyond that contained in the body of the statements. Under cash basis reporting, notes assume even greater importance, because they are the only external source of information concerning the entity's fixed assets, short-term debt, general long-term debt, and other obligations, such as pensions and compensated absences.* The city of Harris has included information concerning fixed assets and various debt obligations in notes to the financial statement. Two of these notes appear as Exhibit 1.

---

* According to "GASB Votes Down Accrual Accounting." *Accounting Today*, June 7, 1993, pp. 1, 61 most local governments fail to accrue as a liability the accumulated sick leaves and vacations of retiring employees.

Exhibit 1   Note 4: Fixed Assets

General fixed asset records have not been maintained since December 31, 1989.

Records are not available providing the historical cost amounts for some fixed assets of the city; therefore, estimates of historical costs have been used. The estimates are based on construction costs indexes applied to estimated current construction or acquisition costs. Any differences between the estimated historical costs and the actual historical costs are not considered material.

The following schedule discloses the amounts of recorded general fixed assets reported on December 31, 1989:

	Estimated historical costs	Actual historical costs	Total
Land	$—	$ 110,195	$110,195
Buildings	—	316,134	316,134
Improvements other than buildings	—	389,991	389,991
Machinery equipment	52,050	385,070	437,120
Totals	$52,050	$1,201,390	$1,253,440

Note 5: Long-Term Debt

Revenue and general obligation bonds

Revenue bonds payable on December 31, 1993 consisted of the following individual issues:

$1,540,000–1955 water revenue bonds due in installments of $45,000 to $70,000, plus interest through July 1, 1994; interest at 3.38%	$45,000
$3,925,000–1986 sewage utility revenue bonds due in installments of $10,000 to $445,000 plus interest through July 1,2013; interest at 5.19–8.32%	$3,820,000
$1,040,000–1966 sewage utility revenue bonds due in installments of $45,000 to $60,000 plus interest through July 1,1998; interest at 4 7/8%	$275,000
$2,075,000–1986 sewage utility revenue bonds due in installments of $45,000 to $120,000, plus interest through July 1, 2013; interest at 5.15%	$1,835,000
Total long-term revenue bonds	$5,975,000

General obligation bonds payable on December 31, 1993 consisted of the following individual issue:

$176,000–general obligation bonds due in installments of $5,000 to $9,000, plus interest through January 1, 1994; interest at 65.%	$5,000

Annual debt service requirements to maturity for revenue and general obligation bonds, including interest of $6,208,067 and $0, respectively, are as follows:

	Revenue	General obligation
Mature unpaid coupons	$85	$5,000
1994	645,672	—
1995	572,011	—
1996	603,634	—

(continued)

Exhibit 1 Continued

1997	603,820	—
1998	603,393	—
Thereafter	9,154,722	—
Totals	$12,183,337	$5,000

Capital leases

The city has entered into various capital leases. Future minimum lease payments and present values of the net minimum lease payments under these capital leases as of December 31, 1993, are as follows:

1994	$134,603
1995	98,268
1996	63,495
1997	14,978
Total minimum lease payments	311,344
Less amount representing interest	37,032
Present value of net minimum	
Lease payments	$274,312

Notes payable

The city has entered into various notes. Annual debt service requirements to maturity for the notes, including interest of $24,948, are as follows:

Matured unpaid	$167
1994	72,064
1995	55,798
1996	35,788
1997	14,320
Totals	$178,137

Changes in long-term debt

During the year ended December 31, 1993, the following changes occurred in long-term debt:

	Balance 1-1-93	1993 additions	1993 deletions	Balance 12-31-93
General obligation bonds	$14,000	$—	$9,000	$5,000
Revenue bonds	6,164,000	—	189,000	5,975,000
Notes payable	192,062	40,000	78,873	153,189
Capital leases	65,817	331,516	123,021	274,312
Totals	$6,435,879	$371,516	$399,894	$6,407,501

RELATION TO BUDGET

One of the combined statements required by GAAP is a comparison of budgeted revenues, expenditures, and changes in fund balances to actual data for the general and special revenue funds. A cash basis annual report may or may not contain such a statement. If omitted, additional sources of information, such as the actual budget document, the annual budget ordinance, or subsidiary ledgers, will have to be consulted in order to obtain budgetary data.

A budget ordinance, also called an appropriation act or ordinance, is issued when the city council or other legislative body formally adopts the annual operating budget. The ordinance covers every fund for which a budget is prepared and gives the amounts the governmental unit is authorized to spend for each function or object of expenditure. The ordinance may be issued in conjunction with a budget order from a state oversight board if there are statutory limitations on the property tax levy. If there is a levy limitation, the order will also restrict the amount the unit is authorized to raise through property taxes.

The amount of property taxes is normally less than the appropriation, because local governments have other sources of income, such as interest on investments, fines, licenses, and permits. There may also be a positive cash or fund balance from the previous year. These sources are not covered in the budget ordinance, because they accrue to the government unit without legal action on its part or are the result of past legal actions.

Once the budget is adopted, it is recorded as part of the accounting system in order to ensure proper budgetary control. In a cash basis system, single-entry rather double-entry accounting is normally used, so there is no set of self-balancing accounts as in a GAAP-basis system. Instead, there are detail cash accounts in a receipts and disbursements ledger along with periodic summaries of receipts and disbursements by fund, department, or object class. In order to incorporate budgetary control, each detail receipt account would be headed by the amount estimated to be received. Actual receipts would then be recorded as negative amounts, with any positive balance representing the amount still expected to be received. Similarly, disbursement accounts would be headed by the appropriated amount, with actual disbursements recorded as negative amounts. In order, to avoid appropriation overruns, encumbrances or purchase commitments should also be entered as negative amounts in the appropriate disbursement account. When the payment is made, the encumbrance would be voided and the disbursement subtracted. The balance of the account, if positive, would represent amounts still available for expenditure.

A brief example will illustrate the use of budgetary accounting in a receipts and disbursements ledger. Assuming that the municipality expected to collect $5,200 in fees during the period from building permits, this amount would be entered in the "licenses and permits—building permits" account under a column entitled "estimated receipts." This amount would also be entered in a "balance" column. If the city subsequently collected $400 in such fees, the $400 would be entered in an adjacent column entitled "receipts." This amount would then be subtracted from the balance column, leaving $4800 as the amount still to be collected from this source. Subsequent receipts would be accounted for in the same manner.

To continue the example, if the city had appropriated $10,000 to purchase materials for road repair, the amount would be recorded in a "highways and streets—supplies" account under a column headed "appropriations." In addition to the appropriations column, there would be three other columns, entitled "encumbrances," "expenditures," and "unencumbered balance." The original appropriation would also be recorded in unencumbered balance, which indicates the amount free to be expended. If, for example, the city ordered $700 in supplies, the $700 would be entered in encumbrances, and then subtracted from the unencumbered balance column, leaving $9300 to be committed or expended. When the supplies were received, $700 would be subtracted from the encumbrances column, eliminating the original encumbrance, and added back to the unencumbered balance, thus restoring it to the previous amount of $10,000. The amount of the actual disbursement, in this case $725, would be recorded under expenditures, and the amount also subtracted from the unencumbered balance column, leaving $9275 to be committed or expended.*

The city of Harris has used this kind of accounting system for several years. Unfortunately, encumbrances have not been recorded on a consistent basis. In some years, this omission has meant that city officials were unaware that they had exceeded the annual appropriation until they were already committed to purchase goods and services, which has caused negative ending balances to build up for cash and investments in some funds. City officials are now in the unenviable position of having to budget to pay for careless purchase commitments of previous administrations as well as current operating needs. In 1993, the city of Harris experienced appropriation overruns in the general fund, the highway and cemetery special revenue funds, and two debt service funds. Late in the year, city officials attempted to alleviate the problem by transferring cash into the general fund from other funds. Disbursements, however, still exceeded appropriations.

SUMMARY AND CONCLUSION

Although GAAP basis financial reporting is gaining wider currency, both cash basis accounting and cash basis financial reporting are still a reality for many local units. Among the attractions of the cash basis are its similarity to nonGAAP budgetary bases, the smaller number and types of accounting entries required during the year, and the relative simplicity of year-end financial statements prepared on this basis. This chapter has provided a general overview of cash basis financial reporting using financial statements and other accounting information of a small city in Indiana to illustrate one possible approach. It has also compared cash basis financial reporting with GAAP.

Although condemned by authoritative bodies, cash basis accounting is not inherently "bad." As with any system of accounting however, its successful operation requires consistent and appropriate recordkeeping, including the use of encumbrances. Unfortunately, this standard of accounting has eluded the city of Harris for several years, and the city's funds have been mismanaged.

Cash basis financial reporting is another matter. Although easier to prepare and understand than GAAP basis financial statements, cash basis statements are also less informative, omitting deferrals and accruals, among other items. Moreover, the notes to the financial statements are often the only external source of information regarding important aspects of the entity's financial position and results of operations. Unlike GAAP basis reporting, there are at present no standards governing cash basis financial reports. Consequently, content and format will vary, making comparisons from year to year and among units difficult.

---

* For further details on the use of subsidiary ledgers and budgetary accounting in general, see Hay and Wilson (1992).

REVIEW QUESTIONS

1. What are some of the differences between cash basis and GAAP basis financial reporting for local governments?
2. How meaningful is cash basis information to users of local government financial statements? In comparison to GAAP basis information?
3. Should the GASB or other authoritative body establish generally accepted standards for cash basis financial reporting? Why or why not? What requirements for content and format should such standards prescribe?
4. How useful is it in cash basis financial reporting to review transactions that occurred after the end of the fiscal year but before issuance of the financial statements? In comparison to GAAP basis financial reporting?
5. In 1993, the city of Harris experienced overdrawn funds and significant appropriation overruns. Is this situation more likely in a cash basis than in a GAAP basis reporting system?
6. How likely is it that the city of Harris will be able to meet principal and interest payments on its long-term debt in future years? Would GAAP basis financial reporting help the city to meet these obligations? Why or why not?

REFERENCES

Bailey, L. P., (1993). *HBJ Miller Comprehensive Governmental GAAP Guide*. San Diego, CA: Harcourt Brace Jovanovich.

Governmental Accounting Standards Board (1991). *Statement No. 14, The Financial Reporting Entity*. Norwalk, CT.

Hay, L. E. and Wilson, E. R. (1992). *Accounting for Governmental and Nonprofit Entities*. Homewood, IL: Richard D. Irwin.

Ingram, R. W. and Robbins, W. A. (1987) *Financial Reporting Practices of Local Governments*. Stamford, CT: Governmental Accounting Standards Board.

27
Changes for Governmental Financial Reporting

Terry K. Patton
University of Wisconsin, Oshkosh, Wisconsin, U.S.A.

Robert J. Freeman
Texas Tech University, Lubbock, Texas, U.S.A.

Governmental accounting and financial reporting are relatively recent developments in the United States. Little need existed for either until the United States moved toward urbanization. By the latter part of the nineteenth century, however, the growing number of cities and widescale graft and corruption in the nation's largest municipalities led to a demand for *financial* (or *fiscal*)* *accountability* (Cleveland, 1909).

Governmental accounting and financial reporting therefore began in a watchdog role—to hold public officials accountable for the financial resources received and used by a government. Accounting systems were designed to gather information necessary to judge whether or not resources were used properly. Uniform financial reports were developed to demonstrate a proper accounting for assets, liabilities, and receipts and uses of cash and other current financial resources. Unquestionably, governmental financial reporting standards—first formalized and adopted in the 1930s—have evolved to play an important role in improving government operations by holding public officials accountable for the financial resources entrusted to their care (Freeman and Shoulders, 1996).

Critics charge, however, that the scope of governmental financial reporting is too narrow, that governmental financial reports currently are designed only to demonstrate compliance with the budget and the sufficiency of current financial resources to meet expenditures during the year. Although compliance and resource sufficiency are important from a *fiscal accountability* perspective, many critics believe governmental financial statements should also emphasize *operational accountability*.[†] They believe that users of government financial statements (particularly citizen groups) need more information than is

---

* "Fiscal accountability is the responsibility of governments to justify that their actions in the current period have complied with public decisions concerning the raising and spending of public moneys in the short term (usually one budgetary cycle or one year)" (GASB, 1997: paragraph 189).

[†] "Operational accountability is the governments' responsibility to report the extent to which they have met their operating objectives efficiently and effectively, using all resources available for that purpose, and whether they can continue to meet their objectives for the foreseeable future" (GASB, 1997: paragraph 198).

currently provided to judge the efficiency and effectiveness of a government's operations and to assess its long-term financial condition.

The Governmental Accounting Standards Board (GASB), formed in 1984 to establish and improve financial reporting standards for state and local governments, is attempting to answer the critics' charges by re-examining the content and format of the basic financial statements to be included in a government's annual financial report. The GASB wants to establish standards that provide users of governmental financial reports (that is, the citizenry, legislative and oversight officials, and investors and creditors) with more relevant information.

Unfortunately, users disagree about the definition of "relevant" information. Some believe that the current financial statements (which emphasize fiscal accountability) provide all the information needed and should not be changed. Others are just as adamant that governmental financial statements are inadequate because they do not emphasize operational accountability. The GASB believes financial statements should emphasize both fiscal and operational accountability, therefore the GASB decided that a compromise between the two views was necessary. In June 1999, the GASB issued statement no. 34, *Basic Financial Statements—and Management's Discussion and Analysis—for State and Local Governments*, which will require governments to include governmentwide financial statements (that emphasize operational accountability) and fund statements (that emphasize fiscal accountability) as basic financial statements (GASB, 1999).

Statement no. 34 has delayed, phased-in effective dates. State and local governments with the most resources—reporting total annual revenues at June 15, 1999, of $100 million or more—will be required to adopt statement no. 34 for periods beginning after June 15, 2001. For governments with total annual revenues of $10 million or more but less than $100 million, statement no. 34 will be effective for periods beginning after June 15, 2002. Finally, governments with total annual revenues of less than $10 million will be required to adopt statement no. 34 for periods beginning after June 15, 2003. Earlier adoption of the statement is encouraged for all governments (GASB, 1999).

The remainder of this chapter examines the development of governmental financial reporting and the financial statements prior to the issuance of statement no. 34. Next, the reasons for and details of some of the major changes required by statement no. 34 are discussed. Finally, some unique features of the operating statements that will be required by statement no. 34 for state and local governments are identified and illustrated.

REPORTING MODEL PRIOR TO GASB STATEMENT NO. 34

The first effort to promulgate governmental accounting standards can be traced to the work of the National Committee on Municipal Accounting (NCMA), which was formed in 1934 by the Municipal (now Government) Finance Officers' Association of the United States and Canada (MFOA). The NCMA was charged with the task of formulating accounting principles, developing standard classifications and terminology for municipal reports, and promulgating standards (1935b). By 1935, the NCMA had published in preliminary documents its principles of municipal accounting and a booklet of municipal accounting terminology (1935a). These principles form the basis of modern-day governmental accounting and reporting.

The NCMA emphasized the importance of reporting revenues and expenditures in governmental financial reports. Expenditures were defined as "amounts paid or incurred for all purposes, including expenses, provision for retirement of debt, and capital outlays" (NCMA, 1936). This definition of expenditures differs from the definition of expenses—the focal point of business operating statements. Expenses are the cost of services (including the cost of generating revenue) during a given period. It is important for businesses to know if revenues exceed expenses to determine net income for a year. Unlike businesses, however, governments exist to provide services without a profit motive. An important question for governments is whether or not enough financial resources exist to continue to provide an expected level of services. The NCMA and subsequent governmental standard setters thus have not concerned themselves with measuring the cost of services (or expenses); rather, they determined that expenditures (or the outflow of current financial resources) should be the focal point of governmental operating statements. This means that current governmental operating statements do not report expenses, such as depreciation, but instead report expenditures, such as the outflow of financial resources for the acquisition of capital assets or to pay principal and interest on long-term debt.

The basis for the governmental financial reporting prior to the issuance of GASB statement no. 34, can be traced to the work of the MFOA's National Council of Governmental Accounting (NCGA), which succeeded the MFOA's National Committee of Governmental Accounting and its predecessor, the NCMA (Freeman, 1976). In March 1979, the NCGA issued statement 1, *Governmental Accounting and Financial Reporting Principles* (NCGA, 1980). That statement defines the measurement focus and basis of accounting for governmental funds and proprietary funds.* The major provisions of NCGA statement 1, which are discussed below, will continue to be followed by governments until they adopt GASB statement no. 34.

The NCGA recommended the continued use of funds for governmental financial reporting. Fund accounting has been described as the most distinctive feature of governmental accounting. Funds are fiscal and accounting entities established to account for the diverse nature of government operations and to ensure legal compliance (Freeman and Shoulders, 1996). Simply stated, a fund can be thought of as a general ledger maintained to account for all the transactions related to a particular part of a government's activities. For example, a debt service fund may be established to account for all the resources accumulated for the payment of principal and interest on a bond issue.

In statement 1, the NCGA classified the fund types into three categories: governmental, proprietary, and fiduciary. Governmental funds are used to account for general governmental activities, such as police and fire protection or street maintenance. Such activities are often expected to be financed from taxes or grants. Governmental fund types include the general, special revenue, debt service, and capital projects funds. Governmental fund types are "expendable" and have a "spending" measurement focus that emphasizes "financial flow" operating data—the sources and uses of "available spendable resources" during a period. With a spending measurement focus, *expenditures* (i.e., financial resources expended) are measured. The *modified accrual basis* of accounting is used to determine when to recognize a transaction (NCGA, 1980). Because governmental funds report only current financial resources, the fixed assets and general long-term liabilities associated with governmental funds are reported in two account groups—the general fixed assets

---

* Soon after the GASB was formed in 1984, it recognized this NCGA pronouncement as authoritative in GASB statement no. 1 (GASB, 1984).

account group and the general long-term debt account group. These account groups are not funds but are accounting records for those noncurrent assets and liabilities.

Proprietary fund types—enterprise funds and internal service funds—are used to account for a government's business-type activities. Activities such as providing electricity or water and sewer services are typically financed from user charges. These "nonexpendable" funds have a "capital maintenance" measurement focus and report *expenses* in their operating statements. Operating statements for proprietary funds are prepared using the *accrual* basis of accounting. The third category of fund types, trust and agency funds, usually are accounted for in the same way as either governmental or proprietary funds, depending on their measurement focus; that is, expendable trust funds have a "spending" measurement focus and report expenditures using the modified accrual basis of accounting, but nonexpendable trust funds have a "capital maintenance" measurement focus and report expenses using the accrual basis of accounting (NCGA, 1980).

FINANCIAL STATEMENTS PRIOR TO GASB STATEMENT NO. 34

NCGA statement 1 introduced the financial reporting pyramid to illustrate the financial section of the comprehensive annual financial report (CAFR)* (Figure 1). The top of the pyramid represents highly condensed summary reports, while the bottom represents highly detailed reports that would include the details of virtually every transaction or event of a government. The financial statements required for a CAFR fall between these two reporting extremes (Freeman and Shoulders, 1996). The CAFR should include general purpose financial statements by fund type and account group (i.e., combined statements), combining statements by fund type and individual fund statements.

The general purpose financial statements (GPFS) required to be presented by NCGA statement 1 are (NCGA, 1980) as follows:

1. Combined balance sheet—all fund types and account groups
2. Combined statement of revenues, expenditures, and changes in fund balances—all governmental fund types and expendable trust funds
3. Combined statement of revenues, expenditures, and changes in fund balances—budget and actual—general and special revenue fund types (and similar governmental fund types for which annual budgets have been legally adopted)
4. Combined statement of revenues, expenses, and changes in retained earnings (or equity)—all proprietary fund types
5. Combined statement of changes in financial position—all proprietary fund types
6. Notes to the financial statements

Before the issuance of GASB statement no. 34, only two significant changes had been made to these statements through the years. First, instead of a combined statement of changes in financial position, GASB statement no. 9 now requires a statement of cash flows for proprietary and nonexpendable trust funds. Second, GASB statement no. 14 may

---

* The CAFR is the government's official annual report and is a matter of public record. In addition to the financial section, the CAFR should include introductory information, schedules necessary to demonstrate compliance with finance-related legal and contractual provisions, and statistical data (GASB, 1996).

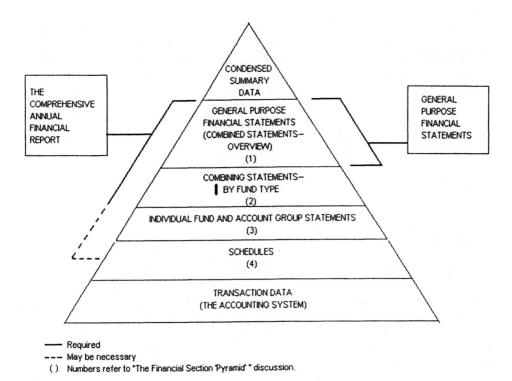

— Required
--- May be necessary
( ) Numbers refer to "The Financial Section 'Pyramid' " discussion.

Figure 1 Financial reporting pyramid. *Source*: Adapted from GASB Codification, section 1900.117.

now cause some governments to report discretely presented component units on the face of their financial statements.

Considering the NCGA's effort in developing financial reporting requirements, its contribution to modern-day governmental accounting cannot be questioned, yet the NCGA statement 1 approach did not provide a satisfactory answer to the critics who believe governmental reporting would be more understandable and useful if it followed commercial accounting principles and reporting guidelines or if it provided information about operational accountability. The dissatisfaction of critics eventually led the GASB to make the changes to governmental financial reporting required by statement no. 34.

GASB STATEMENT NO. 34

Since the GASB's inception in 1984, this financial standard-setting successor to the NCGA was committed to developing a reporting model and related financial statements that would meet the needs of all major groups of users of state and local governmental financial reports. This proved to be an extremely difficult and time-consuming process for the GASB. Although numerous attempts to refocus governmental financial reporting standards were made during the fifteen years prior to the issuance of GASB statement no. 34, none succeeded. The primary reason for this lack of success was the difficulty of designing financial statements that would be useful to diverse groups of users who wanted different types of information reported in governmental financial statements.

The GASB broadly defined users of governmental financial reports as the citizenry, legislative and oversight officials, and investors and creditors. This diversity in user groups leads to a diversity of information needs from governmental financial reports. Information that is relevant to one group—that can make a difference in one user's assessment of a problem or situation—may not be relevant to another (GASB, 1987).

Currently, investors and creditors are the primary users of governmental financial reports. In particular, bond-rating agencies probably use governmental financial reports as much as any other single group. They have developed models to rate governmental general obligation bond issues based on financial statements that are reported by fund types. Some of those funds are reported using a current financial resources flow measurement focus and the modified accrual basis of accounting. Many investors and creditors did not want to lose the detailed information that traditionally has been reported in governmental financial reports. In essence, they probably would have been pleased with a status quo approach to governmental financial reporting.

Nontraditional users of governmental financial reports (e.g., the citizenry and legislative and oversight officials) are believed to have different information needs, however. They want financial information to answer questions that cannot be answered by studying today's governmental financial reports. They want to know about the efficiency and effectiveness of government. They want to know whether current-year revenues are sufficient to pay for current-year expenses or whether a portion of the payment burden for current services is being shifted to future citizens. They want to know whether the government's financial position has improved or deteriorated as a result of the year's operations.

Unfortunately, developing one set of financial statements that would meet the needs of all users was not possible. The GASB therefore, decided to require both fund and governmentwide financial statements. With this approach, traditional users will still be able to glean the disaggregated information reported by funds that they need and currently use to analyze the creditworthiness of governmental entities. Readers of governmental financial reports will still be able to assess the government's fiscal accountability, including whether or not a government is adhering to legal and budgetary restrictions. Nontraditional users will be provided with information that is intended to allow them to assess the costs of providing services and the efficiency and effectiveness of government operations.

FINANCIAL REPORTING REQUIREMENTS

With the issuance of GASB statement no. 34, governmental financial reports will soon be dramatically different from those now issued. The GASB will require including management's discussion and analysis, basic financial statements, and other required supplementary information as the minimum external reporting requirements for state and local governments. The management's discussion and analysis section will introduce the basic financial statements by explaining the objectives of financial reporting from both the governmentwide and fund perspectives. It will also include analytical comments about the government's financial activities that should be useful to those not particularly knowledgeable of governmental accounting (GASB, 1999).

Table 1 Financial Statements Required by Statement No. 34

Governmentwide statements	Fund financial statements		
	Governmental funds	Proprietary funds	Fiduciary funds and component units
Statement of net assets	Balance sheet	Statement of net assets	Statement of fiduciary net assets
Statement of activities	Statement of revenues, expenditures, and changes in fund balances	Statement of revenues, expenses, and changes in net assets	Statement of changes in fiduciary net assets
		Statement of cash flows	

The basic financial statements will be prepared at both the governmentwide and fund levels. Table 1 summarizes the statements required for governmentwide and fund reporting. The governmentwide statements will report financial information at a more aggregated level than the fund statements, and will report the primary government and component unit information in separate columns. Governmental and business-type activities of the primary government will also be reported in separate columns (GASB, 1999).

Governmentwide financial statements are designed to assist users in assessing accountability for economic resources. They will be prepared using an economic resources flow measurement focus and the accrual basis of accounting. Required financial statements will include a statement of net assets and a statement of activities. A schedule of changes in capital assets and long-term obligations will be required to be disclosed in the notes to the financial statements (GASB, 1999).

Fund financial statements will report financial information at a more detailed level than the governmentwide statements. Separate fund financial statements will be prepared for governmental, proprietary, and fiduciary funds and similar component units. The focus of governmental and proprietary fund financial statements is on *major* funds. The measurement focus, basis of accounting, and required financial statements will vary based on fund type.

> Governmental funds will be presented using the current financial resources measurement focus and the modified accrual basis of accounting. Financial statements required for governmental funds would include a balance sheet and a statement of revenues, expenditures, and changes in fund balances. A budgetary comparison schedule or statement would be required for the general fund and other annually budgeted major special revenue funds as required supplementary information (RSI) or as a part of the basic financial statements (GASB, 1999).
>
> Proprietary funds will be presented using an economic resources measurement focus and the accrual basis of accounting. Financial statements required for proprietary funds include a statement of net assets or balance sheet, a statement of revenues, expenses, and changes in fund net assets or fund equity, and a statement of cash flows (GASB, 1999).

Table 2   City of River Falls Government-Wide Statement of Activities

| Functions | Expenses | Program Revenues | | Net (Expense) Revenue |
		Charges for Services	Grants and Contributions	Governmental Activities
General government	$11,172,216	$3,146,915	$3,423,617	$(4,601,684)
Public safety	34,864,749	1,198,855	1,369,993	(32,295,901)
Public works	11,427,121	850,000	2,252,615	(8,324,506)
Engineering services	1,299,645	704,793		(594,852)
Health and sanitation	6,738,672	5,612,267	575,000	(551,405)
Culture and recreation	11,532,350	3,995,199	2,450,000	(5,087,151)
Interest on long-term debt	6,068,121			(6,068,121)
Total	$83,102,874	$15,508,029	$10,071,225	(57,523,620)

General Revenues:	
Taxes	
Property	34,168,449
Other	13,308,487
Grants not restricted to specific programs	1,457,820
Interest and investment earnings	1,885,455
Miscellaneous	884,907
Total general revenues	51,705,118
Excess (deficiency) of revenues over	
expenses before special item	(5,818,502)
Special Item:	
Gain on sale of park land	2,653,488
Changes in net assets	(3,165,014)
Net assets—beginning	124,333,801
Net assets—ending	$121,168,787

This is a government-wide statement prepared using the economic resources flow measurement focus. Revenues and expenses of general government activities of the City of River Falls are summarized. Revenues are recognized in the period they are earned and become measurable, and expenses are recognized when incurred, if measurable. (Statement adapted from GASB "Basic Financial Statements" Exposure Draft, 1997).

COMPARING ILLUSTRATIVE STATEMENTS

Illustrative operating statements prepared for each of the different reporting perspectives are included in Tables 2–4 to highlight the differences in the operating statements.* The illustrative statements are prepared from financial information obtained from the city of River Falls,† which has a population of approximately 80,000. The city is the county seat and the largest city in one of the fastest growing counties in the nation. The city's revenues and expenditures have shown moderate growth during the last ten years, a trend that is expected to continue.

---

* These statements are adapted from the illustrative statements included in the GASB exposure draft that preceded GASB statement no. 34 (GASB, 1997). To simplify the statements, only governmental activities are reported.
† For purposes of anonymity, the actual city's name was changed to the city of River Falls.

Table 3 City of River Falls Governmental Funds Statement of Revenues, Expenditures, and Changes in Fund Balances

	General fund	Road special revenue fund	Debt service fund	Capital projects fund	Total governmental funds
REVENUES					
Property taxes	$28,960,193		$4,925,192		$33,885,385
Other taxes	13,265,300				13,265,300
Fees and fines	687,008				687,008
Licenses and permits	2,287,794				2,287,794
Intergovernmental	6,119,938	$3,951,287		$1,457,820	11,529,045
Charges for services	11,161,964	30,708			11,192,672
Interest	552,325	215,204	146,604	836,589	1,750,722
Miscellaneous	881,874	66,270		2,939	951,083
Total revenues	63,916,396	4,263,469	5,071,796	2,297,348	75,549,009
EXPENDITURES					
Current operating:					
General government	8,630,835	1,634,428	11,820	490,124	10,767,207
Public safety	33,729,623				33,729,623
Public works	4,975,775	5,020,125			9,995,900
Engineering services	1,019,225				1,019,225
Health and sanitation	6,070,032				6,070,032
Culture and recreation	10,411,685				10,411,685
Debt service:					
Principal		75,000	3,375,000		3,450,000
Interest and other charges			5,215,151		5,215,151
Capital outlay	1,280,420			16,718,649	17,999,069
Total expenditures	66,117,595	6,729,553	8,601,971	17,208,773	98,657,892
Excess (deficiency) of revenues over expenditures	(2,201,199)	(2,466,084)	(3,530,175)	(14,911,425)	(23,108,883)
OTHER FINANCING SOURCES (USES)					
Proceeds of refunding bonds			38,045,000		38,045,000
Proceeds of long-term debt				18,829,560	18,829,560
Payment to bond refunding escrow agent			(37,284,144)		(37,284,144)
Transfers in			2,714,856		2,714,856
Transfers out	(2,097,845)	(213,546)		(403,465)	(2,714,856)
Total other financing sources and uses	(2,097,845)	(213,546)	3,475,712	18,426,095	19,590,416
SPECIAL ITEM					
Proceeds from sale of park land	3,476,488				3,476,488
Net change in fund balance	(822,556)	(2,679,630)	(54,463)	3,514,670	(41,979)
Fund balances–beginning	2,177,365	6,225,442	2,930,083	21,539,896	32,872,786
Fund balances–ending	$1,354,809	$ 3,545,812	$2,875,620	$25,054,566	$32,830,807

This statement is presented at the fund level using the flow of current financial resources measurement focus. Revenues are recognized when earned, measurable, and available to finance expenditures. Expenditures are recognized when a fund liability is incurred for goods and services received, capital outlay, or debt service. (Statement adapted from GASB "Basic Financial Statements" Exposure Draft, 1997).

Table 4   City of River Falls Budgetary Comparison Statement—Budgetary Basis General Fund

	Budgeted amounts		Actual amounts (budgetary basis)	Variance with final budget positive (negative)
	Original	Final		
Budgetary Fund Balance, January 1	$2,736,824	$1,264,888	$1,264,888	
Resources (inflows)				
Property taxes	30,124,560	29,959,745	29,280,163	$(679,582)
Franchise taxes	4,546,209	4,528,750	4,055,505	(473,245)
Public service taxes	8,295,000	8,307,274	8,969,887	662,613
Licenses and permits	2,126,600	2,126,600	2,287,794	161,194
Fines and forfeitures	718,800	718,800	606,946	(111,854)
Charges for services	12,392,972	11,202,150	11,374,460	172,310
Grants	6,905,898	6,571,360	6,119,938	(451,422)
Sale of land	1,355,250	3,500,000	3,476,488	(23,512)
Miscellaneous	3,024,292	1,220,991	881,874	(339,117)
Interest received	1,015,945	550,000	552,325	2,325
Transfers from other funds	939,525	130,000	129,323	(677)
Amounts available for appropriation	74,181,875	70,080,558	68,999,591	(1,080,967)
Charges to appropriations (outflows)				
General government				
Legal	665,275	663,677	632,719	30,958
Mayor, legislative, fiduciary and audit	3,058,750	3,192,910	2,658,264	534,646
Finance and accounting	1,932,500	1,912,702	1,852,687	60,015
City clerk and elections	345,860	354,237	341,206	13,031
Employee relations	1,315,500	1,300,498	1,234,232	66,266
Planning and economic development	1,975,600	1,784,314	1,642,575	141,739
Public safety				
Police	19,576,820	20,367,917	20,246,496	121,421
Fire department	9,565,280	9,358,453	9,559,967	(201,514)
EMS	2,323,171	2,470,127	2,459,866	10,261
Inspections	1,602,695	1,585,695	1,533,380	52,315
Public works				
Public works administration	388,500	385,013	383,397	1,616
Street maintenance	2,135,750	2,019,166	2,233,362	(214,196)
Street lighting	762,750	742,540	759,832	(17,292)
Traffic operations	385,945	374,945	360,500	14,436
Mechanical maintenance	1,525,685	1,272,696	1,256,087	16,609
Engineering services				
Engineering administration	1,170,650	1,140,289	1,158,023	(17,734)
Geographical information system	125,625	119,315	138,967	(19,652)
Health and sanitation				
Garbage pickup	5,756,250	5,865,757	6,174,653	(308,896)
Culture and Recreation				
Library	985,230	1,023,465	1,022,167	1,298
Parks and recreation	9,521,560	9,786,397	9,756,618	29,779
Community communications	552,350	558,208	510,361	47,847
Nondepartmental				
Miscellaneous			325,731	(325,731)
Contingency	2,544,049			
Transfers to other funds	2,970,256	2,025,000	2,097,845	(72,845)
Totals	71,186,051	68,303,321	68,338,944	(35,623)
Budgetary Fund Balance, December 31	$2,995,824	$1,777,237	$660,647	$(1,116,590)

This statement is presented for the General Fund using the cash basis, which is the City of River Falls budgetary basis. Resources are recorded when cash is received, and charge are recorded when cash is disbursed. (Statement adapted from GASB "Basic Financial Statements" Exposure Draft, 1997).

Each of the illustrated operating statements has unique features that should make it useful to readers of financial statements. After reviewing the illustrated statements and schedule, you should begin to understand their purposes. The statement of activities is an aggregated statement designed to allow readers to assess the cost of services in a given year and to determine the adequacy of current-year revenues to pay for those services. The fund perspective statements give a more detailed accounting of the current year's operations. The statement of revenues, expenditures, and changes in fund balances gives detailed information about the sources, uses, and balances of current financial resources. The budgetary comparison schedule for the general fund gives detailed information about the government's compliance with the budget.

Statement of Activities

The statement of activities (Table 2) is a new statement designed to allow users to assess whether current-year revenues are sufficient to pay for current-year services. Because this statement is prepared using the economic resources measurement focus and accrual basis of accounting, it provides readers with information about the cost of services and the financing of programs that cannot be found in the fund statements.

For example, the traditional fund operating statement does not report a charge for depreciation. The statement of activities reports depreciation—an annual expense for the expiration of the service life of a fixed asset or infrastructure.* Reporting depreciation expense decreases the value of reported assets and may provide readers with information needed to assess whether or not the government is maintaining and replacing fixed assets and infrastructure and may also help readers make a long-term assessment of the government's operations.

The statement of activities provides the readers with information to assess whether the government's financial position is improving or deteriorating and whether or not the government is generating sufficient revenue to cover the cost of services (GASB, 1999). The net assets for the city of River Falls decreased from $124,333,801 at the beginning of the year to $121,168,787 at year end. This indicates that the city's financial position has deteriorated and should cause interested readers to review the statement of net assets and notes, to make comparisons with previous years, and to ask responsible officials questions.

Another interesting aspect (and potential point of misunderstanding) in this statement is the net expense column, which reports the amount of functional expenses that were not covered by user charges and specific grants or contributions (Patton, 1999). For example, although user charges covered $5,612,267 and grants covered $575,000 of health and sanitation expenses, a net expense of $551,405 had to be financed by general revenues. The net expense amount for health and sanitation should not be understood to mean that the health and sanitation function was poorly managed. Instead, the net expense means that city management has decided to pay for a portion of the services provided by the health and sanitation area with general revenues. General revenues include property taxes of $34,168,449 and other taxes of $13,308,487.

---

* Prior to GASB statement no. 34, state and local governments were not required to report infrastructure assets (e.g., roads, bridges, dams) in their annual financial statements. Reporting infrastructure assets and the cost of maintaining them at an adequate service level is necessary for meaningful cost of service measures.

One purpose of a city government is to provide the services needed by the citizens of a community. This often requires that a city use general revenues to supplement programs. In the health and sanitation area, the city may be supplementing a city clinic that was established to provide basic medical services for individuals not able to pay for the services. The city also may be supplementing the amounts paid by residents for garbage collection. The statement of activities will not provide readers with enough information to determine whether a government is efficiently financing or using its resources in meeting its objectives. The statement of activities, however, provides readers with information that should allow them to begin to ask questions regarding the cost of government services. Also, citizens will be able to ask why the government is supplementing certain programs. For example, some citizens may question why the government is supplementing culture and recreation with over $5 million if they perceive that the city streets are not in good condition and believe more money should be spent on public works.

Fund Statements

The fund statements are of particular interest to readers concerned about the financing of the government's current operations. The statement of revenues, expenditures, and changes in fund balance* (Table 3) provides information about the inflows, outflows, and balances of current financial resources. Because this is a detailed operating statement prepared using a current financial resources measurement focus, readers should be able to gather information about the city's ability to continue to provide services for the coming year that is not in the governmentwide statement of activities.

The statement of revenues, expenditures, and changes in fund balances is reported using *major funds*. Reporting major funds in the fund financial statements provides much more detail about those funds than currently occurs when only reporting by fund type. Nonmajor funds that do not meet the criteria established by the GASB for major funds will be reported in one column in the statement of revenues, expenditures, and changes in fund balances. The illustrated statement in Table 3 assumes that all funds were reported as major funds.

Fund reporting allows the reader to view the financial operations of the government in more detail. The general fund—the city's primary operating fund—is used to account for most of the general activities of the government except for those required to be accounted for in another fund. A reader interested in the availability of financial resources for the coming year would likely want to know that the general fund had an ending fund balance of $1,354,809 and would examine the balance sheet to see how much was available for next year's appropriations.

Special revenue funds are used to account for revenue sources that are legally restricted for a particular purpose (e.g., community development block grants). Debt service funds are used to account for the financing of the general government's long-term debt. Capital project funds are used to account for the acquisition of the general government's major fixed assets or construction of major capital projects.

---

* GASB statement no. 34 requires a highly aggregated reconciliation between the fund financial statements and the governmentwide statements to appear at the bottom of the fund statements or in a separate schedule immediately following the related fund financial statement. The illustrative statement in Appendix II does not include the reconciliation.

The detailed description of revenue sources (e.g., property taxes, other taxes, fines, and fees) should help the reader understand how the city funded its operations and provides information necessary to project the city's ability to pay for services in the next year. The detailed reporting of outlays for principal and interest payments for debt service allows the reader to consider the resources that are necessary for debt repayment. Unlike the statement of activities, this statement reports the amounts that were expended for principal as well as interest for the year. This information is particularly valuable to readers interested in understanding the debt repaying ability of the entity.

The budgetary comparison schedule (Table 4) would be required for the general fund and major special revenue funds and should help readers compare actual results with the legally adopted budget (GASB, 1995). This schedule would be particularly useful to those concerned about budgeting, budgetary management, and compliance with the budget.

Three aspects of the schedule make it particularly useful to readers who are concerned about legal and budgetary compliance. First, the original and final budget amounts are presented. By comparing these amounts, readers may ask why some budget areas increased during the year. Why was the original budget for garbage pickup of $5,756,250 increased to $5,865,757?

Second, differences between budgeted and actual amounts are reported in the variance column.* Because the fire department has an unfavorable variance of $201,514, a reader might question city management's authority for exceeding the budget and might want to know the reason for the additional spending. Were there more fires than expected? Was there mismanagement? In any case, the comparison provides readers with information not provided in other statements that could be useful in their analysis of the city's operations.

Finally, the reporting of expenditures by department level gives the reader a more detailed accounting of actual spending. This level of detail allows the reader to ask questions about departments that would not be possible if reporting were limited to functions or programs.

SUMMARY AND CONCLUSION

Governmental financial reporting has evolved through the years. From its beginning in a watchdog role with a fiscal accountability emphasis it has evolved into a relatively uniform system of financial reporting. Today, governmental fund accounting and financial reporting emphasize the importance of showing compliance with legal and budgetary restrictions and the inflows, outflows, and balances of current financial resources. Readers are provided the information necessary to assess the ability of the government to maintain the current level of services during the next year. Investors and creditors are able to assess the debt-repaying ability of the government.

Many critics believe that the current state of governmental financial reporting is antiquated, however, because it does not provide information to assist users is assessing long-term financial health. The GASB therefore issued statement no. 34 in June of 1999

---

* The actual column in the statement is prepared using the same basis of accounting as is used to prepare the budget. Reporting on the same basis is necessary for meaningful comparisons to be made between budgeted and actual amounts. For the city of River Falls, the budget and actual numbers are presented using the *cash* basis of accounting.

to require state and local governments to provide readers with information to assess operational accountability. The addition of governmentwide financial statements prepared using an economic resources measurement focus and the accrual basis of accounting should provide the information needed to assess long-term financial condition and to evaluate the efficiency and effectiveness of governmental operations. The requirement for governments to continue to report governmental fund-based information using a current resource flows measurement focus and the modified accrual basis of accounting should provide readers with the information needed to assess a government's fiscal accountability.

REVIEW QUESTIONS

1. What are the major features of governmental financial statements (prior to the issuance of GASB statement no. 34)?
2. What is a fund? What types of funds are normally used by governments? Why do governments report by fund types?
3. What are the major changes to governmental financial reporting required by statement no. 34? Why were these changes made?
4. What information do you want from governmental financial statements? What types of information would (1) citizens, (2) investors and creditors, (3) legislative officials, and (4) government financial managers want to find in governmental financial reports?
5. Compare and contrast the three operating statements found in Tables 2–4. What are the major features of each statement? Which statement do you believe best reflects the operating results of the city of River Falls? Do you believe all the statements should be required? Which statement is most important in your assessment of the city's operations?

REFERENCES

Cleveland, F. A. (1909). *Chapters on Municipal Administration and Accounting*. New York: Longmans, Green.

Freeman, R. J. (1976). Governmental accounting research and standards-setting: The role of NCGA. *Governmental Finance, May:* 6–13.

Freeman, R. J. and Shoulders, C. D. (1996) *Governmental and Nonprofit Accounting: Theory and Practice*. 5th ed. Upper Saddle River, NJ: Prentice Hall.

Governmental Accounting Standards Board. (1984). Statement no. 1 of the Governmental Accounting Standards Board. *Authoritative Status of NCGA Pronouncements and AICPA Industry Audit Guide*. Stamford, CT: Governmental Accounting Standards Board.

Governmental Accounting Standards Board. (1987). Concepts Statement no. 1 of the Governmental Accounting Standards Board. *Objectives of Financial Reporting*. Stamford, CT: Governmental Accounting Standards Board.

Governmental Accounting Standards Board. Statement no. 9 of the Governmental Accounting Standards Board. (1989). *Reporting Cash Flows of Proprietary and Nonexpendable Trust Funds and Governmental Entities That Use Proprietary Fund Accounting*. Norwalk, CT: Governmental Accounting Standards Board.

Governmental Accounting Standards Board. (1991). Statement no. 14 of the Governmental Accounting Standards Board. *The Financial Reporting Entity*. Norwalk, CT: Governmental Accounting Standards Board.

Governmental Accounting Standards Board. (1995). *Preliminary Views of the Governmental Accounting Standards Board on Major Issues Related to Governmental Financial Reporting Model: Core Financial Statements*. Norwalk, CT: Governmental Accounting Standards Board.

Governmental Accounting Standards Board. (1996). *Codification of Governmental Accounting and Financial Reporting Standards*. Norwalk, CT: Governmental Accounting Standards Board.

Governmental Accounting Standards Board. (1997). Exposure Draft: Proposed Statement of the Governmental Accounting Standards Board. *Basic Financial Statements and Management's Discussion and Analysis for State and Local Governments*. Norwalk, CT: Governmental Accounting Standards Board.

Governmental Accounting Standards Board. (1999). Statement no. 34 of the Governmental Accounting Standards Board. *Basic Financial Statements—and Management's Discussion and Analysis—for State and Local Governments*. Norwalk, CT: Governmental Accounting Standards Board.

National Committee on Municipal Accounting. (1935a). *Municipal Accounting Terminology for State Municipal and Other Local Governments*. Chicago: Municipal Finance Officers' Association.

National Committee on Municipal Accounting. (1935b). Municipal funds and their balance sheets. Preliminary ed. *Bulletin no. 5*. Chicago: Municipal Finance Officers' Association of the United States and Canada.

National Committee on Municipal Accounting. (1936). Municipal accounting statements. *Bulletin no. 6* Chicago: Municipal Finance Officers' Association of the United States and Canada.

National Council on Governmental Accounting. (1980). *Governmental Accounting, Auditing, and Financial Reporting*. Chicago: Municipal Finance Officers Association of the United States and Canada.

Patton, T. K. (1999). Governmental operating statements: an examination of understandability and usefulness. Ph.D. dissertation, Texas Tech University, Lubbock, TX.

28

Financial Analysis of the City of Mesquite Falls, Texas, Using Comprehensive Annual Financial Reports

Terry K. Patton
University of Wisconsin, Oshkosh, Wisconsin, U.S.A.

Aman Khan
Texas Tech University, Lubbock, Texas, U.S.A.

The city of Mesquite Falls* is located about 130 miles northwest of Dallas in north-central Texas. Incorporated in 1889, Mesquite Falls and its railway network originally served as a center for the area's farming and ranching activities. In the early 1900s, major oil discoveries were made in Mesquite County. Being the county seat of Mesquite County, the city experienced substantial growth as independent oil producers and oil field manufacturing companies established headquarters there. Oil field equipment manufacturers and suppliers remained an important part of the city's economy for several decades. Spurred by rising oil prices in the late 1970s and early 1980s, the city's oil-related businesses expanded, causing the population of Mesquite Falls to reach a high of 104,500 in 1984. Unfortunately for the city, the oil-driven prosperity ended as oil prices began to plummet soon thereafter. By 1989, the city's population had decreased to 95,000.

Because it is the largest city within a 100-mile radius, however, Mesquite Falls continues to be a trade center for southern Oklahoma and North Texas. The city's hospitals and doctors serve as the major regional medical center for a sixteen-county area. Mesquite State University, located within the city's boundaries, has approximately 5000 students in undergraduate and graduate programs. Hoover Air Force Base, located in the northeast corner of the city, has seen substantial growth in the last five years, as many training operations performed at other bases have been consolidated at Hoover. The base is a major training facility for both U.S. and NATO personnel, and it is anticipated that it will continue to be an important military base in the future. In addition, the city has witnessed a surge in manufacturing activity, with Certain Teed and the General Motors AC/Delco division increasing production at local facilities. By 1999, the city's population had rebounded to

---

* For the purpose of anonymity, the actual city and county names as well as other names and details were changed in this case study.

98,600, while its 5.8% unemployment rate was below the state's unemployment rate of 6.5%.

FINANCIAL AND BUDGETARY MANAGEMENT STRUCTURE

The city has a council–manager form of government. The city is governed by a city council that is elected by city residents. The city council hires the city manager, who is responsible for general operations. Nine department heads report to the city manager. These department heads are responsible for the following departments:

    Traffic and transportation
    Finance
    Administrative services
    Housing and community development
    Health
    Police
    Fire
    Parks and recreation
    Public works and utilities.

With the help of department heads and budgeting personnel, the city manager prepares a proposed budget for all departments, divisions, and offices. This budget is presented to the city council prior to the beginning of the fiscal year on October 1. The operating budget is the city's financial plan for the coming fiscal year and includes both proposed expenditures and sources of financing.

After public hearings the city council must approve the budget for the next fiscal year. The budget represents the city manager's legal authority to expend the financial resources of the city. Expenditures must not exceed the legally adopted budgeted amounts at the department level. The city manager must receive council approval before transferring appropriations between departments. The city manager, however, is authorized to transfer appropriated balances from one expenditure account to another within a single department.

The city uses an encumbrance accounting system to ensure that no department exceeds its appropriations. Budgetary control is maintained at the class level within each department. Amounts are encumbered prior to issuing purchase orders to vendors. If the issuance of a purchase order would cause a class-level balance to exceed appropriated amounts, the purchase order will not be issued until additional appropriations are authorized. Department heads oversee the expenditures in their departments and are given periodic reports that detail the amount of appropriations still available for expenditure during the fiscal year. The reports are prepared as part of the normal accounting process in the finance department.

The director of finance heads the finance department. The finance director is directly responsible for the finance, accounting, tax collection, and utility collection functions for the city. Personnel in the finance department are responsible for cash and investment management and are actively involved in risk management for worker's compensation. The city manager and director of finance are responsible for implementing internal accounting controls to ensure the city maintains proper control over resources. These controls are designed to provide reasonable assurance that assets are safeguarded and that the financial records used to prepare financial statements are reliable. City personnel and the external financial auditors have assessed internal accounting controls and indicated they are adequate.

ANALYSIS OF FINANCIAL STATEMENTS

The city of Mesquite Falls has a fiscal year that begins on October 1 and ends on September 30. After the fiscal year ends, the city prepares a comprehensive annual financial report (CAFR) to report the results of operations for the preceding fiscal year. The last five years' worth of CAFRs will form the basis for our examination of the city's financial health. Other sources of information, such as *Moody's Bond Record* (Moody's Investor Services, 1994) and the Government Finance Officers Association's (GFOA's) *Financial Indicators Database: Municipal Governments*,* (GFOA, 1994) will supplement the CAFR analysis. In particular, the GFOA's report of financial indicators will provide a basis for making comparisons between Mesquite Falls and other cities of similar size throughout the country.

A portion of our analysis is based on both horizontal and vertical analyses for each of the city's funds as reported in the last five CAFRs. These analyses consider the variation in accounts over time and within a set of accounts. For the operating statement, a horizontal analysis reveals the rate of change in the factors that affect changes in fund balance or changes in retained earnings over time. In the balance sheet, it provides a dynamic approach to reviewing the increases and decreases that occurred over certain time periods—in our case, five years. A vertical analysis of the balance sheet indicates the quantitative relationships among the data items at a particular time. For the income statement, a vertical analysis indicates how tax and other revenue sources are distributed among the government's programs and the costs to provide them. This type of analysis can also be used to compare one organization with another.

GENERAL FUND

The general operations of the city are accounted for and reported in its general fund. Because the general fund is the largest governmental fund, our analysis begins here. The general fund is used to account for all financial resources except those that are legally or contractually required to be accounted for in another fund.

Cash

A horizontal analysis of the city's general fund balance sheet is presented in Appendix A, schedule 1. An examination of the changes reported in the analysis over the five-

---

* The GFOA published the *Financial Indicators Database: Municipal Governments* in 1992 (GFOA, 1994). The publication includes selected financial ratios for municipalities whose fiscal years ended in 1991. The ratios reported in the publication were taken from the *CAFRs* of municipalities that receive the GFOA's certificate of excellence in financial reporting. This represented 57.07% of cities with populations above 50,000. For cities with populations between 50,000 and 99,999, the database included 190 cities. For cities with populations between 100,000 and 199,999, the database included seventy-eight cities. Although the ratios reported are for the fiscal year ending in 1991, they should still provide an adequate benchmark against which to compare the ratios for the city of Mesquite Falls's fiscal year ending in 1999.

year period yields some interesting observations. Not surprisingly, asset balances have fluctuated over the years. Year-end cash balances have declined by about $1,200,000 from 1995 to 1999. This does not seem to be a cause for alarm, however, because the ending cash balance of $9,688,570 for the fiscal year ending September 30, 1999, was about 35% of the total expenditures of $31,212,658 (Appendix A, schedule 3) made in fiscal year 1998–1999 in the general fund. This means that the city should have had more than adequate resources to cover operating expenses in the subsequent year until property tax collections began in November 1999. Although reserved and designated fund balances will be discussed in detail later, these fund balances do not change our analysis of the adequacy of the cash balance for fiscal year 1999–2000 operations because cash would have had a balance of over $6 million even if the reserved and designated fund balances of $3,265,385 had been subtracted directly from the cash balance. (Of course, this would not be done because reserved and designated fund balances are not a reservation of cash balances, but rather of net assets.)

Property Taxes

Taxes and assessments receivables for property (or ad valorem) taxes showed a steady decline, from $1,203,635 in 1995 to $797,585 in 1999. This may indicate that the city was making a better effort to collect delinquent property taxes in a timely manner. For the fiscal year ending in 1999, the city collected 97% of its current-year assessment during the year. This continued a trend that began in 1995 when the city first collected current-year property taxes at a 97% rate. The statistical tables in the city's CAFR indicate that after including the collection of delinquent property taxes, the total collection of taxes as a percentage of the current-year tax levy had ranged from 98.86–100.34% during the five-year period under consideration.

The statistical tables also report that tax rates showed a slight increase from 1995 to 1999. The property tax rate in 1995 was $.64 per $100 valuation and had increased to $.67 per $100 valuation in 1999. This increase was partially necessary due to a fall in the assessed value of property during the period. The assessed value of property in 1995 was $2,299,242,866, but fell to $2,217,963,473 in 1999. During the same period, taxes assessed increased from $14,664,571 to $14,940,203.

An examination of the largest ten taxpayers from the statistical section of the CAFRs for the years 1995 to 1999 helps to explain the loss in assessed valuation of property during the period. As has been previously discussed, the city saw a major decline in the oil and related manufacturing industry beginning in about 1985. These losses continued throughout the 1980s and early 1990s as more manufacturers and small producers ceased or downsized operations. For example, Texaco, Inc. was the ninth largest taxpayer in 1990, with an assessed valuation of $7,621,544. Texaco had oil storage and other facilities that ceased to be used by 1994. The city also lost a major manufacturer in 1990 when Sprague Electric closed its facility. Sprague Electric's property had an assessed valuation of $16,342,146 in 1995. (The county has recently purchased the Sprague facility for use as a prison.) Retail shopping centers, grocery stores, and utility companies dominated the list of the ten largest taxpayers in 1999, with only one manufacturing firm making the top ten list. Although the expansion of Hoover Air Force Base created new jobs in the area, it only indirectly affected the assessed valuation of property in the city because Hoover is the property of the federal government and not subject to city property tax assessment.

Table 1 Comparison of Property Tax Levies per Capita

Population of city	Total property tax levy per capita (median value)
50,000–99,999	$120.05 (from GFOA)
City of Mesquite Falls 98,600	$151.52 (actual)
100,000–199,999	$162.41 (from GFOA)

Even with manufacturing industry losses in recent years, the city's property tax rate of $.67 per $100 assessed valuation does not seem onerous. Based on its home rule charter, the city is allowed to levy taxes up to $2.25 per $100 of assessed valuation. This means that the city could legally levy up to $34,963,976 in additional tax revenues before reaching its legal tax limit. According to Table 1, based on information reported in the GFOA's *Financial Indicators Database*, Mesquite Falls's total property tax levy per capita for 1999 of $151.52 was comparable to cities of similar size throughout the country.

In summary, the city's property tax collections appear to be reasonable for a city of its size. The city should be able to increase its property tax rate in the future because it is not near its legal tax limit and its total property tax levy per capita is near the median for cities its size. Property tax collection procedures seem to be adequate because the city has been collecting current-year property tax assessments at a rate of 97% or better for the last few years.

Other Receivables and Other Asset Accounts

An examination of the horizontal analysis for the general fund balance sheet (Appendix A, schedule 1) reveals that the receivable from other city funds to the general fund has fluctuated substantially during the period 1995–1999. This is to be expected in any city because this account represents funds that are to be transferred to the general fund from other funds in the city, and these transfers are not made on a regularly scheduled basis. An examination of the vertical analysis for the balance sheet (Appendix A, schedule 2) shows that the receivable from other city funds has not represented more than 4.2% of assets during the five-year period.

The receivable from government agencies showed substantial growth, from $558,700 in 1995 to $1,136,955 in 1999. Although not explicitly stated in the report, this receivable likely represented monies owed to the city from the state of Texas or the federal government. It is interesting to note that the increase in the receivable corresponds with a general increase in intergovernmental revenue during the five-year period. In fiscal year 1994–1995, intergovernmental revenue was $791,383. By fiscal year 1998–1999, intergovernmental revenue had increased to $1,723,190.

An examination of the vertical analysis of the balance sheet for the general fund indicates that other receivables, inventory, prepaid items, and other assets represented an immaterial portion of the overall assets in the general fund. A quick review of the reported balances revealed nothing unusual.

Liabilities

The vertical analysis of the balance sheet for the general fund shows that the balance for current liabilities represents only 25.1% of current assets for the fiscal year ending in

1999. This is up from previous years, but with a current ratio of approximately 4 to 1, the city should easily be able to meet its current operating obligations. Although current liabilities increased by 30.6% for the fiscal year ending in 1999, when compared to the 1998 balances this does not seem unusual, as these fluctuations are common for municipalities. The fluctuations can often be explained by year-end purchases made by department heads who realize they have excess funds in their budgets that will be lost if not spent. Because the CAFR does not explain the fluctuations in current liabilities, this explanation is only speculation. It might be advisable for city management to analyze year-end purchases to ensure that they are appropriate, however.

The horizontal analysis of the general fund balance sheet highlights the fact that no adjustment had been made to the accrued vacation and sick leave account from 1995 to 1999. It seems unusual that no adjustment had been made to this account, because many cities adjust this liability at least periodically if not on an annual basis. Because the CAFR provides only minimal disclosure for accrued vacation and sick leave, it is impossible to assess the adequacy of the liability reported. This could be an underreported liability, however, and should be reassessed by city management.

Long-Term Debt

The general long-term debt of a municipality is not accounted for in the general fund, but rather in the general long-term debt account group. This account group reports all the city's long-term liabilities except for the debts of proprietary funds, which are reported in those funds. Although long-term debt is not reported in the general fund, the discussion of long-term debt at this point seems appropriate because the debt is a general obligation of the city and will be paid largely from general operating revenues.

To assess the amount of debt burden the city placed on its citizens for general obligation debts, it is useful to examine the net general bonded debt per capita amount reported in the statistical section of the city's CAFR. Net general bonded debt is defined as gross general bonded debt less amounts available for the retirement of bonds in the debt service fund. Table 2 compares Mesquite Falls's net general bonded debt per capita to that of comparably sized cities throughout the United States, as reported in the GFOA's *Financial Indicators Database* (GFOA, 1994).

As can be seen in Table 2, Mesquite Falls's net general bonded debt was near the median value for cities its size in the database. Since 1991, the city has maintained its general bonded debt on a per capita basis within about $10 of the 1999 amount of $215.35. Because the size of the city's general obligation debt remained relatively stable on a per capita basis, it seems that city management has attempted to maintain a reasonable debt burden for the community. This is reflected in the Moody's bond rating; the city was

Table 2 Comparison of Net General Bonded Debt per Capita

Population of city	Net general bonded debt per capita (median value)
50,000–99,999	$217.38 (from GFOA)
City of Mesquite Falls—98,600	$215.35
100,000–199,999	$292.47 (from GFOA)

assigned an A1 rating for both the city's general obligation debt and its water and sewer revenue bonds. According to Moody's, the A1 rating is given to bonds that have the strongest investment attributes for A-rated bonds.

Fund Balances

Total fund balance in the general fund showed a general decline over the last five years. Although not reported in the analysis in Appendix A, total fund balances for the general fund showed greater fluctuations over an eight-year period. The fund balance increased for three consecutive years until the fiscal year ending September 30, 1996. The fund balance then decreased by almost $1 million for the fiscal year ending September 30, 1997, before gaining about $380,000 the next year. For the fiscal year ending September 30, 1999, the fund balance declined by over $1 million to an eight-year low of $9,370,406. Two questions should be asked regarding the fund balance for the fiscal year ending in 1999. What contributed to the decline in fund balance? Is the fund balance adequate as of September 30, 1999?

An examination of the horizontal analysis of the general fund statement of revenue, expenditures, and changes in fund balance (Appendix A, schedule 3) does not show any major change in overall revenues or expenditures for the city during the five years being studied. It is evident that the reduction in fund balance for the fiscal year ending in 1999 was due to large operating transfers out. The notes to the financial statements did not explicitly state the destination for the total amount of funds transferred out of the general fund, yet an inference can be made about that transfer. For the fiscal years ending 1995 to 1998, the notes to financial statements reported an operating transfer into the transit fund in the same amount as the operating transfer out of the general fund. It therefore seems safe to assume that a portion of the $2,081,193 in transfers out represents the general fund supplement to the transit fund, which is one of the city's four enterprise funds. The transit fund accounts for the operations of the city's buses. Most cities experience a loss in their transit fund, and it is not unusual for cities to supplement their transit fund with a transfer from general operating funds. It is likely that the city of Mesquite Falls supplemented its transit fund with a transfer from the general fund in the amount of $128,844 during the 1998–1999 fiscal year.

This leaves an unexplained transfer out of the general fund in the amount of $1,952,349. Based on a study of the operating transfer note in the financial statements, it appears that this money was likely transferred to finance a new multipurpose events center. The city's CAFR for the fiscal year ending September 30, 1998, highlights this project. It notes that the city and the county are to contribute $9 million each, with private sources providing the remaining $7 million to finance the center. The center will include a 10,000-seat coliseum, an exhibit hall, meeting rooms, and an agricultural complex.

An examination of the city's budgetary statement, the combined statement of revenues, expenditures, and changes in fund balances—budget and actual—for the fiscal year ending in 1999, shows that the city had budgeted for this amount of operating transfers out of the general fund. It therefore seems that city management intended for the fund balance to be reduced.

The question that still needs to be examined is whether or not the fund balance remaining is adequate. As discussed earlier, the city has more than enough unreserved and undesignated fund balance to meet its current obligations for several months into the

Table 3   Comparison of Unreserved, Undesignated Fund Balance per Capita

Population of city	Unreserved, undesignated fund balance per capita (median)
50,000–100,000	33.51 (from GFOA)
City of Mesquite Falls—98,600	61.92
100,000–199,999	29.73 (from GFOA)

1999–2000 fiscal year. The unreserved, undesignated fund balance of $6,105,021 therefore does appear to be adequate.

As additional evidence that the city's unreserved, undesignated fund balance is adequate, a comparison of the city's balance to that of comparably sized cities throughout the United States is helpful. Table 3 is based on both the GFOA's *Financial Indicators Database* (GFOA, 1994) and actual amounts from the city of Mesquite Falls's 1999 CAFR.

The city of Mesquite Falls's undesignated, unreserved fund balance was clearly better than most cities its size in the database. It is also interesting to note that the city's unreserved, undesignated fund balance *as a percentage of expenditures* was much greater than comparably sized cities. Again, Table 4 was prepared from both data obtained from the GFOA's *Financial Indicators Database* (GFOA, 1994) and actual amounts reported in the city's 1999 CAFR.

This again illustrates the strong financial position of the city and indicates that the city should have no trouble meeting its current financial obligations. Even with the reductions in the fund balance to finance the new multipurpose events center, the city appears to have more than adequate unreserved, undesignated fund balances.

A discussion of fund balance is not complete without an examination of the reserved and designated portions of fund balance. For the fiscal year ending in 1999 a fund balance was reserved for inventory and prepaid items in the amount of $137,733. This is the same amount that is reported for inventory and prepaid items in the assets portion of the general fund's balance sheet. The fund balance was reserved because inventory and prepaid assets are not available as current *financial* resources. The reserve for encumbrance of $127,652 on September 30, 1999, represents amounts that the city is obligated to pay in the 1999–2000 fiscal year. This reserve results from purchase orders issued for goods or services not received by the end of the 1998–1999 fiscal year. The amount reported as a reserve for encumbrances for the last two fiscal years has been quite small (less than 1% of annual expenditures).

Table 4   Comparison of Unreserved, Undesignated Fund Balance as a Percentage of Expenditures

Population of city	Unreserved, undesignated fund balance as a percentage of expenditures
50,000–99,999	9.32 (from GFOA)
City of Mesquite Falls—98,600	19.6
100,000–199,999	7.47 (from GFOA)

An examination of the designated fund balance in Appendix A, schedule 1 found that the city increased its designated fund balance by $250,000 each year during the period from 1995 to 1999. Unfortunately, the notes to the financial statements only state that the designated fund balance represents city management's tentative plans for the use of financial resources in a future period; the actual planned usage for the designated funds is not disclosed. It is assumed city management is planning to make a major expenditure in future years from this designated fund balance.

Revenues

The city's primary source of revenues for the general fund has historically been tax revenues. As can be seen in Appendix A, schedule 4, 82.6% of the city's general fund revenues for the fiscal year ending in 1999 were tax revenues. The city has several sources for tax revenues—property (ad valorem), sales, and franchise tax collections. For the fiscal year ending in 1999, property taxes accounted for approximately 43% of general fund revenues, making it the largest single revenue source for the city. The increase in total revenue of 5.8% from the 1997–1998 fiscal year was primarily due to an increase in tax collections.

Taxes were a more important revenue source for the city of Mesquite Falls than for other cities its size. Comparing information reported in the GFOA's *Financial Indicators Database* (GFOA, 1994) with that of the city of Mesquite Falls, it was found that the median amount of tax revenue reported in the general fund on a per capita basis was $195.60 for other cities the size of Mesquite Falls. Mesquite Falls reported tax revenue in the general fund on a per capita basis of $260.70. This indicates that the city of Mesquite Falls is more dependent upon taxes than other cities its size in the database.

Intergovernmental revenues are resources transferred to the city from other governments, such as the state of Texas and the federal government. The city is less dependent on intergovernmental revenue than other cities its size, however. When compared with other cities its size (using the GFOA's *Financial Indicators Database*), the city reported intergovernmental revenues in the general fund on a per capita basis of $17.48, which was much less than the median value of $37.32 reported for comparably sized cities. Although this revenue source has grown in recent years and is the city's second largest revenue source, it is still only 5.5% of total general fund revenues reported in the 1998–1999 fiscal year.

Given these factors, it appears that the city has a relatively stable revenue source to finance future operations and is not overly dependent on funding from the state and federal governments. As discussed in the receivable section of this chapter, the city could assess substantially more in property taxes without placing a greater tax burden on its citizens than other cities its size.

Expenditures

The majority of expenditures for general operations of the government are reported in the general fund. Appendix A, schedule 4 shows the percentage of expenditures made by each of the nine departments in relation to total expenditures for the general fund.

The police department accounted for almost one-third of total expenditures. A horizontal analysis (Appendix A, schedule 3) reveals that police department expenditures grew substantially each year. The finance director stated in his letter in the CAFR that these increases are the result of increases in staffing. This seems to be a common trend throughout the country.

The fire division, which accounted for nearly 19% of general fund expenditures for the fiscal year ending in 1999, has seen modest expenditure increases over the last five years. The finance director explains that these increases occurred as a result of increased salaries and other costs.

Expenditures for the administrative services division show substantial fluctuation through the years. For the fiscal year ending in 1998, administrative service expenditures declined by 10.6% (Appendix A, schedule 3). The next year the expenditures increased 7.7%. The administrative services division is actively involved in the acquisition of property for city projects. According to the city's finance director, the city acquired a substantial amount of property in fiscal year 1996–1997 in the downtown area to be used for the multipurpose events center. This increased expenditures in the administrative services division. The reduction in expenditures the next year was largely due to a decrease in property acquisition activities. In addition, the data processing and municipal court departments—components of the administrative services division—reduced operating expenditures. The increase in expenditures for fiscal year 1998–1999 was again due to additional expenditures associated with the multipurpose events center.

The health department represented about 8% of total general fund expenditures for the fiscal year ending in 1999. An examination of health department expenditures over a five-year period reveals growth of over 36% during that time. This was the largest percentage growth in any department. Fortunately for the city, the finance director states that much of the increase in expenditures was financed by additional state grants.

Expenditures for the public works division—at 15% of total expenditures—remained relatively stable over the five-year period except for fiscal year 1996–1997, when expenditures increased 17.6% over the previous year. This increase was due to engineering work on a flood control project and work at the water treatment plant. Expenditures in the next fiscal year were reduced to previous years' levels.

Although the other departments showed some fluctuation in expenditures over the five-year period, they were not substantial and do not warrant explanation. Overall it appears that the fluctuations in departmental expenditures can be reasonably explained. One concern, however, is that the public works division's expenditures for the most recent fiscal year are at the same level as the expenditures made in fiscal year 1994–1995. Because the public works division is responsible for capital improvements, the lack of increased expenditures may indicate that the city has failed to maintain its infrastructure. The small amount of expenditures made in the capital projects fund over the five-year period seems to justify this concern and will be discussed in more detail in a later section.

OTHER GOVERNMENTAL FUNDS

The city's general fund accounts for about 80% of total governmental expenditures. The city's other governmental funds report the remaining governmental expenditures and include the special revenue, debt service, and capital projects funds. These governmental funds are analyzed below on a more limited basis. That analysis focuses on each fund's purpose and major points of interest. It is based on a five-year horizontal and vertical analysis for each of the fund's balance sheets and a horizontal analysis of their statements of revenues, expenditures, and changes in fund balances. Because of limited space, however, these statements and related analyses have not been reproduced in this case.

Special Revenue Funds

The city of Mesquite's second largest governmental fund type in terms of both assets and expenditures is the special revenue fund. Special revenue funds are used to account for the proceeds from revenue sources that have been legally designated to be expended for only specific purposes. A separate fund is maintained for each specific purpose. The city of Mesquite Falls had seven special revenue funds reported in fiscal year 1998–1999.

Four special revenue funds are used to account for federal revenues that had been legally restricted for specific usage. These are the community development block grant fund, the Section 8 housing fund, the rental rehabilitation fund, and the home investment partnership agreement fund. Except for the community development block grant fund, which is used to account for federal block grant revenues and expenditures, the remainder of the federally funded special revenue funds is related to lower-income family housing supplements. The remaining three funds are used to report state grants and restricted state revenue sharing programs.

The community development block grant and the Section 8 housing funds accounted for a little over 68% of total special revenue fund expenditures for the fiscal year ending in 1999. These two funds have dominated special revenue fund spending during the past five years. Because the city was required to spend the monies received from the federal government in accordance with federally mandated standards, city management faces the risk that the federal government may disallow certain expenditures and request repayment for them. The notes to the financial statements say that the independent auditors who examined the city's financial statements and reviewed city compliance with federal mandates believe the city has complied with all federal grant requirements. It therefore appears that the city exercised good management control over federal grant expenditures.

Debt Service Funds

Debt service funds are used to account for the accumulation and payment of long-term debt-related expenditures: principal payments, interest payments, and payments for agent fees. The city reports two debt service funds. Our horizontal analysis of balance sheets shows that total assets reported in those funds remained relatively stable over the past five years. Our analysis also shows that debt service expenditures were also relatively stable for the last five years. Debt service expenditures are financed by property tax collections and the interest earned on investments maintained to retire debt. Nothing unusual appears to have occurred in these funds over the five-year period.

Capital Projects Fund

Capital projects funds are used to account for resources received to finance and expenditures made to construct or acquire major capital facilities for the general government. About half of the assets in the city's capital projects funds as of September 30, 1999, are designated for the construction of the multipurpose events center. The only other major project that the city reported in these funds is a flood control project. These two projects

accounted for over 80% of the assets and over 85% of the reported expenditures in the
capital projects funds for the 1998–1999 fiscal year.

The average expenditures in the capital project funds for the last five years were
calculated to be about $1.55 million per year. This appears to be a little low for cities the
size of Mesquite Falls. The adequacy of capital expenditures will be discussed in more
detail at the end of the next section.

TEN-POINT TEST OF FINANCIAL CONDITION

So far the examination of the city's general operations as accounted for in the governmental
funds indicates that Mesquite Falls seems to be in a good financial condition. The city
has an adequate cash balance to meet current operating needs. Property tax levies are
reasonable for a city the size of Mesquite Falls. General obligation debt on a per capita
basis is about the same as for other cities of comparable size. Moody's gave the city a good
bond rating. Although the general fund's fund balance had been reduced, the unreserved,
undesignated fund balance is still more than adequate. The city is not too dependent on
intergovernmental revenues. Finally, the city has had a good collection rate for its property
tax assessments, and the city should be able to levy more taxes if necessary. From all
outward appearances, the city is in a relatively strong financial position. One last test of
the strength of the city's general operations—a ten-point test that compares ten key financial ratios of comparably sized cities—needs to be considered, however.

In 1993, Ken Brown introduced the ten-point test to assess the financial condition
of municipalities with populations of less than 100,000 (Brown, 1993). Brown used the
GFOA's *Financial Indicators Database* for the fiscal year ending in 1989 to calculate the
ratios. The database included the 750 cities in the United States that both had a population
of less than 100,000 and had been awarded the GFOA's certificate of achievement for
excellence in financial reporting for their CAFR.

In general, the first three ratios assess revenues. Ratio 4 considers expenditures.
Ratios 5–7 examine operating position, and ratios 8–10 consider debt structure. Certain
of the components (numerator or denominator) for the ratios are not self-explanatory.
These include the following:

> *Total revenues* is the total revenue for all governmental funds. *Total expenditures*
>   is the expenditure for all governmental funds.
> *Total general fund revenues from own sources* is the total of all revenue reported
>   by the general fund *less* intergovernmental revenues.
> *General fund sources from other funds* is general fund operating transfers in.
> *Total general fund sources* is the total of all revenues and operating transfers in.
> *Operating expenditures* is the total expenditure for the general, special revenue, and
>   debt service funds.
> *Unreserved general fund balances* include both designated and undesignated, unre-
>   served fund balances.
> *Direct long-term debt* is general obligation debt to be repaid from property taxes.

Table 5 shows a comparison of key ratios for the city of Mesquite Falls to comparably
sized towns throughout the United States. (Ken Brown's interpretation of the ten ratios
calculated to assess the financial condition of a city is included after Table 5.)

Table 5 Ten-Point Test Ratios

Ratio	Ratio for Mesquite Falls	Quartile 1 (worst)	Quartile 2	Quartile 3	Quartile 4 (best)
1. Total revenues/Population	$398	$714 or more	$714 to $532	$532 to $429	$429 or less
2. Total general fund revenues/ Total revenues	94.5%	80.2% or less	80.2% to 87.7%	87.7% to 98.8%	98.8% or more
3. General fund sources from other funds/Total general fund sources	3.11%	7.285% or more	7.285% to 2.083%	2.083% to .003%	.003% or less
4. Operating expenditures/Total expenditures	96.0%	95.8% or more	95.8% to 88.9%	88.9% to 81.6%	81.6% or less
5. Total revenues/Total expenditures	.983	.878 or less	.878 to .964	.964 to 1.038	1.038 or more
6. Unreserved general fund balance/ Total general fund revenues	.293	.086 or less	.086 to .180	.180 to .300	.300 or more
7. Total general fund cash and investments/Total general fund liabilities	3.08	.622 or less	.622 to 1.539	1.539 to 3.372	3.372 or more
8. Total general fund liabilities/ Total general fund revenues	.101	.254 or more	.254 to .101	.101 to .069	.069 or less
9. Direct long-term debt/ Population	$223	$413 or more	$413 to $201	$201 to $21	$21 or less
10. Debt service/Total revenues	.065	.134 or more	.134 to .074	.074 to .041	.041 or less

Note: Ken Brown's interpretation of the ten ratios—ratio 1: a low ratio suggests a greater ability to acquire additional revenue; ratio 2: a high ratio suggests the city is not reliant on external governmental organizations; ratio 3: a low ratio suggests the city does not have to rely on operating transfers to finance general government operations in the general fund; ratio 4: a low ratio suggests the infrastructure is being maintained adequately; ratio 5: a high ratio suggests the city experienced a positive interperiod equity; ratio 6: a high ratio suggests the presence of resources that can be used to overcome a temporary shortfall of revenues; ratio 7: a high ratio suggests sufficient cash with which to pay short-term obligations; ratio 8: a low ratio suggests short-term obligations can be easily serviced by the normal flow of annual revenues; ratio 9: a low ratio suggests the city has the ability to repay its general long-term debt; ratio 10: a low ratio suggests the city is able to pay its debt service requirements when due (Brown, 1993).

The ratios in Table 5 are divided into quartiles to make comparisons easier. Quartile 4 always represents the best ratios for a city, thus for ratios that should have a low ratio (i.e., ratios 1, 3, 4, 8–10), the numbers under quartile 4 report the range in ratios for the 25% of the cities examined that had the lowest ratios. For ratios that should be high, the numbers reported under quartile 4 are the ratios reported in the 25% of the cities with the highest ratios. The second best set of ratios is reported in quartile 3, the third best in quartile 2, and the worst in quartile 1.

As can be seen in Table 5, the city of Mesquite Falls compared quite favorably to the cities in the database. Based on the ranking scale used by Ken Brown to categorize the financial health of cities in the database, the city of Mesquite Falls would have been in the best or second best category for six of the ten ratios listed.

The ratios indicate the city does not depend too heavily on other governments for revenue and has the ability to raise additional revenues internally. The city has sufficient cash to pay its short-term obligations and has enough current resources to overcome any temporary revenue shortfalls. Finally, the city has adequate resources to pay general obligation debt service requirements without having to increase revenues. The city does have a higher than average ratio of direct long-term debt to population. This indicates that city management should carefully weigh the issuance of more bonds. Because projects that are financed by debt are settled in future periods often extending to thirty years, the city in effect defers payment on these projects to future generations of taxpayers. Considering the overall financial strength of the city, the city council may wish to consider financing more capital improvements from current revenues. This could be difficult from a political perspective if property taxes rates had to be raised, however.

Only once was the city of Mesquite Falls in the worst quartile. Ratio 4 considers the ratio of operating expenditures compared to total expenditures. This allows the user to assess the adequacy of capital and infrastructure improvement expenditures. Ken Brown includes *as operating expenditures* all expenditures from the general, special revenue, and debt service funds in the numerator of his ratio. Applying this ratio to the city of Mesquite Falls, however, results in including capital expenditures as a part of operating expenditures. This is because certain capital outlays have been reported in the city's special revenue funds. If these capital outlays are excluded, the adjusted ratio would have placed the city in the second quartile.

Concerns remain, however, that the city may not be taking appropriate steps to ensure that it maintains an adequate infrastructure. Because the majority of its fiscal year 1998–1999 capital project expenditures were spent on a new multipurpose event center, there is some question as to whether or not roads and other city assets have been or are being properly maintained or improved. This warrants an explanation, but it is difficult to speculate on the adequacy of capital outlays without additional information.

In the final analysis, it seems that the ten-point test developed by Ken Brown only reinforces the earlier conclusion that the city's general operations are grounded on a strong financial base. There should be little concern over whether or not the city will be able to provide services at the same or a greater level than it has in the past.

PROPRIETARY FUNDS

A discussion of the financial health of the city of Mesquite Falls cannot be complete without a discussion of its proprietary funds. Like most municipalities, the city has two types of proprietary funds: internal service and enterprise.

Internal Service Funds

Internal service funds are used to account for charges by one department of the government to other departments of the government for services or goods provided on a cost-reimbursement basis. The city of Mesquite Falls uses a single internal service fund to account for costs associated with the operation, maintenance, and replacement of city vehicles and equipment. Departments that use vehicles are charged a monthly rental fee to cover the operating costs of vehicles and equipment.

Based on a horizontal analysis of the internal service fund statement of revenues, expenses, and changes in retained earnings, the fund's operating results have declined in recent years. Although the city reported a net loss in the internal service fund for each of the last five years, the loss for the first two years occurred only because operating transfers were made to other funds. The operating losses for the last three years represent an unfavorable trend because in these years operating revenues were not sufficient to cover operating expenses. Also alarming is the rapid deterioration of the internal service fund's retained earnings over the last five years. The fund's retained earnings deficit increased over sixfold from September 30, 1995 to September 30, 1999. This is certainly not a good trend. What contributed to the net loss and deficit retained earnings balance?

The city has reduced its revenues from rents by over $300,000 from the last year that it covered its operating expenses—that is, in fiscal year 1996–1997. At the same time, maintenance costs reported in the internal service fund have increased significantly. Although depreciation expense dropped from its highest level in fiscal year 1996–1997 compared to fiscal year 1998–1999, this set of conditions seems to signal that the city has a large amount of older equipment that is fully depreciated.

Further evidence that the city is not replacing its motor vehicles and equipment at an adequate rate is found by reviewing the horizontal analysis of the city's balance sheet. Only two of the last five years showed significant additions to the balance in the fund's motor vehicles and equipment account. Because we know that the useful life of this type of equipment is relatively short, it appears that the city is failing to replace its vehicles and equipment at a rate necessary to maintain fixed assets' current levels.

What should city management do to reverse the negative trends? City management needs to make an assessment of its motor vehicle and equipment requirements for future years to ensure that these assets are being replaced at an appropriate rate. Even if motor vehicles and equipment *are* being maintained at an adequate level, the city is still failing to set rates that cover depreciation expense. If the city does not recover depreciation expense through rates, it is failing to set aside resources that will be needed to replace those assets in the future. Instead, the city will need to rely on debt financing or transfers from other funds to replace its assets. To maintain positive operating results, the rental fee charged to other departments by the internal service fund probably should be increased. In effect, the internal service fund is supplementing the other funds that use its equipment by setting rental fees too low.

Enterprise Funds

Enterprise funds are used to account for activities of governments that are operated and financed in a manner similar to for-profit business enterprises. The intent is to set prices charged for services at a rate that recovers the cost of providing the services. The city has four enterprise funds: airport, transit, sanitation, and water and sewer funds. These enterprise funds accounted for about 57.6% of the city's assets, excluding the general government's infrastructure assets that the city chooses not to report and about 30% of total city revenues.

Because much information regarding the financial health of the city is lost in an aggregate analysis of enterprise funds, each of the four enterprise funds will be discussed separately. To provide a basis for discussion of the city's enterprise funds, our analysis considers three ratios used by Aman Khan and Theodore Strumm in their analysis of the city of Lubbock's enterprise funds. The first ratio is the current ratio. It considers whether

Table 6 Analysis Ratios for Mesquite Falls'-Enterprise Funds

Fund	For FYE 1995	For FYE 1996	For FYE 1997	For FYE 1998	For FYE 1999
Current ratio					
All enterprise funds (total)	8.21	6.33	7.44	5.83	5.55
Airport	2.69	4.34	6.31	9.19	14.58
Transit	.86	.93	.88	.89	.89
Sanitation	14.43	8.20	16.12	11.96	8.83
Water and sewer	8.56	6.90	7.43	5.56	5.60
Solvency ratio					
All enterprise funds (total)	.30	.31	.43	.42	.41
Airport	.04	.03	.03	.02	.01
Transit	.22	.37	.26	.18	.26
Sanitation	.04	.07	.03	.05	.06
Water and Sewer	.32	.33	.46	.45	.44
Income ratio					
All enterprise funds (total)	.18	.10	.10	.07	.07
Airport	−.60	−.08	−.19	−.29	−.68
Transit	−2.31	−2.78	−3.54	−4.22	−3.70
Sanitation	.15	.01	.06	.02	−.01
Water and sewer	.24	.18	.15	.14	.14

or not an entity has the ability to pay its current liabilities. It is calculated by dividing a fund's current assets by its current liabilities. The second measure of financial health used in our analysis is the solvency ratio. It is calculated by dividing a fund's total liabilities by total assets and measures an entity's ability to repay both its short- and long-term debts. The final ratio is the income ratio. The income ratio is the ratio of a fund's operating income or loss to its operating revenues. Using the techniques of Khan and Strumm, Table 6 shows the calculation of the three ratios for Mesquite Falls's enterprise funds, both in total and individually, for each of the last five years (Khan and Hildreth, 1994: 487–489).

Airport and Transit Funds

The most striking ratios from Table 6 are the negative income ratios for the airport and transit funds. A negative income ratio means that a fund has not generated enough revenue to cover operating expenses. A discussion of the purpose and nature of the activities reported in those funds is warranted, however, before discussion of the losses in those funds.

The airport fund reports the operating revenues and expenses associated with the Mesquite Falls Municipal Airport. City management believes the airport is essential for the economic growth and vitality of Mesquite Falls and the surrounding area. The city is fortunate to have excellent runways and air traffic control facilities that it leases from Hoover Air Force Base The city has a fifty-year lease that runs through May 14, 2009, for which it pays an annual rent of $1. In addition, the city pays a landing fee of about $2 for each scheduled landing at the airport. Landing fees for fiscal years 1997–1998 and 1998–1999 were $9516 and $9096, respectively.

Although the city lost $.68 on every dollar of revenue generated by the airport fund during the 1998–1999 fiscal year, the overall operating loss for the year was only $139,304. Compared with operating losses for other Texas cities, this loss appears quite reasonable. City management, however, should be concerned about a trend that seems to be developing. As shown in Table 6, the operating loss was only $.08 on every dollar for the 1995–1996 fiscal year. In the fiscal year ending on September 30, 1997, the size of the loss had increased 104.3% to $.19 on the dollar. The next year the loss was $.29 on the dollar, and for the fiscal year ending on September 30, 1999, the operating loss increased 127.8% to $.68 for every dollar.

As would be expected, retained earnings for the airport fund showed similar decreases. The airport funds's retained earnings at the end of the 1998–1999 fiscal year showed a deficit balance of $402,353, yet the city was able to adequately operate the airport without an infusion of outside capital. The fund's current ratio also increased steadily over the past five years. How? The statement of cash flows for the airport fund provides an answer. Although the airport fund had an operating loss for each of the last five years, it was able to increase its cash balance from $127,729 for the fiscal year ending in 1995 to $312,866 for the fiscal year ending in 1999. Cash increased even with the operating losses because depreciation expenses (which is a noncash expense) more than offset the losses. Unfortunately, the fiscal year 1998–1999 loss was greater than the depreciation expense for the year, and cash balances declined by roughly the same amount.

Because most of the facilities at the airport are leased, the city's principal capital investment is its airport terminal. Based on the fund financial statements, it appears that the terminal (and other fixed assets) may have been entirely financed by federal airport improvement grants. City management may be operating under the assumption that any new facilities will also be financed by federal grants. If this will not be the case, the city should consider raising airport fees (such as landing fees and rentals) so that financial resources are available to make replacements and improvements.

The other enterprise fund that consistently shows a negative income ratio is the transit fund. The transit fund accounts for the transit system operated by the city of Mesquite Falls. The city uses buses and vans to provide transportation for its citizens and Hoover Air Force Base personnel. The losses experienced by the city are not unusual because most cities experience operating losses from their transit activities, typically recovering less than 25% of their expenses through passenger fares.

One mediating factor concerning the losses must be considered. Many of the transit fund's operating and capital costs are financed by federal operating subsidies from the Urban Mass Transportation Administration. Both of these types of subsidies are excluded from operating income. As a requirement for receiving the federal subsidies, the city must also contribute to transit fund operations through transfers from general operations. After taking into account both the subsidy from the federal government and the operating transfers by the city, the transit fund shows overall net *income* for the past three years.

The transit fund's current ratio has been around .90 for the last five years. A rule of thumb for businesses is that the current ratio should be at least two. A low current ratio would mean that a company would have difficulty paying its current debts. It appears that the city had purposely maintained a small amount of assets *in the fund*, however. The fund cash balance has been less than $2000 for each of the last five years. In addition, the city made equity transfers from the transit fund to the internal service fund in the fiscal years ending in 1998 and 1999. Without these equity transfers, the city would have had positive retained earnings in the transit fund instead of the deficit at September 30, 1999.

In summary, the transit fund's financial condition is not as weak as it would appear at first glance. City management appears to have been purposely maintaining a deficit balance in the fund by removing all cash from the fund before year end. The city actually maintained a small but consistent cash balance over the past five years. It is likely that the city only reports this activity as an enterprise fund to meet federal requirements. The city probably manages the activity more like a governmental fund activity, in which services are provided to its citizens without the expectation of covering all costs through user charges. There is little doubt that city management is well aware of the operating losses incurred by the transit system. It is doubtful that city management would wish to raise revenue in the fund by increasing passenger fares, because the transit system is operated to benefit lower-income residents.

Sanitation Fund

The sanitation and the water and sewer funds are the two utility enterprises operated by the city. The sanitation fund accounts for the revenues and expenses associated with residential and commercial garbage collection and disposal. Although many cities, especially smaller cities, have contracted this service to outside parties in an attempt to avoid federal regulation and potential fines, the city of Mesquite Falls decided to maintain its own landfill and solid waste disposal services.

Currently it appears that the sanitation fund is financially strong. As shown in Table 6, the sanitation fund had a current ratio in excess of 8 to 1 over the last five years. This indicates that the fund should have no trouble in meeting its current liabilities. The fund's solvency ratio of .06 for the fiscal year ending in 1999 was near its average and has shown little fluctuation in the last five years. This provides further evidence that the sanitation fund should be able to meet its debt obligations. A review of the sanitation fund's balance sheet found only long-term liabilities related to landfill closure and postclosure care and more than adequate resources to meet current obligations.

The sanitation fund's income ratio has also been relatively stable over the past five years. The only time in the last five years that the sanitation fund had an operating loss was for the fiscal year ending in 1999. A horizontal analysis of the fund's statement of revenues, expenses, and changes in retained earnings shows that revenues actually increased 6.7% over the past five years. The operating loss resulted from a 16.8% increase in maintenance and repair expenses over the fiscal year 1997–1998 expenses. As seen in the city's other funds, the sanitation fund generally has a trend of increased maintenance costs accompanied with reduced depreciation expenses and no growth in fixed assets. This may again indicate that city assets are becoming worn, but are being repaired instead of replaced. This provides further evidence that city management needs to make an overall assessment of its fixed assets to determine whether or not its capital asset acquisition and maintenance programs need to be revised.

Water and Sewer Fund

The water and sewer fund accounts for the operations of the city's water and sewer utility—the city's water treatment and distribution facilities and wastewater treatment plant. In fiscal year 1998–1999, the water and sewer fund was the city's largest enterprise fund both in terms of total assets and revenues. It accounted for over 93% of total enterprise fund assets and nearly half of the city's reported assets. (As stated earlier, the city does not report general governmental infrastructure assets, such as streets.) For the 1998–1999 fiscal year, the water and sewer fund accounted for over 71% of total enterprise fund revenues and about 23% of all city revenues.

The water and sewer fund appears to be in a very strong financial position. As shown in Table 6, the fund has had a current ratio of about 5.6 for the last two fiscal years and an even higher ratio in previous years. This indicates that the water and sewer fund should be able to meet its current debt obligations. The fund's solvency ratio has been about .44 in each of the last three years, providing evidence that the fund should be able to pay both its short- and long-term debt. One factor contributing to the increase in this ratio is an increase in fixed asset accounts. Unlike the city's other funds, the balance in the buildings, systems, and improvements account in the water and sewer fund increased by over 44% since 1995. This increase is due principally to the cost of constructing a new wastewater treatment plant. Construction began in 1996 and was completed in 1998. The new state-of-the-art wastewater treatment plant represented not only a major capital expenditure, but also a substantial improvement in the city's ability to treat wastewater. This is a major infrastructure asset that should serve the city until about the year 2050.

To finance the new plant, the city issued $20,015,000 of water and sewer revenue bonds. Moody's also gave the city an Al rating for these bonds. Covering the operating, debt, and depreciation expenses related to this new plant caused a decline in the fund's income ratios. For the fiscal year ending in 1999, however, the water and sewer fund still generated 14% more operating revenue than it had in operating expenses. In addition, the city recently increased water and sewer rates charged to customers to ensure sufficient revenues are generated to pay both current operating expenses and debt service requirements.

In summary, the water and sewer fund appears to be in a strong financial position to continue to operate at the same level it has during the past five years. The increase in debt resulted in a slight increase in water and sewer charges, but the new wastewater treatment plant was much needed and should serve the city for many years.

SUMMARY AND CONCLUSION

A financial analysis of the city of Mesquite Falls leads one to the conclusion that the city is in a strong financial position. The examination of the city's general operations as reported in the governmental funds found that the city has adequate financial resources to continue to provide a high level of services to its citizens. The city has sufficient cash balances to pay short-term obligations and enough current resources to overcome any temporary revenue shortfalls. The city does not rely too heavily on intergovernmental revenue and has the ability to raise additional revenues through increased property tax levies. The conclusion that the city is in a strong financial position is verified by Moody's Al bond rating for both the city's general obligation and water and sewer revenue bond debt.

ADDENDUM: NEW FINANCIAL REPORTING REQUIREMENTS

The preceding analysis was based on the CAFR of the city of Mesquite Falls. That CAFR includes financial statements that were issued using generally accepted accounting principles (GAAP), which will soon be changed. The Governmental Accounting Standards Board (GASB), which establishes GAAP for state and local governments, issued statement 34, *Basic Financial Statements—and Management's Discussion and Analysis—for State and Local Governments*, in June 1999. This new standard will modify the existing fund reporting requirements while adding management's discussion and analysis (MD&A) and governmentwide financial statements to a government's annual financial report.

The good news is that the information necessary to perform the type of analysis that we have made in this case will still be available (with few exceptions) in a government's comprehensive annual financial report issued under the new standards. The better news is that the new requirements to include MD&A and governmentwide statements will provide analysts with information that has never been available in a government's annual financial report.

The Good News

GASB statement 34 requires governments to continue to report fund financial statements. The preceding analysis for the city of Mesquite Falls was based on information derived from fund financial statements, the notes to the financial statements, and statistical information that was included in the city's CAFR. GASB statement 34 and subsequently issued standards generally require additional disclosures to the notes to the financial statement rather than reductions to disclosure requirements. For example, an explanation of transfers that do not routinely occur will be added to the notes to the financial statements. Also, statement 34 makes no changes to the content of the statistical section of the CAFR, therefore of the three primary sources of information used in the analysis of the city of Mesquite Falls, only the fund financial statements have been significantly changed.

The major changes to fund-based financial reporting can be classified into three general areas: (1) a change from fund type to major fund reporting, (2) changes in certain fund definitions, and (3) changes in budgetary reporting. Because the city of Mesquite Falls issues a CAFR, the first change should be of minor importance for analysts because they will still be able to obtain the same type of detailed fund information that they have in the past. The changes in fund definitions could have a greater impact on analysts—particularly those who do time series analysis. The changes to fund definitions would have had only a minimal effect on the authors' analysis of the city of Mesquite Falls, however, because the definitions would not have affected the funds examined. Prior to statement 34, budgetary information for all budgeted governmental funds would have been included in a government's financial statements. Statement 34 will limit the disclosure of budgetary information to only the general fund and major special revenue funds. Again, this would not have affected the authors' analysis of the city of Mesquite Falls. The good news is thus that most of the information that analysts have expected from a government's CAFR will still be available.

The Better News

The preface to statement 34 notes that the GASB "developed these new requirements to make annual reports more comprehensive and easier to understand and use." The GASB believes that the changes required by statement 34 will provide financial information that is of interest to those who historically have not shown much interest in a government's financial reports. From an analyst's perspective, the new reporting requirements should provide important information that has not been previously available in governmental financial reports.

One of the more intriguing additions is the new MD&A, which many believe has the potential to interest new users, particularly citizens and taxpayers. The MD&A will precede the basic financial statements of the government and should be an easily readable and fact-based analysis of a government's activities for both the short and long term. A government's financial managers generally should write the analysis because they are the most knowledgeable about the transactions, events, and conditions reflected in the government's financial report. The GASB hopes that financial managers will include charts, graphs, and tables in addition to a narrative to enhance the understandability of the information presented. The MD&A should provide analysts with an informative starting point for their study of a government's financial position and operations.

The basic financial statements will follow the MD&A in a government's annual financial report. Analysts should be particularly interested in the new governmentwide statements. These statements will display financial information about the government as a whole with governmental and business-type activities reported separately. An important aspect of the new statements is their focus on a government's economic resources. This results in a government reporting all of its capital assets, including infrastructure assets, in the governmentwide statement of net assets. As indicated in the analysis of the city of Mesquite Falls, one of the difficulties was making assessments about infrastructure assets. The new reporting requirements should ease these difficulties. Also, prior to statement 34, governmental financial reports were not designed to allow readers to assess the cost of government services. The new governmentwide statements should allow readers to make this assessment because the cost of government services will be reported instead of just the amount expended for government services, as was the case prior to statement 34. For example, depreciation expense—which represents the cost of using capital assets—for police cars will be reported under the new statement 34 requirements, but was not under the previous standards.

When to Expect the New Financial Statements

The date that a government must adopt the new statement 34 reporting requirements will depend on the government's total annual revenues for its first fiscal year ending after June 15, 1999. The city of Mesquite Falls, which had total annual revenues of more than $10 million but less than $100 million, will be required to follow the new reporting requirements for its fiscal year ending September 30, 2003. Governments with total annual revenues of $100 million or more will have to implement the new reporting requirements for its first fiscal year ending after June 15, 2002. Governments with total annual revenues of less than $10 million will not have to implement the new reporting requirements until its first fiscal year ending after June 15, 2004.

REVIEW QUESTIONS

1. What is CAFR? Discuss the role a CAFR plays in government in light of the changes in the financial accounts of the city of Mesquite Falls as reported in this study. Evaluate the major changes the city experienced, in particular the

changes in its receivables, liabilities, and long-term debt, and explain the factors that contributed to that change.

2. What is fund balance? How would you account for the changes in fund balance of the city's general fund accounts? Why did the city change its reserved as well as the designated portions of its fund balance?

3. Most governments maintain several special revenue funds to account for revenues that are legally designated to be expended for special purposes. How many special purpose revenue funds does the city currently maintain? What specific changes have these funds gone through in recent years? Why?

4. What is a financial ratio? What kinds of financial ratios are generally used to analyze the financial condition of a government? Discuss Ken Brown's ten-point test as used in the study to analyze Mesquite's financial condition. What were the results?

5. It appears from the study that the city has been losing revenue from its internal service operations for some time. What in particular contributed to this trend? What can the city do to improve this situation?

6. How many enterprise funds does the city currently maintain? Which of these funds have been most productive? What can the city do to increase its revenue from enterprise fund operations, especially those that are lagging behind?

REFERENCES

Brown, K. (1993). The 10-point test of financial condition: Toward an easy-to-use assessment tool for smaller cities. *Government Finance Review, 9(6)*, 21–26.

Government Finance Officers Association (GFOA). (1994). *Financial Indicators Database: Municipal Governments*. Chicago: GFOA.

Khan, A. and Hildreth, W. (1994). *Case Studies in Public Budgeting and Financial Management*. Dubuque, IA: Kendall/Hunt.

Moody's Investor Services. (1994). *Moody's Bond Record, 61(8)*, 667.

Appendix A, Schedule 1 City of Mesquite Falls General Fund, Horizontal Analysis (1995–1999)

	1995	1996	1995–1996 change (%)	1997	1996–1997 change (%)	1998	1997–1998 change (%)	1999	1998–1999 change (%)
Assets									
Cash and cash equivalents	$10,885,892	$10,855,127	−0.3	$10,011,849	−7.8	$10,602,448	5.9	$9,688,570	−8.6
Receivables (net of allowance for uncollectible):									
Taxes and assessments	$1,203,635	$1,135,317	−5.7	$1,003,575	−11.6	$841,125	−16.2	$797,585	−5.2
Other city funds	$175,775	$538,038	206.1	$372,103	−30.8	$230,626	−38.0	$521,199	126.0
Government agencies	$558,700	$685,790	22.7	$808,074	17.8	$813,321	0.6	$1,136,955	39.8
Other	$225,650	$138,284	−38.7	$142,770	3.2	$310,202	117.3	$235,707	−24.0
Inventory	$31,559	$47,266	49.8	$49,037	3.7	$58,911	20.1	$54,493	−7.5
Prepaid items	$46,389	$194,709	319.7	$90,677	−53.4	$84,532	−6.8	$83,240	−1.5
Restricted assets:									
Government agencies	$166,308								
Other assets	$100	$524	424.0	$2,837	441.4	$100	−96.5	$100	0.0
Total assets	$13,294,008	$13,595,055	2.3	$12,480,922	−8.2	$12,941,265	3.7	$12,517,849	−3.3
Liabilities									
Accounts payable-trade	$661,078	$553,688	−16.2	$416,019	−24.9	$393,843	−5.3	$825,934	109.7
Accrued payroll	$221,920	$245,452	10.6	$304,195	23.9	$449,392	47.7	$527,902	17.5

(continued)

Appendix A, Schedule 1 Continued

	1995	1995–1996 change (%)	1996	1996–1997 change (%)	1997	1997–1998 change (%)	1998	1998–1999 change (%)	1999
Accrued vacation and sick leave	$100,000	0.0	$100,000	0.0	$100,000	0.0	$100,000	0.0	$100,000
Payable to other city funds						–	$72,677	147.0	$179,491
Payable to government agencies	$46,104	43.2	$66,034	5.3	$69,520	12.2	$77,969	−66.6	$26,023
Other liabilities	$481,802	3.1	$496,823	5.5	$524,150	2.3	$536,135	37.3	$736,165
Deferred revenue	$1,121,122	−5.0	$1,065,442	−14.0	$916,211	−14.9	$779,856	−3.6	$751,928
Total liabilities	$2,632,026	−4.0	$2,527,439	−7.8	$2,330,095	3.4	$2,409,872	30.6	$3,147,443
Fund equity (deficit)									
Fund balances (deficit)									
Reserved for encumbrances	$591,512	98.6	$1,174,981	−13.3	$1,018,427	−70.9	$295,860	−56.9	$127,652
Reserved for inventory and prepaid items	$77,948	210.4	$241,975	−42.3	$139,714	2.7	$143,443	−4.0	$137,733
Unreserved									
Designated for									
Subsequent years expenditures	$2,000,000	12.5	$2,250,000	11.1	$2,500,000	10.0	$2,750,000	9.1	$3,000,000
Undesignated	$7,992,522	−7.4	$7,400,660	−12.3	$6,492,686	13.1	$7,342,090	−16.8	$6,105,021
Total fund equity	$10,661,982	3.8	$11,067,616	−8.3	$10,150,827	3.7	$10,531,393	−11.0	$9,370,406
Total liabilities and fund equity	$13,294,008	2.3	$13,595,055	−8.2	$12,480,922	3.7	$12,941,265	−3.3	$12,517,849

Appendix A, Schedule 2 City of Mesquite Falls General Fund Balance Sheet, Vertical Analysis (1995–1999)

	1995 (%)	1996 (%)	1995–1996 change	1997 (%)	1996–1997 change	1998 (%)	1997–1998 change	1999 (%)	1998–1999 change
Assets									
Cash and cash equivalents	81.9	79.8	−2.1	80.2	0.4	81.9	1.7	77.4	−4.5
Receivables (net of allowance for uncollectible):									
Taxes and assessments	9.1	8.4	−0.7	8.0	−0.3	6.5	−1.5	6.4	−0.1
Other city funds	1.3	4.0	2.7	3.0	−1.0	1.8	−1.2	4.2	2.4
Government agencies	4.2	5.0	0.8	6.5	1.5	6.3	−0.2	9.1	2.8
Other	1.7	1.0	−0.7	1.1	0.1	2.4	1.3	1.9	−0.5
Inventory	0.2	0.3	0.1	0.4	0.0	0.5	0.1	0.4	0.0
Prepaid items	0.3	1.4	1.1	0.7	−0.7	0.7	0.0	0.7	0.0
Restricted assets									
Government agencies	1.3	0.0	−1.3	0.0	0.0	0.0	0.0	0.0	0.0
Other assets	0.0	0.0	0.0	0.0	0.0	0.0	0.0	0.0	0.0
Total assets	100.0	100.0		100.0		100.0		100.0	
Liabilities									
Accounts payable—trade	5.0	4.1	−0.9	3.3	−0.8	3.0	−0.3	6.6	3.6
Accrued payroll	1.7	1.8	0.1	2.4	0.6	3.5	1.1	4.2	0.7
Accrued vacation and sick leave	0.8	0.7	−0.1	0.8	0.1	0.8	0.0	0.8	0.0
Payable to other city funds	0.0	0.0	0.0	0.0	0.0	0.6	0.6	1.4	0.8
Payable to government agencies	0.3	0.5	0.2	0.6	0.1	0.6	0.0	0.2	−0.4
Other liabilities	3.6	3.7	0.1	4.2	0.5	4.1	−0.1	5.9	1.8
Deferred revenue	8.4	7.8	−0.6	7.3	−0.5	6.0	−1.3	6.0	0.0
Total liabilities	19.8	18.6	−1.2	18.7	0.1	18.6	−0.1	25.1	6.5
Fund equity (deficit)									
Fund balances (deficit)									
Reserved for encumbrances	4.4	8.6	4.2	8.2	−0.4	2.3	−5.9	1.0	−1.3
Reserved for inventory and prepaid items	0.6	1.8	1.2	1.1	−0.7	1.1	0.0	1.1	0.0
Unreserved									
Designated for									
Subsequent years expenditures	15.0	16.6	1.6	20.0	3.4	21.2	1.2	24.0	2.8
Undesignated	60.1	54.4	−5.7	52.0	−2.4	56.7	4.7	48.8	−8.0
Total fund equity	80.2	81.4	1.2	81.3	−0.1	81.4	0.1	74.9	−6.5
Total liabilities and fund equity	100.0	100.0		100.0		100.0		100.0	

Appendix A, Schedule 3 City of Mesquite Falls General Fund Statement of Revenues, Expenditures, and Changes in Fund Balance, Horizontal Analysis (1995–1999)

	1995	1996	1995–1996 change (%)	1997	1996–1997 change (%)	1998	1997–1998 change (%)	1999	1998–1999 change (%)
Revenues									
Taxes	$23,035,386	$23,736,091	3.0	$23,601,388	−0.6	$24,535,787	4.0	$25,705,065	4.8
Changes for services	$1,261,555	$1,234,406	−2.2	$1,068,713	−13.4	$1,070,926	0.2	$1,111,826	3.8
Licenses and permits	$440,857	$440,088	−0.2	$546,644	24.2	$604,905	10.7	$609,670	0.8
Fines	$834,328	$900,404	7.9	$789,439	−12.3	$904,581	14.6	$1,156,623	27.9
Intergovernmental revenue	$791,383	$779,466	−1.5	$1,225,504	57.2	$1,380,734	12.7	$1,723,190	24.8
Miscellaneous revenue	$1,597,558	$1,453,043	−9.0	$1,255,215	−13.6	$925,466	−26.3	$828,742	−10.5
Total revenue	$27,961,067	$28,543,498	2.1	$28,488,900	−0.2	$29,422,399	3.3	$31,135,116	5.8
Expenditures									
Current									
Administrative services division	$4,514,948	$4,655,580	3.1	$5,037,109	8.2	$4,502,220	−10.6	$4,850,649	7.7
Police division	$7,677,500	$8,359,078	8.9	$8,552,989	2.3	$8,970,402	4.9	9,680,729	7.9
Fire division	$5,240,285	$5,360,935	2.3	$5,393,852	0.6	$5,558,991	3.1	$5,821,934	4.7
Parks and recreation division	$2,478,736	$2,388,480	−3.6	$2,433,579	1.9	$2,555,542	5.0	$2,346,032	−8.2

Accounting/finance division	$418,733	$428,310	2.3	$417,460	-2.5	$462,729	10.8	$381,244	-17.6
Planning division	$336,887	$326,867	-3.0	$269,972	-17.4	$229,485	-15.0	$264,959	15.5
Public works division	$4,232,744	$4,224,499	-0.2	$4,965,920	17.6	$4,243,882	-14.5	$4,246,256	0.1
Health division	$1,830,962	$1,933,354	5.6	$1,955,763	1.2	$2,156,485	10.3	$2,499,686	15.9
Traffic and transportation division	$1,249,506	$1,197,787	-4.1	$1,181,922	-1.3	$1,114,159	-5.7	$1,121,169	0.6
Total expenditures	$27,980,301	$28,874,890	3.2	$30,208,566	4.6	$29,793,895	-1.4	$31,212,658	4.8
Excess of revenues over (under) expenditures	($19,234)	($331,392)	1622.9	($1,719,666)	418.9	($371,496)	-78.4	($77,542)	-79.1
Other financing sources (uses)									
Operating transfers in	$968,100	$950,541	-1.6	$966,084	1.6	$964,505	-0.2	$997,748	3.4
Operating transfers out	($180,558)	($213,515)	18.3	($161,210)	-24.5	($212,443)	31.8	($2,081,193)	879.6
Capitalized leases	$84,970		-100.0						
Total other financing sources (uses)	$870,512	$737,026	-15.3	$804,874	9.2	$752,062	-6.6	($1,083,445)	-244.1
Excess of revenues and other sources over (under) expenditures and other uses	$851,278	$405,634	-52.3	($914,792)	-325.5	$380,566	-141.6	($1,160,987)	-405.1
Fund balance (deficit)—ending	$9,810,704	$10,661,982	8.7	$11,067,616	3.8	$10,150,827	-8.3	$10,531,393	3.7
Fund balance (deficit)—ending	$10,661,982	$11,067,616	3.8	$10,152,824	-8.3	$10,531,393	3.7	$9,370,406	-11.0

Appendix A, Schedule 4 City of Mesquite Falls General Fund Statement of Revenues. Expenditures, and Changes in Fund Balance, Vertical Analysis (1995–1999)

	1995 (%)	1996(%) (%)	1995–1996 change	1997 (%)	1996–1997 change	1998 (%)	1997–1998 change	1999 (%)	1998–1999 change
Revenues									
Taxes	82.4	83.2	0.8	82.8	−0.4	83.4	0.6	82.6	−0.8
Charges for services	4.5	4.3	−0.2	3.8	−0.5	3.6	−0.2	3.6	−0.0
Licenses and permits	1.6	1.5	−0.1	1.9	0.4	2.1	0.2	2.0	−0.1
Fines	3.0	3.2	0.2	2.8	−0.4	3.1	0.3	3.7	0.6
Intergovernmental revenue	2.8	2.7	−0.1	4.3	1.6	4.7	0.4	5.5	0.8
Miscellaneous revenue	5.7	5.1	−0.6	4.4	−0.7	3.1	−1.3	2.7	−0.4
Total revenue	100.0	100.0		100.0		100.0		100.0	
Expenditures									
Current									
Administrative services division	16.1	16.1	0.0	16.7	0.6	15.1	−1.6	15.5	0.4
Police division	27.4	28.9	1.5	28.3	−0.6	30.1	1.8	31.0	0.9
Fire division	18.7	18.6	−0.1	17.9	−0.7	18.7	0.8	18.7	0.0
Parks and recreation division	8.9	8.3	−0.6	8.1	−0.2	8.6	0.5	7.5	−1.1
Accounting/finance division	1.5	1.5	0.0	1.4	−0.1	1.6	0.2	1.2	−0.4
Planning division	1.2	1.1	−0.1	0.9	−0.2	0.8	−0.1	0.8	0.0
Public works division	15.1	14.6	−0.5	16.4	1.8	14.2	−2.2	13.6	−0.6
Health division	6.5	6.7	0.2	6.5	−0.2	7.2	0.8	8.0	0.8
Traffic and transportation division	4.5	4.1	−0.3	3.9	−0.2	3.7	−0.2	3.6	−0.1
Total expenditures	100.0	100.0		100.0		100.0		100.0	

29

Governmental Audit Recommendation Follow-up Systems
Implementing Recommendations Effectively

David B. Pariser and Richard C. Brooks
West Virginia University, Morgantown, West Virginia, U.S.A.

Auditing is an important component of accountability at all levels of government. As an independent appraisal function, auditing provides to the public an independent opinion regarding the extent to which governmental officials carry out their responsibilities in accordance with applicable laws and regulations. A government audit typically consists of an examination of the general purpose financial statements, internal controls, compliance testing, and tests to substantiate account balances. The U.S. General Accounting Office's (1988) *Government Auditing Standards* (commonly called the Yellow Book) requires auditors to communicate their findings to management. The Yellow Book also requires auditors to provide *recommendations* that may improve government operations and programs to management. A system for monitoring the status of these audit recommendations increases the probability of their implementation.

Without a monitoring (follow-up) system to facilitate the implementation of audit recommendations, it is not uncommon for auditors to make the same recommendations year after year because the government failed to implement the recommendations. Furthermore, the lack of an audit follow-up system makes it difficult to measure the impact of audit recommendations on the performance and accomplishments of government programs. The objective of this chapter is to present a framework for audit recommendation follow-up systems. The first section examines the need for audit follow-up systems. The second section presents a framework for an effective audit recommendation follow-up system. The third section provides an overview of existing state, county, and city audit recommendation follow-up systems, based on two survey studies by the present authors (Brooks and Pariser, 1995; Pariser and Brooks, 1997). The fourth section presents a case in which a local government has received the same audit recommendations for two and sometimes three consecutive years. The conclusion asks questions that emphasize the major issues discussed in the chapter.

After completing this chapter, the reader should be able to

Discuss the importance of audit recommendation follow-up systems

469

Explain the basic attributes of an effective audit follow-up system

Describe the characteristics of state, county, and city audit recommendation follow-up systems reported in recent survey studies

Identify the strengths and weaknesses of an audit recommendation follow-up system

THE NEED FOR AUDIT RECOMMENDATION FOLLOW-UP SYSTEMS

Audit recommendation follow-up systems are particularly important to those state and local government entities subject to the requirements of the Single Audit Act (U.S. Congress, 1984). This law requires all governmental entities receiving more than $100,000 in federal financial assistance to have an audit of all federally funded programs. The Single Audit Act also requires state and local officials to take prompt and appropriate action on instances of material noncompliance with applicable laws and regulations that govern federal financial assistance. In the event that a material noncompliance occurs, the Single Audit Act requires state and local officials to submit either a corrective action plan to the appropriate federal agencies or a statement describing the reasons that corrective action is not necessary. State and local government entities failing to comply with the provisions of the Single Audit Act risk certain sanctions, including the reduction or suspension of federal financial assistance.

Beyond the requirements of the Single Audit Act, all states have recognized the need for following up on audit recommendations and have established follow-up procedures. In fact, twenty-eight states have enacted laws or administrative regulations requiring formal follow-up systems and procedures (Brooks and Parisers, 1995: 79). In addition to monitoring the status of recommendations, executive agencies and legislative committees may use an audit follow-up system for various purposes, including the following

Determining current and future budget appropriations

Directing public attention to problem areas via the media

Monitoring compliance with laws and regulations

Identifying areas in need of performance audits

Planning general purpose financial statement audits

Planning single audits

FRAMEWORK FOR AN EFFECTIVE AUDIT RECOMMENDATION FOLLOW-UP SYSTEM

Governmental entities should have in place a method of monitoring the status of audit recommendations. Table 1 illustrates a framework for an audit recommendation follow-up system. The framework structure consists of environmental factors, system procedures, and system uses. The attributes of an effective audit recommendation follow-up system are described below.

According to the U.S. General Accounting Office (GAO) (U.S. General Accounting Office, 1991) a follow-up system should provide answers to questions such as: "What improvements were made as a result of audit work?" and "Did those improvements achieve

Table 1 Framework for an Audit Recommendation Follow-up System

Environmental/organizational factor
   Firm policy basis for following up on audit recommendations
   Single Audit Act
   Clearly written audit recommendations
   Organizational commitment to implementation
   Clear assignment of follow-up responsibilities
System procedure
   Evaluation of recommendations, including budgetary and organizational impact
   Preparation of corrective action plans
   Periodic review to evaluate the adequacy of actions taken on each recommendation
   Special attention to key recommendations
   Preparation and distribution of periodic status reports
System uses
   Budget oversight
   Program review
   Management evaluation
   Single audit planning
   Compliance monitoring
   Performance audit planning

the desired results?" To be effective, an audit recommendation follow-up system should include the following attributes:

    Firm policy basis for following up on audit recommendations
    Organizational commitment to implementation
    Evaluation of recommendations, including budgetary and organizational impact
    Clear assignment of follow-up responsibilities
    Preparation of corrective action plans
    Special attention to key recommendations
    Periodic review to evaluate the adequacy of actions taken on recommendations
    Preparation and distribution of periodic status reports
    Use of status reports for oversight and management evaluation

    A law and/or administrative policy requiring audit recommendation follow-up establishes a firm basis for following up on audit recommendations. The existence of a law and/or administrative policy suggests that a government unit takes audit recommendations seriously and hopes to benefit from those recommendations. Follow-up systems should also be formally documented and incorporated into a policy or procedure manual that describes the operational details of the audit recommendation follow-up system.

    Governmental organizations must be committed to the implementation of audit recommendations. One way an organization can show its commitment to getting audit recommendations implemented is to recognize individuals responsible for implementing recommendations that result in significant benefits. Organizational commitment to the implementation of audit recommendations can be signaled in other ways as well. For example, an organization might provide a training program that teaches managers and auditors how to implement audit recommendations and how to design, use, and maintain follow-up systems. A more drastic approach might include the imposition of a penalty for not implementing audit recommendations (e.g., withholding funds).

Management must evaluate all recommendations in terms of their expected impact on budgetary resources as well as the organization as a whole. The evaluation of a recommendation should determine whether or not the benefits of implementing the recommendation exceed the expected costs of implementation. In the event that an audit recommendation requires a substantial increase in resources that are not currently available to the department, management should bring this fact to the attention of the appropriate legislative committees (e.g., the appropriation committee). If funding is not available, management should consider alternative measures to achieve the same objectives.

Assuming adequate resources are available, assigning the responsibility to monitor the status of audit recommendations to a particular individual or group of individuals may increase the probability of getting recommendations implemented. Assigning responsibility for the implementation of audit recommendations to an individual or team of individuals can increase the probability that recommendations are implemented effectively. According to the Office of Management and Budget (OMB), auditors and agency management should share the responsibility for audit follow-up. The OMB suggests that top management officials oversee audit follow-up, including resolution and corrective action (OMB 1982: 2–3).

Regarding system procedures, the GAO policy document *How to Get Action on Audit Recommendations* identifies several procedures that can enhance the effectiveness of an audit recommendation follow-up system (U.S. GAO, 1991). These procedures are: (1) the preparation of corrective action plans, (2) the periodic review of implementation progress, and (3) the preparation and distribution of periodic status reports.

Corrective action plans are essential because they facilitate follow-up and oversight activities. To encourage the implementation of audit recommendations, a state, county, or city may enact a law or establish an administrative policy requiring the preparation of a corrective action plan prior to taking any action on a particular audit recommendation. Formal corrective action plans are typically written up according to established guidelines for implementing an audit recommendation. Executive department officials, legislative committees, and auditors use corrective action plans to monitor the implementation of audit recommendations. Consequently, corrective action plans play an important oversight role because they allow legislative budget and oversight committees to assess a department's actual performance or progress in implementing a recommendation. For example, a department failing to implement a recommendation according to a corrective action plan may forego cost savings. The legislative budget committee might consider these lost savings during budget hearings prior to approving the department's funding request.

While all recommendations should provide a clear and obvious benefit upon implementation, certain "key" recommendations require special attention because of their potential impact. These include recommendations that have the potential to (1) prevent the loss of significant amounts of money, (2) prevent the loss of life, (3) prevent substantial bodily injury, or (4) prevent environmental damage (U.S. GAO, 1991). A governmental entity should aggressively pursue the implementation of any key recommendations.

A periodic review of actions taken on each recommendation is an essential part of a follow-up system since such a review makes it possible to assess the status of each recommendation. For example, a review might categorize a recommendation as: (1) fully implemented, (2) partially implemented, or (3) not yet implemented. A review might highlight the fact that a recommendation appeared in several previous audit reports. Additional information might include, for example, a note suggesting that a recommendation is no longer valid because of a change in circumstances or a change in public policy. It is helpful to document review results in a standardized format to simplify the compilation and subsequent distribution to interested parties.

A periodic status report, which includes a copy of the standardized follow-up review of each recommendation, should be prepared and distributed to appropriate executive department officials and legislative committees. Potential uses of periodic status reports include budget oversight, program review, management evaluation, single audit planning, compliance monitoring, and performance audit planning, and keep legislative oversight bodies and others informed about the progress made on the implementation of audit recommendations. Periodic status reports typically contain an executive summary and an analysis of the recommendations under review. Status reports typically identify recommendations that have been fully implemented, those in the process of being implemented, and those that have not been addressed.

CHARACTERISTICS OF STATE, COUNTY, AND CITY AUDIT RECOMMENDATION FOLLOW-UP SYSTEMS

This section* provides an overview of the characteristics of state, county, and city audit recommendation follow-up systems based on the results of two surveys conducted by the authors (Brooks and Pariser, 1995; Pariser and Brooks, 1997). The first study (Brooks and Pariser, 1995) described the characteristics of audit recommendation follow-up systems at the state level based on responses to a survey sent to the state auditors of all fifty states. The second study compared and contrasted the characteristics of audit recommendation follow-up systems used by state, county, and city governments (Pariser and Brooks, 1997). The surveys indicated that 82% of the states, 64% of the counties, and 51% of the cities responding to the survey had implemented audit recommendation follow-up systems. Tables 2, 3, and 4 summarize the results of these two surveys with regard to environmental/organizational factors, system procedures, and system uses.

Environmental/Organizational Factors

The data in Table 2 show that a majority of state, county, and city governments have enacted a law and/or adopted an administrative policy requiring audit follow-up. While 56% of states have a statutory and/or administrative requirement to follow up on recommendations, the percentage of cities and counties with such a requirement was considerably higher. Eighty-seven percent of the responding counties had a statutory or administrative requirement to follow up on audit recommendations, while 82% of the responding cities indicated they had such a requirement.

Commitment to Implement Recommendations

According to the surveys, only one state, nine counties, and fifteen cities provided audit recommendation follow-up training programs for their financial managers, program managers, auditors, and soon. While the remaining states, counties, and cities did not offer formal follow-up training, it was possible they provided training through other avenues,

---

* This section is based on two previously published studies by the authors Brooks and Pariser, 1995; Pariser and Brooks, 1997.

Table 2 Incidence of Organizational Factors Conductive to an Effective Audit Recommendation Follow-up System

Organizational factor	States[a] (n = 50)		Counties[b] (n = 297)		Cities[b] (n = 269)	
	Yes	No	Yes	No	Yes	No
1. Statutory and/or administrative requirement to follow up on audit recommendations	28 (56%)	22 (44%)	257 (87%)	40 (13%)	221 (82%)	48 (18%)
2. Has a audit follow-up training program for financial managers, program managers, auditors, etc.	1 (2%)	49 (98%)	9 (3%)	288 (97%)	15 (6%)	254 (94%)
3. Funds can be withheld for failure to take corrective action on audit recommendations	13 (26%)	37 (74%)	119 (40%)	178 (60%)	67 (25%)	202 (75%)

[a] State data previously reported in Brooks and Pariser (1995).
[b] County and city daita previously reported in Pariser and Brooks (1997).

Table 3 Incidence of Audit Recommendation Follow-up Procedures

Follow-up system procedure	States[a] (n = 50)		Counties[b] (n = 297)		Cities[b] (n = 269)	
	Yes	No	Yes	No	Yes	No
1. Have implemented an audit recommendation follow-up system	41 (82%)	9 (18%)	190 (64%)	107 (36%)	137 (51%)	132 (49%)
2. Statutory and/or administrative requirement to prepare a corrective action plan	20 (40%)	30 (60%)	134 (45%)	163 (55%)	143 (53%)	126 (47%)
3. Prepares periodic status reports on audit recommendations	31 (62%)	19 (38%)	158 (53%)	139 (47%)	137 (51%)	132 (49%)
4. Of those answering yes to 3 above, the status report is a matter of public record	28 (90%)	3 (10%)	125 (79%)	33 (21%)	91 (66%)	46 (34%)

[a] State data previously reported in Brooks, Richard C. and David B. Pariser. 1995. "Audit Recommendation Follow-Up Systems: A Survey of the States." *Public Budgeting & Finance* 15 (Spring): 72–83.
[b] County and city data previously reported in Pariser, David B. and Richard C. Brooks. 1997. "A Comparative Study of State, County and City Government Audit Recommendation Follow-up Systems." *Business & Public Affairs* 23 (Spring): 25–30.

Table 4 Uses of Audit Recommendation Follow-up Systems

Follow-up system use	States[a] (N = 50)	Counties[b] (n = 297)	Cities[b] (n = 269)
1. Monitoring compliance with laws and regulations	30 (60%)	143 (48%)	108 (40%)
2. Planning next year's Single Audit Act audit	28 (56%)	96 (32%)	72 (27%)
3. Planning next year's general purpose financial statement audit	22 (44%)	102 (34%)	78 (29%)
4. Testifying at budget and oversight hearings	20 (40%)	16 (5%)	15 (6%)
5. Identifying areas in need of performance audits	18 (36%)	53 (18%)	35 (13%)
6. Directing public attention to problem areas via the media	12 (24%)	18 (6%)	18 (7%)
7. Determining future budget appropriations	10 (20%)	34 (11%)	22 (8%)
8. Monitoring and evaluating service efforts and accomplishments	6 (12%)	34 (11%)	23 (9%)

[a] State data previously reported in Brooks and Pariser (1995).
[b] County and city data previously reported in Pariser and Brooks (1997).

such as supervision of employees, group meetings, on-the-job training, and seminars. Several governments indicated that they had authority to impose penalties on agencies, divisions, or departments that fail to take corrective action on audit recommendations. For example, thirteen states indicated that they had such authority. Six of these thirteen states had actually withheld funds in the past. Sixty-seven of the 269 cities responding to the survey indicated they could withhold funds from a division or department for failing to take corrective action on audit recommendations. Of these sixty-seven cities, five had actually withheld funds. Of the counties responding to the survey, 119 indicated they could withhold funds for not taking corrective action on audit recommendations. Only ten of these counties had actually withheld funds in the past, however.

Assignment of Follow-Up Responsibilities
Thirty-one states assigned responsibility for following up on audit recommendations to the head of the agency or department impacted by the recommendation. In twenty-six of those states, the auditor making a recommendation was responsible for following up. At the county government level, the chief financial officer or finance director and/or the head of the department or division impacted by the recommendation was typically responsible for audit follow-up. With regard to cities, 90% of the cities surveyed assigned audit follow-up responsibility to the chief financial officer/finance director, while 44% assigned this responsibility to the head of the department or division that is impacted by the recommendation.

System Procedures
The surveys provided evidence regarding the procedural aspects of audit recommendation follow-up systems currently used by city and county governments. Table 3 summarizes the incidence of specific system procedures.

Preparation of Corrective Action Plans

Twenty states had either a law or administrative policy requiring the preparation of corrective action plans, while thirty states had no such a law or policy. Forty-five percent of the counties surveyed and 53% of the cities surveyed had either an ordinance or administrative policy that required the preparation of a corrective action plan prior to implementing audit recommendations. It is interesting to note that the incidence of a law or administrative policy requiring the preparation of a corrective action plan was lower for higher levels of government (e.g., states) compared to lower levels of government (e.g., cities).

Preparation and Distribution of Periodic Status Reports

Table 3 shows that thirty-one states prepared periodic status reports on audit recommendations. Twenty-eight of these considered the periodic status reports to be a matter of public record, while the other three did not. The most likely recipients of status reports were the heads of agencies affected by recommendations (nineteen states), legislative oversight bodies (eighteen states), auditors responsible for making recommendations (sixteen states), and audit committee members (thirteen states).

The percentage of cities and counties that prepared periodic status reports was somewhat lower than that of the states. Fifty-three percent of the counties surveyed prepared status reports. A majority of these counties considered their status reports a matter of public record. The most common recipients of these status reports were finance directors (108 counties), followed by local legislative bodies (eighty-eight counties) and the head of the agency impacted by the recommendation (eighty-two counties). With regard to cities, 137 of those surveyed (51%) prepared periodic status reports on audit recommendations, of which ninety-one considered the status reports to be a matter of public record, while the other forty-six cities did not. The recipients of status reports included finance directors (ninety-nine cities), legislative oversight bodies (seventy cities), the heads of the departments affected by recommendations (fifty-nine cities), auditors responsible for making recommendations (fifty-seven cities), and audit committee members (forty-seven cities). Eleven cities indicated that state legislative oversight bodies received copies of the periodic status reports.

System Uses

Table 4 shows how follow-up systems are used by state, county, and city governments. Monitoring compliance with laws and regulations was the most common use of follow-up systems at all three levels of government. Planning next year's single audit was another popular use for audit recommendation follow-up systems. Similarly, a relatively high percentage of government units used their system to plan next year's general purpose financial statement audit.

CASE SETTING

The city of Springdale has a city manager/city council form of government. Springdale has 250,000 residents and total general government expenditures of $106,000,000. The city employs 1480 employees and has an annual payroll of $40,000,000. The city encompasses fifty square miles and has ten community parks. In 1999 the city of Springdale received approximately $3,500,000 in federal financial assistance.

Several articles appearing in the local newspaper note that the past three audit reports repeat many of the same cost-saving recommendations. In fact, six of the fourteen audit recommendations that the city's independent auditor included in the 1999 audit report also appear in the 1996, 1997, and 1998 audit reports.

One newspaper article described the city's existing budgetary and accounting practices and follow-up procedures as informal and charged that the city lacks a credible system for following up on audit recommendations. The article stated that no documentation exists regarding the status of previously issued recommendations or the reasons for not implementing numerous cost-saving recommendations. As a result, citizens are concerned that their taxes may be higher than necessary because of failure to implement potential money-saving audit recommendations. The article also noted that since 1995 significant budgetary cutbacks have occurred within the department of finance. The department's four divisions—treasury, budget, accounting, and internal audit—have been reduced by a number of positions during this period of time, and are currently operating at inadequate staffing levels. This has occurred while growth in financial activities has continued within the city as a whole. As a result of staffing shortages, several part-time employees in the department of finance are responsible for overseeing the accounting records (i.e., maintaining the general ledger) and following up on audit recommendations made by the city's independent auditor. Because of high turnover in these positions there is little interest in keeping current and accurate records. Existing records are often incomplete and are seldom forwarded to the city manager, department heads, or city council for review.

The city has just hired a new city manager. The city council is concerned that an ineffective budget process and the lack of an audit recommendation follow-up system is hampering the city manager's ability to govern effectively. Furthermore, Springdale has not submitted corrective action plans as required by the Single Audit Act, and several federal agencies are beginning to question the city's ability to manage federal monies and comply with applicable laws and regulations. Over the past few years the city has received increasing levels of federal financial assistance. Now the city council worries that failure to comply with the requirements of the Single Audit Act may result in the reduction or elimination of the city's federal financial assistance. At a recent public meeting, the city council discussed the above concerns and asked the new city manager to enlist the cooperation of department heads to design and implement a workable audit recommendation follow-up system.

The fourteen findings and audit recommendations reported in the 1999 audit report of the city's financial statements are reproduced below. The city has not prepared any corrective action plans or made any efforts to implement any of the recommendations.

1. *Finding*: Significant deficiencies exist in the operation of the city's information services department, which provides data processing services to other city departments. Other departments have complained that the information services department was unable to process information correctly and in a timely manner. In addition, several complex computer programs were reported lost and were replaced at substantial cost. These programs process the city's payroll and facilitate the preparation of the city's budget and financial statements. The auditor found information services had not established any internal control policies and procedures to provide reasonable assurance that its objectives will be achieved. One of the basic concepts of effective internal accounting control is the segregation of duties, which is designed to prevent any one individual

from having sufficient capability to perpetrate a fraud. The auditor noted that computer programmers have unrestricted access to data files and application programs. Further, computer operators have unrestricted access to program copies and detailed documentation.

Recommendation The city manager should direct the department of information services to establish and maintain effective internal controls. The objectives of an internal control structure are to provide management with reasonable (but not absolute) assurance that assets are safeguarded against loss from unauthorized use or disposition and that transactions are executed in accordance with management's authorization and recorded properly to permit the preparation of financial reports in accordance with generally accepted accounting principles.

2. *Finding*: The accounting division prepares monthly reports from the city's general ledger accounting system that are distributed to department managers. These reports were often not used by department managers. Department managers frequently requested the accounting division to prepare special reports that were needed for financial management purposes, but that were based on information other than that provided by the city's general ledger system. The accounting division director, who refused to allow his staff to prepare special reports, stated that city policy and procedures did not authorize his division staff to prepare special reports even though they had access to all the necessary data to do so. Consequently, department managers maintained duplicate financial records and computer programs to prepare these special reports, leaving them less time to devote to high-priority management responsibilities. The auditor indicated that accounting division personnel could prepare special reports in less time and at lower costs.

Recommendation: The city manager should direct the accounting division to work closely with department managers to determine the specialized reporting needs of program managers as well as the timing of reports. In addition, the accounting division should adopt reasonable means to produce needed reports and make them available to the appropriate managers in a timely manager. The city manager should periodically review and update the city's operating policies and procedures.

3. *Finding*: The city has not established procedures for reconciling the amount of sales and use taxes due from local businesses against the amounts actually collected. It is the auditor's opinion that a significant amount of sales and use taxes (approximately $5,000,000) are not being collected. The past three annual audits reported this finding.

Recommendation: First, the city manager should direct the treasury and accounting divisions to develop procedures for reconciling the amount of sales and use taxes due from local business against the amounts actually collected. Second, the city manager should direct the treasury division to establish a sales and use tax audit team to audit local businesses that have not paid their total sales and use taxes.

4 *Finding*: The city annually receives $3,000,000 from a federal grant under the Job Training Partnership Act. In accordance with the grant agreement, the city must verify the eligibility of each participant before the training program begins. Each participant's case file must contain verification of eligibility. The

auditor examined several case files and noted that 30% of the files did not contain the appropriate documentation of eligibility. The cause for this lack of documentation is unknown.

Recommendation: A monitor should routinely review all participant files to ensure that all required documentation is included in each participant's file. The city manager should designate an individual who is independent of the training program to be responsible for monitoring these files.

5. *Finding*: The city lacks formal budget preparation procedures at the department level. As a result, department heads use a variety of procedures when they prepare their annual budget requests. For example, the city manager does not require department heads to justify their budget requests in any manner. Furthermore, department heads do not require subordinates (i.e., program managers) to provide expenditure information by function.

    Recommendation: The city manager should require the finance director to establish formal budget preparation procedures. The finance director and the city manager should receive written justification for all budget requests. All program managers should provide a periodic report to the appropriate department head detailing program expenditures by function. The report should compare current expenditure levels by function to (1) expenditure levels of the prior year, and (2) average expenditures over the previous five-year period. An historical analysis of expenditures by function will facilitate departmental performance assessment. (See recommendation 6.)

6. *Finding*: Department managers do not utilize proper budgetary accounting controls (e.g., encumbrance accounting) during the execution of the annual budget. Consequently, the finance director and the city manager cannot rely on periodic budget reports submitted by department heads. These budget reports must be accurate because the finance director and the city manager use them to (1) monitor compliance with the approved budget, (2) provide quarterly summaries to the city council regarding appropriation spending, (3) plan the following year's budget, and (4) evaluate the performance of departmental activities.

    Recommendation: The director of finance should require the accounting division to implement proper budgetary controls (e.g., encumbrance accounting) and must insist that all department heads utilize the encumbrance system. In addition, the periodic budget report format should be uniform to facilitate comparisons across departments. At a minimum, the reports should provide information regarding the department's total budget, the amount of funds encumbered, the amount of funds expended, the percentage of budget expended, and the amount of unencumbered funds. The report should facilitate a comparison of budgeted amounts with actual expenditures to date.

7. *Finding*: An increase in the demand for government services in recent years makes it necessary for the city to develop priorities regarding how it will use its limited financial resources. The city must evaluate the performance of all programs and concentrate its limited resources on those programs that are most effective, economic, and efficient. Currently the city has no formal procedure for evaluating the effectiveness and efficiency of a particular department.

    Recommendation: The director of finance should charge the internal audit division with the responsibility for conducting performance audits designed to identify methods of enhancing the effectiveness and efficiency of departmental programs. In addition, the internal audit division should monitor the implementation of performance audit recommendations.

8. *Finding*: Overdrafts of the city's general fund bank account occur because cash flow projections have not been accurate in determining the amount of funds available for the investment of city funds. The bank covers the deficit so that all checks are paid. At some point the bank could refuse to honor city checks, which could cause problems with vendors and other government entities. For a number of years, the accounting division, has prepared a daily report of checks written, but treasury division personnel responsible for investment of city funds were unaware of this report.

   Recommendation: The director of finance should direct the treasury and accounting divisions to work together to better monitor expected cash needs. Communication between the city's various departments will be necessary on a continual basis to produce reliable cash flow projections.

9. *Finding*: Assessments are authorized to undertake capital projects within a special assessment district. Bonds secured primarily by special assessment revenues are issued and repaid from special assessment collections. Proper accounting for special assessments includes the timely collection of receivables that are used to repay bond debt. The city has not reconciled the special assessment receivable balance, a general ledger account, to the detail special assessment billing registers.

   Recommendation: The division of accounting should regularly reconcile the special assessment receivable amounts to the respective detail billing registers and take appropriate action in correcting any errors or differences.

10. *Finding*: The city has issued revenue bonds that are secured by revenues from the water and sewer system. According to bond covenants, each quarter the city must determine whether or not revenues are sufficient to satisfy specific water rate and debt service covenants. The city does not document these determinations, which are used to ascertain that the city is in compliance with water rate and debt service covenants as specified in various bond ordinances. Failure to determine that rates are adequate to provide mandatory debt service coverage could lead to default by the city under the terms of the relevant bond ordinances.

    Recommendation: The city manager should ensure that proper water rate and debt service covenant determinations are made and that the city is complying with all bond covenants. This compliance should be documented and retained.

11. *Finding*: The department of environmental safety has not responded promptly to its field inspectors' written requests for the issuance of enforcement orders against commercial entities and individuals who continue to violate municipal solid waste and water pollution control regulations. An enforcement order is legally enforceable in a court of law and imposes substantial fines and penalties on violators.

    If a violator refuses to comply with municipal solid waste and water pollution regulations, field inspectors are required to file a written enforcement action request with the department's solid waste division or water pollution division. After division personnel review documentation of the alleged violation they are required to submit a written report and recommendations to the director of environmental safety. The director of environmental safety has sole authority to issue an enforcement order if he or she finds that a local statute or regulation has been violated and appropriate corrective action has not been taken. In 1997 alone, it took the director of environmental safety an average of ninety-six days to issue an enforcement order; in one case 175 days passed before an enforcement order was issued. Recent newspaper articles describing numerous and repeated cases of illegal dumping of solid and hazardous waste materials indicate that the city manager and the city council are concerned that such practices may threaten the quality and safety of the city's drinking water. Municipal statutes and regulations do not require the director of environmental safety to process a written request for issuance of an enforcement order within a specified time period. The absence of formal time guidelines, lack of authority for division personnel to issue enforcement orders, and an inadequate data system for tracking violation and enforcement cases contributed to this delay. Members of the city council and the city manager fear that the slow response by the director of environmental safety may imply a lack of concern about violations and weakens the incentive for violators to comply with municipal solid waste and water pollution regulations.

Recommendation: The department of environmental safety should take steps to improve the timeliness of enforcement actions. Departmental managers should develop and enforce time guidelines for each regulatory area and should periodically review the department's performance in meeting those guidelines and take appropriate corrective action if necessary. The department should develop a data system sufficient to track cases involving enforcement action and compile data to evaluate the status of corrective actions taken. The director of environmental safety and the city manager should consider granting division managers the authority to issue enforcement orders and make recommendations to the city council regarding changes to applicable municipal laws and regulations.

12. *Finding*:   The division of information technology services, a division within the department of administrative services, is responsible for establishing and coordinating a central computer center and a telecommunication system used in delivering services to city agencies. The division is responsible for purchasing computer hardware, computer software, and telecommunication equipment. The division is also responsible for the maintenance of computer hardware, software, and telecommunications equipment. A recent performance audit on the division's activities reported the following findings:

   a. The division does not routinely comparison shop among the authorized hardware and software vendors when making purchases. Division personnel responsible for purchasing do not justify their purchases. There is a general attitude that the city contract with computer hardware, software, and telecommunication equipment vendors provides a guarantee that the lowest price is always paid, regardless of which vendor is selected. As a result, the division may realize substantial savings by purchasing equipment and software from the lowest-priced vendors.

   b. Some costly equipment purchased in the past was of questionable quality and reliability, which led to a high degree of maintenance and downtime for certain brands of equipment.

Recommendation: The purchasing process in the division of information technology services should be modified to require the preparation of a request for proposal (RFP). The RFP should provide detailed specifications for hardware, software, and telecommunications equipment to be supplied by vendors. Vendors should have to submit sealed bids, based on the specifications detailed in the RFP, to the division's purchasing agent. The city can then award the contract to the vendor with the lowest bid. The city council should develop procurement guidelines for all departments to follow when making purchasing decisions. Furthermore, internal auditors should monitor compliance with procurement guidelines and evaluate purchasing personnel performance.

13.   *Finding*:   To ensure that public schools purchase an adequate quantity and quality of textbooks the board of education requires every public school to spend at least 5% of its annual operating budget for textbooks. A recent audit found that some public schools actually allocated less than 5% of their annual operating budget for textbooks even though budget reports prepared by some school administrators indicated compliance with the 5% requirement. The auditor reported that board of education personnel responsible for selecting and purchasing textbooks frequently classified expenditures for computer hardware and compact discs used for instructional purposes as textbooks. The board of education officials reclassified such expenditures as office equipment in accordance with current board expenditure guidelines. These reclassifications made it appear that some schools were spending less than the required minimum amount on textbooks. The guidelines have not been updated to reflect the use of computers and compact discs as substitutes for or supplements to textbooks. In addition, many teachers are not satisfied with the quality of textbooks and compact discs purchased by board of education personnel.

Recommendation: The city's board of education should specify the purpose of the 5% minimum expenditure requirement; assess if the minimum expenditure requirement should continue to be a ratio or if it should be expressed on a perstudent basis or some other basis; determine what actions are appropriate to enforce compliance with the minimum textbook expenditure policy; and develop guidelines that allow teachers to either select textbooks or review and appropriately modify textbook selections by school administrators. Board of education guidelines should be updated to reflect the recent technological advances in education (e.g., computers, compact disks.).

14.   *Finding*:   A performance audit of the city's property tax collection system reported that the city spends nearly $400,000 more than is necessary to collect property taxes. These costs reduce revenues available for education, law enforcement, fire protection, and other general government services. Many stakeholders who should benefit from the property tax collections—especially the city's public schools—are ill served. The system is overly complex, allowing for delays in the collection cycle. Most important, tax dollars intended to fund needed services are diminished by the greater than necessary administrative and overhead expenses attributable to the collection system. In addition, the auditor reported the following findings: (1) collection costs throughout the city vary widely, from $1.25 to more than $10.00 per bill; (2) as of November 1998, delayed property tax collections in three sections of the city amounted to over $3.5 million; (3) interest lost through late tax collections amounts to

approximately $150,000 each fiscal year; and (4) a majority of tax collectors began collecting taxes thirty or more days late in 1997, 1998, and 1999. On average, tax collectors were forty-five days late in beginning tax collection efforts.

Recommendation: The city manager and the city council need to design and implement a tax assessment, collection, and remittance system that allows for the timely receipt of property tax revenues necessary to educate the Springdale's children and to fund essential public services.

SUMMARY AND CONCLUSION

The above discussion clearly indicates that audit recommendation followup is an integral part of public sector financial management and accountability. The auditing function provides evidence regarding whether or not public officials are spending public funds in accordance with applicable laws and regulations. Auditing also assesses the extent to which public sector managers are discharging their responsibilities properly.

Auditors must conduct audits of governmental entities in accordance with the Yellow Book and must communicate their findings and suggest recommendations to improve government operations to management. The implementation of audit recommendations is the only way to realize the benefits of these recommendations. Many audit recommendations are repeated year after year. An audit recommendation follow-up system provides a means to monitor the status of audit recommendations and to ensure the implementation of audit recommendations.

This chapter discusses a framework for audit recommendation follow-up systems. The framework of an effective follow-up system consists of environmental factors, system procedures, and system uses. A properly designed and maintained follow-up system can serve to enhance the performance and accountability of government. The chapter also provides an overview of the characteristics of state, county, and city audit recommendation follow-up systems based on the results of two survey studies conducted by the present authors within the framework for an effective follow-up system. The chapter concludes with a case designed to enhance student understanding of audit recommendation follow-up systems.

REVIEW QUESTIONS

1. Explain the role of auditing in public sector financial management and budgeting.
2. What is the nature and purpose of audit follow-up in public sector financial management and budgeting?
3. Describe the attributes of an effective audit follow-up system.
4. Identify four advantages of an audit follow-up system and explain how these advantages might enhance public sector financial management and accountability. Identify circumstances that might impair the effectiveness of an audit follow-up system.
5. Describe the results of two recent surveys of the characteristics of state, county, and city audit recommendation follow-up systems.

6. Critique Springdale's follow-up system as described by the newspaper articles. How can the system be improved?

7. Assume that you are the city manager of Springdale and are charged with the responsibility of designing and implementing an audit recommendation follow-up system that incorporates the concepts and elements discussed in the chapter. Prepare a proposal describing the framework for a follow-up system to be submitted to the city council at its next meeting. Include an explanation for each element included in the framework.

8. How might the following groups utilize an audit follow-up system?
   a. Legislative budget committees
   b. Audit committees
   c. Program managers
   d. Finance directors
   e. Independent external auditors

9. What actions can a public agency manager take to provide timely and effective implementation of audit recommendations?

10. The case presents fourteen audit recommendations included in Springdale's 1999 audit that have not been implemented. Prepare a corrective action plan for implementing each of these recommendations. How can public sector financial managers and legislative committees use corrective action plans to ensure that recommendations are implemented as intended?

REFERENCES

Brooks, R. C. and Pariser, D. B. (1995). Audit recommendation follow-up systems: A survey of the states. *Public Budgeting & Finance, 15* (spring), 72–83.

Office of Management and Budget. (1982). Circular No. A-50 revised, Audit Follow-up (September 29). Washington, DC: Office of Management and Budget.

Pariser, D. B. and Brooks R. C. (1997). A comparative study of state, county and city government audit recommendation follow-up systems. *Business & Public Affairs, 23* (spring), 25–30.

U. S. Congress. (Oct. 19, 1984). *Single Audit Act of 1984*. P. L. 98–502, 98 Stat. 2327.

U. S. General Accounting Office. (1988). *Government Auditing Standards*. rev. ed. Washington, DC: U.S. Government Printing Office.

U. S. General Accounting Office. (July 1991). *How to Get Action on Audit Recommendations* (OP-9.2.1). Washington, DC: U.S. General Accounting Office.

30

Benchmarking and Cost Accounting
The North Carolina Approach

William C. Rivenbark and K. Lee Carter
University of North Carolina, Chapel Hill, North Carolina, U.S.A.

The North Carolina Local Government Performance Measurement Project (NCLGPMP) originated from a demand of local government administrators who wanted to compare performance and cost data across jurisdictions for the purpose of process improvement.

The Institute of Government at the University of North Carolina–Chapel Hill was selected to manage the project, and the pilot stage of the benchmarking initiative began in September 1995. Three phases of the performance measurement project were completed during the pilot stage, covering a time period of four years and involving thirty-five cities and counties. A performance and cost data report was published after each phase for the city participants and the county participants, containing the areas of service selected for study, the performance measures of workload, efficiency, and effectiveness, and the explanatory information that addressed the level and variations of service. The success of the project prompted an agreement among the Institute of Government, fifteen cities, and five counties to continue the NCLGPMP for five years, beginning in July 1999. The first year of the agreement represents focal year (FY) 1999–2000, collecting performance and cost data from the operating results of fiscal year ended 1998–1999. Performance and cost reports are published on a schedule that allows the participating units to include the information in their following year's budget process.

One of the key components of the NCLGPMP is the cost accounting model used to collect and present the performance and cost data (Coe, 1999). The decision to employ an accounting model that captures full cost was made after a long and deliberate process. The full-cost accounting model was first presented to the steering committee that represented the municipalities participating in the first phase of the performance measurement project. Steering committees are composed of individuals from the participating units, the Institute of Government, the North Carolina League of Municipalities, and the North Carolina Association of County Commissioners, who review performance measures, set policy, and provide the necessary leadership critical to a benchmarking program. The first round of discussion involved costs above the line and costs below the line, representing direct costs and indirect costs, respectively. The path of least resistance was to include

Reprinted from: *Journal of Public Budgeting, Accounting, and Financial Management*, 2000, 12(1), 125–137.
Copyright by PrAcademics Press.

only direct costs. The major issue of the debate, however, focused on the comparability of the performance and cost data. It was determined that the only way to ensure that localities used the same methodology to collect and report the cost data associated with the project was to create a full-cost accounting model.

The lack of a generally accepted methodology to compare costs is not a new issue for local government (Martin, 1992). The individuals involved in the early stages of the NCLGPMP understood this issue and went to great lengths to prevent failure due to the data collection process. In other words, the proper benchmarking mentality was employed (Ammons, 1999). The purpose of this chapter is to present an overview of the full-cost accounting model associated with the NCLGPMP. The development and implementation issues of the model are outlined first, highlighting the necessity to build consensus among participating units. The three components of the model are then presented, addressing direct costs, indirect costs, and capital costs. Other considerations associated with the model are finally discussed to provide additional background on the relationship between benchmarking and cost accounting.

DEVELOPMENT AND IMPLEMENTATION OF MODEL

North Carolina has extensive state oversight of local government finance through the North Carolina Local Government Commission (LGC), which publishes and distributes illustrative charts of accounts that form the foundation of many local government accounting systems. Because of this standardization of accounting systems, the model was designed to incorporate the same categories that are commonly found in the charts of accounts used by the participating units. Emphasis was placed on collecting the needed information at a detailed level to encourage careful consideration of cost data used for performance measurement purposes.

Accuracy and comparability of cost data dominated the pilot stage of the performance measurement project. The steering committee eventually adopted a full-cost accounting model for two reasons. First, several of the participating units wanted to use the information to analyze the costs associated with privatization, responding to the fact that private organizations capture full cost when submitting bids for public sector services. The second and most important reason was that there are no uniform criteria among local governments for classifying direct costs. Governments use fund accounting to account for their activities and have a great deal of discretion over which fund is used to budget and account for a particular activity. Comparing only direct costs would result in many apparent differences that were actually only reflections of different budgeting and accounting systems rather than actual differences in service costs. An example using the risk management functions illustrates this point.

Many of the larger localities account for the risk management function in an internal service fund. The costs associated with risk services are charged directly to the departments and divisions as an operating cost, following general accepted accounting principles. The participating units in the performance measurement project that use propriety fund accounting would clearly include those charges when reporting performance and direct cost data. Some localities account for the risk management function in the general fund, especially the ones that are not self-insured. These units would not show the expenditures associated with risk services when calculating the direct cost of service delivery. As a result, it became necessary to proceed with a full-cost accounting model to capture all costs and to standardize the reporting procedure for cost collection.

The next step involved the allocation of indirect costs. Most of the participating units had cost allocation plans, especially among the county participants. Two of the phase 1 cities created their own plans, allocating indirect costs using the single step-down method. Several of the participating units in phase 3 of the project used an outside vendor, employing the double step-down method that is acceptable under federal grant regulations. It should be noted that a test was conducted at the beginning of the pilot stage that compared the single step-down method with the more sophisticated double step-down method. It was found that the differences were immaterial and did not hinder the comparability of the performance and cost data as long as the participant was inclusive and consistent.

Implementing the full-cost accounting model was difficult and time-consuming. Members of the Institute of Government spent a considerable amount of time communicating with the participating units, ensuring that the methodology of applying the model was uniform. Local government administrators are not as familiar with cost accounting as their counterparts in the private sector. The adjustments required with benchmarking and cost accounting demand time and commitment, but with the completion of the pilot of the NCLGPMP, the participating units are more comfortable with cost accounting and consensus of support has been established for the full-cost accounting model.

COMPONENTS OF MODEL

The full-cost accounting model collects expense data as opposed to expenditure data, capturing the economic condition of a service delivery unit. It is composed of direct costs, indirect costs, and capital costs. The cost data are collected at a detailed level by a collaborative effort of finance, budget, and operational staff in each participating unit. The accounting forms used to record the cost data are in addition to the service profile forms that address workload and service delivery information for each unit under study.

Direct Costs

The first section of the accounting forms is designed for the collection of direct costs. These costs are the personnel and operating expenses associated with a service unit. The information can usually be obtained directly from the general ledger. During the pilot stage of the project, the direct costs were based on audited operating results. This is no longer the case, given the demand for the performance and cost reports. It was felt that audit adjustments associated with expense data are not as numerous and significant as compared to the other areas of the general ledger. In any event most audit adjustments, if any, would be known during the data collection process and included in the final reports. The current model contains approximately thirty-five line items for direct costs. Not all the line items are completed for each service unit, but it was designed to capture the different expense classifications across jurisdictions.

Indirect Costs

The second section of the accounting forms contains the indirect costs. These costs arise primarily from staff functions that support the service delivery units. The city manager's

Table 1 Indirect Costs

Central cost centers	Basis of allocation
City manager's office	FTEs budgeted for fiscal year
Human resources	FTEs budgeted for fiscal year
Finance	Number of accounting transactions
Traffic engineering	Percentage of staff time
Purchasing	Number of purchase orders processed
Economic development	Percentage of staff time
Utilities	Number of square feet occupied
Departmental overhead (all other costs at the departmental level relating to the operation of a service unit; departmental costs, providing the basis)	FTEs assigned to a service unit as percentage of total number of FTEs in the department

office and the finance department are two examples of support units. Operating departments may also have indirect costs that must be addressed, representing managerial and support functions. Table 1 contains examples of central cost centers and departmental costs, providing the basis of allocation for each. It is not an exhaustive list but provides insight of how indirect costs are allocated for the NCLGPMP.

The number of full-time equivalents (FTE) is a very common approach to allocating indirect costs. The accounting model, however, employs a variety of methods in an attempt to link staff functions and operational functions in a sensible and meaningful way. These methods of allocation are consistent with the allocation plans that many of the project participants already use for federal grant reimbursement purposes.

Capital Costs

The majority of services currently under study are accounted for in the general fund; therefore the fixed assets associated with service delivery are recorded in the general fixed assets account group. It should be noted that statement no. 34 of the Governmental Accounting Standards Board (GASB, 1999) will eventually eliminate the general fixed assets account group, requiring state and local governments to record all fixed assets, including infrastructure, in the financial statements. Regardless of the GASB's pronouncement, localities must maintain accurate records of fixed assets to capture the full cost of providing services.

The project's cost-accounting model uses acquisition or construction costs, often referred to as historical costs, as the basis of usage charges for equipment and facilities. Historical costs were chosen over replacement costs for two reasons. The cost data are more reliable with historical costs, and the use of historical costs is consistent with generally accepted accounting principles in both the public and private sectors. Lower costs for older fixed assets also tend to be offset by higher operating and maintenance costs for those assets. If the historical cost of a fixed asset cannot be determined, then a reasonable estimate of the historical cost at the time of acquisition must be made. The project calculates usage charges for all equipment and facilities used in service delivery, whether the fixed

Table 2 Capital Costs

Equipment and facilities costs	Basis of allocation
Furniture and office equipment	10 % of acquisition cost.
Maintenance/construction equipment	12 % of acquisition cost.
Automobiles and light equipment	30% of acquisition cost.
Medium/heavy motor equipment	16% of acquisition cost.
Data processing equipment	20% of acquisition cost.
Light/miscellaneous equipment	10% of acquisition cost.
Other equipment	Based on judgment of useful life.
Equipment rental charges	Including rental payments.
Buildings	The allocation for a facility is square footage. Building costs are based on 2% of the original construction cost plus capitalized renovations.
Building rental charges	Including rental payments.
Financing costs	Do not include debt service payments on capital leases, installment purchase financings, bonds, or certificates of participation.

asset is beyond its estimated useful life or not. Table 2 provides the methodology used by participating units to calculate the usage charges associated with fixed assets.

The calculation of capital usage costs uses a group depreciation method, avoiding the need to calculate charges for individual assets and to calculate gains and losses for service retirements that are greater than or less than estimated useful lives. The depreciation of buildings at 2% assumes an average useful life of fifty years for all facilities involved in providing services. The actual useful life of a facility may be shorter or longer. The fifty-year assumption is low, resulting in a conservative usage charge for buildings. It reflects the tendency for governments to use a facility beyond its useful life, however and is commonly used to calculate depreciation under federal grant programs.

The project's accounting model does not include principal and interest payments on bonds, certificates of participation, or other debt instruments issued in order to finance the acquisition of assets. Fixed assets purchased with debt are placed into the general fixed assets account group for general government assets or proprietary funds for proprietary assets and are subject to usage charges in the NCLGPMP. Including principal expenditures would double count the cost of debt-financed assets since a usage charge is already included. An argument could be made to include interest expense in the calculation. The decision was made to omit interest expense given the fact that all fixed assets used for service delivery are depreciated, regardless of age. Cost accounting methodology typically recommends separating operating and financing costs. Financing methods reflect governmental policy decisions and the amount of available reserves. Project participants chose to omit financing costs so that differences in operating costs would not reflect differences in whether assets had been financed or acquired on a pay-as-you-go basis.

OTHER CONSIDERATIONS OF FULLCOST ACCOUNTING

The fullcost accounting model is designed to ensure that the same methodology is employed across jurisdictions when compiling performance and cost data. Once the informa-

Table 3 Full-Cost Profile

Expenditure types	Amount ($)	Total cost (%)
Personnel services	$231,090	76.0
Operating costs	47,133	15.0
Capital costs	26,122	9.0
Total	$304,345	100.0

tion is collected and forwarded to the Institute of Government, the performance and cost data are subjected to a very rigorous data-cleaning process. Drafts are then produced and returned to the participating units for further review. The goal is to produce materially accurate and comparable data. A datacleaning process cannot be overemphasized with a benchmarking initiative. The work conducted by the Institute of Government prevents the project from waiting on published fiscal year ended audited results, since the performance and cost data reports need to be published before the beginning of the budget cycle for the following fiscal year. The information is materially consistent with the audited financial statements, however.

A key aspect of the performance and cost data reports is the way the cost information is presented. While the model is designed to identify costs at a very detailed level, the costs are presented in an aggregate format in the report. Table 3 provides an example of the full-cost profile contained in a report for a service area under study (Vogt and Few, 1999).

The conversion from detail to aggregate data follows the same reasoning as reporting a locality's financial condition with audited financial statements. The performance and cost data reports present fairly, in all material respects, the performance position of the participating unit. In essence, the inconsistencies found in the detailed information become insignificant when viewing the larger framework of the consolidated reports.

Another aspect of the performance and cost data reports is the way performance data are presented. Figure 1 shows an efficiency measure for residential refuse collection,

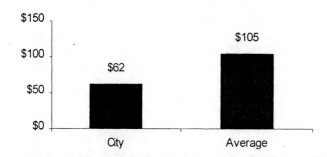

Figure 1 Residential refuse collection efficiency measure.

benchmarking the city's cost per ton collected with the average of the participating units (Few and Vogt, 1997). The alternative is to benchmark all the units on the same graph.

The project's accounting model does not consider any revenues that a service may generate in calculating delivery costs. An example would be fees associated with residential refuse collection. This omission is consistent with fund accounting and avoids reporting an increase in efficiency due to an increase in user fees. Some governmental services lend themselves more readily to charging user fees than other services that are typically financed with general tax revenue. Omitting user fees from cost comparisons allows the focus to be on the cost of providing a service and not on how a service is financed. It also prevents general governmental services from appearing more costly than proprietary-type services. Revenue data are collected for certain service units, such as building inspections and solid waste, and are included in the explanatory section of the performance and cost reports.

As localities become more familiar with benchmarking and cost accounting, the focus is now shifting toward the relationship of performance and cost results. More specifically, the participating units are searching for ways to use the performance measures for process improvement. The contextual reality is that the performance and cost reports are being used differently among the participating units. The Institute of Government sponsors benchmarking meetings on an annual basis to provide the forum for information exchange among the participating units and to provide additional insight on how to make decisions based on the measures of workload, efficiency, and effectiveness. If the performance measurement project is going to withstand the test of time, performance measurement must become a part of the organizational culture.

CONCLUSION

The full-cost accounting model is an integral part of the NCLGPMP, evolving from a collaborative effort of local government officials, faculty, and staff of the Institute of Government, and governmental accounting experts. The involvement of officials from other organizations, including the LGC, the North Carolina Local Government Budget Association, and the North Carolina Government Finance Officers Association, increased the importance of the model and the project. Model construction was driven by the desire of data accuracy and comparability, the fundamental ingredients of benchmarking and performance measurement. Numerous reviews of the performance and cost data were required before publishing the final reports. The success of the project and the full-cost accounting model can be traced directly to this process.

The model includes direct costs, indirect costs, and capital costs, employing a cost allocation plan for the indirect costs. The cost data are collected and reviewed at a detailed level, but are presented at an aggregate level to ensure that the performance measures are materially correct. The data collection process includes extensive analytical review to further address the accuracy of the data and to address the concerns of participating units before the final reports are published. Additional analysis is then required by the participating units for process improvement once the performance and cost reports are finalized and distributed, a step that is often overlooked during a benchmarking initiative.

The process used for the development of the full-cost accounting model still remains critical to the NCLGPMP. Steering committee meetings are held periodically to discuss new service areas for study. When the county steering committee decided to add animal control and fleet services, members of the Institute of Government and local government employees working directly in those service areas developed measures of workload, efficiency, and effectiveness in consideration of how the cost data are collected, reported, and used. The measures were then presented to the steering committee for final review and approval. This process not only builds consensus and ensures comparability, but it provides for the continual examination of the relationship between benchmarking and cost accounting.

ACKNOWLEDGEMENTS

This chapter is based on a workbook being prepared by A. John Vogt, professor of public finance with the Institute of Government at the University of North Carolina–Chapel Hill. Dr. Vogt played a key role in developing the full-cost accounting model and has been principal faculty advisor since the inception of the project. Paula Few, project coordinator, implemented the full-cost accounting model and developed the necessary capacity among the participating units to use it. She continues with the project as data manager.

REVIEW QUESTIONS

1. What is benchmarking? What are its advantages and disadvantages? How would one apply benchmarking in government?
2. What was the special need for using benchmarking in North Carolina? How was the model developed and implemented?
3. One of the key components of the North Carolina experience is the cost-accounting framework used in the development of the model. Discuss the major components of the model and explain the rationale for using them.
4. What other considerations were used by the government to implement the model? Why? How successful was the effort?

REFERENCES

Ammons, D. N. (1999). A proper mentality for benchmarking. *Public Administration Review, 59(2),* 105–109.
Coe, C. (1999). Local government benchmarking: Lessons from two major multigovernment efforts. *Public Administration Review, 59(2),* 110–123.
Few, P. K. and Vogt, A. J. (Oct. 1997). *Performance and Cost Data: Phase I City Services.* Chapel Hill, NC: Institute of Government at the University of North Carolina–Chapel Hill.
Governmental Accounting Standards Board. (June 1999). *Basic Financial Statements—and Management's Discussion and Analysis—for State and Local Governments.* Norwalk, CT.
Martin, L. L. (1992). A proposed methodology for comparing the costs of government versus contract service delivery. In International City Management Association (ed.), *The Municipal Yearbook*, pp. 12–15. Washington, DC: ICMA.
Vogt, A. J. and Few, P. K. (March 1999). *Performance and Cost Data: Phase III County Services.* Chapel Hill, NC: Institute of Government at the University of North Carolina–Chapel Hill.

31

Comparative Analysis of Key Governmental Financial Indicators

Jesse W. Hughes
Old Dominion University, Norfolk, Virginia, U.S.A.

In evaluating an organization's performance, it is useful to compare it with another organization of similar size and characteristics. In the business sector, corporations can be evaluated by comparing their financial data. Earnings per share, return on investments, inventory turnover, and return on sales all present a picture of a corporation's operating results in relation to other corporations. Thus, using various measures of profitability, it is possible to compare one business with another and to rank them on the basis of their performance.

In the governmental sector, on the other hand, the same analyses cannot be used. There are no earnings per share, return on investments, or return on sales. The focus is not on profitability but on serving the community's needs. Governmental accounting systems are designed to prove to the appropriate legislature that moneys have been collected and spent in accordance with the law, but they do not facilitate the evaluation of performance. Various efforts have been made to develop a conceptual framework for financial analysis. These endeavors are described by Groves (1981) and Berne and Schramm (1986).

Since governmental units cannot be measured in absolute terms by their profitability, another way of judging their effectiveness and efficiency is through comparisons to other localities with similar characteristics. Therefore, to evaluate a city's performance, one can compare it with other cities in regard to (1) spending policies, (2) taxing policies, (3) resource management, (4) cash management, and (5) debt management.

This chapter has a threefold objective: (1) to examine the concept of "selective comparability," (2) to describe the financial management practices in Virginia, and (3) to suggest future needs and directions for financial management practices. We begin by discussing the basic concept of "selective comparability."

PROBLEM BACKGROUND AND DISCUSSION

Budgets drive decisions in the public sector. Many researchers have attempted to develop a theory of public budgeting. Key (1940) initially recognized the need for a normative budgetary theory. Applying that need to local governments, Tiebout (1956) developed a descriptive theory and hypothesized that there was competition among local communities for services provided. The essence of Tiebout's hypothesis is that each resident will choose the city that provides the most attractive package of governmental services commensurate with his or her cost-benefit value structure.

Other researchers have concentrated on incremental changes in public budgets to explain the basis for expenditure patterns. Davis et al. (1966) postulated the theory of incrementalism, and it has become one of the main descriptive theories of budgeting in the public sector. This theory postulates that agency requests will result in a net increase over the prior year's appropriation. The agency's request would always be greater than the prior year's appropriation, whereas the current year's appropriation would always be less than the agency's request. The theory recognizes that this year's budget is based on last year's budget, with special attention given to a relatively small range of increases or decreases.

In spite of research efforts, a clear understanding of the expenditure patterns among the local communities does not exist. Hughes (1983) attempts to close that gap by postulating a theory based on comparability in lieu of the traditional theories based on competition or incrementalism. This theory of "selective comparability" notes that there is an identifiable pattern for amounts expended by local governmental units. State laws and local ordinances frequently require that a balanced budget be maintained. In addition, each state will generally set a limit on the amount of debt that each community can incur. Further, taxpayers in one community can be expected to watch the property tax rates in a neighboring community with a view toward keeping their own tax rates in line, and thereby keep a cap on expenditures.

COMPARING THE PERFORMANCE OF TWO VIRGINIA CITIES

To illustrate the concept of "selective comparability," the database of financial factors published by the auditor of public accounts in Virginia is used. Virginia adopted an uniform financial accounting and reporting system in 1981. This system requires that all forty-one cities and forty-two counties report their revenue and expenditure data on a uniform transmittal form. In addition to expressing an opinion on the general purpose financial statement, the external auditor is required to sign the transmittal form indicating that the data agree with the annual financial statements. In Virginia, cities are incorporated separately from counties. Only city data are included in this illustration, since county data would create wider dispersion in the data. Hampton and Newport News (both in Virginia) are used to illustrate the degree of comparability. To depict the trend over time, data are presented for three years, with year 3 being the most recent year.

General Characteristics

To compare the performance of two localities, it must be established that they are comparable in several attributes. Characteristics used to determine the degree of similarity include general population and wealth variables (adjusted gross income and per capita assessed property value). The crime rate per 100,000 population is also used to identify the composition of the population since those communities with younger populations and lower incomes tend toward higher crime rates. Tables 1 through 4 illustrate the degree of compara-

Table 1 General Population

Year	1	2	3
Hampton	129,700	133,793	133,793
Newport News	162,800	170,045	170,045
Virginia city average	55,171	54,912	54,912

Source: Comparative Report of Local Government Revenues and Expenditures, Auditor of Public Accounts.

Table 2 Crime per 100,000 Population

Year	1	2	3
Hampton	5,781	5,935	6,186
Newport News	5,093	5,513	6,912
Virginia city average	4,958	4,912	5,630

Source: Crime in Virginia, Department of State Police.

Table 3 Adjusted Gross Income

Year	1	2	3
Hampton	$18,244	$19,139	$18,930
Newport News	$17,801	$18,652	$18,360
Virginia city average	$17,016	$18,135	$18,093

Source: Distribution of Virginia AGI by income class and locality, University of Virginia.

Table 4 Assessed Property Value (per Capita)

Year	1	2	3
Hampton	$29,434	$30,087	$32,929
Newport News	$31,670	$31,941	$36,337
Virginia city average	$35,957	$39,369	$43,232

Source: Virginia assessment/sales ratio study, Department of Taxation.

bility for Hampton and Newport News along with the average of the forty-one Virginia cities.

Although Hampton's population is smaller than Newport News's, they are both much larger than the average Virginia city. It is noteworthy that in both cities the population has increased, while the average Virginia city has experienced a decline in population of about 5%.

Both cities have somewhat higher crime rates per 100,000 of population than the average Virginia city. Although Hampton's crime rate was larger in the first year, it increased by only 7% during the period. Newport News's crime rate, on the other hand, increased by 36% and is now higher than Hampton's.

Citizens of Hampton have consistently higher adjusted gross incomes (AGI) than citizens of Newport News. Both cities' AGIs are somewhat higher than the average Virginia city's, but they follow the same trend: about 5% increase in the second year, and a 1% (Hampton) to 1.5% (Newport News) decrease in the third year.

Hampton has slightly lower assessed property values than Newport News, and both cities follow the average city's trend of increasing property values (however, at a distinctly slower rate). While the increase from year 1 to year 3 was 12% in Hampton and 15% in Newport News, it was 20% in the average city.

The comparison of these factors show that the two cities are not alike; however, they are sufficiently similar to each other and distinct from the average Virginia city to permit meaningful comparisons of their respective performances and their levels of efficiency and effectiveness.

Spending Policies

The way a local government allocates its resources reflects the government's philosophy of where its priorities and emphases lie. At the same time, local government allocation patterns react to or reflect federal and state spending policies. Whenever the federal or state governments reduce spending in local programs, the local governments either try to find other revenue sources or shift funds around to maintain the same level of services. Tables 5 through 10 reflect the percentage of total expenditures allocated to each functional category (education, public safety, public works, health and welfare, miscellaneous, and transfers to other funds).

In Virginia local governments have control over education services, and the largest portion of local expenditures goes to education. In the first year Hampton's allocation was somewhat lower than both Newport News's and the average city's, but it increased consistently during the period from 32.6–36% in the third year. Newport News spent 36%

Table 5 Education

Year	1	2	3
Hampton	32.6%	34.4%	36.0%
Newport News	36.0%	31.7%	31.4%
Virginia city average	35.9%	33.6%	33.7%

Source: Comparative report of local government revenues and expenditures, Auditor of Public Accounts.

Table 6 Public Safety

Year	1	2	3
Hampton	19.4%	21.0%	19.9%
Newport News	17.7%	20.8%	19.9%
Virginia city average	18.6%	20.0%	20.5%

Source: Comparative report of local government revenues and expenditures, Auditor of Public Accounts.

Table 7 Public Works

Year	1	2	3
Hampton	13.4%	9.1%	8.6%
Newport News	13.0%	13.9%	10.2%
Virginia city average	12.5%	11.1%	10.9%

Source: Comparative report of local government revenues and expenditures, Auditor of Public Accounts.

Table 8 Health and Welfare

Year	1	2	3
Hampton	5.4%	5.1%	5.4%
Newport News	4.1%	3.6%	4.7%
Virginia city average	3.7%	3.9%	5.2%

Source: Comparative report of local government revenues and expenditures, Auditor of Public Accounts.

Table 9 Miscellaneous Expenditures

Year	1	2	3
Hampton	15.4%	18.3%	19.0%
Newport News	18.0%	15.8%	15.6%
Virginia city average	17.5%	16.6%	16.5%

Source: Comparative report of local government revenues and expenditures, Auditor of Public Accounts.

Table 10 Transfers to Other Funds

Year	1	2	3
Hampton	13.8%	12.3%	11.1%
Newport News	11.2%	14.2%	18.2%
Virginia city average	11.8%	14.8%	13.2%

Source: Comparative report of local government revenues and expenditures, Auditor of Public Accounts.

on education in year 1, but since both state and federal funds for education increased during the decade, the city cut back its own education expenditures to 31.4% in year 3, following the overall trend of Virginia cities.

Both cities increased their expenditures for public safety (fire and police protection) from year 1 to year 2, but decreased them in year 3. Hampton's portion was originally higher than Newport News's, but in year 3 both cities allocated 19.9% of their total expenditures on public safety. As mentioned earlier, crime increased during the period in both cities, but expenditures on public safety do not reflect this trend.

The allocation of expenditures for public works (sanitation and road maintenance) decreased in both cities, following the trend of the average Virginia city. Contrary to the average Virginia city, however, whose population has slightly decreased, both Hampton and Newport News grew during the period, calling for more outlays for public works. The cutbacks thus seem to reflect the financial difficulties Virginia cities are facing. Hampton's cutback is more severe: it spent 13.4% in year 1 and is down to 8.6% in year 3, while Newport News spent 13% in year 1 and 10.2% in year 3.

Hampton's allocation for health and welfare expenditures decreased in the second year, but is the same in year 3 as it was in year 1, namely 5.4% Newport News, on the other hand, also decreased its expenditures on health and welfare in the second year, but then increased them in the third year to 4.7%. On average, the trend in Virginia cities was consistently increasing from 3.7% in the first year to 5.2% in the third year.

Hampton's allocation to miscellaneous expenditures (parks, community development, and general administration) has increased over the years from 15.4–19%, but Newport News followed the average Virginia city's trend in the opposite direction, decreasing from 18–15.6%.

While Hampton's transfers to other funds (capital projects, debt services, and enterprise activities) has decreased by 20% during the period. Newport News's transfers in-

Table 11 Assessment Ratio

Year	1	2	3
Hampton	88.3%	90.9%	94.9%
Newport News	91.1%	93.9%	96.0%
Virginia city average	86.5%	86.7%	87.2%

Source: Virginia assessment/sales ratio study, Department of Taxation.

Table 12 Effective Tax Rates: Real Estate

Year	1	2	3
Hampton	$1.01	$1.04	$1.11
Newport News	$0.99	$1.02	$1.10
Virginia city average	$0.90	$0.90	$0.91

Source: Virginia assessment/sales ratio study, Department of Taxation.

creased by more than 60%. The city average was less consistent, increasing in the second year and then decreasing again in the third year.

Taxing Policies

To assure comparability in tax rates, an assessment ratio should be computed. In Virginia, the department of taxation randomly selects properties that have been sold during the past year (Table 11). This selling price divided into the assessed value provides the assessment ratio. For example, property assessed at $80,000 and sold at $100,000 would have an 80% assessment ratio. If the tax rate on real estate is $1 per $100 of assessed value, the effective tax rate is $80.

Both cities assess their property increasingly closer to the market value than Virginia cities on the average, thus approaching the desired assessed real estate value at 100% of market value. Hampton's assessment ratio is consistently slightly lower than Newport News.

Hampton's effective real estate tax rate was consistently slightly higher than Newport News's (Table 12). In both cities the rate itself was higher than in the average Virginia city, and the increase over the three-year period was about 10 cents, while the average city increase was one cent.

In both cities, the effective tax rate for motor vehicles has not been changed for the last several years while it has been slightly increased in the average Virginia city (Table 13). Again, Hampton's tax rate is higher than that of Newport News.

Resource Management

The overall management of resources is best identified by the fund balance available for future appropriations in the general and special revenue funds. The fund balance ratio is

Table 13 Effective Tax Rates: Motor Vehicles

Year	1	2	3
Hampton	$4.40	$4.40	$4.40
Newport News	$4.25	$4.25	$4.25
Virginia city average	$3.23	$3.24	$3.27

Source: Tax rates in Virginia cities, counties, and selected towns, University of Virginia.

Table 14 Fund Balance

Year	1	2[a]	3[a]
Hampton	11.0%	10.0%	12.0%
Newport News	10.0%	11.0%	11.0%
Virginia city average	17.7%	18.2%	18.0%

[a] Data for year 2 and year 3 are estimates.
Source: Financial statements filed by each locality with the Auditor of Public Accounts.

computed by dividing the end-of-year fund balance by the expenditures. Typically, bond rating agencies use a fund balance ratio of 5% to assess the local government's creditworthiness.

The fund balance ratio is very similar for both cities, but lower than the city average. In general, both cities are well above the fund balance ratio required by the bond rating agencies.

Cash Management

Cash management no longer consists only of collecting and disbursing funds, but has become much more sophisticated. By investing idle cash in short-term investments or pooling resources to benefit from higher interest rates, financial managers can improve a locality's financial performance. At the same time, governments are under obligation to safeguard their scarce resources and manage them responsibly and wisely.

The comparison (Tables 14 and 15) shows that both cities follow more conservative cash policies than the average city by investing about 50% of available resources in risk category I (insured or registered or for which the securities are held—in the locality's name). Both cities have also very low percentages of their resources in deposits, thus reflecting much more sophisticated investment policies than average. About 10–13% of Hampton's investments are in category II (collateralized with securities held by the govern-

Table 15 Cash Management

Year	1			2[a]			3[a]		
	Hampton	Newport News	Virginia city average	Hampton	Newport News	Virginia city average	Hampton	Newport News	Virginia city average
Deposits	4.0%	5.0%	54.0%	5.0%	5.0%	56.2%	4.0%	6.0%	52.8%
Category I	49.0%	59.0%	15.0%	50.0%	58.0%	14.7%	52.0%	55.0%	15.5%
Category II	13.0%	0.0%	0.0%	12.0%	0.0%	2.3%	10.0%	0.0%	1.7%
Category III	22.0%	6.0%	23.7%	20.0%	5.0%	17.4%	21.0%	4.0%	20.2%
Pools	12.0%	30.0%	7.1%	13.0%	32.0%	9.4%	13.0%	35.0%	8.3%
Unexplained difference	0.0%	0.0%	−3.6%	0.0%	0.0%	−2.8%	0.0%	0.0%	−2.6%

[a] Data for year 2 and year 3 are estimates.
Source: Financial statements filed by each locality with the Auditor of Public Accounts.

Table 16   Gross Debt Ratio

Year	1	2	3
Hampton	2.6%	3.1%	2.9%
Newport News	4.5%	4.8%	4.5%
Virginia city average	3.0%	3.1%	2.9%

Source: Comparative report of local government revenues and expenditures, Auditor of Public Accounts, Virginia assessment/sales ratio study, Department of Taxation.

ment or its agent in the government's name) and 20–22% in category III (uncollateralized or collateralized with securities held by the pledging financial institution or by its trust department or agent but not in the entity's name). Newport News has no investments in category II, only 4–6% in category III, but it has considerably more funds in pools than Hampton and Virginia cities on average.

The unexplained difference is the difference between the amounts reported on the face of the balance sheet and the amounts reported in the notes to the financial statements. Both cities show no unexplained differences, reflecting the higher than average professional level of their personnel.

Debt Management

During the last decade local governments have been under severe pressure to decrease expenditures while maintaining or increasing services. Increasing revenues through increasing taxes has its limits, and contrary to the federal government, local governments cannot incur deficits. Therefore, city governments have little leeway or latitude for their debt policies.

The legal debt limit for Virginia cities is 10% of assessed property values. Neither the average city nor the two cities in this case study come close to this limit, and thus do not appear to be severely stressed financially. Both cities follow the average trend of slightly increasing the debt ratio in year 2 and then decreasing it again in year 3 (Table 16). Hampton's ratio is consistently lower than Newport News's and has been the same as the Virginia average since year 2.

On average, principal and interest payments of cities account for 6.2–7.3% of total expenditures. Whereas Hampton's performance is very close to this average, Newport News's debt payments comprise a slightly larger share at 7.4–9.1% of its total expenditures (Table 17).

Table 17   Debt Services Ratio

Year	1	2	3
Hampton	6.1%	6.3%	6.9%
Newport News	7.4%	7.4%	9.1%
Virginia city average	6.4%	6.2%	7.3%

Source: Comparative report of local government revenues and expenditures, Auditor of Public Accounts.

SUMMARY AND CONCLUSION

The various comparative data illustrate how different localities allocate their resources and whether or not their emphasis on taxing and spending policies is similar to other Virginia cities'. The comparison of Hampton's and Newport News's performances showed numerous similarities with some differences between the two cities and the average Virginia city. In regard to spending policies, Hampton allocates a larger share of local expenditures to education, as well as health and welfare, than Newport News and the average city. Relative to taxing policies. Hampton's assessment ratio is slightly lower than that of Newport News (though higher than that of the average Virginia city), while its tax rate for real estate and motor vehicles is higher than that of Newport News and the average city. Comparing resource management shows that the fund balance ratio of both cities is above the ratio required by the bond rating agencies but lower than the city average. The comparison of cash management shows that both cities have more sophisticated investment policies than the average city. In regard to debt management, both cities follow the average city's trend of somewhat increasing the debt/assessed property value in year 2 and decreasing it in year 3. Hampton's lower gross debt ratio is reflected in its lower debt services ratio.

This study has analyzed the degree of comparability between two Virginia cities with similar characteristics. Selected key indicators have been identified to assist in this analytical process. Differences noted as a result of this analysis isolate areas for further examination. Recommendations for change should not be made on the basis of this analysis until the reasons for the differences can be identified.

The availability of a central database prepared on a uniform basis is critical to assessing the financial management of any particular governmental unit. Key indicators need to be identified in order to provide the elements of information to include in the database. The database will prove invaluable whenever decision makers become aware of its availability.

REVIEW QUESTIONS

1. How similar are the socioeconomic characteristics used to compare Hampton and Newport News?
2. Are any functional expenditures for Hampton or Newport News out of line with the average of Virginia cities in the allocation of resources?
3. If the answer to question 2 is yes, what action would you recommend to bring them more in line?
4. How comparable are the taxing policies for real estate and personal property between Hampton and Newport News?
5. Based on the funds available for future appropriations, how well have Hampton and Newport News managed their resources?
6. Which city, Hampton or Newport News, places funds in higher-risk investments?
7. How fiscally stressed is Hampton? Newport News?

REFERENCES

Auditor of Public Accounts (various years). *Comparative Report of Local Government Revenues and Expenditures.*

Berne, R. and Schramm, R. (1986). *The Financial Analysis of Governments*. Englewood Cliffs, NJ: Prentice-Hall.

Davis, O. A., Dempster, M. A. H. and Wildavsky, A. (1966). A theory of budgetary process. *American Political Science Review*, *60* (Sept.) 529–47.

Groves, S. M. et al. (1981) Financial indicators for local government. *Public Budgeting & Finance*, *1 (2)*, 15–19.

Hughes, J. W. (1983). *Expenditure Patterns of Local Governments*. dissertation Virginia Tech.

Hughes, J. W. and Laverdiere, R. (1986). Comparative local government financial analyses. *Public Budgeting & Finance*, *6 (4)*, 23–33.

Key, V. O. Jr. (1940). The lack of a budgetary theory. *American Political Science Review*, *34*, 137–44.

Tiebout, C. M. (1956). A pure theory of local expenditures. *Journal of Political Economy*, *64 (Oct.)* 416–24.

32

Financial Performance Monitoring and Customer-Oriented Government
A Case Study

Michael W. Shelton and Troy Albee
Office of Budget and Evaluation, City of Myrtle Beach,
South Carolina, U.S.A.

In the industry of government, which lacks a classic economic bottom line for holding boards and managers responsible to their shareholders, performance monitoring has long been touted as a way to improve a government's accountability to its *stake*holders. By keeping tabs on the resources applied to providing a service and on the effects achieved, a government can amass the information necessary to render to the public a suitable accounting for its activities. According to the Government Finance Officers Association's (1999: 64) statement of recommended practices in local government finance, improved measurement of performance should

> assist government officials and citizens in identifying financial and program results, evaluating past resource decisions, facilitating qualitative improvements in future decisions regarding resource allocation and service delivery options, and *communicating service and program results to the community* [emphasis supplied].[1]

More than simply communicating results *to* their citizens, many local governments have begun to rethink their missions and redefine their goals and objectives with greater consideration of the customers who utilize their services (Osborne and Gaebler, 1992; Syfert, 1995). "Customer-oriented government" has become a popular form to describe a city's or county's efforts to determine its clients' needs and to deliver the services that are relevant for them. Customer-oriented government solicits active community involvement in shaping the public agenda and in crafting the very mission and purpose, goals, and strategies that direct the jurisdiction's operational plans, thus introducing elements of public accountability at each step of the policy process. This is different from conducting activities as usual and then telling the public what the city or county has done. It is involving the community with its elected officials and staff in developing a common set of expectations and the approaches to meeting them (planning), accomplishing results

Reprinted from: *Journal of Public Budgeting, Accounting, and Financial Management*, 2000, 12(1), 87–105.
Copyright by PrAcademics Press.

(performance), determining whether or not the results have met the expectations (evaluation), adjusting expectations and approaches based upon experience (revising the plan), and maintaining active two-way communications with the public during each of these phases (accountability).

Given this orientation toward the policy process, financial planning takes on added significance. By involving its customers more thoroughly in the policy process, the government elevates the importance of their customers' understanding the financial possibilities and boundaries. It is easy to ignore financial issues during a community visioning exercise or to address them as afterthoughts. Financial concerns may be viewed as constraints that would inhibit creative visioning. Alternatively, the participants may complete their visions uninhibited and then turn to the budget and finance people so that they can find the money to implement the dream. The danger is that when financial reality sets in, the visioning process will have raised unrealistic expectations about what can be accomplished and a workable timetable for accomplishments.

What does this shift of viewpoints imply for local government financial planning? GFOA's statement of recommended practices notes that performance measures "should be based on program goals and objectives that tie to a statement of program mission or purpose" (GFOA, 1999: 64). The statement is true of financial planning and performance efforts just as it is of operational performance measures. To effectively facilitate accountability, they must be tied to the organization's mission and must promote the achievement of its service goals and objectives.

One difficulty in trying to integrate financial planning with community visioning efforts stems from the tendency in government to view financial planning as a short-term activity. Most governments are required to adopt budgets covering a period no longer than one year. Even two-year budgets are still something of an oddity. Anything beyond that is practically unheard of. Comprehensive planning exercises, by contrast, usually take a long-term view—twenty years or more.

Interestingly, though, the field of finance can be one of the easiest for which to develop long-term plans and performance monitoring systems. Most areas of governmental operations lack any generally accepted tools to be used in accounting for and reporting on the services they provide, although this may be changing.[2] Financial ratios are common tools of credit analysis, however, and credit rating agencies keep massive data on these ratios to establish benchmarks for communities of various sizes. Moody's Investors Service annually publishes a composite profile of the financial ratios it uses in its credit analysis for cities, counties, and other public agencies (Moody's Investors Service, 1996). With a readily available set of widely accepted tools for measuring financial performance already developed and available to them, governmental organizations can implement quite thorough financial performance monitoring systems with very little adaptation. Then with relative ease, financial plans can become useful tools for implementing a community's strategic objectives.

FINANCIAL PERFORMANCE MONITORING IN MYRTLE BEACH: A CASE STUDY

Many recent innovations in the field of performance monitoring have been spurred by financial distress. They are often discussed in the context of articles on downsizing, right sizing, re-engineering, or privatizing, currently popular options for coping with circumstances of financial distress.[3] Myrtle Beach, South Carolina, has been fortunate that it was the community's financial prosperity that provided the impetus for improving its financial planning and performance—monitoring systems. No longer a sleepy little seaside resort, today this community is the heart of the second fastest growing metropolitan area in the United States, according to *American Demographics* magazine (Myrtle Beach Area Chamber of Commerce, 1997: 3). The city's estimated 1996 population of 30,852 is more than double its 1980 census population.[4] Its service population now *averages* upwards of 100,000. With Myrtle Beach as its heart, the Grand Trand has a peak day population estimated at nearly 900,000. Retail sales reported inside the city have increased from about $550 million in 1987 to nearly $1.4 billion in 1997 (Myrtle Beach Area Chamber of Commerce, 1997: 9, 14). Myrtle Beach's adaptations to this situation include the use of a community planning process that garnered broad-based citizen participation in an effort to tie goals and objectives to community preferences, and employed financial planning to facilitate the achievement of organizational objectives.

A good argument can be made that it is best to prepare for hard times during good times. Objectivity comes more easily when there is less urgency to the decision process. Furthermore, it would be naïve of any community to believe that periods of slow growth or decline will not follow periods of rapid growth sooner or later. This community has seen its share of boom and bust cycles. To understand that, one need only look at the city's building permit statistics over any period of ten years or more. Since 1980, for example, annual permits issued have risen from $25 million to $116 million, and have fallen and risen again—as low as $22 million and as high as $109 million.

In the face of these trends, local elected officials and managers found themselves asking many hard questions. How can we expand our service delivery systems to accommodate such rapid growth without setting ourselves up for a fall when the current cycle passes its peak? How can we be certain that we are providing expanded services at reasonable costs? How can we know that we are maintaining high standards and not allowing service quality to suffer as we attempt to respond to growing demands? Can we better afford to expand in areas of high demand if we cut some services that are no longer essential to the community? How do we know we are providing the public services that meet our citizens' needs?

PLANNING FOR ADAPTATION

In 1993, the city first set the stage for long-range planning and the integration of its plans with the annual budget. Participants at the 1993 budget retreat resolved (1) that they wanted a more customer—oriented government, (2) that they wanted a more adaptable organization, and (3) that they wanted to improve public education about what they were doing. They put together a mission statement for city government and several long-term goals that flowed from the mission. Among the most ambitious goals set at that retreat was the one that stimulated most of the activity described here: *"Develop a strategy for adapting city facilities, service delivery systems, and revenue structures to accommodate rapid growth."*

Staff returned from that retreat and began trying to weave the themes of customer-oriented government, adaptability, and improved public education into a strategic approach to budgeting. The resulting system relies upon financial and operational planning, performance monitoring, and the integration of these items into the annual budget.

Strategic financial planning means looking in a systematic and organized way at an organization's position in its environment. It is an analytical approach that tries to be explicit about the organization's mission and goals and about the strategies it will employ in order to realize them. It is future-oriented and emphasizes the actions necessary to advance the organization toward its vision of itself (Weltzer and Petersen, 1987). Classic strategic financial planning is based upon four central concepts: capital costs, return on investment, risk and return trade-offs, and financial flexibility. With minor modification, these concepts can be adapted to the governmental setting. In Myrtle Beach, the mission of the financial plan was summed up in one statement: "Maintain the financial resiliency necessary to provide continuing high-quality municipal services and to make reasonable and consistent progress toward the vision established in the city's comprehensive plan." In terms of its very purpose, it thus tied financial planning and performance measurement directly to the city's operational mission, goals, and objectives—provision of services and advancement of comprehensive plan interests.

The four concepts of financial planning were translated into four goals having to do with adapting the government's revenue structure to its environment, living within its means, providing value to its customers in the form of uninterrupted service, and ensuring access to long-term credit markets at reasonable borrowing costs. Table 1 summarizes the plan's mission, goals, and strategies. For each strategy, the city employed performance measures to allow it to monitor its progress. It then set out to devise ways of integrating financial planning into an overall comprehensive planning and budgeting process.

If long-term planning is to serve as a blueprint for the development of community assets rather than simply to raise false expectations, the government must plot a financial course to cover the same time horizon as its operational plans. Financial planning establishes a context within which the community can evaluate the affordability of its plans for services and facilities as it is formulating its goals and objectives. Including a financial planning component helps the community to create realistic expectations for the implementation of its vision, develop financing options, or restructure its line of services in order to take on new challenges. Myrtle Beach's strategic financial plan is viewed as a set of long-term goals and broad strategies for maintaining and improving financial resiliency. As with any plan, its success depends upon how it is put into action. Breaking the long-term goals into quantifiable policy guides and milestones that can be used in the short run to advance the interests of the plan, facilitates action and allows evaluation.

MEASURING FINANCIAL PERFORMANCE

City staff decided it needed to measure progress on financial plan goals continuously by means of benchmark comparisons with credit industry standards and specific policy targets developed by staff and council. Where national medians were not available or were deemed inappropriate figures for comparison, the city used a benchmark comparison group of ten southeastern cities. The members of this benchmark group were chosen for similarities in the size and scope of their operations, as well as for the fact that they are some of Myrtle Beach's main competitors in the labor force. The annual budget reports on these comparisons and demonstrates expected performance regarding key financial ratios over the five-year planning period. Some illustrations taken from the 1998–1999 budget follow.

Table 1 Strategic Financial Plan: Mission, Goals, and Strategies

---

Mission: Maintain the financial resiliency necessary to provide continuing high-quality municipal
services and to make reasonable and consistent progress toward the vision established in the city's
comprehensive plan.

Goal 1:   Use a balanced mix of revenues that will ensure reasonable stability for operation at
continuous service levels through economic cycles, but will provide the economic sensitivity
suitable for responding in a rapid-growth, environment.

Strategies

Match funding sources with types of expenditures so that the demand for money is consistent with
the characteristics of the matching funding sources. In general, debt service funds require more
stable revenue sources, capital improvement funds can accumulate more volatile revenues for
future expenditure, and operating funds require a balanced mix of supporting sources.

Utilize user charges for services that are "price excludable" in order to encourage economic
efficiency and reduce the ad valorem tax burden. Devise charges in ways that observe principles
of equity and encourage economic efficiency and that can be administered at reasonable costs.

Goal 2:   Maintain operating expenditures within the city's ability to raise revenues while keeping
tax and rate structures competitive.

Strategies

Balance recurring expenditures/expenses with recurring revenues. Use nonrecurring revenues to
contribute to reserves or to purchase capital equipment.

Isolate volatile components of the revenue base and devise ways of directing them out of the
operating budget and into capital reserves.

Maintain benchmark data on tax and fee rates of comparable municipal organizations and
competitive private service providers.

Goal 3:   Ensure continuity of service without the use of interim borrowing.

Strategies

Maintain fund balances adequate to meet working capital needs (at least 20% of annual
expenditures in each governmental fund, 2 : 1 current ratios in enterprise funds).

Establish reasonable amounts for contingency accounts in the annual budget process.

Control exposure to risk and volatility in capital equipment replacement requirements through the
equipment replacement plan.

Goal 4:   Maintain adequate capital financing sources and low costs of borrowing.

Strategies

Seek new pay-as-you-go sources of capital.

Maintain moderate credit ratios and carefully schedule new debt offerings so as to optimize use of
credit and minimize impacts upon the ad valorem tax rate.

Position the city to be able to take advantage of debt refunding or restructuring opportunities that
offer a minimum net present value savings of 3.0% or a possibility of freeing up debt capacity
for future significant capital projects.

Source: City of Myrtle Beach (1997: 29).

Financial Plan Goal 1—Revenue Mix

A comparison of the 1997–1998 general fund revenue mix with that of 1993–1994 illustrates the city's performance with regard to its goal for the mix of revenues used in various funds (Table 2). The mix of revenues going into the city's major operating fund has grown more responsive to inflation and expanding service demand. Business license revenues, a function of gross receipts from business conducted within the corporate limit, make up

Table 2 Change in Revenue Mix, General and Debt Service Funds (Fiscal Years 1994–1998)

Revenue or financing source	As percentage of total revenue		Percentage change (FY 1994–1998)
	FYear 1994	FYear 1998	
General fund (objective: greater responsiveness to owing demands for service)			
Property taxes	36.3	21.3	−15.0
Business licenses	18.8	25.5	+6.7
Other licenses and permits	7.7	6.8	−0.9
Intergovernmental	12.0	5.5	−6.5
Fines and forfeitures	4.9	5.0	+0.1
Charges for services	11.4	24.3	+12.9
Use of money and property	4.1	2.1	−2.0
Accommodations tax	4.8	9.5	14.7
Total general fund	100.0	100.0	0.0
Debt service fund (objective: greater stability for repayment of known obligations)			
Property taxes	41.3	97.5	+56.2
Business licenses	36.2	—	−36.2
Accommodations tax	22.5	—	−22.5
Intergovernmental	—	2.5	2.5
Total municipal debt service fund	100.0	100.0	0.0

Source: City of Myrtle Beach (1998: 57).

25.5% of the current revenue mix—an increase from 20% (only 18.8%) in 1994. Service charges have increased from 12% (only 11.4%) to 26% (24.3%), primarily as a result of shifting from property taxes to user fees as the source of support for solid waste management.

Property taxes, a relatively stable but stagnant source, accounted for 38% of the general fund revenue mix in 1993–1994. Following implementation of the strategic financial plan, the city relies upon property taxes for only 25% of its governmental operating revenues. A larger share of the property tax levy has been shifted to the debt service fund, where stability in the revenue base was considered an appropriate objective.

Financial Plan Goal 2—Maintaining a Balanced Budget with Competitive Tax and Rate Structures

Each year, Myrtle Beach reports how its tax and utility rates compare with these Southern cities. Similar data are kept for comparing business license rates and solid waste rates with those of private and governmental competitors in the area. Elected officials and managers want to know that their customers are getting competitively priced service, or understand why prices need to be higher than those charged elsewhere. Figure 1 illustrates how benchmark data on taxes and utility rates are reported.

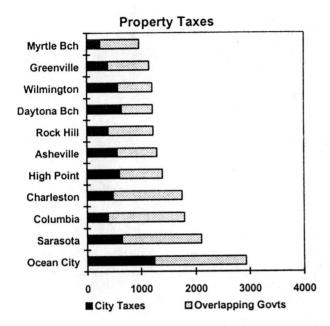

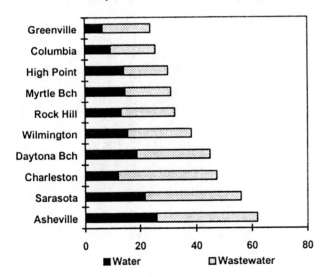

Figure 1 Comparisons of taxes and fees with benchmark sample cities. Source: City of Myrtle Beach (1998: 13).

Financial Plan Goal 3—Ensure Continuity of Service Without Use of Interim Borrowing

The city employs a working capital strategy designed to maintain fund balances adequate to meet working capital needs without interim borrowing. Avoiding the use of tax and revenue anticipation notes saves the cost of interest on the notes, and the cash held in "inventory" for a portion of the year is invested to produce revenue equivalent to almost 5.0% of the general fund tax levy.

For the general fund, city policy provides for the maintenance of fund balance levels at 20.0% of operating expenditures. Financial plans are formulated so as to maintain year-ending fund balance levels as close to 20.0% as possible over the planning horizon.

Figure 2 compares the 20% target for the general fund with the actual ratio of fund balance to operating expenditures from 1988 through 1997. It also shows that the five-year financial plan continues to observe the requirements of the policy (i.e., that fund balances are projected to remain at or slightly above the requisite levels). Notes to the plan explain what additional expenses are anticipated over the period for the costs of new services or the absorption of operating impacts of planned capital projects. They also identify any expected tax or fee increases or decreases that may be necessary in order to sustain the current financial condition.

Financial Plan Goal 4—Maintain Adequate Sources of Capital and Low Costs of Borrowing

Selected ratios are used to show the city's debt position and to estimate how the issuance of new debt, as planned in the five-year CIP, will affect the city's ability to service its debt. Direct net debt includes general obligation (G.O.) debt, as well as capital lease-purchase instruments and debt payable from tax increment revenues or pledged nontax sources.

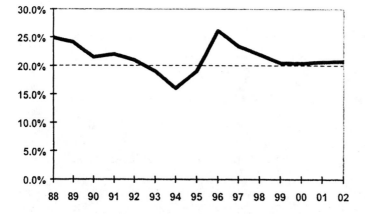

Figure 2 Ratio of fund balance to operating expenditures, general fund. Source: City of Myrtle Beach (1998: 24).

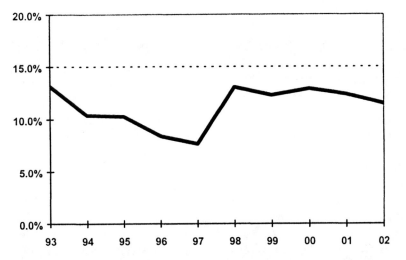

Figure 3 Ratio of direct net debt service to operating expenditures. Source: City of Myrtle Beach (1997: 99).

For direct net debt, the annual budget presents a profile of the city's expected debt position over the five-year planning horizon. The profile is made up of the following six ratios, and typically includes graphic aides, such as that shown in Figure 3, to give both a historical perspective and a sense of how closely the current plan observes each of the objectives. From the 1999 budget, these ratios and benchmark data were

Usage of constitutional G.O. debt capacity (objective: < 90.0%) peaks at 89.7% in 1999.

Unprogrammed G.O. debt margin of about $3.45 million is retained over the period.

Net debt per capita peaks at $1539 for direct net debt, and at $2865 for overall net debt, compared with Moody's 1996 medians of $696 and $1430, respectively.

The ratio of *net debt to estimated full value* over the five-year planning period varies between 1.05–1.13% for direct net debt (median = 1.6%), and between 1.75–2.2% for overall net debt (median = 3.1%).

The ratio of *direct net debt service to operating expenditures* (objective: < 15.0%) varies between 11.0–14.0%.

Overall net debt as a percentage of personal income (objective: < 15.0%) ranges from 10.1–15.0%, with a target ratio of 15.0%.

Figure 3 charts actual and projected direct net debt service as a percentage of operating expenditures. This ratio is a measure of the extent to which a jurisdiction's budget comprises fixed annual expenditures. It reflects the flexibility—or the lack of it—that a government retains in budgeting for its operations. Industry standards favor keeping annual debt service expenditures below 20.0%. The city's objective is < 15.0%. Over the five-year planning period, this measure falls within the 11–14% range, even with the issuance of the $21 million of new debt scheduled in the 1998–2002 CIP.

RESULTS OF FOLLOWING THE PLAN

Using the strategic financial plan and performance monitoring efforts to serve as tools for focusing on certain desired results, the city has accomplished several milestones, as noted in the manager's transmittal letter for the 1999 budget (City of Myrtle Beach, 1998). The city of Myrtle Beach has:

> Developed more demand-responsive revenue structures in its operating funds, and improved stability in its debt service funds
> Maintained A1, A + credit ratings for G.O. debt while making more aggressive use of debt to construct an expanded convention center, a number of new infrastructure items, and public buildings totaling over $32 million
> Improved its underlying credit ratings from Baa, Bbb + to A, A + for waterworks and sewer system revenue debt
> Restructured and refinanced its water and sewer debt (with the cooperation of the financial market), improving the weighted average interest cost from 6.75–4.95%, and the ten-year payout from 49.2% of outstanding debt to 61.9%, while saving over $1 million per year for five years
> Expanded its pay-as-you-go CIP from $500,000 per year to more than $5 million per year
> Improved its overall financial condition

INTEGRATION OF FINANCIAL AND OPERATIONAL PLANNING

As the financial planning component developed, the city was also moving ahead with other aspects of its goal, namely planning for new public facilities and adaptable service delivery systems. In a customer-oriented environment, planning activities are informed, not just by the expertise that professional planners bring or by the policy preferences of a small group who are both willing and able to participate in traditional political processes, but by the needs of individuals and families who buy municipal services. If it expects to get the input it needs from citizens, the government must reach out to them. It must do some accommodating rather than simply rely upon them to show up full of ideas during normal business hours. Myrtle Beach's leaders decided to reach out to the city's citizens in a series of public meetings designed for this specific purpose and scheduled during evening and weekend hours.

Widely publicized under the banner *It's time—A vision for the greater Myrtle Beach community*, the city's public input process involved a series of meetings in every neighborhood inside and immediately surrounding the city. Council, planning commission, and city staff hoped that the process would benefit from greater public input, public ownership of its vision and its goals, and a broad base of support for the implementation of its strategies. The visioning process, completed in May 1997, provided the groundwork for the update of the city's comprehensive plan. According to Myrtle Beach city planner David Fuller, "the visioning process was structured so that the categories of community input parallel the elements of the comprehensive plan. In this way, it is possible for the community's preferences to be fed directly into the comprehensive planning structure."

The annual budget is an ideal vehicle for the integration of these elements into a single document. It serves as a policy document, a one-year financial and operational guide, and a vehicle for public education and accountability.[5] Significant input into the formulation of budgetary policy each year derives from the comprehensive plan. As part of the comprehensive plan update, statutes require the planning commission to prepare and recommend to the city policies, procedures, and strategies to facilitate implementation of planning elements. The budget must clearly show that objectives and performance measures relate directly to the vision statement for a given program. It must provide information on how future budgets anticipate new program costs and the absorption of operating costs of capital projects, many of which flow directly from the comprehensive plan.

CONCLUSION

Myrtle Beach's experience confirms what seems to be a recurring theme in public service today. Accountability will continue to be a paramount issue in the performance of public service, as it should be. In focusing on accountability, however, public servants must be careful not to obscure another very important, and perhaps even prior, question. What do their customers need from them in the first place? Accountability, financial and operational, tends to lose its relevance when this question goes unanswered.

In fact, accountability probably needs to be viewed as a relationship rather than a presentation, a "talking with" rather than a "talking to." You can lead a horse to water, but if he's *hungry* it may not matter to him that your performance measures show consistent improvements in water quality for each of the past several fiscal years. Citizens, customers, constituents—whatever one chooses to call them—need to have access, not just to an *ex post facto* accounting for how their government is performing its objectives, but to the very process of shaping the public policy agenda. Also, local governments need citizen input during all stages of policy development and implementation if they are to provide valuable service to their customers.

As the marketing profession has learned over the past few decades, the most efficient production processes and the most effectively performing products will miss their marks and will eventually fail to sell, unless they are designed to provide what the customer actually needs. Marketing professionals generally teach a different approach today because to the traditional "four P's" of product, price, positioning, and performance, someone added *people* at the head of the list. In much the same way, many local governments are placing a premium on citizen input and creating greater opportunity for public dialogue throughout the policy process. Financial planning and performance monitoring, then, can be made to serve the mission and goals of the community, can adapt with growing and changing community needs, and can help to enable the local government organization to meet realistic and relevant service objectives.

REVIEW QUESTIONS

1. What is a customer-oriented government? How does it differ from a traditional government? Why is financial planning important in a customer-oriented government? Discuss.

2. How did the city of Myrtle Beach use the customer-oriented approach? What efforts did it make to give greater consideration to its citizens?
3. Describe the city's strategic financial plan. What are its major components? How does it fit in the new approach?
4. In monitoring financial performance, what specific measures did the city use? What were the results? Would you attribute the success to the new approach?
5. What is the difference between financial and operational planing? How did the city integrate the two? What were the results of this integration?

NOTES

1. See Government Finance Officers Association (1999), Governmental Accounting Standards Board (1994), Hatry (1990), and Leithe et al. (1997). In fact, performance measurement has become a recommended practice in governmental budgeting and may soon become as much a standard of financial reporting as a balance sheet and an income statement are today.
2. GFOA's recommended practices place emphasis upon development of common definitions of key performance measures to allow intergovernmental comparisons. (See GFOA, 1999: 65.)
3. See Ammons (1995: 1–3), Osborne and Gaebler (1992, and Leithe (1997: 3,4).
4. Waccamaw Regional Planning Council, Conway, South Carolina.
5. These types of service closely parallel the Government Finance Officers Association (GFOA) guidelines for that organization's distinguished budget presentation program. Participation in this program is invaluable because it provides a set of guidelines by which the local government can prepare a budget to serve these four purposes. It allows the city to have its budget document critiqued constructively by three experienced budget and finance professionals, and if a member of staff serves as a reviewer, it gives the city's staff a chance to receive documents regularly from communities around the country. These documents often employ new or different ideas, and thus prompt the reviewers to think creatively about using new approaches in their own budget and financial planning processes. Several of them help devise a budget format that integrates the city's financial plan, comprehensive plan, and performance management interests.

REFERENCES

Ammons, D. N., ed. (1995). *Accountability for Performance: Measurement and Monitoring in Local Government.* Washington, DC: International City/County Managers Association.

City of Myrtle Beach. (1997). *1997–98 Municipal Budget & FY 1997–2002 Financial Plans.* Myrtle Beach, SC.

City of Myrtle Beach. (1998). *1998–99 Municipal Budget & FY 1998–2003 Financial Plans.* Myrtle Beach, SC.

Government Finance Officers Association. (March 1999). *Recommended Practices for State and Local Governments.* Chicago: Government Finance Officers Association.

Governmental Accounting Standards Board. (April 1994). *Service Efforts and Accomplishments Reporting.* GASB concepts statement no. 2. Norwalk, CT.

Hatry, H., Fountain, J. R. Jr., Sullivan, J., and Kremer, L. (1990). *Service Efforts and Accomplishments Reporting: Its Time Has Come.* Norwalk, CT: Governmental Accounting Standards Board.

Leithe, J. (1997). *Implementing Performance Measurement in Government: Illustrations and Resources.* Chicago: Government Finance Officers Association.

Moody's Investors Service. (1996). *Moody's Medians.* New York: Moody's Investors Service.

Myrtle Beach Area Chamber of Commerce, (1997). *Myrtle Beach Area Statistical Abstract. 9th ed., revised.* Myrtle Beach, SC: Myrtle Beach Area Chamber of Commerce.

Osborne, D. and Gaebler, T. (1992). *Reinventing Government: How the Entrepreneurial Spirit Is Transforming the Public Sector.* Reading, MA: Addison-Wesley.

Syfert, P. (1995). Customer-based performance management in Charlotte. In D. N. Ammons (ed.), *Accountability for Performance: Measurement and Monitoring in Local Government*, pp. 169–178. Washington, DC: International City/County Managers Association.

Weltzer, J. W. and Petersen, J. E. (1987). The finance officer as public strategist. In J. I. Chapman (ed.), *Long-Term Financial Planning: Creative Strategies for Local Government*, pp. 11–20. Washington, DC: International City/County Managers Association.

33

Determining the Full Cost of Residential Solid Waste Services

David B. Pariser and Richard C. Brooks
West Virginia University, Morgantown, West Virginia, U.S.A.

Government managers are continuously confronted with financial pressure "to do more with less" and the reluctance of citizens to approve higher taxes and fees to pay for public services. This makes it difficult for governments to add new services and maintain the quality of current services. When managers become aware of the full cost of producing services, they become more informed about the efficiency of operations and the extent to which a fee charged for a given service provides a subsidy to the general fund or whether or not the service is subsidized by the general fund. The full cost of producing a product or service includes both direct and indirect costs. Full cost information allows public administrators and elected officials to make informed decisions on the level of tax subsidies they want to maintain as a matter of public policy. Full cost accounting also helps managers make better decisions on which services should be produced by government employees and which could be produced more efficiently by contracting with private sector firms. The concept of differential costing is appropriate for evaluating such contracting-out decisions. Differential costs are future expected costs that differ between competing decision alternatives.

One of the key principles of cost analysis is the notion that "different costs are used for different decision-making purposes" (Anthony and Young, 1999: 211). Full cost is appropriate for costing services produced by government employees. Full cost includes the cost of all resources utilized in producing a service, including a proportionate share of the government's administrative support costs. Municipal managers of solid waste operations frequently report the components of full costs within a life-cycle framework. Life-cycle costs are grouped into four categorizes: up-front costs, daily operating costs, back-end costs, and overhead costs. These categories are discussed more fully later in the chapter.

This chapter focuses on how municipal governments determine the full cost of residential solid waste services (RSWS), including such activities as collecting residential solid waste (RSW), transporting RSW to transfer stations, recovering recyclable materials, disposing of nonrecyclable waste at landfills, and selling recyclable materials and landfill gas. The costs of producing RSWS have risen steadily over the past decade, primarily due to the increasing cost of complying with stricter federal, state, and local regulations regarding landfill construction and operation. Landfilling is the most common method of solid waste disposal in the United States. The U.S. Environmental Protection Agency (EPA) estimates that over 80% of all municipal solid waste ends up in a landfill. Of the remainder, about 10% is incinerated and about the same percentage is recycled.

The objectives of this chapter are threefold: (1) to introduce full and differential cost concepts within the context of RSWS, (2) to explain the use of fund accounting to determine the full cost of producing RSWS, and (3) to present a case that emphasizes the application of full and differential costing for RSWS. Finally, the case concludes with several questions requiring the application of the cost concepts and issues discussed.

CONCEPTS RELATED TO FULL COSTING OF RESIDENTIAL SOLID WASTE SERVICES

Definition of Cost and Cost Center Budgeting

From an accounting perspective, the word cost is defined as a monetary measurement of the amount of *resources used* to achieve a specific *cost objective* (Horngren et al., 1994). Resources include labor services, materials, equipment, buildings, utilities, and all other inputs required to produce a product or render a service. A *specific* cost objective is defined as anything for which a separate measurement of costs is desired. Examples of a cost objective include a product, a service, a program, and a customer.

Municipal operating budgets are normally prepared on a line-item basis at the departmental level. These budgets focus on the cost of resources or inputs used in producing municipal services. The cost of these resources is normally classified into categories such as salaries and benefits, operating expenditures, supplies used, utilities, rent, and capital equipment (Ingram, 1992: 20–2). A major limitation of line-item budgeting is the focus on the cost of inputs instead of on the cost of the services or "outputs" the government produces and delivers to citizens (Kelley, 1990: 3). This limitation impedes cost analysis. A more effective budgeting approach is cost center budgeting.

According to Anthony and Young (1999: 162) a cost center may be thought of as a "bucket" into which an organization's costs associated with the production of a particular service are accumulated and classified to facilitate full-cost analysis. Cost center budgeting brings together cost and revenue information associated with a particular service to allow a manager to make such decisions as increasing services, decreasing services, eliminating services, or charging a user fee to recover all or part of the cost of producing a service (Kelley, 1990: 3).

Administratively, cost centers are usually organized as departments or divisions. Most municipal governments have two types of cost centers: mission and administrative support (Anthony and Young, 1999: 162). Mission centers carry out the mission of the government and are responsible for performing the central functions associated with producing services for the public. Administrative support centers exist to provide support services to mission centers and other support centers but do not themselves provide services to the public. For example, the police department of the city of Raleigh, North Carolina, is divided into five divisions. Three of the divisions are mission centers (special operations, field operations, and investigations) and two are administrative support centers (police administration and chief's office).[1]

Full Cost Accounting

The full cost of producing a public service consists of both direct and indirect costs. According to the EPA, four states (Florida, Georgia, Indiana, and North Carolina) require local governments to use full cost accounting when reporting the cost of RSWS to citizens.[2] Local governments in other states also use full cost accounting to help manage their solid waste programs (U.S. Environmental Protection Agency, 1997).

Direct Costs

Direct costs can be easily traced to a particular service. Easily traced means that the costs can be assigned by means of a cause-and-effect relationship (Anthony and Young, 1999: 163). For example, the salaries and fringe benefits of municipal employees responsible for collecting and disposing of RSW are direct costs of producing RSWS.

Indirect Costs

Indirect costs, which are also called overhead or shared costs, represent administrative support services that are shared by two or more mission centers in producing public services. Examples of indirect costs include support services, such as accounting and finance, legal services, data processing, and the salaries of supervisors and security guards associated with two or more mission centers. Overhead costs often represent a significant portion of local government expenditures. For example, overhead costs of the city of Flagstaff, Arizona, amounted to about 27% of the city's 1997–1998 operating budget.

The distinguishing characteristic of an indirect cost is that it cannot be directly traced in a straightforward manner to mission centers or to the services they produce. It is this difficulty in assigning indirect costs that gives rise to allocation problems. The process of assigning indirect costs to mission centers is called cost allocation, which is discussed below.

Net Costs

Local governments are interested in the net cost of producing a service. Net cost is equal to the full cost of producing a service minus revenues generated from the sale of by-products generated by the operation. By-products associated with RSWS include recyclables, compost, energy from waste, and landfill gas. When setting user fees, local government managers and elected officials find it helpful to first calculate the net cost per household. This is equal to net cost divided by the total number of households served. (See Figure 1, line 19.) Net cost per household suggests the amount of fees or taxes that must be collected on average from each household served.

If revenues from user fees are inadequate to recover the net cost of producing a service, local government managers and administrators can calculate the revenue shortfall. The shortfall could be financed by a subsidy transfer from the general fund or by transfers from the state and/or federal government. Local government managers and elected officials may choose to subsidize a service such as RSWS as a matter of public policy.

Life-Cycle Costing

In its publication entitled *Full Cost Accounting for Municipal Solid Waste Management: A Handbook*, the EPA indicates that local governments typically summarize and report

Municipality: _____   Fiscal Year: _____

Annual Cost of Operations		Total Solid Waste Budget	Solid Waste Collection	Solid Waste Disposal	Recycling
	Operating Costs				
1	Wages and Benefits of Employees				
2	Maintenance: Operations and Equipment				
3	Power and Fuel				
4	Supplies Used				
5	Landfill Inert Material				
6	Regulatory Compliance Costs				
7	Recycling Costs				
8	Gas Collection				
9	Insurance				
	Up-Front Costs (Capital Expenditures)				
10	Annualized Costs: Pre-development and Construction of Landfill				
11	Annualized Costs: Vehicles/Equipment/Buildings				
	Back-End Costs (Accrued Expenses)				
12	Amortized Closure and Post-Closure Care Costs				
	Overhead Cost (Administrative Support)				
13	Local government Administrative Support				
14	**Total Annual Costs (sum lines 1 - 13)**				
Revenues from Sale of By-Products					
15	Sale of Recyclabes				
16	Sale of Retired Equipment				
17	Other Revenues				
18	**Total Annual Revenues (sum lines 16 - 17)**				
19	**Net Annual Costs (subtract line 14 from line 18)**				
Indicators of Efficiency					
20	Tons of Solid Waste Handled per Year				
21	Number of Households Served				
Cost Per Unit					
22	Cost Per Ton (divide line 19 by line 20)				
23	Cost per Household (divide line 19 by line 21)				

Figure 1 Full cost accounting worksheet—municipal solid waste collection, disposal and recycling.

the full cost of RSWS under four broad life-cycle categories: (1) operating costs, (2) up-front costs, (3) back-end costs, and (4) overhead or shared costs. The first three categories are direct costs and the fourth includes indirect (overhead or shared) costs. Operating costs are associated with the daily production of RSWS. Up-front costs are expenditures for the acquisition of long-term assets essential to production of RSWS. Back-end costs are incurred at the end of a landfill's useful life. Overhead costs represent the cost of adminis-trative support services other departments of a local government provide to RSWS. Figure 1 displays a report format showing the four life-cycle categories and detailed items associ-ated with each category.

One back-end cost that has taken on greater significance in recent years is closure and postclosure care costs. Operators of municipal landfills are legally responsible for properly closing the landfill when it stops accepting waste, as well as monitoring and maintaining the site for thirty years subsequent to closure (Gauthier, 1998: 21). Closure and postclosure costs include construction of on-site leachate treatment facilities, installation of liners and covers, gas monitoring and venting systems, and stormwater and erosion control facilities. Cash outlays for these future costs might not occur for many years, and they are substantial. For example, the city of Flagstaff, Arizona, estimated the total closure and postclosure costs for a currently operating landfill to be $10,122,570, all of which represent future expenses. Regarding this landfill and its associated closure and postclosure costs, the city of Flagstaff made the following disclosure in the notes accompanying financial statements contained in the city's 1997 comprehensive annual financial report:

> The Solid Waste Enterprise Fund ("Solid Waste") currently operates one landfill, the Cinderlake Landfill. Federal and state regulations require that environmental damage caused by landfills be mitigated and that action be taken to prevent future damage. Closure costs, which include the capping of the landfill with soil and installing such items as drainage and monitoring systems, and postclosure cost estimates are based on a study made by an independent consultant, and are subject to change due to inflation, technology changes and applicable legal or regulatory requirements.

> Total closure and postclosure costs for the Cinderlake Landfill, which is still operating, are currently estimated to be $10,122,570, all of which represents future expenses. $6,664,608 has been recorded as a liability in the accompanying financial statements representing costs associated with the cumulative capacity used to date (66% of the total landfill capacity used as of June 30, 1997). The remaining $3,457,962 will be accrued over the remaining life of the landfill, which is currently estimated to be 17 years. The accrual for these closure and postclosure costs for fiscal year 1997 was $1,648,550. The City has pledged its full faith and credit to meet State financial respon-sibility requirements.

Since closure and postclosure care costs occur after a landfill closes and when revenues are no longer being generated, a primary concern is whether or not the local government will have the necessary funds available to pay for closure and postclosure care costs. This concern led Congress to enact Subtitle D of the Resource Conservation and Recovery Act of 1976, which requires owners and operators of municipal solid waste landfills to demonstrate financial assurance that the funds necessary to meet closure and postclosure care costs will be available whenever they are needed. The EPA regulations governing Subtitle D (40 CFR 258.74, revised July 1, 1998) provide local government operators of landfills ten options to choose from to demonstrate financial assurance.[3]

Table 1 Illustration of Landfill Closure and Postclosure Care Costs

	Year 1	Year 2	Year 3
Assumptions			
Landfill opens 1/1/95			
December 31 fiscal year end			
Estimated total cost			
Equipment and facilities	$1,580,000	$1,620,000	$1,777,000
Final cover	1,200,000	1,310,000	1,325,000
Postclosure care	4,120,000	4,228,000	4,977,000
Total	$6,900,000	$7,158,000	$8,079,000
Accumulated usage in cubic yards	65,000	172,000	240,000
Total estimated capacity in millions of cubic yards	3.0	3.0	3.2

Formula

$$\frac{\text{Estimated total current cost} \times \text{Cumulative capacity used}}{\text{Total estimated capacity}} - \text{Amount previously recognized} = \text{Annual allocation}$$

Calculations of annual allocations and liability

Year 1

$$\frac{\$6,900,000 \times 65,000 \text{ yd}^3}{3,000,000 \text{ yd}^3} = \$149,500$$

Liability $=$ $149,500

Year 2

$$\frac{\$7,158,000 \times 172,000 \text{ yd}^3}{3,000,000 \text{ yd}^3} - \$149,500 = \$260,892$$

Liability $=$ $410,392 ($149,500 + 260,892)

Year 3

$$\frac{\$8,079,000 \times 240,000 \text{ yd}^3}{3,200,000 \text{ yd}^3} - \$410,392 = \$195,533$$

Liability $=$ $605,925 ($149,500 + 260,892 + $195,533)

Source: Gauthier (1996: 120–121).

One option is a financial test based on the local government's credit rating and its audited financial statements prepared in compliance with Governmental Accounting Standards Board statement 18 (GASB, 1993). The purpose of GASB statement 18 is to ensure that local government financial statements measure and report landfill closure and postclosure care costs over the useful life of the landfill. Further, GASB statement 18 requires that the estimated total current cost of closure and postclosure care be recognized in proportion to the filled capacity of the landfill. The annual allocated cost is reported as an operating expense each year that the landfill accepts waste. The current cost estimate should be adjusted each year for the effects of inflation or deflation, as well as more stringent regulatory requirements and changes in operating plans, if applicable. Statement

18 mandates the use of the following formula to calculate annual closure and postclosure care costs:

$$\frac{\text{Estimated total cost} \times \text{Cumulative capacity used}}{\text{Total estimated capacity}} - \begin{array}{l}\text{Amount of cost}\\\text{previously}\\\text{recognized}\end{array}$$

$$= \text{Annual cost allocation}$$

Table 1 illustrates the calculation of the annual allocation based on the above formula.

Cost Allocation Methods

As mentioned earlier, both mission and administrative support centers incur costs, but only mission centers produce services for the public. If only the direct costs of a mission center are used to calculate the cost of producing a service, the resulting cost figure would be understated because it does not include the cost of the administrative support services the mission center receives from other departments of the government. To avoid making misleading cost calculations, the cost of administrative support centers must be allocated to each of the mission centers they support. The amount of administrative support costs allocated to a mission center should be related to the amount of administrative support services utilized by the mission center. A variety of allocation bases or cost drivers are used to measure support service utilization. Table 2 shows examples of administrative support costs and related allocation bases frequently used in practice.

Governments use several methods to allocate administrative support costs to mission centers. Three widely used methods are the budget share method, the personnel share method, and the direct method.[4] Each of these methods is discussed below.

Budget Share Method

The budget share method is easy to apply. Each mission center is allocated a percentage share of administrative support costs equal to the mission center's share of the government's total expenditures. The budget share method is a two-step process. In the first step, each mission center calculates its "allocation ratio." The allocation share is equal to the

Table 2 Examples of Administrative Support Costs and Related Allocation Bases

Service and administrative costs	Acceptable bases
Research and development	Estimated time or usage, sales dollars, assets employed, new products developed
Personnel department	Number of employees, payroll, number of new hires
Accounting functions	Estimated time or usage, sales dollars, assets employed, employment data
Purchasing function	Dollar value of purchase orders, number of purchase orders placed, estimated time or usage
Employee health service	Number of employees or office visits
Maintenance and repairs	Number of repair orders or service hours
Warehouse	Square footage used or value of materials stored
Occupancy costs	Square footage occupied

mission center's annual expenditures divided by the government's total expenditures, excluding administrative support costs. The second step calculates the amount of administrative support costs allocated to each mission center by multiplying the mission center's allocation ratio by the government's total expenditures less administrative costs. The budget share method assumes that a mission center utilizes support services in proportion to its share of total government expenditures. This assumption may not always be valid. The following example illustrates the budget share method, using a municipality's solid waste department as an example.

Government's annual budget (expenditures)	$3,000,000
Total administrative support costs	900,000
Solid waste department annual budget	600,000

Step 1:   Calculate solid waste department allocation ratio:

$$\frac{\text{Solid waste department expenditures}}{\text{Total expenditures} - \text{support costs}} = \text{Allocation ratio}$$

$$\frac{\$600,000}{\$3,000,000 - \$900,000} = .2857$$

Step 2:   Determine solid waste department's share of administrative support costs Administrative support costs $\times$ Allocation ratio

$$\$900,000 \times .2857 = \$171,420$$

Solid waste department's total cost	
Department's annual expenditures	$600,000
Share of support costs	171,420
Total cost	$771,420

Personnel Share Method

The personnel share method is similar to the budget share method. The allocation ratio is based on the number of employees (or full-time equivalents) in the solid waste department as a percentage of total government employees. The following example illustrates the personnel share method:

Number of government employees	1875
Number of solid waste department employees	150

Step 1:   Calculate solid waste department allocation ratio:

$$\frac{\text{Solid waste department employees}}{\text{Government employees}} = \text{Allocation ratio}$$

$$\frac{150}{1,875} = .08$$

Step 2: Determine solid waste department's share of administrative support costs:

Administrative support costs × Department's allocation ratio

$900,000 × .08 = $72,000

	Solid waste department's total cost
Department's annual budget	$600,000
Share of support costs	72,000
Total	$672,000

The above illustrations indicate that the budget share and personnel share methods might yield somewhat different results.

Direct Method

This method is more involved than the budget share and personnel share methods, although it is relatively easy and convenient to apply. The direct method typically uses more than one allocation base to assign administrative support center costs to mission centers. Different allocation bases are used in an attempt to more accurately measure the amount of support services utilized by each mission center. Table 3 illustrates the direct method of allocation.

Table 3 Illustration of Direct Allocation Method

	Total	Fire dept.	Police dept.	Solid waste collection dept.
Accounting and finance department				
Base (number of transactions)	100,000	10,000	30,000	60,000
Percentage of total base	100%	10%	30%	60%
Cost allocations	$200,000	$20,000	$60,000	$120,000
Office of city manager				
Base (square footage occupied)	40,000	5,000	15,000	20,000
Percentage of total base	100%	12.5%	37.5%	50%
Cost allocations	$300,000	$37,500	$112,500	$150,000
Purchasing and receiving department				
Base (number of orders placed)	6,000			
Percentage of total base	100%	30%	45%	25%
Cost allocations	$400,000	$120,000	$180,000	$100,000

Cost summary	Accounting and finance	City manager	Purchasing and receiving	Fire	Police	Solid waste collection
Department cost before allocations	$200,000	$300,000	$400,000	$700,000	$800,000	$600,000
Cost allocations						
Accounting and finance department	($200,000)			20,000	60,000	120,000
City manager's office		($300,000)		37,500	112,500	150,000
Purchasing and receiving department			($400,000)	120,000	180,000	100,000
Department costs *after* allocations	$0	$0	$0	$877,500	$1,152,500	$970,000
Full cost per unit of service						
Cost per fire (800 occurrences)				$1,097		
Cost per police case (3500 cases)					$329	
Cost per ton of solid waste collected (38,420 tons)						$25.25
Cost per household (45,200 households)				$19.41	$25.50	$21.46
Cost per household *before* allocations				$15.49	$17.70	$13.27

Suppose a city has three administrative support centers (accounting and finance, office of city manager, and purchasing and receiving) and three mission centers (fire department, police department, and solid waste department). The upper section of Table 3 shows the annual costs of each administrative support center, the allocation base associated with each administrative support center, and each mission center's share of each allocation base. As shown in Table 3, accounting and finance has annual expenditures of $200,000 and uses the number of transactions as an allocation base, the office of the city manager has expenditures of $300,000 and uses square footage occupied as an allocation base, and purchasing and receiving has expenditures of $400,000 and uses the number of orders placed as an allocation base. The lower section of Table 3 shows the details of the allocation process and each mission center's full cost and cost per unit.

Table 3 clearly shows the implications of full costing. If the mission center has calculated its cost per unit *before* taking cost allocations into account, the results would be misleading because administrative support service costs are ignored.

Challenges in Implementing Full Cost Accounting

Full cost accounting offers many potential benefits to local government managers and their communities. In a recent study on full cost accounting for solid waste services published by the International City/county Management Association (ICMA), 98% of the municipal managers surveyed said that full cost accounting is a useful decision-making tool for managing solid waste services. The study reports that municipal solid waste managers use full cost accounting to identify actual costs, establish user fees, explain costs more clearly to citizens, manage costs more efficiently, plan services more effectively, benchmark, target cost-reduction efforts, and improve negotiations with private sector firms (Yuhas, 1998: 7–10).

Realizing the benefits of full cost accounting, however, may not be easy because local government managers must overcome several barriers to implementation. According to the ICMA study, local government managers identified eleven obstacles to implementing full cost accounting. These obstacles (from most frequently to least frequently cited) include: (1) difficulty determining accurate overhead rates, (2) lack of staff time, (3) incomplete records, (4) disagreement on full cost accounting methodology, (5) changes in the existing accounting system, (6) cost of implementation, (7) lack of interdepartmental coordination, (8) concerns about financial disclosure, (9) employee concerns, (10) lack of political support, and (11) lack of management support (Yuhas, 1998:8). It is interesting to note that 35% of the managers reported that no obstacles were encountered when they implemented full cost accounting (Yuhas, 1998: 8).

DIFFERENTIAL COSTING: APPLICATIONS TO RSWS

Many municipalities contract out solid waste services to reduce the cost of service delivery.[5] In a recent study on alternative service delivery choices, ICMA reported that 49% of local governments surveyed contract out RSW collection to private sector firms (Hall, 1998: 2). In practice, however, realized cost savings often fall short of expectations.

Local government managers have come to realize that the decision to contract with private sector firms is complex, frequently requiring government managers to make an inordinate number of estimates and assumptions regarding operating costs, contractor performance, and the cost of monitoring and managing contracts. Contract monitoring—a responsibility of local government contract compliance officers—is the primary means of overseeing performance, ensuring quality, and assuring a competitive price (Eagle, 1997: 11–14). Estimates of contract management increase considerably when all contract administration activities are considered. A study of contracting out in the Los Angeles, California, area calculated the full cost of contract administration to be approximately 25% of the total cost of the contract (Martin, 1992: 13).

When deciding between competing alternative courses of action, government managers should focus their attention on differential costs. Differential costs are future expected costs that differ between alternatives (Titard, 1996: 386). Managers frequently find that contracting-out decisions result in the elimination of certain costs and the creation of new costs, such as contract administration. When considering whether or not to contract out a service it is important to identify relevant costs; that is, those costs that can be avoided by contracting with a private sector firm. It thus makes financial sense for a government not to contract out a service when the government's avoidable costs are less than the contractor's proposed bid price.

When a government contracts out a service, some administrative support costs included in the cost of producing the service will still be incurred by the government, even after the government no longer produces the service. This happens because administrative support departments will continue serving other mission centers. Costs that were allocated to the contracted service will more likely than not be absorbed by other mission centers. Those costs that cannot be avoided must be subtracted from the full cost of public sector production before comparing the government's production cost to the cost of contracting the service out to a private sector firm. In the event that the eliminated service used a major share of administrative support services, some cost savings might actually be realized. This depends on whether or not one or more administrative support departments can be "downsized" without jeopardizing their future ability to provide adequate levels of administrative support to the remaining mission centers. The following example illustrates the use of differential cost analysis.

Suppose a city manager is deciding whether or not to contract out its RSWS. The government's full cost of producing RSWS is $970,000, as shown in Table 3. The city manager would eliminate the RSWS department if the service is contracted out. The city manager estimates that only 10% of the administrative support cost allocated to the RSWS department is avoidable, and that the remaining 90% cannot be avoided. The city manager also estimates that $50,000 of new contract management costs would be incurred annually if the RSWS were contracted out. A private sector firm submits a bid of $675,000 per year. Should the city manager accept the bid? A differential cost analysis follows.

Differential Cost Analysis

	City's avoidable cost
RSWS department's direct cost	$600,000
Allocated cost ($370,000 × 10%)	37,000
Total avoidable cost	$637,000
	Contract-out option
Contractor's bid	$610,000
Contract administration costs	50,000
Total	$660,000
Difference	$23,000

The above differential cost analysis shows that contracting out the RSWS is not financially feasible. The city would save $23,000 a year by continuing to produce RSWS compared to the amount it would spend to contract out the services. If the city chooses to contract out RSWS, it would avoid spending $637,000 to produce the service but would have to pay the contractor $610,000 and spend an additional $50,000 on contract administration. If the contractor's bid plus the new contract administration costs are less than $637,000, contracting out would be financially feasible. Before making a final decision, the city manager should also consider various qualitative factors that could influence the decision. Such factors include the number of competing bidders, the adequacy of contract specifications, the ability to monitor contractor performance, city employee resistance to contracting out, and whether or not citizens will be satisfied with the contractor's quality of service. In the event the contractor fails to provide adequate service or terminates services completely, the local government must either return to producing the service itself or quickly contract out with another private sector firm while resolving legal issues with the previous contractor (Eggers, 1994: 58–59).

FUND ACCOUNTING AND ITS USES IN COSTING PUBLIC SERVICES

Municipal fund accounting systems typically use the general fund or an enterprise fund to account for RSWS. Because the objectives of enterprise funds and the general fund differ markedly they provide managers with different kinds of cost information; consequently, managers must be aware of these differences when setting user fees for services based on the full cost of producing the services. In a 1994 survey of local governments providing solid waste services, the ICMA reports that about 39% of the jurisdictions use the general fund to finance these services and about 45% use user charges to finance these services. The remaining 16% utilize other funding mechanisms (Cimitile and Feinland, 1994: 5–6).

The General Fund

The general fund is used to account for general government activities and focuses on the inflows and outflows of spendable financial resources (i.e., cash and other items that can be expected to be converted into cash in the normal course of operations) using a modified accrual basis of accounting. Because of its focus on spendable financial resources, the general fund does not provide a complete picture of the full cost of producing a service. For example, modified accrual accounting recognizes up-front costs before the periods in which service is produced and recognizes back-end costs after the service has been produced.

Since full cost accounting requires that all costs (i.e., operating costs, up-front costs, back-end costs, and overhead costs) be assigned or allocated to the periods in which the service is produced, the modified accrual method of accounting is unable to meet this requirement. In this regard, managers working with general fund information should give careful consideration to the treatment of up-front and back-end capital outlays associated with the production of a particular service in determining the full cost of producing that service. The modified accrual method does not depreciate up-front capital expenditures or amortize back-end capital expenditures over the years in which services are produced. As a result, the annual cost of production is understated.

Enterprise Funds

In contrast, enterprise funds are used by local governments to account and report activities that can be financed and operated like a private business. Full cost accounting is inherent in the concept and operation of enterprise funds, which focus on all economic resources that are used in the production of services. All assets and liabilities (both long-term and short-term) are reported on the balance sheet of an enterprise fund. Enterprise funds use the accrual method of accounting, which assigns and allocates all costs (operating, up-front, back-end, and overhead) to the periods in which services are produced. Under accrual accounting, revenues are recognized when they are earned regardless when cash in received. Up-front and back-end capital expenditures are recorded as long-term assets of the enterprise fund and depreciated or amortized over the periods in which production occurs.

In early 1998, the Government Finance Officers Association (GFOA) recommended that local governments apply full cost accounting to municipal solid waste activities and use the accrual basis of accounting for determining the cost of producing solid waste services (Gouthie, 1998:19). The GFOA also recommended the use of enterprise funds to account for solid waste services. In light of the GFOA's recommendations, managers of municipal governments that use the general fund to account for solid waste services should become familiar with accrual accounting principles and procedures for establishing an enterprise fund for solid waste services.

Establishing an Enterprise Fund

Eggers describes several important preliminary and ongoing considerations in establishing an enterprise fund (Eggers, 1994: 76–80). These considerations include (1) determining whether or not the government has the authority to impose user charges on activities to be accounted for in a newly established enterprise fund; (2) obtaining political support for establishing a new enterprise fund and user charges from elected officials, administrators, and citizens; (3) determining the amount of user charges necessary to recover the full cost of producing the service; and (4) educating the public about the reasons for the need to establish an enterprise fund and impose user charges to support the fund.

Establishing User Fees: Accrual Versus Modified Accrual Accounting

As discussed earlier, a major difference between the modified accrual and accrual basis is the treatment of up-front and back-end capital outlays; consequently, when solid waste operations are accounted for in the general fund managers may have difficulty calculating the full cost of production. While the recovery of the full cost of production measured on an accrual basis is an important factor in establishing user charges, it should not be the only consideration; the cash flow needs of the solid waste operation must also be considered. In this regard, financial experts caution against using accrual accounting to establish user charges when the use of depreciation expense might lead to revenue shortfalls (Reed-Stowe & Co. et al., 1995; Gauthier, 1998). For example, if a city's solid waste collection facilities are being depreciated over twenty years but are financed with a ten-year revenue bond, the bond's annual principal and interest payments will be greater than the annual depreciation expense. In this case, user charges should reflect debt service requirements rather than depreciation expense to avoid a cash shortfall for the city in the early years and a surplus in the later years. Other adverse consequences could also occur if rates are based on the lower depreciation expense instead of the higher debt service requirements. For example, a revenue shortfall could lead to a city violating loan covenants, which could in turn result in the downgrading of the city's credit rating and possibly putting the city in technical default on its debt.

RESIDENTIAL SOLID WASTE SERVICES: A MUNICIPAL CASE

The city of Chesterville was established in 1889 and has a current population of 300,000. The city uses a council–manager form of government and employs 3500 people. Most public services are produced by municipal employees and are funded by property taxes, various licence fees, user fees, and federal and state grants. The city council has established a goal of maintaining an unobligated fund balance in the general fund equivalent to approximately thirty working days of expenditures. Such an unobligated fund balance is needed to ensure an exemplary credit rating, to guard against unexpected emergencies, and to provide a cash position to avoid short-term borrowing. The year-end unobligated fund balance of the general fund for the previous fiscal year was equivalent to forty-five days of expenditures.

The city uses enterprise funds to account for two businesslike operations: water and sewer utilities and mass transit bus services. The water and sewer utilities enterprise fund is self-supporting. It also transfers some of its surplus each year to the general fund to pay the cost of administrative support services it receives from general administration. The mass transit enterprise fund provides subsidized bus transportation services to the community. Almost 95% of the mass transit fund's contributed capital came from grants provided by the Federal Transit Administration (FTA). As a matter of public policy, the city keeps bus fares substantially below the full cost of producing the service since most users are senior citizens and schoolchildren. The city council intends to continue this policy despite declining FTA grants. The FTA's annual revenue grants have been adequate to cover the operating losses of the mass transit fund.

The city is halfway through the current fiscal year. The city was recently notified that in the next fiscal year it will experience substantial reductions in the state and federal grant monies it has received in the past. The reduced funding level is likely to continue for the foreseeable future. On average, these intergovernmental grants represented about 10–15% of the city's annual revenues. The city has been using virtually all of the grant monies to cover operating losses of the mass transit fund and for funding public education programs in the community. The director of finance and the city council are very concerned that lower intergovernment revenues in the future could potentially lead to (1) lower bond ratings and higher borrowing costs; (2) the inability to maintain the minimum unobligated fund balance in the general fund; and (3) spending a larger portion of general revenues on public education, resulting in a decrease in the amount of general revenues available to support RSWS.

Residential Solid Waste Budget Planning

The residential solid waste services department (RSWSD) is responsible for the collection of RSW, transportation of solid waste to the city-owned landfill, and operation of a recycling program. The RSWSD provides weekly curbside garbage collection and recycling services to all residential households. The RSWSD also is responsible for operating the city-owned landfill facilities in compliance with all federal and state regulations. The department employs 210 people and serves 65,000 households. Administratively, RSWSD is part of the city's general fund operations and prepares an annual operating budget on a modified accrual basis of accounting. The RSWSD is organized into three divisions: solid waste collection, municipal landfill, and recycling.

The RSWSD has proposed an operating budget for the next fiscal year, which begins in six months. The RSWSD's proposed operating budget is shown in Table 4. Proposed

Table 4 City of Chesterville Residential Solid Waste Services Department—Proposed Operating Budget

	Total	Collection division	Landfill division	Recycling division
Number of employees	210	130	55	25
Revenues				
Service fees	$ 3,120,000	$ 780,000	$ 1,560,000	$ 780,000
Sale of recyclables	125,000			125,000
Sale of landfill gas	35,000		35,000	
Total	$ 3,280,000	$ 780,000	$ 1,595,000	$ 905,000
Expenditures				
Wages and benefits	$ 8,560,000	$ 5,000,000	$ 2,400,000	$ 1,160,000
Maintenance	190,000	60,000	85,000	45,000
Power and fuel	427,500	112,000	250,000	65,500
Supplies used	1,055,000	225,000	645,000	185,000
Landfill inert material	175,000		175,000	
Regulatory compliance costs	1,435,000	350,000	950,000	135,000
Recycling	85,500			85,500
Gas collection	15,500		15,500	
Insurance	125,000	35,000	80,000	10,000
Capital outlay—new trucks	285,000	110,000	50,000	125,000
Total	$ 12,353,500	$ 5,892,000	$ 4,650,500	$ 1,811,000
Operating surplus (deficit)	$ (9,073,500)	$ (5,112,000)	$ (3,055,500)	$ (906,000)
Annual subsidy per household	$ (139.59)	?	?	?
Monthly subsidy per household	$ (11.63)	?	?	?
Number of households served	65,000			

	Total pounds	Total tons	Pounds per household
Garbage collected annually	93,000,000	46,500	1500
Material recycled annually	38,440,000	19,220	620

Table 5   Allocation of Citywide Administrative Support Costs to SWSD

Administrative support department	Total expenditures of administrative support departments	Allocation base (citywide total in parentheses)	Allocation base of solid waste collection division	Allocation base of landfill division	Allocation base of recycling division
General administration and management department	$25,000,000	Budgeted expenditures ($510,000,000)	$5,892,000	$4,650,500	$1,811,000
Legal services department	$17,800,000	Hours of legal service (20,800 hours)	2010 hours	3200 hours	4040 hours
Data processing department	$28,000,000	Hours of computer usage (41,800 hours)	4990 hours	2450 hours	580 hours
Accounting and finance department	$18,000,000	Hours of accounting and finance service (72,800 hours)	10,892 hours	3250 hours	1725 hours
Payroll and human resources department	$16,800,000	Number of employees (3000 employees)	100 employees	40 employees	20 employees
Purchasing and warehouse department	$28,200,000	Number of purchase orders (4500 purchase orders)	410 purchase orders	225 purchase orders	115 purchase orders
Building maintenance and security department	$19,200,000	Square feet of building space occupied (240,000 square feet)	15,000 square feet	8000 square feet	10,000 square feet

expenditures do not include allocations of citywide overhead costs (administrative support costs). Municipal departments that provide administrative support services to RSWSD are listed in Table 5.

As a matter of public policy, the city subsidizes RSWS from general revenues, primarily property taxes. Each household is billed a small monthly fee of $4.00 for RSWS ($1.00 for garbage collection, $2.00 for landfill disposal, and $1.00 for recycling). This monthly fee is less than the full cost of producing the services. The service fee revenues shown in RSWSD's proposed operating budget are based on the $4.00 monthly fee per household. In view of the reduction in intergovernment revenues, the city council is evaluating alternative funding sources for RSWS. The city manager has suggested that the RSWSD be self-supporting. She also has suggested that the city council and the director of finance explore the possibility of establishing user charges for RSWS to relieve the financial stress on the city's general revenue system.

In addition to creating new revenue streams, the city manager believes that user charges offer other advantages as well. These advantages include: (1) making citizens aware that public services are not costless, (2) tracking public demand for a service, (3) improving financing equity for those services being subsidized by general tax revenues, and (4) improving operating efficiency by encouraging government employees to place greater emphasis on controlling costs and improving quality of services (Mikesell, 1995:

424–425). The city manager also is aware of two limitations associated with user charges. When imposed on essential public services, user charges may be counterproductive in that they could adversely affect low-income groups. Second, imposition of a user charge may face public opposition from taxpaying citizens who believe that the taxes they are now paying entitle them to the public service without any additional payment of taxes or user charges (Mikesell, 1995:427).

Financing of Capital Assets for Solid Waste Services

For the last three years the city has been disposing RSW at the city-owned landfill. Before that, the city used the county landfill. The city-owned landfill has an expected life of thirty years. Predevelopment and landfill construction costs were financed by general obligation bonds. The general obligation bonds provide considerable flexibility to the city because it can choose any source of revenue for payment of principal and interest.

The city owns a fleet of garbage and recycling trucks. It also owns buildings, transfer stations, and equipment utilized by the RSWSD. The acquisition of these assets was financed with general obligation bonds, which also provide considerable flexibility to the city because they, too, allow the city to choose any source of revenue for payment of principal and interest.

User Charge Option for Solid Waste Services

The city council and the director of finance are interested in exploring the city manager's suggestion of establishing a user charge for RSWS. They are unclear as to how much to charge each household, however. At a recent hearing on the RSWSD's proposed budget for the next fiscal year, members of the city council asked the director of finance several questions about the cost of producing RSWS and related issues. The questions and the finance director's responses follow.

> Question: Is it correct to say that many local governments use full cost accounting to determine the cost of producing solid waste services?
>
> Director of finance: Yes. Many local governments use full cost accounting to set cost-based user charges for solid waste services. In fact, four states have passed laws requiring local governments to use full cost accounting for solid waste services. These laws also require local governments to disclose full cost information to citizens. In a recent study, ICMA identified 400 local governments that use full cost accounting for managing solid waste services [Yuhas, 1998].
>
> Question: Does the city of Chesterville currently use accrual accounting for solid waste services? Does the city have the capability to use full cost accounting for solid waste services?
>
> Director of finance: The city of Chesterville does not use accrual accounting for solid waste services for internal budgeting purposes. Our accounting system was designed to use the modified accrual basis of accounting which is similar to "cash flow" accounting. As you know, the residential solid waste services department has been accounted for in the general fund, which uses the modified accrual basis of accounting. However, we recently completed a special project that converted the department's accounting records to an accrual basis to meet the requirements

of full cost accounting. It took us nine month to complete this project. The conversion gives the department the ability to use full cost accounting to conduct special studies, such as setting cost-based user charges, evaluating the operating efficiency of the department, and assessing proposals for contracting out residential solid waste services.

Question: Please explain the consequences of calculating service fees using modified accrual accounting instead of accrual accounting principles.

Director of finance: As you are aware, accrual accounting is not the same as "cash flow" or "general fund" accounting. When cash flow accounting is used to set user fees, the result is likely to be a distorted picture of the actual cost of producing solid waste services. This distortion occurs because cash flow accounting focuses exclusively on current outlays of funds. However, not all of the costs associated with residential solid waste services result from current outlays of funds. Substantial costs are incurred for past (up-front) and future (back-end) outlays. For example, the garbage trucks, buildings, and the landfill were acquired several years ago. The cash outlays were recorded in the past and those costs have not been allocated to the subsequent periods in determining the cost of services. As a result, the modified accrual method understates the cost of producing residential solid waste services. In contrast, the accrual method gives a more accurate picture of the annual cost of production because it depreciates up-front costs and amortizes back-end costs over the years in which services are produced.

Question: I realize that the recovery of the full cost of production measured on the accrual basis is a crucial consideration in setting user charges for solid waste services. Are the cash flow needs of the solid waste operation ever taken into account?

Director of finance: Yes. The cash flow needs of the solid waste operation must be taken into account when setting user charges. Otherwise, the city runs the risk of not generating adequate revenues. A case in point is the acquisition of long-term assets with the use of debt financing. The debt service may be amortized over a shorter period than the useful life of the assets. In this case, user charges should be established using debt service requirements rather than deprecation expense. However, the city has not followed this practice but may do so in the future.

Question: Obviously, the benefits of full cost accounting do not come free. Please tell us how much effort was involved in designing and implementing a full cost accounting system for residential solid waste services.

Director of finance: A substantial amount of effort was involved in designing and implementing a full cost accounting system, particularly in the beginning. In designing our full cost accounting system we did the following: (1) we identified all direct costs associated with providing solid waste services; (2) we identified all indirect or overhead costs associated with providing the services; and (3) we selected a method of allocating overhead costs to the solid waste department and its three divisions.

Implementing this system required a substantial investment of staff time because our financial records were not in very good shape. For instance, we had to do a lot of research into financial records and spend several months meeting with the residential solid waste services staff as well as other department heads to make sure that we identified all direct and indirect costs. Because of incomplete records, a big challenge was compiling and validating an inventory of all capital expenditures, both past and future outlays. Numerous disagreements among staff over the cost and expected life of several long-term assets had to be reconciled, sometimes with the help of expert consultants. The finance staff spent several weeks identifying and evaluating different methods of allocating overhead costs. A few staff members of the solid waste department initially resisted full cost accounting because they lacked training in overhead allocation methods and their application. With the assistance of outside consultants, we provided all the necessary training to the staff. In my opinion, our staff members learned a great deal working together in designing and implementing the full cost accounting system. And, as a result of their efforts and accomplishments, our accounting records have never been in better shape.

Question: In your opinion, should the city establish an enterprise fund for solid waste services?

Director of finance: Yes, the city should establish an enterprise fund for residential solid waste services.

Question: The city council would like to approve the residential solid waste services department's budget for the coming fiscal year within the next 45 days. Before approving the budget, however, the council would like you and the solid waste department staff to revise the amount of revenue from service fees shown in the department's proposed budget [Table 4]. Instead of basing these revenues on the current $4.00 monthly fee per household, we would like you to base these revenues on the full cost of producing these services.

The city council would like you and the solid waste department staff to prepare and submit a report within the next 30 days. The report should include the following: (1) calculation of the full cost of producing residential solid waste services, including a breakdown by individual services produced by the department; (2) calculation of a user charge based on full cost; (3) a revised budget; and (4) suggested guidelines for establishing an enterprise fund for residential solid waste services. Will you be able to prepare and submit such a report within the next 30 days?

Director of finance: Yes. The residential solid waste services department staff has compiled and summarized all the necessary cost data for determining the full cost of solid waste services and establishing user charges for these services. I see no problems in completing the study within the next 30 days. In fact, I brought along copies of a cost summary data sheet the solid waste staff prepared for members of the city council to review [Table 6]. The staff also developed a worksheet to facilitate the calculation and presentation of the full cost of solid waste services. The worksheet presents the costs in four life-cycle categories. I also brought copies of the worksheet for the city council [Figure 1].

Question: In preparing your report, the city council would also appreciate receiving any recommendations you might have based on the findings of your report.

Director of finance: We would be pleased to include recommendations in our report. We look forward to working with the city council and the city manager on setting user charges for residential solid waste services and establishing an enterprise fund for these services.

Table 6 Summary of Cost Data—Solid Waste Collection, Disposal, and Recycling

I. Operating costs

Operating costs include the following items included in the department's operating budget: wages and benefits, maintenance, power and fuel, supplies used, landfill inert material, regulatory compliance costs, recycling, and gas collection.

II. Up-front costs

Annualized costs: Predevelopment and construction of landfill[a]

1.	Site engineering	$ 545,000
2.	Reports to city council	12,000
3.	Predesign studies	235,000
4.	Land use planning	135,000
5.	Land titles, transfers, and fees	5,500
6.	Permits	75,000
7.	Legal services	625,000
8.	Landfill construction cost	2,400,000
9.	Total cost	$4,032,500
10.	Expected life of landfill	30 years
11.	Amortization (line 8/line 9)	$ 201,625

Annualized cost of trucks/equipment/buildings[b]

Trucks acquired in past years

1.	Trucks used for solid waste collection	$ 760,000
2.	Trucks used in landfill operations	285,000
3.	Trucks used for recycling operations	196,000
4.	Total cost	$1,241,000
5.	Use life of trucks	12 years
6.	Annual depreciation (line 4/line 5)	$ 103,417

New trucks acquired in current fiscal year[c]

1.	Truck used in solid waste collection	$ 110,000
2.	Truck used in recycling operations	125,000
3.	Truck used in landfill operations	50,000
4.	Total cost	$ 285,000
5.	Useful life of trucks	12 years
6.	Annual depreciation (line 4/line 5)	$ 23,750

Equipment acquired in the past years[d]

1.	Equipment used in solid waste collection	$ 650,000
2.	Equipment used in landfill operations	1,225,000
3.	Equipment used in recycling operations	275,000
4.	Total Cost	$ 2,150,000
5.	Useful life of equipment	15 years
6.	Annual depreciation (line 4/line 5)	143,333

Buildings acquired in past years[e]

1.	Buildings used in solid waste collection	$ 920,000
2.	Buildings used in landfill operations	785,000
3.	Buildings used in recycling operations	465,000
4.	Total Cost	2,170,000
5.	Expected useful life of buildings	30 years
6.	Annual depreciation (line 4/line 5)	$ 72,333

(*continued*)

Table 6 Continued

III. Back-end costs	
Amortized closure and postclosure cost	

The landfill opened three years ago. It has an expected life of 25 years. Table 1 lists the assumptions and estimated total costs and annual allocations for the first three years. The estimated total costs in year 4, the forthcoming fiscal year, are shown below.

Estimated total cost	Year 4
Equipment and facilities	$ 1,821,425
Final cover	1,345,000
Postclosure care	5,792,200
Total	$ 8,958,625
Accumulated usage in cubic yards	310,000
Total estimated capacity in millions of cublic yards	3.2

IV. Overhead costs (administrative support)
  See Table 5.

---

[a] The above predevelopment and construction costs were financed by 20-year general obligation bonds. The bonds were issued three years ago upon the completion of landfill construction. The annual principal and interest payment is $320,600. The general obligation bonds provide considerable flexibility to the city because it can choose any source of revenue for payment of the bonds.

[b] The above trucks were financed by 10-year general obligation bonds. The bonds were issued five years ago. The annual principal and interest payment on these bonds is $160,750. The general obligation bonds provide considerable flexibility to the city because it can choose any source of revenue for payment of the bonds.

[c] The above new trucks were purchased with cash.

[d] The above equipment was financed by 10-year general obligation bonds. The bonds were issued six years ago. The annual principal and interest payments on these bonds is $285,200. The general obligation bonds provide considerable flexibility to the city because it can choose any source of revenue for payment of the bonds.

[e] The above buildings were financed by 20-year general obligation bonds. The bonds were issued eight years ago when the buildings were constructed. The annual principal and interest payment on these bonds is $181,500. The general obligation bonds provide considerable flexibility to the city because it can choose any source of revenue for payment of the bonds.

SUMMARY AND CONCLUSION

This chapter discusses concepts and procedures for determining the full cost of providing services in the public sector. Knowing the full cost of providing public services is important because it helps managers make responsible decisions on behalf of the citizens they represent. The chapter describes several concepts related to full costing, including cost centers, direct costs, indirect costs, net full cost, life-cycle costing, and cost allocation methods. Differential costing is discussed within the context of the decision to contract out residential solid waste services versus producing those services with municipal employees.

The chapter also discusses fund accounting and shows how certain funds may be useful for determining the full cost of providing services to the public. More specifically, enterprise funds that utilize the accrual basis of accounting rather than the general fund, which uses the modified accrual basis of accounting, may provide better information regarding the full cost of providing services to the public. Full cost information can then be utilized to set user fees to cover the full cost of providing the service. On the other hand, full cost information can be used to determine the extent to which a service will be subsidized by tax revenues. The chapter concludes with a case and related questions that relate to the provision of residential solid waste services within a municipality.

REVIEW QUESTIONS

1. From a managerial perspective, what are the advantages and limitations of accounting for residential solid waste services in the general fund?
2. From a financial statement user's perspective, what benefits can be obtained from accounting for residential solid waste services in an enterprise fund?
3. What type of government activities should be accounted for in an enterprise fund?
4. How is an enterprise fund for solid waste service established?
5. Should the city of Chesterville establish an enterprise fund for residential solid waste services?
6. What are the benefits and costs of establishing and maintaining an enterprise fund for residential solid waste services?
7. Explain why the EPA encourages, and four states require, local governments to use full cost accounting for managing residential solid waste services. Why would managers of local governments, elected officials, and citizens be interested in knowing the full cost of producing residential solid waste services? Explain.
8. In Table 4, calculate the annual subsidy per household and the monthly subsidy per household for the three residential solid waste divisions.
9. Using Tables 1 and 3–6, complete the full cost accounting worksheet (Figure 1) for the proposed fiscal year using the budget share method to allocate overhead costs.
10. Using Tables 1 and 3–6, complete the full cost accounting worksheet (Figure 1) for the proposed fiscal year using the personnel share method to allocate overhead costs.
11. Using Tables 1 and 3–6, complete the full cost accounting worksheet (Figure 1) for the proposed fiscal year using the direct method to allocate overhead costs.
12. How do the amounts on line 23 of Figure 1 compare with the current service fees charged to each household for the three residential solid waste services?
13. The city wants to set a user charge for each residential solid waste service equal to the full cost of producing each service. Of the three worksheets you prepared in answering questions 9, 10, and 11, which cost per household (line 23, Figure 1) would you recommend the city use for the three residential solid waste services? Explain your answer.
14. How does your answer to question 13 compare to the current monthly fee per household for each residential solid waste service?
15. Using your answer to question 13, revise the proposed operating budget for the city of Chesterville (Table 6).
16. At a recent city council meeting, several citizens expressed concern about the cost of residential solid waste services. According to the city manager, several private sector firms have indicated an interest in submitting bids to provide

residential solid waste services. What is the maximum bid the city would be willing to accept from a private sector firm, assuming that none of the overhead costs can be eliminated if residential solid waste services are contracted out? Explain.

17. How would your answer to question 16 change if 30% of overhead costs could be eliminated if residential solid waste services are contracted out?

18. What qualitative factors should a city consider before making a final decision to contract out residential solid waste services?

NOTES

1. The city of Raleigh's 1998–1999 annual budget describes the purposes of the five divisions as follows. (1) the special operations division is responsible for special enforcement and community services provided by the department. This division works closely with the field operations division to coordinate enforcement activities. (2) The field operations division consists of five rotating platoons whose functions are to provide basic patrol and response to calls for service twenty-four hours per day. (3) The investigations division conducts follow-up investigations, makes arrests, and helps prosecute offenders. (4) The chief's office provides overall supervision, legal counsel, and coordination of the department's operations. (5) The police administrative division provides all administrative services of the police department, which include such functions as evidence control, property management, crime prevention, records, and crime analysis.

2. Several states, including these four, have prepared documents on using full cost accounting for solid waste services. These documents are available on the EPA Website at: http://www.epa.gov/epaoswer/non-hw/muncpl/fullcost/docs.htm.

3. Subpart G (financial assurance criteria) of 40 CFR 258.74 allows owners and operators of municipal solid waste landfills to choose from ten options. They are: (1) a trust fund and annual payments over the life of the landfill; (2) a surety bond guaranteeing payment or performance; (3) irrevocable letter of credit; (4) insurance; (5) corporate financial test comprisus credit rating and financial ratios requirements based on the owner or operator's most recent audited financial statements; (6) local government financial test, comprising credit rating and financial ratios, based on the owner or operator's audited financial statements and compliance with Governmental Accounting Standards Board (GASB) statement no. 18; (7) corporate guarantee; (8) local government guarantee; (9) state-approved mechanism; and (10) state assumption of legal responsibility for an owner or operator's compliance with closure and postclosure care cost requirements.

4. For information on the budget share and personnel share methods, see U.S. Environmental Protection Agency (1997: Chap. 4). For information on the direct and step methods, see Blocher et al., 1999: chap. 14.

5. For example, see Brooks, 1996: 493–514.

REFERENCES

Anthony, R. N. and Young, D. W. (1999) *Management Control in Nonprofit Organizations*. 6th ed. Boston, MA: Irwin/McGraw-Hill.

Blocher, E. J. Chen, K. H. and Lin, T. W. (1999). *Management Accounting: A Strategic Emphasis.* Burr Ridge, Il: Irwin/McGraw-Hill.

Brooks, R. C. (1996). An analysis of residential sanitation collection under alternative delivery arrangements. *Public Budgeting and Financial Management, 7(4).*

Cimitile, C. J. and Feinland, G. (1994). *Cost Factors in Local Government Solid Waste Management.* Baseline data report, vol. 25, no. 3. Washington, DC: International City/County Management Association.

Eagle, K. S. (1997). Contract monitoring for financial and operational performance. *Government Finance Review, 13(3).*

Eggers, D. M. (1994). *Enterprise Funds for Solid Waste Management.* Chapel Hill, NC: Department of Environmental Sciences & Engineering, University of North Carolina.

Gauthier, S. J. (1996). *The GAAFR: Guide to GASB Pronouncements.* Chicago: Government Finance Officers Association.

Gauthier, S. J. (1998). Applying full-cost accounting to solid-waste management operations. *Government Finance Review,* 14(4).

Governmental Accounting Standards Board. (Aug. 1993). Statement number 18. *Accounting for Municipal Solid Waste Landfill Closure and Postclosure Care Costs.* Norwalk, CT: GASB.

Hall, G. R. (1998) *Public Works: Alternative Service Delivery Choices, 1997.* Special data issue, no. 2. Washington, DC: International City/County Management Association.

Horngren, C. T., Foster, G., and Datar, S. M. (1994). *Cost Accounting: A Managenal Emphasis,* 8th ed. Upper Saddle River, NJ: Prentice-Hall.

Ingram R. W. (1992). Cost Evaluation. In N. G. Apostolou and D. L. Crumbley (eds.), *Handbook of Governmental Accounting and Finance.* New York: Wiley.

Kelley J. T. (May 1990). Cost center budgeting. In *Establishing the Cost of Services.* MIS report, vol. 22, number 5. Washington: ICMA.

Martin, L. L. (1992). A proposed methodology for comparing the costs of government versus contract service delivery. In *The Municipal Year Book 1992.* Washington, DC: International City/County Management Association.

Mikesell J. L. (1995). *Fiscal Administration: Analysis and Applications for the Public Sector.* 4th ed. Belmont, CA: Wadsworth.

Reed-Stowe & Co., Camp Dresser & McKee, and Thompson Y. (April 1995). *Municipal Solid Waste Services Full Cost Accounting Workbook,* RG-127. Austin, TX: Texas Natural Resource Conservation Commission.

Titard, P. L. (1996). *Managerial Accounting.* 4th ed. Houston: Dame Publications.

U.S. Environmental Protection Agency. (Sept. 1997). *Full Cost Accounting for Municipal Solid Waste Management: A Handbook.* Washington, DC: EPA. (available on the EPA Website at: http://www.epa.gov/epaoswer/non-hw /muncpl/fullcost/docs/epadocs.htm#fcahandbook).

Yuhas, B. (1998) *Full Cost Accounting for Solid Waste Services.* Local Government Special Report. Washington, DC: International City/County Management Association.

34

Reengineering Financial Management
Pittsburgh's Unisource 2000 Project

Rowan Miranda*
Office of Management and Budget, City of Pittsburgh, Pennsylvania, U.S.A.

Natalee Hillman
University of Pittsburgh, Pittsburgh, Pennsylvania, U.S.A.

Throughout the country, major corporations have sought to reengineer their business processes in an attempt to remain competitive. Reengineering is an organizational change strategy that promises dramatic improvements in performance if standard operating procedures (SOPs) are redesigned from scratch and modern information technology is used in the redesigned processes. Asserting that incremental changes at best lead to incremental results, reengineering consultants stress the need for "discontinuous thinking." Although reengineering can serve as a strategy for downsizing organizations, its aim is to add value to organizations and their customers by applying information technology to streamline processes.

The city of Pittsburgh is a 200-year-old corporation with more than 4500 employees, an operating budget of $350 million, and a six-year capital budget plan of $180 million. Pittsburgh also has lost half of its population over the past twenty years. Unisource 2000 is a major reengineering effort that the city government has established to redesign the city's accounting, budgeting, and control processes by providing managers with timely information that will improve service delivery decisions.

The impetus for this project came in early 1994 from the city's newly elected mayor. Faced with a general fund balance of $-\$20$ million for fiscal year (FY) 1993 and an estimated fund balance of $-\$50$ million after FY 1994, the mayor's office of management and budget (OMB) took steps to address the city's dwindling cash position and sought support for a long-term initiative to rethink the city's fundamental business processes.

The short-term fiscal management strategy relied on traditional tools such as hiring freezes, across-the-board cuts, layoffs, and postponement of major purchases. Because the city had repeatedly faced fiscal problems and previous mayors had responded with similar steps, department heads found it difficult to trim fat from areas that had already faced deep cuts. The OMB supported the information systems director's view that a long-term strategy using information technology to transform department operations was the best vehicle to improve efficiency and ultimately to provide value to residents and businesses.

Reprinted from: Government Finance Review, August 1995, 7–10.
* Current Affiliation: Government Finance Officers Association, Chicago, Illinois, U.S.A.

543

OBSTACLES TO REENGINEERING

In comparison to its use in the private sector, why have governments had difficulty embracing reengineering? The city of Pittsburgh's experiences illustrate that governments face a number of obstacles to the introduction of process reengineering.

Monopoly Bureaus

One reason why the use of reengineering has lagged in the public sector is that bureaus generally exist in an environment without competition, which allows them to operate inefficiently initially and resist innovation. Fiscal limitations ensure that this will not continue forever. Without access to major new sources of revenue, the city of Pittsburgh will have to implement steps to improve the efficiency of government operations if it is to maintain taxpayer and business confidence. The financial situation motivated the mayor and city council to invest in a serious reengineering effort, even if it meant disrupting bureaucratic fiefdoms by consolidating or eliminating departments to accommodate new business processes.

Rigidity of SOPs

Many bureaucratic routines are embedded in legislative statutes and corporate charters that make it difficult to "redesign from scratch." Also, the piecemeal bargaining concessions made to unions over time can lead to work rules that often frustrate financial managers and employees alike. A true reengineering effort, such as the one Pittsburgh is seeking to adopt, may require home rule charters or labor contracts to change. Civic and political leadership is crucial for such efforts to succeed.

Relationships Between Branches of Government

A major impediment to change is the poor relationship among different branches of government. For example, generally accepted accounting principles (GAAP) basis accounting traditionally was viewed as an attempt by the independently elected controller to embarrass the mayor's office. The OMB passed balanced cash basis budgets only to find the controller pointing to GAAP-basis deficits the following year. This led to an annual ritual of one branch of government attempting to discredit the other when audit results were released. Early in the new mayor's tenure, OMB established common ground with the controller's office by adhering to the GAAP basis in its financial projections and by convincing the city council to do the same. Recognizing the importance of professional accounting standards enabled OMB and the controller's office to develop a technical basis for cooperation on the Unisource 2000 project.

Assignment of Financial Information Rights

Informational asymmetries generally exist between oversight agencies and departments. During budget execution for example, departments have a considerable advantage over OMB and council on matters such as uncommitted appropriations. If information is power, a new financial management system can upset prevailing advantages of city departments.

Technology typically improves the timeliness and quantity of information available to oversight authorities, which may threaten some bureaus. Although the mayor's office has formal administrative authority over operations, the independently elected city controller and city council have important roles in the production and dissemination of financial information. The mayor began the reengineering effort by soliciting the participation of the controller and council. Department heads were similarly included in major project decisions. Council and controller participation eased OMB's task of acquiring legislative support to fund Unisource 2000. The city council, in particular, needed to be assured that access to financial information would be maintained or increased under the new system.

Labor Relations

Discussion of change in government spreads fear among public employees that their jobs are in jeopardy. Because the term reengineering is often used loosely, union leaders may equate it with downsizing approaches such as privatization. There are various ways to address union concerns, including retraining, transfers to departments, or reduction of the workforce through attrition. In processes in which technology can substitute for labor, the city of Pittsburgh is committed to a "no layoffs" approach by requesting that unions be flexible in reassignment of existing staff to avoid layoffs.

ORGANIZING A REENGINEERING EFFORT

Unisource 2000 began as a response to the following financial management problems: absence of budgetary controls such as allotments; untimely and inaccurate feedback on encumbrances, expenditures, and revenue to date; poor information on cost centers; proliferation of independent personal computer-based systems; inability to share data among departments; and redundant paperwork/data entry. To address these problems, the project was organized into three phases.

In phase I, a team of upper and middle managers mapped the city's core financial processes and established "must have" requirements for hardware and software. In phase II, select software and hardware were subjected to rigorous testing in a procedure called the "solutions demonstration lab" described below. Phase III will involve hardware and software implementation. All phases are to be managed by a project consultant and a hierarchy of cross-functional teams.

Consultants

An experienced consulting firm is an invaluable part of the reengineering effort because most governments do not possess cutting-edge technical and functional expertise. To serve as project manager, the city of Pittsburgh contracted with a consulting firm that is a leader in corporate reengineering efforts throughout the country.

Leadership Council

Because of the need to institutionalize cooperation across branches and departments, a project leadership council was established as the governance mechanism for major decisions. The leadership council is composed of the budget director, finance director, information systems director, deputy controller, and the assistant city clerk, who represents the city council. It meets weekly for briefings from the consultant and the core team on progress to date and obstacles encountered. Continuous interaction and exchange of departmental perspectives makes collective interests more evident and reduces the time needed for implementation of the redesigned processes.

Core Project Team

The eight-member core project team of upper and middle managers possessing technical and financial expertise guides the project on a daily basis. Team members also were selected on the basis of their ability to be freed of daily responsibilities in city operations. The leadership council also felt it was important to form a core project team with member-ship weighted toward functional concerns rather than one emphasizing the technical ele-gance of the hardware and software. Functional versus technical priorities were a source of recurring tensions in the core team and generally were resolved at the leadership council level. A cross section of professionals on the core team capitalized on synergy and facili-tated the representation of department concerns.

Citywide Team

A citywide team was established from the start to represent the community of users who actually implement the processes—account clerks, data entry staff, and others. Since reen-gineering emphasizes processes, not departments, input from these employees at the front end is an essential aspect of change management and allows the leadership council to assess the fit between the new processes and the organizational culture.

FINANCIAL PROCESS REENGINEERING

The first task of the leadership council was to define the elements of a financial manage-ment system. It was agreed that Unisource 2000 would focus on building an accounting and budgeting system foundation first by limiting its focus to general ledger, accounts receivable, accounts payable, purchase order, asset management, and budget preparation analysis. Although opinions were expressed that human resources, payroll, centralized collections, and activity-based costing were worthy areas to pursue, the leadership council decided against diluting project resources on other areas. Figure 1 presents a flow chart of the elements of the financial reengineering process.

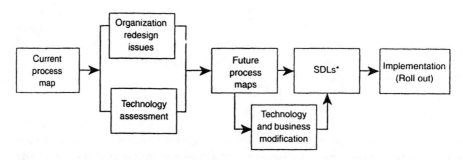

Figure 1   Reengineering financial processes.

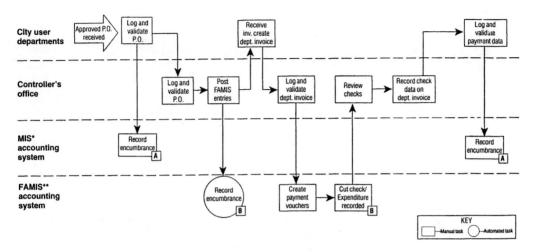

Figure 2 Current process map for encumbrance accounting.
*MIS = management information system.
**FAMIS = financial management information system.

Current Process Maps

Current process maps delineate start-to-end sequences of tasks that define a process. The core project and citywide teams explicitly traced every step of twenty major financial processes, such as operating budget preparation and inventory control. Such maps expose tasks that do not add value and that contribute to a cumbersome financial system. The current process for encumbrances illustrates problems that reengineering can eliminate.

Figure 2 shows that two accounting systems are used in the current encumbrance accounting process. The A boxes show that departments record encumbrance and payment information in the management information system (MIS) accounting system, only to have the controller's office use a separate financial management information system (FAMIS; B boxes). These redundancies not only cause timing differences, making information difficult to reconcile across agencies, they also waste resources. If left as is, departmental records will seldom agree with the controller's records throughout the accounting cycle. Not apparent in Figure 2 are the numerous spreadsheets and independent databases created by departments to determine budget-to-actual variances. This patchwork of financial systems makes budgetary control measures such as allotments difficult to institute and enforce.

Technology as an Enabler

Reengineering relies on information technology to bridge current and future processes. An injection of technology without task redesign simply automates bad processes, which allows them to continue, albeit at a faster pace. With respect to the encumbrance accounting process, for example, technology can be used to perform the following operations in a single step: (1) liquidate pre-encumbrances, (2) validate account codes, (3) perform budget checks, and (4) post amounts to budgetary accounts. In this manner, technology permits an encumbrance process that minimizes steps that pass documents across units (handoffs).

Future Process Maps

Future process maps are used to describe the linkage between technological and organizational restructuring. There are several issues to consider when designing them.

1. *Capture information at the source.* Future process maps seek to eliminate data entry redundancies in current maps. When technology is poor, paper is passed among units, with each unit undertaking separate validations. Technology allows data to be captured at the source initiating a transaction.
2. *Substitute parallel for sequential processes.* At first glance, this practice appears to advocate antispecialization; however, fragmented sequences can entail numerous handoffs that do not add value to the process and that cause delays in information processing, which frustrates users. Parallel processes seek to minimize these shortcomings.
3. *Share information across the organization.* If data are captured only once, the information should be widely accessible; otherwise departments have an incentive to re-enter data that were already entered in other parts of the organization. The resulting centralized information system enhances informed decision making and facilitates budgetary control.

The future process map for encumbrances in Figure 3 illustrates some of these redesign issues. By creating an electronic invoice upon receipt, either by imaging or standard formats, information is captured once at the source (box X). Technology enables users to share, view, and take action without unnecessary handoffs and duplication. Box Y in Figure 3 also shows how technology permits parallel processing. Process redesign will enable the city to eliminate a large number of non-value-adding tasks, as shown in Table 1, without affecting operations. During software implementation, these "high-level" future maps will be broken down further for each subprocess.

Select Financial Software

A series of must have requirements were developed as a consequence of future maps. In addition to meeting basic requirements, such as GAAP-basis accounting and integrated

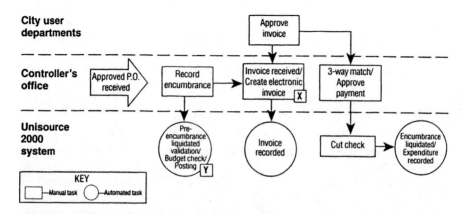

Figure 3   Future process map for encumbrance accounting.

Table 1 Comparing Current and Future Financial Process Maps

Process	Number of steps	
	Current map	Future map
Operating budget	33	10
Capital budget	10	9
Budget transfers	10	7
Inventory control	5	4
Fixed asset management	9	6
Encumbrances/expenditures	12	5
Travel advances	12	5
Cash investment decisions	10	6
Tax collection	17	6
General cash management	8	3
Purchasing explanatory items	15	14
Payroll processing	37	7
Total	178	82

fund accounting the software requirements included online/real-time inquiries, appropriation and budgetary control, and detailed audit trails. A request for proposal process was used to evaluate several software vendors. Software flexibility to support customized solutions and a client-server environment were important criteria in the city's selection process. The software package that was ultimately selected had modules for each of the financial management applications previously discussed.

The main unanticipated problem was the lack of proven client—server software for public-sector financial applications. Of the packages evaluated, most were products originally designed for mainframes making the transition to the clientserver environment. A second problem was the shortage of governmental accounting expertise among software vendors. To compensate for this, the software vendor selected was asked to form a partnership with a national accounting firm with a government service practice during the implementation phase of the project.

Solutions Demonstration Labs (SDLs)

Reengineering consultants compare the task of carrying out an SDL to "changing the tire while the car is moving." SDLs are used in a controlled environment to test not only the software's ability to carry out new business processes but also the interaction between the redefined processes and organizational culture.

The SDL is a tool to quickly assess feasibility of the software and future business processes before an expensive full-scale commitment is made. Pittsburgh's SDL was conducted over a rigorous six-week process involving the project manager, software developers, and the city's core team. Participants in the city's SDL tested seventy-two elementary business processes (EBPs), such as increasing appropriations for a budgetary account, paying an invoice, and initiating an interfund transfer. Any problems encountered while testing EBPs may require software to be modified or must haves to be reconsidered. An

SDL should enable participants to recommend implementation or to continue further systems evaluations.

Implementation

Implementation of the financial software and future business processes are at the beginning stages. None of the major business processes has been fully implemented to date. It is envisioned that implementation of the core financial management system will occur over a two-year period. As implementation of future processes and software solutions begins, technical and functional components of the project will need to be integrated. The task of managing the entire project becomes more difficult due to the large number of actors participating. Issues such as network design, training, pilot-testing, and sequencing of activities need to be addressed. Because reengineering is a process of continuous improvement, participants need to be open to the idea of changing initial solutions.

CONCLUSIONS

Financial process reengineering is one of many organizational change platforms available to state and local governments. The Unisource 2000 project is part of a three-year, $10 million effort to modernize the city's technological infrastructure. Current financial processes are very labor-intensive, which provides a potential for cost savings, although precise estimates of cost savings are difficult to assess. Over the long run, other benefits stemming from the project include performance-based budgeting, GAAP-basis interim financial statements, automated budget preparation, and customized control processes (by department).

Although Pittsburgh is far from completing implementation of its reengineering plan, future process mapping in the financial area has motivated similar efforts in other parts of the organization. Throughout the organization, managers have embraced reengineering because incremental approaches tried in the past simply have not worked. As implementation proceeds, the most critical aspects to project success are each department head's (1) commitment to continue to lend staff support to the project and (2) willingness to question the assumptions underlying prevailing processes. Reengineering, however, also has its critics.

Traditional reform movements embedded accountability in governments by imposing layers of checks and balances on top of the ones already in place. Critics may contend that government reengineering, in its zeal to streamline processes, sacrifices financial control and accountability. As the "reinventing government" brand of thinking emphasizes, however, excessive controls also entail such costs as low productivity and sluggish bureaucratic responsiveness to citizens. The promise of reengineering is that technology and process redesign, used appropriately, can improve the degree of financial control without restricting the actions of public managers to serve the citizenry.

REVIEW QUESTIONS

1. What is reengineering? Why is it necessary to reengineer financial programs and policies? What are the obstacles to reengineering a government?

2. Why did the city of Pittsburgh need reengineering? Could it have used any methods other than rengineering to deal with the problem? How?

3. What is the Unisourse 2000 project? What are its principal components? How was it implemented? Who was involved in the implementation process? Would you consider the project a success? Why?

4. What is a future process map? What role does it play financial reengineering? What issues must one consider when designing a future process map? Discuss.

35

Learning from Experience
Cash Management Practices of a Local Government

Aman Khan
Texas Tech University, Lubbock, Texas, U.S.A.

Cash is central to the operation and management of a financial organization. Like all financial organizations, governments need cash to meet three principal objectives: (1) *transaction* objective, according to which governments need to maintain sufficient funds to meet cash demands resulting from normal transactions, i.e., regular operations of the government, (2) *precautionary* objective, according to which funds must be available to meet cash demands that often result from unanticipated operations or events over which governments have very little or no control, and (3) *speculative* objective, according to which funds are needed to respond to investment opportunities resulting from excess or idle cash. Most governments, especially local governments, receive the bulk of their tax and other revenue during three or four short months in the year, leaving substantial cash, called *idle cash*, for investment. A good cash management program can significantly improve a government's capacity to generate cash to meet cash demands as they occur, provide funds for responding to unanticipated events, and ensure return on investments of idle cash to their maximum potential.

The purpose of this chapter is to briefly discuss the principal cash management activities of a midsized urban community in a rural setting, namely Lubbock, Texas. Located approximately 350 miles northwest of Dallas, with a population close to 200,000 and an annual budget of over $200 million, the city of Lubbock has a reasonably well-placed cash management program with clearly defined goals and objectives. The program has grown in importance in recent years and serves as an important link between the city administration and the local financial community.

The chapter is divided into three sections. The first section presents some background information on the financial operations and management of the city, the second section

The author acknowledges the support and assistance provided by Mr. Robert Massengale, treasurer and assistant city manager in charge of finance, and Mr. Jimmy Rodriguez, assistant treasurer, in the preparation of this study.

provides an analysis of the key elements of the city's cash management program, and the third section makes some suggestions and recommendations that should serve as guidelines for further improving the program.

BACKGROUND INFORMATION

A major agricultural, educational, medical, and commercial center, and serving a regional population of well over a quarter of a million people, the city provides services for its residents through seven administrative divisions, seventeen operating departments, and 10% operating centers or units. All of the operating departments, with the exception of those responsible for providing various enterprise services, are financed through general fund (GF) revenues. These revenues mostly include real estate tax, sales tax, licenses and fees, state and federal grants, and transfer from other funds.

In compliance with the basic GAAP requirements, the city currently maintains three governmental funds, eight enterprise funds, and one trust and agency fund. Most of the enterprise funds, with the exception of the airport and golf course funds, are self-sufficient.* The city also prepares two separate annual budgets—one for the general fund and the other for the capital projects fund—using a combination of program and performance budgeting systems. As with all executive budgets, the budgets process is designed to identify and plan the functions, activities, and accomplishments of the city as well as plan for its future financial needs (City of Lubbot, 1993a). In addition, the city puts together both an interim and a comprehensive annual financial report (CAFR) using the modified accrual basis of accounting for general and special revenue funds, and the full accrual basis for proprietary and trust funds.

Lubbock's cash management program is directed by the assistant city manager in charge of finance with the help and assistance of an interim review committee (IRC) consisting of five members, including the assistant city manager as an ex-officio member, the chief accountant, the assistant treasurer, the director of personnel (or any other qualified city official in lieu of), and a fifth member from outside the city government with experience in cash and treasury management. The members of the committee serve in an advisory capacity and do not have any formal authority to direct or execute the cash management program.

ANALYSIS OF THE CASH MANAGEMENT PROGRAM

A cash management program typically involves a number of distinct but interrelated activities, called the *cash management process*. To a large measure, the success of a program depends on the efficiency with which this process and its component activities are carried out. The following sections present four of the most important activities that constitute the core of this process and analyze them for the city: *cash budgeting, management of cash flows, bank relations*, and *investment of idle cash*.

---

* For a detailed discussion and analysis of these funds, see the chapter by Khan and Stumm in this volume.

Cash Budgeting

Cash budgeting is the key to an effective cash management program. A cash budget makes weekly or monthly estimates of future cash receipts (inflows) and disbursements (outflows) from all operating and nonoperating activities of a government. The estimates are prepared for at least one quarter or as much as one year in advance. Typically, a cash budget starts with the cash balance, called the *beginning balance*, at the beginning of a forecast period. Then all cash receipts expected during the period are added to estimate the total cash available. From this, all cash disbursements are subtracted to yield the adjusted net flow, called the *ending balance*. Estimates of cash receipts and disbursements can be easily made using historical analysis of cash flows. For instance, monthly receipts and disbursements of previous years should reveal patterns and timing of cash flow as well as responsiveness of the revenue structure to fluctuations in the economy. Although ideal cash flow estimates would require several years of data, the pattern exhibited from one year prior should provide a reasonable guide to project current year levels.

Table 1 shows the cash flows of the city for fiscal year (FY) 1992–1993. According to Table 1, the city collects a substantial portion of its cash receipts between October and February, receiving as much as 60% of its total revenue. The expenditures are more or less evenly distributed throughout the year, with the exception of the months when portions of debt service payments become due. By far the largest share of revenue comes from charges for utility and other services, accounting for over 60% of the total receipts, followed by earnings from investments, property taxes, and sales tax, in that order. The collection from charges is high due in part to the fact that Lubbock is one of the handful of cities in the state that provides electric utility for its residents in addition to providing the traditional utility services, such as water, sewer, and solid waste. This adds considerably to the variety and amount of services the city currently provides and the revenue it earns for a community of its size.

Table 1 Patterns of Cash Flow (FY 1992–1993)

Month	Inflow	Outflow	Net flow	Ending balance
Beginning balance				$270,373
October	$23,370,443	$19,039,254	$4,331,189	4,601,562
November	20,653,515	11,284,459	9,369,056	13,970,618
December	21,319,804	13,443,667	7,876,137	21,846,755
January	19,761,372	14,959,084	4,802,288	26,649,043
February	27,701,741	26,772,754	928,987	27,578,030
March	12,109,871	14,317,129	(2,207,258)	25,370,772
April	12,779,151	28,454,564	(15,675,413)	9,695,359
May	13,906,859	14,528,763	(621,904)	9,073,455
June	16,082,602	11,599,179	4,483,423	13,556,678
July	13,833,721	18,630,893	(4,797,172)	8,759,506
August	16,019,169	19,531,525	(3,512,356)	5,247,150
September	14,884,197	15,727,941	(843,744)	4,403,406
Total	$212,422,445	$208,289,212	$4,133,233	$4,403,406

Source: City of Lubbock, Department of Finance Compilation (fall 1993).

Table 2 Estimates of Cash Flow (FY 1993–1994)

Month	Inflow	Outflow	Net flow	Ending balance
Beginning balance				$4,403,406
October	$14,766,696	$19,296,377	$(4,529,681)	126,276
November	16,348,575	11,187,484	5,161,091	5,034,816
December	26,984,885	13,765,104	13,219,781	18,254,597
January	22,275,079	15,508,397	6,766,682	25,021,279
February	27,326,396	27,690,359	(363,963)	24,657,316
March	13,874,943	13,499,976	374,967	25,032,283
April	13,599,334	27,658,986	(14,059,652)	10,972,631
May	15,988,212	13,617,651	(2,370,561)	13,343,192
June	22,216,036	12,204,261	10,011,775	23,354,967
July	21,279,970	18,296,188	2,983,782	26,338,749
August	16,920,721	24,177,786	(7,257,065)	19,081,684
September	13,801,046	17,792,911	(3,991,865)	15,089,819
Total	$225,381,893	$214,695,480	$10,686,413	$15,089,819

Because of the seasonal and other variations in tax collection, and to some extent due to variations in the disbursement of utility and accounts payable, most governments can easily anticipate their future cash flow patterns. (i.e., how much excess cash they will have in future months, for how long) and should have no difficulty in designing a cash management plan that would best utilize the excess cash. In general, the cash flow pattern of the city for FY 1992–93 appears to be consistent with its overall financial picture. The net positive flows for the months in which surpluses are generated are followed by a series of net negative flows, indicating the need for investing the surplus, or for generating additional cash that must be borrowed or withdrawn from current investments to compensate for shortages.

Table 2 presents the estimates of cash flow for FY 1993–1994 based on the most recent monthly series. In order to determine these estimates, three simple time-series methods that best fit the data (given by their mean squared errors) were used. They are: simple percentage change,* Holt–Winters additive seasonal adjustment,† and simple decomposition.‡ These methods were used to estimate the payroll (simple percentage adjustment); accounts payable, utilities, charges for services, and miscellaneous receipts (Holt–Winters); and sales and property taxes (decomposition). Tables 3 and 4 show the details of these estimates. Estimates on two other categories, income from investments

---

* Based on 2% increase in payroll over FY 1992–1993 figures.

† This is an extension of the exponential smoothing combined with Holt's linear-trend updating and is given by the expression $Y_1 = (b_o + b_{1t}) + S_1 + e$ where t and S represent the trend and seasonality factors respectively. The additive structure was used because the magnitudes of the seasonal effects did not show any consistent increase with the series.

‡ This method isolates, measures, and accounts for the effects of each of the four factors that affect the behavior of a series: trend T, seasonal S cyclical C, and random R. The general expression for the decomposition model used here is a familiar one: $Y_1 = T \times S \times C \times R$. The model was used in two stages; the contributions from each factor were calculated individually, and then multiplied to produce the desired estimates.

Table 3 Estimates of Cash Inflow (FY 1993–1994)

Month	Sales tax	Property tax	Misc.	Charges	Investment income
October	$1,249,689	$877,317	$412,420	$12,975,240	$152,030
November	1,725,776	2,071,547	918,483	11,144,860	487,910
December	1,196,645	9,125,800	278,805	12,114,180	4,269,455
January	1,179,845	7,860,821	268,698	12,123,530	842,185
February	2,390,768	10,433,921	846,192	11,401,840	2,253,675
March	1,576,218	404,544	514,861	11,376,840	2,480
April	1,181,502	299,317	356,695	11,686,820	125,000
May	1,923,856	224,044	857,252	12,513,310	469,750
June	1,272,151	255,829	485,186	13,696,120	6,506,750
July	1,336,472	244,374	392,634	13,229,280	6,077,210
August	1,685,927	145,702	886,477	14,020,840	181,775
September	1,455,154	143,201	391,934	11,786,480	24,277
Total	$18,174,003	$32,036,416	$6,609,637	$147,169,340	$21,392,497

Note: Based on twenty-four most recent data series.

and debt service payments, were provided by the city and were simply added to the above estimates (of receipts and disbursements) to produce the total. No attempts were made here to estimate them separately on the assumption that the government policy toward debt service payments and investment earnings would remain unchanged during the forecast period, thus leaving the contributions from these two categories to their respective total the same as they were for FY 1992–1993.

The cash flow estimates of the city provide a good assessment of the projected cash inflows and outflows, indicating the expected cash position for each month of the entire

Table 4 Estimates of Cash Outflow (FY 1993–1994)

Month	Payroll	Utility	Debt services	Accounts payable
October	$2,519,518	$1,336,474	$1,183,985	$14,256,400
November	2,522,168	1,349,378	—	7,315,938
December	4,205,660	1,290,269	—	8,269,175
January	2,532,717	1,217,910	—	11,757,770
February	2,550,053	1,509,3254	15,192,230	8,438,752
March	2,516,825	1,352,168	11,925	9,619,058
April	2,548,163	1,321,208	4,823,985	18,965,630
May	2,487,834	1,264,742	—	9,865,075
June	3,830,479	1,324,774	—	7,049,008
July	2,609,063	1,447,875	—	14,239,250
August	2,538,380	1,604,061	7,672,115	12,363,230
September	2,571,751	1,626,465	101,925	13,492,770
Total	$33,432,611	$16,644,648	$28,986,165	$135,632,056

Note: Based on twenty-four most recent data series.

fiscal year. According to Table 4 the cash shortages and surpluses reveal a pattern identical to that observed for the series used in forecasting: net positive flows in the earlier months (due to a much higher rate of collection in property and sales taxes) followed by net negative flows during months of relatively higher expenditure. Table 4 also depicts a general increase in cash receipts (of about 6%) and disbursements (of about 3%), with a much larger positive beginning balance for FY 1994–1995. As expected, much of the increase will take place in charges for services, property and sales taxes, accounts payable, and to some extent payroll. On the whole, the changes seem reasonable, especially in view of the recent increase in property tax and a conditional half-a-cent sales tax increase that was introduced in FY 1992–1993 to attract a major defense outlet but that did not succeed and was subsequently repealed.

Management of Cash Flows

The positive ending balance throughout the fiscal year 1993–1994 indicates that the city is apparently doing a good job of conducting its cash management program. Nevertheless, efforts can be made to further improve the program by carefully managing its cash flows, in particular by managing its collection and disbursement system. The management of cash flows essentially means the development of procedures to accelerate cash receipts and control disbursements to keep cash available as long as possible. The strategy for efficient cash flow management is simple. Checks must be deposited as soon as possible and payments on vouchers delayed as long as possible without incurring a finance charge or impinging on the legal limits of the state or federal government. This difference between the time when a check is deposited and the payment made on an obligation is called *float*. A good cash management program makes a concerted effort to minimize the float for collection and maximize it for disbursement. Floats are generally measured in dollar-days, but are frequently expressed in dollars.*

Since many receipts and disbursements are predictable, it is not difficult to develop a framework to effectively manage the cash flows of a government. In particular, collection could be accelerated by reducing the time between when the residents receive their bills and when they make payments. Although it does not have it in place, the city can easily institute a policy of early payment discounts or penalties for late payment, or even advance the date of payments, if feasible. Another commonly suggested but not as frequently used method that the city does not presently employ is to have all payments made to the city mailed directly to a bank or to a post office *lock box* controlled by the bank. Payments according to this method can be immediately deposited, thus increasing the cash availability or reducing the float. The city does, however, engage in limited wire transfers averaging between five outgoing and ten incoming transfers a month. Wire transfer is a real-time method of transferring cash from one bank to another using Federal Reserve account

---

* Two types of floats commonly associated with cash flow management are *collection float* for collection of receipts, and *disbursement float* for payments. The dollar float is calculated by taking the difference between the two; that is, (collection float − disbursement float) = [(total collection time × volume) − (total disbursement time × volume)]. For instance, dollar float = [(5 days × \$5 million) − (6 days × \$5 million)] = (\$25 million − \$30 million) = (−) \$5 million. (For more discussion on the subject, see Ramsey and Hackbart, 1993.)

balances.* With a wire transaction, the payor's account is debited and the payee's account is credited the same day. Transaction information flows through a computer network residing in the Fed's twelve district banks. These transfers, for which the *lead bank* charges the city an amount equal to the cost of transfers, significantly contribute to the cash flow management of the government by minimizing the float (i.e., by minimizing the time to mail, process, and clear a transaction).

Like acceleration of collection, the city can control disbursement structure to build up cash flows. According to a policy worked out some time ago, city employees are paid biweekly rather than on a weekly basis, which results in savings in payroll preparation and early payment costs. Currently, the city does not have a specific time for paying its bills since most of them are received throughout the year at different time intervals. With the exception of employee salaries, which are paid every other week, utility bills, which are paid at the end of the month, and insurance premiums, which are paid regularly and on time, all other bills are paid daily or as soon as vouchers are received. Most incoming bills do not contain a discount for early payment, although the city would probably prefer paying all bills within the discount period if such a period was available. Bill payments are approved by respective department heads if the amount does not exceed $15,000. Where the amount exceeds $15,000, council approval is needed.

The payments on long-term obligations, such as bonds, on the other hand, follow a more predictable but somewhat different pattern. Over the years, as bonds were issued debt service payments for both general obligation (GO) and revenue bonds (currently for the airport and electric utility) were scheduled to fall due once a year for the partial payment on the principal and interest, and once for the interest. Apparently, the timing was chosen to permit the city to invest tax receipts before they could be used for debt service payments, thereby expanding the opportunities for investment income for the city.

Bank Relations

Establishing and maintaining strong bank relations are critical to the needs of a well-developed cash management program. Banks have become keenly aware of the benefits of government accounts and in recent years have developed a variety of innovative services designed to attract these accounts. In addition to providing the traditional services, such as establishing checking accounts and securing loans, today most banks provide assistance with securities portfolios and sophisticated information packages and even budget for complex disbursement and centralized cash control—all to help the government maximize daily cash availability and facilitate short-term investing.

As a general rule, governments are encouraged to maintain accounts with more than one depository, one of which must serve as the lead bank. Having multiple depositories has the advantage of receiving services at a competitive price, although there are certain benefits of dealing with a single bank, as the city currently does. The most obvious benefit of dealing with a single depository is that it affords the *pooling* of cash from various subaccounts into one centralized account to smooth out cash flows and to maximize investment opportunities by making larger increments of cash available for investment. For

---

* The wire transfer system currently used by the city is called automated clearing house (ACH). For example, for payroll transactions the city sends a tape of all payroll checks to the lead bank. The bank verifies the totals and notifies the Federal Reserve Bank (FRB, the clearing house) of the amount via modem. The FRB charges the lead bank's account, which in turn charges the city payroll account.

Table 5 Cost of Banking Services

Services provided	Quantity	Unit price	Cost of service
Account Maintenance	27	$10.00	$270.00
Daily Balance Recap	1	25.00	25.00
Deposits & Other Debits	813	0.25	203.25
Checks & Other Debits	6,336	0.20	1,267.20
Check Sorting	6,336	0.02	126.72
Items Deposited	64,560	0.07	4,519.20
Stop Payments	7	17.50	122.50
Wire Transfer-Incoming	19	5.00	95.00
Wire Transfer-Outgoing	9	15.00	135.00
Investment Transactions	0	35.00	0.00
Safekeeping Securities	25	5.00	125.00
Return Items	557	1.25	695.25
Deposit Slip Order	0	Cost	0.00
ACH Origination	—	—	404.00
Total cost			$7,989,12

Source: City of Lubbock, *Account Analysis Statement* (Dec. 2, 1993).

instance, the city currently maintains twenty three (sub)accounts consolidated into one large account. Revenues collected on individual accounts are pooled into this account, from which payments are made to individual accounts. Besides this, pooling has the added advantage of keeping track of the sources of cash being combined so that proper apportionments of earned interest could be made to the respective sources.

In addition to pooling the accounts, the lead bank also provides a host of other services, ranging from account maintenance, to wire transfer, as noted previously, to investment transactions. Table 5 presents a sample of the services the bank currently provides to the city and the costs associated with them. As Table 5 shows, the per unit cost of service varies from $1.25 for a return item to $25.00 for daily balance recap, with the total cost of services running around $8000 a month, depending on the volume of services rendered. In theory, this is the amount the city needs to maintain at a minimum in its accounts with the bank to compensate for its services, commonly known as *compensating balance*. Compensating balances are funds on deposits in the bank that a government must maintain to cover the cost of bank services. Most banks calculate the compensating balance by using a simple procedure in which the annualized service charge is divided by the bank's *earnings credit* rate. The earnings credit rates are usually based on the ninety-day Treasury bill adjusted for reserve requirements, if any, on the deposit. The concept here is that the bank must be able to earn enough on the deposits to equal the service charge.* In practice, the banks apply the earnings credit rate to a government's average deposit balance for a particular month to determine whether or not the service charge would be covered.

---

* There are other more sophisticated methods available to determine the compensating balances. For a discussion of these methods, see Schwartz (1985).

A simple example will help clarify this. Suppose the bank has a reserve requirement of 10% on deposit accounts, which means the bank only has use of 90% of the funds on deposits. Suppose also that the T-bill rate for a given month, say December, is 5.33%. The earnings credit would then be 90% of 5.3%, which is 4.80%. Using the service charge in Table 5 as a case in point, the annualized December service charge will be $95,869 ($7,989.12 × 12), and the compensating balance required will be $1,997,280 ($95,869.44/ 0.0480). This is the balance the city must maintain for one month to compensate the bank for its December service charge. In reality, the lead bank does not currently require the city to maintain a reserve but, nevertheless, expects the city to leave at all times a balance of $6 million on its accounts. In the absence of a reserve requirement, the compensating balance would be even lower at $1,798,675 ($95,689.44/0.0533). In both cases, the present balance of $6 million is much higher than the compensating balance the city should have ideally maintained. The bank may require the city to keep a higher balance in a given month, however, or pay a net fee if the monthly balance falls below an expected level of compensation.

Investment of Idle Cash

Once the cash flow estimates have been made, the compensating balances have been determined, and the amount available in excess cash has been identified, it becomes relatively simple to develop a set of strategies for investing the excess cash. There are two basic strategies a government can adopt to substantially increase its earning potential from investments of idle cash: a passive strategy and an active strategy (Miller, 1991). In a *passive strategy*, the excess cash is placed in a sweep account that earns interest on a daily basis but has no other use for the funds. Such a strategy might be appropriate for a government with poor cash flow estimates and a general paucity of resources to manage an investment portfolio. A more *active strategy*, on the other hand, would involve investments in securities with specific maturities to smooth out cash flows.

Whether or not a government has an active or passive strategy, it remains imperative that it has a written investment policy with clear statements of objectives, in particular the types of investment securitie in which excess cash would be invested, the dealers or brokers to be used in this process, and the dollar amount allowed by security types of maturity. The written statements serve as principal guidelines and also as a means of communicating investment strategies and restrictions to those responsible for managing the city portfolio.

Presently the city operates under a written investment policy that applies to all financial assets and funds over which it exercises financial control. According to this policy, the investment strategies of the city government must be based on (but not entirely restricted to) the following: (1) preservation of capital and the protection of investment principal, (2) maintenance of sufficient liquidity to meet anticipated disbursements and cash flows, (3) diversification to avoid potential risks associated with certain instruments, (4) attainment of a market rate of return equal to or higher than the performance measure established by the assistant city manager, and (5) conformance with all federal, state, and other legal requirements (City of Lubbock, 1993b).

The current policy allows the city to invest its idle funds in any one or a combination of the following portfolios: (1) 100% in U.S., Treasury obligations, (2) 50% in certificates of deposit, (3) 40% in instruments of federal agencies, (4) 30% in repurchase agreements collateralized by federal instruments, (5) 100% in repurchase agreements collateralized by U.S. Treasury obligations, and (6) a maximum of 5% in a qualified investment pool, such as the TexPool, a multijurisdictional concentration under the auspices of the state. The policy also ensures that the maturity of any government investment should not be more than thirty years. In practice, investments over ten years are limited to a maximum of 10% of the portfolio, with provisions that the city at all times maintains 10% of its investments in instruments maturing in 120 days or less to guarantee maximum liquidity. Furthermore, the policy requires that all investment transactions be executed with city authorized dealers who must be selected on a competitive basis.

At least in policy, the city seeks active rather than passive management of its portfolio assets. To some extent, this is reflected in the attempts it has made in recent years to diversify its assets. Table 6 presents a simple percentage breakdown of the city's portfolio assets for FY 1992–1993 and parts of FY 1993–1994, which primarily consist of bank deposits and CDs, money market funds and TexPool, Treasury notes and agency securities, such as those issued by the Federal National Mortgage Association (FNMA), the Federal Home Loan Banks (FHLB). According to Table 6 the city currently maintains over 60% of its portfolio in federal agency securities, which is almost three times as high as the next category. One simple explanation for this apparent preference for federal securities is that the city, like most local governments, finds them attractive because they offer a much higher yield than either the money market funds or Treasury notes. Also, the agency securities have a much stronger secondary market that is easily accessible through security

Table 6 Portfolio Investment and Efficiency Measure (Percent)

Month	MMF and TexPool	Bank deposits and CDs	Treasury securities	Agency securities	Efficiency rate
FY 1992–1993					
October	19.00	.04	19.90	60.60	96.23
November	13.90	.04	19.90	65.70	92.42
December	13.20	.04	18.90	67.50	92.84
January	16.70	.03	22.20	60.80	89.29
February	16.90	.03	22.40	60.30	89.31
March	18.90	.03	21.90	58.90	94.14
April	11.80	.04	23.80	64.00	95.47
May	12.30	.04	23.70	63.70	95.35
June	19.10	.03	22.50	58.10	95.43
July	15.50	.04	23.50	60.60	95.58
August	16.00	.04	23.40	60.30	94.31
September	13.90	.04	23.90	61.80	97.18
Average	15.60	.04	22.17	61.86	93.96
FY 1993–1994					
October	8.20	.04	25.50	66.40	93.85
November	8.20	.04	25.50	65.90	92.38
December	16.90	.04	25.17	63.50	93.24
Average	11.10	.04	25.17	63.50	93.24

Source: Based on City of Lubbock. *Accrued Earnings and Book Value Consolidated*, Department of Finance Compilation (fall 1993).

dealers, thus making them more attractive to investors. The city has not invested for some time in repurchase agreements, a popular instrument, which until recently constituted roughly a third of total city investments. Repurchase agreements generally have a lower rate of return and, as such, do not have the same appeal as agency securities.

Table 6 also shows the efficiency of the city's investment portfolio for the same period. Efficiency of a portfolio is the highest rate of return an investment can earn for a given degree of risk. Since most local governments invest in securities either issued or backed by the federal government, which hardly carry any risk, the conventional notion of efficiency does not quite apply in this context. A more useful notion of efficiency will be to define it in terms of the extent to which a government maximizes the return on investments of excess cash for a given cash balance or by simply taking the ratio of average investment to the total cash balance for a given period.* The latter expression is the one actually used to calculate the efficiency rates presented in Table 6. According to these calculations, the overall efficiency of the city could be rated as good, ranging between 89–97% with an average of 93.96% for the year. The lower efficiency rate is obviously due to city's maintaining a much higher average cash balance for those months than it should have. This is a common problem most governments experience, even those that have a long tradition of cash management. The problem can be greatly reduced by developing cash flow estimates on a regular basis, determining a priori the compensating balances, keeping track of developments in the securities market, and constantly updating the information base.

Like most governments with good cash management history, the city prepares several reports on a monthly, quarterly, and annual basis. The monthly reports include listings of all investments held by the city, the current market valuation of the investments, and transaction summaries. The quarterly reports provide information on investment strategies employed in the most recent quarter and describe the portfolio in terms of investment securities, maturities, risk characteristics and other features. The policy requires that within sixty days after the end of the fiscal year the city prepare a comprehensive annual report on the investment program, showing both monthly and quarterly comparisons of various investment statistics. The policy also recommends a periodic review or amendment of the general investment policy by the assistant city manager as the conditions warrant.

SUGGESTIONS AND RECOMMENDATIONS

Based on the information presented here, it seems that the city is doing a reasonably good job of managing its cash, in particular idle cash. It has a good management and administra-

---

* The following expression was used to calculate the efficiency rate (ER) of a portfolio:

ER = (Average investment in period i)/(Average investment + Average cash balance in period i)] × 100

where i stands for the i-th period, which could be a day, a week, or a month. If the average cash balance for a given period is equal to 0, then ER will be 100%, meaning that there is no idle cash left for that period. If it turns out to be negative, the ER will still be 100% because any negative balance will have to be compensated by transferring an equivalent amount from the investment portfolio of short-term assets. This will obviously leave a lower amount available for investment in the following week or month affecting investment income, which means that negative balance is not a desirable objective even though it may have a higher efficiency rate. As always, the objective should be to maintain as small a cash balance as possible without incurring the problems mentioned earlier.

tive structure with trained individuals and well-defined responsibilities that are vital for running a sound cash management program. The city has a good working relationship with its citizens and the financial community, even though it transacts with one particular financial institution for its cash management operations. The city has for a long time maintained a policy of "fiscal conservatism," which has helped it survive some financial hard times in the past and can easily help it in its cash management efforts in the future. Nevertheless, there is room for additional improvement in its current practice. This final section makes several recommendations which, if properly pursued, could further improve the quality of Lubbock's cash management program.

Recommendation 1. The city should develop an annual cash budgeting system to (1) assist in the management of cash, (2) make monthly, if not weekly, estimates of cash flows, and (3) formulate investment policies. The recent effort by the finance department to develop rough estimates of cash flows is a move in the right direction, but needs formal support and approval of the council. In order to initiate a formal cash budgeting system, before the end of each fiscal year the city should make a full year's projection of cash flows broken down by months, make a full year's projection of investment decisions by months, and update these projections on a regular basis.

Recommendation 2. The city should establish a more structured system of cash collection and disbursement to improve the management of float. Proper guidelines for cash collection, including some provisions for discounts (for early payments) and penalties (for late payments), would considerably reduce the time during which cash remains idle. The current practice of making daily payments or as soon as vouchers are received is rather inefficient in the sense that it drastically reduces the amount of time as well as cash that the city could have earned by simply extending the disbursement float. The city should work out some procedures similar to the ones suggested earlier, to determine the actual amount of float. It should also explore the possibility of introducing a lock-box system to speed up collection and to minimize the collection float.

Recommendation 3. The city should make a serious effort to reconcile the compensating balance it currently holds with the lead bank for its services. Although the bank currently does not have a reserve requirement, the very fact that the city has to maintain a minimum balance of $6 million on its accounts is far more than what it should ideally maintain. Assuming an even more liberal estimate than the $2 million calculated earlier in the chapter, the compensating balance would still be far less than what it presently is. The difference, which should run between 2 million to 5.3 million dollars at least, could easily be invested in short-term securities to generate additional earnings for the city.

Recommendation 4. The city should make a conscious effort to ensure maximum return on its investments by shifting between different maturities based on relative returns and expectations of future rates. The traditional *yield curve* can be used in this regard to provide information on the expected directions of interest rates, in particular in assessing future market conditions and deciding on the maturity of the securities to be purchased. To give an example, a downward-sloping yield curve may be a signal that rates are expected to fall in the future, meaning that short-term maturities should be preferred, as opposed to longer-term maturities.

Recommendation 5. The city should monitor and revise its portfolio on a regular, not a periodic, basis. Monitoring portfolios requires an accurate, up-to-date database that includes information on all securities in a portfolio particularly such as the data on the security purchased, the amount, the maturity, the date and time of transaction, the name of the authorizing person, the dealer, and the delivery information. These data should be maintained in a form that facilitates the generation of regular summary reports. Also, reports of portfolio performance, including the cost of portfolio administration as well as the return on the portfolio, should be carefully monitored by the city. From time to time, perhaps monthly, if not weekly, the city should make sure that it is consistent with the cash flow forecast since actual cash flows often deviate from the forecast.

Recommendation 6. The city should carefully evaluate the bank reports on accrued earnings and book value and, if possible, should develop a formal "recordkeeping procedure" to determine the average daily balance, earnings, charges, and net gain or loss which, in the long run, will form a historical record for setting bank compensation for its services. In the short run, this procedure would indicate if the lead bank's profits were excessive, or if it had suffered a loss. Compensating balances for the months following these accounting procedures, therefore, could be increased or decreased from the projected level in order to reimburse the bank for the previous month's loss or to reduce the earnings to recover excessive profits.

Recommendation 7. The city should develop a more aggressive plan for competition in bank relations. As noted earlier, competition is a key element in getting the most out of bank services and should be explored to the fullest extent. It should attempt to stimulate competition by inviting several banks in the area, including those in the neighboring municipalities, to provide information regarding services and fees. Even though the city may end up selecting the same lead bank, the process of encouraging competition will make it possible to learn more about the breadth of services provided by these banks and to take advantage of any worthwhile services on occasion.

Recommendation 8. The city should develop long-term budgetary forecasts at least five to six years into the future. This would allow the city to assess its future capital needs, determine its resource potential, and improve its ability to adjust to changes in the demands for services in advance. Given the state of local economy and the rising costs of providing services across the board, long-term forecasting has become a must for all governments, large or small. The city does have a good history of budgeting and financial reporting, which should help it develop such forecasts on a regular basis.

Recommendation 9. Finally, the city should make an effort to keep abreast of the legal and nonlegal materials, such as fiscal notes, occasional financial reports, and other documents published by various agencies in the state that have direct implications for its cash management program. These documents are prepared with a view to helping the local communities in the state and frequently focus on such important topics as treasury management, multiyear revenue and expenditure forecasting, fiscal impact assessment, guidelines on municipal borrowing, and investment. Together they provide a wealth of information that could easily add to its current efforts toward building a more effective cash management program.

SUMMARY AND CONCLUSION

Governments generally hold cash to achieve three basic objectives: transaction, precautionary, and speculative. Because cash balances provide no direct return, the precautionary or speculative objective for investing cash is met in part by holding marketable securities. The ultimate objective of cash management, however, is to make certain that enough cash is available on hand to meet payment obligations that arise in the course of normal government operations and try to reduce the government's idle cash balances to a minimum. This chapter has briefly described how and the extent to which these objectives are being realized by a Texas city and the amount of success it has had to this point. It has also presented a set of recommendations that could be realistically implemented by the city to improve its current practice. Although general in scope, these recommendations will not only aid in the continued improvement of the program but will also open up interest in other areas of financial management practice of the city. Much of the responsibility for implementing these recommendations rests with the city management, especially those who are directly in charge of the program with the active cooperation and support of the council. At a minimum, the city can utilize an incremental approach to build on the structure that currently exists to develop a more sound and aggressive program in order to realize much greater benefits of cash management in the future.

EPILOGUE

The city has made several changes in its cash management policy since the publication of this chapter in 1994. For instance, it has developed a five-year budget forecast that allows it to trace its revenue and expenditure growth more carefully, although it still does not have a formal cash budgeting system except for a monthly estimate for capital improvement projects. It has yet to develop a well-designed cash collection and disbursement system. The city has reduced its compensating balance with the lead bank to $600,000 from the $6 million it was maintaining at the time, however. It has also developed a good monitoring system by which the city investment advisors now monitor its portfolio on a daily basis and the bank reports on a monthly basis.

The city is currently in the process of looking into the possibility of doing business with other banks besides the lead bank. If it does, it will increase competition and lower the price of services it receives from the latter. There are also other changes in its cash management policy consistent with the recommendations we made. For instance, the city now revises its investment guidelines annually. In addition to this, it has increased its limit on securities, in particular agency securities and commercial paper. The increase on the limit on agency securities allows for 80% rather than the previously allowed 65%. The percentage of portfolio that can be invested in commercial paper, an alternative the city has not always pursued, also increased from 20–25%.

REVIEW QUESTIONS

1. What objectives does a cash management program serve for a government? Why should a government prefer cash flow data to accounting and other financial data in making financial decisions? Develop an aggregate cash flow scenario for the operations of a government and contrast it with that of a nonprofit organization.
2. Define cash budgeting. Why is it important to prepare cash budgets on a regular basis? What other methods could you suggest for cash flow forecasting besides

the ones suggested here? Discuss the advantages and disadvantages of these methods.

3. Define and distinguish between collection and disbursement float. Explain how a lock box works and how its use can increase the collection float. What are the tangible benefits of a wire transfer system? Discuss the role of the Federal Reserve and the lead bank in this regard.

4. What is excess balance? Why should a government have excess or idle balance even when cash is transferred daily from the field banks? Explain how concentrating cash into a central cash pool is superior to managing funds in many smaller balances at various banks.

5. What is considered to be the most liquid of money market securities? Why? Discuss the factors a government should consider in investing its idle balances in money market securities.

6. Why is it necessary to have a written investment policy? Is this more important for a large or a small government? Explain.

REFERENCES

City of Lubbock, TX. (1993). *The Budget Manual: 1994–1995*. Lubbock, TX: Budget Department of the City of Lubbock.

City of Lubbock, TX (1993). *The Investment Policy*. Lubbock, TX: Finance Department of the City of Lubbock.

Miller, G. L. (1991). Cash management. In J. E. Petersen and D. R. Strachota (eds.), *Local Government Finance: Concepts and Practices*, Chicago: Government Finance Officers Association, 241–262.

Ramsey, J. R. and Hackbart, M. M. (1993). Public funds management: Current practices and future trends. In R. Lamb et al. (eds.), *The Handbook of Municipal Bonds and Public Finance*, pp. 194–224. New York: New York Institute of Finance.

Schwartz, E. M. (1985). Inventory and cash management. In J. R. Aronson and E. Schwartz (eds.), *Management Policies in Local Government Finance*, pp. 342–363. Chicago: International Finance Officers Association.

36

The Evolution of a Debt Management Policy and Program

A Case Study of Kentucky

James R. Ramsey*
Western Kentucky University, Bowling Green, Kentucky, U.S.A.

Merl Hackbart
University of Kentucky, Lexington, Kentucky, U.S.A.

The municipal bond markets grew significantly in volume throughout the decade of the 1980s (Ramsey and Hackbart, 1993). This increase in borrowing by state and local governments can be attributed to many factors. State and local governments showed a renewed interest in infrastructure financing during this period of time. Much has been written about the deteriorating infrastructure of our cities and states. As a result, state and local governments began to concentrate in the 1980s on rebuilding highways, bridges, water and sewer systems, educational facilities, and so on. Adding to state and local governments' commitment to infrastructure financing was the general decline in federal support for many of these activities during this period of time (Ramsey and Hackbart, 1992). Infrastructure projects are suitable for debt financing by state and local governments due to the long-term capital investment nature of these projects.

Second, the changing fiscal federalism of the 1980s, in conjunction with constantly constrained budgets, forced many state and local governments to rely on the capital markets to finance expenditures that might otherwise be financed from current receipts. Computer equipment, other types of major equipment, and cash flow borrowing are examples of the use of the credit markets by state and local governments. Relatedly, economic development became a major public policy issue with both state and local governments during the decade of the 1980s. The recession of 1981–1982 significantly impacted employment growth and personal income growth in the states, and as a result, most states undertook aggressive job creation and industrial development programs during the 1980s. State and local governments have historically been involved in the recruitment of business and industry. The competition between state and local governments in the 1980s, however took on new dimensions as state and local governments relied less on tax abatement incentives and more upon direct and indirect cash subsidies financed through the credit markets (Hackbart and Ramsey, 1993).

---

* Current Affiliation: University of Louisville, Louisville, Kentucky, U.S.A.

State and local governments[1] borrowing increased during the 1980s for other reasons as well. The early 1980s witnessed record high interest rates followed by significant interest rate reductions over the next ten years. These interest rate movements allowed state and local governments to refinance many of their outstanding liabilities. New bonds were often issued throughout the latter part of the 1980s to refund bonds that may have been sold just several years earlier, hence the changing interest rate environment required state and local governments to be active debt managers. In addition, the municipal markets during this period of time witnessed significant innovations in financing techniques. State and local governments faced new financing techniques in the capital markets beyond those that had traditionally existed. For example, a number of short-term borrowing techniques allowed state and local governments to issue debt for cash flow management purposes. Certificates of participation evolved in part, as a means for allowing state and local governments to borrow yet keep the debt incurred as an "off balance sheet item." As a result of these and numerous other innovations, state and local governments became more active in the credit markets throughout this period (Peterson, 1993).

This growth in the municipal markets and the necessity of public entities to actively manage their debt programs resulted in changing state and local government debt management policies and programs. The purpose of this chapter is to present a case study of the evolution of a debt management program in the Commonwealth of Kentucky. This case study focuses upon the creation of a centralized debt management unit, the Office of Investment and Debt Management,* which was mandated by statute to develop an active and centralized debt management program for the state.

This case study focuses on Kentucky for several reasons. First, the authors were an integral part of the development and the management of the office throughout the 1980s. Second, Kentucky's debt management program has been cited in prior research as one of the most centralized debt management functions among the states, and it is this office that has significant oversight and responsibility for all state debt (Hackbart et al., 1990). Many states have attempted to attain more oversight and management of the proliferation of debt by state agencies, boards and so for in. The Kentucky example may be a model to be used by other states in attempting to achieve better oversight and management. Finally, Kentucky's debt management program has been generally regarded in the credit markets as a highly respected and professional debt management program (Yacoe, 1992).

HISTORY

John Y. Brown Jr. was elected governor of Kentucky in 1979 on the pledge to run state government more like a business. Governor Brown had no previous political experience but was a successful entrepreneur in business management. His concept of managing state government was that the principals and practices utilized in business could be adopted in the public sector.

Upon his election, Governor Brown had an efficiency assessment performed of the various business practices of the state. It was determined that Kentucky's financial management programs were not professionally organized and staffed. This applied particularly to the cash management and investment management programs of the state. Several

---

* The name of the office was later changed to the Office of Financial Management and Economic Analysis.

different organizational units within the state had responsibility for the oversight and management of the state's cash assets. Further, approximately twenty-four debt authorities existed, each of which operated independently of each other and in many cases independently of state government. Most of these debt authorities were governed by separate boards, each of which had their own professional staffs who carried out the programmatic aspects of the entities and the financings of the entities. As a result, these debt authorities planned their own debt issues, employed their financing teams, structured their financing transactions, and marketed their transactions with little, if any, input or oversight from the central state government. In the case of many of these boards, commissions, agencies, and so on, the board members were appointed by and served at the pleasure of the governor, and the debt management decisions made reflected the policy initiatives of the executive branch. In many other cases however board members were appointed by prior governors or served in other capacities and the governor and executive branch of government exercised only minimal oversight and control. Due to such decentralization, the state of Kentucky was not able to articulate a state debt policy, effectively manage its outstanding debt, and develop and implement a financially sound infrastructure financing strategy required by the rapidly changing fiscal condition or the state.

Therefore, Governor Brown proposed to the 1980 Kentucky General Assembly the creation of the Office of Investment and Debt Management. Conceptually, the office was designed to provide a centralized organization with broadranging responsibilities to formulate and implement sound debt management policies and practices as well as be responsible for the investment of the state's short-term cash portfolio. The decision to incorporate both functions within the same office was made due to the perception that there were potential staffing and expertise synergies that could be realized by placing both functions in the same office. The specific statutory responsibilities assigned to the new office were the following:

1. The analysis and management of short- and long-term cash flow requirements
2. The maximization of the return on state investments given the cash flow and liquidity requirements
3. The coordination and monitoring of cash needs relative to investment and debt activity
4. The development of a long-term debt plan, including criteria for the issuance of debt and an evaluation of how much total state debt is justified
5. The evaluation of revenue projections relative to proposed revenue bond issues
6. The responsibility for liaison with the general assembly on all investment and debt matters, including but not limited to new bond issues, the status of state debt, and the status of state investments
7. All other functions of the department relative to state investment and debt management including but not limited to making debt service payments, selling bonds, and assisting the State Property and Buildings Commission and the State Investment Commission (Kentucky Revised Statues, 1980)

The statutes went on to further specify that: "all state agencies, authorities, boards, cabinets, commissions, corporations, or other entities of, or representing, the Commonwealth with authority to issue bonds, shall submit all proposed bond issues, bond anticipation notes, or interim debt financing to the Office for Investment and Debt Management for review and approval prior to the issuance of such debt" (Kentucky Revised Statutes, 1980).

The legislation passed during the 1980 session of the Kentucky General Assembly was effective in July 1980. The first executive director was appointed in January 1981. While the legislation establishing the office referred to both debt and cash management, Governor Brown decided to initially focus on enhancing the state's cash management practices. Such a focus was logical due to the fact that in 1981 Kentucky had not been greatly impacted by the changing fiscal federalism and cuts in federal infrastructure support and interest rates were at historical highs. Such interest rates provided opportunities to enhance portfolio earnings and to increase "nontax" revenue during a period of economic decline. Therefore, staff efforts were primarily directed over the next two to three years in this direction. Efforts were made to develop a debt management program during this period of time; however, initially the primary policy focus was on the cash management and investment programs.*

Developing a Centralized Debt Management Program

As the Office of Investment and Debt Management began to develop debt review and approval procedures, significant resistance was encountered from some of these semiautonomous debt entities. For example, in 1981 the debt outstanding of the Kentucky Housing Corporation was approximately equal to the statutory limit of debt authorized by the general assembly for this debt authority. The staff and board of directors of the Kentucky Housing Corporation sought to circumvent this debt ceiling by creating a sister corporation of the Kentucky Housing Corporation and empowering the sister corporation to issue debt. The staff for the Office for Investment and Debt Management believed that the creation of a sister corporation would be a subterfuge of the statutory debt ceiling of the Kentucky Housing Corporation. As a result, an attorney general's opinion was sought by the Office for Investment and Debt Management. In a strongly worded opinion of the attorney general, it was determined that the Kentucky Housing Corporation

> must submit all proposed bond issues in debt financing to the Office for Investment and Debt Management since the legislative intent was to establish a centralized entity in state government to evaluate, review, and approve all proposed note and bond issues of all state agencies, boards, etc. (Opinion of the Attorney General, 1981).

The attorney general's office also ruled that the creation of a sister corporation was not authorized by statute. This attorney general's opinion was significant in the development of a centralized debt policy for the state.†

In 1983, another debt authority of the state raised issues concerning the review and approval procedures of the Office of Debt Management with regard to its debt, and again an attorney general's opinion was sought. Consistent with the 1981 attorney general's opinion, the 1983 attorney general's opinion confirmed the centralized oversight and review responsibilities of the office (Opinion of the Attorney General, 1983).

---

* Prior to this time the cash and investment management functions of the state were divided between the state treasurer, an elected state official, and the executive branch, managed by the governor. The 1982 legislature further clarified the roles and duties of the Treasurer and the executive branch by centralizing most of the cash and investment management functions within this new office. The state treasurer in Kentucky has never played a role in the management of the state's debt.

† The attorney general in Kentucky is an independently elected state official whose opinion is advisory and does not have the effect of law.

The resistance to a centralized debt and cash management model was expected and took several forms. For the most part, however, the new organization' new procedures and operating relationships were implemented by the time Governor Brown left office in December of 1983.

Organization of Debt Function

The Office for Investment and Debt Management was created as a unit within the Finance and Administration Cabinet of the executive branch of Kentucky state government. The secretary of the Finance and Administration Cabinet is appointed to this position by the governor. Further, the secretary of the Finance and Administration Cabinet is the chief financial officer for the Commonwealth of Kentucky, with all the procurement, accounting, communications, information systems, and audit responsibilities of the state. While organizationally cabinet secretaries in the executive branch of government are equals, reality has long dictated that the secretary of the Finance and Administration Cabinet was more "equal" than other cabinet secretaries since all purchases, contracts, and so forth of the commonwealth had to be approved by the secretary of finance. Further, the secretary of the Finance and Administration Cabinet serves as a member of the board of directors of all of the various agencies, boards, commissions, and so on with debt issuing authority. Therefore, the organization of the Office of Investment and Debt Management was strengthened implicitly by the powers granted to the secretary of the Finance and Administration Cabinet.

In 1988, a significant reorganization of state government took place that significantly enhanced the responsibilities of the Office of Investment and Debt Management. At that time, the revenue estimating and economic analysis functions of state government were reorganized from the Revenue Cabinet to the Office for Investment and Debt Management. The office was renamed the Office of Financial Management and Economic Analysis. This reorganization enhanced the analytical capabilities, and this became particularly important as the state enhanced its debt management program in the late 1980s and early 1990s. This will be discussed in greater detail later in the chapter.

Management Philosophy

From the beginning of the formation of the Office for Investment and Debt Management, the management philosophy that evolved was one that the Commonwealth of Kentucky should actively manage its debt management program. Prior to this time, the state's approach could be more described as a passive management style; that is, the secretary of finance and administration would designate the members of the financing team and then these paid consultants (investment bankers, bond counsel, bank trustees, etc.) would structure the forthcoming bond issues and develop the marketing plan for the issue with little review or oversight by the state. The limited staff assigned to debt management issues by the state at that time could do little more than coordinate meeting schedules for the approval of bond resolutions, closings, and so forth.

As a result of the creation of the new centralized debt management office and the increase in the use of debt financing for infrastructure and other purposes, it became economically feasible to employ a professional staff with technical competencies consistent with the broadened debt management mission of the office. With the evolution of the office, a more active management philosophy emerged. The office also took on broadened responsibilities regarding the overall fiscal condition of the state. Specifically, the office believed that the issuer is the most important member of the financing team since the debt to be incurred is its liability. While most members of the financing team collect a fee and move on to other financial transactions at the completion of a bond issue, the issuer must manage the financing over its life. Therefore, it was believed that the issuer should play a very active role in analyzing structuring alternatives and should have the final "sign off" on the financing structure and marketing plan. This change in management philosophy met with some resistance, particularly from those investment banking firms and bond counsel firms who had done the preponderance of the state's bond work over time.

Additionally, the implementation of an active debt management policy required the enhancement of the capabilities of the staff and the enhancement of their computer and other support systems. The original staffing of the office consisted of an executive director and two professional staff members assigned from other areas of state government. In the case of these staff members, a reorientation of management approach needed to occur. In addition, training was required to upgrade their analytical and quantitative skills to implement this active management approach. In many cases, this professional development came from the investment community itself. Many investment banking firms and bond counsel firms were willing to provide training and professional development sessions and other support helpful to upgrading staffing abilities. In other cases, staff became more active in the training opportunities provided through professional organizations such as the Government Finance Officers Association and the National Association of State Treasurers.

It is interesting to note that throughout the 1980s there did not exist one specific professional organization that consisted exclusively of state debt managers. The focus of the professional organizations previously cited have been much broader than debt management. Still, these groups provided valuable professional opportunities. In recent years, a group of debt management professionals from various states have come together to form a debt management network. In its start-up phase, the National Association of State Treasurers has provided staff support to this group. The debt management network's single purpose is to bring together debt managers from state governments to exchange ideas and information and to enhance professional development opportunities for state officials in this area.

In addition to upgrading the capabilities of existing staff, a strong centralized debt management program that pursues an active management philosophy required the addition of staff members. The early 1980s were, in general, a period of budget cuts and reductions for Kentucky state government. Therefore, the addition of staff members was often accomplished through the reallocation of vacant positions from other areas of state government to the debt management function. In particular, one or more positions from the state's budget office were reallocated to the debt management function. In addition, it was discovered that at least in several cases, these quasi-autonomous debt authorities of the state had their own staffs, which were not needed on a full-time basis for the programs that employed them. As a result, consolidation of one or more debt authorities took place, with the staff from these debt authorities being consolidated as part of the staffing of the Office for Investment and Debt Management. Specifically, the Kentucky Pollution Abatement Authority consisted of a one-person office. The workload of that individual was less than full time, so that individual was reassigned to the Office of Investment and Debt Management and assigned additional debt management-related duties in addition to the responsibilities with the Kentucky Pollution Abatement Authority.

Finally, commitment of new funds was required for the technological resources needed to support the active management philosophy of the office. A commitment was made to provide personal computers to each professional staff members. In addition, a commitment was made to network the personal computers so that software and databases could be shared. The computer network installed also permitted direct communication with the state's mainframe computer, which was located in a different building. The state's mainframe computer housed the official debt reports of the commonwealth that were an integral part of the state's comprehensive annual financial report. In addition, accessing the mainframe directly allowed staff the ability to utilize software programs that were run on the mainframe computer.

Concurrent with the effort to upgrade the computer hardware and software capabilities of the office with the debt management staff was an effort to upgrade the technical resources available to the investment staff. In particular, the state began to subscribe to various financial information services utilized by the investment community. These financial information services could also be shared with the debt management staff. Having up-to-date market information on the treasury markets and other markets complimented the work of the debt management staff. More important, the addition of this financial information service added credibility to the state's professionalism. Investment bankers realized that Kentucky was making a commitment to upgrading its debt management program and that Kentucky's debt management staff had access to much of the same information that they had.

As part of the effort to upgrade the office's technology, the state purchased various debt management software packages that allowed the state to size and structure bond issues. Again, this allowed the staff to better understand the advice and alternatives proposed to it by investment bankers. The acquisition of such computer software also enhanced the credibility of the office with investment bankers and other credit market participants.

In 1983, the office developed a procurement procedure for selecting the investment banking, bond counsel, banking firms, and other participants of the financing team. Prior to this Kentucky did not have a procurement process for these types of professionals and the selection of these firms was made by the secretary of the Finance and Administration Cabinet as the state's chief financial officer. The procurement procedures developed were (and continued to be to some degree) somewhat subjective, and the final selection decision continued to rest with the secretary of the Finance and Administration Cabinet. The process required, however the submission of proposals to the professional staff that addressed specific structuring, marketing, experience, and other questions. This again reflected the active management philosophy, as it began to indicate to the members of the financing teams that the professional staff was requiring the investment banks, bond counsels, and so on to do a certain amount of homework prior to their selection and the structuring and marketing of a transaction.

Once the financing team was in place, the staff of the office took the lead in the development of the financing plan. Again, this sometimes created conflict with investment bankers, and at least in some cases with bond counsels, who historically took the lead and made all or most of the financing decisions. Further, "to send a message" to the investment community that the office had the professionalism and capability to understand municipal bond issues, the state on several competitive transactions served as its own financial advisor (i.e., structured the issue and prepared it for market, including writing the official statement). The active management philosophy pursued attempted to convey to the investment community that Kentucky sought professional investment advice, creativity, and analysis of alternatives. At the same time, this active management philosophy said that the ultimate responsibility for such decision making would rest with the state. Most investment banking firms developed an appreciation for this active management approach over time. As a result, most firms began to realize that a significant key to "getting deals" in Kentucky was developing a working professional relationship with the office's staff. It became very common for investment bankers to bring ideas to the staff for review and input well before the request for proposal process. Most investment bankers tried to win the confidence of the staff by proving the investment banking firm's professionalism and by staying in constant communication with the staff so that the investment bankers could be responsive to the state's financing needs.

This active debt management philosophy initially focused on structural issues. Toward the end of the 1980s this philosophy expanded significantly to a gamut of marketing issues. The office initially developed a working relationship with Moody's Investors Service and Standard and Poor's. This relationship, however was always centered or upcoming transactions; that is, when the state was preparing for a transaction, numerous communications were held with the rating agencies to ensure that they had complete information. Visits were periodically made to New York to communicate with the rating agency personnel. On a periodic basis the state did extend to rating agency personnel invitations to visit the state and to meet with a broad array of state government officials. These state visits included briefings on economic, budgetary, and other governmental issues as well as trips to major economic development projects or state facilities.

The relationships with the rating agencies took a significant new direction in 1988 with the merger of the Office of Investment and Debt Management and the Office of Revenue Estimating and Economic Analysis. This merger, as noted before, combined the professionals dealing in the credit markets on a day-to-day basis (the investment and debt management staffs) with the staff that developed the state's short-and long-term revenue forecasts and performed general state economic analysis. These latter skills strengthen the office's understanding of economic, revenue, and budgetary issues and permitted an advanced level of communication with the rating agencies. For example, at the suggestion of Standard and Poor's, the office began the development of a quarterly economic and revenue report to improve the ongoing flow of information on the state to the rating agencies. Kentucky experienced several revenue and budget shortfalls through the early 1980s, and the debt management staff had only a secondary understanding of the reasons for such shortfalls and the implications of such shortfalls. Therefore, in communicating with the rating agencies, the debt management staff could not always address issues and questions raised by the rating agencies. The merger of these two offices changed that significantly. As the debt management professionals worked side by side with the economic analyst, they gained first-hand access to information and data on economic, revenue, and governmental issues for the first time.

In 1988 the office began making quarterly visits to the rating agencies to provide them with these reports and a formal presentation on other budget, legislative, and governmental activities for the quarter. These quarterly visits to the rating agencies then focused on "macro" state issues as opposed to specific bond transactions. In fact, at the quarterly rating visits, a debt calendar for the upcoming quarter was presented to the rating agencies for their planning purposes. These quarterly visits with a macro orientation greatly enhanced the communications between the commonwealth and the rating agencies. The rating agencies had direct access to any information that they requested and as a rule found that they then were not surprised with changes in budget or governmental policy.

In addition, the rating agencies provided guidance to the state with regard to the concerns, questions, and issues that they had. It has generally been believed by the office and the rating agencies that these quarterly visits and informational meetings are a hallmark of Kentucky's debt management program.

In addition, in 1988 the office began for the first time to reach out to the ultimate buyers of Kentucky debt. Prior to this time, the office had worked to develop a relationship with the investment banking community. The investment bankers who underwrite the state debt in the primary market, however then market these bonds to insurance companies, banks, individuals, mutual funds, and so on in the secondary market. The office believed that it would be valuable to attempt to begin direct communication with the ultimate buyers to gain an appreciation for structural and market issues and concerns that they might have. The bottom line for the office was a belief that communication with the ultimate buyers would strengthen the state's standing in the credit markets and thus enhance the marketability of state debt. Also, there was evidence that investment banking firms underwriting state bonds did not always have perfect knowledge or access to information on various credit matters or state governmental issues and that an efficient communication system was one that permitted bond buyers to have direct access to the state for information.*

The first attempt to communicate directly with the buyers of Kentucky bonds was the development of an annual investors' seminar. The first two such seminars were, in fact, not seminars at all but rather receptions that permitted bond buyers to have the opportunity to meet with state policy makers and debt management staff on a somewhat informal basis. At the end of the second investors' seminar in 1989, a survey was distributed to attendees and also representatives of potential bond buyers whom the state sought to attend the seminars. The response received to the survey was that the investors' seminar should be more substantive than a reception. The respondents to the survey indicated a preference for a true seminar to review state economic budget issues and to discuss the upcoming state bond issues.

Credit analysts at bank and insurance companies indicated a willingness to travel to Kentucky to attend such an investors' seminar if the seminar contained a substantive discussion in addition to a reception that allowed them to meet key policy officials. Beginning with the third annual investors' seminar, the format was changed to include an afternoon of discussions on the subjects mentioned in the survey results, which was then followed by a reception.

In addition to this effort to communicate directly with the major bond buying institutions, the state also began a program of meeting with representatives of these firms individually in their offices. Whenever representatives of the state were in New York, meetings were set up with several insurance companies and other large institutional buyers to make economic presentations on the commonwealth. The materials discussed again focused on the state's economy, revenue outlook, budget outlook, and debt outlook. An effort was made to establish an ongoing communication with these individuals. With the assistance of the investment banking community, efforts were made to identify the appropriate bond buyers and the staff at these institutional firms to conduct such meetings. In addition, special trips were made to Chicago and Boston to meet with portfolio managers of institu-

---

* Investment banking firms were generally willing to share with the states names of large institutional buyers the state could contact. More recently, the state has began to develop a marketing program focused on retail buyers.

tional buyers located in these cities. This communication was viewed as a vital link in enhancing the marketability of state bonds.

Debt Review Process

From the beginning, one of the major responsibilities of the office was the review and approval of the debt of all state boards, corporations, commissions, agencies, and so on. It should be noted that over time the office served as the staff to several of the state's debt authorities, including the State Property and Building Commission, the Kentucky Infrastructure Authority (the restructured Kentucky Pollution Abatement Authority), the Kentucky Local Correctional Facilities Construction Commission, and the Kentucky Agricultural Finance Authority. The review of the debt of these authorities could be very straightforward since the office staff was involved in procuring the financing team, structuring the issue, and marketing the issue. In one sense the office was required to review and approve its own work. Two other review processes evolved over time.

The first involved those debt authorities of the state whose credit involved a moral obligation of the commonwealth. These include the Kentucky Housing Corporation, the Kentucky Student Loan Corporation, and the debt issued by the public universities in Kentucky. As a general rule, each of these debt authorities had statutory authority to issue its own debt up to a predetermined statutory amount. The statutes also specified that if for whatever reason it became necessary these debt authorities could petition the governor to petition the general assembly to appropriate debt service to make debt service payments on their debt. This moral obligation pledge was a weak moral obligation since the governor was not obligated to seek an appropriation for debt service and the general assembly was not required to make such an appropriation of debt service. Still, the debt of these authorities was as a practical matter viewed as debt that should be the oversight of the office. Therefore, the office developed a specific set of review procedures for these debt authorities.

Additionally, there were at least two debt authorities of the commonwealth that served as conduit issuers for debt of public entities (i.e., issued industrial revenue bonds). These debt authorities were the Kentucky Development Finance Authority and the Kentucky Infrastructure Authority. (Some of the debt of the Kentucky Infrastructure Authority was supported by appropriations by the general assembly; other debt of the Kentucky Infrastructure Authority was supported by loan repayments from local communities and had a moral obligation backing from the state; still other debt of the Kentucky Infrastructure Authority was issued on the behalf of private entities). In one particular bond issue in the early 1980s, the office attempted to review an industrial revenue bond issued by the Kentucky Development Finance Authority on behalf of a private company. The bond counsel for the company indicated that the office had no review authority. In this particular case, the bond council requested an attorney general's opinion to that effect. In fact, the attorney general confirmed its earlier opinion that the statute created the Office of Investment and Debt Management to implement a strong, centralized debt management program for the commonwealth and that as a result all debt issued by state debt authorities must be reviewed and approved by the Office of Investment and Debt Management. The attorney general's opinion went on to say, however, that the office could not expect private companies using a state debt authority as a conduit issuer to follow the procurement policies and practices of the office. Therefore, the attorney general's opinion limited the review process to two factors: (1) the form and legality of the transaction, and (2) the creditworthiness of the transaction (Opinion of the Attorney General 1983). As a result, the office developed a new procedure format for those debt authorities that serve as conduit issuers for industrial revenue bonds.

All bonds issued in Kentucky by state debt entities over the past decade have been reviewed and approved by the office. In fact, nearly all bond attorneys have required a certification letter to that effect from the executive director of the office. In addition, most bond transcripts include the review and approval letter as part of the official records of the transaction. As a practical matter, the office attempted to be involved in the planning for future debt issues as well as the structure and marketing of such issues so that a situation would not occur where a debt authority got to its closing and a significant disagreement was outstanding with the office on the issue. As a result, the office has not disapproved any state debt issue. There has been at least one case in which the office would not issue an approval letter on an industrial revenue bond and left it up to the bond council to certify that the closing was in compliance with state statutes. Early in the history of the office, some of the debt authorities of the state resisted the involvement of the office in their management affairs. As the professionalism within the office grew and the technical capabilities improved, however, most debt authorities welcomed the involvement of the office on their financing transactions.

The appendix provides an outline of the approval letter format and the debt issuance procedures. These procedures were incorporated by reference to an administrative regulation that was promulgated by the office and approved by the legislature. As a result, these procedures had the force of law and were not merely internal guidelines.

Debt Capacity

One of the statutory responsibilities of the office was the determination of the appropriate level of debt for the commonwealth. Needless to say, this is no easy task; it involves many policy issues beyond the expertise of the professional debt manager. Still, the office developed a statistical model that focused on the relationship between the state's principal debt outstanding and four economic variables that can be quantified and that can be evaluated by the rating agencies in performing their credit analysis of the state. A full discussion of this statistical model is beyond the scope of this presentation; however, Kentucky's debt capacity model provided a source of information to executive and legislative decision making that could assist in the budget decision-making process (Hackbart and Ramsey, 1990).

SUMMARY AND CONCLUSION

The evolution of the Office of Investment and Debt Management (and its successor unit—the Office of Financial Management and Economic Analysis) provides an interesting case for the study of organizational change, change in state government financial management practices in response to outside forces and internal desires to enhance government efficiency and management processes. In its earlier years, the office was principally a response to a governor's desire to change financial management practices and procedures and to prove that private sector financial management practices were transferable to state government.

The success of the initial initiative led to the creation of an office with financial expertise and professional recognition that then took on an everlasting role within the Finance and Administration Cabinet. Prior to this time, the Finance and Administration Cabinet had little capability to manage major finance issues. As the office established greater capability, additional responsibilities were added to the office and greater centralization of activities occurred. At the same time that the capabilities of the office were being expanded internally, external forces were exerting new pressures for enhanced state financial management capabilities. Rating agencies became more demanding for state accountability regarding fiscal and debt management in order for the state to maintain and enhance its credit rating. Reduced federal financial support of the state created the need for the state to issue more debt to finance infrastructure and other public investment. Increased debt levels led to greater legislative scrutiny and concern regarding state debt policy and a greater desire by legislators to be more fully informed regarding state debt management policy and procedures. Greater public understanding of the fiscal conditions and demands facing the state led to greater public scrutiny of financial management practices and more pressure on the state and the office to intelligently respond to questions regarding debt and debt management. The net result of a governor's initiative, the evolution of a professional staff and the demand for greater accountability and public investment led to the establishment of a professional, centralized, innovative office that permits the state to manage this important public policy issue.

REVIEW QUESTIONS

1. What factors led to the establishment of the Office of Investment and Debt Management? How did they interact to enhance the mission and responsibilities of the office?
2. How does the experience of this office contribute to the debate regarding the centralization or decentralization of state program administration?
3. What innovations resulted from the creation of this office? How did they impact the fiscal management processes of the state?
4. How did the addition of the revenue forecasting function alter the overall capabilities and functions of the office?
5. What additional adjustments (of function and mission) would you anticipate for this office? Why?
6. What staff capabilities would you seek in your hiring practices if you were named the director of this office?
7. How does this office contribute to the overall financial management policy of the state of Kentucky?
8. Discuss the pros and cons of a highly centralized state debt management program from the prospective of the state's debt authorities.

APPENDIX: COMMONWEALTH OF KENTUCKY, FINANCE AND ADMINISTRATION CABINET, OFFICE OF FINANCIAL MANAGEMENT AND ECONOMIC ANALYSIS, DEBT ISSUANCE PROCEDURES

Purpose

This procedure is intended to provide coordination, accountability, and oversight pursuant to KRS 42.420. Information as necessary by the Office of Financial Management and

Economic Analysis (OFMEA) to implement KRS 42.420 shall be provided to the OFMEA by the issuing authority and/or the managing underwriter/financial advisor on a continuous, as-occurring basis, throughout the debt-issuing process.

Background Information

I. Documents to be provided (when available)
  A. Preliminary official statement
    1. Official statement
    2. Trust indenture
    3. Bond resolution
    4. Lease agreement
    5. Ratings
    6. Construction schedule/program implementation
    7. Cash needs schedule (drawdown)
II. Timing of issue
  A. Identify expected similar issues and amount
  B. Marketing date proposed relative to
    1. Need for funds
    2. Market trends
III. Rating agency presentation preparation
  A. Information to be provided rating agencies
  B. Designated personnel to make presentation
IV. Structure description
  A. Size of issue
    1. Need
    2. Market reception
    3. Reinvestment
    4. Authorization
  B. Maturity of issue
    1. Project life
    2. Debt service available
  C. Method of sale
  D. Security
  E. Type of financing (note, permanent, line of credit, lease, etc.)
  F. Insurance
  G. Capitalized interest
  H. Discount
  I. Rate structure
  J. Early retirement provisions (refunding, redemption features)
  K. Funds flow (application of proceeds)
  L. Bid instructions
  M. Type of bond
    1. Bearer, coupon
    2. Registered
    3. Book entry
    4. Other

Approval Criteria

The issuing entity will inform OFMEA, on an ongoing basis, information such that the following may be answered.

I. Legal authorization and procedural compliance
   A. Advisors are to be selected as follows: all advisors, consultants will be selected pursuant to competitive bidding (except where existing trust indentures preclude). Such advisors include
     1. Trustee
     2. Paying agent
    The following shall be selected by competitive bidding or, if documented as necessary and approved by the OFMEA competitive negotiation
     1. Bond counsel (must be in the "red book")
     2. Underwriter counsel (*subject to underwriter approval*)
     3. Underwriter/financial advisor
    A minimum of three proposals for each advisor will be solicited. The selection will be determined by an evaluation team made up of at least the chairman of the debt-issuing agency's board of directors or his designee from the board of directors; the staff director of the debt-issuing agency, or his designee from the staff; and the director of the OFMEA or his designee from the staff. The team will document reasons for advisor selection. Underwriter counsel will also be subject to the approval of the managing underwriter.
   B. The proposed bond issue has been legally authorized and/or determined feasible in the biennial *The Budget of the Commonwealth of Kentucky*.
   C. All necessary approvals other than the OFMEA shall be obtained.
   D. There is no pending or anticipated litigation that would materially affect the ability to issue or fund debt service for the proposed debt issue.
   E. The proposed issue does not violate existing parity or other trust indenture restrictions. Specify parity or other unique trust indenture restrictions.
   F. The issuer has obtained an unqualified bond counsel opinion on the proposed debt issue by counsel listed in the most recent Bond Buyer *Director of Municipal Bond Dealers*.
   G. Bond proceeds are dispensed as follows.
    All bond proceeds of state agencies issuing debt are state funds (except as otherwise provided by statute) *pursuant to KRS 446.010*. Consequently, *state* funds will be *deposited in the Treasury pursuant to KRS 56.527 and KRS 42.020, and* invested and reinvested from time to time at the direction of the State Investment Commission, according to the indenture requirements and liquidity needs of the issuing authority *pursuant to KRS 42.500. In certain cases, the* investment function may be delegated *according to statute*. [KRS 164A.560(2) permits the investment of public university funds to be delegated at the option of the university board of trustees or directors.] (*KRS 198A.100 permits the Kentucky Housing Corporation to place bond proceeds with a trustee. KRS 164A.090 permits the Student Loan Corporation to place proceeds with a trustee.*)
    When delegated, that fiduciary will provide the State Investment Commission with quarterly reports indicating the following:
     1. Amount of funds received
     2. Amount of funds disbursed

3. Date of funds disbursed
4. Investment earnings per quarter
5. Investment instruments in which proceeds are held

II. Financial feasibility
   (The initial feasibility will be completed prior to inclusion in the biennial budget.)
   A. There are no pending charges identified by the issuer that would materially affect the issuer's revenues to the extent of jeopardizing his ability to fund (1) projected total operations, maintenance, and debt service, or (2) debt service coverage requirements.
   B. The burden on revenues of the issuer resulting from issuance of the proposed debt will not jeopardize the ability to issue debt to fund other programs (projects) identified in the accepted debt financing plan and approved by the legislature.

III. Costs of issuance
   A. The costs of issuance and/or underwriter spread is not unreasonable compared to similar recent issues. Provide estimated costs from financial advisor/underwriter proposal.
   B. The final costs are not significantly higher than other similar issues in the market. Provide the following to the OFMEA when available:
      1. Costs of issuance (final)—NIC, TIC
      2. Costs compared to similar issues in the market (when possible to determine)

IV. Structure The structural features of the proposed debt issue are
   A. Cost effective. Demonstrate choice quantitatively (see Background Information, Section IV, A-I).
   B. Directed to the needs of the primary market for that type of issue.
   C. Compatible with current marketing methods of other similar issuers.
   D. Compatible with overall marketing methods (policies) of the commonwealth.
   E. Sufficient to obtain a minimum A rating from Moody's and Standard & Poor's.

Approval Letter Format

Documents reviewed
Issuance data:
   Description of the project and financing plan
   Appropriation for debt service
   Size
   Dated date
   Sale date
   Closing date
   Final maturity
   Call provisions
   Security
   NIC
   TIC
   Bond Buyer 20-year A-rated general obligation bond index at week of the sale
   Coupon on last maturity
   Arbitrage yield
   Rating
   Method sale: competitive/negotiated (selling group or syndicate)

Purchaser:
Discount:
For refunding
    A. Nominal dollar savings
    B. B.P.V. savings as %
Professional services (means of selection of each)
    Bond counsel/fee
    Underwriter/fee
    Financial advisor/fee
    Trustee, registrar, paying agent/fee
    Official statement printer/fee
    Bond printer/fee
Sources and uses of funds:
    Sources
    Uses
        Construction and related costs
        Other project costs
        Discount
        Costs of issuance
    Annual fees
Parity requirements
Note any deviations from policy statements or regulations
Record of approval by appropriate authorities
Accounts:

	Debt service schedule		
Calender date Rate	Principal	Interest	Other costs

REFERENCES

Hackbart, M. M., Leigland, J., Riherd, R., and Reid, M. (1990). *Debt and Duty: Accountability and Efficiency in State Debt Management*. Lexington, KY: Council of State Governments.

Hackbart, M. M. and Ramsey, J. R. (spring 1990) State debt level management: A stable credit rating model. *Municipal Finance Journal*, 79–96.

Hackbart, M. M. and Ramsey, J. R. (1993) Debt management and debt capacity. In *The Handbook of Municipal Bonds and Public Finance*, New York: New York Institute of Finance.

Kentucky Revised Statutes, Frankfort, KY: various chapters and various years.

Opinions of the Attorney General, Frankfort, KY: various years.

Peterson, J. E., (1993). Innovations in the tax-exempt markets. In *The Handbook of Municipal Bonds and Public Finance*, New York: New York Institute of Finance.

Ramsey, J. R. and Hackbart, M. M. (April 1992) Financing the capital budget: Change and transition. *International Journal of Public Administration*.

Ramsey, J. R. and Hackbart, M. M. (1993) Managing state debt: Issues and challenges. In *Handbook of Comparative Public Budgeting and Financial Management*. New York: Marcel Dekkei.

Yacoe, D. (June 8, 1992) *Bond Buyer*.

37

The Orange County Debacle
Where Irresponsible Cash and Debt Management Practices Collide

Craig L. Johnson and John L. Mikesell
Indiana University, Bloomington, Indiana, U.S.A.

On December 2, 1994, Orange County, California, shocked the financial markets with the public announcement that it had unrealized losses totaling $1.5 billion in its pooled investment fund. On December 6 the county, one of the wealthiest counties in the nation, dropped another bombshell by filing for bankruptcy protection under Chapter 9 of the U.S. Bankruptcy Code. The county proceeded to default on its taxable pension bonds and subsequently on its taxable arbitrage notes. In addition, the county's actions called into question the repayment of principal and interest on funds of 187 local government agencies that deposited money in the Orange County Investment Pool (OCIP). Much of the money deposited in the OCIP was generated from money borrowed in the municipal securities market for the sole purpose of investing in the investment pool.

After the bankruptcy filing the Orange County treasurer, Robert Citron, resigned and pled guilty to six counts of fraud. As we write, the assistant treasurer, Matthew Raabe, is under state indictment and the market awaits the outcome of a myriad of legal proceedings. These proceedings include Orange County lawsuits for $2.4 billion against MerrillLynch, the investment broker/dealer that facilitated most of the county's investment and borrowing transactions, and for $3 billion against KPMG Peat Marwick, its former auditor (*Bond Buyer*, Dec. 21, 1995). The county just recently worked out a state-imposed postbankruptcy recovery plan that, among other things, lays claim to hundreds of millions of dollars in future revenues from the Orange County Transportation Authority.

This chapter analyzes the Orange County debacle in light of contemporary financial management policy. Specifically, we use this experience to demonstrate the nexus between cash and debt management principles and techniques. We lay out general cash management and debt management principles and policy issues, and critically analyze what happened in Orange County. Then we prescribe general policy advice for the rapidly changing financial marketplace. This will include the application of sophisticated cash and debt management techniques to public investment pools.

Reprinted from: Municipal Finance Journal, 1996, 17(2): 1–15.

STATE AND LOCAL CASH AND DEBT MANAGEMENT

State and local governments issue debt instruments and manage portfolios of investment securities to support the provision of public goods and services. Therefore debt and cash management must ultimately be judged on their ability to help government officials meet the public's demand for services. The Orange County experience is most tragic at this level because services in the county have had to be drastically reduced because officials ignored fundamental cash and debt management principles.

Principles of Cash Management

Operating fund management requires maintaining a balance between a safe return on idle cash and the ability to meet anticipated cash demands (Mikesell, 1995). Governments manage both short-term investment funds and longer-term bond funds. Short-term investment funds should be handled fundamentally differently from long-term funds.* When held in a trust capacity by government, both fund types should be managed to ensure the return of principal; the maintenance of sufficient liquidity; and, *within these constraints*, the maximization of yield. Within those objectives, the primary emphasis for the two funds differs. Short-term cash funds should focus almost exclusively on maintaining liquidity and ensuring return of principal. Longer-term funds may, however, seek higher yields by taking on additional risk in terms of less liquidity and more credit risk exposure than short-term funds accept.

It is tempting to castigate the pool for improperly running a government like a business; that is, for forgetting that there are different standards of prudence between managing a private investment fund seeking to obtain a return from the delegated investment balances of private investors and managing a government cash fund to facilitate the provision of government services. That is not quite where the problem begins, however because the county investment pool, even narrowly evaluated as a business, was a badly run business.

First, the county changed lines of business without informing the owners (or the owners' representatives) and unjustly put the core (even exclusive) reason for the business's existence in jeopardy. The operating funds of local government are collected through tax levies and charges for the provision of services to the public—services of schools, police and fire departments, road maintenance, and so on—and also to cover financing requirements during the year. These operating entities raise funds to finance the primary business of government: the provision of government services. Unlike a private business, however, they do not exist to produce the generically acceptable profit that provides a maximum return for capital invested; they exist to provide specific services that markets cannot adequately provide. They cannot be held to a single test of profit, regardless of how (ethically) raised, in the way that a proprietary firm can be judged. Although an investor in General Motors (GM) might be pleased when GM produces something other than cars to generate a higher yield than would be attainable from the auto business, a person paying taxes for the support of local schools will probably not be pleased if the

---

* This distinction is analogous to the distinction between money market and mutual fund investment companies in the business sector. Money market fund regulations are designed to produce portfolios with low risk and high liquidity. Money market portfolios are limited to an average maturity of no more than 120 days and their stated objective is to maintain a "stable" $1 net asset value per share on a daily marked-to-market basis.

school system goes into the business of garbage collecting, neglecting the provision of education; rather, the taxpayer would probably prefer to have taxes lowered, reflecting less financial assistance needed for schools, thereby letting the individual decide for him- or herself how the extra disposable income is to be used.

Even the GM investor, quite satisfied to earnd profit without regard to the line of business, would certainly want to be informed about the change in line of business so that she could consider whether or not the revised use of resources fit her own investment strategy. Given the inverse relationship between the risk of an investment and the return from an investment, investors reach some satisfactory balance between risk and return in how their resources are used. If the business earns a bit more return by taking some business and investment risks beyond the scope of practices normal for that trade, it must let its owners know so that they can decide whether that balance of risk and profit remains comfortable for them or whether they want to seek a balance more to their liking by moving their funds to another investment. The OCIP—in point of fact, the Orange County treasurer—changed business lines without clear notice. That is not consistent with good business practices (nor is it consistent with public trust, although that is another point).

Second, the county pool violated standard cash investment principles by borrowing short to invest long.* Arbitrage profits are possible because money can be lent at a higher rate than it was borrowed, but a strategy that crosses maturity lengths is always prey to the risk of a change in market interest rates. Rising rates result in sharply lower principal values for long-term fixed income investments, leaving less principal to cover the repayment of short-term loans when they come due and, in the case of cash pool investments, leaving less principal to meet the demands of pool participants when they have operating bills to pay. Falling interest rates make the strategy attractive, but when there are regular cash needs that call on the invested principal, waiting out the market until longer-term investments mature to recover their full face value is not possible. Holding pool securities to maturity works only if the pool does not have participants wanting to cash out—and participants will want their funds from a cash pool, because that pool, in contrast to the long-term profile for endowments, pensions, or even debt service sinking funds, is created because there are intrayear differences between the flow of revenues and the flow of expenditures. The disastrous consequences of maturity mismatching should have been obvious, given the similar but smaller crisis in San Jose, California, in 1984, but somehow it was not.†

Third, the pool invested money needed in the short term in medium-term structured notes and leveraged instruments. The funds were needed to meet expenses within the year. The money was not being set aside to grow over the long term to meet future obligations. The funds were known to be necessary to meet budgeted expenses with the fiscal year. Any long-term investment with such funds runs the risk of loss of principal from adverse movements in market interest rates. Instruments that react swiftly and violently to market interest rate changes simply are not appropriate media for cash fund investment, regardless of ownership of those funds. Market risk from changing interest rates can be insured against, by hedging with derivative instruments, but this standard approach used by profes-

---

* Why a county, operating in its primary line of business, should be permitted to borrow to invest in financial investments is, of course, a distinct problem itself.

† In 1984, San Jose, California, had placed funds in a pool of \$750 million in government bonds with an average maturity of seventeen years. An increase in interest rates caused a loss in portfolio value of \$60 million, endangering the ability of the city to pay its bills (Mikesell, 1995).

sional and skilled investors trades a certain loss of return (effectively an insurance pre-mium) against some of the potential return if the manager guesses market moves correctly. It is a strategy that a business working with a cash pool needed in the short term would use, but the Orange County pool did not. Again, the pool, as a business, was badly managed.

The Orange County tragedy is one of both cash and debt management. The OCIP was designed to be a short-term cash fund but operated as a long-term fund, and as a result, suffered the $1.7 billion (22%) loss in value. Orange County and numerous other local entities issued debt, much of it general obligation, to fund highly speculative invest-ments in the OCIP.

Principles of Debt Management

Neither long-term nor short-term debt should be sold to supply capital to investment pools. Long-term debt should be issued to finance long-term capital investment projects. Short-term debt should be issued to smooth over short-term cash flow mismatches. Because of the large, binding, and often long-term nature of debt obligations, debt issuance and management practices should be guided by a debt policy based on sound public account-ability and financial economic principles.

Specifically, the sale of state and local debt should be guided by four basic principles: accountability, equity, efficiency, and effectiveness (Johnson, 1996). *Public accountability* refers to the basic premise that the people responsible for repaying a debt obligation should have a say in incurring the obligation. There should be effective vehicles for citizen participation in debt issuance decisions that enable taxpayers to hold government officials strictly accountable for debt incurred on their behalf. Violating this accountability principle can result in disastrous consequences for taxpayers and investors, as described below. *Equity* is also a very important guiding principle in selling debt. The equity principle is based on the premise that those not benefiting from a project financed with debt proceeds should not have to pay for it; liability for public debt should be limited to the beneficiaries of the services bought with it. *Efficiency* refers to selling debt at the lowest possible cost, and *effectiveness* refers to generating a sufficient amount of capital when needed.

CASH INFLOWS TO THE OCIP AND FUND MANAGEMENT

Money flowed into the OCIP from more than 100 participants, including sixty school districts, thirty-seven cities, and eleven water districts, as listed in Table 1. The investment return performance of the OCIP was so spectacular, surpassing the return on the much larger state investment pool over a twenty-two-year period, 9.4–8.4% (Jorian, 1995), that municipalities outside Orange County clamored to get in.

The OCIP investment policy allowed for the purchase of a variety of securities, with limitations as to exposure, maturity, and credit rating for each type of security. Money deposited in the pool belonged to participants, based on amounts deposited and average daily balances. The investment pool, in common with twenty-nine similar pools maintained by other state and local governments around the nation, was not regulated by the federal government, as are the mutual funds that the pools so much resemble, but was regulated by state limits on investment instruments.

The advantage of hindsight suggests the importance of the innocuous statement that the pool may enter into various reverse repurchase agreements that are essentially leveraged

Table 1 Orange County Investment Pool (OCIP) Participants

Entity	Amount contributed (millions of dollars)	Share of fund (%)
Orange County	$2,760.3	37.2
Orange County Transportation Authority	1,092.9	14.7
School districts (60 in all),[a] including	1,048.0	14.1
Irvine Unified S.D.	105.8	1.7
North Orange County Community College	98.9	1.6
Newport-Mesa Unified S.D.	82.4	1.3
Capistrano Unified S.D.	75.0	1.2
Cities (37 in all), including	1,043.0	14.1
City of Irvine	198.1	2.7
City of Anaheim	169.6	2.3
City of Santa Ana	150.7	2.0
Water districts (11 in all), including	516.2	7.0
Irvine Ranch W.D.	300.9	4.1
Orange County W.D.	118.4	1.6
Orange County Sanitation District	441.0	6.0
Orange County Employees Retirement System	133.4	1.8
Other districts and agencies	382.6	5.2

Note: Figures are through Nov. 30, 1994.
[a] Includes education-related funds and agencies.
Source: *New York Times*, Dec. 7, 1994

investments; at the time, one might presume that such investments would be used appropriately as defensive measures (hedges) to prevent losses, but that proved not to be the case. The reverse repurchase agreements were used to leverage securities in the portfolio to bolster return. In 1979 the state legislature, ironically with intense lobbying from Robert Citron, amended Cal Gov Code sec. 53601 to give county treasurers' authority, with approval from their board of supervisors, to borrow money through reverse repurchase agreements.

The pool was the responsibility of the Orange County Board of Supervisors, but was really managed by the county treasurer. The board apparently lacked any significant capacity, or will, to supervise complex financial arrangements.* Moreover, the board did not oversee the daily management of the portfolio once allowable investment instruments and general reporting requirements were set. The treasurer was required by law to report officially every month on the status of the fund to the board and pool participants. Over his tenure Citron reported only sporadically, but it appears that even these reports were not reviewed carefully by the board. Had the board understood the principles of fund management, surely it would have raised questions about the arbitrage notes, which are certainly at odds with the fundamentals of good financial management.

---

* Indeed, in a recent report commissioned by the Orange County grand jury, Knoll Associates blasts the board, stating that "the foundations of this financial disaster were clearly built on ineffective management of, and oversight controls over, Treasury operations" (*Bond Buyer*, Sept. 11, 1995).

Table 2   Taxable Arbitrage Notes Sold in Fiscal Year 1994–1995 to Fund the Orange County Investment Pool (OCIP)

Issue date	Amount (in thousands of dollars)	Issuer/purpose	Credit rating	Interest rate structure	Under writer
4/5/94	$95,000	Anaheim TRANS	MIG-1 SP-1+	FR[a]	RPR[b]
6/14/94	42,180	Orange County BOE	SP-1+	N/A	RPR
6/14/94	54,500	Irvine USD TRANs	SP-1+	VR[c]	RPR
6/14/94	46,960	Newport Mesa USD TRANs	SP-1+	VR	RPR
6/14/94	56,285	North-Orange County Community College District TRANs	SP-1+	VR	RPR
7/8/94	600,000	Orange County TRANs	P-1 A-1+	VR	ML[d]
7/20/94	111,000	TEETER PLAN notes	P-1 A-1+	SPA[e]/VR	ML
7/27/94	62,455	Irvine TRANs	P-1+	VR	RPR
8/2/94	100,000	Orange County Flood Control District	P-1 A-1+	VR	SB[f]/ML
8/24/94	100,000	Placentia–Yorba Linda USD TRANs	P-1 A-1+	VR	Citicorp
Total	$1,218,380				

[a] FR: fixed rate; [b] RPR: Rauscher Pierce Refsnes, Inc.; [c] VR: variable rate; [d] ML: Merrill Lynch & Co.; [e] SPA: Standby Purchase Agreement from the Orange County Investment Pool (OCIP); [f] SB: Smith Barney, Inc.
Source: "MuniIRIS," by DPC Data, Inc.

The Arbitrage Notes

Local entities may invest surplus funds in the OCIP (Cal. Gov. Code sec. 53601). Districts and agencies within Orange County were authorized by California law (Cal. Gov. Code sec. 53684), but not required, to place surplus funds on deposit with the county treasurer. In addition to these surplus revenues, many issuers borrowed short-term money in the municipal securities market for the sole purpose of investing the proceeds in the OCIP. Local issuers sold a mix of taxable and tax-exempt securities. Many of these securities, listed in Table 2, were variable rate general obligation taxable arbitrage notes.

The pool received $1.2 billion of taxable arbitrage notes, almost all variable rate, sold from April 1994 through August 1994, during an increasing interest rate environment.* The full cost of these notes was not known in advance, since the interest rate on the notes

---

* The Federal Reserve raised the discount rate from 3.00%, where it had been since July 1992, to 3.50% in May 1994, 4.00% in August, and 4.75% in November. After a long and steep descent from 11% in February 1989 to 5.50% in October 1993, the prime rate increased to 6.25% in February 1994. It increased steeply throughout 1994 to 6.75% in March, 7.25% in May, 7.75% in August, and finally, with one more prime rate hike, to 8.50% in November.

floated. Ironically, as rising rates caused the interest costs of the notes to increase, the market value of the pool declined.

Many pool participants sold taxable notes for the expected arbitrage gains from investing note proceeds in the OCIP. As a matter of debt issuance policy, the sale of notes solely to invest in the OCIP is imprudent. Moreover, the sale of taxable securities, which are much more costly to sell than tax-exempt securities, borders on negligence. In addition, public accountability was absent on the sale of these notes, since the risky arbitrage strategy was undertaken without getting direct voter approval. In prior years many school districts in the county had successfully executed this risky arbitrage strategy, selling securities and investing the proceeds at a higher rate to reduce fiscal pressure on their operating budgets. These issuers, however, were not bonding out future "excess" or "surplus" revenues, they were bonding out revenues already dedicated to essential services. Orange County was also using pool returns to finance basic expenditures. Indeed, in fiscal year 1994–1995 Orange County budgeted $33 million more in investment income than in property tax revenue.

The purchase of the taxable notes is also suspect. Many school district arbitrage notes had a principal value exceeding 40% of annual revenues. As an extreme illustration, the 1994 Newport-Mesa $46,960,000 note issue accounted for 55.9% of its 1993 revenues. Such arbitrage notes, despite being backed by a "GO" repayment pledge, possessed negligible revenue repayment support and served no essential purpose.

Surprisingly enough, both Moody's Investors Service and Standard & Poor's assigned prime quality ratings to the notes, Moody's MIG-1 and Standard & Poor's SP-1 +.* Certainly in hindsight, the school district taxable arbitrage notes were not prime quality investments. In addition, the credit rating agencies unwittingly contributed to the artificial propping up of the fund by requiring borrowers to put note proceeds into the OCIP in order for their notes to receive a prime credit rating (Jorian, 1995).

County of Orange, California, $600,000,000 1994–1995 Taxable Notes

On July 8, 1994, Robert Citron, on behalf of Orange County, sold $600 million of taxable arbitrage notes. The $600 million taxable arbitrage notes received the highest credit rating from both Moody's and Standard & Poor's. According to the official statement accompanying the note issue, a number of investment and legal firms were involved in bringing the issue to market. Leifer Capital provided financial and marketing advice, with Brown & Wood acting as its legal counsel; Merrill Lynch, Pierce, Fenner & Smith, Inc. was the underwriter; and LeBoeuf, Lamb, Greene & MacRae acted as bond counsel.

There were clear indications of serious problems in the OCIP prior to the issuance of the $600 million taxable arbitrage notes. Indeed, it appears that the $600 million taxable notes were sold to provide the OCIP with additional liquidity to meet likely collateral calls in the near future and/or to purchase securities to support additional reverse repurchase agreements in an attempt to bolster yield.

---

* According to Moody's, the MIG-1 rating designation "denotes the best quality. There is strong protection by established cash flows, superior liquidity support or demonstrated broad-based access to the market for refinancing" (Moody's, 1993). According to Standard & Poor's, the SP-1 + rating designation indicates that "the degree of safety regarding timely payment is strong. Those determined to possess extremely strong safety characteristics are denoted with a plus sign (+)" (Standard & Poor's, 1994).

Market interest rates started increasing early in 1994 and began eating away at the market value and liquidity of the OCIP. In March 1994 the fund suffered its first collateral call for $140 million on its reverse repurchase agreements (*Bond Buyer*, April 22, 1994). The pool suffered additional collateral calls of $75 million in April and $515 million in May. At this point the fund still had significant cash reserves. In the rising interest rate environment from August 1994 to the end of November 1994, however, the fund faced $385 million in collateral calls and absorbed approximately a $1 billion loss on structured notes, thus shrinking cash reserves from $1.4 billion to about $350 million. The OCIP faced $1.25 billion in additional collateral calls on December 6, 1995, and decided, rather than come up with the money, to file for bankruptcy protection under Chapter 9 of the U.S. Bankruptcy Code.

DISCLOSURE ON THE TAXABLE NOTES AND DUE DILIGENCE

Disclosure on the $600 million taxable notes appears to be substantial but incomplete. Disclosure is provided to the market through the process of origination. Origination involves all the tasks necessary to get the securities ready for sale, including determining the terms and structure of the issue and developing the official statement. The official statement, or prospectus, is designed to provide potential investors with all the necessary information to make an informed investment decision regarding the securities for sale. It is the issuer's disclosure statement to potential investors, but is usually prepared by the financial advisor or underwriter contracted with by the issuer.

The official statement for the $600 million taxable note issue clearly indicates that proceeds from the sale of the taxable notes were to be used to invest in the OCIP; in other words, the notes were not being used to fund capital improvements, but were sold for arbitrage purposes. The official statement also contained a separate section on the OCIP that lays out a number of items important to potential investors, including the stated buy-and-hold investment policy of the county and the fact that pool assets were valued at original cost on March 31, 1994, and June 16, 1994, at $7.61 billion and $7.71 billion, respectively. Based on the manner of the presentation of this material, the casual observer might infer that the true value of the protfolio had increased from March 1994 to June 1994. Actually, while portfolio holdings did increase, leverage was increasing at a much more rapid pace, from 1.5 in June 1990 to 2.7 in November 1994.*

The official statement also contained an appendix with the county's audited financial statement dated December 14, 1993, covering the July 1, 1992, through June 30, 1993, fiscal year. It showed the value of fund investments to be $15.1 billion. The notes to the financial statements included an itemized listing of investments held in the portfolio, including repurchase agreements and investments held by broker-dealers under *reverse repurchase/securities lending agreements*, which, according to the financial statements, at that point totaled $7.5 billion. So, at the time the $600 million taxable issue went to market, the audited financial statements disclosed that almost 50% of total fund value was

---

* Leveraging involves making a financial investment with borrowed funds. In this case, Jorian defines the leverage ratio as "the total value of securities purchased divided by the capital initially invested." The leverage figures are based on portfolio holdings and borrowing of $3.5 billion and $1.7 billion, respectively, for June 1990, and $7.6 billion and $13 billion for November 1994 (Jorian, 1995).

leveraged in reverse repurchase/securities lending agreements in the custody of private firms, not under the legal control of the OCIP. In spite of what would appear to be a clear element of danger, the rating agencies gave the issue their highest credit rating.

There was no disclosure in the official statement, however, of the $730 million in collateral calls through May 1994, or any disclosure of the likely impact on the fund from future collateral calls if interest rates continued to increase. Clearly, any recent fund transactions that adversely affected the principal value of the fund or its liquidity position, such as large collateral calls, should have been reported in the official statement. It should be noted that at this point the likelihood of the fund experiencing future collateral calls was predictable and highly likely; moreover, their significant adverse impact on fund value and liquidity was quantifiable. Financial disaster from future collateral calls was therefore preventable. Indeed, according to an April 22, 1994, *Bond Buyer* article, almost three months prior to the sale of the $600 million taxable notes, Matthew Raabe, the Orange County assistant treasurer, confidently stated that

> A total of $1.5 billion in liquid investments has been set aside to cover collateral calls. . . . To position for future collateral calls, the fund will expand its liquidity by $500 million to $1 billion in the coming months. . . . This is more liquidity than we normally have. . . . But we want to be ready because we think rates are going to rise a little bit more.

Raabe does not explicitly state the source of the $500 million cash infusion, but the timing and size of the $600 million taxable issue is too close for mere coincidence. With the sale of the notes, Raabe appears to have believed that the fund had unlimited liquidity, despite being clearly counseled in writing to the contrary by Merrill Lynch. In the March 31, 1993, derivative pricing report, Michael Stamenson, director of Merrill Lynch's municipality unit unambiguously warned Citron that due to the leverage in the OCIP a rise in short-term interest rates would devastate the prices of securities in the portfolio.* Unfortunately, Merrill Lynch's warning fell on deaf ears. The following question begs asking, however: as underwriters of the $600 million taxable notes, why didn't Merrill Lynch disclose in the official statement the interest rate risks in the portfolio they illustrated in detail in their February 23, 1994, presentation to Citron?

Practices involved in the sale of municipal securities are covered under the antifraud provisions of Section 17(a) of the Securities Act and Section 10(b) of the Securities Exchange Act. Rule 10b–5(b) of this act prohibits any person, including municipal issuers, brokers, and dealers, from making a false or misleading statement of material fact, or from *omitting* any material facts necessary to make statements made, in light of the circumstances under which they were made, not misleading in connection with the offering, purchase, or sale of any security.

The large and recurring collateral calls prior to the sale of the notes were material events, especially since it was known to all parties involved in the issuance that note proceeds were to be used to fund the OCIP. Significant interest rate risks in a portfolio should be reported along with the composition of the portfolio. Simply providing an itemized listing of the securities in the pool without disclosing recent pool events that provide evidence of the risks of the securities in the pool is misleading.

---

* This memo is included in a package of materials Merrill Lynch released to the public that includes correspondence between Merrill Lynch and Citron.

Merrill Lynch, the underwriter of the issue, argues that it was not involved in preparing the disclosure documents and was awarded the bonds at the last minute after it informed the county that it would buy the bonds at a lower price than Paine Webber, Inc. Even so, SEC Rule 15c2–12 requires underwriters to obtain and review the official statement prior to purchasing the securities. That would seem to require managing underwriters to identify any omission and add any material facts before purchasing the securities.

Moreover, it is standard practice in negotiated offerings for underwriters to perform due diligence investigations. *Due diligence* refers to the underwriter's "diligence" in ascertaining the accuracy of statements made by the issuer during disclosure. According to the SEC, in negotiated offerings underwriters have an affirmative obligation to perform due diligence investigations (Fippinger, 1994). In due diligence investigations, underwriters gather information about the issuer from a variety of sources, including personal interviews and official and unofficial issuer documents. The due diligence investigation sets up an "adversarial" relationship between the underwriter and the issuer that is designed to produce the most complete disclosure of information. Any financial advisor and underwriter involved in bringing the issue to market and selling it to investors has an obligation to perform due diligence and disclose all material risks. The rating agencies also appear to be negligent, because they knew of the collateral calls, but believed that the fund had enough liquidity not to affect debt obligations (*Wall Street Journal*, Dec. 6, 1994). With the benefit of hindsight, we can say they were wrong.

SUMMARY AND CONCLUSION

The municipal market will feel the effects of the Orange County debacle for some time to come. The lessons learned and implemented should help to improve our financial management practices well into the next century. The incident reminds us that cash and debt management are intertwined because the poor execution of one has a direct and potentially adverse impact on the other. Another lesson that we seem to forget is that government financial management is important and prudent financial management cannot be taken for granted; moreover, financial management has a direct and lasting impact on a government's ability to deliver public services.

In reviewing the cash management failings of Orange County officials, it goes without saying that investment managers should pursue the safety of principal first, liquidity second, and then, and only then, yield—unlike Orange County officials, who pursued a yield, yield, and only yield strategy. Moreover, leveraged investments that put operating funds at risk should be *prohibited* for short-term investment pools; there simply is no need for public sector operating funds to be spent on leveraged investments.

Also, investment pools should be marked to market on a frequent, perhaps weekly, basis. Public sector investment pools should be run with the objective of maintaining a stable principal value and should adopt the equivalent of the stable net asset value per share model used in the business sector. Public investment pools should also use more sophisticated risk management techniques, such as the use of duration and convexity to understand and limit portfolio interest rate volatility. In addition, the investment pool should be closely monitored by a third party or parties, such as a knowledgeable investment board, and there should be regular and stringent accounting, auditing, and reporting requirements.

Finally, Orange County violated appropriate debt management practices. Debt sold primarily for arbitrage purchases should be prohibited in all circumstances, and taxable 60 bonds should be prohibited without direct voter approval. On any debt issue, full and complete disclosure of all material events is required and the market should demand nothing less from all parties involved in bringing securities to market.

REVIEW QUESTIONS

1. What are the principles of cash management? Did Orange County adhere to these principles? If not, why not?
2. What are the principles of debt management? Did Orange County adhere to these principles in its debt management activities? If not, why not?
3. Describe the major reasons that led to the bankruptcy of the county and the consequences that resulted from them.
4. To construct a redevelopment plan, what specific courses of action should the government take into consideration? Why?
5. What lessons can be learned from the Orange County experience?

REFERENCES

Altman, B. (1994). California official defends his strategy of managing pooled investment fund. *Bond Buyer* (*April 22*), 1.

Fippinger, R. (1994). *The Securities Law of Public Finance*. New York: Practicing Law Institute.

Johnson, C. (1996). Administering public debt. In J. Perns (ed.), *Handbook of Public Administration*. San Francisco: Jossey Bass.

Jorian, P. (1995). *Big Bets Gone Bad, Derivatives and Bankruptcy in Orange County*. San Diego: Academic.

Mikesell, J. (1995). *Fiscal Administration: Analysis and Applications for the Public Sector*. Belmont, CA: Wadsworth.

Moody's Investors Service. (1993). *An Issuer's Guide to the Rating Process*. New York: Moody's Investors Service.

Standard & Poor's. (1994). *Municipal Finance Criteria*. New York: Standard & Poor's.

Utley, M. (1995a). Supervisors bear brunt of blame for losses, grand jury says. *Bond Buyer* (*Sept. 11*). 2.

Utley, N. (1995b). Peat Marwick sued by Orange County. *Bond Buyer* (*Dec. 21*), 32.

Vogel, T. Jr. (1994). Orange County fund had green ratings light. *Wall Street Journal* (*Dec. 6*), C1.

38

The Gordian Knot of a Project Revenue Bond Default

W. Bartley Hildreth
Wichita State University, Wichita, Kansas, U.S.A.

Revenue bonds finance projects that are designed to yield a specified revenue stream that will cover both operational expenses and periodic debt service. These bond deals involve complex arrangements regarding the generation and dispersal of project-related funds. To ensure that all parties understand these arrangements, the terms are written into the record through bond covenants that legally bind the parties. A project's financial viability is assessed through a reading of these (and other disclosure) documents. What happens when the assumptions upon which the financing is based do not materialize? What happens when the project turns into an unreliable facility with all parties contemplating legal action to minimize their respective liability? This case study is of one such situation. After reviewing the project's financing structure and the default that occurred, as well as the resulting dilemmas facing a new mayor, the case study of a waste-to-energy facility presents the workout as implemented in a financial reorganization.

DEBT AND DEFAULT

A wide array of parties are involved in debt creation and management. The participants include the issuer (or the ultimate risk bearer if different from the issuer), the investors with funds to loan for a price, investment bankers to buy the issuer's bonds and sell them to the investors, a bond counsel willing to issue an opinion on the legality of the debt instruments, a trustee to monitor the issuer on behalf of the bondholders, credit raters to assess the probability of default, and (very infrequently) state and federal government oversight agencies. The ability of the participants to work together in a complex market is not tested just during issuance of the securities but also later, in the course of operating the project which was financed by the bonds that still are being repaid through periodic debt service payments (Hildreth, 1987; 1993).

Debt creation imposes an explicit burden of debt repayment. Sometimes the debt repayment conditions fail to be honored, resulting in default. The general concept of default

I wish to acknowledge the unique contributions of Thomas C. Sawyer to my understanding of this case.

597

is a single, distinct occasion involving nonpayment of a financial obligation. Default is either failure to repay the principal amount borrowed or to pay scheduled interest payments on time. In both cases, a delay in payment by only a few days still meets the definition of a default even though the delay imposes a negligible economic impact on the bondholders. Continuing nonpayment of principal or interest imposes a much more significant burden.

Default is also defined by obligations, duties, and responsibilities that are more procedural than economic. The obligations are usually detailed in specific covenants that bind the debtor to particular practices and policies, and are combined into a document termed an indenture. Covenants include pledges to transfer and retain a specified stock of funds in certain restricted accounts; to maintain levels of property and casualty insurance; to revise rates to levels sufficient to cover all expenses and coverage requirements; and numerous other features designed to protect the assets covering the bondholders' claims. Violation of any single covenant results in an "event of default." According to Spiotto (1993: Section 13.43): "An 'Event of Default' is the agreed upon occurrence that allows the bondholders or their representative (indenture trustee) to take appropriate action, including the institution of the remedies set forth in the indenture." The trustee's remedies include a range of legal action to force the debtor to take the steps contained in the indenture; assert the trustee's control over the project to protect bondholders' interests; and/ or accelerate as due and payable all outstanding bonds. As pointed out by a representative of Moody's Investors Service (Smith, 1979: 245–246), such obligations seek "to prevent default" rather than merely to enforce the payment of delinquencies. In other words, an issuer pledges to follow certain procedural terms and conditions; failure to follow the covenants (often termed a "technical" default) alerts the bondholders to the possibility of repayment problems. The indenture thus serves to anticipate repayment problems before the bondholders incur actual economic loss.

The municipal finance community asserts that a technical default is less significant than a default because of the distinction between the violation of procedural covenants and the nonpayment of principal and interest. (See Advisory Commission on Intergovernmental Relations, 1985; Feldstein, 1983.) While not necessarily differing on the apparent economic difference between the two, the law is more precise and less tied to economic calculations. Spiotto, perhaps the most prominent municipal default legal expert, clarifies that a "default ripens into an Event of Default after notice has been given to the issuer for the commencement of the grace period and, after a lapse of time, the default remains uncured" (Spiotto, 1993: Section 13,42).

While defaults may appear to be distinct and final, Spiotto (1993: Section 13.41) isolates three phases of default. The first phase involves gathering information on the reasons for the default and correcting any questions regarding the security for the debt. For example, if a revenue source appears ineffective, corrective action might be possible to preserve the probability of repayment. The second phase of a default is the workout, where the bondholders and the issuer attempt to resolve their differences. Failure in the second phase leads to what is generally considered the nature of a default. In the third phase of a default, bondholders assert their rights to obtain payment, including calling the bonds due and payable immediately (acceleration of payments) and using the full force of litigation to uphold their interests.

This case study examines a successful use of a workout to resolve a municipal default. This default was labeled technical since all principal and interest payments were made on time, albeit from sources unanticipated in the original financing. A case study such as this one is important because the ability of public officials to resolve financial dilemmas such as a default is critical to governing in resource-scarce environments.

A DEFAULTED WASTE-TO-ENERGY SYSTEM

Communities face solid waste disposal problems due to landfill site and capacity constraints. One alternative embraced by many communities is to burn solid waste to generate energy (either steam or electricity) for sale to business, industry, and other customers. Currently, there are 142 waste-to-energy facilities in operation (Kiser, 1992). At the forefront of this movement was a midwestern city's recycle energy system (RES). The RES was designed to dispose of 1000 tons per day of garbage and trash by shredding, removing ferrous materials for sale, and burning the residue to produce steam for sale as a source of energy. This is termed a refuse-derived fuel facility since it processes and produces fuel on site. There are sixteen in operation throughout the country (Kiser, 1992). Further distinguishing itself, RES was one of the first (and last) strictly public refuse recovery facilities financed solely by revenues generated by the project itself, including fees for dumping garbage into the RES as well as the fees generated from selling the output steam.

The city turned to the RES option for dealing with a looming solid waste disposal problem given its diminishing landfill capacity and increasing environmental regulations. The event that accelerated public debate was a private utility firm's decision in 1971 to abandon its downtown steam system unless it could secure substantial steam rate increases. Steam customers joined the city in opposing the utility's abandonment request. As a result, the city was eventually deeded the physical assets for operation of the existing steam loop. Building on this opportunity, the city decided to build a modern resource recovery plant to dispose of municipal solid waste and generate the steam required for the loop.

The city demonstrated caution in entering into this new venture. It engaged a local engineering firm to conduct a preliminary feasibility study, and public officials conducted field trips to view operating facilities in the United States and Canada. There were even hints the facility might make a profit for use on public services. After inviting nationally known engineering firms to present design proposals, the city awarded a design contract to the same local firm that had prepared the earlier study. These actions solidified the city's May 1974 view that the RES was "an innovative, timely, and financially attractive step into the future for solving the area's solid waste disposal problems." Engineering plans and specifications for the RES were received and let out for bid in late 1974, with bids received in February 1975.

Only after deciding to proceed with the project in 1975 did the city and bond counsel begin to develop financing plans. The city's initial plan was to issue revenue bonds as it had done for its water and sewer systems. This path was squashed by New York City's 1975 fiscal crisis, the resulting calls for better bond disclosure practices, and the near default of a similar waste-to-energy system in another state. These events led the city to seek a state–local partnership with tax-exempt securities issued by a state financial intermediary (or conduit) with the proceeds loaned to the city for constructing the project. Under this arrangement, the city would contractually agree to repay the loan from project revenues, but it would own the facility without a mortgage on the facility securing the loan or the bonds. Unable to secure the conduit agency's bonds with the city's general fund, alternative security was required that included the negotiation of long-term steam contracts and waste disposal assurances.

As is too often found with public power projects (Jones, 1984; Feldstein, 1983), this one faced technological, economic, and operational risks. The technology was unproven, the economics were uncertain, and the managerial ability to deal with the complex system was questionable. On Standard & Poor's (1984) risk assessment scale, this resource recovery facility scored high. The eventual result was a waste-to-energy project that entered into technical default on its state agency-issued municipal securities.

The Project Financing Framework and the Technical Default

In December 1976, a state statutory authority—the state water development authority (WDA)—issued $46 million of municipal bonds to help finance the city's RES. A series of legal agreements secured the bonds. Financing was made pursuant to a *trust indenture* between the WDA and a bank trustee named by WDA. The bank trustee's normal duty was ministerial, merely to process semiannual debt service payments to bondholders. A *cooperative agreement* by and among the WDA, the city, and the county specified that proceeds from the sale of the WDA bonds were loaned by the WDA to the city to construct and operate the RES. The RES was to generate revenues from a tipping fee charged to the city and other haulers to dump solid wastes into the RES and a fee charged to users of steam produced by the RES. The financing was thus premised on expected revenues on the inflow side (tipping fees) and the output side (steam user rates).

Steam customers were classified into three classes: uninterruptible, interruptible, and surplus. Uninterruptible customers were those located on the old steam loop in the central business district (CBD); they had no alternative heating sources. Interruptible customers were a downtown state university and a large nonprofit hospital, each a large user with existing natural gas alternatives. The surplus, or third, class was composed of a single customer, a large international manufacturing firm headquartered in the city (but with little actual manufacturing at the site). A series of contracts entered into by these parties specified that the three classes of customers agreed to pay rates at a level sufficient to cover the operation and maintenance expenses and to provide 1.5 times coverage of annual debt service. The contracts included "take or pay" provisions specifying that the contract customers would pay for their contracted level of steam even if they did not use the steam.

The RES revenues, including tipping fees and steam fees, were earmarked for operational expenses and to make payments on the WDA-to-city loan, which in turn served as the security and funds for the WDA bonds. The city did not extend its full faith and credit guarantee to the WDA bonds; the WDA bonds were state agency-issued project revenue bonds.

To ensure an adequate supply of refuse, both the city and county agreed in the cooperative agreement to enact ordinances requiring all solid waste collected in their respective jurisdictions to be disposed of at the RES after payment of the required tipping fee. As required, the city enacted what is termed a "flow control" ordinance. It was challenged by several private landfill operators and private solid waste haulers as being in violation of federal antitrust laws, the "takings" clause of the 14th Amendment, and other laws. In spite of two appeals to the U.S. Supreme Court, the validity of the city's ordinance was ultimately upheld in 1985. In contrast to the city's affirmative stance in support of the flow control provisions of the cooperative agreement, the county resisted enacting a similar flow control ordinance.

Scheduled to begin operation in 1979, the RES was not totally operational until January 1983. During the delay, steam was generated, but the garbage handling operation did not work as conceived. Major design and mechanical problems required extensive modification. Originally estimated to cost $56,000,000, the financing package included $46,000,000 from the WDA bonds and $5 million each from the city and the county from separately issued general obligation securities. At completion, however, the cost had escalated to almost $100 million.* To make up the difference, the city contributed the proceeds of $8 million more of general obligation bonds, the WDA added $16 million, and a congressionally mandated U.S. Environmental Protection Agency (EPA) grant to the city (a reallocation of an unused grant) added $19.7 million.

The delay in achieving operating status, as well as other problems (some to be reviewed later), led to the situation in which the RES did not produce the revenues required to make all loan payments. This resulted in a continuing series of events of default under the cooperative agreement, triggering corresponding events of default under the indenture. There was no interruption of payments of principal and interest due to the bondholders, however. Instead of project revenues, the debt service reserve fund (stocked by some of the original WDA bond proceeds) was tapped to pay debt payments in 1980. City and WDA contributions made the difference in 1981 and 1982; the EPA grant was used for 1983 and set aside for 1984 payments. This left no clear special source of funds from which to make bond payments in 1985.

Technical default actually occurred in February 1981, when the RES did not have sufficient project funds to make the scheduled loan payment pursuant to the cooperative agreement, although the funds were made available from other sources, as outlined above. The event of default under the cooperative agreement and the event of default under the indenture gave rise to certain remedies under the indenture. During the summer of 1981, the bondholders' bank trustee asserted one remedy by assuming management of the RES in order to preserve the interests of the bondholders and to gain the $16 million infusion from the WDA. In this pressure-packed period, a long-term *operating service agreement* was signed by the trustee, the city, and a private waste management company. The firm agreed to retrofit the RES by making its operations simpler, and once the RES passed a thirty-day performance test (which it did in January 1993), to operate the RES for ten years under a "cost plus fee" contract. The fee was set low in the initial years, but escalated at a rapid pace. An incentive fee also was included in the package.

To assist in its duties, the trustee engaged the services of legal counsel, a consulting engineering firm, and a national accounting firm. The fees for the trustee and this entourage, as well as the operator's fixed fee, received first claim over RES revenues. The costs for the trustee to assume active management and monitoring thus increased the cost structure of the RES. Although modifications to the RES were made and mechanical difficulties were significantly reduced, the system continued to incur operating deficits.

The City's RES Dilemma

In late 1983, a newly elected mayor assessed the realities of the RES. While the RES was an ongoing question in the mayoral campaign, it was not a decisive matter in the voters' rejection of the incumbent. Early in the transition period, the following facts of the city's dilemma were outlined.

---

* A rule of thumb used "within the industry to 'ballpark' the construction cost of waste-to-energy facilities is $100,000 for each ton of daily processing capacity" (National League of Cities, 1986: 59). The RES was designed to handle 1000 tons per day.

The cooperative agreement among the city, county, and WDA required project revenues to provide 150% coverage of WDA debt service. At the time, however, achieving just 100% coverage of the debt service would require steam rate increases of approximately 40% for the uninterruptible customers, 103% for the interruptible customers, and 153% for the surplus sales customer. Even these rate levels assumed that a stock of funds remaining from the special EPA grant would be used to pay all debt service obligations during 1984 since the RES could not generate sufficient funds on its own.

The trustee proposed to force the city to impose rate increases on January 1, 1984—the first day of a new mayoral term. While not sufficient to meet debt service coverage requirements, the proposed rate increases were set at approximately 13% for the uninterruptible customers, 51% for the interruptible customers, and 137% for the surplus sales customer. Tipping fees—the fees paid by both the city and private garbage haulers to dump their loads into the RES—were to increase 10%. This schedule of rate increase also assumed that the remaining federal grant proceeds would cover the year's debt service requirements. The trustee projected that the rate increases were sufficient to get the RES through 1984, given the assumption that all users would continue the current level of services, but at the higher rates—thus assuming no price inelasticity of demand and no flight to substitute energy sources. A further assumption in the scenario was that the RES operation would meet its budget estimates, including no fires or unexpected operational problems (both high-risk assumptions, given past history).

In pursuit of revenue maximization, the RES sought to maximize the composition of the refuse supply. A basic flow of refuse was required to run the plant at the desired level of capacity. By the original financing agreement, the city had to use the facility for its collected garbage and pay a tipping fee to the RES. The city paid the RES the tipping fees for residential garbage collected by the city. Pending final resolution of litigation, the city was not enforcing the flow control ordinance, which required private haulers of commercial wastes to also use the RES and pay the tipping fee. A continuous flow of garbage into the RES was required also to generate an uninterrupted flow of steam. Any break in the garbage flow or any downtime due to mechanical problems resulted in the burning of gas to produce steam—a wasteful and uneconomical energy conversion. The RES reverted to this costly step many times due to mechanical problems.

Given these constraints, the RES had an incentive to attract premium-paying waste dumpers. Accepting out-of-state wastes arranged through brokers was one result. Despite local newspaper headlines, the RES accepted New Jersey waste that did not meet New Jersey disposal laws but complied with state laws governing the RES. A form of such waste was saw-oil, or sawdust laced with certain kinds of oils (including flavors and fragrances, ball bearing and grinding oils, synthetic and organic lubricants, and waste oil bottom sludges). There was a twofold advantage in accepting this waste: it generated a premium payment for the right to dump the waste into the RES, and the oil-based product had a high burning yield—it generated more energy than regular wastes.

Despite the planned rate increases and the attempt to attract high-paying waste, regular and periodic rate increases would be necessary to produce net operating income (operating revenues less operating expenses). Part of the problem was the expense structure. A major RES cost was the contract operator's fixed fee: $130,000 in 1983, $550,000 in 1984, $1 million in 1985, and $1.5 million in 1986. The fixed fee levels agreed to in the long-term operating service agreement were purported to give the private operator a return for assuming the business risk of making the RES operationally viable. Even with modest price increases on utilities and other expenses, the fixed fee levels would require significant increases in operating revenues each year to cover escalating cost factors.

Even if achieved, a positive net operating income was not sufficient to ensure the financial viability of the RES. The loan repayments to WDA and the required stocking of both an equipment and replacement fund and a debt service reserve account constituted additional expenses *not* included within the net operating income calculation. The 1984 debt service on WDA bonds was $4.266 million; stocking the other accounts required more funds.

Under the operator's contract, if the operator budgeted an upcoming year's positive net operating income (NOI) that exceeded the forecasted NOI figure contained in the operating service agreement, the operator would receive an incentive fee set at 60% of the difference between the forecasted NOI and the budgeted NOI. The probability of such an incentive payment was remote, given the financial problems besetting the RES.

Under the contract the operator prepared a budget, formally called an "annual forecast of costs," for submission to the city and the trustee by October 1 of each year. Both the city and the trustee had to give the operator written notice of any budget disputes by November 1—a one-month review period. The contract specified that when the parties could not amicably resolve the dispute by December 1 the monthly payment to the operator "shall, until the dispute is resolved, be prepared, submitted and paid on the basis of the Annual Forecast of Costs as submitted by the Operator." The operator did not have an obligation to submit a budget generating a net operating income or one that necessarily covered debt service. In fact, the operator had no control over setting RES rates, yet the trustee sought to pressure the city to set higher rates to cover budget shortfalls and debt service requirements. The trustee's form of pressure was a threat to call all bonds due and payable immediately if rate increases were not imposed, an act surely to set off all types of legal warfare.

The mayor had no effective budgetary control over the RES budget because of the trustee's assumption of management responsibility. In this strong mayor–council city, neither the mayor nor his appointed finance director were able to monitor costs and, if necessary, make day-to-day, week-to-week, or month-to-month budget cuts to offset revenue shortfalls or expense overruns, neither did the city have control over the RES accounting system, bank accounts, or billing system. All of these controls were taken over by the trustee when the bonds went into technical default. In fact, the city only received monthly variance reports on expected versus actual costs for the preceding month. Since all steam users paid their bills directly to a trustee-controlled bank account, the city did not know the cash flow position of project funds until reported later by the operator and the trustee's financial advisor.

The operator submitted a monthly invoice to the trustee (with a copy to the city) for payment of costs to be incurred in the *ensuing* calendar month, as estimated in the annual forecast of costs. As a result, scarce project funds were used to pay for utility fees (a large monthly cost item) before the service was actually used, billed, or paid. For example, the operator would submit the December invoice by November 15, with the invoice paid from project funds by December 1. The RES would use the gas in December, but the operator would not be billed until January 10, with payment due on February 10. The operator thus enjoyed the cash float from December 1 to February 10. This was during a time when interest rates were in the double digits.

Enterprise operations such as the RES are sensitive to rate and usage changes. If users face RES rates exceeding the cost of alternative energy, the economic signal to them is clear. While many steam users lacked boilers or existing alternative energy sources, the return on a capital investment is justified under certain pricing scenarios. Instead of making the investment, the business might just move from the central business district, striking another blow to a struggling down town. If the RES closed down, similar hardships would occur. Furthermore, the city could face possible liability to customers under the concept of utility service abandonment.

As originally envisioned, the demand-side risk of the RES was reduced through "take-or-pay" contracts. Major users entered into contracts specifying their agreement to use the allotted share of RES steam or pay in lieu thereof. For example, a major international manufacturing firm headquartered in the city had a twenty-five-year contract to buy all the excess steam of the RES. Instead of being a captured buyer, however, this user (and others) considered its obligation as one tied to a gas equivalent rate, that pricing of one energy source could lead to a substitution of energy sources. As shown by the experiences of the Washington Public Power Supply System, as economics clash with take-or-pay contracts, litigation ensues (Jones, 1984). Major RES users had quietly put the city and the trustee on notice that they would legally challenge the validity of the contracts if pressed on the point.

Despite the fact that the WDA bonds did not involve the city's full faith and credit guarantee, the city's taxing power supported part of the total cost of the RES. A long-term city cost was debt service on $13,640,000 in unvoted general obligation bonds—$5 million for the original financial commitment and the rest for subsequent capital repair contributions. The city also paid tipping fees to dispose of city-collected residential solid wastes, the cost of hauling the ash generated by burning waste in the RES, and expenses associated with general city "overhead" (supervisory and monitoring time and expense—not an insignificant amount, given the problems imposed on the city by the RES's financial quagmire).

Under one scenario, the city could become the ultimate risk bearer for the WDA bonds. Under the cooperative agreement (among the city, the county and WDA), the city agreed to pay tipping fees to the RES for disposal of the city's residential solid wastes. Assuming the flow control ordinance and steam contracts were all ultimately held invalid and unenforceable, the city would remain its sole user. This "put-or-pay" feature was designed to ensure an adequate supply of refuse. Under such a scenario, the city would have an obligation to charge residential collection customers a rate necessary to offset the tipping fee, up to the contractually agreed to limit of fees "comparable with competitive charges for such services" (surely a phrase worthy of debate, and litigation, if necessary). In such a worst case scenario, the city had the equally unacceptable option of offsetting the necessary residential fee increases with diverted general tax receipts, a pathway to the city's operating budget.

Still, the city had to have a way to dispose of its garbage. The existing city landfill was projected to reach its limit in approximately five to seven years without the RES; it could last twenty to thirty years with the RES. No other landfill site was programmed and it would take three to five years to conduct all the required tests and acquire the necessary permits to site a new landfill. In addition, the state government was intensifying its regulatory powers over landfill activities. The costs to upgrade the landfill escalated yearly. All of these factors pointed to the need to examine the RES as part of the city's entire solid waste collection and disposal system, and not just a subsystem—albeit a costly and troubled one.

Looming over the city was a state law mandating state supervision over municipalities that failed specific fiscal emergency tests. Default on a debt obligation was one fiscal test, so an argument could be made that the city's failure to make the loan payments to WDA in accordance with the cooperative agreement constituted a fiscal emergency condition. The state auditor had the responsibility to issue the determination, but he had not done so; nor did he during the period covered by this case. Had the state auditor acted, a state-created board would have been appointed to oversee the city's entire financial agenda, not just the RES. To some, the city's financial reputation was at greater risk with a financial emergency declaration (see Advisory Commission on Intergovernmental Relations, 1985) than with a long-term default on RES bonds, since those bonds were clearly project revenue bonds, issued by a state agency, not the city.

The city's general financial condition was improving after an economic restructuring that saw many of the major manufacturing facilities close their doors in the preceding decade with a concomitant loss in the city's population. A city income tax provided the bulk of the tax revenue, with collections reflecting anemic local economic conditions. Significant budget reductions were in force for several years. The city's general obligation bond ratings were downgraded in 1980–1981 to an AA by Standard & Poor's Corporation and an A by Moody's Investors Service, Inc. The city was a yearly borrower of funds to finance a systematic and aggressive capital improvements program for which a share of the local income tax was dedicated. The city's finances were in strong shape, given its economic environment, but it had little room to maneuver. Any attempt to bail out the RES at the expense of general services would be a budget-busting exercise that would be both politically unacceptable and likely to erode the city's general bond ratings.

Shortly after being briefed on these legal, financial, and operational aspects of the RES, the newly elected mayor was called to a city hall meeting. This late November meeting was instigated by the trustee and included the trustee's legal entourage as well as the current (outgoing) mayor and key members of his staff, the private RES contractor, the WDA executive director accompanied by the agency's legal advisor, and the city's bond counsel. With the threat of possibly calling the bonds due and payable as of January 1 the trustee sought a commitment from the new mayor to commit to solving the RES financial predicament within a month. With a term of office not to start until January 1 the not-yet-sworn-in mayor could make no such assurances, even if a decision to avoid default had been decided. Interestingly, the trustee offered to serve as a foil if that would help provide local political cover for a difficult decision. The end result of the meeting was to let the crisis roll into the new year—and a new mayoral term—with a new trustee-imposed deadline of January 31. Adding further drama to the situation, a series of fires and explosions rocked the RES facility just days before the mayor took the oath of office.

A Default Workout

As demonstrated by the structure of the financial dilemma, the city had to balance the risk of a default on state-agency bonds for a city-owned project against the risk of opening the city's treasury to a troubled enterprise operation. Befitting its complexity, the default workout dominated the city's fiscal agenda for over a year.

The goal of the workout was to reorient the RES from its myopic attempt to maximize revenues in the face of significant fixed-cost escalations brought on by the trustee's management of the RES, to a substitute premise of viewing the RES as part of a local solid waste collection and disposal system judged by cost-effective standards. This required developing a solid waste collection and disposal system that would accomplish its responsibilities in a safe manner, and at minimum costs, given local needs. A movement to local control would allow city policymakers (the administration and city council working together) to decide what wastes should be processed into the plant, the price citizens should pay for solid waste handling and disposal, and the price steam customers should pay for access to a dependable energy system.

Politically, the newly elected mayor could have let a financial default occur, and probably successfully placed the blame on the prior political regime. After reviewing the likely impact on the community, however, he proceeded to fashion a resolution to the problem, despite the risk of gaining political ownership over the results if he failed. The newly elected mayor came to view the RES as the city's most troubled fiscal problem and if the bank trustee's fee increase plan was implemented, the legal battles pitting local economic interests against one another was sure to harm the good of the community. The short-term financial focus of the trustee had to be replaced by a long-term solution good for the community, and the bondholders, too. His plan was simple at its core—keep the parties talking, in a status quo manner, until he could build consensus around a financial reorganization that would slice through the complexity of the financial, operational, and legal knot. An atmosphere of cooperation among the major players was needed to replace the prevailing one of adversity.

A drift in policy direction by the thirteen-member city council provided an opportunity for the new mayor. For the first time in over a decade and a half, the mayor and a majority of council members were of the same political party. A signal of cooperation was expressed with one key appointment. The council president was selected to serve as the city's public works director (the office responsible for a city-run RES). He was a fifteen-year veteran council member whose private job was as a manager of facilities support services at the local headquarters of a major international manufacturing firm. Not only was this person well qualified for the job, council members trusted his political instincts. This was important because the council felt they had been led astray by past RES votes for short-term "solutions" that never endured for very long. They thus had to be convinced that a financial reorganization would work for the long term and meet the city's competing needs. The new mayor knew that he could not confront the council; it had to be part of the solution. In fact, early in the first days of the new administration, the trustee pressured for a city council vote on bailing out the RES's 1984 operating deficit with city funds. An agreed-upon script was played out with the council expressing strong objections to a city bailout. The "no" vote was coupled with a demand for a long-term solution, not just an operating subsidy that left the debt (and its structures) overhanging the RES.

During the workout, the contending positions of steam customers and the trustee were used by the city as leverage. The point was to keep the customers from going to court too soon or the trustee from pushing steam rates higher than market rates. A variety of standstill arrangements was employed to freeze each position pending a long-term solution.

To build a consensus that the local community had to resolve the default, the newly elected mayor resurrected an idea previously offered by the council but vetoed by the prior mayor. A nine-member "blue ribbon" commission was appointed, comprising major corporate chief executives, local business leaders, representatives of the major customers, and the top city and county elected officials. The commission brought financial, legal, and political expertise to the table, both through the members themselves and the tasking of their corporate staff experts to serve on special subcommittees. Operational experts identified efficient management procedures while a subcommittee of financial experts worked on both the liquidity problems and the needed financial reorganization. A major result of the commission was the concensus call for a long-term solution. In fact, in its May 1984 report, the commission concluded that the RES was a valuable community investment that provided the only feasible solid waste disposal system available to the area. It also found that the RES could not realistically expect to sustain any debt service. In the short run, the commission kept the major steam customers aware of the RES and its problems and the damage that a single lawsuit could do to a lasting solution. In fact, the interruptible and surplus steam customers agreed to modest (18%) price increases and advanced their payments in some cases to help ease the RES's severe cash flow problems as the workout took shape.

Gaining the confidence of bondholders was important, partly to calm the trustee bank. The WDA bonds were held by about 200 bondholders, with several institutional investors holding about 50% of the outstanding bonds. Any steps taken to increase the probability of repayment is welcomed by bondholders, and this was especially true for RES bondholders who were left holding near-default-rated bonds (with a CC speculative rating by Standard & Poor's Corporation). Their trustee bank was afraid of incurring bondholders' wrath if the bonds were not repaid and the trustee's actions (or lack thereof) became the subject of legal challenge.

A meeting of bondholders was called by the trustee and held late in the first month of the new mayor's term. In the call for the meeting, the trustee concluded, "It is very possible [the plant's] viability cannot be achieved." The purported purpose of the bond-holders meeting was to put pressure on the mayor to agree to steam rate increases by the end-of-month deadline imposed by the trustee. As a fallback position, the trustee wanted explicit bondholder permission not to have to raise rates to those levels. In the meeting, the attending bondholders gave strong support to the workout efforts outlined by the new mayor in his address to the group. Bondholders dismissed the city council's negative vote (of the prior evening) on the trustee's bailout proposal as understandable since it was not a long-term solution. The institutional investors at the meeting were supportive of the mayor's early initiatives, especially the blue ribbon commission and his pledge to make a good faith effort to have a long-term solution in place by year's end. Importantly, the mayor noted that default would not serve the interests of anyone, a calming note to bondholders. In no uncertain terms, the institutional investors instructed the bondholders' trustee to be more cooperative with the mayor's agenda for a long-term solution, not a piecemeal solution. Even when the workout took longer than planned, a private meeting of major institutional investors and bond insurance guarantors assured the mayor of their continued support and pledged to monitor the trustee's increasingly noncooperative stance. Furthermore, the trustee bank was part of a larger regional bank holding company whose leadership had expressed confidence in the mayor's efforts and offered comfort that the trustee bank would not take any precipitous actions.

The WDA was at risk also. The WDA actually issued the bonds that were in technical default, so its credit reputation was at risk. As with any conduit financing agency, the WDA's future was tied to its continued market access. It was thus willing to work with the city as long as the city had a feasible workout plan. Later it helped fund the final workout with a major financial contribution.

The mayor enlisted the city's long-serving (for over thirty years) bond counsel firm to help in the workout. This same firm served as the bond counsel and general legal advisor to the WDA. According to some observers, this legal firm faced a potential conflict of interest charge over the dual representation on the basis that it would be hard for the firm to have maximized the competing interests of both the city and the WDA. At a minimum, the firm stood to have its reputation tarnished if the RES failed and the bonds went into actual default, with all the legal claims that would ensue. As one of the most prominent law firms in the state, its influence in state policy making was widely recognized. In private, one of the firm's senior partners made it clear that it was in the interest of the state, the city, and his law firm to solve the problem, and the firm would help design a financial reorganization. In the end, the law firm was of significant help in clarifying the state's interest in a viable local solid waste disposal solution and the risks to the state from an actual monetary default on the WDA bonds.

The mayor refrained from a public recitation of precise strategies and planned actions. This annoyed the local newspaper but it prevented the various parties from taking hard stances that later would be difficult to reverse. This preserved everyone's flexibility as the fluid negotiations took shape. Furthermore, the outstanding bonds would gain in value as a solution emerged, and as "live securities," insider trader laws were in effect. United States securities laws view insider trading as that based on material information not yet made public if the person has a responsibility to keep the information confidential. All parties to the workout were placed on notice about the personal liability of insider trading.

Financial Reorganization

A financial reorganization of the RES was required to advance the goals embodied in the planned operating premise of a cost-effective solid waste system run by the city. Defeasance of the outstanding WDA bonds was at first dismissed as financially impossible, at least by the original RES investment banking advisor. This led to a quickly examined, but dismissed, look at an open-market purchase of all outstanding bonds. This method was discarded as unlikely to be successful enough to totally remove all the legal baggage of the bonds. Defeasance then emerged as the preferred solution, spurred in part by the bond lawyers settling on this method as the cleanest way to remove the bond indenture and therefore the trustee.

Defeasance is a voluntary financial organization to adjust the pattern of debt service payments and to gain release from the original bond indenture. The concept of defeasing a bond series is to structure a portfolio of government securities, the principal and interest of which is sufficient to meet all future principal and interest payments on the refunded outstanding bonds (Feldstein and Fabozzi, 1987). Through defeasance, the bondholders achieve certainty that their interest and principal payments will be paid on time and in full. Bondholders and their trustee thus have no further interest in the project and its operations. Upon successful defeasance of the outstanding bonds, the trust indenture is removed, as is the need for an active trustee. In fact, the trustee reverts to the traditional role of a paying agent of coupons and maturities.

In the RES situation, defeasance would remove the trust indenture for the WDA bonds, but the cooperative agreement would remain in effect. This results from the state's continuing interest in the project and WDA's prior advances to the system. While the RES would remain responsible for repayment of the WDA advances, those obligations are due at such time as the plant generates excess revenues.*

---

* This latter point was to become a significant issue years later, but is not relevant for the purpose of this case presentation.

Due to the fact that a state conduit financing agency—WDA—issued the original bonds, the city could not directly or legally defease another issuer's bonds. In addition, the city could not borrow funds to provide the required stock of funds to defease the state agency debt.

A plan to acquire federal, state, and city resources to implement defeasance took shape. It required an interwoven set of contingency commitments to make sure that all come to fruition and that no single source would be viewed as causing the plan to fail. The city considered the state government a prime source of funds. In fact, WDA possessed excess funds from interest earnings on several bond issues, but the gubernatorially appointed board was unwilling to apply the funds to help out only one city in the state. Despite meetings between city and gubernatorial representatives, as well as a strong political relationship between the mayor and governor, the importance of the issue was most forcefully made by market experts. The governor went to New York to brief "Wall Street" analysts on the state's fiscal health. Although the state's general credit quality was not directly tied to its conduit financing agency's default, the governor was bluntly reminded that the WDA default—although "technical"—was a point of concern to those interested in the state's credit standing, and would become even more so if the principal and interest payments on the RES bonds were abrogated. The governor's position on using the WDA to help the city became more accommodating thereafter, leading to a called meeting with the mayor. As a result, the WDA voted to make funds available for the RES financial reorganization.

In October of 1984, the city council approved the mayor's financial reorganization plan. This plan provided funding for the defeasance with $13 million from a (new) congressionally enacted special EPA allocation, $15 million from the state's WDA (backed by an implicit state agreement to replenish WDA's coffers) and $6 million from the city. The city also contributed an additional $2 million to cover transition costs. The city's total contribution of $8 million was taken from the city's pay-as-you-go capital budget with the bumped capital projects financed instead by borrowing—merely a matter of fungibility of funds to meet legal requirements. Furthermore, defeasance would release $850,000 held in special RES debt accounts that could be used, if needed.

Actions to secure a special grant of funds from Congress was seeded over several months. In October 1984, grounded in a long-standing trust between key members of Congress, an amendment to the continuing appropriations law specified that the city would receive a special "EPA grant." As a perfunctory condition for the dollars and to avoid having the grant viewed strictly as a porkbarrel project, the city had to allow the RES to serve as a "laboratory facility for municipal waste-to-energy research." The special law also restricted the city's use of the funds to only "refinance the bond debt" of the RES. Furthermore, the congressionally mandated grant specified that no more than 60% of the refinancing could be made up of the federal dollars. Due to the specified percentage requirement, the federal funds had to be the last dollars into the account. To create the proper paper trail concerning the appropriate percentage of funds derived from federal funds, the federal dollars had to be the first ones out of the defeasance account. Defeasance was thus delayed partially in response to the need to ensure that the federal dollars were the last in but the first out.

Defeasing the RES bonds depended upon an adequate stock of funds to buy a sufficient amount of U.S. Treasury securities. Once the funds were acquired, the next step was to use investment bankers for advice on market timing. This talent was needed because defeasance rested on an open market purchase of Treasury securities. Traditionally, defeasance is accomplished by issuing debt, the proceeds of which are invested in a structured portfolio of U.S. government securities specially issued by the U.S. Treasury. The purpose of this arrangement is to achieve an optimum fit between the U.S. Treasury securities and the debt service schedule of the outstanding (defeased) bonds and to avoid making more interest on the investment than is due on the bonds—an illegal arbitrage gain. In the RES defeasance, however, no tax-exempt bonds were issued. An open market purchase was thus required to purchase a set of outstanding securities to make the best possible fit. The constraints involved matching a fixed stock of funds and a fixed debt schedule with an open market purchase of a portfolio of high-yield government securities.

Spreading alarm that the RES might be unmanageable (but not affecting the defeasance per se), the RES was not operational during much of the time of the financial reorganization. An explosion in December 1984 fatally injured three workers and injured seven. A quick investigation confirmed that a New Jersey firm mixed into a regular shipment, by "error," three highly flammable chemical solvents that should have been transported instead to a federally approved hazardous-waste landfill. As these products were being processed in the shredder, they exploded, killing three workers from an independent maintenance contractor working above the pit. In terms of the facility itself, insurance covered its physical damage.

Although negotiations had been ongoing for months, this event galvanized opinion that the operator's role had to come to an end, and the contract, specified in the operating service agreement, had to be bought out. The city recognized that the contract might be upheld in a court of law, but convinced the contractor that it might end up as a Pyrrhic victory. After reflection, the contractor settled the contract on terms favorable to the city.

Implementing the defeasance solution had to await receipt of the federal dollars. On January 17, 1985, the city picked up the $13 million check from the EPA regional office in Chicago. Market drifts made the optimizing decision difficult to achieve for awhile, causing some apprehension by all parties. Finally, in late January, an investment banking firm made a bid to sell the required portfolio of Treasury securities at a slightly higher than anticipated, but still acceptable, price of $34.85 million. The bid was accepted pending verification as to accuracy and accomplishment of the defeasance requirements by an independent accounting firm. The delivery of the purchased securities to WDA occurred about two weeks later. On March 20, 1985, the portfolio of structured securities was transferred to the trustee to defease approximately $42 million of RES revenue bonds, only two months shy of the next debt service due date! The trustee then released the RES back to the city. This allowed the trustee, and soon thereafter the private management firm, to end their involvement with the RES facility.

SUMMARY AND CONCLUSION

As a profit-making enterprise, the RES was a loser. As an integral part of a local solid waste collection and disposal system, however, the RES faced a brighter future. The state of affairs facing a newly elected mayor was bleak, however, with the parties to the bonds in technical default quickly adopting intractable positions, and legal warfare the likely result. The trustee focused on short-term operational concerns, thinking the RES could operate itself out of the financial quagmire. In contrast, the mayor viewed a long-term solution as the only way to proceed, keeping his options open until settling on a path out of the legal and financial conundrum. A workout requiring a steady-hand unraveling of the Gordian knot of interlocking contracts seemed impossible, but a financial reorganization that peeled away the most imposing binds, aided by bold strokes (such as turning bondholders into allies and securing the congressional grant of funds), achieved debt reduction and a return of the RES to local control and management.*

REVIEW QUESTIONS

1. How is a "technical" default different from a "monetary" default? Does it make a difference to government officials, taxpayers, or bondholders?
2. To what degree is a city's general obligation credit rating at risk if taxpayers end up paying more in fees or taxes to bail out a project revenue bond-financed enterprise operation?
3. Outline the legal and economic linkages among and between the various parties involved in the RES. How did the new mayor use this tension to structure a solution to the technical default?
4. A bond trustee's normal ministerial duty is to process bondholders' interest and principal payments. As the threat of default looms, the trustee's duties increase according to the terms of the bond indenture agreement. Prior to an event of default, a trustee only has a good faith responsibility to monitor compliance with the indenture and other factors important to the bondholders' interests. After default, however, a trustee generally must meet a prudent person rule, taking care to act as if the assets are personal ones. The indenture specifies the remedies a trustee can take on behalf of the bondholders. Fundamentally, the trustee's role is to protect the bondholders' repayment mechanism—the ability of the system to continue operation so it can generate funds for bond repayment. Assess the trustee's role in the RES case.
5. What lessons should this city's officials, and public officials generally, gain from this episode in the life of a community?
6. If you were the state auditor, would you have instituted proceedings to issue a determination of a financial emergency? What would have been the likely implications of such actions?
7. What could the city do to avoid default if the special congressional appropriation had been voted down and not enacted? Why should local projects such as this even be able to receive U.S. taxpayer funding given that every community has garbage disposal problems?

REFERENCES

Advisory Commission on Intergovernmental Relations. (1985). *Bankruptcies, Defaults, and Other Local Government Financial Emergencies.* Washington, DC: U.S. Government Printing Office.

---

* Not covered in this default case study is the story of the continuing operation of the RES, but that story is not as interesting!

Feldstein, S. G. (1983). "Waste-to-energy" or resource recovery revenue bonds. In S. G. Feldstein, F. J. Fabozzi, and I. M. Pollack (Eds.) *The Municipal Bond Handbook*, vol. II. pp. 151–162. Homewood, IL: Dow-Jones-Irwin.

Feldstein, S. G. and Fabozzi F. J. (1987). *The Dow Jones-Irwin Guide to Municipal Bonds*. Homewood, IL: Dow Jones-Irwin.

Hildreth, W. B. (1987). The changing roles of municipal market participants. *Public Administration Quarterly, 11*, 314–340.

Hildreth, W. B. (1993). State and local governments as borrowers: Strategic choices and the capital market. *Public Administration Review, 53*, 41–49.

Jones, L. R. (1984). The WPPSS default: Trouble in the municipal bond market. *Public Budgeting and Finance, 4*, 60–77.

Kiser, J. V. L. (1992). Municipal waste combustion in North America: 1992 update. *Waste Age (November)*, 26–36.

National League of Cities. (1986). *Waste-to-Energy Facilities: A Decision-Makers Guide*. Alexandria, VA: National Publishing.

Smith, W. S. (1979). *The Appraisal of Municipal Credit Risk*. New York: Moody's Investors Service.

Spiotto, J. E. (1993). Municipal insolvency: Bankruptcy, receivership, workouts and alternative remedies, in M. David Gelfand, (ed.), *State and Local Government Debt Financing*, vol. 3, pp. 13:01–13:56. Wilmette, IL: Callaghan.

Standard & Poor's Corporation. (1984). Credit comment: Resource recovery ratings approach. *CREDITWEEK (June 4)*, 1–8.

39

Obtaining a Better Bond Rating
A Case Study

Charles Coe
North Carolina State University, Raleigh, North Carolina, U.S.A.

Rating agencies assign to bond issues a credit rating that assesses the risk of nonpayment of borrowed funds. The better the bond rating, the lower the interest costs paid. For example, one rating difference amounts to about $50,000 in interest costs for a $1,000,000 bond issued for twenty years at an interest rate of 5%. Ratings are assigned at the time of the sale of bonds and usually stay in effect until the next sale but may be lowered if the conditions in a government have worsened.

To determine a bond rating, rating analysts examine a wealth of information both supplied by the government and derived independently by the analyst. Rating analysts evaluate a wide array of economic, debt, financial, and governmental considerations.

This chapter asks the research question of what local units can do to improve their likelihood of getting a better bond rating. Rating agencies do not completely explain their reasons for assigning a particular rating, nor do they give a precise formula to get a better rating. Local governments that frequently sell bonds are generally familiar with the bond rating process and how to improve their ratings. In contrast, infrequent bond issuers often are not as familiar with the complexities and nuances of the bond rating process. Consequently, some local units take a passive approach to the rating process, waiting to be upgraded or downgraded by the rating agencies.

In contrast, this chapter advocates a proactive approach. Bond rating agencies evaluate four areas: economic, debt, governmental, and financial. Local units may try to improve themselves in one or more of these four rating areas, but may not have a systematic plan to make comprehensive improvements in all four areas as needed. Further, local officials may not be aware of the importance of maintaining an open and continuing dialogue with bond raters. This chapter proposes a model for proactively improving debt ratings. The case of the city of Asheville, North Carolina, shows a city that actively attempted over a six-year period to improve its general obligation bond rating. Eventually, Asheville received a rating upgrade from the two main bond rating agencies. The case asks the reader to speculate as to why Asheville was upgraded. What did city officials proactively do? What effect did economic development have?

PROBLEM BACKGROUND AND DISCUSSION

Three nationally recognized rating agencies—Moody's Investors Service, Inc. (Moody's), Standard & Poor's Corporation (S&Ps), and Fitch Investor's Service, Inc.—rate a wide variety of bonds: tax-supported, enterprise-supported, lease–rental, hospital revenue, mortgage-backed housing, higher education/university revenue, student loan revenue, and refunded bonds. This chapter focuses on the rating of tax-supported, general obligation (GO) bonds. The property tax is the basic underlying security for GO bonds. General obligation bonds typically finance the construction of general purpose governmental facilities, such as schools, public buildings, roads, criminal justice buildings, and recreational structures.

For a fee, rating agencies assign a bond rating to prospective bond issues. The rating agency assigns a rating analyst to recommend a rating to a bond rating committee. The rating agencies' fees and rating schedules are shown in Table 1.

Table 1   Rating Fees and Rating Schedules Rating Fees for GO Obligation Bonds

	Fees
Issue size	Amount of fee
Under $3,000,000	$1,000–$ 3,000
$ 3,000,000-$ 5,000,000	$ 2,000–$ 4,000
$ 5,000,000-$ 20,000,000	$ 3,000–$ 6,000
$ 20,000,000-$ 50,000,000	$ 4,000–$ 8,000
$ 50,000,000-$ 100,000,000	$ 6,000–$ 12,000
$ 100,000,000 and over	$ 10,000–$ 25,000
	Rating definitions
Fitch Investors Service, Inc.	
AAA	Highest credit quality bonds
AA	Very high credit quality bonds
A	High credit quality bonds
BBB	Satisfactory credit quality bonds
Moody's Investors Service	
Aaa	Best quality bonds
Aa	High quality bonds
A	Upper medium quality bonds
Baa	Medium quality bonds
Standard and Poor's Corporation	
AAA	Highest quality bonds
AA	Very strong quality bonds
A	Strong quality bonds
BBB	Adequate quality bonds
	Bonds in the Aa, A, and Baa groups that possess the strongest investment attributes, in Moody's opinion, are designated by the symbols Aa1, A1, and Baa1. For Fitch and Standard and Poor's (S&P), plus (+) or minus (−) signs are used to indicate upper or lower positions within an assigned rating.

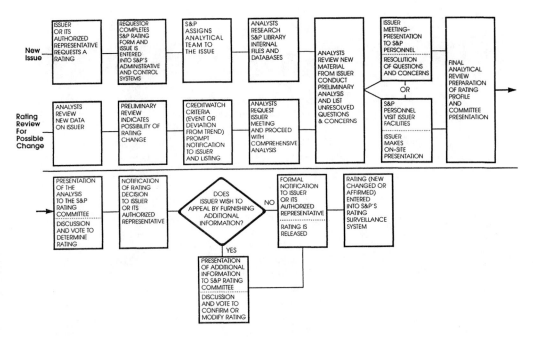

Figure 1   S&Ps bond rating process. *Source*: Standard & Poors Corporation (1989).

The actual bond rating process that S&P goes through is depicted in Figure 1. Moody's and Fitch use similar processes. Rating analysts evaluate new bond issues and maintain surveillance over current ratings. A government is placed on CreditWatch if the lowering of a current bond rating may be forthcoming. The recommendation of rating analysts is reviewed by a rating committee, which assigns the rating. The credit issuer may appeal the assigned rating by furnishing additional information to the rating agency.

To make their credit evaluation, rating agencies require governments to furnish reports and other information. Table 2 is indicative of the type of information needed; more comprehensive discussions of information needs have been produced by the Government Finance Officers Association (GFOA, 1991) and by the National Federation of Municipal Analysts (1992). Rating analysts evaluate four types of information: economic, debt, financial, and governmental.

Economic factors.   Among other criteria, analysts evaluate an area's locational advantages, population, wealth, labor factors, the diversity of employers, and the economic prospects for the area.

Empirical research has found that of the four valuative areas, only economic variables are statistically related to the bond rating received (Wilson, 1986: 20). Economic variables that are significantly related to bond ratings include the percentage of the economy dominated by the ten largest taxpayers (which is intended to measure the concentration and dependence of the local economy); the rate of unemployment; the tax base per capita: and the change in population. Ironically, though most important in the rating process, economic factors are the hardest of the four rating areas to improve. In some communities, economic development

Table 2 Information Required by Bond Rating Analysts

Economic factors	
Natural resources	Economy of the area; geographical and location advantages; land-use characteristics; educational opportunities; medical opportunities
Population, wealth, and labor factors	Population composition; wealth level (family income and per capita income); housing characteristics; new construction values
Economic structure	Principal industries; dates established; and employment
Economic performance and prospect	Prospective expansion and diversification
Debt factors	Information required by rating agencies
Debt policy	Amount authorized and unissued; future debt requirements by purpose and type of debt instruments to be issued
Adequacy of debt structure	Summary schedule of existing and proposed principal requirements; revenue sources for debt service requirements
Debt burden	Gross debt at June 30; date, purpose, amount of original issue; amount of outstanding debt relative to other governments; debt allocable to the jurisdiction
Debt history	Default record; gross debt in 5-year intervals; per capita debt; percentage of assessed valuation of properties; tax rates required for debt service
Prospective borrowing	Amount and nature of debt to be incurred; revenue sources for estimated debt service requirements; approximate date to be issued; computation of legal debt restrictions
Governmental factors	
Organization	Brief history; date incorporated; form of government; powers of key officials
Services	Utility systems owned and operated; capacity and adequacy of systems; recent or planned improvements
Intergovernmental	Overlapping governments, services, and revenues
Administrative performance	Members of governing boards; principal administrative personnel; length of service; professional qualifications; availability of audits, budgets, annual reports, capital planning documents, and land use plans
Financial factors	
Financial practices	Audited financial report to determine the timeliness of financial report; accounting practices employed; and the financial flexibility
Budget trends	Copies of last 3 years' budgets to examine budget trends relative to the growth of the tax base
Revenue and expenditure trends	Copies of last 3 years' budgets
Pension fund trends	Annual benefits payouts; deference of funding benefits

Source: North Carolina State Treasurer (1993).

is simply not possible due to locational disadvantages, inadequate labor supply, or other reasons. In other local units, economic development is possible, but is a very long-term proposition.

Debt factors. Rating analysts examine a local unit's debt policy, debt structure, debt burden, debt history, and prospective borrowing to assess the likelihood of meeting its commitments to bondholders. Analysts are concerned that if public indebtedness becomes too high the community may be unwilling or unable to honor its debt commitments. Moody's has compiled national averages of net debt per capital and the ratio of net debt to estimated full value (EFV) of all taxable property (1992). Such averages are used to evaluate the amount of debt burden. Clearly, communities with high net debt may have cause for concern. On the other hand, low net debt may not necessarily be a good sign if communities with low debt have ignored needed infrastructure improvements by not issuing GO bonds.

Planning for future debt and having a solid infrastructure is looked at favorably by analysts. Local jurisdictions should have a capital improvement program (CIP). The CIP is a comprehensive document that systematically plans for future capital projects and financing. The CIP is usually for five or six years and should tie back to the local unit's land use and transportation plans. Capital improvement programs are simply plans; funding for some of the projected future projects can be counted on, but other funding is only hoped for. Some communities solidify future CIP financing by dedicating taxes and other funds to support capital projects in the CIP.

Governmental factors. Continuity in management and good fiscal control are two important governmental considerations. The analyst assesses whether or not managerial and policymaking powers are clearly delineated; how professional the management team is; how long the professional team has been in place; whether or not the unit has the GFOA Certificate of Achievement for Excellence in Financial Reporting and/or GFOA's Distinguished Budget Presentation Award; and whether or not units are independent of overlapping and conflicting intergovernmental relationships.

Financial factors. Analysts examine past financial reports and budgets to assess existing and future revenue and expenditure trends. Analysts determine whether annual revenues meet or exceed annual expenditures; if there sufficient fund balance available to meet unforeseen contingencies; it the unit follow-generally accepted accounting principles (GAAP) if revenues are sufficiently diversified; what the interfund transfers policies are; if there has been any short-term financing; what the property tax collection rate; and how well-funded pension liabilities are.

A RATING IMPROVEMENT MODEL

Governments can passively wait until rating analysts decide that the unit deserves a better rating or can actively seek a better rating. There are two ways to better a rating: (1) making improvements in one or more of the four areas that analysts evaluate and (2) proactively selling the community to the rating agencies via meetings with rating analysts and through ongoing conversations and correspondence.

Improvements in the four rating areas.   To determine what local officials feel are the most important types of improvements to make, in 1993 a telephone survey was made of nineteen of the forty-nine cities and counties in North Carolina that received rating upgrades during 1987–1992. Nine of nineteen counties (47%) and ten of thirty cities (33%) were contacted. Overall, 39% of the local units were surveyed. Those surveyed generally represented the population sizes of forty-nine local units, which were relatively small in population. For example, fourteen of the cities receiving upgrades were less than 10,000 in population (47% of the total cities), and five of these were contacted (50% of the respondents). Eleven of the counties were less than 60,000 in population (58% of the total counties), and five of these were contacted (56%).

Fourteen (74%) of the local units reported that they had taken steps to improve their bond ratings. The respondents were asked what factors they believed led to receiving a better bond rating. Predictably, economic factors were perceived to be most important, particularly population growth, per capita, income growth, construction growth, and economic diversification. (See Table 3). Having a CIP

Table 3   Perceptions of Factors Leading to a Bond Rating

	Respondents	
	Number	Percent
Economic factors		
Population growth	13	93
Less dependence on the leading taxpayers	2	86
Unemployment decrease	6	43
Growth in construction activity	10	71
Per capital income growth	12	86
Positive labor force trends	2	14
Economic diversification	12	86
Debt factors		
Decrease in debt per capita	6	43
Decrease in net debt	4	29
Capital improvement program available	12	86
Financial factors		
Increase in fund balance	12	86
Low property taxes as a percentage of total revenues	1	7
Increase in sales tax	4	29
Clean auditor's opinion	8	57
Positive changes in accounting procedures	9	64
Management letter	5	36
Governmental factors		
Increase in assessed valuation	4	29
Increase in tax collection rate	3	21
Professional management	7	50
Budgetary improvements	2	14
GFOA award for budget and/or financial report	2	29
Stability of management and of elected board	4	58

Table 4 Bond Rating Improvement Strategies

Rating area	Short-term step	Long-term step
Economic		Encourage industrial development, invest in infrastructure
Debt	Adopt a CIP	When market is right, refinance debt if too much is outstanding
Governmental	Get GFOA recognition for the budget and financial report	Encourage the professional team to stay in place by offering a good pay and benefits package
Financial	Respond to management letter's recommendations, increase the property tax collection rate, follow generally accepted accounting procedures (GAAP), get a clean auditor's opinion, automate the budgeting and accounting systems	Increase the amount of unreserved fund balance

was perceived to be the most important debt factor; professional management the most important governmental factor; and an increase in fund balance the most important financial factor.

Looking at the four rating areas and at the survey responses, what can local units do to improve their chances of getting a better rating? Steps that can be taken fall into short- (one to two years) and long-term steps. (See Table 4). Local units can do little to improve economy in the shortterm, but an economic development effort may increase the likelihood of economic investment. A poor economic location may negate any and all such efforts, however.

Regarding the debt rating area, a local unit can adopt a CIP in the short term, given a commitment on the part of top management to organize and staff for the CIP planning process. Dedicating funding for the CIP further strengthens a unit's hand. Governments with excessive outstanding GO debt may be able to refinance the debt if interest rates fall.

In the governmental area, obtaining GFOA's Certificate of Achievement for Excellence in Financial Reporting and the Distinguished Budget Presentation Award signals professional management and can be accomplished in a one-to-two-year period if the local unit is willing to commit the needed staff time and effort. Both of the GFOA awards also are strong financial indicators. Other evidence of governmental competence is a professionally educated management team that has been in place for some time. Policymakers can try to ensure continuity and professionalism by offering managers attractive pay and fringe benefit package; nonetheless, managers in small-sized communities may be lured away by the higher salaries that larger towns and counties can usually offer.

In the financial rating area, local units can increase the property tax collection rate by taking strong enforcement measures against delinquent taxpayers; can follow GAAP, thereby obtaining a clean auditor's opinion; and can invest in software to automate the budgeting and accounting systems. In the long term, the local unit can increase the amount of unreserved fund balance by underestimating budgeted revenues and overestimating budgeted expenditures.

Proactively selling the community.   Local managers should apprise rating agencies of economic, debt, governmental, and financial improvements in the community. The local jurisdiction should establish a "back and forth" relationship with the rating agency. The city or county should introduce key staffers to the rating analysts (the city or county manager, finance director, treasurer, etc.) and should encourage the rating analysts to ask for information from these persons as needed. The local jurisdiction's staff should familiarize the rating analysts with the government's financial policy; moreover, any changes in financial policy that might affect the credit rating should be first reviewed with rating analysts. To keep the rating agencies abreast of new developments, local managers should submit written material, special reports, and newspaper accounts that highlight changes and improvements.

The New York visit.   Some local units visit the bond rating agencies whenever they are issuing a new bond; others minimize the expense of going to New York by visiting only if seeking a better rating or if there is a possibility of being downgraded. Some governments hire financial advisors to provide a range of services, including making the rating presentation to the rating agency. Financial advisors have extensive experience working with bond agencies and their services can lead to a improved credit rating (Petersen and Watt, 1986: 85).

As one highly respected and experienced fiscal advisor notes, the visit to the bond rating agency is in some ways "an exercise in spin control" because rating analysts have skillfully and thoroughly analyzed the rating documents before the meeting (McLoughlin, 1992). It is therefore very important that the team representing the local jurisdiction be well prepared for the meeting and make a highly professional presentation. No set rules exist as to who should be on the team, but the team should not be unwieldy in number and should be composed of persons who can make a constructive contribution to the dialogue (S&P Corporation, 1989: 7). The rating analysts judge the management capacity of the local unit in part by how professionally the team makes its presentation and how deftly it answers questions.

The analysts are particularly interested in information that cannot be obtained in the rating documents already provided. The staff should check with the analyst to determine whether or not the material that will be presented is complete and relevant. Typically, the team uses a booklet as the basis for its presentation. The booklet should be well crafted. Financial advisors are experienced at preparing a booklet. If not using a financial advisor and if developing a booklet for the first time, local units can refer to a guide distributed by the International City Management Association (ICMA, 1987). Supplementing the written material with overheads, slides or a videotape is a useful strategy.

Standard & Poor's suggests that the issuer make a ten to fifteen-minute introductory statement highlighting the important features in the submitted documents and then let rating analysts ask questions (S&P Corporation, 1989: 7). One expert financial advisor says that the meeting should not last for more than ninety minutes and normally runs for about one hour (McLoughlin, 1992). The "pitch" is less important than the content of the answer. If unsure of an answer, the team should provide additional information later. Finally, after the presentation, the local unit should provide analysts with any further information needed to make their determination.

The on-site rating visit. In lieu of the New York visit, the rating agency may request to visit a community if significant changes have occurred in underlying credit factors, but most on-site visits are initiated by the local jurisdiction. Local managers should give analysts an "on-the-ground," first-hand look at the community. The notion is that a "picture is worth 1000 words." The analyst can refuse a community's request for a visit if he or she deems a visit would not be useful. On the tour of the community, analysts want to see a balanced view of the community. In this spirit, the tour should disclose the community's good features as well as areas deserving improvement. Often the tour combines walking, riding, and an aerial overview. The local unit should emphasize growth, significant changes, previously bond-financed projects, and projects that require future bond funding. During the visit, analysts typically meet with a forum of elected, business, and community leaders at some point in the tour.

THE RATING IMPROVEMENT MODEL: A CASE STUDY

Not all communities actively seek a better bond rating and not all should. For a variety of reasons some communities may have no hope of improving their bond rating. On the other hand, some communities take a totally passive approach when they should be aggressive. Other local units take a limited approach, concentrating on improving one rating area when they should be more systematically addressing rating needs on all fronts. Communities should take active steps to increase their chance of obtaining a better bond rating both by making improvements and by working closely with rating analysts in meetings, on-site visits, and through ongoing communication over time. To see a proactive approach in action, let's examine the case of Asheville, North Carolina, which ultimately received a rating upgrade from both Moody's and S&P.

Background on the City of Asheville, North Carolina

Asheville is located in western North Carolina. The city's population grew from 60,218 to 62,121 from 1980 to 1990. The city has had the council–manager form of government for over sixty years. The city received the GFOA's Distinguished Budget Presentation Award in 1979 and has received it every year since, follows GAAP, has a fully funded pension plan, and enjoys a high property tax collection rate.

In North Carolina, all bonds of local governments are sold by the local government division of the state treasurer's office; therefore few jurisdictions use financial advisors. Most local jurisdictions, Asheville included, market their bonds with the rating agencies without the assistance of a financial advisor.

1984. The finance director, Larry Fisher, came to the city in 1972. For over forty years the city had an A1 rating from Moody's and an A+ rating from S&P. In 1984 the city hired a new city manager who wanted to improve the city's bond rating. The city manager and Fisher assembled a very knowledgeable rating presentation team composed of themselves, the budget director, and the mayor. Moody's did not grant a rating upgrade for the reasons shown in Exhibit A.

In response to the Moody's credit report, the city increased the amount of unreserved fund balance. The city council also adopted a CIP for the first time and dedicated 8 cents of the property tax and 60% of the one-half cent sales tax for capital improvements, thereby ensuring that all projects in the CIP over $7500 in value would be funded over six years.

In 1986 Fisher attended a ratings seminar conducted by S&P staff at which he learned more about rating criteria and established a personal relationship with key S&P managers. As a consequence of this seminar, Fisher prepared a very thorough and readable ratings presentation booklet. Thereafter, Fisher also established a close working relationship with key Moody's managers.

Most significantly, the completion of major interstate highways I-26 and I-40 in the late 1970s began to bear the fruits of economic development: $59 million in economic development and redevelopment projects were completed or underway.

1986. Again, the city applied to Moody's and also to S&P for a rating upgrade. Moody's did not grant a rating upgrade for the reasons shown in Exhibit B. Thereafter, the city voters approved $17 million in GO bonds for streets and sidewalks and $3 million as part of a $17 million cultural arts center project. During this time, unemployment decreased, the tax base increased by 9% due to economic expansion and redevelopment, and two parking facilities were constructed downtown at a cost of $6.4 million

1987. The city applied for another upgrade, having improved its fund balance and experiencing continued economic growth. Moody's again did not grant a rating upgrade for the reasons shown in Exhibit C.

1988. Moody's upgraded the city to Aa, citing the diversifying and growing economic base as evidenced by improved personal income indicators, a lower unemployment rate, and a growing tax base due to increased health care investment, more tourism, and increasing enrollment at the University at North Carolina at Asheville. In 1989 S&P upgraded the city to AA-, citing similar reasons.

SUMMARY AND CONCLUSION

The city of Asheville proactively sought a better bond rating by working closely with the bond rating agencies and by improving areas deemed weak by rating agency personnel. Much of Asheville's economic improvement, however, resulted from events out of city officials' control; namely, the completion of two interstate highways which prompted economic investment. It is a moot question whether or not Asheville would have been upgraded without the added economic investment. Just as moot is whether or not the city would have been upgraded if it had done nothing other than wait for increased investment due to the highway construction.

Local government officials must decide whether actively seeking a better bond rating makes sense for their community. If the decision is yes, this chapter offers a model that can be used to improve the likelihood of achieving a better rating.

Moody's **Municipal** Credit Report

Asheville, North Carolina	November 7, 1984
Review	General Obligation/Special Tax

Moody's rating: A1

opinion: Low debt and very favorable finances provide more than adequate security. However, limited economic growth within city boundaries and looming capital needs pose an element of susceptibility in the years ahead.

key facts:

Debt Burden:	0.8%	Population Change, 1970–80:	–7.1%
Payout, ten years:	94.0%	% Housing Built, 1970–80:	12.0%
Undesignated General Fund Balance as % of FY 1983 Revenue:	10.5%	U.S. Percent Housing Built, 1970–1980:	25.9%
Year–end Cash Surplus as % of FY 1983 General Revenues:	25.7%	Median House Value, 1980:	$32,200
		U.S. Median House Value, 1980:	$47,300

analysis: Asheville has continued to have strong financial operations. It has reduced its debt burden to a very low level. However, while Asheville's economic base demonstrated resilience in the last recession. It shows little evidence of having shared in the growth witnessed in other parts of North Carolina or surrounding Buncombe County.

Except for a short lived burst in the 1960's, Asheville's population has remained unchanged for a half century in spite of a doubling of its land area. In contrast, Buncombe County has increased its population by 30% in 30 years. Moreover, political and geographical factors make annexation or consolidation with Buncombe County unlikely at this time. Asheville has an aging housing stock and has exhibited only moderate growth in its tax base and employment level. In most other economic indicators it does not compare favorably to regional norms. While Asheville can expect to benefit from developments in Buncombe County even there the signs are not uniformly positive; namely, declining growth in retail trade and insignificant employment growth in recent years.

By its own account Asheville has pressing capital needs in its municipal buildings, roadways, and water system. The issuance of BANs in 1983 for $870,000 may presage additional borrowings. A recent offering by Buncombe County for $15.7 million as well as plans for more offerings suggests that overall debt burden may grow.

Exhibit A   1984 credit report.

Moody's **Municipal** Credit Report

Asheville, North Carolina	December 2, 1986
New Issue	General Obligation/Special Tax
sale: $4,800,000	Street and Sidewalk Bonds, Series 1986
date: For bids December 2	

Moody's rating: A1

opinion: Low debt and very favorable finances provide upper medium grade security. However, limited economic growth within city bound-aries and the capital needs which are just beginning to be addressed pose an element of susceptibility in the years ahead.

key facts:

Debt Burden:	1.3%	Population Change, based on		
Payout, ten years:	72.4%	Revised 1970–80 Census:	1.9%	
Property Taxes as % of Current Revenue, FY 1986:	39.6%	1980 Median Family Income, Asheville/Norm:	93.5%	
Sales Taxes as % of Current Revenue, FY 1986:	13.7%	1980 Median Value Housing, Asheville/Norm:	82.7%	
Undesignated General Fund Balance as % of Revenue, FY 1986:	20.3%	Unemployment, 8/86, Asheville: State:	5.9% 5.1%	

analysis: Asheville, an important trade and service center for an extensive 17–county area in western North Carolina, has had favorable tax base increases due primarily to reappraisal and annexations. In 1983 and 1984, annexations added approximately $276 million to taxable values effective in fiscal 1985. Furthermore, discovery of undervalued business inventory contributed approximately $25 to $30 million of assessed value in fiscal 1985; this property was subsequently taken off the fiscal 1986 tax roll after prior year's taxes had been paid.

Future moderate tax base growth of approximately $59 million is expect-ed due to various current development and redevelopment projects. Ashville's 1980 population has been revised by the U.S. Census Bureau and now indicates a slight increase to approximately 59,000 through the 1970s; however, overall population increase, except for the 1960s, has been flat.

In contrast, Buncombe County's population increased 30% from 1950 to 1980 reflecting suburban growth trends. City unemployment has declined from recessionary levels in the early 1980s but remains above county and state levels. City resident income and housing values compare unfavorably to norms.

Exhibit B 1986 credit report.

Asheville continues to have strong finances evidenced by the increasing General Fund balance. Furthermore, the Undesignated General Fund balance has increased to a significant percentage of current revenue, at the same time reserves for capital expenditures have increased.

While financial reserves have strengthened, capital renovation needs have developed. City officials seek to address these needs with proceeds of Series 1986, $15.2 million in bonds to be issued over 1987 and 1988, and accumulated capital reserves. The issuance of Series 1986, as well as proposed bonds for 1987 and 1988 create a moderate debt burden. Payout, although slower due to structure of Series 1986, remains rapid.

details of bond sale:		
	Legal Name of Issuer: City of Asheville, North Carolina.	Registrar/Paying Agent: Branch Banking and Trust Co., Wilson, North Carolina.
	Security: G.O., ULT.	Delivery: On or about December 18, 1986.
	Date of Bonds: December 1, 1986.	
	Denomination: $5,000.	Bond Counsel: Smith, Helms, Mulliss, and Moore, Greensboro, North Carolina.
	Annual Maturities 6/1 ($ 000)	

Year	Amount	Year	Amount
1988-93	$100	1996-03	$400
1994-95	$200	2004-05	$300

Interest Rate: To be determined.

Interest Payable: Beginning June 1, 1987 and semiannually thereafter.

Call Features: Beginning June1, 1996 at 102.

Financial Officer: Larry Fisher, Finance Director.

Advisors: North Carolina Local Government Commission, Raleigh.

Auditor: Price Waterhouse, Greenville, South Carolina (FY 1986).

details of last comparable sale		
	Date of Sale: March 2, 1976.	Interest Cost: 5.7243%
	Amount: $5,175,000	Moody's Index: [1] 7.54%
	Purchaser: First-Citizens Bank & Trust Co., Smithfield.	[1] For A1 rated issues: as of March 4, 1976.

rating history:		
	General obligation bonds:	October 1973 to present: A1
	June 1971: A	

Exhibit B 1986 credit report (continued).

Moody's **Municipal** Credit Report

Asheville, North Carolina	August 31, 1987
Update	General Obligation/Special Tax

Moody's rating: A1

opinion: Low debt and very favorable finances provide upper medium grade security. However, limited economic growth within city boundaries and the capital needs which are just beginning to be addressed pose an element of susceptibility in the years ahead.

key facts:

Debt Burden:	1.5%	Coverage of Maximum Annual Lease Rental Payment by FY 1986 Utility Franchise Taxes:	3.36
Payout, ten years: [1]	58.9%		
Property Taxes as % of Current Revenues, FY 1986:	39.6%	Population Change, Based on Revised 1970-80 Census:	1.9%
Sales Taxes as % of Current Revenues, FY 1986:	13.7%	1980 Median Family Income Asheville/Norm:	93.5%
Franchise Taxes as % of FY 1986 Current Revenue:	10.1%	Per Capita Income, Asheville/State,	
Undesignated General Fund Balance as % of Revenue FY 1986:	20.3%	1969:	115.5%
		1983:	108.0%
Authorized, Unissued Bonds:	$15.2 million	1980 Median Value Housing, Asheville/Norm:	82.7%
Outstanding Bonded Debt:	$12,335,000	Unemployment,	
[1] Includes all bonds and certificates of participation.		Asheville, 5/86:	7.1%
		Asheville, 5/87:	4.9%
		State, 5/87:	4.2%

update: Since our report dated December 2, 1986, fiscal 1987 has closed with continued favorable results including an estimated $1.3 million General Fund operating surplus and related increase in General Fund reserves. The city entered a lease rental agreement to secure $6.4 million certificates of participation issued pursuant to a trust agreement between Wachovia Bank and Trust Company and the Asheville - Buncombe Development corporation to provide funding for construction of parking facilities.

Exhibit C   1987 credit report.

analysis: Asheville, an important trade and service center for an extensive 17-county area in western North Carolina, has had favorable tax base increases due primarily to reappraisal and annexations. In 1983 and 1984. annexations added approximately $276 million to taxable values effective in fiscal 1985. Furthermore, discovery of undervalued business inventory contributed approximately $25 to $30 million of assessed value in fiscal 1985, this property was subsequently taken off the fiscal 1986 tax roll after prior year's taxes had been paid. Future moderate tax base growth is expected due to various current development and redevelopment projects. Asheville's 1980 population has been revised by the U.S. Census Bureau and now indicates a slight increase to approximately 59,000 through the 1970s; however, overall population increase, except for the 1960s, has been flat. In contrast, Buncombe County's population increased 33% from 1950 to 1984 reflecting suburban growth trends. City unemployment has declined from recessionary levels in the early 1980s but remains above county and state levels. City resident income and housing values compare unfavorably to norms.

Asheville continues to have strong finances evidenced by the increasing General Fund balance. Furthermore, the undesignated General Fund balance has increased to a significant percentage of current revenue at the same time reserves for capital expenditures have increased. While financial reserves have strengthened, capital renovation needs have developed. City officials seek to address these needs with proceeds of the Series 1986 issue, $15.2 million in bonds to be issued over the next few years, and accumulated capital reserves.

This update was completed due to the city's unconditional, limited obligation to make lease rental payments, pursuant to a lease agreement dated July 1, 1987 with the Asheville — Buncombe Development Corporation, which secure $6,415,000 certificates of participation executed by Wachovia Bank and Trust Company on July 23, 1987. The certificates will fund construction of two downtown Asheville, municipal parking decks. The city has pledged proceeds of the state-administered utility franchise tax, but may use any available revenue if necessary. Outstanding proposed bonds and the certificates of participation create a moderate debt burden. However, certificates of participation should be easily paid by utility franchise taxes as the fiscal 1986 amount covered maximum annual certificate debt service 3.36 times, reducing the burden on the tax base. Payout including the certificates remains above average.

rating history:	General obligation bonds: June 1971:		A	October 1973 to present:	A1

Exhibit C   1987 credit report (continued).

REVIEW QUESTIONS

To answer these questions, refer to text of the article and to Exhibits A, B, and C.

1. Why did Moody's not upgrade Asheville in 1984, 1986, and 1987? How did Asheville respond to Moody's concerns? What did the city do to improve itself in the four rating areas? Specifically discuss the steps Asheville took to improve itself in the economic, debt, governmental, and financial areas.
2. What did the city do to improve the way it marketed its bonds with the bond rating agencies?
3. Of any of the improvements made, which do you think were the most important?
4. How important a factor was the completion of the two interstate highways? Would the city have received a rating upgrade without the completion of these highways?
5. How important is it for local officials to have a close working relationship with bond rating analysts?
6. Based on the model presented in the chapter, what else could the city have done to improve its chances of getting a better rating?

REFERENCES

Government Finance Officers Association. (1991). *GFOA Disclosure Guidelines for State and Local Government Securities*. Chicago.

International City Management Association. (1987). *G. O. Bonds: Rating Agency Presentation by the City of Fort Worth Texas*. Washington, D.C.

McLoughlin, T. (1992). Vice-president, Government Financial Group. Telephone interviews on Oct 2.

Moody's Investors Service, Inc. (1992). *1992 Medians*. New York.

National Federation of Municipal Analysts. (1992). *Disclosure Handbook for Municipal Securities*. Pittsburgh.

North Carolina Department of State Treasurer. (1992). *Policies Manual: General Obligation Debt*. Raleigh, NC.

Petersen, J. E. and Watt, P. (1986). *The Price of Advice*. Chicago: Government Finance Officers Association.

Standard & Poors Corporation. (1989). *S&P's Municipal Finance Criteria*. New York.

Wilson, S. R. (1986). Credit ratings and general obligation bonds: A statistical alternative. *Government Finance Review* (*June*), 21.

40

Procurement Dilemmas

Social Policies Versus Pure Competition—The Case of Vendor Preferences

Susan A. MacManus
University of South Florida, Tampa, Florida, U.S.A.

Purchasing policies and their ramifications have been thrust into the public finance limelight in the 1990s. More contracting out for goods and services by governments has led the public and the press to pay more attention to who in the private sector gets the contracts—and how.*

Less visible are the tensions *within* government. It is not uncommon for elected officials and purchasing professionals to be at odds over the design and implementation of certain purchasing policies and procedures. Each group tends to have different notions of what the desirable goals of public procurement are. Picture the following scenarios:

A large, vocal group of local business owners in a city with a depressed economy appears before the city council and demands that a local vendor preferences policy be adopted immediately in order to save local businesses.

A candidate for public office runs on a platform calling for the county to adopt a Buy American policy and handily defeats the incumbent who opposed the idea. (The winning candidate has no idea about how to write such a policy or what its fiscal impacts would be.)

In a state with a large African American population, the newly elected governor (whose winning coalition included minority voters) urges the legislature to adopt a policy prohibiting the state from buying anything from vendors who do business in South Africa.

The author would like to thank Theodore J. Grable, Jr., director of Hillsborough County, Florida, Purchasing and Contracts Department. Henry Morbach, principal buyer for the School District of Hillsborough County Florida, and Les Jackson, director of technical services for the National Institute of Governmental Purchasing, for their assistance in gathering materials and examples for this case study. Some of the information in this case study was adapted from the author's *Doing Business With Government* (MacManus, 1992).

* There is a vast literature on the trend toward privatization and contracting out. For excellent overviews, see MacManus, 1992; Donahue, 1989; Irwin, 1988; Morley, 1989; Chi, 1988; Rehfuss, 1989.

629

Following a series of newspaper articles highlighting which firms got the bulk of a school district's contracts (mostly large firms owned by white males), the local Small Business Owners Association demands that the district adopt a small business preference policy. Their request leads to a similar demand from associations representing firms owned by the handicapped, women, and minorities.

In a college town, the well-organized, highly visible environmental community descends upon the city council (with TV cameras whirring) and insists that it's time the city gave preference to vendors selling or using recycled products, even if they cost the taxpayer more.

If the elected officials in each of the above scenarios fail to respond to the demands of the voters who put them in office, are they being unresponsive and contradicting the principles of representative government, or are they being unethical if they adopt vendor preference policies that disadvantage or exclude certain types of firms if such policies seem to violate the very principles of good purchasing?

Welcome to the world of public procurement in the 1990s! It is an arena in which competition and fairness, two goals of public purchasing, increasingly appear to be contradictory. In each of scenarios posed above, the demands for vendor preference policies would almost certainly yield cries of outrage, and in some instances, lawsuits from various vendors, business owners associations, and free market advocacy groups who see preference policies as unfairly restricting competition. The same demands would evoke strong support from those who would benefit from the policies, however. As noted by Jackson (1992:5) of the National Institute of Governmental Purchasing (NTGP), "Preference buying brings some strange bedfellows together. Business[owners], laborers, and politicians are apt to see something good in a preference. Business like the elimination of competition in price and quality, laborers like the prospects of higher local employment, and politicians will try to unseat incumbents who have spoken out for free trade."

Public purchasing professionals frequently, and unavoidably, end up in the middle of these politically explosive frays. As "experts" they are often queried by the elected officials as to whether such preference policies should be adopted. These officials want to know the legality of such preferences, their potential fiscal impacts on government, and their ability to achieve their stated goals and objectives. The purpose of this case study is to give public finance specialists a feel for this issue and the difficulties it often creates by focusing on preference policies at the state and local level.

THE PRINCIPLES OF PUBLIC PURCHASING

The National Association of State Purchasing Officials (NASPO), in its widely cited *State and Local Government Purchasing*, identifies the four fundamentals of public purchasing and contracting as competition, impartiality, efficiency, and openness: "Public business is to be offered for competition; bidders are to be treated alike and contracts administered alike, without favoritism; economy and value are basic aims; and the documents used and actions taken are public information" (National Association of State Purchasing Officials, 1988: 7).

It is also a well-established fact, however, that another goal of government procurement is to promote social and economic objectives. According to *Alijan's Purchasing Handbook* (Farrell, 1982: 205–6)

[Government] procurement involves much more than buying. The process is used extensively to promote such social and economic objectives as interests of small business, use of minority business, fair employment practices, payment of fair wages, safe and healthful working conditions, employment of the handicapped, rehabilitation of prisoners, and use of recycled materials.

Prime examples of purchasing policies that promote social and economic objectives are those that encourage the purchase of American, in-state, or locally produced goods and services and those encouraging purchases from small businesses and firms owned by women, racial and ethnic minorities, and the handicapped.* These are often referred to as "vendor preference" policies and are controversial because they are seen by many as contradictory to the principles of competition, efficiency, and impartiality.

VENDOR PREFERENCE POLICIES: THE VIEW OF THE PURCHASING PROFESSIONALS

Both NASPO and NIGP have adopted resolutions opposing preferences (Jackson, 1992: 5–6). From NASPO's (1988:13–14) perspective, "Preference, accorded one class of vendors over all others, strikes at the basic principles of public purchasing: equity, impartiality, open competition, and the least cost to the taxpayers. The genesis of preference laws and administrative fiat is political, and the trade-off of anticipated socioeconomic goals must be weighed against the demonstrable adverse effect upon other public policies and goals, not the least of which is excellence in public purchasing."

The NIGP resolution (adopted October 7, 1981) is quite similar in its thrust. It reads

Whereas, the National Institute of Governmental Purchasing consistently supports the competitive bidding process as the most effective vehicle for obtaining products and services at the lowest evaluated costs; and

Whereas, the National Institute of Governmental Purchasing encourages an opportunity for all suppliers to compete for Federal, State and Local Government business on an equal basis; and

Whereas, the application of preferences in awarding public contracts restricts suppliers from bidding on an equal basis and thereby increases costs and inhibits competition;

Now Therefore, BE IT RESOLVED that the National Institute of Governmental Purchasing continues to oppose the use of in-state and local bidding preferences in awarding public contracts.

Key Criteria for Awarding a Contract

Without vendor preference policies, government purchasing policies and procedures are tailored to conform to the four principles of public purchasing. Most purchasing statutes or ordinances require governments "to award contracts to the lowest bidder who is determined to be responsible and responsive." According to the NIGP *Dictionary of Purchasing*

---

* Historically, the most common preferences of this type have been extended to firms owned and/or operated by visually or hearing-impaired individuals. More recently, firms specializing in the production and/or distribution of products made by the mentally or emotionally disadvantaged have also been given preferences in some jurisdictions.

Terms (1986:26), a *responsible bidder* is one "whose reputation, past performance, and business and financial capabilities are such that the bidder would be judged by appropriate authority to be capable of satisfying an organization's need for a specific contract." A responsive bidder is one "whose bid does not vary from the specifications and terms set out in the invitation for bids."

These criteria are well established and their purposes clear to purchasing professionals. Several years ago, the staff attorney for the Florida League of Cities summarized these "basic principles" and their intent (1978:10).

> Such requirements are for the purpose of inviting competition, to guard against favoritism, improvidence, extravagance, fraud and corruption in the awarding of municipal contracts, and to secure the best work or supplies at the lowest price practicable, and are enacted for the benefit of property holders and taxpayers, and not for the benefit or enrichment of bidders, and should be so construed and administered as to accomplish such purpose fairly and reasonably with sole reference to the public interest.

The success of the contracting process is often measured in terms of the amount of competition generated. As stated in NASPO's *State and Local Government Purchasing*, "In principle, competition is the centerpiece around which the public contracting process turns ... The importance of competition demands that acquisitions be made under conditions which foster competition among a sufficient number of potential vendors representing a wide spectrum of producers or services or marketplaces" (1988:24). Any condition perceived as creating an artificial barrier to competition is viewed with skepticism by most purchasing professionals.

Cross-Pressures on the Public Purchasing Professional

Without question, preference policies create a dilemma for the public procurer who is professionally trained to vehemently oppose them but often pressured to help draft and/ or defend them by his or her elected official bosses. Frequently, the purchasing agent is also cross-pressured from within as he or she may personally sympathize with the social goals of preference policies. The director of purchasing and supply for a major state university outlined these cross-pressures well in an article published in the *NIGP Technical Bulletin* (Jones 1992:3–4).

> Most of us might hesitate to argue against preferential treatment aimed at awarding contracts to blind industries or sheltered workshops that assist mentally or emotionally disadvantaged people. Many would support specific attention for small businesses struggling to get started. Affirmative action aimed at minority owned and controlled firms that historically got the short end of the stick certainly seems to have merit. After all, these are motherhood and apple pie types of preferences. However, as I researched further I began to realize how deep and broad this purchasing activity extends. I was reminded of a conversation regarding small business preferences: over time the official definition of a small business (measure by maximum number of employees and gross dollars of revenue) has expanded so that more and more vendors qualify. We concluded that ultimately nearly all vendors would be declared small. Effectively, if all are "small" none are small for the purpose of special treatment in awarding contracts. *I'm concerned that institutional and governmental procurement is rapidly approaching that nonproductive state where no net value is derived from special preferences* [author's emphasis].

This purchasing director concluded his article with a call for the elimination of all preference rules and pleads for the return of "straight forward purchasing processes and procedures designed to enable professional buyers to simply search the marketplace and acquire
the goods and services that best fit the needs at the most effective (competitive) prices."

The scenario just presented makes it obvious that a well-informed public financial
manager must be aware of the common types of preference policies, along with their
respective pros and cons.

VENDOR PREFERENCE POLICIES: ADVANTAGED FIRMS
AND FREQUENCY OF USE

The NIGP *Dictionary of Purchasing Terms* (1986:23) defines a preference as "an advantage in consideration for award for a contract granted to a vendor by reason of the vendor's
residence, business location, or business classification (e.g., minority, small business)."

Common Business Classification Definitions

The U.S. Department of Commerce defines business classifications quite specifically. A
small business is "one that, including its affiliates, is independently owned and operated,
and not dominant in the field in which it is bidding on government contracts." A *woman-
owned business* "is at least 51 percent owned, controlled, and operated by a woman or
women." A *minority-owned business* "is at least 51 percent owned, controlled, and operated
by a member of an economically or socially disadvantaged minority group, including
blacks, Hispanics, Native Americans, Asian-Pacific Americans, and Asian-Indian Americans." A *disadvantaged business* is one "owned or controlled by persons who have been
deprived of economic opportunity by social disadvantage" (NIGP, 1986:10). These same
broad definitions are generally used by state and local governments. There are, however,
often variations in how to operationalize (measure) and/or document ownership, control,
and operation.

Frequency of Preference Policies

A 1991 survey by the NIGP examined the frequency with which governments adopted
vendor preferences designed to address six separate social objectives—local vendor, Buy
American, small or disadvantaged business, minority business enterprise (MBE) firm,
South African trade restriction, and recycled products preferences (NIGP, 1992). The
NIGP found that 30% of the jurisdictions and agencies have local vendor, 32% Buy
American, 26% small or disadvantaged business, 27% MBE, 12% South African trade
restriction, and 42% recycled products preferences* (See Table 1). In many instances,
however, the preferences only apply in case of a tie bid.†

---

* While the percentage of jurisdictions having adopted each of these preference policies differs by type of
  governmental entity, caution should be taken in interpreting the results because of the nature of the respondent
  sample. There is a small number of cases in many categories.
† Such policies are perceived much less negatively by staunch opponents of vendor preference policies as they
  do not appear to violate the sacred principle of unrestricted competition.

Table 1 Vendor Preference Policies by Type of Government/Agency

Type of government agency	Local vendor		Buy American		Small/disadvantaged business		Minority business enterprise		South African trade restrictions		Recycled products	
	n	Percent	n	Percent	n	Percent	n	Percent	n	Percent	n	Percent
Federal	1	33	2	100	1	33	1	33	2	67	1	33
State/province	8	32	8	35	6	23	6	24	4	16	20	80
State/provincial agency	8	23	12	34	18	50	17	53	5	14	10	31
City/municipality	60	30	45	25	31	16	38	21	21	11	81	44
County/region	27	26	28	29	14	15	15	17	6	6	33	36
School system	13	28	13	31	9	24	9	23	3	7	13	34
University/college	19	42	19	46	19	44	14	35	8	20	19	46
Special authority	20	37	25	46	21	42	19	49	11	22	18	42
City/county consolidation	3	33	1	11	3	33	2	50	1	13	2	25
Health-related	0	0	3	43	3	50	2	33	1	14	1	14
Prison/correctional	1	100	1	100	1	100	1	100	0	0	0	0
Total responses	160	30	157	32	126	26	124	27	62	12	198	42

Source: National Institute for Governmental Purchasing (1992: 17–20).

In another survey, NIGP found that a number of states have preference policies for in-state firms and their products and/or services. Preference policies may vary even within the *same* state across different types of jurisdictions (state, city, county, school district). (See Table 2.) Most of these state-imposed preference policies are price percentage preferences rather than set-asides—a distinction that will be clarified later in the chapter.

Public purchasing experts predict that there will be an upward trend in preferential policies in the 1990s, especially local vendor and Buy American, if the economy remains anemic (Dimeo, 1992; NIGP, 1991). This forecast is based upon their review of historical data showing that protectionism surfaces in periods of economic decline.

Preferences as Deterrents of Undesirable Behavior or "Regulatory" Instruments

There is a growing body of evidence showing that elected officials now see procurement policies as methods of deterring undesirable behavior on the part of both businesses and individuals. For example, in 1989 the Florida legislature, upon the recommendation of the state attorney general, passed the Public Entity Crime Bill (F.S. 287. 133). It was intended to prevent state and local governments from doing business with companies that have been convicted of certain crimes against public entities, such as collusion (bid-rigging), fraud, theft, bribery, racketeering, conspiracy, or material misrepresentation. The law requires the state of Florida Department of General Services to publish quarterly a "convicted vendor" list consisting of persons and affiliates who are disqualified from the public contracting and purchasing process because they have been found guilty of a public entity crime (Monroe, 1989).*

In other instances, we have observed more aggressive actions by elected officials and the public to adopt procurement policies that are more regulatory in nature. In one Florida county, a commissioner has pushed (unsuccessfully thus far) for legislation requiring county contractors to provide health care benefits to their employees. The commissioner's argument is that contractors who do not provide their employees these types of benefits may have an unfair advantage in the competitive bidding process because of lower personal services costs.* Another proposal in the same county, submitted to the county commission by a local chamber of commerce, has urged the county to require all its contractors to have an *aggressive* drug-free workplace program in place in order to enhance productivity, improve efficiency, and permit the county to get the most for its contracting dollars. (The state already has a preference policy in the case of a tie bid for businesses having implemented drug-free workplace programs—F.S. 287.087.)

---

* According to one purchasing expert, the paperwork and compliance costs for both businesses and government have been considerable. At the same time, the expert estimates that between 1989 and May 1993, fewer than firms have actually been investigated by the state for possible debarment. To his knowledge, only one firm has actually been placed on the disbarred list. From the deterrent perspective, however, one can make the argument that the law may have been more effective than these numbers suggest because businesses that have been convicted of these crimes may simply have stopped attempting to do business with government in Florida (Grable, 1993).

* Relatedly, employees of firms who do not offer health care benefits may very well end up in the county's indigent health care program, which would mean that the county is in effect subsidizing the firms who don't offer benefits.

Table 2 1991 Summary of In-State Preference Practives—States

State	Legal preference	Reciprocal law	Scope of preference and conditions
Alabama	None	No	By law, certain printing is to be kept in Montgomery, Alabama.
Alaska	5%	No	5% applies to state purchases from Alaskan vendors; 7% applies to state-grown
	7%		agricultural, fishery, and timber products. 3–7% applies to products produced
	3–7%		in state on value-added basis.
Arizona	None	No	—
Arkansas	5% (15%)	No	5% preference applies to state, counties, and municipalities for commodities.
	3% (Construction)		Vendor must claim preference. 15% preference against out-of-state prison
			industry bids. 3% preference on construction contracts. Firm must have paid
			Arkansas taxes for two years to qualify for preference.
California	None, except for distressed areas	No	For contracts over $100,000, California-based vendors located in distressed areas and enterprise zones receive a 5% preference. Preference applies to state level for commodities and services.
Colorado	None	Yes	Reciprocal law applies to both state and local governments for construction. Applies to state only for commodities and services. Vendor need not claim preference.
Connecticut	None	No	Never had preference or conditions to keep specific items in state.
Delaware	None	No	Preference law repealed in 1982.
Florida	None	Yes	Reciprocal law applies to counties, municipalities, school districts, and other political subdivisions. Does not apply to state purchases.
Georgia	None (except for forestry products)	Yes	Preference for Georgia vendors to match percentage of preference imposed by other states on Georgia vendors.
Idaho	10% (printing only)	Yes	Printing preference applies to state and counties. Reciprocal law applies to state, counties, municipalities, and other political subdivisions for commodities and construction.
Illinois	None (except for coal)	Yes	Reciprocal law applies to any state agency when contract is awarded to the lowest responsive bidder. Vendor need not claim preference. 10% preference for Illinois coal.
Indiana	Up to 5%	No	Up to 5% preference for Indiana businesses whose product includes 50% of the

Iowa	None (except for coal)	Yes	value of the product added within state. Bidders/offerors must certify their eligibility under penalty of perjury. 10% for ink made from soybeans. Reciprocal law applies to state, counties, municipalities, and other political subdivisions for commodities, services, and construction (including highways). Vendor need not claim preference. 5% preference is given to Iowa firms for coal.
Kansas	None	Yes	Reciprocal law applies to state, counties, municipalities, and other political subdivisions for commodities, services, and construction (including highways). Vendor need not claim preference.
Kentucky	None	No	—
Louisiana	7% 4% 10%	Yes, if over the applied preference	7% for products produced, manufactured, grown, harvested, or assembled in Louisiana. 4% for meat and catfish grown outside Louisiana but further processed in Louisiana. 10% for milk produced in Louisiana. 10% for steel rolled in Louisiana. Vendor can only receive one preference, and the highest applies.
Maine	None	No	—
Maryland	None	Yes	Reciprocal law applies to state level for commodities, services, and construction (including highways). Bidder need not claim preference. All new coal-burning boilers must be able to burn Maryland coal.
Massachusetts	None	No	—
Michigan	None (except for printing)	Yes	All printing is set aside for Michigan printers.
Minnesota	None	Yes	Reciprocal law applies to state level for commodities, services, and construction.
Mississippi	None	Yes	Reciprocal law applies to state level for commodities, services, and construction.
Missouri	None	Yes	Reciprocal law applies to both state and local governments for commodities and construction.
Montana	3% construction 5% commodities 3% commodities	See Note	Preference for Montana-made products applies to state, counties, municipalities, and other political subdivisions for commodities. 5% preference for all Montana-made products sold by Montana vendors or out-of-state vendors. 3% preference for all Montana vendors over out-of-state vendors of non-Montana-made goods.

(continued)

Table 2 Continued

State	Legal preference	Reciprocal law	Scope of preference and conditions
Nebraska	None	Yes	Reciprocal law applies to state level for commodities, services, and construction.
Nevada	None	No	—
New Hampshire	None	No	—
New Jersey	None	Yes	Reciprocal law applies to the state and other entities commodities and services.
New Mexico	5%	No	Preference applies to state, counties, municipalities, and other political subdivisions for commodities, services, and construction. Vendor must claim preference. A manufacturer who offers materials grown, produced, processed or manufactured wholly in New Mexico gets a 5% preference when bidding against a New Mexico business not supplying New Mexico-made goods.
New York	3% (food only)	No	The law allows a preference in the purchase of food products that are either grown or processed in New York State. The percentage of preference is determined by the commissioner of general services. Which food products are to be covered are determined by the commissioner of agriculture and markets.
North Carolina	None	No	—
North Dakota	None	Yes	Reciprocal law applies to state, counties, municipalities, and other political subdivisions for commodities. Vendor need not claim preference.
Ohio	5%	See Scope and Conditions	Preference, by statute, applies to state level for commodities and services. Awards are made to vendors from border states that offer the lowest and best bid and whose state does not impose a preference restriction to Ohio bidders. Reciprocity applies to border states only, except West Virginia.
Oklahoma	5%	Yes (if over 5%)	Preference applies to state, counties, municipalities, and other political subdivisions for commodities produced, grown, or manufactured in Oklahoma. Vendor must claim preference.
Oregon	None (except for printing)	Yes	All printing is set aside for Oregon printers unless in-state printers are unable to supply or price is unreasonable.
Pennsylvania	None	Yes	Reciprocal law applies to commodities. Act 146 of the 1986 legislature did away with Pennsylvania's retaliatory provision. For construction, law provides that contractor's labor force must have resided in Pennsylvania for at least 90 days. Coalfired heating systems installed after 6/8/90 must burn coal mined in Pennsylvania.

State	Reciprocal (Yes/No)	Percent Preference	Comments
Rhode Island	No	None	—
South Carolina	No	2% (under $2.5 mil.) 1% (over $2.5 mil.)	Preference applies to state for commodities. Preference does not apply when the price of a single unit exceeds $10,000, or to either prime contractor or subcontractor as it relates to the construction industry.
South Dakota	Yes	None (except for grade A milk processors)	Reciprocal law applies to state, counties, municipalities, and other political subdivisions for commodities, services, and construction. Grade A milk processors receive a 5% preference.
Tennessee	No	None	—
Texas	Yes	None	Reciprocal law applies to state, counties, municipalities, and other political subdivisions for commodities, services, and construction. Contracts involving federal funds are exempted unless political subdivision's own ordinance is more restrictive.
Utah	Yes	None	Reciprocal law applies to state level and school districts for commodities, services, and construction. If Utah-made product is lowest responsive offered by an out-of-state vendor, in-state bidder must agree to meet low bid price.
Vermont	No	None	—
Virginia	Yes	None (except for coal)	Reciprocal law applies to state level for commodities, services, and construction (including highways). Vendor need not claim preference. Coal mined in Virginia gets 4% preference if price is not more than 4% of the lowest responsive bidder.
Washington	Yes	None	Reciprocal law applies to state level for commodities and services.
West Virginia	Yes	Up to 5%	5% preference for all commodities, printing, and construction. Penalty of up to 5% may be imposed on contractors for incorrect certification.
Wisconsin	Yes	None	—
Wyoming	No	None (except for construction and printing)	For construction, 5% preference is granted if not more than 20% is subcontracted to out-of-state vendors or American-made products. For printing, 10% preference is granted if 75% of the work is done in state.

Note: In tie-bid situations, all states, by law or policy, give a preference to in-state vendors or American-made products over out-of-state vendors or non-American products.
Source: National Institute of Governmental Purchasing (1992).

THE CONTRACT AWARD PROCESS—PREFERENCE:
GRANTING TECHNIQUES

There are two major types of preference-granting techniques that can give an advantage to certain types of firms over others in the contract award process: price percentage preferences and set-asides.

Price Percentage Preference Policies

Often state and local vendor preference policies establish a set percentage of preference to be given to a certain category of vendor. For example, if a local government gives a 10% preference to purchases from local vendors, it means that a local vendor would get the contract if his or her price were equal to or lower than that of the low bidder's price plus 10%, For example, let's say that the lowest bidder overall on a computer system is an out-of-town responsible and responsive firm whose bid was $10,000. The lowest bid by a responsible and responsive local firm bid was $11,000. Under a percentage preference policy, the local firm would get the computer contract because its bid would be equal to the lowest bid overall plus 10% ($10,000 + $1,000 or $11,000). In addition to local vendors, price percentage preferences are often established for other socially and economically disadvantaged firms (e.g., small, minority, women-owned). So too are set-asides.

Set-Asides

The NIGP *Dictionary of Purchasing Terms* (1986: 28) defines a set-aside as "a procedure whereby an established percentage of expenditures is designated for exclusive bidding or purchase from specified (minority, small, disadvantaged, etc.) businesses." As noted by Rice (1991: 114) in his excellent article about government set-asides for minority-owned businesses, there are two types: "(1) pure set-asides which provide that a certain percentage of the total number of government contracts be allotted to minority-owned businesses and (2) subcontractor goal set-asides which require that a certain portion of a prime contractor's fee be spent with minority-owned contractors."

The use of set-asides as a preference-granting technique at the state and local level has diminished considerably following the U.S. Supreme Court's ruling in the *City of Richmond* v. *J. A. Croson Co.* (January 23, 1989). In that case, the Court ruled (6–3) that the city of Richmond's minority set-aside program was unconstitutional, although it did *not* rule that all set-asides were unconstitutional.* Specifically, the Court ruled that the city's set-aside violated the right of white contractors to equal protection of law guaranteed by the 14th Amendment.† The Court also "ruled that state and local governments are

---

* The court said, however, that set-aside programs "must have a well-documented basis to withstand constitutional challenges" (*New York Times*, 1991).

† For discussions and interpretations of the *Croson* ruling, see Bell, 1989; Benjamin, 1989; Cohen, 1989; Davis and Jackson, 1990; Dobrovier, 1990; Fried 1989; Hall, 1990; Hoogland and McGlothlen, 1989; Hoogland, et al, 1989; Lewis, 1989; Mackie, 1989; Moreno, 1992; Norton and Norton, 1989; Ollerman, 1989; Rasnic 1989; Reuben, 1989; Rice, 1991; Rosenfeld, 1989; Sandoval, 1990; Scherer, 1990; Selig, 1990; Suggs, 1990; Weeden, 1989; *Yale Law Journal*, June and October, 1989.

denied the powers that the federal government can employ in deciding to use 'race-conscious' remedies to end so-called societal discrimination" (Moreno, 1992:48).*

The Richmond policy had required white prime contractors who were awarded city construction contracts to subcontract at least 30% of the dollar value of the prime contract to one or more minority business enterprises. The Court ruled that the city's minority business utilization plan was "too broad and not 'narrowly-tailored'—meaning that it used general [minority] population figures that didn't provide a specific statistical justification of the program, documenting the extent to which minority businesses were actually being discriminated against" (Moreno, 1992:48). (The 30% figure was not based on data reflecting the eligible pool of minority contractors.)

Today, if a state or local public entity wishes to adopt a minority set-aside policy or defend one already in place, it must complete a very expensive, time-consuming, difficult "disparity study"† to demonstrate that the policy has been adopted to remedy the effects of past discrimination. (See Rice, 1991; LaNoue, 1991; Moreno, 1992.) The basis for this approach is a statement by Justice Sandra O'Connor in the Court's plurality opinion in the *Croson* case.

> Where there is a significant statistical disparity between the number of qualified minority contractors willing and able to perform a particular service and the number of such contractors actually engaged by the locality or the locality's prime contractors, an inference of discriminatory exclusion could arise.

In his excellent *Minority Business Programs and Disparity Studies*, LeNoue (1991) offers a detailed checklist of decisions that must be made by any government undertaking such a study. These decisions fall into four broad categories: (1) selecting a team; (2) determining the scope of the study; (3) measuring disparity; and (4) determining remedies.

In *Hispanic Business* (1992:48), Moreno states that a disparity study must "develop two predicates justifying the need for remedial action [i.e. preference policies]. The predicates are that the contracting agencies must: (1) avow the remedial purpose of the race-conscious program, and (2) justify such remedial programs with both statistical and anecdotal evidence of the discrimination to be remedied." In other words, "discriminatory business practices must be proved to exist before a government [can] set aside contracts for minority companies, and then the remedial program must be narrowly designed to address the discrimination" (*New York Times*, 1991).

More Voluntary Techniques: Vendor Recruitment, Good Faith, and Shelters

Less controversial are the more *voluntary* "preferential" approaches used by state and local governments to attract certain categories of vendors. In *Black Enterprise*, Gallman (1991: 153–62) identifies these as they have been applied to minority vendors (but the same approaches are used for other categories of vendors as well; e.g., small, women,

---

* According to an article by the *New York Times* (1991; 2E), the *Croson* "ruling did not affect federal set-aside programs, which continue to pump billions of dollars a year into businesses owned by members of minority groups and women. Congress has broad discretion under the Constitution to decide what the country needs to promote racial equality, the court said."
† One estimate is that disparity studies cost between $250,000 and $750,000 each and typically take one to two years to complete (Moreno, 1992:49).

disadvantaged). One common approach for the government is to aggressively recruit the desired, often underrepresented, category of vendor. In such *outreach programs*, "a city or state purchasing office registers minority vendors and distributes the list to majority companies in hopes that they will use the minority businesses as subcontractors."

Another type of voluntary approach is known as "good faith." Governments using this approach ask companies that are awarded contracts (prime contractors) to make a good faith effort to subcontract a certain percentage of business to minority-owned firms.

The *sheltered market* approach, also known as "restrictive bidding," restricts bidding (formal or informal) on a contract to minority vendors. It is limited to areas in when there are substantial numbers of minority businesses (i.e., competition). If the approach does not yield bids or quotes that are within a certain range of the market price, the process is aborted.

Use of informal, or noncompetitive, methods of awarding contracts* are another way to voluntarily promote American, state, or local vendors, small businesses, or businesses owned by women, minorities, or the handicapped. Most commonly used are RFQs (*requests for quotes*), whereby government procurement rules permit purchasing agents to seek oral (telephone) or written quotes from vendors without formal advertising and receipt of sealed bids in certain situations and within specific dollar thresholds.

These voluntary mechanisms for increasing the participation of certain categories of vendors in the procurement process are not as likely to evoke litigation over their constitutionality as mandatory price percentage preferences and set-asides policies (which give categories of businesses a competitive advantage in the actual bidding process). Nonetheless, they elicit the same types of arguments for and against them.

THE "PROS" OF VENDOR PREFERENCE POLICIES

Supporters of vendor preference policies argue vehemently that they promote both competition and impartiality.

Business Classification Preferences

Proponents maintain that without policies promoting small businesses and firms owned by women and minorities, little change will occur in the current vendor pool, the development of new business firms will be stunted, and in the long term competition will suffer and government will pay more for goods and services than it might otherwise. (Compare Cohen, 1989; Norton and Norton, 1989; *Yale Law Journal*, 1989.)

LeNoue (1991:7) summarizes the advantages of preferences for minority-owned firms well: these social preference policies "create jobs, particularly for minority residents,

---

* "Unlike formal methods, informal methods of awarding contracts do not necessarily require public advertising, public opening, or awarding of the contract to the lowest, most responsive and responsible bidder. They are most likely to be used in coping with emergencies, contracting for professional services, contracting for goods and services for which there is only one source, contracting for goods and services falling under certain dollar threshold amounts, and fulfilling policy goals . . . They are seen as ways to make the procurement process more flexible, less bureaucratic, more innovative, and more attractive to vendors. The major drawback is that informal methods may lead some potential private sector suppliers to doubt the impartiality, openness, and competitiveness of the system" (MacManus, 1992:47).

add economic vitality and competition, especially in urban areas, and are necessary to overcome the disadvantages caused by historical and present discrimination against minorities in business."*

Another reason given for using techniques such as preferences to expand the vendor pool is the nation's changing demographic and socioeconomic profile. By the year 2000, projections by the Census Bureau are that minorities will make up a majority of the population in many jurisdictions. Another projection is that by the same year, women will own 50% of all small businesses in the United States. It is important that public purchasing practices promote diversity among its bidders and attract a wider range of firms to compete for government business; otherwise, the basic purchasing principles of competition, efficiency, and impartiality will be violated, say the proponents of preferences.

Business Location Preferences

Preference policies based on a firm's geographical location (i.e., local vendors) are generally promoted on the grounds that they enhance efficiency and can save a jurisdiction money. In defending a local vendor preference policy, one purchasing director outlined the situations in which this claim seems to be most valid (Bruso, 1989:4).

1. Local vendors are better able to provide commodities that rely on the warehouse function (e.g., lumber, paint, hardware items, electrical supplies, plumbing supplies, glass replacement, auto parts, auto tires, and carpet).
2. Local vendors are better able to provide the mobilization function required for commodities such as shell, fill, asphalt, and contract hauling.
3. Local vendors are better able to provide services that may require local resources. Title companies or contracted legal services are examples.
4. Local vendors are sometimes better equipped to provide the "service after the sale" that may be required of some commodities.
5. Local vendors are usually first aware of new or breaking projects that provide a ground floor opportunity to assist in specification development.

Firms currently unable to successfully compete for government contracts, such as small minority-owned firms and local vendors, often see government's failure to adopt preference policies as evidence that the public procurement process is noncompetitive, unfair, and protective of the status quo, but firms currently holding government contracts often view any special efforts by government to bring in new classes of vendors as noncompetitive and unfair as well. Let's examine their arguments against preferences.

THE "CONS" OF VENDOR PREFERENCES

"Most favored customer" policies are generally regarded by opponents as "anticompetitive and self-defeating," primarily because they "have the effect of setting artificial floors on

---

* It should be noted, however, that minority firm owners often oppose preference policies. Among their chief complaints is their being "used" by nonminority firms, either in the prime–subcontractor relationship or in establishing ownership of a firm in order to qualify as a minority-owned business. (See MacManus, 1992; 1993; Green and Pryde, 1990.) Another basic complaint is that they see participation in these programs as too restrictive, limiting the scope of their business and their chances of expansion.

prices and of fixing prices at one level" (NASPO, 1988:26–27). Preference laws, in NASPO's opinion, show "the chilling effect of constituent preference upon competition and unrealized savings" and increase administrative costs to governments. Finally, opponents make the claim that "there has been little substantive demonstration of program effectiveness."

Restricted Competition Yields Higher Costs

Opponents of preferences (price percentage, set-asides) argue that they encourage the "advantaged" vendors to inflate their prices, meaning that government has to pay inflated prices for goods or services it could acquire more cheaply absent preference policies. Preference policies also often increase labor costs as governments need additional personnel to design, implement enforce, and defend such policies. For example, the purchasing agent for the city of Lincoln, Nebraska, "estimated that a 10% Buy American preference would add about $3 million to his government's costs, and would necessitate hiring a professional analyst and a clerk at the cost of about $50,000 a year to search for American suppliers, make determinations as to which products were really American and which were foreign, and to verify vendors' certifications" (Jackson, 1992:3).

Definition Difficulties

The purchasing director for Volusia County, Florida, outlined for his governing board the definition difficulties associated with creating and implementing a relatively "simple" local vendor preference policy (Bruso, 1989:7).* These were as follows:

1. What is the definition of a local vendor?
2. Must the local vendor own or rent property in Volusia County?
3. What are the minimum requirements for the length of time a vendor must have been located in Volusia County to qualify as a local vendor?
4. Do branch offices of firms qualify as local vendors?
5. Are businesses operated from Volusia County residences considered local vendors? Does the home of a sales representative qualify as a local vendor if the correspondence goes there?
6. Does a post office box qualify a company as a local vendor?
7. Does a legal street address qualify a company as a local vendor?
8. Does the holding of a current Volusia County occupational license qualify a company as a local vendor?
9. Does the company do its banking in Volusia County? Would payments made to companies with addresses outside Volusia County disqualify them as local vendors?
10. In construction contracts must a certain percentage of the subs be qualified as local vendors? If the construction company uses a large percentage of local vendor subs will it be required to have its home office in Volusia County? If the construction company is qualified as a local vendor, will any of its subs be required local vendor certification?

---

* The same basic definition issues would have to be resolved with the establishment of any group (classification) based preference policy.

11. What ties to the community will be required to qualify a firm as a local vendor?
12. Should the ownership of a business be local to qualify it as a local vendor?
13. Should the vendor be able to provide the warehouse function as well as the sales function locally to be certified as a local vendor?

In order to arrive at the answers to these questions (particularly ones that would be sustainable in court if litigation were to ensue), it would be necessary to do a lot of background research on the topic. This intensive research effort would cost the county considerably both in terms of time and resources. Some say this whole exercise is unnecessary because "Local vendors already enjoy natural advantages . . . a more intimate knowledge of their state or locality's needs, a competitive advantage in delivery distance, a local sales and service force, and easier access to the purchaser for review of past bids" (Dimeo, 1992:61).

It might be even more difficult to devise a "Buy American" policy: "They simply are not practical in some cases because it is tough to figure out what is American-made these days. Jurisdictions considering [them] may have to look to where the company's profits go or where the workers are employed in order to shape policies" (Dimeo, 1992: 61).

Another fairly common argument against preferences is that in the long term, they may actually reduce the level of competition and increase costs as nonpreferenced vendors decide that bidding for that government's contracts is a waste of time.

Yet another argument against preferences is that they might result in retaliatory legislation being implemented by other jurisdictions. The effect of retalatory legislation would be to restrict a local firm's ability to sell elsewhere, which in turn would negatively impact on that government's local economy and its revenue (tax) stream. (See Bruso, 1989.)

Difficulty in Showing That Preference Programs Yield the Desired Results

Prior to the *Croson* ruling, there was not much evidence that preference policies yielded the desirable results which themselves were rarely articulated in detail.* Even in the post-*Croson* era, effectiveness studies have almost exclusively focused on the "fairness" goal to the exclusion of the "economic" goals.

For example, most of the evaluations of the effectiveness of minority set-aside programs have used a before-and-after-*Croson* design to gather data showing a drop-off in the percentage and/or dollar volume of a government's contracts being award to minority-owned firms. Few have examined the extent to which set-aside policies save the govern-

---

* A 1986 report drafted by the staff for the U.S. Civil Rights Commission (but never officially endorsed by the commission at large) summarized several studies by state and federal agencies that found that minority set-aside programs did not help minority firms compete in the marketplace (*New York Times, 1991*). Post-*Croson* comments by the executive director of the National Association of Minority Contractors seemed to confirm these earlier studies: "Thousands of minority businesses went under or were neutralized, and thousands of strong businesses became weak. Most of the minority community's business comes from government programs, and when these programs are struck down, they no longer have a place to sell their goods and services" (*New York Times*, 1991). Others, however, blamed "the nationwide recession, the tax sqeeze on state and local governments, the persistence of racism and the relative inexperience of many minority entrepreneurs, who set up their companies expressly to take advantage of such programs" (*New York Times*, 1991).

ment money, result in a net growth to the local economy, create net growth in the number of and assets of the "preferred" class of vendors, or result in the retention of businesses and jobs (Dimeo, 1992). These *should* be considered when measuring the effectiveness of preference policies, however, along with the number of preferenced vendors and the volume of contracts awarded to them.

In general, there have been few well-designed cost-benefit studies that incorporate both the economic and social goals associated with public purchasing to test the effectiveness of various preference policies. The closet thing to such an approach was a 1991 survey by the NIGP. In that survey, the respondents were asked to gauge the success of various types of preference policies in their jurisdictions or agencies (NIGP, 1992). (Caution should be taken in interpreting these responses since they are the *opinions* of the respondents rather than the results of rigorous cost–benefit analyses.) The results were mixed. For example, among those governments with local vendor preference policies, 60% reported that local businesses have not grown competitively stronger as a result of the policy. With regard to Buy American preferences, 71% reported that even though their jurisdiction had such a policy, foreign bids were not rejected. Relatedly, for those with policies restricting businesses trading in South Africa, 69% said they rejected no bids on this basis.* Preferences for small/disadvantaged and MBE businesses appeared to be more successful, at least in increasing the number of these firms bidding for government contracts. Where such preferences were in place, 57% increased the number of small/disadvantaged firms bidding and 79% reported an increase in the number of MBE firms bidding on contracts. Even this survey, however, did not *really* examine the overall effectiveness of these policies, the measurement of which was outlined above.

SUMMARY AND CONCLUSION

Public administrators, financial managers, and procurers must be aware that they will often be at odds with elected officials over the design and implementation of certain purchasing policies and procedures because each group tends to have a different notion of what are the primary goals of public purchasing. At the top of the list of potential areas of disagreement are vendor preferences.

For the most part, the public purchasing professional community opposes mandatory vendor preferences on the grounds that they violate several of the principles of good purchasing (competition, impartiality, efficiency). Elected officials often favor them because they are evidence of their responsiveness to their constituencies. Rarely, however, are vendor preference issues so clear cut, even from the perspective of the professional purchasers. This case study has demonstrated that there are equally powerful arguments, even with regard to the principles of competition, impartiality, and efficiency, both for and against vendor preference policies. The study has also shown that more stringent cost-benefit analyses need to be conducted to determine whether or not such policies are effective—in their design, implementation, and evaluation.

---

* Restricting trade with South Africa is no longer a goal of minority groups or government policies aimed at punishing racism following the demise of the all-white South African government and the election of Nelson Mandela as president.

REVIEW QUESTIONS

1. If elected officials press to adopt vendor preference policies, are they being responsive to the demands of voters who put them in office or are they being unfair by effectively excluding or disadvantaging certain types of firms from competing for public business?
2. How do the competition, impartiality, and efficiency goals of public purchasing conflict with the social goals inherent in public procurement policies? Are there any instances in which they complement each other?
3. What is the difference between a vendor who is merely the "lowest" bidder and one who is "responsible" or "responsive?"
4. What are the common types of business classifications that benefit from vendor preference policies or locational classifications?
5. What are the major differences between mandatory preference policies (such as price percentage preferences and set-asides) and the more voluntary approaches (outreach, good faith, shelters, RFOs) to vendor preferences?
6. What are the major arguments in favor of vendor preference policies? Against? Which groups within you state or local government are most likely to support or oppose each type of vendor preference policy if it were proposed or re-examined?

REFERENCES

Bell, A. F. (fall 1989). *City of Richmond v. J. A. Croson Company*: The decision and some of its implications. *School Law Bulletin, 20*, 22–29.

Benjamin, J. H. (April 1989). The Supreme Court decision and the future of race-conscious remedies. *Government Finance Review, 5*, 21–24.

Bruso, C. W. (May 23, 1989). Interdepartment memorandum: Preferential purchasing. DeLand, FL: Volusia County Purchasing Department.

Chi, K. (1988). *Privatization and Contracting for State Service: A Guide*. Lexington, KY: Council of State Governments, Innovation Report RM-777.

Cohen, D. S. (spring–summer 1989). The evidentiary predicate for affirmative action after *Croson*: A proposal for shifting the burdens of proof. *Yale Law & Policy Review, 7*, 489–515.

Davis, C. H. and Jackson, D. D. (1990). The sunset of affirmative action? *City of Richmond v. J.A. Croson Co. National Black Law Journal, 23*, 73–87.

DeHoog, R. H. (1985). Human services contracting: Environmental, behavioral and organizational Conditions. *Administration and Society, 16*(4), 427–454.

Dimeo, J. (July 1992). Buy American, Buy Local. *American City & County, 107*, 61.

Dobrovier, W. (1990). Creating a program that passes the *Croson* test. Minority set-asides and the Court: Was the *Croson* decision the end of affirmative action? *Legal Times, 11*, 32.

Donahue, J. D. (1989). *The Privatization Decision: Public Ends, Private Means*. New York: Basic Books.

Farrell, P. V. ed. (1989). *Alijan's Purchasing Handbook*. 4th ed. New York: McGraw Hill.

Fried, C. Comments: Affirmative action after *City of Richmond v. J. A. Croson Co.* A response to the scholars' statement. *Yale Law Journal, 99* (Oct), 155–162.

Gallman, V. (1991). Winning the government procurement game. *Black Enterprise, 21*, 153–162.

Grable, T. J. Jr. (April 29, 1993). Memorandum: Social/preference programs in government procurement. Tampa, FL: Hillsborough County Department of Purchasing and Contracts.

Green, S. and Pryde, P. (1996). *Black Enterpreneurship in America*. New Brunswick, NJ: Transaction.

Hall, D. (1990). Contradictions, illusions, ironies and inverted realities: The historical relevance of the *Richmond v. Croson* case. *Urban League Review, 14*, 9–16.

Halligan, P. D. (spring 1991). Minority business enterprises: Guidelines for studies by local governments. *Urban Lawyer, 23*, 249–279.

Hoogland, K. A. and McGlothlen, C. (summer 1989). *City of Richmond v. Croson*: A setback for minority set-aside programs. *Employee Relations Law Journal*, 5–19.

Hoogland, K. A., McGlothlen, C. and Rosenfeld, M. (June 1989). Richmond: Affirmative action and the elusive meaning of constitutional equality. *Michigan Law Review, 87*, 1729–1724.

Irwin, D. T. (1988). Privatization in America. In *The Municipal Year Book 1988*, pp. 43–55. Washington, DC: International City Management Association.

Jackson, L. (March/April 1992). Buying American is one thing: Buying dumb is something else. *NIGP Technical Bulletin*, 1–2.

Jackson, L. (Sept./Oct. 1992). Buy American—Buy local. *NIGP Technical Bulletin*, 1–7.

Jacobson, L. (May 8, 1993). Green Giants (recycled products procurement), *National Journal, 25*, 1113–1116.

Jones, R. C. (Nov./Dec. 1992). The red tape of preference buying. *NIGP Technical Bulletin*, 3–4.

LaNoue, G. R. (1991). *Minority Business Programs and Disparity Studies: Responding to the Supreme Court's Mandate in Richmond v. Croson: A Local Official's Guide*. Washington, DC: National League of Cities.

Levinson, D. R. (Nov. 1980). A Study of Preferential Treatment—the evolution of minority business enterprise assistance programs. *George Washington Law Review, 49*, 61–99.

Lewis, A. (April 13, 1989). Now is the time for healing on the race issue. *Los Angeles Daily Journal, 102*, 6.

Lewis, E. and Weltman, E. (Feb. 1993). Government purchasing saves tax dollars and environment. *American City & County, 108*, 34.

Lowinger, T. C. (1976). Discrimination in government procurement of foreign goods in the U.S. and Western Europe. *Southern Economic Journal, 42(3)*, 451–460.

Mackie, S. A. (June 1989). Florida minority business hiring in light of *City of Richmond v. J.A. Croson Co. Florida Bar Journal, 63*, 11–14.

MacManus, S. A. (1990). Minority business contracting with local government. *Urban Affairs Quarterly, 25*, 455–473.

MacManus, S. A. (1991). Why businesses are reluctant to sell to governments. *Public Administration Review, 51*, 328–344.

MacManus, S. A. (1992). *Doing Business with Government: Federal, State, Local & Foreign Government Purchasing Practices For Every Business & Public Institution*. New York: Paragon House.

MacManus, S. A. (Feb. 1993). Minority contractors' views of government purchasing and procurement practices. *Economic Development Quarterly, 7*, 30–49.

Mejer, V. M. (Feb 1992). "Buy American?????????" *NIGP Technical Bulletin*, 1–2.

Monroe, W. O. (July 10, 1989). Memorandum: Public entity crimes. Tallahassee, FL: State of Florida, Department of General Services.

Moreno, R. L. (Oct 1992). Court setback could get worse: Minority set-aside programs forced to shore up their defenses. *Hispanic Business, 14*, 48–50.

Morley, E. (1989). Patterns in the use of alternative service delivery approaches. In *The Municipal Year Book 1989*, pp. 33–44. Washington, DC: International City Management Association.

Mullis, C. L. (Nov. 1978). Competitive bidding law. *Florida Municipal Record*, 10–12.

National Association of State Purchasing Officials (NASPO). (1988). *State and Local Government Purchasing*. 3rd ed. Lexington, KY: Council of State Governments.

National Institute of Governmental Purchasing. (1986). *The Dictionary of Purchasing Terms*. 4th ed. Falls Church, VA: NIGP.

National Institute of Governmental Purchasing. (Jan./Feb. 1991). Are local preference laws in the United States an impediment to world trade? *NIGP Technical Bulletin*, 1–2.

National Institute of Governmental Purchasing (1992). *Results of the 1991 Procurement Survey.* Falls Church, VA: NIGP.

National Institute of Governmental Purchasing. (1992). *1991 Survey of In-State (Buy-Local), Buy-American, and Recycled Product Preferences of Fifty States and Cities Over 500,000 Population.* Falls Church, VA: NIGP.

New York Times. (Dec. 24, 1991). Rulings killing minority-owned businesses. *St. Petersburg Times* 1–2E.

Norton, E. H. and Norton, E. W. (May 1, 1989). A setback for minority businesses: Minority set-asides and the Court: Was the *Croson* decision the end of affirmative action? *Legal Times*, *11*, 31.

Ollerman, C. M. (1989). Recent developments—Constitutional law: Equal protection and affirmative action in local government contracting—*City of Richmond v. J.A. Croson Co. Harvard Journal of Law and Public Policy*, *12*, 1069–1081.

Ostrander, S. (1989). Private social services: Obstacles to the welfare state? *Nonprofit and Voluntary Sector Quarterly*, *18*, 25–46.

Page, H. R. (1987). *Public Purchasing and Materials Management.* Lexington, MA: Lexington Books.

Perlman, E. (Nov. 5–18). Minority set-aside programs back on track. *City & State*, 4.

Premus, R., Karns, D., and Robinson, A. (1985). *Socioeconomic Regulations and the Federal Procurement Market.* Washington, DC: Joint Economic Committee, Congress of the United States.

Rasnic, C. D. (fall 1989). *City of Richmond v. J. A. Croson Co.*: What does it portend for affirmative action? *Creighton Law Review*, *23*, 19–43.

Rehfuss, J. (1989). *Contracting Out in Government.* San Francisco: Jossey-Bass.

Reuben, R. C. (March 7, 1989). U. S. high court sharpens focus on "Set-Aside": "*Croson* Doctrine." *Los Angeles Daily Journal*, *102*, 1.

Rice, M. F. (1991). Government set-asides, minority business enterprises, and the Supreme Court. *Public Administration Review*, *51*, 114–122.

Rosenfeld, M. (1989). Decoding Richmond: Affirmative action and the elusive meaning of constitutional equality. *Michigan Law Review*, *87*, 1729–1794.

Salamon, L. M. (1987). Partners in the public service: The scope and voluntary sector relationship. In W. W. Powell (ed), *The Nonprofit Sector: A Research Handbook.* New Haven, CT: Yale University Press.

Sandoval, R. (Jan 1990). An analysis of the new legal model for establishing set-aside programs for minority business enterprise: The case of *City of Richmond v. J. A. Croson Co. Gonzaga Law Review*, *25*, 141–155.

Savas, E. S. (1982). *Privatizing the Public Sector: How to Shrink Government.* Chatham, NJ: Chatham House.

Scherer, D. D. (Winter 1990). Affirmative action doctrine and the conflicting messages of *Croson*. *University of Kansas Law Review*, *38*, 281–341.

Selig, J. (1990). Affirmative action in employment after *Croson* and *Martin*: The legacy remains intact. *Temple Law Review*, *63*, 1–29.

Simms, M. C. (Sept. 1990). Rebuilding set aside programs. *Black Enterprise*, 33.

Suggs, R. E. (Winter 1990). Rethinking Minority business development strategies. *Harvard Civil Rights—Civil Liberties Law Review*, 101–145.

Taylor, R. L. (1990). The equal protection dilemma of voluntary state and local set-aside programs for minorities and women. *Houston Law Review*, *27*, 45–70.

Van Benthuysen, H. D. (1981). Minority business enterprise set-aside: The reverse discrimination challenge. *Albany Law Review*, *45*, 1139–1176.

Weeden, D. (1989). *City of Richmond v. J.A. Croson* and the aborted affirmative action plan. *Southern University Law Review, 16,* 73–100.

Wilson, M. (1987). Set-asides of local government contracts for minority-owned businesses: Constitutional and state law issues. *New Mexico Law Review, 17,* 337–359.

Yale Law Journal. (June 1989). Joint statement: Constitutional scholars' statement on affirmative action after *City of Richmond v. J.A. Croson Co. Yale Law Journal, 98,* 1711–1716.

Yale Law Journal (Oct. 1989). Scholars' reply to professor fried. *Yale Law Journal, 99,* 163–168.

41
Risk Management
A Case Study

Bernard H. Ross and David H. Rosenbloom
American University, Washington, D.C., U.S.A.

Ask any urban residents, as newspapers frequently do, what the major issues or problems facing their city or county are and they will respond fairly predictably. Their answers in recent years would include most of the following: high crime rates, AIDS, increasing numbers of homeless people living on the streets, unacceptable levels of high school dropouts, excessive traffic congestion, air pollution, mass transit delays, increased use of hard drugs among different levels of the population, unethical and corrupt behavior by local public officials, and a continued deterioration of our bridges, tunnels, highways, railroads, and airport facilities.

While all of these answers represent obvious and serious problems, few, if any, respondents ever think of the municipal liability implications of each of these major contemporary urban problems or the many other areas of risk facing local governments in the course of providing services. Nevertheless, local public officials across the nation continue to worry about the threat of lawsuits against their political jurisdictions growing out of the action or inaction of their employees as well as the inherent risks in government service delivery (Matlock and Woodhouse, 1987).

Our cities, counties, and schools faced a nationwide crisis that threatened the continued existence of some of the smaller jurisdictions. This was the municipal liability crisis that surfaced in the mid-1980s and that continues to concern local government officials as they make decisions about how best to deliver public services. This crisis resulted from rapidly escalating liability insurance premiums.

Both the public and the private sectors were hard hit by this crisis. The private sector always had the option to reduce or discontinue risky ventures if adequate protection was not available, however. On the other hand, local governments faced a much more difficult task. Could they pull police officers off the street because adequate liability insurance was not available or because the law enforcement activity is inherently a risky one? Could they stop incarcerating criminals because their overcrowded, antiquated jails violated the inmates' Eighth Amendment rights? As a general rule the public will not accept these alternatives. Still, some police were removed from the streets,* some inmates were shifted

---

* For a discussion of communities that suspended, disbanded, or abolished their police forces in the wake of skyrocketing liability premiums, see McLean, (1986: 8, 1). See also *U.S.A. Today*, Jan. 10, 1986.

to privatized prisons, and some communities closed recreational areas, pools, parks, and beaches because of the increased exposure to lawsuits* Mayors and councils concerned about loss of their personal assets hesitated to make policy decisions on issues of potential public risk, and in some instances, actually resigned their positions.† This is an unfortunate way to lose local government leaders, and is both damaging and disruptive to local government while undermining our democratic process.

The initial results of this crisis have already had far-reaching effects on the economic and political health of our local communities. If funds have to be diverted from services to pay for escalating insurance premiums, self-insurance, costly litigation, or court judgments, the taxpayers in the end suffer the most. Businesses will assess these factors and then determine whether or not to locate in those jurisdictions with large liability or property losses or where they think property taxes could be increased to pay for a large financial loss. This could reduce a jurisdiction's ability to provide jobs, enhance its tax base, maintain or improve its public service delivery, improve its standard of living, and generally upgrade the quality of life in the community.

WHAT IS RISK MANAGEMENT?

Risk management has been identified as one of the fastest growing fields in local government (Cragg and Kloman, 1985). Historically, risk management has been associated with insurance management, but in the last fifteen years there has been increased attention to the much broader function of effectively managing risks facing state and local governments. The Public Risk Management Association (PRIMA), an association of state and local government risk managers, was created in 1978 with 250 members, but had grown to more than 900 by 1985. In 1997 PRIMA claimed 2000 members. PRIMA is dedicated to increasing risk management professionalism in public agencies and to improving the operation of local governments through proven risk management techniques. More than 1500 people attend PRIMA's annual conference, and several hundred more attend regional specialized training sessions focusing on the enhancement of risk management skills and practices.

By the early 1980s public risk management was gaining acceptance as an important governmental function. Numerous large cities and counties began hiring (or appointing from within) full-time risk managers who could oversee this very important function of government. Today risk managers handle a variety of tasks, including public safety, insurance and claims management, workers' compensation, employee training, employee benefits, litigation management, and emergency preparedness. In any operation in which there is a risk of human or financial loss, risk managers are involved (Roos, Johnson, and Ross).

Although this chapter deals with legal liability, it is important to note that there are several other types of risks to which the core concepts of risk management apply. These are: property loss, as in the case of fires and natural disasters, such as violent storms; unanticipated expenses, such as unavoidable cost overruns; loss of anticipated income;

---

* For a discussion on the impact of soaring liability premiums on local governments' ability to provide athletic and recreational activities see Hanley (1986). For discussion of prison privatization, see Matlock (1995).

† For examples of local public officials resigning from office, see Welch (1985). See also *National Underwriter*, Nov. 15, 1985.

and loss of human resources through death, resignation, accident, illness, and/or labor–management disputes.

In dealing with these types of losses, risk management can be divided into five primary functions. They are exposure identification, risk evaluation, risk control, risk funding, and risk administration.

Cragg and Kloman (1985) have discussed the major elements of risk management, and their views can be summarized as follows. *Exposure identification* requires public officials to assess and identify their jurisdiction's resources as well as the potential loss exposures that could result from the use of those resources. Resources can be physical, human, financial, natural, or intangible. Identification of potential risks facing public agencies includes assessing everything from the classroom teacher to the recreational lake to the local garbage truck to the winter snowstorm, all of which could result in liability losses or affect the ability of the local government to provide services in a noninjurious manner while assuring that income-producing activities continue unabated.

Risk evaluation entails a thorough analysis of the activities previously identified. This includes an historical analysis of past losses for each public activity as well as an assessment of the future frequency and severity of potential losses. This can be a very costly and time-consuming job if accurate records have not been kept or are not available from the jurisdiction's insurers over the years.

Risk managers must be able to assess the value of all of the resources identified, including potential revenues. When combined with loss frequency and severity historical data, risk managers are in a position to evaluate accurately their local community's total potential risk exposure.

Risk control involves the reduction or elimination of risk or loss to the local community. This task logically follows the risk identification and evaluation functions. Risk control is both the most important and most difficult component of risk management to implement. It is important since it seeks only not to reduce loss, but also to minimize and wherever possible eliminate risk. This task is made difficult by the fragmented and departmentalized nature of local government. Some agencies try to coordinate such activities as police, fire, and rescue squads, but local government risk spans the breadth of public sector activities and very few local governments have been successful in trying to coordinate education, health, public works, recreation, public housing, public transit, and senior citizen activities. The difficulties associated with risk management control in local governments are evident in the National Safety Council figures that indicate that in measuring days away from work per year, the public employee rate is more than twice as high as the private sector (Cragg and Kloman, 1985: 13).

The fourth element of risk management is *risk funding*. Simply put, once you have assessed the value of your resources, analyzed the past frequency and severity of your losses, forecast future potential losses, and taken steps to prevent or control them, then the question becomes where the money will come from to protect local government against losses that do occur. The solution is not usually found in one program. Local governments use a combination of internal and external approaches to optimize their use of financial resources to meet any major liability crisis that may arise.

The major funding alternatives available to local governments are self-insurance, pooling arrangements, and commercial insurance. Most local governments use a mix of the available alternatives with a recent tendency to increase their self-insurance commitments.

By the late 1970s pooling was beginning to grow as a way to combat rising insurance premiums. Pooling is a cooperative risk-financing tool used by public agencies to spread and share the costs of financing risk. Participating entities pay a premium, receive coverage, and make claims. Risk pools provide workers' compensation, unemployment, property, liability, life, and health insurance. Pools also save their members money, give them greater control over risk financing, and help them develop better risk management practices. Today, all but two of the states are using pooling arrangements for some types of their insurance protection. Nationwide an estimated 450 pools provide a wide range of coverage to approximately 33% of the general and all purpose governments in the United States. (Brown, 1985; Young, 1988; Johnson and Ross, 1989; interview with Prima official). Pools can be structured statewide, countrywide, or to cover metropolitan areas.

The final aspect of risk management is the administration of the different components. Some individual or department has to be charged with the responsibility of carrying out the risk identification, evaluation, control, and funding activities that note up a comprehensive risk management program. In larger communities there may be a full-time risk manager with a staff to carry out the risk management functions. In smaller communities these responsibilities may devolve upon the finance officer, assistant city manager, personnel director, or one of his or her top aides (Johnson and Ross, 1991).

A risk manager should work closely with the elected governing body to develop and disseminate a comprehensive policy statement of the jurisdiction's risk and insurance management objectives. This can become a key ingredient in overcoming the fragmentation problem in managing risk across agencies. The risk manager needs to open up channels of communication with both the elected officials as well as the department heads, supervisors, and public. Policy statements, changes in policy, guidelines on risk reduction and elimination, and progress reports on how each department is doing should be issued periodically by the risk manager in addition to an annual report to the elected officials.

CASE BACKGROUND

This case and the supporting materials deal with the essence of local government and its ability to deliver services to its citizens. The case points up the difficulty of police officers doing their job without a full understanding of the legal ramifications of their actions.

As the Supreme Court decides cases on the liability of local officials, this information has to be transmitted to the thousands of local governments. Following some rulings officials must be given more, better, or different training. In other cases policy and procedure manuals must be rewritten or amended to account for the new rulings by the court. Failure to do so increases the liability exposure of both the local government and its official agents.

In this chapter, we not only present a case but also show how local government liability has grown and changed in the past two decades. These changes have prompted local governments to hire risk managers who are changed with the responsibility of identifying, managing, and reducing risk for local governments.

THE CASE

On a fall evening in the city of Potluck, Ohio, two police officers were sitting in their cruiser enjoying an uneventful tour of duty. Even as their radio came on indicating a domestic squabble had broken out in another part of Potluck, the two officers, Willie Whackum and Lance Howe, continued to relax.

After three radio messages repeating the incident Whackum and Howe realized all other patrol officers were engaged and they informed the police dispatcher they were responding to the call.

The domestic incident took place in a poor section of Potluck and appeared to involve a physical dispute between a husband and a wife. No weapons were evident, but it did appear that the husband had hit his wife several times, causing her to bleed from the nose. Bruises were also evident on her cheek and shoulder.

Several neighbors had now clustered around the participants and told the police officers tales of periodic disturbances, leading to physical abuse by the husband, Henry. Upon hearing himself identified as an abuser, Henry began screaming and cursing at his neighbors and even took a swing at two of them, who easily avoided his punches.

Officer Whackum, who had gone back to the police cruiser, returned with confirmation that indeed, on five other occasions, Henry and his wife had engaged in actions so loud that the Potluck police had been called to their home to suppress acts of violence that threatened the well-being of one or both of the participants.

By now, Officers Whackum and Howe had quieted everybody down but Henry, who continued to curse at the neighbors, his wife, and the police officers. Outraged that his family problems were now out in public in front of his neighbors, Henry began swinging his fist at the neighbors again and ran across the lawn and tackled Officer Howe. The two officers forced Henry to the ground and handcuffed him. Henry was escorted to the police cruiser and driven to the police station. At the station, Henry was interviewed by a police sergent and then seated in a waiting room, where he promptly fell asleep.

Within an hour Henry awakened and began to cough, sputter, and gasp for air. These episodes would last no more than a few minutes, and once they ended, Henry would fall back asleep.

Over the next hour or so Henry's attacks came more frequently, but each time they passed with no apparent serious aftermath. As the time passed, Henry began asking for medicine, claiming he had asthma.

Since the attacks came and went, Officers Whackum and Howe were not overly concerned about Henry's condition, and they proceeded to lock him up in a detention cell.

Henry's attacks accelerated, but the arresting officers assumed he was faking as a ploy to be released. It was during one of his attacks that Henry's condition attracted the attention of a police officer who was asthmatic. The officer recognized that Henry was having a serious medical emergency. Henry was now perspiring and gasping for air.

The police officer who recognized Henry's condition talked to the arresting police officers and learned neither Officer Whackum nor Howe had ever had a case in which he had to diagnose and then deal with a medical emergency. The police officer then overruled the judgment of Whackum and Howe and immediately called for an emergency medical team to come to Henry's assistance. Clearly the prisoner was having a severe asthmatic attack.

Henry was rushed to a hospital, where the emergency room recognized his symptoms and treated him for his asthmatic condition. Henry recovered from his attack and was released, incurring expenses of over $1500. A few weeks later, Henry was contacted by an attorney who patiently listened to Henry's review of the evening's events on the night he was arrested. The attorney told Henry he would get back to him about the possibility of filing a lawsuit against the police officers for failure to perceive a prisoner in distress. Henry missed a week of work, costing him an additional $550.

Legal Liability: Enter the Courts

Henry's case is not unusual, and prior to the 1970s would not have triggered municipal liability or potential suits against Whackum and Howe, but concomitant with insurance problems came an enormous growth in the legal liabilities of public agencies. Legal changes at the state and federal levels left municipalities uniquely vulnerable to civil suits for money damages.

Not too long ago, it was far more difficult to sue local governments for many of their torts. They enjoyed sovereign immunity within the states under the Anglo-American theory that the king or sovereign could do no wrong, and consequently civil suits against them would be pointless. As the states and federal government increasingly waived their sovereign immunity, we have discovered that not only is the king punishable for his mistakes, but he is also punishable for the mistakes of his policymakers, and sometimes even their agents.

Local governments have become a soft target for litigation, because they have a great deal of daily contact with the public, some mistakes and injuries are inevitable, and it is assumed that they can be made to pay. These tempting "deep pockets" are lined with taxpayers' dollars, which are being diverted to pay excessive premiums or large damages.

In addition to state tort liability, local governments and most of their personnel are subject to civil suits for money damages under the Civil Rights Act of 1871, passed by the 42nd Congress to counter repression of freed men and women in the former Confederate states by the Ku Klux Klan. In terms of municipal liability, the act's most important provision reads as follows:

> Every person who, under color of any statute, ordinance, regulation, custom, usage, of any state or territory subjects or causes to be subjected, any citizen of the United States or other person within the jurisdiction thereof to the deprivation of any rights, privileges, or immunities secured by the Constitution and laws, shall be liable to the party injured in an action at law, suit in equity, or other proper proceeding for redress (42 U.S. Code, section 1983).

Section 1983, as the law is now called, has a broad sweep. It creates a new species of federal "constitutional tort" law and changes federalism by subjecting state and local officials and employees to suits in federal district court for their alleged violations of individuals' federally protected constitutional or statutory rights. The act was essentially moribund for almost a century, however, because the courts bestowed broad common law immunities on most public officials and employees, privileges and immunities were narrowly defined, and in practice individuals had few federally protected constitutional rights vis-à-vis state and local administration. For almost ninety years after passage of the Civil Rights Act, Section 1983 was hardly used. Approximately twenty suits were brought in the first fifty years, and from 1920–1960 most of the suits were for violations of voting rights, not act of municipal liability (Geller, 1986: 9).

Today the picture is drastically changed. Most state and local personnel can be sued personally for compensatory and punitive damages. When exercising discretion, they have a qualified immunity from suit and can only be held liable for violations of "clearly established constitutional or statutory rights of which a reasonable person would have known" (*Harlow* v. *Fitzgerald*, 1982: 457 U.S. 800, 818). If such violations occur, damages may be assessed regardless of whether or not the official or employee acted in good faith. As a general rule, public officials and employees retain absolute immunity when engaging in judicial or legislative functions. Private individuals engaged in governmental action, such as prison guards in privatized prisons, are potentially liable for their constitutional torts and have no immunities (*Richardson* v. *McKnight*, 1997 138 L. Ed. 2d 540).

Municipalities and their agencies face another set of rules. Since the Supreme Court's decision in *Monell* v. *Department of Social Services of the City of New York* (1978, 436 U.S. 656), they are considered "persons" within the meaning of Section 1983, therefore they are suable in federal court for their constitutional torts and violations of federally protected statutory rights. Municipalities are potentially liable for compensatory damages only; no punitive damages can be assessed against them under Section 1983 (*Newport* v. *Fact Concerts*, 1981: 453 U.S. 247). Because these governments and agencies have no qualified immunity, the judiciary has sought to craft a jurisprudence that will protect them from vicarious, *respondeat superior* liability. The task has been to hold them accountable for their own actions, but not for the wayward actions or mistakes of their employees. The resultant jurisprudence is "a highly complex body of interpretive law" (*Board of County Commissioners* v. *Brown*, Justice Breyer dissenting, 1997: 137 L.Ed.2d 626, 658).

Monell established that municipalities or their agencies are liable if their official policies violate individual's constitutional rights. In *Owen* v. *City of Independence* (1980: 445 U.S. 622), the Supreme Court removed the possibility of a municipality raising a good faith defense, finding such a government "will be liable for all of its injurious conduct, whether committed in good faith or not" (p. 651).

What is an "official policy?" In *Pembaur* v. *City of Cincinnati* (1986: 475 U.S. 469), the Court adopted a broad definition.

> To be sure, "official policy" often refers to formal rules or understandings—often but not always committed to writing—that are intended to, and do, establish fixed plans of action to be followed under similar circumstances consistently and over time . . . However . . . a government frequently chooses a course of action tailored to a particular situation, and not intended to control decisions in later situations. If the decision to adopt that particular course of action is properly made by that government's authorized decisionmakers, it surely represents an act of official government "policy" . . . [w]here action is directed by those who establish government policy, the municipality is equally responsible whether that action is to be taken only once or to be taken repeatedly (475 U.S. 480–481).

Under this standard, a municipality may be liable when one of its officials responsible for establishing final policy in a subject area makes a "deliberate choice to follow a course of action . . . from among various alternatives" (475 U.S. 483). In short, municipalities may be liable even for one-shot, verbal decisions of their policymakers. For instance, in *Pembaur*, a county prosecutor's instructions to law enforcement officers to "go in and get" two witnesses from a physician's office triggered potential liability when the officers chopped down the doctor's door with an axe in violation of his Fourth and Fourteenth Amendment rights.

An obvious difficulty in applying this standard lies in determining whether or not a particular official or employee has authority to establish a municipality's policy in a given area. Another problem lies in assessing "the link between the policymaker's inadequate decision and the particular injury alleged" (*Board of County Commissioners* v. *Brown*, 1997: 137 L.Ed.2d 626, 643). Establishing a link sufficient to trigger liability is straightforward in cases in which the municipal policy directly violates an individual's rights. For example, in *Monell* the Department of Social Services had an unconstitutional maternity leave policy and in *Owen*, an employee's procedural due process rights were allegedly violated by his discharge without a hearing.

Sometimes a decision policy does not directly abridge individual rights however, but sets in motion circumstances in which they are subsequently breached. Here, liability will attach to a municipality if the injured individual can show that the "decision reflects deliberate indifference to the risk that a violation of a particular constitutional or statutory right will follow the decision" (*Board of County Commissioners* v. *Brown*, 1997: 13 L.Ed.2d.626, 644). "Deliberate indifference" exists where a reasonable policymaker would conclude that "the plainly obvious" consequence of a decision would be a deprivation of constitutional rights (*Board of County Commissioners* v. *Brown*, 1997: 137 L.Ed.2d626, 644).

Matters are equally complicated when a municipality's lack of a policy leads to a violation of protected rights. In these circumstances, the courts may treat deliberate indifference to an obviously necessary policy as though there is a policy not to have a policy. For instance, in *City of Canton* v. *Harris* (1989; 489 U.S. 378), the Supreme Court held that a municipality's failure to provide training may cause liability under Section 1983 when the need for training is "so obvious, and the inadequacy so likely to result in the violation of constitutional rights, that the city can reasonably be said to have been deliberately indifferent to the need" (*Canton* v. *Harris*, 1989: 390) and the ultimate injury to constitutional rights is closely related to the absence of training. Potluck could thus be liable for violation of Henry's Eighth and Fourteenth Amendment rights to adequate medical care while in custody if it took no steps to train its police to recognize medical emergencies.

The lack of bright lines that characterizes much of the constitutional jurisprudence under Section 1983 also engulfs suits alleging that nonfederal government actors have violated federally protected statutory rights. Many federal statutes establish rights, but not all of them are enforceable via Section 1983. The burden of vindicating federal statutory rights rests on the plaintiff to show: (1) that he or she "is an intended beneficiary of the statute," (2) the "asserted interests are not so vague and amorphous as to be beyond the competence of the judiciary to enforce," and (3) "the statute imposes a binding obligation on the State" (*Blessing* v. *Freestone*, 1997: 137 L.Ed.2d 569, 576). Additionally, Congress can foreclose the use of Section 1983 explicitly in the statute at issue or implicitly "by creating a comprehensive enforcement scheme that is incompatible with individual Section 1983 enforcement" (*Blessing* v. *Freestone*, 1997: 137 L. Ed.2d 569, 576).

In summing up Section 1983 as it applies to municipalities, Justice Stephen Breyer noted that the "basic legal principle" of trying to avoid respondent at superior liability "requires so many distinctions to maintain its legal life [that] it may not deserve such longevity" (*Board of County Commissioners* v. *Brown*, 1997: 137 L. Ed.2d 626, 659). Certainly the distinctions—not to mention tortured reasoning—are difficult to grasp and apply. It is less than encouraging that the majority in *Board of County Commissioners* charges four dissenters with "misunderstanding our approach" (*Board of County Commissioners* v. *Brown*, 1997: 137 L.Ed.2d 626, 645, note 1). Lack of clarity leads to uncertainty, and uncertainty seriously exacerbates the difficulties municipalities face in making rational choices regarding risk management. Rationality is difficult under the best of circumstances; when you have ambiguous assessments of what constitutes acceptable risk, the problems are exacerbated for all public officials.

SUMMARY AND CONCLUSION

In the aftermath of the near financial collapse in New York City and other large metropolitan areas in the mid-and late 1970s, there arose a renewed interest for cities to hire experienced and competent urban managers on all levels. The recessions of 1981–1983 and 1990–1991 tested the skills of many urban mayors, managers, and department heads. On the whole our urban areas weathered the economic storm fairly well and emerged ready to confront the managerial challenges of the 1990s.

The municipal liability crisis of the 1980s and the economic recession posed a whole new array of management problems for cities and their leaders, however.

One of the most serious managerial problems confronting urban managers of the 1990s was how to direct his or her subordinates in the exercise of bureaucratic discretion. With both the courts and insurers concerned about this issue, it has become increasingly difficult for local governments to operate without a carefully drafted set of plans and procedures. Most students of urban bureaucracy are aware of how impossible it is to categorize all of a jurisdiction's policies and then establish a specific set of procedures to be carried out by all departmental employees.

There are some departments in which the plans and procedures manual can be followed fairly easily with a minimum amount of discretion exercised by bureaucrats. In police, fire, health emergencies, and school settings, however, discretion is an integral part of the bureaucratic function. If public employees are trained to be timid in performing their duties because of the potential liability involved, then the city is apt to perform in a less then satisfactory manner in its primary function of delivering services.

Another major problem confronting urban managers today is the hidden risk problem. What is occurring in my jurisdiction that is potentially risky and that I know virtually nothing about? Are my employees, the public, and our financial and property resources at risk? Aside from the dangers involved in apprehending criminals, fighting fires, and treating hospital emergencies, how does an urban manager today deal with the questions of AIDS, drug testing, and emerging workplace health and safety issues? What about such environmental hazards as leaking underground storage tanks, toxic emissions, and hazardous waste transported through or near the city at 2:00 a.m.? Risk managers today are cataloging the potential unseen dangers and developing contingency plans for the unknown ones. Contractors hired by the city need to be checked for liability insurance, past safety performance, and the quality of their workforce. All of these activities represented new challenges for the urban management profession in the 1990s.

Increasingly risk managers in the 1990s have found themselves on the cutting edge of the financial management function. As risks are uncovered and assessed, costs of liability insurance will surely increase. Risk administration will not only include the basic functions mentioned above, but will expand to include a thorough knowledge of the national economy, changing demographics, workforce skill requirements, and intergovernmental fiscal transfers, all of which have a tremendous impact on local government resources.

In addition, risk managers will also find themselves much more involved in intergovernmental programs. Since local governments are so dependent on state and federal funding for much of their revenues, risk managers need to become thoroughly familiar with these programs. This is important not only because of their resources, but also because of the state and federal regulations and mandates that require government expenditures and actions. Even with passage of the Unfunded Mandates Act there will still be state and federally mandated expenditures. The federal government's commitment to devolve more financial and program administration responsibility on the states will also increase the challenges for local governments and their risk managers. Risk managers will need to assess all of these programs much more carefully in the future.

Finally, there is the rapidly expanding role of the risk manager in urban areas. As the municipal liability crisis heightened more and more cities and counties began hiring risk managers to assess the jurisdiction's potential risk and to provide a mix of risk control and risk financing to ensure the preservation of limited public resources (Johnson and Ross, 1989).

A risk manager needs data on the public entity's total risk exposure to make the timely decisions that help to contain costs and minimize risks, yet accomplishing this is an arduous task. Local governments are departmentalized and fragmented. Obtaining information from numerous departments is time-consuming and the information is often uneven in quality. Risk managers are therefore called upon to coordinate activities across a broad spectrum of agencies, personnel, and activities and to make major decisions about municipal liability with less than complete data on potential risk.

The field of public risk management is a growth field. Cities and counties are moving gradually to reduce or eliminate risks and uncover hidden or potential risks. The ability of risk managers to marshal the necessary resources to coordinate risk management activities in a timely and a professional manner may well determine the future of the municipal liability issues confronting local governments now and into the next century.

REVIEW QUESTIONS

1. What is risk management? Why is risk management so important? Especially in the 1990s?
2. What are the principal components of the risk management function in state and local government? How critical are they in determining the risk management policies of a government?
3. Why have so many state and local governments turned to insurance pools and self-insurance as a means for minimizing risk exposure?
4. How have the courts helped to heighten our awareness of risk management?
5. Why should the person responsible for risk management within an organization be a high-level local official?
6. What are some of the major issues facing risk managers in local government?

BIBLIOGRAPHIC CASES

Blessing v. *Freestone*, 137 L. Ed. 2d 569 (1997).
Board of County Commissioners v. *Brown*, 137 L. Ed. 2d 626 (1997).
City of Canton v. *Harris*, 489 U.S. 378 (1989).
Harlow v. *Fitzgerald*, 457 U.S. 800 (1982).
Monell v. *Department of Social Services of the City of New York*, 436 U.S. 658 (1978).
Newport v. *Fact Concerts*, 453 U.S. 247 (1981).
Owen v. *City of Independence*, 445 U.S. 622 (1980).
Pembaur v. *City of Cincinnati*, 475 U.S. 469 (1986).
Richardson v. *McKnight*, 138 L. Ed. 2d 540 (1997).

REFERENCES

Arnold, D. S. (1997). Purchasing and risk management. In R. J. Aronson and E. Schwartz (eds), In *Management Policies in Local Government Finance*, pp. 364–382. Washington DC: International City Management Association.

Brown, A. (1985). Self-insurance pooling arrives in Colorado. In N. Wasseman and D. G. Phelus (eds.), *Risk Management Today*, pp. 65–73. Washington, DC: International City Management Association.

Cragg, L. C. and Kloman, H. F. (1985). Risk management: A developed discipline. In N. Wasseman and D. G. Phelus (eds.), *Risk Management Today*, p. 7. Washington, DC: International City Management Association.

Elliott, C. J. (1985–86). Police misconduct: Municipal liability under section 1983. *Kentucky Law Journal, 743*, 651–666.

Galanter, M. (1988). Beyond the litigation panic. In W. Olson (ed.), *New Directions in Liability Law*, pp. 18–24. New York: Academy of Political Science.

Geller, K. S. (Nov. 1986). Municipal liability under section 1983: A thumbnail sketch. *Public Management, 68*, 9–12.

Hanlen, R. (1986). Insurance costs impact recreation industry. *New York Times, May 12*, Al, B4.

Hildreth, W. B. and Miller, G. A. (1985). State and local officials and their personal liability. In J. Rabin and D. Dodd (eds.), *State and Local Government Administration*, pp. 245–264. New York: Marcel Dekker.

Johnson, R. B. and Ross, B. H. (1989). Risk management in the public sector. In *Municipal Year book*, pp. 1–11. Washington, DC: International City Management Association.

Johnson, R. B. and Ross, B. H. (1991). Risk management, In J. E. Peterson and D. R. Strachota (eds.), *Local Government Finance*. pp. 355–367. Chicago: Government Finance Officers Association.

LaBrec, D. J. and Kurt, F. (1987). Public official's liability: The loss Exposure, In N. Wasserman and D. G. Phelus (eds.), *Risk Management Today*, pp. 77–87. Washington, DC: International City Management Association.

Lee, Y. S. (March/April 1987). Civil liability of state and local governments: Myth and reality. *Public Administration Review, 47*, 160–170.

McLean, G. (1986). Ohio feeling the severity of the liability crunch. *National Underwriters, July 11*, 8, 13.

Matolock, L. M. and Woodhouse, L. R. (Aug. 1987). *The State of the Small Cities: A Survey of the Nation's Cities and Towns Under 50,000*. Washington, DC: National League of Cities.

Hock, C. (1995). Prison Paradox. *Government Executive, 27*, 60–63.

Meyer, W. E. (Nov. 1986). The morning after: Emerging from the hard market. *Public Management, 68*, 6–8.

Muzychenko, J. (1987). Local governments at risk: The crisis in liability insurance. In *The Municipal Yearbook 1987*, pp. 3–7. Washington, DC: International City Management Association.

Muzychecnko, J. (Jan./Feb. 1987). PRIMA survey reflects insurance trends. *Public Risk, 67*, 8, 17.

Muzychenko, J. (Nov. 1986). Where did all the insurance go? *Public Management, 68*, 3–5.

Nahmod, S. (July 1987). *Municipal Liability: What Should Be Done About Section 1983?* Washington, DC: League of Cities.

National Community Reporter. (Jan.–Feb. 1987). Washington, DC: National Association of Towns and Townships.

Risk Watch. (March 23, 1988). *Special Report*. Washington, DC: Public Risk and Insurance Management Association.

Roos, N. (Feb. 1982). Risk management: Selected characteristics for individual cities and counties, *Urban Data Service Reports, 14*(2).

Rosenbloom, D. H. and O'Leary, R. (1997). *Public Administration and Law*. New York: Marcel Dekker.

Shapira, Z. (1997). *Risk Taking A Managerial Perspective*. New York: Russell Sage Foundation.

Smith, W. C. (Sept. 1997). Defining acceptable police practices. *Public Risk*, 23–25.

Sylvester, K. (Oct. 1987). Do-it-yourself insurance (or learning to live with risk). *Governing*, 56–63.

Task Force on Liability Insurance. (Aug. 1987). *Report to the National Governors' Association*. Washington, DC: National Governors' Association.

U.S. Congress, Committee on the Judiciary, Subcommittee on Antitrust, Monopoly and Business Rights, (1987). Hearings on the McCarran–Ferguson Act, 100th Cong., 1st sess., June 2.

Walsh, S. W. and Mayer, C. S. (1986). 8 states sue U.S., British insurers. *Washington Post*, March 23, p. B1, B5.

Wasseman, N. and Phelus, D. G. eds. (1985). *Risk Management Today: A How-to Guide for Local Government*. Washington, DC: ICMA.

Williams, C. A. Jr., Smith, M. L. and Young, P. C. (1995). *Risk Management and Insurance*, 7th ed. New York: McGraw Hill.

Young, P. C. (May–June, 1988). Survey results: Pools a significant risk-financing option. *Public Risk*, 26, 31.

Hazardous Waste: Issues Surrounding Insurance Availability U.S. General Accounting Office. (Oct. 1987). Report RCED 88–2. Washington, DC.

Welch, W. (1985). Sky high insurance hurts cities. *The State*, Aug. 19.

42

The Politics of Pension Investment Returns

W. Bartley Hildreth
Wichita State University, Wichita, Kansas, U.S.A.

Laurie W. Adams
Louisiana State University, Baton Rouge, Louisiana, U.S.A.

In the fourth quarter of 1992, the State Employees Retirement System (SERS) posted a $43 million loss. Accusations, reprisals, and memos flew back and forth between the director of the SERS and the elected state treasurer, an ex-officio member of the SERS board of trustees. The issue became a political hot potato, and while the loss did hold serious implications for the already largely unfunded state pension system, it also brings to mind a difficult question. What are the implications for a public pension system when it has poor investment returns?

To set the context, an overview of the entire state pension system is provided. Then, the case turns to the nature of the loss. This case study identifies the types of securities purchased for the SERS internally managed portfolio, the one posting the loss. Fundamentally, the case addresses the pension system's delegation of investment decisions to an internal money manager. Overall, the case highlights the implications of pension investment decisions.

This chapter examines the loss in the SERS pension system from the fourth quarter of 1992 to the second quarter of 1993, but with particular focus on the fourth quarter of 1992. It is the reporting of the fourth quarter losses of 1992 that caused the political fallout for the pension system.

STATUS OF THE STATE'S PENSION SYSTEMS

Over the years, the state government created thirteen pension systems to serve a total of 282,000 members (both active and retired). Of these systems, the SERS was the second largest, with 114,060 members. Of that membership total, 59.4% represented active vested

The authors acknowledge the help of participants and market experts in conveying the events and context of this case study.

Table 1 State Employees Retirement System Membership at June 30

		1988	1989	1990	1991	1992
A.	Retirees and beneficiaries currently receiving benefits and terminated employees entitled to benefits but not yet receiving benefits	37,426	39,328	38,964	38,842	46,262
B.	Current active employees					
	Vested	62,144	62,566	66,711	28,451	30,554
	Nonvested	NA	NA	NA	42,476	37,244
C.	Total members	99,570	101,894	105,675	109,769	114,060
	Current active employees (B) as a percentage of total membership (C)	62.4%	61.4%	63.1%	64.6%	59.4%

Note: NA means "not available."
Source: State's comprehensive annual financial report (year).

and nonvested employees, a sharp drop from that of recent years caused by a large increase in member retirements in response to special incentives and an aging workforce (Table 1). As a single-employer public employee retirement system, SERS was organized to provide retirement benefits for employees of the state and various departments and agencies and their beneficiaries. The other state pension systems represented schoolteachers, university faculty, law enforcement, and other assorted specialized groupings. The SERS is governed by an eleven-member board of trustees, partially elected from the membership.

The system's income is derived from employer and member contributions as well as investment income. The employer's contribution rate, established annually based upon pension forecasting assumptions and state law, was increased to 11.9% in 1992. Member contribution rates, established by statute, are deducted from members' salaries. The majority of the members pay at the rate of 7.5% of their salary, while several other groups within the system pay at rates from 8.5–11.5%.

The financial strength of a retirement system is the degree to which current assets are estimated to cover the long-term value of benefit obligations. Surveys reveal that many public pensions systems have an unfunded pension obligation, meaning that the present value of all future benefits exceeds the present value of all assets, including expected future contributions (U.S. General Accounting Office, 1992). Actuarial estimates of future contributions are based on assumptions regarding potential investment returns, the projected rate of inflation, the demographic composition of the covered workforce, mortality and disability rates, and expected career paths.

The unfunded pension benefit obligation when placed in some perspective can be used to gauge the financial standing of a public pension system. The sheer dollar size of the pension liability is one negative measure. As shown in Table 2, the unfunded pension benefit obligation grew to $2 billion by 1992. Another way of looking at the unfunded pension obligation is as a percentage of the payroll of all covered employees. The lower the percentage, the stronger the system, with a fully funded (no accrued liability) pension

Table 2 Assets in Excess of Pension Benefit (Unfunded Pension Benefit Obligation) as a Percentage of Annual Covered Payroll and Employer Contributions as a Percentage of Annual Covered Payroll (Amounts in Millions)

	1988	1989	1990	1991	1992
Unfunded pension benefit obligation	$1,786.6	$1,883.3	$1,961.5	$2,018.3	$2,080.9
Annual covered payroll	$1,111.0	$1,141.1	$1,226.1	$1,368.5	$1,454.4
Unfunded pension obligation as a percentage of covered payroll	160.8%	165.0%	160.0%	147.5%	143.1%
Employer contributions	$125.4	$127.1	$93.7	$143.0	$205.1
Employer contributions as a percentage of covered payroll	11.3%	11.1%	7.6%	10.4%	14.1%

Source: State's comprehensive annual financial report (year).

system having a zero coverage ratio. In 1992, SERS had a very high ratio of 143.1%, but it had declined from a figure of 161% in 1988 (Table 2).

Pension systems, if they are of the actuarial funding type, receive more revenues in a year than expenses; the positive difference adds to the asset base to generate sufficient funding for future benefits. Total SERS revenue in 1992 was $602 million. The SERS took in $109 million from member contributions, $205 million from employer contributions, $278 from investment income, and $10 million other income. Investment income represented about 46% of the total system revenues. In 1992, SERS expenses totaled $279.6 million, including benefits paid to members ($248 million), refunds to members leaving the system ($23.8 million), and administrative costs. Administrative expenses increased at a compound annual rate of 28% from 1988 through 1992 (reflecting the increased use of external investment managers), while investment income increased at a compound growth rate of 14.5%. The SERS system ended the 1992 fiscal year with a fund balance of $2.8 billion.

Even with net assets available for benefits of $2.8 billion the SERS pension system was largely unfunded. The SERS system's actuarial accrued liability, or total pension benefit obligation, totaled $4.88 billion. Only 57.4% of the pension benefit obligation was funded in 1992, but the percentages funded increased in recent years. (See Table 3.) After subtracting assets of $2.8 billion from the total actuarial accrued liability of $4.88 billion, the SERS was left with an unfunded pension liability of $2.08 billion. To address this

Table 3 Net Assets Available For Benefits as a Percentage of Pension Benefit of Obligation (Amounts in Millions)

	1988	1989	1990	1991	1992
Net assets available for benefits	$1,999.6	$2,133.6	$2,268.6	$2,481.0	$2,803.6
Pension benefit obligation	$3,786.2	$4,021.9	$4,210.1	$4,499.3	$4,884.5
Percentage funded	52.8%	53.1%	53.9%	55.1%	57.4%

Source: State's comprehensive annual financial report (year).

liability, the state legislature passed an act in 1990 requiring state pension systems to amortize the unfunded liability over a foury-year period. It also required the state to make the appropriations that are required, not what the state might choose to fund, as had occurred in the past. The law further prohibited the state and the various pension boards from incurring any further unfunded accrued liability. An added layer of employer contribution rates resulted, meaning that the state's pension costs escalated, putting pressure on an already strapped state budget. The state's concern stemmed from the fact that if a state-operated pension system should fiscally collapse, the pension systems enjoyed constitutional authority to draw the necessary funds out of the state treasury to cover benefit payments. This large unfunded pension liability made the public even more sensitive to any controversy regarding investment results, because any shortfall would require taxpayers to ante up the difference.

INVESTMENTS GONE SOUR

The SERS chief investing officer (CIO) was vested with responsibility by the board of trustees to guide all investment decisions pursuant to board policy and state law. The CIO maintained direct investment control over a board-approved "in-house" account of investment funds with investment goals and a list of allowable securities for investment. The remainder of SERS's investable funds were managed externally by private money managers under contract terms specifying investment goals and allowable securities. The in-house account was initially approved as an interim investment pool until external managers could be chosen for some new investment styles the SERS board was interested in pursuing. The avowed plan was that as external managers were chosen, the in-house portfolio would then be liquidated. In 1988, however, the CIO decided, and the board approved, investing these funds in mortgage-backed securities. As a point of reference, mortgage-backed securities are treated and purchased with ease by many institutional investors; however, the derivatives of mortgage-backed securities (i.e., inverse floaters, principal-only strips, interest-only strips) are extremely complex. These derivative securities carry market risk since in certain economic environments they are difficult to liquidate.

By late 1991, the state treasurer's office became concerned about the SERS investment strategy after several of the treasurer's Wall Street contacts alerted her to the system's heavy investment in derivatives of mortgage-backed securities. As an ex-officio member of the SERS board, however, the state treasurer, or her designee, was in attendance at board/committee meetings and received the same reports as other trustees and voted on the same motions regarding the funding of the in-house account. The treasurer formally expressed her new concern in a letter to the SERS board in March of 1992. The letter stated, "It appears that the SERS owns in excess of $570 million of these securities (mortgage-backed). Very few institutions own comparable amounts. Generally speaking, these institutions have far greater assets and much larger support staffs than does SERS . . . (The investment is) totally inappropriate for SERS."

When confronted, the CIO revealed that not only were investments made in mortgage-backed securities, an acceptable investment category, but also in their derivatives, a much less understood type of investment. In April 1992, the CIO announced that he would be retiring in a month. At this point, the board of trustees instructed him to begin selling off the securities in the in-house account. In early 1992, interest rates dropped, homeowners refinanced their mortgages, and the mortgage-backed securities lost value. Unable to sell the "interest-only" (IO) derivatives of mortgage-backed securities, which made up 25% of the portfolio and which had lost half of their value, the CIO began to sell off the "principal-only" derivatives, which had gained in value as the interest rates had dropped. As the portfolio was liquidated, losses totalling $43 million were posted in the fourth quarter of 1992, and with these losses came an onslaught of criticism and inquiry.

COMPOSITION OF THE PORTFOLIO

There were two major categories of investment in the in-house account: U.S. government securities and U.S. federal agency securities. U.S. governments, as the former ones are termed, represent direct debt obligations of the U.S. Treasury, widely recognized as the safest investment in the world. In contrast, agency securities are issued by creatures of the U.S. government, and some carry no federal guarantee of repayment, although the general perception is that the federal government would not allow agency securities to default. Three of these federally sponsored agencies stimulate the development of private mortgage activity by buying single-family mortgages from the original lender (such as a local bank or savings and loan) and pooling them into a new security instrument so investors can buy a share of the entire pool rather than a single mortgage. In turn, the agency guarantees repayment of each mortgage. This means that the creditworthiness of the agency is substituted for the individual mortgagee. Given that federal agency securities have a relatively higher default risk than a direct Treasury security, these bonds offer a higher return. While default risk is covered, an investment can lose value if traded prior to maturity. An added problem emerges with some derivatives, such as IO strips, which represent the interest portion of monthly payments from a group of mortgages. Interest-only strips drop in value when the underlying mortgages are refinanced since interest payments cease to exist.

Mortgage securities have become the focus of very sophisticated financial engineering, with the ability to fashion various cash flows from traditional mortgage securities. One mortgage security can turn into many investment options. Since they are unique, they are hard to value. This calls into question price transparency, a matter critical for an efficient market system. A benchmark is the stock market, with almost instantaneous posting and dissemination of trades. Derivatives of mortage obligations operate without price transparency. Such a situation opens the door to the mispricing of trades, with attendant high commissions that buyers cannot detect.

The composition of the in-house portfolio from July 1991 through May 1993 reveals its investment philosophy. As shown in Table 4, from July 1991 until March 1992, the majority of the in-house portfolio was invested in federal agency issues, which would include mortgage-backed securities. In April 1992 a diversification of investments took place, resulting in a shift to a much larger share (25%) of the portfolio invested in U.S. government securities. The share invested in U.S. securities increased until October/November 1992, when the CIO began trying to liquidate the portfolio. He had difficulty selling the IO strips, so he sold off the more liquid, U.S. Treasury securities and principal-only securities.

The CIO was not alone in misjudging the stability of the mortgage-backed securities. A bond rating analyst, quoted in the financial press about this story,* said that "mortgage-

---

* In order to mask the actual pension system from which these facts were taken, it is also necessary to avoid citing specific references that might pierce this scholarly veil. The authors acknowledge such help and will provide source documents to other scholars.

Table 4 In-House Portfolio Composition (July 1991–May 1993)

Month/year	U.S. government securities (%)	U.S. federal agencies (%)	Other (%)
July 1991	0.00%	97.43%	2.57%
August 1991	4.92	84.99	10.09
September 1991	7.02	88.98	4.00
October 1991	1.79	93.78	4.43
November 1991	9.44	81.27	9.29
December 1991	5.92	87.57	6.51
January 1992	0.00	84.59	15.11
February 1992	1.09	86.55	12.36
March 1992	1.14	87.19	11.67
April 1992	25.19	67.84	6.97
May 1992	31.07	58.52	10.41
June 1992	NA	NA	NA
July 1992	33.50	46.39	20.11
August 1992	38.83	49.04	12.13
September 1992	40.02	46.57	13.41
October 1992	NA	NA	NA
November 1992	NA	NA	NA
December 1992	9.87	75.43	14.70
January 1993	9.31	51.03	39.66
February 1993	49.47	46.42	4.11
March 1993	NA	NA	NA
April 1993	59.46	39.75	0.79
May 1993	66.25	31.63	2.12

Note: NA = Not available.
Source: Monthly spreadsheets for SERS board members.

backed securities come in dozens of structures that require complex computer models to analyze . . . as a result even the most sophisticated market players can fall into traps caused by unexpected rate gyrations, or by misjudging the length, depth or direction of interest rate changes." He went on to state, "The (mortgage-backed securities) that were the riskiest in 1992 and 1993 have been the (interest-only securities) . . . they've lost the most in market value and they're very (difficult to sell)."

By June 1993, the in-house portfolio of $300 million had been transferred to an external manager. The portfolio contained U.S. government securities and almost $100 million in IO securities that could only be sold at a price that would mean a substantial loss for the system. In a memo in early May, the retiring CIO recommended to the board that it hold on to the IO securities. He justified this advice by saying that he understood market experts to be predicting higher interest rates, and as interest rates rise, IO securities increase in value.*

At the time of the loss, the in-house portfolio had $600 million in assets, comprising about 20% of the system's total assets. The in-house account contained highly speculative

---

* In fact, long-term interest rates dropped to their lowest level in twenty-five years.

IO securities, which pay the interest from a pool of mortgages. When interest rates fall, people refinance their homes and the value of the securities fall. The CIO had these investments hedged with another type of mortgage-backed security, inverse floaters. Inverse floaters rise in value as interest rates fall, so theoretically the inverse floaters help to protect the portfolio from losing substantial value. As it happened, however, there were not enough of the inverse floaters in the portfolio to prevent a loss of the magnitude posted.

It helps to compare the investment returns of the in-house portfolio to a comparable one both in size and bond investment strategy, but managed externally by a nationally recognized pension investment manager. As shown in Table 5, the in-house account enjoyed higher investment returns than the externally managed account in the year prior to the liquidation process. The mean monthly return from July 1991 through September 1992 was 1.44% for the in-house portfolio versus 1.18% for the external managers. In October/November 1992, however, the CIO began selling off the principal-only securities, and the

Table 5 Comparative Investment Returns, with Portfolio Size Indicators

Month/year[a]	External management percentage change[b]	In-house management percentage change	In-house size	Total system assets	In-house as percentage of total system assets
7/91	1.37%	.61%	$425,926,971	$2,582,269,372	16.49%
8/91	2.34%	1.24%	$431,187,838	$2,635,900,800	16.36%
9/91	1.09%	.60%	$447,265,276	$2,663,401,834	16.79%
10/91	1.14%	2.19%	$457,076,788	$2,716,151,760	16.83%
11/91	.95%	.43%	$464,383,652	$2,691,317,556	17.25%
12/91	3.21%	4.93%	$571,355,791	$2,869,656,888	19.91%
1/92	−1.60%	1.98%	$589,201,164	$2,870,891,185	20.52%
2/92	.53%	.65%	$599,217,876	$2,889,905,590	20.73%
3/92	−.28%	−.24%	$586,645,004	$2,847,578,950	20.60%
4/92	.60%	.98%	$597,590,913	$2,875,304,611	20.78%
5/92	1.93%	.38%	$599,857,754	$2,092,208,775	20.67%
6/92	1.58%	3.35%	$619,982,719	$2,913,244,712	21.28%
7/92	2.28%	1.92%	$631,217,888	$2,975,251,066	21.22%
8/92	1.11%	2.08%	$644,364,224	$2,972,691,956	21.68%
9/92	1.40%	.47%	$647,361,238	$2,995,142,556	21.61%
10–11/92	−1.64%	−47.33%	$352,450,265	$3,052,550,961	11.55%
12/92	1.61%	−2.22%	$333,111,729	$3,080,190,636	10.81%
1/93	2.34%	−1.99%	$323,475,541	$3,111,702,420	10.40%
2/93	1.85%	−1.00%	$323,144,798	$3,098,278,251	10.43%
3/93	.47%	−5.98%	$303,807,046	$3,138,248,124	9.68%
4/93	.68%	.74%	$305,145,975	$3,137,367,989	9.73%
5/93	−.04%	−.62%	$315,561,456	$3,215,763,348	9.81%

[a] Information for 10/92 and 11/92 were not available. The data shown as 10–11/92 were derived from 9/92 and 12/92 figures and therefore cover a two-month period.

[b] The external account refers to a SERS portfolio of comparable size managed by external money managers that followed a bond investment strategy. These results tracked, but were slightly less than, a commonly used market benchmark (the Lehman Brothers Government/Corporate Bond index).

Source: Monthly SERS spreadsheets for SERS board members.

IO securities began dropping in value. During the October/November period over 54% of the total in-house portfolio was either liquidated or lost due to poor investment performance. Accordingly, the portfolio's percentage of the system's total assets was reduced from 21.6% to 11.55% in two months.

The in-house portfolio continued to lose money in the first quarter of 1993. The losses for the first quarter of 1993 totaled $24 million, and the losses continued into the second quarter of 1993, but as of the writing of this chapter, the extent of those losses are unclear.

RISK AND RETURN

Were these securities suitable for use by a public pension system? Risk-related questions increasingly bedevil investment officers. Historically, most pension funds invested in long-term bonds, with the purchase of equity ownership in publicly traded corporations (i.e., the "stock market") prohibited by many governments. As years passed and inflation increased, bond rates could not keep up with inflation. Besides, equity ownership investment became more acceptable. Investment firms also designed many new complex securities for purchase by pension fund managers. One problem with such investment instruments is that there is no easy way to continually price their value, such as there is with the stock market. This means that the prices charged to engage in such trading is even more difficult to distill for use in comparative shopping of suitable investments. An advantage, however, that pension systems have over other institutional investors is their long investment horizon. This is often referred to as patient capital.

Investors willing to assume more risk do so expecting a greater return. Even when a share of the portfolio is lost in a higher risk investment, the overall yield may compensate. A review of the composite yield of the in-house portfolio as of March 31, 1992, shows that different conclusions can be drawn depending upon the time period of analysis.

Quarter ending March 1993	Last half year	Last year	Last 2 years	From September 1988
−7.37%	−15.73%	−10.38%	2.36%	7.92%

Even with a 15.73% loss for the six months covering the end of 1992 and the beginning quarter of 1993, the overall yield for the fund since its inception in 1988 was 7.92%. This is a quarter of a percentage point under the SERS actuarially assumed return on investments of 8.25% (the target rate of return used in calculating the amount of the unfunded pension benefit obligation figure), making the in-house portfolio the poorest performer of all the SERS portfolios. The fund's performance was much brighter one year earlier, as of March 1992.

Quarter ending March 1992	Last half year	Last year	Last 2 years	From September 1988
2.67%	9.83%	15.97%	16.00%	13.80%

Table 6   Total SERS Investment Income

Year	Investment income (in millions)[a]	Percentage of total revenues
1982	$103.771	37.60%
1983	$109.111	37.12%
1984	$115.687	38.01%
1985	$143.987	41.57%
1986	$183.677	46.85%
1987	$183.843	47.54%
1988	$160.912	41.79%
1989	$181.179	45.59%
1990	$206.633	51.85%
1991	$225.267	47.01%
1992	$273.259	45.67%

Source: 1992 Actuarial Report on the State Public Retirement Systems by the Legislative Auditor and the 1992 Actuarial Report by SERS.

[a] Acturial reporting reflects external professional investment advisory expenses as a reduction of investment income which differs from the financial statements (referred to in an earlier section) which reflects such fees in administrative expenses. In 1992, for example, the financial statements show $278 million of investment income; the difference represents fees paid to external managers.

As shown, the first quarter of 1992 recorded a 2.67% return, further enhancing returns posted in earlier time periods analyzed. Unfortunately, commendable returns during earlier quarters were not enough to offset the late 1992 and early 1993 losses and keep the portfolio as a reasonable performer. The added risk associated with the in-house investment strategy caused a smaller gain than a more conservative investment approach would have yielded, but this result cannot always be guaranteed.

The loss of $43 million represented 59.97% of the investment income for the fourth quarter of 1992 and 15.7% of the total 1992 investment income for SERS. (See Table 6.) Since investment income represented over 45% of the total revenues for SERS, the impact of such a loss is noteworthy, at a minimum.

CHARGE AND COUNTERCHARGE: THE POLITICAL IMPACT OF THE LOSS

The reporting of the SERS loss caused heated public exchanges to take place between the state treasurer and the director of the SERS. The state treasurer and the director of the state retirement system were accustomed to being in opposition. Several years earlier the two ran against each other for state treasurer. After the election, the newly elected state treasurer employed her former opponent (then the acting state treasurer after years as the assistant state treasurer) for a few weeks prior to his appointment as director of the state retirement system. The treasurer was quick to issue a press release implying that she had a major part in the appointment, upsetting the board and the newly appointed director, who knew of no such help. As the investment controversy grew, the history between the two public officials only exacerbated an already tense situation. In addition the state treasurer was frequently viewed as a leading candidate in the next election for governor.

In a memo to the employer members of the pension system the director of the retirement systems wrote, "In the last quarter of 1992, the plan enjoyed a gain of $71.7 million through investment performance according to [an external portfolio evaluation service]." The state treasurer responded to this in a memo to state legislators by writing, "SERS did have a net gain of $71.7 million for the quarter ending December 31, 1992. Had the 'in-House' account not lost $43 million the net gain for the system would have been $112 million."

These officials disagreed on whether the events would amount to a loss for the taxpayer or not. The director of the retirement systems claimed, "The taxpayers will not 'get a bill', they will get a credit.* This means a savings to the taxpayer. Since 1988, SERS investment earnings have resulted in a credit to the state of $204,952,000." In her memo to the state legislators, the state treasurer disagreed: "It is important to understand that whatever money is not made through investment of the system's assets the difference must be made up by contributions by employees and employer (taxpayer). Over the next 34 years the taxpayers of this state will spend approximately $8.7 billion to correct the financial situation."

The director of the state retirement system further asserted that media reports were unfair because they only concentrated on one quarter: "in the quarter ended 3/31/92, the realized gain/loss portion had gains of $39 million, while the interest component had losses of $25 million, for a net profit of $14 million. In the next quarter, the realized gain/loss component was down $33 million, while the interest portion was up $51 million, for a net profit of $14 million. . . . (see how misleading it could be to look at only one component for only one quarter?)."

With battle lines drawn, the public was left confused between the competing statements. What is clear, however, is that SERS changed the management of the so-called in-house account and hired legal counsel to investigate the entire issue.

INTERNAL OR EXTERNAL MANAGEMENT OF FUNDS

After deciding to sell what it could of the troubled mortgage securities portfolio, the pension system board had to decide whether or not to keep an internally managed portfolio. It decided to discontinue the internally managed portfolio and in June of 1993 the remaining in-house securities were transferred to an external money manager. If in the money manager's opinion it is advantageous to the system to sell, then the money manager has the full discretion to do so.

In *The Public Money Manager's Handbook*, Michael Clowes (1981) outlines the advantages and disadvantages of having internal management of a portfolio. Public entities, more than private ones, use internal management of investments. An advantage to internal management is that the pension system's trustees have direct control over the assets and can be involved on a day-to-day basis. The second reason for internal management is

---

* The director uses "credit" to refer to how state law requires that SERS credit the state with the investment earnings in excess of the actuarial assumption rate. State government uses these credits to reduce the future employer share of contributions to SERS.

cost-effectiveness. For the larger pension fund systems, it is less expensive to maintain an internal staff than to pay fees for many outside managers. In terms of disadvantages to an internal staff, the first one is the opportunity for political interference by politicians looking to earn recognition as reformers by tapping pension funds as the source of funds to accomplish social purposes. Second, there is difficulty in obtaining a diversity of management styles with an internal management team, and diversification is crucial to reducing risk. It is also very difficult for an internal staff to be familiar with all investment management styles. Besides, market complexity may demand that fixed-income portfolio management be handled by experts (Miller, 1992).

Clowes believes that many small and medium-sized pension systems turn to external management firms for cost reasons. Many times it is less expensive to contract for several firms to manage different types of portfolios than to pay salaries to several experts to manage the same types of portfolios internally. It is also much easier for the external firm to hire talent and fire ineffective managers, while it can be very difficult to get rid of a public servant. External management can also reduce the temptation for political interference in the buying and selling of securities.

External management also offers opportunities to instill some competition in the investment of pension assets. In order to retain their position, external investment managers have to produce yields within stated parameters and against market benchmarks. There are always other investment managers waiting to garner the business of those who fail to achieve the desired investment returns.

Establishment of the in-house account was tied to the movement of the CIO from his prior position as SERS executive director. At the time of his retirement from the executive position, he was quite involved in daily trading decisions, so upon his retirement, the new position of CIO was created for him. Management of the in-house account was viewed as a significant part of his new job, as was giving investment advice to the new executive director, as called upon.

Following revelation of the in-house account's problems but consistent with the (above) advice for a medium-size pension system, the SERS board decided as of June 1993 to invest all of its funds with external managers. This was also in keeping with the SERS director's statement during the controversy that SERS "selects its money managers from among the top performers in the nation on a highly competitive basis. The performance of these managers is monitored on a monthly basis." Since the director attributed the increase in investment income to the strategy of using external managers, it was easy to try to end the debate over investments by turning away from in-house portfolio management.

SELECTION, INVESTMENT, AND MONITORING OF FUNDS

The in-house account's loss raised questions about the pension system investment strategy. First, such questions are not unique to this pension system, but they emerged as a result of dramatic public questioning of this pension system's management. What types of investments should be made by the trustees of public pension systems? Fundamentally, like other state pension systems the investment power of SERS is derived from state statutes and board policy. Investment rules specify limits on the types and amount of investments. A general outline of the restrictions placed on the capital of SERS, as taken from its annual report, shows that

No more than 55% of its total portfolio can be invested in common stock.

No more than 5% of total assets at market value may be invested in the debt securities of any one issuer. This does not apply to the U.S. government and federal agencies.

Corporate bonds—no more than 50%, with limits per issuer of 8% if rated AAA, 6% if rated AA3 or AA-, and 4% if rated A3 or A-.

Equity securities—No one holding shall account for more than 10% of the allowable equity portion of the portfolio at market value or more than 5% of the outstanding common stock of any one corporation.

Commercial paper and short-term investments—Only U.S. dollar denominated paper of domestic companies will be used. Paper must be rated either P-1 by Moody's or A-1 by Standard & Poor's. No more than $10 million is to be invested in commercial paper of any one issuer.

Real estate—Investments in commingled real estate pools may be made only upon specific approval of the board and initially may not exceed 10% of total investments at book value.

Repurchase agreements—Funds may be invested in repurchase agreements, which are fully collateralized by U.S. Treasury issues.

Recognizing these investment restrictions, the SERS's assets were in the following types of investments:

Money market investments	5.14%
Treasury issues	24.66%
Federal agencies	10.66%
Corporate issues	5.26%
Common stock	32.13%
Foreign equities	9.88%
Foreign bonds	8.30%
Accrued interest	.74%
Real estate	3.13%
Misc assets	.11%
	100.00%

The market value rate of return on these investments for 1992 was 10.92%. In 1991, the return was 9.9%. These returns exceeded the stated assumption that investments should yield a return of 8.25%. The majority of SERS investments were in common stock, which is considered riskier than government securities but usually produces a higher return. The second largest investment in U.S. Treasury securities represented a very safe investment with a predictable yield, if held to maturity.

Any SERS person, contractor, or trustee who exercises any discretionary authority or control is subject to what is termed fiduciary responsibility, because he or she holds assets in trust for a beneficiary. State investment law states that the fiduciary shall use the "prudent person rule." The statutory definition of this rule means that fiduciaries shall exercise the judgment and care under the circumstances then prevailing that an institutional advisor of ordinary prudence, discretion, and intelligence exercises in the management of large investments entrusted to it, not in regard to speculation but in regard to the permanent disposition of funds considering probable safety of capital as well as probable income.

Establishing and maintaining investment policies and procedures is vital to a public pension fund. The Government Finance Officers Association (GFOA) of the United States of America and Canada recommends that the following fundamentals be kept in mind when designing investment policy. First, the investment operations must be long-term in scope, with the initial inflow of money providing more than ample funds for current payments. Of concern is "the predictability and durability of net cash flow in the future." This information requires the expertise of an actuary and an investment advisor. The GFOA (1977) goes on to state that the "primary objective of the investment program is a reasonable, long-range total rate of return" and the preservation of capital.

As is common with pension systems, all investment activity is supposed to be processed through the services of a custodian—an institution such as a large bank or trust company. The custodian provides custody, settlement notice, and reporting services to the client pension system. The SERS utilized a custodian and employed a nationally recognized private evaluation service to organize the custodian's data into a comparative performance-ranking report. This report was then used by the SERS as its monitoring tool. While the performance reports revealed gains or losses, it combined straight mortgage-backed securities with the more volatile derivatives. Later, this lack of disclosure brought the private evaluation service's role into question, at least by the SERS board.

The 1992 annual independent auditor's report on the SERS financial statements contained component discussions on internal accounting controls and compliance with laws and regulations, as well as a separate letter to management. In none of these attestations did the independent auditor isolate any concerns about the mortgage-backed securities. The only points of slight relationship were a general call for an internal auditor and the need to test daily securities transaction confirmation slips against monthly reports from the custodians.

As expected, the SERS had a comprehensive, written investment policy. The investment policy actually authorized the purchase of mortgage-backed securities, but investment in their derivatives is the subject of legal inquiry at this point. This underscores the concern that what may be an approved investment may be inappropriate for yielding desired results (Miller, 1986). It also raises a concern over the use of derivatives, a growing line of financial products. Whether or not such investments met the fiduciary responsibility of the board of trustees has not been decided.

SUMMARY AND CONCLUSION

Investing funds for a single individual carries risk, so being charged with the responsibility for thousands of state employees' pension funds is no less so. Evaluation of a public pension fund's investment results goes beyond composite rates of return and into the relative risks involved in the choice of investments. This case highlights the political implications of a loss. A careful evaluation of the situation, however, may not assure an investment officer of how public officials will respond to results that deviate from anything but the most rosy results. Investing is a subjective profession, with each investment officer using a philosophy of his or her own with guidance from investment policies and generally accepted practices. When investments are made in the public arena, however, economic risk taking carries at a minimum, political risk, as the SERS system found out to its chagrin.

REVIEW QUESTIONS

1. Evaluate the financial standing of the State Employees Retirement System.
2. How should a pension system's financial status influence its investment policy?
3. Why should taxpayers care about the management of a public pension system?
4. What was and what should have been the role of the board of trustees in the decision-making process to invest and disinvest? Did it meet its fiduciary responsibilities?
5. Should a "hold" rather than a "sell" strategy have been employed for dealing with the derivatives?
6. Were SERS investment decisions made on sound financial information or political pressure? Explain.
7. What impact do you think news coverage of this controversy might have had on SERS retirees (or those soon to reach retirement age)?
8. Would you side with the director of the state retirement system in his arguments or would you lean toward the arguments of the state treasurer? Why?
9. Should SERS have invested in mortgage-backed securities? Why or why not?
10. Do you think the members of the board of trustees understood the risks associated with derivatives?
11. Should funds be internally or externally managed? Why? Would it have mattered if the losses had been made by an external manager? Why?
12. What benchmarks could be used to evaluate the work of a state pension system's board of trustees?

REFERENCES

Clowes, M. (1981). *The Public Money Manager's Handbook*. Chicago: Crain.
Government [Municipal] Finance Officers Association. (1977). *Public Employee Retirement Administration*. Chicago.
Miller, G. (1986). *Investing Public Funds*. Chicago: Government Finance Officers Association.
Miller, G. (1992). Using a fixed-income money manager. [*Fidelity Investments*] Investment Exchange (June), pp. 1–2.
U.S. General Accounting Office. (1992). Letter to chairman, Select Committee on Aging, House of Representatives, from associate director, (HRD-93–9R, Dec. 3).

43

Promises and Pitfalls of Contracting for Public Services
The LAWA Case

Sandra M. Emerson
California State University, Pomona, California, U.S.A.

Had advocates for privatization prevailed in 1989, Article 1, Section 8 of the U.S. Constitution would have empowered the Congress to delegate the coining of money and Indian affairs to the lowest, most qualified bidder. Historically, public services were provided by public institutions because it was seen as either the best-insulated (e.g., national bank) or most sensitive to public sentiments (e.g., public education by the states). Today the fusing of public responsibility with private expertise draws on research and theory building stretching from Taylor's scientific management to Osborne and Gaebler's re-engineering of government.

Reflecting on 100 years of history demonstrates that public administration has evolved in a context of competing demands. Historically the pendulum has swung back and forth between demands for efficiency and demands for equity. Today successful administrators must avoid the endless swings of the pendulum. They must balance efficiency with equity.

This chapter focuses on the historical promises and pitfalls that have come to define public service contracting in the twenty-first century. It describes the experiences of the Los Angeles World Airport (LAWA) with purchase of service contracts. The exploration of LAWA's approach provides insight on how managers are meeting a community's needs for efficiency and equity by capitalizing on contracting for public services.

OUT OF THE PAST—AN HISTORICAL PERSPECTIVE

The Promise of Effortlessness

Modern management theory began with the application of studies on efficiency and effectiveness pioneered by Taylor, Gilbreth, and Fayol. Their basic premise was that management achieved specified goals using tested and proven means. During this early period,

Reprinted from: *Journal of Public Budgeting, Accounting, and Financial Management*, 2000, 12(2), 307–332.
Copyright by PrAcademics Press.

the field of management was dominated by private sector issues and engineering models. The engineering ideal was to employ *the least amount of time and effort on an activity*. The greater the efficiency, then the greater the productivity, profitability, and remuneration to workers. Time–motion studies enabled organizations to structure work into fundamental steps. The goal was to identify the *one best way* to do a task and integrate it with related tasks for the greatest level of production (Harmon and Mayer, 1989; Taylor, 1996)

This period of scientific management would provide later practitioners interested in contracting for services with two lasting legacies: first, an understanding that tasks could be itemized and measured in a meaningful way, and second, that those who engaged in governing an effort need not be engaged in executing a task (Shafritz and Ott, 1996).

The Pitfall of Peddling Political Influence

While management theory and innovations developed in the private sector during the Industrial Revolution, government languished in the spoils system. Political party bosses brokered jobs for immigrants and lucrative public projects for businesses. Public revenues paid for jobs and public works contracts. Campaign contributions to political party bosses paid the expenses of candidates and party regulars to get out the vote. Each pool of money greased the wheels for conducting the public's business (Osborne and Gaebler, 1993).

The reform efforts of the Progressives did not eliminate the spoils system, but it did ameliorate some of the most egregious abuses. Progressive reforms led to public contracts being awarded to the most qualified lowest bidder. Civil service systems ended the wholesale replacement of public employees with political appointees. Jobs were defined by tasks and filled by persons holding the requisite knowledge, skills, and abilities. Public jobs or contracts ceased to be a payment for campaign contributions or voter turnout in specified precincts (Wolfinger, 1972). The attention to identifying persons and businesses of merit rather than those with political influence would be a lasting legacy for contracting of services in decades to come.

The Promise of Accountability

Reforms at the federal level included the Pendleton Act (1885), which established a federal civil service system, and the Budget and Accounting Act (1921), which established the Bureau of the Budget, the precursor to the Office of Management and Budget (Wildavsky and Caiden, 1997). Even though the Congress passes thirteen appropriations annually, there is a single accounting of all revenue and expenditures in the president's budget message to Congress. This practice has constrained the fragmented funding system that had prevailed among government bureau chiefs, interest groups and high-ranking members of congressional appropriations committees.[1] Similar reforms followed at the state and local levels. The Progressives popularized the idea of fiscal accountability by the executive, a premise basic to utilizing contracts to secure public services.

The Promise of the New Deal

The Progressives sought to deal with efficiency in terms of specified goods and services. The model was the well-managed firm. Nothing would prepare them for the economic tsunami of the Great Depression, however, when stock prices fell 40%, 86,000 businesses failed, wages dropped by 60%, and unemployment rose to 25% (Heilbroner, 1975).

Incorporation of management theories into daily governmental activities was driven by a growth in government under Franklin D. Roosevelt and by nearly three decades of Progressive reforms. In the 1930s and 1940s administrative science was defined by Urlick's and Gulick's basic functions: planning, organizing, staffing, directing, coordinating, reporting, and budgeting (POSDCoRB). POSDCoRB pulled into a coherent whole the purpose, systems, accountability, and coordination of activities and specialties.

In the hands of the Brownlow commission (1936–1937) the executive branch was modernized. Presidential staff provided pertinent information but remained anonymous. They were neither decision makers nor intermediaries between the president and the heads of the departments. The Brownlow commission's view of the executive and FDR's style of governing complemented one another. Staff members close to FDR had few fixed assignments and were jacks-of-all-trades. They were unspecialized and moved from one ad hoc assignment to another. Staff positions required close relationships and often operated with staff "jostling" one another. This *managed conflict* provided the president with multiple channels of feedback and ideas on the effectiveness and equity of policies run by his administration (Neustadt, 1963).

FDR used Gulick's and Urwick's "managerial" language to justify his administrative structure, but he employed a Madisonian approach to competition among dissident interests to address political concerns. The FDR legacy for the development of contracting for public services was the introduction of the role of management *generalist* who served as troubleshooter or monitor for the executive while remaining unencumbered by any direct responsibility for implementation.

The Promise of Employee Competence

In the postwar era, the human relation's school defined the manager as one who taught, supported employees, and provided the context needed to achieve results. The principle watchwords for managers were decentralization and customization. The objective was redefined from process-driven to outcome-oriented. Employees thrived on empowerment, responsibility, and meeting or exceeding standards of performance. The contribution of the human relation's school for contracting of services was the idea that employees could be trusted and been best suited to serve clients once a context for their role had been provided. It would take another four decades to link employee empowerment to the mechanics of contacting for services to reach this labor pool through nonprofit and for-profit organizations.

The Pitfall of Sacrificing Equity for Efficiency

Should the independence and variability of the private sector be replicated in the public sector? Is not the public sector qualitatively a different instrument of decision making? In a democracy no practice or policy is immune from public scrutiny or debate. Democratic managers must by "attitude" be inclusive in their views of who the client is. Public administration had an unmistakable duality. On the one hand it was the most "expeditious and economical" means for implementing the public will. On the other hand it was incorporated inside the state with obligations to protect private rights, develop civic capacity, respect public opinion, and provide for the general welfare (Appleby, 1996). The basic values of public administration were representativeness, political neutrality, and executive leadership. What some failed to recognize was that the greater the representativeness the less political neutrality in the system, and the greater the demand for neutrality the less representative a system would be. The discipline needed to err either on the side of neutrality or representativeness. By 1971 Fredrickson took on the challenge and argued that government needed to err on the side of *social equity*. This meant government was skewed on behalf of the disadvantaged, the ill, or anyone who lacked political and economic resources (Fredrickson, 1996).

Maximizing social equity was to be employed by the public sector in the same way that maximizing of profits was used in the private sector. Policies that enhanced equity (among individuals) were to be the guideposts for public administration rather than the institutional model of the past. The new public administration was a product of the turbulent 1960s. It sought to carve out for administrators the same agenda, energy, and enthusiasm as had been the hallmark of the Warren Supreme Court. It also laid down a burden for those who would contract for services in the future. That burden would be to temper demands for efficiency with concerns for social equity.

The Pitfall of Promising Too Much

The idealism of the 1960s soon diminished. An inability to improve the quality of life, a stalemate in Viet Nam, and the Watergate scandal dominated public policy and administration in the 1970s. In this turbulent era both governmental outcomes and means were questioned. Had government become too big and by extension too arrogant?

Dissatisfaction with government's efforts and the high cost of services erupted with initiatives in eleven states from California to Michigan. Voter anger took on almost biblical proportions. For example, in Kalkaska, Michigan, the 1993 school year ended in March rather than in June. The voters would not approve any property tax increase to keep schools open (Straayer, et al., 1998). Achieving Frederickson's (1996) balance between efficiency and equity would not be easy; those reformers interested in contracting for services would need additional tools.

The Promise of the Tailor-Made Solution

The antigovernment malaise gave rise to advocates for the re-engineering of government. Beginning with Osborne and Gaebler (1993), the re-engineering advocates proposed purchasing services, using vouchers and related reforms. They drew on theories of market behavior. In less than a decade the model would focus anew on the most enduring demand of public administration—providing goods and services in the most effective and efficient manner available. Social equity remained an academic interest rather than a practical consideration.

The gurus of the reinventing government movement would define their approach as one that challenged an underlying assumption of implementation (Osborne and Plastrik, 1997; Savas, 2000). Did the public's *will* require a public provider? *Reinventors* believed the answer was no.

Reformers, such as Savas, argued public services could be customized for target neighborhoods. Clients could be better served through a decentralized administration and entrepreneurial innovations spurred on by competition.

Savas defined "privatization" as anything that was not government, therefore privatization included volunteers, self-help efforts by citizens, not-for-profit agencies, and for-profit-firms (Savas, 2000). Markets provided freedom. Decision makers pursue their own interests, generate goods and services, and minimize waste. Market mechanisms are more reliable and diligent in weeding out inefficiency than are government regulators. Markets require decision makers to focus on the end users of goods and services. Markets are flexible in meeting the ever-changing demands of customers and rewarding proactive innovators. Government decisions, like other monopoly systems, are less able to optimize performance. In the absence of competition, governments are more apt to expand budgetary demands (Friedman, 1999; Niskanen, 1968). Contracting for public services, once an anathema, had now found its way into the political mainstream as an instrument for delivering public programs. The history of this evolutionary development is summarized in Table 1.

Table 1 Historic and Theoretical Roots of Purchasing of Services Contracting

Historical roots	Contributions to purchase of service contracting
Scientific management era	Enables managers to identify, quantify, and measure task efficiency, thereby reducing waste of resources; separates the "doing of a task" (in realm of engineering effort and output) from integration or administration of functions
Progressive reform era; civil service, competitive bidding, executive budget	Establishes skill, knowledge, and task capability of labor for providing public sector goods and services; establishes competitive bid system for contracting; establishes single comprehensive budget process to replace fragmented legislative committee appropriations approach
Administrative science era—Brownlow and FDR; defines common administrative functions, role of administrative generalists	Identifies administrative functions central for provision of goods and services, such as planning, coordination, reporting, and budgeting; expands staff functions to include monitoring, evaluating, and troubleshooting
Human relations school era; challenges mechanistic principles view; emergence of structure based on capable employee and supportive manager	Encourages organizational structures to be more flexible, less hierarchical, and more decentralized; manager acts as coach not as controller; less structure and more support for front line employees to make decisions effectively on behalf of customer
"New" PA era; advance idea of fostering democratic access and social equity; shifts to focus on impact on client of policy/program	Challenges economic market models as framework for viewing public practices; calls for social equity; suggests markets can be tweaked to accommodate disparities in equity that are not well addressed by government programs
Reengineering government movement and taxpayer revolts; addresses disparity between quality and cost of services; experimentation with new methods for improving service and reducing bureaucracy	Introduces multiplicity of means for meeting public demand; emphasis on providers based on capabilities, cooperation, and partnerships between sectors
	Expansion of "market means" to include vouchers, loan guarantees, privatization, contracted services; reliance on markets, in lieu of government monopolies, for the provision of services; provides means for optimizing performance while minimizing stress on public budgets

CRITICISM CONCERNING CONTRACTING FOR PUBLIC SERVICES

Labor Concerns

Contracting for services and other re-engineering mechanisms have had their critics. They come from a variety of perspectives, including organized labor, business, and populists. One enduring criticism of privatization is that it depresses wages and hobbles labor unions (Kuttner, 1997). Proponents of purchasing of services contest this view, but their data are not supportive. Private contractors employ fewer unionized workers and have a younger workforce with less job tenure than their public sector counterparts. Each of these factors contributes to lower wages, fewer benefits, and fewer union members (Savas, 2000). While the wage and benefits for labor decrease, there are some increases in capital equipment (computers) and "incentive" programs for labor (performance bonuses). What is missing from this discussion is adequate data as to what happens to the labor pool that is downsized. Also missing is an accounting of how much of the incentive plans are actually paid out to labor for goods and services once provided by public employees.

Business Concerns

Generally, businesses champion the purchase of a service idea as it broadens their opportunities. They are less enthusiastic when contracts go to competitors. The reality and appearance of a fair process is essential to assure the business sector's support. The degree to which communities fall short of an impartial process is the degree to which support wanes and bidder participation declines.

Equity

Finally, having private sector experts provide services is less appealing to some citizens and community groups than is empowering persons to take on civic roles and responsibilities themselves. Do we want to contract out education or encourage parents to home-school their children? There is no requirement that purchasing a service per se diminishes opportunities for citizens to provide for themselves. There is a concern, however, that contracting services precludes governments from seeking alternatives that are for nonmarket objectives (Mintzberg, 1986). For example, recycling is more ecologically sound but requires multiple bins for trash collectors to pick up and sort. It is therefore more costly than single bin systems. Does the community give up on an ecological objective due to cost-efficient standards?[2]

Presumption of Public Neutrality

Independent of the management issues, other critics are concerned that the balance provided by the separation of sectors is neutralized when funds and interests are commingled. In 1787 James Madison argued that government has an obligation to be functionally neutral: "No man is allowed to be a judge in his own cause, because his interests would certainly bias his judgement and . . . corrupt his integrity. Men are unfit to be both judges and parties at the same time" (Madison, 1961: 79).

Can government contract with a business and be indifferent about the impact of tax, labor, and environmental policies on these businesses? For these critics the hint of bias results in a loss of integrity. Government, under these circumstances, cannot be the effective instrument of justice in the community (Derber, 1998).

A citizen's expectations of fairness from government are more demanding than the customer's expectations of fairness from a business. When a citizen's relationship to a public service is similar to a pure market relationship (e.g., janitorial services, data entry), then the citizen functions primarily as a customer. Some public functions, however (e.g., addiction treatment and incarceration), are less like a pure market. For example, the rights of a prisoner as a citizen (constitutional protections that are costly and hard to quantify) differ from the view of the prisoner as client requiring physical constraints. The appellate court system assumes intolerance for errors that deny citizens their liberty. This community standard is based on civic, rather than market, reasons.

In cases with "less than perfect market" scenarios there are often multiple "customers" with competing interests. There are different perspectives held by the mental health patient, the mental health practitioner, and the taxpayer. How much care does a facility need to provide, what the taxpayer is willing to spend, what the practitioner's experience deems is quality care, or what the patient sees as necessary? Market systems are efficient because *individuals* can maximize their self-interest. Which "self" (practitioner, patient, or taxpayer) does one rely on? When services are of this nature, then success for diverse and competing interests is more *about equity* in representation than an issue of self-maximization. Under such circumstances accountability from elected officials for the quality of community life is also a constituent concern.

Accountability in these circumstances is highly subjective and not easily measured. Savas makes a distinction between "hard services" involving tangible, measurable, physical outputs versus "soft" services provided by social workers or other intermediaries (Savas, 2000). While vouchers are one means of contracting for soft services, who gets to be the "customer with the voucher" significantly influences the service provided. The need to make contracted service outcomes clear and unequivocal is more difficult with soft services. It is not easy to define a mentally healthy adult. Is the patient the best judge of whether he or she is mentally healthy? Should the *customer* in these soft service cases be the judge or health professional?

The worst case scenario is when customers are discouraged or diverted from services. This occurs when a contractor sees some clients as more costly to train and place in jobs or less likely to meet performance goals in the contract. There is a tension between the certainty of standards and the scope of the contractor's responsibilities when circumstances and outcomes vary among clients (Behn and Kant, 1999).

THE LOS ANGELES WORLD AIRPORTS (LAWA): A CASE STUDY

The LAWA is a proprietary department of the city of Los Angeles that manages four facilities: Los Angeles International Airport (LAX), Ontario International Airport, the general aviation airport in Van Nuys, and a regional airport in Palmdale. A general manager and nine assistant general managers for such areas as facilities, business development, and financial services run the airport. The airport has about 2300 employees, a $400 million operating budget, and a $600 million capital improvement budget. The four facilities serve approximately 61.2 million passengers and move 2 million tons of cargo annually (Guevara, 2000; Winfrey, 1999).

The largest service contracts are for parking (a $21 million contract that yields $58.7 million in revenue) and ground transportation (at $8.4 million). The director of operations manages both of these services. Approximately 90% of the telecommunication's $13.7 million budget is contracted out, as is $3.3 to $4.4 million for janitorial services. Special one-time expenses, such as buying an up-to-date financial computer system, will be contracted out for an estimated $7 to $10 million. In all, the airport contracts out or spends a total of $126 million annually. It receives an estimated $227 million in income from most of its contracts, including parking, rent-a-cars, concessions, food, retail sales, and phones (K. Van Ness, LAWA budget director, personal communication, Feb. 19, 2000).

Political Issues

While purchasing services have moved from the status of public ridicule, to strong opposition, to self-evident truth in many parts of the United States, it has been a time-honored tradition at LAWA. While the broader concerns about soft services (health care, prisons) are outside the scope of this chapter, there remain significant political issues for those public services in cases in which measures are relatively easy to quantify and the citizen's relationship to the service is most like that found in a market.

A five-person board of commissioners appointed by the mayor and approved by city council governs LAWA. Board decisions may be subject to review by and approval of the city council. LAWA personnel are city employees. This structure provides opportunities for political issues to dominate LAWA operations.

Labor

Reforms in Los Angeles are directed at real and perceived drawbacks of contracting. For example, there was a small but persistent movement to require contractors to pay employees a living wage as defined by local statute. On January 14, 1999, the city of Los Angeles's living wage ordinance took effect. By law, contractors pay a minimum of $7.51/hour with health benefits or $8.76/hour without benefits. This rate is $1.75 to 3.00 higher than the $5.75 federal minimum wage standard. The following factors contributed to political support for living wage legislation:

> Most of the airport contractors provide services that are "elastic," or what economists call *price sensitive*. As the costs for services go up, consumer demand declines, therefore, increases in costs cannot be passed on to consumers. When employers who pay low wages are compared with those who pay a living wage in the same industry, the customer's price differential is low. Burger King employs a unionized workforce and pays a living wage, as defined by the Los Angeles statute, while McDonalds does not. The cost for a hamburger at Burger King is $2.49 while it is $2.37 at McDonalds. Even within the same firm, local ordinances can increase hourly labor costs by 50% with no price difference for consumers. The Radisson Hotel is another case in point. Its housekeeper wages range from $820/month in one city to $1934/month in another city. The Radisson's king size room daily rate is $189 at both locations. There is virtually no impact on consumers.[3]
> Stockholder share value does not differ significantly between McDonalds and Burger King. McDonalds' fifty-two-week stock price ranged from $37.87 to $49.56, while Pillsbury (owner of Burger King) ranged from $29.66 to $49.56. While the impact on small "mom and pop" operations may be significant, the economic difference between corporate giants is minimal. The impact on their shareholders is also minimal.

The sustained economic vitality in communities and the growing support for federal programs, such as the Temporary Assistance to Needy Families (TANF), has led to expectations that persons should work rather than rely on public assistance. Welfare reform also leads to expectations that full-time employees should receive a wage that meets basic needs, however. When wages from full-time employment are insufficient, major corporations touting prosperity to prospective shareholders draw unwanted attention from community churches, foundations, public agencies, and unions seeking economic relief for working families.

The living wage resonates with politicians. It improves conditions for working families and limits demands on tax revenue by reducing the number of households dependent on public relief. In addition, it's inconsequential to customers and has a minimal impact on corporate share value. If legislation distinguishes between large and small providers, it can protect small businesses, nonprofits, and government agencies. It is not a burden to contract administrators who review contract records as part of their standard audit responsibility.

Small Business

Another political hot button is the equitable distribution of contracts to small and big businesses. Access to lucrative contracts is sustained through "minority business enterprise, women business enterprise, and disabled business enterprise" (MBE/WBE/DBE) regulations. Despite efforts in California (Proposition 209) to rid agencies of this regulatory role, equity issues and practices endure. This issue has become less a function of government than a responsibility of prime contractors. Small, eligible firms seeking to do business with the city apply for certification from the city's bureau of contract administration. Prime contractors may consult lists of certified minority firms to include in their proposals. The city is responsible for assuring the firm meets the business ownership standards of MBE/WBE/DBE. The prime contractors conduct outreach efforts, however, such as advertising in newspapers and contacting minority business associations. The prime contractor is responsible for assuring the MBE/WBE/DBE's quality of work. The city contract administrators have the best of all possible worlds. They meet the responsibility of quality of work by making the prime contractor responsible for all contract work, by monitoring performance, and by *not distinguishing* between tasks of primes and subcontractors. In addition, administrators leave the fostering of business cooperation and distribution of tasks and funds to subcontractors to the prime. Consequently the city stands to get the most qualified and capable and least costly MBE/WBE/DBE. Even when this is not the case, the consequences of poor choices are shouldered by the prime, not the city. The city can and will get drawn into disputes between primes and subcontractors.

The city's living wage requirement does not extend to small firms of fewer than fifty employees or to those with limited contracts or spending caps. Consequently, it is not an issue that divides or unites large and small firms operating under service contracts.

Scrutiny by Political Appointees and Elected Officials

Finally, the most consistent and unsurprising aspect of the purchase of service contracting lies in the influence that elected and political appointees seek to have in determining who will be awarded the contract. In the past, LAWA relied primarily on bids. Under the bid process, awards went to firms with the lowest cost for the specified good or service.

The bid process sent the message to competing firms that price was the determining factor. The consequences to LAWA soon became self-evident. To meet the competition based solely on price, firms skimped on toilet paper and towels used by the traveling public; inconsistently staffed parking booths, creating unnecessary delays; cut corners regarding maintenance; and delayed or miscalculated employee pay. Today, nearly all LAWA contracts are through proposals that specify in detail performance measures, working relations between the firm and airport, and expectations regarding subcontractors and employees, as well as price. The introduction of qualitative concerns created opportunities for subjective considerations. Subjectivity opened the door for political interests.

The airport's board of commissioners, executives, and city council representatives contact administrators suggesting that one firm or anther would be a fine candidate for an outstanding contract. Administrators have learned to listen and provide applicants with information and opportunities to ask questions regarding the proposals. The same support is extended to firms championed by appointed and elected leaders as to other bidders, however. Consequently, intense politicking occurs when administrators publicly announce their recommendation to the board. It is here that the board (or city council) is free to raise issues of process or the criteria for comparing bidders. Also raised through the political process are concerns regarding a firm's business practices, labor relations, or service record, both real and rumored.

In Los Angeles, city council or board dissatisfaction is manifest by delay. Political decision makers will postpone a decision and request additional consideration and investigation by the department or agency. Another option is to defer the decision to a later board/council meeting. Airport administrators pay attention to and resolve issues of award criteria, policy guidelines, or the accuracy of information as soon as possible. Legislative delays generated by officials trying to avoid unpopular decisions or due to court actions require that airport administrators make interim arrangements. In such cases they may continue existing contracts on a monthly basis or use a temporary provider until a contract is awarded.

The long-term consequences of political interest are that criteria are widely distributed and more explicitly defined. In some instances non-airport administrators (airline representatives) have served on review panels for airport-contracted services. This opens up the process, sustains cost-conscious efforts, and has had some unexpected benefits. For example, including the airlines on review panels for selecting concessionaires provided an opportunity to better understand airline concerns and to build a better working relationship between the airlines and the airport.

The issue of government's monopoly power concerning public goods and services is not fully resolved by contracting out services. Government's role has evolved from that of monopoly provider (with production inefficiencies) to monopoly consumer (with inefficiencies in patterns of consumption). As sole "consumer of record" there is a temptation to place a number of nonpricing requirements and responsibilities on the service contract. Primarily these have concerned accountability back to elected officials regarding economic equity to employees and/or small businesses. The other concern to representatives is the subjectivity and discretionary factors that influence the recommendation of one bidder over another. Any decision that has an aspect of subjectivity invites public debate. Administrators, interest groups, and elected and appointed decision makers each vie to be the spokesperson for the public.

Economic Issues

Cost Control and Containment
Significant reductions in the costs of goods and services have been found through purchasing services. This is the consensus in the literature (Savas, 2000; Osborne and Gaebler,

1993). Contracted service costs have not changed significantly over the past five years for LAWA. Nearly all requests for proposals (RFP) are put out for bid every three to five years. While rates have gone up and down, there has been no significant shift in either direction. Increases are assumed to be tied to higher labor costs (especially with regard to the city's living wage ordinance) and to higher costs for technology. Declines in costs are associated with more competitors in the market and funding down capital costs. The cost savings or increases are largely invisible to the administrators for a variety of reasons.

> There has been a significant growth in passenger and cargo traffic, as noted above. These translate into higher demands on services. For example, janitorial services once had a seven-hour period with little to no passenger traffic. Currently, terminals have few low-traffic periods and janitorial services are continuously needed. How much of the cost increase is due to increases in service demand and how much is due to increased labor costs is hard to isolate.
>
> Contract administrators do not account for the cost of auditors, attorneys, and adjunct staff who assist with purchases of services but are outside their departments.
>
> Contract costs that are within the department are primarily concerned with contract monitoring. These monitoring hours are part of a blend of staff responsibilities and are not accounted for as much as they are broadly estimated.
>
> The airport has a line-item budget, therefore it tracks changes in inputs but not in outputs or outcomes.

Since a significant portion of the costs are in hidden staff expenses (e.g., legal fees, contract administration, program monitoring), the full cost of contracting for services is neither documented nor quantified.

Cost Shifting

Low-skill contract positions often received no health or retirement benefits. New costs and coverage through Medicaid or public emergency room services may have offset a cost reduction in contracted services. Such cost reductions are shifts from one agency to another (Uchitelle, 1999). A pay increase due to a living wage with a health insurance provision may again shift costs from Medicaid to airport operations, but increases in contract costs do not necessarily result in higher costs to travelers, airlines, or taxpayers.

LAWA has miles of corridors. Maintaining public walkways constitutes a large portion of the janitorial contract. Faced with a certain increase in wages, the airport looked for alternative means to contain costs. One option is to employ floor scrubbers that janitors ride on rather than relying on slower, handheld equipment. This leveraging of labor with capital investments enables the airport to pay higher wages and increase productivity while minimizing costs. The riding scrubbers can be bought to maximize the efficiency of janitorial teams made up of public employees. Scrubbers increase the number of miles and quality of cleanliness of a janitorial shift. Also, they become the basis for establishing savings for contracts with private firms. Rather than face a rise in costs and decline in service, the airport can meet or exceed standards while containing costs.

Embracing Social Equity Costs

Airport administrators have become expert at using capital for addressing Fredrickson's (1996) social equity issue. The use of capital for janitorial services addresses the equity issues of a living wage. The on-site shuttle services uses *alternative fuel* buses owned by the airport. Alternative fuel vehicles are less damaging to the environment. While the service contractor provides drivers, cleaning crews, and mechanics, LAWA provides a fleet of buses. Each bus uses low-polluting alternative fuel and LAWA provides the alternative fuel. In the shuttle business, fuel is a considerable portion of the firm's costs. Because the airport absorbs the capital and fuel costs, private firms can submit competitive bids while the airport minimizes ground transportation pollution. A similar pollution concern defines the overland ground service between the main airport in Los Angeles and its general aviation airport in Van Nuys. The cost for the traveling public between the two airports, some twenty plus miles apart, is $6.00 for a round trip. No market could provide fares this low in a busy metropolitan area. The issue is not lowest market price, however, but equity concerns of congestion on the ground and pollution in the air (J. Christian, LAWA landside operations, personal communication, Jan. 7, 2000).

In the telecommunications area, the airport installed a state-of-the-art video system. The airport recognized it served as a guinea pig for working out the problems with a new video monitoring system. The initial high cost for introducing the technology, however, leveled out over the years as adaptations met the specific needs of airport security and communications. In this case there was no underlying social equity need. The airport operated as any trustee of a service, investing more resources in areas that are core to its mission. In other situations, the airport waits for technologies to be more developed. Airport administrators view their role as being the expert on new technologies and their applicability to the airport's needs (K. Wong, LAWA telecommunications area, personal communication, Jan. 19, 2000).

Monitoring Contracts: Balancing Need Against Costs

The most significant economic issue regarding *contracting for services* concerns monitoring. Currently, there is no on-site monitoring program of the retail and food trade at the airport. A monitoring plan is being developed. LAWA analysts check to assure there is no price gouging and that the airport's portion of revenues is accurately accounted for by concessionaires. In this area the citizen/customer is operating in a pure market environment. Market competition serves this area well.

The shuttle and janitorial services are pure public goods where travelers pay nothing for the services they use. Pure public goods are extensively monitored. This means there are designated monitors and that 40% or more of their time is allocated solely to monitoring (J. Christian, LAWA, personal communication, Jan. 7, 2000; C. Sipple, LAWA, personal communication, Jan. 14, 2000). Monitoring of pure public goods means standing in the shoes of the citizen. There are site inspections of public areas, on-time surveys of bus service, and considerable weight given to citizen complaints. Monitoring can be as frequent as on a daily basis, and feedback to contractors is continuous.

Services that fall between pure market and public service realms require less intense monitoring efforts. The overland bus service, telecommunications, and parking/security services lie somewhere between pure market and pure public goods. The intensity of monitoring efforts directly follows the extent to which a service is a market-driven good versus a pure public good. The complexity of the technology attached to a service also contributes to the intensity of monitoring. Midrange services (a blend of public good and private funds) require fewer on-site staff monitors but rely on monitoring devices, monitoring by exception or surrogate methods (service tickets for repairs) to assess service. While citizen complaints are important, they are evaluated within the context of the public objective and capacity of the agency's technology.

Contracted services with well-known consultant groups arise in response to pressure from elected officials to use the services of prominent experts. Unlike contracts for hard services, strategic plans or benefit–cost analysis is less quantifiable. In practice, the high-skilled experts touted by firms are often substituted with lower-level, younger and less knowledgeable employees of the firm who do data collection and analysis by tapping the expertise of the agency's staff. Consequently, LAWA contracts call for authorization from LAWA prior to adding or removing consultant staff from projects (K. Van Ness, finance, LAWA, personal communication, Feb. 12, 2000). Enforcement is difficult in some cases.

The quality and utility of high-skilled consultant services is more ambiguous. Project deadlines and outcome specifications are more broadly stated in the contract. Specifications evolve during the course of the project. Outside consultants are a cost to the agency. Major contracts can require the agency to invest upwards of 5% of the total contract for its own staff and overhead needs associated with a project (K. Van Ness, finance, LAWA, personal communication, Feb. 12, 2000). These agency costs are largely unaccounted for in the full cost of the project.

At the heart of purchasing services are their economic justifications. The dilemma for practitioners has been that every advantage appears coupled with an equal disadvantage. Table 2 lists the promises and pitfalls in light of the LAWA's experience.[4]

CONCLUSION

Monitoring Obligation Increases As Public-ness of Service Increases

Services for which citizens are not true consumers require detailed contract specifications and frequent monitoring. Here public administrators need to stand in the shoes of the citizen/customer to assure quality services. These services will attract administrators, citizens, and interest groups demanding specifications regarding service requirements and restrictions. It is this category in which monitoring is more extensive and administrators need to be prepared to shoulder this responsibility.

Assess Political and Economic Value of Contract Requirements

Administrators need to identify and evaluate the impact of adding restrictions or requirements to service contracts. Typically these requirements serve to correct some perceived deficiency in the "market." These limitations need to be viewed as issues of representativeness not surely in terms of efficiency. For example, can the higher costs of labor due to a living wage ordinance be mitigated with technology, and further decentralization? If so, then implementation should reflect this capacity and remain largely transparent to citizens.

If the negative consequence cannot be assuaged then administrators need to clarify the most probable consequences of new requirements. They need to examine if a service contract approach is still consistent with the community's broader agenda. Services once seen as purely private (airfields) have become largely public arenas (airports). Services once solely in the public sector (post offices) now operate largely in the private sector (FedEx and UPS). The boundary lines between sectors are not rigid and can shift in either direction.

Buyer Beware

Caveat emptor. There is a balance between market forces and community demands for representative government. When the citizen operates primarily as a customer, then market forces will provide quality while keeping costs down.

Table 2 Managing the Promises and Pitfalls of Purchasing of Services

Promises	Pitfalls	LAWA experiences
Eliminates political influence	Corrupt practices in awards	Discretionary decision making fuels political interests and influence; balancing clear expectations with price considerations eliminates much of this problem.
Mobilizes expertise	Adverse effect on veterans, minorities, low-skilled workers	Consequence of purchasing services is that labor mobilizes opposition around its its impact on employment groups. Neither labor nor management has sufficient information about the impact to judge its full effect. Agency retains experts to adequately identify projects and hire qualified consultant support.
Quick response and flexible	Limits flexibility in responding to emergencies	Provides flexibility when response times and expectations are specified and agreed to in the contract.
Avoids capital outlays	Doesn't eliminate, but restructures capital outlays	Neither increases nor decreases capital outlays; does provide opportunities to use capital outlays for social and environmental equity.
Greater economies of scale	Limits economies of scale	Single contractor expands economies of scale opportunities but limits diversity and variety; multiple contracts increase diversity of opportunity but limits economies of scale.
Provides yardstick for comparing costs	Pays for high profits in private sector	Provides yardstick for comparing costs both inside government and among bidders; profitability of firm is not a consideration, only viability of firm to execute the contract.
Fosters good management	Monitoring contributes to high cost of contracting	Care in contract specifications and monitoring contributes to good management and high (largely invisible) cost of contract administration.
Reduces dependency; less vulnerable to disruptions in services;	Shortage of qualified suppliers and at mercy of few contractors	Size of contract (cost, technology) limits number of bidders due to financial risk. Some risks can be lowered through insurance and contract guarantees. Political gamesmanship will discourage bidders and increase dependency of government on few bidders.
Creates opportunities for entrepreneurs	Leaves public vulnerable to strikes, slowdowns, etc.	Creates opportunities for large corporations as primes. Opportunities for small businesses needed to be nurtured by government policies.
Limits the size of government	Loss of government accountability and control	The public holds government accountable for services provided by nongovernment agencies, therefore governments exercise control and assume responsibility for scope and quality of services.
Spurs private sector research and innovation	Few incentives for innovation or efficiencies	Innovations of private sector providers are limited. Public administrators obtain information on the most effective market technologies for their areas. Administrators see identifying and assessing innovation as their responsibility.

Finally, administrators need to look for the value added by service contracts in qualitative terms regarding community life. Does the contract for services afford the government an opportunity to invest in social equity such as an improved environment, economic justice, or citizen participation? Not all benefits of purchasing services are economic. Administrators can use this opportunity to address broader considerations.

ACKNOWLEDGMENT

This chapter would not have been possible without the cooperation, collaboration, and support of Dr. Kathy Van Ness of the Los Angeles World Airport's Finance Bureau. Her contribution is gratefully acknowledged.

REVIEW QUESTIONS

1. Contracting for services is based on a wide range of promises, some of which are overly optimistic. What are these promises? Are they reasonable? Why?
2. What is the relationship between equity and efficiency? Why is it necessary to maintain a balance between efficiency and equity in government? At what point must one trade off one for the other?
3. There is an ongoing debate in public finance literature on contracting as an alternative means for providing public services. What is the essence of this debate?
4. What were the political and economic issues that called for contracting LAWA services? Did the policy help? Could the city have dealt with the problem in some other ways?
5. What does the LAWA experience tell us about the promises and pitfalls of contracting for services in the public sector?

NOTES

1. Today this network of congressional committees, public bureaucracies, and interest groups/clientele is referred to as "iron triangles." They wield considerable policy influence but do not have the unconstrained access they had at the beginning of the twentieth century.
2. New Hanover Township in Montgomery County, Pennsylvania, provides a 96-gallon container and/or a 36-gallon "toter" for weekly trash collection. Yard waste is bagged and picked up by designated collectors each month. Costs of bags are borne separately and independently by residents. The explanation for increased costs and less service is that the single bin approach increases control, [assures] less damage to "roads, increases health, safety and welfare" (New Hanover Township Web site www. newhanover.pa.org/waste.htm).
3. V. Carrelezes, spokesperson for Los Angles Living Wage Coalition, presentation at CSU–Pomona on January 27, 2000.
4. Interviews at LAWA were conducted with the following administrators: J. Christian (transportation), K. Wong (telecommunications), K. Van Ness (finance),

C. Sipple (custodial services), R. Yoneda and G. Harris (parking services), R. Olivares (concession management), C. William (MBE/WBE/DBE), and N. Duca (contract administration) during January and February 2000.

REFERENCES

Appleby, P. (1996). Government is different? In J. M. Shafritz and J. S. Ott (eds.), *Classics of Public Administration*. 4th ed., pp. 122–126. Fort Worth, TX: Harcourt, Brace.

Behn, R. and Kant, P. (1999). Strategies for avoiding the pitfalls of performance contracting. *Public Productivity and Management Review, 22(4)*, 470–489.

Derber, C. (1998). *Corporation Nation*. New York: St. Martin's.

Frederickson, H. G. (1996). Toward a new public administration. In J. M. Shafritz and J. S. Ott (eds.), *Classics of Public Administration*. 4th ed., pp. 329–339. Fort Worth, TX: Harcourt, Brace.

Friedman, M. (1999). Capitalism and freedom. In B. Miroff, R. Seldelman, and T. Swanstrom (eds.), *Debating Democracy*. 2nd ed., pp. 67–77. Boston: Houghton Mifflin.

Guevara, C. (2000). *Mayor Rirodan Names Lydia Kennard Executive Director of Los Angeles World Airports*. Los Angeles: Office of the Mayor; available at http://www.lawa.org/html/ LAWA—show—news.asps/news = 84.

Harmon, M. M. and Mayer, R. T. (1989). *Organization Theory for Public Administration*. Burke, VA: Chatalaine.

Heilbroner, R. L. (1975). *The Making of Economic Society*. Englewood Cliffs, NJ: Prentice–Hall.

Kuttner, R. (1997). *Everything for Sale*. New York: Knopf.

Madison, J. (1961). Federalist Paper 10. In A. Hamilton, J. Jay, and J. Madison (eds.), (with introduction by C. Rossiter), *The Federalist Papers*, New York: Mentor Books.

Mintzberg, H. (1996). Managing government/governing management. *Harvard Business Review, 74(3)*, 75–83.

Neustadt, R. E. (1963). Approaches to staffing the presidency: Notes on FDR and JFK. *American Political Science Review, 57(4)*, 855–864.

Niskanen, W. A. (1968). The peculiar economics of bureaucracy. *American Economic Review, 58(2)*, 293–305.

Osborne, D. and Gaebler, T. (1993). *Reinventing Government: How the Entrepreneurial Spirit Is Transforming the Public Sector*. New York: Plume.

Osborne, D. and Plastrik, P. (1997). *Banishing Bureaucracy: The Five Strategies for Reinventing Government*. Reading, MA: Addison-Wesley.

Savas, E. S. (2000). *Privatization and Public Private Partnerships*. New York: Chatham House.

Shafritz, J. M. and Ott, J. S. (1996). *Classics in Organizational Theory*. 4th ed. Orlando, FL: Harcourt Brace.

Straayer, J. A., Wrinkle, R. D., and Polinard, J. L. (1998). *State and Local Politics*. 2nd ed., New York: St. Martins.

Taylor, F. W. (1996). The principles of scientific management. In J. M. Shafritz and J. S. Ott (eds.), *Classics of Organization Theory*. 4th ed., pp. 66–79. Orlando, FL: Harcourt Brace.

Uchitelle, L. (Oct. 18, 1999). Devising new math to define poverty. *New York Times*, A, 1.

Wildavsky, A. and Caiden, N. (1997). *The New Politics of the Budgetary Process*. 3rd ed., New York: Longman.

Winfrey, T. (1999). *LAWA Addresses Regional Needs During 1999–2000*. Los Angeles: LAWA; available at http://www.lawa.org/html/LAWA show news.asps/news =56.

Wolfinger, R. E. (1972). Why political machines have not withered away and other revisionist thoughts. *Journal of Politics, 34(2)*, 365–398.

44

Enterprise Fund Operation in a West Texas City

Aman Khan and Theodore J. Stumm
Texas Tech University, Lubbock, Texas, U.S.A.

Enterprise funds are often used by governments as a means of providing goods and services to their citizens in a businesslike manner; that is, citizens may purchase desired goods and services and pay for them at the time or on a regular, usually monthly, basis. Enterprise funds thus relieve the government from having to provide these goods and services from general fund revenues. This is especially important today when citizens are more and more reluctant to approve higher taxes. Meanwhile, they continue to demand a high level of services, while the services themselves are becoming increasingly costly. Enterprise funds have also traditionally provided goods and services that the private sector cannot provide or is less willing to provide. This is usually because of the high capital investment required and the need to provide a minimum level of some essential services to all, regardless of their ability to pay on a par with other users.

Cities operate a variety of enterprise funds. These include utilities such as electricity, water, sewer, and solid waste. They also include service-type enterprises, such as parking facilities and bus lines. Enterprise funds are also established to operate facilities such as convention centers and airports to facilitate passenger and cargo movement and to draw visitors and businesses to the city. In addition, cities may also provide a wide range of recreational facilities, such as golf courses, swimming pools, marinas, and stadiums, through enterprise funds.

While enterprise funds have traditionally been thought of as self-contained, charging user fees to cover the cost of services, maintaining their own capital equipment, and even securing their own financing, this view is changing. Many cities now charge their enterprise funds payments in lieu of taxes, franchise fees, and other fees and charges, just as if they were private sector businesses. Also, some enterprises provide goods and services to city agencies at minimum rates or as services in kind. These practices increase the cost of goods and services to the consumer, while in effect subsidizing the city's general fund. Enterprise revenues in excess of costs are transferred to the general fund in many cities. On the other hand, some cities subsidize their enterprise activities from their general fund in order to cover costs not recouped by user fees. In other words, enterprise activities interact with other financial entities of the city and have a significant effect on how the city manages its finances (Khan and Stumm, 1994).

693

This chapter will examine the enterprise operations of one city that uses a variety of enterprise funds to provide a wide range of goods and services to its residents. It will first review the city's enterprise fund structure and operations. Next, it will examine these enterprise operations in more detail in order to determine whether or not problem areas exist, and if so, to isolate possible causes. Finally, some options for solving these problems will be explored, along with some considerations that may affect the choice of solutions.

ENTERPRISE FUND ACTIVITIES IN LUBBOCK, TEXAS

The west Texas city of Lubbock provides an excellent example of a moderate-sized city that provides many services to its citizens through the use of enterprise funds. The city operates eight enterprise activities, including utilities, services, municipal improvement, and recreation.

Lubbock is nearly equidistant from Dallas and El Paso, Texas, Oklahoma City, Oklahoma, and Albuquerque, New Mexico, on the high south plains of west Texas. It is a city of 187,000 residents that is the focal point for a bistate area largely dependent upon agriculture, oil, light manufacturing, and retail businesses for its economic well-being. The city has a council–manager form of government. The council consists of the mayor and six council members elected by district.

The city has three universities and colleges: Texas Tech University, Lubbock Christian University, and South Plains College. It also hosts the largest medical complex between Dallas and the West Coast with seven hospitals, including Texas Tech's University Medical Center. These facilities draw a large number of students and visitors from the tristate area and provide a strong base of support to the city's private sector.

Like most cities over the past several years, Lubbock has been affected by the national recession. It has also had to work its way through economic difficulties caused by uncertain oil prices and several years of adverse weather that hurt agriculture production. By early 1993 most of the city's economic indicators were positive and the area's economy now seems to be expanding, albeit slowly. It is within this demographic and economic setting that we will examine the city's enterprise fund operations.

Lubbock operates eight enterprise funds, four of which are utility enterprises. These funds provide electricity, water, sewer, and solid waste services for the city's residents and some private, industrial, and municipal customers outside the city. The water, sewer, and electric utilities are operated by the city's utility division, while the solid waste utility falls under the public safety and services division. These enterprises derive nearly all of their operating revenue from charges for services. In a somewhat unusual arrangement, the electric utility, Lubbock Power and Light (LP&L), competes directly with a private electric utility, Southwestern Public Service (SPS).* In this arrangement, consumers may elect to use either utility and pay the same rates. Competition for the consumers' business is based largely on quality of service, the convenience of making a single payment for all utilities, and the customer's interest in having profits go to the city's general fund rather than to private stockholders. In order to provide a uniform financial environment for these competitors, the city charges LP&L both payments in lieu of taxes and franchise

---

* One small residential area is serviced only by South Plains Electric Cooperative, Inc., which buys its power from SPS.

fees. These fees are basically those that would be charged a private electric utility with the same plant, property, and equipment assets. Franchise fees are set at 3% of gross revenues, and payments in lieu of property taxes are based on the estimated value of the enterprise's property multiplied by the city property tax rate.

Two of the city's other enterprise funds are used to provide transportation to the city's residents and visitors. The first of these is the city's airport. It provides much needed facilities for commercial airlines to move passengers and cargo into and out of this relatively isolated city. The airport collects most of its operating revenue from landing and parking fees and the rental of airport space to private enterprises such as restaurants, airline provisioning firms, and automobile rental companies. The other transportation enterprise is the Citibus fund. This fund provides bus service to the city and surrounding area. Actual bus operation is done under contract by a private transportation company. All of this enterprise's operating revenue comes from service charges. Both of these enterprises are overseen by the city's development services division.

Civic Lubbock, Inc., is a city enterprise that promotes the use of the city's civic center for cultural and educational activities. This facility attracts many conventions, shows, and cultural events. Accordingly, it provides an important means of attracting visitors and businesses to the city. Its operating revenues are gained entirely from service charges.

Lubbock's only recreational enterprise is its golf fund, which is operated by the parks and recreation department. Its function is to operate a complete golf facility for public use. Its features include two eighteenth-hole courses at a single location, a pro shop, a driving range, and related services. Operational revenue comes mainly from user fees and equipment rentals.

ANALYSIS OF ENTERPRISE FUND OPERATIONS

Because enterprise funds are essentially businesses operated by the city, we may use performance measures similar to the private sector to measure their financial accomplishments. Table 1 summarizes enterprise fund operations for the four most recently completed

Table 1   Lubbock, Texas: Combined Enterprise Funds Operation (in Thousands of Dollars)

	1988–1989	1989–1990	1990–1991	1991–1992	1992–1993	1993–1994
Operating revenues	$87,242	$92,705	$94,832	$96,002	$99,124	$102,356
Operating expenses	(66,862)	(66,839)	(70,436)	(72,054)	(73,890)	(75,773)
Operating income (loss)	20,380	25,866	24,396	23,948	25,234	26,583
Nonoperating revenues (expenditures)	(2,510)	(3,059)	408	(211)	(253)	(304)
Income (loss) before operating transfers	17,870	22,807	24,804	23,737	24,981	26,279
Operating transfers in (out)	(5,590)	(6,675)	(7,539)	(8,282)	(9,447)	(10,776)
Net income (loss)	$12,280	$16,132	$17,265	$15,455	$15,534	$15,503

[a] Forecast amounts projected using the average percentage change computed for the preceding fiscal years in the table.

fiscal years (FY) and includes a forecast for FY 1993 and 1994. As Table 1 shows, Lubbock's enterprise funds seem to be on solid ground. Operating revenues show steady increases, reflecting the city's slow but fairly constant growth over the past four years. Over all, both operating income and net income show healthy growth, and the city's enterprises appear to be prospering. In fact, the net income of the city's enterprise funds is approximately equal to its sales tax revenues and is exceeded only by property tax receipts. In FY 1992, the city's enterprise funds transferred over $13.5 million to the general fund, providing just over 22% of the city's general fund revenues (City of Lubbock, Tx, 1993–1994). These transfers were in the form of payments in lieu of franchise and property taxes, assessments to cover a share of the city's indirect costs, the provision of services in kind (street lighting), and allocations for general debt service.

As is frequently the case, however, aggregate analyses can be misleading. In fact, the overall success of Lubbock's enterprise activities is due primarily to the four utility enterprises—electricity, water, sewer, and solid waste—which operate very profitably. As we shall see, its other enterprises are not doing as well. In order to fully understand the condition of Lubbock's enterprise activities, each will be examined in more detail.

Three measures, or ratios, will be used in this examination—the current ratio, the solvency ratio, and the income ratio. The current ratio is a measure of financial condition. It is the ratio of a fund's current assets to its current liabilities. It measures a fund's ability to cover its short-term obligations using readily available assets such as cash and inventory. The second measure to be used is a solvency ratio—the ratio of a fund's total liabilities to its total assets. This ratio shows whether or not a fund is capable of covering its long- and short-term obligations from the fund's existing resources. Finally, we will look at each fund's income ratio—the ratio of operating income or loss to its operating revenue. This is a measure of how much operating income is generated by each dollar taken in. The income ratio is a measure of profitability of the enterprise (Anthony and Reece, 1989; Berne and Schramm, 1986; Pierce and Rust, 1991).

Table 2 presents the three ratios computed for each city enterprise for the past four years. The current ratios show that four of the city's enterprise funds are unable to cover their current liabilities using only current assets. This may not be too great a problem since the city as a whole has the assets to assure that current obligations can be met. The large decrease in the current ratio for the airport fund comes from the acquisition of a large liability due to other funds in FY 1991 and 1992. Similarly, the sewer fund showed a large decrease in accounts receivable in FY 1990 and subsequent years that reduced its current ratio. The trend for most funds is down, however, as is the trend for the funds as a whole. This should be an item of concern for city officials because it indicates decreased revenues, increased costs, or both, and reduces the city's ability to cover current obligations without using long-term resources.

The solvency ratios indicate that all of the enterprises except the golf fund can satisfy their short- and long-term obligations with existing resources. The golf fund shows an increasing trend toward an unsatisfactory solvency ratio because of decreasing revenues and sharp increases in payments due to other funds. Although golf fees have been raised, it is uncertain whether or not this will increase revenues sufficiently to reverse this trend.

It is not until we examine the income ratios of the various enterprises that we begin to see serious problems in the ability of some of the enterprises to generate operating income. Although the city's enterprise funds generate an average of $0.25 for every dollar they take in, most of the resultant revenue is produced by the four utility enterprises. The remaining enterprises all break even or lose money and will be discussed in more detail.

Table 2 Table of Ratios for Enterprise Activities, Lubbock, Texas (FY 1990–1992)

Activities	1988–1989	1989–1990	1990–1991	1991–1992
		Current Ratio		
Enterprise fund total	1.61	1.74	1.39	1.31
Electric fund	3.30	4.27	3.86	4.85
Water fund	0.42	0.77	0.41	0.37
Sewer fund	1.51	0.48	0.60	0.52
Solid waste fund	0.39	0.42	0.36	0.30
Airport fund	13.61	9.65	1.43	1.36
Golf fund	0.22	0.15	0.11	0.19
Civic Lubbock, Inc.	4.32	2.59	1.40	1.68
Citibus fund	1.20	1.14	1.13	1.16
	−0.06	−0.05	−1.60	−2.11
		Solvency ratio		
Enterprise fund total	0.41	0.39	0.46	0.48
Electric fund	0.46	0.40	0.39	0.34
Water fund	0.48	0.52	0.63	0.61
Sewer fund	0.40	0.36	0.33	0.58
Solid waste fund	0.34	0.46	0.40	0.54
Airport fund	0.03	0.02	0.03	0.05
Golf fund	0.67	0.74	0.83	1.06
Civic Lubbock, Inc.	0.22	0.47	0.54	0.46
Citibus fund	0.21	0.25	0.25	0.17
		Income ratio		
Enterprise Fund Total	0.23	0.28	0.26	0.25
Electric fund	0.24	0.26	0.26	0.26
Water fund	0.38	0.46	0.46	0.42
Sewer fund	0.40	0.47	0.44	0.39
Solid waste fund	0.02	0.11	0.09	0.15
Airport fund	−0.39	−0.16	−0.24	−0.21
Golf fund	0.01	−0.11	−0.12	−0.10
Civic Lubbock, Inc.	0.13	−0.03	0.04	0.01
Citibus fund	−0.06	−0.05	−1.60	−2.11

Civic Lubbock is essentially a break-even fund. Its function is one of facilitating events and activities that draw participation from city residents and visitors. As such, the city gains in revenues through other levies, such as sales and hotel/motel taxes. Another benefit to be gained from Civic Lubbock is the attraction of investors and new businesses to the area. Success in this endeavor results in greater employment, new residents, and industrial or commercial expansion. All of these create more tax revenues for the city and new consumers for other enterprise fund goods and services. This fund's failure to maintain a continuous positive income ratio is consistent with its purpose. In fact, this fund has remained relatively stable at a point very close to a break-even income ratio of 0.00.

The negative income ratio generated by airport operations may in part be justified by logic similar to that associated with Civic Lubbock. Without an airport capable of providing the necessary passenger and cargo movement required by a city of Lubbock's size, business would be greatly handicapped. By providing a modern air terminal and supporting facilities, the city supports existing businesses and attracts new ones. The benefit to the citizens and the city may well more than offset the loss incurred by unprofitable operations. Its three-year income ratio average of -0.25, or a loss of $0.25 for every dollar of operating revenue generated, however, is a warning sign that cannot be ignored by city officials.

The inability of the other two funds, the golf fund and Citibus, to generate operating revenue should also be of concern to city officials. First, the golf fund incurs an operating loss of approximately 10% on every dollar taken in. It has maintained this ratio for the past three fiscal years as operating revenues have steadily declined. This has been due to declining pro-shop sales and concession revenues, even though revenues from greens fees had increased steadily until unusually wet weather in 1992 resulted in a slight decrease. Although operating expenses have decreased in both years since 1990, these decreases did not prevent sizable operating losses.

Second, the Citibus operation appears to have taken a severe downward tumble in 1991 and 1992 as the income ratio fell to a negative 2.11. In reality, however, this is not the case. Citibus has had a sustained record of steadily increasing operating losses for the past four fiscal years. In FY 1989 and 1990, cash grants and reimbursements of approximately $1.4 million and $1.9 million, respectively, were included as part of the total operating revenues for Citibus. When these sums are removed to make the figures for those years compatible with the two latter years, the income ratios for these years are -2.04 and -2.31. These figures, while still a cause for grave concern, particularly in view of a sharp decline in ridership in 1992 after two years of rapid growth, are not new.

In order to appreciate the magnitude of the losses associated with these income ratios, the income statements for each enterprise must be examined. These are contained in Tables 3 and 4. The net operating loss for the four nonutility enterprises for FY 1992 is over $3.1 million. This is a sizable amount for a city the size of Lubbock, but operating income or loss does not tell the whole story.

Some enterprise activities are the recipients of grants or payments from other governmental agencies. This is the case for mass transit enterprises. Federal grants for the city's bus system are based on equal support by the city and state. In FY 1991–1992, federal grants to Citibus totaled nearly $1.4 million. The state contributed another $221,00 and the city provided nearly $650,000 worth of support. Altogether, this nonoperating income resulted in a net loss for Citibus of about $218,000, despite an operating loss of over $2 million.

The airport's operating loss of $887,000 for the same year was transposed into a net loss of over $1.25 million, largely because of transfers out of over $400,000. These transfers were for grounds maintenance, indirect cost allocation, and partial payment for debt service. Because of the large amount of property, runways, taxiways, and other operating facilities, however, the airport incurs a disproportionately high amount of depreciation expense. The amount of depreciation in FY 1991–1992 was over $1.5 million. Without depreciation, the airport generated an operating income of $667,000. Federal support to airports is also very different from that for mass transit. The Federal Aviation Agency (FAA) provides 90% of funding for operations related capital projects. Since these are capital contributions, they are not reflected in net income figures. The Lubbock International Airport received $1.2 million in capital contributions in FY 1991–1992, about the size of its net loss. These capital contributions are earmarked for specific projects,

Table 3   Utility Enterprise Fund Data for Lubbock, Texas; FY 1990–1992 (FY 1993 Forecasted)

	1989	1990	1991	1992	1993 (Forecast)
Electric fund					
Total operating revenues	49,285,975	49,271,634	49,142,119	50,196,280	50,506,354
Total operating expenses	37,335,311	36,642,933	36,287,020	36,999,831	36,893,590
Operating income (loss)	11,950,664	12,628,701	12,855,099	13,196,449	13,612,764
Total nonoper, revenues (expend.)	110,559	(707,386)	302,839	1,357,330	1,900,000[a]
Income (loss) before oper. transf.	12,061,221	11,921,315	13,157,938	14,553,779	15,512,764
Total transfers in (out)	(3,520,751)	(4,621,684)	(5,087,836)	(5,328,261)	(6,146,709)
Net income (loss)	8,540,472	7,299,631	8,070,102	9,225,518	9,366,055
Water fund					
Total operating revenues	16,660,193	19,668,087	21,821,722	20,765,507	22,438,104
Total operating expenses	10,323,225	10,658,193	11,815,664	11,995,785	12,620,731
Operating income (loss)	6,336,968	9,009,894	10,006,058	8,769,722	9,817,373
Total nonoper, revenues (expend.)	(2,135,201)	(1,969,922)	(1,693,977)	(2,561,375)	(2,812,870)
Income (loss) before oper. transf.	4,201,767	7,039,972	8,312,081	6,208,347	7,004,503
Total transfers in (out)	(1,052,256)	(1,309,188)	(1,768,916)	(2,035,351)	(2,541,440)
Net income (loss)	3,149,511	5,730,784	6,543,165	4,172,996	4,463,064
Sewer fund					
Total operating revenues	8,518,054	9,571,277	9,696,057	10,275,402	10,948,213
Total operating expenses	5,104,560	5,056,042	5,448,701	6,251,328	6,700,304
Operating income (loss)	3,413,494	4,515,235	4,247,356	4,024,074	4,247,909
Total nonoper. revenues (expend)	(428,411)	(622,740)	(248,300)	(371,492)	(414,643)
Income (loss) before oper. transf.	2,985,083	3,892,495	3,999,056	3,652,582	3,833,266
Total transfers in (out)	(497,905)	(181,049)	(572,398)	(883,106)	(1,491,861)
Net income (loss)	2,487,178	3,711,446	3,426,658	2,769,476	2,341,405
Solid waste fund					
Total operating revenues	5,240,173	5,630,037	6,340,137	7,153,729	7,937,897
Total operating expenses	5,139,495	5,026,208	5,764,240	6,057,070	6,411,601
Operating income (loss)	100,678	603,829	575,897	1,096,659	1,526,296
Total nonoper, revenues (expend)	24,028	158,154	319,148	65,932	193,546
Income (loss) before oper. transf.	124,706	761,983	895,045	1,162,591	1,719,842
Total transfers in (out)	(227,713)	(175,226)	(186,822)	(198,873)	(192,256)
Net income (loss)	(103,007)	586,757	708,223	963,718	1,527,586

[a] Estimated graphically because of large variation in values.
Source: City of Lubbock, TX, Comprehensive Annual Financial Reports, FY 1990–1992.

Table 4 Nonutility Enterprise Fund Data for Lubbock, Texas; FY 1990–1992 (FY 1993 Forecasted)

	1989	1990	1991	1992	1993 (Forecast)
Airport fund					
Total operating revenues	3,617,038	3,810,316	4,064,177	4,130,487	4,318,225
Total operating expenses	5,038,789	4,423,389	5,043,168	5,007,673	5,025,940
Operating income (loss)	(1,421,749)	(613,073)	(978,991)	(877,206)	(707,715)
Total nonoper. revenues (expend)	4,787	167,295	228,703	45,030	247,000
Income (loss) before oper. transf.	(1,416,962)	(445,778)	(750,288)	(832,176)	(460,715)
Total transfers in (out)	(286,214)	(387,300)	(421,490)	(436,199)	(505,461)
Net income (loss)	(1,703,176)	(833,078)	(1,171,778)	(1,268,375)	(966,176)
Golf fund					
Total operating revenues	840,475	885,485	853,926	787,030	771,177
Total operating expenses	835,486	984,533	960,283	868,580	885,450
Operating income (loss)	4,989	(99,048)	(106,357)	(81,550)	(114,273)
Total nonoper. revenues (expend)	(85,248)	(80,574)	(57,301)	(83,616)	(86,837)
Income (loss) before oper. transf.	(80,259)	(179,622)	(163,658)	(165,166)	(201,110)
Total transfers in (out)	(5,340)	(509)	0	0	0
Net income (loss)	(85,599)	(180,131)	(163,658)	(165,166)	(201,110)
Civic Lubbock fund					
Total operating revenues	972,440	1,102,455	1,498,859	1,421,509	1,630,783
Total operating expenses	846,054	1,139,428	1,444,314	1,409,627	1,687,003
Operating income (loss)	126,386	(36,973)	54,545	11,882	(56,220)
Total nonoper. revenues (expend)	8,574	5,369	144	(3,043)	(6,500)
Income (loss) before oper. transf.	134,960	(31,604)	54,689	8,839	(62,720)
Total transfers in (out)	0	0	0	0	0
Net income (loss)	134,960	(31,604)	54,689	8,839	(62,720)
Citibus fund (corrected)					
Total operating revenues	734,398	877,853	1,269,103	1,020,853	1,172,421
Total operating expenses	2,238,800	2,907,977	3,299,622	3,178,497	3,598,981
Operating income (loss)	(1,504,402)	(2,030,124)	(2,030,519)	(2,157,644)	(2,426,560)
Total nonoper. revenues (expend)	1,363,956	1,879,064	1,472,010	1,339,888	1,358,479
Income (loss) before oper. transf.	(140,446)	(151,060)	(558,509)	(817,756)	(1,068,081)
Total transfers in (out)	0	0	409,658	599,980	878,723
Net income (loss)	(140,446)	(151,060)	(148,851)	(217,776)	(189,358)

Source: City of Lubbock, TX, Comprehensive Annual Financial Reports, FY 1990–1992.

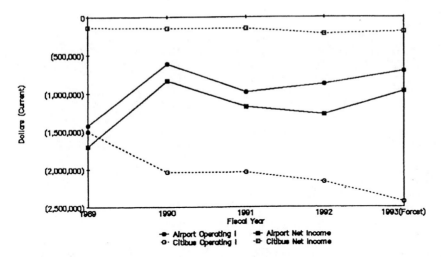

Figure 1   Airport and Citibus operations and net income (FY 1990–1992).

however, and cannot be considered to offset any portion of the airport's loss. In fact, as the value of capital airport property, plant, and equipment increases, so does depreciation expense, requiring larger operating revenues to offset the increase.

These points are summarized graphically in Figure 1. The differences between the operating and net incomes are startling for the Citibus fund, and the effects of grants and transfers in are clearly evident. The divergence between the operating and net income for the airport fund between FY 1990–1991 and 1991–1992 may signal the beginning of an adverse trend. Since the forecast figures are based on average annual change, they will not reflect a new trend at its inception.

The golf fund presents a slightly different situation. Despite falling revenues from play, reduced maintenance costs for FY 1992 brought about a $25,000 reduction in the fund's operating loss. Like the airport fund, depreciation also has a significant effect on the operating expenses of the golf fund ($131,523). The reduction in operating loss was more than offset, however, by increased interest expenditures and losses on property disposition. These two factors have been this fund's largest nonoperating expense for the past four years. As a result, the golf fund continues to lose over $165,000 per year after transfers to the general fund of $84,000 for general debt service. While this is a small amount compared to larger enterprises, it is a significant amount and carries implications that losses in the other funds do not.

A DIFFERENT VIEW

The ratios presented above were selected for ease of use and understanding. There are, of course, many other ratios which may be used (Ingram, et al., 1991; Moody's, 1992). Moody's annually presents a set of national medians for selected ratios of profitability and debt repayment ability for electric, water, sewer, and airport enterprises. These ratios

Table 5 Comparison of Selected Ratios, Lubbock vs. Moody's Enterprise Performance Medians (Lubbock/Moody's Median)

Enterprise	Operating ratio (%)	Net takedown (%)	Interest coverage (X)	Debt service coverage (X)	Debt service safety margin (%)
Electric	67.5/76.3	34.2/29.1	6.48/3.13	2.61/2.29	21.1/15.6
Water	47.5/64.6	45.9/41.7	1.24/3.33	0.76/2.20	−14.8/19.1
Sewer	45.9/62.4	52.4/44.4	4.16/4.00	2.44/2.07	30.9/24.6
Airport	83.8/54.0	17.1/49.8	21.55/–*	6.03/1.71	14.2/21.4

[a] Not provided.

Source: City of Lubbock Comprehensive Annual Financial Report, FY 1991–1992: Moody's 1992 enterprise performance medians.

provide a means of comparing Lubbock's performance in these areas with the national average in Table 5. The definitions of each ratio are provided in Table 6.

The operating and net takedown ratios are measures of profitability, with a smaller percentage indicating higher profitability for the operating ratio. With the exception of the airport, Lubbock's enterprises are more profitable than the national median. This finding is confirmed by Lubbock's higher net takedown ratios for its three utility enterprises.

The three debt repayment ratios indicate that Lubbock's electric and sewer enterprises have above-average debt repayment capability. The water enterprise debt repayment ratio reflects the construction of a new water treatment facility and does not at this point necessarily indicate a lack of creditworthiness (Moody's, 1992). The airport shows-above-average ability to repay its current debt, but a below-average safety margin.

While these ratios are helpful, they are primarily intended to indicate the creditworthiness of a city's enterprises. They are presented here to illustrate that different ratios are available and may be of interest to various stakeholders. The current, solvency, and income

Table 6 Moody's Enterprise Performance Median Definitions (From Moody's 1992 Enterprise Performance Medians)

Gross revenue and income	Operating revenue plus nonoperating revenue
Operating and maintenance expenses	Operating and maintenance expenses net of depreciation, amortization, and interest requirements
Net revenues	Gross revenue and income less operating and maintenance expenses
Operating ratio (%)	Operating and maintenance expenses divided by total operating revenues
Net takedown (%)	Net revenues divided by gross revenue and income
Interest coverage (x)	Net revenues divided by interest, requirements for year
Debt service coverage (x)	Net revenues divided by principal and interest requirements for year
Debt service safety margin (%)	Net revenues less principal and interest requirements for year divided by gross revenue and income

ratios however, provide sound indications of enterprise performance and will serve most analytical needs well while being easier to use.

OPTIONS FOR CHANGE

Clearly, no one solution will meet the needs of all enterprise funds in all cities. The needs of each city are different. So are their management methods and objectives. Some cities are enjoying a period of growth and others are declining in population. Some are attracting new commerce and industry and others are experiencing changes in the nature of their economy. Still others must struggle to retain their industrial and commercial bases. All, however, share a growing resistance among their voters to increased taxes, as well as continued demands for city services. Enterprise funds present one way of continuing a given level of municipal services in a constrained fiscal environment. Accordingly, various options are presented here as possible partial or total solutions to the problems being experienced by Lubbock's airport, bus, and golf enterprise funds. By analogy, these may also be helpful in other cities and in other enterprise activities.

Airport Revenue Fund

Lubbock's airport enterprise will be the first fund to be considered. The first option, clearly, is to do nothing. That option carries some implications that may not be acceptable to either city officials or to residents, however. As mentioned earlier, the airport provides an essential service to the city and surrounding area. Accepting the status quo implies that the airport is sufficiently important to the city that the approximate $1 million annual loss is acceptable. The burden of that loss is borne by the city and its residents, but not all of the benefits are being reaped by the city. The airport also benefits residents of nearby cities, although the degree to which each benefits is hard to determine. Under this option the city continues to take the full loss without receiving the full benefit.

An increase in rental fees and charges for services would be one means of spreading the costs among the beneficiaries. Increased rents for hangars and agricultural and industrial areas would put more of the cost on those who benefit directly from using these facilities. The amount of increase that can be reasonably charged, however, is limited by the returns that users can expect to gain from the use of these areas. Increased rents for landing fees and terminal areas would affect the servicing airlines, and these increased costs would presumably be passed on to those who actually use the airlines' services. This would place more of the burden of operating the airport on those who actually benefit, but again there are practical limits to such increases in an era in which airlines are suffering from their own financial woes. In fact, Lubbock is increasing some rents and airline charges for FY 1993–1994, but these increases are moderate. At the same time, some airlines are modifying service by reverting to turboprop aircraft rather than the jets that they have operated in Lubbock for many years.

In May 1993, Lubbock voters approved a $2.5 million bond issue to repair the airport terminal roof and its heating and air conditioning system. The funds needed for these repairs were not available from other sources. This action by the voters signals a commitment to maintain attractive and functional airport facilities even at the cost of a $0.50 increase in the property tax rate. Subsidization of an enterprise fund in this manner may not be a viable option in cities that have more or better transportation facilities, however. This option also puts the onus for airport support only on Lubbock citizens rather than all of those who stand to directly benefit.

Another change in airport charges approved by the city council and the FAA but not yet implemented is the imposition of a passenger facility charge of $6 for one-way tickets and $12 for round-trip tickets. This charge may be collected by the next two airports that the traveler transits if the originating airport does not collect it. Based on an average annual passenger load of 580,000, this charge could bring in about $7 million annually to Lubbock. This amount would certainly correct the airport's net loss, if it could. These funds may only be used for safety and service expansions, however. Even so, it would seem that some creative uses of these funds might ease the load in other areas and result in improved net income figures. This charge also has the advantage that it is paid only by those who actually use the airport's facilities.

Another option that might be considered would be to reduce the airport's share of transfers to the general fund for indirect cost allocation, general debt service, and grounds maintenance. It would seem, first, that the grounds maintenance charge should be an operating expense and not a transfer to the general fund. Reducing the other two transfers, however, would involve a major policy decision on the part of the city. All enterprise activities except Citibus, which is operated under contract, are charged general debt service and their share of the city's indirect costs for administration and other expenses not directly attributable to any specific activity or operation. Exempting the airport fund might result in a need for deliberations on the contributions to be made by each of the other enterprises and require renewed deliberations on a year-by-year basis. Under the current system, a strong argument can be made for the fairness of the process and the efficiency of the budget process.

These options are not all-inclusive, but they do provide some ideas for improving the net income figures for the airport fund. The amount of improvement needed is a political question as well as a financial one. Obviously, it would be ideal for each enterprise fund to at least operate on a break-even basis, but, as we have seen, there may be valid reasons why they do not. The decision ultimately rests in the hands of the city's elected policy-making officials. The financial manager's role is to provide the best options possible for their consideration.

Transit Enterprise Fund

Lubbock's Citibus enterprise presents some different challenges for the city's elected and appointed leaders. Lubbock is widely spread out for a city of its size, and a mass transit system is a necessity for many workers, students, shoppers, and the elderly and disabled. An affordable means of transportation is required for these persons to get to work, school, and medical facilities, as well as to be able to purchase needed goods and services. Citibus fills this need by providing both route service and on-demand transportation. It also provides a special service to the Texas Tech campus, which covers several square miles.

The fact remains, however, that Citibus has experienced operating losses of over $2 million in each of the last three years. Federal and state subsidies, along with city support, have reduced this figure to a net loss of only $150,000 in FY 1989–1990 and 1990–1991. In FY 1991–1992, operating revenues dropped nearly $250,000, and despite reduced maintenance costs and increased city support, the enterprise's net loss was over $200,000.

As discussed earlier, this level of annual loss may be acceptable in view of the benefits received. A majority of the riders are lower-income persons who might otherwise not be able to work, and an increasing number of riders are disabled and elderly persons who are finding the demand response service required by the Americans with Disabilities Act a good way to accomplish their shopping and get to their medical appointments. The current level of support by the city for these services is nearly $600,000, however. This is a hefty price for the city's taxpayers to pay in support of the relatively small segment of the population that use Citibus services on a regular basis.

Maintenance costs for an enterprise such as Citibus tend to fall more slowly than operating revenues when services are reduced because of the high level of fixed costs for equipment and facilities. Conversely, they also tend to rise more slowly as service is expanded. One alternative would then be to expand services to the extent possible. Lubbock is doing this by extending service into new areas in the southwest section of town and providing special "trolley" transportation for conventions and special events. Service improvement and attracting more riders are also the goals of the new downtown transfer plaza now under construction with both federal and city funds. There is a relatively fixed number of potential riders in any given population, however, which results in practical limits on expansion.

Fare increases encounter similar limits. The current basic fare is $0.75. Increasing this fare could impose significant hardships on those who must use the service daily to get to work. The fare for demand service is $1.50. Many of the people who use this service are on fixed incomes, however, and may have to cut their ridership frequency, negating the benefits of any fare increase. Increasing the charge for the service to Texas Tech is another fare increase possibility. This service has already been reduced to some degree however, because of its cost and the financial pressures being experienced by the university. The positive side of fare increases, where they can reasonably be used, is that federal support is based on the total of revenue received form the city and state and from operating revenues Increasing revenues from fares would thus bring matching federal support—at least as long as the current rules remain in effect.

Another possibility for reducing the city's load in providing mass transportation may be to negotiate revised requirements with the company operating the service. Contracts providing profit incentives and penalties based upon agreed-upon levels of performance are becoming increasingly common and may prove useful in this regard, as might shorter contracts, which would provide the city more control over performance. Of course, city operation may at some time become more attractive than contracting out operations.

Cutting costs by reducing or eliminating service on less productive routes may also be an attractive option, but such decisions must be based upon more than numbers. In some cases eliminating service to some areas could be counterproductive to the goal of providing reliable and affordable transportation to assist lower-income citizens in staying employed. Another cost-cutting option is to reduce equipment that is no longer needed. In addition to reducing higher maintenance and operating costs associated with older equipment, insurance and other indirect costs are also reduced. Lubbock is pursuing this latter approach by selling off some older buses at auction.

All of the options outlined above, and many others, can probably be used individually or in various combinations to improve the financial performance of Citibus and other similar enterprises. As has been shown, however, there are both practical and political limits to many of them that must be considered.

Golf Fund

As a recreational fund, the golf fund does not present as many social and economic benefits for the city as the airport and Citibus funds. Recreational enterprise funds are usually provided strictly for the benefit of the users and often compete with private sector providers. This is particularly true of golf courses, and Lubbock is no exception. There are four public courses in Lubbock, including the city's thirty-six-hole Meadowbrook course. Combined with the city's private courses there is one course for approximately every 21,000 residents in Lubbock compared with an average of one course per 50,000 residents statewide.* This provides a more competitive environment for those in pursuit of the golfer's dollar, including the city.

One way of improving operating revenues would be to provide the best facilities for golfers at a competitive price. It is assumed that golfers prefer to play the most attractive and best maintained course provided the cost to them is not significantly greater. Using this assumption, course improvements and enhanced maintenance should improve operating revenues from greens fees, memberships, and pro-shop sales. Lubbock is pursuing this option through a golf development plan.

Fee increases are another obvious means of increasing operating revenue and may be made more possible by course improvements. Meadowbrook's fees were increased in FY 1992–1993, and the city is examining the possibility of an increase of another $1.00 per round of golf and an increase of $0.75 in electric cart rental fees. These increases will result in weekday greens fees of $10.00, weekend fees of $12.00, and a $9.00 electric cart rental fee, however, As a result Mead owbrook players would pay $1.00 more on weekdays and $1.00 per electric cart more than the next most expensive privately operated public courses. Whether or not golfers will support these changes remains to be seen.

Another option is to contract golf course operation and maintenance to the private sector. As with Citibus, emphasis should probably be on shorter-term contracts and performance bonuses and penalties. Lubbock has already contracted out operation of the Meadowbrook driving range. Short of contracting out the entire operation, it may also be possible to contract out course maintenance. Here again, emphasis on performance would be paramount.

There may also be economies to be achieved in the area of golf course maintenance by combining that function with the city's other grounds maintenance function on a reimbursable basis. This option could result in a reduction of equipment required by the golf course, with a corresponding reduction in depreciation expense. Personnel costs may also be reduced under such an arrangement.

The ultimate cost saving measure, especially in view of the comparatively low ratio of golfers per course in Lubbock, may be to close the golf enterprise entirely. Should the continued losses resulting from golf course operation become an issue, it is more difficult to defend these losses to the city's taxpayers. Social and economic benefits to be achieved by the airport and Citibus fund do not exist in the golf fund, nor can continued losses be justified based on the basis of providing recreational alternatives as a counter to youth unemployment and gang prevention, as is the case with many of the recreational programs that the city provides out of general fund revenues. In this instance equity tends to demand that those who use the facility pay for it.

---

* Figures cited by city budget research personnel.

SUMMARY AND CONCLUSION

This study has looked at the enterprise funds operated by the city of Lubbock, Texas, as an aid to understanding what enterprise funds are and how they operate. They are very flexible financial tools for cities that often enable them to offer goods and services to residents that otherwise would not be available from general fund revenues. Enterprise funds also offer a means of augmenting general fund revenues under certain conditions and interact with the city's other funds.

Because they are self-contained, businesslike financial entities, enterprise funds may be analyzed using methods similar to those used in the private sector. This chapter examined Lubbock's enterprise funds using the current ratio, solvency ratio, and income ratio. These ratios may not be appropriate for use in every situation, but other, similarly easy to use ratios may be found in most basic accounting and management texts.

Our analysis of Lubbock's enterprise funds revealed three that may be considered to be experiencing financial difficulty. Two of these are critical to the city's social and economic well-being the airport and Citibus funds. The other fund having difficulty is the golf fund, a recreational fund. In considering various options that may help to alleviate the financial difficulties these funds are having, we saw that the solutions may need to be as much political as financial and that there are very real constraints based upon equity and social values.

Which of these options, or others, are recommended for use in Lubbock or any other city under similar circumstances is left to the individual analyst's judgment, depending on his or her evaluation of the economic and social environment at the time. The purpose of this study was to provide information and stimulate thought about how enterprise funds may be used to best advantage. As financial analysts and managers, we may only propose methods and measures that we believe will be effective based on our knowledge and experience. The final decisions must still be made by our elected policy makers.

ACKNOWLEDGMENT

The authors would like to thank Mr. Mark Hindman, director of budget and research for the city of Lubbock for his invaluable assistance in the preparation of this study, especially with researching questions and data collection.

REVIEW QUESTIONS

1. Enterprise funds may be used for a variety of purposes and to fill many needs. How are enterprise funds used to enhance the quality of life for the residents of your city?
2. There are some who would argue that enterprise funds should only be used to cover the costs of providing goods and services, not to subsidize the city's general fund. What costs should then be included? Should payments in lieu of taxes, franchise fees, and other transfers to the general fund be included as costs under this concept?

3. Where city enterprise funds compete directly with the private sector, such as in Lubbock's electric and golf enterprises, is the city obligated to "level the playing field" to provide equal opportunity to the private sector? If so, how?
4. When considering enterprise fund policies, how much weight should be given to social and economic factors versus strictly financial considerations? How might this vary, depending on fund type or purpose?
5. How does the concept of equity affect enterprise fund operations? Is it realistic to expect to be able to observe the concept of equity and achieve financially sound results?
6. Should enterprise funds be established strictly as revenue generators for the general fund? If so, under what circumstances, and what types of enterprises should be used?

REFERENCES

Anthony, R. N., and Reece, J. S. (1989). *Accounting: Text and Cases*. 8th ed. Homewood, IL: Richard D. Irwin.

Berne, R. and Schramm, R. (1986). *The Financial Analysis of Governments*. Englewood Cliffs, NJ: Prentice-Hall.

City of Lubbock, TX. (1991–92). *Annual Program of Services*. Enterprise Funds.

City of Lubbock, TX. (1992–93). *Annual Program of Services*. Enterprise Funds.

City of Lubbock, TX. (FY 1989–90). *Comprehensive Annual Financial Report*. Enterprise Funds.

City of Lubbock, TX. (FY 1990–91). *Comprehensive Annual Financial Report*.

City of Lubbock, TX. (FY 1991–92). *Comprehensive Annual Financial Report*.

City of Lubbock, TX. (FY 1993–94). *Preliminary Budget*.

Ingram, Robert W., Petersen R. J. and Martin, S. W. (1991). *Accounting and Financial Reporting for Governmental and Nonprofit Organizations: Basic Concepts*. New York: McGraw-Hill.

Khan, A. and Stumm T. J. (summer 1994). On the tax and expenditure effects of subsidization by municipal utility enterprises. *Municipal Finance Journal, 15 (2)*, 68–81.

Moody's Investor's Service (1992). *Selected Indicators of Municipal Performance*. New York.

Pierce, L. W. and Rust K. L. (1991). Government enterprises, in *Local Government Finance*. eds., J. E. Petersen and D. R. Strachota Chicago: Government Finance Officers Association of the United States and Canada.

45

Ethical Issues Facing Private, Not-for-Profit Hospitals in the United States

The Case of the Methodist Hospital System

Alan Blankley
Western Michigan University, Kalamazoo, Michigan, U.S.A.

Dana Forgione
University of Baltimore, Baltimore, Maryland, U.S.A.

Almost any discussion of health care today leads inevitably to a discussion of specific moral choices that must be faced along several different dimensions: medically, families and physicians must often choose if and when to discontinue artificial life-support treatment to unresponsive patients; technologically, scientists must decide whether or not certain innovative treatments are ethically acceptable; economically, administrators must decide how to allocate scarce and costly resources among patients in need. Indeed, one of the principal ethical dilemmas facing both society in general and hospitals in particular is the economic problem of how, and among whom, to distribute scarce medical resources. The underlying question, of course, is whether or not one has a God-given or constitutional "right" to costly medical care. The issue, while often debated, is beyond the scope of this chapter. If we assume for the sake of argument that one does,[1] then several attendant questions arise. How does society decide between competing claims on (i.e., effectively ration, whether explicitly or implicitly) scarce medical resources? If all persons have this right, then presumably one's ability to pay for medical care does not affect one's right to medical care. If so, who bears the redistribution of the costs?

One way society addresses this problem in the United States is through tax-exempt status for not-for-profit (NP) hospitals. The general idea is that the hospital will be economically able to provide health care services, including charity care[2] to those unable to pay for it up to the value of its tax exemption. In other words, through exemptions from U.S. federal, state, and property taxes,[3] the government encourages private pursuit of "charitable purpose." These charitable purposes, according to U.S. Internal Revenue Code section 501(c)(3), are to include activities that "promote health." While this includes such activities as providing charity care, it may also consist of activities that further the hospital's charitable purpose.[4] Therefore, activities such as operating gift shops coffee shops, and cafeterias

Reprinted from: Public Budgeting and Financial Management, 1996, 8(3), 334–353. Copyright by PrAcademics Press.

within the hospital; selling the silver by product of X-ray film; operating a community health club; providing scanner services to other health care providers; or providing collection services for radiologists may constitute charitable activities (Baldwin, 1987). In order to maintain tax-exempt status, a hospital must be considered NP, must have a charitable purpose, and must conduct health-promotion activities.

The somewhat ambiguous nature of the tax exempt status for not-for-profit private hospitals in the United States gives rise to certain ethical considerations. It is clear that it is in the government's economic interest to encourage private provision of charity care for indigent patients lest the entire cost of treating such patients fall within the domain of the public budget. In pursuit of this interest, federal and state governments agree to forgo taxes, if providers of equity capital (donors) forgo extracting dividends, so that NP hospitals can use the combined funds to offer such care. In effect, a de facto contract exists among the providers of investment capital for the hospital, the government, and the hospital. It is based on a cost-sharing principle by which the major portion of the capital for health care is provided voluntarily by the private sector, alleviating the need for the government to procure 100% of the capital through unpopular taxes or public debt. On the other hand, the government recognizes that hospitals must use at least part of their profits to fund other essential health-related products or services.

To what *extent*, then, are private NP hospitals morally obligated to provide charity care under this "contract?" To what extent does the government have the right to enforce charity care? To what extent does the government have strong economic incentive to enforce specific levels of private charity care? Increasing public and private pressures to contain costs give private hospitals the economic incentive to reduce provision of charity care services, shifting the burden onto the governmental hospitals. Those same pressures at the governmental budgetary level give the government strong incentive to resist any shift of the burden of charity patients. If the tax exemption gives government the right to require charity care over and above other health services, then what is the appropriate level or "fair share" of charity care to require from the private sector?

These ethical issues make such cases as the *Methodist Hospital System, St. Luke's Hospital*, and *Hamot Medical Center* timely and characteristic studies. In these cases, states sued the hospitals for failing to provide enough charity care; in some cases, the state challenged the hospital's tax-exempt status. These cases are not unique; many NP hospitals find themselves in similar circumstances. Indeed, challenges to the tax-exempt status of hospitals have recently occurred in thirty-two states—with Pennsylvania presenting the greatest frequency of cases. About half of Pennsylvania's sixty-seven counties are involved in legal tax challenges of NP organizations, and approximately 95% of those challenges are against hospitals (Winslow, 1990; Hudson, 1992).

What makes the *Methodist Hospital System* particularly interesting to the accounting profession is the fact that much of the dilemma in the case centers on accounting numbers and theory; in fact, what we find in the current lawsuit brought by the state of Texas (*State of Texas* v. *The Methodist Hospital*, 1990) against the Methodist Hospital System is an almost classic moral hazard situation. The government expects a certain (unspecified) level of charity care to be performed in exchange for tax exemptions; hospital management, purportedly acting in its own interest, spends additional resources on perquisites, not ("enough") charity care. In the resultant lawsuit, both sides use accounting numbers to defend their positions; the attorney general uses accounting numbers to support his contention of managerial opportunism, and management uses accounting numbers to defend its charity care practices.

The rest of the chapter will be organized as follows: the next section will outline the financial environment many NP hospitals currently face in the United States and their responses to financial difficulty; the following section summarizes agency theory; the subsequent section details the state's case against the Methodist Hospital System and analyzes the ethical issues involved; and the final section contains concluding comments and implications for further study.

BACKGROUND

Some background concerning the financial environment facing hospitals seems necessary to a full understanding of the problems involved in this specific case. Like most hospitals, private NPs face rising costs and decreasing revenues. Unlike large public hospitals, however, private hospitals cannot expect direct support from federal or state governments. Instead, private hospitals must rely principally upon cost containment measures in order to effectively utilize scarce resources.

Revenues, however, are being threatened from a variety of sources. First, the sheer numbers of uncompensated services is staggering. Mowll (1988) reports that in 1988, U.S. hospitals provided $11.5 billion of service for which there was no compensation. While large public hospitals accounted for much of the uncompensated service, private hospitals bore a large part of the burden as well. Catholic Health Corporation's statement of revenues and expenses asserts that it alone provided $9, 788, 160 in charitable care for 1988.[5] Many researchers believe that the loss of revenue due to charity care threatens the financial survival of some hospitals (Mowll, 1988).

Second, with increasing numbers of elderly patients, especially those with no insurance but federally provided Medicare, hospitals are facing shrinking payments for expanded services. Weaver (1990) notes that nearly half of all Medicare payments occur during the last ninety days of life. While the hospital incurs higher costs due to more extensive treatments for the elderly, Medicare only pays a calculated mean value for some 490-plus diagnostic related group (DRG) categories. Thus, if a patient is admitted with, say, pneumonia, the hospital would be paid a prospective amount based on the mean cost and length of stay for other patients with similar respiratory illnesses around the country. There are some regional and other adjustments to the payment rate, and the intent is to provide hospitals with economic incentive to hold costs down. If the patient is discharged within the estimated length of stay period, the hospital might make money: if not, the hospital will lose money. The *Wall Street Journal* ("Hospitals Win Medicare Patient Dispute with Federal Health Agency," May 30, 1990) reports that for some 6000 hospitals under question, Medicare typically paid 23%–50% less than their standard charges ("full retail prices"). Terris (1990) writes that Medicare only covers 40% of the health costs for the aged. In addition, Medicare has paid 85% of hospital capital costs, and there have been proposals to reduce the amount to 75% (Clarke and Weiss, 1988). As the federal government grows increasingly concerned about the national debt, lawmakers look for ways to offset the growing annual deficit balances. One of the current methods is to "fold" the Medicare capital reimbursement program into the DRG prospective payment plan. This, according to Bernie Brown, president of Kennerstone Regional Health Care System, will "limit payment to an inadequate amount based on budget capabilities" (Johnsson, 1990). Finally, in a study comparing solvent and insolvent Catholic hospitals, Kwon et al determined that hospitals remaining dependent on Medicare and Medicaid payments were significantly more likely to experience financial distress and insolvency than hospitals not dependent on Medicare and Medicaid (Kwon et al., 1988).

While revenues are getting more difficult to maintain, costs are increasing steadily. Not only are the obvious costs of purchasing and maintaining the necessary medical technology growing, but the costs of nonprice competition are growing as well. Higgins (1989) claims that U.S. hospitals compete for patients indirectly by competing for physicians. This, he claims, leads to "redundant and unnecessary services and technology by hospitals." It also leads to adding amenities, other "marginal" medical services, and advertising budgets, increasing total costs.

Finally, the costs associated with malpractice and litigation are onerous. Weaver (1990) estimates that litigation costs are between 10–15% of the total cost of medical care. Not only are hospitals named as defendants in malpractice suits, but they also face significant challenges from governmental officials. The *Wall Street Journal* reported, for example, that Hamot Medical Center was sued by the city of Erie despite the fact that it provided close to $16 million in charity care each year and its nonprofit affiliates paid more than $200,000 a year in property tax. The bases for the suit were that the hospital had $6.9 million in profits for fiscal 1989; the CEO had a $200,000 salary, plus perquisites; the hospital used its money to restore part of the depressed downtown area and to buy real estate including a marina; and that it owned an adjacent office complex, which contained a restaurant (Swasy, 1990). The article further notes that the city of Erie's suit against Hamot Medical Center, a private NP, is likely to prompt further challenges to tax-exempt status in "scores of cities."

Even when hospitals prevail in such suits, they often incur substantial costs. In a case challenging the tax-exempt status of St. Luke's Hospital in Bethlehem, Pennsylvania, the hospital retained its exempt status, but as part of the decision, the presiding court of common pleas judge Robert K. Young devised a formula to test "substantial charitable care," and obtained an agreement from St. Luke's to provide specific charitable services in settlement of the case (Hudson, 1992). Given the rather hostile financial environment—rising costs, decreasing revenues, and potentially large political costs due to "excessive" revenues, or "inadequate levels of charity care," NP hospitals in the United States must balance their strategic needs against governmental requirements for "charitable purposes," as well as donor mandates and their own moral imperative for charitable care.

SYNOPSIS OF AGENCY THEORY

Agency theory provides a useful framework for analysis of the economic incentives and management choices with respect to real-valued and accounting decisions. A brief synopsis of the agency model will help frame the subsequent discussion. The basic economic agency model posits a principal and an agent. The principal (business owner) provides economic resources such as equity capital, and delegates stewardship of those resources to an agent (management). The theory assumes that the principal seeks to maximize the return on capital investment while the agent seeks to maximize personal "wealth"—broadly defined to include nonpecuniary benefits i.e., valued executive perquisites). In order to align the economic self-interest of both parties, the principal will enter into a profit-sharing, incentive-compensation contract with the agent. The terms of this contract will make the maximization of profit to the principal in the direct economic self-interest of the agent by giving the agent a share of any profits earned.

Such a contract demands the production of accounting information that accurately measures profit. Since the agent possesses asymmetric (inside) information regarding the economic performance of the business enterprise and is responsible for generating the accounting measures upon which the profit sharing is based, the agent is in a situation of "moral hazard"; that is, the agent has an economic incentive to manipulate two categories of variables: (1) the real-valued financing, investment, and production decisions that underlie the specific constructs measured by accounting "profit," and (2) the specific accounting methodology used to measure profit. In order to reduce the costs to the principal of such potential manipulation, the principal will expend considerable resources in monitoring the agent. Such monitoring costs in turn increase the total costs of the business and thereby reduce the profit earned by both principal and agent. In order to reduce these agency costs for the benefit of both parties and to ensure "full and fair accounting disclosure," a regular independent audit of the accounting records will be contracted with an outside public accounting firm. To the extent that the deterrent and corrective features of the independent audit provide a net reduction in total agency costs, the demand for and value of audit services is established.

Agency theory has been adapted to NP organizations, and specifically to hospital organizations. (See Foster, 1987: Wallace, 1987; Forgione and Giroux, 1989.) The principal in the NP health care setting is essentially the donor of equity capital. Donors of large amounts of resources frequently are members of the board of directors of a hospital and receive both tax benefits from their donations as well as valued goodwill (e.g., satisfaction of personal moral imperatives, or less altruistically, notoriety from named facilities or research sponsorship, or consequent referral business). Hospital management functions as agent.

The Methodist Hospital System case in particular serves well to illustrate the ethical dilemma a large, private NP hospital might face within an agency context. Given the financial pressures on hospitals, management seeks ways to reduce costs and increase revenues. At the same time, its mission as a charitable institution and its responsibility to the government requires it to undertake activity that raises costs and lowers revenues: charity care. Complicating matters is the agency-theoretic expectation that economic incentives may exist for management to act in its own interest and manage both real-valued and financial accounting choices in order to do so (Watts and Zimmerman, 1986). If management's income cannot lawfully be based on earnings (profit) numbers under Internal Revenue Code Section 501(c)3, then under a situation of limited monitoring by donors or other stakeholders one might expect to see management channel excess revenues away from charity care for which there is no tangible reward, toward perquisites, for which there is. In addition, one might also expect to find managerial attempts to limit the scope of services offered to treatments that are not frequently demanded by indigent patients i.e., avoid offering prenatal and emergency room services) and also control reported financial information to their own advantage. In this case, that might be lowered revenue figures in keeping with the political cost hypothesis (Watts and Zimmerman, 1986) or higher reported charity care numbers. Some evidence that hospital management will actively lobby for changes in accounting standards in a manner consistent with their specific economic circumstances has been observed in a sample of NP hospitals by Forgione and Garrets (1989).

In fairness, and in keeping with the agency-monitoring hypothesis, under a situation of limited monitoring by constituents one might also expect regulators or politicians to act in their own best interests. This may take the form of highly visible pronouncements or accusing large, profitable enterprises of financial misconduct of some sort, ostensibly in an effort to redress public wrongs—but also in keeping with an effort to replenish the public coffers and foster the political profile and career of the public official in question. Citing Joseph Letnaunchyn (1992), a vice president of the Hospital Association of Pennsylvania, Hudson (1992) reports: "Local governments' need for money, and the fact that hospitals are big users of real estate space, make them natural targets."

In its capacity as a sanctioning body, the Internal Revenue Service (IRS) has ongoing audits of about forty-five NP hospitals, colleges, universities, and other charitable organizations nationally. Approximately twenty of those audits are of hospitals, and the Internal Revenue Service (IRS) expects revocation of exempt status for one or two of the hospitals (Ford, 1993). Indeed, the Methodist Hospital System was recently audited by the IRS, but was not specifically challenged on its tax-exempt status. Hamot Medical Center, on the other hand, lost its exempt status in 1992, paid nearly $4 million in back taxes, then reorganized and reapplied for exempt status (Hudson, 1992). Marcus Owens, director of the IRS's exempt organizations technical division has indicated that integrated health care delivery systems (a hybrid arrangement involving members of a hospital's medical staff who combine to form a substantial group practice) can cause problems with exempt status—evidently on issues of inurement of assets to private individuals, which is unlawful. The IRS is also concerned that the existence of medical clinics structured as stock corporations carries implications about diversion of profits and ownership of the assets (Ford, 1993).

METHODIST HOSPITAL SYSTEM CASE

Within this political, legal, economic, and social setting of perceived entitlements as well as scarce resources, with conflicting constituent groups and economic incentives, we observe the case of the Methodist Hospital System. The Methodist Hospital System includes as its primary operating entity a large[6] private NP hospital incorporated in the state of Texas for, "charitable, educational, and scientific purposes" (Methodist Hospital System and Related Corporations, 1984a). In keeping with Texas laws, the corporation is prohibited from allowing any part of net earnings to profit any individual, carry on propaganda, participate in a political campaign, or influence the outcome of any election. In addition, the hospital's *Bylaws* (Methodist Hospital System and Related Corporations, 1984b) state that it shall "charge reasonably for services, education, training facilities . . . to those able to pay, and shall furnish and provide services . . . free of charge to those unable to pay."

In November 1990, the attorney general for the state of Texas, Jim Mattox, filed suit against the Methodist Hospital and the Methodist Hospital System, alleging that it failed as a charity hospital "to provide its required share of health care for poor people." The suit further alleges that the hospital has the duty under law to provide "charity care in an amount commensurate with its resources, the tax-exempt benefits received, and the needs of the community," but that the hospital has failed in this duty. It had allegedly failed to provide "a factually or meaningful degree of charity care." In order to determine that the hospital management and directors were in breach of their legal fiduciary responsibility, the suit cites accounting numbers: "From 1985 through 1989, the Hospital System, including the Methodist Hospital, had gross revenues of more than $2 billion yet provided less than $17 million in charity care, which equals less than one percent of gross revenues for charity care." Furthermore, the suit cites realized profits (revenues less expenses) of

$250 million over the same period, and a $330 million cash reserve fund at the end of 1989.

Key Ethical Aspects of the Case

There are two particularly interesting ethical aspects to the suit. First, does the state have the right to specify not only that a hospital must provide charity care, but that it must provide an *acceptable level* of charity care based not on some value of its tax exemption but on its available resources and the need of the community? Should charity care take precedence over other essential health-related services, for which the hospital receives tax-exempt status as well? If so, what is an acceptable level or "fair share" of charity care? Second, note the use of accounting numbers to support the contention. Charity care of less than 1% of gross revenue indeed appears small. An alternative ratio, charity care expressed as a percentage of net revenues (6.8%), is not stressed.

   If the suit filed by the attorney general's office raises some interesting ethical questions, the actions taken by management reveal dubious ethical activity. Like the Hamot Medical Center, the Methodist Hospital System also dabbled in real estate and restaurant ventures, as well as providing generous perquisites. The top members of management were paid $300,000 salaries, and the hospital's "institute of preventative medicine" included an exclusive health club complete with swimming, racquet ball, indoor jogging, massages, weight room, whirlpool, and sauna. The hospital's decor and amenities rivaled that of exclusive hotels, including a concierge, valet parking, bellmen for luggage, an elegant gourmet restaurant (menu items include sautéed prawns, poached Norwegian salmon, and ricotta cheesecake), and patient room suites complete with wet bar. In contrast, charity care patients, even those offering to put down a cash deposit, were frequently turned away and refused treatment. Members of health maintenance organizations (HMOs) were also denied admission. The hospital's response to the lawsuit was to argue that they had no legal obligation to provide charity care (Morales, 1993).

Failure to Follow GAAP

Most significantly, hospital management went against promulgated industry accounting standards and reported accounting numbers that grossly inflated the reported value of its "free, uncompensated care." Until recently, on the revenues and expenses statement hospitals essentially reported three adjustments to gross revenues: (1) "contractual allowances," which are the differences between hospital charges and the amount paid by Medicare or other insurance companies by regulation or contract agreement; (2) 'bad debts," which are amounts due from patients deemed to be able but *unwilling* to pay; and (3) "charity care," which represents amounts due from patients deemed to be *unable* to pay, and hence no collection effort is made (Healthcare Financial Management Association's, 1978; 1986). The Healthcare Financial Management Association's (HFMA's) principles and practices board (P&PB) issued statements of position no. 2 and no. 7, prescribing industry guidance on accounting for charity care. These pronouncements specifically exclude from charity care any item except services provided to those patients deemed unable to pay. They further require contractual services, such as those provided for Medicare patients, to be recorded only at amounts the patient is legally obligated to pay. Recording such services at gross charges ("full retail prices," which are frequently not realized) is explicitly identified as an overstatement of both revenues and discounts.

The American Institute of Certified Public Accountants (AICPA) has recognized P&PB statements as part of the authoritative hierarchy of generally accepted accounting principles (AICPA, 1990b). The AICPA, in consultation with the Financial Accounting Standards Board, then went on to take an even more stringent position on accounting for charity care. Since publication of the revised AICPA audit guide for health care providers, and in the face of vigorous industry opposition (Kovener, 1990), reported charity care is no longer permitted as either a revenue or as a deduction from revenue (AICPA, 1990a). Charity care is now relegated to footnote disclosure only.

In the particular accounting procedure used by the Methodist Hospital System, the hospital classified the amount of gross charges less Medicare payments as "free, uncompensated care." In a similar manner it also included what are known as courtesy discounts and bad debts, as well as charity care amounts. These amounts were alleged by the attorney general to be more than 600% overstatements of actual charity care provided by the hospital, yet they were presented in the hospital's argument as demonstrating fulfillment of its obligation to patients unable to pay for health services (Morales, 1993). Gross charges are rarely realized, and such accounting treatment of discounts is contrary to the HFMA's P&PB statements of position nos. 2 and 7. It is conceivable, though, that Medicare payments, even though below gross charges, could represent profitable cases (however unlikely), because neither gross charges nor Medicare payments represent the actual treatment costs incurred by the hospital.

Related-Party Transactions

The notes to the 1987 audited financial statements (*Note F—Related Party Transactions*) disclose that in 1986 a member of the board of directors sold twelve and one-half acres of land to San Jacinto Methodist Hospital, a subsidiary of the Methodist Hospital System, for $2.4 million, or $192,000/acre (Methodist Hospital System and Related Corporations, 1987). Even if the deal were an arm's-length transaction (it was conducted through a trustee), and the price per acre consistent with prevailing market conditions, one might still question the appearance and appropriateness of such an undertaking, since the IRS has prohibitions against inurement of hospital resources to private individuals (Silverberg, 1988). In addition, part of the Methodist Hospital System real estate holdings at the time of the suit included a $2 million duck hunting lodge. Two weeks after the attorney general's lawsuit was filed, the hospital system sold the property, claiming that it did not fit the mission of the hospital, which was to provide health care (SoRelle, 1991). Finally, the gourmet restaurant owned by the hospital system reported annual losses of nearly $250,000 in each of the years 1986, 1987, and 1988, while maintaining a $600,000 payroll. This suggests less than optimal use of the hospital's resources.

Questionable Transactions

Furthermore, upon careful study of the notes (*Note A: Organization*, and *Note H: Commitments and Contingencies*) to the combined audited financial statements for 1987, management of the Methodist Hospital System disclosed that a complex real estate transaction had been set up utilizing the system's elaborate organizational structure of multiple subsidiaries. The transaction provided what appears to be an essentially risk-free return on a multimillion dollar real estate venture to a group of private investors.

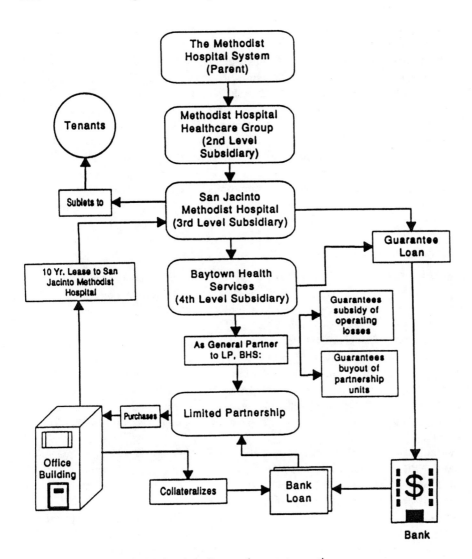

Figure 1 Baytown Health Services, Inc., real estate transaction.

The real estate venture was structured as follows, and is diagrammed in Figure 1. Baytown Health Services, Inc. (BHS), a fourth-level subsidiary of the Methodist Hospital System, served as general partner of a limited partnership. The partnership invested in an office building. The building was financed by $7,400,000 in debt, plus an undisclosed amount of equity investment by the partners. The loan was guaranteed by both BHS and its immediate parent organization, San Jacinto Methodist Hospital (SJMH). The outside partners were thus relieved of default-risk on the loan.

Next, the building was leased for ten years to SJMH, which then sublet the building to tenants. Baytown Health Services guaranteed subsidization of any operating losses on the rental activity, thus relieving the outside partners of operating-loss risk on the rental operations. Finally, BHS guaranteed buyout of all partnership units for $15,562,000 at the end of the ten year period, evidently relieving the outside partners of any market-decline risk on the value of the building.

Assuming an original equity investment of 20% of the building cost, with 80% bank financing, the limited partners would enjoy an approximately 24% compound annual internal rate of return for ten years, virtually risk-free. If the outside partners contributed less than a 20% original equity investment, that annual rate of return would be even higher.

While one could make the argument that capital is difficult to obtain and such arrangements for investors are a practical necessity to raise funds, an effectively risk-free, approximately 24% compound, annual internal rate of return for ten years is highly attractive in almost any market. It raises the question of whether or not the charitable mission of a hospital to provide health services is compromised by providing what appears to be a "sweetheart deal" for investors, while at the same time overstating reported "free care" to the indigent.

A Question of Mission

While when taken in isolation each of the issues discussed above may not seem significant in and of themselves, when taken together, they form a pattern of what appears to reflect management opportunism at the neglect of the hospital's charitable mission—the heart of the attorney general's lawsuit. Several ethical issues thus seem worth exploring.

First, in spite of its charitable purpose and tax-exempt status, hospital management engaged in apparent consumption of perquisites to the detriment of resource provision for charity care. Should a hospital, under similar circumstances, avoid any profitable investment not in keeping with its charitable mission whether in fact or appearance? If the hospital engages in real estate speculation (or any other seemingly unrelated activity) should the hospital lose its tax exemption? If so, would it be punitively obligated to provide care to the indigent?

Second, in an apparent effort to avoid political costs, management employed accounting procedures at variance with promulgated industry standards. The accounting procedures at best defined free care so liberally that the ensuing information presented an overstated, if not grossly misleading, display with respect to the actual charity care services. Should financial information be more strictly regulated to avoid such liberal interpretations of free care, purportedly demonstrating fulfillment of charity care obligations? The AICPA seemed to think more stringent guidance was necessary when it resisted industry opposition and deleted charity care from revenues altogether, and relegated the required reporting of charity care to footnote disclosure only (AICPA, 1990a). Third, the external auditors gave the financial statements clean opinions. Does this constitute a form of audit failure i.e., Are NP clients overly regarded as low risk-exposure engagements by CPA firms? Perhaps the reported free, uncompensated care and its subcomponents were regarded as constituting adequate disclosure, or perhaps they were not considered material dollar amounts in relation to the financial statements taken as a whole, in which case, it would be prima facie evidence of an insignificant dollar amount of charity care being provided—which itself was only about 6% of the total free, uncompensated care that was reported.

CONCLUSION

The case of the Methodist Hospital System raises many difficult ethical questions. Is there an ethical obligation for NP hospitals to provide charity care? Established levels of charity care? What should such levels be based upon? Who should establish the formulas? If resources allow should the required levels be greater than some value of the tax exemption? Should NP hospitals be permitted to make investments in areas clearly outside their charitable purposes and still be allowed to maintain their tax exemptions? To what extent? How is this clouded by complex joint ventures with private for-profit (FP) organizations? What if such investments occur after considerable charity care has already been given? Does the financial reporting of NP hospitals in the United States need further monitoring or regulation? Which agency should conduct the monitoring or regulating?

By using the agency theory perspective, it is possible to develop an approach to studying such issues. In fact, the ethical issues involved in this case may be studied on a larger scale by considering not a single NP hospital, but a sample of NP hospitals. One might look, for example, for any observable differences between the investing behavior or the financial reporting behavior of NP hospital managers and those of FP hospitals, or between NP private and NP public hospitals. It is possible to formulate hypotheses for empirical tests between these groups, but it is a more difficult task to formulate normative conclusions concerning the ethical issues involved. Still, this case provides opportunity to examine some of the questions that need to be addressed.

REVIEW QUESTIONS

1. What are the basic ethical problems facing private, not-for-profit hospitals in the United States? How is society trying to address the problem?
2. What is the typical financial environment faced by many not-for-profit hospitals? What measures are they taking to correct the financial challenges?
3. What is agency theory? How does the agency theory contribute to the discussion of health care and relevant ethical issues? Discuss.
4. In the case of the Methodist Hospital System, what were the key ethical issues? What kinds of problems did they create for the system? What role did different stakeholders play in this conflict?
5. Using the agency theory, develop a number of hypotheses that would allow a greater understanding of the ethical issues involved in the current context.

NOTES

1. Many factions within the United States believe universal health care, or some form of guaranteed health care, is a right, attending not only to citizens, but also to illegal immigrants. They often cite the Canadian model of health care. The Clinton administration, for example, devoted a great deal of attention and effort toward passing a universal health care bill. Many others believe that no such universal "right" to health care exists and that scarce medical resources should be allocated no differently than other scarce resources. We do not intend to support either position in this chapter; we assume a right to health care for the sake of argument *only*, which allows us to raise the questions and issues that arise under such an assumption more conveniently.
2. Charity care is generally defined as care extended to those *unable* to pay for it because they are either medically or financially indigent. It *does not include*

contractual or regulatory allowances, courtesy discounts, or amounts attributable to patients able to pay but whose accounts are later deemed to be uncollectible due to *unwillingness* to pay.

3. Such incentives may also include access to low-cost financing through tax-exempt bond issues.

4. A 1969 Internal Revenue Service (IRS) ruling as well as a series of private letter rulings established this definition of charitable purpose.

5. Catholic Health Corporation is a private NP corporation consisting of seventy-two health care institutions throughout fourteen states. This information was taken from Catholic Health Corporation, *Official Statement: Statement of Revenues and Expenses*, March 1, 1990.

6. Hospital size is usually measured by the number of beds maintained. Methodist Hospital has 1218 beds, according to the lawsuit (*petition no. 494,212*) filed by the attorney general against the hospital. According to the attorney general's task force commissioned to study NP hospitals, it has 1172 beds. According to the *Houston Chronicle* (Sorelle, 1991), it has 1527 beds. In spite of the disagreement over the actual number of beds, it is considered to be the largest hospital in Texas, and one of the largest, if not richest, hospitals in the United States.

REFERENCES

American Institute of Certified Public Accountants. (1990a). *AICPA Audit and Accounting Guide: Audits of Providers of Health Care Services*, 2nd ed. New York.

American Institute of Certified Public Accountants. (1990b). *AICPA Audit Risk Alerts: Health Care Industry Developments—1990*, New York.

Baldwin, M. F. (May 1987). Legislatures, agencies debating whether not-for-profit hospitals deserve their tax-exempt status. *Modern Healthcare*, 34–46.

Clarke, R. and Weiss, L. (1988). High capital costs could trigger losses. *Healthcare Financial Management*, 60–71.

Ford, S. (Feb. 3 1993). Hospitals may lose exemptions following audits Owens warns, *Tax Notes Today*, 25–27.

Forgione, D. and Giroux, G. (1989). Fund accounting in nonprofit hospitals: A lobbying perspective. *Financial Accountability & Management*, 5, 233–244.

Foster, R. W. (1987). Hospitals and the choice of organizational form. *Financial Accountability & Management*, 3, 343–365.

Healthcare Financial Management Association. (July 1978). *P&PB Statement No. 2: Defining Charity Service as Contrasted to Bad Debts* Westchester, Il.

Healthcare Financial Management Association. (April 1986) *P&PB Statement No. 7: The Presentation of Patient Service Revenue and Related Issues*. Westchester, Il.

Higgins, C. W. (1989). Competitive reform and nonprice competition: Implications for the hospital industry. *Health Care Management Review*, 14, 57–66.

Hospitals win medicare payment dispute with federal health agency. (May 30, 1990), *Wall Street Journal*.

Hudson, T. (Nov. 5, 1992). Tax-exempt challenges continue. *Hospitals*, 66, 40–42.

Johnson, J. (Aug. 1990). CEOs: Keep capital fold-in out of budget politics. *Hospitals*, 64, 25.

Kovener, R. R. (Oct. 1990). New rules affect bad debt, charity care reporting. *Healthcare Financial Management*, 44, 48–57.

Kwon, I., Martin, D., and Walker, W. (1988). Causes of financial difficulty in Catholic hospitals. *Health Care Management Review*, 13, 29–37.

Methodist Hospital System and Related Corporations. (1984a). *Articles of Incorporation of the Methodist Hospital*. Houston.

Methodist Hospital System and Related Corporations. (1987). *Combined Financial Statements and Other Financial Information (Audited)*.

Methodist Hospital System and Related Corporations. (1984b). *Bylaws of the Methodist Hospital*. Houston.

Morales, D. (Feb. 11 1993). *Corrected State's Opposition to Defendant's Motion for Summary Judgment and to Dismiss for Want of Jurisdiction*, petition no. 494,212 district court, 126th Judicial District, Travis County, TX.

Mowll, C. A. (Aug. 1988). The search for solutions to the indigent care crisis. *Healthcare Financial Management, 42*, 10–24.

Silverberg, K. H. (1988). Obtaining and maintaining exempt status. *Health Care Financing, 14*, 9–14.

SoRelle, R. (Jan 24, 1991). Methodist Hospital, facing charity suit, sells Duck Lodge. *Houston Chronicle*.

State of Texas v The Methodist Hospital; The Methodist Hospital System; and [Members of the Board of Directors]. (Nov. 1990). no. 494,212, district court, 126th Judicial District, Travis County, TX.

Swasy, A. (Feb 16, 1990). Challenge to Erie Hospital's tax status gains attention of cash-poor U.S. cities. *Wall Street Journal*.

Terris, M. (Summer 1990). Lessons from Canada's health program. *Journal of Public Health Policy*, 151–160.

U.S. Internal Revenue Code. Section 501(c)(3).

Wallace, W. A. (1987). Agency theory and governmental and non-profit sector research. In J. L. Chan (ed.) *Research in Governmental and Non-Profit Accounting*, pp. 51–70.

Watts, R. L. and Zimmerman, J. (1986). *Positive Accounting Theory*. Englewood Cliffs, NJ: Prentice-Hall.

Weaver, F. J. (July 20, 1990). Large hospitals: Challenges. In *Proceedings of the Health Care Conference*. Dallas: Texas Society of Certified Public Accountants.

Winslow, R. (March 30, 1990). Nonprofit hospital facilities feeling pinch in New York. *Wall Street Journal*.

46

Financial Management Under Budgetary Stress

C. Kurt Zorn
Indiana University, Bloomington, Indiana, U.S.A.

The early 1990s were difficult times for many states due to the ravages of a prolonged national recession coupled with increased service commitments. Despite the inevitable slowdown in revenue growth due to the recession, pressure continued on the expenditure side due to growing service demands from the citizenry, federal mandates, and other factors. Many states were faced with a looming budget deficit that forced them to search for remedies to their projected shortfalls. Not surprisingly the approaches varied from state to state, but generally involved a combination of spending cuts and revenue enhancements to close the projected gap.

One state, Indiana, placed considerable emphasis on expenditure reduction as a way to close its projected gap in the 1991–1993 biennium. A key component of its expenditure reduction plan was the implementation of a policy of agency-specific financial management plans. These plans were constructed by the subject agency, in consultation with the State Budget Agency, to meet reversion targets set by Governor Evan Bayh and the State Budget Agency.* In other words, Governor Bayh and the State Budget Agency mandated each agency return a percentage of its 1991–1993 biennial appropriation back to the state general fund. Each agency was allowed to determine how it best could meet the reversion target through the development of its financial management plans.

This chapter discusses the general fiscal problems faced by the state of Indiana in the 1991–93 biennium and how its financial management initiative assisted in controlling state expenditures. Specifically, it describes a number of expenditure reduction initiatives adopted by the governor and the State Budget Agency, emphasizing the financial management plan initiative. To illustrate how these policies were implemented on the agency level, the financial management plan prepared by one agency, the State Board of Tax Commissioners, is discussed.

---

* A reversion is a "give back" of dollars already appropriated to an agency by the state legislature. It reduces the amount of the appropriation by some amount, meaning the agency has less money available for obligation during the 1991–93 biennium than was appropriated by the legislature.

A GROWING FISCAL PROBLEM

While it may be debatable exactly when the recession of the 1990s began and it certainly is debatable when the recession ended, the effect of the recession on state finances is clear. The early 1990s were difficult times for states, as revenues fell far short of projections and expenditures seemed to increase unabated. Adding to the effects of the recession were concerns about the federal budget deficit and the threat of war in the Persian Gulf due to Iraq's aggression against Kuwait.

General Fund Revenue

The effects on the state of Indiana from the deteriorating national economy and other exogenous forces became evident during the latter part of the 1991 fiscal year.* During the first 8 months of 1990, state general fund revenues were running approximately $108.8 million, or 2.8% below forecast for the year and approximately 10.4% below forecast during the May through August period (State Budget Agency, Sept. 5, 1990).

Things did not improve as fiscal year 1992 got underway. Revisions in the official state revenue forecast in December 1990, April 1991, and December 1991 indicated the ravages of the national recession on state revenues were continuing as each successive forecast revised state general fund revenue collections downward. By the time the December 1991 forecast was issued it was estimated general fund revenues for fiscal year 1992 would only increase a paltry 0.7% over fiscal year 1991 revenues.† For fiscal years 1991 through 1993, it was estimated over $1.2 billion in revenue would be lost to the recession‡ (State Budget Agency, July 15, 1992).

State Expenditures

At the same time the recession was constraining general fund revenue growth, the state of Indiana was experiencing mounting pressure on the spending side of the ledger. In May 1992 it was estimated the increase in annual spending between fiscal year 1989 and fiscal year 1993 would amount to approximately $1.2 billion, or a compound annual growth rate of 5.45%, while inflation was estimated to be approximately 3.5%. Major components of this increased spending were tuition support for schools growing at a 5.56% compound annual rate; medicaid increasing at a 15.3% rate; higher education increasing at a 4.7% rate; and corrections increasing at a 14.0% rate (State Budget Agency, May 27, 1992).

---

* Indiana's fiscal year runs from July 1 through June 30. It has a biennial budget process that covers two fiscal years commencing on July 1 of the odd calendar year. For example, the state legislature approves a budget during its 1991 session for fiscal year 1992 (beginning July 1, 1991) and fiscal year 1993 (ending June 30, 1993).

† Actual fiscal year 1992 general fund revenue collections ended up 2.2% above fiscal year 1991 collections.

‡ The gap is the difference between forecast revenues for fiscal years 1991 through 1993 using an assumed 5% growth rate and the revenues actually being forecast for the period. In other words, before the recession state general fund revenue collections had been increasing approximately 5% per year. Therefore, in the absence of recession, it was reasonable to assume state revenues would continue to grow at an approximate 5% rate during the 1991–93 period.

ADDRESSING THE FISCAL PROBLEM

Given the forecast divergence between revenues and expenditures, it was imperative action be taken to close the projected budget gap.* While there were reserve balances (general fund, tuition reserve, and rainy day fund) available to help close the gap, Governor Bayh and the State Budget Agency were reluctant to rely on these as the primary instruments for closing the gap. Admittedly the reserve balances would have been large enough to cover the shortfall between estimated revenues and expenditures during the 1991–93 biennium, but the result would be reserve balances insufficient to protect against a prolonged recession or another downturn in the economy occurring soon after the end of the current recession.

In the face of deteriorating revenue collections, a reluctance to exhaust reserve balances, a commitment not to raise taxes, and a constitutional requirement to balance the state budget, Governor Bayh and the State Budget Agency took bold steps to reduce the increase in state expenditures. These policy initiatives included among other things a hiring freeze, a moratorium on pay increases for state employees, restrictions on travel, restrictions on other operating expenditures, mandatory reversions, and agency-specific financial management plans.

Overall Approach

On September 5, 1990 the Bayh administration issued a financial management circular outlining spending reductions to be implemented by the executive branch of government for the remainder of the 1991 fiscal year (State Budget Agency, Sept. 5, 1990). Noting the effect the deteriorating national economy was having on state revenue collections, the uncertainty surrounding the federal budget, and the looming crisis in the Persian Gulf, all state agencies were requested to redouble their efforts to reduce spending on a voluntary basis.

When Governor Bayh took office January 9, 1989, he had urged all agencies to identify ways to eliminate wasteful spending and control increases in spending. This voluntary restraint had proven successful in reducing the growth in state spending but was insufficient by itself to meet the fiscal challenge posed by the recession. The governor therefore ordered a number of additional measures in the financial management circular.

First, a series of personnel actions were taken: a hiring freeze was implemented effective immediately; no reclassification of positions was allowed; and no exceptions would be granted to standard policies governing personnel transactions while the freeze was in effect.

Second, restrictions were placed on other operating expenses. A moratorium was placed on the purchase of new equipment unless the equipment was intended to replace existing equipment at or close to the end of its useful life. The intent of this provision was to extend the time horizon for planned replacement of equipment, including vehicles. A number of restrictions were placed on contracts, including increased scrutiny by the budget agency with regard to the essential nature of the contract. Finally, the budget agency was instructed to reduce by 50% each agency's general and dedicated fund quarterly allotment for out-of-state travel.

---

* Like a number of other states, Indiana is required by its state constitution to have a balanced budget.

Third, a moratorium was placed on state construction unless the construction satisfied one or more of a number of criteria. Exceptions to the prohibition on construction included projects that would expand prison bed capacity; projects needed to meet compliance requirements; highway projects; preventive maintenance projects; and projects that would result in substantial savings to the state if not postponed.

Fourth, allotment amounts placed in reserve by the state budget agency would not be allotted.* It was a long-standing policy to place a small percentage of each agency's allotment in a reserve account to ensure a cushion at year end if that agency was spending at an accelerated rate. This reserve was a mechanism to obviate—or at least reduce—the need for a supplemental appropriation.

The financial management circular contained a safety value. A committee was established consisting of the state commissioner of administration, the state budget director, and the governor's deputy chief of staff. It had the ability to consider exceptions to the aforementioned restrictions on a case by case basis. The criteria for granting exceptions included: protecting the health, safety, or welfare of Indiana citizens; providing for the efficient administration of government; serving Indiana citizens adversely affected by prevailing economic conditions; creating or collecting additional revenue to support state government services; and implementing or continuing high-priority state services or programs. If any of the exceptions allowed the hiring of additional personnel, however it had to occur at the minimum salary level for any classification or position (State Budget Agency, Sept. 5, 1990).

While the majority of the provisions contained in the financial management circular were in effect until June 30, 1991, the restriction on personnel actions initially was only in effect until December 1, 1990. As subsequent forecasts of state revenue collections continued to be dismal, the restriction on personnel actions was extended first to March 1, 1991 (State Budget Agency, Nov. 26, 1990) and then to July 1, 1991 (State Budget Agency, Feb. 22, 1991). A final extension of all the provisions contained in financial management circular 90–2 was made lasting until July 31, 1991 (State Budget Agency, June 30, 1991).

The actions taken to control expenditures were significant. It was estimated that the provisions resulted in total savings of $74.1 million during the September 5, 1990 to June 30, 1991 period (State Budget Agency, Aug. 1, 1991).†

July 1, 1991 ushered in a new fiscal year and a new biennium budget. The new fiscal year and the new budget failed to "solve" the fiscal problems facing the state of Indiana, however. While the national economy was showing signs of recovery, there was substantial talk among economists regarding the possibility of a "double-dip" recession. Also, the erosion suffered by the state's general fund revenue base in fiscal year 1991 left projected expenditures for fiscal 1992 significantly above projected revenues. Therefore, on August 1, 1991 a new financial management circular was issued containing a modified spending reduction plan (State Budget Agency, Aug. 1, 1991).

The modified spending reduction plan acknowledged agency management and personnel understood the importance of and were committed to restraining spending. It delegated increased responsibility to agencies to reduce spending and reduced the importance of the centralized review and approval procedure set up by the previous reduction plan.

---

* An allotment is an authorization by the State Budget Agency to incur obligations up to a certain dollar limit during a particular time period. In this case, allotments were made on a quarterly basis.
† These savings reverted to the state general fund. They were commonly referred to as reversions.

While the provisions of the previous plan formally expired on July 31, 1991, the new spending reduction plan contained some of the same elements. The restriction on out-of-state travel was retained, effectively reducing each agency's quarterly allotment by 50%. The hiring freeze was lifted, but restrictions were placed on the speed with which the vacancies could be filled. In effect, agencies could only fill one-twelfth of existing vacancies per month, resulting in a phased-in filling of positions.

Financial Management Plans

A cornerstone of the new spending reduction plan were financial management plans, a policy implemented in March 1991 (State Budget Agency, March 20, 1991). The Bayh administration was interested in improving financial management in Indiana state government to ensure state agencies operate within the tight budgets imposed on them, to ensure state agencies do not make commitments of state resources not anticipated in the state budget, and to increase the accountability of state agencies for the administration of their day-to-day financial affairs while reducing the role of the budget agency in those matters.

The financial management plan initiative contained two parts—a budget administration plan and a financial management improvement plan. Each agency was required to prepare a 1991–1993 budget administration plan that contained the following components: a list of positions that would be filled and left vacant and the effect on the operation of the agency's program; detail on grants and distributions the agency would make; and a listing of base reductions and a timetable for these reductions that would enable the agency to meet appropriation targets.*

The financial management improvement plan prepared by each agency was to give consideration to the following initiatives: delegation of management of program budgets to program managers; training for substantive program managers in budget management techniques; ensuring the long-term fiscal impact of policies is considered; requiring that both substantive managers and financial managers approve all decisions that have a fiscal impact before requesting approval of the agency head; and establishing an ongoing monitoring system to enable top management in an agency to review actual spending with budgeted spending and trace through fiscal impacts associated with various policy decisions.

These financial management initiatives were particularly important given the uncertainty of the economy and the precarious balancing of the state budget that resulted from the 1991 legislative session. In fact, all agencies were required to submit an amendment to their budget administration plans specifying how they would retain an amount equal to 290 of the agency's general fund budget for the 1992 fiscal year (State Budget Agency, Aug. 1, 1991). This reserve amount was increased to 390 at a later date.

ONE AGENCY'S APPROACH

As could be expected, the response of the executive branch of state government to Governor Bayh's and the State Budget Agency's financial management initiatives was swift and

---

* The financial management initiative was occurring simultaneously with the 1991–1993 biennial budget's being considered by the state legislature. While the exact appropriations were unknown at the time, the executive budget request had included, with a few exceptions, agency appropriations for the 1991–1993 biennium exactly the same as those for the preceding biennium.

serious. While each agency undertook budget management plans and financial management improvement plans best suited to its particular situation, it is instructive to discuss the approach taken by one agency in order to provide a more robust understanding of the financial management initiative.

The Agency

The State Board of Tax Commissioners (tax board) is a small to medium-sized state agency. Its primary purpose is to construe the property tax laws and administer a system that provides for the uniform and equitable distribution of the property tax burden in the state of Indiana. Property taxes are a central source of revenue for funding schools and local units in the state and it is important these revenues are stable, predictable, and sufficient.

The tax board accomplishes its tasks through the adoption and promulgation of rules and regulations for the assessment of real estate, personal property, public utilities, and mobile homes. These rules and regulations promote a uniform and consistent assessment of property throughout the state by the 1100 locally elected assessors.

Additionally, the tax board is charged with reviewing and certifying budgets, tax rates, and levies for approximately 2280 units of local government. Without tax board review of budgets, levies, and certification of property tax rates, state law forbids local units to levy and collect local property taxes.

More than half of the tax board's employees "work in the field," meaning they are given various geographic assignments and handle budgets, appeals, audits, and other matters associated with their assigned region.

The tax board had 105 authorized positions during the 1989–91 biennium and an annual general fund appropriation of more than $4 million per fiscal year. Of that amount, approximately 80% went to personal services (salaries and wages and fringe benefits), approximately 8% was spent on in-state travel by the tax board's fifty-plus-person field staff, and the remainder of the appropriation was spent on other operating expenses, such as materials and supplies, contracts, and equipment.

The Financial Management Plan

On August 31, 1991 the tax board submitted its final financial management plan to the state budget director (State Board of Tax Commissioners, Aug. 31, 1991). In order to fulfill the 2% reserve requirement, the tax board was required to identify savings of slightly more than $90,000 in its budget management plan.* It planned to accomplish this by leaving three positions vacant (saving over $66,500 in salaries and fringe benefits) and placing restrictions on in-state travel with projected savings of more than $23,000.

Along with the budget management plan, the tax board submitted its financial management improvement plan. Highlights of the plan included: implementation of monthly meetings of the tax board's five program directors to review goals, accomplishments, status of work assignments, and problems; development of a stringent monitoring system of in-state travel funds providing a monthly accounting of actual versus budgeted travel by individual employees; approval of all nonroutine expenditures by the program director

---

* The requirement was increased to 3% at a subsequent date.

and the agency fiscal officer; and careful monitoring of computer-related charges incurred with the State Information Services Division.

Results of Improved Financial Management

In its 1993–1995 biennium budget transmittal letter, the tax board recounted the success it had meeting the 3% required reserve target, largely due to its budget management plan and financial management improvement plan (State Board of Tax Commissioners, Sept. 14, 1992). The mandated 3% reversion amounted to $135,200 on an annual appropriation of $4,505,695, but the tax board reverted an additional $294,110 for a total reversion of $429,310 (9.5% of the annual appropriation).

The savings were realized in two major areas. Despite having 105 positions funded, the tax board was operating at times during the 1992 fiscal year with as few as ninety-three positions filled. These unfilled vacancies resulted in savings of $247,456. The restrictions on in-state travel and the enhanced monitoring ability developed as part of the financial management improvement plan resulted in savings of $193,722 compared to the budgeted amount.*

Of course these savings were not "costless." In order to realize such substantial savings both in personal service expenditures and in-state travel expenditures, it had to reduce the service the tax board provided to its constituents—mainly the taxpayer and local government officials.

Historically, the tax board provided substantial assistance to local government units and its officials in budget preparation and execution, adhering to the levy limits mandated by the 1974 property tax control program and administering the property tax system. The adoption of the financial management plan and its cost saving measures reduced the direct "hands-on" assistance the tax board's field staff could offer to local units and officials. In response to this scaling back of direct assistance, however, a centralized system of providing assistance was developed.

Specifically, tax board field staff used to visit their assigned counties on a regular basis—generally each county was visited four or five times a month. During these visits, tax board staff would be available to answer questions and address concerns raised by local officials in that county. In order to reduce travel expenditures and to operate with a reduced number of field staff, the practice of regular visitation of each county was suspended. Tax board field staff would visit counties only on an "as-needed" basis. Local officials were instructed to direct their questions and inquiries to the central office in Indianapolis and the central office would respond to the question or contact the appropriate field staff and ask the staff to contact the local official.

Initially, local government officials disliked the fact that tax board staff would not be visiting their county on a regular basis. A number of complaints were lodged, but as time passed and everyone got acquainted with the new procedure, the complaints stopped. As a result, tax board field staff were making more efficient use of their time, travel costs were reduced, and service to local units and officials was not significantly degraded.

Clearly, the reduction in staff and the pressure to reduce costs forced the State Board of Tax Commissioners to carefully evaluate the way it had historically done its job. Long-

---

* The careful reader will note that these savings should amount to $441,178 in savings and only $429,310 was reverted to the general fund. The difference of $11,868 is accounted for by spending over budgeted amounts in other budget lines.

standing procedures and policies were reviewed in an attempt to determine whether or not the procedure or policy was necessary or being implemented in the most efficient manner.

SUMMARY AND CONCLUSION

The recession of the early 1990s created significant hardships for state finances. Every state was impacted slightly differently by the national recession, the uncertainty surrounding the federal budget deficit, and the impending war in the Persian Gulf. Individual states chose from a number of options as they attempted to close the gap between revenues and expenditures created by these exogenous forces. Some states chose to raise taxes, some chose to look for alternative revenue sources, some states chose to cut state expenditures, and some states chose various combinations of the three approaches.

Like most states Indiana was faced with a growing disparity between revenues and expenditures during the latter part of fiscal year 1991 and the 1991–1993 biennium. It chose as the cornerstone of its expenditure reduction efforts a financial management initiative. This initiative placed more day-to-day financial responsibility with the specific state agency and its divisions, effectively decentralizing financial management in the executive branch. The goal was to involve agency management and personnel more closely in the financial management process, there instilling a sense of ownership. It was hoped the result would be more significant and achieve "smarter" savings than those realized through a more centralized approach.

As was the case with one agency, the State Board of Tax Commissioners, overall savings and reversions by all agencies to the state general fund in fiscal year 1992 were significantly above the 3% targeted amount.* Clearly, the specific financial management initiatives developed by each individual agency in consultation with the State Budget Agency had the success intended and assisted the state of Indiana in dealing with its budget gap for fiscal 1992.

REVIEW QUESTIONS

1. What were the effects of the 1990s recession on state finances in general? Pick one state adversely affected by the recession and prepare a brief overview of the way it handled its fiscal crisis.
2. How reliable are revenue and expenditure forecasts in general? Given the inevitable forecast error associated with these types of projections, how much attention should governors and state legislators pay to forecasted gaps? What alternatives, in lieu of forecasts, are available to ensure fiscal responsibility?
3. What options are available to states when they are faced by a budget deficit but are required to balance the budget?
4. What are the advantages of centralized financial management versus decentralized financial management? What are the disadvantages?

---

* The reversion target was $64,900,000, with actual reversions of $99,186,153, savings over 50% higher than the targeted amount (State Budget Agency, July 15, 1992).

5. Are mandatory reserves and reversions good financial management tools? What are their advantages and disadvantages?

REFERENCES

State Board of Tax Commissioners. (July 29, 1991). *Improving Financial Management.* memorandum.

State Board of Tax Commissioners. (Aug. 31, 1991). *Amended Budget Plan* memorandum, Indiapapolis, IN.

State Board of Tax Commissioners. (Sept. 14, 1992). *Budget Transmittal Letter.* letter. Indianapolis, IN.

State Budget Agency. (Sept. 5, 1996). *Financial Management Circular #90–2.* Indianapolis, IN.

State Budget Agency. (Nov. 26, 1990). *Financial Management Circular #90–4.* Indianapolis, IN.

State Budget Agency. (Feb. 22, 1991). *Financial Management Circular #91–1.* Indianapolis, IN.

State Budget Agency. (March 20, 1991). *Improving Financial Management.* Indianapolis, IN.

State Budget Agency. (June 30, 1991). *Financial Management Circular #91–2.* Indianapolis, IN.

State Budget Agency. (Aug. 1, 1991). *Financial Management Circular #91–3.* Indianapolis, IN.

State Budget Agency. (July 15, 1992). *Fiscal Overview.* Indianapolis, IN.

State Budget Agency. (Jan. 9, 1992). *Governor's Spending Reduction Program.* Indianapolis, IN.

47

The Richmond Unified School District Default

COPs, Bankruptcy, Default, State Intervention, and Epilogue

Craig L. Johnson and John L. Mikesell
Indiana University, Bloomington, Indiana, U.S.A.

The ability of a government to meet its obligations to the public depends on how well it can manage its financial resources. One critical concern is the handling of debt obligations, because the need to service debt (i.e., to meet requirements for periodic payments of principal and interest) can strain resources needed to deliver current services and because careless management can impede the government's ability to borrow in the future. Borrowing provides resources for service delivery, but the debt creates an obligation to make payments out of resources in the future (Mikesell, 1991). Sustained fiscal viability—indeed, the fiscal independence of the government—hinges on the planning and balanced execution of debt strategies. New financial instruments, including special varieties of debt and leasing, provide governments with additional flexibility in an era of revenue constraints and increased service demands. As the following case illustrates, they also bring considerable fiscal and political danger when not carefully managed.

PROBLEM BACKGROUND AND DISCUSSION

This case involves financial management decisions made by the Richmond (California) Unified School District in the use of certificates of participation (COPs), securities that combine features of both borrowing and leasing. To understand the problems requires some special background about the school district, the nature of local government finance in California, and the nature of municipal (state and local) debt finance.

The Richmond Unified School District

Richmond Unified School District (the district) serves 31,000 students (the fifteenth largest of the state's 1100 districts) in Contra Costa County, about twenty-five miles east of San

---

The authors are grateful for the able research assistance of Craig LeFeber.

Francisco. Cities within its boundaries include Richmond, El Cerrito, Kensington, San Pablo, Hercules, Pinole, and El Sobrante. Communities served range from "working-class inner-city" neighborhoods in Richmond to "affluent suburbs" of Contra Costa County. Its ethnic distribution is 37% African American, 33% Anglo, 16% Asian, and 13% Latin.

To serve this population the district operated fifty schools and employed around 1400 teachers and counselors. Its total expenditures in 1986–1987 equaled $98.8 million, almost $2.5 million more than its revenue. Of its total revenue, 70.8% came from state aid and 4.9% from the federal government. District taxes produced 22.8% of revenue.

Through the early 1980s, the schools in the district produced low standardized test scores and high dropout rates. In 1987, the school board hired a new superintendent, Walter Marks, to change the system. Marks had achieved national recognition for the systems of school choice he had developed in Montclair, New Jersey, and Wake County, North Carolina. The district wanted him to create a model urban school district.

Marks set up the district's "system for choice." He established magnet schools with specialized programs throughout the district, hired new teachers, upgraded equipment, and allowed parents and students great flexibility in choosing what school the student would attend. The choice and magnet programs induced minority students to suburban schools and white students to inner-city schools. Schools became more flexible and accountable to the student-parent-customers.

On the surface, Richmond did indeed become a model urban school district. In the first two years of the new system, district enrollment rose, unexcused absences fell 50%, suspensions declined by 60%, and achievement scores improved. In the California Assessment Program standardized test for eighth graders released in 1989, Richmond students scored an average of 241 points. This was below the statewide average of 263, but the improvement since implementation of the choice program was startling: 29 points against the statewide average growth of 16 points. Other grade levels showed similar improvement (Merl, 1989). Campuses offered classical studies, future studies, applied arts, international studies, language, visual and performing arts, mathematics, science and technology, and "alternative education" programs. All schools offered reading and language arts, math, sciences, and social studies. District schools could boast of waiting lists for enrollment spaces and of bringing students back from private schools.

Unfortunately, the district lacked a financial management system able to account for and control its money. In an audit a few years later, California State Comptroller Grey Davis called the district a "financial nightmare" without "even the most rudimentary form of financial control." According to the audit, no single person (e.g., treasurer, finance director) was in charge of managing district day-to-day financial affairs. Other critical violations of basic financial management principles included the following:

1. A governing school board that did not review expenditures.
2. An accounting system with no limit on expenditures.
3. Administrators who did not know how much money they received, how much money they spent, or how much money was left over. (For example, the district once sold two properties but collected for only one.)
4. A financial system that duplicated payments to vendors and authorized checks that were never seen by the administrator whose name appeared on them.

Local Government Finance in California

School districts in California are independent governments with their own elected governing boards. As with virtually all school governments in the United States, taxes on property represent the predominant locally determined revenue source at their disposal. California public schools, however, receive nearly three-fourths of their total revenue from the state, the highest percentage in the nation (the median across all states is 51%). A limit on local school taxes, to be described shortly, prevents this unusually high state assistance from producing relatively high education expenditure; state expenditure per pupil is close to the national median.

Two constitutional provisions help define the financial limitations the district faced. First, California school districts must obtain the approval of two-thirds of their voters for the creation of any new indebtedness (Article XI, Sec. 18). This referendum requirement reduces the ease of district borrowing, particularly in light of the supermajority requirement for approval. Second, in 1978 California voters approved the Jarvis–Gann Amendment (Proposition 13) to the state constitution. That amendment (1) restricted the local property tax rate to no more than 1% of assessed value, (2) set assessed value for real property at its 1975–1976 fair market value plus 2% (compounded) each year or its acquisition value if the property has sold since that date, and (3) required new local taxes or increases in existing local taxes (except property taxes) to receive a two-thirds approval from voters. These provisions both reduced the growth of the local property tax base and made it more difficult to enact new revenue sources.

Debt and Certificates of Participation

State and local governments regularly borrow to acquire assets that will provide a return over many years or to manage a temporary imbalance between spending and revenue flows. Private lenders are, however, willing to loan only if they have reasonable prospects of repayment with sufficient interest to compensate for the delayed use of the funds and the risk of default. As perceived risk is greater, interest rates must be higher.

Of critical importance to potential lenders is the pledge for repayment; in other words, what the borrower intends to commit for paying principal and interest on the loan. The municipal market is now characterized by many debt forms with complex risks and security structures. For the present purposes, three types of financial transfers across periods should be differentiated.

1. General obligation bonds: bonds backed by the general taxing authority of the municipality
2. Revenue (limited obligation) bonds: bonds payable from a specific stream of revenue, often the stream generated by the project financed by the bond issue
3. Certificates of participation: certificates backed by annual lease payments on a mortgaged real property parcel or piece of equipment

General governmental capital projects are usually financed through the issuance of general obligation bonds. These bonds, virtually the only kind of municipal debt until the 1960s, are called full faith and credit bonds, because they are supported by the general taxing power of the debt issuer. Tax-supported bonds have traditionally been viewed as the most secure of all municipal bond investments. Revenue bonds, now the predominant type of municipal bond, are generally supported by the revenue generated by a specific project. They include three broad categories: (1) those payable solely from the revenues of a government-owned enterprise, such as a publicly owned water and sewer utility; (2) those payable solely from the income or revenue of private entities or individuals; and

(3) those primarily payable from the income or revenue of private entities but ultimately backed by a sponsoring government.

The COP does not clearly fit into those debt categories. Certificates of participation are leases generally secured by the property being leased, not a specific revenue stream or general obligation pledge.* Certificates of participation were developed in California in the late 1970s, largely in response to restrictions imposed by Proposition 13 on the ability of local governments to raise taxes to support general obligation bonds. Since then COP issuance has grown dramatically; in 1990 total market volume was estimated to exceed $10 billion.

California local governments frequently use COPs because, as in many other states, the lease payments backing the certificates are legally a current expense and not a long-term debt obligation. The lease is therefore not subject to constitutional or statutory debt limitations, provided the lease agreement contains certain provisions. In California, to not be considered debt, lease agreements must conform to the so-called Offner rule [*City of Los Angeles* v. *Offner*, 19 Cal. 2d483, 122P.2d14 (1942)]. The rule requires the lease agreement to contain an abatement clause that prohibits the lessee (tenant) from making a lease payment for property for which it does not have the full use. Any annual lease payment is therefore for the actual use of the facilities during the year.

THE USE OF COPs IN RICHMOND—A BRIDGE TO BANKRUPTCY

The Richmond district had deficits, an administration with a mandate to innovate, constraints on its capacity to increase revenue, and interesting security options. A chronological review of the financial policies it adopted, starting with 1988, illustrates many critical issues of government finance: the problem of operating deficits, the use of COPs in a fiscal management plan, the implications of state responsibility and control, the nature of default and bankruptcy, and the general consequences of failure to maintain close control of finances.

The Certificate Issue: 1988

In the spring of 1988, the bills from the urban model school system became impossible to conceal. The district faced an operating deficit of $6.7 million. California fiscal restrictions made it difficult to levy new taxes. Balancing the budget by cutting expenditures would almost certainly harm the magnet schools so essential to the choice program, and because so much of district spending was for personnel, would require teacher layoffs or

---

* Certificate of participation leases usually have one of three security features: (1) firm appropriation, (2) nonappropriation-out, or (3) enterprise (Illyes, 1990). Firm appropriation leases extend for the life of the bond issue, but payment of the debt service depends upon annual appropriations. Nonappropriation-out leases, used primarily to finance equipment, allow the lessee to terminate the lease at the end of the current period simply by not making an appropriation for the next period. This pledge may be less secure than that of a firm appropriation. Enterprise leases, generally supported by self-sustaining revenue projects, do not rely on an annual appropriation from a general governmental unit. None of these pledges would ordinarily be as strong as that in a traditional general obligation or revenue municipal bond.

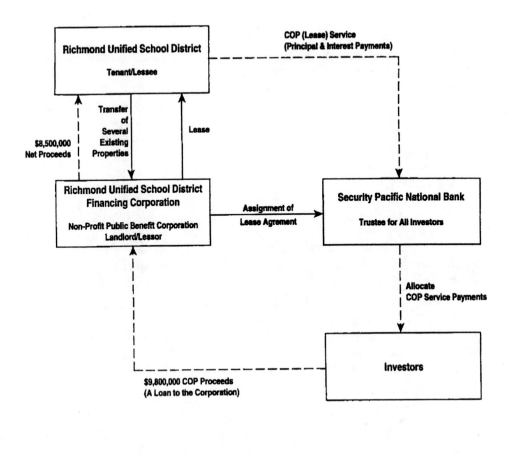

Exhibit 1. The structure of the Richmond Unified School District COP transaction.

salary reductions.* These options were difficult; Superintendent Marks and the school board took another route.

Rather than adjust expenditures to available resources, the district chose to borrow to finance the deficits. That decision to fund an operating deficit by issuing a long-term obligation turned the short-term problem into the start of long-term disaster. California law ordinarily constrained the ability of local governments to borrow; they could only issue debt after obtaining the approval of two-thirds of the voters. The district, however, issued COPs.

The transaction involved the entities linked in Exhibit 1.†

---

* The high share for personnel costs in state and local spending is common.

† These descriptions come from the preliminary official statement, Richmond Unified School District, Contra Costa County, California, for $9,800,000 COPs (1988 financing project) dated April 27, 1988, as prepared by the underwriter Rauscher Pierce Refsnes, Inc.

1. The district operated the school system and initially owned the buildings (the administration building, the central kitchen, and six other warehouses and maintenance facilities) involved in the transaction. After the transfer, the district would pay rent to use those buildings.
2. The Richmond Unified School District Financing Corporation (the corporation), a nonprofit public benefit corporation, accepted the transfer of the buildings and paid the district $8,500,000 for these assets. The corporation leases the buildings to the district for a fixed period, at the end of which the buildings return to district ownership.
3. Private investors, people, and businesses attracted to tax-exempt interest, loan $9,800,000 to the corporation to cover the payment to the district and other costs associated with the transaction. The investors will receive the proportionate share of lease payments (interest and return of principal) during the life of the lease.
4. Security Pacific National Bank, the trustee, represents the interests of all investors. The bank receives the lease payments from the district and distributes the appropriate share to each investor.

The proceeds from the transaction would resolve district fiscal problems for the year, as well as allow it to finance some other activities.

Three critical specifics about the 1988 COPs—what would be borrowed and for how long, how the proceeds would be used, and what the basis would be for repaying the loan—appear in the official statement issued by the district.

1. The loan and its maturity. The total principal amount to be borrowed equaled $9,800,000, with repayments made throughout the ten years of the issue.

Maturity (Aug. 1)	Principal	Interest	Debt service
1989	705,000	873,271	1,578,271
1990	745,000	658,080	1,403,080
1991	795,000	611,518	1,406,518
1992	850,000	559,843	1,409,843
1993	915,000	502,467	1,417,467
1994	985,000	438,417	1,423,417
1995	1,060,000	367,005	1,427,005
1996	1,150,000	288,565	1,438,565
1997	1,245,000	201,165	1,446,165
1998	1,350,000	105,300	1,455,300
Total	9,800,000	4,605,631	14,405,631

The certificates were to be issued in denominations of $5000 or multiples with interest payable on February 1 and August 1 of each year, beginning February 1, 1989. Interest would accrue from the issue date, May 1, 1988. The COPs had a 7.81% NIC (net interest cost), 9 basis points above the *Bond Buyer* index. The district applied for a credit rating from Moody's Investors Service, Inc., but withdrew the request because it expected the certificates to be rated below investment grade.

2. The use of the proceeds. The district outlined the following use of the funds from the issue:

Construction of multipurpose rooms in three schools.	$1,000,000
Acquisition of computerized management system.	800,000
Deposit in district's general fund.	6,700,000
Delivery costs (administrative costs associated with the issue).	124,529
Underwriting discount.	
(This discount, the difference between the face value of the issue and what the underwriter paid, is the firm's gross margin.)	254,800
Deposit to reserve fund.	
(Part of the issue is held by the trustee for distribution in the event the district does not make payment when due.)	954,520
Total uses	$9,833,849*

3. The basis for repayment. Certificates of participation investors needed some assurance that the district would make lease payments. That legal agreement, or covenant, appeared in the offering statement.

> The District has covenanted in the Lease to include all Lease Payments in its annual budgets. Lease Payments are an obligation of the District's General Fund. Should the District default under the Lease, the Trustee, as assignee of the Corporation under the Lease, may terminate the Lease and re-let the sites, or may retain the Lease and hold the District liable for all Lease Payments thereunder on an annual basis.

In other words, the district will annually appropriate from its general fund money to make the lease payments, and if that does not work, the corporation may lease the properties to some other client. The offering statement notes the risk.

> The District has not pledged the full faith and credit of the District, the State of California or any political subdivision there of to the payment of the Lease Payments or any other payments due under the Lease. The District is not obligated to levy any form of taxation to pay Lease Payments. Neither Lease Payments nor the Certificates constitutes a debt of the District, the State of California or any political subdivision thereof. In the event the District's revenue sources are less than its total obligations, the District could choose to fund other services before making the Lease Payments and the other payments due under the Lease. The same result could occur if, because of State constitutional limits on expenditures, the District is not permitted to appropriate and spend all of its available revenues.

The Emergency Loan and a State Trustee: 1990

By 1990 the district's current operating deficit had grown to $9 million. The deficit was primarily a result of overly optimistic revenue projections involving state aid and federal

---

* The additional $33,849 represents accrued interest on the face amount of the issue.

grants and the failure to sell a piece of district property expected to bring in $2.5 million. In addition, the district lost a lawsuit requiring it to grant a two-year, 16.9% salary increase to teachers, which was estimated to cost the district $10 million in 1990 alone. On June 22, with the district unable to meet its June payroll, Governor George Deukmejian signed into law a $9.525 million emergency state loan. The loan had an interest rate of 6.1% and a seven-year term; repayment would begin in fiscal year (FY) 1991–1992. The bailout loan enabled the district to meet its June payroll, but under the terms of the bailout, the district had to accept the appointment of a state trustee to oversee its financial affairs.

What about Superintendent Marks, the person responsible for both the success of the system of school choice and the financial problems of the district? He blamed the fiscal problems on state aid that did not materialize and noted that the school board had approved each of his budgets. Others blamed him for overly ambitious plans for innovation without much regard for where the money would come from. The president of the United Teachers of Richmond union, Gabrielle Moore, criticized the plans as "a Cadillac program for a Chevrolet district" (Hallissy, 1990). Whatever the division of responsibility, the school board believed that Marks had to leave if the district was to receive additional state loans. His contract was therefore bought out and his administration ended with the beginning of the new year.

Bankruptcy Petition, State Control, and Default: 1991

The district faced a $29 million deficit and was on the verge of financial collapse in the spring of 1991. The school year was scheduled to end on June 14, but the district lacked funds to operate past May 1. Faced with this educational and financial disaster, on April 19, 1991 the district petitioned for bankruptcy protection under Chapter 9 of the federal bankruptcy code. The Chapter 9 filing was intended to provide the district with a temporary shield from creditors while it negotiated additional emergency bailout funds from the state and reorganized its debt structure. In one effort, Assemblyman Bob Campbell of Richmond (Democrat) sponsored legislation for a $29 million bailout for the district. Governor Wilson (Republican), however, faced with a $12.6 billion FY 1991–1992 state budget deficit, threatened to veto the bill unless union contracts in the district were suspended for three years. The legislation did not pass.

Parents of students attending district schools sued to force the state of California to keep the schools open. Contra Costa judge Ellen James sided with the parents and ordered the state to provide the necessary funds to keep the district operating through the regular school year. Judge James unequivocally gave the state ultimate responsibility for keeping California public schools operating throughout the normal school year by ruling that the "education of children is *the* function of the state." Moreover, Judge James reasoned that the state had to respond, "by *whatever* means they (the state) deem appropriate" (Superior Court of Contra Costa County, no. C91–01645) if a school district could not provide the same educational opportunities received by children in neighboring districts.*

Faced with the superior court order, on April 31, 1991 state officials agreed to provide the district with a $19 million loan to keep it operating throughout the remainder

---

* Other states, including Ohio and New Jersey, have voluntarily provided emergency funding to local school systems or taken over those systems that were unable to manage their own financial affairs, but it is the first time a state has been ordered by the courts to rescue a local school district.

of the school year. The money came from a transfer of a $10 million loan intended for, but not distributed to, Oakland, and $9 million from a state program that provided educational and job training to welfare recipients. The emergency bailout loan, however, carried stiff terms: an 8.5% interest rate over its ten year term with payments beginning in FY 1992–1993. The loan was to be repaid from property taxes and state aid, but the district faced a projected $28.6 million deficit in FY 1992–1993. Furthermore, the loan required that the district surrender any remaining autonomy. The state-appointed trustee was given total control over the district, including the power to set the salaries of teachers and other school employees. Among other things, the trustee could impose a new pay scale on the union if the administration and union could not reach agreement on a new contract.

Bill Honig, California superintendent of public instruction, and Gray Davis, California state controller, both Democrats, arranged the bailout loan. They both believed the district's situation was the result of internal fiscal mismanagement, but wanted to carry out the superior court order expeditiously to put the affair behind the state. On the other hand, Governor Wilson (Republican) did not want to comply with the superior court order to bail out the district. Indeed, Governor Wilson, through California attorney general Dan Lungren, petitioned the state supreme court to immediately stop payment on the $19 million bailout loan. Governor Wilson believed the lower court ruling set an ominous precedent, as described in his appeal to the state supreme court: "the message that will be sent to the other districts is clear—you can stubbornly and irresponsibility [sic] spend yourselves into bankruptcy . . . with the realization that the [state] must continue your district in operation."

On May 8, the California supreme court permitted the district to stay open throughout the school year by denying Governor Wilson's request to block the $19 million emergency loan. The court did agree to review the case directly instead of requiring the state court of appeals to hear the case first. The general constitutional appeal of the lower court order requiring state officials to keep schools open—by all possible means—would therefore be heard quickly and possibly overturned. The schools remained open, but in August 1991 the district missed its $1.1 million lease payment, putting the COPs in default. The trustee, however, paid the certificate holders from reserve funds.

On October 3, 1991, federal bankruptcy judge Edward Jellen removed the district from bankruptcy because the district's state-appointed trustee withdrew the bankruptcy petition. Municipal bankruptcy, unlike business bankruptcy, is a voluntary procedure and municipalities cannot be forced by creditors or the court to remain in bankruptcy or liquidate their property. The judge therefore dismissed the bankruptcy petition, despite the inability of the district to develop a plan to pay off creditors and despite objections from creditors and unions.*

Constitutional Transactions, Empty Covenants, and State Responsibility: 1992

The district released its financial recovery plan in January. The budget drafted by the state-appointed trustee provided for full payment of the $29 million of state loans, but

---

* *In Re Richmond Unified School District, Debtor*, no. 91–42434J, U.S. Bankruptcy Court for the Northern District of California, decided Nov. 4, 1991.

made no provision for COPs debt service.* On February 4, 1992, the district missed the second payment on its defaulted certificates. Because reserve funds were gone, certificate holders received no money. At this point it became clear to investors that the district intended no more debt service payments on the certificates.

The initial offering statement clearly identified the potential risks of the certificates in a separate section entitled "Risk Factors." The section noted the district's serious financial troubles and that it might choose to fund other services rather than make debt service payments if it faced a future operating deficit. Given the district's historical financial performance, this was a significant admonishment. The operating deficit in 1988 was $6.7 million, 7% of the FY 1986–1987 budget, and the district had run operating deficits in three of the last four years. The investment community did not realize the full extent of the potential problem it faced, however. Not only was the district unwilling to make timely debt service payments, but the state sought to nullify the entire COPs deal.

On July 14, 1992, Attorney General Lungren petitioned the Contra Costa Superior Court to invalidate the district's defaulted COPs. He argued that the certificates were unconstitutional because they created long-term debt that had not been approved by the electorate. The issue was a debt financing scheme, not a true lease, because it intended to produce cash to cover an operating deficit. A half century of judicial rulings created a lease exemption for financing the construction or acquisition (capital projects) and subsequent lease of the property being leased, not the "continued" use of property already owned and in operation. Mortgaging the district's property to fund an operating deficit was illegal, as well as bad public policy (about two-thirds of the COP proceeds were used to close an operating deficit). Moreover, Lungren argued that the lease/leaseback financing arrangement had not been authorized by the state legislature for operating purposes. Accordingly, the certificates did not fall within the "lease exception" to the voter approval requirement for debt.

On December 11, 1992 the court disagreed. Superior court judge John F. Van de Poel discounted the attorney general's argument that the certificates were long-term debt in disguise, and ruled that the lease agreement supporting the COPs did not constitute a long-term debt obligation because the "payments are due only in the year when the site was used, and the payments could not be accelerated." Moreover, in response to the attorney general's argument that the leasing structure was not authorized by state law because it was used to finance an operating deficit, Judge Van de Poel tersely ruled that "the use to which the proceeds of the site lease was made is irrelevant to the issue of the constitutional debt limit." Accordingly, the COPs are legal and the district could not avoid its liability for the certificates by blaming other parties (i.e., the state of California, the bond counsel, the underwriters) for its actions.

Judge Van de Poel dismissed earlier, however, a motion to force the district to resume payments on the defaulted COPs. He ruled that the budgetary and appropriations covenant in the official statement did not compel the district to budget COP service payments. Although bond counsel had argued that the statement legally bound the district, Judge Van de Poel ruled that the language was "not in furtherance of any statute and

---

* In contrast, the San Jose School District continued to make interest payments when it filed for bankruptcy protection in 1983.

cannot be enforced."* The COPs therefore were constitutional, but the covenant statement did not force the district to appropriate funds to cover the lease payments.

Finally, the last day of the year, the state supreme court completed the cycle that had kept district schools open in 1991. The court held that the state had a constitutional duty to intervene to prevent the premature end to that school year. The action was required to ensure that students in Richmond receive the same basic education as other pupils in the state: "The state itself . . . had a duty to protect district students against loss of their right to basic educational equality."† The supreme court did rule, however, that the diversion of state funds to the emergency loan from appropriations made for other purposes was improper. This circuit court action violated the constitutional separation of powers between the judiciary and the legislative and executive branches of government. In sum, the state takeover was required, but the means of financing the loan would have to be changed.

A Way Out?: 1993

Did the district have any financial obligation to the corporation? On April 22, Judge Van de Poel of the Contra Costa County Superior Court ruled that the district owed past-due lease payments. The district had argued that the offering statement warning that financial difficulties might lead to interruptions in lease payments removed its legal obligations. In essence, the district was required to make payments only when it had sufficient money in its general fund to do so—and there was no money available. The risk factor was clear in the offering statement. The trustee, when negotiating a lease contract that did not recognize this risk, acted in bad faith, therefore the district was not required to make rental payments in tough fiscal times.

Judge Van de Poel ruled otherwise. The risk factors in the offering statement did not provide an excuse for default. The district owed the lease payments in default when the lawsuit was filed (April 1992), so the trustee could collect past-due rent. The judge again did not order enforcement of the covenants: "The court cannot grant specific enforcement as to future years since the district's obligation to make lease payments under the lease is dependent on future events such as the usability of the site." The trustee viewed the ruling as a victory, although almost certain to be appealed. The state wondered how a judgment could ever be collected, given that the court had ruled itself unable to force a district to budget money.

While arguments continued in the judicial system, the California legislature was in session. Early in the year, Governor Pete Wilson and Assemblyman Tom Bates (D–Berkeley) reached tentative agreement on a Richmond bailout, which the legislature eventually passed and the governor signed on June 30, 1993. Assembly bill 535, as amended and ultimately approved, (1) consolidated the existing state loans of $9.525 and $19 million into one loan, (2) adjusted the interest rate on the loan to prevailing rates earned by the state investment pool on January 1, 1993,‡ and (3) extended debt repayments over the

---

* Budgetary and appropriation covenants are common in California, and according to Standard & Poors, they give lease financings there higher ratings than lease issues in states in which issuers retain the right to not appropriate lease payments annually.

† *Butt* v. *California*, 4 Cal. 4th 668 (Dec. 31, 1992).

‡ That rate was 4.543%.

period from 1995 through 2007. The new consolidated debt repayment schedule, including interest, became the following:

Payment Date	Amount
February 1, 1993	$0
February 1, 1994	$0
February 1, 1995	$5,570,443
February 1, 1996	$1,870,443
February 1, 1997	$1,870,443
February 1, 1998	$5,570,443
February 1, 1999	$1,870,443
February 1, 2000	$1,870,443
February 1, 2001	$5,570,443
February 1, 2002	$1,870,443
February 1, 2003	$1,870,443
February 1, 2004	$5,570,443
February 1, 2005	$1,870,443
February 1, 2006	$1,870,443
February 1, 2007	$5,287,705

The law made no provision for the defaulted COPs. Furthermore, it immediately changed the name of the district to the West Contra Costa Unified School District. In the period from 1988 to 1993, the Richmond Unified School District thus went from being a model urban school district to being a district that no longer existed under that name, and COPs provided a vehicle for that journey!

SUMMARY AND CONCLUSION

Financial administration matters for the delivery of government services. The fiscal choices made by the Richmond Unified School District allowed the district to deliver a model urban school program. Certificates of participation permitted an apparently easy bridge over operating deficits and around apparently rigid popular oversight of borrowing. The certificates did not, however, change the reality that the program was not within the basic resources available to the district.

When economic reality could no longer be denied, the district proposed to shut down early. By legal action school parents reminded the state of California of its constitutional responsibility for ensuring the education of all of its children. The state assumed control of the district and made emergency loans to allow operations to continue. Soon thereafter, in an effort to reduce expenditures, lease payments to COP holders stopped. This act awakened all market participants to the true risks inherent in COPs and served as a reminder of the high costs of fiscal mismanagement.

This default raised questions about the constitutionality of the COPs, the power of bond covenants, the meaning of statements of risk in offering statements, and the proper role of the state in managing the financial affairs of substate governments. There are no clear answers to these questions, either in law or in terms of municipal credit market operations.

EPILOGUE

The West Contra Costa Unified School District survives. The leadership and financial management changes made following the default and bankruptcy crisis have led to fiscal solvency. The district's ability to fund educational programs is still hampered because the settlement required the district to sell some schools and unimproved land parcels, and the debt load is very high. Academic performance has not improved. The crisis is over, but the district is still not able to deliver a high-quality educational program (Mecoy, 1997).

On a more macro level, the Richmond Unified School District crisis represents a watershed in school finance in California. California school district debt payments will never again be viewed as invulnerable to default and bankruptcy, and municipal investors will no longer believe that the California state government will ultimately bail out local governments.

Richmond did prompt state legislation to improve the financial management and monitoring structure of school districts in California. First, school districts may no longer use COPs to fund current operating expenses (Section 43133.5 of the California Education Code). Second, the state may now take over financially troubled school districts (AB 1200). School districts must report their financial condition twice a year to the county department of education. Any district in danger of not being able to pay its bills is monitored by county school officials and placed on a statewide list of having a financial condition certified to be either negative or qualified. Such districts may be subject to the imposition of a state-supported roving "fiscal crisis and management assistance team" to help the district put its affairs in order. A district that must get a loan from the state is automatically placed under the control of a trustee appointed by the state superintendent. The local superintendent and school board become advisors to the state-appointed trustee.

These reforms leave California school districts better prepared to face the fiscal limitations imposed by Proposition 218, which was passed by California voters on November 6, 1996. One of the positive consequences that may come out of the Richmond Unified School District financial crisis is a stronger intergovernmental financial management system that is more capable of prudent local financial management.

REVIEW QUESTIONS

1. What should a local government do when faced with an operating deficit? What options did the district have? Is issuance of long-term debt to finance these deficits ever justifiable?
2. What should a state government do when one of its local governmental units faces a fiscal crisis of the type experienced in Richmond? Are there fundamental responsibilities for the state to come to the aid of or to restrain troubled localities?
3. Given that interest rates may be expected to compensate lenders for risks of default, what case is there for state assistance to make district COP holders whole? Did the premium here appropriately capture the risks?
4. What responsibility does a public financial manager have to accommodate operating decisions that may have adverse future consequences (i.e., is there a valid "Nuremberg defense" in government finance)?
5. The National Association of Bond Lawyers has recommended that brokers be required to print the following on confirmations of purchases of nonrated bonds:

"The security you have purchased has not, to our knowledge, received a rating from any national credit rating agency. Absence of a rating may involve special circumstances of which the purchaser should be aware." What do you think of this proposal in light of what you now know of the Richmond case?

6. Trace the role of the state through the case, taking care to distinguish actions by state officials (as opposed to the district and the corporation) and the interests and apparent motives of those officials.

7. What negative externalities did the second emergency loan generate?

8. Are there any other actions after AB 535 the state government should take?

REFERENCES

Public Securities Association. (1991) *A Guide To Certificates of Participation.*

Butt v. *California*, 4 Cal. 4th 668 (Dec. 31, 1992).

City of Los Angeles v. *Offner*, 19 Cal. 2d483, 122 P.2d14 (1942).

Hallissy, E. (Dec. 7, 1990). Richmond schools chief ousted—fiscal crisis. *San Francisco Chronicle*, A1.

Hill, P. (Oct. 4, 1991). Judge dismisses Richmond, California, school district's bankruptcy filling. *Bond Buyer.*

Hill, P. (Feb. 4, 1992). California district defaults on COP issue, unveils budget plan with no payments set. *The Bond Buyer.*

Hill, P. (Feb. 11, 1992). California, hoping to avert future bailouts, makes example of Richmond School District. *Bond Buyer.*

Hill, P. (Oct. 12, 1992). California judge refuses to force district to budget COPs payments. *Bond Buyer.*

Hill, P. (Dec. 14, 1992). California court backs validity of Richmond lease in blow to state. *Bond Buyer.*

Hill, P. (April 1993). California court says Richmond must pay COPs investor. *Bond Buyer.*

Illyes, J. W. (Jan. 1990). *COPs and Lease-Backed Bonds in Major Leasing States: California, Indiana, New Jersey, and Kentucky* Nuveen Research.

Illyes, J. W. (June 1991). *California School COPs and Bonds After Richmond.* Nuveen Research.

In Re Richmond Unified School District, Debtor, no. 91-42434J, U.S. Bankruptcy Court for the Northern District of California, decided Nov. 4, 1991.

Mecoy, L. (June 15, 1997). State-run schools get mixed marks. *Sacramento Bee.*

Merl, J. (Nov. 29, 1989). Free-choice schooling gets an A in Richmond. *Los Angeles Times*, 3.

Mikesell, J. L. (1991). *Fiscal Administration.* 3rd ed. Pacific Grove, CA: Brooks/Cole.

Walters, D. (April 19, 1991). California school district to seek Chapter 9: Outstanding COPs have unclear future. *Bond Buyer.*

48

Property Tax Abatement
A Case Study of San Marcos, Texas

Kay Hofer
Southwest Texas State University, San Marcos, Texas, U.S.A.

Property taxes have long been the primary revenue source for local governments. During the 1980s, however, state control over local revenue sources generally increased, and nearly all states placed a limit on local property tax rates or the levy. With the declining fiscal situation, local governments were forced to seek new revenue sources or reduce or eliminate services. As property taxes are sensitive to economic development, state and local governments turned to tax concessions and other financial incentives to attract business and industry hoping to expand or stabilize the tax base. Although considerable variety in tax incentives exists, property tax abatement remains one of the most frequently used concessions (*Director of Incentives for Business Investment*, 1991). Tax abatements are designed to modify taxpayer behavior or to achieve particular economic goals, such as attracting business and industry, stimulating local employment, or improving the local economy.

Local governments may adopt tax abatement policies based on the assumption that the outcome will be unquestionably positive without a prior, thorough analysis of the economic outcome that can reasonably be expected. The initial costs of abatement may appear negligible, while the actual costs are hidden or diffused. Property tax abatement can be a two-edged sword, and local governments that adopt tax abatement policies without sound analysis of appropriate net benefits and costs may discover the result is an adverse fiscal situation in the future. Tax abatements may have a substantial effect on both revenues and expenditures of local governments. Rapid economic growth may result in a negative situation in which property taxes must be increased beyond existing levels to cover the cost of the temporary abatement as well as increased infrastructure and service demands. Issues of equity and distribution of the tax burden between business and residential owners which are already factors in property assessment can be raised. Any change in the property tax has significant economic and political implications; the more narrow a local government's tax base, the more susceptible that base is to a change. The property tax is the most sensitive of all taxes to a change in population; property values fall quickly in response to a rapid decrease in population. The alternative side of the issue is that rapid growth in population and resulting infrastructure and service demands are more difficult to finance in smaller, more rural communities, often requiring a greatly increased tax effort. The size of a community may also be a factor in successful tax abatement policies. Most local governments that report successful use of tax abatement have populations between 10,000 and 50,000 and use this concession in combination with other diversified strategies to encourage economic development.

This case study examines the tax abatement policies of San Marcos, Texas. San Marcos has a population of 35,959 permanent residents and 21,320 university students and falls within the size range of communities reporting success with tax abatement policies. The potential for a more significant impact on property taxes and economic development exists as well, due to the size of the existing tax base; the community is a midsized rural area with a significant amount of exempt property. The objective of the case study is to identify factors that are both essential and realistic and that can be used to evaluate tax abatement and to examine the interrelationship of property tax abatement and assessment.

TAX ABATEMENT: WHAT IT IS AND HOW IT WORKS

Tax abatement is a method of allocating resources through the tax system rather than by direct expenditures: "Tax abatements are enacted under state enabling legislation and local ordinance and provide for the foregoing of revenue due to special tax exemptions, exclusions, deductions, credits, deferrals, or preferential tax rates" (Benker, 1986). The source of finance for property tax abatement is a change in the local tax base that may not immediately be reflected in a tax rate change. Tax concessions are found in all states and in the federal tax code and include, but are not limited to, sales, property, and income tax abatements. Property tax abatement currently is the most frequently utilized economic development tool. All states allowing property tax abatement have provisions for concessions of up to 100%, and the years of exemption vary from a minimum of five to a maximum of thirty, with ten being the most frequent. Eleven states legislatively target property tax abatement to specific industries, such as timber, mining, manufacturing, textile mills, railroads, and blighted areas. If all other factors such as workforce, transportation, and business operating costs are equal, tax abatement may be a factor in business location, and business location in an area generally is thought to mean jobs, property tax revenue, and other economically positive results (Edwards, 1988; *Director of Incentives for Business Investment*, 1991).

Measurement of the net impact of tax abatement is difficult, as the revenue loss or gain depends on the abatement provisions as well as taxpayer behavior. The interactive effect of net job changes and net changes in other taxes may result in increased or decreased revenues. The most commonly used methods to compute the costs of abatements rely on actual face values and do not measure this interactive effect on other revenues and costs. Measures of cost-effectiveness of property tax abatement also depend on the method and accuracy of assessing property value. If arbitrary or inaccurate assessments are used, an inaccurate estimate of revenue loss or gain may result (Edwards, 1988).

Studies of property tax assessment across the states have revealed a declining percentage of areas with coefficients of dispersion (CD) within the recommended range of 5 to 20 dependent upon the type of property. The coefficient of dispersion measures the extent of uniformity in assessment ratios, and hence the extent to which effective property tax rates vary within a taxing jurisdiction. As the analysis of costs or benefits of tax abatement are directly related to the accuracy and method of property tax assessment, the topic is worth examining more closely. Property tax abatement may present a further impediment to effective and accurate property tax assessment. Errors in abatement benefit/ cost estimates will be magnified in proportion to the variability in assessment practice.

Property tax assessment is an area already replete with problems that may be exacerbated by tax abatement policies. As property value is seldom based on current market transactions between willing buyers and sellers under no pressure to sell, the value-estimation procedure (assessment) becomes a critical factor in the determination of effective tax rates. The assessed value is the base for the property tax levy, and property tax assessment policies vary widely across the states. In some cases, assessment is on the basis of current use; in others, replacement costs may form the assessment basis; and for some, the income approach (estimating the net income flow capitalized at an interest rate related to risk) is used to estimate real property value. If assessed value is not objectively related to real value on an equitable basis, property tax burdens may be shifted in such a manner that gross differences in taxable values of comparable properties occurs, raising a constitutional issue under the Equal Protection Clause of the U.S. Constitution (Mikesell, 1991). Without systematic analysis, the net economic impact of tax abatements remains in question; moreover, the impact of tax abatement on assessed value and tax levies may also remain unmeasured. Property tax abatement is an area worthy of more interest due to the issues of validity and liability that are raised within the context of property tax assessment and the uncertain net impact on economic development.

Tax Abatement in Texas

Until 1987, Texas law had limited tax abatements to blighted areas; the law was amended in 1987 to allow abatements that would contribute employment or major investment and enhance the economic development of a locality. The maximum abatement period is fifteen years, and counties and municipalities are not restricted by type of industry or business (Bland, 1989). With the exception of enterprise zones, which automatically qualify for sales tax rebates and property tax abatement, Texas does not mandate the type of local government tax concession policy. Local governments must apply for enterprise zone designation and receive approval from the Department of Commerce.

States such as Texas have increasingly allowed local governments more discretion in determining the appropriate combination of economic development incentives. Discretion carries with it, however, increased responsibilities for the financial outcomes that result from such decisions. Recently studies have pointed to the net financial loss resulting from preferential tax rates and concessions; Texas was among the states registering the most significant revenue loss as a result of tax concessions (Edwards, 1986). In the 1990s, economic development inducements have moved from assistance driven primarily by tax concessions to an assortment of nontax incentive programs that include direct loans, job training, write downs of market value, long-term leases and encouragement of foreign investment (*Directory of Incentives for Business Investments*, 1991). Of those Texas cities responding to an ICMA survey designed to measure the results of local government use of economic development incentives, McAllen was determined to be the most successful. McAllen is diversified and aggressive with regard to the tools of economic development utilizing tax abatement in combination with such nontax incentives as loan guarantees, loan subsidies, direct loans to private business, in-kind services, employment training, and centralized management (*Meeting Business Attraction*, 1990).

To project the image of a favorable business environment, local governments seem increasingly to be pushed to adopt some type of economic development tool. Today, property tax abatement is the most frequently utilized economic development incentive in Texas (*Directory of Incentives for Business Investment*, 1991). How do local governments determine if the revenue foregone from a tax abatement is worth the benefits derived from any economic development that results? Under what conditions is tax abatement an appropriate economic development incentive? As San Marcos, Texas, has only recently initiated a tax abatement policy, the community provided an ideal setting for a case study to examine factors that might be used to evaluate the net economic impact of property tax abatement and answer the foregoing questions.

CURRENT STATE OF TAX ABATEMENT IN SAN MARCOS, TEXAS

San Marcos is located along Interstate 35 (the only major north/south route) approximately an equal distance (32 miles) from two major metropolitan areas, San Antonio and Austin. In the early 1980s, San Marcos adopted a number of municipal ordinances designed to control the amount, type, and direction of economic growth. The ordinances are targeted to encourage growth north and south along the I-35 corridor and away from the western side of the city due to the sensitive nature of the Edwards aquifer recharge zone, the primary source of water for the area. Development permits are very difficult to obtain in areas in which growth is not desired. Other ordinances were passed to assure that infrastructure needs would not be outpaced by growth and that the rate and type of growth would fit with the master plan and capital improvement plan (Gilley, 1993).

Like many other small cities San Marcos relies heavily on property tax revenues. Other sources of revenue include a 1.5% sales tax, permits, licenses, fees, franchise taxes, and income from municipally owned utilities. The recessions of 1982 and 1986 and the real estate bust of 1986 took their toll on the financial health of the city, which was faced with declining property values and a significant loss of property tax revenue with already strained spending needs. Infrastructure, school, police, and fire protection were at capacity and in need of improvement and expansion. The city also has a relatively significant proportion of exempt property due to the location of a large university, numerous churches, medical facilities, a federal Job Corps facility, schools, and nonprofit entities, thereby reducing the tax base under city control and increasing the property tax burden on commercial and residential real estate. The single largest employer in the city is Southwest Texas State University. Manufacturing, city government, retail trade, a variety of small businesses, and agriculture form the remaining economic base.

In 1989, San Marcos applied for an enterprise zone designation, which was approved by the Texas Department of Commerce. The enterprise zone program was developed by the state to promote job opportunities and investment incentives in areas of high unemployment. The enterprise zone covers 5.05 square miles and is authorized through September 1, 1997. The primary purpose is to create jobs for residents of the zone. In such zones, investments automatically qualify for property tax abatement, including a city sales tax rebate related to the number of employees hired, and the city has no control over such revenue concessions. CTEC, located in the enterprise zone, was the first enterprise to apply for a property tax abatement.

With CTEC's application, San Marcos turned to the development of a general policy on tax abatement as an incentive to provide employment and encourage further economic development for the city. San Marcos's policy on tax abatement was adopted by local ordinance in 1990. The essential factors that were to be considered in abatement decisions were agreed upon in advance by elected officials and city administrators and were included in the abatement policy. The ordinance provides that tax abatement and other economic development incentives be considered on an individual basis. The following criteria must be met in San Marcos to receive a property tax abatement: the proposed development and/or redevelopment must create and maintain at least five jobs, and the investment by the applicant of at least $50,000 in property improvements is required. The project must meet the requirements of the city's master plan, zoning ordinances, building codes, and other applicable city ordinances. The final tax concessions and abatement agreement must be in the form of a formal contract. The contract must include provisions "for the recovery of property tax revenues and all waived fees and costs which are lost as a result of the agreement" if specified obligations are not met by the business (*Policy on Tax Abatement*, 1993).

The city considers these additional criteria, which are not included in the ordinance: expansion of the local tax base, costs of infrastructure improvements the city will have to provide, type of industry or firm, recapture of tax abatement revenue loss, and the time the business will become operational. Preference is given to "businesses which use local suppliers, contractors, local labor force, and require no new public facilities." Although abatement decisions are made on a case by case basis, such abatements are to be generally limited to no more than ten years. Additionally, the city council has the discretion to reduce or eliminate impact, building permit, inspection, contractor, subdivision, zoning, and land use fees and to provide special utility rates (*Policy on Tax Abatement*, 1993).

A development coordinator was hired and is involved in the review process prior to granting an abatement and monitoring of business performance and compliance after the contract is granted. According to the development coordinator, the majority of decisions to grant an abatement were made on the basis of consideration of new full-time jobs created and the commitment to use local suppliers. Tax abatements have been denied to businesses that are high water users or generate hazardous waste. None of the industries that applied for and were denied a property tax abatement moved to this location. In no cases have impact fees been waived in order to assure that infrastructure capacity can continue to be aligned with the growth that occurs; however, most permit fees are waived (Ronson, 1993). Table 1 provides a listing of the current San Marcos tax abatement contracts, including the required job creation, contract value of new property, and current assessed value of the property.

By the end of 1993, San Marcos had approved nine abatement contracts since adoption of the local ordinance. The number of jobs to be created totaled 1673, and the contract value of property to be created was $23,650,000, excluding the Vanity Fair Factory Outlet and the San Marcos Factory Stores, large retail outlets. The retail outlet contracts required an increase in sales tax revenue of an annual fixed dollar amount based on a progressive sliding scale in order to retain the property tax abatements of 100% of assessed value. The contract value is the amount of property value at full market assessed value that was to be added. The required documentation of actual investment value has been provided by the businesses to the San Marcos development coordinator. For five of the properties, however, the actual assessed value is approximately 60% below contract value; property assessment is centralized and administered by the Hays County Tax Appraisal District.

Table 1 San Marcos's Property Tax Abatement Contracts

Type of firm	Percentage of abatement	Years granted	Jobs required	Contract value	Assessed value
CTEC manufacturing	100%	4	400	$6,000,000	$4,200,000
HEB-wholesale	50%	2	135	3,100,000	2,000,000
HTA aerostructures/ ROHR	100%	5	468	8,000,000	3,400,000
Harper's Hall Retail	100%	5	15	350,000	229,000
Parkview Metals[c]	100%	3	200	2,000,000	1,200,000
San Marcos Factory Stores[a,c]	100%	5	401	[d]	5,900,000
Best Western motel	100%	2	10	2,200,000	2,200,000
Vanity Fair Factory Outlet[a,c]	100%	5	44	[b]	(unknown)
Central Texas Medical Center	100%	1	0	4,000,000	4,000,000

[a] To retain the rebate, a sliding scale of sales tax revenues was required that increased over the term of the contract. For San Marcos Factory Stores, the terms of the contract required sales tax revenue of $270,000 (year 1), $853,125 (year 2), $1,552,875 (year 3), and $2,252,625 (year 4); these revenue requirements have been exceeded.

[b] The abatement contract expired during the first year, as the business failed to report and provide documentation required.

[c] Denotes a phased-in job creation that increases over the life of the abatement contract to the total shown in the table.

[d] No contract value was specified for new property value to be created.

Source: Interview with economic director, city of San Marcos review of current San Marcos tax abatement contracts.

Factors Relevant to Tax Abatement

The availability and use of tax abatement as an economic development incentive can readily be assessed; it is the magnitude and direction of the net impact that is difficult to determine. Tax abatement has not been discussed or examined very much in the literature. The studies of the impact of tax abatement that do exist fail to systematically address the interrelationship of property tax abatement and assessment, and there has been virtually no attempt to use cost-effectiveness analysis to measure the nonmonetary impact of abatement. The interactive impact of tax abatement and economic development on jobs, net revenues, and relative tax burden is seldom systematically measured. Numerous studies have pointed to the lack of systematic analysis for measurement of the net impact of property tax abatement, and empirical evidence remains inconclusive. From an examination of the literature that specifically addresses property tax abatement, factors that might be used to more thoroughly analyze the impact were selected on the basis of three criteria: (1) the frequency with which economists and political scientists have suggested their importance; (2) the potential for enhancing the measurement of the net economic impact; and (3) nonmonetary factors with the potential for a negative or positive impact on expenditures and revenues dependent upon the outcome of economic development.

Factors that can be readily converted to monetary values for purposes of benefit/cost tax abatement analysis include assessment of the current tax base, net job creation, net revenue impact, interjurisdictional economic impact, current economic environment, interjurisdictional property tax rate differential, and infrastructure service capacity. Other factors, such as targeted contracts specific to the results of abatement analysis and the use of combined economic development incentives, can be directly determined. Spillover benefits and costs and environmental impact/utility demand are factors either directly or indirectly related to economic development that can, and should, be imputed, as they have the potential for a direct impact on expenditures and revenues as well as the quality of community life. Cost-effectiveness analysis, which imputes values to nonmonetary factors, can make explicit the intuitive reasoning of decision makers, improve outcomes, and allow a more accurate assessment.

While criteria for tax abatement decisions that are established by city ordinance (creation of five jobs, minimum of $50,000 property investment, recovery of property tax revenue, and conformance with the city's master plan) or state statute (enterprise zone automatic property and sales tax abatements) take precedence over other assessment factors, the factors currently in use in San Marcos seem somewhat limited in scope. Analysis of nonmonetary benefits is more difficult than those for which monetary values can easily be determined. The absence of direct monetary values, however, does not preclude the application of systematic analysis that will provide assistance in tax abatement decisions.

Application of Factors to San Marcos's Abatement Policies

The factors considered relevant for comprehensive analysis of the net impact of property tax abatement policies are now applied to San Marcos in order to evaluate their usefulness for assessment of benefits and costs of the property tax abatement and any resulting economic development.

Assessment of the current tax base status. The tax base is the source from which a city extracts all of its revenues; generally property taxes and sales taxes form the largest portions of a local tax base. As bond ratings for local communities are directly related to the size of the property tax base (measured by the assessed value), the accompanying debt to assessed property value ratio of all jurisdictions taxing the same base is a relevant factor. An increasing total debt to total assessed property value ratio for overlapping tax districts signals a declining economic situation. Unsuccessful abatement programs are more costly for localities with a declining tax base. The measurement of change with regard to property, income, sales, and revenue generation capabilities across time are also relevant to assessment of the current tax base status. Declining personal income levels may be a harbinger of decreasing property and sales tax revenues in the future.

In fiscal year FY 1990–1991, San Marcos's property values had fallen by $83 million, and property taxes were 31.8% of the revenue base. Sales taxes were 41.8% of the base. During the late 1980s, the city faced a declining property tax revenue situation, an increasing debt to assessed property value ratio, and even or declining sales tax revenues. Since initiation of the tax abatements, property taxes have not been increased, and the resulting economic growth has allowed the city to lower the effective property tax rate for 1993. By FY 1992–1993, property taxes had fallen to 19.6% of the revenue base, and sales taxes had increased to 52.68%, becoming the primary source of revenue for the city (City of San Marcos budget, 1993). The elasticity of the sales tax is higher than that of property taxes. The increased reliance on the sales tax creates a situation in which San Marcos's tax base will be more vulnerable in the future to a downturn in the macroeconomy.

The portion of San Marcos's property tax revenues going to debt service for infrastructure development has been reduced from 90–40% over the past 4 years, resulting in a significantly improved debt to assessed property value ratio. The change in effective city property tax rates may, however, have masked a significant change in the total effective tax rates created by the combined tax burdens of other overlapping jurisdictions, such as the San Marcos Consolidated Independent School District (SMCISD) and Hays County. The SMCISD has increased property taxes an average of 120% for 1993; county property taxes increased an average of 83% for 1993, producing an increased total debt to assessed property value ratio for the overlapping tax jurisdictions for 1994.

Assessment of the net job impact. For tax abatement to produce a net benefit, the net labor/capital ratio must change within the locality (i.e., the net jobs created must be measured as well as the net change in income per capita). Job offsets may occur when existing businesses lay off workers or close, producing no net change in jobs, or when low-wage jobs replace higher-wage positions, resulting in decreased capital in the community. The types of jobs created and salary levels are directly related to revenue change. Rather than increasing revenues, low-wage jobs may increase the fiscal burden due to a change in demand for social services.

The current level and trend in unemployment is also a relevant factor; attraction of firms that are labor-intensive will result in higher net economic gains in areas in which unemployment is high or increasing, offsetting abatement costs. Unemployment was high enough in San Marcos to receive the designation of an enterprise zone. CTEC, a manufacturing firm located in the designated enterprise zone, was required to create 400 jobs (with a minimum of 25% provided to enterprise zone residents) over the four-year life of the abatement contract. Over half of the current abatement contracts involve industries that are labor-intensive; the total CTEC job requirement constitutes 23.9% of all jobs created over the life of current San Marcos abatement contracts, constituting a labor-intensive enterprise in a high-unemployment area; the remainder involve retail trade, not considered labor-intensive industries and often involving low-wage positions. There is currently no mechanism in place to estimate jobs that are offsets to existing business layoffs or to determine the net wage impact, hence the net labor/capital ratio currently remains unmeasured. One way to measure the net job impact would be to use the Department of Commerce and Department of Labor unemployment, per capita income, and total jobs by sector of the economy data to estimate the net change in the labor/capital ratio.

Assessment of net revenue impact. Net revenue impact is the absolute change in tax revenue from all sources for the community. Effective property tax rates may mask the net revenue impact, and econometric models must be used to estimate the interactive effect of a change in the tax base relative to revenues from future property taxes, sales taxes, user fees, and other revenue sources. The benefits of the tax abatement should exceed the benefits of not granting the abatement measured in terms of net revenue change. Abatement analysis is also dependent upon the accuracy of assessment of property values; if inaccurate or arbitrary assessments are used, the estimate of net revenue loss or benefit will also be inaccurate.

When the surface cost of property tax revenues foregone is used as an indicator of outcome, the estimated cost of the property tax abatement contracts constitutes 5.1% of assessed value removed from the 1993 property tax base of $615,427,340 for nonexempt property in San Marcos. If all new properties are included at total contract, the cost of all abatements would be $1,906,561. A significant problem may occur in the future, however, when such abatements expire and property is again placed on the tax rolls. For the seven existing abatement contracts, five have been assessed at approximately 60% of the guaranteed contract value; the assessed valuation of the five properties is $17,029,000 below the actual investment and would result in an estimated revenue loss of $221,126 or 40% in future years. The CD for the five properties is 12.19, and the ratio of assessed to contract value ranges from a low of 0.425 for HTA to a high of 0.7 for CTEC. The variability of the assessments prohibits the accurate computation of benefit and cost estimates of the net impact on revenues.

At the current time, San Marcos has not performed a systematic analysis of the shift in tax burden that results from tax abatement. The equity of the tax burden is a relative measure of the business versus individual share and the balance of regressive versus progressive taxes as a source of revenue for the city. The increased city sales tax revenues have more than exceeded abatement contract specifications. Since the sales tax is generally regarded as substantially more regressive than the property tax, the increase in sales tax as a proportion of city revenue from 31.8% of the base in FY 1990–1991 to 52.68 in FY 1992–1993 would appear to indicate a shift toward a more regressive revenue burden.

For all but one of the contracts, San Marcos retains local control over the provisions and extent of tax abatement granted. For CTEC, the property tax abatement as well as the sales tax abatement and rebate is automatic due to the location of the business within the enterprise zone. There is currently no mechanism in place to determine the net revenue impact of CTEC's abatement. San Marcos used Bleakly's model to estimate the interactive impact on revenue prior to project approval and abatement, but net revenue change after abatement remains unmeasured.

Interjurisdictional economic impact analysis. The expected impact of tax abatement on interarea economic development is a relevant factor; economic development may be a zero sum game (i.e., what one jurisdiction loses, another gains), producing no net effect on the total welfare of the area and possibly resulting in a lack of cooperation with neighboring jurisdictions. Tax abatement may not be the appropriate tool in such circumstances. To measure the interjurisdictional economic impact the per capita income of the population, net change in the tax base, net jobs gained and lost, and number of new businesses/business closures for neighboring jurisdictions can be compared over several years before and after abatement contracts.

The San Marcos retail outlets are responsible for generating 27.5% of all new jobs required by the current abatement contracts. A large retail outlet mall located in New Braunfels, 16 miles from San Marcos, is in direct competition with the San Marcos Factory Stores for customers. Numerous stores are duplicated in both cities. For example, Welcome Home, a home decor shop, is located in the San Marcos Factory Stores, the San Marcos Tanger Outlet, and the New Braunfels outlet; Leggs/Hanes and Corning Revere as well as other stores are duplicated in the two communities. The interjurisdictional impact of San Marcos tax abatement policies has not been measured, but the foregoing would seem to indicate that some interjurisdictional transfer of revenues has occurred. It is clear that San Marcos has gained in sales tax revenue from the abatements granted to the large retail chains. What is not clear is whether or not nearby communities have lost an equivalent amount of sales tax resulting in a zero sum situation for the local area in general. Surface analysis of a tax base change fails to measure the exportability of the sales tax burden.

Interjuristictional property tax rate differential analysis. The tax rate differential is the standard deviation of tax rates of communities in close proximity to each other (i.e., with a range of 30 miles or less). The greater the tax differential between localities, the more likely a tax abatement program is to affect business location decisions if all other factors are relatively equal. If tax rates are relatively similar in nearby areas, however, abatement may not be the most effective economic development tool. Additionally, if the interlocational tax differentials are not quantitatively greater than the sum of differentials among other cost factors, such as labor, energy, and transportation, tax abatement may not be a significant factor influencing business location decisions.

Without tax abatement, the interjurisdictional property tax rates of the communities within the area (New Braunfels, Sequin, and San Marcos) vary less than $.05 per $100 of assessed value. On the surface, property tax abatement appears to increase the attractiveness of the business environment in San Marcos; however, the low interjurisdictional tax rate differential indicates that cost factors other than tax differentials should be examined, as they may be more important than abatement in the decision of a business to locate in San Marcos. Tax abatement may not be the most appropriate economic development tool when all factors are considered.

Evaluation of current local economic environment. The critical analysis involves weighing the assessment of how much the taxing jurisdiction can afford in abatement against the severity of the need for economic development. Assessment of the local economic environment can determine if the basis exists for development of an agglomeration economy that would attract particular types of business or industry; agglomeration economies are those with similar labor forces and support systems for a particular type of business. Agglomeration economies were found to be more significant than tax abatement as a factor relevant to economic development.

San Marcos uses highly sophisticated economic impact analysis (Bleakly's model) prior to making a tax abatement decision. The model is interactive and measures the direct and indirect impact of a project on a local economy as well as providing an estimate of the interactive tax impact (Bleakly, 1993; Ronson, 1993). Clear evidence exists of a greater diversification of services, jobs, and tax base in San Macros. It will take more time to determine the long-term net effects on the local economy. Assessment of the city's basis for development of an agglomeration economy currently is not formalized. A formalized assessment could provide a more accurate evaluation of the local economic environment and enhance the development of targeted abatement contracts.

Assessment of infrastructure service capacity. Projections of the level of traffic congestion, current and future growth patterns, demand for utilities, education facilities, police and fire protection, and other infrastructure and service capacity needs are relevant factors in computing the net costs or benefits of abatement policies. If the infrastructure and services are currently underutilized, a locality is in a better position to gain benefits from economic development. If the system is at maximum utilization levels, the additional demands may cause a net increase in property taxes. The smaller the property tax base, the more enhanced the impact of increased taxes will be.

Although the city makes every attempt to relate the demand for infrastructure and service to the expected development associated with an abatement contract, problems related to a strain on the existing San Marcos infrastructure have surfaced in recent months. Numerous letters have appeared in the daily paper indicating unacceptable levels of traffic congestion. The schools are at capacity, and a bond election for $17.3 million to build new schools and remodel existing facilities was passed in April of 1993, significantly increasing property taxes. The county (Hays) held a bond election for $18 million in November 1993 to finance needed renovations of existing roads and public buildings that are in a declining state of repair and maintenance in addition to building a new county records building, as current capacity is inadequate. These taxes will also increase significantly, as $13.4 of the bond issue (all parts except the new county records building) passed.

Clearly, San Marcos is not in a situation in which capacity of the infrastructure is underutilized, and present value analysis at various levels to estimate the cost for infrastructure and service development in the future is not part of the formalized abatement evaluation process. As overlapping jurisdictions compete for the revenues from the same tax base, a potential exists for the increase in tax burdens to outpace the ability of the revenue base to fund future infrastructure and service demands for the city, county, and school district. Revenue generation is more difficult in smaller, more rural communities with a high level of exempt property and numerous demands on the same tax base.

Estimate of spillover benefits/costs. Spillover benefits and costs are indirect or third-party costs that may be either tangible or intangible. The tangible or direct costs and benefits are more easily determined than are indirect benefits and costs, which must be estimated by some process. The desired level and type of development, the relationship to the master plan of the locality, the potential for attraction of other related economic development, the level of community change desired, and current and future growth patterns are relevant factors in computing the net costs or benefits of abatement policies. The absence of an absolute market value or efficiency measure should not preclude attempts to conceptualize tertiary effects that might occur as a result of economic development. Because of measurement difficulty, such spillover costs often are overlooked when assessing the net cost or benefit from tax abatement.

Economic development that results from tax abatement policies may be paid for by a lower level of public services or higher taxes. If a local jurisdiction reduces service levels as abatements are granted, the cost of the reduced service levels is a relevant factor. Indicators to measure potential spillover benefits and costs, such as changes in property usage, growth rates, and patterns, and demand for such government services as education and social assistance can be derived through cost-effectiveness analysis (i.e., imputing values on the basis of market prices for similar products at varying expectation levels). Weights can used to indicate the relative importance of the benefits and costs. Cost-benefit analysis can be used to estimate spillover benefits readily convertible to monetary values.

San Marcos informally evaluates the spillover benefits and costs of abatement decisions by requiring that projects mesh in objective, design, and public service demand with the master plan of the city. While the framework for cost-effectiveness analysis is in place, the process of estimating values not readily converted to a monetary value and providing a systematic ranking system for proposed projects has not been formalized to date. If estimates of the need for pubic service were formalized prior to evaluation of abatement decisions, cost/benefit projections could be considered in relation to future financing ability and the level of development desired. While benefits such as increased jobs, property improvements, and development that meets long-term city goals are considered by San Marcos when granting abatements, nonquantifiable spillover benefits and costs are not included systematically in the evaluation process.

Assessment of utility capacity and environmental impact. Economic development will affect the existing environmental balance and demand for utilities, particularly if energy is in short supply or the water supply is at risk. Rapid economic development of the wrong type can produce a negative outcome when demand for energy outpaces a city's current generation capacity or environmental factors produce an undesirable negative impact. Utility costs relative to other nearby locations can be readily determined and compared; changes in demand for utilities and the costs of meeting those demands can be estimated relative to the level and type of development that will be permitted or encouraged. The current capacity of solid landfills can be determined, and projections for capacity changes required to meet future needs can be estimated and evaluated relative to the costs associated with the type of development expected.

Cost-effectiveness analysis can be used to impute values and weight environmental factors that should be considered in assessing the impact of economic development. The level and type of economic development will have a potential impact on water quality, air pollution, hazardous or toxic waste levels, noise levels, and the use of natural resources such as parks and recreation areas. City officials, members of the community, and elected officials can identify all factors related to environmental impact that are considered to be important. The relative worth of each factor can be determined and a mathematical ranking of importance (a weight) assigned for each factor. The total weight of all factors should equal 100%. The acceptable level of risk can be predecided, and an assessment method can be developed and formally adopted. For example, any associated costs or benefits can be estimated at varying levels to reflect worst, expected, and best possible outcome that may result from economic development. If a positive benefit/cost ratio results for all estimation levels, the likelihood of a net positive outcome increases. The formal assessment process might require that positive benefit/cost ratios at all three levels are required prior to approval of an abatement contract. Having a formalized process for the assessment of environmental impact and a cost limitation for utility development can mitigate the potential for a negative outcome in the future as well as political problems that might develop.

San Marcos uses zoning ordinances to discourage development to the west of the city due to the environmentally sensitive nature of the Edwards aquifer recharge zone. The Edwards aquifer provides the primary source of water for the area and is at risk if too much development or the wrong type occurs. The energy supply is sufficient for most development, and concessions in utility rates are possible for certain abatement contracts. San Marcos also has ordinances in place to prevent development that involves hazardous waste that could adversely affect the water supply. Most recently, new city user fees were implemented to control environmentally sensitive waste. San Marcos also discourages the development of industries that involve intensive water usage. The request for tax abatement by DARE, a Canadian cookie and candy manufacturer requiring high water usage was denied by the city; the Toronto-based firm elected not to locate in San Marcos. No firm denied a tax abatement has located in San Marcos. While San Marcos computes the surface costs of increased utility requirements and considers the impact of development on the environment, cost-effectiveness analysis has not been formalized to assess the net impact of economic development on the local environment, and acceptable utility development cost schedules have not been adopted as part of the assessment process.

Targeted contract specific to the results of the analysis. If city abatement policy ordinances permit flexibility, contracts can be customized on the basis of benefit/ cost and cost-effectiveness analysis to enhance the possibility of a net gain from tax abatement. A targeted contract that tailors each abatement contract to a community's specific attributes to attract a particular type of industry or economic development has been found to be more effective than uniform abatement policies. The high cost of obtaining accurate information regarding business location sites is often overlooked by communities. The ability to bear such costs increases with a firm's size. A city can tailor recruitment efforts to attract the desired type of industry and development and may attract the desired businesses by lowering the cost of locational choice.

San Marcos's abatement ordinance does permit flexibility and the development of targeted abatement contracts. City officials preselect and target firms for recruitment on the basis of SIC codes, the percentage of income generated, the number of employees, and the type of industry. Generally, the targeted industries are those that would mesh with the master plan, provide the most new jobs, and reak the least environmental impact or hazardous waste. Abatement contracts are customized on a firm- or industry-specific basis on the basis of systematic analysis and use of Bleakly's interactive model.

Use of combined economic development incentives. Evidence indicates that tax abatement is a more effective tool when used in conjunction with targeting, recruitment teams, and a combination of economic development incentives. Tax abatement policies alone may not significantly influence business locational decisions. Although the property tax rate may affect firm locational choice, other factors, such as workforce size and price, safety, public services, education, agglomeration economies, population density, and per capita income, may be more important.

San Marcos has been actively engaged in economic development, particularly promoting tourism with the establishment of a local tourist bureau and other

connected services in 1987, hiring a development coordinator in 1991, and contracting with the chamber of commerce to actively pursue and carry out business
recruitment activities. San Marcos combines targeting, active recruitment, customized abatement contracts, and enterprise zone designation in pursuit of economic
development. City recruitment teams also work in cooperation with other organizations, such as the Lower Colorado River Authority (LCRA) and the Association
of Wholesale Customers, visiting firms targeted for recruitment. The mayor and
city manager often serve on the recruitment teams. Most of this recruitment activity occurs in the Northeast and on the West Coast. Clearly, the efforts have been
successful in attracting the type of business desired by the city (i.e., retail trade
and clean manufacturing) (Ronson, May 23 and June 1, 1993; Gilley, 1993).

SUMMARY AND CONCLUSION

The current case study revealed that the net impact of San Marcos tax abatement policies
cannot be readily determined from assessment of the criteria of number of new jobs,
investment, and coordination with the master plan included in the city ordinance. More
comprehensive criteria coupled with cost-effectiveness analysis would enhance the analysis of the potential impact of tax abatement decisions. In San Marcos, the framework
exists for the application of cost-effectiveness analysis to factors not easily converted to
monetary values; such analysis could increase the possibility that local tax abatement
produced net gains for the community over time and that the local citizens would be
satisfied with both the level and type of development. Although the city considers abatement contracts in light of the master plan, the failure to systematically assess spillover
benefits and costs, net job impact, infrastructure and service demands at varying expectation levels, and net revenue impact increases the risk of an adverse situation developing
in the future.

The case study revealed that the sales tax has greatly expanded and the required
number of jobs were created. The net job impact and change in labor/capital ratio, however,
is unmeasured. The city property tax base is improving with regard to the debt to assessed
value ratio and effective tax rates. The impact on interjurisdictional competition and the
overlapping tax base is currently unmeasured. In the San Marcos case, the competition
of the school district and county for the same tax base and accompanying infrastructure
service demands may produce a debt to assessed property value ratio that improves for
the city while increasing the property tax burden in general in other overlapping jurisdictions. The underassessment of the majority of property included in the city abatement
contracts precludes compilation of accurate benefit cost measures and creates a potentially
negative impact on property tax revenues when those properties are once again included
on city tax rolls. Expansion of the revenue base through job creation and investment may,
however, continue to stabilize or improve the tax base.

San Marcos has accomplished a significant diversification of the tax and job base
through the use of a variety of economic development activities and targeting of abatement
contracts. San Marcos is also in good shape with regard to local control of abatement as
the state enabling legislation allows broad local discretion rather than providing uniform
abatement provisions. Local control allows cities to make the most judicious use of tax
concessions. Tax abatement decisions can be customized on the basis of thorough analysis;
clearly the city is on the right track with regard to targeted abatement decisions and

contracts. Evaluation of the potential impact of the economic development relative to the capital improvement or master plan for infrastructure is critical to a city the size of San Marcos, and the city is clearly on the right track in this area. Although cost-effectiveness analysis is not systematically used by San Marcos to evaluate spillover costs and benefits in abatement decisions, planning and budgeting decisions could more effectively be combined with economic development decisions as additional criteria are formalized.

While the empirical jury remains out and one cannot generalize from a case study, tax abatement does appear to be a cost-effective economic development tool when coupled with other economic incentives and awarded on a case-specific basis after thorough analysis. With the broad local discretion allowed, cities such as San Marcos are limited in their approaches to economic development only by the level of their creative ability and current fiscal status. Systematic evaluation coupled with cost-effectiveness analysis and a diversified and innovative approach to encourage economic development can assure that the current fiscal status remains solid, allowing for the most productive use of economic development incentives matched to community need.

REVIEW QUESTIONS

1. What would you judge are the most significant factors that should be included in a conceptual framework for evaluation of the impact of tax abatement on economic development?
2. Where should future evaluation efforts and empirical studies be directed to provide a greater understanding of the impact of tax abatements and concessions on economic development?
3. Are the factors included in this case study valid benefit and cost or cost-effectiveness criteria for evaluation of the net impact of tax abatement?
4. How can tax abatement policies further impede the property tax assessment process, and what problems may result?
5. What additional factors should San Marcos include in the tax abatement evaluation process to improve the analysis and decision making and avoid the potential for future problems?
6. What benefits or costs can be associated with the failure to use systematic analysis as a basis for tax abatement decisions?

REFERENCES

Benker, K. M. (Dec. 1986). Tax expenditure reporting: Closing the loophole in state budget Oversight. *National Tax Journal, 39,* 403–417.

Bland, R. L. (1989). *A Revenue Guide for Local Government.* Washington, DC: ICMA. See especially Chapter 9, "Taxes and Economic Development: Finding the Balance, pp. 153–180.

Bleakly, K. D. Jr. (1993). *Economic Impact Analysis: Assessing a Project's Value to a Community.* Rosemont, IL: American Economic Development Council.

City of San Marcos 1992–93 Budget.

Directory of Incentives for Business Investment and Development in the United States. (1991). Washington, DC: Urban Institute Press.

Edwards, K. K. (Aug. 1988). "Reporting for tax expenditures and tax abatement." *Government Finance Review, 4,* 13–17.

Enterprise Zone Program. (1989). City of San Marcos.

Gilley, L. (June 1, 1993). City Manager, San Marcos. interview.

Taylor M. and Ash, D. B. eds. (1990). *Meeting Business Attraction, Business Retention, and industrial Development Goals: Tools That Work.* Washington, DC: ICMA.

Mikesell, J. (1991). *Fiscal Administration Analysis and Applications for the Public Sector.* Pacific Grove, CA: Brooks/Cole.

Policy on Tax Abatement and other Economic Development Incentives for the City of San Marcos, Texas (1993).

Ronson, B. (1993). Economic director, City of San Marcos. interviews. May 23 and June.

49

Financing a Recycling Facility Through a Public–Private Partnership

Patrick W. Manion†
City of Phoenix, Arizona, U.S.A.

Many municipalities across the United States are implementing recycling programs in response to public concerns about the environment. Through recycling programs, citizens can help select which materials can be remanufactured and recirculated in the marketplace. Through their participation in recycling programs, citizens also are able to reduce the amount of refuse that must be sent to solid waste disposal facilities. These recycling programs, however, are expensive to operate.

When the city of Phoenix decided to implement a citywide curbside recycling program in January 1991, the Public Works Department recommended a state-of-the-art system requiring residents only to separate perishable items from nonperishable items. All source separation would be done through a high technology process at a materials recycling facility. As part of its plans for this facility, the Public Works Department suggested a public–private partnership to keep costs to a minimum. Under this partnership concept, the city of Phoenix would contract with a private firm to build and operate the materials recycling facility and pay a fee to the private firm to process the recyclable materials, but also share in the revenues generated through sale of the recyclable products.

The planned implementation of the recycling program over a five-year period was linked to the scheduled closing of the city's 27th Avenue landfill in fiscal year 1993–1994. Following the closure of the landfill, the Public Works Department will bring solid waste material from the southern half of Phoenix to a new transfer station. The solid waste then would be hauled by tractor-trailer from the transfer station to more remote landfills. By timing the start-up of the citywide recycling program to coincide generally with the opening of the transfer station, the Public Works Department will be able to reduce significantly the amount of solid waste that must be long hauled to distant landfills.

This case study will follow the development of the public–private partnership through a competitive request for proposals (RFP) process leading to the selection of New England CRInc. as the firm offering to build and operate the most cost-effective materials recycling facility. The negotiation process and final contract with New England CRInc. will be analyzed to determine the net financial impact to the city of Phoenix. The specific terms of the agreement will be examined to focus on the operational stipulations that help ensure that the facility can be profitable, while safeguarding the city of Phoenix revenue

---

† Deceased.

stream from extreme fluctuations in the market. Finally, the case study will review the total cost of the city of Phoenix's recycling program as it affects the overall solid waste collection and disposal system and its net impact on the service fee paid by residents.

EVALUATING THE PROPOSALS

The RFP process was designed to allow continuing review and negotiation by a multidisciplinary evaluation team, comprising representatives of the Public Works Department, Finance Department, Budget and Research Department, Community and Economic Development Department, Law Department, and citizen members. The various city department representatives were selected for their detailed knowledge of the solid waste collection and disposal operations, expertise in evaluating the economic benefits of public—private partnerships, understanding of the city's financial and budgeting systems, and experience in preparing legal contracts. The citizen members, representing the general public, previously had served on the Solid Waste Subcommittee of the 1988 Citizens Bond Committee that had successfully promoted a $1 billion citywide capital improvement program approved by the voters.

Narrowing the Field

Five private firms responded to the RFP: Browning-Ferris Inc. (BFI), Multi-Compact, New England CRInc., Waste Management, and Why Waste America. After the initial review of the five proposals, two firms, Multi-Compact and Why Waste America, were eliminated from further consideration by the evaluation team. The evaluation team concluded that these two firms did not meet the base criteria of having sufficient experience and expertise in running large-scale recycling programs, and proven financial resources to undertake building and operating a materials recycling facility. The remaining three firms all scored high on these criteria.

The evaluation team then requested the remaining three firms to respond to a series of questions to provide additional information and clarify their proposals. At this stage of the process, the evaluation team focused their review on the following seven criteria:

Processing fee.   The firms offered competitive rates for processing the recyclable materials sent to the processing facility. This rate formed the primary cost charged to the city of Phoenix.

Guaranteed minimum floor prices.   When projecting the revenues that would be generated from the sale of recyclable products, the proposals included a guaranteed minimum floor price. This guarantee established the base revenues that the city of Phoenix could receive even if there were a sharp drop in the recyclable products market prices.

Net operating cost to the city of Phoenix.   The proposals required that the city of Phoenix would get 25% of all revenues. The net revenues gained will be determined by fixing the processing fee minus the revenue generated. The revenues will be calculated by showing a range from the anticipated level of sales to the guaranteed minimum floor price.

Residue.   The firms were asked in their proposals to try and meet a residue level of 1% or less. This level refers to the amount of recyclable materials that cannot be sorted and marketed.

Type of sorting equipment.   The proposals included a description of the technology that would be used in the recycling materials facility.

Facility availability.   The firms were asked to include in their proposals when they could have an interim facility in place, how quickly they could build a permanent facility, and when it could be ready for full operation.

Educational component.   The firms were asked to include an educational component in their proposals. Specifically, they were asked to include a viewing room and educational opportunities for free tours by schools and public groups at the permanent facility.

Comparing the Finalists

Following the detailed examination of the remaining three proposals, the evaluation team further narrowed the field by eliminating Waste Management, primarily due to an inadequate financial package offer.

The evaluation team asked the final two firms, BFI and New England CRInc., to submit their "best and final" offer. The evaluation of the best and final offers emphasized the net financial impact to the city of Phoenix. Both firms' proposals were judged to offer quality materials recycling facility operations. While the two firms prepared their revised proposals, members of the evaluation team toured existing BFI and New England CRInc. recycling facilities in other cities.

The financial analysis of the two best and final offers for the first five years of operation are summarized in Table 1.

Even though they offered much higher guaranteed minimum floor prices, assuring the city of Phoenix more revenues for recyclable products when market prices were down, BFI's basic processing fee was substantially greater than the New England CRInc. proposal. For the five-year period, the processing fee charged by New England CRInc, including inflation allowances, averaged $16.46 per ton, compared to $31.53 per ton for BFI. The cost difference was so significant that the net operating costs became the dominant criteria used in the evaluation. Other major differences between the two bids showed an

Table 1   Phoenix Materials Recycling Facility Cost Comparison of Final Proposals for First Five Years of Operation (in Thousands of Dollars)

Operating costs	BFI		New England CRInc.	
	Projected revenues	Minimum revenues	Projected revenues	Minimum revenues
Processing costs based on 272,000 tons of material	$8,602	$8,602	$4,489	$4,489
City revenues based on 25% share and 80% of materials sold:				
Projected revenues	3,105		3,141	
Guaranteed minimum		2,279		508
Net processing costs	$5,497	$6,323	$1,348	$3,981
Other facility expenses	289	289	344	344
Total operating costs	$5,786	$6,612	$1,692	$4,325

advantage for the BFI proposal that called for building a permanent facility in 180 days, compared to 322 days for New England CRInc.; and an edge to the New England CRInc. proposal that included installation of the more automated high technology Bezner sorting equipment.

Based on the overall superiority of its proposal in meeting the established criteria, the evaluation team recommended that the city of Phoenix contract with New England CRInc. to build and operate the materials recycling facility.

NEGOTIATING THE FINAL CONTRACT

In July 1991, the Phoenix City Council authorized the Public Works Department to negotiate with New England CRInc. to develop a final contract for the materials recycling facility. The contract negotiations took several months to complete. In October 1991, the Natural Resources Subcommittee approved the basic terms of an agreement with New England CRInc. This agreement was completed and ratified by the full Phoenix City Council in January 1992.

The final agreement differed slightly from the earlier RFP. During the negotiation process, as terms became more specific, adjustments were made to the final contract language. The net operating costs, however, were within 5% of the original RFP offer.

Establishing Basic Terms of the Agreement

The terms of the agreement provided for an initial contract period of five and one-half years, ending in June 1997. Two five-year renewal options are included. If the city of Phoenix does not exercise the first five-year option, however, a buyout clause would be activated. This provision was set so New England CRInc. has the ability to amortize its equipment costs. The buyout clause requires the city of Phoenix to pay New England CRInc. a lease cost estimated at $200,000 annually, or buyout of the lease for an estimated $1.2 million. The city of Phoenix also would pay $3.76 million for New England CRInc.'s equipment if the average of three appraisals is within 15% of this amount; otherwise the payment would be the average appraisal.

The agreement set the location of the facility in a south Phoenix industrial area with proper zoning. The agreement also called for an interim facility to be in operation within fifteen weeks after the contract was signed and to have a permanent facility with a required investment of $5 million in equipment in place eight months later. The facility has been built to handle a maximum capacity of 90,000 tons of recyclable materials annually. The city of Phoenix committed to bringing a minimum of 13,250 tons to this facility annually, but projected sending near-capacity amounts by the end of the first five-year period. The city will pay a processing fee beginning at $51 per ton and decreasing to $9.79 per ton as the amount of materials increase.

The recyclable materials that will be accepted for processing at the materials recycling facility are specified. They include such items as cardboard, aluminum, ferrous metals, bulk metal, plastic milk and water jugs, soda bottles, plastic food containers, paper, textiles, polystyrene, and glass.

The agreement differentiates among rejects, residue, and potentially recyclable materials. Rejects include all material that is contaminated or otherwise cannot be processed. The city of Phoenix agreed that rejects delivered to the center would be decreased from a maximum of 20–10% over the first few years of operation. Residue refers to recyclable materials that are not processed or marketed. New England CRInc. stipulated that residue would be kept to 1% or less. It will pay a penalty for residue exceeding this level. Potentially recyclable materials were defined in the agreement as that which may be recyclable but has no known market. The city of Phoenix will pay New England CRInc. a fee to collect this material while efforts are made to find a suitable market for the products.

Other key terms included in the agreement are as follows:

Commodity sales price. The city of Phoenix will receive 25% of the sales revenues, estimated to be $55 per ton. During the first and second five-year renewal option periods, the 25% share figure may be negotiated up or down, depending on market conditions.

Guaranteed minimum floor prices. The agreement includes a minimum floor price for certain key commodities that guarantees the city of Phoenix a base revenue stream regardless of fluctuations in the marketplace.

Restricted use of facility. The city of Phoenix has exclusive use of the facility to process its recyclable products. With the permission of the city of Phoenix, New England CRInc. may accept materials from other cities or commercial haulers. If it does, however, the city will receive a credit of $2.50 per ton for materials deposited from other cities and $5.00 per ton for material received from commercial operations.

Performance bond. New England CRInc. was required by the agreement to post an irrevocable letter of credit by a bank approved by the city of Phoenix for $3 million.

Educational center. New England CRInc. will provide a visitor and viewing area at the permanent facility, and personnel on a limited basis to conduct tours for school groups and other interested parties.

ANALYZING THE FINANCIAL IMPACT

Detailed cost projections were prepared showing the operating costs and revenues for a ten-year period ending in 2001. The processing costs charged to the city of Phoenix for this period are estimated of $9.94 million. These costs will be offset by revenues ranging from $2.14 million to $7.5 million. The wide range in revenue estimates stems from the minimum guaranteed to the projected level, assuming reasonable market prices being available for the recyclable products. These cost and revenue projections are displayed in Figure 1.

As part of the financial analysis for this facility, Public Works calculated the impact the materials recycling facility will have on landfill expenses. This analysis projected the cost of continuing to dispose of the solid waste materials through landfilling. As discussed earlier, the costs of landfill disposal will increase sharply with the scheduled closure of the 27th Avenue landfill requiring the solid waste material to be processed first at the new transfer station before being finally transported to remote landfills. The cost avoidance for *not* transporting the recyclable material to the landfill through the transfer station was estimated at $14.6 million. Figure 2 compares the net city minimum and projected costs of operating the materials recycling facility to the estimated landfilling costs.

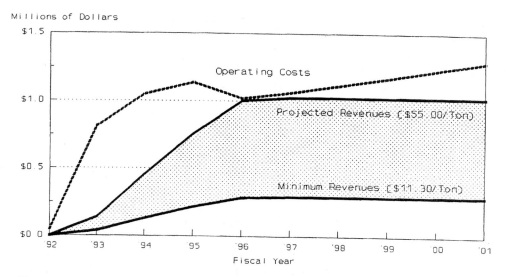

Figure 1 Operating costs compared to minimum and projected revenues, Phoenix Material Recycling Facility.

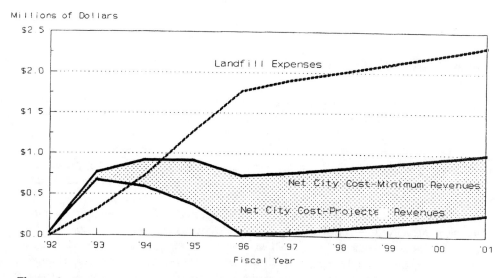

Figure 2 Net operating costs compared to landfilling expenses, Phoenix Materials Recycling Facility.

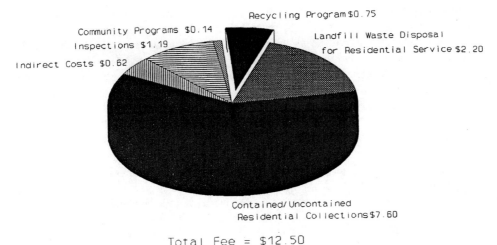

Figure 3 Impact of cost of recycling program on Phoenix solid waste residential fee.

Reviewing the Residential Fee

A primary objective for entering the public–private partnership with New England CRInc. was to keep the net operating costs for the materials recycling facility to a minimum. The overall recycling program was estimated to cost $2.6 million in 1992–1993. Of this total, between $676,000 and $774,000 will be attributable to the materials recycling facility. The total residential solid waste collection and disposal program will cost $43.7 million. This equates to a $12.50 residential fee to fully recover all costs. The recycling portion of the cost, as shown in Figure 3, is $.75, or 6% of the total. The net operating cost of the materials recycling facility represents $.21 of this fee.

ADDRESSING IMPLEMENTATION ISSUES

Following the opening of the permanent materials recycling facility in April 1993, Public Works began addressing some implementation problems that were occurring. The new high technology equipment in the permanent facility, while operating properly and efficiently, is very sensitive and requires the recyclable material to have low levels of contamination.

The level of recyclable materials contamination from the residents in the first several phases of the recycling program was higher than anticipated. Based on results from extended pilot area tests, Public Works had predicted a contamination level of 15% or less. While a number of the neighborhoods were recording levels of contamination of 3% or less, some neighborhoods were experiencing 40–50%. The issue of contamination has created some contractual disputes between New England CRInc. and the city of Phoenix that are still being negotiated at press time.

The problem areas primarily were less affluent, older neighborhoods with alley pickup. Under the Phoenix mechanized collection system, residents having alley pickup are serviced by 300-gallon containers that are shared by three or four homes. Residents having street pickup have individual 90 or 60-gallon containers. Compliance with the recycling guidelines has proven to be much easier with street pickup routes. A possible solution to this problem will be to shift some alley pickup to street pickup, but this is more costly and unpopular with some residents.

Another problem emerging from the implementation of the recycling program is the issue of the nonparticipant fee. The original program financial projections anticipated that residents who chose not to participate in the recycling program would be charged an extra $3.50 per month. This charge would cover the cost of sending a special truck to make a second pickup. Residents in the recycling program receive each week one pickup using a green barrel for nonrecyclable goods and a second pickup using a blue barrel for recyclable material. Residents who want two nonrecyclable (green barrel) pickups cause Public Works to schedule additional routes.

The implementation of the nonparticipant fee was dropped, pending further review after a number of residents expressed concern at public hearings related to proposed changes in the city's solid waste ordinance. After considering the public reaction, Public Works decided that it would be better to emphasize education to encourage participation rather than use punitive measures calling for increased fees for nonparticipants. Suspension of the fee, however, has reduced the revenue estimates by over $100,000 in 1992–1993. One solution to this problem under consideration is to offer an incentive discount to those who *do* participate in the recycling program at the time of the next solid waste increase.

SUMMARY AND CONCLUSION

The case study documents how the city of Phoenix used a public–private partnership to build and operate a materials recycling facility. Through an innovative application of guaranteed minimum floor prices. Phoenix was able to determine fairly accurately a base level of revenues that would be realized from the facility operations. This enabled city management to be able to predict maximum operating costs to compare with expenses otherwise required to dispose of the same material through traditional landfilling. This level of accuracy in financial projections helped to assure elected officials that the proposed system would provide a significant cost avoidance for the solid waste fund.

Additional experience with the implementation of more homes as part of the recycling program will help address any potential problems with contamination. Through better education and enforcement efforts, combined with residents becoming more familiar and comfortable with the recycling procedures, the problems in time may be mitigated, at least partially. It is apparent, however, that more inspectors probably will be needed to fully monitor the problem and control the contamination of recyclable materials. If this happens, the cost estimates will have to be increased by up to $200,000 annually.

REVIEW QUESTIONS

1. What type of expertise did the department representatives on the evaluation team have that helped them to critique all aspects of the proposals from the private firms to build and operate the materials recycling facility?
2. What were the key criteria used to evaluate the proposals?

3. What is the importance of the guaranteed floor prices in evaluating the financial feasibility of the project?
4. What are the terms of the buyout clause and why is it important for New England CRInc. to have this provision in the contract?
5. Why is there a cost avoidance achieved by taking recyclable products to the materials recycling facility rather than to landfills?
6. What is the net operating cost of the materials recycling facility and how does this compare to the overall cost of the recycling program and to the total solid waste fee paid by residents?
7. What are some of the problems that are being addressed during implementation of the recycling program, and what are some possible solutions to these problems?

REFERENCE

Jensen, R. W. (Jan. 15, 1992). Recyclable materials processing facility agreement. *City of Phoenix City Council Report.*

50

The Chickens Come Home to Roost
The Publicization of Private Infrastructure

Ellen Rosell*
University of Central Florida, Orlando, Florida, U.S.A.

Infrastructure partnerships with developers are powerful incentives in political arenas. For governments driven by fiscal constraints, partnerships provide viable resources for funding the infrastructure that supports community and economic development. For political office-holders and government managers intent on "reinventing government," they offer opportunities for demonstrating entrepreneurial leadership. For both public and private partners, the partnership alludes to increased value in property taxes and in real estate profits from the developed land.

This case study is about a thirty-year public–private partnership in infrastructure that failed its community. The private partner, frequently described by the national media as "one of Florida's most respected and reputable developers," declared bankruptcy and abandoned its infrastructure commitments. The public partner, Palm Bay, Florida, has inherited 580 miles of deteriorating roads and an erratically developed water and sewer system. The majority of the developer's 83,000 home sites depend upon onsite sewage disposal systems that are contributing to high levels of pollutants in groundwaters and canals flowing into a nearby river (Sherman, 1991; Worzalla, 1991).

The extensive theoretical and empirical literature on privatization pays scant attention to the reversal of responsibility for service delivery from private suppliers back to the public partner. There is no term available in the literature for the public undertaking or publicization of a private delivery system. How does a public partner, a municipality, assume responsibility for a failed private infrastructure enterprise? What strategies evolve as municipal leaders negotiate with tax-resistant yet service-demanding citizens in a growing community?

The study initially outlines the historical and contextual underpinnings of public–private partnerships in infrastructure development. The following section describes the evolution of the city's partnership with the private developer, the impacts of county and state policy decisions on the partnership, and the private partner's legacies. The concluding section discusses the challenges to the city in undertaking its former partner's delivery system.

---

* Current Affiliation: New Mexico State University, Las Cruce, New Mexico, U.S.A.

UNDERPINNINGS OF PUBLIC–PRIVATE INFRASTRUCTURE PARTNERSHIPS

Public works, or the more current term, infrastructure, has long been publicly provided by local governments and privately produced by developers. Residents of early cities relied on privately owned wells and privies with "sewage disposal left to the Almighty—who had thoughtfully provided rain, gravity, and buzzards" (Aldrich, 1979: F.23). In the late 1800s increasing population density and outbreaks of typhoid, cholera, and other diseases prodded concerns with public health and pressured municipalities into constructing water-works and sewer systems. By the early 1900s municipalities owned and operated the urban core infrastructure: streets, roads, bridges, water and sewer systems, and sewage treatment facilities. Suburban growth in the 1920s prompted localities into enacting zoning ordinances and subdivision regulations to cope with exurban infrastructure demands (Aldrich, 1979; Tarr, 1984).

The courts and the federal government blessed local controls over land use policy in the interest of providing for the community's health, safety, and welfare. In *Village of Euclid* v. *Ambler Realty Company* (1926), the Supreme Court upheld zoning as within municipal police powers "to determine their own desired land use patterns as long as it stood the test of being reasonable for the public interest" (Smith, 1991: 80). Model enabling acts proposed in the late 1920s by Herbert Hoover while secretary of commerce encouraged states to delegate planning and zoning controls to local boards and recommended requiring physical improvements to the land as prerequisites to plot approval.

Physical improvements to the land, commonly referred to as exactions, emerged in conjunction with the local land regulations of the 1920s. Exactions have generally included physical facilities that the developer constructs or dedicates land to or makes payments for in lieu of their building. Developers have come to expect communities to demand exactions as quid pro quo for project approvals. Nelson (1988: 118) noted the development of municipal–developer partnerships as early as the 1940s: "the community would provide central facilities, main lines, and roads to an area, while the developer would extend services to each lot or home in the development at his cost."

In the past three decades declining federal funding, minimal state involvement, and a tax-resistant public have pressured local governments into a variety of infrastructure arrangements with developers to support community development and redevelopment projects. Current local exaction policies either mandate or negotiate nonfiscal and fiscal infrastructure provisions ranging from physical improvements and franchises to land dedications for schools and parks, impact fees for off-site public facilities, and linkages for social welfare projects (Alter man, 1988; Catanese, 1988). The majority of communities, 88% of cities, counties, and common entities, rely on partnerships with private developers to supply their new roads, water and sewer lines, and drainage systems (Purdum and Frank, 1987).

THE PALM BAY PARTNERSHIP

Located on Florida's east coast, Palm Bay dates to an 1850s river village, but it experienced little growth until General Development Corporation (GDC) began its real estate development project in the area. GDC's Palm Bay development was one of 115 new communities emerging in Florida during the 1950s. Typically located on undeveloped land in areas outlying municipal boundaries, they encompassed approximately 1 million acres and were projected to contain over 2 million dwellings and an estimated 6 million residents by 1985. GDC planned the development of the largest number of acres, 236,450, involving nine communities for over a million people ("New Community," 1974).

Targeting the retiree market, particularly military personnel and residents of the Northeast, GDC offered free house hunting trips with one-stop shopping for lots, homes, mortgages, and appraisals. Attracted by land, housing opportunities, and sunshine, Palm Bay's population grew from 6750 in 1970 to 18,560 in 1980. By the early 1990s Palm Bay was the largest city in the county, in land size with over 65 square miles and in population with over 70,000 residents. Today Palm Bay's population is second only to Orlando in the central Florida area.

Local Provision/Public Production

As had older American cities of the 1920s, Palm Bay assumed responsibility for land use and infrastructure early in its history. The town of Palm Bay appointed a building committee at its first council meeting in September 1956 and a zoning committee at the second meeting in October. By November it was delivering basic infrastructure services: "four trucks, a grader and a drag line (were) ready to move marl for the necessary repair of rain damaged streets. A sum of fifty loads were hauled and graded into the various locations, free of charge to the property owners" (Palm Bay Town/City Council Meeting [PBT/CCM], Nov. 8, 1956). The free services certainly attracted good community relations as a resident "reported that people on his street, who were originally against the incorporation of the Town of Palm Bay, were inquiring as to who was repairing the street, and was informed that the Town of Palm Bay was repairing said street" (PBT/CCM, Nov. 8, 1956). The zoning and planning committee soon recommended the purchase of "additional maps showing subdivisions and plats within the city limits in order that we may intelligently recommend commercial and industrial sites" (PBT/CCM, July 18, 1957). The town's earliest ordinances focused on electrical and plumbing codes and construction standards for "water closets."

Local Provision/Private Production

Palm Bay's partnership with GDC began in May 1959 when the mayor reported a visit from a GDC representative who was "very agreeable and would like the whole area to be included in the Town of Palm Bay, approximately 100,000 acres to be developed" (PBT/CCM, May 7, 1959). In November 1959 the town council granted a thirty-year franchise to GDC with "the exclusive right and privilege to erect, construct, operate, and maintain a water and sewage collection and disposal" (Palm Bay Ordinance no. 31). The agreement specified "the town" would "fix rates and charges." The council meetings reflected early, amiable relationships between the city and its private partner. The city approved GDC subdivision projects and accepted its streets for permanent maintenance. The developer sold land at cost to the city for a "disposal area" and set aside over 1000 acres of land for parks and schools.

In the mid-1960s tensions in the partnership began surfacing due to the growing community. The private utility refused to expand water services to areas not included in the original franchise agreement and requested increases in water rates, claiming operating deficits. The city threatened to take over the private utility or to contract with a nearby city for water services due to complaints about the water quality and "extremely high water rates" (PBT/CCM, Nov. 18, 1965). The city initiated a condemnation case against the utility company in late 1965 that it eventually withdrew after negotiations with the corporation (GDC, Feb. 8, 1967) and the election of city council members who evidently were more favorably inclined toward GDC interests (Diamond, 1991). City council meetings and internal documents cite inquiries into the 1980s from property owners requesting hookups to the GDC water and sewage systems.

County Provision/Private Production

In 1963 the state legislature passed a special act authorizing the county to regulate privately owned water and sewage utility companies operating in the county's unincorporated areas (Chapter 63–699). The county initiated its regulatory program in 1965, but acknowledged "the program has met strong opposition from several utility companies" (Dept. of Environmental Health, 1965). In 1968 the county health department and GDC negotiated an agreement allowing the delay of sewer system installation until two-thirds of the lots on a block had septic tanks.

GDC could then selectively concentrate on providing services. Deeds with owners, often planning their lots for retirement homes, committed the company to physical improvements at future dates, generally at ten-to-fifteen-year time periods. GDC grouped its lot sales according to commitment years on deeds and dispersed its home sales among blocks within the county's two-thirds limitation for septic tank usage. The scattered growth patterns, ranging from a single home in a ten-block area to subdivisions with 100% lot occupancy, enabled GDC to leapfrog its water and sewer lines to predetermined sites while bypassing or jumping over other areas.

Future commitments with lot owners for utility services were not always honored. A GDC representative commented: "There are some platted units with commitment years that have passed and in which GDU [General Development Utilities] does not serve any customers. Where this is the case, it is due to the fact that no service has been requested in those areas" (Palm Bay Comprehensive Plan [PBCP], 1981: 6–6). In lieu of GDC-provided water and sewer systems, the majority of home sites came to rely on private wells and septic tanks.

State Provision/Private Production

In the 1970s and 1980s Florida passed ambitious legislation intending to regulate and coordinate land use with population growth and infrastructure needs. The Environmental Land and Water Management Act of 1972 (Land Management Act, Chapter 380) required reviews by regional planning agencies of developments with regional impact (DRI) on the environment or on local public services. Comprehensive land use plans addressing growth and infrastructure problems and needs were mandated for the state in 1972, for counties and municipalities in 1975, and for regional areas in 1980. Revisions in 1985 to the Local Government Comprehensive Planning Act of 1975 (LGCPA) mandating local comprehensive land use plans required that all necessary infrastructure be in place concurrent with new development.

The Land Management Act of 1972, however, had included a major loophole for private developers. Any project authorized by registration, recordation, or building permit prior to the act's July 1973 implementation date was exempted from DRI provisions. The

LGCPA of 1975 also referred to the act in defining developments and excused these projects from consistency with local comprehensive plans. GDC's Palm Bay community, along with its other statewide projects initiated prior to July 1973, qualified for these provisions. Exempted from compliance with Florida's growth management legislation and Palm Bay's comprehensive land use plans and blessed by its agreement with the county health department, GDC maintained its policy of delaying or leapfrogging the city's roads and water and sewer delivery system throughout the 1980s.

Demise of the Private Partner

In 1990 GDC claimed Chapter 11 bankruptcy protection after federal prosecutors charged the company with fraud and conspiracy in its Florida real estate projects. Described as "one of the largest and most complex bankruptcies in U.S. history" ("Scaled-down," 1992), GDC's bankruptcy reorganization plan was approved with provisions that the company would pay off its creditors with notes and stock in its newly organized corporation, Atlantic Gulf Communities. Banks could expect 78 cents on the dollar; homeowners, 27.8 cents; bondholders, 2.4 cents; and former stockholders, nothing. Cities, counties, and water districts with more than $400 million in claims for back taxes, liens, stromwater fees, and repairs for unfinished roads and sewer and drainage problems objected to the reorganization plan as the Florida Constitution barred them from accepting stock. Their objections were overruled as the federal bankruptcy law was held supreme over state law. The governmental entities then had to negotiate individual settlements with the corporation that cut their claims to less than $100 million.

Former GDC executives were convicted on forty counts of defrauding home buyers through high-pressure sales techniques, false appraisals, and conspiracy. The corporation has emerged from bankruptcy under a new name and is back in the business of buying and selling homes A GDC legacy of unpaved roads and incomplete sewer and drainage systems haunts the agendas of nine Florida communities, now home to 225,000 people. A resident in one of those communities reflects: "It didn't get magically fixed when the company came out of bankruptcy or when these guys got convicted. It's simply the heritage" ["Lawyers: Land Fraud," 1992: 16(C)].

Palm Bay's Infrastructure Legacy

Palm Bay has inherited over 580 miles of unfinished and deteriorating roads and over 1000 miles of drainage swales. The developer repaired the roads with marl, a mixture of lime, clay, and sand. Rains loosen the marl that then runs into ditches clogging culverts and backlogging drainage. The city receives over 1500 drainage complaints annually from residents. Many of the roads also lack stop signs and street signs, complicating liability issues in traffic accidents and slowing the city's response to citizens' calls for fire and police services.

The majority of the city's 70,000 residents live in GDC-built homes that rely on onsite sewage disposal systems and private wells. The region's soils and water table characteristics limit adequate treatment of septic tank sewage "resulting in ground and surface water pollution" (Worzalla, 1991: 15). Studies in a Palm Bay subdivision have found significant and consistent levels of fecal micro-organisms in monitoring wells and canal waters and high levels of nitrate pollution in groundwaters flowing into the nearby Indian River Lagoon (Sherman, 1991).

The Partnership Legacy

Palm Bay's experience with a private partner reflects the vulnerability of local authority in the politicized arena of exaction policy making and of citizen participation in partnerships. As in other scenarios of urban development and redevelopment partnership projects (Feagin and Parker, 1990; Squires, 1989), the private partner in the Palm Bay—GDC partnership dominated the political arrangements underlying the partnership.

The developer's goal of a 100,000-acre city obviously enticed the town council. Attracted by visions of increased property taxes and booming economic activity, the council was certainly mindful of the political significance of its leadership role in the project. The developer offered nationwide marketing to promote the city and the infrastructure package to support its growth in exchange for use of the land that was regulated by the council. GDC, however, was intent on immediate real estate profits to justify its investment of time and money in the project and to secure additional funds from investors.

The city's regulatory process offered opportunities for deal making and concessions to the developer. The project approval process was piecemeal and occurred over a long period of time, with elections shifting the actors on the city councils and zoning committees and their agendas. The city lacked the professional staff to develop detailed construction standards and to monitor the developer's projects (Diamond, 1993). GDC's capacity to exit the partnership and leave infrastructure development to the city translated "into greater power in negotiations" (Cummings, et al., 1989: 217). Relying on informal negotiations, the election of empathetic council members, and muted threats of operating deficits and potential insolvency, the developer undermined the city's efforts to exert its authority.

The partnership did not offer opportunities for citizen participation. Citizen input into infrastructure policy making was limited to city council meetings. Citizens voiced their complaints about the quality and cost of GDC services, but they were "captured consumers." The sole provider infrastructure delivery system offered only two options to residents with complaints: sell their homes and move or rely on their own infrastructure system, wells, and septic tanks.

GDC monopolized the city's infrastructure policy-making process and service delivery. Palm Bay's 1981 comprehensive plan conceded that "availability of utilities, market forces, and choices by the private sector" (PBCP, 1981: 1–42) steered the city's early development. County and state intervention in the latter stages of the partnership did usurp Palm Bay's land use and partnership authority. However, GDC's early co-optation of the partnership dynamics and the city's reliance on a single provider for its infrastructure portended that the private developer's interests would prevail in the partnership. GDC's objective, incremental development of infrastructure to accommodate immediate real estate sales is the public partner's heritage. Disintegrating roads, clogged drainage systems, and a leapfrogging system of water and sewer lines haunt the city, not the developer.

THE PUBLICIZATION OF PRIVATE INFRASTRUCTURE

The "publicizing" or reversal of infrastructure responsibilities entailed legal, management, and financial issues in unraveling the partnership and presented three challenges to the city: (1) purchasing GDC's waste and wastewater utility system, (2) settling its claims with GDC, and (3) financing repairs to the deteriorating infrastructure. The first two challenges encompassed negotiations with its former partner over ownership of the infrastructure and stymied infrastructure responsibility and service delivery for several years. The third challenge is straining the city's resources, yet provides an opportunity for the city to embark on a different partnership.

Provision and Production in Limbo

The 1959 franchise agreement had given Palm Bay the option of purchasing the GDU water and wastewater system after operation by GDC for 30 years. In 1989 GDC rejected the city's initial offer of $35 million for the utility and tied up the legality of the agreement with appeals in district courts for 3 years. During that time GDU raised water rates by 21% and sewer rates by 71%, the first rate increases in 10 years. At hearings before the Florida Public Service Commission, the city argued that the rate increases were deliberate attempts to drive up the utility's book value. The commission issued an order postponing the utility's rate increases until after arbitration hearings to determine the selling price of the utility to the city. Palm Bay finally acquired the utility system in late 1992 for $31.9 million. The city has mandated that new home builders must connect to its waste and wastewater services. Hookups are optional for existing homeowners. The hookup fees of $3,000 to $4,000 are generally discouraging requests for city water and sewer services.

Negotiations over settling the city's claims against its former partner took 2 years. The city sued GDC for $83 million to cover back taxes, liens, stormwater fees, and repairs for unfinished roads and sewer and drainage problems. GDC had put up corporate bonds to guarantee the promised physical improvements. When the corporation declared bankruptcy, these bonds became unredeemable. They were also twenty years old, so the amounts of the bonds did not reflect today's costs (Diamond, 1993).

Complaints about deteriorating roads and clogged drainage systems went unheeded as responsibility for the infrastructure system was in limbo during the negotiations. The city's attorney advised that fixing the road and drainage problems would jeopardize the city's suit against the corporation. The Veterans Administration and local financial institutions halted mortgage loans in several neighborhoods, as the city could not assure maintenance of the former GDC, owned infrastructure. Citizens' frustrations with the road and drainage problems contributed to the ousting of the former city manager. The city ultimately accepted 800 acres of land worth $11.7 million, $700,000 ($453,00 is for back taxes), and responsibility for GDC roads and related drainage projects in exchange for dropping its claim against GDC.

Rediscovering Citizens

Financing the repairs of the deteriorating roads and clogged drainage systems has presented the city with its most difficult challenge. The citizens of Palm Bay are no different from citizens of other cities; they demand services yet are reluctant to pay for them. Long-term residents argue against paying for new streets; new residents against fixing other people's roads. All residents question "why the city didn't do something about those potholed roads and overflowing ditches before it got to be such a mess." Three strategies evolved in the negotiations between the municipal leaders and citizens: (1) imposing a referendum, (2) involving the citizens, and (3) developing another referendum proposal from citizen input.

Developing a five-year program to rehabilitate and maintain the community's 880-mile road system, the city called for a referendum to increase property taxes and expected its citizens to acquiesce to the inevitable road problem solution. The new city manager pointed out: "Everybody knows the road problem has gotten completely out of hand, and this is the most practical way of handling it" (Rowe, 1992a). The voters resoundingly defeated the referendum to add a 1-mill property tax and renew current sidewalk (1-mill) and capital improvements (1.5-mill) taxes, with all revenues directed toward funding the $31 million program. The owner of a $70,000 home with the standard $25,000 state homestead exemption would have paid an additional $45 in annual property taxes.

Although publicly advocating the practicalities of taxes, the city manager was also initiating broader problem-solving strategies. Dimock's (1990: 24) contention that "citizenship is the best way to deal with crises" appropriately describes the city manager's efforts to reorient Palm Bay's governing arrangement with its citizens. He has launched Vision 2005, a process of involving citizens in policy making and educating residents in citizenship.

Palm Bay's Vision 2005 began with meetings with residents and community leaders focusing on how to improve the city's quality of life. Teams of volunteer citizens were organized, with city staff as facilitators. They were charged with designing long-term goals for their specific area, developing yearly objectives, and submitting proposals. Each team had material provided as to how to write goals and objectives and had access to city and departmental data.

In the first phase of the visioning plan, the teams presented their specific area goals. The citizens' roads advisory committee proposed improving city roads and utilities to attract businesses and increase property value. The plan's second phase resulted in three road improvement financing proposals from the committee to the city council: (1) splitting the costs among the owners of 87,000 properties, (2) shifting all costs to owners of developed properties, or (3) shifting a greater share of costs to commercial land owners. The council decided on the first proposal: a flat three-year fee of $97 for all property owners for repairs and $75 thereafter annually for maintenance. In the November 1993 referendum voters approved the road repair proposal that was packaged with increased taxes for fire and police services (from .25 to 1 mill).

Evaluation of the Visioning process and its impact is somewhat premature, but several observations can be noted. Involving the public entails a time-consuming process that delays vital decisions. The city's public works director has pointed out that the ongoing deterioration of the city streets is increasing the costs of the long-term maintenance plan. He did acknowledge that "maybe we're too close to the problem, and bringing in the residents will show us something we haven't seen yet" (Rowe, 1993).

The city manager and his staff have been concerned with the lack of broad citizen representation in the process (Abels, 1993). Approximately seventy citizens are participating, but developers and realtors are somewhat overly represented, indicating the need to identify and solicit participation from unrepresented groups. A resident concurs: "In order to make this dream a reality, every citizen needs to be contacted. It's our city and the dream will only lay dormant if each voice does not get a say" (Rowe, 1992b).

Not all the council members wholeheartedly endorsed citizen involvement in their traditional decision-making authority. Concerns with their specific constituents' interests, the time the process is taking, and with reconciling the recommendations with budget and mandate realities foreshadowed the possibility of hesitating council support. Referendum workshops involving citizens, elected officials, and city staff improved understanding of the infrastructure problems and built support for the referendum.

Aligning citizen input with elected officials' political agenda and with public officials' administrative agenda certainly complicates the city's road repair agenda. The legacy of the city's previous partner, however, strongly supports "elevating citizen choice" (Bellone and Goerl, 1992: 133). The city is embarking on a new partnership, one aspiring to be citizen-driven. Its Vision 2005 process anticipates that public involvement in infrastructure decision making offers greater citizen understanding of the city's infrastructure problems and voter acceptance of taxes.

SUMMARY AND CONCLUSION

Driven by fiscal constraints local governments are engaging in a variety of infrastructure arrangements with developers to support urban development and redevelopment projects. The Palm Bay partnership experience emphasizes that local governments can underestimate the capacity of the private entrepreneur to control the dynamics of the partnership. Developers inherently have several advantages in the politicized arena of exaction policy making. Their capacity to exit by taking their projects elsewhere inclines the municipality to yield concessions in opportunities to bargain over exactions, negotiate zoning ordinances, or relax project specifications. They also benefit from a capacity to alter the rules of the partnership. Driven by market demands, developers are oriented toward incrementally developing infrastructure to accommodate the sale of lots. Local governments may be hesitant to bind their private partners to their original agreements when challenged with changes in the housing market or threats of operating deficits. Developers operating across state and national markets have broader political arenas to exercise their options. Dialogues and negotiations with political allies at regional and state levels can disrupt local agreements.

A partnership driven by developer interests is risky government. If the partnership is unworkable or unprofitable, the private entrepreneur can exit and renege on agreements. Local governments simply do not have that option. Untangling the legal, management, and financial webs of a partnership can consume years and complicate service delivery. Fixing the infrastructure problems left over from a failed partnership shifts resources, staff, and policy focus away from current service demands. The intent of exaction policies is to avoid taxation by privatizing the financing of local public services (Netzer, 1988). Ultimately citizens in Palm Bay will pay to fix the developer's legacy.

A partnership driven by a vision of a community with citizens relying on land use decisions to protect the health and safety of their neighborhoods is simply good partnership governance. As Dimmock (1990: 21) cognizantly observes: "The starting point and center of the administrative art is the citizen being served." Long before citizens move into a development, the partnership has arranged installation and financing of the community's streets, utilities, and water and sewage systems. Citizens have every right to expect their interests are the most powerful incentives in public–private partnerships.

REVIEW QUESTIONS

1. What budgeting and financial management tools are available to public partners for controlling private producers of public services?
2. How can budgeting and financial management tools be integrated into the infrastructure planning process and into negotiations with developers for exactions?

3. Did overlapping local land use controls with county and state regulations balance private–public participation in the partnership?
4. Did the city have to accept responsibility for its former partner's deteriorating roads and leapfrogging system of water and sewer lines?
5. What are the advantages and disadvantages of privatizing infrastructure?
6. Do you think the citizens of Palm Bay would have approved the referendum to increase their property taxes to repair and maintain the roads if it had not been packaged with the public safety taxes?

REFERENCES

Abels, M. (1992–1993). City manager of Palm Bay. interview.

Aldrich, M. (1979). A history of public works in the United States, 1790–1970. In CONSAD Research Corporation, *A Study of Public Works Investment in the United States*, pp. Fi-F105. Washington, DC: U.S. Government Printing Office.

Alterman, R. (1988). Exactions American style: The context for evaluation. In R. Alterman (ed), *Private Supply of Public Services*, pp. 3–21. New York: New York University Press.

Bellone, C. J. and Goerl, F. (March/April 1992). Reconciling public entrepreneurship and democracy: *Public Administration Review, 52*, 130–134.

Catanese, A. J. (1988). Planning infrastructure for urban development. In J. M. Stein (ed), *Public Infrastructure Planning and Management*, Newbury Park, CA: Sage. pp. 81–93.

Cummings, S. C., Koebel, T. and Whitt, J. A. (1989). Redevelopment in downtown Louisville: Public investments, private profits, and shared risks. In G. D. Squires, (ed), *Unequal Partnerships: The Political Economy of Urban Redevelopment in Postwar America*, pp. 202–221. New Brunswick, NJ: Rutgers University Press.

Department of Environmental Health Survey of Brevard County, Florida, Nov. 1–6, 1965. (1965). Tallahassee, Fl: Florida Board of Health, Bureau of Local Services, Division of Sanitation.

Diamond, R. (1991–1993). former city manager of Palm Bay. interviews.

Dimock, M. (Jan/Feb 1990). The restorative qualities of citizenship. *Public Administration Review, 50*, 21–25.

Feagin, J. R. and Parker, R. (1996). *Building American Cities: The Urban Real Estate Game.* Englewood Cliffs, NJ: Prentice Hall.

General Development Corporation. (Feb. 8 1967). Letter to the city council city of Palm Bay.

Lawyers: Land fraud case sends message to firms. (1992). *Florida Today, Aug. 10*, 16(C).

Nelson, A. C. (1988). Financing new infrastructure with development impact fees. In J. M. Stein (ed.), *Public Infrastructure Planning and Management*, pp. 17–130. Newbury Park, CA: Sage.

Netzer, D. (1988). Exactions in the public finance context. In R. Alterman (ed.), *Private Supply of Public Services*, pp. 35–49. New York: New York University Press.

New community developments in Florida (1974). *Florida Environmental and Urban Issues, 1 (March)*, 8–11.

Palm Bay Comprehensive Plan (1981). Palm Bay, Fl.

Palm Bay Town/City Council Meeting minutes (1956–1993). Palm Bay, FL: City Clerk's Office.

Purdum, E. D. and Frank, J. E. (1987). Community use of exactions: Results of a national survey. In J. E. Frank and R. M. Rhodes (eds). *Development Exactions*, pp. 123–152. Washington, DC: American Planning Association.

Rowe, S. (1992a). Palm Bay votes today on a road tax. *Florida Today, July 7*, 1(B).

Rowe, S. (1992b). Planners commit to high quality of life. *Florida Today, July 1*, 1(B).

Rowe, S. (1993). Citizens group hopes to offer road improvement plan votes will approve. *Florida Today, Jan. 1*, 1(B).

Scaled-down GDC to leave Chapter 11. (1992). *Florida Today*, 28 *(March)*, 14(C).

Sherman, K. M. (1991). The scientific basis for requiring adherence to density agreements in Brevard County, Florida. unpublished report.

Smith, H. H. (1991). *Planning America's Communities: Paradise Found? Paradise Lost?* Chicago: Planners Press.

Squires, G. D. (1989). *Unequal Partnerships: The Political Economy of Urban Redevelopment in Postwar America*. New Brunswick, NJ: Rutgers University Press.

Tarr, J. A. (1984). Evolution of the urban infrastructure in the nineteenth and twentieth centuries. In R. Hanson (ed), *Perspectives on Urban Infrastructure*, (pp. 4–60). Washington, DC: National Academy Press.

Worzalla, D. (Nov. 1991). A tale of two cities: A case study. *Florida Journal of Environmental Health*, 14–18.

Index